HANDBOOK ON TRANSPORT AND DEVELOPMENT

Handbook on Transport and Development

Edited by

Robin Hickman

University College London, UK

Moshe Givoni

Tel-Aviv University, Israel

David Bonilla

Universidad Nacional Autonoma de Mexico (UNAM), Mexico

David Banister

University of Oxford, UK

Edward Elgar
PUBLISHING

Cheltenham, UK • Northampton, MA, USA

Published by
Edward Elgar Publishing Limited
The Lypiatts
15 Lansdown Road
Cheltenham
Glos GL50 2JA
UK

Edward Elgar Publishing, Inc.
William Pratt House
9 Dewey Court
Northampton
Massachusetts 01060
USA

Paperback edition 2017

A catalogue record for this book
is available from the British Library

Library of Congress Control Number: 2015935879

This book is available electronically in the **Elgar**online
Economics subject collection
DOI 10.4337/9780857937261

ISBN 978 0 85793 725 4 (cased)
ISBN 978 0 85793 726 1 (eBook)
ISBN 978 1 78643 844 7 (paperback)

Typeset by Servis Filmsetting Ltd, Stockport, Cheshire
Printed and bound in Great Britain by TJ International Ltd, Padstow, Cornwall

Two people in particular have influenced our thinking over the years on the transport and development topic, helping to shape our work in this area – Professor Sir Peter Hall and Professor Piet Rietveld. We were hugely privileged to work with both of them, always offering great knowledge, entertaining debate, encouragement to develop and publish our thoughts, and huge inspiration. Peter and Piet unfortunately passed away in 2014 and 2013, just as this book was reaching its last stages of production. We dedicate the book to them.

Robin Hickman, Moshe Givoni, David Bonilla, David Banister
London, Tel-Aviv and Oxford

Contents

Editors and contributors

All of the contributors are recognized authorities with a strong reputation in research or practice for the issues on which they contribute. Short biographies are given below.

EDITORS

Robin Hickman is a Senior Lecturer at the Bartlett School of Planning, University College London, and a Visiting Research Associate at the Transport Studies Unit, University of Oxford. He has research interests in urban structure and travel, transport and climate change, the affective dimensions of travel, integrated transport and urban planning strategies, and transport planning practice in Europe, Asia and South America. He leads the MSc in Transport and City Planning at UCL. He gained his PhD on urban structure and travel at the Bartlett School of Planning, UCL, in 2007. His most recent book is *Transport, Climate Change and the City*, with David Banister, published by Routledge in 2014.

Moshe Givoni is Head of the Transport Research Unit (TRU) and a Senior Lecturer at the Department of Geography and Human Environment, Tel-Aviv University. He is also a Visiting Research Associate at the Transport Studies Unit, University of Oxford, and an Associate Editor for the journal *Transport Reviews*. He gained his PhD at the Bartlett School of Planning, UCL, and received a Marie Curie postdoctoral fellowship, which was undertaken at the VU University, Amsterdam. His academic background also includes degrees in Economics and Geography (BA) and Business Administration (MBA) from Tel-Aviv University. He is co-editor of the book *Towards Low Carbon Mobility*, together with David Banister, published by Edward Elgar in 2013.

David Bonilla holds joint appointments at the Transport Studies Unit (Senior Researcher in Transport) and at the Oxford Martin School (James Martin Fellow), both at the University of Oxford. He obtained degrees at London University (Economics) and at the Tokyo University of Agriculture and Technology. He was an energy economist at the Asia Pacific Energy Research Center in Tokyo and at Cambridge University. He has been a recipient of several research grants from the European Commission and from the Japanese government. He has also contributed to the World Economic Forum in China. He sits on the executive committee of the University Transport Studies Group of the UK and is a past member of the Japan Society of Energy and Resources.

David Banister is Professor of Transport Studies at the School of Geography and the Environment (SoGE) and Director of the Transport Studies Unit, University of Oxford. He is a Fellow of St Anne's College. During 2009–10 he was also Acting Director of the Environmental Change Institute in SoGE. Until 2006, he was Professor of Transport Planning at UCL. He has been Research Fellow at the Warren Centre in the University of Sydney (2001–2) on the Sustainable Transport for a Sustainable City project and was

Visiting VSB Professor at the Tinbergen Institute in Amsterdam (1994–7). He was a Visiting Professor at the University of Bodenkultur in Vienna in 2007. He was the first Benelux BIVET-GIBET Transport Chair (2012–13). He has published (as author and editor) 23 research books.

CONTRIBUTORS

Jan Anne Annema is Assistant Professor of Transport Policy at Delft University of Technology. He works at the Department of Engineering Systems and Services, in Transport and Logistics. He has research interests in ex-ante transport policy evaluation (e.g., scenarios, cost-benefit analysis), pricing policy implementation issues and environmental policies. His recent book is *The Transport System and Transport Policy* with Bert van Wee and David Banister, published by Edward Elgar in 2013.

Flor Avelino is a Senior Researcher and Lecturer at the Dutch Research Institute for Transitions (DRIFT), Erasmus University Rotterdam, focusing on the power of people to realize sustainability transitions. Her fields of interest are transitions management, social innovation, the role of power, self-organization and sustainability. As the Academic Director of the Transition Academy, she strives to co-create new learning environments to challenge people to think and act for radical change. She holds a PhD (cum laude) from the Erasmus University Rotterdam.

Frank Bruinsma is Associate Professor in Transport and Regional Economics at the Department of Spatial Economics at the VU University Amsterdam. He has research interests in the impact of transport development on urban and regional development and spatial planning policies. He gained his PhD on the impact of transport infrastructure on spatial patterns of economic activities in 1994. Since 2006, he has taught on the interdisciplinary programme Earth and Economics, a joint Bachelor and Masters programme of the Faculty of Earth Sciences and the Faculty of Economics at the VU University.

Chantal C. Cantarelli is a Research Fellow at Oxford University's Saïd Business School. Her research focuses on the performance of large infrastructure projects. Her main research areas are decision-making, escalation of commitment, project ownership and financing of major programmes. Prior to her research at Saïd Business School, she received her PhD from Delft University of Technology in 2011 on theoretical and empirical notions of cost overruns in transport infrastructure projects in the Netherlands and worldwide.

Xinyu (Jason) Cao is Associate Professor of Urban and Regional Planning at the Humphrey School of Public Affairs, University of Minnesota, Twin Cities. His research interests include the relationship between the built environment and travel behaviour, particularly the role of residential self-selection, planning for quality of life, telecommunications and travel behaviour. He received his PhD in the Department of Civil and Environmental Engineering, University of California, Davis, in 2006 and his Bachelor's and Master's degrees from Tsinghua University, China. He served as the Vice-Chair of International Association for China Planning in 2013–15 and will be the Chair for the next two years.

Chia-Lin Chen is a Research Associate at the Bartlett School of Planning, UCL. Her research concerns the relationship between transport and territorial dynamism at different spatial scales with particular interests on the role of design, integrated planning, and multi-level institutional governance. Her PhD research looked at the wider impacts of high-speed rail on regional development. She is currently working on the EU Interreg IVB SINTROPHER project, looking at the reframing of public transport appraisal and decision-making for urban transformation in deprived towns.

Galit Cohen-Blankshtain is a Senior Lecturer at the School of Public Policy and Governance and at the Department of Geography at the Hebrew University. She is the head of the Master's honour programme of the School of Public Policy. She holds an MA in Geography from the Hebrew University and gained her PhD on Spatial Economics at the Free University of Amsterdam. Her research interests are transport policy, beliefs and emotions regarding different transport modes, urban ICTs policy and public participation in policy processes.

Carey Curtis is Professor of City Planning and Transport at Curtin University, Western Australia. She is Visiting Professor, University of Amsterdam. Her research interests cover land-use planning and transport planning, including a focus on city form and structure, transit-oriented development, personal travel behaviour, accessibility planning, institutional barriers to sustainable transport, governance and transport policy. She has published more than 80 papers, book chapters and books, including *Institutional Barriers for Sustainable Transport* (2012) with Nicholas Low, and *Transit Oriented Development: Making it Happen* (2009) with John Renne and Luca Bertolini – both published by Ashgate.

Gamze Dane is a Postdoctoral Researcher at the Urban Planning Group, Department of the Built Environment, Eindhoven University of Technology. She has research interests in travel behaviour analysis, activity based modelling and time-use research. She gained her PhD at the Eindhoven University of Technology on a model of the trade-off between time use and expenditure. She is currently working on a project about the impact of the economic crisis on housing mobility.

Jago Dodson is Director of the Centre for Urban Research and Professor of Urban Policy at RMIT University. He has a longstanding interest in transport problems particularly in the links between transport policy and planning, urban land-use and development and the social consequences of transport access and cost differentials. Much of his recent work has examined the problem of 'oil vulnerability' in Australian cities. He has a record of more than 60 publications, including three books, many of which address transport questions, and has received major grants examining transport issues.

Alastair Donald was a Postgraduate Researcher at the Martin Centre for Architectural and Urban Studies, University of Cambridge, where he worked on mobility and space as part of the EPSRC-funded SOLUTIONS programme. He is Project Director for the British Pavilion for Venice Architecture Biennale, 2014. He is Associate Director of the Future Cities Project and co-editor of *The Lure of the City: From Slums to Suburbs* (Pluto, 2011).

Robyn Dowling is Professor of Human Geography at Macquarie University, Australia. She received her PhD from the University of British Columbia, which provided the foundations for her long-term research on suburban lives and identities. With Alison Blunt she is the co-author of *Home* (Routledge, 2006). She is the recipient of a number of Australian Research Council grants, with the most recent focusing on the mobility practices associated with car-sharing and electric bikes.

Marcial Echenique is a Fellow of Churchill College and Professor Emeritus of Land Use and Transport Studies and former Head of Architecture at the University of Cambridge. He is accredited, in particular, with early work on the integration of land-use and transport planning. He has acted as a consultant to numerous government and local authorities and has directed major planning studies financed by international institutions such as the World Bank and the United Nations. He directed the influential study of Cambridge Futures (Royal Town Planning Institute award for planning innovation in 2000). In 2009 he was awarded an OBE for services to Urban and Regional Planning.

Ahmed El-Geneidy is an Associate Professor at the School of Urban Planning, McGill University. El-Geneidy's research interests include land-use and transportation planning, transit operations and planning, travel behaviour analysis including both motorized (auto and transit) and non-motorized (bicycle and pedestrian) modes of transportation, travel behaviour of disadvantaged populations (seniors and people with disabilities) and measurements of accessibility and mobility in urban contexts.

Reid Ewing is Professor of City and Metropolitan Planning at the University of Utah, Director of the Metropolitan Research Center, Associate Editor of the *Journal of the American Planning Association*, and columnist for *Planning* magazine, writing the bi-monthly column 'Research you can use'. He holds Master's degrees in Engineering and City Planning from Harvard University and a PhD in Urban Planning and Transportation Systems from the Massachusetts Institute of Technology. His work is aimed at planning practitioners. His eight books include *Pedestrian and Transit Oriented Design*, co-published by the Urban Land Institute and American Planning Association; *Growing Cooler – Evidence on Urban Development and Climate Change*, published by the Urban Land Institute; and *Best Development Practices*, listed by the American Planning Association as one of the 100 'essential' books in planning over the past 100 years.

Eran Feitelson is Professor at the Hebrew University of Jerusalem. A former chair of the Department of Geography, he was for five years the head of the Federmann School of Public Policy and Government. Currently he is head of the Advanced School for Environmental Studies. He holds an MA in Geography and Economics from the Hebrew University of Jerusalem and a PhD from the John Hopkins University. In 2009–10 he was a Visiting Professor at the Transport Studies Unit, Oxford University. He has edited or co-edited three books, and published more than 70 papers in refereed journals and edited volumes in the fields of transport policy, land-use planning, environmental policies and water policy. In addition to his academic work, Feitelson has participated in several national planning teams and has been a member of many national committees. He has also served as chair of the Israeli Nature Reserves and National Parks Commission for ten years.

Bent Flyvbjerg is the first BT Professor and Founding Chair of Major Programme Management at Oxford University's Saïd Business School and Director of the University's BT Centre for Major Programme Management. He was twice a Visiting Fulbright Scholar to the USA, where he did research at UCLA, UC Berkeley and Harvard. His books include *Megaprojects and Risk: An Anatomy of Ambition*, Making *Social Science Matter: Why Social Inquiry Fails and How It Can Succeed Again* and *Rationality and Power: Democracy in Practice*. His publications have been translated into 19 languages. Flyvbjerg has served as advisor to the United Nations, the EU Commission and to governments and companies around the world.

Norman Garrick is an Associate Professor of Civil Engineering at the University of Connecticut. He is also a member of the national board of the Congress for the New Urbanism (CNU). He specializes in the planning and design of urban transportation systems especially as they relate to sustainability, placemaking and urban revitalization. His writing has appeared in *Atlantic Cities*, *Planetizen*, *New Urban News*, the *Denver Post* and the *Hartford Courant*. He has worked as transportation consultant on a number of design charrettes including urban revitalization projects with the Prince of Wales Foundation in Jamaica and Sierra Leone. He is a recipient of the Transportation Research Board's Wootan Award for best paper in policy and organization and a Fulbright Fellowship to Kingston, Jamaica. He has also been a Visiting Professor at the Swiss Federal Institute of Technology (ETH) Zurich and a lecturer in both MIT's Department of Urban Studies and Planning and Oxford University's (UK) Masters of Sustainable Urban Planning Programme.

Harry Geerlings is Professor in Governance and Sustainable Mobility at the Department of Public Administration of the Erasmus University Rotterdam and a 'Port Professor' of Erasmus Smart Port Rotterdam, an initiative between the Port community and the Erasmus University Rotterdam. Most of this research is related to the interaction between transport, environment and spatial planning. He holds a PhD in Economics from the Vrije Universiteit Amsterdam. He is a member of the PhD-school TRAIL (Transport, Infrastructure and Logistics).

Karst Geurs is Professor of Transport Planning at the Centre for Transport Studies, Faculty of Engineering Technology, University of Twente, the Netherlands. His research focuses on accessibility analysis and modelling, land-use and transport interactions, transport policy evaluation and sustainable transport. He gained his PhD at the Faculty of Geosciences, Utrecht University, the Netherlands, on accessibility appraisal of land-use and transport policy strategies. He is the current president of the Network of European Communications and Transport Activities Research (NECTAR). His most recent book is *Accessibility and Transport Planning: Challenges for Europe and North America* with Aura Reggiani and Kevin J. Krizek, published by Edward Elgar in 2012.

Andrew R. Goetz is Professor in the Department of Geography and the Environment and a faculty member in the Intermodal Transportation Institute at the University of Denver, USA. He is co-editor of *The Geographies of Air Transport* (2014) and co-author of two other air transport books, as well as numerous publications on topics including transportation infrastructure and urban/economic growth, air transportation and airports, globalization, sustainability, intermodal transportation, transport geography, high-speed rail, smart growth planning, rail transit systems and transit-oriented development. He received the 2010 Edward L. Ullman Award from the Association of American Geographers for Significant Contributions to Transportation Geography.

Peter Gordon was Professor in the University of Southern California's Price School of Public Policy until his retirement at the end of 2013. He is now Professor Emeritus. His research interests are in applied urban economics. With colleagues, he has developed various economic impact models which have been applied to the study of the effects of infrastructure investments or disruptions from natural events or terrorist attacks. In addition, he continues to be interested in urban structure and economic growth along with the associated policy implications. He has published in most of the major urban planning, urban transportation and regional science journals and is a Fellow of the Regional Science Association International. He has consulted for local, state and federal agencies, the World Bank, the United Nations and many private groups. He received his PhD from the University of Pennsylvania in 1971.

Anna Grigolon is a Postdoctoral Researcher at the Urban Planning Group, Department of the Built Environment, Eindhoven University of Technology. She has research interest in tourism analysis, travel behaviour analysis and logistics. She gained her PhD at the Eindhoven University of Technology on a model of the influence of lifecycle on tourism behaviour. She is currently working on a project about the impact of the economic crisis on housing mobility.

Derek Halden is Director of DHC, a company he founded in 1996 after spending ten years in the UK civil service working for the Scottish Office and the Transport Research Laboratory. His research in the 1990s on the use of accessibility concepts in planning helped to pave the way for the introduction of more user-focused transport planning in the UK, and since 2002 he has been supporting the UK Department for Transport with the planning of national policies and programmes to improve access to services. His research on the future of transport and logistics includes the review *Access, Information and Flexibility* published by the British Council of Shopping Centres, which has been used as a blueprint for smart travel delivery. Halden is a Civil Engineer, was Chair of the Chartered Institute of Logistics and Transport in Scotland from 2011 to 2013, and is a member of the Polish Academy of Science. He has directed and managed more than 300 projects to strengthen links between transport and the wider economy and society across Europe and in New Zealand.

Peter Hall was Bartlett Professor of Planning and Regeneration at the Bartlett School of Planning, UCL, President of the Regional Studies Association and President of the Town and Country Planning Association. He was author, co-author or editor of 50 books including *The World Cities, Urban and Regional Planning, Cities of Tomorrow, Cities in Civilization, The Polycentric Metropolis* and *Good Cities, Better Lives*. Since 2009, he directed SINTROPHER (Sustainable Integrated Tram-Based Transport Options for Peripheral European Regions), an EU Interreg IVB project. Peter Hall sadly died in July 2014.

Iqbal Hamiduddin is a Lecturer in Transport Planning and Housing at the Bartlett School of Planning, UCL. His research specialisms are in transport, housing and particularly the interface of transport and housing policies in residential design. His PhD thesis on the 'Social implications of residential car reduction' was based largely on detailed comparative field research undertaken in different neighbourhoods of Freiburg. He has also investigated different elements of transport planning and housing delivery separately in a variety of projects for organizations including the Royal Institution of Chartered Surveyors, the Regional Studies Association and the European Union.

Susan Handy is Chair of the Department of Environmental Science and Policy and the Director of the National Center for Sustainable Transportation at the University of California, Davis. Her research interests centre on the relationships between transportation and land use, particularly the impact of neighbourhood design on travel behaviour. She is currently working on several studies of bicycling as a mode of transportation. She is a member of the Committee on Women's Issues in Transportation of the Transportation Research Board and is an associate editor of the newly launched *Journal of Transport and Health*.

Peter Headicar is an Associate at the Department of Planning, Oxford Brookes University where he was Reader in Transport and leader of the Department's Transport MSc programme until his retirement in 2011. He continues to research spatial demographic trends in England and their implications for travel and on the inter-relationships in policy and practice between land-use and transport planning. He is the author of *Transport Policy and Planning in Great Britain*, published by Routledge in 2009. He received the PTRC Lifetime Achievement Award in 2012 and was appointed a member of the UK Independent Transport Commission in 2013.

David A. Hensher is Professor of Management, and Founding Director of the Institute of Transport and Logistics Studies (ITLS) at the University of Sydney. A Fellow of the Australian Academy of Social Sciences, recipient of the 2009 International Association of Travel Behaviour Research (IATBR) Lifetime Achievement Award in recognition for his longstanding and exceptional contribution to IATBR as well as to the wider travel behaviour community; recipient of the 2006 Engineers Australia Transport Medal for lifelong contribution to transportation. Hensher is also the recipient of the Smart 2013 Premier Award for Excellence in Supply Chain Management. Honorary Fellow of Singapore Land Transport Authority, and a past President of the International Association of Travel Behaviour Research. He has published extensively (more than 550 papers) in the leading international transport journals and key journals in economics as well as 12 books. David has advised numerous government and industry agencies in many countries (notably Australia, New Zealand, the UK, the USA and the Netherlands), with a recent appointment to Infrastructure Australia's reference panel on public transport, and is called upon regularly by the media for commentary.

Darío Hidalgo is the Director of Research and Practice of EMBARQ, the transport initiative of the WRI Ross Center for Sustainable Cities, where he is involved in projects in India, Mexico, Brazil, Turkey, the Andean Region and China. He also coordinates the Observatory of the BRT Centre of Excellence. He has 23 years of experience as a transport expert, consultant, and government official in more than ten countries of Latin America, Asia and Africa. He has also been a Lecturer in Urban Planning and a researcher, focusing on documenting bus systems implementation and operations. He holds PhD and MSc degrees in Transportation Planning from Ohio State University, and a Civil Engineering degree from Universidad de los Andes, Colombia.

Mayer Hillman was an Architect and Town Planner in private practice from 1954. The lack of attention paid at the time to environmental considerations led him to leave it and to write his doctoral thesis at Edinburgh University and then to join the Policy Studies Institute in 1970 as Head of its Environment and Quality of Life Research Programme. He has written more than 50 books on transport, urban planning, energy conservation, health promotion and environment policies. Now, as Senior Fellow Emeritus of the Institute, his work is focused on the awesome implications of climate change. He proposed personal carbon rationing in 1990, citing it as 'the only realistic way by which catastrophic climate change can be prevented'.

Randi Hjorthol is Chief Research Sociologist at the Institute of Transport Economics in Oslo, Norway. She is leading the Strategic Institute Program of Mobility and Travel Behaviour. In the past decade she has managed several projects on ageing and mobility. She was a member of the Scientific Advisory Board of CASE (Centre for Ageing and Supportive Environments) at the University of Lund. She has served as a leader of the programme Committee for Research on Transport and Infrastructure, Danish Agency for Science, Technology and Innovation. She was member of the Advisory Board of TRANSGEN-project (transport and gender) at the University of Copenhagen, member of the Advisory Board of SAMOT (service and market oriented transport research) at the University of Karlstad, and was a member of an Expert Group in OECD on mobility needs for an ageing society.

Erling Holden is Professor in Renewable Energy at Sogn and Fjordane University College, Faculty of Engineering and Sciences. He has a Master's Degree in Mechanical Engineering from the Department of Energy and Process Engineering, Norwegian University of Science and Technology (NTNU). He gained his doctoral degree in Urban Planning at the Department of Urban Design and Planning, NTNU; and has worked with issues related to energy, transport and sustainable development since 1988. In his work, Holden combines one or more of three different theoretical perspectives: technological-oriented environmental studies, sociological and socio-psychological behavioural studies, and physical planning studies. His most recent book is *Achieving Sustainable Mobility*, published by Ashgate in 2007.

Torben Holvad is Economic Adviser at the European Railway Agency (France), Senior Research Associate at the Transport Studies Unit (University of Oxford), Research Associate at École Polytechnique Fédérale de Lausanne (EPFL), and external Associate Professor at the Department of Transport (Danish Technical University). He obtained Economics degrees from Copenhagen University (MSc) and the European University Institute in Florence (MA and PhD).

Helmut Holzapfel is Professor of Transport and Urbanism at the faculty of Architecture, Urban and Landscape Planning at the University of Kassel. He studied civil engineering and had leading positions from 1980 to 1993 as Transport Scientist in research groups and later as an official at the Transport Ministry of North Rhine Westphalia. Between

1995 and 1998 he was leading transport planning in the German 'Land' of Sachsen-Anhalt. Since 2009, he has contributed to the EU SINTROPHER research project in close collaboration with Professor Sir Peter Hall. He has had positions as a Visiting Professor in Vienna (Austria) and in Alessandria (Italy). He has published many books and articles; his most recent book is *Urbanism and Transport* (Routledge, 2015).

Michael Iacono is a Research Fellow in the Department of Civil, Environmental and Geo-Engineering at the University of Minnesota and a member of the NEXUS research group. His research interests cover a variety of topics related to the interaction between transportation networks and the people and places they serve. Much of his recent work has been focused on evaluating and applying methods to understand the economic impacts of transportation network improvements, as well as investigating the role of demographic transitions in travel behaviour change.

Ole B. Jensen is Professor of Urban Theory at the Department of Architecture, Design and Media Technology, Aalborg University (Denmark). He holds a BA in Political Science, an MA in Sociology and a PhD in Planning. He is co-founder and board member at the Center for Mobilities and Urban Studies (C-MUS). His main research interests are within urban mobilities and urban networked technologies. He is the co-author of *Making European Space: Mobility, Power and Territorial Identity* (Routledge, 2004, with Tim Richardson), and author of *Staging Mobilities* (Routledge, 2013) and *Designing Mobilities* (Aalborg University Press, 2014).

Peter Jones is Professor of Transport and Sustainable Development in the Centre for Transport Studies, UCL; previously he was Director of the Transport Studies Group at the University of Westminster. He has a wide range of transport research and teaching interests, including traveller attitudes and behaviour, travel trends and the determinants of travel demand, activity patterns and lifestyles, traffic restraint, accessibility studies, policy option generation, major transport economic and social impact studies, public engagement, development of new survey and appraisal methods, and advances in urban street planning and design. He is a member of the Independent Transport Commission and the DfT's Science Advisory Council; and has a Visiting Professorship at the China Academy of Transportation Sciences.

Jeff Kenworthy has spent 35 years in the transport and urban planning field. His research focuses on large international comparisons of cities from a transport and land-use perspective. He is author/co-author of a number of books as well as more than 200 book chapters and journal publications in the area of urban planning, transport and sustainability. He has received two awards from the German government for his research and teaching in the field, including a Mercator Guest Professorship (Goethe University) and is currently a Guest Professor at the Frankfurt University of Applied Sciences.

Susan Kenyon began her career in transport research in 1998. Her research interests focus on travel behaviour and influences on behaviour, including travel behaviour change; and on the links between transport, social policy and the functioning of society. In 2013, she moved from academia to the policy environment. Her academic background includes a Bachelor's in Politics, a Master's in Environmental Politics and a PhD examining the influence of virtual mobility on travel behaviour and social exclusion.

Christian A. Klöckner is Professor in Social Psychology and Quantitative Methods at the Norwegian University of Science and Technology (NTNU) in Trondheim. He took his education at Ruhr-University Bochum, Germany, where he also received his PhD with the influence of habits on travel mode choice as a topic. Since 2007 he is affiliated to NTNU where he does research on determinants of environmentally relevant behaviour on all levels from everyday behaviour like travel mode choice or food purchase to big investment decisions like buying a car (including electric cars) or insulating a house. He is furthermore interested in modelling behaviour change and innovative environmental communication through means of art, games or modern communication technology.

Kevin J. Krizek is Professor of Transport in the Programs of Environmental Design and Environment Studies at the University of Colorado Boulder. He is a 2013–14 Fellow of the Leopold Leadership Program and was awarded a 2014 US-Italy Fulbright Scholarship. He also serves as the Visiting Professor of 'Cycling in Changing Urban Regions' at Radboud University in the Netherlands (2015–2018). He co-heads the Active Communities/Transportation (ACT) Research Group and is appointed to the bicycle transportation committee of the Transportation Research Board of the National Academies, and is the Senior Transportation Fellow for the Environmental Center at CU.

Bumsoo Lee is an Associate Professor in the Department of Urban and Regional Planning at the University of Illinois, Urbana-Champaign. His research interests include urban spatial structure, travel behaviour, sustainable transportation and economic impact analysis. He earned his PhD in Planning at the University of Southern California.

Steen Leleur is Professor of Decision Support Systems and Planning at the Department of Transport at the Technical University of Denmark. He is an experienced transport planner, who has participated in numerous activities especially in the fields of national and international strategic transport planning and transport investment appraisal. He has worked out several textbooks such as *Road Infrastructure Planning: A Decision Oriented Approach*, published in 2000 by Polyteknisk (2nd edition), and *Complex Strategic Choices: Applying Systemic Planning for Strategic Decision Making*, published in 2012 by Springer. His most recent research concerns uncertainty of appraisal methodology and the formulation of comprehensive assessment frameworks for sustainable transport development.

David Levinson serves on the faculty of the Department of Civil, Environmental, and Geo-Engineering at the University of Minnesota and Director of the Networks, Economics, and Urban Systems (NEXUS) research group. He holds the Richard P. Braun/CTS Chair in Transportation. He also serves on the graduate faculty of the Applied Economics and Urban and Regional Planning programs at the University of Minnesota. In academic year 2006–7 he was a Visiting Academic at Imperial College in London.

Terry Li is a Research Fellow at the Urban Research Program at Griffith University. His research focus is on developing spatial understanding of urban and transport systems in Australian and international urban environment. Much of his research lies in the application of quantitative geographical methods for urban and transport modelling and analysis, which covers a broad range of urban and regional issues, including questions of journey to work dynamics, transport impacts of employment decentralization, urban vehicle fleet fuel efficiency, and transport vulnerability. He has published more than 20 journal articles. He is also a guest editor for the special issue of *Journal of Transport Geography* on public bike-sharing programmes.

Zheng Li is a Senior Research Fellow in Transportation at the Institute of Transport and Logistics Studies (ITLS) in the University of Sydney Business School. Li's main research interests include willingness to pay valuation, advanced non-linear travel choice models, and transport policy. Li has published more than 23 journal articles, the majority of which are published in the top transportation and logistics journals (e.g. *Transportation Research, Parts A, B, D and E, Transportation Science, Transportation*), and has presented papers at a number of international conferences. In 2010, he was awarded the Institute of Transport and Logistics Studies Prize for research excellence in transport or logistics. In 2013 he took up a new appointment in the Department of Transportation, Southwest Jiaotong University Hope College, Jintang University City, Chengdu, China.

Kristin Linnerud is a Senior Research Fellow at the Center for International Climate and Environmental Research – Oslo (CICERO). Linnerud has a Master's Degree (1990) in finance from the London School of Economics and a Doctoral Degree in Economics from the Norwegian School of Economics (2008). Linnerud has done research on issues related to energy, transport and sustainable development since 2007. Her work is based upon microeconomics, behavioural economics, econometrics and finance. Some recent publications are 'Sustainable development: *Our Common Future* revisited' (*Global Environmental Change*), 'Sustainable passenger transport: back to Brundtland' (*Transportation Research Part A: Policy and Practice*) and 'Troublesome leisure travel: the contradictions of three sustainable transport policies' (*Urban Studies*).

Stephen Marshall is Reader in Urban Morphology and Planning at the Bartlett School of Planning, UCL. He has more than 20 years of experience in the built environment fields, initially in consultancy and subsequently in academia. His principal research interests are in urban morphology and street layout, and their relationships with urban formative processes, including urban design, coding and planning. He has written and edited several books, including *Streets and Patterns* (2005), *Cities, Design and Evolution* (2009) and *Urban Coding and Planning* (2011). He was Chair of the Editorial Board of *Urban Design and Planning*, from its launch to 2012; and is now co-editor of *Built Environment*.

Wesley Marshall is an Assistant Professor at the University of Colorado Denver, Program Director of the UCD University Transportation Center through the Mountain Plains Consortium, and co-director of the Active Communities/Transportation (ACT) research group. He received his Professional Engineering licence in 2003 and conducts transportation teaching and research dedicated to creating more sustainable infrastructures, particularly in terms of road safety, active transportation and transit-oriented communities. Other recent teaching and research topics involve resiliency, parking and street networks. Having spent time with Sasaki Associates and Clough, Harbour and Associates, he has been working on issues related to transportation for the past 15 years. A native of Watertown, Massachusetts, he graduated with honours from the University of Virginia and received his Master's and Doctoral degrees from the University of Connecticut. He is a recipient of the Dwight Eisenhower Transportation Fellowship and winner of the Charley V. Wootan Award for Outstanding TRB Paper.

Ellen Matthies is Professor of Environmental Psychology at Otto von Guericke University Magdeburg (Germany). From 2009 to 2011 she was Professor of Environmental Psychology at the Norwegian University of Science and Technology, Trondheim (Norway). She accomplished her habilitation in 2001 with the topic 'Coping with environmental threats and global environmental change' at the Psychology department at Ruhr-University Bochum where she also received her PhD. Her main research field is man–environment interactions with a focus on environmentally relevant behaviours and decisions (mainly electricity use and car use) and theory driven development and evaluation of intervention measures to promote sustainable consumption.

Lucia Mejia Dorantes works at the Fraunhofer Institute for Systems and Innovation Research in the Sustainability and Infrastructure System Unit in Germany. She gained her PhD in the University of Madrid (UPM), in the Transport Research Centre (TRANSyT) in 2011 with the analysis of impacts on house prices and firms' location due to new transport infrastructure (Cum-Laude, Doctor Europeus, and also honoured with the extraordinary doctoral thesis award of the UPM). She has collaborated with different institutions and research centres in Europe and America. Her research interests are related to efficient transport planning strategies, transport economics, long-term effects of transportation, transport policy and transport equity, using both qualitative and quantitative techniques.

Rainer Meyfahrt is Honorary Professor of Public Transport at the Department of Architecture, Urban and Landscape Planning at the University of Kassel. From 1974 to 1989 he was Lecturer and Professor of Urban Development at the University of Kassel, and from 1982 to 1986 he was Vice-President. From 1990 to 2009 he was member of the staff of the public transport company of Kassel (KVG), responsible for corporate planning and the development of the tram and RegioTram system. From 2004 to 2009 he was a member of the executive board of the company and Director of the Regionalbahn Kassel (RBK). Since 2009, he has worked on the EU SINTROPHER project. He is member of the German Academy of Urban and Regional Spatial Planning.

Patricia Mokhtarian is Professor of Civil and Environmental Engineering at the Georgia Institute of Technology in Atlanta. Prior to joining Ga Tech in 2013, she spent 23 years on the faculty of the University of California, Davis. Her research interests include the impacts of land use on travel behaviour (particularly residential location and residential self-selection issues), the impact of telecommunications technology on travel behaviour, commuters' responses to congestion or to system disruptions, attitudes toward mobility and travel multitasking. She is an editor of *Transportation*, and serves on the editorial boards of six other transportation journals. She is currently Vice-Chair/Chair-Elect of the International Association for Travel Behaviour Research.

Juan Carlos Muñoz is Director of the Department of Transport Engineering and Logistics and Deputy Director of the Sustainable Urban Development Centre at Pontificia Universidad Católica de Chile, and leader of the Bus Rapid Transit Centre of Excellence. He has provided advice to the Chilean Ministry of Transport and the Santiago Metropolitan Urban Transport Directorate, and has been member of the board of the Metro systems in Valparaiso and Santiago. His research includes optimization of crew assignment, advanced control for transit systems, improved planning mechanisms for bus and metro systems, and measurement of transit performance. He holds PhD and MSc degrees from the University of California at Berkeley, and MSc and Civil Engineering Degrees from Pontificia Universidad Católica de Chile.

Petter Næss is Dr. Ing., Architect and Professor in Planning in Urban Regions at the Norwegian University of Life Sciences, where he is Head of the Doctoral School of Society, Development and Planning. Combining qualitative and quantitative research methods, he has for more than 25 years carried out research into urban sustainability topics, with a particular focus on influences of urban structures on travel behaviour. Other research interests are driving forces of urban development, planning theory and philosophy of science. He has published widely within all these areas.

Peter Newman is Professor of Sustainability at Curtin University in Perth, Australia where he is the Director of the CUSP research institute, which has 80 PhD students. He is the author of 15 books and 280 papers and with Jeff Kenworthy invented the term 'automobile dependence' in the 1980s. He is a lead author for transport on the IPCC and is on the board of Infrastructure Australia. In 2014 he was awarded the Order of Australia for his contribution to sustainable transport and urban design.

Susanne Nordbakke is a Senior Research Sociologist at the Institute of Transport Economics. Her research interests include the influence of social and spatial phenomena on individuals' travel behaviour and decisions, and the analysis of wellbeing effects of travel and activities in different socio-demographic groups. She gained her PhD on mobility and well-being among older people at the University of Oslo in 2014.

Susan Petheram is a PhD candidate in City and Metropolitan Planning at the University of Utah, and an Associate Principal with CRSA, a planning and architecture firm in Salt Lake City, Utah. Her research interests include the impacts of light rail systems on surrounding land uses, the value of arts and culture in neighbourhoods and how past relationships between transportation and the built environment affect present-day urban form characteristics.

Soora Rasouli is Assistant Professor of the Urban Planning Group of the Eindhoven University of Technology, the Netherlands. She has research interests in activity-based models of travel demand, modelling of choice processes under uncertainty and complex systems. She serves on the editorial board of several transportation journals and is a member of TRB and WCTR committees on demand forecasting.

Piet Rietveld was Professor in Transport Economics and Head of the Department of Spatial Economics at the VU University Amsterdam (the Netherlands). His main research interests were in transport economics, regional development, and evaluation methods. He obtained his PhD in 1980 from the VU University Amsterdam. In the 1980s, he was Research Fellow at the International Institute for Applied Systems Analysis (Laxenburg, Austria) and research coordinator at the Universitas Kritsen Satya Wacana (Salatiga, Indonesia). He was a member of numerous advisory boards. He was also chairman of network organizations such as RSA Netherlands (the Dutch branch of the Regional Science Association International) and NECTAR (the worldwide network of transport researchers, 2003–7). In addition, he was a fellow of several organizations, most notably the Tinbergen Institute (the graduate school of Erasmus University Rotterdam, the University of Amsterdam and VU University Amsterdam) and NAKE (Dutch Network for General and Quantitative Economics), and member of the Royal Netherlands Academy of Arts and Sciences (KNAW). He published more than 400 articles and 250 book contributions. Piet Rietveld sadly died in November 2013.

Orit Rotem-Mindali is a Lecturer at the Department of Geography and Environment, Bar-Ilan University. She gained her PhD at The Hebrew University of Jerusalem on spatial, and transport implications of households' consumption patterns in the e-commerce age. Her academic background includes also degrees in Life Science and Environmental Studies (BSc) and Geography and Environmental Management Planning and Policy program (MA) from the Hebrew University of Jerusalem. Her research interests include spatial behaviour in urban environments. Her research emphasizes individual spatial behaviour while focusing on the reciprocal relationship of this behaviour with urban, economic and social processes in the presence of technological changes.

Tim Schwanen is Departmental Research Lecturer and Associate Professor in Transport Studies and Human Geography at the School of Geography and the Environment, University of Oxford. He holds a PhD in Human Geography (2003, cum laude) from Utrecht University where he also worked as a post-doctoral researcher and lecturer in Urban Geography (2003–9). He is currently the Editor-in-Chief of the *Journal of Transport Geography*.

Neil Sipe is Professor and Head of the Planning Program at the University of Queensland. He was previously Deputy Director of the Urban Research Program at Griffith University and served as Head of the Griffith University's Urban Planning Program for more than ten years. He has been an active researcher in the area of transport planning and has collaborated with Jago Dodson on a body of research related to oil vulnerability in the transport sector. He currently serves on the US Transportation Research Board Ferry Committee and the Social and Economic Effects of Transportation Committee and is the editor of *Australian Planner*, the peer-reviewed journal serving the Australian planning community.

Dominic Stead is Associate Professor in the Faculty of Architecture and the Built Environment, Delft University of Technology, and Honorary Research Fellow at the Bartlett School of Planning, UCL. He has published more than 25 book chapters and more than 60 journal articles. He has also co-edited three books. He is a member of the editorial board of four international journals – *European Journal of Transport and Infrastructure Research*, *European Planning Studies*, *Journal of Planning Education and Research* and *Planning Practice and Research*.

Philip Stoker is PhD Candidate in the Department of City and Metropolitan Planning at the University of Utah. Philip has a Master's degree in Resource and Environmental Management from Simon Fraser University, Vancouver, and a Bachelor of Science in Environmental Management from the University of Redlands, California. He has conducted environmental and social science research internationally, including work with the World Health Organization, Parks Canada, the National Park Service, the Kenyan Wildlife Service and the Vancouver 2010 Olympic Games. Currently, he is an iUTAH graduate research fellow investigating urban water use.

Gordon Stokes is a Visiting Research Associate at the Transport Studies Unit, University of Oxford. He has done research for the UK government at the Transport and Road Research Laboratory, for Oxford University, for consultancies and the government's Countryside Agency and Commission for Rural Communities. His worked has generally been concerned with social, environmental and rural transport issues, and has involved analysing large-scale datasets and panel surveys, in particular the UK's National Travel Survey. He was responsible for the 'State of the Countryside' reports while at the Commission for Rural Communities and was an author of *Transport, the New Realism* in the early 1990s while working for Transport Studies Unit.

Harry Timmermans is Head of the Urban Planning Group of the Eindhoven University of Technology, the Netherlands. He has research interests in modelling decision-making processes and decision support systems in a variety of application domains, including transportation. His main current research project is concerned with the development of a dynamic model of activity-travel behaviour. He is Co-Chair of the International Association of Travel Behaviour Research.

Bert van Wee is Professor of Transport Policy at Delft University of Technology, the Netherlands, in the Faculty of Technology, Policy and Management. In addition he is scientific director of TRAIL research school. His main interests are in long-term developments in transport, in particular in the areas of accessibility, land-use transport interaction, (evaluation of) large infrastructure projects, the environment, safety, policy analyses and ethics. He gained his PhD in Economics and Econometrics at the University of Amsterdam, and his masters in Geography at Utrecht University. In 2014 the Transport Geography Specialty Group of the Association of American Geographers offered him the Edward L. Ullman Award.

Ryan Wilson is a registered Professional Engineer and member of the American Institute of Certified Planners. Ryan works currently at the Minnesota Department of Transportation, Metro District Transit Section, as a Transit Corridor Engineer focused on the region's light rail transit system. He previously served as project manager for the Minnesota 20-year State Highway Investment Plan 2013 update. He has worked at MnDOT in the areas of highway planning, investment analysis, construction, and design and has prior experience in research and construction. Ryan holds a Master of Science in Civil Engineering and Master of Urban and Regional Planning from the University of Minnesota, Twin Cities as well as a Bachelor of Science in Civil Engineering from the University of Wisconsin, Madison.

Dujuan Yang is a PhD Candidate in the Urban Planning Group, Department of the Built Environment, Eindhoven University of Technology. She received her MSc from Harbin Institute of Technology, China. Her PhD is concerned with a model of energy consumption related to activity-travel patterns and consumer response to increasing energy prices. Her publications have appeared in *Transportation, Journal of Transport Geography* and *Transportation Research Record*.

PART I

AN INTRODUCTION TO TRANSPORT AND DEVELOPMENT

1 The transport and development relationship

Robin Hickman, Moshe Givoni, David Bonilla and David Banister

UNDERSTANDING THE LINKAGES BETWEEN TRANSPORT AND DEVELOPMENT

Arthur Miller's ([1949] 2000: 12) famous prose on the aspiration for life in suburbia, sometimes followed by the diffidence with it, nicely encapsulates the focus of this edited collection:

> Linda: We should've bought the land next door.
> Willy: The street is lined with cars. There's not a breath of fresh air in the neighbourhood. The grass don't grow anymore, you can't raise a carrot in the backyard. They should've had a law against apartment houses. Remember those two beautiful elm trees out there? When I and Biff hung the swing between them?
> Linda: Yeah, like being a million miles from the city.

There has been much discussion about the relationships between the built form and travel, and between transport investment and development, with many differences in opinion offered. There are wider factors that influence the relationships, such as individual and societal attitudes, and changes also occur over time. This area of research – the changing nexus between transport and development – has been examined and debated since at least the late 1800s, from the building of the early railway systems in Europe; through to the development of the major highway and motorway networks in the United States and Europe from the 1920s onwards, and continuing in many contexts. Major infrastructure projects are considered and carefully examined in relation to their likely developmental impacts; and, more recently, the psychological and cultural factors surrounding travel have been examined alongside the infrastructural and developmental aspects. Often it seems the development form follows the transport investment, from the Victorian suburbs of London built around the early railway and Underground lines; to the dispersed suburbia following the newly developed highway networks in the United States. But the causality is rarely in one direction and often the development form helps shape the transport infrastructure investments. This means that the dispersed city requires more highway investments, the compact centre(s) requires public transport, walking and cycling improvements. The linkages are often complex, sometimes easy to understand and sometimes difficult and subtle. They are often debated – and it is this debate that is the focus of the *Handbook on Transport and Development*.

First, we define what we mean by 'transport and development', to help the reader in the discussion that follows. From the *Oxford English Dictionary* (2014) we can obtain the following definitions:

- Transport (verb): 'to carry, convey, or remove from one place or person to another; to convey across'; or, transport (noun): 'the action of carrying or conveying a thing or person from one place to another; conveyance'.
- Development (noun): 'the process or fact of developing', 'a gradual unfolding, a bringing into fuller view' and 'the act or process of developing a tract of land'.

We understand the focus of the edited collection is to cover all of these dimensions, but also the integrative element, concerning the different means and systems of transport and how these are related to the change in land use, and also the wider aspects, such as the changed situation of the economy, environment, social equity and well-being. The idea for the book was similarly wide-ranging, arising from various conversations that the editors had while researching at the Transport Studies Unit, University of Oxford, and continuing in our later careers. It seemed that we all tackled the same broad topic from different directions – as urban planners we were interested in which transport investments worked 'best' for the city, and how urban planning might help encourage greater sustainability in travel behaviours; as economists we were interested in the impacts that infrastructure investment might have on the economy and wider societal issues; and all of us were interested in the cultural factors, including the psychology and sociology of travel, and the role that these factors might play in urban development. The book therefore attempts to cover all of these areas, and is organized in three main sections, as outlined below.

PART II   URBAN STRUCTURE AND TRAVEL

Part II contains 13 chapters, each presenting research on the built environment and its relationship with travel, from an international perspective. The chapters explore the main debates, such as the key built form variables, the influence of urban structure at different scales, the changes over time; the locational and contextual dimensions; and the roles of attitudes, including the concept of 'self-selection' (the choice of residential, and indeed employment and other activities, based on an individual's travel and other attitudinal preferences).

The first chapter, from Philip Stoker, Susan Petheram and Reid Ewing, opens with an overview of the topic, arguing that the built environment is an important factor in travel behaviour, with the relationship evident at different scales, such as the regional (macro) and neighbourhood (mezzo) scales. Measures of sprawl are defined and discussed, with significant relationships associated with vehicle miles travelled (VMT) and mode share. Elasticities are then derived from the most common built environment factors – using the '3Ds' (density, diversity and design) and '5Ds' typologies (destination accessibility and distance to transit). Individual elasticities are fairly small, but combined effects can be quite large – hence the case is made for shaping the built environment to help reduce private motor car-based travel.

Peter Newman and Jeff Kenworthy present the patterns of transport carbon dioxide (CO_2) emissions and energy consumption in cities globally. They discuss the large variation in transport emissions between cities, such as 100kg CO_2 in Ho Chi Minh City, 3,000kg CO_2 in New York, rising to 7,500kg CO_2 in Atlanta; and the varied mode shares for the private car, public transport and non-motorized transport contributing to this. The relationships between transport and built environment characteristics are then explored, again with great difference in city densities, such as Ho Chi Minh City with more than 350 persons per hectare and Atlanta at a density of six persons per hectare. Equity is brought out as an important issue, with different contexts developing very different transport systems and urban forms, resulting in a huge variation in emissions and energy consumption.

Peter Headicar, using a case study of Oxfordshire (UK), considers the relationships between homes, jobs and commuting, arguing that the strategic dimension of commuting outside the home settlement is overlooked in policymaking – and that there is a strong locational element within the urban structure and travel relationship. A lack of workplaces in the surrounding area and poor public transport availability means that some neighbourhoods have higher than average car mode shares (such as Bicester); whereas others with more local employment opportunities and better public transport connections have much greater usage of public transport (Didcot). The spreading of housing allocations across these different settlements produces very uneven travel outcomes.

Robin Hickman and David Banister examine new households in Surrey (UK), using longitudinal analysis to assess the temporal relationships between the built environment, socio-economic characteristics and the commute to work. A residential typology is developed: with 'stayers' (households remaining over the three year survey time period), 'outmovers' (those moving away from the original residence), and 'inmovers' (those moving in). The stayers experience the least transport energy consumption relative to the other cohorts – 9 per cent lower than the sample average in 1998. However, energy consumption increases over time, by 3 per cent from 1998 to 2001. This reflects trends that move in different directions: journey distance and journey time reduce, yet car mode share increases. A number of variables are significantly correlated with transport energy consumption, such as residential population density, distance from London, public transport accessibility and household income. There are important changes over the period 1998–2001, such as the lower residential densities increasing their transport energy consumption and the higher densities reducing their transport energy consumption. Locational and temporal issues thus seem to be a critical feature in the urban structure and travel relationship.

Peter Gordon and Bumsoo Lee assess city size, spatial organization and commuting and non-commuting trends in US metropolitan areas. They ask whether the impacts of the built environment on travel are large enough to justify land-use policies to help influence travel behaviours. The analysis seeks to understand whether metropolitan level spatial restructuring, towards more dispersed forms, is linked to reduced travel times. Average commuting times appear to rise with metropolitan size, but as cities continue to increase in size and sprawl, the commuting time and non-work travel remain fairly static. The locations of homes, workplaces and other activities appear to be chosen for a variety of reasons, including some level of 'mutual accessibility'.

Marcial Echenique and Alastair Donald analyse commuting and non-work travel in Greater London and the south-east of the UK, considering the role of mixed use development and density in reducing travel distance and private car mode share. Residential, employment areas and more mixed residential and employment areas are compared in terms of their travel patterns, including inflows, outflows and total flows. The areas with high employment concentrations attract longer average trip distances for the journey to work (total flows), but there is little difference between suburban and mixed residential/employment areas in terms of trip distance. There is a similar trend for non-work trips and also for mode share – only the high employment concentrations demonstrate a significant public transport mode share. Correlations between density and private car usage are also weak, with the higher employment densities leading to longer trip distances.

Petter Næss gives a more positive view on the urban structure and travel relationships, using case studies of Hangzhou (China) and Copenhagen (Denmark). The case study contexts are of course very different; for example, car ownership and mobility levels in Copenhagen are much greater than in Hangzhou. The location relative to the main centre of the urban area appears to be the most important urban characteristic. An important point is made: that considering the self-selection effect may help underestimate the influence of the built environment on travel. For example, inner cities residents who do not value proximity to public transport, employment or shopping opportunities as criteria for locational choice travel much less by car than suburban respondents who do value these criteria (the dissonance factor). If attitudes were more important than location, we might expect the reverse effect. Travel distances seem to depend more on the location of the dwelling to the main concentration of activities, but are modified by factors such as specialized job skills, leisure interests, 'exclusive' cultural tastes, time availability, etc.

Carey Curtis considers the role of public transport accessibility, alongside changes to the built form, in achieving greater sustainability in travel. A GIS-based accessibility modelling tool is developed and applied in Perth (Australia), assessing centrality, impacts of network modifications, catchment, speed and network connectivity. Activity centres around public transport nodes are then developed – the tool helping to consider which centres should be developed at the regional and local levels and where the public transport investment should be prioritized. Network connectivity and improved service frequencies are seen as critical factors in gaining higher public transport mode shares.

Xinyu (Jason) Cao examines the role of attitudes in the relationship between neighbourhood type and travel (vehicle miles driven), using a case study of Northern California (US). He considers whether people living in walkable neighbourhoods walk more because the built environment 'invites' them to do so, or whether people who like to walk choose these types of neighbourhoods, i.e., he explores the role of the self-selection effect and potential directions of causality. A theoretical model is developed to assess the possible interactions: attitudes as antecedent, intervening or of little or no importance. In reality, there are likely to be multiple directions of causality and, in the North Californian data, the impact of neighbourhood type accounts for 13 per cent of average driving distance after controlling for attitudinal aspects.

Bert van Wee and Patricia Mokhtarian also discuss the role of attitudes, in terms of residential self-selection and travel, arguing that there is heterogeneity between respondents that is not fully captured by socio-economic and demographic variables, and consequently there is always a risk of self-selection based on those other (attitudinal) variables. A number of methodologies that have been used to account for residential self-selection are reviewed. The measurement of attitudes and the relevance of attitude-related self-selection for travel behaviour are discussed, distinguishing between residential choice, other spatial choices (such as work location) and non-spatial choices relevant for travel behaviour. It is suggested that 'perfectly' measuring attitudes might come at a cost of accuracy in measuring travel behaviour or a lower response rate in surveys.

Kevin J. Krizek, Ahmed El-Geneidy and Ryan Wilson use data from the Twin Cities (Minnesota, US) to analyse the consistency of preferences for neighbourhood types among intra-county movers. The analysis employs factor and cluster analysis to define eight neighbourhood types and finds 54 per cent of respondents moving to new neighbourhoods embodied similar features to their previous neighbourhood. The determinants of moves within neighbourhood types are also discussed, together with implications for land use and transportation policy.

Susan Handy examines the evidence on the impact of community design on active travel and finds that various elements, covering functional, aesthetic and natural dimensions, are important in influencing the use of walking and cycling. She also discusses the practical implications, such as asking what policies, investments or mechanisms communities can use to create environments that are more supportive of walking and cycling.

Wesley Marshall, Norman Garrick and Stephen Marshall conclude this section by considering what makes a good street network. The characteristics of street networks are examined relative to the amount of driving by private car, the tendency to walk or bike and levels of community safety and health. A dataset is collected for 24 Californian cities with populations ranging from 30,000 to around 100,000 residents. The analysis asks whether the three fundamental characteristics of street design – street connectivity, street network density and street patterns – are associated with residents driving fewer miles and also walking and cycling more.

PART III   TRANSPORT AND SPATIAL IMPACTS

In Part III, the chapters shift focus to examine the varied perspectives on the spatial impacts of transport investments. Sixteen chapters are presented, with the analysis exploring the debates in the literature from the standpoints of different modes, types of 'impact' and empirical approaches. We can see that most research studies, in this book and in the wider literature, are ex-ante in nature (before the event) and there is little analysis that is ex-post (after the event). Much of the research emphasizes, explicitly or implicitly, that 'development' and 'impact' are perceived mainly in economic terms. This is challenged towards the end of Part III, and continues into Part IV, where a much wider perspective of transport and development is taken. These areas, of course, reflect many of the key debates within the topic of transport and development, i.e., what is meant by development and how this might be effectively measured.

The first chapter, from Piet Rietveld and Frank Bruinsma, gives a brief historical overview of transport as a main driving force in urban development, and revisits the theory on how transport (investments) could affect spatial change and economic development. They highlight the challenge of determining the spatial scale at which impacts are measured, since, in most cases, what might be a positive development impact at a certain (local) scale is potentially a redistribution impact when looked at on a wider scale (regional or national). The impacts from transport investment can be varied and are likely to be both positive and negative at the same time in different locations. This

creates substantial difficulties in empirical analysis and conflicting results in the literature depending on the assumptions taken in the research.

Michael Iacono and David Levinson examine the basic methods of evaluating the
impacts of transport investment, such as the common use of cost-benefit analysis (CBA)
and the limitation of such approaches, for example when it is obvious that the impacts
will not be confined to the immediate area around the project. They suggest tools used
in regional economic analysis should be applied. Changes in land values may also better
capture the impacts of transport investment to also account for induced demand that
may, in some instances, be seen as a negative impact as it contributes to congestion and
the erosion of the benefits from investments.

Torben Holvad and Steen Leleur review the theoretical and empirical evidence regarding the linkages between transport projects and the economy. They consider the possible
solutions concerning how the wider economic impacts can be integrated into project
appraisal, notably through cost-benefit analysis. The role of computable general equilibrium (CGE) modelling is also highlighted to provide information about the effects of
improved accessibility on the economy.

David Hensher and Zheng Li look at urban freight distribution as a critical part of
the city economy, viewing the biggest challenge facing urban freight distribution as
traffic congestion on roads and at key transfer locations such as ports and consolidation
terminals. The role of government is seen as important to articulate and facilitate the
linkages between short-term and long-term policies on land-use planning, environmental
externalities and the transport task. Within the urban environment, a strategy is required
for the location of rail hubs serving the road–rail interface, focused on integrated multimodal service provision.

Eran Feitelson and Orit Rotem-Mindali consider the role of public transport
investments in metropolitan areas and ask to what extent there is an effect on the car-
dominated metropolitan structure. They briefly review the historical timeline of rail and
suburban development, and comment on the current empirical difficulties in assessing
the impacts of light rapid transit (LRT) and bus rapid transit (BRT) schemes in a car-
dominated landscape. The evidence of impacts is mixed, with little impact at the macro
scale, and impacts mostly occurring at the micro level, in close proximity to stations. Any
effects, however, are determined by local economic trends, the socio-economic structure
of the area, the associated planning strategy, the existing built stock and the physical
context around stations. Hence, the micro effects vary between cities, different parts of
the city, different sections of the LRT or BRT corridor and by different types of activity.

Chia-Lin Chen and Peter Hall present a comparative analysis of the wider impacts of
high-speed trains (HSTs) in Britain and France, asking whether, to what extent, and in
what ways, HSTs could reduce inter- and intra-regional inequality. A review of the literature finds that the contradictory evidence is often due to the specificities of the context
and that understanding the interregional competition between cities is particularly difficult, and poorly understood, as many of the benefits are relative in nature. Qualitative
in-depth interviews and policy analysis offer insights into the wider spatial-economic
outcomes. A number of critical factors are suggested for the differential effects, including the national political economy (the perception and exploitation of the HST opportunity, macro economy), governance approaches (level of devolved decision-making,
resource allocation and financial levers available), planning approach (including level of

integration between development and transport investment), local political leadership and city type (local economy, employment sectors, city attractiveness and competition). The contrast between the UK's market-led approach and the French interventionist approach is examined and proves highly instructive, with very different impacts following the transport investments.

Peter Jones provides a rare example of ex-post analysis of transport investment, reporting on an in-depth study of the wider impacts of the Jubilee Line Extension (JLE) in East London (UK). The JLE is an interesting example, built despite a low cost-benefit ratio, largely for the aspiration of supporting regeneration in East London. The real challenge in such analysis is not only to measure and quantify the impacts that have followed, but to estimate the counterfactual (what would have happened without the project) and to attribute causation to the transport intervention. A range of impacts are examined, including: transport and accessibility changes; residential and commercial development, land value; employment and changes in the economy; and impacts on incumbent and migrant residents and their travel patterns. The evidence suggests that the JLE has raised land values and property prices in the surrounding area and has stimulated faster development than might otherwise have been expected. But, there was little positive impact on employment among the incumbent populations, either in terms of higher levels or in the character of employment (occupation and industry); instead, aggregate benefits are largely the result of the different profile arising from in-movers. A long lead time is required to assess many impacts; for example, several decades might be required to allow the full effects of the project on land-use patterns.

Lucia Mejia-Dorantes uses a spatial-statistical approach with micro-level data to evaluate the effects of Madrid's (Spain) Metrosur expansion on retail businesses location patterns. The analysis uses point pattern density surfaces to show where firms have increased or decreased their levels of activity. It is argued that the increase in accessibility brought about by the new Metro line is not associated with an increase in retail activity around the station areas, although the probability of location of economic activity is greater in Getafe and Leganes relative to Fuenlabrada. Much of this may be due to the location of Fuenlabrada, which is the furthest from the centre of Madrid.

Darío Hidalgo and Juan Carlos Muñoz provide a global overview of the development of bus rapid transit (BRT) and bus of high level of service (BHLS), rapidly emerging in practice in South America and Asia, with more limited experience in Africa, North America and Europe. The commentary includes the well-known upgrade of busways in Curitiba, Brazil, to fully specified BRT in 1982, and the implementation of TransMilenio in Bogotá, Colombia, in 2000; and also the wider global experience from cities such Jakarta and Guangzhou. In 2014, there were around 180 cities with BRT or similar types of systems globally, serving more than 31.5 million passengers per day, with 152 cities developing systems since 2001 – an incredible growth in the past decade or so. The transport benefits of the systems are made clear – in terms of reliability, comfort and low-cost urban mobility. There are also impacts in developmental terms, with some studies citing development pattern and land value changes, although the evidence here is much less, and the causal chains often unclear or indirect.

Andrew R. Goetz examines the growth in air passenger and cargo transport as a major element of global commerce, including air-based tourism, trade, logistics and producer services. He considers the developmental impact of Denver International Airport, reflecting the wider aspiration of many cities to develop the 'aerotropolis' model of new poles of economic activities and development around their airports. Thus airports not only connect cities and provide accessibility to markets, placing them on the global map; they can also become hubs for new city development, with enlarged agglomeration economies. While this impact is noticeable in the many expanding aerotropolises, and is generally viewed positively in economic terms, there are major concerns over the environmental sustainability of these airport cities, and these problems have yet to be resolved.

Chantal C. Cantarelli and Bent Flyvbjerg consider the decision-making process for major infrastructure projects, examining the high level of 'misinformation' concerning the estimation of costs and benefits in the appraisal of projects. They discuss the problems involved with this process of misinformation and the potential reasons for this happening. They examine how mega-project performance, in terms of the accuracy of the cost forecast, is influenced by project ownership (with the private or the public sector as promoters). They conclude that ownership is not a significant issue in project performance, and that there is little evidence that private projects perform better than public ones. A case study of the HSL-South railway line in the Netherlands demonstrates that the contracting strategy and the amount of private financing are better determinants of project performance. Again, there is seen to be a relative scarcity of ex-post analysis, with economic and wider dimensions, for transport investments.

The issue of externalities, and mainly those related to congestion, are central in the chapter by Jan Anne Annema, who considers how effective the various road pricing schemes are in 'reducing' congestion and thus can alleviate some of the negative impacts of investing in road infrastructure. The various international studies of road pricing schemes are compared, with a marked difference in results demonstrated according to context and methodological approach. Experience in the Netherlands is then examined, and despite the apparent effectiveness of some of the potential pricing schemes (some more than others), the long and difficult political struggle with road pricing in the Netherlands and the accompanying controversy has still not resulted in implementation of any of the potential approaches. This angle in the debate on the spatial development impacts of transport investments connects back to the first chapter in the section, where Rietveld and Bruinsma suggest there is evidence that political considerations, such as the desire to be re-elected, can be a main driving force behind investment decisions.

Gordon Stokes widens the consideration of 'impacts' from transport, examining the relationship between travel behaviour and poverty. In particular, he argues that low incomes and poor accessibility can lead to disproportionate spending on transport to access basic services or to suppression of some trips. He notes that low-income people, on average, travel less than those on higher incomes and are much less likely to have access to cars. However, the link between (lack of) transport and poverty is not straightforward to assess, since poverty is influenced by an array of factors. Nevertheless, there is evidence that poorer people in rural areas (and other areas without travel alternatives) suffer through reliance on cars when they have difficulty affording them. Accessibility planning is offered as an approach to help consider the equity dimension within transport, alongside more effective public transport provision, land-use planning to ensure transport poverty is not 'built in' to lifestyles and innovative means of car access, such as car clubs and car share schemes, for areas which remain with low public transport accessibility.

Susan Kenyon considers the role of transport in social development. The discourses of 'too little mobility' and 'too much mobility' are explored relative to their impacts on social well-being. A case study of access to education in the UK is used to demonstrate how important transport and mobility can be to participation and to the educational experience. It is argued that the link is sometimes so strong that transport must be considered as a social policy in some cases – with inadequate transport often acting as a barrier to the improvement of social well-being.

Iqbal Hamiduddin reviews the impact of the car at the neighbourhood scale. First, the history of the Garden City Movement (UK), and competing approaches such as found in Radburn (New Jersey, US), are reviewed in terms of their treatment of the car and the design of the street. Second, case studies in Freiburg and Tübingen (Germany) are explored, including the use of mixed use development, pedestrian and cycling priority, high-quality public realm and 'home zones', good public transport access, reduced car parking provision and also the Baugruppe approach to development (community-designed housing), all of which encourage very strong community bonds within the neighbourhoods examined.

Karst Geurs and Derek Halden conclude the section with a review of accessibility planning, in theory and practice, in the Netherlands and UK. Accessibility can be measured in a number of ways, including location-based, person-based and utility-based measures. Various levels of disaggregation can also be employed, either spatially or by population cohort, and levels of accessibility can also be related to policy objectives, such as social goals. In practice, in the Netherlands, there has been a gradual move from using accessibility indicators covering the transport provider perspective (e.g., the transport performance of infrastructure links) to a 'transport user' perspective (e.g., travel time and delay). In the UK, accessibility indicators have become central to transport planning appraisal since the late 1990s, often as a means of measuring progress against social objectives such as regeneration. The choice of accessibility measures (and the manner in which the evidence is used) strongly affects the related strategies and investments and, consequently, the impacts of accessibility changes on the spatial economy and social change. Hence, as always, the empirical approach used in the research remains critical to results.

PART IV   WIDER DIMENSIONS IN TRANSPORT AND DEVELOPMENT

Part IV contains 14 chapters examining wider dimensions that may affect the transport and development relationship, as previously conceived. The chapters explore the wider non-physical context that influences mobility patterns, such as the means by which society and culture might impact on travel, or how changes in technology, such as e-commerce, may influence the need for travel. Each of these themes represents new analytical challenges to transport researchers. The chapters reveal research that intersects with economic, demographic and wider social concerns related to, mainly, personal travel. As with the previous sections, Part IV reveals the breadth of academic research within the transport and development field, covering transport geography, sociology, economics and wider disciplines.

The first chapter, from Ole B. Jensen, opens by highlighting the key issue that travel is more than a 'derived demand' – that there is more to travel than the 'journey from A to B'. He reviews the emerging research on mobilities, including features such as culture, affect, habits, norms and emotions; hence widening our understanding of the potential rationales for travel. This is compared to the more conventional standpoints within transport planning, of rational choice in movement and reducing friction (in distance, time and cost). 'Staging mobilities' are discussed – the proposition that mobilities are staged from above in planning and regulation terms, and below from everyday life. The debate is thus widened greatly, to help us understand that there are built environment impacts on travel, that travel has impacts spatially and over time – but also that there are greater psychological, sociological and cultural contexts to travel and development.

Ellen Matthies and Christian A. Klöckner explore the phenomenon of habit in travel behaviour, arguing that 'car-fixation' is a possible explanation for the limited success in reducing car usage. Cognitive mechanisms for habitual behaviours are discussed, including possibilities of script-based and connectionist processes. Socialization processes (early influences, family, school, media and peer group) appear to contribute to car-fixation, and particular groups of car users are more prone to fixation than others (e.g., men more than women, those living in rural areas more than urban). Strategies for preventing and overcoming car fixation, drawing again from psychological models, are also proposed, including situational changes (e.g., moving home or employment location) or temporary interventions to break habitual use (e.g., free travel card for public transport).

Galit Cohen-Blankshtain examines the role of information and communication technologies (ICTs) and their potential for changing travel behaviours, including the substitution of physical travel but also modification and generation. The 'death of distance' hypothesis is explored, with telecommuting replacing commuting and e-retailing replacing walk-in retailing. The potential conclusion is that ICT networks might play the same role in the twenty-first century that streets and highways played in the twentieth century – with ICTs changing the shape of the city similar to the private car in earlier years. However, the 'friction reducing' effects of ICTs are largely discounted, for two main reasons: ICTs are being introduced into the car-dependent city and do not directly replace the role of the private car. In addition, different technologies tend to have varied effects on travel behaviour. For example, mobile phones tend to compliment face-to-face activities, while the Internet substitutes some physical activities. In recent years, the technologies have merged, hence the smartphone allows both functions. The relationships are hence complex and evolving over time.

Orit Rotem-Mindali develops an analysis of e-retailing (both business to consumer, B2C, and consumer to consumer, C2C) and its impact on travel. She considers the recent locational and organizational changes in retailing, from small retail stores in inner urban locations to larger footprint out-of-town stores – and perhaps back again as fuel prices rise, e-retailing becomes more frequently used and the out-of-town bulk shop becomes less popular. The travel behaviour implications are often complex and heavily dependent on the context. For example, the mode and trip distance of the 'original' shopping trip and any substitution activities are important to estimates the change in transport energy consumption. The take up of e-retailing is also heavily dependent on the type of product and the consumer; indeed there is some evidence that a greater use of the Internet and e-shopping online is also associated with more shopping trips.

Robyn Dowling focuses on automobilities and travel with children, perceiving the private motor car as a 'daily management' tool, an important facilitator in managing family life, and deeply associated with aspirations for and relationships with children. The car is used to facilitate 'good parenting', particularly during the school run, with the car used to access educational and other activities, and enable busy schedules. The time in the car is often seen as family time. Much of this discussion perhaps reflects the Australian context, which is reported on, where there is often little alternative to the car to access activities. The objective of good mothering is so highly valued by some respondents that many were willing to make considerable sacrifices for its achievement, including, for example, overlooking any disenchantment with driving as an activity.

Randi Hjorthol and Susanne Nordbakke take a different angle, assessing car driving patterns among the older population, including the often critical role of the car in accessing everyday activities. Using National Travel Survey cohort data from Norway, Denmark and Sweden, they focus on lifecycle changes and find that the growth in the elderly population will influence mobility patterns in Europe considerably. They use in-depth interviews and surveys to further examine the perceived utility of the car for older people, asking whether use of the car contributes to well-being and whether the car/ability to drive has an impact on participation in activities that generate well-being. For example, the loss of the use of the car in later life often leads to reductions in freedom, independence, the pleasure of driving and control of life.

Gamze Dane, Anna Grigolon, Soora Rasouli, Harry Timmermans and Dujuan Yang explore activity participation, vacations, travel behaviours and travel expenditures of the elderly in the Netherlands. The analyses suggest that the elderly (over 65 years of age) have less 'compulsory' activity-travel behaviour (i.e., working), although for maintenance and leisure activities, both travel time and travel distances are slightly higher than the overall average. Travel time and travel distance of ageing people by car is higher for compulsory activities, but these mobility indicators decrease rapidly with increasing age. The start time of activities of the ageing population is later than average, except for maintenance activities. Hence, as constraints and commitments are relaxed (such as travelling to work), activity-travel patterns become more flexible and tend to shift to off-peak hours.

Jago Dodson, Neil Sipe and Terry Li explore the problem of combined volatile oil prices and housing mortgage cost pressures within a large, dispersed city region, using Brisbane, Australia, as a case study. The problem of 'oil vulnerability' is examined, i.e., the socio-economic exposure of households to rising oil and motor vehicle fuel prices, based on their socio-economic status, car-dependence and access to alternative modes. Using two indices of vulnerability, the distributional impact of higher oil prices is shown to be greater for lower-income households, with high levels of car dependence and relatively poorer access to alternative travel modes such as public transport – and often these households are concentrated in the suburbs.

Erling Holden and Kristin Linnerud explore the difficult problem that sustainable passenger transport policies are most often directed towards everyday travel, but ignore the large and expanding amount of leisure travel. They examine whether policies aimed at reducing energy consumption and CO_2 emissions for everyday travel may have an opposite effect on leisure travel by assessing the impacts of three sustainable passenger transport policies: developing more compact cities, building pro-environment awareness and attitudes, and promoting the growth of information and communication technologies. It is found that the policies used may indeed have unintended effects. Several mechanisms, such as moral accounting, are suggested that might explain why this occurs. The potential for developing more comprehensive sustainable transport policies is also considered, including limiting densification policies and improving environmental awareness among the population.

Mayer Hillman reminds us that the spreading and intensifying addiction to fossil fuel-dependent lifestyles around the world will inevitably lead to huge ecological problems from climate change. Current policymaking and patterns of development will not deliver the very low-carbon footprints essential to preventing such problems. It is argued that a large-scale programme to educate the public on the links between energy-intensive lifestyles and carbon emissions is required, alongside the introduction of personal carbon allowances and a cap on aggregate emissions – the latter shared equally on a per capita basis globally, and following contraction and convergence principles. Finally, that all of us have a responsibility to make the necessary changes to our lifestyles to limit the impacts of climate change on the planet. In particular, professions such as transport and urban planning have a critical role to play.

Harry Geerlings and Flor Avelino examine the role of transition management, as a new mode of governance that may help move towards sustainable development, involving a transformation process in which society changes in a fundamental way over a generation or more. A case study from the Dutch transport sector is used: the Transumo A15-Maasvlakte sustainable freight project. The multi-level perspective is employed, including the different scales of landscape (macro-level), regime (meso-level) and niche (micro-level). Consideration is given to understanding the likely 'frontrunners': individuals that are 'ahead' with developing new structures, cultures and practices in sustainable transport – and then to scaling these up wherever this is possible. The case study demonstrates the difficulty that many important stakeholders seem to be locked into conventional visions on port and business development, and that it is difficult to find leaders of change in such contexts.

Helmut Holzapfel and Rainer Meyfahrt examine the renaissance of the regional tram-train system in Kassel, Germany, and in particular consider the importance of strong regional government in delivery. Responsibility for planning, the fare system and the design of transport schemes was transferred to regional institutions from the 1970s onwards in Kassel, and the RegioTram was gradually expanded and enhanced. The process, however, was difficult, involving the coordination of many different interests within local, regional, national and transnational institutions, including with Deutsche Bahn. The investment has had a large impact on the redevelopment of central Kassel and the wider region – strengthening the functions of the central city (including education, administration, higher order shopping) and promoted accessibility to the smaller municipalities throughout the region.

Dominic Stead discusses the development of transport policy at the European Union level, from the 1950s to the present date. There have been a number of treaties (Paris, Rome, Amsterdam, Lisbon) and attempts to develop a common European transport policy, but this been difficult to agree at the national level, with many different perspectives, priorities and interests proving impossible to bring together. Key dilemmas are discussed within European transport policy, such as the reconciliation of the free movement of people and goods, one of the basic pillars of the European Union, while at the same time protecting the environment and improving the health and safety of citizens. Major initiatives and investments, such as the liberalization of transport markets and investment in the Trans-European Transport Network, are highlighted as emerging from lobbying efforts from industry organizations, often with little regard for sustainability ambitions, and leading to a major focus on road-building.

Tim Schwanen brings Part IV to a close in assessing the practice of transport research in terms of the dynamics of relationships. Reflecting on the philosophy of Alfred Whitehead, it is argued that understanding temporality is critical to research on transport and development. The conventional practice of drawing inferences from cross-sectional data is often problematic, with assumptions made on relationships staying current or changing in a linear fashion, replicating closed systems, with very simple cause and effect relationships – and often leading to the 'fallacy of misplaced concreteness'. For example, understanding the use of a car, the competency required for cycling, a pro-environmental attitude, or the environmental, social or economic impacts of investment, cannot be assigned to a specifiable point in space and time. This critiques much of the previous research in this area, for these are the assumptions that are made in much of the work, and there are important implications that lead from this. However, a direction forward for research is also offered: exploring process and the different ways of understanding this, might help us to develop a deeper understanding of the transport and development field in future years.

PART V   SUMMARY AND CONCLUSIONS

In Part V, the final chapter brings the edited collection to a close, attempting to synthesize a very wide-ranging field, including the changes experienced in urban development – in retrospect and also in prospect. Comments are made on the development of the research field in transport and development over the past 30 years, and the potential avenues forward.

This edited book hence forms an extensive review of the debate surrounding the transport and development topic. We are delighted to have assembled such a fine collection of authors, and we think this is a remarkable collection of different, often competing, viewpoints that sit happily side-by-side, competing for attention. We have journeyed a long way in understanding how urban development might interact with travel and how transport might interact with urban development – and the varied forms in-between. We hope you enjoy the debate, and of course you can decide which positions you agree with, to what extent and for how long – before you modify your views.

REFERENCES

Miller, A. ([1949] 2000), *Death of a Salesman*, London: Penguin Books.
Oxford English Dictionary (2014), Oxford: Oxford University Press, www.oed.com (accessed December 2014).

PART II

URBAN STRUCTURE AND TRAVEL

2   Urban structure and travel
Philip Stoker, Susan Petheram and Reid Ewing

1.   INTRODUCTION

Does urban structure influence travel? The theory of environmental or architectural determinism ascribes great importance to the physical environment as a determinant of travel behavior. The counter view is that social and economic factors are the main, or even exclusive, drivers of travel behavior. If urban structure plays a role in determining travel behavior patterns, then the way we design and build neighborhoods, cities, and regions are contributing factors.

The degree to which urban structure determines human travel behavior, however, remains a long-running debate in urban planning research. Recent and historic advances reflect the complexity of the relationship between urban structure and travel. This chapter presents a review of the literature, major findings, remaining questions, and conclusions. We first synthesize findings regarding the impacts of urban structure on travel at the regional (macro) scale, followed by those at the neighborhood (mezzo) scale. The hypothesis of this chapter is decidedly environmental and deterministic in its outlook: urban structure significantly influences travel. The objective of synthesizing the historic and current literature is to offer perspectives on the scale of urban structure's influence and the conditions under which its impact is greatest. While most of the literature and examples are from the US, relevant international literature is drawn upon when available, including studies from the United Kingdom and Australia.

The potential to moderate travel demand by changing the built environment has become one of the most heavily researched subjects in urban planning. Since just 2000, there are at least 14 surveys of the literature on urban structure and travel (Badoe and Miller, 2000; Brownstone 2008; Cao et al., 2009; Cervero, 2003; Crane, 2000; Ewing and Cervero, 2001; Handy et al., 2005; Heath et al., 2006; McMillan, 2005, 2007; Pont et al., 2009; Saelens et al., 2003; Salon et al., 2012; Stead and Marshall, 2001). There are another 14 surveys of the literature on the built environment and physical activity, including walking and biking (Badland and Schofield, 2005; Cunningham and Michael, 2004; Frank, 2000; Frank and Engelke, 2001; Humpel et al., 2002; Kahn et al., 2002; Krahnstoever-Davison and Lawson, 2006; Lee and Moudon, 2004; McCormack et al., 2004; National Research Council, 2005; Owen et al., 2004; Saelens and Handy, 2008; Trost et al., 2002; Wendel-Vos et al., 2004). Considerable overlap is present among these reviews, particularly where they share authorship. The literature is now so vast it has produced three reviews of the many reviews (Bauman and Bull, 2007; Gebel et al., 2007; Ding and Gebel, 2012).

2.   URBAN STRUCTURE AT THE REGIONAL SCALE

The costs and benefits of one development pattern versus another are of ultimate interest to urban planners. While there may be no inherently good or bad patterns, the outcomes related to development patterns have been shown to be either positive or negative. These outcomes include travel behavior and associated environmental costs, as well as physical health and well-being.

At the regional scale, development patterns are often characterized as either sprawling or compact. As the costs of sprawl have become more apparent, the term "urban sprawl" (or "suburban sprawl") has been transformed from an urban planning construct to a matter of popular concern.

In the early 1990s, four prototypical urban form patterns characterizing sprawl were developed as the state of Florida tackled growth management issues and desired a definition of sprawl (Ewing, 1997). The definition included the following four urban form patterns (see Figure 2.1): (1) leapfrog or scattered development, (2) commercial strip development, (3) expanses of low-density development, or (4) expanses of single-use development (as in sprawling bedroom communities). The definition was supplemented with two primary indicators of sprawl that could be measured and made subject to regulation for growth management purposes. The indicators included: (1) poor accessibility

(1) Leapfrog or scattered development   (2) Commercial strip development

(3) Expanses of low-density development   (4) Expanses of single-use development

Figure 2.1   Four prototypical sprawl patterns

and (2) lack of functional open space. All four prototypical patterns are character-ized by these two indicators and the potential link to travel is clear. In sprawl, poor accessibility between land uses may leave residents with no alternative but to travel by automobile.

However, even the specificity of Florida's regulatory definitions fell short of an opera-tional definition of sprawl. Before something can be studied quantitatively, it must be measured. So it was with sprawl.

3.   EARLY ATTEMPTS TO MEASURE SPRAWL

Around 2000, researchers began to measure sprawl. The early attempts to measure the extent of urban sprawl were crude. Several researchers created measures of urban sprawl that focused on density (Fulton et al., 2001; Malpezzi and Guo, 2001; Nasser and Overberg, 2001; Lopez and Hynes, 2003; Burchfield et al., 2005). Density, as a measure of sprawl, has the advantage of being easy to quantify with available data. Population density is relatively easy to measure, and hence served as the sole indicator of sprawl in several studies.

Three notable features characterized these early sprawl studies. The most notable feature was their failure to define sprawl in all its complexity. The Florida definition has four elements, and others have defined sprawl even more broadly (Burchell et al., 2002).

A second notable feature of these studies was the wildly different sprawl ratings given to different metropolitan areas by different analysts. With the exception of Atlanta, which always seems to rank as one of the worst, the different variables used to opera-tionalize sprawl led to very different results. For example, in one study Portland was listed as the most compact region and Los Angeles was ranked among the most sprawl-ing. In another, their rankings were essentially reversed (Glaeser et al., 2001; Nasser and Overberg, 2001). If average population density is all you are measuring, Los Angeles looks compact; it is the endless, uniform character of LA's density that makes it seem so sprawling.

A third notable feature of the studies was how little attention was paid to the impacts of sprawl. With the exception of a few studies focusing on individual outcomes, sprawl was either presumed to have negative impacts or presumed to be free of them, depending on the viewpoint of the author.

4.   REFINED MEASURES OF SPRAWL

The unsatisfying results of these studies led some scholars to develop more complete measures of urban sprawl. Galster et al. (2001) disaggregated land-use patterns into eight dimensions: density, continuity, concentration, clustering, centrality, nuclearity, hetero-geneity (mixing), and proximity. The researchers operationally defined each dimension and successfully quantified six of the eight measures for 13 urbanized areas. Sprawl was defined as a pattern of land use with low values in one or more of these dimensions. New York and Philadelphia ranked as the least sprawling of the 13, and Atlanta and Miami as the most sprawling.

Since then, Galster and his colleagues have extended their sprawl measures to more than 50 metropolitan areas, confirming the multidimensional nature of sprawl. In one study, they ranked metropolitan areas using 14 different dimensions measuring both jobs and housing (Cutsinger et al. 2005). However, the 14 dimensions, reduced to seven factors through principal component analysis, tended to cancel each other out. Metropolitan areas ranking near the top on one factor were likely to rank near the bottom on another. Los Angeles, for example, ranked second on both "mixed use" and "housing centrality," but 48th on "proximity" and 49th on "nuclearity." With so many overlapping variables, the analysis became confused.

Ewing, Pendall, and Chen (2003a) also developed sprawl indices that, like Galster's, were multidimensional, but were more focused and demonstrated wider degrees of variability among metropolitan areas. They defined sprawl as any environment with the following four factors: (1) a population widely dispersed in low-density residential development; (2) a rigid separation of homes, shops, and workplaces; (3) a lack of major employment and population concentrations downtown and in suburban town centers and other activity centers; and (4) a network of roads marked by very large block sizes and poor access from one place to another.

These conceptual definitions were operationalized using principal component analysis, which extracted common factors from multiple measurements of each construct. The result of this effort is a set of four sprawl factors for 83 of the nation's largest metropolitan areas. All four factors were standardized with mean values of 100 and standard deviations of 25. The factors are:

> *denfac – density factor* for 2000 (a weighted combination of seven density variables)
> *mixfac – mix factor* for 2000 (a weighted combination of six mixed-use variables)
> *cenfac – centers factor* for 2000 (a weighted combination of six center-related variables)
> *strfac – streets factor* for 2000 (a weighted combination of three street-related variables)

These four factors were combined to create and overall compactness/sprawl index, also standardized with a mean value of 100 and standard deviation of 25.

> *index* – overall compactness/sprawl index (linear sum of four sprawl factors)

Using these composite measures, the more compact a metropolitan region, the larger its index value. More sprawling metropolitan regions had smaller index values. Thus, in the year 2000, the relatively compact Portland, Oregon metropolitan area had an index value of 126, while the slightly smaller Raleigh-Durham metropolitan area had an index value of 54 (see Figure 2.2). Los Angeles ended up near the middle of the 83 metropolitan regions classified, with an index of 102.

Source: www.maps.google.com

Figure 2.2   Aerial images of Portland and Raleigh at the same scale

5.   RELATIONSHIP OF SPRAWL TO TRANSPORTATION OUTCOMES

With sprawl indices in hand, Ewing et al. (2003a) studied the relationship between sprawl, as they measured it, and a set of transportation outcome measures (Table 2.1). The outcome measures were:

Table 2.1   Transportation outcomes vs. sprawl factors (2000)

	Transportation outcomes							
	vehph	*transhr*	*walkshr*	*mntime*	*dlycap*	*vmtcap*	*facap*	*oz8h*
constant	−0.382	−14.11	0.566	4.77	−119.4	2.24	20.16	0.112
denfac	−0.00534	0.118	0.0315	−0.0245	−0.110	−0.215	−0.105	−0.0006
	(−4.7)***	(3.9)***	(2.6)**	(−0.9)	(−0.9)	(−3.0)**	(−2.5)*	(−3.8)***
mixfac	0.000659	−0.00924	0.00046	−0.0242	0.00728	0.00023	−0.041	0.00012
	(1.5)	(−0.8)	(0.1)	(−2.2)*	(0.2)	(0.0)	(−2.5)*	(2.0)*
cenfac	−0.00117	0.0351	0.0199	−0.0181	−0.110	−0.0462	−0.037	−0.00012
	(−2.7)**	(3.0)**	(4.3)***	(−1.6)	(−2.2)*	(−2.0)	(−2.3)*	(−1.9)
strfac	0.000492	0.00347	−0.00272	0.0424	0.130	0.0128	0.0149	−0.00014
	(0.9)	(0.2)	(−0.5)	(3.2)**	(3.0)**	(0.5)	(0.8)	(−2.0)
metpop	−1.5E-08	4.64E-07	−1.7E-08	8.53E-07	2.05E-06	8.72E-07	−9.4E-08	4.27E-09
	(−1.7)	(2.0)*	(−0.2)	(4.0)***	(2.2)*	(1.6)	(−0.3)	(3.5)***
hhsize	0.412	−1.68	−0.678	4.32	14.77	1.76	0.667	0.00305
	(7.0)***	(−1.1)	(−1.1)	(3.0)**	(2.9)**	(0.6)	(0.3)	(0.4)
pwkage	0.0246	−0.0207	−0.0268	0.0576	1.47	0.667	0.226	0.00047
	(4.5)***	(−0.1)	(−0.5)	(0.4)	(3.0)**	(2.4)*	(1.1)	(0.6)
pcinc	4.06E-06	0.00036	2.6E-05	0.00029	0.00075	3.01E-06	−0.00032	6.22E-08
	(1.2)	(4.0)***	(0.7)	(3.4)***	(2.0)	(0.0)	(−2.6)*	(0.1)
adjusted R2	0.56	0.67	0.36	0.61	0.63	0.28	0.44	0.40

Note:
  *   .05 probability level
 **   .01 probability level
***   .001 probability level

vehph – average vehicles per household
transhr – percentage of commuters using public transportation (including taxi)
walkshr – percentage of commuters walking to work
mntime – mean journey-to-work time in minutes
dlycap – annual hours of delay per capita
vmtcap – daily VMT per capita
facap – annual highway fatalities per 100,000 persons
oz8h – fourth highest daily maximum eight-hour average ozone level

Control variables included:

metpop – metropolitan area population (MSA or PMSA)
hhsize – average household size for the metro area
pwkage – percentage of population of working age in the metro area (20–64 years)
pcinc – per capita income in the metro area

At first, all four sprawl factors were included in the analysis. Each outcome was regressed on the four factors plus the standard set of control variables. Results for 2000 are presented in Table 2.1. Regression coefficients and t-statistics appear across from their respective independent variables (with the t-statistics in parentheses). Adjusted R^2 statistics appear at the bottom of the table.

The strongest and most significant variable related to travel and transportation outcomes was the *density factor*. It had a significant inverse relationship to average vehicle ownership, VMT per capita, traffic fatality rate, and maximum ozone level, and a significant direct relationship to public transportation and walk shares of commute trips. To illustrate the importance of the density relationships, consider that a 25-unit increase in the *density factor* is associated with a 2.95 percentage point rise (25 × 0.118) in public transportation mode share on the journey to work. Each additional increase in standard deviation increases public transportation mode share by almost 3 percentage points. Intuitively, this makes sense; low-density metropolitan areas cannot support public transportation to the same degree that dense metropolitan areas can.

The second most important factor for travel outcomes was the *centers factor*. Metropolitan areas with clearly defined centers, as opposed to un-centered low-density development, were related to lower annual delay per capita and traffic fatality rate, while directly related to higher public transportation and walk shares of commute trips.

Surprisingly, land-use mix did not significantly affect public transportation or walk mode shares for commute trips. The *mix factor* was significant in only three cases, as a mitigating influence on travel time to work and fatal accidents, and an aggravating influence on the maximum ozone level. There are two possible explanations, related to one another. Perhaps land-use mix was not successfully operationalized due to problems with the underlying datasets. Alternatively, land-use mix may have been successfully operationalized, but at a scale inappropriate for walk trips.

The *streets factor* was just barely significant in only two cases (average travel for commute trips and annual traffic delay per capita) and with unexpected signs. Higher values of this factor correspond to finer meshed street networks, and shorter travel times and less delay was expected. The potential for shorter trips is one argument (made by New Urbanists and

Table 2.2   Transportation outcomes vs. overall sprawl index (2000)

	vehph	transhr	walkshr	mntime	dlycap	vmtcap	facap	oz8h
				Transportation outcomes				
constant	−0.117	−19.9	−0.543	−0.281	−103.3	−0.452	16.13	0.162
index	−0.0019	0.0568	0.0219	−0.0170	−0.027	−0.079	−0.081	−0.0003
	(−4.2)***	(4.8)***	(4.8)***	(−1.6)	(−0.6)	(−3.6)***	(−5.4)***	(−4.9)***
metpop	−3.4E-08	8.82E-07	3.16E-08	9.48E-07	2.84E-06	3.74E-07	−4.0E-07	1.51E-09
	(−4.6)***	(4.7)***	(0.4)	(5.4)***	(3.1)**	(0.8)	(−1.6)	(1.5)
hhsize	0.306	0.959	−0.128	4.10	11.96	−2.51	−2.54	−0.012
	(5.3)***	(0.6)	(−0.2)	(2.9)**	(2.4)*	(−0.9)	(−1.3)	(−1.5)
wkage	0.0215	0.0516	0.00456	0.144	1.18	0.707	0.371	−6.8E-05
	(3.9)***	(0.4)	(0.1)	(1.1)	(2.4)*	(2.8)**	(2.0)*	(−0.1)
pcinc	−6E-07	0.000476	4.3E-05	0.00027	0.000807	−0.00016	−0.0005	−6.1E-07
	(−0.2)	(5.9)***	(1.4)	(3.6)***	(2.2)*	(−1.0)	(−4.8)***	(−1.4)
adjusted R2	0.43	0.59	0.22	0.51	0.52	0.21	0.41	0.24

Note:
* .05 probability level
** .01 probability level
*** .001 probability level

others) for development of dense, interconnected street networks. Interestingly, the simple correlations between the streets factors and transportation outcomes were significant and had the expected signs. However, when the density factor was controlled, the correlation between the two factors caused the signs on the streets factor to flip and street accessibility to become insignificant. Such is the dominance of the density factor.

Ewing et al. (2003a) also regressed each of the outcome variables on the overall compactness/sprawl index, plus the standard set of control variables (Table 2.2). The overall compactness/sprawl index showed strong and statistically significant relationships to six outcome variables. All relationships were in the expected directions. As the index increases (compactness increases), average vehicle ownership, daily VMT per capita, annual traffic fatality rate, and maximum ozone level decrease to a significant extent. At the same time, shares of work trips by transit and walk modes increase to a significant extent.

It is generally assumed that larger metropolitan regions generate long commute trips and high levels of traffic congestion. However, the index did not show a significant relationship to either average commute time or annual travel delay per capita after controlling for population size and the other socio-demographic variables. Gordon and Richardson (1997) offer arguments for why a relationship between each of these two variables and sprawl are not significant. Further discussion on this perspective can be found in Chapter 6 of this *Handbook*, authored by Gordon and Lee.

6.   OTHER COSTS OF SPRAWL

The term "sprawl" has been so heavily researched precisely because of documented negative outcomes related to those types of development patterns. These extend beyond travel behavior to physical health and well-being.

Since development of the index, sprawl, as measured by Ewing et al. (2003a), has been linked to lower physical activity, higher obesity, worsened air quality, higher residential energy use, longer emergency response times, lower social capital, and other outcomes (Ewing et al., 2003b, 2003c, 2006; Kelly-Schwartz et al., 2004; Sturm and Cohen, 2004; Cho et al., 2006; Doyle et al., 2006; Kahn, 2006; Plantinga and Bernell, 2007; Ewing and Rong, 2008; Joshu et al., 2008; Stone, 2008; Trowbridge and McDonald, 2008; Fan and Song, 2009; Trowbridge et al., 2009; Lee et al., 2009; Nguyen, 2010; Stone et al., 2010; Schweitzer and Zhou, 2010; Zolnik, 2011).

Similar to academics in transportation and urban planning, public health researchers relate physical activity, rather than travel, to features of urban structure such as accessibility to parks (Kaczynski and Henderson, 2007); street characteristics (Heath et al., 2006) and connectivity of streets (Frank and Engelke, 2005). These reviews of published papers in public health stress the importance of further study yet conclude that physical activity is associated with the built environment, and accessibility to parks and destinations can have an impact on physical activity. The most frequently reported correlates for physical activity are a combination of urban structure and travel factors: traffic speed/volume, access/proximity to recreation facilities, mixed land use, residential density, and walkability as well as land-use mix and residential density (Ding et al., 2011).

7.   URBAN STRUCTURE AT THE NEIGHBORHOOD LEVEL

The urban structure of sprawl and the previously presented measures of it are tailored to larger areas, such as metropolitan areas and counties. For smaller areas, such as neighborhoods, corresponding urban structure measures are characterized by words starting with the letter D. The term "3Ds" was coined by Cervero and Kockelman (1997) to describe the built environment at the neighborhood level in relation to density, diversity, and design. As the studies on neighborhoods advanced, urban structure measures evolved to include a total of five D variables, with density, diversity, and design supplemented by destination accessibility and distance to transit (Ewing and Cervero, 2001, 2010; Ewing et al., 2011). The D variables are a framework for organizing measurements of urban structure.

Table 2.3 defines the D variables and describes how they are typically measured. While these are rough categories with somewhat fuzzy boundaries, they provide a useful framework for organizing the empirical literature and providing insights into how urban structure affects travel at the neighborhood level.

8.   RELATING THE DS TO TRANSPORTATION OUTCOMES

The study of neighborhood structure's impact on travel behavior began in earnest around 1990, with the first research focusing on the impact density had on travel. Subsequent studies became more sophisticated in characterizing urban structure in terms of all the D variables. The Ds are important because they affect the accessibility of trip productions to trip attractions. This, in turn, affects the utility of different travel choices. For example, destinations that are closer as a result of higher density or greater diversity

Table 2.3   The D variables

D variable	Measurement
Density	Density is always measured as the variable of interest per unit of area. The area can be gross or net, and the variable of interest can be population, dwelling units, employment, or building floor area. Population and employment are sometimes summed to compute an overall activity density per areal unit.
Diversity	Diversity measures pertain to the number of different land uses in a given area and the degree to which they are balanced in land area, floor area, or employment. Entropy measures of diversity, wherein low values indicate single-use environments and higher values more varied land uses, are widely used in travel studies. Jobs-to-housing or jobs-to-population ratios are less frequently used.
Design	Design measures include average block size, proportion of four-way intersections, and number of intersections per square mile. Design is also occasionally measured as sidewalk coverage (share of block faces with sidewalks); average building setbacks; average street widths; or numbers of pedestrian crossings, street trees, or other physical variables that differentiate pedestrian-oriented environments from auto-oriented ones.
Destination accessibility	Destination accessibility measures ease of access to trip attractions. It may be regional or local (Handy, 1993). In some studies, regional accessibility is simply distance to the central business district. In others, it is the number of jobs or other attractions reachable within a given travel time, which tends to be highest at central locations and lowest at peripheral ones. The gravity model of trip attraction measures destination accessibility. Local accessibility is a different animal.
Distance to transit	Distance to transit is usually measured as an average of the shortest street routes from the residences or workplaces to the nearest rail station or bus stop. Alternatively, it may be measured as transit route density, distance between transit stops, or the number of stations per unit area. In this literature, frequency and quality of transit service are overlooked.

are easier to walk to than distant destinations. In general, as distance to transit decreases and the other Ds increase, the generalized cost of travel by alternative modes decreases, relative utility increases, and mode shifts occur.

In a meta-analysis, Ewing and Cervero (2010) computed weighted averages of results from more than 60 studies (see Tables 2.4–6). A meta-analysis is valuable to researchers as it synthesizes and reports the findings of many studies. Ewing and Cervero (2010) examined three common travel outcomes modeled in the literature – VMT, walking, and transit use – and related them to dimensions of the built environment as characterized by the D variables. The Ds that significantly related to travel were population and job density; diversity measured in term of jobs-population balance and land-use entropy; design measured in terms of intersection density and street connectivity; destination accessibility measured in terms of jobs reachable within a given travel time by auto and transit; and distance to transit measured directly.

The meta-study produced a set of elasticities quantifying the effects of the D variables on travel outcomes. An elasticity is the change in the value of one variable for a one

Table 2.4   Weighted average elasticities of VMT with respect to built environment variables

	n total (n with controls for self-selection)	e
DENSITY		
household/population density	9 (1)	−0.04
job density	5 (1)	0.0
DIVERSITY		
land-use mix (entropy index)	10 (0)	−0.09
job–housing balance	4 (0)	−0.02
DESIGN		
intersection/street density	6 (0)	−0.12
% four-way intersections	3 (1)	−0.12
DESTINATION ACCESSIBILITY		
job accessibility by auto	5 (0)	−0.20
job accessibility by transit	3 (0)	−0.05
distance to downtown	3 (1)	−0.22
DISTANCE TO TRANSIT		
distance to nearest transit stop	6 (1)	−0.05

Table 2.5   Weighted average elasticities of walking with respect to built environment variables

	n total (n with controls for self-selection)	e
DENSITY		
household/population density	10 (0)	0.07
job density	6 (0)	0.04
commercial FAR	3 (0)	0.07
DIVERSITY		
land-use mix (entropy index)	8 (1)	0.15
job–housing balance	4 (0)	0.19
distance to store	5 (3)	0.25
DESIGN		
intersection/street density	7 (2)	0.39
% four-way intersections	5 (1)	−0.06
DESTINATION ACCESSIBILITY		
jobs within one mile	3 (0)	0.15
DISTANCE TO TRANSIT		
distance to nearest transit stop	3 (2)	0.14

Table 2.6   Weighted average elasticities of transit use with respect to built environment variables

	n total (n with controls for self-selection)	e
DENSITY		
household/population density	10 (0)	0.07
job density	6 (0)	0.01
DIVERSITY		
land-use mix (entropy index)	6 (0)	0.12
DESIGN		
intersection/street density	4 (0)	0.23
% four-way intersections	5 (2)	0.29
DISTANCE		
distance to nearest transit stop	3 (1)	0.29

unit change in a second variable. The value of the elasticity tells you the direction and strength of change.

For all travel variables and D variables, the relationships are inelastic, which means they have absolute values less than one. The weighted average elasticity with the greatest absolute magnitude was 0.39; most elasticities were much smaller. Still, the combined effect of several built environmental variables on travel is potentially quite large. A dense neighborhood with good accessibility should have higher walk and transit trips, and thus lower VMT. All D variables should be considered as possible predictors of travel in a multivariate study.

The D variable most strongly associated with VMT was destination accessibility. The elasticity from the earlier meta study, −0.20, was confirmed by this meta-analysis (based on "job accessibility by auto"). In fact, the −0.19 VMT elasticity was nearly as large as the highest elasticities of the first three D variables – density, diversity, and design — combined. This too was consistent with the earlier meta study (Ewing and Cervero, 2001). Neighborhoods with mixed commercial and residential uses are expected to have lower VMT, because residents have opportunities for shorter trips, trip chaining, and multiple destinations nearby.

The D variables most strongly associated with mode share and likelihood of walk trips were the design and diversity dimensions of urban structure. Intersection density and jobs–housing balance appeared to be most strongly associated with higher rates of walking. A doubling of intersection density was accompanied by a 39 percent increase in walking, all else being equal. This reflects that smaller blocks are easier to walk than longer blocks. Where street connectivity is good for accessibility, if the blocks are too large, walkability may be reduced. Also of interest was the fact that jobs–housing balance had a stronger relationship to walking than the more commonly used land use mix (entropy) variable. Finally, Table 2.5 shows that as with VMT, job density is less strongly related to walking than is population density.

Transit access had a strong effect on mode share and likelihood of transit trips, no surprise. Living near a bus stop is related to transit riding, supporting the transit industry's standard of running buses within a quarter mile of most residents. Most transit riders would intuitively agree with this finding, if it's too far to a transit stop, and you have a choice, you won't ride.

Perhaps what can be said with the highest degree of confidence is that destination accessibility is most strongly related to both motorized (i.e., VMT) and non-motorized (i.e., walking) travel. The primacy of destination accessibility may be due to confounders like auto ownership and auto dependence. Almost any centrally located development is likely to generate less automobile travel than the best-designed, compact, mixed-use development in a remote location.

The relatively weak relationships between density and travel likely reflect density's role as an intermediate variable that ultimately gets expressed by the other Ds – i.e., dense settings usually have mixed uses with small blocks and plentiful intersections that shorten trips and encourage walking. Among design variables, intersection density more strongly sways the decision to walk or take transit than street connectivity. This suggests that block size matters more than gridded designs if significant numbers residents are to be lured out of their cars. And among diversity variables, jobs–housing balance is a stronger predictor of non-auto mode choice than land-use mix measures. Linking where people live and work allows more to commute by foot and by transit, which appears to shape mode choice more than sprinkling a multiplicity of land uses within a neighborhood.

9.   THE RESIDENTIAL SELF-SELECTION CAVEAT

Despite all the empirical evidence regarding environmental determinism, we are left with the question of how influential residential self-selection is on travel behavior. Should we ignore the fact that people choose which neighborhoods they live in, we would be overstating the influence of compact development patterns. Indeed, this is a common source of statistical bias in many studies to date.

However, at least 38 studies have attempted to control for residential self-selection via nine different research approaches (Mokhtarian and Cao, 2008; Cao et al., 2009). While nearly all found that residential self-selection attenuates the effect of the built environment on travel, they also found the associations between travel behavior and the built environment remain a larger, statistically significant influence. For example, in studies evaluating a diversity of areas, from New York City to Raleigh, North Carolina, the influence on travel behavior attributed to the built environment was estimated to range in influence from 48 percent to 98 percent, with the balance attributed to residential self-selection (Salon, 2006; Zhou and Kockelman, 2008; Cao, 2010; Cao et al., 2010; Bhat and Eluru, 2009). Others have found that self-selection is more likely to enhance rather than diminish built environment influences (Chatman, 2009: 1087). This is an intuitive finding. If people choose to live in compact communities for the improved accessibility, the built environment facilitates their propensity for walking, short auto trips, and transit riding.

10.   CONCLUSIONS

While sprawl is principally considered to be an American phenomena, global urbani-zation and rapid population growth have made sprawl an international development form. Historically, cities shaped before development of modern transport systems grew primarily as a function of population growth. As a result, they had a dense historical core that was compact in structure. Changing lifestyles, increasing automobile owner-ship worldwide, and global socio-economic factors are causing cities to grow in new ways (European Environment Agency, 2006). For example, in Europe the amount of space consumed per person has more than doubled over the past 50 years (European Environment Agency, 2006).

Likely for the first time in history, an Iranian student is studying "toseh kam tarakom," a Chinese researcher is reporting on "cheng shi man yan," a Columbian biolo-gist is investigating tree cover in "urbanización por derrame" on surface temperatures; and a Korean city planner is identifying strategies to minimize the impacts of "dosi hwaksan hyunsang." It is because the impacts of sprawl are felt globally. For example, in the sprawling urban fringe of Beijing, low density and dispersed development have increased trip distances and car use (Zhao, 2010). In Yazd, Iran, and Magalore, India, sprawling urban growth is consuming natural resources and land at rates that outpace population growth (Sudhira et al., 2004; Shahraki et al., 2011). In Barcelona, urban sprawl is transforming the traditional urban character of the region; however, unlike in North America, the historical development of numerous medium sized towns surrounding Barcelona has proved to be a deterrent of excessive sprawl (Catalán et al., 2008). The European Environment Agency (2006: 5) went so far as to say that "sprawl threatens the very culture of Europe, as it creates environmental, social and economic impacts."

Sprawl will have impacts, regardless of where in the world it takes place. It may take different shapes and forms. The average density even in "sprawling" European cities will likely still be higher than sprawling American cities, so the unique characteristics of regions must be accounted for. The existing literature on the impacts of sprawl will greatly benefit from further studies that examine the effects of sprawl in countries outside of the US.

This chapter began with the question: does urban structure influence travel? The liter-ature offers extreme views, from it having no importance to it being critically important. Existing evidence suggests a more moderate view. While findings do vary, as methods for classifying and operationalizing urban structure evolve, much of the evidence leans toward environmental determinism having a greater influence than self-selection. In urban planning, where studies of urban structure effects on travel dominate the field, the call for further study is qualified by a need for improved measurement and methodolo-gies (Handy et al., 2002; Crane, 2000; Cervero, 2003; Badoe and Miller, 2000).

Despite potential shortcomings, research on the impacts of urban form on travel sug-gests that while the effect of the built environment on travel may be small, it is indeed sig-nificant (Ewing and Cervero, 2001; Cao et al., 2009). The most common travel outcomes modeled are trip frequency, trip length, mode choice, and VMT (as a composite measure of travel demand). Hence, we can describe measured associations between so-called D variables (density, diversity, design, destination accessibility, and distance to transit) and these outcomes with more confidence than we could for outcomes studied less often, like trip chaining in multipurpose tours or internal capture of trips within mixed use developments.

The current understanding of the complex relationship between urban structure and travel has some agreement: there is agreement with regard to the questions that need to be answered; there is also agreement in regard to what data should be investigated. Thus, while much has been accomplished, we conclude there is room for additional research.

REFERENCES

Badland, H. and Schofield, G. (2005), Transport, urban design, and physical activity: an evidence-based update, *Transportation Research Part D*, **10**, 177–96.

Badoe, D.A. and Miller, E.J. (2000), Transportation – land-use interaction: empirical findings in North America, and their implications for modeling, *Transportation Research Part D*, **5**(4), 235–63.

Bauman, A.E. and Bull, F.C. (2007), *Environmental Correlates of Physical Activity and Walking in Adults and Children: A Review of Reviews*, London: National Institute of Health and Clinical Excellence.

Bhat, C.R. and Eluru, N. (2009), A copula-based approach to accommodate residential self-selection effects in travel behavior modeling, *Transportation Research Part B*, **43**(7), 749–65.

Brownstone, D. (2008), Key relationships between the built environment and VMT, Department of Economics, University of California, Irvine.

Burchell, R.W., Lowenstein, G., Dophin, W., Galley, C., Downs, A., Seskin, S., Gray Still, K., and Moore, T. (2000), *Costs of Sprawl – 2000*, TCRP Report 74, Transportation Research Board, http://onlinepubs.trb.org/onlinepubs/tcrp/tcrp_rpt_74-a.pdf.

Burchfield, M., Overmans, H.G., Puga, D. and Turner, M.A. (2006), Causes of Sprawl: A portrait from space, *The Quarterly Journal of Economics*, **121**(2), May, pp. 587–633.

Cao, X. (2010), Exploring causal effects of neighborhood type on walking behavior using stratification on the propensity score. *Environment and Planning A*, **42**(2), 487–504.

Cao, X., Mokhtarian, P.L., and Handy, S.L. (2009), Examining the impacts of residential self-selection on travel behaviour: a focus on empirical findings, *Transport Reviews*, **29**(3), 359–95.

Cao, X., Xu, Z., and Fan, Y. (2010), Exploring the connections among residential location, self-selection, and driving: propensity score matching with multiple treatments, *Transportation Research A*, **44**(10), 797–805.

Catalán, B., Saurí, D., and Serra, P. (2008), Urban sprawl in the Mediterranean? Patterns of growth and change in the Barcelona Metropolitan Region 1993–2000, *Landscape and Urban Planning*, **85**, 174–84.

Cervero, R. (2003), The built environment and travel: evidence from the United States, *EJTIR*, **3**(2), 119–37.

Cervero, R. and Kockelman, K. (1997), Travel demand and the 3Ds: density, diversity, and design, *Transportation Research D*, **2**(3), 199–219.

Chatman, D. (2009), Residential choice, the built environment, and nonwork travel: evidence using new data and methods, *Environment and Planning A*, **41**, 1072–89.

Cho, S., Chen, Z., Yen, S.T., and Eastwood, D.B. (2006), *The Effects of Urban Sprawl on Body Mass Index: Where People Live Does Matter*, 52nd Annual ACCI Conference, Baltimore, Maryland, March 15–18.

Crane, R. (2000), The influence of urban form on travel: an interpretive review, *Journal of Planning Literature*, **15**(1), 3–25.

Cunningham, G. and Michael, Y. (2004), Concepts guiding the study of the impact of the built environment on physical activity for older adults: a review of the literature, *American Journal of Health Promotion*, **18**(6), 435–43.

Cutsinger, J. and Galster, G. (2006), There is no sprawl syndrome: a new typology of metropolitan land use patterns, *Urban Geography*, **27**(3), 228–52.

Cutsinger, J., Galster, G., Wolman, H., Hanson, R., and Towns, D. (2005), Verifying the multi-dimensional nature of metropolitan land use: Advancing the understanding and measurement of sprawl, *Journal of Urban Affairs*, **27**(3), pp. 235–59.

Ding, D. and Gebel, K. (2012), Built environment, physical activity, and obesity: what have we learned from reviewing the literature? *Health & Place*, **18**(1): 100–105.

Ding, C. and Zhao, X. (2011), Assessment of urban spatial-growth patterns in China during rapid urbanization, *The Chinese Economy*, **44**(1), pp. 46–71.

Doyle, S., Kelly-Schwartz, A., Schlossberg, M., and Stockard, J. (2006), Active community environments and health: the relationship of walkable and safe communities to individual health, *Journal of the American Planning Association*, **72**(1), 19–31.

European Environment Agency (2006), *Urban Sprawl in Europe: The Ignored Challenge*, www.ecologic. eu/1886.

Ewing, R. (1997), Is Los Angeles-style sprawl desirable? *Journal of the American Planning Association*, **63**, 107–26.

Ewing, R. and Cervero, R. (2001), Travel and the built environment: a synthesis, *Transportation Research Record: Journal of the Transportation Board*, **1780**, 87–114.

Ewing, R. and Cervero, R. (2010), Travel and the built environment: a meta-analysis *Journal of the American Planning Association*, **76**(3), 265–94.

Ewing, R. and Rong, F. (2008), Impact of urban form on US residential energy use, *Housing Policy Debate*, **19**, 1–30.

Ewing, R., Pendall, R., and Chen, D. (2003a), Measuring sprawl and its transportation impacts, *Transportation Research Record*, **1832**, 175–83.

Ewing, R., Schieber, R., and Zegeer, C. (2003b), Urban sprawl as a risk factor in motor vehicle occupant and pedestrian fatalities, *American Journal of Public Health*, **93**, 1541–5.

Ewing R., Schmid, T., Killingsworth, R., Zlot, A., and Raudenbush, S. (2003c), Relationship between urban sprawl and physical activity, obesity, and morbidity, *American Journal of Health Promotion*, **18**, 47–57.

Ewing R., Brownson, R., and Berrigan, D. (2006), Relationship between urban sprawl and weight of US youth, *American Journal of Preventive Medicine*, **31**, 464–74.

Ewing, R., Greenwald, M., Zhang, M., Walters, J., Feldman, M., Cervero, R., Frank, L., and Thomas, J. (2011), Traffic generated by mixed-use developments – six-region study using consistent built environment measures, *Journal of Urban Planning and Development*, **137**(3), 248–61.

Fan, Y. and Song, Y. (2009), Is sprawl associated with a widening urban–suburban mortality gap? *Journal of Urban Health: Bulletin of the New York Academy of Medicine*, **86**(5), 708–28.

Frank, L.D. (2000), Land use and transportation interaction: implications on public health and quality of life, *Journal of Planning Education and Research*, **20**(1), 6–22.

Frank, L.D. and Engelke, P. (2001), The built environment and human activity patterns: exploring the impacts of urban form on public health, *Journal of Planning Literature*, **16**(2), 202–18.

Frank, L. and Engelke, P. (2005), Multiple impacts of the built environment on public health: walkable places and the exposure to air pollution, *International Regional Science Review*, **28**(2), 193–216.

Fulton, W., Pendall, R., Nguyen, M., and Harrison, A. (2001), *Who Sprawls Most? How Growth Patterns Differ Across the US*, Washington, DC: Center for Urban and Metropolitan Policy, the Brookings Institution.

Galster, G., Hanson, R., Ratcliffe, M., Wolman, H., Coleman, S., and Freihage, J. (2001), Wrestling sprawl to the ground: defining and measuring an elusive concept, *Housing Policy Debate*, **12**(4), 681–717.

Gebel, K., Bauman, A., and Petticrew, M. (2007), The physical environment and physical activity: a critical appraisal of review articles, *American Journal of Preventive Medicine*, **32**(5), 361–9.

Glaeser, E., Kahn, M., and Chu, C. (2001), *Job Sprawl: Employment Location in US Metropolitan Areas*, Washington, DC: Center for Urban and Metropolitan Policy, the Brookings Institution.

Gordon, P. and Richardson, H. (1997), Are compact cities a desirable planning goal? *Journal of the American Planning Association*, **63**(1), 95–106.

Handy, S. (1993), Regional versus local accessibility: Implications for non-work travel, Transportation Research Record No. 1400, 58–66.

Handy, S., Boarnet, M., Ewing, R., and Killingsworth, R. (2002), How the built environment affects physical activity: views from urban planning, *American Journal of Preventative Medicine*, **23**(2S), 64–73.

Handy, S.L., Cao, X., and Mokhtarian, P.L. (2005), Correlation or causality between the built environment and travel behavior? Evidence from Northern California, *Transportation Research D*, **10**(6), 427–44.

Heath, G., Brownson, R., Kruger, J., Miles, R., Powell, K., Ramsey, L., and the Task Force on Community Preventative Services (2006), The effectiveness of urban design and land use and transport policies and practices to increase physical activity: a systematic review, *Journal of Physical Activity and Health*, **3**(1), 55–76.

Humpel, N., Owen, N., and Leslie, E. (2002), Environmental factors associated with adults' participation in physical activity: a review. *American Journal of Preventative Medicine*, **22**(3), 188–99.

Joshu, C.E., Boehmer, T.K., Brownson, R.C., and Ewing, R. (2008), Personal, neighbourhood and urban factors associated with obesity in the United States, *Journal of Epidemiology and Community Health*, **62**, 202–8.

Kaczynski, A. and Henderson, K. (2007), Environmental correlates of physical activity: a review of evidence about parks and recreation, *Leisure Sciences*, **29**, 315–54.

Kahn, E.B., Ramsey, L.T., Brownson, R.C., Heath, G.W., Howze, E.H., Powell, K., and Stone, E. (2002), The effectiveness of interventions to increase physical activity: a systematic review, *American Journal of Preventive Medicine*, **22**(4), 73–107.

Kahn, M.E. (2006), *The Quality of Life in Sprawled versus Compact Cities*, prepared for the OECD ECMT Regional Round, Berkeley, California, March 2006, Table 137, pp. 27–8.

Kelly-Schwartz, A., Stockard, J., Doyle, S., and Schlossberg, M. (2004), Is sprawl unhealthy? A multilevel analysis of the relationship of metropolitan sprawl to the health of individuals, *Journal of Planning Education and Research*, **24**, 184–96.

Krahnstoever-Davison, K. and Lawson, C.T. (2006), Do attributes in the physical environment influence children's physical activity? A review of the literature, *International Journal of Behavioral Nutrition and Physical Activity*, **3**(19).

Lee, C. and Moudon, A.V. (2004), Physical activity and environment research in the health field: implications for urban and transportation planning practice and research, *Journal of Planning Literature*, **19**(2), 147–81.

Lee, I.M., Ewing, R., and Sesso, H.D. (2009), The built environment and physical activity levels: the Harvard alumni health study, *American Journal of Preventive Medicine*, **37**(4): 293–8.

Lopez, R. and Hynes, H.P. (2003), Sprawl in the 1990s: measurement and trends, *Urban Affairs Review*, **38**(3), 325–55.

Malpezzi, S. and Guo, W.-K. (2001), *Measuring "Sprawl": Alternative Measures of Urban Form in US Metropolitan Areas*, Madison, WI: Center for Urban Land Economics Research, University of Wisconsin.

McCormack, G., Giles-Corti, B., Lange, A., Smith, T., Martin, K., and Pikora, T.J. (2004), An update of recent evidence of the relationship between objective and self-report measures of the physical environment and physical activity behaviours, *Journal of Science and Medicine in Sport*, **7**(1), 81–92.

McMillan, T.E. (2005), Urban form and a child's trip to school: the current literature and a framework for future research, *Journal of Planning Literature*, **19**(4), 440–56.

McMillan, T.E. (2007), The relative influence of urban form on a child's travel mode to school, *Transportation Research A*, **41**(1), 69–79.

Mokhtarian, P.L. and Cao, X. (2008), Examining the impacts of residential self-selection on travel behavior: a focus on methodologies, *Transportation Research Part B*, **42**, 204–8.

Nasser, H.E. and Overberg, P. (2001), A comprehensive look at sprawl in America, *USA Today*, http://usatoday30.usatoday.com/news/sprawl/main.htm.

National Research Council (2005), *Does the Built Environment Influence Physical Activity? Examining the Evidence*, Special Report 282, National Academies Press.

Nguyen, D. (2010), Evidence of the impacts of urban sprawl on social capital, *Environment and Planning B: Planning and Design*, **37**(4): 610–27.

Owen, N., Humpel, N., Leslie, E., Bauman, A., and Sallis, J.F. (2004), Understanding environmental influences on walking: review and research agenda, *American Journal of Preventive Medicine*, **27**(1), 67–76.

Plantinga, A. and Bernell, S. (2007), The association between urban sprawl and obesity: is it a two-way street? *Journal of Regional Science*, **47**(5): 857–79.

Pont, K., Ziviani, J., Wadley, D., Bennett, S., and Abbott, R. (2009), Environmental correlates of children's active transportation: a systematic literature review, *Health & Place*, **15**(3), 827–40.

Saelens, B.E. and Handy, S. (2008), Built environment correlates of walking: a review, *Medicine & Science in Sports & Exercise*, **40**(S), S550–67.

Saelens, B.E., Sallis, J.F., and Frank, L.D. (2003), Environmental correlates of walking and cycling: findings from the transportation, urban design, and planning literatures, *Annals of Behavioral Medicine*, **25**, 80–91.

Salon, D. (2006), *Cars and the City: An Investigation of Transportation and Residential Location Choices in New York City*, PhD dissertation, University of California, Davis.

Salon, D., Boarnet, M., Handy, S., Spears, S., and Tal, G. (2012), How do local actions affect VMT? A critical review of the empirical evidence, *Transportation Research Part D*, **17**(7), 495–508.

Schweitzer, L. and Zhou, J. (2010), Neighborhood air quality outcomes in compact and sprawled regions, *Journal of the American Planning Association*, **76**(3): 363–71.

Shahraki, S., Sauri, D., Serra, P., Modugno, S., Seifolddini, F., and Pourahmad, A. (2011), Urban sprawl pattern and land-use change detection in Yazd, Iran, *Habitat International*, **35**(4), 521–8.

Stead, D. and Marshall, S. (2001), The relationships between urban form and travel patterns: an international review and evaluation, *European Journal of Transport and Infrastructure Research*, **1**(2), 113–41.

Stone, B. (2008), Urban sprawl and air quality in large US cities, *Journal of Environmental Management*, **86**, 688–98.

Stone, B., Hess, J., and Frumkin, H. (2010), Urban form and extreme heat events: are sprawling cities more vulnerable to climate change than compact cities? *Environmental Health Perspectives*, **118**(10), 1425–8.

Sturm, R. and Cohen, D. (2004), Suburban sprawl and physical and mental health, *Public Health*, **118**(7): 488–96.

Sudhira, H., Ramachandra, T., and Jagadish, K. (2004), Urban sprawl; metrics, dynamics and modeling using GIS, *International Journal of Applied Earth Observation*, **5**, 29–39.

Trost, S.G., Owen, N., Bauman, A.E., Sallis, J.F., and Brown, W. (2002), Correlates of adults' participation in physical activity: review and update, *Medicine & Science in Sports & Exercise*, **34**(12), 1996–2001.

Trowbridge, M.J. and McDonald, N.C. (2008), Urban sprawl and miles driven daily by teenagers in the United States, *American Journal of Preventive Medicine*, **34**(3): 202–6.

Trowbridge, M.J., Gurka, M.J., and O'Connor, R. (2009), Urban sprawl and delayed ambulance arrival in the United States, *American Journal of Preventive Medicine*, **37**(5), 428–32.

Wendel-Vos, G.C., Schuit, A.J., Feskens, E.J., Boshuizen, H.C., Verschuren, W.M., Saris, W.H., and Kromhout, D. (2004), Physical activity and stroke: a meta-analysis of observational data, *International Journal of Epidemiology*, **33**(4), 787–98.

Zhao, P. (2010), Sustainable urban expansion and transportation in a growing megacity: consequences of urban sprawl for mobility on the urban fringe of Beijing, *Habitat International*, **34**(2), 236–43.

Zhou, B. and Kockelman, K. (2008), Self-selection in home choice: use of treatment effects in evaluating the relationship between the built environment and travel behavior, Transportation Research Record No. 2077, 54–61.

Zolnik, E.J. (2011), The effect of sprawl on private-vehicle commuting outcomes, *Environment and Planning*, **43**(8), 1875–93.

3 Urban passenger transport energy consumption and carbon dioxide emissions: a global review and assessment of some reduction strategies
Peter Newman and Jeff Kenworthy

1. INTRODUCTION

Transport accounts for 22 per cent of global energy use and within the sector passenger transport accounts for roughly two-thirds of this, with freight transport accounting roughly for the other third (InterAcademy Council, 2007). Table 3.1 from the World Business Council for Sustainable Development shows in more detail how the global transport sector consumes its energy.

Virtually all energy for transportation comes from petroleum-based fuels (InterAcademy Council, 2007). According to the IPCC, in 2004 the global transportation sector was responsible for 23 per cent of world energy-related CO_2 emissions (IPCC, 2007). The growth rate of greenhouse gas emissions in the transport sector is the highest among all the energy end-user sectors (IPCC, 2007). Reducing these emissions from transport must therefore be an important part of climate change mitigation programmes both at the city and national levels across the world. The focus of this chapter is on cities and in this we attempt to address several questions:

1. What are the patterns of carbon dioxide emissions from private and public transport in cities worldwide? To answer this question we present detailed per capita data on

Table 3.1 World transport energy use by mode

Mode	Energy use (EJ[5])	Share (%)
Passenger transport		
Cars	34.20	44.5
Buses	4.76	6.2
Air	8.95	11.6
Other (motorbikes, rickshaws etc.)	1.20	1.6
Passenger and freight transport		
Rail	1.19	1.5
Freight transport		
Heavy freight trucks	12.48	16.2
Medium freight trucks	6.77	8.8
Shipping	7.32	9.5
Total	76.85	100.0

Source: WBCSD (2004)

84 cities in the USA, Canada, Australia, Western and Eastern Europe, the wealthy and poorer parts of Asia, the Middle East, Africa, Latin America and China. Without such data, which show the vast range in per capita carbon dioxide emissions from transport in cities, it is difficult to see just how profligate or frugal different cities are, or to what levels these factors may be able to be reduced under different policies.

2. How do different modes in cities perform in terms of their energy consumption per passenger kilometre and carbon dioxide-generating potential? Transport in cities involves many different types of motorised modes, which vary greatly in their rates of energy use and carbon dioxide emissions. It is important to show these patterns in detail with sound empirical data, since they vary a lot between cities and highlight which modes offer the best potential for reducing energy and carbon dioxide.

3. What relationships can we find between transport energy use (and by inference carbon dioxide emissions) and other urban characteristics? Transport energy conservation and carbon dioxide reduction policies need to be based on a sound understanding of some key factors that underpin the large differences between cities in energy use and carbon dioxide generation.

4. What policies seem to be important in addressing carbon dioxide emissions from urban passenger transport? With the comparative insights generated in the previous sections in mind, we then examine three commonly found approaches to transport energy reduction: vehicle technology approaches versus urban and transport planning strategies, the issue of congestion and free-flowing traffic and the potential of public transport to reduce energy use and carbon dioxide emissions.

The chapter now examines these questions by presenting and discussing a series of key data and other evidence from a variety of sources.

2. WHAT ARE THE PATTERNS OF CARBON DIOXIDE EMISSIONS FROM PRIVATE AND PUBLIC TRANSPORT IN CITIES WORLDWIDE?

There is enormous variation in the amount of transport fuel used per capita and thus carbon dioxide produced across the world's cities. The data below are drawn from *The Millennium Cities Database for Sustainable Transport* compiled over three years by Kenworthy and Laube (2001) for the International Union (Association) of Public Transport (UITP) in Brussels. The database provides data on 100 cities (metropolitan regions) on all continents. Data summarised here represent averages from 84 of these fully completed cities (Table 3.2) in the USA, Australia and New Zealand, Canada, Western Europe, Asia (high- and low-income areas), Eastern Europe, the Middle East, Latin America, Africa and China. The population of each of the metropolitan regions in 1995/6 is also shown. The 58 higher income cities, defined here on the basis of their metropolitan GDP per capita being over $US12,000 (1995 US dollars), are shown in the top half of the table. Although these data are now dated, an ongoing update of these global cities data by Kenworthy suggests that the 'big picture' differences between the cities

Table 3.2 Eighty-four cities in *The Millennium Cities Database for Sustainable Transport* by high-income and low-income region (with populations)

USA	CANADA	AUST/NZ	WESTERN EUROPE	WESTERN EUROPE (continued)	HIGH-INCOME ASIA
Atlanta (2.90)	Calgary (0.77)	Brisbane (1.49)	Graz (0.24)	Athens (3.46)	Osaka (16.83)
Chicago (7.52)	Montreal (3.22)	Melbourne (3.14)	Vienna (1.59)	Milan (2.46)	Sapporo (1.76)
Denver (1.98)	Ottawa (0.97)	Perth (1.24)	Brussels (0.95)	Bologna (0.45)	Tokyo (32.34)
Houston (3.92)	Toronto (4.63)	Sydney (3.74)	Copenhagen (1.74)	Rome (2.65)	Hong Kong (6.31)
Los Angeles (9.08)	Vancouver (1.90)	Wellington (0.37)	Helsinki (0.89)	Amsterdam (0.83)	Singapore (2.99)
New York (19.23)			Lyon (1.15)	Oslo (0.92)	Taipei (5.96)
Phoenix (2.53)			Nantes (0.53)	Barcelona (2.78)	
San Diego (2.63)			Paris (11.00)	Madrid (5.18)	
S. Francisco (3.84)			Marseilles (0.80)	Stockholm (1.73)	
Washington (3.74)			Berlin (3.47)	Bern (0.30)	
			Frankfurt (0.65)	Geneva (0.40)	
			Hamburg (1.70)	Zurich (0.79)	
			Dusseldorf (0.57)	London (7.01)	
			Munich (1.32)	Manchester (2.58)	
			Ruhr (7.36)	Newcastle (1.13)	
			Stuttgart (0.59)	Glasgow (2.18)	
Av. Pop. 5.74	**Av. Pop. 2.30**	**Av. Pop. 2.00**	continued	**Av. Pop. 2.17**	**Av. Pop. 11.03**

EASTERN EUROPE	MIDDLE EAST	AFRICA	LATIN AMERICA	LOW-INCOME ASIA	CHINA
Prague (1.21)	Tel Aviv (2.46)	Dakar (1.94)	Curitiba (2.43)	Manila (9.45)	Beijing (8.16)
Budapest (1.91)	Teheran (6.80)	Cape Town (2.90)	S. Paulo (15.56)	Bangkok (6.68)	Shanghai (9.57)
Krakow (0.74)	Riyadh (3.12)	Jo'burg (2.25)	Bogota (5.57)	Mumbai (17.07)	Guangzhou (3.85)
	Cairo (13.14)	Harare (1.43)		Chennai (6.08)	
	Tunis (1.87)			K. Lumpur (3.77)	
				Jakarta (9.16)	
				Seoul (20.58)	
				HCM City (4.81)	
Av. Pop. 1.29	**Av. Pop. 5.48**	**Av. Pop. 2.13**	**Av. Pop. 7.85**	**Av. Pop. 9.70**	**Av. Pop. 7.19**

38

have been largely retained and this is explained in Priester, Kenworthy and Wulfhorst (2013).

Figure 3.1 shows how the carbon dioxide emissions from passenger transport vary in all 84 cities in this study, from the US cities with just over 3,000kg in New York to nearly 7,500kg per annum of CO_2 per person in Atlanta, through to the most extreme low emitting developing cities with less than 100kg (Ho Chi Minh City, 71kg). In order to see more clearly how this varies by region, the data are sorted into 11 regional groupings of cities in Tables 3.2 and 3.3 and are discussed further under these regional city variations in sections below. Methodological details on the development of the data in Figure 3.1 and Tables 3.3 and 3.4 can be found in Kenworthy (2008). The codes used in ensuing tables are:

HIGHER INCOME

USA	US cities
ANZ	Australia/New Zealand cities
CAN	Canadian cities
WEU	Western European cities
HIA	High-income Asian cities

LOWER INCOME

EEU	Eastern European cities
MEA	Middle Eastern cities
LAM	Latin American cities
AFR	African cities
LIA	Low-income Asian cities
CHN	Chinese cities

US cities generated on average 4,405kg of CO_2 per person from passenger transport in 1995, while, the Canadian cities, produced about half that level (2,422kg),and Australian cities a fraction lower (2,226 kg). Starting with the Western European cities (1,269kg), the figures decline rapidly to the high-income Asian cities (825kg). In the lower-income cities, there were 812kg per person in Middle Eastern cities, down to a meagre 213kg in Chinese cities. US cities produced in 1995, 21 times more CO_2 per capita from passenger transport than the Chinese cities.

In terms of the proportion of CO_2 that is attributable to public transport, the US cities had the lowest at only 1.9 per cent, while the Eastern European cities had the highest at 30.8 per cent due to the fact that they had in 1995 the most extensive and well-utilised public transport systems in the world (Kenworthy and Laube, 2001) and the update of the data already mentioned has shown that Prague in 2005 had even grown in public transport use per capita (along with car use). The other high-income regions, excluding the USA, have cities where public transport contributed on average only 10 per cent to passenger transport CO_2 emissions, while the average for the lower-income cities, excluding Eastern Europe, is 18 per cent. In most cities public transport is by far the minor player in CO_2 emissions, due partly to its comparatively low share of trips, but also because of its greater efficiency in moving people, which is shown in the next section.

A close examination of Figure 3.1 shows, however, that in some cities public transport was one half or more of the total per capita CO_2 figure (Manila, Dakar, Bogota and

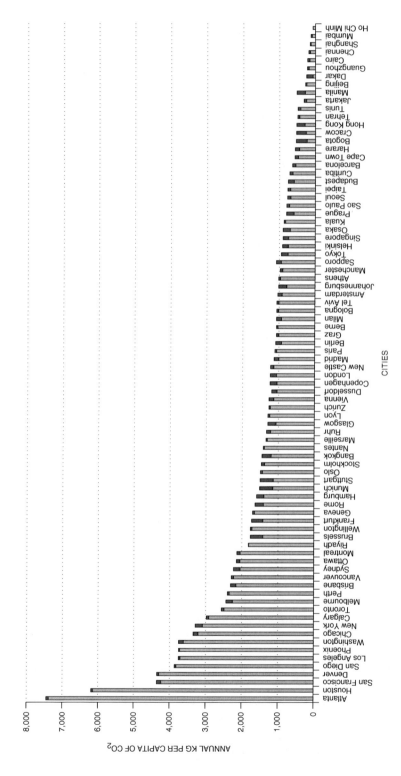

Source: Kenworthy (2008)

Figure 3.1 Per capita emissions of carbon dioxide from private and public passenger transport in 84 cities (1995)

Table 3.3   Carbon dioxide emissions per capita from transport in low-income cities, 1995

Greenhouse indicators		EEU	MEA	LAM	AFR	LIA	CHN
Total passenger transport CO_2 per capita	kg/person	694	812	678	592	509	213
Total private transport CO_2 per capita	kg/person	480	761	524	443	441	180
Total public transport CO_2 per capita	kg/person	214	51	154	149	96	33
% of passenger transport CO_2 from public transport	%	30.8	6.2	22.7	25.2	18.8	15.5

Source: Kenworthy (2008)

Table 3.4   Carbon dioxide emissions per capita from transport in high-income cities

Greenhouse indicators		USA	ANZ	CAN	WEU	HIA
Total passenger transport CO_2 per capita	kg/person	4,405	2,226	2,422	1,269	825
Total private transport CO_2 per capita	kg/person	4,322	2,107	2,348	1,133	688
Total public transport CO_2 per capita	kg/person	83	119	74	134	162
% of passenger transport CO_2 from public transport	%	1.9	5.3	3.1	10.6	19.7

Source: Kenworthy (2008)

Cracow all had between 51 per cent and 78 per cent of total CO_2 emissions from passenger transport coming from public transport). Riyadh and a handful of US cities, on the other hand, had only 0.5–0.6 per cent.

3.   HOW DO DIFFERENT MODES IN CITIES PERFORM IN TERMS OF THEIR ENERGY CONSUMPTION PER PASSENGER KILOMETRE AND CARBON DIOXIDE-GENERATING POTENTIAL?

Modal energy use can be examined on a per vehicle kilometre or per passenger kilometre basis. The former is an indication of the inherent energy use of the particular vehicle, the technology it exploits and the environment in which it operates (congestion, etc.). Energy use per passenger kilometre is an indication of the mode's efficiency in carrying people, based on the kind of loadings that the mode achieves in different cities. Each city has a different set of conditions that impact on how much energy is consumed per kilometre by the different modes. It depends on the technologies used for each mode, the conditions under which they operate in terms of congestion, the distances they need to travel to service their demand and the occupancies achieved by both private and public transport. For the CO_2 emissions that this travel generates, this further depends on the source and type of fuel used to make electricity where electric traction is involved. We explore the end result of these many variations in cities by examining the energy consumed per passenger kilometre for all transport modes in the 11 groups of cities previously detailed.

Table 3.5   Energy consumption per passenger kilometre by mode in low-income cities

Transport energy indicators	UNITS	EEU	MEA	LAM	AFR	LIA	CHN
Energy use per private passenger km	MJ/p.km	2.35	2.56	2.27	1.86	1.78	1.69
Energy use per public transport passenger km	MJ/p.km	0.40	0.67	0.76	0.51	0.64	0.28
Energy use per bus passenger km	MJ/p.km	0.56	0.74	0.75	0.57	0.66	0.26
Energy use per tram passenger km	MJ/p.km	0.74	0.13	–	–	–	–
Energy use per light rail passenger km	MJ/p.km	1.71	0.20	–	–	0.05	–
Energy use per metro passenger km	MJ/p.km	0.21	–	0.19	–	0.46	0.05
Energy use per suburban rail passenger km	MJ/p.km	0.18	0.56	0.15	0.49	0.25	–
Energy use per ferry passenger km	MJ/p.km	4.87	2.32	–	–	2.34	4.90
Overall energy use per passenger km	MJ/p.km	1.31	1.99	1.60	1.26	1.20	0.87

Source: Kenworthy (2008)

The data are contained in Tables 3.4 and 3.5, and again the details of the methodology can be found in Kenworthy (2008). All energy data are based on end use or actual delivered operating energy. Vehicle occupancies are based on actual empirical data collected in each city. Private passenger vehicle occupancies are 24 hours a day/seven days a week and were multiplied by annual private passenger vehicle kilometres of travel to derive passenger kilometres. For public transport, actual passenger kilometres of travel were collected for each mode and for every operator in every city.

In no case other than a few ferry systems does public transport ever become more energy intensive and CO_2 emitting than private transport (mainly cars and motorcycles). Energy consumed per passenger kilometre in public transport in all cities is between one-fifth and one-third that of private transport, the only exception being in the US cities. In US cities, public transport energy use per passenger kilometre stands at 65 per cent that of cars. Part of the reason for this is that in US cities the public transport vehicles have the highest use of energy per vehicle kilometre of all cities (26MJ/km, with most other regions under about 16 to 17MJ/km, or as low as 10MJ/km in African cities) and their buses have to chase passengers in suburbs designed principally around the car (Kenworthy, 2008).

Tables 3.5 and 3.6 also contain energy consumption data for buses, trams, light rail (LRT), metro systems, suburban rail and ferries. Not all modes are present in some regions and the averages for a particular mode are taken from the cities in the region where the mode is found. Table 3.7 summarises the average energy consumption for all the modes for the entire 84 cities.

The following points summarise the comparative energy use for the different modes.

1. Except for trams and light rail in Eastern European cities, rail modes use less than about half the energy of buses per passenger km in each region and overall there is not a huge difference in energy consumption between the different rail modes.
2. Urban rail modes, taken together across regions, are on average 4.6 times less energy consuming than the average car (0.54 compared to 2.45MJ/passenger kilometre).

Table 3.6   Energy consumption per passenger kilometre by mode in high-income cities

Transport energy indicators	UNITS	USA	ANZ	CAN	WEU	HIA
Energy use per private passenger km	MJ/p.km	3.25	2.56	3.79	2.49	2.33
Energy use per public passenger km	MJ/p.km	2.13	0.92	1.14	0.83	0.48
Energy use per bus passenger km	MJ/p.km	2.85	1.66	1.50	1.17	0.84
Energy use per tram passenger km	MJ/p.km	0.99	0.36	0.31	0.72	0.36
Energy use per light rail passenger km	MJ/p.km	0.67	–	0.25	0.69	0.34
Energy use per metro passenger km	MJ/p.km	1.65	–	0.49	0.48	0.19
Energy use per suburban rail passenger km	MJ/p.km	1.39	0.53	1.31	0.96	0.24
Energy use per ferry passenger km	MJ/p.km	5.41	2.49	3.62	5.66	3.64
Overall energy use per passenger km	MJ/p.km	3.20	2.43	3.52	2.17	1.40

Source: Kenworthy (2008)

Table 3.7   Energy consumption by mode (MJ per pass.km) averaged over 84 global cities incorporating actual vehicle occupancies

Mode	Energy consumption (MJ per pass.km)
Car	2.45
Bus	1.05
Metro	0.46
Suburban rail	0.61
Light rail	0.56
Tram	0.52

3. The above averages do, however, mask some exceptional energy performance by specific rail modes in particular regions. For example, light rail in low-income Asian cities and metro systems in Chinese cities consume only 0.05MJ/passenger km. This is 57 times more efficient than an American urban bus and 76 times more efficient than a Canadian car per passenger kilometre. These high efficiencies are mainly due to some exceptional loading levels on Chinese systems.
4. In every region, ferries are by far the most energy consumptive public transport mode, often exceeding private transport.
5. In policy terms, rail modes are clearly the most energy-efficient, they have the greatest potential to run on renewable energies and should be prioritised in urban transport infrastructure development where cities are facing a coming oil crisis and a requirement to reduce carbon dioxide emissions. They are also best suited to serving dense nodes and linear strips of urban development and thus fit well with increasing urban densities, discussed later in the chapter.

Examining the overall modal energy consumption of motorised transport in cities (private and public transport combined), Canadian cities are the least efficient at 3.5MJ per passenger kilometre, followed closely by US cities at 3.2MJ per passenger kilometre.

This reflects the large vehicles in use in North American cities, especially 4WD sports utility vehicles, their low use of motorcycles and their high levels of private versus public mobility. The private vehicles in US and Canadian cities consume about 5MJ/km, whereas most other regions are under 4 or even 3MJ/km, despite generally worse levels of congestion in these latter areas.

By contrast to North America, Australia and New Zealand cities average 2.4MJ per passenger kilometre for their total motorised passenger transport system, while the lower-income regions range between 0.9 (China) and 2.0MJ per passenger kilometre. All these lower-income cities have a more significant role for energy-efficient public transport, some have high use of low fuel-consuming motorcycles and many operate fleets of mini-buses, which are relatively energy-efficient (especially with high loadings).

4.   WHAT RELATIONSHIPS CAN WE FIND BETWEEN TRANSPORT ENERGY USE (AND BY INFERENCE CARBON DIOXIDE EMISSIONS) AND OTHER URBAN CHARACTERISTICS?

This section takes another look at the global cities data in terms of transport energy use per capita and its relationship with some other key factors in cities. The variation in how much transport energy is used by private and public passenger motor vehicles is outlined for the 84 cities across the world in Figure 3.2.

These data show:

1.   US cities dominate the other world cities in their transport energy use, but there are significant differences within the sample of ten cities, with Atlanta at 103GJ/person, Houston 75GJ/person and New York with 'only' 44GJ/person.
2.   Australian, Canadian and New Zealand cities follow this with 30–40GJ/person.
3.   All Western European cities bar Geneva used 20GJ/person or less and reached to less than 10GJ/person in Barcelona; Eastern European cities were even lower between 5 and 10GJ/person, with Cracow lowest at 2GJ/person.
4.   Wealthy Asian cities (Sapporo, Taipei, Tokyo, Osaka, Seoul, Hong Kong and Singapore) were also extremely low with 5 to 10GJ/person.
5.   Cities in developing countries are scattered throughout this array but apart from Riyadh and Tel Aviv were less than about 8GJ/person and mostly were less than a few GJ/person. Thus, the developing cities to the right of the graph (Jakarta, Beijing, Bogota, Guangzhou, Cairo, Chennai, Shanghai, Mumbai, Dakar and Ho Chi Minh City) are hardly measurable on the same scale as those to the left of the graph.

The variation is seen dramatically in the previous numbers where Atlanta used 103GJ per person of fuel in transport, whereas Barcelona used 8GJ. Yet the US and European cities had very similar levels of per capita wealth at the time (Kenworthy and Laube, 2001). In order to help explain such differences, other factors must be considered. The remainder of this section therefore examines some important other carefully collected data from the *Millennium Database* for these 84 cities to gain an insight into factors that may help to reduce urban transport energy use and carbon dioxide production.

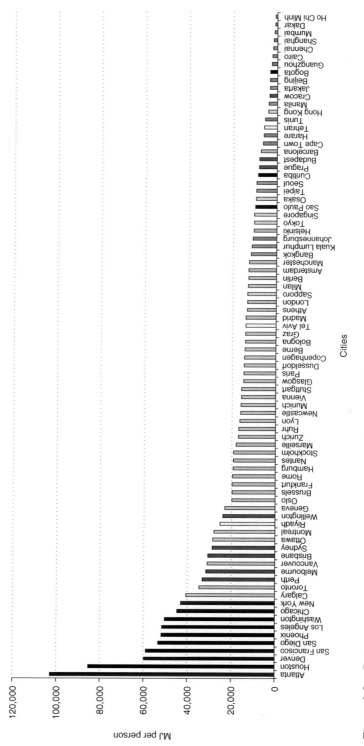

Figure 3.2   Private passenger transport energy use in 84 cities, 1995

First of all it is important to understand the apparent differences in transport priorities demonstrated in different cities. This can at least be partly shown in the comparative role of public transport in the 84 cities. Figure 3.3 sets out the proportion of motorised transport accounted for by public transport. The order of the cities has been fixed according to Figure 3.2 on private passenger transport energy use per capita in order to better see the relationship between the two variables. The data reveal the following key points:

1. The US cities, to the left of the graph, like Atlanta, Denver, San Diego, Houston and Phoenix have vanishingly small levels of transit at less than 1 per cent of total motorised passenger transport, with Washington, San Francisco and Chicago at 5 per cent and the best US city, New York, with still only 9 per cent.
2. Australian, Canadian and New Zealand cities are just a little better varying from 5 per cent in Perth to 12 per cent in Sydney and 14 per cent in Toronto.
3. European cities mostly had around 20 per cent of motorised movement on public transport, with Barcelona and Rome at about 35 per cent. However, some Western European cities performed more poorly, such as Glasgow, Marseille and Geneva at about 10 per cent and Lyon and Bologna less than 10 per cent. The three Eastern European cities (Prague, Budapest and Cracow) were all around 50 per cent public transport.
4. The wealthy Asian cities are very high in public transport (apart from the smaller Japanese city of Sapporo at 21 per cent and Taipei at 25 per cent). Singapore and Seoul had 40 per cent of motorised travel on public transport, Tokyo and Osaka were around 60 per cent and Hong Kong 73 per cent.
5. The less wealthy cities were highly scattered with Mumbai at 84 per cent winning the public transport prize in this global study. Dakar, Chennai and Shanghai achieved around 70 per cent, Beijing and Tunis about 50 per cent, Tel Aviv 20 per cent, Kuala Lumpur 11 per cent, Ho Chi Minh City 8 per cent and Riyadh only 1 per cent.
6. Despite there being some scatter in the data in Figure 3.3, it is clear that there is a general trend of increasing importance of public transport from left to right.

None of these patterns seem to follow per capita wealth levels. Some cities appear to invest in public transport and create systems that are highly attractive and perform a major role in the transport system and others don't (Kenworthy and Laube, 2001; Newman and Kenworthy, 1999).

Another indicator of key significance is density of population (people per hectare of urban land), as shown in Figure 3.4. These data are related to the above transport and energy patterns with higher density cities having the most public transport and the least car use, energy use and carbon dioxide emissions and vice versa. For example, Atlanta has a density of six people per hectare and Barcelona has a density of 200 per hectare, which helps to explain the huge variation in transport energy use between cities of similar wealth. Figure 3.5 shows very clearly the strong relationship between private passenger transport energy use and urban density. The graph also shows the general positioning of the regional groupings of cities by including the names of many key cities.

Figure 3.6 shows that this relationship is also apparent within cities, in this case the variation in total passenger transport energy use with activity density (population and jobs per urban hectare) across Sydney's suburbs in 2002. The density of activity is very

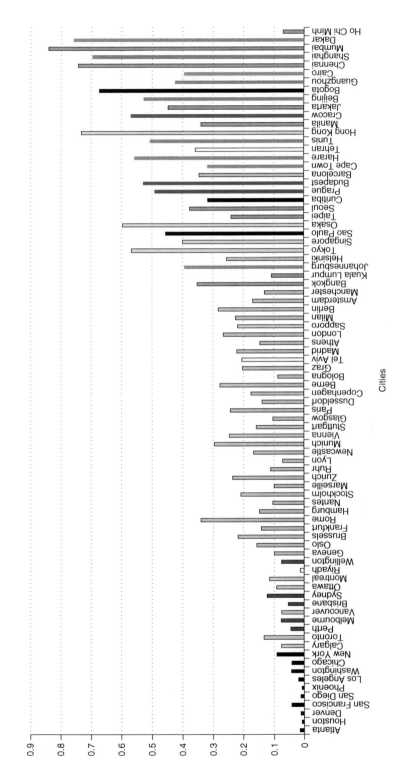

Figure 3.3   Proportion of motorised passenger kilometres on public transport in 84 cities, 1995

47

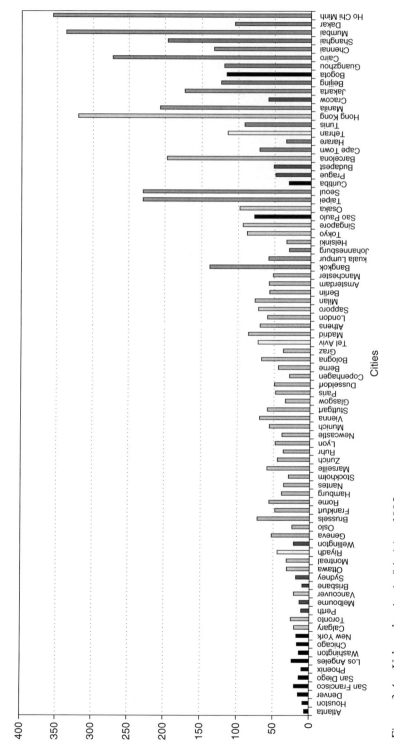

Figure 3.4   Urban density in 84 cities, 1995

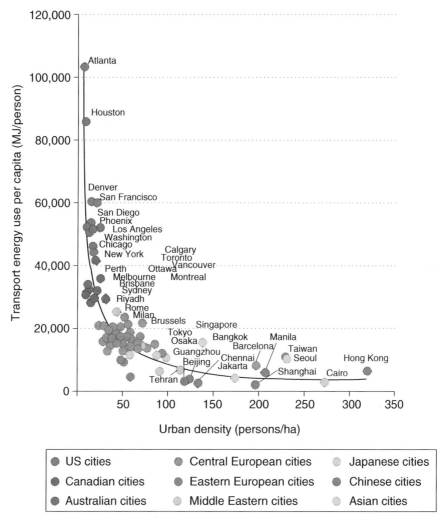

Figure 3.5   Private passenger transport energy use and urban density in cities, 1995

high in the centre and there the passenger transport energy use per capita of residents is similar to Asian cities or even Cracow, the inner suburbs are like Western European cities and the outer suburbs are like Phoenix and Houston. Income is not driving these patterns as Sydney, like all Australian cities, declines uniformly in wealth from the centre to the fringe (Dodson and Sipe, 2006).

We can also see that there is a link between urban density and how much walking and cycling occurs in cities. In Table 3.8, the patterns of urban density are summarised in the regional groups of cities alongside the percentage of total daily trips by walking and biking (non-motorised transportation). Obviously, patterns of non-motorised transport can be determined by many factors, including qualitative matters such as the quality of public environments, street layout, history and culture, but it is clear from Table 3.8 that

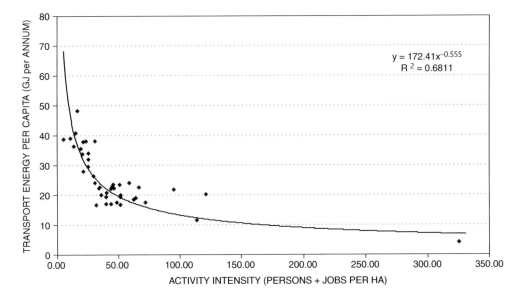

Figure 3.6   Passenger transport energy use per capita versus activity density across the Sydney metropolitan area, 2002

Table 3.8   Percentage of daily trips by non-motorised transport and urban density in global cities, 1995

Cities	Non-motorised transport use (percentage of daily trips)	Urban density (people per urban ha)
American cities	8.1	14.9
Australian/New Zealand cities	15.8	15.0
Canadian cities	10.4	26.2
Western European cities	31.3	54.9
Asian high-income cities	28.5	150.3
Eastern European cities	26.2	52.9
Middle Eastern cities	26.6	118.8
Latin American cities	30.7	74.7
African cities	41.4	59.9
Asian low-income cities	32.4	204.1
Chinese cities	65.0	146.2

low density development, as epitomised in the USA, Australia and Canada, never supports high levels of walking or cycling. These variations in the amount of non-motorised mode use contribute to the picture shown in the previous discussions about density and transport energy use.

5. WHAT POLICIES SEEM TO BE IMPORTANT IN ADDRESSING CARBON DIOXIDE EMISSIONS FROM URBAN PASSENGER TRANSPORT?

Having examined in some detail the picture of transport energy use and carbon dioxide emissions from passenger transport in cities, we now turn to the important question of how these may be reduced. Here we examine three key issues:

1. The role of vehicle and fuel technology.
2. The role of fuel-efficient, freer flowing traffic (versus fuel-efficient cities).
3. The role of modal shifts to public transport.

Will Technological Improvements in Vehicles and Fuels be Sufficient?

There has been exponential growth in private car ownership, with the 200 million cars in operation in 1970 expected to reach 12 billion by 2030, and much of the pressure of this growth is felt by cities (WBCSD, 2004). Recent trends suggested for a while that this may have been an overestimate, with passenger vehicle manufacture (including light duty trucks) dropping from 69 million units in 2007 to 60 million in 2009, but then rejuvenating in 2010 to a record 75 million (Renner, 2011). There have, on the other hand, been reductions in car use per capita and rapid increases in public transport use in many cities across the US and Australia, which have traditionally been the most car dependent and car using. In at least eight major industrialised nations there is evidence of 'peak travel', combining all modes (summarised in Newman and Kenworthy, 2011). The data on developing cities is not yet suggesting a similar pattern, although it is still an open question, as the data is not yet as reliable or extensive as that provided in Europe, the US and Australia.

Overall, however, despite significant advances in energy productivity, the levels of current achievements in energy demand reduction of various transportation modes, such as cars and aeroplanes (Davidson, 2005), are not keeping pace with the rapid growth of these modes. In 2001 road transport via cars (light duty vehicles) and freight trucks accounted for the majority of total transport CO_2 emissions, some 74 per cent, with air travel close behind (IPCC, 2007). Figure 3.7 from the World Business Council for Sustainable Development (WBCSD), shows this graphically and extended into the future. Hence, both at the city level and the national level, strategies that intend to reduce energy and carbon dioxide in the transportation sector will need to include a strong focus on both light vehicles and trucks.

The seemingly most obvious way to reduce vehicle fuel consumption is through improving the vehicle technology itself. Technology is powerful and must be part of the solution to this problem. However, engineering does not work in a vacuum, but with people making real choices. Not only may the new more fuel-efficient vehicles not be chosen (e.g., the growth in SUVs washed out all fuel efficiency gains for nearly 20 years), but drivers may just use the money they saved to drive further. For example, Leggett (2006) suggested that US dependence on Middle Eastern oil would be reduced to zero if fuel efficiency was improved in the US vehicle fleet by just 2.7 miles per gallon. This assumed that if the fuel efficiency of cars is doubled, then the US will need half the fuel.

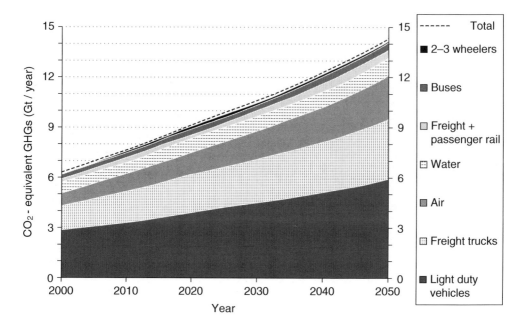

Source: World Business Council for Sustainable Development (2004)

Figure 3.7   *Transport-related Well-To-Wheels CO$_2$ emissions*

The problem is that simple economics does complicate this and more efficient vehicles means they are used more. This is called the Jevons Effect after the nineteenth-century economist who predicted that more efficient coal-fired electricity would mean more coal was needed not less.

The different innovations that are occurring in vehicle technology and fuels are set out in Salter, Dhar and Newman (2011), with an emphasis on the developing world. These technologies will all be needed but unless there is a simultaneous emphasis on how to reduce the growth in light vehicles and trucks, then the innovations will be simply swept away by the sheer growth in numbers of vehicles.

Can Improving Traffic Flow Reduce Energy and Carbon Dioxide Emissions?

Freeways and overpasses are usually proposed to help free up congestion and in the process this is considered to help save time, fuel and emissions. Speeding up traffic will save time (for a while) and thus is considered to save fuel and emissions because vehicles are involved in less stop-start driving, which is inefficient on fuel use. Traffic planners use benefit-cost analyses based on these simple ideas to justify the large capital cost of freeways (Newman and Kenworthy, 1988). However, the data do not support these contentions. Figure 3.8 shows how increasing provision of freeways in US cities does not save time.

In order to understand whether freeing up traffic saves fuel it is necessary to understand the trade-off between making vehicles fuel-efficient and making whole cities

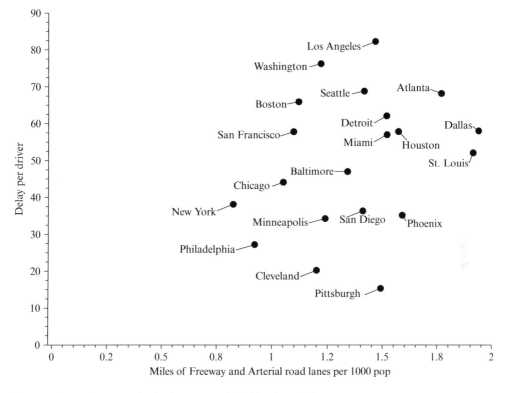

Source: Texas Transportation Institute, quoted in Richardson (n.d.)

Figure 3.8 *The non-correlation between miles of freeway and delay in US cities*

fuel-efficient. Figure 3.9 shows that as traffic congestion lessens with distance from the CBD in Perth, Western Australia, vehicles did become more fuel-efficient but their fuel savings were less than the extra fuel they consumed in driving more. The basis of this seeming paradox can be seen in the conceptual diagrams in Figure 3.10 that show how linear or reductionist assumptions about freeing up traffic are not able to explain the complete fuel consumption story; the only way to consider the matter from a holistic perspective is to see the feedback loops between how cities respond in all their modes and land use patterns as transport infrastructure is built. Congestion in a total urban system sense leads to less fuel use and freeing up traffic leads to greater fuel use.

Empirical evidence for this is provided in Figure 3.11, which shows that those cities with higher congestion, as reflected in lower average speed of traffic, have lower fuel use. Cities with the least congestion, as reflected in high average traffic speeds, use the most fuel. This supports the concepts shown in Figure 3.10 where although individual vehicles in less congested cities are moving more efficiently and using less fuel on a per kilometre basis, they are being used much more and for longer distances, while greener modes are being used less (Newman and Kenworthy, 1984, 1988).

In order to save fuel and reduce carbon dioxide emissions, there must be a balance between enabling personal vehicle travel and enabling greener modes. If congestion

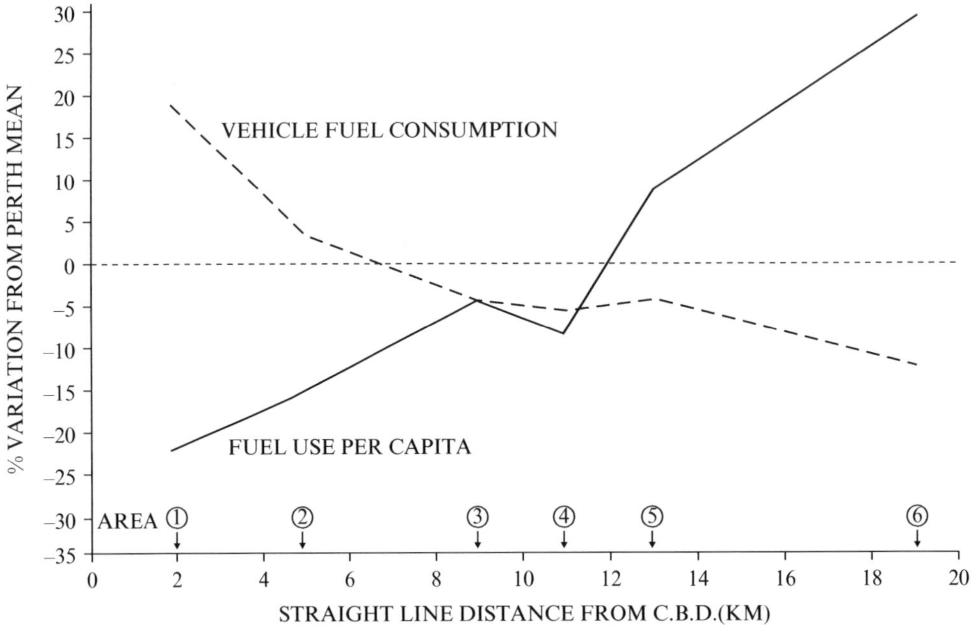

Source: Newman and Kenworthy (1988)

Figure 3.9   *The trade-off between fuel-efficient vehicles and actual fuel use per capita across the Perth metropolitan area*

can be reduced by car use being reduced, then a city has a more sustainable solution to congestion and fuel use. London put in a congestion tax to reduce congestion and pay for the external costs of motor vehicles. Singapore, Oslo and Stockholm had also done this, but London was the first big city to attempt a more city-wide approach. The London initiative ringed the central city with sensors that enabled people to pay automatically or to fine those who did not pay when they crossed the cordon into the centre of London. Most importantly they put the money raised back into better public transport. The result was a 15 per cent reduction in traffic and much better bus services, both because they were able to meet their schedules more easily and because they had more buses. The 60,000 fewer vehicles per day was much preferred by those who chose to continue driving and 50–60 per cent of those who stopped driving changed to public transport (http://en.wikipedia.org/wiki/London_congestion_charge). For the cities of the world, it showed that such intervention can be done, that you can tax the car to make greener urban transportation work. Other cities are now moving to a congestion tax; Stockholm found that there was a reduction in congestion of 25 per cent at the morning rush and 40 per cent in the evening, about half the people moved to transit with a 4.5 per cent increase in public transport patronage from a very high base (Expert Group, 2006).

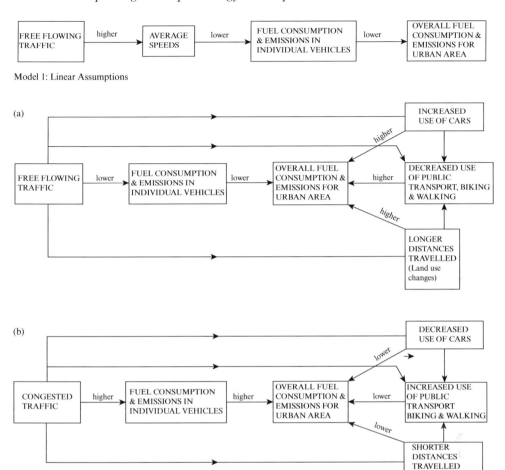

Model 1: Linear Assumptions

Model 2: Feedback Assumptions (a) Freeflowing Traffic, & (b) Congested Traffic

Source: Newman and Kenworthy (1988)

Figure 3.10   Reductionist (linear) and holistic (feedback loop) explanations of transport energy use in cities

Can Energy and Carbon Dioxide Emissions be Saved by Switching to Public Transport and by How Much?

The data presented in Tables 3.4–6 show how much more energy efficient public transport is per passenger kilometre travelled compared to cars – across all the cities, in the order of 50–80 per cent more efficient. However, experience with studying the impact of delivering public transport has showed that it appears to do even better at saving fuel – especially if it is a rail system. It appears that it is not just a case of comparing modal efficiencies on the assumption that people will replace 1km of travel by car with 1km of travel on, for example, a new train. Indeed it appears that a train could mean savings of

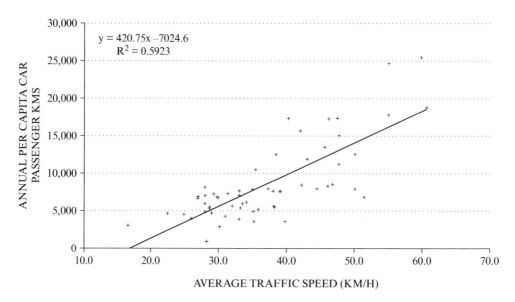

Source: From data in Kenworthy and Laube (2001)

Figure 3.11   Average road traffic speed versus per capita car use in 58 cities, 1995

seven passenger kilometres of car use for each one passenger kilometre of train use. Why is this?

Figure 3.12 shows the relationship between car passenger kilometres and public transport passenger kilometres from the *Millennium Cities Database for Sustainable Transport*. The most important thing about this relationship is that as the use of public transport increases linearly, the car passenger kilometres decrease exponentially. This is due to the phenomenon called *Transit Leverage* whereby one pass km of transit use replaces between three and seven passenger kilometres in a car (Neff, 1996) due to:

- more direct travel (especially in trains);
- trip chaining (doing various other things like shopping or service visits associated with a commute);
- giving up one car in a household (a common occurrence that reduces many solo trips); and
- changes in where people live or work near transit (Newman et al., 2008).

The lower end of the transit leverage seems to be associated with buses as they don't have the same direct speed (unless BRT is being used) and they don't facilitate land-use change as easily. These calculations can mean a very significant change in carbon dioxide emissions is possible when public transport policies are being considered. This kind of dramatic reduction in car use, as new rail systems are built and transit-oriented development becomes the focus in the city, can be seen in a number of places (Newman and Kenworthy, 1999). On this basis, one can argue that the kind of dramatic improvements

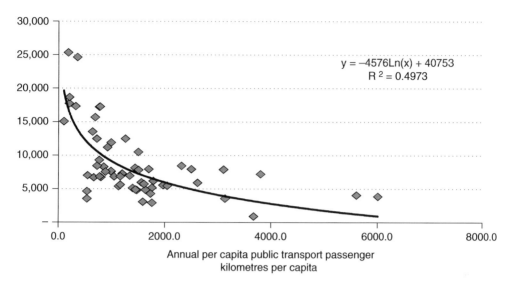

$$y = -4576 \text{Ln}(x) + 40753$$
$$R^2 = 0.4973$$

Figure 3.12 *The exponential decline in car use that follows the increase in public transport*

in public transport being built in Chinese and Indian cities (e.g., the massive subway systems in Shanghai and Beijing) are likely to significantly suppress private motorised transport growth in these emerging city economies.

6. CONCLUSIONS

The data on cities around the world in this chapter has demonstrated the vast range in per capita transport energy use and carbon dioxide emissions, from the massive levels shown in cities such as Atlanta and Houston, through the very much lower levels in European cities, to the infinitesimally small levels often found in the very dense, low income places such as Ho Chi Minh City and even in much wealthier Hong Kong. It has also shown how public transport modes are universally more energy-efficient than private passenger transport and that within the public transport modes, rail is clearly the best.

Using carefully collected data for the same cities, we have investigated some key relationships between private passenger transport energy use per capita and other factors such as the level of public transport use, urban density and the use of non-motorised transport. The work has shown the key role played by urban density and these other factors in helping to determine passenger transport energy per capita, as opposed to the more usual explanation that wealth is the key determinant. Higher urban densities, and greater use of public transport and non-motorised transport all work together, and apparently synergistically, to help achieve some very low levels of passenger transport energy use.

Reducing transport energy use and carbon dioxide are likely to become greater planning imperatives as we move further into this century. The analyses here have attempted to examine three commonly found approaches to achieving these aims. The results suggest that:

1. Transport technological improvements will be needed, but will probably not be enough due to the tendency for increasing vehicle use to consume the gains made in individual vehicles.
2. Transport management that simply frees up the movement of traffic will be counterproductive, as induced car use and land-use changes simply create more traffic. The building of large new highways and freeways will be totally counterproductive to reducing transport energy use and their resulting carbon dioxide emissions.
3. Transport policy that improves public transport options has the potential for dramatic impacts on fuel use and carbon dioxide emissions, since public transport has been shown capable of reducing car use exponentially.

REFERENCES

Davidson, S. (2005), Air transport impacts take off, *ECOS: Towards a Sustainable Future*, **123**.

Dodson, J. and Sipe, N. (2006), *The Suburbs: Urban Location, Housing Debt and Oil Vulnerability in the Australian City*, Urban Research Program, Research Paper 8, Brisbane: Griffith University.

Expert Group (2006), *The Stockholm Congestion Charging Trial – What Happened?* City of Stockholm, www.stockholmsforsoket.se.

InterAcademy Council (2007), *Lighting the Way: Toward a Sustainable Energy*, Amsterdam: InterAcademy Council.

IPCC (2007), *Climate Change 2007: Mitigation of Climate Change*, Contribution of Working Group III to the Fourth Assessment Report of the Intergovernmental Panel on Climate, Cambridge: Cambridge University Press.

Kenworthy, J. (2008), Energy use and CO_2 production in the urban passenger transport systems of 84 international cities: findings and policy implications, in P. Droege (ed.), *Urban Energy Transitions*, Amsterdam: Elsevier, pp. 211–36.

Kenworthy, J. and Laube, F. (2001), *The Millennium Cities Database for Sustainable Transport*, Brussels: UITP and Perth: ISTP, Murdoch University.

Leggett, J. (2006), *Half Gone: Oil, Gas, Hot Air and the Global Energy Crisis*, London: Portobello Books.

Neff, J.W. (1996), *Substitution Rates between Transit and Automobile Travel*, paper presented at the Association of American Geographers' Annual Meeting, Charlotte, NC, April.

Newman, P. and Kenworthy, J. (1984), The use and abuse of driving cycle research: clarifying the relationship between traffic congestion, energy and emissions, *Transportation Quarterly*, **38**(4), 615–35.

Newman, P. and Kenworthy, J. (1988), The transport energy trade-off: fuel efficient traffic vs fuel efficient cities, *Transportation Research*, **22A**(3), 163–74.

Newman, P. and Kenworthy, J. (1999), *Sustainability and Cities: Overcoming Automobile Dependence*, Washington, DC: Island Press.

Newman, P. and Kenworthy, J. (2011), 'Peak car use': understanding the demise of automobile dependence, *World Transport Policy and Practice*, **17**(2), 31–42.

Newman, P., Kenworthy, J. and Glazebrook, G. (2008), How to create exponential decline in car use in Australian cities, *Australian Planner*, also published on AdaptNet Policy Forum 08-06-E-Ad, 8 July.

Priester, R., Kenworthy, J. and Wulfhorst, G. (2013), The diversity of megacities worldwide: challenges for the future of mobility, in Institute for Mobility Research (ed.), *Megacity Mobility Culture: How Cities Move on in a Diverse World*, Munich: Springer, pp. 23–54.

Renner, M. (2011), Auto industry stages comeback from near-death experience, *Worldwatch Institute Vital Signs*, http://vitalsigns.worldwatch.org/vs-trend/auto-industry-stages-comeback-near-death-experience.

Richardson, E. (n.d.) *Integrated Transport Planning: Affordable and Supportable Solutions for Perth Communities*, Sinclair Knight Merz Technical Paper, www.skmconsulting.com/Site-Documents/Technical-Papers/Intergrated%20transport%20planning.pdf.

Salter, R., Dhar, S. and Newman, P. (2011), *Technologies for Climate Change Mitigation: Transport Sector*, UNEP Risoe Centre, www.tech-action.org/guidebooks.asp.

WBCSD (2004), *Mobility 2030 Report: Meeting the Challenges to Sustainability*, Geneva: World Business Council for Sustainable Development.

4 Homes, jobs and commuting: development location and travel outcomes

Peter Headicar

1. INTRODUCTION

In the mid-1990s planning policies towards transport and development in the UK were comprehensively revised to fulfil the government's commitment to the then novel concept of sustainable development. The particular objectives sought were to reduce the need to travel and to ensure a choice of modes so as to obviate car dependence (DoE and DoT, 1994). Coincidentally the same point in time marked a break in the long-run trend of increasing car use. Over the subsequent decade (before the economic recession) car mileage per head levelled off entirely (DfT, 2011).

The sustainability problem that the revised planning policies were designed to address nevertheless remains and indeed has become more acute in two respects. Population growth has come to assume much greater significance in projections of future traffic levels. (National road traffic forecasts published in 2011 assume an 18 per cent population growth over 25 years whereas the equivalent figure underpinning forecasts made in 1997 was just 4 per cent). Yet under the Climate Change Act 2008 the UK government has committed itself to a *greater* long-term reduction in CO_2 emissions, 80 per cent below 1990 levels by 2050. The overall volume of road traffic is now projected to be 44 per cent higher in 2035 than in 2010 with barely any expected reduction in associated CO_2 emissions (DfT, 2011). Meanwhile traffic growth threatens to exacerbate congestion in the nation's more urbanised regions, which have come to be recognised as critical to its economic prospects (Eddington, 2006).

Addressing these issues is especially problematic in south-east England because of greater than average rates of population and economic growth. Here the role that development planning might play in contributing to less car use is also made more difficult because of highly politicised battles over urbanisation generally – battles that long precede, and operate independently of, any concerns over traffic growth from a sustainability perspective.

This chapter explores the relationship between planning policy and travel outcomes using Central Oxfordshire, a sub-region within the outer south-east, as a case study. It is argued that, in respect of development location, application of the policy has neglected the strategic dimension represented by commuting outside the home settlement (i.e., as a component of *inter-urban* travel). The culture of car dependence that characterises suburban developments in smaller expanded towns adds to the already formidable institutional and practical barriers facing any attempt to reduce car use for these medium and longer distance trips.

2.   PLANNING POLICY

The UK's comprehensive system of development planning and control introduced in 1947 owes its existence in part to the desire to counter the adverse effects of motorisation – specifically the trend towards fragmented, low density urban sprawl that had accompanied increasing vehicle use in the inter-war years. The twin objectives of urban containment and countryside protection have been prominent in planning policy throughout the period since.

These policies of physical restriction had to be complemented by others aimed at positive provision for new development within surrounding regions. Initial programmes redistributing population and employment to publicly promoted new and expanded towns were later succeeded by more spontaneous processes of counter-urbanisation within development frameworks prepared by local authorities (Cervero, 1995; Champion, 1989). Although the growing settlements retained traditional urban forms and densities, their functioning changed markedly over time as increasing car ownership and investment in the inter-urban road network facilitated commuting between towns and over longer distances (Breheny et al., 1993).

In the mid-1990s the guidance issued to local planning authorities was revised to help reduce the growth in the length and number of motorised journeys and thus contribute to the government's Sustainable Development Strategy (DoE and DoT, 1994). Authorities were originally asked to 'allocate the maximum amount of housing to existing larger urban areas' (DoE and DoT, 1994: para 3.2) although this was later amended to a more nuanced search sequence starting with the reuse of land within urban areas, then urban extensions and finally new development around nodes in 'good' public transport corridors (DETR, 2001: para 14). Thereafter potential sites were to be assessed for their accessibility to jobs, shops and services by modes other than the car and the potential for improving such accessibility.

It is a feature of this policy framework that it focuses on the *opportunities* available for using modes other than the car and on ensuring that centres of employment and other facilities are accessible by them. Little emphasis is placed on actual travel outcomes. Even the requirement to undertake Transport Assessments of major developments which was added in 2001 prescribes that these should be presented in terms of mode share, rather than *the resulting volume of car mileage* (DETR, 2001: para 23). Such advice has the effect of being almost counterproductive since in practice the journeys whose mode it is easiest to influence are typically the shortest!

3.   THE RESEARCH CONTEXT

Investigating the effect of any aspect of national policy guidance is extremely challenging because of the long time-lag between publication of the guidance, the execution of local planning and development processes and eventual travel outcomes.[1] In this case there is the additional difficulty of data availability. Although development outcomes can be identified from databases maintained by local planning authorities, travel outcomes cannot. Travel behaviour generally is monitored annually through the National Travel Survey but the sampled household records cannot be analysed individually and linked to specific locations (of which 'recent developments' would in any case represent only a very small share). Data on household car ownership and journey to work distance and mode can be obtained from the National Population Census and related to specific localities. (The smallest output area level contains 125 households on average.) However, this is only conducted every ten years and at the time of writing data from the 2011 Census on commuting distances had not been published.

An alternative proposition is to undertake bespoke household surveys and to analyse the resulting travel data in relation to specific local land use and transport features. This is the approach adopted in a recent UK Research Council funded project (Susilo et al., 2012). The project focuses on the design aspects of individual developments, reflecting the dominant orientation of planning practice (since it is this aspect over which planning authorities can exert most direct influence). Bespoke surveys have also been used in the Oxfordshire research to be described here, which is concerned with the strategic location of new residential development.

Central Oxfordshire is a relatively self-contained sub-region about 30 miles across centred on the city of Oxford some 60 miles north-west of London. As an administrative entity the city is relatively small (152,000 in 2011) but it functions as the main concentration of employment and more specialised services for about 550,000 people in the wider area. Outside the city the settlement pattern is characterised by historic market towns interspersed with villages, both tending to have larger suburban additions the closer they are to Oxford. As with much of outer south-east England the area has experienced rapid growth in recent decades with a 60 per cent increase in the number of households over the past 40 years.

Since the 1950s peripheral expansion of Oxford has deliberately been halted by the designation of a Green Belt about five miles wide, closely drawn around the edge of the city's built-up area. Until the 1980s, new residential development was widely distributed in settlements within and beyond this belt and took the form of modest extensions to smaller towns plus infilling within the boundaries of settlements generally. Thereafter the pattern of growth was modified to reflect what was termed the 'country towns' strategy adopted by Oxfordshire County Council, which at the time had overall planning responsibility for the area. The significance of the strategy in the present context is that it anticipated the 'urban concentration' prescribed in the later national planning guidance while maintaining restriction on the expansion of Oxford itself in order to preserve the Green Belt.

Under the strategy the bulk of new housing land required in the county was to be found at a limited number of towns beyond the Green Belt of which three – Bicester, Didcot and Witney – fall within Central Oxfordshire. Transport connections were a consideration in their selection. Bicester and Didcot lie at opposite ends of the A34 trunk road which forms a dual carriageway spine north-south through the area (see Figure 4.1). Since 1991 Bicester has also been served by the M40 motorway between London and Birmingham. Bicester and Didcot are both linked by rail to London but only Didcot benefits from a good rail service to Oxford. Otherwise connections to the city are provided by commercial bus services.

The 'country towns' strategy has been maintained over the past 30 years, during which time the population of the three towns has more than doubled (to an average of around 30,000). Despite complementary growth in local jobs and services the historic imbalance of employment in favour of Oxford remains. However a combination of growth and

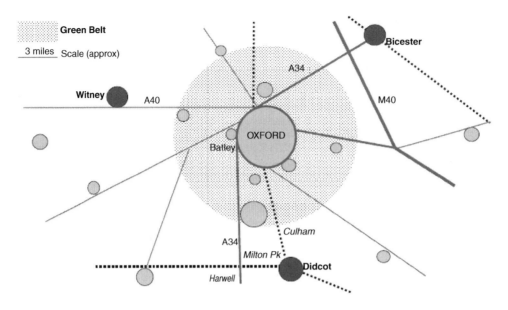

Figure 4.1   Central Oxfordshire showing the three 'country towns' that have undergone major planned expansion

relocation means that a half of all workplaces in the city are now located in its outer suburban ring close to the ring road.

Significantly – reflecting the chance element of historical legacy that planners also have to contend with – three of the most important centres of employment outside the urban areas mentioned originated as former government scientific research stations (Harwell and Culham) and a military depot (Milton Park). These lie in the south central part of the county, close to the A34 and initially were deliberately located well away from the main centres of population!

The situation in Central Oxfordshire therefore exemplifies a planning predicament common to many city regions arising from the interplay of two opposing trends – regional concentration of major employment in or around the core city on the one hand and a centrifugal pattern of housing demand extending over the surrounding hinterland on the other (WSP and Arup, 2005).

4.   CHARACTERISTICS OF THE OXFORDSHIRE ESTATES

The estates studied in the Oxfordshire towns were built as planned neighbourhoods of around 2,500 dwellings on the edge of the established urban areas. They are physically distinct, bounded by main roads and incorporate a small shopping centre, primary schools and other local facilities within easy walking distance. Local employment is concentrated in the respective town centres (0.7–1.1 miles away) and in segregated light industrial areas. Residential densities are relatively high by traditional English suburban standards (30–8 dwellings per hectare net) but consistent with the minimum of 30dph set more recently in planning guidance.

Household travel surveys were first conducted on the estates in the three country towns in 1993 when the properties were only a few years old. For the purpose of comparison a smaller development of a similar age and character was also surveyed at Botley – a traditional suburban district immediately to the west of Oxford City (Headicar and Curtis, 1998). These four areas were re-surveyed in 2011. Together with data from the 2001 Census they provide insights into how the composition and travel behaviour of residents has 'matured' in the intervening years. The country town estates also now act as useful exemplars of contemporary lifestyles in 'suburban' areas away from cities that are a distinctive product of counter-urbanisation.

In terms of tenure almost all the properties on the estates are either privately owned or rented (their date of construction precedes the national policy to include a proportion of 'affordable' housing in new developments). This is reflected in a socio-economic profile that, relative to the parent towns and to Oxfordshire as a whole, is skewed towards economically active adults and professional/managerial occupations (Table 4.1). Consistent with this, car ownership is higher, although average household size is similar. Oxford City has a similar occupational profile but a conspicuously lower proportion of owner-occupied properties and level of household car ownership.

Between the estates average house prices at Botley are 44 per cent higher than in the country towns, although this reduces to 35 per cent if viewed in terms of cost (£) per habitable room (Table 4.2).[2] The difference reflects the premium enjoyed by places in or close to Oxford. There are much smaller differences between the individual towns.

Table 4.1   Socio-economic characteristics of the Oxfordshire estates

		Country towns avg		Botley		Oxford City	Oxfordshire*
		Estates	Towns	Estate	Suburb		
Tenure	% owner-occ	82	78	94	80	55	71
Economic activity	% 16–74 EA	82	75	75	68	53	66
Occupational category**	% SEC 1 & 2 (prof/man)	52	41	53	49	51	46
Household size	Persons per h'hold	2.40	2.45	2.37	2.35	2.32	2.41
Vehicle Ownership	Cars & vans per h'hold	1.45	1.32	1.44	1.22	0.94	1.33
Age of residents	% 0–15	26	22	21	18	16	20
	% 16–24	8	10	9	9	23	12
	% 25–44	48	36	32	28	30	30
	% 45–64	14	20	28	24	18	23
	% 65+	4	11	10	21	13	15

Notes:
*   Oxfordshire includes Oxford city
**   Among economically active adults

Source: Census of Population, 2001

Table 4.2   Contemporary house prices, household incomes and household composition on the Oxfordshire estates

	Bicester Langford Village	**Didcot** Ladygrove	**Witney** Deer Park	*Average of country town estates*	**Botley** Fogwell Road
Average property price £k	240.5	200.1	221.6	*220.7*	319.3
Average number of habitable rooms	5.59	5.15	5.07	*5.27*	5.67
£k per habitable room	43.0	38.8	43.7	*41.9*	56.3
Average household annual income £k	52.3	46.6	49.4	*49.4*	53.7
% single adult households	23	37	21	*27*	27
% households with dependent children	40	30	53	*41*	43

Although the physical attributes of the estates are similar variations in the character of the parent towns is reflected in differences in their socio-economic composition. Witney – most obviously conforming to the image of a 'country town' – contains a much higher proportion of households with children, while Didcot – more urban and industrial in character – has a higher proportion of single adult and/or childless households.

5.   TRAVEL OUTCOMES: COMMUTING

The more recent Oxfordshire research has focused on commuting and the factors surrounding it. This is because the earlier survey had demonstrated that among journeys made regularly (taken to be the ones over which development planning was most likely to be able to exert an influence) commuting accounted for the majority (76 per cent) of the travel mileage. It was also the source of the greatest variation in *car* mileage between the surveyed locations. Other research using English evidence has concluded that land-use factors exert a greater influence on journey to work distance than travel generally (Stead, 2001). In addition the Department for Transport (DfT) has identified the significance of commuting among non-discretionary (i.e., non social/leisure) journeys in contributing to car-based CO_2 emissions (DfT, 2009). Almost 90 per cent of the adults in work on the surveyed estates are involved in a regular commuting journey. Table 4.3 shows the average length and proportion of these trips by mode from each of the estates.

The average work trip length on the country town estates (11.8 miles) is 37 per cent higher than the current national average but 14 per cent less than when surveyed in 1993.[3] Similarly the car driver mode share (74 per cent) is seven percentage points higher than the national average but four points lower than in 1993.

As a single measure incorporating both trip length and mode share distributions Table 4.3 also shows the average car miles per commuter trip (i.e., the total car driver mileage divided by the number of commuters). As in 1993, the country town estates exhibit remarkable differences, given that they have such fundamental similarities in terms of density, socio-economic composition, size of parent settlement and distance from

Table 4.3   Average distance and mode share of commuting trips

		Bicester Langford Village	**Didcot** Ladygrove	**Witney** Deer Park	*Average of country town estates*	**Botley** Fogwell Road
Adults with commuting journeys n =		79	67	77		79
Average one-way trip length (miles)		15.5	10.4	9.6	*11.8*	11.2
% mode	Car driver	81	66	74	*74*	55
share	Car passenger	4	2	4	*3*	4
	Public transport	6	19	8	*11*	21
	Walk/cycle/other	9	13	14	*12*	20
Car miles per commuter trip		12.0	5.9	8.6	*8.8*	7.3

Oxford city. The high figure for the Bicester estate is due to two factors in combination – the lack of workplaces in the area near to the town (resulting in 60 per cent of residents commuting more than ten miles) plus public transport being used for barely 10 per cent of these longer distance journeys. At the other end of the scale, Didcot benefits from significant workplaces in its immediate hinterland – the former government establishments referred to earlier – with the result that only 40 per cent of its residents commute more than ten miles. In addition, public transport (almost exclusively rail) is used for 40 per cent of these longer-distance journeys. Witney is in an intermediate position. A relatively high proportion of trips are to workplaces within the town itself, such that, like Didcot, a minority of workers are involved in travelling more than ten miles. In this case, however (with no rail option available) almost all such journeys are made by car.

Hence what has superficially been an 'even-handed' policy of spreading overall requirements for housing development between established towns of a similar size has in practice produced thoroughly uneven and often undesirable travel outcomes as far as commuting is concerned. Worse, the country town estates collectively have a combination of dependence on external workplaces and high levels of car use that results in 84 per cent of all car commuting mileage arising from trips of more than ten miles (Figure 4.2). A policy of 'urban concentration', without explicitly discriminating in

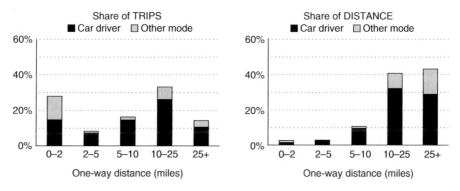

Figure 4.2   Distribution of commuting trips by distance and car driver/other modes (average of country town estates)

favour of sub-regional cities like Oxford, therefore has the perverse effect of denying the exceptional potential of such places for lessening car mileage while simultaneously 'building in' car dependence elsewhere.[4]

6.   FACTORS CONTRIBUTING TO LONGER-DISTANCE CAR COMMUTING

The relationship between the spatial patterning of housing and employment opportunities on the one hand and observed commuting behaviour on the other depends on the balancing of choices made by households (Jarvis, 2001). Why do people opt for longer-distance commuting and why in the majority of cases do they choose to do so by car?

A fundamental point to establish is that longer-distance commuting is not regarded as a desirable activity in itself. In the 2011 survey, respondents were asked to score their journey to work on six criteria using a five-point scale in each. Each person's responses were then amalgamated to form a single rating from +2 to −2. Unsurprisingly there was a negative correlation overall between rating and distance (r = 0.543 p<.001); people with journeys of less than two miles had an average rating of +1.16, those of more than 25 miles −0.60.

In accepting the negative attributes of longer-distance commuting, people are trading these off against the advantages of obtaining or retaining a particular job on the one hand and those of obtaining or maintaining a particular type of property or home location on the other (and avoiding the costs and upheaval that would otherwise be involved in moving). Many of the respondents who were involved in the longest commuting journeys had very specific personal reasons for doing so. Examples were retaining an established (relatively well-paid) job with a firm that had relocated further afield or reluctantly moving house (necessitating a long commute) in order to live with or near an elderly relative requiring care.

More generally it is useful to examine whether certain basic socio-economic attributes characterise different categories of commuter. Table 4.4 compares commuters who drive more than ten miles to work (essentially 'inter-urban' journeys in the Oxfordshire context) with those who drive less than ten miles and those who use other modes for journeys above and below this distance. (In practice 'other' modes beyond ten miles is almost exclusively by rail.)

Longer-distance commuters as a whole are more likely to be male, working full-time, in professional or managerial occupations and members of higher-income households. Such features are as expected. More surprisingly, given the constraints on moving associated with families, they are also more likely to be members of *childless* households. One reason for this apparent anomaly is that many older workers are 'childless' in the sense that their grown-up children no longer live at home and they have become accustomed to living in a particular property or neighbourhood (and commuting to a particular workplace) in a pattern established during previous years as a family.

It is also notable that commuters from single adult households have *shorter* work journeys. One reason for this is likely to be the greater flexibility they possess over home location by not having the interests of partners or children to consider (since almost all are childless). However economic factors also come into play as their lower incomes impinge on their purchasing power in the housing market and on their ability to sustain

Table 4.4   Characteristics of commuters by mode and trip length (all four survey areas)

		ALL	Non-car driver modes		Car driver mode	
		(N= 301)	<10 miles	10+ miles	<10 miles	10+ miles
% of commuters			23	11	35	32
Household	% owner-occupied	74	61	71	73	83
	% 1 adult householder	18	29	19	16	14
	% 0 children	55	59	77	43	56
	Mean h'hold income £k	54.0	47.1	58.4	50.8	60.3
	Mean years resident	8.4	8.1	8.2	9.0	7.9
Individual	% male	48	39	65	43	55
	% in full-time work	83	83	94	76	87
	% prof/managerial occup'n	66	61	78	59	73
	% with sole use of car/van	74	39	42	85	97
	% escort child to school	12	20	0	22	9
	Mean age	42.0	40.2	40.1	42.7	42.7

Table 4.5   Importance of factors prompting commuters to move home and influencing their eventual choice of house (average of four estates N = 190)

Move prompt	Avg score*	% very imp't**	Choice of house	Avg score *	% very imp't**
Different type of property	0.40	34	Price of property	0.73	60
Forming new household	0.32	31	Character of neighbourhood	0.63	46
Change in family size	0.27	24	Access to workplace	0.53	38
Different type of area	0.26	20	Character of property	0.40	20
Change of job	0.17	17	Access to family	0.38	22
Change in income	0.13	7	Able to make quick purchase	0.36	23
Required to move	0.12	10	Access to rail station	0.24	15
			Access to M40/A34	0.23	14
			Access to bus service	0.22	13

Notes:
*   On a scale from 0 (not important) to 1 (very important)
**   Percent respondents answering 'very important' (each factor was considered separately; hence figures sum to >100)

the costs of car ownership and longer-distance commuting. Significantly the estate with the lowest house prices (Didcot) is also the one with the highest representation of single adult households. Of the three country towns, it is also the one where the availability of jobs in the immediate area is greatest.

Further insight into the source of commuting behaviour can be found in the circumstances surrounding people's house move (i.e., to their current home) and its impact on travel distances. Table 4.5 identifies the importance of factors prompting their move and influencing their eventual choice of house using a scale from 0 (not important) to 1 (very important). Securing a change in the type of property was the dominant prompt – the proportion of respondents living in detached and owner-occupied properties as a consequence of moving increased by 28 and 25 percentage points respectively. A broader range of factors had a significant bearing on the eventual choice of house with access to workplace coming third after relative price and character of neighbourhood.

Particular transport features were less important than the other factors mentioned in influencing the eventual choice of house but there were significant differences between the estates reflecting their local attributes. For example 'access to rail station' scored an average of 0.52 at Didcot and access to A34/M40 0.48 at Bicester. This invites speculation that people choosing to live in these places were 'self-selecting' as far as their subsequent commuting behaviour is concerned (Næss, 2009). There are individual cases where this applies but it is not a pervasive phenomenon. For example at Didcot only 16 per cent of all commuters actually travel by rail and most householders who registered access to the rail station as very important in their house choice did not use it for commuting themselves. (There are of course other reasons why it may be regarded as important and factors influencing a household's choice do not necessarily apply to all its members.)

Most people who previously lived in their hometown did not consider moving to places outside it. For them the character of the neighbourhood and access to/quality of schools was registered as more important than access to workplace, although this has to be interpreted in the light of the fact that their house move would not alter this significantly. People who previously lived outside their hometown (or who lived within it but had considered moving elsewhere) placed access to workplace on a par with neighbourhood character and more important than access to schools, friends and family.

In the country town estates, almost half of respondents had previously lived within their hometown. At Botley three-quarters had done so (including Oxford City within the definition of 'hometown'). In both situations, people moving from elsewhere were disproportionately likely to come from similar kinds of places. The net result is that 86 per cent of respondents in the country towns had previously lived in small or medium sized towns or in rural areas. By contrast almost the same proportion at Botley had previously lived in a large town or city. Hence, although the estates have a similar suburban appearance, the backgrounds of the people currently living in them – and by implication their 'lifestyles' – is very different. This is reflected in their current levels of car ownership and use.

The 2011 survey did not ask about commuting distances before people's house moves but it did identify their previous commuting time. For the three country town estates, average commuting times have barely altered since before residents' house move (increasing by one minute to 37 minutes). This compares with an increase of eight minutes (to 36 minutes) in the 1993 survey, which was associated with an increase in long-distance commuting among the majority of people coming to live on the then newly built estates from outside the town (Headicar and Curtis, 1996).

Further analysis shows that the present figure in fact masks an important difference between people moving within their home town and those continuing to move in from elsewhere. Commuting times for the former have *decreased* by an average of four minutes (to 30) whereas the latter have increased by five (to 45). The current national average is 28 minutes.

Comparison can also be made with the earlier survey in terms of workplace destinations and mode of travel. Figure 4.3 shows that the overall proportion of travel to places beyond

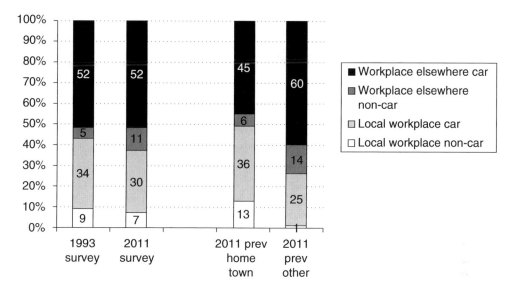

Figure 4.3   Workplace location and commuting mode 1993 and 2011 plus 2011 by previous residence

the hometown and its immediate hinterland has increased a little since 1993, although the share by car to these places has remained the same. However subdivision of the 2011 data again highlights the difference between people previously living in or outside the home town. Roundly a half of the former work locally but only a quarter of the latter do so.

Just over 80 per cent of respondents who commute outside their local area do so by car. The fact that almost all of these people have sole use of their vehicle would imply that they had a 'choice' of mode as conventionally understood. Objectively most do – only a few travel to remote or distant places where public transport is not a practicable alternative. It was therefore surprising to find that, when asked whether they had a choice of mode for their commuting journey, almost two-thirds of these people said that they did not. The interpretation that respondents placed upon this question is highly significant. With the exception of a small proportion who had other reasons for needing to drive (e.g., as part of their work or in order to convey children to/from school) the explanation was almost always some perceived deficiency in public transport which they interpreted as leaving them with 'no choice'. Even in getting to workplaces in Oxford City (which is relatively well-served) 41 per cent of otherwise unconstrained drivers responded in this way.

7.   CONCLUDING DISCUSSION

Throughout its existence planning policy in the UK has been framed in terms of the contrasting characteristics of 'town' versus 'country' or 'urban' versus 'rural'. Over recent decades the phenomenon of counter-urbanisation has undermined this distinction in functional terms although, as a prime objective of policy, the physical differentiation is as strong – or possibly stronger – than ever. The term 'suburban' is now used by the Office of National Statistics in its cluster analysis of Census data at ward level to describe areas that have socio-economic characteristics typical of the traditional outer residential parts of cities and industrial towns but that are now also widely found in and around the expanding 'country towns' of city regions in growth areas.

In these places much of the out-commuting to employment centres that is a feature of suburban areas now takes place at the inter-urban scale. The Oxfordshire case illustrates the significance of these commuting movements and the way in which they have been added to as a consequence of severely restrictive development policies in the area immediately around the core city.

The research conducted on the country town estates has shown that since their completion 20 or so years ago the proportion of longer-distance car commuting has reduced among those residents who have since moved to them from within the same town. This can be regarded as a form of 'naturalising' adjustment over time similar to that observed amongst residents moving to the Surrey commuter belt south of London (Hickman and Banister, 2007). In overall terms, however, this reduction is negated by an increase in longer-distance car commuting amongst those people who have continued to move in from elsewhere (45 per cent of the present total).

Arguably more serious is the accumulation of an increasing share of the county's population within settlements that are nominally 'urban' but in fact have high car ownership levels and extensive commuting patterns very little different from neighbouring 'rural' areas. This is in marked contrast to the situation on the Botley estate, which has attributes more in common with neighbouring Oxford City.

Since the physical design and socio-economic attributes of all the estates conformed to a similar 'suburban' mould, this leads one to suggest that in planning terms it would be helpful to distinguish between the two types of location – 'suburban (city-within)' as distinct from 'suburban (city-without)'. Certainly it is clear that continuing to phrase planning policy guidance for new housing sites simply in terms of 'urban' extensions and minimum development densities will not prevent the proliferation of further development at locations where high volumes of car use will be generated.

Likewise phrases such a 'ensuring access to a choice of modes' and 'development around nodes in good public transport corridors' deserve to be scrutinised in terms of their implications for the *actual* travel behaviour of people with the option of car use. All the estates studied in Central Oxfordshire would conform with these criteria and yet, except in the few instances where a rail option is available, the use of public transport for commuting outside the home town is virtually non-existent.

The principal impediment (aside from a basic antipathy to bus use) is the geographical relationship of homes to workplaces. Most journeys, if made by public transport, would require separate access and/or egress legs to connect with the main inter-urban service in the home and destination town respectively. The delay, inconvenience and potential unreliability involved in the necessary interchanges are inherent disadvantages that could only be offset by some compensating package of 'stick' and 'carrot' measures of the kind that at present only operates in Inner Oxford. However the possible extension of such a package – particularly if it involved some element of road user or parking charge to fund the necessary improvements – would be viewed as penal by many people living and working in the 'new' suburban areas. For them a direct commute by car is the 'natural', indeed only, option to enable them to fulfil the longer distance journeys that they have to make by virtue of a combination of family circumstances, local settlement geography and the housing market.

The strategic location of new development and the management of transport networks in pressurised areas are both highly contentious issues. To date local planning authorities have not been under any obligation to marry the two, i.e., to identify and adequately account for the overall amount of car mileage likely to arise from their development plan proposals. For them following planning guidance framed in terms of 'reducing the need to travel' and 'ensuring modal choice', *applied locally*, provides a means by which sustainability can appear to be served in a way which is feasible politically and practically. Unfortunately in the circumstances described in this chapter this does not deliver the travel outcomes consistent with major reductions in car-based CO_2 emissions. The uncomfortable connection between environmental, transport and development policies at the strategic scale necessary to achieve this reduction has yet to be made.

NOTES

1. The only systematic attempt to do this is in England was as part of research project commissioned by the Department for Transport (WSP and Arup, 2005). In addition a series of case studies were undertaken as part of a project undertaken for the Commission for Integrated Transport (Halcrow Group et al., 2009). The author participated in both these exercises and their evidence informs the more general observations made here.
2. The estimates of house prices are obtained from the commercial site www.Zoopla.co.uk, which uses an algorithm based on actual sale prices in the locality held by the Land Registry coupled with data on trends on prices generally and the characteristics of individual properties. The number of habitable rooms is obtained from the 2001 Population Census for the relevant output areas. Household information is derived from the 2011 survey and excludes households with no one in work during the last year. Household incomes are before tax and are estimates derived from the mid-point of national decile bands used in the survey. Dependent children are all aged 0–15 plus 16–18 in full-time education.
3. The comparisons with 1993 are made solely in respect of commuting householders within two-adult households in order to match the sampling criteria of the earlier survey. Some of the reduction noted may be due to a small increase in the proportion of high-income males who work from home and a greater proportion of women within the workforce.
4. Belatedly the case for some expansion of Oxford at its periphery was accepted in the *South-East Plan* (DCLG, 2009) during a short-lived period between abolition of County Structure Plans under the 2004 Planning and Compulsory Purchase Act and the coalition government's abolition of these successor Regional Spatial Strategies under the 2011 Localism Act. As a consequence decisions on the amount and location of new housing development in the sub-region now fall entirely to individual local planning authorities. For a commentary on the immediate repercussions of this in relation to the employment area of South Central Oxfordshire (now branded as 'Science Vale') see Valler et al. (2012). The proposed extension of the city's built-up area southwards into the Green Belt (fiercely contested by neighbouring South Oxfordshire District Council in whose administrative area it falls) has been abandoned.

REFERENCES

Breheny, M., Gent, T. and Lock, D. (1993), *Alternative Development Patterns: New Settlements*, report for Department of Environment, London: HMSO.
Cervero, R. (1995), Planned communities, self-containment and commuting – a cross-national perspective, *Urban Studies*, **32**(7), 1135–61.
Champion, A. (1989), *Counter-urbanisation: The Changing Pace and Nature of Population De-concentration*, London: Edward Arnold.

DCLG (2009), *The South-East Plan*, London: TSO.

DETR (2001), *Planning Policy Guidance Note 13: Transport*, London: TSO.

DfT (2009), *Low Carbon Transport: A Greener Future*, London: TSO.

DfT (2011), *National Travel Survey 2010*, London: TSO.

DoE and DoT (1994), *Planning Policy Guidance Note 13: Transport*, London: HMSO.

Eddington, R. (2006), *The Eddington Transport Study: Transport's Role in Sustaining the UK's Productivity and Competitivenerss*, report to HM Treasury and Department for Transport, London: TSO.

Halcrow Group, Oxford Brookes University and Oxford University Transport Studies Unit (2009), *Planning for Sustainable Travel*, report to the Commission for Integrated Transport, www.plan4sustainabletravel.org.

Headicar, P. and Curtis, C. (1996), *The Influence of Previous Experience on Current Travel Behaviour and Attitudes*, Economic and Social Research Council Research Project R 000221599.

Headicar, P. and Curtis, C. (1998), The location of new residential development – its influence on car-based travel, in D. Banister (ed.), *Transport and the Environment*, London: E. & F.N. Spon.

Hickman, R. and Banister, D. (2007), *Transport and Energy Consumption: Does Co-location of Housing and Workplaces Occur Over Time?* Working Paper no. 1027, Transport Studies Unit, Oxford University.

Jarvis, H. (2001), Urban sustainability as a function of compromises households make deciding where and how to live: Portland and Seattle compared, *Local Environment*, **6**(3): 239–56.

Næss, P. (2009), Residential self-selection and appropriate control variables in land use: travel studies, *Transport Reviews*, **29**(3), 293–324.

Stead, D. (2001), Relationships between land use, socio-economic factors and travel patterns in Britain, *Environment and Planning B*, **28**(4), 499–528.

Susilo, Y., Williams, K., Lindsay, M. and Dair, C. (2012), The influence of individual's environmental attitudes and urban design features on their travel patterns in sustainable neighbourhoods in the UK, *Transportation Research Part D*, **17**(3), 190–200.

Valler, D., Phelps, N. and Wood, A. (2012), Planning for growth? The implications of localism for 'Science Vale', Oxfordshire, *Town Planning Review*, **83**(4), 457–88.

WSP and Arup (2005), *Impacts of Land Use Planning Policy on Transport Demand and Congestion*, research report for Department for Transport, Cambridge: WSP Policy and Research, www.wspgroup.com/upload/documents/PDF/news%20attachments/PPG13_Final_Report.pdf

5 New household location and the commute to work: changes over time
Robin Hickman and David Banister

1. INTRODUCTION

The relationship between urban form and travel has been subject to a huge amount of research over the past three decades, perhaps representing one of the most intensively researched fields within urban planning. It is an attractive topic for policymakers – with the engaging possibility that shaping the built environment in a certain way, if this can be defined, will mean that our travel behaviours will be made more sustainable. The literature has developed from exploring simplistic relationships, such as density and travel, to a more sophisticated understanding of multiple and multi-directional influences, including various built environment features, socio-economic and attitudinal and cultural factors. The built environment 'independent' factors have been broken down into more detailed variables, such as the '3 Ds' of density, diversity and design (Cervero and Kockelman, 1997); the '5 Ds', with destination accessibility and distance to transit added (Ewing and Cervero, 2001); and even the '7 Ds', with demand management and demographics added (Ewing and Cervero, 2010). The travel 'dependent' factors have been explored in terms of travel distance and time, mode share, and even composite indicators such as transport energy consumption and carbon dioxide (CO_2). The overriding interest is to understand the most effective urban form(s) – in terms of new development, redevelopment and retrofit – which may help achieve greater sustainability in transport. To an extent, the policymakers have taken the research as being more definitive than it is, and the compact city ideal (or variants such as the polycentric region) has been seen as the most desirable urban form (OECD, 2013).

This chapter examines a small part of this debate, but perhaps quite an important one. Most of the empirical research tends to be from the North American context and developed through one-off surveys or cross-sectional surveys (different individuals with similar characteristics), representing 'snapshots' in time. There is only a little longitudinal analysis developed (the same individuals tracked over time). There are very few datasets that allow for a systematic tracking of change over time, and this is an important reason for the lack of understanding of the complexity of changes over time. 'Matched pair' analysis is one form of longitudinal analysis where the tracking of new household location and travel behaviour for the same respondents is undertaken over time. It is from this perspective that we consider the urban structure and travel relationship, with a focus on how journey to work travel patterns change over time, with the same matched pair households surveyed in 1998 and 2001. The households are all taken from new developments in Surrey, UK.[1]

2. THE PREVIOUS LITERATURE: SPATIO-TEMPORALITY

The inspiration for the research was taken from the multiple studies considering the urban structure and travel relationship, with different variables and scales employed, gradually introducing new elements to the complex relationship, from density (Newman and Kenworthy, 1989, 1999; Banister et al., 1997), mixed use or jobs-housing balance (Cervero, 1989, 1996), location (Headicar and Curtis, 1998), socio-economic characteristics (Stead, 2001) and attitudes (Kitamura et al., 1997); leading to the more recent analysis that debates the influence of many of these built environment, attitudinal and socio-economic variables on travel (Boarnet and Crane, 1999; Ewing and Cervero, 2001, 2010; Krizek, 2003; Schwanen and Mokhtarian, 2005; Cao et al., 2006; Næss, 2009; Bohte et al., 2009; Hickman et al., 2009). Also of interest are authors, such as Gordon and Richardson (1989, 1995, 1997), in offering very different viewpoints from the empirical analysis and the controversial policy prescription put forward. They speculate that co-location may occur in low-density suburban areas, whereby firms and households periodically readjust spatially to achieve balanced average commuting distances and duration. There appears to be little empirical evidence behind this argument, beyond the Californian context, and little systematic tracking of individual household travel behaviours over time. Certainly in the UK, it is far from clear that suburbanisation trends lead to an 'efficient' location of activities. Indeed, traffic volumes (mainly based on increased travel distances) increase over time as people choose to access working and other activities that are not the closest to home. This can be seen as a 'discernment factor' and it is likely to be very important in many contexts.

3. THE RESEARCH FRAMEWORK AND CASE STUDY

To help test some of these issues in the literature, new households were surveyed in Surrey, a county to the south-west of London in the UK. A New Household Occupier Survey (NHOS) was sent as a postal survey in September 1998 and September 2001, with new households derived from those newly registering for the Council Tax in 1998. The NHOS 1998 is used as the basis for the analysis, with respondents who replied in 1998 resurveyed in 2001. Additional, complementary data on the built environment (such as density, mixed use, accessibility, etc.) is added using local authority datasets. Descriptive data from the survey is described in Table 5.1.

Table 5.1 NHOS descriptive statistics

NHOS	1998	2001
Number of surveys	2,920	1,568
Response rate	54%	39%
Total households returned	1,568	607
Total adult respondents	2,865	1,103
Total working respondents	1,916	698
'Stayers' working respondents	376	376

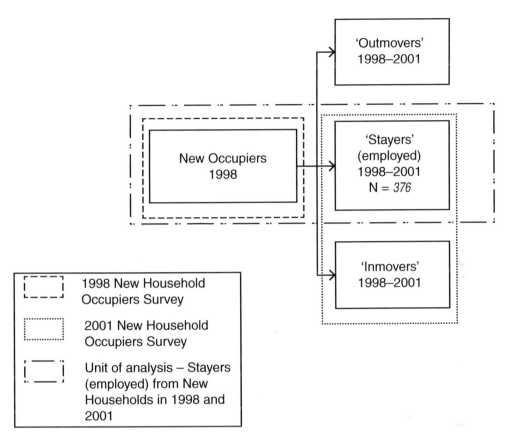

Figure 5.1   NHOS resident typology

A resident typology is developed to assess the differential travel behaviour of new house-holds, in terms of 'stayers' (individuals remaining in the new households from 1998 to 2001), 'inmovers' (individuals moving into new households between 1998 and 2001), and 'outmovers' (individuals moving out of new households between 1998 and 2001) (see Figure 5.1). Longitudinal analysis is used to provide analysis of the matched pair stayers, assessing how individuals within households adapt their travel behaviour to their new residential locations over a three-year period. The analysis systematically tracks travel behaviour from the same households over the time period. It focuses on the stayers' data (N = 376), and uses employed residents only.[2]

The matched pair approach attempts to reduce attritional problems in the survey analysis, where changes in behaviour may be due to the loss of survey respondents from one survey to another (rather than changes in the variables themselves). The level of attrition between the surveys is fairly high, as only 39 per cent of residents responded in the second survey. However, this still represents a very good response rate for a postal survey. The NHOS sample is also non-representative of the wider Surrey population, with the '25–44' age group, 'employed full time', 'retired' and 'car driver' cohorts slightly overrepresented.

Surrey is used as the case study, a county representing London urban fringe and suburbia in Epsom, Esher and Staines, with other self-standing settlements in more rural settings such as Guildford and Woking. The county is generally relatively affluent – although isolated areas have high multiple deprivation ratings, for example, parts of Woking or Guildford – and it has good rail linkages into London, hence has a strong commuting relationship with central London.

Individual characteristics and built environment variables act as the 'independent' variables; and the 'dependent' variable in the analysis is travel, as represented by energy consumption in the journey to work[3] (a composite of journey length, time, mode share and occupancy). Commuting trips were used rather than all trip types to highlight the strong relationship between housing and employment location, and also to limit the range of the analysis. Independent variables cover a range of urban structure characteristics including resident population density, resident population size, distance from urban centres and strategic transport networks, jobs–housing balance, resident location (relative to the urban area), neighbourhood streetscape layout, public transport accessibility and also a range of socio-economic and attitudinal characteristics.

4.   COMPLEXITY OF TRAVEL BEHAVIOURS

The research findings are discussed in terms of two key themes: individual volatility and resident typology. This aims to illustrate the complexity of travel behaviour and the subtlety of the relationships with urban structure and change over time. Figure 5.2 shows the locations of new household residences and workplaces in 1998 in Surrey (new households as dots). The changes in workplace by 2001, just for one new housing development in north Horley, are given by the arrows. We can see that the changes over time are very significant. Some commutes become longer, some shorter, others stay the same distance; some commuters change modes, others use the same mode. The individual volatility is huge – a 'travel kurtosis effect' hidden below the aggregate trends analysis. The example shown illustrates the complexity of the changes within households over even a short period of time. Commutes to London, Croydon and Gatwick in 1998 remain the same in 2001. Others change, for example, a former London commute in 1998 modifies to a local commute to Horley in 2001. Some of the changes are unexpected, for example, a Dorking commute in 1998 modifies to Ealing in 2001, a Whyteleafe commute in 1998 modifies to Oxford in 2001. These latter two changes are facilitated by M25 access.

At the aggregate NHOS level, the pattern of commuting by the survey respondents has changed markedly, with the radial commute into the key towns or London becoming less important, as one or more members of the household find employment more locally. This perhaps represents the typical lifecycle of moving into Surrey – the 30-plus age group who partner up, have a family and move out of London for more space. Unfortunately, the public transport network in Surrey, particularly by rail, remains largely radial in nature, and has difficulty in responding to these rapidly changing demands. This is the multiple origins and destinations problem – it is very difficult to serve dispersed development patterns (residential, employment and other facilities) by public transport.

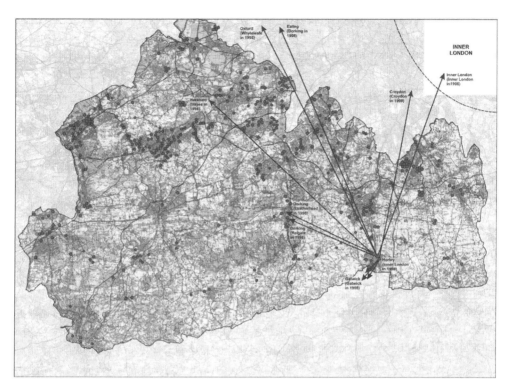

Figure 5.2   Residence and workplace location change: individual volatility in Surrey

Table 5.2   Resident typology and travel

Resident typology	Energy consumption (MJ/JTW)	Journey distance (km)	Journey time (mins)	Car mode share
All 1998	60.1	30.1	41.9	72%
Stayers 1998	54.9	29.5	40.5	70%
Stayers 2001	56.8	28.4	39.9	73%
Outmovers 1998	59.4	30.7	41.0	75%
Inmovers 2001	62.6	29.8	39.3	74%

People periodically change their travel patterns, with both home and workplace location changes, and this is largely facilitated by a road network that allows access to a wide area. Hence car dependency becomes more and more entrenched in people's lifestyles.

If the data is disaggregated by respondent typology (Table 5.2), a number of trends are apparent:

- The stayers are the least energy consuming of the cohorts (9 per cent lower than the sample average in 1998). However, energy consumption increases over time, by 3 per cent from 1998 to 2001. This reflects trends that move in different directions – journey distance and journey time are reduced by 4 per cent, yet car mode share increases by 3 per cent. This point can often be missed if the travel metric used is travel distance or mode share.

- The outmovers are the most mobile grouping in terms of journey distance travelled (4 per cent greater distance than the stayers in 1998), have the highest car mode share (at 75 per cent) and account for 8 per cent more in energy consumption than the stayers in 1998.
- The inmovers are more mobile than the stayers, but less mobile than the outmovers. They account for the greatest in energy consumption, 14 per cent more than the stayers in 2001. The difference in energy consumption between inmovers and outmovers is accounted for by the high car mode share.

These findings are potentially very important for this field of research, as travel behaviour varies by resident type and over time. The location of new households, and the modelling of likely future travel behaviour, should recognise this likely difference in segmentation. Most analysis assumes a uniform traveller profile.

5.   DISAGGREGATE LEVEL ANALYSIS OF THE STAYERS DATA

Table 5.3 highlights the aggregate level change in the stayers data. It appears that the stayers co-locate their resident and workplace locations, albeit marginally (a reduction in distance travelled of 4 per cent). However a focus on journey distance co-location masks the increase in car dependency as represented by car mode share (an increase in car mode share of 3 per cent). Most importantly, the composite indicator of transport energy consumption increases over time (by 3.5 per cent).

Hence it appears that, typically, a long distance rail commute into London is replaced by a shorter distance car commute; or a local commute by bus, foot or cycle is replaced by a longer distance car commute; or a short-distance car commute is replaced by a longer-distance car commute. Critically, this local travel modification results in an aggregate increase in energy consumption. The results show only relatively marginal

Table 5.3   Changing travel behaviour[4] over time

Changing travel behaviour 'Stayers' data	Count		Average of energy consumption (MJ/jtw)			Average of journey to work distance (km)		
	1998	2001	1998	2001	% change	1998	2001	% change
Total	376	376	54.9	56.8	3.5%	29.5	28.4	−3.7%

Average of journey to work time (mins)			Car mode share		
1998	2001	% Change	1998	2001	% Change
40.5	39.9	−1.5%	70%	73%	+3%

Source: *Data:* Surrey New Occupiers Survey 1998 and 2001; stayers data only

Table 5.4   Correlation analysis (stayers)

Socio-economic variable	Correlation	Energy consumption 1998	Energy consumption 2001
Residential population density	Pearson correlation	−0.092	−0.137**
	Sig. (two-tailed)	0.076	0.008
Residential population size	Kendall's tau	0.65	0.105**
	Sig. (two-tailed)	0.104	0.009
Distance from London	Pearson correlation	0.173**	0.237**
	Sig. (two-tailed)	0.001	0.000
Jobs–housing balance	Pearson correlation	0.021	0.017
	Sig. (two-tailed)	0.680	0.747
Public transport accessibility	Pearson correlation	0.122*	0.181**
	Sig. (two-tailed)	0.019	0.001
Household income	Pearson correlation	0.129*	0.186**
	Sig. (two-tailed)	0.029	0.002
N		376	376

Note: NB. Significance at the 5 per cent level is shown by * and at the 1 per cent level by **

changes, yet only a short time period is considered. They are partially consistent with the argument of the Gordon and Richardson (1989) distance co-location thesis, but this offers only a selective analysis of a complex picture. The aggregate increase in energy consumption seems to be the more important figure in sustainability terms.

Correlation analysis gives an indication of the strength of the relationships within the stayers data. Pearson's product moment correlation is used to examine interval data and Kendall's tau for ordinal data (Table 5.4). Residential population density, distance from London, public transport accessibility and household income all show significant relationships, reflecting the findings from the full Surrey NHOS analysis (Hickman, 2007), and each of these is discussed in the next section.

Cross-tabulated analysis of the data is also useful, and this is given below in terms of the various urban structure and travel behaviour relationships and the impact of time on these. Not all of the variables are given, and more detail can be found in Hickman (2007), but some of the more interesting variables are discussed, covering some the issues not often considered in this type of research.

Residential Population Density

Broadly we might expect that, as the density of development increases, average energy consumption and journey distance decreases for any given year. However, from the previous literature we do not know how this density and travel relationship develops over time. The 'stayers' data broadly supports the expected general trend. There is an inverse linear relationship between the household location, the density of the surrounding area (at ward level) and travel. As density increases, travel reduces in energy consumption – with the exception of the 20–35 persons/hectare cohort, which has a higher than expected energy consumption pattern (Table 5.5). Over time, the density ranges are affected

Table 5.5 Residential population density and JTW energy consumption (stayers)

Residential population density (persons/ha)	Travel behaviour	1998	2001	% Change	Count
0–1	EC	71.0	69.8	−2%	16
	JD	33.0	32.9	0%	
	Car mode share (%)	81%	88%	7%	
1–10	EC	59.9	64.4	8%	153
	JD	30.3	29.6	−2%	
	Car mode share (%)	73%	76%	3%	
10–20	EC	45.2	49.5	9%	107
	JD	28.3	28.6	1%	
	Car mode share (%)	61%	63%	2%	
20–35	EC	60.6	56.2	−7%	74
	JD	29.4	25.2	−14%	
	Car mode share (%)	76%	78%	2%	
>35	EC	37.8	34.9	−8%	26
	JD	27.5	26.4	−4%	
	Car mode share (%)	65%	69%	4%	
NHOS Stayers Total	EC	54.9	56.8	3%	376
	JD	29.5	28.4	−4%	
	Car mode share (%)	70%	73%	3%	

Note: EC = energy consumption; JD = journey distance. Dark shading = at least 5 per cent > than sample average; light shading = at least 5 per cent < sample average

Source: NHOS 1998 and 2001 data. Usually resident population/hectare, Census 2001, Office for National Statistics

differently. Households over the 20–35 persons/hectare threshold modify their behaviour by reducing their energy consumption (a 7 per cent reduction in energy consumption from 1998 to 2001). This reflects reduced travel distance and an increase in car mode share over time. Below the 20 persons/hectare threshold, energy consumption increases over time (with the exception of a marginal decrease in the 0–1 persons/hectare cohort). Perhaps there is a further nuance to the co-location hypothesis in terms of density. Within the Surrey data there appears to be an important threshold effect. Co-location in terms of travel distance and energy consumption occurs at the higher population densities. At the lower population densities, only travel distance co-location occurs, and this is outweighed by the increase in energy consumption.

Residential Location

We might expect that household location is important to energy consumption and change over time. If this is considered in terms of a town centre-rest of urban area-rural classification (Table 5.6), it can be seen that households in rural locations consume 25 per cent more energy than the stayers sample average in 1998. This reflects an increased car dependency rather than increased journey length. This is partly due to the particularities of the Surrey context. For example, households in town centre locations,

Table 5.6 *Town centre-urban area-rural classification and JTW energy consumption (stayers)*

Urban classification	Travel behaviour	1998	2001	% Change	Count
Town centre	EC	41.4	46.5	12%	43
	JD	30.7	29.1	−5%	
	Car mode share (%)	53%	56%	3%	
Rest of urban area	EC	52.3	54.3	4%	248
	JD	28.8	27.8	−4%	
	Car mode share (%)	71%	73%	2%	
Rural	EC	68.9	68.8	0%	85
	JD	30.9	29.7	−4%	
	Car mode share (%)	74%	81%	7%	

Note: EC = energy consumption; JD = journey distance. Dark shading = at least 5 per cent > than sample average; light shading = at least 5 per cent < sample average

Source: NHOS, 1998 and 2001 data. Urban classification from Surrey County Council, (1994)

in places such as Woking, Guildford or Epsom, are very well placed for commuting lengthy distances into London. Many of these 30–60km journeys by rail are more consumptive in energy than a short commute by car. Over time households in all the urban classifications (town centre, rest of urban area and rural) reduce their average journey length, however car mode share increases in all. This means that composite energy consumption increases, with the exception of the rural locations which remain at a similar level of energy consumption.

Public Transport Accessibility

Public transport accessibility is not often considered in the urban structure and travel relationship. A variable covering distance to public transport is more prevalent, yet clearly we would expect the availability and quality of the public transport provision to have some impact on travel behaviour. This may explain some of the weak relationships being found in the US research. Higher densities and mixed uses, by themselves, will have limited impacts on travel if there is little availability of public transport. The quality of the public transport service is important in terms of the connections and journey times to various destinations, as well as the experience of the public transport journey itself. In the Surrey data, residential location relative to public transport accessibility (Table 5.7) shows quite clear trends. The stayers data supports the argument that energy consumption rises as public transport accessibility to the town centres in Surrey reduces. This reflects mainly an increasingly lengthy average travel distance, and also, to a certain extent, higher car mode shares. The trends over time show that households in locations with good public transport accessibility (0–30 minutes journey time to the town centres in Surrey) reduce their average journey length, meaning that average energy consumption reduces by 2–4 per cent over the period 1998–2001. Conversely, households in locations with poor public transport accessibility (taken as >30 minutes journey time to the town centres in Surrey) increase their average journey length

Table 5.7   Public transport accessibility and JTW energy consumption (stayers)

Public transport accessibility	Travel behaviour	1998	2001	% Change	Count
0–10 mins	EC	47.3	44.9	−5%	67
	JD	26.8	23.8	−11%	
	Car mode share (%)	63%	66%	3%	
10–25 mins	EC	49.0	48.1	−2%	77
	JD	27.3	25.4	−7%	
	Car mode share (%)	74%	74%	–	
25–30 mins	EC	52.4	50.5	−4%	51
	JD	26.3	24.2	−8%	
	Car mode share (%)	67%	73%	6%	
30–45 mins	EC	60.7	65.9	9%	84
	JD	34.6	33.3	−4%	
	Car mode share (%)	68%	71%	3%	
>45 mins	EC	63.1	66.8	6%	86
	JD	30.7	32.5	6%	
	Car mode share (%)	77%	80%	3%	

Note: Public transport accessibility shows journey times through the public transport network to the nearest town centre, with 28 town centres in Surrey, using PTAM software. EC = energy consumption; JD = journey distance. Dark shading = at least 5 per cent > than sample average; light shading = at least 5 per cent < sample average

Source: NHOS, 1998 and 2001 data

and/or their car mode share, meaning that average energy consumption increases by 6–9 per cent.

Household Income

Many socio-economic (and attitudinal) characteristics are associated with travel (Hickman, 2007), but in particular energy consumption rises with increasing household income. The stayers data supports this, with the >£100k household income cohort consuming 22 per cent more energy in their commutes to work in 1998 than the sample average (Table 5.8). This reflects much higher average travel distance, but, importantly, not higher car mode shares. In Surrey, it is the lower household income groups (<£35k) that are more car dependent. This illustrates the peculiarities of the Surrey location, with a high dependence on commuting into London by rail for higher-income jobs, and the typically lower-income jobs in the county served largely by car. Over time, all income groups increase their energy consumption. However, within this, there are a number of countervailing trends. The lower household income groups (<£100k) appear to co-locate homes and workplaces and reduce their commute distance, yet they increase their car mode share. In composite terms, energy consumption rises marginally (by 2 per cent). It is the highest earners (>£100k household incomes) that increase both their average journey distances and car mode shares, and hence their composite energy consumption to a large degree, with an increase of 27 per cent from 1998 to 2001.

Table 5.8   Household income and JTW energy consumption (stayers)

Household income 'stayers' data	Travel behaviour	1998	2001	% change	Count
<£35k	EC	53.4	54.5	2%	54
	JD	22.2	21.8	−2%	
	Car mode share (%)	78%	83%	5%	
£35–100k	EC	58.5	58.7	0%	200
	JD	31.7	30.0	−5%	
	Car mode share (%)	70%	73%	3%	
>£100k	EC	67.1	85.0	27%	34
	JD	42.9	46.2	8%	
	Car mode share (%)	56%	65%	9%	

Note: EC = energy consumption; JD = journey distance. Dark shading = at least 5 per cent > than sample average; light shading = at least 5 per cent < sample average

Source: NHOS, 1998 and 2001 data

Many of the subtleties in the data may be peculiar to the Surrey context, but they do provide new interpretations of the co-location (and dis-location) debate. For example, the co-location thesis appears to have a series of large caveats to it in terms of income disaggregation. The lower-income groups co-locate in distance terms, but this is out-weighed, in terms of composite energy consumption, by increases in car dependency. The higher-income groups dis-locate in terms of journey distance and become more reliant on the car, and they experience large increases in composite energy consumption over time. Note that for Gordon and Richardson, and others researching the US context, modal split is not so important, as the commute in their analysis is primarily by car, and public transport is usually only of marginal importance. This means that the usual metric ana-lysed is vehicle miles travelled (VMT).

6.   CONCLUSIONS

Kostof (1992: 280) draws to our attention that 'in cities, only change endures' and we can see that temporal aspects seem to be an important part of the urban structure and travel relationship. Recent research and much of the current debate in urban structure and travel research has concentrated on the role of attitudes and self-selection in this relationship. This is the debate over whether people choose the built environment in which they live, and then travel according to this individual preference, together with the extent to which the built environment shapes travel itself. Perhaps there are other issues that deserve more careful consideration, and we have examined some in the Surrey context, namely temporal change and the wider contextual factors such as density, resi-dential location and distance from the core city (London), public transport accessibility and income. It is also argued that the different metrics for travel are important, such as distance, mode share, energy consumption and the choice of these can affect the results in the analysis of urban structure and travel.

It is very useful to set up longitudinal analysis, tracking the same residents over time. We can see that the changes in travel patterns over time are subtle and complex. The individual volatility is large, even over a three-year time period, and represents a travel kurtosis effect hidden in any aggregate analysis. It is possible to consider the different travel behaviour patterns of the 'stayers', 'outmovers' and 'inmovers'. All of these groups appear to have different travel behaviours, with the stayers being the least energy consuming (9 per cent less than the sample average in 1998). However, energy consumption increases over time, by 3.5 per cent from 1998 to 2001. This reflects trends which move in different directions: journey distance and journey time reduce (co-locate) by 4 per cent, yet car mode share increases (dis-locates) by 3 per cent.

A number of variables are significantly correlated with transport energy consumption, including residential population density, population size, distance from London, public transport accessibility and household income. The cross tabulated analysis reveals a number of nuanced trends:

- In terms of density, and within the Surrey data, there appears to be an important threshold effect. Co-location in travel distance and energy consumption occurs at the higher population densities. At the lower population densities, only travel distance co-location occurs, and is outweighed by the increase in energy consumption.
- Over time households in the rural locations increase their average journey length and car mode share, meaning that average energy consumption increases by 11 per cent. Only the households in the smaller towns in Surrey reduce their energy consumption over time.
- Households in locations with good public transport accessibility (0–30 minutes journey time to the town centres in Surrey) reduce their average journey length, meaning that average energy consumption reduces by 2–5 per cent from 1998 to 2001. Conversely, households in locations with poor public transport accessibility (>30 minutes journey time to the town centres in Surrey) increase their average journey length and/or their car mode share, meaning that average energy consumption increases by 6–9 per cent.
- The lower-income groups co-locate in distance terms, but this is outweighed, in terms of composite energy consumption, by increases in car dependency. The higher-income groups dis-locate in terms of journey distance and become more reliant on the car, hence experience large increases in composite energy consumption over time.

When people choose to move, 'transport' as an issue appears to enter the decision-making process at a number of levels. Sometimes the workplace location dictates the choice of resident location, in others the resident location dictates the workplace location. These factors work alongside a wide combination of factors, including the desire for a bigger house; a good environment; relationship changes; a location close to family, friends or schools; and often the 'transport' element is a minor part of locational decisions (Hickman, 2007). These individual decisions manifest themselves into large movement flows at the aggregate level. This chapter adds a systematic, longitudinal and disaggregated analysis of the urban structure and travel relationship over time. It shows that co-location and dis-location occur – at the same time – in different ways depending on what level and type of analysis is used in terms of dependent variable (land use) and independent variable (travel behaviour/energy consumption indicator).

There are many recent trends that may affect these findings – such as the recent slowing, and perhaps reversal, of the growth in motor car usage, and the levels of housing affordability, in the south-east of the UK. We have seen a glimpse of changes in travel behaviours over time, and how these might be related to the built environment. But it would be very useful to explore these contextual issues in more detail. Perhaps there is one point that will be of most interest to the policymakers. Changes to the built form will only affect travel if they are complemented by significant public transport improvements, investments in walking and cycling, and the implementation of traffic demand management measures. Transport planning is best carried out when closely integrated with urban planning – indeed travel behaviours are unlikely to be affected without this. This leads us to a requirement for integrated transport and urban planning mechanisms – and within the UK these are currently weak at best and non-existent at worst. Change might endure – but our planning frameworks are not strong enough to push this in sustainable directions.

ACKNOWLEDGEMENTS

Many thanks to Surrey County Council (Jim Storrar and Steve Howard) for help in assembling data and providing transport model runs. The views expressed in this chapter are of course from the authors and do not necessarily reflect those of Surrey County Council.

NOTES

1. More detailed analysis is given in Hickman (2007).
2. Returned household surveys in each survey year are higher, at N = 1,568 in 1998 and N = 607 in 2001.
3. The method used for calculating energy consumption is as derived in Banister et al. (1997). Aggregate transport energy consumption factors are used for each mode of travel, using peak occupancy factors for the journey to work. More details can be found in Hickman (2007).
4. Note that there is no adjustment for changes in the car stock – vehicles are assumed not to change – this means that all the change identified is due to distance and modal choice influences. Car occupancy is also assumed to remain constant over time.

REFERENCES

Banister, D., Watson, S. and Wood, C. (1997), Sustainable cities, transport, energy and urban form, *Environment and Planning B*, **24**, 125–43.
Boarnet, M. and Crane, R. (1999), *Travel by Design: The Influence of Urban Form on Travel*, New York: Oxford University Press.
Bohte, W., Maat, K. and van Wee, B. (2009), Measuring attitudes in research on residential self selection and travel behaviour: a review of theories and empirical research, *Transport Reviews*, **29**, 325–57.
Cao, X., Mokhtarian, P. and Handy, S.L. (2006), Neighborhood design and vehicle type choice: evidence from Northern California, *Transportation Research D*, **11**, 133–45.
Cervero, R. (1989), Jobs–housing balancing and regional mobility, *Journal of the American Planning Association*, **55**, 136–50.

Cervero, R. (1996), Jobs–housing balancing revisited, *Journal of the American Planning Association*, **62**, 492–511.

Cervero, R. and Kockelman, K. (1997), Traffic demand and the 3Ds: Density, diversity, and design. *Transportation Research D*, **2**, 199–219.

Ewing, R. and Cervero, R. (2001), Travel and the built environment: a synthesis, *Transportation Research Record*, **1780**, 87–114.

Ewing, R. and Cervero, R. (2010), Travel and the built environment: a meta analysis, *Journal of the American Planning Association*, **76**(3), 265–94.

Gordon, P. and Richardson, H. (1989), Gasoline consumption and cities: a reply, *Journal of American Planning Association*, **55**, 342–5.

Gordon, P. and Richardson, H. (1995), Sustainable congestion, in J. Brotchie, M. Batty, E. Blakely, P. Hall and P. Newton (eds), *Cities in Competition: Productive and Sustainable Cities for the 21st Century*, Melbourne: Longman.

Gordon, P. and Richardson, H. (1997), Are compact cities a desirable planning goal? *Journal of the American Planning Association*, **63**, 95–106.

Headicar, P. and Curtis, C. (1998), The location of new residential developments: its influence on car-based travel, in D. Banister (ed.), *Transport Policy and the Environment*, London: Spon.

Hickman, R. (2007), *Reducing the Need to Travel: A Micro Analysis of New Housing Location and the Commute to Work*, unpublished PhD thesis, University College London.

Hickman, R., Seaborn, C., Headicar, P. and Banister, D. (2009), *Planning for Sustainable Travel*, London: Halcrow and CfIT.

Kitamura, R., Mokhtarian, P. and Laidet, L. (1997), A micro-analysis of land use and travel in five neighbourhoods in the San Francisco Bay Area, *Transportation*, **24**, 125–58.

Kostof, S. (1992), *The City Assembled: The Elements of Urban Form Through History*, Boston: Bullfinch Press.

Krizek, K. (2003), Residential relocation and changes in urban travel: does neighbourhood-scale urban form matter? *Journal of the American Planning Association*, **69**(3), 265–81.

Næss, P. (2009), Residential self selection and appropriate control variables in land use: travel studies, *Transport Reviews*, **29**, 293–324.

Newman, P. and Kenworthy, J. (1989), Gasoline consumption and cities: a comparison of US cities with a global survey, *Journal of the American Planning Association*, **5**, 24–37.

Newman, P. and Kenworthy, J. (1999), *Sustainability and Cities: Overcoming Automobile Dependence*, Washington, DC: Island Press.

OECD (2013), *Compact Citites: A Comparative Study*, OECD Green Growth and Strategy Series, Paris: OECD.

Office for National Statistics (2001), Census 2001.

Schwanen, T. and Mokhtarian, P. (2005), What if you live in the wrong neighborhood? The impact of residential neighborhood type dissonance on distance traveled, *Transportation Research D*, **10**, 127–51.

Stead, D. (2001), Relationships between land use, socioeconomic factors and travel patterns in Britain, *Environment and Planning B*, **28**, 499–528.

Surrey County Council (1994), *Surrey Structure Plan*, Kingston: Surrey County Council.

6 Spatial structure and travel: trends in commuting and non-commuting travels in US metropolitan areas

Peter Gordon and Bumsoo Lee

1. INTRODUCTION

The economist Robert Lucas famously noted that, once you start thinking about economic growth, it's hard to think about anything else. Those who think about cities also think about economic growth, to the point that describing cities as the "engines of growth" is almost a cliché. Paul Romer, perhaps the father of modern economic growth theory, has launched his Charter Cities project, which recognizes that the most promising option for lagging economies is successful cities. He seeks to foster well-run big cities as "opportunity zones especially for the working poor."[1]

Human capital, entrepreneurship and creativity, Julian Simon's (1995) "ultimate resource,"[2] are most potent when ideas can be exchanged. But some analysts simply tout the advantages of proximity to a "knowledge base" found in cities. This is misleading. Knowledge is highly fragmented, specialized, and dispersed. Various locators seek the peculiar benefits of interactions with highly specialized sources of ideas. Urban districts and clusters of specialized firms and outlets are well known. Matt Ridley (2010) has famously discussed human progress this way: "I believe that at some point in human history, ideas began to meet and mate, to have sex with each other." This was surely not casual or random sex. It refers to specific interactions involving specific proximities. But this denotes complex spatial organization.

Tyler Cowen and Alex Tabarrok (2010) have summarized much of what we know about growth economics in one schematic (Figure 6.1). Whereas they cited the importance of "organization" at the center of his chart, they did not cite *spatial* organization. Our analysis in this chapter addresses spatial organization which many commentators seemingly over-simplify when they apply generic urban form types such as "urban sprawl" or "compact development." But even these are not easily defined.[3]

Does city size or the city's spatial organization matter with respect to productivity, competitiveness and growth? Both matter and you cannot have one without the other. When activities are concentrated in space, there is an opportunity for economizing with respect to transactions costs *and* at the same time with respect to many *realized* positive and negative externalities.[4] But both types of interactions are vis-à-vis many activities spread over many locations. In fact, cities exist and survive because they manage to find the spatial organization whereby the positive advantages, including those transacted as well as those not (the positive externalities), dominate. Whereas analysts contrast and compare Marshallian specialization externalities (between firms in the same industry) with Jacobsian diversification externalities (between firms not necessarily in the same

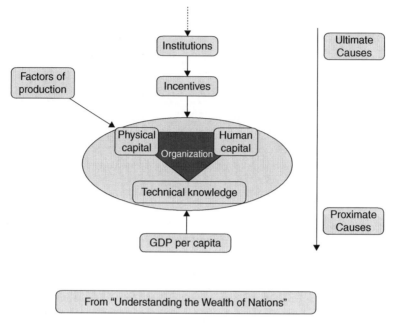

Figure 6.1   The causes of economic growth

industry) (Glaeser et al., 1992), both of them occur and land markets sort out which ones are best *realized* in which situations.

Within the US, the near stability at the top of city-size rankings suggests that the big metropolitan areas manage to get even bigger. Table 6.1 compares population rankings from seven decennial cross-sections of US urbanized areas. There is a strong link between size and ability to maintain rank. Among the top five areas there are 30 possible rank changes, but only five occurred. Among the next five, there are also 30 possible, but 22 occurred. How is it that the biggest places manage to get even bigger? It is well-known that they grow outward. But they must do so in ways that are not costly to the point of undermining the metropolitan area's economic advantage. Size and scale economies are achieved via the proper spatial organization.

Data on urban travel have been widely used to address some of these questions. There are many urbanization benefits and costs beyond travel costs, but trip patterns denote spatial organization and we are trying to identify modes of spatial organization that are selected in a context of competition between metropolitan areas. Labor and capital are quite mobile within most modern economies and can be expected to be economic in their selection of locations.

Table 6.1 Rankings of top-ten US urbanized areas, census years 1950–2010

Rank	1950	1960	1970	1980	1990	2000	2010	Changes
1	New York	New York	New York	New York	New York	New York	New York	0
2	Chicago	Los Angeles	Los Angeles	Los Angeles	Los Angeles	Los Angeles	Los Angeles	1
3	Los Angeles	Chicago	Chicago	Chicago	Chicago	Chicago	Chicago	1
4	Philadelphia	Philadelphia	Philadelphia	Philadelphia	Philadelphia	Philadelphia	Miami	1
5	Detroit	Detroit	Detroit	Detroit	Detroit	Miami	Philadelphia	2
6	Boston	San Francisco	San Francisco	San Francisco	San Francisco	Dallas	Dallas	2
7	San Francisco	Boston	Boston	Wash D.C.	Wash D.C.	Boston	Houston	4
8	Pittsburg	Wash D.C.	Wash D.C.	Boston	Dallas	Wash D.C.	Wash D.C.	4
9	Knoxville	Pittsburgh	Cleveland	Dallas	Houston	Detroit	Atlanta	6
10	St. Louis	Cleveland	St. Louis	Houston	Boston	Houston	Boston	6

Source: Author calculations; data from http://demographia.com

89

2.   LITERATURE: URBAN SPATIAL STRUCTURE AND TRAVEL

The relationships between urban form (or land use) and transportation have been among the most debated topics among planning researchers in recent years. Extensive research has been done in this area and various surveys of the literature (Badoe and Miller, 2000; Crane, 2000; Ewing and Cervero, 2001; Handy, 2005) have been published. An up-to-date and comprehensive meta-analysis of the literature concludes that travel behaviors such as vehicle miles traveled (VMT) and travel mode choices are generally inelastic with respect to changes in individual urban form variables (Ewing and Cervero, 2010). But, this report also shows that the combined effects of simultaneous changes in various urban form measures can be substantial. The travel impacts of neighborhood characteristics are found to be significant in many studies even after controlling for the influence of residential self-selection. It still remains to be clarified whether the autonomous effects of neighborhood-scale built environments are large enough to justify land-use policies designed to change people's travel behavior (Cao et al., 2009).

Much less is known about the links between metropolitan level spatial structure and transportation because most research to date has focused on the (especially residential) neighborhood-scale built environment. We are particularly interested in metropolitan level studies because spatial structure at the metropolitan scale has profound implications for the efficiency of urban agglomerations. Moreover, neighborhood-scale travel impacts may be contingent on metropolitan spatial contexts. Cervero and Gorham (1995) showed that distinct transit ridership rates between auto-oriented and transit-oriented neighborhoods observed in the San Francisco metropolitan area were not found in the Los Angeles area.

This chapter will focus on the question whether metropolitan-level spatial restructuring towards more polycentric and dispersed forms is linked to reduced or increased (especially commute) travel times. Urban economists and planners generally hold contrasting views on the commuting impacts of metropolitan level spatial changes. Most urban economists view the spatial transformation from monocentric to polycentric structures as an adjustment process that mitigates some of the negative externalities that may accompany urban growth, including congestion, whereas many urban planners blame excessive decentralization and sprawl for more congestion and longer commuting distances and durations.

Workers' behavior to economize on commuting trips is an important foundation in many theoretical urban models. Spatial adjustments in cities occur in such a way as to mitigate congestion and shorten workers' commute time as a city grows, according to these urban economic models. One of the most studied spatial evolutions is the transformation from monocentric to polycentric structure (Fujita and Ogawa, 1982). McMillen and Smith (2003) demonstrated empirically that the number of urban employment subcenters increases with population and commuting costs. Wheaton's (2004) urban model, which includes land-use mix, implied that jobs dispersal also leads to lower commuting costs and distances.

Gordon and Richardson and their colleagues published a series of empirical studies in the 1980s that show polycentric or dispersed spatial structure was associated with shorter commute times (Gordon and Wong, 1985; Gordon et al., 1989). The seeming paradox, constant average commute time in spite of increased congestion and commuting distance, led them to suggest that many individual households and firms "co-locate" to reduce commute time and that this spatial adjustment can be more easily made in dispersed metropolitan space with many alternative employment centers and residential location choices (Gordon et al., 1991; Levinson and Kumar, 1994). A more recent empirical study using panel data also found that jobs decentralization in the context of suburbanized population contributes to shorter average commutes (Crane and Chatman, 2003).

Kim's (2008) recent empirical study of location choices and commuting behavior in the Seattle metropolitan area highlights the co-location mechanism by using a unique panel data set. He shows that relocators choose their residence and workplace locations in commuting zones (in terms of commute time and distance) similar to the one before their relocation. As a result, the average commute time and distance in the region remain stable despite rapid regional growth and high residential and workplace mobility.

An interesting computable general equilibrium (CGE) simulation study of the Chicago metropolitan area by Anas (2011) also demonstrates that average commute time and personal travel time per day would remain remarkably stable over long periods, in this case between 2000 and 2030. In this model, workers and firms make economizing adjustments in their location choices and mode choice (increased public transit ridership) in response to population growth and the rise of congestion and gasoline price.

In spite of these findings, it appears that most urban planners believe that the dispersion of jobs and population, or sprawl-type development, causes more frequent and longer travels, more auto uses, and hence more congestion (Sarzynski et al., 2006). Cervero and Landis (1992) argued that the co-location process may not work properly, producing short commutes due to the growing number of two-earner households, location barriers and restricted residential and job mobility, and increased auto dependency. Cervero and Wu (1998) showed that both commute time and distance increased with employment sub-centering and decentralization in the San Francisco Bay Area in the 1980s. But a case study of this kind has limitations in properly controlling for the effects of other relevant factors, such as increased wealth.

More recent studies have employed cross section regression analysis utilizing various urban structure and land-use measures. A study of the links between four sprawl indicators and transportation outcomes in 83 US metropolitan areas (Ewing et al., 2003) found that higher residential density and more centering were associated with higher transit and walk shares of commute trips, but not with greater average commute time. Rather, denser and finer street layouts were associated with longer commute times and more congestion delays. It was land-use mix that contributed to reducing commute durations in their analysis.

Sarzynski et al. (2006) significantly advanced cross-sectional research on commuting by using more elaborate urban form variables (sprawl indices) and addressing potential endogeneity and time-lag effects between urban structure and congestion. Their regression analysis, with a sample of the 50 largest urban areas, provides mixed results. Controlling for the 1990 congestion level and other demographic and transportation supply changes, density/contiguity, and housing centrality were associated with more congestion while housing–job proximity were related with less congestion in 2000.

In sum, there was some support for the co-location hypothesis in the literature. Polycentric spatial structure seems to be more accommodating of urban growth while mitigating commute time growth. On the other hand, more centralized structures with higher density appear to encourage more public transportation use and lower VMT (Bento et al., 2005). Therefore, spatial evolution may have different implications for efficiency and the area's future prospects.

3.   WORK TRIPS

Urban Structure and Commute Time

Descriptive analysis

This section presents results from an empirical analysis of the determinants of average commute time after briefly reviewing descriptive statistics on average commute time by different intra-urban locations in US metropolitan areas. Lee (2006) examined the 79 largest US metro areas and compared commute times by drive-alone mode with job location in each area. Figure 6.2 shows how average commuting times rise with metro-

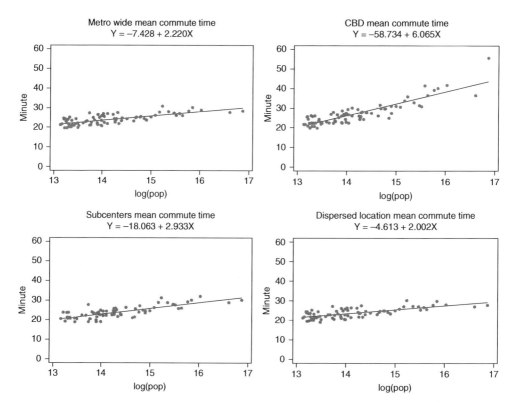

Note: Mean commuting time was calculated only for the drive-alone mode

Source: Lee and Gordon (2011)

Figure 6.2   Mean commute time by workplace type vs. metro population size

politan area size. There are metropolitan area advantages associated with polycentric structures and jobs dispersion; they accommodate continued growth in the largest metropolitan areas. Lee placed all commuters as either working in the traditional center, the various sub-centers or outside of either, namely dispersed. The proportions for the largest (three million or more population) metropolitan areas were 18, 14, and 68 percent, respectively. The first panel shows a linear relationship between average commuting time and the natural log of metropolitan population size. The other three panels show the same relationship for downtown (CBD), sub-center, and dispersed commuters. The steepest slope describes the CBD commuters, while the least steep slope describes the dispersed workplace commuters.

These relationships hold up when control variables are added to the analysis. In multivariate analysis, Lee found that a doubling metro of area population size results in average commute time increases of approximately 2.2 minutes. However, the commute time penalty of metropolitan population size is much larger for CBD workers (6.1 minutes) and smaller for workers in sub-centers (2.9 minutes) and dispersed locations (2.0 minutes). These differential effects of city size by different types of locations demonstrate that polycentric and dispersed employment distributions have an edge in mitigating congestion in large metropolitan areas.

Recent work by Lee and Gordon (2007) looks for the urban growth effects of spatial structure via its impact on commuting; growth is the most easily accessible proxy for productivity. The finding is that urban forms evolve to accommodate growth; spatial patterns emerge that accommodate and limit the road and highway congestion that comes with greater urban scale. This view places a premium on flexible land markets and the open-ended evolution of urban structure. Dispersion and jobs sprawl is more likely to be the traffic solution than the traffic problem in large metropolitan areas with massive population already suburbanized. In fact, problems are intensified when downtowns and central locations gain in size. This makes sense in light of our understanding of how land markets work. It is standard practice to model traffic flows to reflect adjustments to temporary disequilibria; but land markets are similarly a dynamic process energized by various disequilibria. This view also undermines the conventional wisdom that links more development to more traffic.

Tables 6.2 and 6.3 show some of Lee's results – the various travel times and the workplace locations of the corresponding groups Looking at the drive-alone travel times, the two tables indicate that the more concentrated the workplaces, the longer the commutes; CBD workers have the longest trips while those working in dispersed locations enjoy the shortest trips. These data are consistent with three plausible ideas: (1) where there are the most agglomeration economies, there are likely to be the highest wages, which compensate commuters for the longer trips; (2) the co-location of workers and employers ("dispersed" column) favors the greatest number of workers; (3) the idea that the latter is a chaotic and wasteful "sprawl" does not stand up.

Multivariate analysis
In this section, we report the results of multivariate analyses that examine the impacts of urban spatial structure on average commute time in 79 largest metropolitan areas in the US. As Sarzynski et al. (2006) correctly pointed out, the relationship between commute time and urban spatial structure can be simultaneous. On the one hand, congestion or

Table 6.2 Mean commute time by workplace type in largest metropolitan areas

MSA Name	Population	All modes				Drive-alone mode			
		Metro	CBD	Sub-centers	Dispersed	Metro	CBD	Sub-centers	Dispersed
New York	21,199,865	34.3	51.1	38.6	31.6	28.5	55.6	30.2	27.8
Los Angeles	16,369,949	29.0	39.0	30.0	28.1	27.8	36.6	28.9	27.0
Chicago	9,157,540	31.3	46.4	33.3	29.7	28.9	41.8	32.1	28.0
Washington	7,608,070	32.1	42.0	32.2	31.2	30.3	40.2	30.2	29.8
San Francisco	7,039,362	30.4	40.9	30.7	29.4	28.4	39.3	29.3	27.8
Philadelphia	6,188,463	27.7	38.8	26.4	26.6	26.1	36.6	26.1	25.7
Boston	5,828,672	28.3	42.3	26.5	27.2	27.1	41.6	25.9	26.7
Detroit	5,456,428	26.6	32.0	27.7	25.9	26.2	31.0	27.7	25.4
Dallas	5,221,801	28.1	33.3	28.5	27.6	27.4	31.5	28.0	27.1
Houston	4,669,571	29.2	35.8	30.0	28.2	28.1	32.9	28.9	27.3
Atlanta	4,112,198	31.9	37.8	32.4	31.3	30.9	36.0	31.4	30.3
Miami	3,876,380	28.9	35.8	29.6	28.0	27.9	33.8	28.9	27.1
Seattle	3,554,760	27.9	35.1	27.5	27.1	26.2	30.7	26.3	25.8
Phoenix	3,251,876	26.2	32.2	25.6	25.7	25.4	31.1	24.7	25.0
3 million and plus		29.4	38.8	29.9	28.4	27.8	37.1	28.5	27.2
1 to 3 million	—	24.8	28.0	23.9	24.4	24.1	26.9	23.4	23.8
half to 1 million		22.9	23.8	22.2	22.8	22.3	23.3	21.7	22.2

Table 6.3 *Employment shares by location type in 2000*

MSA name	Employment	No. of Sub-centers	Employment			Share of employment (%)			
			CBD	Sub-centers	Dispersed	All centers	CBD	Sub-centers	Disperse
			A	B	C				
New York	9,418,124	33	937,055	1,057,297	7,423,772	21.2	9.9	11.2	78.8
Los Angeles	6,716,766	53	190,100	1,931,988	4,594,678	31.6	2.8	28.8	68.4
Chicago	4,248,475	17	297,755	504,732	3,445,988	18.9	7.0	11.9	81.1
Washington	3,815,240	16	283,341	449,488	3,082,411	19.2	7.4	11.8	80.8
San Francisco	3,512,570	22	205,553	849,021	2,457,996	30.0	5.9	24.2	70.0
Philadelphia	2,780,802	6	239,735	125,190	2,415,877	13.1	8.6	4.5	86.9
Boston	2,974,428	12	238,092	239,257	2,497,079	16.0	8.0	8.0	84.0
Detroit	2,508,594	22	129,845	557,776	1,820,973	27.4	5.2	22.2	72.6
Dallas	2,565,884	10	126,010	404,365	2,035,509	20.7	4.9	15.8	79.3
Houston	2,076,285	14	165,525	432,101	1,478,659	28.8	8.0	20.8	71.2
Atlanta	2,088,215	6	166,946	223,168	1,698,101	18.7	8.0	10.7	81.3
Miami	1,623,892	6	121,045	243,970	1,258,877	22.5	7.5	150.	77.5
Seattle	1,745,407	7	163,051	207,542	1,374,814	21.2	9.3	11.9	78.8
Phoenix	1,463,581	9	104,417	189,071	1,170,093	20.1	7.1	12.9	79.9
3 million and plus		17.0				22.1	7.1	15.0	77.9
1 to 3 million		2.6				17.8	10.8	7.0	82.2
half to 1 million		0.9				17.4	12.2	5.2	82.6

longer commute time facilitates jobs decentralization and dispersion given population size and other conditions. On the other hand, more spatial adjustment may contribute to mitigating congestion all else being equal. Thus, we used two-stage least square (2SLS) regression models as well as ordinary least square (OLS) regressions.

Our regression model is specified as in the equation below and descriptions of variables are shown in Table 6.4. The dependent variable for all the regression models is the

Table 6.4   Variables used in regression models

Variables	Descriptions
Dependent	
Commute time	Log mean commute time by drive alone mode (min)
Spatial structure variables	
Decentralization	1) Share of metropolitan employment outside CBD (%)
	2) Factor score from three decentralization indices (modified Wheaton index, area based centralization index and weighted average distance from the CBD) and employment share outside CBD
	3) Share of metropolitan employment outside all centers (%)
Dispersion	4) Factor score from three concentration indices (Gini coefficient, Theil index, and Delta index) and employment share outside all centers
Instrument variables for spatial structure	
Metropolitan age	Median housing age
Industrial structure	Four factor scores (principal component analysis) from employment shares by two digit industrial sectors
Region dummy	Three dummy variables indicating Census Region
Central city incorporation	Percentage population in the core central city
Number of municipality	Number of cities with 10,000 people and more/100k population
Rail dummy	Dummy indicating the presence of rail transit
Independent variables	
Population size	Natural log of population
Population density	Population per acre excluding tracts with 0.15 persons/acre
Population decentralization	Factor score from three population decentralization indices
Percentage transit use	Percentage workers who commute by public transportation
Highway	Highway lane miles/1,000 population
Income	Median household income ($10k)
Bay dummy	Dummy indicating the presence of bay
Housing market flexibility	Housing permits in the 1990s/1990 stock – population growth
Household with children	Percentage households with children
Multi-worker family	Percentage multi-worker family
Female workers	Percentage female share of workers

Note: Log (Mean commute time) = f (P, Spatial structure, R, X), where P denotes log population size; R vector of variables indicating population distribution (density and decentralization); X vector of covariates

Source: See Lee (2007), for detailed explanations for these spatial structure variables

natural log of mean one-way commute time by drive-alone mode from 2000 Census data. On the right-hand side, we include population size, spatial structure variables, population distribution and other covariates. For population distribution, we have population density and a decentralization factor score derived from three different decentralization indices via a principal components analysis. Other covariates include transit use, highway facility, income, an indicator of the presence of a bay, housing supply, and other demographic variables.

We define two dimensions of spatial structure—decentralization and dispersion—and used two alternative measures for each spatial dimension. The first measure of decentralization is the percent share of metropolitan employment located outside the CBD and the second is a factor score that is derived from the first measure and the other three decentralization indices: a modified Wheaton index, an area-based centralization index, and weighted average distance from the CBD.[5] In a similar fashion, dispersion is represented by two measures, employment share outside all centers and a factor score extracted from the dispersed job shares and three concentration indices, Spatial Gini, Theil index, and Delta index. See Lee (2007) for detailed explanations of these indices and how we defined CBD and employment sub-centers.

Because spatial variables are endogenous to the model, we used instrument variables in 2SLS regressions. The instrument variables include median housing age, four factor scores presenting industrial structure, Census region dummies, the percent share of metro population in the core central city, the number of cities, and a dummy variable indicating the presence of rail transit. In the first-stage regression models we also included population size and distribution, and a presence of a nearby bay as well as instrument variables.

Tables 6.5 and 6.6 present OLS and 2SLS regression results, respectively. The most consistently significant control variable was the presence of a bay; median household income was significant in some of OLS models. Both variables were positively associated with average commute time when they were significant. The presence of a bay in such areas as San Francisco and Seattle was associated with about a 5 percent longer average commute time (about 1.2 minutes in an average metropolitan area). The percent transit commuting variable was significant only in the decentralization models, indicating that more transit use may shorten drivers' commute time by mitigating congestion to some extent. However, freeway density was not significant in most of the estimations, perhaps may be due to measurement issues. This variable was measured for core urbanized areas while all the other variables were for metropolitan areas.

Turning to the population variables, population size was highly significant in all the estimated models: average commute time increases by about 10 percent with doubling metropolitan population size. This is the same result as reported by Anas (2011). Population decentralization was significant and associated with longer commute times in both the OLS and 2SLS results except for only one specification. Because our decentralization variable is a factor score, the variable unit is a standard deviation. Commuting time effects of one standard deviation change in the extent of population decentralization were smaller than 6 percent in OLS results and 13 percent in the 2SLS results. Population decentralization and other variables being controlled, population density was not significant in most specifications except for only two 2SLS models with employment dispersion.

Spatial structure variables presenting employment decentralization and dispersion were significant in all but one model. Given the population size and suburbanization,

Table 6.5   Ordinary least square regression results

	Model 1			Model 2			Model 3			Model 4		
	Beta	t		Beta	t		Beta	t		Beta	t	
Intercept	2.206	4.41	***	1.678	3.60	***	2.161	4.16	***	1.896	3.77	***
Spatial structure[1]	−0.004	−1.93	*	−0.060	−4.08	***	−0.001	−0.72		−0.025	−2.04	**
Log (population)	0.104	5.16	***	0.110	6.16	***	0.089	4.65	***	0.092	4.93	***
Pop density	−0.007	−0.60		−0.009	−0.79		−0.009	−0.69		−0.015	−1.19	
Pop decentralization	0.019	1.95	*	0.059	4.10	***	0.011	1.24		0.026	2.24	**
% transit use	−0.005	−1.37		−0.006	−1.69	*	−0.003	−0.76		−0.002	−0.63	
Freeway lane miles/1k pop	0.043	0.93		−0.003	−0.08		0.063	1.35		0.030	0.62	
Median HH income($10k)	0.048	1.58		0.051	1.87	*	0.048	1.53		0.050	1.67	*
D Bay	0.050	2.02	**	0.042	1.84	*	0.050	1.96	*	0.044	1.75	*
Housing supply	0.000	0.08		0.000	0.59		0.000	−0.11		0.000	0.46	
% HH with children	0.001	0.35		0.000	0.09		0.001	0.32		0.001	0.43	
% Multi-worker family	−0.005	−1.44		−0.005	−1.53		−0.005	−1.44		−0.005	−1.53	
% Female workers	−0.002	−0.21		0.001	0.11		−0.002	−0.25		0.001	0.15	
R-square	0.647			0.702			0.630			0.649		
Adj R sq	0.583			0.648			0.563			0.586		

Note: * Spatial structure variables:
Model 1: Share of metropolitan employment outside CBD (%)
Model 2: Decentralization factor score
Model 3: Share of metropolitan employment outside all centers (%)
Model 4: Dispersion factor score
** Dependent variable: Natural log of commute time by drive alone mode

more decentralized and dispersed employment distribution was associated with shorter average commute time. In Models 2 and 4 of Tables 6.5 and 6.6, the two dimensions of spatial structure were measured by factor scores. Thus, the estimated coefficients are comparable to the coefficients of population decentralization. The coefficients of employment distribution variables were slightly larger than those of population decentralization in 2SLS models while the size of coefficients was similar to the OLS results.

Stability of Commute Time in the 2000s

ACS commuting data are available for the years 2000, and 2005–9. Table 6.7 (minutes, one-way, all modes) shows that for the US as a whole, the average trip times barely moved, although they were greater than in 1990. Our previous paper (Lee et al., 2009) did show that there was a post-1995 effect on commuting times resulting from slow rates of road construction and growing affluence which prompted more non-work travel. For the years since 2005, the data are available by metropolitan as well as micropolitan areas as well their principal cities.[6] Each row of Table 6.7 shows remarkable inter-temporal stability. And, corroborating the other two studies citied, the shortest commutes are by people living in the principal cities of micropolitan areas, the "edge cities."

The other principal source of commuting data for the US is the Nationwide Household Travel Survey (NHTS). The latest two iterations of this survey were for 2001 and 2009.

Table 6.6   Two stage least square regression results

	Model 1			Model 2			Model 3			Model 4		
	Beta	t		Beta	t		Beta	t		Beta	t	
Intercept	2.492	4.26	***	1.127	1.93	*	2.957	3.97	***	1.268	1.85	*
Spatial structure	−0.014	−2.84	***	−0.142	−4.96	***	−0.012	−2.90	***	−0.110	−3.75	***
Log (population)	0.139	5.04	***	0.138	6.02	***	0.084	3.30	***	0.101	4.11	***
Pop density	−0.010	−0.72		−0.012	−0.92		−0.038	−1.91	*	−0.046	−2.43	**
Pop decentralization	0.041	2.79	***	0.126	4.99	***	0.025	1.97	*	0.082	3.69	***
% transit use	−0.009	−1.96	*	−0.009	−2.11	**	0.003	0.49		0.001	0.31	
Freeway lane miles/1k pop	−0.032	−0.52		−0.110	−1.82	*	−0.055	−0.74		−0.122	−1.59	
Median HH income ($10k)	0.032	0.92		0.047	1.42		−0.011	−0.23		0.035	0.88	
D Bay	0.050	1.77	*	0.031	1.10		0.047	1.38		0.022	0.66	
Housing supply	0.000	0.56		0.001	1.33		0.000	0.34		0.002	1.77	*
% HH with children	0.001	0.33		−0.001	−0.23		0.001	0.15		0.002	0.57	
% Multi-worker family	−0.003	−0.69		−0.004	−0.88		0.001	0.27		−0.003	−0.66	
% Female workers	0.000	0.02		0.005	0.59		0.002	0.22		0.013	1.23	
R-square	0.597			0.643			0.517			0.556		
Adj R sq	0.524			0.579			0.429			0.475		

Note: * Spatial structure variables:
Model 1: Share of metropolitan employment outside CBD (%)
Model 2: Decentralization factor score
Model 3: Share of metropolitan employment outside all centers (%)
Model 4: Dispersion factor score
** Dependent variable: Natural log of commute time by drive alone mode

These two are distinctive because they include slightly greater spatial detail than the previous surveys. NHTS now aggregates data for three types of metropolitan location, "urban," "suburban," and "second city." Table 6.8 shows the two surveys' mean travel times for these places for the two years mentioned. Once again, changes over the time span were very minor; the metropolitan average had increased by just one minute, from 24 minutes in 2001 to 25 minutes in 2009, even though the relevant population had increased by 12 percent. Looking at the three sub-area types, the changes were also minor with no change for "suburban" and only one-minute increases for the other two area types. And here too, the "suburban" and "second-city" averages were lower than the urban averages.

Most of these results corroborate the idea that employers and employees have chosen locations that favor mutual accessibility. Location choice involves numerous trade-offs, but important among these is continued mutual accessibility.

4.   NON-WORK TRAVEL

In our recent paper on non-work travel we compared data from the 1990 and 2001 NHTS surveys (Lee et al., 2006). We found that whereas the US population had grown by 16 percent in these years, and number of workers had grown by 20 percent, the

Table 6.7   Commuting times from US Census and American Community Surveys, 1990–2009

	Census		ACS					% Change		
	1990	2000	2005	2006	2007	2008	2009	1990–2000	2000–9	2005–9
US	22.4	25.5	25.1	25.0	25.3	25.5	25.1	13.8%	−1.6%	0.0%
Metropolitan or micropolitan statistical area*			25.2	25.1	25.5	25.6	25.3			0.4%
Metropolitan statistical area	26.1	25.7	25.6	25.9	26	25.7		−1.5%	0.0%
In principal city**	24.8	24.4	24.2	24.6	24.6	24.2		−2.4%	−0.8%
Not in principal city	26.9	26.5	26.4	26.8	26.9	26.7		−0.7%	0.8%
Micropolitan statistical area	21.1	21.1	21.6	21.8	21.5			
In principal city	16.4	16.5	17	17	16.8			
Not in principal city	23.4	23.3	23.8	24.2	23.8			
Not in metropolitan or micropolitan statistical area	22.9	22.8	22.8	22.8	23.2	22.8		−0.4%	0.0%

Table 6.8   Mean commute times (minutes, one-way, all modes), 2001 and 2009

	Urban	Suburban	Second city	Town & country	All metro	
2001	**28.1**	**24.3**	**20.8**	**24.0**	**24.2**	
Population (thousands)*	39,757	61,105	43,140	60,757	204,050	253,131
Prop of US pop	15.7%	24.1%	17.0%	24.0%	80.6%	
2009	**27.9**	**24.2**	**21.9**	**24.8**	**24.7**	
Population (thousands)*	49,563	69,223	45,322	65,532	229,639	283,017
Prop of US pop	17.5%	24.5%	16.0%	23.2%	81.1%	

Note: NHTS defines an "urban continuum" from "urban" to "suburban" to "second city" to "town and country"
* Excludes ages 0–4

Source: Author calculations from 2001 and 2009 NHTS

volume of non-work travel (person-trips) grew by 30 percent (while work trips grew by 23 percent). We also found that in the Monday–Thursday AM-peak 62 percent of all person-trips were for non-work purposes. In the Monday–Thursday PM-peak it was 76 percent. We speculated that the absence of peak-period pricing explained some of this.

Having suggested that there is some seeming rationality in US urban land market outcomes, as corroborated by the 2001 and 2009 data on commuting, what about other travel? Most of the literature on urban travel focuses on commuting. But most urban travel is not for work. The 2009 NHTS shows that 79 percent of all person-trips, 61 percent of all person-miles, and 70 percent of all person-minutes (population of age

Table 6.9   Mean non-work travel times (minutes, one-way, all modes), 2001 and 2009

	Urban	Suburban	Second city	Town & country	All metro
2001 non-work	**18.9**	**16.9**	**17.1**	**17.9**	**17.6**
Family/personal	16.8	15.1	15.3	15.9	15.7
School/church	18.6	16.1	15.9	17.6	17.0
Social/recreational	22.7	20.1	20.6	21.6	21.1
2009 non-work	**19.2**	**16.8**	**17.4**	**18.4**	**17.8**
Family/personal	16.9	14.7	15.4	16.4	15.8
School/church	19.8	16.6	17.1	18.7	17.9
Social/recreational	22.8	20.0	20.8	21.2	21.1

Note: NHTS defines an "urban continuum" from "urban" to "suburban" to "second city" to "town and country"
* Excludes ages 0–4

Source: Author calculations from 2001 and 2009 NHTS

five and up) were for non-work purposes. To be sure, while most travel is for other purposes, most work trips occur during peak periods and are the most regular.

Table 6.9 shows NHTS travel times for non-work trip types presented in the same format as the commuting data in Table 6.8. Remarkably, there was little change between the two surveys, again even though there had been significant population growth. And suburban as well as second-city non-work trips were slightly less time-consuming than urban trips in all three categories.

The International Council of Shopping Centers reports that in 2010 there were 106,752 shopping centers of all types in the US, and that these accounted for one-half of all the retail space in the country.[7] Many of these centers were more than simply places to shop because they also included places to socialize and be otherwise entertained. Some include medical, legal, insurance, and other outlets. In other words, these places account for many of the non-work trips. Our analysis shows that, no matter where people reside, their accessibility to these many destinations is remarkably similar. As in the case of workplaces, buyers and sellers have found ways to locate that enables them to keep doing business with each other. Once again, as with our discussion of work trips, we ascribe these benign results to flexible and accommodative land markets.

5.   CONCLUSIONS

Whether we consider commuting or non-work travel, the data and findings we described reveal that, in spite of the continued spreading out of cities, the effect on traffic conditions (measured by average travel times) is remarkably benign. Transportation economists often point to the absence of peak-load pricing on most urban roads and the non-price rationing (crowding) that results. Indeed, traffic congestion is cited as a major complaint by many Americans. But in spite of all this, it is interesting that aggregate travel time measures show no significant deterioration as the population grows and as cities spread. These results are perhaps counterintuitive unless we consider the possibility that land markets are able to accommodate the co-locations of many origins and destinations so that reasonable travel times remain available to most people. In a world of second-best (many "market failures" and many "policy failures"), these results will comfort some and surprise others.

NOTES

1. http://chartercities.org/blog/212/vox-talk-romesh-vaitilingam-interviews-paul-about-charter-cities.
2. "[N]atural resources are not finite in any meaningful economic sense, mind-boggling though this assertion may be. The stocks of them are not fixed but rather are expanding through human ingenuity" (see Simon, 1995).
3. See, for example, Burchfield et al. (2006). We prefer the less pejorative and less vague "auto-oriented development," but will use "sprawl" in this discussion with that reservation.
4. Many of the trade-offs involved can be specified in terms of discrete programming models, as in Gordon and Moore (1989).
5. Modified Wheaton index (Wheaton, 2004): $MWI = (\sum_{i=1}^{n} E_{i-1} DCBD_i - \sum_{i=1}^{n} E_i DCBD_{i-1})/DCBD^*$ area-based centralization index (Massey and Denton, 1988): $ACI = \sum_{i=1}^{n} E_{i-1} A_i - \sum_{i=1}^{n} E_i A_{i-1}$; weighted average distance from CBD (Galster et al., 2001): $ADC = \sum_{i=1}^{n} e_i DCBD_i/E$; Gini coefficient (Gordon et al., 1986): $GINI = \sum_{i=1}^{n} E_i A_{i-1} - \sum_{i=1}^{n} E_{i-1} A_i$; Delta index (Massey and Denton, 1988): $DELTA = \frac{1}{2}\sum_{i=1}^{N} |\frac{e_i}{E} - \frac{a_i}{A}|$. e_i: number of employment at zone i; E_i: cumulative proportion of employment at zone i; E: total metropolitan employment; e_i/E: share of employment at zone i; a_i: land area at zone i; A_i: cumulative proportion of land area at zone i; A: total metropolitan land area; a_i/A: share of land area at zone i; $DCBD_i$: the distance of zone i from CBD; $DCBD^*$: metropolitan radius; n: number of zones.
6. Since 2003, the US data have been presented for metropolitan as well as micropolitan areas. Together, they make up the "core-based statistical areas" (CBSAs). The former contain an urban core of at least 50,000 population; the latter have an urban core of at least 10,000.
7. www.icsc.org/srch/lib/2010%20S-C%20Classification.pdf.

REFERENCES

Anas, A. (2011), *Metropolitan Decentralization and the Stability of Travel Time*, working paper, University of Buffalo.
Badoe, D.A. and Miller, E.J. (2000), Transportation-land-use interaction: empirical findings in North America, and their implications for modeling, *Transportation Research D*, **5**, 235–63.
Bento, A.M., Cropper, M.L., Mobarak, A.M., and Vinha, K. (2005), The effects of urban spatial structure on travel demand in the United States, *Review of Economics and Statistics*, **87**(3), 466–78.
Burchfield, M., Overman, H., Puga, D., and Turner, M. (2006), Causes of sprawl: a portrait from space, *The Quarterly Journal of Economics*, **121**(2), 587–633.
Cao, X.Y., Mokhtarian, P.L., and Handy, S.L. (2009), Examining the impacts of residential self-selection on travel behaviour: a focus on empirical findings, *Transport Reviews*, **29**(3), 359–95.
Cervero, R. and Gorham, R. (1995), Commuting in transit versus automobile neighborhoods, *Journal of the American Planning Association*, **61**(2), 210–25.
Cervero, R. and Landis, J. (1992), Suburbanization of jobs and the journey to work: a submarket analysis of commuting in the San Francisco Bay Area, *Journal of Advanced Transportation*, **26**(3), 275–98.
Cervero, R. and Wu, K.-L. (1998), Sub-centring and commuting: evidence from the San Francisco Bay Area, 1980–90, *Urban Studies*, **35**(7), 1059–76.
Cowen, T. and Tabarrok, A. (2010), *Modern Principles of Macroeconomics*, 2nd edn, New York: Worth Publishers.
Crane, R. (2000), The influence of urban form on travel: an interpretive review, *Journal of Planning Literature*, **15**(1), 3–23.
Crane, R. and Chatman, D. (2003), Traffic and sprawl: evidence from US commuting, 1985 to 1997, *Planning and Markets*, **6**(1), 14–22.
Ewing, R. and Cervero, R. (2001), Travel and the built environment: a synthesis, *Transportation Research Record*, **1780**, 87–114.

Ewing, R. and Cervero, R. (2010), Travel and the built environment: a meta analysis, *Journal of the American Planning Association*, **76**(3), 265–94.

Ewing, R., Pendall, R., and Chen, D. (2003), Measuring sprawl and its transportation impacts, *Transportation Research Record*, **1931**, 175–83.

Fujita, M. and Ogawa, H. (1982), Multiple equilibria and structural transition of nonmonocentric urban configurations, *Regional Science and Urban Economics*, **12**, 161–96.

Galster, G., Hanson, R., Ratcliffe, M.R., Wolman, H., Coleman, S., and Freihage, J. (2001), Wrestling sprawl to the ground: defining and measuring an elusive concept, *Housing Policy Debate*, **12**(4), 681–717.

Glaeser, E.L., Kallal, H.D., Scheinkman, J.A., and Shleifer, A. (1992), Growth in cities, *Journal of Political Economy*, **100**, 1126–52.

Gordon, P. and Moore, J.E. (1989), Endogenizing the rise and fall of urban subcenters using discrete programming models, *Environment and Planning A*, **21**, 1195–203.

Gordon, P. and Wong, H.L. (1985), The cost of urban sprawl: some new evidence, *Environment and Planning A*, 17, 661–6.

Gordon, P., Richardson, H.W., and Wong, H.L. (1986), The distribution of population and employment in a polycentric city: the case of Los Angeles, *Environment and Planning A*, **18**, 161–73.

Gordon, P., Kumar, A., and Richardson, H.W. (1989), The influence of metropolitan spatial structure on commuting time, *Journal of Urban Economics*, **26**, 138–51.

Gordon, P., Richardson, H.W., and Jun, M.J. (1991), The commuting paradox: evidence from the top twenty, *Journal of American Planning Association*, **57**(4), 416–20.

Handy, S. (2005), Smart growth and the transportation–land use connection: what does the research tell us? *International Regional Science Review*, **28**(2), 146–67.

Kim, C. (2008), Commuting time stability: a test of a co-location hypothesis, *Transportation Research Part A: Policy and Practice*, **42**(3), 524–44.

Lee, B. (2006), *Urban Spatial Structure and Commuting in US Metropolitan Areas*, paper presented at the Western Regional Science Association 45th Annual Conference, Santa Fe, New Mexico.

Lee, B. (2007), "Edge" or "edgeless" cities? Urban spatial structure in US metropolitan areas, 1980 to 2000, *Journal of Regional Science*, **47**(3), 479–515.

Lee, B. and Gordon, P. (2007), *Urban Spatial Structure and Economic Growth in US Metropolitan Areas*, paper presented at the the 46th Annual Meetings of the Western Regional Science Association, Newport Beach, CA.

Lee, B. and Gordon, P. (2011), Urban structure: its role in urban growth, net new business formation and industrial churn, *Région et Développement*, **33**, 137–59.

Lee, B., Gordon, P., Moore, J.E., and Richardson, H.W. (2006), *Non-work Trips Revisited: A Neglected Issue in Urban Transportation*, paper presented at the Western Regional Science Association 45th Annual Conference, Santa Fe, New Mexico.

Lee, B., Gordon, P., Richardson, H.W., and Moore, J.E. (2009), Commuting trends in US cities in the 1990s, *Journal of Planning Education and Research*, **29**, 78–89.

Levinson, D.M. and Kumar, A. (1994), The rational locator: why travel times have remained stable, *Journal of American Planning Association*, **60**(3), 319–32.

Massey, D.S. and Denton, N. (1988), The dimensions of residential segregation, *Social Forces*, **67**, 281–313.

McMillen, D.P. and Smith, S.C. (2003), The number of subcenters in large urban areas, *Journal of Urban Economics*, **53**, 321–38.

Ridley, M. (2010), *The Rational Optimist: How Prosperity Evolves*, New York: HarperCollins Publishers.

Sarzynski, A., Wolman, H.L., Galster, G., and Hanson, R. (2006), Testing the conventional wisdom about land use and traffic congestion: the more we sprawl, the less we move? *Urban Studies*, **43**(3), 601–26.

Simon, J.L. (1995), *The State of Humanity*, Oxford: Blackwell Publishers.

Wheaton, W.C. (2004), Commuting, congestion, and employment dispersal in cities with mixed land use, *Journal of Urban Economics*, **55**, 417–38.

7 New urbanism and travel
Marcial Echenique and Alastair Donald

1. INTRODUCTION

For some time, urban and transport policies have promoted urban containment as a means to create balanced communities, and supported reductions in the use of cars in order to promote enhanced urban vitality. These objectives have been translated into physical proposals by many designers in the form of increased densities, mixed-use development and restrictions on mobility. Such plans, which have been promoted in the UK under the banner of Urban Renaissance (Department of Environment, Transport and the Regions, 2000) and across the Atlantic as New Urbanism (Duany and Plater-Zyberk, 1991; Calthorpe, 1993: Katz, 1994), appear to fly in the face of trends around the world towards increased personal mobility and greater specialisation of land uses.

The main argument for increasing density and creating mixed-use development is that it will help reduce the use of cars by diminishing the distances between where people live and where they work and access services. Such compaction will, in the view of the proposers, encourage the use of more sustainable forms of transport such as walking, cycling and the use of public transport.

Taking as a case study the Greater London area of England,[1] this chapter explores whether there is any empirical evidence to support the claims by the proponents of an Urban Renaissance and supporters of New Urbanism that higher densities and mixed-use development will help to reduce the distance travelled, especially by car. The empirical work to test the hypothesis uses data from the 2001 Census (Office for National Statistics, 2001) of population, which records the work trip origins and destinations for all the population of the UK. In addition it uses the 2001 London Area Travel Survey (LATS; Transport for London and Research International, 2002), which records not only work trips but all the other trips undertaken by a sample of residents of Greater London area. This information on travel is cross related to the Generalised Land Use Database (GLUD; Communities and Local Government, 2007), which records the uses of all parcels of land within England.

2 METHOD

The method utilised the 633 zones into which Greater London area is subdivided. These zones are census wards. The GLUD data was aggregated to the same zones and used to define two main characteristics – mixed-use and density – and these characteristics were then related to travel information tabulated at the same zone level. It must be stressed, however, that while the population of Greater London area in 2001 was over seven million, it sits within a wider region of over 20 million people,[2] with considerable interaction across the wider region for the purposes of travel to work and services.

The adopted definition of 'mixed-use' is very simple. It classifies the zones with respect of how they differ from the regional average in terms of the proportion of employment land versus housing and employment land combined. If the zone has a similar proportion to the regional average of employment to housing and employment land combined, it is considered to be a balanced zone. If a zone has a higher proportion of housing than the regional average, the zone is classified as transitional residential, and where the proportion is substantially higher, it is classed as a specialised residential zone. If the contrary is the case, with more employment land than the average, it is classified as transitional employment reaching in the extreme a specialised employment zone. To work out the regional average, individual zone proportion is weighted by the population of the zone to reduce the bias caused by the difference in size of zones.

Thus the measure is the ratio of land use for employment in relation to employment and housing uses combined, i.e.,

$$x_i = e_i / (e_i + h_i) \tag{1}$$

where x_i = ratio of the mix of use for zone i, e_i = land of all employment uses in zone i (including industry, offices and services) and h_i = land for housing uses in zone i (including gardens).

A regional average ratio weighted by population is calculated as,

$$x_w = \Sigma_i (x_i \, p_i) / \Sigma_i \, p_i \tag{2}$$

where x_w = weighted regional mean mixed use ratio and p_i = population of zone i.

The score for each zone is brought into a systematic relationship by expressing it as a product of its deviation from the weighted regional mean.

$$IMU_i = 100 * ((x_i - x_w) / x_w) \tag{3}$$

where IMU_i = Index of Mixed Use for zone i.

The result is an index with a directional quality indicating the land use character of the zone. Places with a balance of employment to residential uses approximating the mix within the wider region score close to zero. Increasingly positive scores reflect higher levels of employment specialisation associated with centrality, while negative scores indicate greater specialisation in housing associated with suburbanisation. Figure 7.1 illustrates the distribution of the scores for the Greater London area. In the main, the specialised employment zones are concentrated in the west at Heathrow Airport and follow the River Thames, passing through West London, the City and the industrial areas to the east. Specialised residential zones concentrate on the periphery, while the balanced zones are intermediate zones near transitional employment zones.

According to their score on Index of Mixed Use (IMU), zones are allocated to one of five urban types ranging from 'specialised residential' via 'balanced combination' to 'specialised employment'. Zones scoring between −25 and +25 on the IMU were considered to be balanced zones. Scores of between −25 and −75 meant the zone was classified as a transitional residential zone and those scoring below −75 were considered specialised residential zones. Zones with positive values of between +25 and + 75 were considered

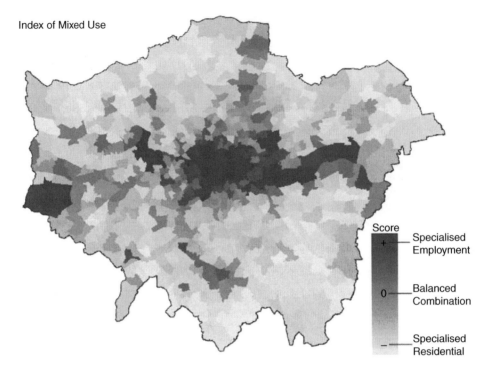

Index of Mixed Use

Figure 7.1   Greater London map illustrating the Index of Mixed Use for each zone

transitional employment zones and a score of above +75 meant a zone was ranked as a specialised employment zone. Within the study region, 117 zones exhibited a balance of residential and employment uses that approximated the regional norm. The majority of zones were in the transitional residential category, while the remaining zones were highly specialised, either dominated by employment uses or where most of the urban footprint was given over to housing land uses (see Figure 7.2).

Density is defined for two types of uses: residential and employment. The density is a net density measure, which for residential is defined as the number of people residing in a zone divided by the residential land including domestic gardens. The employment density is also a net density defined as the number of jobs divided by the employment land. Streets and other land uses are excluded from the calculations.

Travel is analysed in two categories: work trips and non-work trips. The latter includes travel for the purposes of shopping, leisure and entertainment, personal business and services. The analysis reports the average trip distance and modal share of total passenger kilometres travelled against each type of zone as derived from the IMU. Travel data is drawn from the 2001 Census statistics (Office for National Statistics, 2001), with straight line distances measured between zone centroids. Analysis of non-work travel is based upon the 2001 London Area Travel Survey (LATS; Transport for London and Research International, 2002) with straight line distances in this analysis recorded from the geographical coordinates of trip origin and destination.

The trips are classified into three types: outflows, inflows and total flows. The first

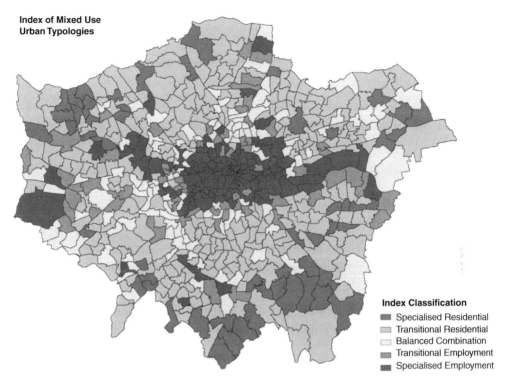

**Index of Mixed Use
Urban Typologies**

Index Classification

- ▓ Specialised Residential
- ▒ Transitional Residential
- ░ Balanced Combination
- ▤ Transitional Employment
- ■ Specialised Employment

Figure 7.2   Zones allocated to classifications according to Index of Mixed Use

category represents trips of residents that originate within the zone and that correspond with zones as places of residence. Inflows represent the trips where the zone is the destination and correspond to employment places. Inflows and outflows are added to give the total travel associated with a zone.

One of the difficulties encountered with the available data is that, although the census reports the travel to work for all of England thus making it possible to calculate all the outflows and inflows associated with a zone, the LATS data is based on only a sample survey of residents within the Greater London area. Consequently, while the latter adequately reports all the outflows (see Figure 7.3) it fails to fully capture the inflows from travellers whose journeys originate outside the area.

Comparing the census and LATS data, it is estimated that the under reporting of outflow commuting distances by LATS is 3 per cent overall. The under-reporting of LATS inflow commuting distances is estimated as 51 per cent (see Figure 7.4) by comparison to the Census values. This is understandable as LATS is only a sample survey of Greater London area residents and thus the people coming from outside the study area who often work in specialised employment areas are not recorded.

Figure 7.5 illustrates the difference in terms of average distance travelled for the total outflows and inflows combined. It can be observed that for the zones denoted as specialised residential, the overall difference between the two data sources is relatively minor. However, the difference increases to 14 per cent under-reporting for transitional

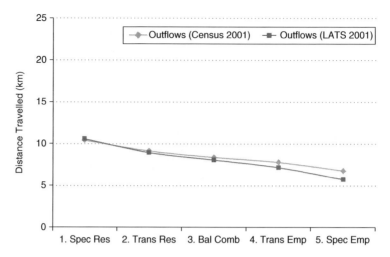

*Figure 7.3   Comparison of results for trip distances using Census and LATS data:
outflows*

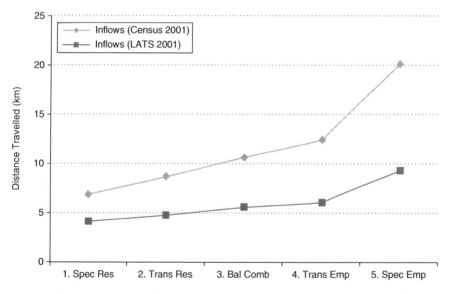

*Figure 7.4   Comparison of results for trip distances using Census and LATS data:
inflows*

residential zones and 25 per cent for balanced zones. The under-reporting of trip distances associated with transitional employment and specialised employment zones register 36 per cent and 51 per cent respectively.

While it is suspected that a similar under-reporting of distance travelled is present for the
non-work trips surveyed by LATS, there is no comparable source to the census for checking
non-work trips. It is likely that the sub-estimation for travel to services such as education

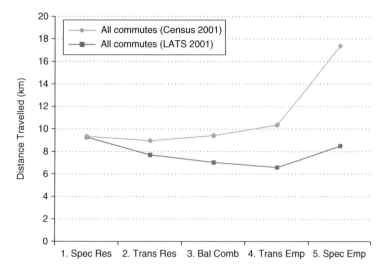

Figure 7.5 Comparison of results for trip distances using Census and LATS data: outflows and inflows

will be relatively minor. However, for shopping, leisure and entertainment, and personal business, there may exist within the data a substantial under-reporting of inflow distances. Consequently, the reporting results below should be treated with care, as the travel distances for non-work trips reported may not exhibit a slight reduction with balanced zones.

3. RESULTS

Figure 7.6 reports for each classification of zones, the average travel to work trip distances for outflows, that is to say from residential places to employment zones. For the

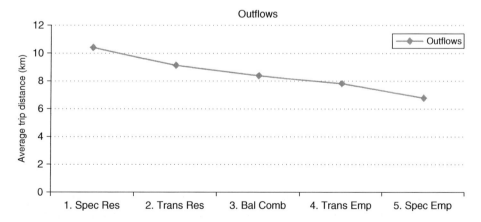

Figure 7.6 Travel to work: average trip distance for residents living in the zones

outflows trips of residents, as expected, the longest trip distances are associated with specialised residential zones. Distances steadily decrease as zones incorporate more employment within mixed zones. The shortest distances generated by residents of zones predominantly given to employment, which tend to be in central locations with comparatively few people living in them.

However, the outflows tell only half the story. The analysis of inflow trips – people arriving to work in the zone – reveals trip distances increase as zones incorporate higher shares of services and employment, most notably in specialised employment areas that act as a magnet for labour drawn from beyond the administrative boundaries of Greater London region (see Figure 7.7).

When all trips (inflows and outflows) are considered in Figure 7.8, it is clear that the

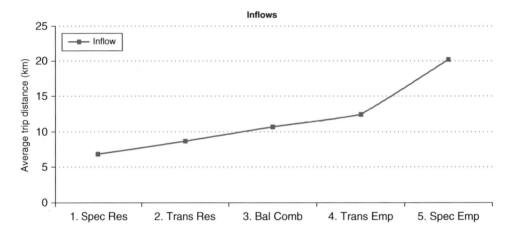

Figure 7.7   Travel to work: average trip distance for employees working in zones

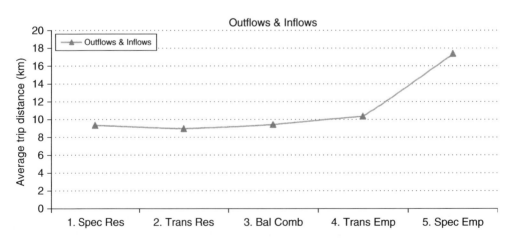

Figure 7.8   Travel to work: total average trip distance for residents living and employees working in the zones

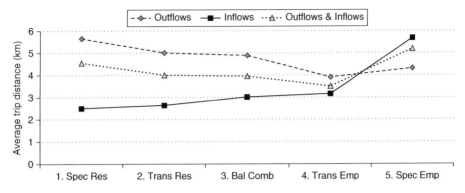

Figure 7.9   Non-work travel: average trip distances for all zonal travel

specialised employment zones generate by far the longest distances. This is understand-able as those zones attract workers undertaking highly specialised jobs who travel from localities within a large catchment area. In addition these employment zones are acces-sible by public transport systems such as the London Underground and over-ground commuter rail. Across all other classes of zones, however, little difference exists in terms of average trip distance. The important comparison between mixed areas and specialised suburban areas reveals that the average trip distance associated with suburban residents and workers is slightly lower.

The results from repeating the above tests for non-work travel carry less certainty as they are based on data from LATS. As explained above, LATS reports only on the travel by residents living within the Greater London area and thus is not able to take account of those residing outside the region whose activity destination is within London. If all inflows were taken into account, then in a similar manner as has been demonstrated above for travel to work, it seems likely that the average distance would increase, espe-cially in the more mixed and specialised employment zones. However, this analysis makes no attempt to correct for the under-reporting of inflows.

Figure 7.9 reveals that the residents of mixed areas travel less distance than their coun-terparts living in more specialised residential zones (outflows). However, the analysis of inflows to mixed areas shows increased distances compared with suburban areas. The result is that, when all non-work travel is considered, here too there is relatively little difference in trip distances when averaged across outflows and inflows. Even the most specialised residential areas appear to generate only marginally longer average trips than those generated by mixed areas.

If creating a balance of uses is not associated with a significant reduction in trip distance, it might be expected that the greater benefits would result from a shift in the modal choices of travellers. However, as shown in Figure 7.10, which reports travel to work by the modal share for cars of total passenger distance travelled (PkmT), here too there appears to be only a marginal reduction in car use when the combined inflows and outflows of areas with a balance of uses are compared with those of more suburban specialised residential zones.

As can be seen, the only zones that have a substantial reduction of car share are those highly specialised employment zones. Those zones, as explained above, have a very high index of public transport accessibility and because of this fact they attract high-level

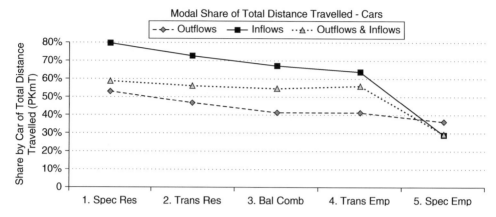

Figure 7.10   Travel to work: modal share by car of passenger kilometres travelled

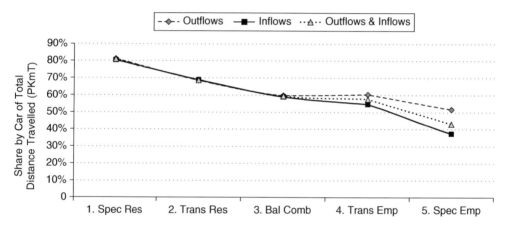

Figure 7.11   Non-work travel: modal share by car of passenger kilometres travelled

employees from a large catchment area that extends well beyond the boundary of Greater London region. Commuter rail is the most convenient way to enter these congested centres that has the effect of reducing car use.

When the above analysis is repeated for non-work travel in Figure 7.11, the reduction in car use when suburban areas are compared to mixed areas becomes much more pronounced with the share of total distance travelled by car falling from 81 to 59 per cent.

Here, again the proviso explained above should be repeated and thus the inflows from people living outside the Greater London area travelling to shopping, entertainment, personal business and to services within the region are not accounted for. It seems reasonable to assume that, should travel from outside London be taken into account, then the pattern is likely to be similar to that for travel to work. In such a scenario, the car modal share for each of the classes of zones might be expected to equalise, with the exception of the specialised employment zones where use of public transport could be anticipated to remain much higher.

The results of this analysis highlight that, when assessing trip distances and modal share of total distance travelled, the inclusion of inflows into the analysis serves to significantly alter results that are obtained when only outflows are considered. While for outflow trips, the distances for work and non-work travel of residents show a reduction when suburban areas are compared to those with a balanced combination of uses, inflow trips show an opposite trend. Consequently, when all trips are considered together, mixed use areas show little or no benefit in terms of shorter trip distances. When modal shares are considered, the share taken by cars shows a small reduction for travel to work. Therefore the main benefit offered in areas with a balance of uses would appear to be associated with non-work travel, although here the average trip lengths are much shorter than those generated by trips to work. As has been stressed, however, the results for non-work travel are open to question as the inflow trips do not include the trips of residents from outside the area.

It is widely understood, of course, that highly specialised employment areas attract long-distance commuters. However, it is clear from this analysis that a considerable impact also exists in areas of mixed use. When all trips (outflows and inflows) are considered, for balanced combination areas, average trip distances for LATS are about 30 per cent below those reported using the data from the non-geographically limited census. Consequently, when suburban areas are compared with a balance of residential and employment uses, Figure 7.4 shows a reduction in travel to work distances for trips recorded under LATS data. However, when trips are analysed from the census 2001 data, trip distances are relatively stable when suburban areas are compared to mixed areas.

Figure 7.12 plots all individual zones at the corresponding zone IMU. It can be observed that there is relatively low level of variation of total work trip distances (inflows plus outflows) in the ranges −100 to 100, representing the zone types of specialised residential passing through balanced (0) to transitional employment zones. Only the scores above 100, representing the specialised employment zones, increases the average distance travelled with increased positive scores of IMU.

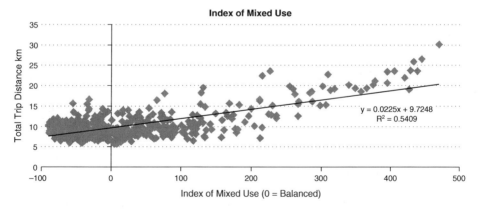

Figure 7.12   Work travel: average total distance travelled (outflows and inflows) with respect to index of mixed use

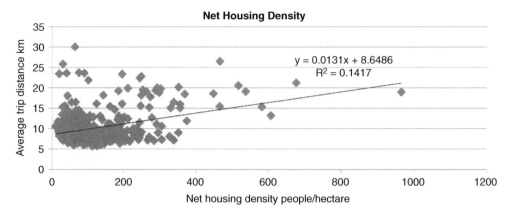

Figure 7.13   Work travel: average trip distance (inflows and outflows) and net housing density

4.   DENSITY

For the 633 zones, the net residential density can be estimated by using the 2001 census of population and the Generalised Land Use Data (GLUD, Communities and Local Government, 2007). This characteristic of each zone can be related to the average distance for work trips flowing out and inflowing into the zone. This is illustrated in Figure 7.13. It can be observed that there is little or no correlation between the net housing density and the average total trip distance from trips departing or arriving to the zone. In general it can be said that zones with high residential density are also zones with high concentration of employment. On balance, the concentration of employment tends to receive longer trips, mainly by public transport, more than offsetting shorter trips emanating from the zone.

Figure 7.14 illustrates that increased employment density is associated with an increase in the average trip distance to work. Zones with high employment density tend to be specialised areas of tertiary services, which require a highly specialised work force travelling from a large catchment area.

Although higher densities correlate with increased trip distances, Figures 7.15 and 7.16 show that they are also associated with a reduced share of travel by car. This result reflects the increased costs and reduced speeds that come with driving to and from higher density areas, and also the greater accessibility to public transport, which is more likely to serve higher density urban areas.

In general, it can be said that the correlation between reduction of car use and density is not as strong as it is assumed by proponents of densification. Furthermore, there is substantial evidence that densification increases congestion because the reduction in share of all travellers who choose to drive does not compensate the increase in numbers of cars within a given space. In Figure 7.15 it can be seen that doubling the density of housing from 100 to 200 people per hectare in London, leads to a reduction in use of cars from 50 per cent to 42 per cent, which means an increase of cars of 84 per cent within the same space (elasticity of −0.16). The results here confirm other work by

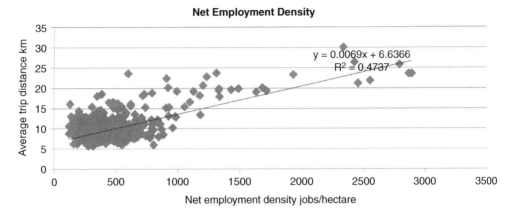

Figure 7.14   *Work travel: average trip distance (inflows and outflows) and net employment density*

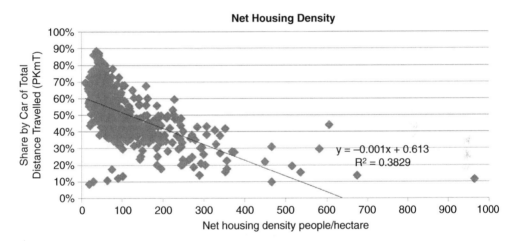

Figure 7.15   *Work travel: share of total distance travelled (inflows and outflows) and net housing density*

Echenique et al. (2012), which also reports that increasing density by compacting urban areas marginally reduces the use of car but increases congestion. The report of The Transportation Research Board (2009) also concluded that density plays a modest role in reducing car travel.

It is more common to see that the high density of employment is the product of good public transport accessibility which reduces the travel by car. But this phenomenon occurs at very high employment densities of more than 500 jobs/hectare. The availability of high capacity public transport in the form of underground or over-ground rail services is a necessary requirement and leads to high-rise office blocks. Below this threshold there is little correlation between density and car use (see Figure 7.16).

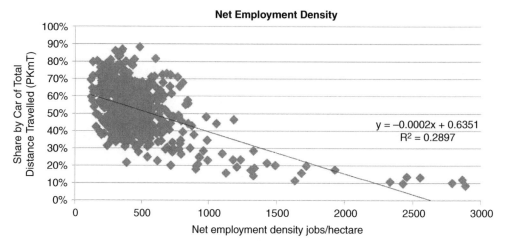

Figure 7.16   Work travel: share of total distance travelled (inflows and outflows) and net employment density

5.   CONCLUSION

There are a number of qualifications to place on this analysis. In developing land-use classifications, no attempt has been made to take account of the social characteristics of the traveller or to distinguish between different types of employment.

With the above qualifications in place, two main conclusions can be drawn from this analysis. First, results demonstrate that, as well as taking account of the outflows trips of residents, it is vital to also include in any analysis the inflow trips of workers, shoppers or people coming into a place for leisure or personal business. Once this occurs, the benefits in terms of trip distance and modal share of mixed areas compared to suburban areas are subject to considerable modification, and in many cases the result is to eradicate the benefits. Second, if inflows are to be considered, then it must be recognised that geographically circumscribed travel surveys will be prone to under-reporting of trip distances as they fail to take account of longer trips from outside the survey area. Evidence from London reported here suggests a significant difference when results are analysed with different data. The influence of longer trips is such that for places that incorporate a mix of employment and residential, the benefits of reduced trip distances shown through analysis of travel survey data are no longer apparent when a national travel data is employed.

With respect to density, the results demonstrate that there is no obvious reduction of trip distances with increased residential density. What is clear is that employment density leads to longer trip distances. While there is a reduction of car use with increased density, it is not sufficient to compensate the increase numbers of cars in the area which leads to increase congestion. The elasticity of demand for car use with respect to density is of the order of −0.16, which is consistent with other studies in the UK and USA.[3]

The overall conclusion is that there is no clear cut evidence to support the New Urbanism or Urban Renaissance belief that increase density and mixed-use development will produce more sustainable travel reducing distances and car share of total travel.

NOTES

1. The area covered by the 32 London boroughs plus the City of London.
2. The wider region includes three regions: Greater London, south-east and east of England regions.
3. See Echenique et al. (2012) and Transportation Research Board (2009).

REFERENCES

Calthorpe, P. (1993), *The Next American Metropolis: Ecology, Community and the American Dream*, New York: Princeton Architectural Press.

Communities and Local Government (2007), *Generalised Land Use Database Statistics for England, 2005*, London: Department for Communities and Local Government.

Department of Environment, Transport and the Regions (2000), *Our Towns and Cities: Delivering an Urban Renaissance*, Norwich: Department of the Environment, Transport and the Regions, HMSO.

Duany, A. and Plater-Zyberk, E. (1991), *Towns and Town-making Principles*, New York: Rizzolli.

Echenique, M.H., Hargreaves, A.J., Mitchell, G. and Namdeo, A. (2012), Growing cities sustainably: does urban form really matter? *Journal of the American Planning Association*, **78**(2), 121–37.

Katz, P. (1994), *The New Urbanism: Towards Architecture of Community*, New York: McGraw-Hill.

Office for National Statistics (2001), *Census 2001, Origin – Destination Matrices Table W203: Method of Travel to Work*, www.ons.gov.uk/ons/guide-method/census/census-2001/index.html.

Transport for London and Research International (2002), *London Area Travel Survey: Household Survey*.

Transportation Research Board (2009), *Driving and the Built Environment: The Effects of Compact Development on Motorized Travel, Energy Use and CO_2 Emissions*, Special Report 298 by the Transportation Research Board and the Board on Energy and Environmental Systems, of the National Research Council of the National Academies, Washington, DC.

8. Residential location and travel: Hangzhou and Copenhagen compared to studies in cities worldwide
Petter Næss

1. INTRODUCTION

The aspect of urban form that has attracted the greatest amount of research on its impacts on travel behaviour is arguably the location of residential areas. In the United States, research into land use and transport relationships during recent years has to a high extent been directed towards the influence of local-scale urban structural conditions on travel behaviour, comparing traditional suburban residential areas with areas developed according to the so-called 'New Urbanism' or 'Transit Oriented Development' principles (Boarnet and Crane, 2001; Ewing and Cervero, 2010). In a European context, research into relationships between land use and travel has focused much more on the location of the residence relative to the main metropolitan centre and sub-centres within the metropolitan-scale spatial structure. This also applies to some recent studies in Asian and South American countries. A few studies have also sought to compare the influences on travel behaviour from neighbourhood-scale and city-scale characteristics. This chapter will discuss the state of knowledge on this topic, comparing findings in two selected case urban regions (the metropolitan areas of Hangzhou, China, and Copenhagen, Denmark) with the results of studies in other cities and city regions in Europe and America.

Copenhagen Metropolitan Area is one of the largest urban areas in Northern Europe and a major node for international air and rail transport. While making up only 3.4 per cent of the spatial extension of Copenhagen Metropolitan Area, the central municipalities of Copenhagen and Frederiksberg have one-third of the inhabitants and an even higher proportion of the workplaces (Næss, 2006). The whole metropolitan area has around 1.8 million inhabitants, of which 1.2 million live in the continuous urban area of Copenhagen. The metropolitan centre structure could be characterized as hierarchic, with downtown Copenhagen as the main centre, the central parts of five once independent outer-area towns as second-order centres along with certain other concentrations of regionally oriented retail stores, and more local centre formations in connection with, among others, urban rail stations and smaller-size municipal centres at a third level.

Hangzhou is the capital and the economic and political centre of the Zhejiang province in China, located 180km south-west of Shanghai. Hangzhou Metropolitan Area has five million inhabitants, about half of whom live in the continuously built-up urban area of the city of Hangzhou. Similar to European cities, the historical urban cores of Chinese cities are usually the areas with the highest concentration of workplaces, retail stores and other service facilities. Hangzhou Metropolitan Area is no exception. The inner city of Hangzhou has an unchallenged status as the dominating centre of the metropolitan area. The population density in this part of the region is considerably higher than in the outer parts of the region. In addition to the major centre, the metropolitan area includes three second-order centres (one of which is being developed) and six third-order centres. These centres, too, include a more or less comprehensive set of centre functions, but with a more narrow range and with a lower number of facilities within each category than in the main city centre.

The two case cities differ considerably in terms of affluence level, population densities, cultural traditions and political conditions. The average population density within the urbanized parts of Copenhagen Metropolitan Area is 28 persons per hectare, compared to 70 persons per hectare in Hangzhou Metropolitan Area. In Copenhagen Metropolitan Area, the mobility level has been relatively high for decades, although car ownership has been and is lower than in the other Nordic capital regions. In 2008, half of the households in Copenhagen Metropolitan Area had one or more private cars at their disposal. Distinct from this, motor vehicle ownership has until recently been very low in Hangzhou, where sales of automobiles were restricted before 2004. Since then there has been an almost explosive growth in car ownership as well as ownership of other motor vehicles. Car ownership increased from 0.7 private cars per 100 households in 2000 to 17.8 cars per 100 households in 2008. At the time of our investigation (2005), 6 per cent of the respondents belonged to a household with a car.

In spite of these differences, there are, as we shall see, considerable similarities in the relationships between residential location and travel found in the two studies.

2.   METHODS

The studies in the metropolitan areas of Copenhagen and Hangzhou were both carried out by means of a combination of qualitative and quantitative research methods. Besides recording urban structural conditions from maps, aerial photographs and visits to the investigated urban districts and residential areas, the investigation was based on a number of qualitative interviews (17 in the Copenhagen case and 28 in the Hangzhou case) and answers from individuals participating in questionnaire surveys (1,932 in the main survey of the Copenhagen study and 3,155 in the survey of the Hangzhou study). The questionnaires included questions about, among others, the respondents' travel behaviour (travel modes and distances for each day during the week of investigation, business travel and holiday travel), activity participation, socio-economic characteristics, residential preferences and attitudes to transport and environmental issues. The respondents in each metropolitan area were recruited from residential areas varying in their urban structural situation in terms of distance to the main city centres of Hangzhou and Copenhagen as well as to local centres, and with differences in density, availability of local facilities, etc. Figure 8.1 shows the locations of the investigated residential areas in each of the studies (notice the different scales of the maps).

The qualitative interviews were semi-structured, focusing on the interviewees' reasons for choosing activities and their locations, travel modes and routes as well as the meaning attached to living in or visiting various parts of the city. The interviewees in each metropolitan area were recruited from five of the investigated residential areas, representing typical inner-city neighbourhoods, suburban locations close to rail stations as well as a

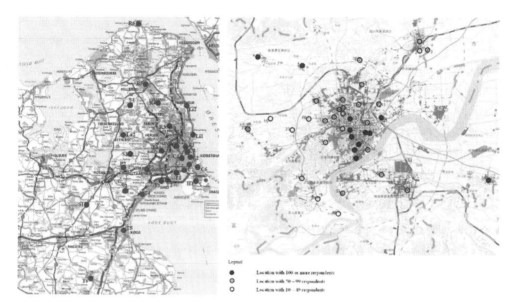

Figure 8.1   Investigated residential areas in the two metropolitan areas: Copenhagen (left, scale 1/1.48 million) and Hangzhou (right, scale 1/0.49 million). The city centre of Copenhagen is located close to the residential area C1. In Hangzhou, the city centre is located close to the north-eastern end of the lake. In Copenhagen, the number of respondents from each area varied from approximately 45 to approximately 100, with a total of 1932. In Hangzhou, there was a greater variation in the number of respondents (see the legend)

suburban neighbourhoods poorly serviced by public transport. As an important tool for the analyses interpretation schemes were developed. By requiring the research teams to make written interpretations of each interview in light of each of the detailed research questions, the interpretation schemes made us read and penetrate the transcribed interview texts more thoroughly than we would probably have done otherwise. More detailed information about the methods and results of the two studies is available in Næss (2005, 2006, 2010, 2011, 2013).

3.   RESULTS

Figure 8.2 shows average distances travelled by car, non-motorized modes, public transport and (in the case of Hangzhou) electric bike among respondents living in different distance belts from the city centres of Copenhagen (to the left) and Hangzhou (to the right). In both metropolitan areas, each distance belt includes about one quarter of the total number of respondents. Reflecting the very different overall mobility levels in the two city regions, the scale of the vertical axis of the graph of Copenhagen is ten times that of Hangzhou.

In Copenhagen as well as in Hangzhou, travel by motorized modes is generally lower

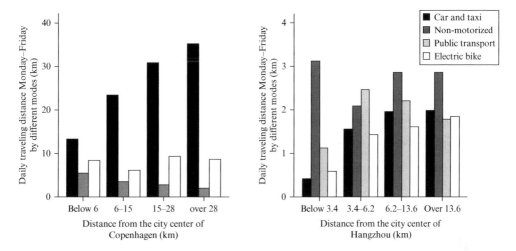

Figure 8.2 *Mean daily travelling distances by modes among respondents living at different distances from the city centre. N = 1804 (Copenhagen) and 2829 (Hangzhou). Notice the different scales of the vertical axes of the two graphs*

among inner-city respondents than among suburbanites. This reflects the fact that a high proportion of the respondents living in the outer distance belts have to travel to destinations beyond acceptable walking or biking distance in order to reach the facilities they use on weekdays, in particular workplaces and places of education. In Hangzhou, suburbanites travel longer distances than inner-city respondents by car and taxi, public transport as well as by electric bike. In Copenhagen, respondents living less than 6km from the city centre travel on average about equally long distances by public transport as those living in the two outer distance belts. This reflects that, on the one hand, the availability of public transport opportunities is highest in the central parts of the metropolitan area. On the other hand, inner-city residents can reach a large number of facilities within walking or biking distance and are thus less dependent on motorized travel. In both metropolitan areas, inner-city residents travel longer distances by non-motorized modes than the suburbanites do. Combined with their lower amount of motorized travel, this implies that the proportion of distance travelled by non-motorized modes is considerably higher among those respondents living close to the city centre.

We also see that travelling distances are generally much longer in Copenhagen than in Hangzhou (again, the scale of the vertical axis is ten times as high in the diagram for Copenhagen as for Hangzhou). This reflects the much higher mobility level in Copenhagen.

Travel behaviour has been shown as depending on the location of the dwelling relative to the main centre of the metropolitan area. There are also relationships in both metropolitan areas between travel behaviour and the location of the residence relative to lower-order centres and more local neighbourhood characteristics. These relationships are, however, considerably weaker than the relationships with the location of the dwelling relative to the main centre. This has been demonstrated by means of multivariate statistical analyses, where all investigated factors of influence were kept constant apart from those variables whose effects we wanted to examine. In addition to comparing the influences of different urban structural characteristics of the dwelling, the multi-variate analyses also included a number of demographic, socio-economic and attitudinal variables.

As could be seen in Figure 8.2, outer-area respondents in both metropolitan areas travel considerably longer by energy-demanding travel modes than their inner-city counterparts do. Below, results of multivariate analyses of factors influencing the respondents' energy use[1] for transport will be shown (Table 8.1). Besides its obvious relevance to the discussion on environmentally sustainable urban structures, energy use is a variable summarizing key aspects of travel behaviour, as it depends on both travelling distances and travel modes. The urban structural variables of the analyses include the location of the dwelling relative to the main city centre, the closest second-order centre and the closest third-order centre, and in Copenhagen also the density of population and jobs in the local neighbourhood. The control variables include sex, age, number of children younger than seven years of age in the household, number of children aged 7–17 in the household, number of adult persons in the household, education level or type, personal income, driver's licence for car, whether or not the respondent is a workforce participant, whether or not the respondent is a student, transport-related residential preferences and a few variables indicating particular activities, obligations or circumstances that may influence travelling distances. In both metropolitan areas we also included car availability in the household and transport attitudes as control variables due to their strong influence on energy use as well as their association with place of residence. However, as argued elsewhere (Næss, 2009), this tends to result in underestimation of the effects of residential location on travel behaviour and its associated energy use, since car ownership as well as transport attitudes are considerably influenced by residential location: the need for owning a car (or a second car in the household) is much lower if you live in the inner city with high public transport accessibility and a large number of facilities within walking or biking distance than if you live in a suburb where public transport services as well as the availability of local facilities are poor. Similarly, respondents living in areas where they feel strongly dependent on car travel in daily life are likely to develop more positive attitudes towards the car than inner-city residents who do not need to use the car in their daily life but are exposed to traffic noise and emissions in their neighbourhoods. The estimates of the effects of residential location on transport energy use shown in the following must therefore be considered as conservative.

Figure 8.3 shows how daily energy use for transport varies with the distance from the dwelling to the city centres of Copenhagen and Hangzhou, respectively, when controlling for the demographic, socio-economic and attitudinal characteristics of the respondents.

In both metropolitan areas, inner-city living is associated with considerably lower energy use for transport, also when a number of individual characteristics of the respondents are taken into consideration. We also notice a very large general difference in transport energy use between the Danish and the Chinese context (the scale of the vertical axis is 20 times larger for Copenhagen than for Hangzhou). In addition to the effect of proximity to the main city centre, a slight tendency of decreasing energy use when living close to a third-order centre is found in both metropolitan areas, but not any effects of other neighbourhood characteristics.

Table 8.1   Effects of investigated variables on energy use for transport (kWh) during one week among respondents from the metropolitan areas of Copenhagen and Hangzhou

	Unstandardized coefficients		Standardized coefficients		Level of significance (p values)	
	Copenhagen	Hangzhou	Copenhagen	Hangzhou	Copenhagen	Hangzhou
Residential location variables:						
Location of the dwelling relative to the main city centre (non-linear distance functions, values ranging from 0.66 to 3.80 in Copenhagen and from −0.23 to 1.00 in Hangzhou)	1.823	0.968	0.106	0.098	0.0000	0.0000
Location of the dwelling relative to the closest third-order centre (logarithmically measured in Copenhagen, non-linear function in Hangzhou with values ranging from −0.93 to 1.00)	2.138	0.267	0.056	0.045	0.0124	0.0096
Location of the dwelling relative to the closest second-order centre (logarithmically measured in Copenhagen, non-linear function in Hangzhou with values ranging from −0.94 to 1.00)					N. S. (p = 0.554)	N. S. (p = 0.907)
Density of population and jobs within the local neighbourhood (persons per hectare, only included in Copenhagen)					N. S. (p = 0.471)	
Control variables:						
Whether the respondent has been outside the metropolitan area during week (yes = 1, no = 0)	24.71	1.026	0.422	0.091	0.0000	0.0000

Table 8.1 (continued)

	Unstandardized coefficients		Standardized coefficients		Level of significance (p values)	
	Copenhagen	Hangzhou	Copenhagen	Hangzhou	Copenhagen	Hangzhou
Control variables:						
Availability of private car in the household (in Copenhagen: cars per adult household member; in Hangzhou: yes = 1, no = 0)	13.67	4.445	0.241	0.348	0.0000	0.0000
Attitudes to transportation issues (car-oriented = high value, range: in Copenhagen −17 to 11, in Hangzhou −17 to 6)	0.554	0.070	0.177	0.079	0.0000	0.0000
Whether the respondent holds a driver's licence for car (yes = 1, no = 0)		1.434		0.202	N. S. (p = 0.805)	0.0000
LAMBDA[2] (only in Hangzhou)		0.609		0.109		0.0000
Personal annual income (in Copenhagen: measured in 1,000 DKK, in Hangzhou: logarithmically measured in yuan)		0.642		0.105	N. S. (p = 0.683)	0.0000
Sex (female = 1, male = 0)	−3.181		−0.075		0.0002	N. S. (p = 0.948)
Age (deviation from being middle-aged, logarithmically measured)	−4.762		−0.072		0.0010	N. S. (p = 0.869)
Number of household members above 18 years of age	2.266		0.065		0.0015	N. S. (p = 0.988)
Workforce participation (yes = 1, no = 0)	2.950		0.058		0.0081	N. S. (p = 0.848)
Education level (Hangzhou) or type (Copenhagen), binary variables	3.720		0.056		0.0051	N. S. (p = 0.854)

Number of household members under seven years old	−2.109	−0.055	0.0056	N. S. (p = 0.984)
Whether the respondent had moved to the present dwelling less than five years ago (yes = 1, no = 0)	0.394	0.052	N. S. (p = 0.901)	0.0024
Overnight stay away from home four or more nights during the week of investigation	3.290	0.041	0.0437	N. S. (p = 0.711)
Attitudes to environmental issues			N. S. (p = 0.633)	N. S. (p = 0.807)
Regular transport of children to school or kindergarten (yes = 1, no = 0)			N. S. (p = 0.642)	N. S. (p = 0.967)
Whether the respondent is a student/pupil (yes = 1, no = 0)			N. S. (p = 0.876)	N. S. (p = 0.973)
Transport-related residential preferences (index values)			N. S. (p = 0.951)	N. S. (p = 0.973)
Number of household members aged 7–18			N. S. (p = 0.802)	N. S. (p = 0.976)
Constant	2.182	−1.245	0.5544	0.0000

Note: N = 1,466 in Copenhagen Metropolitan Area and 2,156 in Hangzhou Metropolitan Area. Adjusted R^2: 0.447 in Copenhagen Metropolitan Area and 0.395 in Hangzhou Metropolitan Area. Only variables meeting a required significance level of 0.05 were included in the final regression model. N. S. = not significant at the 0.05 level

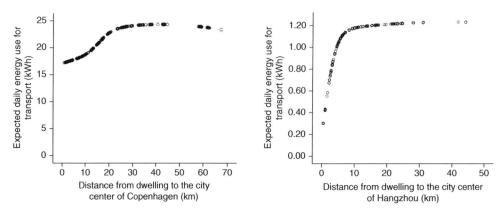

Figure 8.3   *Expected daily energy use for transport among respondents living at different distances from the city centres of Copenhagen and Hangzhou. N = 1567 and 2156, respectively. P = 0.0000 in both cases. Notice the different scales of the vertical axes of the two graphs*

In both the Copenhagen and the Hangzhou study, special attention was given to the so-called 'self-selection problem' (Cao et al., 2009), among other things by including transport-related residential preferences as a control variable (see Table 8.1). Moreover, a comparison was made of the relationship between residential location and travel among respondents emphasizing versus not emphasizing proximity to daily destinations or public transport stops as an important characteristic of the dwelling. In both metropolitan areas, inner-area respondents who do not emphasize proximity to public transport, employment or shopping opportunities among their prioritized residential choice criteria travel considerably less by car, on average, than suburban respondents who do emphasize these characteristics as important for choice of residence. If self-selection were the main reason for geographical differences in travel, the former group of residents would have been expected to travel more by car than the latter (Næss, 2009, 2011).

Among the non-urban-structural variables, we find, as might be expected, tendencies in both metropolitan areas of increasing energy use among respondents with car availability and car-oriented transport attitudes. As mentioned earlier, the inclusion of these control variables results in a certain underestimation of the impact of residential location on energy use for transportation. If car availability and transport attitudes are excluded from the analyses, the differential in daily energy use between the most energy-demanding suburban locations compared to inner-city locations increases from 7.1kWh to 9.8kWh in Copenhagen Metropolitan Area, and from 0.93kWh to 2.0kWh in Hangzhou Metropolitan Area. In the latter case region, car ownership was at the time of investigation (2005) considerably lower than in Western countries, and car availability might therefore influence the residential location of the relatively few car-owning households to a stronger extent than the influence of their residential location on their car ownership. For Hangzhou, therefore, excluding car ownership (and transport attitudes) from the control variables arguably produces an exaggerated estimate of the effect of residential location on transport energy use, while this effect may be somewhat underestimated when including these control variables. In Copenhagen Metropolitan Area, the inclusion of car availability and transport attitudes as control variables probably leads to a considerable underestimation in Table 8.1 and Figure 8.3 of the effect of residential location on energy use.

Needless to say, people who have been on trips outside the metropolitan area during the investigated week tend to use more energy for transport than those who have not. The remaining non-urban-structural variables show weaker effects on energy use and are either statistically significant in only one of the metropolitan areas or non-significant in both. The significant effects are, however, in accordance with what could be expected from theoretical considerations. The proportions of variance accounted for by the investigated variables (the adjusted R2 figures of 0.45 in Copenhagen and 0.40 in Hangzhou) must be considered high for this type of disaggregate studies (with individual persons as units of analysis and covering only a limited time span), since there will always be substantial random variation depending on particular individual and temporal circumstances that cannot be translated into measurable variables.

4.   RATIONALES INFLUENCING TRAVEL BEHAVIOUR

Why does travel behaviour in the two case city regions depend more on metropolitan-scale than on local-scale built environment characteristics? Material from the qualitative interviews has illuminated some important rationales on which people base their travel behaviour (Næss, 2005, 2013). The relative importance of metropolitan-scale and neighbourhood-scale built environment characteristics to travel behaviour depends in particular on people's rationales for location of the activities in which they participate.

For most travel purposes, most interviewees do not necessarily choose the closest facility, but rather they travel a bit further if they can then find a better facility. They thus tend to emphasize a rationale of choosing the best facilities above a rationale of minimizing the friction of distance. This is especially true as regards workplaces, and it holds true both for the Danish and the Chinese context. Travel distances therefore depend more on the location of the dwelling relative to large concentrations of facilities than on the distance to the closest facilities. Interviewees who live close to the city centre have a large number of facilities within a short distance from the dwelling and therefore do not have to travel long distances, even if they are very selective as to the quality of the facility. Since most of their destinations are within easy reach, inner-city residents carry out a higher proportion of trips by bike or on foot.

Among the interviewees, the following circumstances tend to contribute to a high priority attached to the rationale of choosing the best facility, compared to distance minimizing: specialized job skills, specialized leisure interests and 'exclusive' cultural taste, a lot of time available, high mobility resources, many facilities available in the local area of the dwelling and short distance from the local facilities to the closest competing concentration of facilities.

Our material from both case cities suggests that the propensity for using local facilities depends partly on which facilities exist in the proximity of the dwelling, and partly on the competition from non-local facilities. In the districts next to the downtown area, a relatively broad supply of local facilities often exists, but at the same time there is a strong competition from facilities in the city centre. Conversely, the local supply of facilities is often more modest in the outer parts of the metropolitan area, but the long distance to the concentration of facilities found in the central city at the same time weakens the competition from the latter facilities.

The interviewees' choices of travel modes are influenced by a number of different and interconnected rationales. These rationales could be classified into two main groups: rationales concerning the efficiency of the movement from origin to destination and rationales concerning the process of moving from origin to destination.

The first of these two groups includes concerns related to time consumption, economic costs and accessibility benefits of travelling by different modes. The second group includes concerns related to physically, psychologically and socially positive or negative aspects associated with travelling by a particular mode. Several of the rationales are hinted at indirectly through a criterion of trip distance as an important condition influencing the interviewees' choices of travel modes. Since long trips will be very time-consuming as well as physically exhausting if they are made by non-motorized modes (in particular by foot), rationales of time-saving and limitation of physical efforts will logically imply a dependence of travel modes on trip distances. Living close to relevant trip destinations thus does not only contribute to shorter travelling distances, but also implies a higher propensity of using non-motorized modes.

5.   INFLUENCES OF RESIDENTIAL LOCATION ON OTHER TRAVEL BEHAVIOUR VARIABLES

Table 8.2 shows the impacts of the location of the dwelling relative to different categories of urban centres in the metropolitan areas of Hangzhou and Copenhagen, respectively, on five main transport variables: total travel distances on weekdays and in the weekend, commuting distances and the proportions of non-motorized travel on weekdays and in the weekend. The magnitudes of the effects have been stated verbally as well as in terms of crude percentages. The crudeness of the latter estimates must be underscored, due to the non-linearity of most of the relationships referred to as well as to the interdependency between the urban structural variables. Due to downward-sloping density gradients from the centre towards the periphery in both regions, the density of lower-order centres is lower in the outskirts than in the inner parts of the metropolitan areas. In the estimates, the fact that proximity to a second- or third-order centre is influenced by the location of a residential area relative to the main city centre has been taken into account.

For Copenhagen Metropolitan Area, the influences of the location of the dwelling relative to the main city centre and the local area density have been combined in order to make the Copenhagen results more comparable to those of Hangzhou. There is considerable overlap between the local area density and the distance from the dwelling to downtown Copenhagen, as most of the high-density areas are located in the inner city or relatively close to it. It should still be kept in mind that the residential locational variables of the Copenhagen area study are differing somewhat those of the Hangzhou area study. For example, both the second-order and the third-order centres of the Copenhagen area study should probably be considered more local (i.e., belonging to a somewhat lower order in the hierarchy of centres) than the second- and third-order centres of Hangzhou

Table 8.2 *Main effects of different residential location variables in Hangzhou and Copenhagen on selected transport variables (approximate percentage differences, compared to situations far away from the respective centre types, are shown in parentheses)*

	Proximity to the main centre of the metropolitan area		Proximity to a second-order centre		Proximity to a third-order centre	
	Hangzhou Metropolitan Area	Copenhagen Metropolitan Area	Hangzhou Metropolitan Area	Copenhagen Metropolitan Area	Hangzhou Metropolitan Area	Copenhagen Metropolitan Area
Total daily travelling distance on weekdays	Shorter (30%)	Considerably shorter (50%)	No clear effect	Somewhat shorter (20%)	Slightly longer (10%)	Somewhat shorter (15%)
Total daily travelling distance in the weekend	Shorter (40%)	Slightly shorter (10%)	No clear effect	No clear effect	No clear effect	No clear effect
Commuting distance	Shorter (40%)	Very much shorter (75%)	Somewhat shorter (20%)	No clear effect	Longer (30%)	No clear effect
Non-motorized share of travel on weekdays	Higher (45%)	Much higher (130%)	No clear effect	Considerably higher (80%)	No clear effect	No clear effect
Non-motorized share of travel in the weekend	Considerably higher (70%)	Considerably higher (65%)	Higher (35%)	Considerably higher (65%)	Somewhat higher (20%)	No clear effect

Metropolitan Area, as nearly 20 second-order and almost 80 third-order centres were defined in the Copenhagen Metropolitan Area study, compared to only two second-order and six third-order centres in Hangzhou Metropolitan Area. We still think that the juxtaposition of results from the two studies shown in Table 8.2 provides a useful background for comparison of the findings.

In general, there are considerable similarities between the findings of the two studies. Both in Hangzhou Metropolitan Area and in Copenhagen Metropolitan Area, living in the central parts of the region contributes to shorter overall travelling distances, shorter commuting distances and a higher share of non-motorized travel. In particular, the location of the dwelling relative to the main centre of the region appears to influence travelling distances and modes in very similar ways. Moreover, in both metropolitan areas, the influences of the location of the residence relative to lower-order centres are weaker and less unambiguous than those of the location of the dwelling relative to the main city centres of the two urban regions.

Notwithstanding the above many similarities between the results of the studies in Hangzhou Metropolitan Area and Copenhagen Metropolitan Area, residents of Hangzhou Metropolitan Area travel in general only a small fraction of the distance travelled by Copenhagen Metropolitan Area residents. Thus, inner-city respondents of Copenhagen travel on average nearly four times as long on weekdays as the outer-area respondents of Hangzhou Metropolitan Area. While energy use for transport does not appear to increase to any extent worth mentioning when the distance from the dwelling to downtown Hangzhou increases beyond some 8–10km (see Figure 8.3), the curve of Copenhagen Metropolitan Area levels out at a distance from the city centre of more than 40km.

These differences obviously reflect the far higher car ownership rates in Denmark than in China. Although car ownership as well as the availability of company cars for private use is increasing rapidly in China, currently with a doubling of the car ownership rate each five years, there is still a considerable difference between China and Denmark in terms of car ownership and use. Since the rationales influencing travel behaviour were found to be pretty much the same among the interviewees of the two studies, we might, however, expect that the curve in Figure 8.3 showing the relationship between residential location and energy use in Hangzhou will be lifted upward as car ownership increases, and the distance from the city centre of Hangzhou at which the curve begins to level out will be moved to the right in the figure. Needless to say, such a development is of course problematic in a sustainability perspective. In order to avoid the forecasted rapid growth in car traffic in Hangzhou, an energy-conscious spatial planning should be combined with transport policy measures to limit urban motoring while improving accessibility by public transport.

6.   COMPARISON WITH OTHER CITIES

The results of the Hangzhou and Copenhagen studies are in accordance with findings in a large number of studies worldwide and across city sizes. Similar centre-periphery gradient has been found, among others, in Paris (Mogridge, 1985; Fouchier, 1998), London (Mogridge, 1985), Athens (Milakis et al., 2008), New York (Newman and Kenworthy, 1989), San Francisco (Schipper et al., 1994), Austin (Pushkar et al., 2000), Portland

Table 8.3   Effects of residential location variables on travel distances found in selected studies where multivariate control has been exercised

City/metropolitan area (present number of inhabitants within the city's continuous urban area in parenthesis)	Residential location variables influencing travel distances, with standardized regression coefficients	Reference
Santiago de Chile (5,040,000), car transport only	Distance to main city centre (0.109***) Distance to metro station (0.074**) Location in Andes foothills (0.035*)	Zegras (2010)
Athens (3,070,000), mean trip length by car	Distance to main city centre (0.487***) Net residential density (−0.215)	Milakis et al. (2008)
Hangzhou (1,920,000 in the six core districts)	Distance to main city centre (0.091***)	This study
Portland (1,850,000), non-work vehicle miles travelled	Distance to main city centre (0.147***) Local density of road intersections (−0.109***)	Boarnet et al. (2004)
Copenhagen (1,230,000)	Distance to main city centre (0.145***) Distance to second-order centre (0.055) Distance to urban rail station (0.046)	This study
Oporto (1,100,000)	Local population and job density (−0.160***)	Næss et al. (2011)
Oslo (910,000), motorized transport only	Distance to main city centre (0.472***) Mean distance to local services (0.158**)	Næss et al. (1995)
Aalborg (125,000)	Distance to main city centre (0.202***) Distance to second-order centre (0.097***)	Nielsen (2002)
Frederikshavn (25,000)	Distance to main city centre (0.240***)	Næss and Jensen (2004)

Note: Standardized regression coefficients are shown in parentheses. Levels of significance are indicated by asterisks: * = <0.05; ** = <0.01; *** = <0.001. Unless specified otherwise, the dependent variable is daily or weekly travel distance regardless of travel mode

(Boarnet et al., 2004), Santiago de Chile (Zegras, 2010), Melbourne (Newman and Kenworthy, 1989), Greater Oslo (Næss et al., 1995; Røe, 2001), the Norwegian cities of Bergen (Duun, 1994) and Trondheim (Synnes, 1990), the Helsinki region (Lahti, 1994), Gävle, Sweden (Tillberg, 2001) and the Danish cities of Århus (Hartoft-Nielsen, 2001), Aalborg (Nielsen, 2002) and Frederikshavn (Næss and Jensen, 2004).[3] Table 8.3 summarizes the effects of residential location found in selected studies where multivariate control has been exercised and standardized regression coefficients are available. In nearly all these studies, the location of the dwelling relative to the main city centre was the urban form characteristic found to exert the strongest influence on travel behaviour. The size of the standardized regression coefficients varies considerably, however. This may be partly due to differences between the studies in whether or not trips outside the urban region have been included in the analyses. If such trips have been excluded (like in the Oslo study by Næss et al., 1995), the variation of the dependent variable will be smaller, and a greater proportion of the variance can then be attributed to the investigated urban form and socio-economic variables. In another study (the case of Athens), the analysis was based on a comparison of mean values for 82 municipalities within the metropolitan area, levelling out individual variations in travelling distances within each municipality and again increasing the proportion of variance accounted for by the investigated variables. Apart from this, there seems to be a tendency for the standardized regression coefficients to be higher in smaller cities than in large metropolitan areas (where the variability in intra-urban trip distances is likely to be greater), and in cities with a high level of motorization than in cities with a low level of car ownership. In the latter cities, people could be expected to use available local facilities to a higher extent, resulting in a reduced effect of the inner city as attractor of suburban commuters.

Some influence of proximity to local centres or local service facilities on travel behaviour has also been found in many studies, but in cities with a monocentric or hierarchical centre structure this influence has generally been found to be weaker than that of distance to the main city centre. The Copenhagen study also encompassed a sub-study comparing the travel behaviour effects of metropolitan-scale and neighbourhood-scale built environment characteristics, including seven variables measuring the density of the local area and the neighbourhood, 12 variables measuring different aspects of service facility accessibility in the proximity of the dwelling, two variables measuring the availability of local green recreational areas, and one variable indicating the type of local street structure (Næss, 2011). Interestingly, some local-scale variables often described as influential in the literature, such as neighbourhood street pattern, showed no significant effect on travel behaviour when provisions were made to control for the location of the dwelling relative to the city centre. Generally, the effects of neighbourhood-level variables were found to be weaker than those of the location of the dwelling in relation to the metropolitan-level centre structure. However, in cities with a more polycentric structure, like Oporto, the influence of the distance to the city centre itself may be weaker, with travel behaviour more closely related to local-area density (Næss et al., 2011).

Apart from travelling shorter overall distances as well as distances by car, inner-city dwellers tend to travel more by non-motorized modes. Travel by public transport differs less between suburbanites and residents of central areas; although the latter are usually blessed with the highest level of public transport service, proximity to trip destinations often makes motorized travel unnecessary. Among suburbanites, there is still a tendency of higher use of public transport among those who live in areas with a high level of public transport accessibility.

7.   CONCLUSION

The studies in Hangzhou and Copenhagen both show that the location of the dwelling relative to the centre structure of the metropolitan area exerts a considerable influence on the travel behaviour of the respondents. On average, living close to downtown contributes to a lower total amount of travel, a higher share of trips by bike or on foot, and lower energy use for transport. The location of the dwelling relative to the closest second-order and third-order centre also influences travel, but not to the same extent as the location of the residence relative to the main city centre. The geographical differences in travel behaviour within each metropolitan area exist independently of residential preferences and attitudes to transport and environmental issues and cannot be explained by residential self-selection (Næss, 2009, 2011). Instead, a number of rationales for travel behaviour identified in qualitative interviews show important links in the causal mechanisms by which residential location influences travel (Næss, 2005, 2013).

The results of the Hangzhou and Copenhagen studies are in line with findings in a large number of cities worldwide (cited above). In both city regions, avoiding low-density urban spatial expansion seems indispensable in order to minimize the need for motorized transportation in general and car travel particularly. Densification close to the main centre of the urban region is especially conducive to reducing the amount of travel and enhancing non-motorized modes. In Copenhagen metropolitan area there has during recent years been a change towards a more concentrated urban development after several decades of more or less strong urban sprawl. In Hangzhou metropolitan area, economizing on land consumption for urban development has for a long time been high on the agenda in order to protect farmland resources. However, Hangzhou's land-use development in the past decade shows a tendency to loosening these urban containment policies (Xue et al., 2011).

Due to the relatively low density of its urban structure (apart from the inner city), the potential for densification is considerable in Copenhagen Metropolitan Area. In Hangzhou Metropolitan Area (and other similar Chinese urban areas), the challenge is maybe not to make the built-up areas even denser than they are already (although such density increases may also be relevant), but first and foremost to avoid adopting the low-density, sprawling form of development typical for American, and in a more moderate form also European, urban regions during the second half of the twentieth century.

NOTES

1. In the calculations of energy use for car travel, considerations were made about the influence of travel speeds on fuel consumption per vehicle kilometre. Since inner-city dwellers that have got a car mainly use their cars for trips to suburban and exurban locations, while suburban commuters often drive a considerable part of their daily journeys under congested conditions, we do not consider it likely that energy use per vehicle kilometre by car will be significantly higher among inner-city residents than among their suburban counterparts. In the Copenhagen study, energy use per vehicle kilometre by car for all respondents was thus calculated as a weighted average of fuel consumption figures for driving under 'urban' and 'highway' conditions, based on information from the Danish Road Directorate (for more details, see Næss, 2006: 236.) In the Hangzhou study, energy use per vehicle kilometre for cars was based on the average of figures from two different Chinese sources (Committee on the Future of Personal Transport Vehicles in China et al., 2003 and Wu, 2008). Energy use for different types of public transport in the two studies was calculated from figures based on Danish/Scandinavian and Chinese sources, respectively.
2. A Heckman sample selection correction factor was used in the Hangzhou study, where a high proportion of respondents used only non-motorized modes and hence had a zero value on energy use. The Lambda factor reflects the portion of the unmeasured characteristics of the residential choice/transport decision (i.e., whether to be a motorized traveller). The coefficient of this factor therefore captures the portion of the effect of these characteristics that is related to energy use for transport.
3. See Næss (2012) for an overview with an emphasis on Nordic studies.

REFERENCES

Boarnet, M.G. and Crane, R. (2001), *Travel by Design: The Influence of Urban Form on Travel*, Oxford and New York: Oxford University Press.

Boarnet, M.G., Nesami, K.S. and Smith, C.S. (2004), *Comparing the Influence of Land Use on Nonwork Trip Generation and Vehicle Distance Traveled: An Analysis using Travel Diary Data*, paper presented at the 83rd annual meeting of the Transportation Research Board, Washington, DC.

Cao, X., Mokhtarian, P.L. and Handy, S.L. (2009), Examining the impacts of residential self-selection on travel behaviour: a focus on empirical findings, *Transport Reviews*, **29**, 359–95.

Committee on the Future of Personal Transport Vehicles in China et al. (2003), *Personal Cars in China*, Washington, DC: The National Academies Press.

Duun, H.P. (1994), *Byutviklingens transportvirkninger. En studie av transporteffekter, energibruk og utslipp til luft ved alternative byutviklingsstrategier i Bergen*, Bergen: West Norwegian Planning Group.

Ewing, R. and Cervero, R. (2010), Travel and the built environment, *Journal of the American Planning Association*, **76**, 1–30.

Fouchier, V. (1998), *Urban Density and Mobility in Ile-de France Region*, paper presented at the UN-ECE 8th conference on Urban and Regional Research, Madrid, 8–11 June.

Hartoft-Nielsen, P. (2001), *Boliglokalisering og transportadfærd*, Hørsholm: Danish Forest and Landscape Research Institute.

Lahti, P. (1994), *Ecology, Economy, Energy and other E-lements in Urban Future*, paper for a Nordic research workshop in Espoo, Finland, 17–18 February.

Milakis, D., Vlastos, T. and Barbopoplos, N. (2008), "Relationships between urban form and travel behaviour in Athens, Greece: a comparison with Western European and North American results", *European Journal of Transport and Infrastructure Research*, **8**, 201–15.

Mogridge, M.H.J. (1985), Transport, land use and energy interaction, *Urban Studies*, **22**, 481–92.

Næss, P. (2005), Residential location affects travel behaviour – but how and why? The case of Copenhagen Metropolitan Area, *Progress in Planning*, **63**, 167–257.

Næss, P. (2006), *Urban Structure Matters: Residential Location, Car Dependence and Travel Behaviour*, New York and London: Routledge.

Næss, P. (2009), Residential self-selection and appropriate control variables in land use–travel studies, *Transport Reviews*, **29**, 293–324.

Næss, P. (2010), Residential location, travel and energy use: the case of Hangzhou Metropolitan Area, *Journal of Transport and Land Use*, **3**, pp. 27–59.

Næss, P. (2011), 'New Urbanism' or metropolitan-level centralization? A comparison of the influences of metropolitan-level and neighbourhood-level urban form characteristics on travel behaviour, *Journal of Transport and Land Use*, **4**, pp. 25–44.

Næss, P. (2012), Urban form and travel behaviour: experience from a Nordic context, *Journal of Transport and Land Use*, **5**, 21–45.

Næss, P. (2013), Residential location, transport rationales and daily-life travel behaviour: the case of Hangzhou Metropolitan Area, China, *Progress in Planning*, **79**, 1–50.

Næss, P. and Jensen, O.B. (2004), Urban structure matters, even in a small town, *Journal of Environmental Planning and Management*, **47**, 35–56.

Næss, P., Røe, P.G. and Larsen, S.L. (1995), Travelling distances, modal split and transportation energy in thirty residential areas in Oslo, *Journal of Environmental Planning and Management*, **38**, 349–70.

Næss, P., Silva, C. and Pinho, P. (2011), *Residential Location and Travel in a Polycentric City*, paper presented at the World Symposium on Transport and Land Use Research, Whistler, Canada, 28 July.

Newman, P.W.G. and Kenworthy, J.R. (1989), *Cities and Automobile Dependence*, Aldershot: Gower Publications.

Nielsen, T.S. (2002), *Boliglokalisering og transport i Aalborg*, PhD dissertation, Aalborg: Aalborg University.

Pushkar, A.O., Hollingworth, B.J. and Miller, E.J. (2000), *A Multivariate Regression Model for Estimating Greenhouse Gas Emissions from Alternative Neighbourhood Designs*, paper presented at the 79th annual meeting of the Transportation Research Board, Washington, DC.

Røe, P.G. (2001), *Storbymenneskets hverdagsreiser. Sammenhenger mellom bosted, livsstil og hverdagsreisepraksis i et senmoderne perspektiv*, Dr Polit. dissertation, Norwegian University of Technology and Science.

Schipper, L., Deakin, E. and Spearling, D. (1994), *Sustainable Transportation: The Future of the Automobile in an Environmentally Constrained World*, paper presented at a research seminar arranged by the Board of Communications Research, Stockholm, 23 September.

Synnes, H. (1990), *Reisevaner i Trondheim 1990*, unpublished MSc dissertation, Norwegian Institute of Technology.

Tillberg, K. (2001), *Barnfamiljers dagliga fritidsresor i bilsamhället – ett tidspussel med geografiska och könsmässiga variationer*, Geografiska regionstudier no. 43, Uppsala: Uppsala University.

Wu, Z. (2008), *Introduction of Transportation Energy Situation and Challenges in China*, presentation materials, www.acus.org/docs/WU_Transport.ppt.

Xue, J., Næss, P., Yao, Y. and Li, F. (2011), The challenge of sustainable mobility in urban planning and development: a comparative study of the Copenhagen and Hangzhou metropolitan areas, *International Journal of Urban Sustainable Development*, **3**, 185–206.

Zegras, C. (2010), The built environment and motor vehicle ownership and use: evidence from Santiago de Chile, *Urban Studies*, **47**, 1793–817.

9 Public transport-orientated development and network effects
Carey Curtis

1. INTRODUCTION

There is an interest, in cities worldwide, in a more coordinated approach to growth management aimed at achieving a more sustainable urban form that in turn can provide the opportunity to achieve sustainable transport outcomes. A popular planning strategy has been to strive for public transport-oriented development (PTOD), more commonly referred to as transit-oriented development. At the heart of this approach is a need to consider both land-use planning and transport planning in an integrated way. If city planning is to be framed around public transport, it is necessary to address both the form and structure of the city as well as the quality of the public transport network to ensure each are mutually supportive and provide for improved accessibility.

The chapter draws together the different ideas about PTOD. First, PTOD is positioned within the longstanding academic debate about urban structure, intensity of land use and the relationship with public transport efficiency and accessibility. Second, the planning practice response to these ideas is charted by drawing on a case study of Perth, Western Australia. It is evident that while Perth has had a longstanding planning policy focus on PTOD, it is only in the past decade that strategic planning practice has begun to directly engage in land use–public transport integration as a practice rather than simply a policy aspiration. The case study demonstrates how a public transport accessibility tool played a critical role in moving policy aspirations forward, both for future urban growth and for public transport investment.

2. URBAN STRUCTURE AND THE RELATIONSHIP WITH PUBLIC TRANSPORT EFFICIENCY

The idea that different urban forms can result in more sustainable transport outcomes has its roots in the understanding that land use and transport are inextricably linked, and that accessibility is determined both by the proximity of land uses to each other and to the transport network (Webber, 1964; Keyes, 1982; Kelly, 1994; Westerman, 1998). Changes then in either land use and/or transport infrastructure impact on travel patterns.

A considerable body of academic research has attempted to analyse this relationship through empirical studies and through modelling simulations. The 1970s 'oil shock' provided the initial context with a focus on transport energy use (Owens, 1984). North American simulation studies concluded that a 'polycentric' urban form (an urban area comprising small, compact sub-centres arranged in transport corridors) was the least transport energy consumptive (Keyes, 1982; Van Til, 1979; Brindle, 1992). In the period following the Brundtland Report (United Nations General Assembly, 1987) these kind of research studies mushroomed – here the search was for an efficient urban form focused on transport's contribution to the sustainable city. Most researchers concluded that urban form has an impact on travel behaviour, but the extent of this impact has been inconclusive and there is no consensus as to the ideal urban form (Sorenson, 2001; Williams et al, 2000; Hickman and Banister, 2002). The most widely agreed urban form for sustainable transport outcomes in cities is where there are multiple nodes of concentrated activity, connected both physically and by telecommunications (Srinivasan, 2002: Sorenson, 2001; Lloyd Jones et al., 2001; Filion, 2001; Healey, 2000; Newton, 2000; Frey, 1999; Brotchie, 1992; Newman and Kenworthy, 1999; Van der Valk and Faludi, 1992; Kumar, 1990; Van Til, 1979).

There have been many ideas for the development of a multi-centred city based on a network of mutually dependent sub-centres linked by transport corridors (see Lynch's 'Urban Star', 1961; de Wolfe's 1971 'Civilia' cited in Breheny, 1996; concepts by Rickaby, 1991; Duany and Plater-Zyberk, 1994; Wood et al., 1994; Frey, 1999; Roberts et al., 1999; Calthorpe and Fulton, 2001). The main benefit of this form of development is that, by accommodating urban population growth within higher-density centres along transport corridors, urban sprawl is contained and land is used more efficiently. Locating land uses that are major traffic generators (employment and service uses) at nodes within these corridors and close to residential population serves to support an efficient public transport service. It also provides the opportunity for transport mode shift where travel distance and travel time are reduced through development concentration. Providing a competitive public transport alternative provides a means to reduce road congestion and also reduces the road transport investment requirement at the urban fringe as the city spreads.

3.   PLANNING PRACTICE AND PTOD

This urban form debate has been captured in planning practice through many city planning strategies; the backlash against suburban sprawl has seen the rise of New Urbanism as an alternative. The OECD has reinforced recommendations for compact cities where PTOD forms the backbone of a recommended strategy for providing accessibility to local shops and services (OECD, 2012). Many metropolitan strategies focus on creating a polycentric city where PTOD is regarded as means of creating an urban structure that can better support public transport, as well as supporting walking and cycling, and thus provide transport choice as an alternative to the car. Examples of planning strategies that aim at such a networked city can be seen worldwide (for example Copenhagen, the Randstad (Netherlands) and Cape Town). The Dutch 5th national policy on Spatial Planning 2001 advocated progression from the traditional compact city to a network of compact cities where transport infrastructure was seen as the main structuring device connecting these (Priemus and Zonneveld, 2003). Local Urban Activity Corridors formed the key to Cape Town's metropolitan planning strategy with the expectation that these could provide for integration across different spatially segregated populations and promote economic growth outside the CBD (Cape Metropolitan Council, 1996). The transit-oriented development corridor concept is promoted by Ontario and New Jersey transit planners (Ministry of Transportation and Ministry of Municipal Affairs, 1995; New Jersey Transit et al., n.d.). Australian cities have also embraced PTOD during this past decade, including the concept in metropolitan strategies for Adelaide, Brisbane, Gold Coast, Melbourne, Sydney and Perth.

Clearly these planning strategies represent policy aspirations. Attempts to implement them in reality present a considerable challenge to the current development direction. Indeed, this was recognised in the US New Urbanism's Charter, 'the reconfiguration of sprawling suburbs into communities of real neighbourhoods and diverse districts' will require 'coherent' metropolitan planning (CNU, [1998] 2001; Katz, 1994). It is not, however, simply a problem of governance and planning process, creating such a polycentric city based on public transport poses a challenge to the existing urban structure, which is predicated on car-based catchments. Walkable catchments developed around public transport nodes are promoted, but this is at odds with the approach that designated sub-regional city centres assuming access by car. Today, both individual travel patterns and the activities of business are now complex and diverse. Neither is suited to such a simple dichotomy of walking or car-based travel. Instead, at different points in time, activities span the neighbourhood, district, sub-region, CBD and beyond (Cuthbert, 2003; Bertolini and Dijst, 2003; Madanipour, 2001; Graham and Marvin, 2001; Lloyd-Jones et al., 2001; Calthorpe and Fulton, 2001; Bertolini, 1999; Healey, 2000; Feitelson and Salomon, 2000; Webber, 1964). A spatial planning strategy must cater for this by designing a land-use and transport network with the capability of providing accessibility at all spatial scales in a sustainable way (Gehl, 1987: 85), 'accessibility must be ranked as the dominant criterion against which alternative settlement patterns must be judged. The spatial form and density pattern that makes for the most access . . . should be the structure most worth striving for' (Webber, 1998: 204).

So, while policy aspirations place PTOD in the forefront as a physical planning concept, a clear understanding of the underlying policy objective lies at the heart of actually planning for PTOD. If city planners are to deliver genuine accessibility they will need to develop both a transport strategy and a land-use strategy that together integrate the concept for the whole city. As Webber intimates, accessibility must be the dominant measure against which these strategies are judged. In planning practice it is clear to the author that these are new skills required of planners. Rarely has a strategic land-use plan been developed in symbiosis with a public transport plan. It is more usual for conventional road-based four-step transport modelling to be employed, where land-use plans are tested to see their effect on road congestion. Accessibility by public transport has not been the metric applied. Where planning strategies have aspired to PTOD, in many cases of implementation the new PTOD developments have been isolated islands in a city where car-travel dominates, PTOD has rarely been implemented as a coherent strategic package.

To move from the policy aspiration of PTOD to planning reality, land-use change must be accompanied by changes to transport operations to be effective. A focus on efficient public transport as a means of urban structuring is a key. Efficient in this case means that accessibility is delivered as well as patronage – again the metric must change. Equally, where development change is envisaged, the transport needs and impacts of those accessing this development must be planned for. This is captured by the term 'land use–transport integration' (LUTI).

LUTI requires the 'need to deal simultaneously with both transport and urban development issues' (Bertolini and Spit, 1998: 17). Where accessibility forms the core metric in LUTI, new planning perspectives are highlighted. From a transport perspective, as well as simply considering the reach of any given public transport network, the 'network effect' must also be considered. Sometimes been referred to as 'transport integration', this concerns the need to address the factors that, together, can enhance accessibility by public transport. These factors include the integration between public transport services and timetable coordination (train to train, train to bus, train to tram and ferry and so on), and between public transport and other modes of transport (car, bicycle, walking); the quality of interchange facilities (walking distances between transport modes and to land uses, legibility, safety, amenity, etc.); and service frequencies.

From a land-use perspective, factors include considering how to locate development in order to support public transport; the density and intensity of land use in relation to public transport capacity and efficiency of use. Development location must be considered at both a strategic and local level – in the former considering the optimum arrangement of centres across the network to support public transport, the latter considering the orientation of development towards public transport for ease of access. Planning in this way also provides a rationale for proposing a particular intensity of use at given development locations. In so doing, resolution can be provided for the criticism that the existing pattern of development is not energy efficient in that public transport systems are designed to meet peak-direction peak-hour flows (Lloyd-Jones et al., 2001; Tanner, 2003) running empty on the opposite direction. The approach acknowledges that the structure of the urban network, the relationship of corridors to the CBD and other activity centres, is a more important consideration than development density since it determines travel patterns (March, 1969; Gordon et al., 1991; Brindle, 1996; Schwanen et al., 2001; Næss and Jensen, 2002). An urban structure capable of supporting an efficient public transport service suggests particular parameters for the composition, size and location of centres within the network of activity and transport corridors. Separation of employment locations from housing has made inefficient demands on transport infrastructure and services. If half of the workforce has local employment, this reduces transport inefficiency since the transport system benefits from two-way flows, providing employment at centres across the network. Even if all the local residents work elsewhere, there will still be an exchange of employees that will result in transport efficiencies (Klassen, 1990, cited in Westerman, 1998). There is a need to develop a hierarchy of urban centres designed to provide a high level of public transport accessibility.

4.   PUBLIC TRANSPORT ACCESSIBILITY TOOLS

Translating policy aspirations for PTOD into practical action presents a formidable technical challenge. It is evident that there has been an absence of such an approach designed to usefully inform key policy objectives about the future public transport network in relation to accessibility improvements (Curtis et al., 2010). Instead, as will be shown below, strategic planning for public transport has often been unambitious, with most proposals offering incremental improvements to the existing network based on demand forecasting rather than future planning in the context of meeting a policy objective to provide public transport accessibility for all (Curtis et al., 2010). To meet an objective where public transport can offer a real alternative transport mode choice to the car requires a new approach for planning and evaluating public transport accessibility. It requires a method that can also serve stakeholders and decision-makers as they deliberate on the best public transport network configuration, service levels and capacity upgrades. In this respect, accessibility tools have a critical role in examining ways of integrating transport and in integrating transport with land use. These accessibility tools can provide a new planning technique that enables land-use and transport planners to engage with the PTOD policy approach. Such a public transport accessibility tool has been applied in Perth, Western Australia and its contribution to both metropolitan land-use planning and public transport infrastructure planning is described below.

Policy goals formulated by Australian federal and state governments have begun to emphasise the desirability and importance of increasing public transport mode share since the mid-1990s (DOT, 1995; DOI, 2002). These are set within a new understanding of the need for transport planning to deliver accessibility rather than simply mobility. The development and establishment in practice of methodologically robust and user-friendly accessibility tools for LUTI planning in Australian cities is therefore a timely endeavour in the context of recent changes to policy priorities at federal and state level (SSCRRAT, 2009). The Spatial Network Analysis for Multimodal Urban Transport Systems (SNAMUTS) tool has been developed to serve this purpose. It is a GIS tool designed to assess the accessibility of a public transport network in its land-use context. SNAMUTS endeavours to identify and visualise a land use-public transport system's strengths and weaknesses of geographical coverage; the ability and efficiency to connect places of activity; the strategic significance of routes and network nodes; and the speed competitiveness between public transport and car travel in a coherent mapping exercise. The tool is intended to aid discussion and to lend weight to decision-making within the fields of land-use planning and transport planning, particularly where outcomes leading to more sustainable transport options are needed. A full explanation of the components of the tool and its method can be found in Curtis and Scheurer (2010), in this chapter the focus is on its application in planning practice.

The tool is designed to reflect a vision of world best practice in public transport most comprehensively documented in the European Union HiTrans project (Nielsen et al., 2005). The success factors most frequently discussed include: network coverage and service frequencies that offer a viable alternative to the car for most travel purposes (Laube, 1998; Nielsen et al., 2005; Mees and Dodson, 2011); a legible network structure that is efficient to operate, easy to navigate and offers a choice of routes wherever possible (Mees, 2000, 2010; Mees and Dodson, 2011; Vuchic, 2005); a speed advantage over road traffic along a city's main corridors (Newman, 2009; Newman et al., 2009); the integration of public transport facilities with supportive urban development (Bernick and Cervero, 1997; Cervero, 1998; Dittmar and Ohland, 2004; Curtis et al., 2009).

SNAMUTS breaks down the land use–transport system into a set of activity nodes and route segments derived from strategic planning documents and public transport timetables. The accessibility of the system is determined from the perspective of a public transport user who also has a choice of using a car for any given journey. In this respect the following parameters are set:

- Minimum service standard: inclusion of a public transport route into the analysed network, normally requiring a service frequency of 20 minutes (or better) during the weekday inter-peak period (about 10:00 to 15:00) and 30 minutes (or better) during the day on Saturdays and Sundays. This level has been chosen as it reflects the minimum for public transport to be perceived as having a full-time presence and attracting usage for a variety of both planned and spontaneous journey purposes.
- Activity nodes: higher-order activity centres that appear in strategic planning documents or have been identified by on-site observation, in order to capture major transfer points. Each activity node is assigned an exclusive catchment of residents and jobs located within walking distance from the associated rail station(s) (800m) or tram/bus corridors (400m).
- Travel impediment: spatial separation (a proxy value for distance) is measured closest to the user experience, namely travel time and service frequency. Each route segment is labelled with an impediment value consisting of the average travel time divided by the number of services per hour, separately for each direction. The travel impediment (proxy distance) between any two activity nodes on the network is thus made up of the sum of the impediment values on each route segment traversed along the path.
- Weekday inter-peak: Routes are included for the service offered during the weekday inter-peak period (roughly between 10:00 and 15:00, Monday to Friday). This is considered to be the time when the greatest diversity of travel purposes over a daily and weekly cycle coincide, and when the potential of public transport to offer a viable alternative (or not) to the car is critical.

A set of seven SNAMUTS indicators provide the possibility to measure accessibility from several perspectives:

1. Closeness centrality measures the average minimum cumulative impediment (travel time divided by service frequency per segment) for all network paths, and from each node to reach any other node on the network.
2. Degree centrality measures the average minimum number of transfers required for all network paths, and from each node to reach any other node on the network.
3. Efficiency change measures the before and after effect of network modifications.
4. Contour catchment measures the number of residents and jobs in activity nodes accessible within 30 minutes from the reference node, and the average size of all 30-minute contour catchments across the network.
5. Betweenness centrality measures the percentage of all preferred network paths (weighted by cumulative impediment and combined activity node size) that flow through each route segment.
6. Speed competitiveness measures the ratio of lowest available public transport travel time with road travel time in congested conditions for all network paths, and from each node to reach any other node on the network.
7. Network connectivity measures the propensity of each activity node to act as a transfer hub (and thus attract potential activities to service transferring passengers), and includes a cumulative count across the network.

Finally a composite indicator for overall public transport accessibility is compiled for each activity node drawing on six of the above indicators (Scheurer and Curtis, 2008; Curtis and Scheurer, 2009). There are a wide range of different accessibility tools now in use on planning practice (see for example Hull et al., 2012). Many are based on measuring access from/to one location to the rest of the urban area (see, for example, the UK's Accession Tool as used by West Sussex County Council, n.d.).

Metropolitan Spatial Planning to Deliver Land Use – Transport Integration

Perth's long term strategic planning now has LUTI at its heart. The Network City metropolitan strategy (WAPC, 2004) aimed to increase the efficiency of the use of urban land, to strengthen local sense of place and employment opportunities, and to encourage public over private transport. A more prominent role for activity centres and corridors is the strategy's prime means of achieving these goals. Formulating an implementation strategy, however, where land for 375,000 houses could be identified in accordance with these policy aspirations, required a clearer identification of the role of each activity centre in a regional hierarchy, as well as a more detailed assessment of multimodal accessibility than had been previously provided. The SNAMUTS tool was used to examine a range of future scenarios concerning public transport infrastructure and service initiatives and corresponding land-use priorities.

Two stakeholder participant workshops were conducted where SNAMUTS was employed as an interactive decision tool to assist in the examination of scenarios for activity centres framed around the accessibility of the transport network and the accessibility of place. Testing these factors through a scenario approach enabled three planning questions to be examined: which activity centres could best be intensified; which centres should perform a regional role and which ones a local role; and where public transport investment (infrastructure, service improvement) should go. Clearly, in addition to the factors addressed in this example, there are other (non-transport) factors that are important to the choice of which centres to intensify, such as quality of the urban fabric, attractiveness to the population, opportunity for redevelopment and funding opportunities.

The scenarios developed were agreed through a discursive and collaborative process with officers from the state planning, public transport and main roads agencies. The data and ideas being fed into SNAMUTS were drawn from work in progress within the agencies. The starting point was a workshop comprising two mapping games designed to capture data and short- and long-term thinking within and across the agencies and to assist in ascertaining a collective view on scenarios to be tested. The outputs from both games were then used to inform the scenarios that SNAMUTS modelled. A total of five future scenarios were developed to assess different assumptions for priorities in public transport service and infrastructure improvements and for the spatial distribution of urban growth. One scenario focused simply on boosting public transport frequencies, others included different configurations of heavy and light public transport networks and different configurations of development types (high intensity central city development; development along transport corridors; development of the middle ring; development at the urban fringe). The workshop reconvened to deliberate on the accessibility outputs from these scenarios and to workshop a composite strategy. This resulted in a final scenario – the Composite Wishbone – a combination of those elements of the previous scenarios that had the greatest positive effect on network performance. The key aspects of the urban development configuration were the development of strategic activity centres in the middle ring and along new light rail corridors. The light rail corridor took the shape of a wishbone centred on the Perth central area, hence the name of the scenario. This scenario demonstrated how limited any significant urban fringe development would be on improving accessibility by public transport to all residents across the metropolitan area.

The comparison of accessibility improvements to service intensity proved a powerful measure in generating a strong understanding among practitioners of the costs of different growth management options in a way not previously conceived. It was evident that using the accessibility tool had enhanced practitioners understanding of LUTI and planning for accessibility.

This first application demonstrates the capability of SNAMUTS to provide a set of quantitative measures to analyse the impact of alternative visions for transport and land-use integration, comparing the results against common benchmarks and each other. It also showed the capability of the tool to visualise and communicate the outputs. It is significant that both elements were developed iteratively and discursively: the content and methodology of SNAMUTS were gradually refined as the tool was used to engage stakeholders in an important debate on urban development priorities in Perth during the next 25 years. The outputs informed the next iteration of the metropolitan planning strategy (WAPC, 2009).

Evaluating Public Transport Investment Proposals

In the second application, SNAMUTS was employed to evaluate the proposals by the state Public Transport Authority (PTA) for the next 20 years investment in public transport for greater metropolitan Perth. In developing their strategy, the PTA wanted to test how well the proposed network and service performed in relation to enhanced public transport accessibility to key activity centres. The PTA supplied the proposed public transport network for the 2031 reference year. They also requested changes to three of the standard SNAMUTS measures. First, use of the inter-peak service was changed to the morning peak. Second, the 'contour catchment' measure was increased from 30 minutes to 45 minutes, thus extending the potential accessibility of the area 'on paper'. Third, only accessibility to 14 key activity centres was assessed, not the full set of 94 public transport-accessible activity centres identified in the earlier metropolitan strategy (WAPC, 2004). These were important changes with far reaching implications for the competitiveness of public transport to the car for the individual traveller and demonstrate the lag between policy aspirations (public transport for all), political reality and current public transport planning practice (demand led).

The evaluation of the PTA network focused on three objectives, based on the metropolitan planning aim of improving public transport access (WAPC, 2009): the extent to which potential accessibility of quality public transport was expanded to a larger proportion of metropolitan residents; the extent to which accessibility was enhanced across the 14 key activity centres; and the public transport 'effort' (performance of different transport modes and across corridors). For the construction of the scenario, the number of residents, jobs and students in metropolitan Perth was projected to increase by 39 per cent between 2009 and 2031. By 2031 it was proposed to extend one rail line to meet city expansion plans and to develop a rail branch line to the airport; additional stations were proposed along the southern suburbs rail line; initiatives proposed to improve service levels in the bus network included the establishment of a priority busway running into the Perth CBD and the provision of high-frequency express services between the CBD and a key activity centre. In total, the requirement for operational input in 2031 was 60 per cent higher than in 2009.

The PTA scenario was assessed using the SNAMUTS tool and compared to the existing situation. On average, it was found that composite accessibility across the network increased by about three points on the 45-point scale between 2009 and 2031, thus demonstrating some improvement in the context of the accessibility policy aspiration. Concerns were raised as to whether the rate of growth was sufficient to meet the aspirational target for mode shifting set in the 1996 Metropolitan Transport Strategy and in relation to future (2031) likely mandatory standards for accessibility and carbon emissions, as well as possible constraints in the availability and affordability of transport fuels. Further, it was apparent that important centres with a metropolitan-wide function had not benefited from the proposed measures to the extent necessary to ensure they were very well served by public transport.

Improvements were largely achieved by increased service frequencies; the basic structure of the network in existing areas was not altered significantly. Changes to the infrastructure network served to consolidate rail's domination, even though only three rail extensions are proposed by 2031. Further, the rail extensions were located in areas where they could not play a role in relieving existing rail routes. The busway added a radial corridor of critical significance, but doubts were raised as to whether the capacity of a bus system was the most efficient solution. The focus of the PTA proposals was on incremental improvements to the existing radial, mono-centric network. There were lost opportunities where additional orbital links could help network strategic centres and take pressure off the central city. New constraints emerged on some radial bus routes with some buses carrying in excess of 30 buses per hour during the morning peak (equivalent to a two-minute frequency). The accessibility analysis alerted PTA to other network choices – either rerouting some services away from the high-frequency corridor and to other destinations or replacing bus with a higher capacity mode such as light rail. The former choice creates new transfer-free links that may relieve pressure from the central area and thus addresses the goal of polycentric accessibility.

This case exposed the broader institutional barriers to the achievement of the future vision. The proposed network was tempered by views on the preferred mode and by a vision based on the existing city and public transport network structure rather than futures thinking. Replacement of buses by light rail was considered to be the '2050 Plan'. Two factors appeared to constrain the future thinking, both influenced by the traditional ways of transport modelling and forecasting: first that these proposals would be costly and would not be funded by the Treasury; second, that while these proposals would offer public transport accessibility for residents in line with policy objectives, the current demand (6 per cent mode share across the metropolitan area) meant it would be difficult to justify finance. Decision-makers were relying on transport forecasts based on past demand rather than supplying a network in line with the policy aspiration.

5. CONCLUSION

While there have been aspirational planning policies seeking to increase use of public transport through targeted land development and infrastructure investment since the mid-1990s, planning action has been unambitious and produced little more than incremental improvements based on traditional demand forecasting. A new tool was required that focused on improving accessibility by public transport and this led to the development of SNAMUTS, an interactive decision tool capable of measuring accessibility of a city's public transport network from the traveller's perspective. SNAMUTS calculates seven different accessibility measures and combines them into one overall composite indicator, enabling scenario testing of measures such as land-use intensity and development location, public transport network coverage and service frequency. SNAMUTS has been extensively utilised in Perth (as described above), Melbourne and Adelaide to test the effects of both land-use and public transport network options. The process and results have informed refinement of the tool, enhanced participants understanding of LUTI and uncovered entrenched limitations to current thinking about future planning of public transport.

In relation to the SNAMUTS accessibility tool, work is now progressing to test its application to a wide range of city types throughout the world. This project is funded by the Australian Research Council.[1] Not only will this add further insights into the value of the various indicators employed, but more important this enables a consideration of whether it is possible to benchmark cities for public transport. If this is possible, it will provide a useful metric for planning practice and assist in directing funding towards public transport and urban development to support this infrastructure in a way not yet experienced. Further work in developing such accessibility tools should also go beyond simply addressing the physical measures of accessibility. Attention is also needed on the social aspects of accessibility, here focussing on access for low income households, who increasingly in Australia are located at the urban fringe (where housing is cheaper) distant from employment and public transport.

There are now increasing developments in the range and focus of accessibility tools. Not many of these directly address the need to assist in the delivery of public transport oriented development. Where such tools are employed they highlight the value of the network effect in developing robust public transport systems to offer accessibility by public transport competitive to the car. The next steps for research and for practice are to focus on how to move quickly from policy aspirations of public agencies for PTOD to implementation of development on the ground.

NOTE

1. Australian Research Council Discovery Grant DP110104884.

REFERENCES

Bernick, M. and Cervero, R. (1997), *Transit Villages in the 21st Century*, New York: McGraw Hill.

Bertolini, L. (1999), Spatial development patterns and public transport: the application of an analytical model in the Netherlands, *Planning Practice and Research*, **14**(2), 199–210.

Bertolini, L. and Dijst, M.J. (2003), Mobility environments and network cities, *Journal of Urban Design*, **8**(1), 27–43.

Bertolini, L. and Spit, T. (1998), *Cities on Rails: The Redevelopment of Railway Station Areas*, London: Spon.

Breheny, M. (1996), Centrists, decentrists and compromisers: views on the future of urban form, in M. Jenks, E. Burton and K. Williams (eds), *The Compact City: A Sustainable Urban Form?* London: E. & F.N. Spon.

Brindle, R. (1992), Toronto – paradigm lost? *Australian Planner*, September, pp. 123–30.

Brindle, R. (1996), Urban densities and travel behaviour – mind gap!, *Issues*, **36**.

Brotchie, J.F. (1992), Urban land use, transport and the information economy: metropolitan employment, journey to work trends and implications for transport, *Urban Futures*, **17**.

Calthorpe, P. and Fulton, W. (2001), *The Regional City: Planning for the End of Sprawl*, Washington, DC: Island Press.

Cape Metropolitan Council (1996), *Metropolitan Spatial Development Framework: A Guide for Spatial Development in the Cape Metropolitan Functional Region*, Cape Town: Cape Metropolitan Council.

Cervero, R. (1998), *The Transit Metropolis: A Global Inquiry*, Washington, DC: Island Press.

CNU ([1998] 2001), *Charter of the New Urbanism*, San Francisco: Congress for New Urbanism.

Curtis, C. and Scheurer, J. (2010), Planning for sustainable accessibility: developing tools to aid discussion and decision making, *Progress in Planning*, **74**, 53–106.

Curtis, C., Renne, J.L. and Bertolini, L. (eds) (2009), *Transit-Oriented Development – Making it Happen*, Farnham: Ashgate.

Curtis, C., Scheurer, J. and Burke, M. (2010), The dead end of demand modelling: supplying a futures-based public transport plan, in P. Ache and M. Ilmonen (eds), *Space is Luxury: Selected Proceedings of the 24th AESOP Annual Conference*, http://lib.tkk.fi/Reports/2010/isbn9789526031309.pdf.

Cuthbert, A.R. (ed.) (2003), *Designing Cities: Critical Readings in Urban Design*, Oxford: Blackwell.

Dittmar, H. and Ohland, G. (2004), *The New Transit Town: Best Practices in Transit-Oriented Development*, Washington, DC: Island Press.

DOI (2002), *Melbourne 2030: Planning for Sustainable Growth*, Melbourne: Department of Infrastructure.

DOT (1995), *Perth Metropolitan Transport Strategy 1995–2029*, Perth: Department of Transport.

Duany, A. and Plater-Zyberk, E. (1994), The neighbourhood, the district and the corridor, in P. Katz (ed.), *The New Urbanism: Toward an Architecture of Community*, New York: McGraw-Hill.

Feitelson, E. and Salomon, I. (2000), The implications of differential network flexibility for spatial structures, *Transportation Research A*, **34**, 459–79.

Filion, P. (2001), Suburban mixed-use centres and urban dispersion: what difference do they make? *Environment and Planning A*, **33**, 141–60.

Frey, H. (1999), *Designing the City: Towards a More Sustainable Form*, London: E. & F.N. Spon.

Gehl, J. (1987), *Life Between Buildings: Using Public Space*, New York: Van Nostrand Reinhold.

Gordon, P., Richardson, H. and Jun, M. (1991), The commuting paradox: evidence from the top twenty, *Journal of the American Planning Association*, **57**(4), 416–21.

Graham, S. and Marvin, S. (2001), *Splintering Urbanism: Networked Infrastructures, Technological Mobilities and the Urban Condition*, London: Routledge.

Healey, P. (2000), Connected cities, *Town and Country Planning*, pp. 55–7.

Hickman, R. and Banister, D. (2002), Reducing travel by design: what happens over time? in *5th Symposium of the International Urban Planning and Environment Association Conference*, Oxford.

Hull, A., Silva, C. and Bertolini, L. (2012), *COST Action TU1002 – Accessibility Instruments for Planning Practice: Report One*, www.accessibilityplanning.eu/reports/report-1-accessibility-instruments-in-practice.

Katz, P. (1994), *The New Urbanism: Toward an Architecture of Community*, New York: McGraw-Hill.

Kelly, E. (1994), The transportation–land use link, *Journal of Planning Literature*, **9**(2), 128–45.

Keyes, D. (1982), Reducing travel and fuel use through urban planning, in R. Burchell and D. Listokin (eds), *Energy and Land Use*, New Brunswick, NJ: Center for Urban Policy Research, Rutgers University.

Kumar, A. (1990), Impact of technological developments on urban form and travel behaviour, *Regional Studies*, **24**, 137–48.

Laube, F. (1998), *Optimising Urban Passenger Transport*, PhD Thesis, Murdoch University.

Lloyd-Jones, T., Erickson, B., Roberts, M. and Nice, S. (2001), The integrated metropolis: a strategy for the networked multi-centred city, in A. Madanipour, A. Hull and P. Healey (eds), *The Governance of Place: Space and Planning Processes*, Aldershot: Ashgate, pp. 102–23.

Lynch, K. (1961), The pattern of metropolis, in A. Blowers, C. Hamnett and P. Sarre (eds), *The Future of Cities*, London: Hutchinson Educational.

Madanipour, A. (2001), How relevant is 'planning by neighbourhoods' today? *Town Planning Review*, **72**(2), 171–91.

March, L. (1969), Homes beyond the fringe, in A. Blowers, C. Hamnett and P. Sarre (eds), *The Future of Cities*, London: Hutchinson Educational.

Mees, P. (2000), *A Very Public Solution: Transport in the Dispersed City*, Melbourne: Melbourne University Press.

Mees, P. (2010), *Transport for Suburbia: Beyond the Automobile Age*, London: Earthscan.

Mees, P. and Dodson, J. (2011), *Public Transport Network Planning in Australia: Assessing Current Practice in Australia's Five Largest Cities*, Research Paper 34, Urban Research Program, Brisbane: Griffith University.

Ministry of Transportation and Ministry of Municipal Affairs (1995), *Transit-Supportive Land Use Planning Guidelines*, Ontario: Ministry of Transportation and Ministry of Municipal Affairs.

Næss, P. and Jensen, O.B. (2002), Urban land use, mobility and theory of science: exploring the potential of critical realism in empirical research, *Journal of Environmental Policy and Planning*, **4**, 295–311.

New Jersey Transit, New Jersey Office of Smart Growth, Downtown New Jersey Inc., New Jersey Future, Project for Public Spaces Inc., Regional Plan Association, Rutgers State University of New Jersey and Alan M. Vorhees Transportation Policy Institute (n.d.), *Building a Transit-Friendly Community: Place, Access, Development, Parking, Partnerships*.

Newman, P. (2009), Planning for transit-oriented development: strategic principles, C. Curtis, J.L. Renne and L. Bertolini (eds), *Transit-Oriented Development – Making it Happen*, Farnham: Ashgate.

Newman, P. and Kenworthy, J. (1999), *Sustainability and Cities: Overcoming Automobile Dependence*, Washington, DC: Island Press.

Newman, P., Beatley, T. and Boyer, H. (2009), *Resilient Cities: Responding to Peak Oil and Climate Change*, Washington, DC: Island Press.

Newton, P. (2000), Urban form and environmental performance, in K. Williams, E. Burton and M. Jenks (eds) *Achieving Sustainable Urban Form*, London: E. & F.N. Spon.

Nielsen, G., Nelson, J.D., Mulley, C., Tegnér, G., Lind, G. and Lange, T. (2005), *Public Transport – Planning the Networks*, HiTrans Best Practice Guide 2, Oslo: Civitas Consultants.

OECD (2012), *OECD Green Growth Studies: Compact City Policies: A Comparative Assessment*, Paris: OECD Publishing.

Owens, S. (1984), Spatial structure and energy demand, in D. Cope, P. Hills and P. James (eds), *Energy Policy and Land Use*, Oxford: Pergamon Press.

Priemus, H. and Zonneveld, W. (2003), What are corridors and what are the issues? Introduction to special issue: the governance of corridors, *Journal of Transport Geography*, **11**, 167–77.

Rickaby, P. (1991), Energy and urban development in an archetypal English town, *Environment and Planning B*, **18**, 153–75.

Roberts, M., Lloyd-Jones, T., Erickson, B. and Nice, S. (1999), Place and space in the networked city: conceptualising the integrated metropolis, *Journal of Urban Design*, **4**(1), 51–65.

Scheurer, J. and Curtis, C. (2008), *Spatial Network Analysis of Multimodal Transport Systems: Developing a Strategic Planning Tool to Assess the Congruence of Movement and Urban Structure – A Case Study of Perth before and after the Perth-to-Mandurah Railway*, research monograph, GAMUT, Melbourne, www.abp.unimelb.edu.au/gamut/publications-media/gamut-papers/gamut-papers-zero-eight.html.

Schwanen, T., Dieleman, F.M. and Dijst, M.J. (2001), Travel behaviour in Dutch monocentric and policentric urban systems, *Journal of Transport Geography*, **9**, 173–86.

Sorenson, A. (2001), Subcentres and satellite cities: Tokyo's 20th century experience of planned polycentrism, *International Planning Studies*, **6**(1), 9–32.

Srinivasan, S. (2002), Quantifying spatial characteristics of cities, *Urban Studies*, **39**(11), 2005–28.

SSCRRAT (2009), *Investment of Commonwealth and State Funds in Public Passenger Transport Infrastructure and Services*, Canberra (ACT): Commonwealth of Australia, Senate Standing Committee on Rural and Regional Affairs and Transport.

Tanner, R. (2003), Tanner on . . . best models for town layouts to ease congestion, *Planning*, 19 December, p. 9.

United Nations General Assembly (1987), *Our Common Future: Report of the World Commission on Environment and Development*, published as Annex to General Assembly document A/42/427, Development and International Co-operation: Environment, 2 August.

Van der Valk, A. and Faludi, A. (1992), Growth regions and the future of Dutch planning doctrine, in M. Breheny (ed.), *Sustainable Development and Urban Form*, London: Pion, pp. 122–37.

Van Til, J. (1979), Spatial form and structure in a possible future, *American Planning Association Journal*, July, pp. 318–28.

Vuchic, V.R. (2005), *Urban Transit: Operation, Planning and Economics*, Hoboken, NJ: Wiley.

WAPC (2004), *Network City. A Community Planning Strategy for Perth and Peel*, Perth: Government of Western Australia, Western Australian Planning Commission.

WAPC (2009), *Directions 2031:Draft Spatial Framework for Perth and Peel*, Perth: Government of Western Australia, Western Australian Planning Commission.

Webber, M. (1964), The urban place and the non-place urban realm, in M. Webber, W. Dyckman, D. Foley, A. Guttenburg, W. Wheaton and C. Baner Wurster (eds), *Explorations into Urban Structure*, Philadelphia: University of Pennsylvania Press, pp. 79–153.

Webber, M. (1998), The joys of the spread city, *Urban Design International*, **3**(4), 201–6.

Westerman, H.L. (1998), *Cities for Tomorrow: Integrating Land Use, Transport and the Environment. Better Practice Guide*, Haymarket, NSW: Austroads Incorporated.

West Sussex County Council (n.d.), www.westsussex.gov.uk/your_council/plans_projects_reports_and/plans/west_sussex_transport_plan/west_sussex_transport_plan_mon/west_sussex_public_transport_a.aspx.

Williams, K., Burton, E. and Jenks, M. (2000), *Achieving Sustainable Urban Form*, London: E. & F.N. Spon.

Wood, C., Watson, S. and Banister, D. (1994), *The Relationship between Energy Use in Transport and Urban Form*, paper presented at the Universities Transport Studies Group 1994 Conference, University of Leeds.

10 The effects of neighbourhood type and self-selection on driving: a case study of Northern California

Xinyu (Jason) Cao

1. INTRODUCTION

Urban sprawl has been widely criticized for causing auto-dependence and its negative consequences on modern society: climate change, air pollution and oil reliance. Recently, federal, state and local governments in the US have been promoting a variety of land-use and transportation policies to counter to the impacts of sprawl development. In 2008, the California Senate passed Bill 375 to reduce driving and greenhouse gases through regional sustainable community strategies; the 2009 US HUD-DOT-EPA Interagency Partnership for Sustainable Communities recommended directing federal funding toward existing communities – through strategies like transit-oriented, mixed-use development and land recycling, and providing more transportation choices; in 2010, Portland adopted its 2030 Bicycle Plan to invest $613 million on bike infrastructure in the next 20 years.

An open question emerges: if we develop metropolitan areas in an alternative way, will people reduce their driving and increase their use of transit and non-motorized transportation? That is, is there a form of neighbourhood development that makes urban development more sustainable than sprawl development? Many studies have explored the relationships between the built environment and travel behaviour since the 1990s. Collectively, these studies have found that residents living in traditional neighbourhoods (characterized as high density, mixed land uses, high street connectivity and so on) tend to drive less and walk more than suburbanites (Ewing and Cervero, 2001, 2010; Crane, 2000; Frank and Engelke, 2001). However, scholars widely agree that research has yet to establish the predominant causal link: do people living in 'walkable' neighbourhoods walk more because the built environment itself 'invites' them to do so, or because people who like to walk tend to choose residential neighbourhoods conducive to exercising that preference? The latter phenomenon is referred to as 'self-selection'. It is a potential explanation for observed differences between groups whenever individuals 'select' themselves into those groups rather than being randomly distributed between them. In this context, self-selection refers to 'the tendency of people to choose locations based on their travel abilities, needs and preferences' (Litman, 2005: 6). Residential self-selection generally results from two sources: attitudes and demographic attributes (Mokhtarian and Cao, 2008; Bohte et al., 2009).

A number of studies have addressed the issue of residential self-selection in the connections between the built environment and travel behaviour. After reviewing 38 empirical studies, Cao, Mokhtarian and Handy (2009a) concluded that self-selection plays an important role in influencing travel behaviour and that the built environment

149

has a separate effect beyond self-selection. Therefore, the observed influence of the built environment on travel behaviour (without controlling for residential self-selection) generally constitutes two components: the influence of the built environment itself and self-selection effect. This finding intrigues planners in knowing if the observed influence of the built environment on travel behaviour diminishes substantially once we control for self-selection. In other words, because many studies did not control for residential self-selection (especially that resulting from attitudinal factors), it is important for planners to know to what extent the impact of the built environment itself on travel behaviour could have been overestimated. However, among hundreds of studies on the connections between the built environment and travel behaviour, few have explicitly answered the question and hence researchers recommended future studies to fill the gap (Mokhtarian and Cao, 2008).

This chapter discusses the role of attitudes in the relationships between the built environment and travel behaviour, applies propensity score matching to Northern California data to investigate the extent to which the observed impact of the built environment on travel behaviour can be attributable to the environment itself, and compares and contrasts propensity score matching with sample selection models and the statistical control approach.

2.   ATTITUDE-INDUCED SELF-SELECTION

As indicated above, previous studies have consistently found a significant association between the built environment and travel behaviour. However, association itself is insufficient to establish causality. To robustly infer causality, scientific research generally requires at least four kinds of evidence (Schutt, 2004; Singleton and Straits, 2005): association (a statistically significant relationship), non-spuriousness (a relationship that cannot be attributed to another variable), time precedence (cause precedes effect) and causal mechanism (a theoretical/logical explanation for why the alleged cause should produce the observed effect). Transportation economists have offered an underlying mechanism: the built environment influences travel behaviour through its influence on the prices of travel (Boarnet and Crane, 2001). Longitudinal data can provide relatively robust evidence for time precedence whereas cross-sectional data can infer only the direction of an influence, depending on the availability of attitudinal factors in the data. Accordingly, a great deal of effort has been invested to fulfil the non-spuriousness requirement by controlling for confounding factors. Since most data contain demographic characteristics but not attitudinal factors, attitude-induced self-selection has become a key issue in the causality debate between the built environment and travel behaviour (Bohte et al., 2009; Mokhtarian and Cao, 2008).

If the built environment is significantly associated with travel behaviour, attitudes may interact with them in at least four ways, as discussed in Mokhtarian and Cao (2008). Figure 10.1 presents the possible interactions, using driving preference, auto-oriented neighbourhood and driving behaviour as an example. Figure 10.1a illustrates a potentially spurious relationship between auto-oriented neighbourhoods and driving behaviour, which can be addressed by controlling for driving preference. In Figure 10.1b, a large amount of driving (which may or may not have very much to do with the built

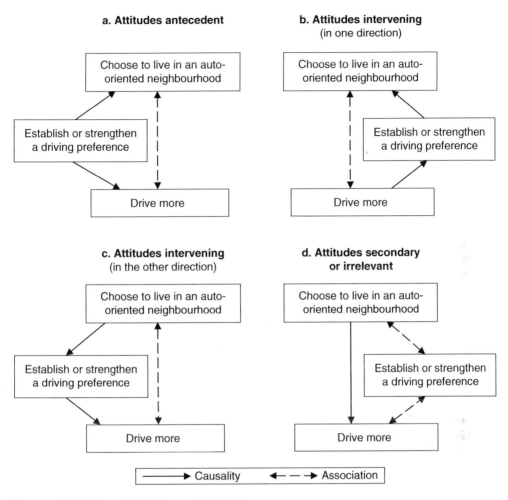

Source: Adapted from Mokhtarian and Cao (2008)

Figure 10.1 *Some potential relationships among travel attitudes, built environment and travel behaviour*

environment) may stimulate or reinforce an individual's preference for driving, which may in turn encourage her choice of highly-auto-oriented neighbourhoods. In other words, driving behaviour (in that model) is likely to be a proxy for driving preference. If we explicitly account for the influence of driving preference, the influence of the driving behaviour on the choice of auto-oriented neighbourhood is likely to diminish. Further, an individual's current travel behaviour is not a logical indicator of her previous residential choice.

Therefore, when only cross-sectional data on the built environment and travel behaviour are available, the influence from the (previously chosen) built environment to (presently chosen) travel behaviour is generally inferred more strongly than that from

travel behaviour to the built environment. In that situation, two roles of driving preference can be distinguished. Travel attitudes may again serve as an intervening variable
but in the other direction, as shown in Figure 10.1c. In particular, if travel attitudes are
measured at the current time, these attitudes may be more a function of prior residential
choice than the reverse (Chatman, 2009; Chen, et al., 2009). Alternatively, as shown in
Figure 10.1d, the built environment may have a primary and direct causal influence on
travel behaviour while travel attitudes may be secondary or irrelevant to this link, as
most previous studies that did not control for self-selection have implicitly or explicitly
assumed.

Therefore, the specific relationships among the built environment, travel behaviour
and attitudes depend on the way in which attitudes are measured and the assumption
between previous and current attitudes. If the attitudes are measured prior to residential
choice, or they are measured at the present time and they are highly correlated with the
prior attitudes, the relationships in Figure 10.1a and 10.1b are likely to exist. If the attitudes are measured at the present time, the relationships in Figure 10.1c and 10.1d may
apply. In the field, it is very rare that researchers measure attitudes before residential
move. Therefore, the hypothesis that attitudes are antecedent to residential choice is
implicitly based on the assumption that attitudes before and after the move are highly
correlated, which lacks empirical substantiation. Some surveys asked respondents'
attitudes retrospectively. However, their responses may also be contaminated by
their (previously chosen) residential environment, in response to cognitive dissonance
(Chatman, 2009).

If attitudes are antecedent to both residential choice and travel behaviour (Figure 10.1a),
what is the consequence if the self-selection is not controlled for? Although empirical
studies overwhelmingly conclude the overestimation of the impact of the built environment on travel behaviour, both overestimation and underestimation are likely to happen
(see Cao, 2010 for a conceptual illustration) Further, the dominance of overestimation
in empirical studies may result from the unmet demand of alternative development (such
as New Urbanism and smart growth communities) in the current real estate market (Cao
and Chatman, forthcoming).

3.   METHODOLOGY

A variety of methodological approaches have been used in recent studies to address
the self-selection in the relationships between the built environment and travel behaviour. Cao et al. (2009a) and Mokhtarian and Cao (2008) classified the approaches into
nine categories: direct questioning, statistical control, instrumental variables models,
sample selection models, propensity score, joint discrete choice models, structural
equations models, mutually dependent discrete choice models and longitudinal designs.
Specifically, some scholars adopted focus group to directly ask interviewees whether
their travel and land use predispositions influenced their choice of residential neighbourhood and travel behaviour (Handy and Clifton, 2001). The method of statistical
control explicitly accounts for the influences of attitudinal factors by measuring them
and including them in the models of travel behaviour (Frank et al., 2007; Joh et al.,
2008; Cao et al., 2009b). Several studies modelled a built environment variable as a

function of instruments and then replaced the observed built environment variable in the travel behaviour equation with its predicted value from that instrument model to account for the influence of self-selection (Boarnet and Sarmiento, 1998; Vance and Hedel, 2007). Zhou and Kockelman (2008) and Cao (2009) applied a sample selection model (first using a discrete choice model to predict residential choice and then inserting the selection correction factor into travel behaviour models) to control for potential self-selection. Recently, researchers have applied three types of joint models to simultaneously account for multiple endogenous choices among residential choice, travel behaviour and/or attitudes: joint discrete choice models involving nominal and/ or ordinal endogenous variables (Bhat and Guo, 2007), structural equations models involving continuous endogenous variables (Scheiner, 2010) and mutually dependent discrete choice models (Chen et al., 2008). Using longitudinal (or quasi-longitudinal) data, a few researchers studied the relationship between changes in the built environment and changes in travel behaviour (Cao et al., 2007; Krizek, 2003; Meurs and Haaijer, 2001). Propensity score matching (PSM) was recently introduced in the field (Boer et al., 2007; Cao et al., 2010). This study adopts this approach and compares it with statistical control and sample-selection model.

Propensity score matching has been widely used to overcome non-random assignment of treatment in the evaluation of social programmes (Oakes and Johnson, 2006). Evaluation studies are often based on observational data, in which the assignment of treatment is not random. Accordingly, individuals in the treatment group are likely to differ systematically from those in the control group. In the context of land use and travel, suburbanites tend to have more cars, live in a larger household, be more auto-oriented and prefer larger space than their counterparts in urban areas, a result of residential self-selection. Therefore, the observed difference in behavioural outcomes between the groups is confounded by the self-selection. Statistically, it is a biased estimate of treatment effect.

Conceptually, if we can find an almost 'identical' observation in the control group for an observation in the treatment group, this matching is approximately equivalent to the process in which one of the two 'same' observations is assigned into a treatment group and the other is assigned into a control group. If we repeat this process for all observations in the treatment group, observations in the matched treatment group should not differ from those in the matched control group. That is, the matching roughly resembles an experiment with random assignment of treatment. Then, the average treatment effect (ATE) is the difference in mean outcomes between the matched treatment and matched control groups (D'Agostino, 1998).

When a treatment group differs in many characteristics from a control group, the matching should be based on a scalar that can integrate all of these characteristics (Rosenbaum and Rubin, 1984). The propensity score (PS) is a scalar function that can be used to balance multiple characteristics. The PS in this context is the conditional probability that an individual lives in one type of neighbourhoods given her observed characteristics such as demographics and attitudes. This probability can be estimated using discrete choice models such as binary logit model in this study. Using large and small sample theory, Rosenbaum and Rubin (1983: 41) have proved that 'adjustment for the scalar propensity score is sufficient to remove bias due to all observed covariates [characteristics/variables]'.

4. EMPIRICAL CONTEXT

The data came from a self-administered survey mailed in two rounds in late 2003 to residents of eight neighbourhoods in Northern California. The neighbourhoods were selected to vary systematically on neighbourhood type, size of the metropolitan area and region of the state. Neighbourhood type was differentiated as 'traditional' for areas built mostly in the pre-World War II era, and 'suburban' for areas built more recently. Using data from the US Census, potential neighbourhoods were screened to ensure that average income and other characteristics were near the average for the region. The traditional neighbourhoods included Mountain View (downtown), Sacramento (midtown), Santa Rosa (Junior College area) and Modesto (central). The suburban neighbourhoods were Sunnyvale (I-280 area), Sacramento (Natomas area), Santa Rosa (Rincon Valley area) and Modesto (suburban area). The four traditional neighbourhoods differ in visible ways from the four suburbs – the layout of the street network, the age and style of the houses, and the location and design of commercial centres (Figure 10.2).

The original database (purchased from New Neighbors Contact Service, www.nncs.com) consisted of 8,000 addresses but only 6,746 valid addresses. The data contained 1,682 respondents, and the response rate is about 25 per cent based on the valid addresses only. This response rate is considered quite good for a survey of 14 pages, since the response rate for a survey administered to the general population is typically 10–40 per cent (Sommer and Sommer, 1997). A comparison of sample characteristics to population characteristics, based on the 2000 US Census (Table 10.1), shows that survey respondents tend to be older than residents of their neighbourhood as a whole, and that the percentage of households with children is lower for the sample for most neighbourhoods. In addition, median household income for survey respondents was higher than the census median for all but one neighbourhood, a typical result for voluntary self-administered surveys. However, since the focus of our study is on identifying the causal effect, these differences are not a concern.

The dependent variable is weekly vehicle miles driven (VMD). In the survey, respondents were asked to report the approximate miles they drove in a typical week including weekends. On average, individuals in this data drove 160.1 miles per week. People observed living in traditional neighbourhoods on average drove 150.5 miles, 28.0 miles less than suburban residents. This difference is statistically significant at the 0.001 level. However, this does not mean the causal effect of neighbourhood type on driving distance is 28.0 miles because respondents' choice of neighbourhoods is not a random assignment.

The explanatory variables are classified into three groups: residential preferences, travel attitudes and socio-demographics. Respondents were asked to indicate the importance of 34 attributes regarding their residence and neighbourhood when/if they were looking for a new place to live, on a four-point scale from 1 ('not at all important') to 4 ('extremely important'). A factor analysis reduced these items to six factors: accessibility, physical activity options, safety, socializing, attractiveness and outdoor spaciousness (Table 10.2). To measure attitudes regarding travel, the survey asked respondents whether they agreed or disagreed with a series of 32 statements on a five-point scale from 1 ('strongly disagree') to 5 ('strongly agree'). Factor analysis was then used to extract the relatively uncorrelated fundamental dimensions spanned by these 32 items. Six underlying dimensions were identified: pro-bike/walk, pro-transit, pro-travel, travel

Sacramento – traditional   Sacramento – suburban

Street network

Residential streets

Commercial centres

Figure 10.2   Comparison of traditional and suburban neighbourhoods – Sacramento

Table 10.1　Sample versus population characteristics

	Traditional				Suburban			
	Mountain View	SR Junior College	MD Central	SC Mid-town	Sunny vale	SR Rincon Valley	MD Sub-urban	SC Natomas
Sample characteristics								
Number	228	215	184	271	217	165	220	182
Percent of females	47.3	54.3	56.3	58.2	46.9	50.9	50.9	54.9
Average auto ownership	1.80	1.63	1.59	1.50	1.79	1.66	1.88	1.68
Age	43.3	47.0	51.3	43.4	47.1	54.7	53.2	45.6
Average HH size	2.08	2.03	2.13	1.78	2.58	2.19	2.41	2.35
Percent of HHs w/kids	21.1	18.6	21.7	8.9	42.4	24.8	25.5	31.9
Percent of home owners	51.1	57.8	75.6	47.0	61.1	68.7	81.0	82.4
Median HH income (k$)	98.7	55.5	45.5	64.2	95.0	49.5	55.5	55.3
Population characteristics								
Age	36.1	36.3	36.5	42.7	35.9	38.3	38.1	31.7
Average HH size	2.08	2.21	2.46	1.79	2.66	2.48	2.51	2.57
Percent of HHs w/kids	19.3	20.3	32.9	12.4	35.3	35.4	34.2	41.7
Percent of home owners	34.3	31.2	58.8	34.3	53.2	63.5	61.4	55.2
Median HH income (k$)	74.3	40.2	42.5	43.8	88.4	49.6	40.2	46.2

Notes:　SR = Santa Rosa, MD = Modesto, SC = Sacramento, HH = household

minimizing, car dependent and safety of car (Table 10.2). Finally, the survey contained a list of socio-demographic variables that help to explain residential choice and travel behaviour. These variables include gender, age, employment status, educational background, household income, household size, the number of children in the household, mobility constraints and so on.

5.　ESTIMATION AND RESULTS

The PSM was implemented in STATA 11. First, a binary logit model is developed to estimate the PS of living in a traditional neighbourhood. For a PS model, independent variables should be exogenous to and should not be determined by residential location

Table 10.2   Loading on residential preference and travel attitude factors

Factor	Statement
Residential Preferences	
Accessibility	Easy access to a regional shopping mall (0.854); easy access to downtown (0.830); other amenities such as a pool or a community centre available nearby (0.667); shopping areas within walking distance (0.652); easy access to the freeway (0.528); good public transit service (bus or rail) (0.437)
Physical activity options	Good bicycle routes beyond the neighbourhood (0.882); sidewalks throughout the neighbourhood (0.707); parks and open spaces nearby (0.637); good public transit service (bus or rail) (0.353)
Safety	Quiet neighbourhood (0.780); low crime rate within neighbourhood (0.759); low level of car traffic on neighbourhood streets (0.752); safe neighbourhood for walking (0.741); safe neighbourhood for kids to play outdoors (0.634); good street lighting (0.751)
Socializing	Diverse neighbours in terms of ethnicity, race and age (0.789); lots of people out and about within the neighbourhood (0.785); lots of interaction among neighbours (0.614); economic level of neighbours similar to my level (0.476)
Attractiveness	Attractive appearance of neighbourhood (0.780); high level of upkeep in neighbourhood (0.723); variety in housing styles (0.680); big street trees (0.451)
Outdoor spaciousness	Large backyards (0.876); large front yards (0.858); lots of off-street parking (garages or driveways) (0.562); big street trees (0.404)
Travel Attitudes	
Pro-bike/walk	I like riding a bike (0.880); I prefer to bike rather than drive whenever possible (0.865); biking can sometimes be easier for me than driving (0.818); I prefer to walk rather than drive whenever possible (0.461); I like walking (0.400); walking can sometimes be easier for me than driving (0.339)
Pro-transit	I like taking transit (0.778); I prefer to take transit rather than drive whenever possible (0.771); public transit can sometimes be easier for me than driving (0.757); I like walking (0.363); walking can sometimes be easier for me than driving (0.344); travelling by car is safer overall than riding a bicycle (0.338)
Pro-travel	The trip to/from work is a useful transition between home and work (0.683); travel time is generally wasted time (−0.681); I use my trip to/from work productively (0.616); The only good thing about travelling is arriving at your destination (−0.563); I like driving (0.479)
Travel minimizing	Fuel efficiency is an important factor for me in choosing a vehicle (0.679); I prefer to organize my errands so that I make as few trips as possible (0.671); I often use the telephone or the Internet to avoid having to travel somewhere (0.514); the price of gasoline affects the choices I make about my daily travel (0.513); I try to limit my driving to help improve air quality (0.458); vehicles should be taxed on the basis of the amount of pollution they produce (0.426); when I need to buy something, I usually prefer to get it at the closest store possible (0.332)
Safety of car	Travelling by car is safer overall than riding a bicycle (0.489); travelling by car is safer overall than walking (0.753); travelling by car is safer overall than taking transit (0.633); the region needs to build more highways to reduce traffic congestion (0.444); the price of gasoline affects the choices I make about my daily travel (0.357)
Car dependent	I need a car to do many of the things I like to do (0.612); getting to work without a car is a hassle (0.524); we could manage pretty well with one fewer car than we have (or with no car) (−0.418); travelling by car is safer overall than riding a bicycle (0.402); I like driving (0.356)

Note: The numbers in parentheses are the pattern matrix loadings for the obliquely rotated factors

Table 10.3   Binary logit model for the choice of traditional neighbourhoods

	Coefficients	P-value
Constant	0.602	0.202
Demographics		
Education	−0.002	0.966
Female	0.282	0.027
Worker	−0.113	0.532
Age	−0.006	0.282
Renter	0.795	0.000
Household size	−0.206	0.031
Number of children under 18	−0.228	0.076
Household income (k$)	0.006	0.009
Number of cars	−0.016	0.855
Residential preferences		
Accessibility	0.053	0.528
Physical activity options	−0.101	0.229
Safety	−0.558	0.000
Socializing	0.231	0.001
Outdoor spaciousness	0.080	0.275
Attractiveness	0.314	0.000
Travel attitudes		
Pro-bike/walk	0.337	0.000
Pro-transit	0.048	0.489
Pro-travel	−0.055	0.369
Travel minimizing	−0.040	0.536
Car dependent	−0.084	0.199
Safety of car	−0.453	0.000
N	1 475	
Pseudo R-square	0.162	

choices. Here, we chose socio-demographics and residential preferences because they are potential sources of residential self-selection. Furthermore, because the PS model is a prediction model, we do not need to check the statistical significance of independent variables. In fact, many studies do not even report the results of the model (D'Agostino, 1998). For illustration purpose, Table 10.3 presents the binary logit model for the choice of traditional neighbourhoods.

Second, we attempted to find an 'identical' person from those living in suburbs to match each person living in traditional neighbourhoods. Specifically, based on the PS, we matched observations in the treatment and control groups using the command 'PSMATCH2'. We chose the following options 'non-replacement', 'common' and 'calliper (0.01)'. Non-replacement performs a one-to-one match without replacement (thus an observation in the control group can be used at most once); common means that before matching we drop treatment observations whose PSs are outside of the range of the PS of control observations; and calliper (0.01) indicates for a treatment observation, we search a match in control observations whose PSs are within 0.01 of the PS of the treatment observation (the calliper length of 0.01 or 0.02 is commonly adopted in empirical studies). It is likely that we cannot find matches for some treatment observations because of these chosen options. Therefore, we may discard some treatments in the matching process. Further, if the data are ordered based on some rules, the order of the observations may influence the outcome because of the non-replacement one-to-one match. To reduce potential bias, the data were sorted randomly before matching.

Third, we evaluated whether the matched residents (through the matching process above) in the suburbs are systematically different from those in traditional neighbourhoods. If they are different in terms of demographics and attitudes, self-selection is still a concern. In particular, we used 'PSTEST' to assess whether demographics and attitudes are balanced between the matched groups. The following equation was used to calculate the standard difference δ (D'Agostino, 1998):

$$\delta = \frac{100(\bar{x}_T - \bar{x}_C)}{\sqrt{\dfrac{s_T^2 + s_C^2}{2}}},$$

where $\bar{x}_T$ and S_T are the mean and standard deviation of a confounding variable for the treatment group, respectively; $\bar{x}_C$ and S_C are the mean and standard deviation of the variable for the control group, respectively. It was suggested that $\delta \leq 10$ per cent is an acceptable difference between groups, a rule of thumb in epidemiology (Oakes and Johnson, 2006). Table 10.4 shows standard differences of socio-demographics and attitudinal factors before and after matching. Before matching, residents in the two types of neighbourhoods differ by a number of factors such as age, household size, preferences for neighbourhood safety and non-motorized modes. After matching, the standard differences of all variables reduced to the acceptable level of 10 per cent (as shown in the last column of Table 10.4). Overall, characteristics of residents in the matched treatment and control groups are not statistically different.

For the sample, the matching process is complete using the PS derived from our initial model specification shown in Table 10.3. Sometimes, however, we are not able to successfully balance confounding variables in the first attempt. We need to modify the PS model specification and repeat previous three steps. Specifically, the unbalanced variable, its high-order form (such as polynomial terms), and its interaction with other variables can enter the PS model until the balance of all confounding variables is achieved (Rosenbaum and Rubin, 1984).

The final goal of PSM is to compute the 'true' impact of the built environment on travel behaviour. Once the matching was complete, we calculated the ATE of neighbourhood type on VMD (i.e., the effect of neighbourhood type on VMD while controlling for self-selection). It is computed as the difference in mean VMD between the *matched* residents in traditional and suburban neighbourhoods. According to the STATA output, the point estimate of the ATE is 20.9 miles with a standard error of 11.4 miles. Thus, the ATE is significantly different from zero at the 0.1 level (Z = 1.84). The observed influence of neighbourhood type on VMD is the difference in mean VMD between the *unmatched* residents in traditional and suburban neighbourhoods, which is 28.0 miles as presented in the previous section. Therefore, about three quarters (= 20.9/28.0) of the observed difference can be attributable to neighbourhood type itself. Furthermore,

Table 10.4   Standard differences of observed covariates between traditional and suburban neighbourhoods

	Unmatched sample			Matched sample		
	Trad.	Suburb	Std. Diff.	Trad.	Suburb	Std. Diff.
Demographics						
Education	4.29	4.09	15.0%	4.17	4.09	5.6%
Female	53.5%	48.6%	9.8%	50.9%	47.9%	6.2%
Worker	84.4%	79.6%	12.4%	77.7%	81.3%	−9.3%
Age	44.5	48.6	−27.6%	48.9	47.5	9.6%
Renter	43.4%	26.3%	36.4%	31.0%	32.7%	−3.5%
Household size	2.03	2.46	−36.8%	2.26	2.28	−2.2%
Number of children under 18	0.29	0.56	−33.5%	0.42	0.46	−4.1%
Household income (k$)	72.3	69.2	8.6%	69.9	69.7	0.3%
Number of cars	1.68	1.84	−18.8%	1.78	1.77	0.9%
Residential preferences						
Accessibility	−0.38	−0.43	4.9%	−0.39	−0.45	6.9%
Physical activity options	−0.32	−0.33	1.2%	−0.33	−0.32	−0.9%
Safety	0.21	0.60	−49.8%	0.52	0.50	3.4%
Socializing	−0.22	−0.31	8.6%	−0.24	−0.25	1.2%
Outdoor spaciousness	−0.11	−0.00	−11.2%	0.04	0.03	0.5%
Attractiveness	0.07	0.01	7.0%	0.04	0.05	−1.9%
Travel attitudes						
Pro-bike/walk	0.22	−0.22	44.9%	−0.13	−0.08	−5.4%
Pro-transit	0.11	−0.16	28.4%	−0.06	−0.07	1.4%
Pro-travel	−0.03	0.00	−3.7%	−0.01	0.00	−1.4%
Travel minimizing	0.02	−0.02	3.5%	−0.01	−0.04	2.5%
Car dependent	0.02	0.10	12.5%	0.13	0.12	1.0%
Safety of car	−0.27	0.29	−58.4%	0.10	0.11	−1.0%

the ATE accounts for about 13 per cent of the average VMD for the whole sample (= 20.9/160.1). This effect is non-trivial in practice.

6.   DISCUSSIONS

The impact of neighbourhood type itself on VMD is 20.9 miles, based on the PSM approach. Cao (2009) applied a sample selection model in the same dataset and concluded a neighbourhood type impact of 25.8 miles. A linear regression model for VMD was also developed by controlling for all of the demographic and attitudinal factors shown in Table 10.3. The coefficient for neighbourhood type was estimated at 22.2 miles (the model is not shown). Given that standard deviations of these estimates are at the size of ten miles, the three point estimates are not statistically different from each other at the 0.05 level. It seems that all three approaches produced equivalent outcomes although the estimates vary.

What are the differences among the three approaches? The sample selection model for a binary endogenous variable is essentially a generalized propensity score approach, although the application of the former is earlier than that of the latter (Winship and Morgan, 1999). The difference between the two approaches is that the sample selection model requires a strong normality assumption and inserts a correction factor into the behaviour equation, but the application of a propensity score as a regressor inserts the estimated propensity score into the behaviour equation (Winship and Morgan, 1999). Empirically, the Heckman sample selection models offer only point estimates of the ATE (Heckman et al., 2001). Therefore, we are unable to test whether the ATE differs from zero. Further, some scholars questioned the reliability of sample selection model speci-fication (Zhou and Kockelman, 2008; Brownstone and Golob, 2009), thus the model should be used with caution.

Although both statistical control and PSM address the bias resulting from observed characteristics, they are different. Conceptually, PSM controls for the observed charac-teristics that affect whether an individual is assigned to a treatment group or a control group. The attention is directed to the imbalance in the values of confounding variables between treatment and control groups. Statistical control identifies the determinants of travel behaviour through incorporating them directly into the behaviour equation, so that we can account for all differences between treatment and control groups that affect the behaviour. The attention is directed to the behavioural outcome (Winship and Morgan, 1999).

Empirically, first, a model estimating propensity scores is a prediction model so it is not necessary to evaluate multi-colinearity and statistical significance of explana-tory variables (Oakes and Johnson, 2006). However, multi-colinearity and statistical significance are important for an explanatory model in the statistical control approach. Thus, if multi-colinearity among independent variables is a potential problem in the data, it seems that PSM is superior to statistical control. Second, the PSM approach generally requires a discrete classification (binary, nominal or ordinal) of treatments and controls although there are some applications with continuous treatment (Guido and Keisuke, 2004). Therefore, we need to transform continuous measurements of the built environment into discrete scales. This transformation may lead to a loss in efficiency. In contrast, statistical control can accommodate both continuous and discrete variables. Third, unlike statistical control, PSM does not extrapolate, especially when the option of common support is chosen. Fourth, statistical control may require data to follow a certain distribution, depending on the model used, whereas PSM does not have a distri-bution requirement. Fifth, PSM will discard some observations if no match is found for some treatment observations or if control observations are not close (in terms of propen-sity score) to any treatment observations. This may not be desirable because resources are wasted. Finally, with the same set of variables, the statistical control approach will produce a unique outcome if the model converges. However, the outcome of PSM depends on many factors. For example, when the calliper width is set as different values, the outcome varies (Table 10.5). Therefore, a sensitivity analysis is required for propen-sity score matching. Empirically, the following factors may also influence the outcome: matching method (calliper, K-nearest neighbour, kernel, etc.), one-to-one matching or one-to-more matching, replacement or non-replacement of controls, and the order of respondents in the data.

Table 10.5   Sensitivity analysis of propensity score matching

Calliper width	ATE
0.05	20.50
0.045	24.96
0.04	18.68
0.035	21.68
0.03	24.95
0.025	20.21
0.02	20.34
0.015	19.66
0.01	20.90
0.075	19.55
0.005	13.50

7.   CONCLUSIONS

There are several alternative explanations for the significant association between the built environment and travel behaviour. This study discusses the role of attitudes in the association. Given the scarcity of longitudinal data with attitudinal measurements, conceptual and empirical evidence suggests that attitudes are either antecedent to both residential choice and travel behaviour, or intervening variables from the (previously chosen) built environment to (presently chosen) travel behaviour. Most studies assume the former. If the latter is true, we are likely to misestimate the impact of the built environment on travel behaviour. In reality, it is likely that both the antecedent and intervening roles of attitudes are true. However, this threat is not worse than many demographic characteristics that are already in the models. For example, in cross-sectional data, auto ownership may not be a predictor of residential choice, but its outcome; household structure may have changed since respondents move to their current neighbourhoods. On the other hand, if we do not control for attitudes, self-selection bias may arise.

This study adopts the propensity score matching approach to address residential self-selection resulting from travel attitudes, residential preferences and demographics. After controlling for self-selection, the impact of neighbourhood type on vehicle miles driven is estimated at 20.9 miles per week. This accounts for 13 per cent of respondents' average driving distance. Thus, neighbourhood design seems to be able to produce meaningful changes in driving behaviour. Furthermore, 75 per cent of the observed influence of neighbourhood type on driving distance results from neighbourhood type itself and self-selection accounts for a quarter. Accordingly, neighbourhood type plays a more important role in affecting travel behaviour than residential self-selection.

Statistical control, propensity score matching and sample selection model produced consistent results in this study. Without substantiated knowledge on reliability, however, sample selection models are not recommended for addressing residential self-selection. Both statistical control and propensity score matching have their strengths and weaknesses (Table 10.6). Overall, propensity score matching is recommended if the endog-

Table 10.6   Approach comparison

	Propensity score	Statistical control	Sample selection
Do travel behaviour data need to follow a distribution?	No	Yes, depending on regression method used	Multivariate normal distribution
Is there any requirement on the measurement scale of endogenous built environment variables?	Often discrete, occasionally continuous	Discrete and continuous	Binary
Can it control for unobserved factors?	No	No	No
Reliability	Sensitivity analysis is required	No requirements	Sensitivity analysis is required
Is multi-colinearity a concern?	No	Yes	Yes
Does statistical significance matter for confounding correlates?	No	Yes	Yes
Does it offer interval estimates?	Yes	Yes	No, only point estimate
Does it discard some data?	Possibly	No	No
Does it extrapolate?	No	Yes	Yes

enous built environment can be measured in a discrete scale and sensitive analysis indicates the results are stable.

The relationships between the built environment and attitude merits further investigation to better understand their relative impacts on travel behaviour. If the built environment and attitude interact with each other, attitude influences travel behaviour directly and indirectly through the built environment. Similarly the built environment affects travel behaviour directly and indirectly through attitude. In this case, structural equations models are required to test the interactions between the built environment and attitude. Further, qualitative analysis (such as focus group) may offer insights on their dynamic interactions: is attitude stable over time? Does attitude adapt to the chosen built environment and the resulting behaviour in response to cognitive dissonance? To what extent is the current attitude attributable to the adaptation? What factors does the extent depend on? What are the implications of the answers to the questions for the relative impacts of the built environment and attitude on travel behaviour?

ACKNOWLEDGEMENTS

The data collection was funded by the UC Davis-Caltrans Air Quality Project, the Robert Wood Johnson Foundation and the University of California Transportation Center. The survey was designed by Susan Handy and Patricia Mokhtarian.

REFERENCES

Bhat, C.R. and Guo, J.Y. (2007), A comprehensive analysis of built environment characteristics on household residential choice and auto ownership levels, *Transportation Research Part B: Methodological*, **41**(5), 506–26.

Boarnet, M. and Crane, R. (2001), *Travel by Design: The Influence of Urban Form on Travel*, Spatial Information Systems, New York: Oxford University Press.

Boarnet, M.G. and Sarmiento, S. (1998), Can land-use policy really affect travel behaviour? A study of the link between non-work travel and land-use characteristics, *Urban Studies*, **35**(7), 1155–69.

Boer, R., Zheng, Y., Overton, A., Ridgeway, G.K. and Cohen, D.A. (2007), Neighbourhood design and walking trips in ten US metropolitan areas, *American Journal of Preventive Medicine*, **32**(4), 298–304.

Bohte, W., Maat, K. and van Wee, B. (2009), Measuring attitudes in research on residential self-selection and travel behaviour: a review of theories and empirical research, *Transport Reviews*, **29**(3), 325–57.

Brownstone, D. and Golob, T.F. (2009), The impact of residential density on vehicle usage and energy consumption, *Journal of Urban Economics*, **65**(1), 91–8.

Cao, X. (2009), Disentangling the influence of neighbourhood type and self-selection on driving behaviour: an application of sample selection model, *Transportation*, **36**(2), 207–22.

Cao, X. (2010), Exploring causal effects of neighbourhood type on walking behaviour using stratification on the propensity score, *Environment and Planning A*, **42**(2), 487–504.

Cao, X. and Chatman, D.G. (forthcoming), How will Smart Growth land use policies affect travel? A theoretical discussion on the importance of residential sorting. *Environment and Planning B*.

Cao, X., Mokhtarian, P. and Handy, S. (2007), Do changes in neighbourhood characteristics lead to changes in travel behaviour? A structural equations modeling approach, *Transportation*, **34**(5), 535–56.

Cao, X., Mokhtarian, P. and Handy, S. (2009a), Examining the impacts of residential self-selection on travel behaviour: a focus on empirical findings, *Transport Reviews*, **29**(3), 359–95.

Cao, X., Mokhtarian, P. and Handy, S. (2009b), The relationship between the built environment and nonwork travel: a case study of Northern California, *Transportation Research Part A: Policy and Practice*, **43**(5), 548–59.

Cao, X., Xu, Z. and Fan, Y. (2010), Exploring the connections among residential location, self-selection, and driving: propensity score matching with multiple treatments, *Transportation Research Part A: Policy and Practice*, **44**(10), 797–805.

Chatman, D.G. (2009), Residential choice, the built environment, and nonwork travel: evidence using new data and methods, *Environment and Planning A*, **41**, 1072–89.

Chen, C., Gong, H. and Paaswell, R. (2008), Role of the built environment on mode choice decisions: additional evidence on the impact of density, *Transportation*, **35**(3), 285–99.

Chen, C., Chen, J. and Timmermans, H. (2009), Historical deposition influence in residential location decisions: a distance-based GEV model for spatial correlation, *Environment and Planning A*, **41**(11), 2760–77.

Crane, R. (2000), The influence of urban form on travel: an interpretive review, *Journal of Planning Literature*, **15**(1), 3–23.

D'Agostino, R.B. (1998), Propensity score methods for bias reduction in the comparison of a treatment to a non-randomized control group, *Statistics in Medicine*, **17**(19), 2265–81.

Ewing, R. and Cervero, R. (2001), Travel and the built environment: a synthesis, *Transportation Research Record: Journal of the Transportation Research Board*, **1780**, 87–114.

Ewing, R. and Cervero, R. (2010), Travel and the built environment – a meta-analysis, *Journal of the American Planning Association*, **76**(3), 265–94.

Frank, L.D. and Engelke, P.O. (2001), The built environment and human activity patterns: exploring the impacts of urban form on public health, *Journal of Planning Literature*, **16**(2), 202–18.

Frank, L.D., Saelens, B.E., Powell, K.E. and Chapman, J.E. (2007), Stepping towards causation: do built environments or neighbourhood and travel preferences explain physical activity, driving, and obesity? *Social Science & Medicine*, **65**(9), 1898–914.

Guido, I. and Keisuke, H. (2004), The propensity score with continuous treatments, in A. Gelman and X.-L. Meng (eds), *Applied Bayesian Modelling and Causal Inference from Missing Data Perspectives*, Chichester: Wiley.

Handy, S.L. and Clifton, K.J. (2001), Local shopping as a strategy for reducing automobile travel, *Transportation*, **28**(4), 317–46.

Heckman, J., Tobias, J.L. and Vytlacil, E. (2001), Four parameters of interest in the evaluation of social programs, *Southern Economic Journal*, **68**(2), 210.

Joh, K., Boarnet, M., Nguyen, M., Fulton, W., Siembab, W. and Weaver, S. (2008), Accessibility, Travel behaviour, and new urbanism: case study of mixed-use centers and auto-oriented corridors in the South Bay region of Los Angeles, California, *Transportation Research Record: Journal of the Transportation Research Board*, **2082**, 81–9.

Krizek, K.J. (2003), Residential relocation and changes in urban travel: does neighbourhood-scale urban form matter? *Journal of the American Planning Association*, **69**(3), 265–81.

Litman, T.A. (2005), *Land Use Impacts on Transport: How Land Use Factors Affect Travel Behaviour*, Victoria, BC: Victoria Transport Institute.

Meurs, H. and Haaijer, R. (2001), Spatial structure and mobility, *Transportation Research Part D-Transport and Environment*, **6**(6), 429–46.

Mokhtarian, P.L. and Cao, X. (2008), Examining the impacts of residential self-selection on travel behaviour: a focus on methodologies, *Transportation Research Part B: Methodological*, **42**(3), 204–28.

Oakes, M.J. and Johnson, P.J. (2006), Propensity score matching for social epidemiology, in M.J. Oakes and J.S. Kaufman (eds), *Methods in Epidemiology*, New York: John Wiley & Sons, Inc.

Rosenbaum, P.R. and Rubin, D.B. (1983), The central role of the propensity score in observational studies for causal effects, *Biometrika*, **70**(1), 41–55.

Rosenbaum, P.R. and Rubin, D.B (1984), Reducing bias in observational studies using subclassification on the propensity score, *Journal of the American Statistical Association*, **79**(387), 516–24.

Scheiner, J. (2010), Social inequalities in travel behaviour: trip distances in the context of residential self-selection and lifestyles, *Journal of Transport Geography*, **18**(6), 679–90.

Schutt, R.K. (2004), *Investigating the Social World: The Process and Practice of Research*, 4th edn, Thousand Oaks, CA: Pine Forge Press.

Singleton, R. and Straits, B.C. (2005), *Approaches to Social Research*, 4th edn, New York: Oxford University Press.

Sommer, B.B. and Sommer, R. (1997), *A Practical Guide to Behavioral Research: Tools and Techniques*, 4th edn, New York: Oxford University Press.

Vance, C. and Hedel, R. (2007), The impact of urban form on automobile travel: disentangling causation from correlation, *Transportation*, **34**(5), 575–88.

Winship, C. and Morgan, S.L. (1999), The estimation of causal effects from observational data, *Annual Review of Sociology*, **25**, 659–706.

Zhou, B. and Kockelman, K. (2008), Self-selection in home choice: use of treatment effects in evaluating relationship between built environment and travel behaviour, *Transportation Research Record: Journal of the Transportation Research Board*, **2077**, 54–61.

11 The role of attitudes in accounting for self-selection effects

Bert van Wee and Patricia Mokhtarian

1. INTRODUCTION

The combined transport and land-use system allows people to travel between activity locations (home, work, family and friends, sports and other recreational locations, etc.). And it allows companies to transport goods in their several stages of production and distribution between related locations. But transport comes at high costs. First, transport costs time and money. In most Western countries people spend 10–15 percent of their income on transport (Schafer and Victor, 2000). On average, and at the aggregate level (e.g., all persons in one country), people travel between 60 and 75 minutes per person per day, in almost all countries worldwide (Mokhtarian and Chen, 2004; Zahavi and Talvitie, 1980; Szalai, 1972). Second, the transport system causes negative impacts on society. Impacts include travel time losses to other users in case of congestion, safety impacts, and environmental impacts. Even for a small country like the Netherlands the costs of congestion, safety and the environment are as large as 14.8–25.3 billion euros (KiM, 2009), around 1.9–3.3 percent of GDP. In the United States the cost of congestion alone in 2010 was estimated to exceed \$100 billion (Schrank et al., 2011). Third, transport infrastructure is expensive. Large infrastructure projects often costs billions of euros, and budgets of Ministries of Transport constitute a large share of government budgets in many EU member states and elsewhere.

Changes in the transport system in almost all countries are highly influenced by transport policies; for example, related to infrastructure, public transport services, subsidies on public transport, and levies on vehicles and fuels. The impact of policies on changes in land use vary strongly between countries, ranging in polarity from (former) communist planning doctrines dictating urbanization on the one hand, to 'free market' development such as in large parts of the USA on the other, European countries having an intermediate position.

The land-use and transport systems interact: locations for urbanization are partly chosen (both in the case of governmental decisions as well as in the case of the 'free market') based on the location of transport infrastructure, and new infrastructure often follows new urbanization. This phenomenon is referred to in the literature as land use–transport interaction (LUTI). In addition, the wants and needs of people have an impact on their location choices (residential locations and destinations) and their choices with respect to travel behavior, as well as vice versa. Figure 11.1 conceptualizes the relationships between locations of desired and needed activities, travel impedance (resulting from the transport system) and the land-use system, making clear that all three components influence each other in all directions.

Because land use has an impact on travel behavior, it seems logical that in many

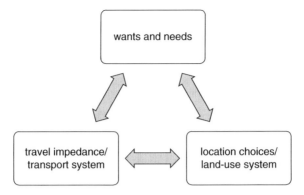

Source: Revised from van Wee (2002)

Figure 11.1   *Interactions between wants and needs of people, location choices and travel impedance*

countries governments try to influence travel behavior via land-use planning, the New Urbanism movement in the USA being a well-known example. The reasons behind such policies often relate to the environment: 'better' planning may contribute to less car use and consequently to lower emissions of pollutants and CO_2, and less noise nuisance.

Partly inspired by such policies researchers have studied the impact of land use and built environment on travel behavior for decades, and far more than 100 studies can be found in the academic literature. This literature generally recognizes that land-use characteristics and socio-economic and demographic variables are all relevant and should be included in such research, often leading to regression models of travel behavior that include those variables as explanatory factors. Probably the most cited study that did not include socio-economic and demographic variables is the study of Newman and Kenworthy (1988) on the impact of urban densities on energy use per capita for passenger transport. They concluded that density had a very strong relationship on energy use for travel per capita, with the USA and Canadian cities having high energy use per capita, Asian cities low values, and European cities being positioned in the middle. In response to the criticism of ignoring other variables, they re-estimated their models with corrections for differences in income and fuel prices, after which the explanatory power of density about halved (Newman and Kenworthy, 1999; see also Kenworthy and Laube, 1999). Since their 1988 work, to the best of our knowledge no studies focusing solely on the impact of land use on travel behavior and ignoring other variables have been published in journals. However, despite all the research, the debate over the impact of land use on travel behavior is still going on, the most important reason being a methodological discussion on how to disentangle complex relationships between categories of variables. The recent debate is concentrated around two important and interrelated topics. The first is residential self-selection, the other is attitudes towards travel and residential preferences.

Self-selection, in this case residential self-selection (RSS), can be defined in (at least) two ways. The general definition is "the tendency of people to choose locations based on their travel abilities, needs and preferences" (Litman, 2005: 6). This is a very broad definition and includes, for example, the tendency of high-income people to live in more expensive houses. According to this expansive definition, RSS includes that which is induced by socio-economic and demographic variables among others. These types of RSS are generally recognized adequately in older studies in this area (assuming that socio-economic and demographic variables, as well as land-use and travel behavior variables, are measured adequately). Therefore we consider this broad definition as less relevant for our chapter. The model structure assumed, however, is not always adequate, as discussed below. Our more narrow definition is limited to "the tendency of people to choose locations based on their residential and travel preferences and other attitudes." Since the mid-1990s the importance of RSS-related attitudes to understanding the impact of land-use on travel behavior has increasingly gained attention, but the debate is certainly not closed, mainly for methodological reasons.

The basic problem of ignoring attitude-related residential self-selection, as linked to the more limited definition as presented above, is relatively simple.

> People's choices are based on (1) variables included in a model (including interactions between the variables); (2) variables not included in the model ("omitted variables") (including their mutual interactions); and (3) interactions between the variables from (1) and (2). A problem is that (3) can exist: the unobserved variables can be correlated with the observed variables. In this case, the estimated effects attributed to the observed variables might in fact be partly or completely due to the unobserved variables with which they are correlated. This can be illustrated if we consider the impact of the built environment on travel behavior. To understand the impact we might include the characteristics of the built environment (e.g. densities, variables for mixed use, distance to railway stations), socio-demographic variables (such as age, sex, income), but fail to measure the preferences to travel with certain modes. However, the preferences for modes may be correlated to residential choice: people with a preference for travelling by train will, on average, live closer to railway stations. Ignoring this preference leads to an overestimation of the impact of the distance to railway stations on travel behavior. In this case, attitudes may play a role both directly in travel behavior, but may also indirectly influence the impact of land-use variables on travel behavior. Another problem is that the dependent variable can influence an explanatory variable.
>
> (van Wee, 2009: 280–81)

For example, the experience of having traveled by train may have an impact on people's attitude – in this case the preference to travel by train (Bohte, 2010). After having traveled by train, people might have a better estimation of the real train travel times, might have experienced traveling by train to be relaxing, and might have experienced the option to work or read in the train, reducing the "net time loss." All in all, after having traveled by train, people's preference to travel by train might have increased. In trying to capture the influence of train attitude on travel behavior with a single equation then, the coefficient of train attitude is partly reflecting the opposite direction of causality, from behavior to attitude. At the extreme, it may *only* reflect the behavior-to-attitude direction of causality, since it is possible for attitudes to change *without* influencing behavior (perhaps constraints intervene; perhaps the individual is willing to tolerate cognitive dissonance). Accordingly, it would be a mistake to use that coefficient to predict the influence of a change in attitude on behavior. Figure 11.2 presents one conceptualization of the influence of attitudes and residential self-selection on travel behavior. Numerous other variations on the figure are plausible.

The aim of this chapter is to discuss the importance of attitudes to understanding residential self-selection and travel behavior.

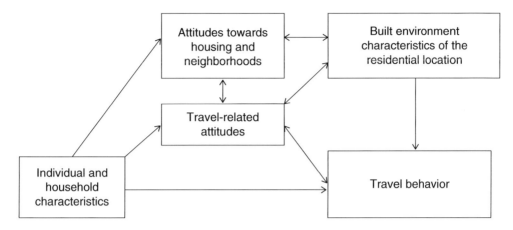

Source: Revised version of Bohte (2010)

Figure 11.2 *A conceptual model of the influence of attitudes and residential self-selection on travel behavior*

The remainder of the chapter is organized as follows. Section 2 gives an overview of the role of attitudes in methods of accounting for self-selection. Section 3 elaborates on several issues related to the measurement and modeling of attitude-related self-selection. Section 4 argues that self-selection is not limited to residential self-selection, but is probably present also in other spatial and non-spatial choices. Section 5 discusses the implications of our chapter for future research and policymaking.

2.   THE ROLE OF ATTITUDES IN METHODS OF ACCOUNTING FOR SELF-SELECTION

We will use the following notation: ATT = attitudes, BEH = the behavior of interest, ENV = measures of the environment (in the broad sense) expected to influence BEH, and SED = socio-economic and demographic traits. In the transportation literature, a common example is that BEH is a measure of travel behavior such as distance traveled or the choice of auto versus non-auto modes, and ENV comprises measures of the built environment (e.g., the traveler's residential location). As discussed in Section 4, however, the self-selection issue extends far beyond this single example, and thus we attempt to keep the notation more general, even while the discussion will inevitably draw upon the sizable literature regarding the influence of residential self-selection (RSS) on travel behavior in particular.

   As mentioned in the Introduction, "self-selection" (SS) in the transportation literature most often refers to the biased and inconsistent estimation of parameters that occurs when unmeasured variables, typically ATT, influence both BEH (the dependent variable of the model) and ENV. In simplified form, the model can be expressed as:

$$BEH = f(ENV(ATT), SED) + \varepsilon(ATT).$$

It is also quite possible to have attitudes influenced by the environment, i.e.,

$$BEH = f(ENV, SED) + \varepsilon(ATT(ENV)).$$

In either case, the problem is the same: unobserved variables (ATT) are correlated with observed variables (ENV), in contradiction to the assumption required for consistent parameter estimation using conventional techniques.

Mokhtarian and Cao (2008) provide an overview of seven approaches to accounting for SS; Cao et al. (2011) extend it to nine approaches. Space does not permit a separate treatment of each approach, so the present discussion necessarily assumes acquaintance with those methods. Table 11.1 summarizes the way each method deals with the unmeasured attitudes in the equations above.

It can be seen that in some methods attitudes must be explicitly measured, while in others attitudes may or may not be observed (and most often are not). The explicit inclusion of attitudes is by no means a panacea for all problems – issues of endogeneity and measurement error remain in most practical applications – but we suggest that careful measurement and incorporation of attitudes into models provides deeper, more specific, and more reliable insights into behavior than neglecting them altogether. Section 3 discusses the implications of Table 11.1 for future research.

3.   THE IMPORTANCE OF ATTITUDE-RELATED RESIDENTIAL SELF-SELECTION FOR MODELING AND EMPIRICAL RESULTS

This section further discusses the importance of including these attitudes, focusing on a selection of dominant topics.

The "True" Impact of Land Use on Travel Behavior

The general problem of ignoring attitude-related RSS is that the research may draw "wrong" conclusions with respect to which land-use variables have a significant effect on travel behavior, and how strong the impact of (significant) variables is. In general the risk of overestimation of this impact dominates, because some of the estimated impact of land-use variables will be caused by attitudes, not by land-use characteristics. In specific cases ignoring attitude-related RSS may also lead to an underestimation of the impact of land-use variables, depending on the share of people with travel preferences that do not match their residential location.

It is easier to conclude that attitude-related RSS matters than to produce a "perfect" method to tackle the precise impact of attitude-related RSS. Attitudes and location choice are likely to be very closely related and, with other factors, be associated with travel, with complex, multidirectional relationships. And even if attitudes explain residential choice and then travel behavior, this does not mean land-use characteristics are not important for travel behavior. For example, a compact/high-density residential area needs to be there to attract people with attitudes preferring such locations. None of the methods available perfectly reflect the complexity of the issues at hand – which all vary

Table 11.1 Methods of accounting for self-selection

Method of accounting for SS	Role of attitudes
1. Direct questioning	Existence and qualitative impact of ATT on BEH is elicited through interviews. Does not permit quantification of the respective roles of ATT and ENV on BEH.
2. Statistical control	ATTs are directly measured (either as simple responses or through factor analysis or related techniques combining related responses) and incorporated into the equation for BEH, thereby moving them from unobserved (ε) to observed and thus reducing or eliminating the correlation of ε with ENV. With cross-sectional data, there can be a temporal mismatch problem, in that ATTs are generally modeled as influencing BEH, yet they are measured after the BEH has occurred, and thus the *measured* ATTs may already be influenced *by* the BEH.
3. Instrumental variables (IV) models	ENV is purged of its correlation with ε(ATT) by first modeling it as a function of instrumental variables that are (ideally) highly correlated with ENV but uncorrelated with ε(ATT). The resulting predicted $E\hat{N}V$ is then "safe" to include in the equation for BEH. In theory, permits assessment of the "true" impact of ENV on BEH. In practice, suitable instruments are difficult to find. They may either fail to account for all of the variation in BEH that is due to the true impact of ENV (and thus probably *underestimate* the impact of ENV on BEH), or fail to completely avoid correlation with ATT (and thus perhaps *overestimate* the impact of ENV on BEH) – or both (with an unknown net bias). Also, because the impacts of ATT on ENV are in principle purged away, the IV method does not permit a rigorous comparison of the separated impacts of ATT and ENV on BEH. Comparing the coefficient of ENV itself in the BEH model, to that of $E\hat{N}V$ in the otherwise identically specified BEH model, can provide a heuristic assessment.
4. Sample selection models	Individuals are observed to be in one and only one of a set of discrete environmental states, where $DENV_k = 1$ if the person is in the kth state and 0 else, $k = 1, 2, \ldots$ K. K models, of BEH_k conditional on being in state k (the *outcome* equations), are estimated together with a discrete response model of the probability of being in each state (the *selection*, or *participation*, model). Those probabilities are generally functions of ENV variables: for example, DENV could be a traditional versus a suburban residential neighborhood, while ENV could be various measures of the built environment (such as density, land-use mix, and pedestrian-friendliness). The predicted BEH for a randomly-selected member of the population, then, is: $$B\hat{E}H = \sum_{k=1}^{K} B\hat{E}H_k \hat{P}r[DENV_k = 1],$$ where $B\hat{E}H_k$ contains a correction term (the inverse Mills ratio) derived from the participation model.

Table 11.1 (continued)

Method of accounting for SS	Role of attitudes
	The models of BEH_k and $DENV_k$ *could* contain ATT, but seldom do in practice. ATTs are generally considered to be implicitly accounted for through the inclusion of ATT-influenced ENV variables in the participation model. The error terms of all equations are allowed to be correlated in this method. However, without the explicit incorporation of attitudes into the participation model, $\hat{P}r[DENV_k = 1]$ may not be very high for the chosen state (i.e., the model does a poor job of predicting which state is selected), and thus the estimation of $B\hat{E}H_k$ could be rather noisy.
5. Propensity score methods	Each individual receives a propensity score, indicating the probability she receives a treatment – such as living in a traditional neighborhood – given explanatory variables (ENV, SED, and possibly, but not usually, ATT; Cao, 2010 is one exception). In propensity score matching, for example, individuals in the treatment group are matched with people in the control group who have similar propensity scores (mimicking the random assignment of individuals to states), and differences in BEH between people in the treatment group and those in the control group are computed. If unmeasured ATTs remain a source of SS, however, the "assignment" of individuals to treatment versus control states is *not* random, and this method does not control for them.
6. Joint discrete choice models	Conceptually similar to sample selection models, except that here, BEH is discrete as well as DENV, and a model of the joint probability of {DENV, BEH} pairs is estimated. Error terms of the two equations are allowed to be correlated, and the correlation can be parameterized as a function of observed variables (e.g. Pinjari et al., 2007). For example, the error can include a term such as w ENV, where w is an individually specific sensitivity to ENV that can be presumed to be due to ATT. Var(w) can be estimated simultaneously with the other parameters.
	Although ATTs can be measured and explicitly included in such models, in applications to date they have remained unmeasured, and in such cases the specific role of ATTs must be inferred.
7. Structural equations models (SEMs) with continuous endogenous variables	In principle, allows multiple directions of causality among ATT, ENV, and BEH. In practice, having enough exogenous variables to identify all hypothesized relationships can be challenging. Also, with cross-sectional data there is the same temporal mismatch as in the single-equation statistical control method.
	In non-recursive SEMs (i.e., those with feedback loops), it is difficult or impossible to isolate the effects of ATT on BEH from those of ENV, because it is impossible to change the one while holding the other constant: changing one leads to a change in the other.
8. Mutually-dependent discrete choice models	Seldom-applied (Cher et al., 2008), and so far not including ATT. Conceptually, the role of ATT can be similar to that of SEMs with continuous endogenous variables.
9. Longitudinal designs	If ATTs do not change over time, then they are ruled out as a cause if a change in ENV is followed by a change in BEH. However, it may in fact be a change in ATT (or dissonance between ATT and ENV) that prompts a change in ENV, in which case SS is at work. Also, across time, ENV and BEH may affect ATT, and these feedback loops should be taken into account in longitudinal studies (i.e., longitudinal SEMs).

by individual. For further discussion we refer to Cao (2010) who has a good illustration of how under- or overestimation can happen; see also Pinjari et al. (2008).

Attitudes Partly Follow from Residential Choice

It is important to realize that attitudes are not only a *cause* of residential choice (and other choices relevant for travel behavior – see Section 4), but also an *effect* of the experiences resulting from that choice. For example, the characteristics of the residential area can have an impact on attitudes. This reversed causality emphasizes the importance of assumptions with respect to the model structure, and with respect to when attitudes are measured: at the time of decision-making (e.g., residential choice) or after these choices are made. An impact due to the reverse causality was found in Bohte (2010).

Which Method Should be Used?

Each of the methods described in Table 11.1 has its advantages and disadvantages, and each has its supporters and detractors. In many cases, the selection of which method to use is constrained or even dictated by the nature of the data available. Assuming that the data are quantitative in nature and that the sample size is adequate, the two main issues are (1) whether they include attitudes, and (2) whether they are longitudinal. If both these conditions are true, then any of the quantitative methods is feasible. If attitudes are *not* available then the statistical controls method is not feasible, and if attitudes *are* available, then the instrumental variables approach is probably not necessary. All of the remaining approaches are feasible and useful with or without attitudes – although, as commented earlier, we would argue that they are *more* useful *with* attitudes.

Clearly, the maximum analysis flexibility is provided by longitudinal data that includes attitudes (and other variables) measured at multiple time points, and Mokhtarian and Cao (2008) argue that longitudinal structural equations modeling including attitudes is the methodology permitting the strongest causal inferences. Suppose, however, that the researcher possesses a cross-sectional dataset, with attitudes. Is one of the approaches presented in Table 11.1 better than the others? This is an open research question. It would be highly desirable to systematically compare each of the cross-sectional methods on the same dataset, on their explanatory power and their conclusions with respect to the role of self-selection. For example, two models could be developed for each method: the first one controlling as much as possible for model specification, i.e., including the same variables for each approach, and the second one constituting the "best" model specification for each method, where the significant explanatory variables could differ by method. One could also do a parallel analysis with and without attitudes, to ascertain how explanatory power and SS conclusions might differ when attitudes are not available.

4.   SELF-SELECTION AND OTHER SPATIAL AND NON-SPATIAL CHOICES

So far we have only discussed *residential* self-selection. In this section we argue that self-selection also can occur with respect to other location choices. The section is largely based on van Wee (2009) – for more discussion we refer to that paper. Below we first discuss self-selection with respect to destination choice (work locations; other locations), followed by a table summarizing self-selection in a variety of travel-related choice contexts.

Work Location

People might self-select with respect to work locations. A person with a strong preference for traveling by public transport ("public transport lover") might prefer a job near a railway station, all other factors remaining equal. On the other hand, a car lover might dislike a downtown job location with poor car access. A person with a preference for eating lunch outdoors, or for doing some shopping during the lunch hour or after work might prefer to work in an inner city or suburban center.

Other Destinations

People might also self-select with respect to destinations for non-work related trips, based on characteristics of the destinations. Consider two statistically equivalent people (based on observed characteristics) who live next-door to each other. The one who loves public transport is more likely to choose the restaurant that is well-served by transit, while the one who loves driving is more likely to choose the equally distant restaurant that has plenty of parking and easy automobile access.

The relevance of ignoring this form of self-selection is comparable to that of ignoring self-selection with respect to residential location. The outcome in both cases is misprediction of behavior, and particularly of responses to policies intended to influence behavior in socially desirable ways. In neither case is it safe to assume that a randomly selected person who finds herself to be in a new choice context (e.g., because of a policy incentive or regulation) will behave the same way (on average) as those who chose to be in that context of their own accord.

In addition to destination-related self-selection, van Wee (2009) argues that self-selection can occur in other respects as well, as summarized in Table 11.2. The column 'importance' gives an indication of the importance of each type of self-selection, based on the authors' impression.

We conclude that the research area of attitude-related RSS has matured over the past decade and a half, but that research into other forms of self-selection (destination related and non-destination related forms as presented in Table 11.2) is still in its infancy, or even completely absent. We think that a better understanding of these types of self-selection can be very relevant for understanding travel behavior and its externalities. And we think that the methodological discussion as presented in Section 3 is also relevant for these types of self-selection.

5.   DISCUSSION

The key message of our chapter is that both measuring attitudes adequately as well as selections with respect to model structure and specifications are very important for

Table 11.2   Self-selection in a variety of travel-related choice contexts

Type of self-selection	Explanation	Importance
Work-related		
Employment characteristics	E.g., job-hoppers might be less willing to adapt residential location or travel mode	Probably less important than residential self-selection: lower share in travel, less important for quality of life
Job type	Impact on job location Can be linked to a preference for a leased car	Probably less important than residential self-selection (see above)
Travel modes, travel behavior and driving behavior related		
Use of cars, public transport, bicycle	Car lovers, public transport lovers – may have an impact on all spatial choices (residential choices, work location choice, other destinations)	Probably very important: can affect all travel
Number of trips	Can have an impact on residential choice	Uncertain, we think this is less important
Trip distances and trip travel times	Can have an impact on all spatial choices and travel behavior	Uncertain, probably more important than the number of trips, but less important than residential self-selection
Car ownership level (number of cars in the household)	Can have an impact on residential choice and maybe work locations	Probably quite important
Car type choice (e.g., SUV, sedan, station car, convertible), engine and fuel choice	Generally recognized by car insurance companies Relevant for safety and environmental impact	Important for environmental impacts
Engine and fuel choice	Relevant for environmental impacts and for test cycles for emissions	Important for environmental impacts
Other trip characteristics	E.g., ticket class, scenery type, road type	Probably less important
Driving behavior (style of driving, e.g., aggressively)	Relevant for road safety and the environment	Important for environmental characteristics and safety
Driving under the influence of alcohol and/or drugs	Relevant for road safety	Important for safety – alcohol is probably more important than drugs
Driving in bad weather conditions	Relevant for road safety	Probably marginally important for safety
Related to exposure to safety levels and impact of externalities		
Noise exposure	Relevant for understanding noise nuisance	Nijland et al. (2007) did not find a significant impact of noise sensitivity on residential choice

Table 11.2   (continued)

Type of self-selection	Explanation	Importance
Related to exposure to safety levels and impact of externalities		
Air pollution exposure	Relevant for understanding health impacts of pollution	Uncertain
Exposure to third-party risks	Relevant for safety	Uncertain
Safety preferences	Relevant for safety	Uncertain
Congestion	Relevant for marginal value of time, benefits of infrastructure improvements	Potentially very important and potentially large effects on benefits of new road infrastructure

answering the specific research questions when SS is present. In this section we extend the discussion focusing on a few related topics.

The Importance of Residential Self-Selection for Future Research

Trade-off measuring attitudes, other variables and response rate

With respect to measuring attitudes a dilemma exists. On the one hand the researcher may wish to measure attitudes as comprehensively as possible. But this would require many questions in a questionnaire. These questions may come at the cost of (1) asking other questions, such as those related to travel behavior and socio-economic and demographic variables, or (2) the response rate. Note that research in this area generally is based on quite extensive questionnaires. The researcher typically wants to include several travel behavior-related questions, socio-economic and demographic variables, and maybe also some questions related to land-use variables, though the latter types of variables are often at least partly based on other data sources. So in practice we think the researcher should carefully trade off asking questions about attitudes, asking other questions and response rates. We think it is an important research challenge to find out how 'well' attitudes should be measured, and the impact of options for this measurement on the explanatory power of a model, as well as on the values of the coefficients and significance of variables.

An even more narrow definition of self-selection: remaining unobserved self-selection

Above we presented two definitions of (residential) self-selection. Van Wee (2009: 280) proposes an even more narrow definition in which self-selection is "limited to only those factors that are not included in the variables under consideration, and – in our case – are relevant for travel behavior." He argues that the variables included in a travel behavior models always only partly explain travel behavior – unobserved heterogeneity will always remain – and that there is always a risk of non-random heterogeneity in choices and behavior over people. This non-random behavior can result in several types of (residential) self-selection and interact with the impact of land use on travel behavior.

Self-selection and land-use policies

Even though it seems that residential self-selection reduces the independent impact of land use on travel behavior we would not suggest this is a reason not to build 'favorable' neighborhoods (e.g., with higher densities and mixed use, located near railway stations). First, even if people with a preference for slow modes, public transport, and short travel distances would self-select into such areas, they need to be built, to allow such people to travel as they prefer. Without providing those options people will be 'mismatched' and be forced to drive more than they wish. And as explained in Section 3 the characteristics of the residential area can have an impact on attitudes, so 'favorable' neighborhoods can change attitudes. Second, it is important to realize that policy choices with respect to land use should not be based on travel behavior (and its impacts such as on the environment) only – a wide range of evaluation criteria play a role, including environmental and safety impacts, preferences of people, wider accessibility impacts, costs of policy options and more (van Wee, 2002). We next discuss the interaction between impacts on travel behavior (and related environmental impacts) versus accessibility impacts.

Discussion on Travel Behavior Versus Accessibility Impacts

As explained in the Introduction, the most important reason why researchers and policymakers are interested in research into the impact of land use on travel behavior is the impact of travel behavior on the environment, in the context of policies promoting a reduction in car use. In general it seems that the "better" methodologies for studying the impact of land use on travel behavior suggest a lower impact of land use. What if even better methodologies than those currently applied, as discussed in Sections 2 and 3, would suggest an even lower "real" impact of land use on travel behavior? Would the conclusion then be that related policies, such as new urbanism, would not make sense? We think this would be a wrong conclusion. Van Wee (2011) argues that if land use potentially could decrease motorized mobility (including car use) but in practice people do not travel less using motorized modes, there must be accessibility gains that at least equal the potential gains in savings of generalized transport costs (GTC). He argues that the general way of evaluating land-use impacts, on travel behavior and environmental gains, is insufficient: accessibility benefits should be added. In other words, the researcher and policymaker should be careful in rejecting land-use concepts if these would, after controlling for other variables and RSS, influence travel behavior relatively little – there might be good reasons for such policies from an accessibility perspective. In addition, the depletion of oil and possibly stringent future climate change policies might increase the value societies place on reducing the oil consumption of travel and related "favorable" land-use policies.

REFERENCES

Bohte, W. (2010), *Residential Self-selection and Travel: The Relationship between Travel-related Attitudes, Built Environment Characteristics and Travel Behavior*, Delft: Delft University of Technology.

Cao, X. (2010), Exploring causal effects of neighborhood type on walking behavior using stratification on the propensity score, *Environment and Planning A*, **42**(2), 487–504.

Cao, X., Mokhtarian, P.L., and Handy, S.L. (2011), Examining the impacts of residential self-selection on travel behavior: methodologies and empirical findings, in Elisabetta Venezia (ed.), *Urban Sustainable Mobility*, Milan: Franco Angeli, pp. 15–100.

Chen, C., Gong, H., and Paaswell, R. (2008), Role of the built environment on mode choice decisions: additional evidence on the impact of density, *Transportation*, **35**, 285–99.

Kenworthy, J. and Laube, F. (1999), A global review of energy use in urban transport systems and its implications for urban transport and land-use policy, *Transportation Quarterly*, **53**(4), 23–48.

KiM (2010), *Mobiliteitsbalans 2010*, The Hague: Kennisinstituut voor Mobiliteitsbeleid.

Litman, T.A. (2005), Land use impacts on transport: how land use factors affect travel behavior, www.vtpi.org/landtravel.pfd (accessed January 13, 2006).

Mokhtarian, P. and Cao, X. (2008), Examining the impacts of residential self-selection on travel behavior: a focus on methodologies, *Transportation Research Part B*, **43**(3), 204–28.

Mokhtarian, P. and Chen, C. (2004), TTB or not TTB, that is the question: a review and analysis of the empirical literature on travel time (and money) budgets, *Transportation Research Part A*, **38**(9–10), 643–75.

Newman, P. and Kenworthy, J. (1988), The transport energy trade-off: fuel efficient traffic versus fuel-efficient cities, *Transportation Research A*, **22**(3), 163–74.

Newman, P. and Kenworthy, J. (1999), *Sustainability and Cities: Overcoming Automobile Dependence*, Washington, DC: Island Press.

Nijland, H., Hartemink, S., van Kamp, I., and van Wee, B. (2007), The influence of sensitivity for road traffic noise on residential location: does it trigger a process of spatial selection? *Journal of the Acoustical Society of America*, **122**(3), 1595–601.

Pinjari, A.R., Pendyala, R.M., Bhat, C.R., and Waddell, P.A. (2007), Modeling residential sorting effects to understand the impact of the built environment on commute mode choice, *Transportation*, **34**(5), 557–73.

Pinjari, A., Eluru, N., Bhat, C., Pendyala R., and Spissu, E. (2008), Joint model of choice of residential neighborhood and bicycle ownership: accounting for self-selection and unobserved heterogeneity, *Transportation Research Record*, **2082**, 17–26.

Schafer, A. and Victor, D.G. (2000), The future mobility of the world population, *Transportation Research Part A*, **34**(3), 171–205.

Schrank, B., Lomax, T., and Eisele, B. (2011), *TTI's 2011 Urban Mobility Report*, Texas: Texas Transportation Institute, Texas A&M University, http://mobility.tamu.edu/ums (accessed December 19, 2011).

Szalai, A. (ed.) (1972), *The Use of Time: Daily Activities of Urban and Suburban Populations in Twelve Counties*, The Hague: Mouton.

van Wee, B. (2002), Land use and transport: research and policy challenges, *Journal of Transport Geography*, **10**(4), 259–71.

van Wee, B. (2009), Self-selection: a key to a better understanding of location choices, travel behaviour and transport externalities? *Transport Reviews*, **29**(3), 279–92.

van Wee, B. (2011), Evaluating the impact of land use on travel behaviour: the environment versus accessibility, *Journal of Transport Geography*, **19**, 1530–33.

Zahavi, Y. and Talvitie, A. (1980), Regularities in travel time and money expenditures, *Transportation Research Record*, **750**, 13–19.

12 How stable are preferences for neighbourhood type and design in residential moves?
Kevin J. Krizek, Ahmed El-Geneidy and Ryan Wilson

1. INTRODUCTION

Active discussions in land-use and transportation planning circles continue to revolve around three related dimensions of travel behavior, neighborhood design and preferences. The bulk of this literature clearly focuses on the strength and magnitude of correlations between neighborhood design and travel behavior; many literature reviews have been published (Badoe and Miller, 2000; Crane, 2000; Ewing and Cervero, 2010) and more appear each year focusing on different dimensions or contexts such as walkable environments or different measures of accessibility (van Wee, 2002; Saelens et al., 2003; Geurs and van Wee, 2004; Saelens and Handy, 2008; Transportation Research Board, 2009). An outstanding question arising from this research relates to the issue commonly referred to as "self-selection". Attitudes and preferences for neighborhood design may influence travel more than the neighborhood design itself. In other words, showing correlations that people living in higher density/mixed-use developments walk more tells an incomplete story; it does not necessarily mean developing additional communities of this type will lead to more walking. Subsequently, an active body of literature aims to better understand the role of preferences. For almost a dozen years now, research has aimed to differentiate between the factors influencing one's inclination to walk from their residential choice to live in neighborhoods that support walking.

Neighborhood design characteristics are one of many factors affecting residential location decisions. Others include housing price and type, access to destinations, household characteristics, school quality, changing lifecycle and lifestyle considerations. The list goes on. One issue, however, is that it is difficult to measure what is meant by "neighborhood design." Many studies individually treat different characteristics of a neighborhood: street patterns, land-use mix, density, landscaping, type of retail or age of structures. In reality, however, most consumers approach these characteristics in a combined manner; the important aspect to measure is how these disaggregate dimensions combine to form attributes or characteristics of a neighborhood.

This research first creates a taxonomy of neighborhood types that is based on relevant design characteristics to land use–transportation research. Employing this taxonomy, we assess the degree to which households change their type of neighborhood when they move. By examining the consistency of preferences for neighborhood types among a sample of intra-county relocations in Hennepin County, Minnesota (US), this research advances our understanding of issues surrounding residential self-selection.

Importance for Policy and Research

While there is much enthusiasm from urban planners and others about using land use to modify the demand for travel, there is increasing evidence to suggest that self-selection might play a role in curtailing the expected impact of such initiatives. The reason is that the characteristics of a person or household might determine travel behavior and/or housing choice more than the characteristics of the neighborhood itself. For instance, a "walker" might choose to move to a community that supports walking, suggesting any change in travel behavior should not be credited to neighborhood design alone. Thus, any effort to analyze the factors affecting travel behavior and residential location decisions must consider self-selection.

This research aims to inform this discussion via two advancements. We first propose an approach to more suitably capture a neighborhood's overall character (as opposed to discrete and individual characteristics). Second, we employ this taxonomy to examine the stability of preferences among residents for different neighborhood types when they move. Our analysis therefore provides a straightforward response to a question often conjectured in land use–transportation research – to what degree do households change their neighborhood type – which is an important dimension to the self-selection discussion.

2.   RECAP OF RESIDENTIAL RELOCATION DECISIONS

Understanding household moves is important for transportation planning for two reasons. First, the attractive availability of travel choices (e.g., rail) largely depends on the location of where one lives. Second, moves occur relatively frequently. Given the overall context of the paper, we briefly highlight some primary aspects of residential relocation decisions. US data from 1996 estimated that half of the population had moved within the last five years (Schachter and Kuenzi, 2002). The predominant trend has favored urban to suburban moves or those within suburban areas, evidenced generally by US county-level analysis (Manson and Groop, 2000) and in other contexts – Chattanooga, Tennessee (Regional Planning Agency Information and Research, 2003) or in Boston, Massachusetts, Dallas, Texas, and in Philadelphia, Pennsylvania (Kasarda et al., 1997). Most moves between locations, at least in the US, are also relatively short. One study found that 73 percent of moves were less than 50km[1] and 46 percent less than 10km among those who had relocated once during the past three years (Long et al., 1988). Additionally, longitudinal studies estimating migration patterns estimated roughly two-thirds of a new-born's moves during their lifetime will be intra-county (Wilber, 1963; Long, 1973; Kulkarni and Louis, 1994).

Factors Influencing Residential Relocations

The reasons people move are myriad. Pioneering work (Rossi, 1955) spotlighted the role of changing lifecycle and lifestyle factors such as age, tenure type, tenure length and household size – considerations that have since been summarized in literature reviews on relocation patterns from the 1960s–1970s (Ritchey, 1976), 1970s–1980s

(Greenwood, 1985) and 1980s–1990s (Dieleman, 2001). Younger generations move more frequently and for different reasons than families and retirees (Boehm and Ihlanfeldt, 1986; Plane and Heins, 2003). Moves vary by race; blacks are more likely than whites to remain in and move to urban centers (South and Crowder, 1997). Tenure length, household income and education can have varying effects on renters and owners (Boehm and Ihlanfeldt, 1986).

Housing and job related reasons also are important to consider. A US study estimated 51.6 percent of moves to be for housing related reasons (e.g., a different home (36 percent) or not to rent (22 percent)), 26.3 percent for family and 16.2 percent for work. Housing reasons explained 65 percent of intra-county compared to 32 percent of inter-county relocations (Schachter, 2001). Additional research supports variation in reasons for intra-county and inter-county moves; for example, employment is more likely to stimulate long distance relocations (Boehm et al., 1991; Dieleman, 2001). Housing reasons can vary between household and socio-demographic groups and can result from differences in perceived and actual neighborhood quality (Boehm and Ihlanfeldt, 1986; Schwanen and Mokhtarian, 2004). Discontent with current residence may even be a predecessor of neighborhood dissatisfaction (Parkes et al., 2002), although another found housing satisfaction insignificant relative to lifecycle and socio-demographic characteristics (Varady, 1993).

The role of neighborhood characteristics and design has been less studied and its impact is therefore less clear. Weisbrod et al. (1980) brought forth the idea that households make trade-offs between transportation and public services in relocation decisions, though their role was pale in comparison to socio-economic and demographic considerations. Relying on a Belgian context, accessibility and neighborhood attributes (e.g., parking, amount of traffic, privacy, safety) were less important than housing attributes (e.g., number of rooms, type of house, mortgage/rent) among consumers (Molin and Timmermans, 2003). Another study found the effect of accessibility insignificant relative to other variables (Zondag and Pieters, 2005). Other recent work specifically focused on neighborhood design characteristics. A choice-based analysis in Columbus (Ohio, US) found that households prefer suburban street layouts and lower housing densities, although also desire open space and shorter commute times. Improving school quality and neighborhood safety helped to make urban environments competitive (in choice) with suburban ones (Morrow-Jones et al., 2004). A survey in a Dallas (Texas, US) neighborhood found that residents were generally dissatisfied with the physical aspects of suburban development, but at the same time, the survey found residents lacking support for higher density/mixed-use neighborhoods (Talen, 2001).

Neighborhood Classification

The concept of neighborhood classification is not new. A study based in Los Angeles (California) was perhaps the earliest attempt to classify residential areas using aerial data across a large geography. Measuring housing (type, cost, age, tenure), land use and demographic (age and ethnicity) Census variables, the study employed cluster analysis to classify the city's 727 census tracts into 11 neighborhood types that matched, at least somewhat, residential patterns (Kendig, 1976). Respondents in Minneapolis

(Minnesota, US) organized into neighborhoods of similar social class (Adams and Gilder, 1976). A recent technique combines factor analysis (to relate various characteristics) and cluster analysis (to uncover group differences using the factor scores) (Krizek and Waddell, 2002).

The most relevant method was based on a case study of Portland (Oregon, US). The authors, who more extensively review approaches for classifying neighborhoods than what is provided here, measure physical properties of the built environment (street and lot design, density, land-use mix, accessibility and natural environment) in a one-quarter mile buffer around each new single-family home, defining this as "neighborhood." The study uses factor and cluster analysis to classify six neighborhood types (Song and Knaap, 2007). Notwithstanding the advancements of this research, a key question remained unanswered. Because the analysis heavily weighed overall accessibility, it leaves open the question of the role of neighborhood classification in which regional location is held relatively constant.

3. RESEARCH APPROACH

Household Survey

Our analysis employs data from a household survey to map household moves and GIS data to classify neighborhoods. We began by administering a household survey to approximately 1,000 randomly selected households in Hennepin County (Minnesota, US). The survey used a clustered sampling strategy, drawing from three geographically stratified areas representing locations that were urban (City of Minneapolis), inner suburban (first ring suburbs immediately to the west of Minneapolis), and outer suburban (second ring suburbs further west). The survey queried household travel patterns, perceptions of residential location, lifestyle attributes and basic demographics. The surveys were mailed in mid-July of 2005 and followed with three reminder mailings (Dillman, 2000). Excluding surveys returned as undeliverable, we received a response rate of over 40 percent.

We restricted our sample for analysis using two criteria. First, we removed households who formerly lived outside of Hennepin County. Acquiring and operationalizing detailed design characteristics at a regional scale was beyond the scope of this research.[2] Second, we removed households who did not relocate in the past ten years. The primary rationale for this second filter was to control, loosely, for major changes that may have taken place in these areas. While most urban and some inner suburban Hennepin County locations are "built-in," the characteristics in some inner suburban and many outer suburban areas have changed substantially in recent years. Based on these constraints and accounting for missing data, the final sample was reduced to 278 observations. The final sample is slightly better educated, younger, has a greater percentage of renters than owners and a lower percentage of married individuals compared to the original sample. Figure 12.1 depicts the location of the former and current address of each respondent in the context of the three geographic areas.[3]

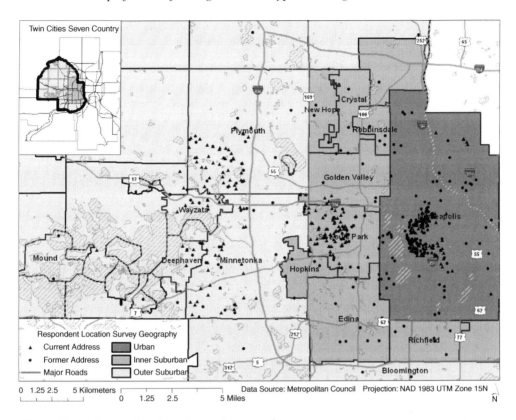

Figure 12.1 Respondent location and geographic areas

Operationalizing Neighborhood Design Characteristics

People perceive neighborhoods in different ways. Part of the confusion stems from issues of geography. How big (or small) is a neighborhood? For example, 32 percent of Seattle respondents defined their neighborhood as an area between one square block and a 0.80km radius and 18.6 percent consider it larger, while 25 percent describe their neighborhood as no larger than one block and 14.3 percent define it as their block or cul-de-sac (Guest and Lee, 1984). Central issues are detecting subtle differences in design characteristics and using an appropriate unit of analysis. Units range from municipal boundary to Census tract to simple buffer around a home. Defining units of analysis that are too large or small may fail to match a resident's perception of space or neighborhood description (Moudon et al., 1997; Coulton et al., 2001; Krizek, 2003; Guo, 2004). Furthermore, employing units of analysis drawn along sometimes arbitrary lines such as Census tracts or transportation analysis zones may obscure subtle variations in how persons perceive different neighborhood features.

We combined approaches that have been used previously and divide the study area into 300m grid cells, informed largely by previous research (Krizek, 2003). We consider each cell to be a "neighborhood." However, in defining neighborhood types, we hypothesize the character of each cell is not determined by the attributes of that cell alone; it is influenced by nearby neighborhoods. To best operationalize the neighborhood characteristics, we treat each grid cell as the "immediate neighborhood" and the adjacent cells as the "surrounding neighborhood."

We use ArcGIS v9.1 to operationalize a range of readily available neighborhood characteristics often used in past research at the grid cell level. Measures include the physical built environment, accessibility to various destinations, and socio-demographic and economic conditions (Bagley et al., 2002; Bhat and Guo, 2007; Guo and Bhat, 2007; Song and Knaap, 2007). Table 12.1 displays summary measures for 24 neighborhood characteristics and provides summary statistics. The demographic variables are from the 2000 US Census and the neighborhood variables are from the Metropolitan Council (Twin Cities metropolitan planning organization) Datafinder, year 2000 or later.

4. RESULTS

We present our results along three dimensions that relate to: (1) general relocation trends of our sample, (2) the results of the individual neighborhood taxonomies/types and (3) the stability of preferences for neighborhood types.

General Relocation Trends

Average tenure length at current residence is 4.2 years with increasing rates of home-ownership. Those who rented characterize 58 percent former residences compared to 28 percent of current residences. Most former owners remain owners (92 percent) while 57 percent of former renters currently own. As renters comprise a larger percentage of the final sample, this change would have likely been less using the full sample. Examining moves broadly among urban, inner suburban and outer suburban areas finds two-thirds of households moving within their geographic area. Moves of this type are also of shorter distance than moves between areas. Of the households moving from an urban area, 89 percent moved to another urban area. Of those moving form an inner suburban area, 49 percent moved to another inner suburban area. The same analysis yields 53 percent for outer suburban respondents. Moves between areas are generally outward, from urban to inner suburban to outer suburban.

Factor Analysis

Broadly defined, geographic areas fail to capture more nuanced elements of neighborhood character and design. We therefore employ principal component factor analysis to better understand the relationship among the detailed neighborhood design characteristics. Factor analysis extracts a small number of dimensions (factors) from the larger set of correlated characteristics, measuring different aspects of those characteristics (Garson, n.d.). We extract ten dimensions (factors with eigenvalues greater than one) to explain 81.5 percent of the variation in the total sample. Table 12.2 sorts the characteristics according to factor loading size and then sequential factor order and compares immediate and surrounding grid cell factor scores. Immediate and surrounding neighborhood areas factor scores fall into the same factor for each neighborhood design characteristic.

Table 12.1   Summary of variable measures in each grid cell

Variable	Unit of Measure for Each Grid Cell	Mean	Std. dev.	Min.	Max.
Bicycle trail length	Sum of length (meters)	53.5	145.6	0.0	1679.1
Water area	Area (hectares)	0.5	1.8	0.0	9.0
Park area	Area (hectares)	0.7	1.8	0.0	9.0
Open space	Area (hectares)	2.9	3.5	0.0	9.0
SFDU density	Single familing dwelling units per acre	2.4	2.8	0.0	29.9
Retail stores	Count	0.3	2.6	0.0	148.0
Number of residential lots	Count	23.0	30.0	0.0	194.0
Residential lot size	Average size of residential lots (hectares)	6.2	7.3	0.0	22.4
Estimated market value	Assessor's estimated value	382716	264681	0	2119565
Weekday bus service	Sum of weekday bus trips (count)	19.8	122.0	0.0	5400.0
Grade 3 school quality	Minnesota standardized test scores	3117.5	131.1	2546.0	3545.0
Local roads	Network length (meters)	438.6	437.8	0.0	2000.9
Non-local roads	Network length (meters)	130.5	293.9	0.0	4641.4
Street connectivity	(# 4-way intersections)/ (culsdesacs+4-way)	0.2	0.4	0.0	1.0
Violent crime	Count	1456.5	1790.3	0.0	7665.0
Distance to downtown Minneapolis	Network distance (kilometers)	23.5	10.8	0.0	45.6
Population density	Area weighted average of census tract	2051.2	2521.4	81.6	61633.7
Percent black	Area weighted average of census tract	3.4	7.1	0.1	66.8
Percent white	Area weighted average of census tract	90.7	11.8	8.3	98.0
Median household income	Area weighted average of census tract	69872.5	18519.9	124.1	113850.0
Percent own housing unit	Area weighted average of census tract	81.2	18.4	0.2	99.6
Percent with kids less than 18	Area weighted average of census tract	39.2	11.5	0.1	69.3
Household size	Area weighted average of census tract	2.7	0.4	0.0	3.8
Percent high school graduates	Area weighted average of census tract	93.5	5.1	51.1	99.4

Table 12.2 Principal component factor loadings defining neighborhood dimensions

Variable[a]		Factor 1 Street Design & Land Use	Factor 2 Race	Factor 3 Household Structure	Factor 4 Retail & Transit	Factor 5 Parks	Factor 6 Non-local Roads	Factor 7 Estimated Market Value	Factor 8 Lake Area	Factor 9 School Quality	Factor 10 Bicycle Trails
Residential lot size	IN SN	**-0.678**	0.109	0.324	-0.007	-0.179	0.400	-0.086	-0.170	-0.135	-0.187
		-0.682	0.111	0.328	-0.007	-0.182	0.400	-0.087	-0.171	-0.134	-0.188
Open space	IN SN	**-0.626**	0.099	0.267	-0.045	-0.380	0.313	0.047	-0.294	-0.120	-0.100
		-0.666	0.114	0.308	-0.043	-0.369	0.328	0.029	-0.267	-0.112	-0.126
Dist. to downtown Minneapolis	IN SN	**-0.654**	0.306	0.406	-0.086	-0.147	0.340	-0.061	0.048	0.116	-0.112
		-0.655	0.307	0.406	-0.085	-0.149	0.338	-0.061	0.048	0.116	-0.112
SFDU density	IN SN	**0.440**	-0.037	-0.062	-0.002	-0.167	0.232	-0.101	0.062	-0.099	0.111
		0.690	-0.096	-0.105	0.000	-0.146	0.191	-0.140	0.035	-0.139	0.062
Violent crime	IN SN	**0.571**	-0.395	-0.237	0.091	0.219	-0.127	-0.039	-0.058	-0.274	0.117
		0.577	-0.394	-0.243	0.093	0.220	-0.127	-0.040	-0.058	-0.277	0.118
Population density	IN SN	**0.606**	-0.485	-0.302	0.186	0.019	-0.044	-0.016	0.005	-0.152	0.053
		0.624	-0.495	-0.316	0.195	0.028	-0.059	-0.017	0.006	-0.167	0.058
Street connectivity	IN SN	**0.609**	-0.229	-0.159	0.183	-0.085	0.046	-0.053	-0.134	-0.104	-0.047
		0.727	-0.336	-0.252	0.193	-0.051	-0.014	-0.087	-0.095	-0.190	-0.040
Local roads	IN SN	**0.810**	-0.163	-0.148	0.097	-0.074	-0.008	-0.091	-0.156	0.046	0.002
		0.868	-0.217	-0.213	0.104	-0.025	-0.092	-0.114	-0.079	-0.023	0.040
Number of residential lots	IN SN	**0.872**	-0.064	-0.024	-0.037	-0.063	0.136	-0.113	-0.087	-0.023	-0.066
		0.918	-0.096	-0.058	-0.021	-0.010	0.073	-0.133	-0.038	-0.087	-0.017
Percent black	IN SN	0.254	**-0.913**	-0.040	0.105	0.030	-0.110	-0.015	-0.016	-0.015	0.030
		0.271	**-0.910**	-0.050	0.117	0.033	-0.115	-0.018	0.017	-0.037	0.031
Percent high school graduates	IN SN	-0.076	**0.841**	0.146	-0.054	0.079	-0.041	0.200	0.015	0.216	0.134
		-0.089	**-0.842**	0.146	-0.067	0.079	-0.038	0.201	0.017	0.242	0.138
Percent white	IN SN	-0.303	**0.905**	0.089	-0.094	-0.051	0.141	0.057	0.029	0.067	-0.067
		-0.320	**0.896**	0.101	-0.103	-0.054	0.148	0.060	0.030	0.088	-0.068
Median household income	IN SN	-0.164	0.544	**0.639**	-0.066	0.052	-0.022	0.336	0.002	0.221	0.086
		-0.181	0.546	**0.632**	-0.072	0.049	-0.015	0.333	0.002	0.234	0.089

Percent own housing unit	IN	-0.094	0.477	**0.757**	-0.165	-0.002	0.092	0.014	-0.011	-0.089	-0.109
	SN	-0.118	0.479	**0.761**	-0.174	-0.007	0.103	0.008	-0.013	-0.081	-0.109
Household size	IN	-0.321	-0.030	**0.894**	-0.115	-0.067	0.146	0.014	-0.058	-0.003	-0.046
	SN	-0.346	-0.021	**0.888**	-0.120	-0.075	0.153	0.007	-0.063	-0.010	-0.046
Percent with kids less than 18	IN	-0.297	0.026	**0.913**	-0.114	-0.043	0.108	0.003	-0.037	0.055	0.025
	SN	-0.314	0.038	**0.905**	-0.116	-0.048	0.114	-0.002	-0.041	0.050	0.027
Retail stores	IN	0.026	-0.001	-0.057	**0.687**	-0.014	-0.105	-0.087	0.021	0.064	-0.001
	SN	0.075	-0.069	-0.197	**0.776**	-0.030	-0.140	-0.047	-0.020	0.013	0.017
Weekday bus service	IN	0.105	-0.166	-0.095	**0.807**	0.006	0.018	0.037	-0.025	-0.110	-0.010
	SN	0.148	-0.265	-0.173	**0.792**	-0.002	-0.002	0.055	-0.036	-0.165	-0.004
Park area	IN	-0.062	-0.003	-0.049	-0.025	**0.871**	0.102	-0.021	0.015	-0.043	0.131
	SN	-0.011	0.008	-0.049	-0.028	**0.891**	0.065	-0.025	0.080	-0.023	0.111
Non–local roads	IN	-0.047	-0.090	-0.149	0.102	-0.122	**-0.703**	-0.076	-0.060	-0.105	0.057
	SN	0.017	-0.194	-0.271	0.155	-0.102	**-0.702**	-0.092	-0.078	-0.050	0.065
Estimated market value	IN	-0.217	0.217	0.054	-0.037	-0.036	0.075	**0.894**	0.160	0.092	-0.049
	SN	-0.223	0.223	0.055	-0.037	-0.038	0.080	**0.890**	0.161	0.106	-0.052
Lake area	IN	-0.073	0.026	-0.048	-0.020	0.023	0.044	0.086	**0.914**	-0.006	-0.006
	SN	-0.069	0.050	-0.077	-0.024	0.085	0.062	0.169	**0.890**	0.031	-0.009
Grade 3 school quality	IN	-0.238	0.443	0.017	-0.096	-0.041	0.096	0.142	0.020	**0.781**	0.007
	SN	-0.248	0.460	0.020	-0.100	-0.042	0.095	0.151	0.023	**0.774**	0.008
Bicycle trail length	IN	0.057	0.017	-0.038	-0.001	0.097	-0.025	-0.025	-0.022	-0.028	**0.874**
	SN	0.149	0.027	-0.032	0.000	0.155	-0.109	-0.045	0.013	0.036	**0.849**
Percent of Variance Explained		**38.2**	**10.5**	**7.9**	**5.6**	**4.4**	**4.4**	**3.4**	**2.6**	**2.4**	**2.2**

Note:
a   Two neighborhood measures: 1) Immediate neighborhood (individual cell) & 2) SN - surrounding neighborhood (adjacent cells)

The first factor, street design and land use, captures the following variables: residential lot size, open space, distance to downtown Minneapolis, single-family home density, crime, population density, street connectivity, local roads and number of residential lots. Race and high school graduation rate are associated strongly with the second factor. The third factor reflects homeownership and the presence of children. The number of retail stores and weekday bus stops are associated strongly with factor four. The last six factors each represent single measures: park area, non-local roads, estimated (home) market value, lake area, elementary school quality and bicycle trail length.

Cluster Analysis

K-means cluster analysis combines the neighborhood dimensions to form unique neighborhood types.[4] Cluster analysis classifies grid cells into neighborhood types using the ten dimensions, ensuring the degree of association is maximal between types and maximal within types (Garson, n.d.). The best fit for this data is an eight cluster (neighborhood type) model, based on statistics from the cluster analysis and ease of interpretation.[5] The magnitude of the ten dimensions (cluster centers) in each of the eight clusters is presented in Table 12.3 and graphically in Figure 12.2.

Five of the neighborhood types, "Commercial Centers," "Low Density Home Ownership," "Urban Commercial Core," "Parks & Trail Residential," and "Lake Lots" are relatively specialized and are few in number. For example, "Commercial Centers" reflect areas high in traffic, retail stores and transit service and low in homeownership, children and median household income.

Distinguishing among the final three neighborhood types, "Suburban Residential," "Mix Urban Residential" and "Family Urban Residential," is a bit more nuanced. These neighborhoods share some similarities, such as grid streets and small lots. The difficulty is identifying subtle – but important, in terms of feel – differences between areas of primarily single family land use. Suburban Residential is best characterized by higher quality schools and the presences of parks. Mix Urban Residential has lower quality schools and a greater number of non-local roads. Family Urban Residential can be best identified by higher family size and a relatively high percentage of black households.

The spatial distribution of these three neighborhood types across Hennepin County adds further differentiation (see Figure 12.3). Family Urban Residential, Mix Urban Residential and Suburban Residential neighborhoods were the first to fully develop before growth spread to the large lot residential areas, helping to explain differences in street pattern, demographics, school quality and residential lot size. This analysis underscores the value of local knowledge of the built environment when interpreting factor scores and more importantly, evaluating each possible cluster solution.

Figure 12.3 maps current and former home locations for the 278 respondents.[6] While not clearly evident from this figure, detailed inspection finds some short-distance relocations are to different neighborhood types, while some long-distance relocations are to the same neighborhood type. Other definitions of neighborhood (e.g., Census tract or geographic area) would not likely quantify this change. Table 12.4 lists the number of respondents in each neighborhood type. Nearly 39 percent of former residences are in both the Suburban Residential and Mix Urban Residential neighborhoods compared to

Table 12.3 Final cluster center values for each neighborhood type

Neighborhood Dimension	Commercial Center	Surburban Residential	Mix Urban Residential	Family Urban Residential	Lake Lots	Urban Commercial Core	Park & Trail Residential	Large Lot Residential
Street Design & Land Use	-0.147	0.477	1.409	0.659	-0.234	-0.941	0.251	-0.814
Race	-0.363	0.161	-0.182	-5.070	0.146	0.654	0.155	0.146
Household Structure	-1.272	-0.281	-0.948	0.684	-0.141	0.170	0.189	0.394
Retail & Transit	6.176	-0.122	0.148	0.189	-0.060	27.766	-0.051	-0.044
Parks	-0.154	0.363	-0.023	-0.104	-0.121	1.147	0.254	-0.391
Non-local Roads	-1.129	-0.480	0.282	-0.253	0.177	0.798	-0.140	0.440
Estimated Market Value	-0.261	-0.229	0.081	0.380	0.416	0.069	-0.157	0.153
Lake Area	-0.072	-0.145	-0.149	-0.004	3.150	0.457	-0.092	-0.384
School Quality	-0.072	0.452	-1.995	0.237	0.169	0.363	0.347	-0.181
Bicycle Trails	-0.018	-0.427	0.013	-0.091	-0.225	-0.621	2.091	-0.246
% to total grid cells (N=16424)	0.55%	34.25%	7.42%	2.41%	6.73%	0.07%	12.09%	36.48%

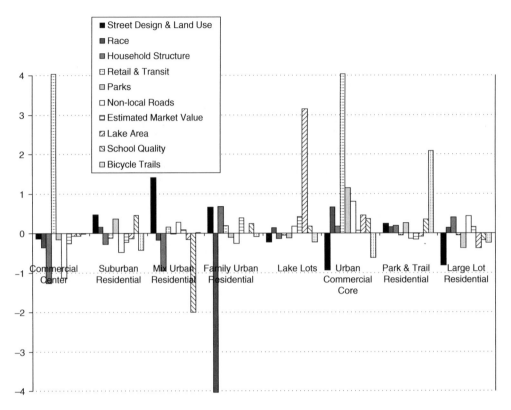

Figure 12.2   Final cluster center values for each neighborhood type

45 percent of current residences in the Suburban Residential and 32.4 percent in the Mix Urban Residential neighborhoods.

Stability of Preferences for Neighborhood Types

Having assigned each address a neighborhood type, we turn to discussing the frequency of moves between each. Our most pointed conclusion is that over one-half of the respondents (53.6 percent) moved within the same neighborhood type (Table 12.5). Among households, 27.4 percent moved within the Suburban Residential type (not a totally surprising finding, given this is the neighborhood type of largest total area). Twenty-three percent moved within Mix Urban Residential and 1.4 percent within both Park & Trail Residential and Family Urban Residential neighborhoods. The largest number of moves between neighborhoods was from Mix Urban Residential to Suburban Residential. Most moves of this type were – although not exclusively – from urban to suburban areas.

The last part aims to better understand the factors – both neighborhood design and respondent characteristics – that influence moves within neighborhood types. We employ a binary logistic regression (Table 12.6) to predict if respondents moved within the same neighborhood type. The model includes 16 independent variables; seven describe values

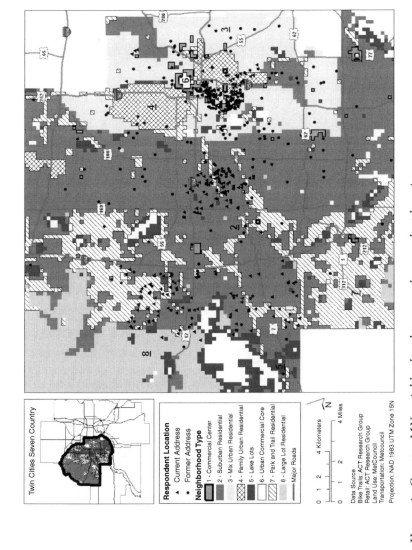

Figure 12.3   Hennepin County, MN, neighborhood types and respondent locations

Table 12.4   Number of respondent residences in each neighborhood type

Neighborhood Type	Former Residence	Current Residence
	% (n=278)	% (n=278)
Commercial Center	5.8	1.1
Suburban Residential	39.6	45.3
Mix Urban Residential	39.9	32.4
Family Urban Residential	6.1	6.8
Lake Lots	1.1	0.4
Urban Core	0.0	0.0
Park & Trail Residential	7.2	12.9
Large Lot Residential	0.4	1.1

Table 12.5   Moves between and within neighborhood types

Move Direction (Former to Current)	% (n=278)[a]
Suburban Residential to Suburban Residential	27.4
Mix Urban Residential to Mix Urban Residential	23.4
Mix Urban Residential to Suburban Residential	9.6
Suburban Residential to Park & Trail Residential	8.6
Park & Trail Residential to Suburban Residential	3.6
Commercial Center to Mix Urban Residential	3.2
Mix Urban Residential to Family Urban Residential	3.2
Mix Urban Residential to Park & Trail Residential	2.9
Suburban Residential to Mix Urban Residential	2.5
Family Urban Residential to Mix Urban Residential	2.5
Family Urban Residential to Suburban Residential	1.8
Park & Trail Residential to Park & Trail Residential	1.4
Family Urban Residential to Family Urban Residential	1.4
Commercial Center to Suburban Residential	1.4
Commercial Center to Family Urban Residential	1.1
Lake Lots to Suburban Residential	0.7
Park & Trail Residential to Family Urban Residential	0.7
Park & Trail Residential to Large Lot Residential	0.7
Mix Urban Residential to Commercial Center	0.7
Suburban Residential to Family Urban Residential	0.4
Suburban Residential to Lake Lots	0.4
Suburban Residential to Large Lot Residential	0.4
Family Urban Residential to Commercial Center	0.4
Lake Lots to Mix Urban Residential	0.4
Park & Trail Residential to Mix Urban Residential	0.4
Large Lot Residential to Suburban Residential	0.4

Note:
a   Combinations with zero moves not reported

Table 12.6   Logistic regression predicting moves within neighborhood types

Variable	Beta	Odds Ratio	p-value	95% C.I. for Odds Ratio	
				Lower	Upper
Current Neighborhood Characteristics					
Residential lot size	−0.031	0.970	0.859	0.690	1.362
Percent white	0.040	1.041	0.003	1.014	1.069
Percent own housing unit	−0.019	0.981	0.038	0.963	0.999
Retail stores	−0.147	0.863	0.178	0.696	1.070
Lake area	0.467	1.595	0.068	0.966	2.635
Estimated Market Value (per $10,000)	−0.022	0.978	0.022	0.960	0.997
Grade 3 school quality	−0.001	0.999	0.676	0.996	1.002
Respondent Characteristics					
Age	−0.014	0.986	0.227	0.964	1.009
Have kids at home (Dummy, 1=Yes)	0.252	1.287	0.476	0.643	2.576
Owned at former address (Dummy, 1=Yes)	0.391	1.478	0.295	0.712	3.068
Walker (Dummy, 1=Yes)	0.050	1.051	0.875	0.562	1.967
Biker (Dummy, 1=Yes)	0.805	2.237	0.016	1.159	4.317
Distance moved from downtown	−0.189	0.827	0.000	0.763	0.898
Most Important Factors in Choosing New Home Location (Attitude) (Dummy, 1=Yes)					
Closeness to work, short commute time	0.796	2.216	0.039	1.040	4.722
Cost of housing	−0.497	0.608	0.127	0.321	1.153
Quality of home and others around it	0.031	1.032	0.926	0.534	1.992
Constant	1.668	5.304	0.683		
Nagelkerke R-squared	0.273				n = 278

of neighborhood design characteristics at the respondent's current address; six measure characteristics of the respondent and three show responses to attitudinal questions. We code the attitudinal variables as a dummy indicating whether the respondent selected the three most common responses, among 18 choices, as the most important factor in choosing their current home location.

The model suggests six variables are statistically significant at the 0.05 level. Each helps to predict whether respondents move within the same type of neighborhood. Examining the odds ratio (probability of an event/probability of non-event), reveals the influence of each variable. A ratio greater than one indicates the odds of moving to the same neighborhood type are increased and vice versa.[7]

The model reveals that the odds of a household moving to the same neighborhood type are higher if that respondent: (1) chooses their home location for a shorter commute, (2) is a cyclist, and (3) currently lives in a neighborhood with a higher percentage of white neighbors. A respondent who is a cyclist[8] and one who chooses their home location for a shorter commute has 2.2 times the odds of moving to the same neighborhood type. This finding shows a stronger relation between cycling and self-selection, cautioning us about the notion that building new cycling facilities will lead to changes to active modes. In other words, cyclists tend to move to areas that are similar to where they lived in the past.

Second, a shorter commute is a desirable goal among movers and movers aim to find the same type of neighborhood when they move nearer to their jobs. Each unit (1 percent) increase of white neighbors in the current neighborhood improves the odds by 1.041. Each 1 percent increase in homeowners reduces the odds by a factor of 0.981. The odds also decrease for each $10,000 increase in the estimated market value and with each additional 1.6 kilometers moved from downtown, measured as the difference between current and former distance from downtown. In addition, households moving farther from downtown have greater odds of changing neighborhood types.[9]

5.   FURTHER RESEARCH AND IMPLICATIONS

We demonstrated that a detailed taxonomy of neighborhood types reveals nuances in neighborhood location and character that an analysis at a more geographically aggregate scale failed to detect. For example, 53.6 percent of respondents moved within their neighborhood type compared to 66 percent within their broad geographic area. Particularly, the detailed analysis shows moves between geographic areas are not all to locations with similar design characteristics and moves within geographic areas could be to neighborhoods with differences in neighborhood design. In fact, at least five different neighborhood types comprise each geographic area in Hennepin County. For these 53.6 percent of the respondents, isolating the role of neighborhood factors in influencing travel behavior from that of self-selection (preferences and habits) is a complex endeavor. The built environment is expected to have a strong and significant impact on travel behavior for these individuals if regular methods (ignoring self-selection) are used in quantifying these impacts. This can, in turn, lead to exaggerating the impacts of built environment on travel behavior.

Being cognizant of the role of self-selection for these individuals is valuable when trying to measure the neighborhood impacts, especially among cyclists. For 46.4 percent of respondents, these are the best candidates to conduct studies that measure the impacts of built environment on travel behavior. Of course, other control variables – such as work location, culture, lifecycle, etc. – should be included in any study, yet the built environment impacts among these individuals would be closer to reality, if self-selection variables are not present, compared to the other group of movers. Many studies use travel behavior data from the Census and link back to neighborhood characteristics, generating causal relations while ignoring self-selection since it is not included in the Census data. Such studies tend to leave the reader with overestimated correlations and causations. Accordingly, our work cautions one to form policies strictly on the basis of such studies, especially for cyclists as they show a higher than normal tendency to stay in the same type of neighborhoods. In other words, if new cycling facilities are built in an area, these areas are more likely to attract existing cyclists from similar neighborhoods who will move for various reasons. A more in-depth analysis is recommended especially for cyclists to understand the impacts of their values and preference on home location choice as well as their travel behavior.

Several factors help further inform some implications and caveats of this analyses. First, we draw our sample from one county within a large metropolitan area; this obviously limits the options available in terms of neighborhood type. Second, our conclusions tie closely to both the taxonomy of neighborhoods created and the geographic scale of analysis. While the 24 neighborhood design characteristics are relatively comprehensive and adequately capture the overall "feel" of a neighborhood, more nuanced and qualitative factors could certainly be introduced. The decision to use 300-meter grid cells involved much discussion and experimenting as few guiding studies were available. What unit of analysis is appropriate and how many different types of neighborhoods are important to account for? This remains an open question.

Third, the logit model, admittedly, does not fully account for the variety of possible reasons one's preferences may change (e.g., change in job or household composition). We are also unable to account for the location and volume of available housing. We only know that preferences for neighborhood type are stable for roughly half the population and, while this is an important conclusion in its own right, there is ample opportunity for more robust analysis.

The taxonomy of neighborhood types could have great utility in future research. The methodology, while somewhat laborious, was able to identify subtle differences among relatively similar residential neighborhoods. Future research can operationalize the methodology on a broader scale or in multiple metropolitan areas. With a survey instrument designed to fully consider the range of factors that might affect residential location — for example, housing type and tenure, lifecycle and lifestyle changes, previous neighborhood type – the influence of neighborhood design characteristics can be properly uncovered. Such a survey could also ask respondents to identify their neighborhood from a range of "types" and examine differences in perceived and actual neighborhood type.

Overall, the results hold a potentially important message for land-use and transportation policy. This research adds value to discussions that increasingly focus attention on preferences and the possible mitigating extent to which urban design alone can influence housing choice and/or travel behavior. One-half of households show stability in their preference for neighborhood type, suggesting less interest in other neighborhood designs. Alternatively, nearly half the respondents demonstrated willingness to change neighborhood types. If developers and policymakers can better identify the preferences of this population, they can develop a stronger idea of the market for different styles of neighborhood development, especially the ones that encourage the use of active transportation modes.

Satisfying this task through further study will help planners, policymakers and developers in two respects. It will help determine the neighborhood characteristics that households prize and neighborhoods that better satisfy people's preferences. In so doing it will also help moderate the demand for travel.

NOTES

1. The distance of 50km excludes international moves or those from or within Alaska and Hawaii.
2. Regional data would be necessary to include respondents who have former addresses outside Hennepin County.
3. Several outlying respondents are not shown for purposes of map clarity.
4. In general, employing factor then cluster analysis is a useful technique to classify many variables into a smaller set of meaningful groups.

5. Cluster analysis also balances spatial interpretation of the clusters.
6. Strong associations with some factors may lead to unexpected values in others. For instance, Urban Commercial Core neighborhoods are strongly associated with concentrations of retail and bus service, which may help explain the lower than unexpected value of the factor street design and land use (falsely suggesting low density and curvilinear streets).
7. If the 95 percent confidence interval contains the value of one, meaning the independent variable is not related with a change in odds of the dependent for a given household, then that variable is not a helpful predictor of the binary logistic model.
8. A cyclist is defined as a person who cycles at least once per week for recreation or maintenance activities. This information was gleaned from the survey.
9. The relationship is linear, though the squared distance from downtown (not included) would be nearly significant at the 90 percent level. Had the squared distance been significant, a likely explanation would be related to the concentration of cluster values. A respondent moving 3km from downtown is more likely to change neighborhood types than one moving 3km farther from Suburban Residential or Low Density Home Ownership.

REFERENCES

Adams, J.S. and Gilder, K.A. (1976), Household location and intra-urban migration, in D.T. Herbert, and R.J. Johnston (eds), *Social Areas in Cities, Volume 1: Spatial Processes and Form*, New York: John Wiley & Sons, pp. 159–92.

Badoe, D. and Miller, E. (2000), Transportation–land-use interaction: empirical findings in North America, and their implications for modeling, *Transportation Research Part D*, 5(4), pp. 235–63.

Bagley, M.N., Mokhtarian, P.L. and Kitamura, R. (2002), A methodology for the disaggregate, multidimensional measurement of residential neighborhood type, *Urban Studies*, 39, 689–704.

Bhat, C.R. and Guo, J.Y. (2007), A comprehensive analysis of built environment characteristics on household residential choice and auto ownership levels, *Transportation Research Part B: Methodological*, 41(5), 506–26.

Boehm, T.P. and Ihlanfeldt, K.R. (1986), Residential mobility and neighborhood quality, *Journal of Regional Science*, 26(2), 411–24.

Boehm, T.P., Herzog, H.W. and Schlottmann, A.M. (1991), Intra-urban mobility, migration and tenure choice, *The Review of Economics and Statistics*, 73(1), 59–68.

Coulton, C.J., Korbin, J., Chan, T. and Su, M. (2001), Mapping residents' perceptions of neighbourhood boundaries: a methodological note, *American Journal of Community Psychology*, 29(2), 371–83.

Crane, R. (2000), The influence of urban form on travel: an interpretative review, *Journal of Planning Education and Research*, 15(1), pp. 3–23.

Dieleman, F.M. (2001), Modeling residential mobility: a review of recent trends in research, *Journal of Housing and the Built Environment*, 16, 249–65.

Dillman, D.A. (2000), *Mail and Internet Surveys: The Tailored Design Method*, New York: John Wiley & Sons, Inc.

Ewing, R. and Cervero, R. (2010), Travel and the built environment: a meta-analysis, *Journal of the American Planning Association*, 76, 265–94.

Garson, G.D. (n.d.), *Statnotes: Topics in Multivariate Analysis*, www2.chass.ncsu.edu/garson/pa765/statnote.htm.

Geurs, K. and van Wee, B. (2004), Accessibility evaluation of land-use and transport strategies: review and research directions, *Journal of Transport Geography*, 12(2), pp. 127–40.

Greenwood, M.J. (1985), Human migration: theory, models and empirical studies, *Journal of Regional Science*, 25(4), 521–44.

Guest, A.M. and Lee, B.A. (1984), How urbanites define their neighbourhoods, *Population and Environment*, 7(1), 32–56.

Guo, J.Y. (2004), *Addressing Spatial Complexities in Residential Location Choice Models*, PhD dissertation, University of Texas.

Guo, J.Y. and Bhat, C.R. (2007), Operationalizing the concept of neighbourhood: application to residential location choice analysis, *Journal of Transport Geography*, 15(1), 31–45.

Kasarda, J.D., Appold, S.J., Sweeney, S.H. and Sieff, E. (1997), Central-city and suburban migration patterns: is a turnaround on the horizon? *Housing Policy Debate*, 8(2), 307–58.

Kendig, H. (1976), Cluster analysis to classify residential areas: a Los Angeles application, *Journal of the American Planning Association*, 42(3), 286–94.

Krizek, K.J. (2003), Operationalizing neighbourhood accessibility for land use-travel behaviour research and regional modeling, *Journal of Planning Education and Research*, **22**, 270–87.

Krizek, K.J. and Waddell, P. (2002), Analysis of lifestyle choices: neighbourhood type, travel patterns, and activity participation, *Transportation Research Record, Journal of the Transportation Research Board*, **1807**, 119–28.

Kulkarni, M. and Louis, G.P. (1994), Migration expectancy revisited: results for the 1970s, 1980s, and 1990s, *Population Research and Policy Review*, **13**, 195–202.

Long, L. (1973), New estimates of migration expectancy in the United States, *Journal of the American Statistical Association*, **68**(341), 37–43.

Long, L., Tucker, C.J. and Urton, W.L. (1988), Migration distances: an international comparison, *Demography*, **25**(4), 633–40.

Manson, G.A. and Groop, R.E. (2000), US intercounty migration in the 1990s: people and income move down the urban hierarchy, *Professional Geographer*, **52**(3), 493–504.

Molin, E. and Timmermans, H. (2003), *Accessibility Considerations in Residential Choice Decisions: Accumulated Evidence from the Benelux*, paper presented at the Annual Transportation Research Board Meeting, Washington, DC, www.ltrc.lsu.edu/TRB_82/TRB2003-000142.pdf.

Morrow-Jones, H.A., Irwin, E.G. and Roe, B. (2004), Consumer preference for neotraditional neighbourhood characteristics, *Housing Policy Debate*, **15**(1), 171–202.

Moudon, A.V., Hess, P.M., Snyder, M.C. and Staniov, K. (1997), Effects of site design on pedestrian travel in mixed use, medium-density environments, *Transportation Research Record*, **1578**, 48–55.

Parkes, A., Kearns, A. and Atkinson, R. (2002), What makes people dissatisfied with their neighbourhoods? *Urban Studies*, **39**(13), 2413–38.

Plane, D.A. and Heins, F. (2003), Age articulation of US inter-metropolitan migration flows, *The Annals of Regional Science*, 37, 107–30.

Regional Planning Agency Information and Research (2003), Inter-County Commuting Patterns and Migration Trends: Hamilton County, Chattanooga, TN: 22.

Ritchey, P.N. (1976), Explanations of migration, *Annual Review of Sociology*, **2**, 363–404.

Rossi, P.H. (1955), *Why Families Move: A Study in the Social Psychology of Urban Residential Mobility*, Glencoe, IL: Free Press.

Saelens, B. and Handy, S. (2008), Built Environment Correlates of Walking: A Review, *Medicine & Science in Sports & Exercise*, **40**, pp. S550–66.

Saelens, B.E., Sallis, J.F. and Frank, L.D. (2003), Environmental correlates of walking and cycling: findings from the transportation, urban design, and planning literatures, *Annals of Behavioral Medicine*, **25**(2), pp. 80–91.

Schachter, J. (2001), *Why People Move: Exploring the March 2000 Current Population Survey*, Washington, DC: US Census Bureau.

Schachter, J.P. and Kuenzi, J.J. (2002), *Seasonality of Moves and the Duration and Tenure of Residence: 1996*, Washington, DC: Population Division, US Census Bureau, www.census.gov/population/www/documentation/twps0069/twps0069.html.

Schwanen, T. and Mokhtarian, P.L. (2004), The extent and determinants of dissonance between actual and preferred residential neighbourhood type, *Environment and Planning B: Planning and Design*, **31**(5), 759–84.

Song, Y. and Knaap, G.-J. (2007), Quantitative classification of neighbourhoods: the neighbourhoods of new single-family homes in the Portland Metropolitan Area, *Journal of Urban Design*, **12**(1), 1–24.

South, S.J. and Crowder, K.D. (1997), Residential mobility between cities and suburbs: race, suburbanization, and back-to-the-city moves, *Demography*, **34**(4), 525–38.

Talen, E. (2001), Traditional urbanism meets residential affluence: an analysis of the variability of suburban preference, *Journal of the American Planning Association*, **67**(2), 199–216.

Transportation Research Board (2009), *Driving and the Built Environment: The Effects of Compact Development on Motorized Travel, Energy Use, and CO_2 Emissions*, Special Report 298, National Research Council of the National Academies, Washington, DC.

Van Wee, B. (2002), Land use and transport: research and policy challenges, *Journal of Transport Geography*, **10**(4), pp. 259–71.

Varady, D.P. (1993), Determinants of residential mobility decisions, *Journal of the American Planning Association*, **49**, 184–99.

Weisbrod, G., Ben-Akiva, M. and Lerman, S. (1980), Tradeoffs in Residential location decisions: transportation versus other factors, *Transportation Policy and Decision-Making*, **1**(1), 13–26.

Wilber, G.L. (1963), Migration expectancy in the United States, *Journal of the American Statistical Association*, **58**(302), 444–53.

Zondag, B. and Pieters, M. (2005), Influence of accessibility on residential location choice, *Transportation Research Record*, **1902**, 63–70.

13 Community design and active travel
Susan Handy

1. INTRODUCTION

Active travel modes – walking and cycling and other self-propelled modes used for transportation – are low-cost, low-polluting, low-carbon, calorie-burning, health-improving alternatives to driving. Recognizing these advantages, the World Health Organization in 2002 published a special report on active travel arguing that:

> Walking and cycling as part of daily activities should become a major pillar of the strategy to increase levels of physical activity as part of reducing the risk of coronary heart diseases, diabetes, hypertension, obesity and some forms of cancer. Increasing non-motorized transport will also reduce air and noise pollution and improve the quality of urban life.
>
> (Racioppi et al., 2002)

In some places, active modes are already a pillar of the transportation system. In the Netherlands and Denmark, walking and biking accounted for about 51 percent and 34 percent of daily trips as of 2008, respectively (Pucher and Buehler, 2010). In comparison, the share of daily trips by active modes in the United States was 12 percent, and the share of commute trips by active modes was less than 4 percent. Australia and Canada fared somewhat better, with active modes accounting for 6 percent and 12 percent of commute trips, respectively. Bringing these numbers closer to those of northern European would clearly yield considerable benefits in these countries.

Indeed, communities throughout the US are increasingly adopting strategies designed to support active travel. In the US, New York, Chicago and San Francisco are investing in bicycle infrastructure in hopes of matching the success of Portland, Oregon, where the number of cyclists crossing bridges into downtown increased by 369 percent from 1992 to 2008 (Pucher and Buehler, 2010). Even the city of Copenhagen is aggressively pushing to increase its already substantial 35 percent cycling mode share for commuting to 50 percent by 2015 (City of Copenhagen, 2010). Programs to increase walking as a mode of transportation are also increasingly common.

Although the most visible aspect of these efforts is investments in infrastructure – sidewalks, cycle tracks, off-street paths – it is widely recognized that their success depends on other aspects of the built environment as well. More generally, the design of the community influences both the feasibility and the desirability of active travel modes. This chapter offers a conceptual framework for understanding the link between community design and active travel, reviews the available evidence on the influence of community design on active travel, proposes a set of principles for measuring community design and concludes with an overview of strategies for achieving community designs that support active travel.

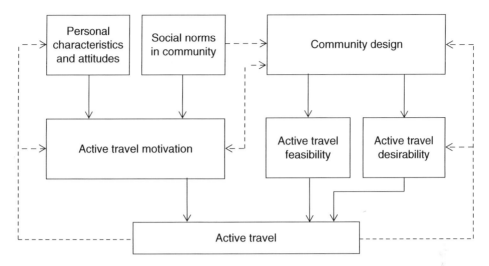

Figure 13.1   Conceptual framework

2.   CONCEPTUAL FRAMEWORK

Whether an individual chooses to walk or bicycle as a mode of transportation, when other options are available, depends on two critical factors (Figure 13.1): first, on whether he or she is motivated to walk, and second, on the degree to which the environment makes that choice both feasible and desirable (Handy, 1996, 2010).

The motivation to walk or bicycle for transportation depends on personal characteristics — ability, comfort, confidence, preferences, habits and perceptions. Individual motivation is also likely to be influenced by community norms, both the degree to which walking and cycling are seen as normal modes of transportation and whether an individual feels peer pressure to conform to predominant behavior. Without motivation, an individual is not likely to walk or cycle unless this is his or her only option.

For those who are motivated, community design may be the determining factor in their choice to walk or bicycle through its influence on both the feasibility and desirability of these modes. The quality of the environment for walking and cycling depends on several elements (Table 13.1). The functional elements of community design influence the feasibility of walking and bicycling: what activities are located where, referred to as land-use patterns, and how these locations are linked, given the configuration of the network. The aesthetic qualities of both locations and network links influence the desirability of walking and cycling. Aesthetic qualities depend on design details, including sidewalk widths, pavement textures, building setbacks, building materials and so forth. These physical details translate into perceptual urban design qualities, such as enclosure, human-scale, transparency, imageability, and complexity (Ewing and Handy, 2009). Finally, natural features, particularly weather, topography and vegetation, influence both the feasibility and desirability of walking and cycling.

The direct and indirect paths by which these factors influence active travel are important to consider. For example, land-use patterns and network configuration together

Table 13.1   Community design factors influencing active travel

Category	Element	Definition	Importance
Functional	Land-use pattern	The arrangement of land uses such as housing, shops, offices, etc., across the community	Determines the straight-line distance among different activities, such as housing, shopping, and offices Influences feasibility
	Network configuration	The layout of streets and trails throughout the community	Determines the actual distance based on how direct the connections from one place to another are Influences feasibility
Aesthetic	Design details	Characteristics of streets, including presence of sidewalks and bike lanes, widths, pavement conditions, crosswalks, signals, etc.	Influence how comfortable, safe, and attractive it is to walk or bicycle that route Contribute to urban design qualities Influence desirability
	Urban design qualities	Imageability, enclosure, human-scale, transparency, complexity, legibility, linkage, coherence	Influence how comfortable, safe, and attractive it is to walk or bicycle that route Influence desirability
Natural	Topography Weather Vegetation		Influence energy needed to walk or bicycle as well as comfort and enjoyment Influence feasibility and desirability

Source: Adapted from Handy (2010) and Ewing and Handy (2009)

determine travel distance from one place to another. Distance in turn determines the travel time and physical exertion required. The combination of the required time and physical exertion then influence how far most people are willing or able to walk or bicycle. Topography, too, influences the feasibility of walking and cycling by influencing the level of physical exertion required. In contrast, aesthetic qualities contribute to the sense of safety, comfort, and level of interest that active travelers feel (Ewing and Handy, 2009). These feelings then influence the desirability of walking.

Note that community design can also influence walking and cycling indirectly by influencing motivation. A desirable walking environment, for example, can increase enjoyment of and thus preference for walking over time. Over time, it is also possible that motivation influences community design, as when motivated community members push local officials to invest in bicycle infrastructure. The web of influences, direct and indirect, including feedback, is ultimately complex (Handy, 2005; Carlson et al., 2012).

Community design – its functional, aesthetic, and natural elements – matters more for active travel than for driving. Walking and cycling are more sensitive to small differences in distance than motorized modes: slower speeds mean that each additional increment of distance is a greater additional increment of time, and self-propulsion means that each additional increment of distance is a greater additional increment of physical exertion. Given their direct physical exposure to the environment, pedestrians and cyclists are also more sensitive to design details and urban design qualities and to the natural elements than are drivers. Community design is critical for making active travel both feasible and desirable.

Research, planning, and policy efforts often lump walking and cycling together as active travel modes, non-motorized modes or other labels. But cycling and cyclists are different from walking and walkers (Forsyth and Krizek, 2012). Walking has more "people potential" than cycling in that more people are able and willing to walk than bicycle, while many people do not know how to or are not comfortable cycling or do not own a bicycle (Handy, 2010). Cycling, on the other hand, has more "trip potential" than walking, given that its greater speed brings more destinations within reach within a given period of time. The different needs of pedestrians and cyclists are evident in studies of the influence of community design on active travel.

3.   EXISTING EVIDENCE

Evidence on the link between community design and active travel comes from both the travel behavior and physical activity fields. While the evidence is extensive for some pieces of the conceptual framework presented in the previous section, it is limited for others. Overall, the research on walking is far more extensive than the research on cycling.

Studies on walking for transportation consistently point to density, mixed land use, and distance to destinations as key elements of community design (Saelens and Handy, 2008; Forsyth and Krizek, 2010; Durand et al., 2011; Ewing and Cervero, 2010). The importance of these elements is not surprising, given the close relationships between them. Higher population densities support higher densities of commercial activity, which mean a greater mix of land uses within a given area, which in turn means shorter distances to potential destinations. In one study, for example, longer distances to specific land uses, such as banks, grocery stores and restaurants, contributed to less walking for transportation, while the intensities of specific land uses as well as overall land-use mix contributed to more walking (McConville et al., 2010). In another, the number of businesses in a neighborhood and the distances to businesses both influenced walking (Carlson et al., 2012).

Distance to destinations is also determined by network configuration, but evidence on the importance of this element is more mixed. Some studies but not all show that network connectivity is tied to walking (Saelens and Handy, 2008; Forsyth and Krizek, 2010; Ewing and Cervero 2010). One study, for example, found that street connectivity, measured as the number of intersections per square mile, was correlated with walking to destinations (Carlson et al., 2012). But another one found that block size, another measure of street connectivity, was not related to average miles of walking per day (Oakes et al., 2007).

Evidence on the influence of design details and urban design qualities is also not so clear or consistent (Saelens and Handy, 2008). The significance of density and land-use mix might in part reflect the association of these elements with design details that also support walking and cycling, for example, shorter building setbacks and wider side-walks. But sorting this out is difficult without direct evidence on each of these details. As with network configuration, some studies suggest that more and better quality sidewalks mean a higher likelihood of walking, but not all find a significant effect of sidewalks (Ewing and Cervero, 2010). A review of the evidence concluded that proximity to destinations and higher population densities matter more than infrastructure, at least for adults (Forsyth and Krizek (2010). Indeed, one study that looked at relatively modifiable attributes of community design found that parking difficulty was positively related to walking for transportation but sidewalks, walkways, trails were not (Rodriguez et al., 2008). Pedestrian amenities and aesthetics do not consistently emerge as important influences on walking (Lin and Moudon, 2010).

For cycling, distance to destinations is also a critical factor (Forsyth and Krizek, 2010; Handy et al., 2010; Handy and Xing, 2011). Like walking, cycling is correlated with population density and land-use mix, both of which influence distances (Cervero and Duncan, 2003; Stinson and Bhat, 2004; Kamphuis et al., 2008). At the same time, evidence suggests some willingness on the part of cyclists to take longer but safer routes (Dill, 2009; Parkin et al., 2007). Indeed, the availability and to some extent the quality of bicycle infrastructure, such as on-street bike lanes and off-street bike paths, also has a critical effect on bicycle use (Forsyth and Krizek, 2010). For US cities, the correlation between supply of facilities and the share of bicycle commuting is strong, though this may reflect bi-directional causality (Pucher and Buehler, 2012). Infrastructure appears to be more important for cycling than for walking (Forsyth and Krizek, 2010). Research on the importance of design details for bicyclists is limited, and the importance of separated versus on-street facilities remains a matter of debate.

Supportive community design is a necessary but not sufficient condition for walking and cycling. Studies of cycling, for example, show that comfort with cycling and liking to bicycle are key factors explaining who does and doesn't bicycle given good infrastructure (Handy et al. 2010; Handy and Xing, 2011). Not everyone travels actively, even in communities that are well designed for active travel. But it is also true that some people will travel actively even when conditions are only minimally supportive, simply because they have to. Thus, households with more mobility choices are more sensitive to the environment than those with fewer mobility choices (Manaugh and El-Geneidy, 2011).

Other evidence also suggests that elements of the built environment matter differently to different segments of the population, although maybe less so than one would expect. In one study, all demographic subgroups walked more for transportation in high density areas, suggesting a similar effect of the built environment on each (Forsyth et al., 2009). A review of the evidence on walking for transportation among older people found similar effects of community design as for adults more generally: results were similarly mixed with respect to the importance of sidewalks, less clear about the importance of density and land-use mix, but suggestive of a greater importance of crime-related safety (Van Cauwenberg et al., 2011). People with substantial mobility impairments are likely to need better infrastructure, such as wider and smoother sidewalks and better lighting (Forsyth and Krizek, 2010). Similarly, sidewalks are clearly important for children walking to school (Forsyth and Krizek, 2010), and distance may be even more important for them than it is for adults (Wong et al., 2011).

Evidence on the influence of community design on active travel is strong enough that the World Health Organization, the US Centers for Disease Control and Prevention and other global and national institutions advocate policies to improve community design. Still, there are notable limitations of the research so far. For example, while most studies examine a number of elements of community design, few have examined potential inter-actions between characteristics. It is likely, for one, that the quality of the environment interacts with actual distances to influence the distances that travelers perceive and thus their willingness to walk or bicycle; a nicer walk feels shorter than an unpleasant walk. Most importantly, the majority of studies employ cross-sectional designs, which cannot establish that changes in environment lead to changes in walking and cycling. A growing number of studies have given attention to the issue of self-selection, i.e., the possibility that those who are more inclined to walk or bicycle tend to live in places that are more conducive to walking and cycling. So far, studies that address this issue almost all show an effect of community design after accounting for self-selection (Cao et al., 2009).

4.   MEASURING COMMUNITY DESIGN

Some of the murkiness of the evidence on the influence of community design on active travel stems from differences in the ways that researchers measure different aspects of community design. A wide variety of techniques has been developed to measure com-munity design for the purposes of assessing walking and cycling conditions, including at least 19 survey instruments and 20 audit tools as of 2009 (Brownson et al., 2009). Some of these tools are useful for research aimed at understanding or predicting walking and cycling behavior. Others are more appropriate for use in planning practice; for example, to evaluate current conditions and to identify areas in need of improvements. Techniques used in research tend to produce more detailed measures of the environment than those used in practice, but several important considerations are common to both.

One important consideration is whether it is sufficient to rely on measures that can be derived from existing data. For example, the widespread use of measures of popula-tion density as an indicator of the pedestrian environment reflects the ease with which density measures can be derived from existing data, particularly when a large number of areas are included in the analysis or assessment. As noted earlier, however, the importance of density for walking and cycling is primarily its influence on distances to destinations. Thus, accessibility measures such as distance to the nearest store or the number of stores with a specified distance are a more direct indicator of the feasibility of walking or cycling than is density (Handy et al., 2006; Lee and Moudon, 2006). A second example is the common practice of relying on existing street network files when calculat-ing distances using geographic information systems (GIS). But these files generally do not include pedestrian and/or bicycle-only facilities. Short connections between streets, sometimes called "cut-throughs," can substantially reduce travel distances for pedes-trians and bicyclists (Tal and Handy, 2012). Similarly, pedestrians and bicyclists may be prohibited or prevented from using selected segments of the street network, thereby substantially increasing travel distances for these modes relative to driving.

If existing data are not sufficient for the purposes of the research or planning effort at hand, then two options remain: data collection through observation using an audit instrument of some sort, or data collection through the administration of a survey of residents or others who use or occupy the area of interest. In general, observational approaches produce what is considered objective data, while surveys produce what is considered subjective data. However, the lines between "objective" and "subjective" are not always clear. On one hand, observational data collection often involves subjective evaluations by those carrying out the audit; for example, the degree of variety in the design of buildings along a street segment. On the other, surveys often ask respondents to report on objective characteristics of the environment, for example, whether or not there is a sidewalk. Which approach is most appropriate for a particular study depends on the purpose of the study as well as practical considerations. Although theory would suggest that subjective measures are better predictors of active travel than objective measures, some studies show a stronger correlation for the latter (e.g., Lin and Moudon, 2010).

Most studies focus on measuring characteristics of residential environments, in other words, community design surrounding home locations. Because many trips start from home, these home-based measures are important. But not all trips do start from home, so a growing number of studies have examined the effect of community design around work locations (e.g., Handy and Xing, 2011). For example, having a restaurant or bank within walking distance of offices can increase the likelihood that employees will walk rather than drive during their lunch hour. A number of studies also look at the environment around schools (e.g., Boarnet et al., 2005). In addition, community design along the route between the origin and destination of the trip also influences whether an individual will choose to walk or bicycle (Lee and Moudon, 2006). Neighborhood-scale measures of community design may capture the entire environment relevant for walking, given the relatively short distance of these trips, but for cycling a different approach that captures the qualities of the environment for the entire length of the trip is more relevant. These measures can be objective, subjective or both.

Spatial scale is yet another consideration. Community design can be evaluated or measured at the building, street/block level, the neighborhood level, the district level or the regional level (Handy, 2005). At each spatial scale, different characteristics are more or less relevant for active travel, with design details generally measured at the smaller spatial scales, and functional characteristics measured at the larger spatial scales. Typical walking and bicycling distances can be used as a guide to determining the appropriate scale for measuring community design, but even regional-scale characteristics, such as the regional transit network, can influence the decision to walk or cycle.

Studies differ in their use of measures of specific community design characteristics or aggregate indices reflecting combinations of characteristics. Because specific elements of community design tend to cluster together, the latter approach may produce more robust statistical results. Examples include a walkability index that combines residential density, land-use mix and intersection density (a measure of network configuration) into one measure, used in several research studies (Frank et al., 2005), as well as various bicycle and pedestrian "level-of-service" measures, increasingly used in practice. Some studies classify communities into categories that reflect overall differences in community design, for example "high-walkable" and "low-walkable" communities, or distinguishing "bicycle-friendly" communities from those that aren't. The categorization approach can simplify analysis and account for synergistic effects between different elements of community design but provides little insight into the specific elements that are most important to walking and cycling.

Finally, the role of GIS should also be considered. The capabilities of GIS can be used to derive many different measures from the same raw data. For example, network files can be used to estimate distances, the density of roadways, the number of intersections in a given area, or the proportion of intersections of different types (e.g., four-way versus three-way). Although data on design details are increasingly available in publicly available datasets in GIS form, a thorough assessment of the active travel environment may still involve extensive observational data collection in the field. GIS is an effective tool for managing the voluminous data that are collected using audit instruments, which often use block-length street segments as the unit for which data are collected. Other technologies such geographic positioning systems (GPS) and smartphones are also expanding the possibilities for data collection, both through observation and through surveys. At the same time, new data sources are coming online that may reduce the need for audits. One study showed that Google Earth can be used to produce measures comparable to those derived from observational data, at least for the more readily observed design details (Clarke et al., 2010). As important a tool as GIS is, however, GIS-based measures "are only as useful as their data inputs and the conceptual frameworks that guide their development" (McKinnon et al., 2009).

5. CONCLUSIONS

With strong evidence of the influence of community design on active travel, the question becomes more practical: what policies, investments or mechanisms can communities use to create environments that are more supportive of walking and cycling? The answer to this question is not straightforward. Some aspects of the physical environment are influenced by policy, but others, like topography, are not. Of those that are, some can be changed quickly, others only over long periods of time. The most promising policies, investments or mechanisms are also likely to vary from community to community, depending on existing community design as well as the political, social and economic context of each.

For active travel, "the devil is in the details." To promote active travel, planners must pay attention to the minutiae of community design. The policies and standards that guide both public investments and private development determine the feasibility and desirability of active travel. First and foremost, pedestrians and bicyclists are highly sensitive to distance, and both land uses and street networks must be configured to bring destinations as close as possible. With respect to land use, policies that permit and encourage mixed-use development are critical, as are programs to bring new land uses into existing areas; for example, establishing retail businesses within residential areas. With respect to the network, communities should consider the strategic placement of "cut-throughs" as well as bridges and tunnels to reduce pedestrian and bicycle distances, and they should seek to eliminate physical barriers that increase distances. Some evidence supports the common assumption that the typical adult is willing to walk about 400m (Forsyth and Krizek, 2010), and this standard can serve as a guide to investment decisions. Pedestrians and cyclists are also sensitive, although to a lesser degree, to aesthetic qualities. Communities should thus focus on improvements to design details that increase the sense of safety and comfort that pedestrians and cyclists feel.

Communities can also benefit from regular assessments of the built environment. Such assessments can help to identify parts of the community where the pedestrian and cycling environments fall short of community standards and where new investments would provide the greatest benefit. To carry out such assessments, communities must select appropriate measures of community design and develop methods for either deriving these measures from existing data sources or collecting new data through audits or surveys. Although the measures currently in use vary widely, some standardization may occur as more and more communities turn their attention to encouraging active travel.

Despite the challenges, a growing number of cities have succeeded in increasing active travel. Their success comes from improvements to community design with respect to functional elements, both land-use patterns and network configuration, as well as to aesthetic qualities. But their success also comes from complementary "soft measures" such as social marketing campaigns, promotional and educational events, and restrictions on driving that help to increase the motivation to walk or bicycle (Pucher et al., 2010; Forsyth and Krizek, 2010). The experiences of these communities show that good community design is critical for enhancing both the feasibility and the desirability of active travel, and that when active travel is both feasible and desirable, it is possible to motivate more of the population on more occasions to travel actively.

REFERENCES

Boarnet M.G., Anderson, C.L., Day, K., McMillan, T. and Alfonzo, M. (2005), Evaluation of the California Safe Routes to School legislation: urban form changes and children's active transportation to school. *American Journal of Preventive Medicine*, **28**, 134–40.

Brownson, R.C., Hoehner, C.M., Day, K., Forsyth, A., and Sallis, J.F. (2009), Measuring the built environment for physical activity: state of the science, *American Journal of Preventive Medicine*, **36**(4S): S99–123.

Cao, X., Mokhtarian, P. and Handy, S. (2009), Examining the impacts of residential self-selection on travel behaviour: a focus on empirical findings, *Transport Reviews*, **29**(3), 359–95.

Carlson, C., Aytur, S. Gardner, K. and Rogers, S. (2012), Complexity in built environment, health, and destination walking: a neighborhood-scale analysis, *Journal of Urban Health*, **89**(2), 270–84.

Cervero, R. and Duncan, M. (2003), Walking, bicycling, and urban landscapes: evidence from the San Francisco Bay Area, *American Journal of Public Health*, **93**, 1478–83.

City of Copenhagen (2010), *Copenhagen City of Cyclists: Bicycle Account 2010*, www.sfbike.org/download/copenhagen/bicycle_account_2010.pdf.

Clarke, P., Ailshire, J., Melendez, R., Bader, M. and Morenoff, J. (2010), Using Google Earth to conduct a neighborhood audit: reliability of a virtual audit instrument, *Health and Place*, **16**, 1224–9.

Dill, J. (2009), Bicycling for transportation and health: the role of infrastructure, *Journal of Health Policy*, **30**, S95–110.

Durand, C.P., Andalib, M., Dunton, G.F., Wolch, J. and Pentz, M.A. (2011), A systematic review of built environment factors related to physical activity and obesity risk: implications for smart growth urban planning, *Obesity Reviews*, **12**(5), 173–82.

Ewing, R. and Handy, S. (2009), Measuring the unmeasurable: urban design qualities related to walkability, *Urban Design*, **14**(1), 65–84.

Ewing, R. and Cervero, R. (2010), Travel and the built environment: a meta-analysis, *Journal of the American Planning Association*, **76**(3), 265–94.

Forsyth, A. and Krizek, K. (2010), Promoting walking and bicycling: assessing the evidence to assist planners, *Built Environment*, **36**(4), 429–46.

Forsyth, A. and Krizek, K. (2012), Urban design: is there a distinctive view from the bicycle? *Journal of Urban Design*, **16**(4): 531–49.

Forsyth, A., Oakes, J.M., Lee, B. and Schmitz, K.H. (2009), The built environment, walking, and physical activity: is the environment more important to some people than others? *Transportation Research D*, **14**, 42–9.

Frank, L., Schmid, T., Sallis, J., Chapman, J. and Saelens, B. (2005), Linking objectively measured physical activity with objectively measured urban form: findings from SMARTRAQ, *American Journal of Preventive Medicine*, **28**, 117–25.

Handy, S. (1996), Urban form and pedestrian choices: a study of Austin neighborhoods, *Transportation Research Record*, **1552**, 135–44.

Handy, S. (2005), *Critical Assessment of the Literature on the Relationships Among Transportation, Land Use, and Physical Activity*, prepared for the Transportation Research Board and the Institute of Medicine Committee on Physical Activity, Health, Transportation, and Land Use as a resource paper for *Does the Built Environment Influence Physical Activity? Examining the Evidence – Special Report 282*, January.

Handy, S. (2010), Walking, bicycling, and health, in S. Malekafzali (ed.), *Healthy, Equitable Transportation Policy*, Oakland, CA: PolicyLink.

Handy, S. and Xing, Y. (2011), Factors correlated with bicycle commuting: a study of six small US cities, *International Journal of Sustainable Transportation*, **5**(2), 91–110.

Handy, S., Cao, X. and Mokhtarian, P.L. (2006), Does self-selection explain the relationship between built environment and walking behavior? Empirical evidence from Northern California, *Journal of the American Planning Association*, **72**(1), 55–74.

Handy, S., Xing, Y. and Buehler, T. (2010), Factors associated with bicycle ownership and use: a study of six small US cities, *Transportation*, **37**, 967–85.

Institute of Medicine (2009), *Local Government Actions to Prevent Childhood Obesity*, Washington, DC: The National Academies Press.

Kamphuis, C.B., Giskes, K., Kavanagh, A.M., Thornton, L.E., Thomas, L.R., van Lenthe, F.J., Mackenbach, J.P. and Turrell, G. (2008), Area variation in recreational cycling in Melbourne: a compositional or contextual effect? *Journal of Epidemiology and Community Health*, **62**, 890–8.

Lee, C. and Moudon, A.V. (2006), The 3Ds + R: quantifying land use and urban form correlates of walking, *Transportation Research D*, **11**, 204–15.

Lin, L. and Moudon, A.V. (2010), Objective versus subjective measures of the built environment, which are most effective in capturing associations with walking? *Health and Place*, **16**, 339–48.

Manaugh, K. and El-Geneidy, A. (2011), Validating walkability indices: how do different households respond to the walkability of their neighborhood? *Transportation Research D*, **16**, 309–15.

McConville, M.E., Rodriguez, D.A., Clifton, K., Cho, G. and Fleischhacker, S. (2010), Disaggregate land uses and walking, *American Journal of Preventive Medicine*, **40**(1), 25–32.

McKinnon, R.A., Reedy, J., Handy, S. and Rodgers, A.B. (2009), Measuring the food and physical activity environments: shaping the research agenda, *American Journal of Preventive Medicine*, **36**(43), S81–4.

Oakes, J.M., Forsyth, A. and Schmitz, K.H. (2007), The effects of neighborhood density and street connectivity on walking behavior: the Twin Cities walking study, *Epidemiologic Perspectives & Innovations*, **4**(16).

Parkin, J., Wardman, M. and Page, M. (2007), Models of perceived cycling risk and route acceptability, *Accident Analysis & Prevention*, **39**: 364–71.

Pucher, J. and Buehler, R. (2010), Walking and cycling for healthy cities, *Built Environment*, **36**(4), 391–414.

Pucher, J. and Buehler, R. (2012), Cycling to work in 90 large American cities: new evidence on the role of bike paths and lanes, *Transportation*, **29**: 409–32.

Pucher, J., Dill, J. and Handy, S. (2010), Infrastructure, programs, and policies to increase bicycling: an international review, *Preventive Medicine*, **50**, S106–25.

Racioppi, F., Dora, C., Krech, R. and von Ehrenstein, O. (2002), *A Physically Active Life through Everyday Transport with a Special Focus on Children and Older People and Examples and Approaches from Europe*, Copenhagen: World Health Organization Regional Office for Europe.

Rodriguez, D.A., Aytur, S., Forsyth, A., Oakes, J.M. and Clifton, K.J. (2008), Relation of modifiable neighborhood attributes to walking, *Preventive Medicine*, **47**, 260–4.

Saelens, B. and Handy, S. (2008), Built environment correlates of walking: a review, *Medicine & Science in Sports & Exercise*, **40**(7S), S550–66.

Stinson, M.A. and Bhat, C.R. (2004), Frequency of bicycle commuting: internet-based survey analysis, *Transportation Research Record*, **1878**, 122–30.

Tal, G. and Handy, S. (2012), Measuring non-motorized accessibility and connectivity in a robust pedestrian network, *Transportation Research Record*, **2299**, 48–56.

Van Cauwenberg, J., De Bourdeaudhuij, I., De Meester, F., Van Dyck, D., Salmon, J., Clarys, P. and Deforche, B. (2011), Relationship between the physical environment and physical activity in older adults: a systematic review, *Health and Place*, **17**, 458–69.

Wong, B.Y-M., Faulkner, G. and Buliung, R. (2011), GIS measured environmental correlates of active school transport: a systematic review of 14 studies, *International Journal of Behavioral Nutrition and Physical Activity*, **8**, 39.

14 Street networks
Wesley Marshall, Norman Garrick and Stephen Marshall

1. INTRODUCTION

The design and planning of street networks is a lost art in contemporary transportation studies. For much of the past 60 years, the focus in transportation has been on optimizing the performance of individual transportation links. However, this is beginning to change with a growing awareness of the important role that the overall street network plays for efficient and sustainable transportation performance as well as placemaking. This renewed awareness is reflected with an increasing attention of this subject by scholars in such fields as urban planning, geography, and, to a lesser extent, transportation engineering.

The emerging interest in street networks is not just limited to professionals – it is also spreading across the general population. For example, the story of the Manhattan street network was the subject of a major exhibition at the Museum of the City of New York in 2011 and 2012. This broad-based reawakening of the subject of street networks illustrates the larger point that street networks are not just about transportation; they influence almost all aspects of urban life. Academic research on this subject is beginning to support long-held beliefs by urban planners that a good street network is a necessary foundation for building strong and vital cities.

But this line of thinking also begs the question: what is a good street network? Cities around the world that are praised for having good street networks, in fact, come in many different configurations – ranging from the medieval patterns of cities like Prague and Florence, to the organic networks of Boston and London, and the planned grids of Washington DC and Savannah, Georgia. Based on the research done over the past decade, some answers are beginning to emerge about the key characteristics of great street networks. In this chapter, we will look at a set of studies on how the characteristics of street networks affect factors such as the amount of driving we do, the tendency to walk or bike, the safety of our communities, and the health outcomes of our populations.

2. A BRIEF OVERVIEW OF THE EVOLUTION OF THE STREET NETWORK

Starting from the earliest known existence of what has been described as a gridded street network pattern in the city of Mehenjo-Daro, New Delhi, from at least 2500 BC (Stanislawski, 1946), compact and connected street networks have seen a long and varied history. From the gridiron plans of the ancient Greeks and Romans to the organic, meandering, medieval patterns found across Europe and eventually in the New World, beliefs regarding the best configuration of streets upon which to build a city tended to evolve with the times. The Renaissance helped bring orthogonal, rectilinear networks back into vogue, and these same street network patterns also found their way into early US planning with cities such as New Haven and Philadelphia in the mid-1600s. The trend continued and eventually expanded to the suburban areas, particularly during the late 1800s and early 1900s in conjunction with the burgeoning use of streetcars.

Despite the network modifications over the years – and the ostensibly dissimilar patterns – the compact and connected nature of the networks endured as a common foundation. However, this dependable approach to assembling the bones of our transportation infrastructure underwent a major shift over the course of the twentieth century. In other words, the 1900s saw a complete overhaul in street network design from the way that we have built our cities and towns for the past few *thousand* years.

By 1915, most roads were now being designed with horses and carriages in mind, but by that time, more than two-thirds of all vehicles in the US were motorized (Hall and Turner, 1998). Roads were now being forced to accommodate road users unlike any others before. The Good Roads Movement in the US, which was originally founded by bicycle enthusiasts in the early 1880s, gained much momentum as interest in automobiles increased. This increased attention to automobiles, however, did not directly influence street network design, as most of the initial work focused more on issues such as paving and geometric design. The fundamental shift in street network design philosophies was likely unforeseen at the time because it was a product of a broad range of influences intended to solve other design issues.

Eventually, the traditional gridded street layouts gave way to a new paradigm of transportation design focused on vehicular mobility and a hierarchical approach to road typology. One example emerges from what is known as the functional classification system, which is the basis for current US design guidelines and have proliferated around the world. The functional classification system, as characterized by the American Association of State Highway and Transportation Officials (AASHTO), is intended to help engineers determine design criteria for a particular roadway though a categorization of that proposed roadway by type. Two factors comprise this organizational structure: facility type and land use. The combination of the two supposedly indicates the level of mobility or accessibility one would expect on the road. The basic facility types include: highways, arterials, collectors, and local roads; which are found in one of two land use types: urban and rural. The goal of providing a straightforward methodology for roadway classification and, in turn, design criteria for that roadway is an admirable one. However, this approach in practice tends to generate a systematic bias toward tree-like street network designs because of the way that the system encourages the channelization of vehicle trips from the arterial highways to the collector roads and then finally to the local roads.

Other influences – such as those related to the coding of these cities as well as the approach to the financing of them – also played a role in helping push street networks toward, not just more dendritic design morphologies, but sparser networks as well (Southworth and Ben-Joseph, 1997; Ben-Joseph, 2005; Talen, 2012). Figure 14.1 illustrates this transition from more compact and connected networks to less street connectivity as well as less street network density, which was commonplace not just in the US but around the world.

While our collective thinking on street networks continues to evolve, the last decade has finally seen an influx of academic research – on topics ranging from vehicle miles

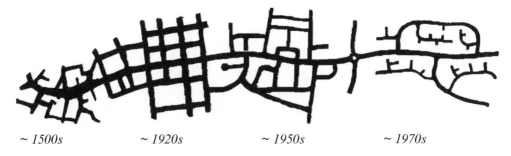

~ *1500s*   ~ *1920s*   ~ *1950s*   ~ *1970s*

Source: Adapted from Marshall (2005)

Figure 14.1   Evolution of street patterns

traveled and active transportation to those related to road safety and broader health outcomes. In this chapter we will explore our own strand of research that has taken an in-depth look into these issues and their relationships with street network design.

3.   OVERVIEW OF RESEARCH STRAND

The goals of the research that will be highlighted in this chapter were to explore the complex relationships between street network design and key indicators of sustainability such as mode choice and road safety. The work was based on an extensive dataset collected for 24 California cities with populations ranging from 30,000 residents to just over 100,000. California is the most populous US state and home to one out of every eight Americans. In terms of area, it is the third largest state and located along the Pacific Ocean on the western coast of the US. The cities are all from a single US state because we wanted to ensure that the data, especially for traffic safety, was collected on a relatively consistent basis.

The street network aspects of community design became a central focus for this research after we observed a noteworthy relationship between the year of incorporation of a city and road safety outcomes. In the initial dataset of more than 150 California cities, many of the post-1950s cities were experiencing significantly higher fatality rates. Since the 1950s represented a transition period in the US when typical street network design shifted from a highly connected gridded system into a sparser, more dendritic arrangement, the concept that differences related to the street network might play a role in these outcomes started to take shape. With so many California cities having been founded both before and after this street network transition period, this single state presented us with a good opportunity to study these issues.

The following cities were selected from the overall database of more than 150 California cities to best represent a geographically diverse collection of 12 medium-sized cities with good safety records and 12 with poor safety records:

Safer cities   Less safe cities
Alameda   Antioch

Berkeley	Apple Valley
Chico	Carlsbad
Cupertino	Madera
Danville	Morgan Hill
Davis	Perris
La Habra	Redding
Palo Alto	Rialto
San Luis Obispor	Temecula
San Mateo	Turlock
Santa Barbara	Victorville
Santa Cruz	West Sacramento

Street network measures – including measures of street network density, street connectivity, and street patterns – were combined with street design characteristics, travel behavior data from the Census as well as the American Community Survey, the California Health Interview Survey, socio-economic data, traffic flow information, and more than 230,000 individual crash records from 11 years of crash data. This information was geo-coded in a GIS database in order to conduct a comprehensive spatial analysis. The spatial analysis was performed primarily at the Census block group level of geography. According to the US Census, a Census block group is intended to average 250 to 500 housing units and to vary in area depending on housing density. The results in this study are based on more than 1,000 block groups at an average of approximately 43.5 in each of our 24 cities.

One additional item of interest that we developed was an estimate of when various parts of the road network were built. Adapted from a methodology by James Spero of the California Fire and Resource Assessment Program for the purposes of assessing fire protection risk and Tim Duane of UC Berkeley to assess the historic levels and spatial distribution of human settlement in the Sierra Nevada region, we estimated the road network development decade of our cities (Duane, 1996; Office of Environmental Health Hazard Assessment, 2002). Using the "Year Structure Built" on the Census long form, we were able to tally the approximate percentage of housing units built by decade. Figure 14.2 depicts the breakdown of development for Davis, California, which typifies the many cities built around an older downtown with a compact and connected gridded network that were expanded upon with more contemporary, dendritic networks.

Trying to better understand the evolution of the street network led us in the direction of needing to figure out a way to better measure such differences. While many factions now point to both increased network density and connectivity as desirable, few successfully differentiate between these two mutually exclusive, but often related, qualities with quantifiable measures. In some cases, such measures were mistakenly used interchangeably (Marshall and Garrick, 2012). And in most cases, actual pattern types were ignored altogether. So in order to best characterize street network differences, we focused on creating a straightforward set of proxy measures for the three fundamental street network items of interest:

1. Street connectivity
2. Street network density
3. Street configuration

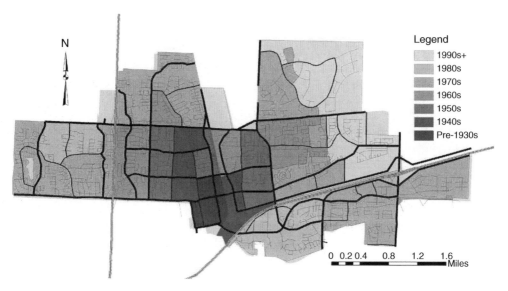

Figure 14.2   Approximate street network year of development for Davis, California

While there are abundant indices, ranging from very simple to overly complex, available to measure both connectivity and network density, our repeated statistical analyses using greedy maximization helped us settle on the link to node ratio for street connectivity and intersection density for street network density. The link to node ratio divides the total number of links (i.e., road segments between intersections) by the total number of nodes (i.e., intersections) (Ewing, 1996; Litman, 2005). Most researchers and practitioners use a score of 1.4 as the threshold of high connectivity with higher values indicating better connectivity (Handy et al., 2003). Intersection density tallies the total number of nodes or intersections, including dead ends, and divides it by the area. Higher values signify higher network densities.

Measures such as the link to node ratio and intersection density are not uncommon; however, neither measure begins to impart any sense of configuration. Consequently, we adapted a chart from Stephen Marshall's book *Streets and Patterns* that emphasizes the macro-level street network structure, or citywide network in our own vernacular, separately from the micro-level street network, which we labeled the "neighborhood network" (Marshall, 2005). Figure 14.3 depicts the adaptation of Marshall's scheme. While arterial and collector roads based upon the functional classification system generally differ from local roads in terms of various elements such as the number of lanes, lane widths, and traffic volumes, the macro-level network in this classification scheme focuses more on the role of the street with respect to network structure. This differentiation between functional classification and network structure allows us to better convey some of the complexities that distinguish street networks and communities in general. This includes the difference between neighborhood and citywide connectivity and the relative densities and connectivities of those elements.

Although Marshall's chart cross-classifying four citywide categories and two neighborhood categories does not accommodate every possible pattern, it does establish a

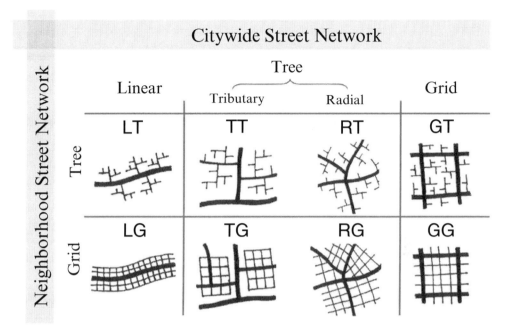

Source: Adapted from Marshall (2005)

Figure 14.3   Street configuration classifications

straightforward visual classification system that can help differentiate between the most common configuration types. Applying the scheme is fairly simple and intuitive, beginning with the selection of citywide streets that are generally continuous across a substantial portion of the city. Understanding the role of the macro-level streets in the network helps facilitate the classification of each block group into one of the eight representative configuration types. Actual city patterns are generally more complex than the representative configurations; so while actual street networks were not always exact replicas of the representative diagrams, there were only a handful of the more than 1,000 block groups that were not able to be confidently classified.

Combining the street network density and connectivity measures described earlier with configuration types results in a more complete understanding of street networks than can conventionally be achieved using functional classification. The next section describes the association of street networks with travel behavior outcomes such as the amount of driving we do and the relative amount of utilitarian active transportation, followed by our results in terms of road safety outcomes and human health.

Street Networks and Driving

From the time motor vehicles became a common fixture on our roads up until the economic downturn, vehicles miles traveled (VMT) has consistently increased at an extraordinary rate. More specifically in the US, VMT has outpaced population growth

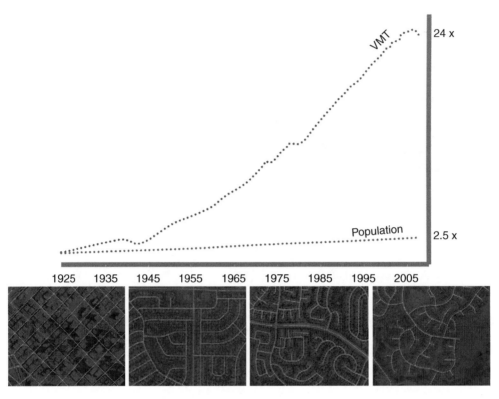

Source: VMT data derived from FHWA and Moeller (1992)

*Figure 14.4   VMT and population (1925–2008) with respect to the evolution of street
           networks in the US*

by a factor of nearly ten to one over the course of the last century. Figure 14.4 illustrates
the relative increases in VMT and population growth since 1925 in conjunction with the
representative street network design common in each time period.

Common sense dictates that the amount of driving people continue to do on a day-
to-day basis is likely related to many factors beyond street network design. One key,
therefore, with this first study was to account for potentially confounding factors such as
income, the degree of mixed land uses, the distance from the city center, and whether or
not one lives near a limited access highway. We also took into consideration differences
in street designs – such as the total number of lanes, and the presence of features such as
sidewalks, bike lanes, on-street parking, shoulders, and medians – in order to help truly
discern the connection to the street network design.

The premise that people living in compact and more connected street networks drive
less was then put to the test. Table 14.1 graphically depicts the results of the statistical
analysis in a way where all variables are held constant at the mean for the dataset so
that we can begin to understand the influence of each factor individually. For instance,
the first image suggests that people tend to drive about 21 miles per day when they live
a half-mile from the city center, which increases to 24 miles per day when they live five

Table 14.1 Expected change in VMT by street network type

	TT		RT		GT		TG		RG		GG		Average VMT	
Base VMT per person (≥18) per day by Street Network Configuration (mi):	22.72		24.99		22.25		20.55		19.56		19.19		21.31	
Intersection Density (i.e. Street Network Density)														
81 int/mi²	24.66	8.56%	26.61	6.49%	24.85	11.73%	25.33	23.25%	26.43	35.10%	27.78	44.79%	25.95	21.76%
144 int/mi²	22.59	-0.57%	24.53	-1.84%	22.78	2.40%	23.26	13.15%	24.35	24.46%	24.84	29.47%	23.72	11.34%
225 int/mi²	19.91	-12.36%	21.86	-12.53%	20.10	-9.64%	20.59	0.15%	21.67	10.80%	21.06	9.78%	20.87	-2.08%
324 int/mi²	16.65	-26.72%	18.59	-25.61%	16.84	-24.30%	17.32	-15.75%	18.41	-5.91%	16.45	-14.25%	17.38	-18.46%
Link to Node Ratio (i.e. Street Connectivity)														
1.1	22.48	-1.04%	24.60	-1.57%	21.62	-2.82%	19.62	-4.53%	18.32	-6.32%	17.78	-7.32%	20.74	-2.67%
1.25	23.17	2.00%	25.29	1.19%	22.31	0.37%	20.20	-1.72%	19.01	-2.80%	18.48	-3.69%	21.41	0.49%
1.4	23.87	5.06%	25.99	3.98%	23.00	3.41%	20.78	1.12%	19.71	0.76%	19.17	-0.10%	22.09	3.65%
1.55	24.56	8.12%	26.68	6.76%	23.70	6.54%	21.36	3.93%	20.41	4.32%	19.87	3.53%	22.76	6.83%
Curvilinear Street Network (0, 1)														
0	22.41	-1.34%	24.38	-2.46%	22.16	-0.39%	20.47	-0.39%	19.52	-0.22%	19.19	0.00%	21.35	0.22%
1	23.51	3.50%	25.47	1.91%	23.25	4.53%	21.57	4.93%	20.62	5.40%	20.29	5.73%	22.45	5.36%
Avg. No. of Lanes on Citywide Streets														
2	20.57	-9.44%	21.46	-14.12%	19.16	-13.85%	18.31	-10.91%	18.74	-4.19%	17.21	-10.30%	19.24	-9.69%
4	25.54	12.45%	26.44	5.79%	24.14	8.52%	23.29	13.30%	21.77	11.28%	22.18	15.61%	23.89	12.13%
6	30.52	34.35%	31.41	25.68%	29.11	30.87%	28.26	37.48%	24.80	26.78%	27.15	41.52%	28.54	33.95%
Block Group Distance from City Center														
0.5 mi.	21.89	-3.64%	23.38	-6.44%	21.59	-2.96%	20.16	-1.90%	19.11	-2.32%	18.96	-1.17%	20.85	-2.15%
2.0 mi.	22.69	-0.14%	24.18	-3.23%	22.38	0.61%	20.97	2.00%	19.90	1.75%	19.76	2.98%	21.65	1.59%
3.5 mi.	23.49	3.39%	24.98	-0.05%	23.18	4.19%	21.76	5.86%	20.70	5.84%	20.55	7.12%	22.44	5.33%
5.0 mi.	24.28	6.89%	25.77	3.13%	23.97	7.77%	22.56	9.73%	21.50	9.91%	21.36	11.30%	23.24	9.07%
Degree of Mixed Land Use														
Low (0.3)	23.63	4.02%	25.79	3.21%	22.95	3.18%	21.38	3.99%	20.42	4.42%	20.11	4.79%	22.38	5.03%
Medium (0.4)	23.05	1.46%	25.22	0.92%	22.38	0.61%	20.80	1.21%	19.85	1.49%	19.54	1.81%	21.81	2.35%
High (0.5)	22.48	-1.04%	24.65	-1.37%	21.81	-1.96%	20.23	-1.57%	19.28	-1.43%	18.96	-1.20%	21.24	-0.34%
Bisecting or Adjacent to Limited Access Highway (0, 1)														
0	22.30	-1.83%	24.70	-1.17%	21.98	-1.20%	20.15	-1.96%	19.37	-0.95%	18.97	-1.13%	21.25	-0.29%
1	23.52	3.53%	25.92	3.70%	23.20	4.27%	21.37	3.96%	20.59	5.27%	20.19	5.21%	22.46	5.42%
% of Citywide Street Length with On-Street Parking														
0%	22.95	1.04%	25.17	0.72%	22.54	1.34%	20.87	1.54%	20.02	2.35%	19.69	2.62%	21.88	2.66%
50%	22.65	-0.30%	24.86	-0.52%	22.23	-0.06%	20.56	0.03%	19.71	0.76%	19.38	1.00%	21.57	1.21%
100%	22.34	-1.67%	24.55	-1.77%	21.93	-1.42%	20.26	-1.45%	19.40	-0.83%	19.07	-0.62%	21.26	-0.24%

Source: Marshall and Garrick (2012)

215

miles from the nearest city center. With all other factors held constant, this result makes sense intuitively. Moving on to our street network variables, we see that that increased street network density seems to play a much larger role in lower driving outcomes than increasing street connectivity. In fact, increased street connectivity was actually associated with an increased amount of driving. However, when we look deeper into the results and consider configuration – as well as how these various patterns have been built in practice – the results suggest that the gridded networks result in reduced driving. These results have also been found, typically at larger levels of geography, by other researchers (Ewing and Cervero, 2010; Marshall and Garrick, 2012).

It is important to consider that even relatively small individual VMT reductions are promising, especially when averaged for the full population over a longer period of time. Take for example the reduction of a single mile per person per day for a city with a population of 60,000, which is approximately the average size for the cities in our study, The reduction of a single mile per person per day would result in 21.9 million fewer miles driven each year. In turn, a reduction in driving by a single mile per person per day would save well over one million gallons of gasoline annually, which could keep over 20 million pounds of CO_2 from being emitted into the atmosphere each year in a single city. Using EPA guidelines for calculating emissions, this is the equivalent of taking more than 1,000 cars off the road for a full year (EPA, 2011).

Street Networks and Active Transportation

Less driving is one thing, but a related question has to do with whether people are actually substituting more active modes of transportation for this drop in automobile usage — or are the shorter trips sometimes found in a more compact street network the root of this reduction in driving? In other words, compact and connected street network designs have long been known to provide greater accessibility through more direct routes as well as increase overall network efficiency and reliability, in part through the added redundancy (Kulash, 1990; Southworth and Ben-Joseph, 1997; Handy et al., 2003; Marshall, 2005); however, do residents of more compact communities simply drive fewer miles or do they also walk and bike more?

This inquiry was designed to learn more about how street networks influence the diversity of modes in a transportation system, and what we found was that all three of the fundamental measures of a street network – street connectivity, street network density, and street patterns – are highly significant and associated with influencing the choice to walk or bike to work. Similarly to the driving study, we controlled for a range of factors including vehicle volumes, activity levels, income levels, and proximity to limited access highways or the downtown area. Fundamentally, both increased street connectivity and street network density were associated with more walking and biking. Since street pattern configurations were also significant across the board, along with a number of interaction terms, the roles of the various street network measures were difficult to interpret individually.

At a basic level, we found that the denser and more connected places resulted in four times more walking and biking. However, the most interesting results turned out to be layered in the variable order of magnitudes of the effect of street connectivity and street network density measures for the different street configuration. For example, Table 14.2

depicts the differing influence of increased intersection density in the fully gridded network versus that in the completely tree-like network (Marshall and Garrick, 2010a). Holding all other variables at their mean, we find that increasing network density has a much bigger association with more active transportation, especially walking, in the fully gridded network than in the tree-like network. In other words, no matter what the street network density is, it is difficult to fully achieve some of the active transportation benefits that we might be looking for in a hierarchical, dendritic street network.

Delving a bit deeper into some of the more interesting results, Table 14.2 also illustrates average mode share for each of the six most common pattern types. Here, we can really begin to see the interesting roles of citywide versus neighborhood connectivity. For example when comparing the fully gridded configuration type to the pattern with a gridded neighborhood pattern combined with the tree-like citywide pattern, we found that the fully gridded network has a much lower driving mode share and higher walking and biking mode shares.

Street Networks and Road Safety

In terms of mode choice, the street pattern outcomes indicated that the dense, gridded street networks with more urban street features were associated with much more walking and biking. Conventional thinking about road safety would suggest that the outcome of lower road fatality rates with more pedestrians and bicyclists would be unlikely since, in general, active transportation modes experience a much higher fatality rate per mile traveled than do drivers in the US (Pucher and Dijkstra, 2000). Take for example the alternative case of substituting transit for driving. Transit is considered one of the safest forms of transportation on a per-mile basis; thus, these former drivers would now have reduced fatality risk. Fittingly, a city with high transit use should be safer than a city with a high mode share for driving. On the other hand, cities with high levels of walking and/or biking should, in theory, be riskier places. The problem with this theory is that the numbers do little to support it; on the contrary, the very places with these high levels of walking and biking are also turning out to be safer places to live. Our models suggested that the denser and more compact places not only resulted in four times more walking and biking, but we also found a population three times less likely to be involved in a fatal crash (Marshall and Garrick, 2010b).

In terms of the fundamental elements of street network design, high intersection density turned out to have the strongest association with fewer crashes across all severity levels. It is also interesting to note that increasing intersection density from an average to high value, while holding all other variables at their mean, was associated with an expected 30 percent drop in total crashes but with more than a 70 percent decrease in fatal crashes. In other words, the effect of increased intersection density was much more pronounced for fatalities than for less severe injuries. This suggests that one factor at work might be lower vehicle speeds on the street networks with higher intersection densities and denser, more urban environments.

Conversely, we found that increased street connectivity is associated with an increase in all types of crashes. The negative effect of the link to node ratio may be due to increased traffic conflicts associated with more connectivity; however, it is important to keep in mind that the places in our study with highly connected street networks tended

Table 14.2   Expected change in mode share by street network type

	TT				RT				GT			
	Transit	Walking	Biking	Driving	Transit	Walking	Biking	Driving	Transit	Walking	Biking	Driving
Avg. Mode Share by Street Pattern Type	**3.66%**	**2.28%**	**1.71%**	**92.35%**	**1.80%**	**0.95%**	**0.54%**	**96.71%**	**2.35%**	**2.01%**	**0.98%**	**94.66%**
Intersection Density (i.e. Street Network Density)												
81	3.81%	1.94%	1.29%	92.96%	1.80%	0.82%	0.38%	97.00%	2.49%	1.65%	0.65%	95.21%
144	3.65%	2.30%	1.74%	92.31%	1.80%	0.99%	0.60%	96.62%	2.38%	1.93%	0.90%	94.79%
225	3.44%	2.85%	2.56%	91.15%	1.79%	1.25%	1.05%	95.91%	2.24%	2.36%	1.37%	94.03%
324	3.18%	3.69%	4.06%	89.07%	1.76%	1.66%	2.10%	94.47%	2.07%	3.00%	2.29%	92.65%
Link to Node Ratio (i.e. Street Connectivity)												
1.1	3.42%	2.40%	1.74%	92.44%	1.60%	1.05%	0.62%	96.74%	1.88%	1.96%	1.04%	95.12%
1.25	4.17%	2.05%	1.65%	92.13%	1.97%	0.88%	0.48%	96.67%	2.41%	2.02%	0.97%	94.60%
1.4	5.06%	1.75%	1.55%	91.63%	2.43%	0.74%	0.38%	96.46%	3.08%	2.08%	0.90%	93.94%
1.55	6.14%	1.50%	1.46%	90.91%	2.99%	0.62%	0.29%	96.10%	3.93%	2.13%	0.84%	93.10%
Avg. No. of Lanes on Citywide Streets												
2	4.48%	2.34%	1.72%	91.46%	2.33%	0.90%	0.80%	95.97%	3.44%	2.01%	1.19%	93.36%
4	2.80%	2.19%	1.68%	93.32%	1.62%	0.97%	0.46%	96.96%	1.86%	2.01%	0.86%	95.27%
6	1.74%	2.05%	1.63%	94.58%	1.12%	1.04%	0.26%	97.58%	1.00%	1.99%	0.62%	96.40%
Block Group Distance from City Center												
0.0 mi.	3.30%	4.03%	3.18%	89.49%	1.55%	2.59%	1.61%	94.24%	2.17%	3.29%	1.67%	92.86%
1.0 mi.	3.48%	3.06%	2.36%	91.11%	1.62%	1.96%	1.19%	95.24%	2.28%	2.49%	1.23%	94.01%
2.0 mi.	3.65%	2.31%	1.74%	92.30%	1.69%	1.47%	0.87%	95.97%	2.38%	1.87%	0.90%	94.85%
3.0 mi.	3.82%	1.74%	1.27%	93.17%	1.76%	1.10%	0.64%	96.50%	2.48%	1.40%	0.66%	95.45%
4.0 mi.	3.98%	1.31%	0.93%	93.78%	1.83%	0.82%	0.46%	96.88%	2.58%	1.05%	0.48%	95.88%
Degree of Mixed-Use Use												
Low (0.3)	0.54%	0.53%	0.15%	98.77%	0.32%	0.26%	0.06%	99.36%	0.53%	0.64%	0.15%	98.68%
Medium (0.4)	1.82%	1.35%	0.71%	96.12%	1.10%	0.65%	0.29%	97.96%	1.77%	1.62%	0.68%	95.93%
High (0.5)	5.77%	3.19%	3.06%	87.98%	3.63%	1.61%	1.31%	93.45%	5.60%	3.84%	2.94%	87.62%
Bisecting or Adjacent to Limited Access Highway (0, 1)												
0	3.99%	2.36%	1.86%	91.79%	1.92%	0.97%	0.57%	96.54%	2.49%	2.06%	1.03%	94.41%
1	3.09%	2.12%	1.45%	93.34%	1.47%	0.87%	0.44%	97.22%	1.92%	1.84%	0.80%	95.44%
% of Citywide Street Length with On-Street Parking												
0%	3.24%	2.10%	1.44%	93.22%	1.63%	0.89%	0.47%	97.01%	2.01%	1.81%	0.79%	95.39%
50%	3.79%	2.33%	1.79%	92.08%	1.93%	0.99%	0.59%	96.49%	2.37%	2.02%	0.99%	94.63%
100%	4.43%	2.59%	2.23%	90.75%	2.27%	1.11%	0.74%	95.88%	2.78%	2.25%	1.23%	93.74%
% of Citywide Street Length with Bike Lanes												
0%	3.61%	2.15%	1.42%	92.81%	1.76%	0.88%	0.42%	96.93%	2.33%	1.93%	0.85%	94.90%
50%	3.69%	2.36%	1.92%	92.03%	1.81%	0.97%	0.58%	96.64%	2.38%	2.11%	1.15%	94.35%
100%	3.76%	2.58%	2.59%	91.07%	1.86%	1.07%	0.79%	96.29%	2.44%	2.32%	1.56%	93.68%
% of Citywide Street Length with Curbs												
0%	2.97%	1.48%	1.73%	93.82%	1.45%	0.61%	0.54%	97.40%	1.89%	1.27%	0.98%	95.86%
50%	3.39%	1.94%	1.72%	92.95%	1.66%	0.81%	0.54%	96.99%	2.15%	1.68%	0.98%	95.19%
100%	3.86%	2.54%	1.70%	91.90%	1.90%	1.06%	0.54%	96.50%	2.46%	2.20%	0.98%	94.36%
% of Citywide Street Length with Raised Medians												
0%	3.46%	2.51%	1.45%	92.59%	1.68%	1.06%	0.44%	96.82%	2.22%	2.21%	0.82%	94.74%
50%	3.65%	2.29%	1.69%	92.37%	1.77%	0.97%	0.51%	96.74%	2.34%	2.03%	0.96%	94.67%
100%	3.84%	2.10%	1.97%	92.09%	1.87%	0.89%	0.60%	96.64%	2.47%	1.86%	1.12%	94.55%
% of Citywide Street Length with Painted Medians												
0%	3.91%	2.52%	1.92%	91.65%	1.91%	1.04%	0.60%	96.44%	2.54%	2.26%	1.12%	94.09%
50%	3.66%	2.27%	1.71%	92.36%	1.78%	0.94%	0.53%	96.75%	2.37%	2.03%	0.99%	94.61%
100%	3.42%	2.05%	1.51%	93.02%	1.66%	0.84%	0.47%	97.03%	2.21%	1.83%	0.87%	95.09%

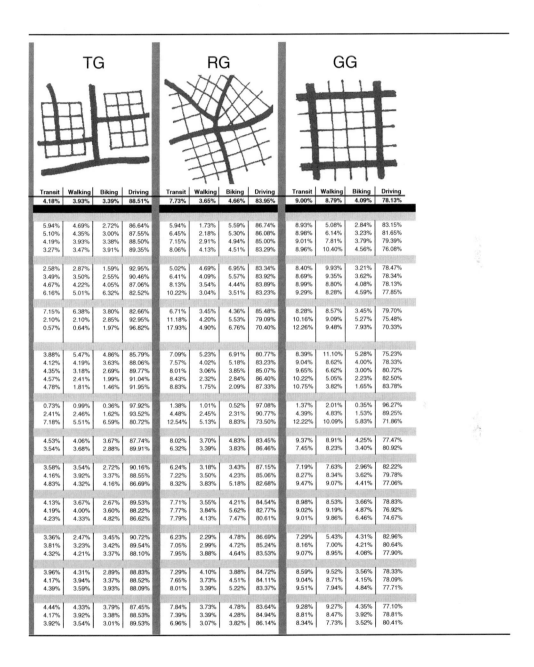

TG				RG				GG			
Transit	Walking	Biking	Driving	Transit	Walking	Biking	Driving	Transit	Walking	Biking	Driving
4.18%	**3.93%**	**3.39%**	**88.51%**	**7.73%**	**3.65%**	**4.66%**	**83.95%**	**9.00%**	**8.79%**	**4.09%**	**78.13%**
5.94%	4.69%	2.72%	86.64%	5.94%	1.73%	5.59%	86.74%	8.93%	5.08%	2.84%	83.15%
5.10%	4.35%	3.00%	87.55%	6.45%	2.18%	5.30%	86.08%	8.98%	6.14%	3.23%	81.65%
4.19%	3.93%	3.38%	88.50%	7.15%	2.91%	4.94%	85.00%	9.01%	7.81%	3.79%	79.39%
3.27%	3.47%	3.91%	89.35%	8.06%	4.13%	4.51%	83.29%	8.96%	10.40%	4.56%	76.08%
2.58%	2.87%	1.59%	92.95%	5.02%	4.69%	6.95%	83.34%	8.40%	9.93%	3.21%	78.47%
3.49%	3.50%	2.55%	90.46%	6.41%	4.09%	5.57%	83.92%	8.69%	9.35%	3.62%	78.34%
4.67%	4.22%	4.05%	87.06%	8.13%	3.54%	4.44%	83.89%	8.99%	8.80%	4.08%	78.13%
6.16%	5.01%	6.32%	82.52%	10.22%	3.04%	3.51%	83.23%	9.29%	8.28%	4.59%	77.85%
7.15%	6.38%	3.80%	82.66%	6.71%	3.45%	4.36%	85.48%	8.28%	8.57%	3.45%	79.70%
2.10%	2.10%	2.85%	92.95%	11.18%	4.20%	5.53%	79.09%	10.16%	9.09%	5.27%	75.48%
0.57%	0.64%	1.97%	96.82%	17.93%	4.90%	6.76%	70.40%	12.26%	9.48%	7.93%	70.33%
3.88%	5.47%	4.86%	85.79%	7.09%	5.23%	6.91%	80.77%	8.39%	11.10%	5.28%	75.23%
4.12%	4.19%	3.63%	88.06%	7.57%	4.02%	5.18%	83.23%	9.04%	8.62%	4.00%	78.33%
4.35%	3.18%	2.69%	89.77%	8.01%	3.06%	3.85%	85.07%	9.65%	6.62%	3.00%	80.72%
4.57%	2.41%	1.99%	91.04%	8.43%	2.32%	2.84%	86.40%	10.22%	5.05%	2.23%	82.50%
4.78%	1.81%	1.46%	91.95%	8.83%	1.75%	2.09%	87.33%	10.75%	3.82%	1.65%	83.78%
0.73%	0.99%	0.36%	97.92%	1.38%	1.01%	0.52%	97.08%	1.37%	2.01%	0.35%	96.27%
2.41%	2.46%	1.62%	93.52%	4.48%	2.45%	2.31%	90.77%	4.39%	4.83%	1.53%	89.25%
7.18%	5.51%	6.59%	80.72%	12.54%	5.13%	8.83%	73.50%	12.22%	10.09%	5.83%	71.86%
4.53%	4.06%	3.67%	87.74%	8.02%	3.70%	4.83%	83.45%	9.37%	8.91%	4.25%	77.47%
3.54%	3.68%	2.88%	89.91%	6.32%	3.39%	3.83%	86.46%	7.45%	8.23%	3.40%	80.92%
3.58%	3.54%	2.72%	90.16%	6.24%	3.18%	3.43%	87.15%	7.19%	7.63%	2.96%	82.22%
4.16%	3.92%	3.37%	88.55%	7.22%	3.50%	4.23%	85.06%	8.27%	8.34%	3.62%	79.78%
4.83%	4.32%	4.16%	86.69%	8.32%	3.83%	5.18%	82.68%	9.47%	9.07%	4.41%	77.06%
4.13%	3.67%	2.67%	89.53%	7.71%	3.55%	4.21%	84.54%	8.98%	8.53%	3.66%	78.83%
4.19%	4.00%	3.60%	88.22%	7.77%	3.84%	5.62%	82.77%	9.02%	9.19%	4.87%	76.92%
4.23%	4.33%	4.82%	86.62%	7.79%	4.13%	7.47%	80.61%	9.01%	9.86%	6.46%	74.67%
3.36%	2.47%	3.45%	90.72%	6.23%	2.29%	4.78%	86.69%	7.29%	5.43%	4.31%	82.96%
3.81%	3.23%	3.42%	89.54%	7.05%	2.99%	4.72%	85.24%	8.16%	7.00%	4.21%	80.64%
4.32%	4.21%	3.37%	88.10%	7.95%	3.88%	4.64%	83.53%	9.07%	8.95%	4.08%	77.90%
3.96%	4.31%	2.89%	88.83%	7.29%	4.10%	3.88%	84.72%	8.59%	9.52%	3.56%	78.33%
4.17%	3.94%	3.37%	88.52%	7.65%	3.73%	4.51%	84.11%	9.04%	8.71%	4.15%	78.09%
4.39%	3.59%	3.93%	88.09%	8.01%	3.39%	5.22%	83.37%	9.51%	7.94%	4.84%	77.71%
4.44%	4.33%	3.79%	87.45%	7.84%	3.73%	4.78%	83.64%	9.28%	9.27%	4.35%	77.10%
4.17%	3.92%	3.38%	88.53%	7.39%	3.39%	4.28%	84.94%	8.81%	8.47%	3.92%	78.81%
3.92%	3.54%	3.01%	89.53%	6.96%	3.07%	3.82%	86.14%	8.34%	7.73%	3.52%	80.41%

to almost always have complementary design features that were found to *increase* safety, such as higher street network densities and less vehicle travel. Moreover, it was typically only the more connected street networks that have the capacity to dissipate congestion from arterials, which allows cities to build arterials with fewer travel lanes. This is important since fewer travel lanes on the major roads tended to be associated with far better crash outcomes. Street network characteristics played a key role in safety outcomes on the streets in our study. In fact we also found that, in terms of how these networks are built in practice, the safest street patterns of all were those that had fully connected street networks.

So why does this seem to be the case, and what have we been missing all these years? One problem is that road safety researchers typically direct their efforts at the various individual features of intersections or road segments. At the same time, communities often focus their road safety interventions on fixing known trouble sports. In both cases, we rarely consider the big picture and the idea that we might be able to build safer places by building places that help minimize unnecessary travel or that allow people to travel by a mode other than the automobile. The bottom line is that when it comes to building safer and more sustainable places, we need to look not only at what features make a good street or intersection but also at the street network designs that tie these places together. The design of the network seems to helps influence travel decisions, driver behavior, and vehicle speeds – all of which are factors that affect the total number of crashes and the severity of these crashes. Street networks are an important piece of this puzzle and examining our transportation system from a more comprehensive perspective can help inform transportation planning policies and put us on a path toward a more complete understanding of how community design affects travel behavior as well as road safety.

Street Networks and Health Outcomes

Well-designed street networks do not directly improve public health; however, communities shaped in ways that enable people to drive less, facilitate more active transportation, and help reduce the number of injuries and fatalities in the transportation system mean we are moving in the right direction. For instance, data from the Centers for Disease Control and Prevention suggests that more than half of the US adult population fails to meet the minimum daily amount of recommended physical activity and that this percentage is higher than it was a generation ago (Centers for Disease Control and Prevention, 2005, 2011). Insufficient physical activity has been shown to be a significant risk factor in contributing to the current obesity epidemic, as well as with diabetes, heart disease, stroke, and other chronic health conditions (Centers for Disease Control and Prevention, 2011). For instance, a person developing diabetes before the age of 40 has a significantly shorter life expectancy on the order of almost 15 fewer years (Jackson and Sinclair, 2011). Obesity-related health issues have also become pressing economic concerns. In 1960 and 1980, the US spent 5.2 percent and 9.2 percent of GDP on healthcare, respectively (Centers for Medicare & Medicaid Services, 2009). This percentage of GDP currently spent on healthcare is now at 17.7 percent (Keehan et al., 2008) while the costs to treat obesity-related health problems are now range between 12 and 13 percent of US healthcare expenditures (Moreno et al., 2011). Thus, the US now spends more than 2 percent of GDP simply treating the health costs borne though the obesity epidemic. Based upon current trends, this is a number is projected to continually increase (Finkelstein et al., 2003; Wang et al., 2008).

US workers drive an average of 25.2 minutes each day as compared to 21.7 minutes per day in 1990 (Pisarski, 2006), and the amount of time spent driving was found to be a key factor impacting obesity risk that was cited in another study (Jacobson et al., 2011). Today, more than 68 percent of Americans over the age of 20 are overweight or obese; this number has increased from just 31.5 percent in 1960 (Ogden and Carroll, 2010b). Perhaps more critically, this issue now affects one in three children, which triples the percentage of overweight or obese children from just a generation ago (Ogden and Carroll, 2010a). Thus, this is likely to be the first generation with a shorter expected lifespan than their parents. The good news is that even modest increases in physical activity have shown to positively impact obesity rates, risk for certain chronic diseases, as well as mortality rates (Warburton et al., 2006; Wen et al., 2011).

The role of the street network with respect to health outcomes should not be overlooked as poorly designed networks, and the associated streets, can inhibit active transportation while well-designed systems permit and perhaps even encourage active transportation (Marshall et al., 2014). Our results suggest that increased intersection density is significantly linked to reductions in rates of obesity, diabetes, high blood pressure, and heart disease. The more compact the street network, the lower the disease rates. While it is possible to lead an active, healthy lifestyle in most any type of neighborhood, our findings suggest that people living in more compact cities do tend to partake in more utilitarian active transportation within their daily lives, and in turn, they tend to have better health outcomes (Marshall et al., 2014).

This is not just true in the US but in cities around the world. Even though the built environment might only be a piece of the puzzle when it comes to understanding health risks, researchers continue to link certain built environments with various levels of driving and active transportation (Handy et al., 2002; Frank et al., 2007; Pendola and Gen, 2007).

4. SYNTHESIZING THE RESEARCH INTO FUNDAMENTAL PRINCIPLES

Given the wide variation in successful street network patterns, it is hard to be prescriptive about the optimal form and configuration of the network. However, there are a number of design patterns that widely admired networks have in common, and such elements can serve as guiding principles for developing and modifying networks for enduring performance. Three essential patterns for good urban street networks include:

1. Create a network consisting of a diverse set of urban street types.
2. Create a connected network with no limitations on what types of streets should connect.
3. Create a human-scale network with a dense pattern of streets and intersections.

A Network of Urban Streets

The most important function of a good street network is that it forms an effective and flexible framework for building a community. The network should provide opportunities for commercial hustle and bustle, as well as opportunities for quiet living, and should also have a host of variations in the middle. The streets in the network should be designed to accommodate this range of desired outcomes. Some streets should be designed to attract traffic of all types, including vehicles and pedestrians, while others should be designed to be very quiet and only see the occasional vehicle or pedestrian. This range of performance is achieved by having variations both in the design of the network and the design of the streets themselves. However, all streets in an urban network should have the character of urban facilities accommodating urban land-use patterns and catering to pedestrians.

According to the Lexicon of the New Urbanism, acceptable facility types in a good urban street network include boulevards, avenues, streets, drives, alleys, lanes, mews, passages, and paths. These facilities should vary in cross-section design, with boulevards occupying the widest right of way with multiple traffic lanes, medians, and wide sidewalks. The key point is that these facilities should also vary in terms of their configuration in the network. Boulevards and avenues should be designed to connect multiple neighborhoods and, as such, they should be continuous across large sections of a city with relatively little break in continuity or deflection in alignment. Streets and drives should generally be less continuous than boulevards and avenues, but connectivity may differ by mode. This lesser continuity can be achieved by a number of design variations in the network pattern including the use of T-intersections for terminating a street segment, the use of offset intersections, or incorporating kinks or deflection in the alignment. Examples, of such variations are illustrated in Figure 14.5, which shows street network for Savannah, GA and Prenzlauer Berg, Berlin, Germany.

Connecting All Types of Streets

The amount and types of connections in the network are key factors in determining both how the community functions and the character of the individual streets themselves. Most streets in a good street network should connect at both ends. A high level of connectivity provides an efficient template for dispersing traffic, facilitating route choice, and creating a more comfortable condition for travel by foot, bike, or transit.

However, it is not just the number of connections that are important to the function of the network but also the patterns and type of connections. Within a neighborhood, connections should be made between all types of facilities. This is the opposite of contemporary practice where arterials and local streets only connect to collectors and rarely to each other. These restrictions create highly specialized facilities that enable high volumes and high speeds on the arterial system and correspondingly low volumes (but not necessarily low speeds) on the local facilities. Good urban street networks enable connections between roads such as boulevards and mews, between avenues and alleys, and between all other possible combinations. This results in individual facilities that are less specialized, and an overall network that is much more efficient.

The pattern of connections is also important in determining whether or not a city functions as a coherent whole or as a collection of islands with a few streets serving as bridges.

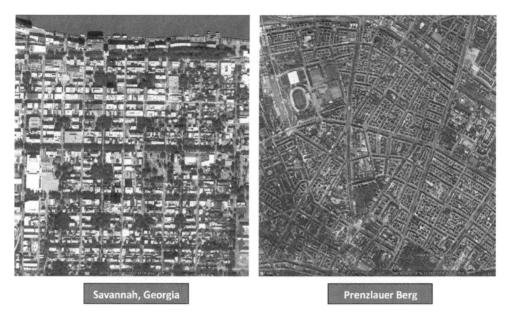

Figure 14.5   Savannah, GA and Prenzlauer Berg, Berlin, Germany

In order to achieve a coherent citywide pattern, a full range of connections should be made, not just within a given neighborhood, but also between surrounding neighborhoods. Boulevards and avenues should always create connections between neighborhoods, but many streets and drives should also bridge across adjacent neighborhoods.

Human-scale Networks

Good street networks need to be attractive and convenient to pedestrians and serve as good templates for development. This is achieved by ensuring that there is a fine grain of pathways and connections in the network. American street network intersection densities typically range from as little as 60 intersections per square mile (one example is the street network in downtown Salt Lake City) to more than 500 (such as the network in downtown Portland, OR). Smaller blocks (or more intersections per square miles) are typically much more comfortable for pedestrians, providing more direct paths to destinations and generally creating the template for a more human scale environment.

The context is often different when trying to understand international cities where human-scale tends to be more prevalent and historical structures more influential; however, the fact that pedestrians still respond well to human scale design is nearly universal (Gehl, 2010; Gehl and Svarre, 2013). This idea of a more human-scale environment also relates to the idea that we should be trying to build places where people enjoy spending time. When you close your eyes and think about the types of urban places that you love to walk or bike around in, consider the sort of street networks that support the places you are picturing. Of course everyone might not be able to have access to a beach or even a picturesque view of the mountains; however, everyone should have safe places to walk, safe places to ride bikes, and even safe places to drive. Focusing on designing communities with streets and street networks working together and purpose-fully designed to evoke such positive emotions can be can a fundamental step in the right direction as good street network design can better support a community that drives less, participates more in active transportation, and is healthier – both in terms of road safety impacts as well as those related to obesity-related health outcomes.

5.   CONCLUDING REMARKS

Around the world, well-loved, high-performing street networks come in many shapes, sizes, and configurations. Within each pattern, there are numerous permutations — many of which have provided an enduring template for great placemaking while sup-porting excellent living and working environments. An important trait of a good street network is that it should help shape a flexible and sustainable framework for building a community. Over generations, good street network patterns can help communities evolve over time with respect to land uses. Purely residential neighborhoods, depending upon the flexibility of the infrastructure, have the capacity to diversify and develop in ways that were perhaps unforeseen when originally planned. Such flexibility in street networks also helps facilitate multiple travel options, not simply with respect to mode, but also by providing redundancy. Diversity should not be limited to modes and routes, but networks should afford opportunities for commercial hustle and bustle as well as the chance for quiet living and all the variations in between. Networks alone cannot achieve all the desired outcomes as there must be a coordinated system of streets designed to facilities the desired outcomes. This requires that some streets be designed to accom-modate all modes – including automobiles, transit, bicycles, and pedestrians — while other streets should only handle the occasional automobile while prioritizing other modes. Such a range of street types and road users, from rushing emergency vehicles to meandering schoolchildren, can only be made possible through good, efficient network design.

Related to street network design, the growing body of research has started to show that in places with a more fine-grained network, more people drive less and utilize active transportation more. The research also suggests that these more human scale networks are much safer for *all* users of the road. In particular, accident severity is drastically reduced, suggesting that such fine-grained networks promote lower vehicular speeds. Fewer injuries and fatalities in the transportation system should be considered a health benefit, but if certain street network designs can also help promote reduced obesity, dia-betes, and heart disease, this more complete understanding of the impacts of community design can go a long way toward building safer, more sustainable, and healthier places.

Although the functional classification system remains ubiquitous in the US and ver-sions of it have proliferated in cities around the world, the twenty-first century is seeing another major shift in thinking about street network design. In essence, the twentieth century evolution toward a hierarchical and sparse street network as the ideal pattern is being supplanted by a revolution focused on more traditional, compact, and connected street pattern morphologies.

REFERENCES

Ben-Joseph, E. (2005), *The Code of the City, Standards and the Hidden Language of Place Making*, Cambridge, MA: MIT Press.

Centers for Disease Control and Prevention (2005), Trends in leisure-time physical inactivity by age, sex, and race/ethnicity – United States, 1994–2004, *Morbidity and Mortality Weekly Report*, **21**(6), 991–4.

Centers for Disease Control and Prevention (2011), *CDC Recommendations for Improving Health through Transportation Policy*, Washington, DC: CDC.

Centers for Medicare & Medicaid Services (2009), *National Health Expenditure Data. S. Research, Data and Systems*, Baltimore, MD: Centers for Medicare & Medicaid Services.

Duane, T. (1996), Human settlement, 1850–2040, in *Sierra Nevada Ecosystem Project, Final Report to Congress*, University of California, Davis, **II**, 235–360.

EPA (2011), *Emission Facts: Greenhouse Gas Emissions from a Typical Passenger Vehicle*, Washington, DC: Environmental Protection Agency.

Ewing, R. (1996), *Best Development Practices: Doing the Right Thing and Making Money at the Same Time*, Washington, DC: APA Planners Press.

Ewing, R. and Cervero, R. (2010), Travel and the built environment, *Journal of the American Planning Association*, **76**(3), 265–94.

Finkelstein, E.A., Fiebelkorn, I.C., and Wang, G. (2003), National medical spending attributable to overweight and obesity: how much, and who's paying? *Health Affairs*, **W3**, 219–26.

Frank, L.D., Andresen, M.A., and Schmid, T.L. (2004), Obesity relationships with community design, physical activity, and time spent in cars, *American Journal of Preventive Medicine*, **27**, 87–96.

Frank, L.D., Saelens, B.E., Powell, K.E., and Chapman, J.E. (2007), Stepping towards causation: do built environments or neighbourhood and travel preferences explain physical activity, driving, and obesity? *Social Science & Medicine*, **65**(9), 1898–914.

Gehl, J. (2010), *Cities for People*, Washington, DC: Island Press.

Gehl, J. and Svarre, B. (2013), *How to Study Public Life*, Washington, DC: Island Press.

Hall, J.W. and Turner, D.S. (1998), Development and adoption of early AASHO design criteria, *Transportation Research Record: Journal of the Transportation Research Board*, **1612**, 26–33.

Handy, S., Boarnet, M.G., Ewing, R., and Killingsworth, R.E. (2002), How the built environment affects physical activity, *American Journal of Preventive Medicine*, **23**(2S), 64–73.

Handy, S., Paterson, R., and Butler, K. (2003), *Planning for Street Connectivity: Getting from Here to There*, Planning Advisory Service Report 515, American Planning Association.

Jackson, R.J. and Sinclair, S. (2011), *Designing Healthy Communities*, San Francisco, CA: Jossey-Bass.

Jacobson, S.H., King, D.M., and Yuan, R. (2011), A note on the relationship between obesity and driving, *Transport Policy*, **18**(5), 772–6.

Keehan, S., Sisko, A., Truffer, C., Smith, S., Cowan, C., Poisal, J., and Clemens, M.K. (2008), Health spending projections through 2017: the baby-boom generation is coming to Medicare, *Health Affairs*, **27**(2), 145–55.

Kulash, W. (1990), *Traditional Neighbourhood Development: Will the Traffic Work?* http://user.gru.net/domz/kulash.htm.

Litman, T. (2005), *Roadway Connectivity: Creating More Connected Roadway and Pathway Networks*, www.vtpi.org/tdm/tdm116.htm.

Marshall, S. (2005), *Streets and Patterns*, New York: Spon Press.

Marshall, W. and Garrick, N. (2010a), The effect of street network design on walking and biking, *Transportation Research Record: Journal of the Transportation Research Board*, **2198**, 103–15.

Marshall, W. and Garrick, N. (2010b), Considering the role of the street network in road safety: a case study of 24 California cities, *Urban Design International Journal*, **15**(3), 133–47.

Marshall, W. and Garrick, N. (2011), Does street network design affect traffic safety? *Accident Analysis and Prevention*, **43**(3), 769–81.

Marshall, W. and Garrick, N. (2012), Community design & how much we drive, *The Journal of Transport & Land Use*, **5**(2), 5–12.

Marshall, W.E., Piatkowski, D.P., and Garrick, N.W. (2014), Community design, street networks and public health, *Journal of Transport and Health*, **1**(4), pp. 326–40.

Moeller, D. (1992), *Environmental Health*, Cambridge, MA: Harvard University Press.

Moreno, L.A., Pigeot, I., and Ahrens, W. (eds) (2011), *Epidemiology of Obesity in Children and Adolescents: Prevalence and Etiology*, New York: Springer.

Office of Environmental Health Hazard Assessment (2002), *Environmental Protection Indicators for California (EPIC)*, Sacramento, CA: California Environmental Protection Agency & California Resources Agency.

Ogden, C.L. and Carroll, M.D. (2010a), *Prevalence of Obesity Among Children and Adolescents: United States, Trends 1963–1965 Through 2007–2008*, Atlanta, GA: National Center for Health Statistics.

Ogden, C.L. and Carroll, M.D. (2010b), *Prevalence of Overweight, Obesity, and Extreme Obesity Among Adults: United States, Trends 1960–1962 Through 2007–2008*, Atlanta, GA: National Center for Health Statistics.

Pendola, R. and Gen, S. (2007), BMI, auto use, and the urban environment in San Francisco, *Health & Place*, **13**(2), 551–6.

Pisarski, A. (2006), *Commuting in America III: The Third National Report on Commuting Patterns and Trends*, National Cooperative Highway Research Program (NCHRP) Report 550, Transit Cooperative Research Program (TCRP) Report 110, Washington, DC: Transportation Research Board.

Pucher, J. and Dijkstra, L. (2000), Making walking and cycling safer: lessons from Europe, *Transportation Quarterly*, **54**(3), 25–50.

Southworth, M. and Ben-Joseph, E. (1997), *Streets and the Shaping of Towns and Cities*, New York: McGraw-Hill.

Stanislawski, D. (1946), The grid-pattern town, *Geographical Review*, **36**(1), 105–20.

Talen, E. (2012), *City Rules: How Regulations Affect Urban Form*, Washington, DC: Island Press.

Wang, Y., Beydoun, M.A., Liang, L., Caballero, B., and Kumanyika, S.K. (2008), Will all Americans become overweight or obese? Estimating the progression and cost of the US obesity epidemic, *Obesity*, **16**(10).

Warburton, D.E.R., Nicol, C.W., and Bredin, S.S.D. (2006), Health benefits of physical activity: the evidence, *Canadian Medical Association Journal*, **174**(6), 801–9.

Wen, C.P., Wai, J.P.M., Tsai, M.K., Yang, C., Cheng, T.Y.D., Lee, M.-C., Chan, H.T., Tsao, C.K., Tsai, S.P., and Wu, X. (2011), Minimum amount of physical activity for reduced mortality and extended life expectancy: a prospective cohort study, *The Lancet*, **378**(9798), 1244–53.

PART III

TRANSPORT AND SPATIAL IMPACTS

15 Transport and urban development
Piet Rietveld and Frank Bruinsma

1. INTRODUCTION

Transport is one of the key factors that influence urban development in the long run. For example, Clark (1958) indicates that transport can be both a 'maker and breaker' of cities. We therefore start this chapter with a short introduction on the long-run trends in transport. A remarkable development in both passenger and freight transport is that costs decreased substantially in the long run, whereas speeds increased over time. For example, for ocean shipping, Crafts and Venables (2001) indicate that real costs fell by about 83 per cent between 1750 and 1990. A similar development can be observed in passenger transport. Moreover, speeds have increased in all major transport modes during the last centuries (Rietveld and Vickerman, 2004). These speeds relate to the average speed for trips, based on total travel time, including access and egress time of the various modes (bus, train, car, motorcycle, plane). Since access and egress modes are slow, the average speed will increase when travel distances increase. Thus, a certain part of the speed increases are due to increases of travel distances. However, most of the speed increases will be related to improvements of infrastructures, network design, vehicle power, frequencies and transport system innovations. An example of a transport system innovation is the introduction and increased use of containers during the past 50 years. A major consequence of the containerization has been the increase in the speed of loading and unloading in seaports. There is, of course, also a negative rebound effect on speeds when quality improvements lead to higher demand and hence to congestion, but in the present context the positive effects tend to dominate the negative effect.

The cost of intra- and inter-urban movements has been and still is a major driver behind urban growth. The generalized costs of transport are defined as the sum of monetary costs and time-related costs ($gc = mc + tc$). The time-related costs are represented by means of the so-called value of time on which an extensive literature exists (Small and Verhoef, 2007). The long-run trend in transport is that technological change and investments have made it faster and cheaper so that one expects that gc has decreased. However, when values of time are taken into account, the situation becomes more complex. Consider the following scheme to explore long-run trends for time costs per kilometre. Suppose that speeds increase with a rate β per year. Further, when the value of time would have an income elasticity of γ and income increases with a rate λ per year. Then the time related generalized costs change with $-\beta + \gamma\lambda$ per year. It is not so clear whether $-\beta + \gamma\lambda$ is positive or negative. Typical values one may obtain for these parameters would be $\beta = .01$, $\gamma = .5$ and $\lambda = .02$ per cent, which would lead to a zero outcome. A source for an income elasticity of travel time of about .5 is Gunn (2001). In countries with high economic growth λ, or with serious congestion problems (β may even be negative or close to zero) one may arrive at increasing time-related costs. These considerations become more complex when both monetary and time-related costs are considered:

the effects of the increase in value of time may outweigh the price decreases in transport mentioned above, but now the final result depends even more on the specific values of parameters. We conclude that for most of freight transport, the long-term trend in generalized costs will be declining, but for passenger transport the time-related costs play a countervailing force because of the increase in the value of time. In particular within metropolitan areas where opportunities for speed increases are limited, one may well find a tendency of increasing generalized costs.

A useful concept to analyse the link between generalized transport costs and spatial development is accessibility. Following Geurs and van Wee (2004: 128), we define accessibility as '[t]he extent to which land-use and transport systems enable (groups of) individuals to reach activities or destinations by means of a (combination of) transport mode(s)'. There are various ways to operationalize the accessibility concept. A commonly used one is to define accessibility ACC of a place i in terms of the mass M of destinations j taking into account the transport costs to go to the destinations:

$$ACC = \textstyle\sum_j M_j \cdot f(d_{ij}).$$

In this formulation $f(d_{ij})$ is the distance decay function – a declining function of distance – used in spatial interaction modelling, thus providing a strong link between the accessibility concept and theories of spatial interaction. Note that where in the standard formulation distance is used as the main concept here, in reality it is not distance as such that matters, but the generalized costs per kilometre, as outlined above. Thus, ideally, the accessibility measure should not be based on distance, but on transport costs.

There are two ways to interpret accessibility as defined above. First, it can be loosely interpreted as a distance weighted destination market potential – more precisely, the weights are not distances themselves, but $f(d_{ij})$. The other interpretation is that accessibility is the market potential weighted average distance to destinations. Note that also this interpretation is somewhat imprecise because again $f(d_{ij})$ figures in the definition, not d_{ij} itself. A closer inspection makes clear that there is a direct link between the accessibility concept and the logsum formulation in welfare analysis, again based on preferences underlying spatial interaction (Small and Rosen, 1981).

As we will see in this contribution the accessibility concept will arise at several places as a useful way to link transport and land use within cities.

We start our review with giving historical perspectives on the relationship between transport and urban development and show developments in the transport domain have had decisive impacts on urban developments: both at the level of cities as a whole (section 2) and within cities (section 3). Then we continue with an analysis of the role of transport in concentration versus de-concentration in urban and regional development (section 4). In section 5 we discuss the theme of local versus broader effects of transport infrastructure. Finally, network formation aspects are discussed in section 6. In section 7 we conclude that cities have to invest in their relative position in the infrastructure network to secure their position in the global urban system.

2.   TRANSPORT AND URBAN DEVELOPMENT: A HISTORICAL PERSPECTIVE OF LOGISTICAL REVOLUTIONS

Over the past 1,000 years, the development of trade was the major driver behind urban growth. In its turn the development of trade is strongly correlated with the development of transport infrastructure networks and systems. Throughout urban history, four major eras of rapid and fundamental changes in the infrastructure system took place which had major impacts on the development of the urban system. Andersson (1986) described them as 'four logistical revolutions'. His hypothesis was that the great structural changes of production, location, trade, culture and institutions are triggered by slow but steady changes in the logistical network. For an update see Karlsson et al. (2009).

The first logistical revolution took place in the period 1000–1500 and was based upon improvements in particular in sea transportation on the one hand and the creation of a basic infrastructure for trade on the other. The development of larger vessels, new sea routes and new ports led to integration of trade between the city states along the coast of the Mediterranean and the Hanseatic cities along the coasts of Northern Europe. The emerging city system formed the basis for this increased trade. Due to larger vessels and the organization of trade fairs, transport costs and trade barriers were reduced. Large economic trade centres in this period were Venice, Florence, Bruges and Lubeck. The population size of those cities grew till they reached around 100,000 inhabitants. Key developments in this era were the emergence of cities, merchants and specialization of production.

The second logistical revolution (1500–1800) was again based on sea transportation and on the development of institutional innovations. The Portuguese and later the Dutch were able to build ocean-crossing merchant ships and an efficient banking and credit system was developed. Both transport costs and trade barriers were further reduced by those developments. Initially Antwerp and, somewhat later, Amsterdam were the central nodes, but all the large capital cities in Europe were engaged in international trade (Braudel, 1994). By the end of this era, London became the commercial and financial centre of the world (Karlsson et al., 2009). London had about 800,000 inhabitants at that time. Key developments in this era were the introduction of central banking systems, science and arts.

The third logistical revolution (1800–2000) results from the Industrial Revolution. Driven by technological innovations, the infrastructure network expanded from sea transport towards land transport: first canals and later on rail, and finally road. The new and relatively large-scale transportation systems made it possible to establish vertical integration between the raw materials in Northern America and the large scale manufacturing industries in the port cities of Western Europe. Division of labour, mass production, standardized products and multinational companies were the main developments in this era. Large new industrial cities developed: Manchester, Liverpool, Detroit, Chicago and, later on, cities all over the world. The size of cities grew from Manchester's 0.5 million inhabitants up to more than ten million inhabitants in Chinese industrial cities.

The current fourth era of logistical revolution manifested itself in a number of knowledge-intensive often high-tech urban regions and corridors. It is based on a rapid extension of motorways and air connections and on an increased capacity and speed of information processing and transmission (Karlsson et al., 2009). Main developments in this era are knowledge workers, R&D investments, out-sourcing, just-in-time-systems and customized production. Main drivers behind this development have been the liberalization of international trade, international capital flows and foreign direct investments. It is in particular in the fourth phase that the travel of persons has become the dominant factor as opposed to the transport of goods, and this implies in increasing weight of the time component in the generalized costs of transport.

Karlsson et al. (2009) conclude that each revolution has been fuelled by successive technological revolutions, in particular in advances that have cut the costs of transportation of goods, people and information. Moreover they state that 'new means of and systems of transportation and communication have reduced transportation and communication costs and time, which have brought different parts of the world closer to each other' (Karlsson et al., 2009: 8). Linking these developments with the discussion in section 1, we observe a long-term decrease in both monetary transport costs and time-related costs, where the weight of time related costs increases. This development led to a concomitant increase of accessibility of cities within urban systems. This also holds for the development of less developed countries.

This has increased the degree of competition between cities which all are part of the 'worldwide' urban system. Thus, cities have to invest in their relative position in the infrastructure network to get their share of the economic opportunities offered by the urban system they are part of.

3.   INTERNAL TRANSPORT AND URBAN DEVELOPMENT

In the preceding section we focused on the effects of changes in interurban transport on urban developments. In the present section we will now concentrate on the relevance of internal transport within metropolitan areas. In his interesting contribution, Clark (1958) indicates how changes in transport costs have always played a role in urban dynamics. Up to the nineteenth century the costs of transport of agricultural products were so high that they put a limit on the size of the urban centres. With the rise of the railways this situation came to an end. It then became feasible to exploit economies of scale in manufacturing production and this led to a period of urban growth. This led to new bottlenecks, since railways had mainly been constructed for long-distance freight transport so that passenger transport of the increasing number of workers to the workplaces became problematic. Thus, cities remained compact and limited in size. The emergence of tramways in the second part of the nineteenth century finally enabled a process of spatial expansion of cities (Hall, 1994), and this was further reinforced by the entry of the electric tram at the beginning of the twentieth century. The coming of the bus and car led to a further growth of urban agglomerations, but now this was mainly an increase of surface area, not of population size. Gradients of density and rents started to level off. An extreme example is Los Angeles, where the centre-supporting role of rail was broken down and a large area with about homogeneous densities of workplaces and residences emerged.

Clark expected, in 1958, a similar development for the large European agglomerations: not only suburbanization of residences, but also of work. However, this expectation did not come true. Examples of cities where there are still strong concentration of work in the centres and where public transport plays a dominant role in commuting are London and New York. Although indeed a certain trend can be observed of de-concentration of work places towards the city fringes, this tendency remained limited in many cases. In addition, it appears that in those cases that jobs moved towards the fringes of the cities this often led again to concentrations of employment. For this phenomenon, Garreau (1988) introduced the concept of edge cities. Researchers such as Henderson and Mitra (1996), Lucas and Rossi-Hansberg (2002) and Glaeser and Kahn (1993) developed new models for this purpose, in which explicit attention is paid to agglomeration advantages for firms. The centre is ultimately restricted in its growth by high transport costs from the residential areas located further away. The formation of sub-centres allows the further growth of urban economies. The underlying trade-off concerns the advantages of a reduction of total transport costs of employed persons and the lower productivity that follows from the spread of economic activities in the region.

Figure 15.1 illustrates the development of the urban structure with a focus on the distribution of employment within metropolitan areas. In *A* we have the classical model of complete concentration of employment in the centre and dispersion of the population around it. On the line *BC* we have a complete dispersion of employment. In *C* employers

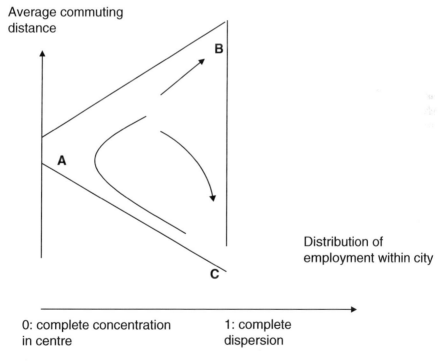

Source: Brotchie et al. (1996)

Figure 15.1 Relationship between the distribution of employment in urban regions, and mean commuting distance

find their job at a local level, whereas in *B* there are many criss-cross connections, 'wasteful commuting' in the terminology of Hamilton (1982). The historical path that was outlined above started near *C* given the high transport costs at the time. The rail based structure led to growth and concentration of the city into the direction of *A*. The present development moves into the direction of the line *BC*, where both the direction of the development and the degree of dispersion from city to city may vary. The extent to which *C* will be the direction of the developments depends among others on the future level of transport costs. Further the spatial distribution of employment in cities will be affected by spatial planning and zoning, and by agglomeration advantages.

The literature on urban land use that developed after the seminal work of Alonso (1964) during the period of 1960 to 1990 concentrated on the urban housing market (Fujita, 1989) and on location choice of households. An aspect that has received relatively little attention has been the theme of vertical transport in cities: the most direct way of reaping agglomeration advantages is by building higher and higher office buildings. Since the invention of safe elevator systems in the nineteenth century, offices have indeed become higher and higher. Consistent with the Alonso model, developers facing high per square metre costs in CBDs will optimize the use of the land by making buildings higher and higher. Skyscrapers have become the landmarks of large metropolitan areas such as Chicago and New York since the 1890s (Barr, 2010). An interesting subject of debate has been whether skyscrapers have become too tall, meaning that they have been made taller than actually justified on the basis of the price of land. The debate has not been settled yet. Helsley and Strange (2008) use game theoretical approaches to analyse the desire to build the tallest building in a city because of reputation effects: the inherent value of being the tallest. Thus, a contest may lead to overbuilding in the real estate market. Barr (2010) gives an empirical analysis for Manhattan and finds support for height competition that increases during boom times, implying that height competition is not a permanent phenomenon, but takes place from time to time, in particular when economic conditions are favourable. This subject of building heights is an important theme for urban development since high-rise buildings may have strong implications for the spatial structure of cities and the necessary transport infrastructures in terms of public transport and parking in metropolitan areas.

The introduction of the vertical dimension has greatly contributed to opportunities to decrease generalized costs of transport and increase accessibility levels in urban areas. It has been instrumental in the shift of cities as places specializing in manufacturing activities to places focusing on command and control activities, R&D and, of course, the production of consumer and producer services.

Agglomeration Economies in Cities

This emerging literature on productivity effects of high-rise buildings ties in with the broader literature on agglomeration economies. A useful review is given in Melo et al. (2009). A key indicator of agglomeration economies is the elasticity of productivity with respect to urban size or density. Typical values for this elasticity obtained in a rather broad range of literature are in the range of 3 to 8 per cent, the median value being about 4 per cent. Thus, an increase of employment density in an urban area of say 10 per cent leads to an increase in productivity of some 0.4 per cent. This may seem rather unnoticeable for a given city that is gradually growing or declining, it would of course have larger impacts when a large city with say an employment size of 1 million jobs would be compared with a smaller city with say 50,000 jobs. Then the difference in productivity would be some $1 - (1000/50)^{04} = 13$ per cent, a factor that may well affect the location decisions of firms and workers who are looking for productive locations and well-paid jobs.

A notable aspect of the literature on the subject is that it remains rather implicit on the transport dimension. Comparing two cities A and B of the same size and density, city A with a well-functioning transport system and B with a bad transport system, one would expect that city A has a higher productivity than city B. For an assessment of the effect of an improvement of the transport system on productivity the accessibility measure mentioned in section 1 may be used to give an indication. Thus, we employ the accessibility concept introduced in section 1: $ACC = \sum_j M_j \cdot f(c_{ij})$, where c_{ij} denotes generalized costs. An often used form for the decay function $f(c_{ij})$ is $f(c_{ij}) = c_{ij}^{-\alpha}$. Where $\alpha = 1$ is often used as a reference value (Rietveld and Bruinsma, 1998). In that case accessibility would be proportional to the level of c_{ij}, implying that the relative increase in accessibility in both cities would be the same when transport costs would improve uniformly within the cities *by a given percentage*. However, the exponential form $f(c_{ij}) = -\beta.\exp(c_{ij})$ appears to be a more adequate form for intra urban transport (Fotheringham and O Kelly, 1989), and in that case an overall tendency will be found that in relative terms city B with the high initial transport costs will experience a stronger increase in accessibility than city A with a better initial transport system. This would imply decreasing economies of transport infrastructure in urban areas.

The accessibility concept can also be used to study the effect of increasing density. An increase in density would imply in increase in the masses M in the accessibility expression $\sum_j M_j \cdot f(c_{ij})$. Then it is immediately clear that a uniform increase in M in all zones in a metropolitan area with a rate z will lead to an increase in accessibility of the same rate z, irrespective of the shape of the decay functions and the urban structure. This would lead to the conclusion that the elasticity of productivity with respect to density would not depend on the transport costs in the city as long as we consider a uniform increase in density. The background of this result is that in this case the accessibility expression is separable in terms of the masses M and the transport costs related interaction intensities $f(c_{ij})$. This holds true as long as the density increase is uniform; when it is not uniform, but, for example, mainly concentrated in the centre, the decay functions again will matter for the possible effect on overall accessibility in cities A and B, and hence on productivity.

A complicating factor is that transport infrastructure will most probably have an impact on density. In particular cities with a strong orientation on rail tend to be considerably denser than cities with a strong orientation on roads (Newman and Kenworthy, 1989). Although there may well be some causality issues here, an important implication is that investments in rail create conditions for a higher density and this in turn leads to a higher productivity in an urban agglomeration. Note also the link with the literature on vertical transport: the construction of high-rise buildings based on vertical transport will strongly affect densities in urban areas and this again increases urban productivity.

Thus, transport infrastructure, although not explicitly mentioned in most of the literature on agglomeration advantages as reviewed by Melo et al. (2009), implicitly plays an important role here. An interesting development in the literature is that an increasing part of the studies uses an accessibility measure (also termed 'market potential') to take into account the spatial structure. This is indeed an important step to incorporate transport dimensions in the analysis of urban productivity. However, the usual way is to measure the distance element just in kilometres, so that the quality of the networks in terms of travel time is not taken into account. An important exception to the above is the study by Rice et al. (2006), who carry out an analysis in terms of travel time bands. They find that in the UK a doubling of the working population within a range of 30 minutes travel time increases productivity with 3.5 per cent. A doubling of the working population between 30 and 60 minutes leads to a productivity increase of 1.5 per cent. Between 60 and 80 minutes the increase is 0.5 per cent and beyond 80 minutes no increase is notable. A specification of agglomeration advantages in this manner is of much help to assess the potential productivity effects of improvements in transport infrastructure.

4.   CONCENTRATION VERSUS DE-CONCENTRATION AT INTER-URBAN LEVEL

Metropolitan areas develop as the result of the interplay of concentration and de-concentration tendencies. In this approach centrifugal and centripetal forces are distinguished. The factor land, which is essential for agriculture, is immobile and contributes to centrifugal forces. Labour is much more mobile and provides opportunities for spatial concentration. This holds even more for capital that is more mobile, although even here there may be a tendency that due to market imperfections such as asymmetric information, capital is not perfectly mobile (Ridhwan, 2011). A necessary condition for concentration is the existence of scale economies within individual firms; otherwise firms could simply spread their production towards individual consumers. Marshall (1920) distinguished three main types of agglomeration economies: concentration of labour markets, face-to-face knowledge exchange and a large local market. The latter of these has received most attention in the current line of models. When a certain location reaches a critical size because of a certain initial advantage, this leads to a lasting advantage since both consumers and delivering firms locate close saving transport costs. These advantages are not unlimited, however, since when the market grows, the centrifugal forces at some stage induce that urban developments will emerge at other places.

Based on the relevance of large local markets, Krugman (1991) developed his well-known core periphery model that leads to the pattern described in Figure 15.2. During the initial phases of economic development when transport is still very expensive, the distribution of economic activities between core and periphery tends to be spread. High transport costs simply hamper the exploitation of economies of scale in the core region. Manufacturing takes place in both core and peripheral regions.

When transport costs decline, gradually manufacturing starts to be concentrated in the core given the agglomeration advantages in this place. This is what typically happened during the period of the industrial revolution in the nineteenth century. Further decreases of transport costs have induced a countervailing shift in manufacturing locations away from core regions towards peripheral regions where costs of production are relatively low. This analysis leads to two important conclusions. First, the theme of whether or not transport system improvements such as building toll roads, high speed

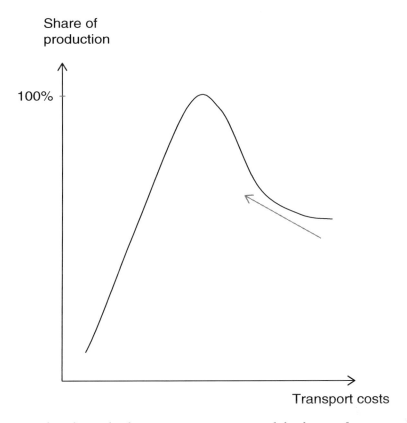

Figure 15.2   The relationship between transport costs and the degree of concentration of manufacturing production

rail connections or airports lead to a concentration versus de-concentration tendency does not have a simple answer in terms of yes or no. In particular the non-monotonous relationship in Figure 15.2 shows that the current level of transport costs and the current level of concentration matter. The second important implication is that lifecycle aspects have to be taken into account in these studies. This does not only hold for lifecycle developments in transport networks (for example: canals were an extremely important investment target in the nineteenth century, but nowadays canals are considered to be no longer of a large importance), but also for lifecycles in economic sectors. The urban-rural manufacturing shift discussed above took place during a period in which many core regions made a major shift from manufacturing regions to service oriented regions. In terms of transport, the driving factors behind this shift have led to a strong reorientation towards passenger transport (both within metropolitan areas and between).

Therefore there is reason in the present situation to focus on the two other agglomeration advantages mentioned by Marshall. The functioning of labour markets remains of undiminished importance in urban development: concentration of labour in a certain area has advantages for both workers and employees in matching processes. Also the advantage of local knowledge spillovers is important. This is an example of positive external effects or non-market interaction in the terminology of Glaeser (1999), where proximity and low transport costs are essential. This conclusion is fully in line with the results of section 2, where these elements were identified as the main drivers for current urbanization tendencies.

5.   LOCAL VERSUS BROADER EFFECTS OF TRANSPORT NETWORKS

An important aspect of transport network developments is the spatial specificity of their effects. Transport networks consist of links and nodes. Network developments usually take place in rather discrete steps (adding or upgrading major links, expanding a congested airport with additional runway capacity, etc.). This process has already been described by Hirschman (1958). The spatial range of the impact of an improvement will differ from investment project to investment project. Consider the case of an improvement of a rail network leading to more frequent and faster trains. This makes the proximity of the stations concerned more attractive, leading to an expansion of office space and/or higher office prices around the station (Willigers, 2006; Debrezion, 2006). Banister and Thurstain-Goodwin (2011) show for the Jubilee Line Extension (JLE) in London that property values around Southwark and Canary Wharf underground stations increased for residential and commercial (both offices and shops) properties. However, for Southwark the greatest effects of JLE were found on existing residential property values, whereas Canary Wharf the attributable effect on new commercial property is much greater. Thus, in the case of network improvements with multimodal transport, transport nodes may well be expected to be places where substantial effects take place. However, there might be differences in the kind of effects that show up. To what extent this also leads to large effects at a higher spatial level is not evident, however (see also Bruinsma et al., 2008). It is probable that competition effects will be substantial: some stations may benefit, but not necessarily all of them will benefit and, probably more important, competition takes place between locations close to railway stations and locations further away.

This leads to the important result that railway infrastructure investments may have visible effects close to railway stations, but the shift away from other places towards station areas may remain mainly invisible, because the negative effect is 'thinned' across a much larger area. As a consequence, the effects of transport infrastructure improvements are often much easier to establish at the local level compared with broader urban or regional level. In other words, transport network changes may well lead to clearly visible relocations, but these relocations often are mainly redistributive in nature. The broader, generative, effects of network improvements are usually small.

This result may even also be found for investments in road networks. Since road networks are essentially unimodal networks, transfer points such as motorway exits will not necessarily play a large role in the formation of spatial patterns. Firms might as well invest in locations further away from major motorway exits of a new expressway. Yet, even here tendencies can be observed that effects of expressways are rather local and difficult to trace at the broader spatial level. For example Rietveld and Bruinsma (1998) find that the effects of the construction of a major international expressway (A1) between the

Netherlands and Germany was mainly visible in a narrow band of around 1km around the expressway, whereas there were only limited employment responses in the broader regions affected. The explanation is probably the combination of two factors: developers prefer locations near to expressways (not necessarily close to exit points) because of visibility effects. The second factor is probably that the public sector that plays a strong role in physical planning preferred the development of locations that were close to the expressway. An advantage of developing employment sites close to highways is that the noise nuisance resulting from the new highways can be spread to work locations; for residential locations the nuisance standards are tighter than for employment locations.

When we use the concept of accessibility based on the notion of generalized costs of transport, it is clear that changes in networks lead to changes in accessibility in a spatially distinct way. Thus, an upgrade of a railway line leading to higher speeds will have its strongest impacts close to the railway stations affected (Geurs, 2006). Thus, in the case of networks with links and nodes accessibility profiles may show rather distinct differences. A zone at a distance of 200m from a railway station may have a considerably higher accessibility level compared with a zone 3km away. From this perspective, accessibility based on speeds and frequencies of services will show larger spatial variations than accessibility based on the monetary costs of transport. The point is that the costs of transport are about proportional with distances. Thus a change in fuel costs would have a proportional effect on travel costs per kilometre. As a consequence, an investment in a network link will have a clearly stronger spatially differentiating effect on accessibility maps compared with a shock in fuel prices. This will make spatial relocation effects less pronounced in the latter case.

6.   NETWORK EVOLUTION IN TRANSPORT NETWORKS: WELFARE ECONOMICS VERSUS POLITICAL ECONOMICS

Most studies in this domain focus on the impacts of transport network developments on urban development. There is of course also a reverse direction of causality that has received less attention: the impact of urban and regional conditions on network developments. The central question addressed here is what factors dominate the evolution of networks. There are two opposing approaches here, i.e., a standard economic approach that assumes that investment decisions are based on long-run profits in the case of private network suppliers or social cost-benefit analysis in the case of public suppliers. The alternative is provided by the public choice and political economics literature which assumes that political considerations like the desire to be re-elected is a main driving force (Persson and Tabellini, 2000).

Important contributions to the economics of network formation can be found in Economides (1996) and Bala and Goyal (2000). However, surprisingly enough, these contributions did not lead to a considerable response of researchers on the empirical side of the economics of transport network formation. This may well become an important field of research in this domain. Recent contributions can be found for example in Levinson (2008) and Jacobs-Grisioni et al. (2012).

A nice example of the public choice approach is given by Cadot et al. (2006) who estimate production functions for French regions jointly with investment volumes in the public capital stock. They find that public choice related factors such as the political colour of the region, the congruence between national and regional political colour and the presence of lobby groups indeed play a significant role in investment decisions. Another part is explained by the development of nationwide high-speed rail network. An economics related criterion (rate of return on public investment), has a negative (but limited) effect on the regional volume of public investments. Hence it seems that in France the regional allocation of public investments is mainly driven by political factors and that efficiency considerations play a limited role. A similar result was found for decision-making about road construction projects in Norway (Fridstrom and Elvik, 1997). This combination of economics and public choice elements in the analysis of infrastructure impacts is apparently an interesting field of analysis. It shows that the economics-based approach, which is often used in the context of cost-benefit analysis, with its normative orientation towards selecting the welfare maximizing alternative is not necessarily the most appropriate tool to analyse the factors that determine actual decisions governing the evolution of networks.

7. CONCLUSIONS

In this chapter we have discussed the impact of the development of transport systems on urban growth both at the inter-urban and intra-urban level. We observed a long-term decrease in transportation costs and time due to new systems of transportation. This development led to an increase of accessibility of cities within urban systems. However, it also led to an increased degree of competition between cities which are all part of the 'worldwide' urban system. Cities have to invest in their relative position in the infrastructure network to secure their share of the economic opportunities offered by the urban system they are part of.

Several studies suggest that transport infrastructure has an impact on urban density. Although there may well be some causality issues, investments in particular in rail infrastructure create conditions for a higher urban density and this in turn leads to a higher productivity in an agglomeration. There exists a strong correlation with literature on vertical transport (elevators): the construction of high-rise buildings based on vertical transport strongly affects urban density and this again increases urban productivity. The recent use of accessibility measures to take into account the spatial structure is an important step to incorporate transport dimensions in the analysis of urban productivity.

At the inter-urban level, much attention is given to the size of the market as agglomeration advantage. We find that the current literature on agglomeration advantages is rather silent on the transport dimension within cities. We argue that a more explicit treatment of transport in the analysis of agglomeration advantages is a promising direction of research.

Considering the spatial range of the impact of an infrastructure improvement, we conclude that local effects tend to be most visible. There is considerable evidence that these local effects are mainly distributive effects: at other places further away from where the network developments take place there is a – limited – decline of economic activity.

Finally, we pay attention to the factors driving investment decisions in transport networks. We argue that not only standard economic approaches – such as social cost-benefit analysis in case of public suppliers – lay behind investment decisions. There is evidence that also political considerations, like the desire to be re-elected, can be a main driving force behind investment decisions. Also this combination of economics and public choice elements in the analysis of infrastructure impacts is an interesting field for ongoing research.

REFERENCES

Alonso, W. (1964), *Location and Land Use*, Cambridge, MA: Harvard University Press.

Andersson, A.E. (1986), The four logistical revolutions, *Papers in Regional Science*, **59**(1), 1–12.

Bala, V. and Goyal, S. (2000), A noncooperative model of network formation, *Econometrica*, **68**(5), 1181–229.

Banister, D. and Thurstain-Goodwin, M. (2011), Quantification of the non-transport benefits resulting from rail investment, *Journal of Transport Geography*, **19**, 212–23.

Barr, J. (2010), Skyscrapers and the skyline: Manhattan, *Real Estate Economics*, **38**(3), 567–97.

Braudel, F. (1994), *A History of Civilizations*, New York: A. Lane.

Brotchie, J.F., Anderson, M., Gipps, G.P. and McNamara, C. (1996), Urban productivity and sustainability, in Y. Hayashi and J. Roy, (eds), *Transport, Land Use and the Environment*, Dordrecht: Kluwer, pp. 81–102.

Bruinsma, F.R., Pels, E., Priemus, H., Rietveld, P. and van Wee, B. (eds) (2008), *Railway Development: Impacts on Urban Dynamics*, Heidelberg: Physica Verlag.

Cadot, O., Röller, L.H. and Stephan, A. (2006), Contribution to productivity or pork barrel? The two faces of infrastructure investment, *Journal of Public Economics*, **90**, 1133–53.

Clark, C. (1958), Transport – maker and breaker of cities, *Town Planning Review*, **28**(4), 237–50.

Crafts, N. and Venables, A. (2001), *Globalization in History: A Geographical Perspective*, paper prepared for the NBER conference on Globalization in Historical Perspective.

Debrezion, G. (2006), *Railway Impacts on Real Estate Prices*, PhD dissertation, VU University, Amsterdam.

Economides, N. (1996), The economics of networks, *International Journal of Industrial Organisation*, **14**, 673–99.

Fotheringham, S. and O'Kelly, M.E. (1989), *Spatial Interaction Models: Formulations and Applications*, Dordrecht: Kluwer.

Fridstrom, L. and Elvik, R. (1997), The barely revealed preference behind road investment priorities, *Public Choice*, **92**(1), 145–68.

Fujita, M. (1989), *Urban Economic Theory: Land Use and City Size*, Cambridge: Cambridge University Press.

Garreau, D. (1988), *Edge City*, New York: Anchor Books.

Geurs, K.T. (2006), *Accessibility, Land Use and Transport*, Delft: Eburon.

Geurs, K.T. and van Wee, B. (2004), Accessibility evaluation of land-use and transport strategies: review and research directions, *Journal of Transport Geography*, **12**(2), 127–40.

Glaeser, E. (1999), *The Future of Urban Research: Non-market Interactions*, mimeo, Harvard University.

Glaeser, E. and Kahn, M.E. (1993), Sprawl and urban growth, in *Handbook of Urban and Regional Economics*, North Holland, Amsterdam.

Gunn, H.F. (2001), Spatial and temporal transferability of relationships between travel demand, trip cost and travel time, *Transportaion Research*, **37**(E), 163–89.

Hall, P. (1994), Squaring the circle: can we resolve the Clarkian paradox? *Environment and Planning B*, **21**(7), 79–94.

Hamilton, B.W. (1982), Wasteful commuting, *Journal of Political Economy*, **90**, 1035–53.

Helsley, R.W. and Strange, W.C. (2008), A game-theoretic analysis of skyscrapers, *Journal of Urban Economics*, **64**(1), 49–64.

Henderson, V. and Mitra, A. (1996), The new urban landscape developers and edge cities, *Regional Science and Urban Economics*, **26**, 613–43.

Hirschman, A.O. (1958), *The Strategy of Economic Development*, Boulder, CO: Westview Press.

Jacobs-Grisioni, C., Koopmans, C.C. and Rietveld, P. (2012), *The Business Of Shinking Distance, Railway Network Evolution in a Mixed Private and Public Playing Field*, VU University. Amsterdam.

Karlsson, C., Andersson, B. and Stough, R. (2009), *Entrepreneurship and Development: Local Processes and Global Patterns*, CESIS Electronic Working Paper Series 160.

Krugman, P. (1991), *The Self-organizing Economy*, Oxford: Blackwell Publishers.

Levinson, D.M. (2008), Density and dispersion: the co-development of land use and rail in London, *Journal of Economic Geography*, **8**, 55–77.

Lucas, R.E. and Rossi-Hansberg, E. (2002), On the internal structure of cities, *Econometrica*, **70**(4), 1445–76.

Marshall, A. (1920), *Principles of Economics*, London: Macmillan and Co.

Melo, P.C., Graham, D.J. and Noland, R.B. (2009), A meta-analysis of estimates of urban agglomeration economies, *Regional Science and Urban Economics*, **39**(3), 332–42.

Newman, P.W.G. and Kenworthy, J.R. (1989), *Cities and Automobile Dependence: An International Sourcebook*, Brookfield: Gower.

Persson, T. and Tabellini, G. (2000), *Political Economics: Explaining Economic Policy*, Cambridge, MA: MIT Press.

Rice, P., Venables, A.J. and Patacchini, E. (2006), Spatial determinants of productivity: analysis for the regions of Great Britain, *Regional Science and Urban Economics*, **36**(6), 727–52.

Ridhwan, M.M. (2011), *Regional Dimensions of Monetary Policy in Indonesia*, PhD dissertation, VU University, Amsterdam.

Rietveld, P. and Bruinsma, F. (1998), *Is Transport Infrastructure Effective? Transport Infrastructure and Accessibility: Impacts on the Space Economy*, Berlin: Springer Verlag.

Rietveld, P. and Vickerman, R. (2004), Transport in regional science: the death of distance is premature, *Papers in Regional Science*, **83**(1), 229–48.

Small, K.A. and Rosen, H.S. (1981), Applied welfare economics with discrete choice models, *Econometrica*, **49**(1), 105–30.

Small, K.A. and Verhoef, E.T. (2007), *Urban Transportation Economics*, London: Routledge.

Willigers, J. (2006), *Impact of High-speed Railway Accessibility on the Location Choices of Office Establishments*, PhD dissertation, Utrecht University.

16 Methods for estimating the economic impact of transportation improvements: an interpretive review
Michael Iacono and David Levinson

1. INTRODUCTION

Transportation network improvements remain a politically popular means for the promotion of economic growth, even though in most developed countries the opportunities for projects that yield exceptionally large returns are becoming more and more scarce. There are other factors at play, including macroeconomic conditions, education and skills levels, which tend to be more important than transport investment. Hence, from the analyst's perspective, estimating the economic impacts from transportation improvements can prove to be a fairly complicated matter, even for projects that are not very large in scope. This chapter reviews some of the more common methods that have been used by practitioners and researchers to analyze transportation improvements of varying scale. We move from basic project-based evaluation techniques like benefit-cost analysis to larger, regional-scale types of analysis that make use of regional economic models, and eventually to aggregate analysis techniques that shift focus from the effect of individual projects to the larger-scale and longer-term relationships between transportation infrastructure and economic growth.

Our discussion of project-based evaluation methods is extended to focus on the unique difficulties of directly estimating the user benefits for a given project over its useful life. Apart from traditional sources of uncertainty encountered in forecasting the demand for a project, the effects of induced demand and the dynamic relationship between transportation network improvement, accessibility changes, and development patterns introduce additional sources of uncertainty that may affect estimates of user benefits. We therefore discuss the possibility of using alternate methods to infer user benefits, such as changes in land values. In the concluding section of this chapter, we discuss some of the practical issues involved with the use of this method and also offer some comments on the merits of the regional and aggregate scale approaches discussed herein.

2. PROJECT-BASED EVALUATION

State of Practice and Limitations

The majority of economic impact studies are undertaken using conventional, project-based methods. These methods tend to focus on the direct user impacts of individual projects in terms of travel costs and outcomes, and compare sums of quantifiable, discounted benefits and costs. Inputs to benefit-cost analyses can typically be obtained from readily available data sources or model outputs (such as construction and maintenance costs, and before-and-after estimates of travel demand, by vehicle class, along with associated travel times). Valuation of changes in external costs of travel (e.g., air pollution and crash injury) can usually be accommodated by using *shadow price* estimates, and many government agencies prescribe a single, standard value based on evidence from recent empirical studies.

The primary benefits included in such studies are those related to reductions in user cost, such as travel time savings and vehicle operating costs (e.g. fuel costs, vehicle depreciation, etc.). Additional benefits may stem from reductions in crash rates, vehicle emissions, noise, and other costs associated with vehicle travel. Project costs are typically confined to expenditures on capital investment, along with ongoing operations and maintenance costs.

Project-based evaluation methods, especially benefit-cost analysis, are favored due to their relative ease of use and employment of readily available or easily acquired data. However, several characteristics inherently limit their effectiveness in practice.

First, there is the general criticism of methods based on benefit-cost analysis that they cannot account for all possible impacts of a project. Project-based methods generally do not describe the economic effects of a project on different user or non-user groups, which are an inevitable outcome of such investments. Winners and losers from a new capacity project cannot be effectively identified and differentiated (Levinson, 2002). Moreover, there is often little consideration given to the extent to which such investments alter patterns of social exclusion, another important distributional concern (Church et al., 2000). There are also concerns that some impacts cannot effectively be quantified, such as impacts on the environment, valued landscapes, and urban environments.

Second, a significant amount of uncertainty and risk is involved in the employment of project-based methods. Methods that use benefit-cost techniques to calculate B/C ratios, rates of return, and/or net present values are often sensitive to certain assumptions and inputs (Ashley, 1980). With transportation infrastructure projects, the choice of discount rate is often critical, due to the long life of projects and large up-front costs. Also, the presumed value of travel time savings is often pivotal, since it typically reflects the majority of project benefits. Valuations of travel time savings vary dramatically across the traveler population as a function of trip purpose, travel mode, traveler wage, household income, and time of day (Hensher, 2001; Brownstone et al., 2003; Hensher and Rose, 2007; Abrantes and Wardman, 2011). It is often useful to test several plausible values. More recently, interest has also extended to other dimensions of travel behavior, such as the reliability of travel time (Noland and Polak, 2002; Brownstone and Small, 2005; Carrion and Levinson, 2012), which may figure in to the estimation of project benefits.

Two of the most important inputs to any project evaluation, forecasts of demand and project costs, are also among the primary sources of risk. Reviews of forecast versus actual traffic volumes for road projects have shown evidence of both systematic over-prediction (Flyvbjerg et al., 2005) and under-prediction (Parthasarathi and Levinson, 2010) of traffic volumes, often by large margins. Evidence of demand forecasts for urban rail projects have shown a consistent trend toward over-prediction of demand, both in the USA and internationally (Pickrell, 1992; Richmond, 2001; Flyvbjerg et al., 2005). Perhaps more worrisome, the evidence suggests that these errors become amplified in the case of large-scale infrastructure projects, or "mega-projects" (Flyvbjerg et al., 2003).

Uncertainty and risk may also arise from other sources apart from the technical analysis components of project evaluation. For example, Mackie and Preston (1998) identify 21 distinct sources of error in project evaluation. Some of these include the sources listed above, both others are more broadly embedded in the planning process itself, such as unclear objectives, prior political commitments, and optimism bias.

Induced Demand and Induced Development

One particular challenge that confronts nearly all evaluations of projects of any significant size, and hence merits additional attention, is the response of travelers, firms, and households to network improvements over extended periods of time. Short-run travel behavior responses, often characterized as "induced demand" and longer-term location decisions in response to new patterns of accessibility may complicate the estimation of project benefits over the economic life of a project.

Induced demand

Since so many assessments of project benefits are based on travel-time savings, the issue of induced or "elastic" demand merits special attention. Since Hansen and Huang (1997) provided evidence of an elasticity of 0.9 between road supply (capacity) and the demand for road use (VMT) among California's counties, there has been a great deal of concern over how the provision of new highway capacity might affect travel behavior and whether new capacity policies might be self-defeating. Such findings may have important implications for the long-term economic and social effects of highway capacity provision.

However, there is still a great deal that is not known about the fundamental causal structure underlying the phenomenon of induced demand. Research attempting to decompose the complex issue of induced demand (Hills, 1996; Lee et al., 1999) has emphasized that there are both short-run and long-run effects of highway capacity additions. Specifically, in the short run, movements along the demand curve for road use are observed, as travelers may switch routes or substitute destinations. In the longer term, fixed adjustments by travelers and location decisions by households and firms in response to changes in travel time and accessibility may affect levels of overall travel, leading to an overall *shift* in the demand curve. Recent research has only begun to address these issues in practice by substituting micro-level data and methods for macroscopic analyses (Goodwin et al., 1998; Levinson and Kanchi, 2002; Mokhtarian et al., 2002; Parthasarathi et al., 2003) and addressing the reciprocal relationship between supply and demand (Cervero, 2002; Levinson and Karamalaputi, 2003; Levinson and Chen, 2005).

Perhaps the greatest difficulty in substantiating and quantifying the effects of induced demand is the task of estimating the amount of "latent" demand that may emerge from a network improvement. The concept of latent demand was popularized by Downs (1962, 1992), along with the related concept of "triple convergence," which suggests that there are (at least) three types of substitution effects that may lead to greater flows on an improved road link following the introduction of the improvement. As its name implies, latent demand is particularly difficult to estimate due to the absence of knowledge about which types of substitutions are most likely to materialize, and in what magnitude. One may also hypothesize further types of behavioral response, such as changes in trip generation and destination choice, in response to lower generalized costs of travel. To the extent that these types of adjustments cannot be modeled accurately, they may lead to overestimates of travel time savings and hence user benefits.

Induced development

Over the course of its lifetime, a project may generate secondary impacts beyond its direct, short-term effects on travel. By changing the level of accessibility of locations served by the improved network link, a project may bring about additional development in those locations. This spatial reorganization of activities may then feed back to the demand for travel and alter network flows accordingly. We might call this process "induced development" in order to differentiate it from induced demand. This process is illustrated in Figure 16.1.

Figure 16.1 provides a conceptual sketch of the process of induced development by illustrating the process of interaction between transportation network development and land development through time. At time t there is some base amount of development at a given location. The introduction of a new road link at time $t + 1$ leads to a set of short-term behavioral responses by travelers as a reaction to the improvement. In the short term, there is some travel time savings on existing links and rerouting, as travelers adjust their route choices to take advantage of lower travel costs. Some additional trips may also be made (induced demand) at previously congested times.

At time $t + 2$, the improved road link leads to a higher level of accessibility, and hence the location becomes more attractive to firms and households. Over time, this additional development increases the demand for travel, as more trips have origins or destinations in the given location. Thus, at time $t + 3$, an additional link is built to serve the location and improve connections with neighboring locations. This process might be called "induced supply" (Levinson and Karamalaputi, 2003), as it is the counterpart to induced demand in the feedback process of transportation network growth and land development.

The recursive process of transportation network growth and land development suggests that efforts to evaluate the effects of larger projects will require model systems

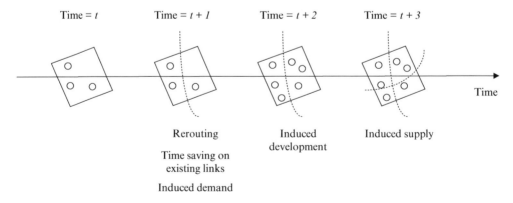

Figure 16.1   Conceptual representation of co-evolution of transportation networks and land use

capable of replicating the dynamics of this process over time. Indeed, there are ongoing projects to develop integrated urban modeling systems that combine transportation models with models of urban land markets and, in some cases, economic production and exchange.[1] Of course, the additional complexity these more sophisticated model structures introduce also contribute additional sources of forecast error, and there continue to be investigations into the likely range of uncertainty associated with their predictions (Clay and Johnston, 2006; Sevcikova et al., 2007).

3. ACCESSIBILITY AS A PERFORMANCE MEASURE

As the previous discussion suggested, estimating user benefits from transportation projects (especially larger ones) is a difficult task. Apart from the inherent sources of uncertainty in travel forecasting and economic analysis, user benefits depend on network flows over time, which may change in response to shifts in travel patterns. Longer-term locational shifts may also contribute to the degradation of network performance and user benefit.

Complicating matters, it is not clear that network improvements that lower the generalized cost of travel necessarily translate into real time savings in the sense that they result in people spending less time on travel as opposed to other activities. The literature on travel time budgets (Zahavi and Talvitie, 1980; Mokhtarian and Chen, 2004) lends some support to the proposition that individuals spend a more or less fixed amount of time traveling during a given day.

In light of these issues, it may be sensible to consider an alternative method of estimating user benefits from a transportation improvement. As discussed in the preceding section, over longer periods of time changes to transportation networks result in altered patterns of accessibility.[2] These patterns of accessibility strongly influence the location of new development, with land markets serving an intermediary function by conveying information about prices. Thus, the price of land in a given location is a function of (among other things) the relative accessibility of that location to various types of opportunities such as employment and shopping. To the extent that there is a consistent relationship observed between these variables, changes to land prices may serve as a substitute for the direct estimation of user benefits from a given project. The empirical implementation of these methods generally makes use of one of two types of techniques: hedonic price functions and repeat sales methods.

Hedonic Price Functions

Models that use hedonic pricing methods are widely adopted for studying the effect of transportation improvements on the value of real property. Regardless of whether prices for raw land or improved properties are available, hedonic pricing models allow the user to decompose the determinants of prices into a set of attributes, each of which has an implicit price associated with it. The theoretical foundations of hedonic analysis of housing markets are widely attributed to the work of Lancaster (1966) that linked consumer utility to the *characteristics* of goods, rather than the goods themselves, and also to a paper by Rosen (1974), which demonstrated how consumers and producers interact in implicit markets for goods, such as housing characteristics. This approach turns out to be quite useful for analysis of the effects of transportation improvements, since data are more often available for developed properties than for the value of undeveloped land. Hedonic pricing methods allow the user to introduce statistical controls for characteristics of properties that influence the property's value.

The basic hedonic price function assumes that the price (or rent) of a property is a function of several sets of characteristics that collectively describe the quality (and quantity) of building features, the neighborhood in which the property is situated, and the property's location within the relevant real estate market. Malpezzi (2003) writes the basic hedonic function using the expression:

$$R = f(S, N, L, C, T)$$

where R represents the rental price of a property (value can be substituted for owner-occupied properties), S is a set of structural characteristics of the property, N is a set of characteristics describing the neighborhood where the property is located, L describes of the location of the property within the market (e.g., distance to CBD, distance to nearest highway, regional accessibility, etc.), C is a set of contract characteristics or conditions (for rental properties), and T is a variable or variables representing the time when the rent or sale was observed, such as a month or year-specific variable.

Together, these variables provide a more or less complete description of a given property. The associated parameters for each variable can then be estimated to give an approximation of their implicit value, as revealed by the consumption decisions of buyers or renters of houses or commercial property. The theoretical literature on hedonic price functions does not specify a particular functional form for the hedonic model, although many empirical studies adopt specifications that are nonlinear in prices but can be transformed to more easily estimable forms (Halvorsen and Pollakowski, 1981). Data on home sales tend to be more readily available than for other types of property, and this is where much of the evidence from hedonic price models has been accumulated. The effects of transportation improvements are usually specified in terms of the distance or travel time to some transportation facility, such as a highway link or public transit station. Where distance or travel time cannot be specified as a continuous variable, researchers sometimes adopt an approach of defining an "impact zone" within which property values are assumed to be influenced by a transportation improvement (Mohring, 1961).

Repeat Sales Methods

Some of the early studies of the effects of transportation improvements on property values used fairly simple test-control methods that looked at changes in land or property prices near a new transportation link before and after an improvement, and compared these changes to those observed for a control site not near the improved link (Ryan, 1999). One weakness of this approach is that the composition of the sample may change over time if new development takes place near the improved link, especially if this new development is quantitatively or qualitatively different from existing properties. Also, this method does not account for any improvements made to the observed properties during the period of study.

A refinement on this method, and an alternative to the hedonic pricing method, is to use repeat sales of properties to estimate annualized changes in price for a given study period. Historically, a more common use for repeat sales methods has been the creation of constant-quality house price indices for entire urban areas (Bailey et al., 1963; Case and Shiller, 1989). However, some more recent applications of the repeat sales approach have generalized the basic equation to allow for the testing of differences in appreciation between different submarkets. This method was used by Archer et al. (1996) to study locational differences in house price appreciation between various segments of the Miami housing market between 1971 and 1992, and by Smersh and Smith (2000) to study differences in rates of appreciation associated with accessibility increases brought about by the opening of a new bridge in Jacksonville, Florida (USA).

Where rich datasets containing extensive attribute information on structure and neighborhood characteristics are not available, repeat sales methods present an appealing alternative for measuring location effects on changes in property prices. In principle, measuring the sale of the same unit at different points in time alleviates the problem of attempting to construct a model that accounts for all sources of variation in prices. However, the usefulness of the repeat sales method relies on the assumption that no significant changes are made to the properties under observation during the period between sales. Also, unless a fairly long time series of observations on sales are available, finding properties that sold multiple times may prove difficult. This may be especially true if a submarket under consideration contains only properties near an improved transportation link or node. A further issue with using this method is that by using only properties that sell more than once during a given study period, much of the information provided in data sets of property sales is lost. More recently, researchers studying house price index construction have begun to establish "hybrid" methods that combine data on repeat sales of unchanged properties with repeat sales of improved properties *and* with single sales, all in one joint estimation procedure (Case and Quigley, 1991).

4.   REGIONAL ECONOMIC MODELS

Up to this point, the emphasis has been placed on the evaluation of individual projects and the degree to which they can be effectively assessed using conventional methods such as benefit-cost analysis. Many such projects are deployed at an intra-urban or at least intra-regional scale. However, some projects are large enough in scale (for example, the Channel Tunnel across the English Channel) that they may generate impacts beyond their immediate area and hence require tools of analysis that are broader in scope.

One approach to measuring the effects of transportation investment at a regional level is to apply macroeconomic simulation modeling methods to represent the effects of cost savings and productivity enhancements due to transportation infrastructure investment. Economic impacts from such a model are measured in terms of employment, income and value added. A basic method for estimating the impacts of investment in a transportation project would involve estimating user benefits from the project, translating these benefits into economic consequences, allocating benefits to specific economic sectors, and finally estimating the additional impact due to changes in logistics and product markets (Weisbrod and Grovak, 1998).

Regional input–output models, such as IMPLAN and RIMS II, have seen extensive application in the transportation sector to issues such as the economic impact of highway and bridge construction (Babcock and Bratsberg, 1998) and regional estimates of commodity flows (Vilain et al., 1999). Weiss and Figura (2003) have noted a more recent shift in economic impact modeling toward the REMI (Regional Economic Models, Inc.) regional economic model (Treyz et al., 1992). This has been attributed to the fact that while IMPLAN and RIMS II are largely expenditure-driven (implying that, from a local perspective, a larger project is invariably a better project), the REMI model is able to translate the results of an analysis of the transportation impacts of a project into regional economic performance via its effects on business costs and productivity. For example, since trucking costs are an important input to most economic sectors, any cost savings attributable to a project can be traced through the local economy.

Regional and inter-regional input–output models are closely related to another type of regional economic model, computable general equilibrium (CGE) models, which can be used to simulate the wider effects of large projects or packages of transportation improvements (Bröcker, 2004). CGE models simulate the behavior of supply, demand, and prices in interacting markets within the economy. As applied to transportation, CGE models are given an explicitly spatial component, where changes to transportation networks are transmitted in the form of changes in spatially differentiated prices among locations, which affect production and household welfare. Accordingly, this type of model is typically referred to as a *spatial* computable general equilibrium (SCGE) model. Bröcker et al. (2010) note that SCGE models offer improvements over other types of analysis techniques in that they allow for simulations involving market imperfections, such as monopolistic competition, which underpin many New Economic Geography models. They also allow for the estimation of distributional consequences across locations, which Bröcker et al. (2010) illustrate with a simulation of the effects of a package of improvements that are part of the Trans-European Transport network (TEN-T) initiative.

Regional economic models are gaining in popularity due not only to their ability to simulate the effects of large intra- or inter-regional transportation improvements, but also due to their ability to be adapted to emerging theories and concepts in urban and regional economies, as well as transportation. The preceding discussion of SCGE models noted their adaptability to regimes of monopolistic competition, which help explain patterns of specialization and trade (Krugman, 1991). Transportation costs, especially where they are falling, are also considered to be an important factor in the emergence of agglomeration economies and associated productivity gains. Venables (2007) provides a theoretical framework for incorporating productivity improvements due to agglomeration into the evaluation of transportation improvements. Recent empirical work on this topic has suggested that transportation costs may figure prominently into the realization of agglomeration benefits at both the urban and regional levels (Rice et al., 2006; Graham and Kim, 2008), although the gains may not be evenly distributed across industries. Agglomeration effects may prove to be an important consideration in the evaluation of projects designed to enhance integration within the European Community.

A related concept that is relevant to regional modeling is that of *network effects*.

Laird et al. (2005) distinguish between two types of network effects: those relating to the network itself and its associated set of flows, and effects in the economic sectors linked by transportation networks. The former type of network effect relates more to the physical flows on the network, and so may be captured mostly within a transportation network model that is coupled with a regional economic model, while the latter relates more closely to patterns of production and exchange enabled by the transportation network. This latter type of network effect, the ability of transportation network changes to alter patterns of trade and production, may be more important in the long run and at the regional level. Thus, they may become a priority for the development of extensions to input–output and SCGE modeling systems (Vickerman, 2007).

5.   AGGREGATE ANALYSIS METHODS

At larger scales of analysis, there are several types of empirical methods available for estimating the contribution of transportation infrastructure to economic growth. The regional economic models discussed in the previous section can be extended to national levels, although this often adds considerably to the computational and data require-ments of the effort. In this section, we will explore a few examples of simpler econometric approaches to estimating the relationship between transportation and economic growth at more aggregate levels. These studies tend to move away from the analysis of individual projects and instead evaluate the cumulative effects of transportation network growth over time. Many of the examples presented here are drawn from the United States, since these approaches have tended to be more popular there.

Production Functions

During the early 1990s, there was a resurgence of interest in research attempting to measure the contribution of public capital to economic productivity, following the publication of work by Aschauer (1989) and Munnell (1990). Both of these researchers estimated econometric production functions for national productivity using time series data and treating public capital stocks as a separate input. Both studies found enormous returns to public capital and suggested that declines in spending on infrastructure as a share of GDP during the 1970s and 1980s might have been a cause for the decline in pro-ductivity observed during that period. This immediately prompted national debate over whether there was an "infrastructure shortfall," a debate recently reignited by the collapse of the I-35W Mississippi River Bridge in Minneapolis, Minnesota (USA). Subsequent research largely dispelled these claims. For example, federal spending on public nonmili-tary capital was shown to be roughly constant from 1950 to 1990, while state and local capital stocks (which tend to be much larger), grew considerably (Gramlich, 1994). Also, research that focused on industry-specific and state-level production functions, while controlling for unobservable differences in state-specific conditions, found much lower (and in some cases, statistically indistinguishable) rates of return (Holtz-Eakin, 1994; Garcia-Mila et al., 1996).

Nadiri and Mamuneas (1998) estimated the benefits of highway investment at the national level between the 1950s and the 1980s and concluded that in the early years returns were as high as 35 percent per year, but that by late in the years of the construction of the Interstate system that contribution had dropped to roughly the same as the return from private capital, about 11 percent.

One of the benefits that has been associated with transportation improvements is the impact that increased accessibility has on agglomeration of urban areas. *Agglomeration economies* are an external benefit that arises from the interaction and co-location of productive factors within an economy, such as infrastructure, suppliers, and customers, as well as a pool of labor with the needed skills. This process can provide added economic value to an economy. Agglomeration economies are offset to some extent by various diseconomies, such as congestion, that may also occur. Recent research by Graham (2007) has examined these impacts, which may affect different industry sectors in different ways.

The flurry of economic research into the role of public capital and, in particular, highway infrastructure capital, shed light on an important way to measure the economic returns from transportation infrastructure investment, albeit at a highly aggregate level. With the aid of time series data, public infrastructure capital can be specified as a factor of production, and its contribution to productivity tracked over time. This information is critically important at a time when the US National Highway System is essentially complete, and marginal improvements to the network must be evaluated. Care needs to be taken, however, in the specification and interpretation of the results from aggregate production function research. Definitions of public capital and other factors of production need to be rigorous (e.g., separating public highway capital from schools, airports, water systems, etc.). Also, the geographic scale of the research (local, state, national) needs to be clearly defined.

Other Econometric Methods

An alternative to using aggregate production functions is to specify econometric models relating levels of highway capital spending to economic indices such as employment, income, or various forms of output. Some of the later production function studies noted that, at smaller geographic scales, the effect of highway capital spending was to redistribute, rather than generate, economic activity (Boarnet, 1997). A related finding was that there were spillover effects from the provision of new highway infrastructure (Boarnet, 1998; Haughwout, 1998; Williams and Mullen, 1998). These findings were not necessarily new – previous research had examined spatially differentiated effects of highway capital spending (Stephanedes and Eagle, 1986, 1987; Stephanedes, 1990), but they did signal a new direction for econometric research into the economic effects of highway capital.

The contribution of much of the recent research into the relationships between transportation infrastructure provision and economic performance has been to refine methods of analysis. New methodologies aim to correct for potential temporal and/or spatial autocorrelation in datasets (Duffy-Deno and Eberts, 1991; Boarnet, 1998; Berechman et al., 2006). Finally, new conceptualizations of the link between transportation investment and economic performance have been suggested, such as relationships between improved accessibility and employment outcomes (Berechman and Paaswell, 2001; Ozbay et al., 2006), firm inventory behavior as a way to measure the returns from highway infrastructure (Shirley and Winston, 2004), and hybrid economic evaluation approaches that attempt to bridge the project-specific and macroeconomic approaches described herein (Weisbrod and Treyz, 1998).

Cliometric Methods

Economic historians, utilizing so-called cliometric methods (after Clio, the muse of history), have assessed the long-term retrospective impacts of major infrastructure investments. Among the more noted of these is the assessment by Fogel (1964) of railroads and economic growth in the nineteenth century, which sought to estimate the incremental economic contribution of railroads compared with its precursor system of canals. Fogel concluded that railroads contributed an increment of only 0.4 percent per year of growth in economic output, compared with competing estimates as high as 4 percent per year (Fishlow, 1965). Fogel later won a Nobel Prize in Economics for his work.

What is noteworthy about the economic history assessments of infrastructure assessments is that they underscore the profound difficulty of a deep assessment of the impact of major infrastructure system implementations even a century after the fact. Of course, investments at a smaller scale pose less daunting challenges for analysis.

The larger point is that the scale of investment is in many respects inversely proportionate to the difficulty of measuring impacts. Thus, assessing the effects of a Washington Beltway is an order of magnitude more difficult that assessing the impact of adding a single link to an already deployed network.

6.   CONCLUSION

This review has documented a variety of approaches that might be employed to analyze the economic impacts of transportation improvements. As should be clear by now, the matter of geographic scale is critical to selecting the appropriate type of analysis (Banister and Berechman, 2001). Matters of geographic context and resource distribution also figure prominently.

We reviewed project-based evaluation methods, where benefit-cost analysis is the predominant technique of analysis in most developed countries. This approach may be appropriate for many urban and even regional-scale projects. We also suggested that, given the difficulty of measuring direct user benefits and the dynamic nature of the relationship between transportation networks and patterns of development, analysts might consider using changes in land prices as an alternative measure of benefit. Other researchers have suggested using this method in order to capture the local, micro-scale effects of a transportation improvement (Banister and Thurstain-Goodwin, 2011). However, its consistent application may require the resolution of some remaining issues.

First, there is the nature of land values as a measure of benefits. As Mohring (1993) points out, the spillover effects of transportation projects are, in a sense, transfers of benefits initially received by users to those who provide services complementary to the use of the network. Thus, land price changes cannot be counted in addition to direct user benefits, as this would result in double-counting. Second, many of the spillover benefits arise due to mispricing of transportation facilities. Prices set closer to marginal cost would reduce the incidence of such spillovers. Third, if land values are to be used for the analysis of a project at a local level, there may be some underestimation of benefits if some users of the improved link have neither an origin nor a destination in the local area (i.e., pass-through traffic). These benefits will likely not be capitalized into local land values. Fourth, if an *ex ante* analysis of a project seeks to use accessibility changes as the primary driver of user benefit (through the medium of land value changes), the estimation of accessibility change may encounter some of the same issues associated with uncertainty in the estimation of user benefits in congested networks, since travel time estimates play an important role in all types of accessibility measures. As a related matter, such calculations may also need to take into account the effect of emerging technological trends, such as the availability of smartphones and small computing devices, on users' perception and valuation of their travel time. While this is already an area of active research for those studying the habits of public transport users, it may eventually also apply to private automobile users with the advent of autonomous vehicle technologies. These issues may represent fruitful areas for future research.

The aggregate-scale analyses discussed in this chapter seem to have a different purpose than the other project-level techniques discussed earlier. The literature on production functions and the growth effects of public infrastructure initially became popular due to the intense interest in the hypothesis of public capital shortfalls as a possible explanation for the slowdown in productivity growth during the 1970s and 1980s in the United States (and to a lesser extent, Europe). While the many papers produced on this topic since then have gradually refined the methodology for conducting such analysis, the reality is that the results of these studies are often not policy sensitive enough to be terribly useful in terms of policy analysis. The geographic scale of analysis and the treatment of transportation are too aggregate to provide much direction as to which types of investment to pursue, where, and how much. Nonetheless, these studies have helped to provide some rough evidence of the scale of returns from additional infrastructure investment in countries with already mature, well-developed networks (Vickerman, 2000; Banister and Berechman, 2001).

Similarly, cliometric methods represent a fascinating line of research, especially where the historical development of transportation networks is concerned, but is often not relevant to much current analysis. They do, however, often provide fodder for rich debates about the role of certain historical developments, as in the works cited here on the economic contribution of the railroads in the United States, in addition to offering useful frameworks for the analysis of such topics.

Regional analysis of transportation improvements and the economy will likely remain the target of much research in transportation economics and planning in the coming years. Opportunities remain for developing regional economic models in such ways that they can incorporate some of the key developments in urban and regional economics from recent decades. Probing network effects on production and supply chains, as well as interactions with agglomerative forces, will prove to be considerable challenges.

Perhaps as important, however, is the need to develop tools that are practical, as well as theoretically consistent. Modeling transportation flows accurately has historically been a challenging enough endeavor. Coupling these models with large-scale economic models introduces additional layers of complexity and uncertainty. One other important criticism of these models is that they lack transparency, that is, that they retain a certain "black box" character. This presents an inherent limitation to their usefulness in terms of policy analysis. Thus, the designers and users of such tools must be mindful that they are developing tools that not only give meaningful answers, but also understandable ones.

ACKNOWLEDGEMENTS

The authors would like to acknowledge the helpful comments of the anonymous reviewers that contributed to the improvement of this chapter.

NOTES

1. For recent reviews of operational model systems, see Wegener (2004), Hunt et al. (2005), Chang (2006), and Iacono et al. (2008).
2. For a more thorough discussion of the concept of accessibility and various types of accessibility measures, see Liu and Zhu (2004) or the collection of papers in Levinson and Krizek (2005).

REFERENCES

Abrantes, P.A. and Wardman, M.R. (2011), Meta-analysis of UK values of travel time: an update, *Transportation Research, Part A: Policy and Practice*, **45**(1), 1–17.
Archer, W., Gatzlaff, D. and Ling, D. (1996), Measuring the importance of location in house price appreciation, *Journal of Urban Economics*, **40**(3), 334–53.
Aschauer, D. (1989), Is public expenditure productive? *Journal of Monetary Economics*, **23**, 177–200.
Ashley, D. (1980), Uncertainty in the context of highway appraisal, *Transportation*, **9**(3), 249–67.
Babcock, M.W. and Bratsberg, B. (1998), Measurement of economic impact of highway and bridge construction, *Journal of the Transportation Research Forum*, **37**(2), 52–66.
Bailey, M.J., Muth, R.F. and Nourse, H.O. (1963), A regression method for real estate price index construction, *Journal of the American Statistical Association*, **58**, 933–42.
Banister, D. and Berechman, Y. (2001), Transport investment and the promotion of economic growth, *Journal of Transport Geography*, **9**(3), 209–18.
Banister, D. and Thurstain-Goodwin, M. (2011), Quantification of the non-transport benefits resulting from rail investment, *Journal of Transport Geography*, **19**(2), 212–23.
Berechman, J. and Paaswell, R.E. (2001), Accessibility improvements and local employment: an empirical analysis, *Journal of Transportation and Statistics*, **4**(2/3), 49–66.
Berechman, J., Ozmen, D. and Ozbay, K. (2006), Empirical analysis of transportation investment and economic development at state, county and municipality levels, *Transportation*, **33**(6), 537–51.
Boarnet, M.G. (1997), Infrastructure services and the productivity of public capital: the case of streets and highways, *National Tax Journal*, **50**(1), 39–57.
Boarnet, M.G. (1998), Spillovers and the locational effects of public infrastructure, *Journal of Regional Science*, **38**(3), 381–400.
Bröcker, J. (2004), Computable general equilibrium analysis in transportation economics, in D.A. Hensher, K.J. Button, K. Haynes and P. Stopher (eds), *Handbook of Transport Geography and Spatial Systems*, Amsterdam: Pergamon, pp. 269–92.
Bröcker, J., Korzhenevych, A. and Schürmann, C. (2010), Assessing spatial equity and efficiency impacts of transport infrastructure projects, *Transportation Research, Part B: Methodological*, **44**, 795–811.
Brownstone, D. and Small, K.A. (2005), Valuing time and reliability: assessing the evidence from road pricing demonstrations, *Transportation Research, Part A: Policy and Practice*, **39**(4), 279–93.
Brownstone, D., Ghosh, A., Golob, T.F., Kazimi, C. and van Amelsfort, D. (2003), Drivers' willingness-to-pay to reduce travel time: evidence from the San Diego I-15 congestion pricing project, *Transportation Research, Part A: Policy and Practice*, **37**(4), 373–87.
Carrion, C. and Levinson, D.M. (2012), Value of travel time reliability: a review of current evidence, *Transportation Research, Part A: Policy and Practice*, **46**(4), 720–41.

Case, B. and Quigley, J.M. (1991), The dynamics of real estate prices, *Review of Economics and Statistics*, **73**(1), 50–8.

Case, K.E. and Shiller, R.J. (1989), The efficiency of the market for single-family homes, *American Economic Review*, **79**(1), 125–37.

Cervero, R. (2002), Induced travel demand: research design, empirical evidence, and normative policies, *Journal of Planning Literature*, **17**(1), 3–20.

Chang, J.S. (2006), Models of the relationship between transport and land-use: a review, *Transport Reviews*, **26**(3), 325–50.

Church, A., Frost, M. and Sullivan, K. (2000), Transport and social exclusion in London, *Transport Policy*, **7**(3), 195–205.

Clay, M.J. and Johnston, R.A. (2006), Multivariate uncertainty analysis of an integrated land use and transportation model: MEPLAN, *Transportation Research Part D*, **11**, 191–203.

Downs, A. (1962), The law of peak-hour expressway congestion, *Traffic Quarterly*, **16**, 393–409.

Downs, A. (1992), *Stuck in Traffic: Coping with Peak-Hour Traffic Congestion*, Washington, DC: Brookings Institution Press.

Duffy-Deno, K.T. and Eberts, R.W. (1991), Public infrastructure and regional economic development: a simultaneous equations approach, *Journal of Urban Economics*, **30**, 329–43.

Fishlow, A. (1965), *American Railroads and the Transformation of the Antebellum Economy*, Cambridge, MA: Harvard University Press.

Flyvbjerg, B., Bruzelius, N. and Rothengatter, W. (2003), *Megaprojects and Risk: An Anatomy of Ambition*, New York: Cambridge University Press.

Flyvbjerg, B., Skamris Holm, M.K. and Buhl, S.L. (2005), How inaccurate are demand forecasts in public works projects? *Journal of the American Planning Association*, **71**(2), 131–46.

Fogel, R. (1964), *Railroads and American Economic Growth: Essays in Econometric History*, Baltimore, MD: Johns Hopkins Press.

Garcia-Mila, T., McGuire, T.J. and Porter, R.H. (1996), The effect of public capital in state-level production functions reconsidered, *Review of Economics and Statistics*, **78**(1), 177–80.

Goodwin, P., Hass-Klau, C. and Cairns, S. (1998), Evidence on the effects of road capacity reductions on traffic levels, *Traffic Engineering and Control*, **39**(6), 348–54.

Graham, D.J. (2007), Variable returns to agglomeration and the effect of road traffic congestion, *Journal of Urban Economics*, **62**(1), 102–20.

Graham, D.J. and Kim, H.Y. (2008), An empirical analytical framework for agglomeration economies, *Annals of Regional Science*, **42**, 267–89.

Gramlich, E. (1994), Infrastructure investment: a review essay, *Journal of Economic Literature*, **32**, 1176–96.

Halvorsen, R. and Pollakowski, H. (1981), Choice of functional form for hedonic price functions, *Journal of Urban Economics*, **10**, 37–49.

Hansen, M. and Huang, Y. (1997), Road supply and traffic in California urban areas, *Transportation Research Part A*, **31A**(3), 205–18.

Haughwout, A.F. (1998), Aggregate production functions, interregional equilibrium, and the measurement of infrastructure productivity, *Journal of Urban Economics*, **44**, 216–27.

Hensher, D.A. (2001), Measurement of the valuation of travel time savings, *Journal of Transport Economics and Policy*, **35**(1), 71–98.

Hensher, D.A. and Rose, J.M. (2007), Development of commuter and non-commuter mode choice models for the assessment of new public transport infrastructure projects: a case study, *Transportation Research Part A: Policy and Practice*, **41**(5), 428–43.

Hills, P.J. (1996), What is induced traffic? *Transportation*, **23**(1), 5–16.

Holtz-Eakin, D. (1994), Public sector capital and the productivity puzzle, *Review of Economics and Statistics*, **76**, 12–21.

Hunt, J.D., Kriger, D.S. and Miller, E.J. (2005), Current operational land-use-transport modeling frameworks: a review, *Transport Reviews*, **25**(3), 329–76.

Iacono, M.J., Levinson, D.M. and El-Geneidy, A.M. (2008), Models of transportation and land use change: a guide to the territory, *Journal of Planning Literature*, **22**(4), 323–40.

Krugman, P. (1991), Increasing returns and economic geography, *Journal of Political Economy*, **99**(3), 483–99.

Laird, J.J., Nellthorp, J. and Mackie, P.J. (2005), Network effects and total economic impact in transport appraisal, *Transport Policy*, **12**, 537–44.

Lancaster, K. (1966), A new approach to consumer theory, *Journal of Political Economy*, **74**, 132–57.

Lee, D.B., Klein, L.A. and Camus, G. (1999), Induced traffic and induced demand, *Transportation Research Record*, **1659**, 68–75.

Levinson, D.M. (2002), Identifying winners and losers in transportation, *Transportation Research Record*, **1812**, 179–85.

Levinson, D.M. and Chen, W. (2005), Paving new ground, in D.M. Levinson and K.J. Krizek (eds), *Access to Destinations*, Amsterdam: Elsevier.

Levinson, D.M. and Kanchi, S. (2002), Road capacity and the allocation of time, *Journal of Transportation and Statistics*, **5**(1), 25–46.

Levinson, D.M. and Karamalaputi, R. (2003), Induced supply: a model of highway network expansion at the microscopic level, *Journal of Transport Economics and Policy*, **37**(3), 297–318.

Levinson, D.M. and Krizek, K.J. (eds) (2005), *Access to Destinations*, Amsterdam: Elsevier.

Liu, S. and Zhu, X. (2004), Accessibility analyst: an integrated GIS tool for accessibility analysis in urban transportation planning, *Environment and Planning B: Planning and Design*, **31**, 105–24.

Mackie, P.J. and Preston, J. (1998), Twenty-one sources of error and bias in transport project appraisal, *Transport Policy*, **5**, 1–7.

Malpezzi, S. (2003), Hedonic pricing models: a selective and applied review, in T. O'Sullivan and K. Gibb (eds), *Housing Economics and Public Policy: Essays in Honour of Duncan MacLennan*, Oxford: Blackwell Science, pp. 67–89.

Mohring, H. (1961), Land values and the measurement of highway benefits, *Journal of Political Economy*, **69**(2), 216–49.

Mohring, H. (1993), Maximizing, measuring, and *not* double counting transportation-improvement benefits: a primer on closed- and open-economy cost-benefit analysis, *Transportation Research Part B*, **27**(6), 413–24.

Mokhtarian, P.L. and Chen, C. (2004), TTB or not TTB, that is the question: a review and analysis of the empirical literature on travel time (and money) budgets, *Transportation Research Part A: Policy and Practice*, **38A**, 643–75.

Mokhtarian, P.L., Samaniego, F., Shumway, R. and Willits, N. (2002), Revisiting the notion of induced traffic through a matched-pairs study, *Transportation*, **29**(2), 193–220.

Munnell, A. (1990), Why has productivity growth declined? Productivity and public investment, *New England Economic Review*, January/February, 3–22.

Nadiri, M.I. and Mamuneas, T. (1998), *Contribution of Highway Capital to Output and Productivity Growth in the US Economy and Industries*, Washington, DC: Federal Highway Administration.

Noland, R.B. and Polak, J.W. (2002), Travel time variability: a review of theoretical and empirical issues, *Transport Reviews*, **22**(1), 39–54.

Ozbay, K., Ozmen, D. and Berechman, J. (2006), Modeling and analysis of the link between accessibility and employment growth, *ASCE Journal of Transportation Engineering*, **132**(5), 385–93.

Parthasarathi, P. and Levinson, D.M. (2010), Post-construction evaluation of traffic forecast accuracy, *Transport Policy*, **17**(6), 428–43.

Parthasarathi, P., Levinson, D.M. and Karamalaputi, R. (2003), Induced demand: a microscopic perspective, *Urban Studies*, **40**(7), 1335–51.

Pickrell, D.H. (1992), A desire named streetcar: fantasy and fact in rail transit planning, *Journal of the American Planning Association*, **58**(2), 158–76.

Rice, P., Venables, A.J. and Patacchini, E. (2006), Spatial determinants of productivity: analysis for the regions of Great Britain, *Regional Science and Urban Economics*, **36**, 727–52.

Richmond, J. (2001), A whole-system approach to evaluating urban transit investments, *Transport Reviews*, **21**, 141–79.

Rosen, S. (1974), Hedonic prices and implicit markets: product differentiation in pure competition, *Journal of Political Economy*, **82**, 34–55.

Ryan, S. (1999), Property values and transportation facilities: finding the transportation land-use connection, *Journal of Planning Literature*, **13**(4), 412–27.

Sevcikova, H., Raftery, A.E. and Waddell, P.A. (2007), Assessing uncertainty in urban simulations using Bayesian melding, *Transportation Research Part B: Methodological*, **41**, 652–69.

Shirley, C. and Winston, C. (2004), Firm inventory behavior and the returns from highway infrastructure investments, *Journal of Urban Economics*, **55**, 398–415.

Smersh, G.T. and Smith, M.T. (2000), Accessibility changes and urban house price appreciation: a constrained optimization approach to determining distance effects, *Journal of Housing Economics*, **9**, 187–96.

Stephanedes, Y.J. (1990), Distributional effects of state highway investment on local and regional development, *Transportation Research Record*, **1274**, 156–64.

Stephanedes, Y.J. and Eagle, D.M. (1986), Highway expenditures and non-metropolitan employment, *Journal of Advanced Transportation*, **20**(1), 43–61.

Stephanedes, Y.J. and Eagle, D.M. (1987), Highway impacts on regional employment, *Journal of Advanced Transportation*, **21**(1), 67–79.

Treyz, G.I., Rickman, D. and Shao, G. (1992), The REMI economic-demographic forecasting and simulation model, *International Regional Science Review*, **14**, 221–53.

Venables, A.J. (2007), Cost-benefit analysis in the presence of agglomeration and income taxation, *Journal of Transport Economics and Policy*, **41**(2), 173–88.

Vickerman, R.W. (2000), Evaluation methodologies for transport projects in the United Kingdom, *Transport Policy*, **7**, 7–16.

Vickerman, R.W. (2007), Cost-benefit analysis and large-scale infrastructure projects: state of the art and challenges, *Environment and Planning B: Planning and Design*, **34**, 598–610.

Vilain, P., Liu, L.N. and Aimen, D. (1999), Estimate of commodity inflows to a substate region: an input–output based approach, *Transportation Research Record*, **1653**, 17–26.

Wegener, M. (2004), Overview of land use transport models, in D.A. Hensher, K.J. Button, K.E. Haynes and P.R. Stopher (eds), *Handbook of Transport Geography and Spatial Systems*, Amsterdam: Pergamon, pp. 127–46.

Weisbrod, G.E. and Grovak, M. (1998), Comparing approaches for valuing economic development benefits of transportation projects, *Transportation Research Record*, **1649**, 86–94.

Weisbrod, G.E. and Treyz, F. (1998), Productivity and accessibility: bridging project-specific and macro-economic analyses of transportation investment, *Journal of Transportation and Statistics*, **1**(3), 65–79.

Weiss, M. and Figura, R. (2003), Provisional typology of highway economic development projects, *Transportation Research Record*, **1839**, 115–19.

Williams, M. and Mullen, J. (1998), Highway capacity spillover and interstate manufacturing activity, *International Journal of Transport Economics*, **25**(3), 287–95.

Zahavi, Y. and Talvitie, A. (1980), Regularities in travel time and money expenditures, *Transportation Research Record*, **750**, 13–19.

17 Transport projects and wider economic impacts
Torben Holvad and Steen Leleur

1. INTRODUCTION

A major weakness of much of current appraisal practice of transport infrastructure projects is its basis on partial equilibrium analysis. The partial equilibrium approach implies that only the changes within the transport market are taken into account in the assessment of a given infrastructure project (e.g., time savings for transport users, reduced operating costs for transport producers and infrastructure construction costs), whereas linkages between the transport market and other markets (notably goods and labour markets) are to a large extent ignored. The importance of ignoring other markets in transport appraisal has been subject to much analysis in the available literature (see, e.g., SACTRA, 1999).

A key research question is whether such wider economic impacts are additional to the time and cost savings generated from transport policy interventions. If such impacts are additional it could change the overall assessment of whether transport projects are worthwhile or not. Three principle issues are relevant (Goodwin and Persson, 2001):

- Traditional economic theory suggests that wider economic benefits are mostly not additional to the time and cost savings that generated them, but only a change in the form and incidence of these benefits. Inclusion of wider economic impacts in a cost benefit analysis (CBA) would therefore create double-counting.
- Newer economic theories dispute this, suggesting that there can be wider economic effects with additional value – but these can involve benefits or disbenefits.
- Even if there is an overall benefit to the economy as a whole, and even if this benefit is additional to CBA results, local areas may be disadvantaged.

The condition under which wider economic effects are additional to a standard transport CBA is the extent to which the economy departs from the economic model of perfect competition. If imperfect competition dominates then it is possible that the wider economic effects can be additional to the CBA result. The context in which perfect competition is not a valid assumption involves imperfectly competitive output and input markets (e.g., due to market concentration) and/or existence of subsidies and taxes. In both cases this would result in prices not being set at marginal costs. It therefore becomes critical to examine the extent to which the different markets in an economy are working (approximately) according to perfect competition or not.

As such, departures from perfect competition, while relying on a partial equilibrium approach in CBA, would affect the appraisal of projects within any economic sector. However, given the importance of well-functioning transportation systems for the overall performance of economies, wider economic effects are likely to be of higher relevance.

It should be pointed out that even if wider economic effects are not additional to the standard transport CBA benefits, it would still be of interest to assess these effects in order to determine the winners and losers of a transport infrastructure projects.

From an empirical perspective, available evidence suggests that there is a possibility for wider economic benefits to add to the order of 40 per cent to the CBA transport benefit-cost ratio (Oosterhaven and Knaap, 2000). However, substantial variation regarding the magnitude of the additional benefits is present such that the actual size should be determined on a case-by-case basis rather than on standard up rate rules (Joint Transport Research Centre, 2008).

This chapter will review the theoretical and empirical evidence regarding the linkages between transport projects and the economy and set out the scope for additionality with respect to the wider economic impacts compared to those items that are included in traditional transport project appraisal. The chapter will also consider the possible solutions to how these wider economic impacts can be integrated into project appraisal, notably cost-benefit analysis. This will also highlight the role of CGE models to provide information about the effects of improved accessibility on the economy as a whole in terms of output, prices and employment.

The remaining part of this chapter is structured as follows. Section 2 sets out the theoretical evidence for wider economic effects with particular focus on specifying the transmission mechanisms of the effects. Empirical evidence is reviewed in section 3, covering results for both individual infrastructure projects as well as outlining findings regarding the implications of changes in the total infrastructure at macroeconomic level. In section 4 the possible solutions towards measurement of wider economic effects within transport project appraisal will be outlined. Section 5 contains conclusions and outlines areas of further research.

2.   THEORETICAL EVIDENCE FOR WIDER ECONOMIC EFFECTS OF TRANSPORT INFRASTRUCTURE PROJECTS

The starting point for understanding the possibility for wider economic effects of transport infrastructure projects is to look at the big picture and consider the importance of a good transport network on performance of modern economies. Indeed, society is dependent on accessibility that is the 'ease of reaching' for households and business in terms of employment, education, supply and delivery of goods/services and leisure activities, etc. The transport network and its characteristics have a critical influence on accessibility in relation to support connectivity within and between countries. Therefore, changes to the available transport network through transport infrastructure projects and other transport policy interventions may affect economic performance in terms of implications on overall output, i.e., gross domestic product (GDP). It should be noticed that infrastructure improvements often also have implications on welfare that are not necessarily captured through changes in GDP (e.g., benefits for commuters or leisure travel). The importance of transport infrastructure for economic growth is, for example, critical in W.W. Rostow's model for economic development in terms of preconditions for take-off (Rostow, 1971). Transport improvements could lead to changes in GDP due to impacts on: (1) the number of inputs used and (2) the efficiency of input usage, i.e., productivity implications. First, transport improvements may facilitate access to labour or the creation of new firms, which could lead to increases in employment and in turn lead to a higher GDP. Second, influences on productivity from transport improvements could occur directly through reduced journey times (for example, due to reduced costs for staff to transport products to customers or bring materials from suppliers). This type of effect is taken into account in standard transport cost-benefit appraisal through monetary valuation of time savings. Other more indirect influences on productivity are not taken into account, although these could be significant for major transport infrastructure projects such as:

- Enhanced profitability of private investment; for example, due to transport improvements that allow companies to extend the geographical area of their output markets, which could imply that investment not profitable before now becomes financially worthwhile because of higher revenue.
- Improved labour mobility; transport infrastructure investment could allow persons in a given region to consider better paid employment opportunities in locations further away that before were not accessible. This may in turn stimulate investment in skills.
- Stronger competition: transport improvements could imply that companies in the same sector but at different locations become competitors if the reduced transport costs allow these companies to deliver goods in each other's local market. In turn, stronger competition is one of the main drivers of productivity (see, for example, Office of Fair Trading, 2007).

An important distinction regarding productivity changes from transport is whether these occur as one-off effects or whether productivity growth can continue over longer periods. Sustained productivity growth could be the outcome if there are positive effects on innovation, although it is rather difficult to identify the mechanisms through which transport may influence extent of innovation within a geographical area or industrial sector.

It should be noticed that, although our focus is on how transport improvements are generating economic growth, there are likely also to be important feedback links from economic growth to transport improvements (Berechman, 2001). In particular, it has been put forward that higher-income countries can easier provide the required funding towards transport infrastructure projects compared to other countries.

A couple of historic examples to demonstrate the importance of transport improvements on economic growth will be given below. The importance of railways in the nineteenth century and early twentieth century for delivering economic growth have been studied by several authors, for example Fogel (1964) in the case of the US and Hawke (1970) for England and Wales. In the case of freight transport in England and Wales, Crafts and Leunig (2006) estimate that welfare benefits of the railway investments in 1865 amounted to 4.1 per cent of gross national product (GNP). At the more project-specific level (and with a more current perspective), the opening of the high-speed rail station in Northern France (Lille) with fast connections to Paris, Brussels and London has been a substantial boost to the local economy within the Lille Metropolitan Area, although partly at the expense of economic performance in more peripheral areas of the region (Mann, 2006).

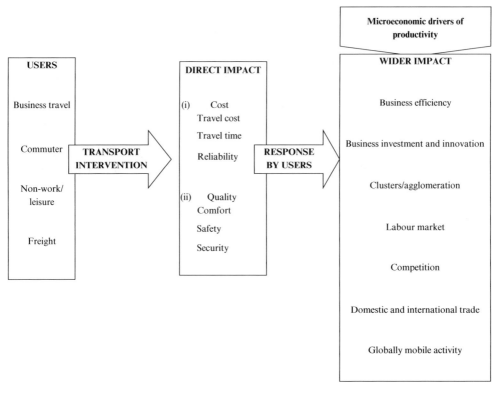

Figure 17.1   Links between transport and economic performance

A graphical illustration of the linkage between transport infrastructure improvement and the economy is included in Figure 17.1. The figure highlights two key elements in order for transport interventions to result in wider impacts: (1) the direct impacts of a given transport intervention; (2) response by users (business travel, commuter, non-work leisure and freight), which may in turn influence productivity according to how they value the changes to the characteristics of the transport system. Some seven microeconomic drivers of productivity are included in Figure 17.1. Below, each of these will be briefly described:

- Business efficiency: the influence of transport improvements on business efficiency occurs if these result in changes to the cost, time or reliability of business/freight traffic. This could then result in cost savings for industry. In general, effects on business efficiency are taken into account in current appraisal of transport infrastructure projects through valuating changes to travel time, vehicle operating costs and reliability.
- Business investment and innovation: transport improvements that contribute to higher business investment or a larger level of innovative activities would as

a result have a positive effect on productivity. Higher investment level could be due to the direct transport cost savings obtained, which may trigger reorganization among companies covering the complete logistics process. The main effect, however, is due to increased size of output markets with higher sales to cover fixed costs and the possibility for lower unit costs in production as the scale of operation expands. These effects may result in additional business investment schemes becoming financially feasible and hence be taken forward. Similarly, it could be argued that innovative activity could be positive influenced. Other mechanisms for productivity effects are linked to the possibility that transport improvements may encourage the formation of clusters which could stimulate technology transfer among firms from the same sector (SACTRA, 1999). However, in practice it is very difficult to identify specific links between transport improvements and innovative activity among businesses.

- Clusters/agglomeration: economies of agglomerations are linked to the existence of external scale economies for certain locations due to (e.g., large urban areas): (1) better matching of people to jobs; (2) wider range of suppliers to choose from by companies; (3) availability of external services (e.g., public transport, restaurants and conference facilities); (4) information spillovers between firms. This means that firms deciding to locate in such locations are more productive than in other locations, especially since unit costs for inputs are likely to be higher in large urban areas compared to other regions. At the general level, the role of transport improvements in the context of agglomeration economies is that these improvements may contribute to secure productivity benefits through reduced travel time and costs that can bring companies, employees and consumers in these areas closer. However, until recently it has been very difficult to determine this linkage at the project-specific level. This is, however, one of the areas where progress is now being made regarding the understanding of the linkages and how these can be measured (Graham, 2007). As such, this is important because available evidence suggests that the contribution from large-scale projects on productivity via agglomeration economies can indeed be substantial.

- Labour market: transport improvements can support the functioning of the labour market as the improved accessibility can enlarge the search area for persons looking for employment opportunities. In addition, employers may also get advantages through larger and more diversified pools of applicants. It should be noted that this effect is relevant both for agglomeration (discussed above) and for less densely populated areas. The reduction in commuting costs could be of particular importance for low-income groups, thereby supporting social inclusion, although important coordination with the housing market is required to prevent that such groups will be disadvantaged from increases in house prices/rents normally associated with transport improvements. An example of recent work on the role of transport improvements on the labour market is Gibbons and Machin (2006).

- Competition: reduced transport costs and improved accessibility can facilitate competition as it extends market areas for companies and thereby increases the possibility that several firms will or can be present in the same markets as competitors. In turn, increased competitive pressure is one of the main drivers of productivity improvements (Office of Fair Trading, 2007) due to low-cost (high-productivity) companies increasing their market share and cost-cutting initiatives; for example, because incumbents attempt to pre-empt market entry.

- Domestic and international trade: transport improvements can facilitate trade through reduced transport costs, implying fewer barriers to trade. In turn, productivity could be influenced positively through higher trade: increased export may facilitate specialization and utilization of economies of scale in production and import growth may facilitate technology transfer between countries (Frankel and Romer, 1999). In this context, airport and port infrastructures play a critical role but also surface transport links. Furthermore, it should be emphasized that transport improvements will not only support international trade but also domestic trade due to lower transport costs.

- Globally mobile activity: the main linkage between transport improvements and global mobile activity is through influences on business location and foreign direct investments (FDIs) for companies working on a global scale. As such there are indications that transport links is one of the factors that are taken into account in the decision of where global businesses locate or take FDIs forward. On the other hand there are mixed evidence regarding the contribution of FDIs on economic growth and productivity. Recent work suggests that the positive growth effects from FDIs are dependent on other factors such as a well-developed local financial markets (Alfaro et. al., 2010).

However, there are also a number of important caveats and counterarguments regarding wider economic effects. Much of the impact of transport improvements may be redistributive rather than generative. This is highlighted by the two-way road argument where a transport infrastructure project linking a backward peripheral region with an advanced core region may lead to economic activity migrating from the peripheral region to the core, contrary to the intended impact of the intervention to promote the migration of activity from the core to the periphery (see, e.g., Vickerman et al., 1997). Further issues relate to crowding out. Excessive public investment can result in higher tax rates and or interest rates, thus reducing private investment. Moreover excessive investment in road transport may reduce public investments in other sectors that may have additional economic benefits. This includes non-road transport investments and direct grants to industry. There is also the related issue of leakage into higher costs. Where investment projects are procured in non-competitive situations there is a risk that the investments may merely leak into higher unit costs for construction and maintenance. Overall, it is concluded that transport investment may be a necessary condition for economic development but it is not a sufficient condition.

Indeed, the recent Eddington Study mentions that there are examples of countries and regions have experienced economic growth without significant changes in the transport network (Eddington, 2006). On the other hand, it is also pointed out that economic growth without transport improvements may sooner or later result in constraints on further economic development as congestion and other transport-related bottlenecks start to become significant. This may also highlight that in developed economies where the different economic centres are, in general, already well-connected there may be less scope for significant impacts on economic growth through entirely new transport links; rather emphasis should be on infrastructure projects that can deal with capacity problems, such as those caused by significant traffic growth and urbanization.

3.   EMPIRICAL EVIDENCE ON THE LINKAGE BETWEEN TRANSPORT INFRASTRUCTURE PROJECTS AND WIDER ECONOMIC EFFECTS

A number of empirical approaches have been utilized over the past couple of decades regarding assessing the contribution from transport infrastructure on economic performance. In particular, the following three groups of analyses have been applied: (1) macroeconomic approaches based on production and cost functions; (2) general equilibrium approaches; (3) microeconomic approaches based mainly on studies at the local/regional regarding employment and land values. Below, these approaches will be reviewed in terms of key results.

Production and Cost Functions

This approach involves econometric estimation of macro production functions (or cost functions), where variation in output (e.g., measured by GDP) is explained by changes in production factors available (such as labour and private capital) as well as changes in infrastructure capital (including transport). The approach covers studies at different geographical scales (national or regional level) depending on the availability of national accounts data at regional level. Estimation of these aggregated production functions can be based on time-series, cross-section or pooled datasets. Variables used in the estimation process show variation, especially with respect to infrastructure capital where some studies include all (public) infrastructure capital while others focus on transport infrastructure capital alone or even mode-specific infrastructure capital. A key output from the estimation is the so-called output elasticity that determines how much output (e.g., GDP) will increase (in percentage) for a 1 per cent increase in available infrastructure capital.

The starting point for much of this work is David Aschauer, whose estimates for output elasticity for the US indicated that a 1 per cent increase in the stock of public sector capital would increase GDP by 0.38 to 0.56 per cent annually (Aschauer, 1989). However, these results have subsequently been found to overstate the impact due to statistical estimation problems, missing variables and data quality (Gramlich, 1994). More recent studies have found much lower values, with Quinet and Vickerman (2004: 28) summarizing the evidence and conclude that a plausible range of the elasticity of output with respect to public capital is 0.05 to 0.30. Table 17.1 provides an overview of output and cost elasticities for a selection of countries (it should be noticed that negative cost elasticities imply that increased infrastructure capital is associated with lower costs, i.e., consistent with positive output elasticities). As such the macroeconomic evidence in Table 17.1 suggests that transport infrastructure has a positive influence on economic growth albeit relatively small and variable depending on the specific context.

Overall, aggregate production functions can provide useful information about the contribution from infrastructure improvements to economic performance. However,

Table 17.1   Summary of output and cost elasticities of highway and other public capital in various countries

Country	Sample	Infrastructure measure	Elasticity range
United States	Aggregate (ts)	Public capital	Output: 0.05 to 0.39
	States (xs)	Public capital	Output: 0.19 to 0.26
	States (ts/xs)	Highway capital	Output: 0.04 to 0.15
	Regions, trucking industry (ts/xs)	Highway capital	Cost: 0.044 to −0.07
Japan	Regions (ts/xs)	Transportation and communication infrastructure	Output: 0.35 to 0.42
United Kingdom	Aggregate (ts)	Public capital	Cost: negative, statically significant
France	Regions (xs)	Public capital	Cost: positive, statically significant
Germany	Industry (ts/xs)	Public capital, highway capital	Cost: negative, statically significant
India	Aggregate (ts) States (xs)	Economic infrastructure: roads, rail, electric capacity	Cost: −0.01 to −0.47
Mexico	National, 26 industries	Transportation, communication & electricity, public capital	Returns to public capital: 5.4–7.3%

Note: ts = time series; xs = cross-section

Source: Lakshmanan (2007)

other tools are required to complement this information in order to get a deeper understanding of the linkages.

CGE Models

Before considering the findings from recent studies regarding the magnitude of wider economic impacts, a brief summary of the key aspects of CGE modelling is included below (for further details see Kehoe and Kehoe, 1994). A CGE model is an abstraction of an economic system encompassing consumers, producers and eventually a government for one or several regions/countries. This group of models is formulated within the microeconomic tradition of comparative static equilibrium analysis with typically utility maximizing consumers and profit maximizing producers. For a given economy (or several economies) utility functions for consumers (or groups of consumers), which determine demand functions, and production and cost functions for specific goods or groups of goods are specified, combined with computational algorithms to determine equilibria between supply and demand. The outcome of the CGE analysis would determine the total net-benefits of a transport improvement and, combined with information about the net-benefits from a transport CBA, this could determine the extent of additional wider economic effects. These models are not designed specifically to examine how

Table 17.2   Evidence on multipliers

Author	Model	Market structure	Multiplier
Jara Diaz (1986)	Partial	Monopoly	1.5
Venables and Gasiorek (1999)	Partial – regional trade	Monopolistic competition	1.28–1.42
Venables and Gasiorek (1999)	General – regional trade	Monopolistic competition	1.35–1.44
Newbery (1998)	Partial	Oligopolistic competition	1.03–1.08
Davies (1999)	Partial	Oligopoly	1.12
Bröcker et al. (2002)	General – CGEurope	Monopolistic competition	1.20
Venables (2007)	General – urban commuting	Monopolistic competition	1.60–2.52*
Oosterhaven and Elhorst (2008)	General – RAEM	Monopolistic competition	1.20 (urban) 1.80 (inter-urban)

Note: * If commuter traffic represents 20 per cent of urban traffic and for the rest of urban traffic a multiplier of 1 applies then a multiplier of around 1.3 applies

Source: Holvad and Preston (2005)

transport improvements influence the economy (via reduced transport costs) but can be used for a whole range of economic instruments.

Our focus on presenting the findings from CGE models will be on the extent to which wider economic effects appear to be additional to the standard benefits from transport cost-benefit analysis. This issue can be examined through the so-called total benefit multiplier, which measures how much the direct transport benefits should be multiplied in order to take full account of wider economic impacts. Table 17.2 provides an overview of the multiplier values from recent studies.

The overall indication from Table 17.2 suggests that the multiplier for wider economic effects is in excess of 1, implying that these types of effects are additional to the benefits traditionally considered. Indeed, the eight studies and 13 values in Table 17.2 suggest a multiplier in the region of 1.4 but with considerable variation around this (standard deviation of 0.4). Without going into the details of CGE modelling, the findings suggest that the assumptions regarding market structure in the transport using sectors have implications for the value of the multiplier identified (highest in the case of monopoly and monopolistic competition and lowest for oligopolistic competition). The variation in the value of the multiplier highlights the need to consider wider economic effects on a case-by-case basis rather than using general multipliers.

Ex-post Monitoring

The third set of evidence is based on ex-post monitoring of investment schemes. These usually focus on the impact of road investments on the location of employment and population and on land prices. There is a substantial literature both with respect to the impact of public transport and private transport oriented interventions. For example, ODPM/RICS (2003) identified 150 references on the topic of land value and public transport, with 18 key references examined. They concluded that 'the expected effect on both the residential and commercial property markets is positive but the range of impacts is very variable – from marginal to over 100% in the commercial sector in North America'.

A review regarding the influence of highways on metropolitan development in the US (Boarnet and Haughwhat, 2000: 6–10) identified some 20 references that revealed empirical evidence. They conclude: 'In sum, the evidence suggests that highways influence land prices, population and employment changes near the project, and that the land use effects are likely at the expense of losses elsewhere.' The finding would suggest that land-use effects tend to be redistributive rather than generative. This work also highlights that highway investments may have negative spillovers by promoting decentralization and suburban sprawl and thus offsetting the economic benefits of agglomeration and the social benefits of integrated communities.

4.   INCLUSION OF WIDER ECONOMIC EFFECTS IN TRANSPORT INFRASTRUCTURE PROJECT APPRAISAL: POSSIBLE APPROACHES

One of the main recent contributions towards the analysis of how transport can contribute to economic growth and productivity is SACTRA (1999). The analyses highlighted the scope for additional benefits through market imperfections/existence of externalities and also illustrated the scale of these benefits through simulation modelling. As part of the recommendations it emphasized the role that CGE models could play in terms of assessment of the linkages between transport and the wider economy. Other approaches towards inclusion of wider economic effects in transport project appraisal include frameworks that identify/quantify specific (additional) effects not included in current appraisal and then add these into the standard transport cost-benefit outcome (Department for Transport, 2005).

The main advantage of the CGE modelling approach is that it facilitates analysis of imperfect competition, location decisions of firms, economies of scale and agglomeration effects and substitution concerning input choices for firms and consumption goods for households, all of which are important in relation to the possible presence of wider economic effects. Furthermore, the general equilibrium approach implies that effects on all markets are considered, thereby – in the case of transport projects – allowing for assessment of non-transport benefits and costs. An important strength of CGE models is the scope for comparison of outcomes of different equilibrium states due to its comparative static equilibrium structure (Tavasszy et al., 2002). This form of analysis is not possible within partial equilibrium models. A number of disadvantages/problems are, however, relevant with respect to CGE models, including:

- potential lack of sufficient detail of transport system;
- potential lack of sufficient detail concerning the spatial dimension;
- extensive analytical and data requirements;

- necessary to make assumptions concerning the precise form of imperfect competition adopted;
- specification of functional forms cannot be definitive;
- the degree of industrial sector disaggregation;
- lack of any basis for statistical diagnostics to validate the whole model.

The majority of these problems are empirical and computational rather than theoretical, in particular concerning lack of detail in the description of the transport system, sectors, household types, etc. (Oosterhaven and Knaap, 2000). It should be noted that general equilibrium considerations matter more for the analysis of macro transport policy or infrastructure projects with large network implications that may have significant impact on transport costs and accessibility. This implies that CGE models are not necessarily appropriate to examine all forms of transport policy interventions, including smaller infrastructure schemes (Gunn, 2004).

In recent years there have been several practical advances regarding the use of CGE models to study the linkage between transport improvements and economic performance, for example the IASON model (Bröcker, 2002) regarding the economic effects of the Trans-European Network Transport priority projects.

More flexible and less resource demanding approaches than CGE models may be required to assess wider economic effects for a broader range of transport infrastructure projects. A recent study by the UK Department for Transport (2005) examined the possibilities for estimating a list of wider economic effects without reliance on CGE models. The study distinguishes between economic impacts that result in welfare changes and those that influence GDP. It is noted that impacts on GDP cannot simply be added to the welfare impacts due to possible double-counting. The following impacts are considered in the study:

- agglomeration economies (see section 2);
- increased competition as a result of better transport;
- increased output in imperfectly competitive markets;
- economic welfare benefits arising from improved labour supply.

For the first three categories, impacts on economic welfare are identical to GDP impacts. For the latter one, GDP and economic welfare gains are different where the GDP effects would relate to additional output due to more persons in employment while the welfare impacts would be a proportion of these arising from higher tax revenues for the Treasury due to increased GDP.

This model framework is placed between partial and general equilibrium analysis by allowing for consideration to impacts in other markets without the requirement of detailed modelling of how the different sectors/markets are structured.

The study guidelines were used in practice for the Crossrail scheme in London. Results from this application are shown in Table 17.3. This table shows the potential significance of additional wider economic effects, in the case of the Crossrail scheme representing some 35 per cent of the total benefits.

Further details regarding the development of the economic appraisal of the Crossrail scheme with inclusion of wider economic effects are set out in Worsley (2011).

Table 17.3   Welfare and GDP effects of Crossrail scheme

	Welfare (mln £)	GDP (mln £)
Business time savings	4,847	4,847
Commuting time savings	4,152	
Leisure time savings	3,833	
Total transport user benefits – conventional appraisal	**12,832**	
Increase in labour force participation		872
People working longer		0
Move to more productive jobs		10,772
Agglomeration benefits	3,094	3,094
Increased competition	0	0
Imperfect competition	485	485
Treasury consequences of increased GDP	3,580	
Additional to conventional appraisal	**7,159**	
Total (excluding financing, social and environmental costs and benefits)	**19,991**	**20,069**

Note: Zero values included in the table for this particular scheme are based on assumptions

Source: Department for Transport (2005)

5.   CONCLUSIONS

Transport project appraisal has developed significantly over the past 30 years, both in terms of the basis for assessing the traditional CBA effects (such as time savings and safety benefits) as well as the extension of the impacts considered, especially concerning environmental aspects such as local air pollution. In recent years, progress regarding the inclusion of wider economic effects has been achieved, although it is not yet established practice to include these in appraisals.

Available theoretical and empirical findings support the hypothesis that wider economic impacts can be rather substantial; for example, the SACTRA work suggested that the true benefits (with inclusion of direct and indirect impacts) could be between 30 and 50 per cent greater than the benefits calculated in a standard cost-benefit analysis (Venables and Gasiorek, 1999). The problem, however, is that the magnitude of these (potentially) additional impacts can only be determined on a case-by-case basis.

Modelling tools such as CGE models are geared to assess these impacts that are caused by the interaction between transport sector and the rest of the economy allowing for consideration to agglomeration economies, imperfect competition in product market and inefficient labour markets. However, CGE models are best suited in the context of large scale transport improvements and therefore complementary tools may be required for other types of tools such as extended transport cost-benefit analysis.

The alternative to these types of approaches would be that important impacts, associated with transport infrastructure investment, would be left out of the examination. This then could lead to biases and wrong decisions concerning transport infrastructure investment priorities.

There are significant gaps in the evidence base regarding wider economic effects such as (Mann, 2006):

- The majority of studies regarding economic benefits of transport improvements have been focusing on the local/regional level and there is a need to examine further whether and how local benefits also result in benefits at the national level.
- Limited assessment of wider economic impacts in specific project appraisals to date, although modelling based studies of schemes and programmes are emerging.
- Most examples of transport project appraisal are ex-ante based with fewer ex-post evaluations, especially regarding consideration to wider economic impacts.
- Most studies available regarding wider economic impacts have so far focused on rail, especially high-speed links. There is then a need to develop studies for other modes.

Further work on specific types of wider economic impacts is also required, i.e., how can these be explained and what are the specific conditions needed for benefits to emerge. This puts emphasis on improving the understanding of the behavioural responses to transport infrastructure projects since these would be the drivers of the economic effects generated.

However, the most important point is that significant progress is currently being made in this area and it is therefore likely that in future it will be possible to assess transport infrastructure schemes more comprehensively and with less bias, thereby providing the basis for improved decision-making within the transport sector (although it is likely that appraisal will remain partial, since all significant impacts cannot be monetized, particularly on an ex-ante basis).

REFERENCES

Alfaro, L., Chanda, A., Kalemli-Ozcan, S. and Sayek, S. (2010), How does foreign direct investment promote economic growth? Exploring the effects of financial markets on linkages, *Journal of Development Economics*, **91**(2), 242–56.

Aschauer, D.A. (1989), 'Is public expenditure productive?' *Journal of Monetary Economics*, **23**(2), 177–200.

Berechman, J. (2001), Transport investment and economic development: is there a link, in ECMT, *Transport and Economic Development*, Report of the 119th Roundtable on Transport Economics, Paris: OECD Publications Service.

Boarnet, M.G. and Haughwout, A.F. (2000), *Do Highways Matter? Evidence and Policy Implications of Highways' Influence on Metropolitan Development*, discussion paper prepared for the Brookings Institution Center on Urban and Metropolitan, Washington DC.

Bröcker, J. (2002), Spatial effects of European transport policy: a CGE approach, in G.J. Hewings, M. Sonis and D. Boyce (eds), *Trade, Networks, and Hierarchies*, New York: Springer.

Crafts, N. and Leunig, T. (2006), *The Historical Significance of Transport for Economic Growth and Productivity*, research annex for the UK Eddington Study, London.

Davies, S. (1999), Review of the evidence on the incidence of imperfect competition in the UK. Report to the UK Standing Advisory Committee on Trunk Road Assessment (SACTRA), October 1999.

Department for Transport (2005), *Transport, Wider Economic Benefits, and Impacts on GDP*, London: HMSO.

Eddington, R. (2006), *The Eddington Transport Study – Transport's Role in Sustaining the UK's Productivity and Competitiveness*, main report from the Eddington Transport Study, London: HMSO.

Fogel, R.W. (1964), *Railroads and American Economic Growth*, Baltimore: Johns Hopkins University Press.

Frankel, J. and Romer, D. (1999), Does trade cause growth? *American Economic Review*, **LIXXXX**, 379–99.

Gibbons, S. and Machin, S. (2006), *Transport and Labour Market Linkages: Empirical Evidence – Implications for Policy and Scope for Further UK Research*, report to the UK Eddington Study.

Goodwin, P. and Persson, S. (2001), *Assessing the Benefits of Transport*, ECMT report, Paris: OECD Publications Service.

Graham, D. (2007), *Transport Investment and Agglomeration Economies*, International Transport Forum Discussion Paper Series, paper no. 2007-11, Paris: OECD Publications Service.

Gramlich, E.M. (1994), Infrastructure investment: a review essay, *Journal of Economic Literature*, **32**(3), 1176–96.

Gunn, H. (2004), *SCGE Models: Relevance and Accessibility for Use in the UK, with Emphasis on Implications for Evaluation of Transport Investments*, report prepared by RAND Europe Cambridge for the UK Department for Transport.

Hawke, G.R. (1970), *Railways and Economic Growth in England and Wales, 1840–1870*, Oxford: Clarendon Press.

Holvad, T. and Preston, J. (2005), *Road Transport Investment Projects and Additional Economic Benefits*, 45th Congress of the European Regional Science Association, Amsterdam, the Netherlands.

Jara-Diaz, S.R. (1986), On the relations between users' benefits and the economic effects of transportation activities, *Journal of Regional Science*, **26**, 379–91.

Joint Transport Research Centre (2008), *The Wider Economic Benefits of Transport: Macro, Meso and Micro Transport Planning and Investment Tools: Summary and Conclusions of Round Table, 25–26 October 2007*, Boston, OECD Joint Transport Research Centre Discussion Paper Series, paper no. 2008-06, Paris: OECD Publications Service.

Kehoe, P.J. and Kehoe, T.J. (1994), A primer on static applied general equilibrium models, *Federal Reserve Bank of Minneapolis Quarterly Review*, **18**(2), 2–16.

Lakshmanan, T.R. (2007), *The Wider Economic Benefits of Transportation: An Overview*, OECD Joint Transport Research Centre Discussion Paper Series, paper no. 2007-8, Paris: OECD Publications Service.

Mann, M. (2006), *Step Change Transport Improvements: An Assessment of the Potential for Step Change*, research annex for the UK Eddington Study.

Newbery, D.M. (1998), *Measuring the Indirect Benefits of Transport Costs Reductions*, report for Marcial Echenique & Partners Ltd.

ODPM/RICS (2003), *Land Value and Public Transport*, study commissioned by Office of the Deputy Prime Minister (ODPM) and Royal Institution of Chartered Surveyors (RICS), London.

Office of Fair Trading (2007), *Productivity and Competition: An OFT Perspective on the Productivity Debate*, OFT Publication, London: HMSO.

Oosterhaven, J. and Elhorst, J.P. (2008), Modelling the economy, transport and environment triangle, with an application to Dutch Maglev Projects, in C. Jensen-Butler et al. (eds), *Road Pricing, The Economy and the Environment*, Advances in Spatial Science Series, Berlin and Heidelberg: Springer Verlag.

Oosterhaven, J. and Knaap, T. (2000), *Spatial Economic Impact of Transport Infrastructure Investments*, paper presented for the TRANS-TALK Thematic Network, Brussels, November.

Quinet, E. and Vickerman, R. (2004), *Principles of Transport Economics*, Cheltenham, UK and Northampton, MA: Edward Elgar Publishing.

Rostow, W.W. (1971), *The Stages of Economic Growth: A Non Communist Manifesto*, Cambridge: Cambridge University Press.

SACTRA (1999), *Transport and the Economy, Final Report*, London: The Standing Advisory Committee on Trunk Road Assessment.

Tavasszy, L.A., Thissen, M., Muskens, J. and Oosterhaven, J. (2002), *Pitfalls and Solutions in the Applications of Spatial Computable General Equilibrium Models for Transport Appraisal*, proceedings of the 42nd ERSA Conference, Dortmund, Germany.

Venables, A. (2007), Evaluating Urban Transport Improvements: Cost–Benefit Analysis in the Presence of Agglomeration and Income Taxation, *Journal of Transport Economics and Policy*, **41**(2), 173–88.

Venables, A.J. and Gasiorek, M. (1999), *The Welfare Implications of Transport Improvements in the Presence of Market Failure*, report to SACTRA study on Transport and the Economy, London.

Vickerman, R., Spiekermann, K. and Wegener, M. (1999), Accessibility and economic development in Europe, *Regional Studies*, **33**(1), 1–15.

Worsley, T. (2011), *The Evolution of London's Crossrail Scheme and the Development of the Department for Transport's Economic Appraisal Methods*, International Transport Forum Discussion Paper Series, paper no. 2011-2732, Paris: OECD Publications Service.

18 Urban freight: freight strategy, transport movements and the urban spatial economy
David A. Hensher and Zheng Li

1. INTRODUCTION

The urban economy is heavily dependent on freight distribution supply chains to ensure that goods and services are available at a time and place where their consumption value is optimised. Sources of inefficiency throughout the distribution chain become sources of lost productivity (Danielis et al., 2010). Transport costs incurred in urban freight distribution are the biggest contributor to the overall logistics costs of many organisations involved in the supply of goods and services into urban locations. Trends in the logistics and business environment that increase the urban freight transport delivery problem include tighter time windows, more shipments, in smaller lot sizes, increasing traffic volumes, increasing congestion and limits on the class of vehicle allowed on specific classes of road (D'Este, 2001).

Some trends in the industry are evolving to cope with growing levels of congestion and risks to productivity growth, such as greater consolidation of freight distribution, pressures to ensure distribution can occur around the clock instead of being restricted by specific constraints at a point in the supply chain (e.g., the opening hours of delivery points) and the inevitable role that new access pricing regimes will play that are focused on the concept of user pays. In this chapter we draw on empirical evidence, as appropriate, to illustrate a number of these themes in the context of urban freight movement. In addition, where possible, we comment on the likely wider economy benefits associated with greater investment in urban transport infrastructure; however, much of the focus is on an urban freight strategy as a way of emphasising the institutional context in which government might seriously develop policy and practice to support the real contributors to productivity in the urban economy. Examples are drawn from Australia, the USA and Europe in order to illustrate the challenges and progress made in urban freight distribution.

With the high demand for transport supplied by road – an expensive solution for certain products and geographic areas, even for urban freight that often begins or finishes its journey outside of the urban precinct, the presence of a growing amount of truck activity is creating a significant negative impact on the quality of road infrastructure to all users, predominantly through congestion, resulting in lost time, extra vehicle capacity to undertake the task and hence lost productivity. Environmental costs such as the carbon footprint are also emerging more strongly as a concern (McKinnon et al. 2010).

Given the focus on urban freight, broadly defined to represent freight distribution that begins or ends in an urban area, or movements that begin and end in an urban area, the role of specific modes becomes very clear. Rather than allocate space to provide a descriptive profile of the incidence of freight modal activity, we will simply note that intra-urban freight distribution is dominated by road transport, with vehicles varying in size from small rigid vans to large articulated vehicles. The use of rail is limited in the main to container movements from a port on the periphery of an urban area to an intermodal terminal, although in many metropolitan areas goods classified as full truckload (FTL) and less than truckload (LTL) are unstuffed at the port and distributed to their urban destination by road. We do not see this changing in the forecastable future.

The economic downturn has challenged logistics providers to contend with factors such as unpredictable demand, volatility in fuel costs and currency valuation, and excess inventory. Overcoming these obstacles in the near-term, shippers are employing two key tactics: cutting operating costs and improving forecasting and inventory management. But they are also using the downturn as an opportunity to assess the strengths and weaknesses of their supply chains and make changes designed to increase agility, be more responsive and reduce costs. Strategies here include network redesign and creative collaboration with logistics providers and even competitors to weather the storm, using steps such as sharing assets across multiple customers in order to reduce risk. These types of initiatives are well aligned to increased transport productivity and associated economy-wide benefits in the form of improved accessibility to markets.

No matter what freight distribution strategies enterprises adopt to improve their performance and become more competitive, the biggest challenge facing urban freight distribution that contributes significant negative impacts on the performance of freight transport movements, is traffic congestion on roads and at key transfer locations such as ports and consolidation terminals. Li and Hensher (2009) predicted that total Australian road freight would increase by around 30 per cent between 2005 and 2012. Australia's urban road freight task is expected to grow by 56 per cent from 2005 to 2020, reflecting the transport consequences of economic growth, increased disposable income and structural changes in the economy, such as growth in services. Importantly, 'unlike the urban passenger task, growth in the urban freight task is showing no signs of abating' (BITRE, 2006: 34). Increasing, urban freight demand has become a major contributor to traffic congestion and negative environmental externalities such as greenhouse gas emissions, pollution and noise (Taniguchi and Thompson 2002). The growth in freight movements (in particular urban freight) would lead to more severe traffic congestion. Associated with the growing levels of road congestion is the substantial challenge for the sector in coping with the complex nature of freight distribution and the substantial amount of heterogeneity in vehicle types required (which in itself adds to costs), products and services being moved, and mixes of load in terms of freight composition and origin-destination patterns (see Table 18.1).

2.   WHAT ARE THE MAJOR ISSUES THAT SHOULD DRIVE AN ACTION-BASED URBAN FREIGHT MOVEMENT STRATEGY?

An urban freight movement strategy (UFMS) must be encapsulated within the broader domain of the supply chain and logistics task. Logistics performance measures are the best indicators of the success of a freight strategy and identifying performance capabilities for business success are central to a meaningful UFMS. Such measures include

Table 18.1 Key characteristics of market sectors

Market sector	Truck type	Commodity	Load type	Route	Trip type
Courier	Small	Mixed	LTL	Variable	Very complex linked trips
General carrier	Intermediate size	Mixed	LTL or FTL	Variable	Variable – simple or linked trips
Specialist commodities (e.g., container, bulk liquid)	Large	Specific	FTL	Regular	Mostly simple trips
Oversized/hazardous	Large	Specific	FTL	Fixed	Simple trips
External	Large	Mixed or specific	FTL	Regular	Simple trips – external to/from a single point

Source: D'Este (2001)

transport dependability, customer service, low logistics costs, delivery flexibility and delivery speed.

Transportation capabilities as interpreted through transport policy traditionally embrace the '4Cs' of capacity, congestion, condition and connectivity. The instruments available are usually infrastructure development, management and maintenance of infrastructure, inter-modal connectors and market reform (e.g., economic deregulation, safety and training regulation). Physical interpretations include transport networks such as rights of way, hubs, ports, access connectors, transfer points and permissible operations. Transport users take the 4Cs as inputs into facilitating the fifth 'C' of logistical capabilities (e.g., mode availability, distribution coverage, carrying capacity, delivery speed, dependability, flexibility, customer responsiveness, expedited delivery and inter-modal transfer and e-commerce). Other matters to consider as interpretations of the 5Cs include building codes (dock and off-loading facilities and freight elevators), incentives to retrofit docks and manage the final link in the supply chain – the drop off to the end customer, improvements in road maintenance, provision of accurate signage, use of intelligent transport systems to actively manage parking in commercial zones and monitoring freight deliveries to prevent theft and vandalism.

Government Should Facilitate an Appropriate Investment Environment

To encourage meaningful commitment from industry, government has a major role in facilitating the environment for such participation. Increasingly the spotlight is cast on the government's role as a facilitator in contrast to a provider. This role transformation means focusing much more on clearer and consistent directions (and informed guidance) that can accommodate more than one election cycle. The challenge is to match strategic and political time frames and to work out a performance synthesis of the two arenas. Informed guidance should include clear statements on the linkages between short-term and long-term policies on land use planning, environmental externalities and the transport task. The interfaces are all too often seen by industry as poorly articulated and translated into action-based policy that can benefit the freight task. An example of a most notable concern is the often lack of standardisation of local government regulations. A common point of frustration in the industry can be summarised as 'try building a terminal in Sydney!' In short, the effectiveness of the government's facilitation role should be measured by its ability to work out an appropriate policy for the development of an investment environment. This is totally consistent with the overarching commitment by government for sustained financial strength described as code for a balanced state budget and maintenance of AAA credit rating.[1]

Freight Transport Hubs

Within the urban environment, a carefully crafted review of the location of rail hubs that service the road–rail interface in the interests of the set of performance capabilities is a high agenda theme in many countries. It is consistent with the industry's experiences in what the customer really wants but that cannot be delivered by rail in isolation. We must tune down reference to the future of rail and replace it with the future of integrated multimodal service provision (critically focused on road–hub–rail configurations). The focus on rail per se misses the real point of a freight strategy. This alternative focus highlights more effectively many concerns raised about curfews, B-double restricted access, turnaround inefficiencies, shortage of sites for distribution centres, shortage of sites to store containers (full and empty) and improved access points to rail and road networks.

Better Utilisation of Existing Networks

The long recognised distinction between investment in new infrastructure and the maintenance of the existing infrastructure continues as a major challenge to many governments. This distinction is increasingly conditioned on the need to focus on better utilisation of networks. Transport demand and supply management offers a large number of instruments to assist in facilitating more efficient use of the existing network. The phrase 'existing network' has been chosen carefully in preference to 'existing infrastructure' to emphasise that a major concern is the inter-connectivity efficiency between the services provided by the road network, for example, and the terminal throughput processing at other stages in the logistics chain. This is where the interface relationship between current government services and private sector services is often at its weakest and most frustrating.

We can cite numerous examples of the inefficiencies created by this weak link (alternatively referred to as the inadequacy of vertical integration). Bottlenecks at port facilities, in particular, are a dominating theme. Major infrastructure projects in many cities throughout the world – such as the Australian examples of the inland freight railway (between Melbourne and Brisbane, bypassing Sydney) – designed to take pressure off large urban areas are in part a response to this major hub deficiency. Yet, at the same time such railway investments open up opportunities for complementary trucking activity to hub off the railway and connect back into urban metropolises. Table 18.2 provides a summary of how the various issues discussed above might involve the private and public sector and contribute to productivity improvements in urban freight distribution. Some of these issues are more tactical than strategic, but are nevertheless useful

Table 18.2   A summary of key issues

Key issue	Role of the private sector	Role of the government sector
Land availability	Advice to government on what is an efficient system	Plan for sites located for rail and major roads
Time restrictions	Address pay rates, reduce the noise of vehicles and improve the design of stores and depots, consider implementing new practices encouraging alternative, off-peak, operating hours	Local government in particular to establish efficient and standardised regulation in contrast to archaic and unproductive restrictions
B-doubles and weights	Develop a code of practice and funded monitoring programme	Establish efficient and equitable charges based on (at least) road maintenance costs
E-commerce	Take responsibility for standardisation	Act as a catalyst to encourage industry participation and establish suitable regulatory framework
Traffic congestion and reliability	Location of terminals to improve performance on the road, and consider implementing new practices encouraging alternative, off-peak, operating hours	Identify and facilitate investment and management strategies (e.g., incident management)
Trucks on roads	Location of depots	Ensure location of terminals is appropriate, encourage greater reliability of all modes, especially rail
Prices and overloading	Improved documentation, self-regulation and accountability	Ensure fair pricing for all modes, and review permits for overloading

Source: Hensher and Brewer (2001)

illustrations of where agendas may be actioned. The potential for partnership options through public–private partnerships should also be considered, an example being the investment in an inter-modal distribution centre in which both government and private investors contribute (see Hensher and Brewer, 2001 for further details).

Pricing Challenges and Market Responses

The pressures to promote competitive neutrality in respect of freight movements by road and by rail has often got in the way of establishing efficient prices for access regimes associated with freight movements. Strictly establishing an appropriate pricing regime that supports a move to true competitiveness must represent recognition of an efficient mapping of the prices or rates charged with the avoidable costs of service delivery, plus appropriate allocation of shared costs according to what each market will bear (Hensher and Brewer, 2000). Any shortfall due to government capping of prices, or even imposing inefficient charges on the use of infrastructure, may then be assessed as a potential case for a community service obligation (CSO), and treated explicitly as such. Subsidy under the guise of CSO payments that compensates for cost inefficiency[2] should be unacceptable. The vagaries of level playing fields are unacceptable outside of this regime. Until one has established a level playing field on how one should properly establish costs and prices, it is very difficult to even contemplate a rational discussion on suitable levels of prices to access the rail (and road) network. Access pricing is often a continuing concern by rail operators given the under-pricing of heavy vehicle activity, and the consequence it has on trucking's contribution to road congestion, especially where access charging fails to recognise opportunities for time-of-day pricing to make better use of the road system, and at the key hubs such as ports at all times of day.

The impact of congestion (and absence of efficient access charging) of the performance of the supply chain is well illustrated by a few recent breeches of the security of supply chains. On 13 December 2004, *Fortune* magazine reported that:

> It's hard to overstate the ripple effects of the chaos [caused by congestion at ports and access to ports]. Just ask Toys 'R' Us which has to build ten extra days into its supply chain; or Sharp Electronics, which had to fly in television parts from China; or toymaker MGA Entertainment, which lost some $40 million in revenues when it couldn't deliver its bestselling Bratz dolls on time to big retailers. Sharper Image even blamed a third-quarter loss in part on reduced inventory from the port backlog. It also cited higher air freight costs to by-pass ports.
>
> (Gimbel, 2004: 164)

In many urban areas, there is a port capacity crisis linked to environmental concerns and limited terminal yard capacity that exacerbates congestion around the port. Coping strategies can include rerouting traffic to less congested ports. For example, on the west coast of North America, Oakland could support extra movements given an estimated 1.3 million TEU (20-foot equivalent unit) excess capacity in 2008 as can Vancouver and Seattle (500K TEU surplus capacity). Coping strategies through improved crane utilisation, improved terminal yard container density and improve terminal gate throughput, can deliver non-marginal productivity gains at currently constrained ports.

Variable user access road pricing, however, is probably the key, applicable beyond trucking, and the challenge will be to discourage excess car use without burdening the economy with greatly increased freight transport costs. One of the difficulties will be to combine car disincentives with upgraded, accessible, reliable and quick public transport. The important message here is that reduced congestion associated with efficient user charges that impact particularly on car use will deliver massive efficiency gains to freight distribution. Figure 18.1 illustrates the vicious cycle of waste associated with congestion.

Unpublished research by the authors has empirically identified the elasticity of probability of vehicle class (for 16 classes of trucks), vehicle use and tonne kilometres of activity with respect to the access charge regimes in Figure 18.2.[3] The elasticity of probability of vehicle class with respect to access charge (i.e., distance-based charging defined in terms of charge per kilometre or mile) is defined as the ratio of the percentage change

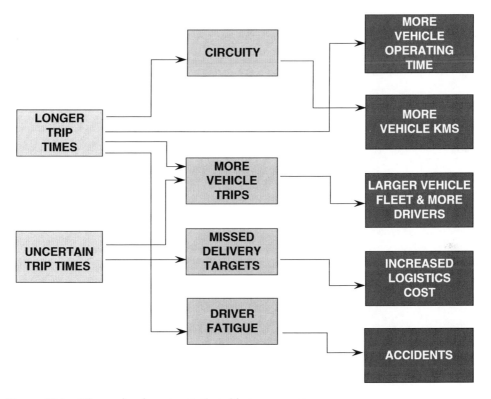

Figure 18.1   The cycle of waste attributable to congestion

in the probability of choosing a vehicle class to the percentage change in the charging level. The findings are summarised in Table 18.3.

It is not easy to establish external support for the empirical evidence herein. We are unaware of any freight study that has looked at access charges at this level of detail (in respect of vehicle classes and range of pricing regimes). What we are able to do is provide some broad based evidence from one of the better studies, summarised in Small and Winston (1999) (see Table 18.4). In all cases, price appears to be the freight rate, so it is not a useful measure for fuel prices or access charges. Despite concerns about comparability, it is encouraging to see the mean estimate of elasticity for total tonne kilometres with respect to access charge of −0.58 in Table 18.3 being similar to evidence elsewhere (we might refer to it as in the ballpark). The price elasticity of freight transport (measured in ton-miles) in Denmark is calculated to be −0.47.

In the existing freight literature, we only found one study which can be directly compared with some of the evidence in Table 18.3. Parry (2008) reported a vehicle mile elasticity with regard to mileage tax (distance-based charging) for the USA truck freight of −0.19 in urban areas, −0.28 in the rural areas and −0.24 for both urban and rural areas. These estimates are lower than −0.373 reported in Table 18.3, where a simulation model was used to produce elasticities. With regard to economy-wide benefits, Parry (2008) estimated welfare gains from various taxes to address truck externalities including congestion, accidents, noise, pollution, energy security and road damage. For

Model Option	Model Option	Explanation
Fuel based charges	PAYGO (current system)	The current road charging system (PAYGO), which includes an annual registration fee and a fuel excise based charge.
	Flat charges	Similar to the current PAYGO system, this option would apply a fixed fuel excise for all heavy vehicles. The new charge has been recalculated to better align fuel excise and the associated cost caused by heavy vehicles.
	Differentiated charges	This option involves a flat fuel charge per litre differentiated for rigid vehicles without a trailer and other heavy vehicles.
Distance based charges	by vehicle	This option is a distance based charge that charges all heavy vehicles using the same flat per kilometre charge.
	by module	This option is a distance based charge that charges differentiated rate for articulated vehicles and rigid vehicles. In addition to this differentiation, the charge also considers the number of modules that each vehicle has. For example, if an operator had a truck and dog combination they would pay the rigid charge twice to reflect both the truck and trailer.
	number of axles	This option charges heavy vehicles based on the total number of axles the vehicle has. The more axles a vehicle has, the higher the charge the vehicle is required to pay.
	by axle group	This option is a distance based charge that charges heavy vehicles according to the number and type of axles it has. In addition to considering the number of axles a vehicle has, it also considers the type of axle groups that a vehicle has.
Distance-location		For each Austroad vehicle type, this option charges heavy vehicles based on the kilometers it has travelled and the road types that it has used. This option charges a different price for 5 major road categories, which are Freeways, Major Urban Arterials, Major Rural Arterials, Local Collector and Local Access.
Distance-mass		For each Austroad vehicle type, this option charges heavy vehicles based on the mass it carries and the kilometers it travels. The charge could be either based on nominated maximum mass or could be dynamically adjusted according to the actual load that is on the vehicle.
Mass- distance –location		This option is a pricing scheme that charges heavy vehicles according to the mass carried and road types used by the heavy vehicle. This option most aligns the price charged to the heavy vehicle and the associated cost of operating the vehicle.

Source: Hensher et al. (2013)

Figure 18.2   Alternative access charging regimes

example, implementing a flat mileage tax with an optimal rate calculated to be 14.6 US cents per mile (equivalent to 85 US cents per gallon), is predicted to increase welfare by US$1.59 billion per annum, which is US$0.25 billion higher than implementing the optimised fuel tax (i.e., US$1.12 per gallon, 2.5 times the current tax) alone. Moreover, the mileage charge has a more direct impact on the reduction of mileage related externalities than the fuel tax.

Table 18.3 Aggregate summary of direct freight distribution elasticities with respect to access charge ($/km): Australia

Elasticity context	Mean direct elasticity
Probability of vehicle class:	
Overall	−0.522
Fuel	
Distance	N/A
Distance-location	−0.149
Distance-mass	−0.007
Distance-mass-location	0.141
Total VKM:	
Freeway/arterial	−0.388
Local roads	−0.759
Total VKM all roads	−0.373
Total tonne kilometres:	
Freeway/arterial	−0.386
Local roads	−0.064
Total tonne VKM all roads	−0.586

Source: Hensher et al. (2013)

Table 18.4 Freight transport elasticities

Model for producing elasticities	Rail	Truck
Aggregate mode split model, price	−0.25 to −0.35	−0.25 to −0.35
Aggregate model from Translog cost function, price	−0.37 to −1.16	−0.58 to −1.81
Disaggregate mode choice model, price	−0.08 to −2.68	−0.04 to −2.97

Note: These elasticities vary depending on commodity group

Source: Small and Winston (1999: Table 2-2)

3. LOGISTICS AND BUSINESS ENVIRONMENT TRENDS

> [I]n future it will be supply chains that compete with each other, not individual companies.
> (Martin Christopher, *The Economist*, 17 June 2006: 4)

There are four key stakeholders involved in urban freight distribution: shippers, freight carriers, residents and administrators/governments, and their interrelationships are given in Figure 18.3, in which freight carriers and administrators are the media of freight flows from shippers to consumers, and the whole process would be affected by a tiny move in one part.

In this section we draw on research over the past ten years in Australia in which we have conducted in-depth interviews with key stakeholders in all of the four boxes in Figure 18.3, to gain a better understanding of what are the key response strategies being

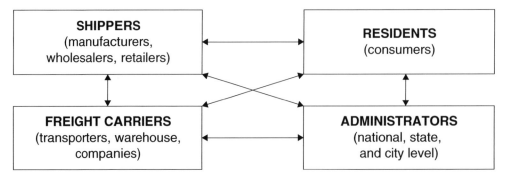

Source: Taniguchi et al. (2001)

Figure 18.3   Key stakeholders in urban freight distribution

adopted to build competitiveness and financial viability in urban freight distribution. In such interviews we sought opinions on the following business and logistics trends:

- consolidation/decentralisation in distribution;
- availability and competitiveness of rail and intermodal service;
- growth in global sourcing or global markets;
- plant consolidation;
- product and service customisation;
- information technology;
- adoption of JIT or Quick Response;
- outsourcing;
- alliances and partnerships.

We now discuss those topics that were dominant during the interviews that have particular relevance to the urban delivery element of the supply chain. Although the interviews were with enterprises in Australia, many are global players, and the evidence has relevance in most urban jurisdictions throughout the world. For example, our findings are in line with the idea of 'city logistics' proposed by some researchers (e.g., Ruske 1994; Kohler 1997; Taniguchi and van der Heijden 2000) to develop better urban freight distribution systems using advanced information systems, cooperative freight transport systems and load factor control. Danielis et al. (2010) suggested the promotion of urban transhipment and consolidation as two important policies to improve the urban freight system in Italy.

Consolidation/Decentralisation in Distribution

Consolidation of distribution facilities occurs when there are economies to be gained in holding inventory, and in transportation. There is a strong and growing urban consolidation trend that has an important impact on transportation needs and demand for transport infrastructure. For example, in the case of Telstra, the dominant Australian telecommunications provider, the consolidation of warehouses resulted in improving turn rates from 1 to 2½ times, and reduced inventory from $126 million to $86 million per annum. Consolidation also reduced the fleet size from 62 to 22 vehicles, but increased the proportion of articulated semi-trailer units. Under the consolidated system, a single location was responsible for more destinations and more products, which enabled consolidation of urban freight. Thus larger vehicles were making more stops with more freight. The current consolidation of the overseas division inventories resulted in the elimination of eight out of nine vehicles currently used by that division, made possible through the consolidation of additional freight on existing routes. Such consolidation has made it possible to ship larger shipments with fewer vehicle kilometres in larger vehicles, both inbound and outbound.

Another example is Woolworths, which has an explicit strategy for meeting its store customer needs, at least distribution and transportation cost, through consolidation. At the very end of the supply chain are a large number of grocery stores that are generally larger than their competitors, have little storage space and have rapid turnover of product. Traditionally from 30 to 50 deliveries are received daily at a retail store directly from suppliers (or their agents) using small 1- to 3-tonne vehicles. This is in addition to the deliveries from the distribution centres (DCs). The result is dock congestion at the store's dock every day, and many unscheduled arrivals at different times, which are often inconvenient to the store manager. At many stores there are too many vendors making deliveries at the backdoor. Many stores have two personnel constantly unloading vehicles and the docks are congested, and vendors often do not arrive on a schedule or arrive at times convenient to them. This results in inefficiency at the store.

The new strategy was to consolidate all vendor deliveries to the DC where freight is consolidated, to produce one or two large truck deliveries per store with mixed loads at a time convenient to the store manager. This changed the transport pattern for many of the vendors as well; whereas they previously had a fleet of small trucks delivering small quantities (e.g., one pallet load), they now need the capability to deliver 20 pallets at a time to the Woolworths DC. The impact on service and transport costs is as follows. First, local vendors who are making milk runs have little control over how fast they can make a specific delivery, since a delay at any stop or between stops (caused by congestion for example), would change the delivery time for all stops remaining. Scheduled delivery reliability is hard to control. Direct deliveries from the Woolworths DC only involves one stop and using time and motion studies, Woolworths can now make a delivery in a ±15 minute window, enabling stores to plan for the arrival of a Woolworths scheduled vehicle.

This system has reduced the number of vehicle trips substantially. For example, one store now takes at least one pallet from each vendor, with deliveries from DCs on 20 pallet vehicles. Thus instead of 40 one-pallet deliveries daily, two 20-pallet deliveries are substituted. For every 20 stores, this means that each vendor must make one delivery to the DC. Thus on a daily basis, a best case scenario comparison is:

● Old system – 40 one-pallet deliveries direct from suppliers × 20 stores = 800 trips in small vehicles.
● New system – (two 20-pallet deliveries a day from DC × 20 stores) + (40 20-pallet trips to DC by suppliers) = 80 large vehicle trips.

In this scenario, up to 720 smaller vehicle trips have been eliminated in favour of 80 larger vehicle trips. The benefit, however, is less than 720 trips saved, since small trucks may be making a number of milk runs. Woolworth operates 185 retail stores in NSW; hence it is possible that more than 6,000 deliveries and a similar number of vehicle trips (depending on the milk run structure of the suppliers) can be eliminated per day. The number of vehicle kilometres travelled could in the future be substantially reduced, assuming that the DC was located centrally (e.g., at the centre of gravity) relative to the suppliers and the grocery stores. On the assumption that each trip is 20km. and all parties operate 312 days a year (six days a week), 6,000 avoided trips per day results in a saving of more than 37 million vehicle kilometres per year.

The primary objective of transportation operations is to deliver the product at least cost, which is translated into kilograms per vehicle kilometre. Currently, Woolworths pays their transportation suppliers by the vehicle kilometre. Reduced kilometres travelled are the direct result of consolidating larger loads. Although the rate per kilometre travelled for larger vehicles is higher, the economics of large vehicles favour using the larger vehicles. The consolidation strategy also considers facility and inventory costs. The capital cost of DC automation creates breakeven throughput volumes that can only be achieved by consolidation.

In summary, consolidation of distribution can lead to substantial reduction in vehicle kilometres travelled by facilitating the consolidation of freight for deliveries in larger vehicles. From a private cost perspective, the benefits of using larger vehicles clearly favour the use of articulated units. However, this ignores the social impact of large trucks that must be considered by the public authorities whose decisions have constrained or limited the operation of larger vehicles.

Plant Consolidation

Plant consolidation is a trend around the world that seeks to take advantage of economies of scale in production. However the products are produced further from market, increasing transport costs and time to market. FJ Walker Foods, the supplier to McDonald's outlets, has suggested that the size of the market encourages plant consolidation for certain products it deals with. For example, all French fries for all stores are produced in Tasmania, and all beef and pork products are processed at a plant in the urban areas where site specific and operating costs are lower. Plant consolidation that results in a new Sydney facility will increase demand for components of the transport system that provide access to other interstate markets or interstate sources of raw materials. Conversely, plant consolidation that results in the loss of an existing Sydney facility will decrease demand for components of the transport system that provide access to raw materials.

Allied, a large freight distribution transport company, argues that since marketplace contact is still important, firms that consolidate outside of a large metropolitan area need faster delivery to compensate for added distance to customers. For example, a paint distributor that consolidated from 20 to 11 sites contracted Allied to enhance the transport service to markets from site locations further away. The importance of transport costs is demonstrated by the partnership between KSFL, a logistics company, and a building materials company. The building company's Sydney plant was operating at 68 per cent capacity utilisation. KSFL set up a transport system/distribution system that made products competitive in markets further away, allowing the plant to increase the volume of production and obtain 98 per cent capacity utilisation. Effective transport made it feasible to expand the market in order to utilise plant capacity.

Growth in Global Sourcing and Global Markets

Increased global activity places pressure on the transport networks of many urban economies. For example, the national meat processing and packing facilities in Sydney supply a number of Asian countries (e.g., McDonald's franchises) with meat patties. These are containerised and shipped out of Port Botany. The growing Asian consumer market, the high quality of the Australian product and the availability of beef products in Australia makes this is a growth area for export. Currently the supplier outsources both the container loading and the local transportation to the port. As the volume grows, the firm has taken over the container processing and plans in the future to leave transportation to third-party transportation providers.

In the retail sector, Woolworths (one of two dominant players in the grocery market) offers an example where the majority of grocery products are sourced within Australia. Their procurement policy is to source overseas only if that source is at least 10 per cent less expensive, otherwise Australian sources are used. The most significant factor is the value of the Australian dollar; and with its increasing value (above parity with the US dollar in 2013), imported goods are less expensive and become a more attractive proposition moving activity away from the hinterland to the port. The growth in transport and logistics suppliers to respond to the growth in port movements in the international supply chain results in greater receipt of ocean containers, unloading and subsequent distribution of freight throughout the urban economy and beyond, impacting heavily on major roads through inner city suburbs rather than the immediate access to Port Botany in Sydney.

Adoption of JIT or Quick Response Delivery Strategies

Just-in-time (JIT) and Quick Response (QR) are management strategies adopted by manufacturing and retailing respectively to minimise inventory and other resource consuming activities by coordinating the sequence of activities in sequential processes. The trend in urban freight distribution is towards greater adoption of JIT and QR strategies as key ways to improve the quality of services (Tseng et al., 2005). In production, this may be the arrival of raw materials just as they are needed on the production line. In retailing, this may be the arrival of finished goods just as they are needed for stocking on the floor rather than in backroom storage. JIT/QR customers generally seek to decrease inventory by ordering smaller quantities for delivery more frequently.

A primary impetus is the lack of storage space at the final destination. Where the core process is selling or producing products, and not storing products, this points to an essential trade-off between storage and transport inputs in the operations processes of all firms involved. A firm can choose to have more storage capacity, which will enable products to be received in large lots less frequently, or in less storage capacity, which will require the delivery of smaller lots more frequently. The latter means more vehicle trips and kilometres travelled. Firms that adopt JIT/QR find that savings in other logistics costs more than offset transportation costs associated with more frequent delivery. Stores, in general, are willing to reduce their inventories only if there is consistent delivery of product, made possible by controlling warehouse and transportation processes.

Transport and logistics providers must have the capability to serve their customers who are adopting JIT/QR strategies, by setting up (or contracting) cross dock operations to transfer full load lots in linehaul to less-than-full-load pallet delivery in final distribution. The JIT market segment is growing, and time-sensitive couriers will be increasingly used to fill product needs unfilled by regular delivery. The increased demand for express shipments will increase the traffic density and increase the ability of many organisations to move multiple shipments per trip. The most significant impact of JIT/QR is an increase in fixed (structured or milk) runs on a daily or more frequent basis. To some degree, this is mitigated by consolidation of deliveries from various suppliers. Hensher and Puckett (2005) suggest that deliveries may be consolidated at an intermediate point (e.g., a DC) and then carried to the final destination so as to maximise the efficiency of a JIT strategy.

4.   CONCLUSIONS

The literature on urban freight distribution highlights the following ten issues as the most important in the minds of both the private and public sector, whether the stakeholder is active in a distribution supply chain or a regulator of the transport network:

- Increased reliability (linked to traffic congestion)
- Increased safety
- Reduced delivery (turnaround and opening hours) times
- Increased vehicle utilisation (backhaul issues)
- Reduced freight costs through the logistics chain (increased productivity)
- Reduced externality costs (noise, vehicle emissions, air quality, local amenity)
- Uniformity of regulations across jurisdictions
- Long-term robustness
- Increased efficiency of all inputs
- Reduced energy consumption (linked to input efficiency)

The focus on travel time variability, terminal time and safety, is informative and reflects what is increasingly understood as the key influences in shippers' decisions to go with one transport supplier (be it a freight forwarder or another form of third- or fourth-party logistics provider).

Too much focus on competition between road and rail may miss an opportunity to improve the performance of the existing road and rail network, without necessarily adding to that network. A primary refocus should be on the efficiency of hubs as interfaces to improve the efficiency and effectiveness of current intermodal activity and to enable future opportunities. This reinforces the view that modal competition is overemphasised to the neglect of the greater gain from viewing transport modes as complementary within the supply chain. It also suggests that the location of existing major hubs needs to be reappraised, be they intermodal terminals or warehouses. It may be more effective and less expensive to relocate such hubs than invest heavily in transport infrastructure to resolve a problem created in the first instance by the location of the hub.

Government commitment to additional investment in network infrastructure (road, rail and hubs) must be reinforced. Although the necessity to ensure that the existing network assets are maintained in good working order, this should not be to the cost of providing the missing links in an integrated road and rail network. Such an infrastructure plan must be fully integrated within a land-use plan and the opportunity to relocate major hubs (and terminals) that are the ultimate drivers of traffic, must be seen as real.

Most transport companies should no longer be seen as transport firms only, but value-added logistics services directly or through affiliates. The benefit of a firm outsourcing to these new transport suppliers is that the outside supplier can do it better, resulting in the least-cost distribution system being used. This should result in the fewest vehicle kilometres travelled as shippers and carriers seek individually and collectively to maximise vehicle trip utilisation, delivering productivity gains to the urban economy. In some cases, the corporate rationale of concentrating on the core business is sufficient justification. In other cases, it must be demonstrated that outsourcing is cost-effective without compromising customer service. The primary reasons an external supplier of transport may be more cost-effective are better operating systems, a lower cost (in particular labour) structure and an ability to utilise assets across many customers. Very large firms, however, can have sufficient volume of traffic to utilise an in-house fleet as effectively as an outside supplier.

NOTES

1. The technical framework for government appraisal and prioritising remains benefit-cost analysis in its broadest interpretation, but it must be implemented in a much more comprehensive way than at present, ensuring inclusion of a wider set of benefits including urban amenity (interpreted to include quality of life or well-being – see Stanley et al. 2012), and employment agglomeration impacts. In addition, an economic impact analysis that complements benefit-cost analysis is necessary to reveal other gains. Economic impacts are the effects a project or policy has on the economy of the surrounding region, measured with the following variables: jobs; business output (i.e., total amount of money flowing through an industry in a year); value added (defined by gross regional product (GRP) as the most basic measure of wealth creation in an economy, commonly used as a bottom-line performance measure in economic impact analysis; and compensation (i.e., the wages and benefits to employees and business owners in a year). Compensation is commonly used in combination with jobs to show whether an investment or policy creates high-wage or low-wage jobs. This broader focus must provide a greater focus on an integrated land use plan and accompanying development approval/facilitation processes.
2. Strictly, cost efficiency is defined as the use of all inputs to produce a *given* level of service at the lowest cost. Importantly, the service level is predefined and not eroded.
3. Austroads vehicle type classification is given in the Appendix.

REFERENCES

BITRE (2006), *Review of Urban Congestion Trends, Impacts and Solutions*, Bureau of Infrastructure, Transport and Regional Economics, Australia: Australian Government.

Danielis, R., Rotaris, L. and Marcucci, E. (2010), Urban freight policies and distribution channels, *European Transport/Trasporti Europei*, **46**, 114–16.

D'Este, G. (2001), Freight and logistics modelling, in A.M. Brewer, K.J. Button and D.A. Hensher (eds), *Handbook of Logistics and Supply-Chain Management*, Oxford: Pergamon Press, pp. 521–34.

Gimbel, B. (2004), Yule log jam: the holiday shipping season was chaos at the biggest US container port. Globalization means it will happen again, *Fortune*, 13 December, p. 164.

Hensher, D.A. and Brewer, A.M. (2000), *Transport Economics and Management*, Oxford: Oxford University Press.

Hensher, D.A. and Brewer, A.M. (2001), Developing a freight strategy: the use of a collaborative learning process to secure stakeholder input, *Transport Policy*, **8**(1), 1–10.

Hensher D.A. and Puckett, S.M. (2005), Refocusing the modelling of freight distribution: development of an economic-based framework to evaluate supply chain behaviour in response to congestion charging, *Transportation*, **32**(6), 573–602.

Hensher, D.A., Collins, A.M., Rose, J.M. and Smith, N.C. (2013), Access charge elasticities for freight distribution by vehicle class, vehicle kilometres and tonne vehicle kilometres *Transportation Research Part E*, **56**(C), 1–21.

Kohler, U. (1997), *An Innovating Concept for City-Logistics*, 4th World Congress on Intelligent Transport Systems, Berlin, Germany.

Li, Z. and Hensher, D.A. (2009), Road freight demand in Australia: key drivers and forecasts, *Road and Transport Research*, **18**(2), 15–26.

McKinnon, A., Cullinane, S., Browne, M. and Whiteing, A. (2010), *Green Logistics*, London: Kogan Page.

Parry, I.W.H. (2008), How should heavy-duty trucks be taxed? *Journal of Urban Economics*, **63**(2), 651–68.

Ruske, W. (1994), *City Logistics: Solutions for Urban Commercial Transport by Cooperative Operation Management*, OECD Seminar on Advanced Road Transport Technologies, Omiya, Japan.

Small, K. and Winston, C. (1999), The demand for transportation: models and applications, in J. Gomez-Ibanez, W.B. Tye and C. Winston (eds), *Essays in Transportation Economics and Policy: A Handbook in Honor of John R. Meyer*, Washington, DC: Brookings Institution Press, pp. 11–55.

Stanley, J.K., Stanley, J. and Hensher, D.A. (2012), Mobility, social capital and sense of community: what value? *Urban Studies* **49**(16), 3595–609.

Taniguchi, E. and Thompson, R.G. (2002), Modeling city logistics, *Transportation Research Record*, **1790**, 45–51.

Taniguchi, E. and van der Heijden, R.E.C.M. (2000), An evaluation methodology for city logistics, *Transport Reviews*, **20**(1), 65–90.

Taniguchi, E., Thompson, R.G., Yamada, T. and Duin, R. (2001), *City Logistics: Network Modelling and Intelligent Transport Systems*, Oxford: Pergamon.

Tseng Y., Yue, W.L. and Taylor, M.A.P. (2005), The role of transportation in logistics chain, *Proceedings of the Eastern Asia Society for Transportation Studies*, **5**, 1657–72.

APPENDIX: AUSTROADS VEHICLE TYPE CLASSIFICATION

Length	Axles	Groups	Description	Class	Parameters	Typical Configurations
Medium 5.5m to 14.5m	2	2	Two Axle Truck or Bus	3	d(1) > 3.2m and axles = 2	
	3	2	Three Axle Truck or Bus	4	axles = 3 and groups = 2	
	>3	2	Four Axle Truck	5	axles > 3 and groups = 2	
Long 11.5m to 19.0m	3	3	Three Axle Articulated Three axle articulated or Rigid vehicle and trailer	6	d(1) > 3.2m, axles = 3 and groups = 3	
	4	>2	Four Axle Articulated Four axle articulated or Rigid vehicle and trailer	7	d(2) < 2.1m or d(1) < 2.1m or d(1) > 3.2m	
	5	>2	Five Axle Articulated Five axle articulated, or Rigid vehicle and trailer	8	d(2) < 2.1m or d(1) < 2.1m or d(1) > 3.2m axles = 5 and groups > 2	
	>6	>2	Six Axle Articulated Six axle articulated or Rigid vehicle and trailer	9	axles = 6 and groups > 2 or axles > 6 and groups = 3	
Medium Combination 17.5m to 36.5m	>6	4	B Double B Double, or Heavy truck and trailer	10	groups = 4 and axles > 6	
	>6	5 or 6	Double Road Train Double road train, or Medium articulated and one dog trailer (M.A.D.)	11	groups = 5 or 6 and axles > 6	
Large Combination Over 33.0m	>6	>6	Triple road train, or Heavy truck and three trailers	12	groups > 6 and axles > 6	

19 Spatial implications of public transport investments in metropolitan areas: some empirical evidence regarding light rail and bus rapid transit

Eran Feitelson and Orit Rotem-Mindali

1. INTRODUCTION

Public transport investments and particularly the development of street cars and light rail have historically been seen as major factors in determining the spatial patterns of development in American and European metropolitan areas (Vance, 1991; Muller, 1995). However, the era in which they were most influential was a century ago, before cars became ubiquitous. In the past 50 years, the car has been the major transport mode that affects the metropolitan structure (Muller, 1995), leading Colin Clark (1958) to make his famous observation of transport as 'the maker and breaker of cities'. Yet, surface public transit systems, particularly light rail, have had something of a comeback in the past 20 years. Hence the question arises – to what extent do such systems exert an effect on the car-dominated metropolitan structure?

This chapter reviews the emerging evidence regarding the effects of transit, mainly light rail (LRT), on spatial development patterns in developed countries in the current car-dominated era. However, as the literature does not always differentiate between light rail, metro and suburban rail, and as these systems are often interlinked, we extend our discussions to the effects of these forms of rail in some points. In addition, as bus rapid transit (BRT) systems have increasingly proffered in the past few years (Hensher and Reyes, 2000; Deng and Nelson, 2011), we extend the discussion to this emerging mode, although the empirical evidence on the effects of BRT systems is still sparse. Hence, we also tentatively extend the review to cities in Latin America, where the advent of BRT systems is most evident.

After a very brief review of the historical, pre-car, effects, we review the empirical evidence on such effects in the car era (focusing on the past 30 years) in America and Western Europe. However, in a multi-network world, the empirical elicitation of the spatial effect of LRT or BRT becomes more difficult, particularly given the long lead time of both infrastructure and urban development. Hence, after the historical review we briefly discuss the methodological difficulties that impede assessments of the spatial impacts of LRT (and BRT). Then we review the studies that attempt to assess the spatial implications at the macro (metropolitan or city-wide) level and at the micro level (the effects around stations). In the last section the variables that seem to affect the relationship between LRT and BRT investments and the spatial pattern of urban development are discerned on the basis of the empirical evidence reviewed and some policy implications drawn.

2.   A BRIEF HISTORICAL OVERVIEW

Rail was a major factor in spawning decentralization and suburbanization in nineteenth-century industrial cities, on both sides of the Atlantic. By allowing for separation between spaces of production and spaces of consumption it allowed the bourgeois of the nineteenth century to escape the horrors of the industrial city core to a seemingly rural idyll, the suburbs (Fishman, 1987; Hunt, 2004). However, with the decline in cost of travel in Britain following the Cheap Train Act of 1883, working-class suburbs followed. Consequently, rail became the major transport mode used for long-range commutes (i.e., beyond walking distance), leading Warner (1970) to term the resulting new building estates in Boston 'streetcar suburbs'.

In North America, the urban form of the late nineteenth-century city largely conformed to the radial structure of rail development, with suburbs concentrated around the suburban rail stations (Muller, 1995). These stations became the focal point of the suburbs as public institutions were often built in their vicinity (Vance, 1991; Fielding, 1995). Thus, rail had major social effects. Due to the greater access it afforded to the countryside, it allowed the upper classes and increasingly also the middle classes in the Anglo-Saxon world, and later also the working classes, to pursue the rural idyll that permeates these societies, thereby generating a greater spatial differentiation among classes (Warner, 1970; Fishman, 1987). Moreover, as Vitiello (2008) shows for Philadelphia, rail was also instrumental in the decentralization of industries and hence in initiating the deconcentration of production too.

While most of the studies focus on the North American city, similar processes were evident in Britain, particularly in the large metropolitan areas of Manchester and London (Freeman, 1999). Although the social stratification implications of rail differed across the English Channel, rail had also a profound effect on cities in Continental Europe, allowing for working-class suburbanization as the upper classes tended to remain in the city centre (Fishman, 1987). But as car use grew, surface rail services in many metropolitan areas were dismantled. Thus, it is only with the so-called renaissance of light rail since the 1980s (Pucher, 2002) that the question of the spatial effects of LRT arose again – but now in the context of the motorized city.

3.   THE DIFFICULTIES IN ASSESSING TRANSIT'S SPATIAL IMPLICATIONS IN THE CAR ERA

Analyses of rail's historical impacts on urban structure are usually case studies of particular cities and regions. As rail was the main medium- and long-range transport mode at the end of the nineteenth century and beginning of the twentieth century, the metropolitan changes that occurred along the tracks could be safely attributed to it. At present, however, LRT and BRT services are being (re-)introduced into the car-dominated metropolis. Thus analyses of the spatial implications of such systems face challenges that were not as pertinent a century ago.

The first challenge is discerning the effects of rail from all other factors that affect metropolitan development. Cohen-Blankshtain and Feitelson (2011) argue that LRT development largely pursues two goals: development of central and/or underdeveloped parts of the city and provision of high-capacity transit along high-demand corridors. In their empirical analysis, they find that in most cases the second goal predominates, as high use is sought to justify the investments. But to attract high ridership, LRT is aligned in high-density corridors where there are often high development pressures. Hence separating out the implications of the LRT (or BRT) project from the development that would have taken place along these corridors without the transit investments faces a simultaneity problem.

A second challenge is the long lead time both of infrastructure development and of changes in urban form. Discussions of LRT development usually take several years and receive wide publicity. Hence, developers can prepare the ground for taking advantage of such projects well in advance of the commencement of LRT services. To this end they will acquire land and/or development rights along the proposed corridors. Such acquisitions will be reflected in the land market, where a competitive land market exists. These effects, however, are often limited to the immediate vicinity of the proposed LRT or BRT lines. Analyses of macro-level effects require a longer lead time, as they will only be felt if there are spillover effects beyond the immediate vicinity of the rail line, or in shifts in land use. Yet, during this long period other factors come into play, such as economic development trends, which may confound efforts to discern the net impacts of transit (Giuliano, 1995).

Finally, LRT or BRT projects are often advanced in conjunction with land-use and auxiliary policies intended to increase their use. These may take the form of parking policies, additional development rights along the corridors and various policies intended to better integrate the public transport system (Givoni and Banister, 2010). Such integrative policy initiatives may have direct and indirect effects on the way space is viewed by developers. In cases where such policy packages are enacted judgement is needed to determine what exactly is the LRT (or BRT) project – is it only the alignment and operation of the LRT or BRT, or does it include all the supporting policies, some of which may have preceded the LRT/BRT line, or may have been enacted also without it.

These issues are of particular concern in analyses of macro effects. However, they are relevant also in analyses of micro effects. Timing of price and development impacts, multi-colinearity between transit development and supporting policies and other market forces are of concern in hedonic price studies of micro-level effects, discussed later in this chapter.

4.   THE METROPOLITAN/CITY LEVEL (MACRO-LEVEL) EFFECTS

Macro-level effects of suburban rail, LRT and BRT systems are the spatial impacts at the metropolitan or city level. The main expectation is that radial systems will encourage the formation of a compact and dense urban configuration. This expectation is based on the assumption that rail increases the accessibility towards the centre in comparison to other parts of the metropolitan area (Boyce, 1972; Knight and Trygg, 1977; Bajic, 1983; Landis et al., 1995).

Empirical evidence on the impact of rail transit at the metropolitan level is scarce as changes in land-use patterns on a large scale are slower than changes in travel behavior pattern. As discussed earlier, there are various methodological difficulties that preclude the isolation of rail transit impacts from other exogenous variables on land use pattern (Fulford, 1996; Ewing, 1997).

In North America, research on the impacts of rail transit investments on land use present diverse and equivocal conclusions. In an early study analysing changes in land-use pattern in Toronto, a two-phase model demonstrated that the distance from the city centre and from the central rail station were the two main significant variables in fore-casting residential and offices development projects (Bourne, 1969). Similar results were concluded for major cities in Illinois and in particular Chicago, showing that railroad vicinity had a significant effect on the development of residential land use (McMillen, 1989). In Green and Jones' (1993) study on rail transit in Washington, rail was found to have substantial impact on urban development. The effects were particularly high along rail transit corridors and near rail stations (Badoe and Miller, 2000). In Montreal, the local Metro system had major implications for the CBD, while other variables such as availability of land were also noted as important in urban renewal of the CBD (Knight and Trygg, 1977). Nonetheless, in areas beyond the CBD lesser impacts were found. In Boston, rail line extensions had mixed effects on land use. In one part of the city the rail extension had a large effect on land development initiatives, although various confound-ing variables, such as real-estate prices and land availability intensified this effect. On the other hand, in other parts of the city only limited micro effects around rail station were observed (Knight and Trygg, 1977).

The development of LRT in the post-industrial period has increasingly been inter-twined with land-use planning (Wegener and Fürst, 1999). Rail investments have often been advanced as part of efforts to rejuvenate the CBD or foster development in a part of town seen to be under-developed (Cohen-Blankshtain and Feitelson, 2011). The combination of land use and transit has been found to be critical in successful 'transit metropolis', metropolitan areas geared around their transit services, that thus enjoy high ridership (Cervero, 1998). This is also known as transit-oriented development (TOD), where land use is encouraged to be developed in clustered areas around key transit hubs the produce islands of high density (Pucher, 2004).

Portland and Toronto are two examples where planning was used to steer devel-opment in conjunction with the construction of the rail system. The planning policy attempted to direct development to rail corridors, next to railroad stations, and adjacent to city centre rail stations (Pill, 1988; Rothblatt, 1994; Cervero, 1998; Post, 1998; Filion, 2000). In Toronto, financial bonuses were offered for intensive construction near transit centres, while implementing limitations for 'park and ride' facilities to control disperse residential development. In comparison, rail projects in Miami and Atlanta failed despite the large capital invested, mainly due to the lack of supportive land-use regulation and widespread suburban expansion (Catanese, 1988).

In Europe, land-use and public transport system are generally better regulated and coordinated, often with the goal of strengthening the urban centre. In many European countries, it is usual to find planning regulations that direct urban development toward rail transit corridors and to city centres (Pucher and Lefevre, 1996; Cervero, 1998). However, land-use regulations are only one factor that affects the spatial effects. Timing of transit improvements is another. Based on a study of 12 European cities Gospodini (2005) shows that timing is important in determining whether the potential effects of transit improvements on development, redevelopment or rejuvenation of urban areas materializes.

In Stockholm, long-term policy to purchase land for development and to steer growth along desired growth axes has been crucial in mediating between transit and urban development. Stockholm's investment in radial rail lines has given rise to a 'string of pearls' urban form with a balanced use of land for work and housing, based on vicinity to rail stations (Cervero, 2009). Similarly, in Montpelier public ownership of land in adjacent to rail stations and corridors enabled intensive office and residential development (Steer Davis Gleave, 2005).

Munich is an example for creating a coordinated planning system between transport and urban planning institutions: MVV is the central management organization for public transport in Munich and its surrounding areas. MVV is responsible for planning urban development and coordinating between different statutory bodies. MVV has aided in solving various transport problems, and has formulated a comprehensive regional policy to manage and direct market demand for land-use development towards radial rail corridors (Pucher and Kurth, 1996). However, empirical evidence shows that rail in Munich had a bidirectional effect on urban form. On the one hand, rail had a strong influence on strengthening the metropolitan centre and intensifying residential density near rail corridors (Cervero, 1998). On the other hand, rail has accelerated the suburbanization processes. Residential growth was also observed along rail corridors, deep in the rural hinterland (Kreibich, 1978). Similar conclusions were found for suburban rail in studies of the Tel Aviv metropolitan area (Israel and Cohen-Blankshtain, 2010) and in Latin America. Urban sprawl and suburbanization processes due to rail development were observed in Bogota and Mexico City (Davis, 1994; Cervero, 1998; Rodriguez and Targa, 2004).

The Curitiba (Brazil) transit plan is perhaps the best-known example for an integrated approach to co-develop BRT and land use. Essentially, Curitiba promoted linear high-density development along the BRT lines (Rabinovitch, 1996; Rabinovitch and Leitman, 1996; Smith and Hensher, 1998). Other Latin American cities that are based on rail, such as Buenos Aires, Caracas, Mexico City and Santiago, exhibit growth in the area surrounding of rail stations, but mainly in the city centre, thus strengthening the CBD (Fouracre et al., 2003).

5.   TRANSIT EFFECTS AT THE LOCAL (MICRO) LEVEL

Accessibility is a major factor in household and business location. As the introduction or improvement of mass transit can increase accessibility to employment, residential and commercial land use, land and property values are likely to be affected, particularly near transit stations (Du and Mulley, 2007; Pagliara and Papa, 2011). These shifts in land and property values are likely to be reflected in development patterns and land-use change. For example, new transit services may attract retail activity to the neighborhood of the transit stations, thereby raising the value of nearby properties and leading to higher densities (Czamanski, 1966; Knight and Trygg, 1977; Pagliara and Papa, 2011). Micro-level spatial impacts are thus the effects on the built environment in the close proximity to mass transit corridors and stations (Bowes and Ihlanfeldt, 2001).

Studies analysing micro-level impacts often take a cross-sectional or longitudinal hedonic price approach, assuming that price effects lead to development impacts. Other studies take a quasi-experimental or before-and-after approach to analyse directly the micro-level impacts. A few studies employ stated preference approaches to elicit the responses of households and businesses to transit improvements as a basis for assessing the spatial implications of new transit services. Most of these studies were conducted in North America.

The results of empirical studies discussing the effects of transit improvements on land and property values are mixed (Bowes and Ihlanfeldt, 2001; Debrezion et al., 2007). These differences can be partially attributed to differences in the specification of dependent and independent variables. While some studies analyse the effect on commercial property values, other focus on residential properties, and some analyse land values irrespective of zoning.

The most consistent effects of transit are expected to be on commercial property values near stations. Yet, the magnitude of such effects varies greatly. Cervero and Duncan (2002) report a 23 per cent capitalization of benefits for a typical commercial parcel near a LRT stop in fast-growing Santa Clara, California. It seems, however, that the circumstances in this case were particularly favorable. Ryan (2005), in a longitudinal hedonic study over a period from 1986 to 1995, found that access to LRT had no effect on office property rents in the San Diego metropolitan area, as firms in this region seem to value only highway access. An earlier study, using a quasi-experiment approach, compared the effects of rail stations on real estate market in Washington and Atlanta. The results show that proximity to stations had a positive effect on office prices and they tend to lease somewhat faster. Nevertheless, these benefits tend to be quite small and less significant than hypothesized (Cervero and Landis, 1993).

Other studies analyse the effects on residential areas. Based on a stated-preference study in Calgary, Hunt et al., (1994) suggest that LRT is a major attractor for residents. But hedonic price studies do not necessarily support this hypothesis. Gatzlaff and Smith (1993), for example, found that the new Metrorail system in Miami had very little effects on residential prices. However, positive effects of transit's stations on property values were observed near metro stations in Philadelphia (Knight and Trygg, 1977) and in San Francisco (Workman and Bord, 1997). Chatman et al. (2012), in a study of the impacts of the River Line of southern New Jersey, found that, while there were small appreciations of values in low-income neighbourhoods near stations, the overall effect on property values along the line was negative. These inconsistent results may be partially accounted for by the variability of the two opposing effects on residential property values – the accessibility effect vis-à-vis the nuisance effect (Chen et al., 1998). Banister and Thurstain-Goodwin (2011) identify the micro-level property value effects of large scale investment in transport infrastructure by using available data on the Jubilee Line Extension (JLE) in London's Docklands Light Rail. The study shows that change in accessibility is the key element in determining residential and commercial price value change, but not in a consistent manner. In stations located in a close proximity to central London, accessibility had a lesser impact, since the proximity to central London meant that accessibility was less fundamentally changed than in relation to other stations' catchment areas (Banister and Thurstain-Goodwin, 2011).

However, the price effects of transit on residential properties are mediated by additional variables. In a study of the impact of proximity to LRT on home values in Buffalo, Hess and Almeida (2007) found that these effects are mediated by income (with premiums being positive in high-income areas and negative in low-income areas) and the actual walking time (rather than distance).

Several studies analyse both business and residential location effects concurrently. Nelson and Sanchez (1997), for example, found that in Atlanta, employment within 800m of the stations rose by 13 per cent, indicating the magnitude of influence the stations' areas have. However, the population within 800m of MARTA (Metropolitan Atlanta Rapid Transit Authority) stations fell by more than 11 per cent.

Some of these studies focus on the impacts on the central cities. However, as Batholomew and Ewing (2011) show, the effects on the CBD is often a result of the combination of transit improvements and amenity provision, such as pedestrianization schemes. Hence, the direct accessibility effects are less than the effect of the full set of policies implemented, combining the LRT with amenity provision.

Research on the micro-level effect of transit in Europe is somewhat more limited. However, also in Europe mixed results are found in different studies. Forrest et al. (1996), using a longitudinal hedonic price methodology, found that the new Metrolink line in Manchester actually depreciated property values, and that the opening of the new transit line did not alter this effect. They suggest that this reflects the persistent pattern of residential structures along the line, which originally dates from the nineteenth century. A study on the short-term impacts of a rail transit extension on property values in Sunderland (UK), also failed to identify positive effects. This finding was explained by the lack of significant opportunities for development in Sunderland, which does not enjoy favorable regional economic trends or favourable social and physical structures (Du and Mulley, 2007). Wegener and Fürst (1999) note an earlier study by Gentlemen et al. (1983) in which they analysed the effects of two rail systems in Glasgow (Scotland), before and after opening. The research concluded that alongside an increase in demand for planning new construction projects near rail stations, there was also a decrease in nearby population size. New rail infrastructure probably had limited marginal effect since it replaced an older system that has already affected urban design (Wegener and Fürst, 1999).

In Naples (Italy), a new LRT system added to the existing system in 1993 generated an increase in property value and density in proximity to rail stations in comparison to control areas (Papa, 2005). A subsequent study summarizing the finding on micro-level impacts of the rail system in Naples between 2001 and 2008 emphasizes the positive effect of rail on land-use value. The outcome of this research underlines that values tend to be higher in station catchment areas than in control areas. The extent of the effect on property values and residents' location depends on several factors such as location, local property market trend and connectivity given by the new metro line to the city centre (Pagliara and Papa, 2011).

Studies in South America focus largely on the effects of BRT systems. In Bogota, a citywide econometric hedonic analysis of 2000 to 2004 data across different walking distances was conducted. The research shows that middle-income properties were valued more if they were closer to the BRT system, while the opposite was true for low-income housing (Munoz-Raskin, 2010). In Curitiba, population density increased along the BRT corridors. Nevertheless, social segregation also occurred, where low income sectors were driven to residential areas with lower accessibility (Smith and Raemaekers, 1998). Simultaneously, higher-density development ensued in the CBD (Cervero, 1998). Social segregation was observed also in Mexico City in relation to the Metro system. Low income population reallocated to the suburban areas (Davis, 1994). A World Bank report indicates that in Bogota higher commercial property value can be observed near transit stations (World Bank, 2005b). However, a different study asserts that there is no evidence to an increase in real-estate prices in proximity to stations (Rodriguez, 2004). Also, in Quito, no correlation between accessibility to transit stations and real-estate development was found (World Bank, 2005a).

6. CONCLUSIONS

In multi-network car-dominated cities, LRTs and BRTs have limited spatial effects on city structures in themselves. The effects that can be perceived are mostly at the micro-level, in close proximity to stations. Yet, also these effects are mediated by the local economic trends, the existing built stock, the socio-economic structure of the area and the physical particularities around the stations (particularly the extent to which they are accessible by foot). Hence, these micro effects vary between cities, different parts of the city and between different sections of the LRT or BRT corridor. Moreover, different effects can be expected for residential and commercial activities. While commercial activities are affected by the ridership alighting or embarking in the station, residential preferences are affected by both the accessibility offered by the transit service and the nuisances emanating from the transit line. The larger effects of transit systems on land use at both the micro- and especially at the macro-level are mostly of suburban rail or metro systems. This is not surprising since suburban and metro rail systems are faster than LRT and BRT, and stations are further apart and hence have more distinctive effects.

The North American and European literature tends to focus on rail transit rather than bus rapid transit, since buses were not operated as mass transit systems in cities where rail transit was first introduced. In contrast, South American studies discuss the impacts of BRTs, as BRTs play a more prominent role there. Although the number of analyses of BRT systems is limited, it is important to examine the effects of BRT systems on land use, as BRT systems are currently rapidly diffusing worldwide (Deng and Nelson, 2011).

While the net effects of enhanced accessibility due to LRT or BRT improvements may be small, particularly at the macro-level, LRT or BRT may have discernible effects when coupled with other measures (Cervero, 1998; Filion, 2000; Bartholomew and Ewing, 2011). This is often the case, as LRT and BRT systems are bundled with other measures as part of wider policy packages. Such policy packages are advanced in order to make an effect on the urban or metropolitan structure, as planners increasingly realize that no single measure can make a substantial impact on complex policy areas such as developing the urban structure. Thus, while it may be possible to try and discern the net effect of transit systems on the urban and metropolitan structure, the utility of doing so can be questioned. As transit use is enhanced by coupling the improvement of such systems with complementary measures, its spatial effects are likely to be enhanced by the combination with synergic measures. The emphasis should thus be on identifying the synergic measures that will augment the desired effects on the urban structure rather than on discerning the net effects of LRT or BRT systems (Bartholomew and Ewing, 2011).

In order to identify the measures that may indeed affect urban structures, which is the goal of many transit improvements, it is necessary to focus on the measures that were identified as mediating the macro effects of transit systems. These include land-use policies (Cervero, 1998; Filion, 2000), provision of amenities, particularly pedestrianization schemes (Bartholomew and Ewing, 2011); complementary transport policies (Giuliano, 1995) and economic tools. How combinations of such policies with transit policies affect land use and urban structures is the next challenge in this field.

REFERENCES

Badoe, D.A. and Miller, E.J. (2000), Transportation–land-use interaction: empirical findings in North America, and their implications for modeling, *Transportation Research Part D: Transport and Environment*, **5**(4), 235–63.

Bajic, V. (1983), The effects of new subway line on housing pricing in metropolitan Toronto, *Urban Studies*, **20**, 147–58.

Banister, D. and Thurstain-Goodwin, M. (2011), Quantification of non-transport benefits resulting from rail investments, *Journal of Transport Geography*, **19**, 212–23.

Bartholomew, K. and Ewing, R. (2011), Hedonic price effects of pedestrian and transit-oriented development, *Journal of Planning Literature*, **26**, 18–34.

Bourne, L. (1969), A spatial allocation–land use conversion model of urban growth, *Journal of Regional Science*, **9**, 261–72.

Bowes, D.R. and Ihlanfeldt, K.R. (2001), Identifying the impacts of rail transit stations on residential property values, *Journal of Urban Economics*, **50**, 1–25.

Boyce, D.E. (1972), *Impact of Rapid Transit on Suburban Residential Property Values and Land Development*, University of Pennsylvania.

Catanese, A.J. (1988), Transit, life and development in the Sunbelt, in W. Attoe (ed.), *Transit, Land Use and Form*, Austin: University of Texas Center for the Study of American Architecture, pp. 47–54.

Cervero, R. (1998), *The Transit Metropolis: A Global Inquiry*, Washington, Island Press.

Cervero, R. (2009), Urban Development on Railway-Served Land: Lessons and Opportunities for the Developing World, working paper from the UC Berkeley Center for Future Urban Transport, UCB-ITS-VWP-2009-13.

Cervero, R. and Duncan, M. (2002), Transit's value-added effects: light and commuter rail services and commercial land values, *Transportation Research Record*, **1805**, 8–15.

Cervero, R. and Landis, J. (1993), Assessing the impacts of urban rail transit on local real estate markets using quasi-experimental comparisons, *Transportation Research A*, **27**(1), 13–22.

Chatman, D.G., Tulach, N.K. and Kim, K. (2012), Evaluating the economic impacts of light rail by measuring home appreciation: a first look at New Jersey's River Line, *Urban Studies*, **49**, 467–87.

Chen, H., Rufolo, A. and Dueker, K.J. (1998), Measuring the impact of light rail systems on single-family homes: a hedonic approach with geographic information system application, *Transportation Research Record*, **1617**, 38–43.

Clark, C. (1958), Transport: maker and breaker of cities, *Town Planning Review*, **28**, 237–50.

Cohen-Blankshtain, G. and Feitelson, E. (2011), Light rail routing: do goals matter? *Transportation*, **38**, 343–61.

Czamanski, S. (1966), Effects of public investments on urban land values, *Journal of the American Institute of Planners*, **32**(4), 204–17.

Davis, D.E. (1994), *Urban Leviathan: Mexico City in the Twentieth Century*, Philadelphia: Temple University Press.

Debrezion, G., Pels, E. and Rietveld, P. (2007), The impact of railway stations on residential and commercial property value: a meta-analysis, *The Journal of Real Estate Finance and Economics*, **35**(2), 161–80.

Deng, T.T. and Nelson, J.D. (2011), Recent development is bus rapid transit: a review of the literature, *Transport Reviews*, **31**, 69–96.

Du, H. and Mulley, C. (2007), The short-term land value impacts of urban rail transit: quantitative evidence from Sunderland, UK, *Land Use Policy*, **24**(1), 223–33.

Ewing, R. (1997), Is Los Angeles-style sprawl desirable? *Journal of the American Planning Association*, **63**, 107–26.

Fielding, G.J. (1995), *Transit in American Cities*, New York and London: The Guilford Press.

Filion, P. (2000), Balancing concentration and dispersion? Public policy and urban structure in Toronto, *Environment and Planning C*, **18**, 163–89.

Fishman, R. (1987), *Bourgeois Utopias*, New York: Basic Books.

Forrest, D., Glen, J. and Ward, R. (1996), The impact of a light rail system on the structure of house prices, *Journal of Transport Economics and Policy*, **30**(1), 15–29.

Freeman, M. (1999), *Railways and the Victorian Imagination*, Connecticut: Yale University Press.

Fulford, C. (1996), The compact city and the market in M. Jenks, E. Burton and K. Williams (eds), *The Compact City: A Sustainable Urban Form?* London and New York: E. & F.N. Spon, pp. 122–33.

Fouracre, P., Dunkerley, C. and Gardner, G. (2003), Mass rapid transit systems for cities in the developing world, *Transport Reviews*, **23**, 299–310.

Gatzlaff, D.H. and Smith, M.T. (1993), The impact of Miami Metrorail on value of residences near station locations, *Land Economics*, **69**, 54–66.

Giuliano, G. (1995), Land use impacts of transportation investments: highway and transit, in S. Hanson (ed.), *The Geography of Urban Transportation*, New York and London: The Guilford Press, pp. 305–86.

Givoni, M. and Banister, D. (eds) (2010), *Integrated Transport: From Policy to Practice*, London and New York: Routledge.

Gospodini, A. (2005), Urban development, redevelopment and regeneration encouraged by transport infrastructure projects: the case study of 12 European cities, *European Planning Studies*, **13**(7), 1083–111.

Green, R.D. and Jones, D.M. (1993), *Rail Transit Station Area Development: Small Modeling in Washington, DC*, New York: Armmonk.

Hensher, D.A. and Reyes, A. J. (2000), Trip chaining as a barrier to the propensity to use public transport, *Transportation*, **27**(4), 341–61.

Hess, D.B. and Almeida, T.M. (2007), Impact of proximity to light rail rapid transit on station-area property values in Buffalo, New York, *Urban Studies*, **44**(5/6), 1041–68.

Hunt, J.D., McMillan, J.D.P. and Abraham, J. E. (1994), Stated preferences investigation of influences on attractiveness of residential location, *Transportation Research Record*, **1466**, 79–87.

Hunt, T. (2004), *Building Jerusalem: The Rise and Fall of the Victorian City*, New York: Metropolitan Books.

Israel, E. and Cohen-Blankshtain, G. (2010), Testing decentralization effects of rail systems: empirical findings from Israel, *Transportation Research A*, **44**, 523–36.

Knight, R.L. and Trygg, L.L. (1977), Evidence of land use impacts of rapid transit systems, *Transportation*, **6**, 231–47.

Kreibich, V. (1978), The successful transportation system and the regional planning problem: an evolution of the Munich rapid transit system in the context of urban and regional planning, *Transportation*, **7**, 137–45.

Landis, J., Guhathakurta, S., Haung, W. and M.Z. (1995), *Rail Transit Investments, Real Estate Values, and Land Changes: A Comparative Analysis of Five California Rail Transit System*, working paper UCTC Berkeley, University of California, Transportation Center, No. 285.

McMillen, D.P. (1989), An empirical model of urban fringe land use, *Land Economics*, **65**(2), 138–45.

Muller, P.O. (1995), Transportation and urban form: stages in the spatial evolution of the American metropolis, in S. Hanson and G. Giuliano (eds), *The Geography of Urban Transportation*, New York and London: The Guilford Press, pp. 26–52.

Munoz-Raskin, R. (2010), Walking accessibility to bus rapid transit: does it affect property values? The case of Bogota, Colombia, *Transport Policy*, **17**(2), 72–84.

Nelson, A.C. and Sanchez, T.L. (1997), *The Influence of MARTA on Population and Employment Location*, paper presented at the 76th Annual Meeting of the Transportation Research Board, Washington, DC.

Pagliara, F. and Papa, E. (2011), Urban rail systems investments: an analysis of the impacts on property values and residents' location, *Journal of Transport Geography*, **19**(2), 200–11.

Papa, E. (2005), *Urban Transformation and Rail Stations System: The Study Case of Naples*, paper presented at 45th Congress of the European Regional Science Association, Amsterdam.

Pill, J. (1988), Toronto: thirty years of transit development, in W. Attoe (ed.), *Transit, Land Use and Form*, Austin: University of Texas Center for the Study of American Architecture, pp. 57–62.

Post, J.R. (1998), The Portland light rail experience, in W. Attoe (ed.), *Transit, Land Use and Form*, Austin: University of Texas Center for the Study of American Architecture, pp. 63–80.

Pucher, J. (2002), Renaissance of public transport in the United States? *Transportation Quarterly*, **56**, 33–49.

Pucher, J. (2004), Public transportation, in S. Hanson and G. Giuliano (eds), *The Geography of Urban Transportation*, New York and London: The Guilford Press, pp. 199–236.

Pucher, J. and Kurth, S. (1996), Verkehrsverbund: the success of regional public transport in Germany, Austria and Switzerland, *Transport Policy*, **2**(4), 279–91.

Pucher J. and Lefevre C. (1996), *The Urban Transportation Crisis in Europe and North America*, London: Macmillan.

Rabinovitch, J. (1996), Innovative land use and public transport policy: the case of Curitiba, Brazil, *Land Use Policy*, **13**(1), 51–67.

Rabinovitch, J. and Leitman, J. (1996), Urban planning in Curitiba, *Scientific American*, **274**(3), 46–53.

Rodriguez, D.A. (2004), Spatial choices and excess commuting: a case study of bank tellers in Bogotá, Colombia, *Journal of Transport Geography*, **12**, 49–61.

Rodriguez, D.A. and Targa, F. (2004), Value of accessibility to Bogota's bus rapid transit system, *Transport Reviews*, **24**(5), 587–610.

Rothblatt, D.N. (1994), North American metropolitan planning, *Journal of the American Planning Association*, **60**(4), 501–20.

Ryan, S. (2005), The value of access to highways and light rail transit: evidence for industrial and office firms, *Urban Studies*, **42**, 751–64.

Smith, H. and Raemaekers, J. (1998), Land use pattern and transport in Curitiba, *Land Use Policy*, **15**(3), 233–51.

Smith, N. and Hensher, D. (1998), The future of exclusive busways: the Brazilian experience, *Transport Reviews*, **18**(2), 131–52.

Steer Davis Gleave (2005), *What Light Rail can do for Cities*, London: Passenger Transport Executive Group.

Vance, J.E. (1991), Human mobility and the shaping of our cities, in J.F. Hart (ed.), *Our Changing Cities*, Baltimore: Johns Hopkins University Press, pp. 67–85.

Vitiello, D. (2008), Machine building and city building: urban planning and industrial restructuring in Philadelphia 1894–1928, *Journal of Urban History*, **34**, 399–434.

Warner, S.B. (1970), *Streetcar Suburbs*, Cambridge, MA: Harvard University Press.

Wegener, M. and Fürst, F. (1999), *Land-Use Transport Interaction: State of the Art*, Dortmund: Institut für Raumplanung.

Workman, S.L. and Bord, D. (1997), *Measuring the Neighborhood Benefits of Rail Transit Accessibility*, paper presented at the 76th Annual Meeting of the Transportation Research Board, Washington, DC.

World Bank (2005a), *Quito, Busways, Equadorm*, http://web.worldbank.org.

World Bank (2005b), *Transmilenio Busway-based Mass Transit, Bogotá, Colombia*, http://web.worldbank.org.

20 High-speed trains and spatial-economic impacts: a British–French comparison on two scales: intra- and inter-regional
Chia-Lin Chen and Peter Hall

1. INTRODUCTION

High-speed trains (HSTs), bringing unprecedented time-space shrinkages in the second half of the twentieth century, have been termed 'The Second Railway Age' (Banister and Hall, 1993), giving a new meaning to Colin Clark's verdict on transport as 'the maker and breaker of cities' (Clark, 1958). HST can potentially trigger wider impacts at multiple spatial levels. This chapter focuses on the wider effects of HST at inter- and intra-regional scales in the European context. Inter-regionally, HSTs offer competitive centre-to-centre accessibility over medium- to long-distance journeys in competition with air and conventional rail. Thus, HST services can greatly enhance inter-regional connectivity between major regional cities. And, as they successfully replace short-haul flights, HST services increasingly need to make good airport connections with long-haul flights, as successfully demonstrated at Paris Charles de Gaulle, Amsterdam Schiphol and Frankfurt International airports. Intra-regionally, since HSTs can inter-operate on conventional tracks, they can potentially run at lower speeds to serve smaller sub-centres within a wider regional territory.

The development of HST networks has coincided with the profound economic restructuring of European economies away from manufacturing and into the knowledge economy (Hall, 2007), placing a premium on major agglomeration economies for very high-valued 'knowledge economy' activities, while others decentralize into ever-spreading 'mega-city regions' (Hall and Pain, 2006). Although HST offers a major opportunity to reshape spatial-economic development, uneven development between places has increased. Particularly in recent decades, many countries have experienced deepening divides between successful central regions and unsuccessful peripheral ones, and also within the peripheral regions (Hall, 2002).

Existing literature on wider impacts of HST has presented a mixed picture, largely based on ex-ante modelling approaches, quantitatively led ex-post studies and analysis of individual cities. So far, a multi-scale perspective including an interrelation between different spatial scales has not been adequately adopted. Given that transport is a necessary but not sufficient condition for urban and regional development, wider impacts require strategic planning that extends beyond transport, and that varies with different contexts and conditions. Few HST studies have been designed to unpack the complexity of dynamic urban development. Wider impacts of HST on reducing regional inequality thus remain contentious. Thus, this chapter seeks to shed light on the wider impacts of HST by drawing on recently completed ex-post area-based studies from a comparison between the British and French experiences: whether, to what extent and in what ways

HSTs could reduce inter- and intra-regional inequality. During the 1980s and 2000s, the UK and France have presented two contrasting national approaches towards HST (the UK: upgrading old lines to operate at 200kph and France: building new dedicated lines for 300kph operation). Comparison between these approaches can make a critical contribution to the HST debate.

This chapter has three main sections. In section 2, a brief literature review is presented to illustrate the competitiveness of HST, a brief summary of the two HST approaches in the UK and France, and the controversial relationship between HST and urban/regional development from the existing impact studies. Second, the empirical evidence is reviewed of inter-regional HST impacts over the past 30 years on changes of the British economic geography and French territorial development. Third, the empirical evidence is reviewed on intra-regional HST impacts on two post-industrial regions: the upgraded West Coast Main Line (WCML) on Manchester and its sub-regions in north-west England versus the TGV-Nord on Lille and its sub-regions in Nord-Pas-de-Calais, France. This commentary embraces both quantitative and qualitative findings. A 'planning standpoint' is employed in examining key factors in seizing opportunities presented by HST during the transformation process. Finally, concluding remarks and implications for HS2 in the UK are drawn in the conclusion.

2.   LITERATURE REVIEW

The Competitiveness of HST and the Fear of Peripheralization of the Periphery

The definition of HST in this paper follows the European Union Directive 96/48: a speed of at least 250kph on specially built lines and 200kph on upgraded high-speed lines. Expert operator analysis suggests that for distances up to 150km, HST provides no advantage over conventional trains; between 150km and 400km, rail is faster than air between city centres; between 400km and 800km, HST offers the fastest mode for personal travel up to 4.5 hours; beyond 800km, air travel is faster (Steer Davies Gleave, 2004; Pepy and Leboeuf, 2005). Thus HST should obtain 80–90 per cent of traffic up to about 500km and about 50 per cent up to about 800km. At the maximum practicable present speed of 350kph, the competitive rail range in Europe could potentially extend to 1500km, embracing journeys like Paris–Madrid or London–Zürich (Hall, 2009). However, in practice, the range is limited by speed restrictions in densely populated areas or in tunnels or long bridges. Also, low-cost airlines continue to compete through aggressive price competition and smart marketing.

Since the first European HST service over upgraded track opened in the UK in 1976 and the first *Train à Grande Vitesse* (TGV) on dedicated track in France in 1981, Europe has been experiencing the process of 'the shrinking continent' (Spiekermann and Wegener, 1994), developing an extensive HST network[1] connecting major cities, which is still being extended. The total HST network in operation reached 6,637km in 2011, expected to be 17,769km by 2025 (International Union of Railways, 2011). However, there is a growing worry that the larger the HST range extends, the higher the possibility that HST services will serve larger urban centres and bypass smaller and less profitable places, which tend to be the ones most seriously affected by deindustrialization (Hall, 2009).

Two HST Approaches

Although modern HST development began in Japan as long ago as 1964, the UK and France were the first two European countries to develop HST systems, but in different ways over a 30-year period. The UK maintained its incremental approach by upgrading mainline services for major inter-city links. In 1976, the UK InterCity125 (achieving 125mph, the equivalent of 200kph) with diesel traction operated at a maximum speed of 200kph from London to Swansea on the Great Western Main Line, designed by the far-seeing engineer Isambard Kingdom Brunel in the 1830s. The East Coast Main Line, the Midland Main Line and West Coast Main Line (WCML) were subsequently upgraded. Due to the fiasco of the APT project in 1982 (Barnett, 1993) and later privatization, high-speed service on the busiest WCML was postponed and not completed until December 2008. The first new dedicated 300kph HST line (the Channel Tunnel Rail Link, later called HS1) arrived in 2007.

In contrast, France has been the first European country to build a dedicated HST network over the same period of time. The arrival of the TGV-*Sud-Est* in 1981, linking Paris with Lyon, over 419km, in two hours, was a big success and triggered a progressive expansion of the TGV network (the TGV-*Atlantique* (1989/90), the TGV-*Nord* (1993), the TGV-*Méditerranée* (2001), the TGV-*Est* (2007) and the *Perpignan-Figueres* line (2010)). Beyond building individual HST lines, an integrated network had emerged by the early 1990s with added interconnection lines and new multi-modal TGV hubs (at Charles de Gaulle airport and Disneyland Paris) around the Paris fringes, allowing direct services to operate between provincial cities without the need to change at terminal stations in central Paris. As Thompson (1994) highlighted, the French HST approach is not an isolated system but is integrated with other high-speed systems, evolving to best serve an unevenly and thinly populated national territory. Also, TGV seats could be effectively used by two successive travellers with lengthy routes (Pepy and Leboeuf, 2005). Furthermore, the TGV network has expanded not only on a national scale, but also on a European scale to UK, Belgium, the Netherlands, Germany, Switzerland, Italy and Spain.

Existing Evidence for Wider HST Impact Studies

Spatially, HST transports people at high speeds on fixed tracks from one city to another, interchanging at stations, so three spatial patterns, i.e., node (point), corridor (line) and a wider geographical area (territory) can be identified, meaning that HST potentially has wider effects simultaneously on three major spatial scales, namely local (station area), intra-regional and inter-regional. The review here pinpoints wider impacts of HST on the inter- and intra-regional scales.

Inter-regional impacts
Inter-regionally, the existing literature on HST impacts falls into distinct groups. Early studies used accessibility-potential models suggesting that HST investment would benefit major cities at the expense of smaller cities, thus widening regional inequalities. Thus Puga (2008) suggested that the Paris–Lyon HST line led to relocation of headquarters from Lyon to Paris, contradicting Bonnafous (1987), who had suggested that it had

strengthened Lyon's business base. But this failed to consider the complexities of the real world (Vickerman et al., 1999). Ex-post case studies could be of importance, but there have been few such studies and they tend to be conducted over a short period soon after opening the services, and they do not always agree. In Europe, ex-post findings suggested that HSTs appeared to reinforce large regional cities (Harman, 2006; Steer Davies Gleave, 2008), like Lyon (Bonnafous, 1987; Payre, 2010), whereas in smaller HST cities impacts differed. Ciudad Real, within one hour of Madrid by HST, transformed itself from a previously isolated small regional city to a sub-centre within a polycentric megacity functional region (Garmendia et al., 2008), but in Ashford, south-east England, economic effects were modest and there was a fear that the HST service would further draw the town into London's commuting belt (Preston and Wall, 2008).

Intra-regional impacts
There is an acute shortage of empirical research on the intra-regional impacts. A few warnings have been given regarding possible polarization within regions. Troin (1995) and Menerault and Barre (1997) suggested that the arrival of HSTs sharply reduced the frequency of conventional long-distance train services, disadvantageous for intra-regional relationships. Bruyelle and Thomas (1994) likewise predicted that regional polarization was likely to worsen due to a limited number of well-served, nodal locations. But, most importantly, empirical evidence has not yet proven these assertions. A qualitative-led method was applied in Ureña et al. (2009), which deepened the understanding through a comparative case study of three HST cities at multiple levels. However, at the regional level, the investigation focused on the relationship between small regional cities and the national capital within the same region, rather than the inequality and interaction within the region.

Four major issues arise in the paucity of empirical evidence. First, the majority of research consists of ex-ante forecasting studies. It is difficult to understand the complexity of the wider effects of HST through these modelling approaches, which are concerned with limited and simplified factors such as transport cost, and fail to differentiate the dynamic uneven nature of development over time. As a result, the forecasts tend to favour the dominance of agglomeration economies in large cities and, thus, no positive implication is available for regional policy with regard to poorer disadvantaged cities. Second, ex-post studies have been few and have tended to adopt largely quantitative-led methods. These studies generally measured socio-economic changes through the effects of HST through a time series featuring before and after HST, and a distinction between HST and non-HST cities. In addition, in some studies, the typology of HST cities (the size and time-space effects brought about by HST) is taken into account to evaluate the development effect of HST. However, the latest UIC (2011) worldwide sample study of the impact of HST has confirmed the difficulty of generalization. Third, there has been a lack of multiple-scale perspectives in examining the wider impacts of HST. The investigation and focus have been placed on individual cities rather than groups of cities including disadvantaged peripheral cities within the country or within regions. Fourth, it has been widely reiterated that public intervention is needed to address regional inequality and that transport is a necessary, but not sufficient condition. The specificities of the context are important and that understanding the interregional competition between cities is particularly difficult as many of the benefits are relative in nature.

In-depth qualitative case studies for unveiling the complexities of HST impact have been lacking.

Thus, a planning perspective underlying new ex-post studies of both quantitative and qualitative evidence on different spatial scales is vital. The aim is not only to try to measure whether and to what extent HST results in a wider impact, but also to understand other factors attributed to a mixed picture of wider impacts of HST.

3.   EMPIRICAL EVIDENCE

Inter-regional Impacts

The evidence below draws on findings of recent individual studies associated with potential time-space effects of HST from the UK and France. Three train time zones – namely, towns within one-hour, one to two-hour and over two-hour journey-times (from London and Paris) were identified to make the comparison.

The UK experience

The upgraded HST IC125/225 services have been largely ignored because they have relatively modest effects in time-space shrinkage compared with newly built HST lines. Chen and Hall (2011) researched their long-term wider impacts on the UK's economic geography. Six London-outbound routes, embracing 26 local authority areas, were selected as units of analysis, all over 150km in length: two HST lines (the Great Western Main Line and East Coast Main Line) and four non-HST lines. The observation emphasized the difference in the effects on local economic strength and knowledge-intensive development between HST and non-HST towns, and potential time-space effects among each group of towns.

Within one hour of London, spillover effects appeared favourable in places with HST services. These were decentralized locations such as Reading, Swindon and Peterborough. Non-HST towns, such as Chelmsford, Colchester, Basingstoke, Winchester and Ashford, largely showed an attraction to high-income commuters rather than directly triggering economic development. Cambridge was the exception, demonstrating the effects of electrification. Within two hours of London, different HST effects were present. Well-established regional capitals – Bristol, Leeds, Cardiff – revived from decline with growth in high-GVA activities and aggregated highly knowledge-intensive industries. But there were exceptions: Doncaster and Newport, both old industrial towns, continued to suffer economically and the industrial decline has been difficult to turn around. Non-HST towns were characterized by weaker economic performance. But Southampton and Bournemouth were exceptions, partly because these places are within two hours from London with high-frequency train services and have established a long-lasting close economic relationship with London prior to the arrival of IC125/225. Beyond the two-hour limit, HST effects appear weaker: Darlington, Swansea and Newcastle-upon-Tyne showed relative economic weakness; while Edinburgh, more than three hours from London by HST, showed strong economic performance, along with significant growth in air travel to London.

The French experience
Although a comprehensive inter-regional study is yet to be conducted for France, the existing literature suggests that the spatial-economic impacts of TGV at the inter-regional scale are important. Within one hour from Paris, HST cities have demonstrated a demand for commuting to and from Paris. According to statistics for 2010, the top nine TGV cities that were the busiest routes with daily travellers are all reachable within one hour from Paris. The Lille–Paris route has the largest base of customers, exceeding the second TGV city (Le Mans) by 35 per cent (SNCF, 2011). Lille is the only large metropolitan city within one hour from Paris by TGV, halving previous journey times. With high train frequencies and high percentages of daily customers, Chen and Hall (2012) found that Lille demonstrated the largest increase in knowledge-intensive employment above the national average and continued to grow its public services. This shows that the arrival of the TGV-Nord and the interconnection with Paris Charles de Gaulle airport not only assisted Lille to develop its knowledge economy, but also drew Lille into a wider Parisian region within a one-hour commuting distance. This was reflected in the growth in public services. Within two hours from Paris, Lyon is the example with the most evident spatial-economic impacts. The two-hour journey time by TGV from Paris is particularly suitable for the commercial operation of HSTs in competition with air. Lyon's economic base has been strengthened. Several studies have been demonstrated the impacts of TGV on Lyon (Bonnafous, 1987; Payre, 2010). However, for other large metropolitan cities like Marseille, Bordeaux and Toulouse, the time-space effect of the TGV is not competitive with air. These cities are located in southern France, more than 500km from Paris, and neither Bordeaux nor Toulouse yet enjoys a direct high-speed service. For Toulouse, the journey time by rail presently takes around five hours 30 minutes, although this will be cut by one hour when a direct high-speed line from Paris to Bordeaux opens in 2019. For Marseille, more than 750km from Paris, the quickest journey time by TGV has improved significantly but is still about three hours 30 minutes. Since southern France has popular tourist destinations, rail journeys over three hours could be still attractive for tourism purposes.

Apart from the reduction of rail journey time, the location of new HST stations in proximity to city centres is a relevant factor, contributing to the positive wider impacts of Lyon and Lille. Based on the current HST experience in France, it is important to avoid *Gares des Betteraves* (Beetroot Stations) – distant from major populated centres (Pepy and Leboeuf, 2005; *Le Monde, 2004*; Hall, 2009). A classic example is the decision to locate the new TGV-Nord station, Lille-Europe, in the Lille city centre. A post-industrial textile city, Lille had suffered from economic decline. In order to seize the opportunities of the TGV in developing the knowledge economy, the former Prime Minister, and then Mayor of Lille, Pierre Mauroy, successfully persuaded SNCF to change the location of its new TGV station from the outskirts to the city core (Fraser and Baert, 2003; Paris and Mons, 2009).

In brief, building upon evidence from both the British and French experiences, HST has had demonstrable and varied effects on cities within one hour and two hours from the capital city, thus helped to generate renewed economies. Towns within one-hour HST accessibility from the national capital could benefit from exploiting both commuting and economic functions, while two-hour HST accessibility from the national capital could benefit mainly from exploiting economic functions. Beyond a two-hour distance, the effect appears weak (here, the one-hour or two-hour classification could be slightly different in specific contexts). However, these effects have not been automatic or universal. Transport accessibility seems to be an important factor in economic performance, and this is enhanced with faster services, but wider macroeconomic and social factors for each particular urban area are also important. Many languishing urban centres that have lost their traditional industrial roles have failed so far to make a full transition to the new knowledge economy. That said, at the very least, there appears to be a strong case for a further analysis of the potential of rail improvement as an agent of change at an intra-regional level.

Intra-regional Impacts

Understanding the wider intra-regional impacts of HST is challenging. A finer-grained comparative case study of two regions was conducted to gain insight (Chen and Hall, 2012; Chen, 2013). Manchester and its sub-regions in north-west England (hereafter NWE) and Lille and its sub-regions in Nord-Pas-de-Calais, France (hereafter NPDC) were chosen – both with similar industrial trajectories and opportunities associated with two different HST approaches (the West Coast Main Line (WCML) modernization versus the new dedicated TGV-Nord). A brief background of transport and economic conditions before the arrival of the HSTs is helpful in interpreting the impacts. In NWE, the spatial-economic landscape had already been significantly changed by well-established and extensive motorway systems. Economic growth was taking place in places with less-pronounced industrial legacy and good road transport accessibility. In NPDC, unlike NWE, the economic turning point had not yet occurred and transport infrastructure was still deficient for this border region. The opening of the Channel Tunnel triggered the construction of the TGV-Nord as well as two major motorways (the A26 and A16), making the whole region much better served by TGV and motorway.

This study involved both quantitative and qualitative analyses to tease out HST impacts through the examination of the 'before' and 'after' situations. Figures 20.1 and 20.2 show the railway networks, main stations and sub-regions in both regions.

Based on two different HST approaches and two spatial-economic effects, two-hour (London–Manchester) and one-hour (Paris–Lille) respectively, the quantitative comparison shows that the transformation of two post-industrial regions and sub-regions towards a knowledge economy, brought by HST, has proved to be a complex and difficult process, but the similarities and differences between these two case study regions are manifest (Figure 20.3). The similarity lies in the fact that both regions have strengthened their representation of knowledge-intensive industries, and the connection with the national capital by faster train services did economically strengthen Manchester and Lille, but did not necessarily have the same effect for nearby sub-regions, especially former industrial sub-regions. The difference is that the overall regional disparity between NPDC and the Île-de-France has been progressively reduced, although a big gap remains, whereas uneven regional development between NWE and Greater London has actually widened.

A critical distinction needs to be made between directly served HST-sub-regions and non-HST sub-regions. The findings from this intra-regional study suggest that HST could facilitate decentralization at the national level with the revival of regional cities

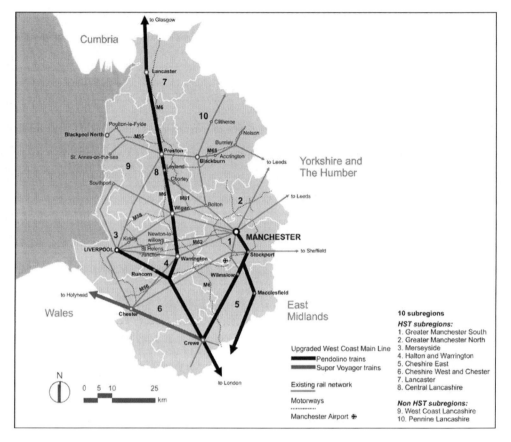

Note: The motorway network is supplementary in this diagram

Figure 20.1   The railway network, main stations, and sub-regions in north-west England

through efficient and much improved inter-city connectivity by HST within one-hour and two-hour ranges from the national capitals. At the same time, HST tends to trigger centralization at the regional level around the regional capitals. Although there could be several other HST sub-regions within a region, their HST services usually do not have the same level as the regional capital, unless there are additional interventions at work to widely spread the benefits. Most importantly, it is not necessarily a zero-sum game because both inter- and intra-regional connectivity are essential. Therefore, for non-metropolitan sub-regions, intra-regional accessibility with the regional capital could prove to be more critical and practical than inter-regional connectivity. This suggests that strategic regional intervention would be needed to exploit the HST opportunity at the regional level. To understand further, all these depend very much on specific contexts with qualitative investigation required.

Further qualitative in-depth interviews and policy analysis offered insights into the wider spatial-economic outcomes. Five critical factors are suggested for their contribution to the differential effects.

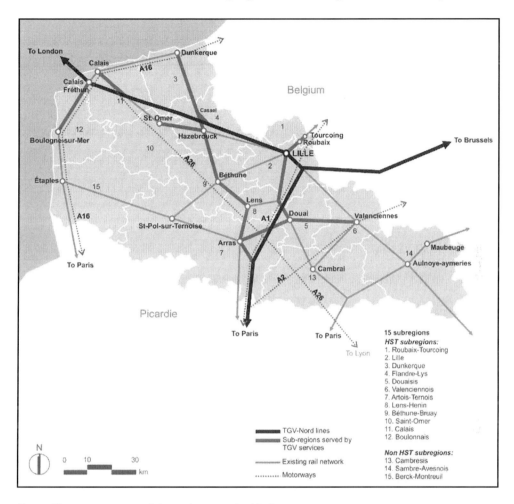

Note: The motorway network is supplementary in this diagram

Figure 20.2   The railway network, main stations, and sub-regions in Nord-Pas-de-Calais, France

National political economy: the perception of the HST opportunity

First, the national political economy proves to be the most fundamental condition. During the 1980s and 2000s, the UK and France had presented distinctive political culture and modes of capitalism: the UK's market-led and France's state-led approaches. This difference could explain a fundamental distinction of perception towards the two HST opportunities. The British ideology signified minimum public intervention, deregulation and privatization of transport investment. The process of the WCML modernization illustrated a lack of coordinated government involvement. Therefore, the WCML upgrade encountered serious technical obstacles, which were perceived and treated as a problem rather than an opportunity with an overextended

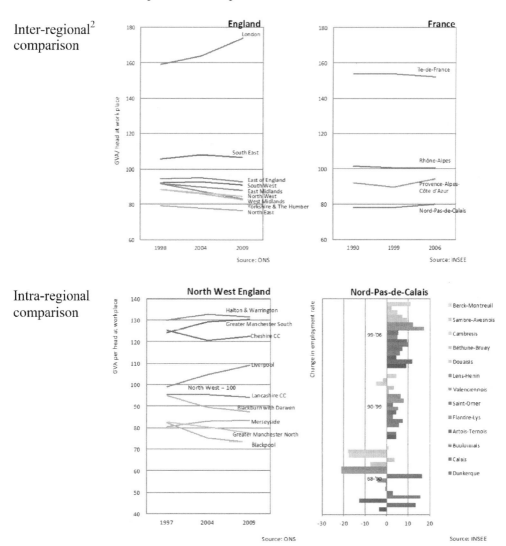

Source: Chen (2013: 196); Chen and Hall (2013: 356)

Figure 20.3 A comparison between the two case studies

construction period, cost overruns, reduction of the planned journey speed and extremely unreliable services during construction: an approach that was 'troublesome and costly' (Chen and Wray, 2011). In addition, an upgrade approach involving modest transport improvement without physical transformation of new routes or stations seems to raise little awareness of the opportunity that was being opened up. In NPDC, the state-led approach has been reinforced with a combination of state-enhanced and decentralized features. The TGV-Nord was not only fully supported by the state as part of the long-term national high-speed network, but also gained wide consensus among regional and local actors who valued it as a great opportunity for the area to transform its manufacturing economy towards '*la turbine tertiaire*' (the tertiary sector of service industries).

Constitutional capacities: market-led versus 'irrigation' approaches

Second, different national political-economic perspectives determined governance approaches which were associated with central-local governmental restructuring and competence, and critically shaped national and local interventions. In NWE, first, rail privatization led to worsening regional inequality. The WCML modernization took place when British Rail had just been privatized and state-led transport investment in the UK had been constrained. WCML service patterns, which were proposed by the private train operator Virgin Trains and agreed by the state, demonstrated a market-led (profit-oriented) approach. Virgin Trains served existing popular places but skipped unprofitable ones. This point could be best exemplified by the differential service patterns for Blackpool and Chester. Despite the fact that both are located on non-electrified conventional lines, through services to and from Blackpool were cancelled in 2001, in contrast to Chester, which continued to be served by Virgin Voyager diesel trains, because Chester is a more buoyant business and tourist destination than Blackpool. Furthermore, Virgin Pendolino services are prioritized for London-oriented inter-city travel in order to compete with air, squeezing the overloaded capacity for intra-regional commuting services. Second, a fragmented regional planning mechanism and competence proved problematic and ineffective, even though attempts were made to strengthen regional development after the Labour government was re-elected in 1997. First, the operation of three non-elected regional bodies has been ineffective amid institutional conflicts (Wray, 2011). The situation was worsened when the pilot referendum of directly elected regional governments outside London was rejected in 2004 by a large margin in north-east England. Next, the centralized state in the UK still controlled the majority of funding resources. Although the priority for transport investment was identified and agreed collectively by three regional agencies, the effect was limited since the Department for Transport had the final decision-making power, taken from a national perspective.

In NPDC, the experience of the TGV-Nord has demonstrated how the regional government exerted its decentralized power and competence to exploit HST to irrigate lagging sub-regions. First, the regional government has gained more power and responsibility from the state since 1982. Although the TGV-Nord enhanced the dominant position of Lille, the regional government meanwhile funded electrification of existing conventional lines to serve the region more widely. The time reduction by the interoperability between dedicated HST lines and electrified conventional lines for sub-regions is evident. Peripheral sub-regions (e.g., Dunkirk) were directly linked by HSTs to Paris. Second, after the responsibility of regional rail passenger services was decentralized to the hand of regional governments, the intra-regional network was further improved through the progressive improvement of regional train services (TER) and the introduction of regional TGV services (TERGV) for which the NPDC regional government pays a subsidy to SNCF. Thus, from 2000 onwards, pure Paris-oriented HST services have been largely modified into Lille-oriented services, in particular for the connection of peripheral coastal areas and Arras with Lille.

Planning priority and resources
Third, similar to constitutional capacity, national political economies influence planning priority and resources that are used to exploit the HST opportunity by strategic planning with a combination of transport and non-transport initiatives. British planning priority and resources demonstrate a period of massive reductions in public spending (including transport) with guidance-led, competition-led, metropolitan-led approaches. In contrast, French approaches have showed a revival of public transport investment with a concern to remedy inequalities. Moreover, progressive decentralization has brought equivalent resources to multi-level local governments with a contractual-led approach for capacity building at the local level. Again, this significantly influences national and local interventions during the process.

Transport resources in the UK have been largely controlled by the state. In contrast, in France, a critical hypothecated tax (*Versement Transport*, VT) was implemented from the 1970s, which has proven to be significant in granting local authorities the power and resources to invest in and transform local transport systems.

A conducive constitutional capacity, with planning priority and resources are necessary but not sufficient conditions. Although the VT became available for local transport planning authorities to organize urban transport systems, it would not be possible to exploit the wider impact of HST without strong leadership and governance (discussed further below). Good examples in NPDC are Lille Metropolis, Valenciennes and Dunkirk. The former two developed their own urban transit systems to connect with TGV stations whereas other coal mining areas around Lens and Bethune did not manage to reach the consensus. Similarly, although tougher institutional constraints in the British context were found, Greater Manchester managed to overcome its constraints and progressively enhanced its competitiveness.

Political leadership and governance
Fourth, political leadership determined whether the HST opportunity could be seized strategically or just dissipated. Strong leadership was demonstrated in both cases with proactive initiatives to integrate HST with a wider local economic strategy and a local transport network. But only inclusive and coordinated governance could possibly address inequality.

In NWE, Manchester established its hegemony through an airport/HST hub strategy that gained enhanced importance beyond the regional boundary within a bigger northern framework. The delayed WCML modernization occurred in parallel with Manchester City Council's entrepreneurial efforts of developing Manchester International Airport from the 1980s to promote its external accessibility to the outside world as well as its rail link with Manchester Piccadilly and beyond, in order to expand the catchment of the airport. From 1998 onwards, train operators TransPennine Express and Northern Rail have explored this airport connection market beyond the regional boundary into Leeds, York, Newcastle and north Wales. The WCML modernization was completed to serve Manchester Piccadilly station in 2008, producing a journey time of around two hours to London, and resulting in a noticeable decline in the London–Manchester air market. In turn, the reduction of domestic flights further provided available space for the growth of long-haul flights. As Manchester International Airport has emerged as an indispensable asset for the whole of northern England, an outward-looking cross-city-regional growth strategy, 'The Northern Way', was further promoted to combat the north/south regional inequality. However, in the discourse of 'The Northern Way', inter-regional inequality was emphasized at the expense of intra-regional inequality. Disadvantaged peripheral sub-regions like Pennine Lancashire or West Coast Lancashire were excluded.

In contrast, in NPDC, rather than exploiting its own international airport, the HST hub of Lille, which is well-connected with the Paris and Brussels international airports, has grown its European status and reinforced its centripetal attraction for the neighbouring area beyond Lille Metropolis, including both the French and the Belgian part. With the promotion of *Coopération Métropolitaine* by the national spatial strategic agency, DATAR, the Lille metropolitan cooperation area was encouraged by the then president of Lille metropolis, Pierre Mauroy, to embrace the former coal-mining area and non-industrial sub-regions such as Arras, and also to include neighbouring Belgian partners. This enlarged Lille metropolitan area involved 23 partners, nearly 500 municipalities and 3.4 million inhabitants, within a territory of 75,000km² (SPIRE, 2005). Under this inclusive governance framework, development projects could be discussed in a broader scale around transport and other infrastructure, economic development and planning strategy, etc. (Colomb, 2007) to help the disadvantaged coal-mining sub-regions. Although this initiative was suspended later on by DATAR, Lille's metropolitan cooperation structure has been well-recognized among stakeholders and continues to assist for mutual benefit. Of course an inclusive and coordinated governance framework is difficult to develop in a partisan and parochial territory.

City type and economic trajectory
Fifth, the economic trajectory of cities denotes the type of city and its particular transport need. For post-industrial metropolitan cities where agglomeration economies tend to develop, a HST hub station could potentially recast their city-image to embrace the knowledge economy and reinforce their urban dynamics. For sub-regions that are still dominated by manufacturing activities, HST connectivity is not as useful as a motorway for transporting goods and an improved intra-regional network for people to access jobs outside their place of residence. For isolated sub-regions, despite abundant local regeneration initiatives (education, housing and physical transformation), intra-regional transport accessibility into nearby HST hubs could be essential to open up any opportunity for redevelopment. A better economic performance depends on a good combination of these local conditions.

In NWE, only a few major destinations are served by Virgin Pendolinos. Three sets of local transformation processes were found and variations in local factors help to explain the resulting economic conditions. First, for two metropolitan cities, a strong leadership capacity resulted in a recentralization regional hegemony around Manchester, which indirectly benefited from a contrasting weak performance by its rival metropolitan city, Liverpool. Second, there was a lack of awareness of opportunities in the non-metropolitan HST sub-regions. The faster link with London did not benefit the Warrington and Preston sub-regions, which already enjoyed good motorway accessibility, because the local leadership was not strong enough to strive for potential transformation. This partly helps to explain why the performance of Warrington sub-region was overtaken by the Manchester sub-region. Third, an arduous but frustrated process was experienced in non-HST sub-regions. Despite the efforts to implement regeneration projects, both peripheral Pennine Lancashire and West Coast Lancashire were relatively powerless and suffered from poor transport accessibility. Political leadership in this context includes the actual characters involved, but also the development of an ambitious vision for the area and mobilization of resources (including lobbying) to help effectively implement it.

In NPDC, most sub-regions are served by TGV. Three different kinds of local transformation processes were identified, with differential interventions. First, Lille has rebuilt its role as a regional centre through an international HST hub with its strong leadership to integrate local economic transformation and the urban public transit network. Second, there has been an active process of exploiting HST for non-metropolitan sub-regions over the long term. For instance, Dunkirk and Valenciennes are performing actively to make the most of the TGV link. Despite its large industrial base, Dunkirk has progressively improved its attractiveness through urban regeneration projects and a local transport network through a BRT system. Similarly, Valenciennes implemented a tramway project and urban regeneration projects along the routes to connect with the main TGV station. However, the transformation of the manufacturing economy with the arrival of TGV is not as apparent as Lille and needs further long-term observation. Third, active initiatives were lacking in other former coal-mining sub-regions. The state had intervened in the 1960s to impose the car industry, resulting in a regional economic cluster of the industry in northern France from then on. In the 1990s, the central government assisted in setting up a new university with multiple campuses for coal mining areas and Arras. Despite being served by TGV, these local authorities lack local initiatives to capitalize the HST opportunity, so transformation effects are limited.

This brings out a critical judgement on the role of government intervention: whether or not assistance to the most disadvantaged places is worthwhile. In both regions, both active and inactive local authorities could be found in capitalizing the opportunities that HST brought. The difference between the British and French experiences is that in France the regional council would help the disadvantaged sub-regions with funding and prestigious projects; while in the UK, the same weak sub-regions are largely less capable to prove their regeneration potential and consequently are further suffering from decline. The best examples are Blackpool in NWE, versus Lens in NPDC. Blackpool lost its casino bid in 2005 because of the ideology from the state 'regeneration benefits of the proposal before us are unproven' (Casino Advisory Panel, 2007). While regarding the branch of Le Louvre, this was decided to locate in Lens, because 'the challenge was the biggest and the most difficult!'[3] There are of course further issues, including moral questions that largely remain unanswered – whether it is 'right' to leave particular areas in decline or support only partially. Also the type of regeneration is also important. In Blackpool's case, whether developing a casino-led regeneration and resulting gambling culture on a vulnerable population was the best route for redevelopment is controversial. These are all difficult questions and there are no common answers that can be applied across different contexts. Often in the weak industrial areas the choices for governmental implementation are very limited and the results are usually sub-optimal. Again transport is one area that investment can be applied to help open potential opportunities, but is unlikely to be sufficient in its own right.

4.   CONCLUSIONS: IMPLICATIONS FOR HS2 IN THE UK

Concerning the uneven inter- and intra-regional HST impacts posed at the outset, this chapter suggests that, inter-regionally, HST could have spillover effects in reviving large regional cities within a two-hour travel limit from the national capital. Within one-hour travel time, HST cities could have characteristics of both commuting functions and economic development in the knowledge economy. But the effects have not been automatic or universal. There is a natural conflict between the national and regional perspective, because a HST network constructs a national urban hierarchy that is oriented towards the national capital. Far-seeing interventions are critical to trigger spillover effects of HST for a region. The contrast between the UK's market-led approach and the French interventionist approach is highly instructive in this regard.

This British–French comparison provides invaluable implications for the UK's HS2 proposal for both inter-regional and intra-regional development. Regarding the inter-regional effects, HS2 is critical because it will serve major urban areas in the Midlands (Birmingham) and northern England (Manchester, Liverpool, Leeds, Sheffield). It will relieve capacity problems on existing main lines, freeing space for growth in freight usage and shorter-haul commuter journeys. But an emerging key issue is its potential impact on the economies of regional cities (Hall, 2013). Here the French experience is relevant but, in many respects, needs to be adapted for the UK.

Outside London, the HS2 stations are limited to a few large regional cities. Special attention needs to be paid to the location of new HST stations in city centres and their relationship to the existing regional rail network; otherwise, the potential may not be maximized. The HS2 station in Birmingham is located at Curzon Street, 800m from the existing Birmingham New Street station, and so seems poorly designed to serve as a regional super-hub. Here Lille provides a relevant lesson: the 400m transition between Lille Europe and Lille Flandres stations, although not perfect, has been carefully designed to make interchange as smooth as possible.

For the intra-regional impacts, the irrigation approach of NPDC should be treated as an exemplar for future regional development in the UK. In NWE, for example, the experience of WCML suggests that a market-led approach has resulted in negative impacts on intra-regional development. Therefore, HS2 should not be treated in isolation (Hall and Wray, 2011): the 'high-speed high-speed' HS2, the existing 'low-speed high-speed' WCML and the north-west rail electrification project approved by the British government in 2011 (and to be completed by December 2016) need to be closely integrated. Even then, further improvements to the regional network are required if the region is to be fully 'irrigated' by HS2 (SYNAPTIC, 2013).

Even this will not be enough in itself: transport investments cannot themselves guarantee the transformation of post-industrial towns that have suffered from poor economic performance for decades and a lack of indigenous innovative capacity. The experience of Lens in NPDC illustrates this point. Therefore, there needs to be an emphasis on social change in parallel with economic change in these peripheral areas. As Hall (2012) points out with 'the endless unaltered people' who find it difficult to adapt to changes even if transport improvements are made, other conditions are needed. The same lesson could be learned from NPDC. An inclusive and effective governance structure and a concern for reducing inequality are very important for any possible transformations.

NOTES

1. The Trans-European Transport Network (TEN-T) was defined in 1996 (Directive 96/48/EC). The core PBKAL HST network, connecting several capital cities (Paris-Brussels-Köln (Cologne)-Amsterdam-London), to which was added Frankfurt, becoming a PBKFAL network after the arrival of the LGV (*Ligne à Grande Vitesse) Est-Europe* in 2007. This PBKFAL network was completed when Amsterdam and Cologne were further connected in 2009.
2. 'Inter-regional' comparison here is defined as the comparison between regions as a whole, whereas elsewhere data is provided at the city or city-regional levels.
3. Interview with Yves Dhau Decuypere (CEO of Mission Bassin Minier).

REFERENCES

Banister, D. and Hall, P. (1993), The Second Railway Age, *Built Environment*, **19**, 157–62.
Barnett, R. (1993), British Rail's InterCity 125 and 225, *Built Environment*, **19**, 163–82.
Bonnafous, A. (1987), The regional impact of the TGV, *Transportation*, **14**, 127–37.
Bruyelle, P. and Thomas, P.R. (1994), The impact of the Channel Tunnel on Nord-Pas-de-Calais, *Applied Geography*, **14**, 87–104.
Casino Advisory Panel (2007), *Final Report of the Casino Advisory Panel*, London: Department for Culture Media and Sport.
Chen, C.-L. (2013), *The Spatial-Economic Impact of High-Speed Trains: Nationally (the UK IC125) and Regionally (a British–French Comparison)*, PhD thesis, University College London.
Chen, C.-L. and Hall, P. (2011), The impacts of high-speed trains on British economic geography: a study of the UK's InterCity 125/225 and its effects, *Journal of Transport Geography*, **19**, 689–704.
Chen, C.-L. and Hall, P. (2012), The wider spatial-economic impacts of high-speed trains: a comparative case study of Manchester and Lille sub-regions, *Journal of Transport Geography*, **24**, 89–110.
Chen, C.-L. and Hall, P. (2013), Using high speed two to irrigate the regions, *Built Environment*, **39**, 355–68.
Chen, C.-L. and Wray, I. (2011), Can high-speed rail save the regions? *Town and Country Planning*, **80**, 119–27.
Clark, C. (1958), Transport: maker and breaker of cities, *The Town Planning Review*, **28**, 237–50.
Colomb, C. (2007), *Making Connections: Transforming People and Places in Europe – Case Study of Roubaix, Lille (France)*, York: Urbed.
Fraser, C. and Baert, T. (2003), Lille: from textile giant to tertiary turbine, in C. Couch, C. Fraser and S. Percy (eds), *Urban Regeneration in Europe*, Oxford: Blackwell.
Garmendia, M., De Ureña, J.M., Ribalaygua, C., Leal, J. and Coronado, J.M. (2008), Urban residential development in isolated small cities that are partially integrated in metropolitan areas by high speed train, *European Urban and Regional Studies*, **15**, 249–64.
Hall, P. (2002), *Urban and Regional Planning*, London: Routledge.
Hall, P. (2007), Delineating urban territories: is this a relevant issue? in N. Cattan (ed.), *Cities and Networks in Europe: A Critical Approach of Polycentrism*, Montrouge: John Libbey Eurotext.
Hall, P. (2009), Magic carpets and seamless webs: opportunities and constraints for high-speed trains in Europe, *Built Environment*, **35**, 59–69.
Hall, P. (2012), The endless unaltered people, *Town and Country Planning*, **81**, 7–9.
Hall, P. (2013), High-speed two: the great debate, *Built Environment*, **39**(3).
Hall, P. and Pain, K. (2006), *The Polycentric Metropolis: Learning from Mega-city Regions in Europe*, London, Earthscan.
Hall, P. and Wray, I. (2011), High-speed gateways? *Town and Country Planning*, **80**, 322–27.
Harman, R. (2006), *High Speed Trains and the Development and Regeneration of Cities*, London: Greengauge21.
International Union of Railways (2011), *High Speed Rail as A Tool for Regional Development: In-Depth Study*, Frankfurt: International Union of Railways.
Le Monde (2004), La SNCF Va Renoncer aux 'Gares-Betteraves' pour les Futurs TGV, *Le Monde*.
Menerault, P. and Barre, A. (1997), TGV et Recomposition des Relations Ferroviaires Interrégionales: L'Exemple des Relations Nord-Pas-de-Calais/Picardie, *Nord-Pas-de-Calais: Changement Régional et Dynamique des Territoires*, Lille.
Paris, D. and Mons, D. (eds) (2009), *Lille Métropole, Laboratoire du Renouveau Urbain*, Marseille: Parenthèses.
Payre, R. (2010), The importance of being connected: city networks and urban government: Lyon and Eurocities (1990–2005), *International Journal of Urban and Regional Research*, **34**, 260–80.

Pepy, G. and Leboeuf, M. (2005), Le TGV au XXIème Siècle: Rompre sans Dénaturer, *Revue Générale des Chemins de Fer*, May, 7–27.

Preston, J. and Wall, G. (2008), The ex-ante and ex-post economic and social impacts of the introduction of high-speed trains in south east England, *Planning, Practice & Research*, **23**, 403–22.

Puga, D. (2008), *Agglomeration and Crossborder Infrastructure*, Luxembourg: European Investment Bank.

SNCF (2011), Les Infos Hors-série, 30 Ans de TGV, in *1981–2011 Trois décennies d'expériences à grande vitesse*, Paris: SNCF.

Spiekermann, K. and Wegener, M. (1994), The shrinking continent: new time–space maps of Europe, *Environment and Planning B: Planning and Design*, **21**, 653–73.

SPIRE (2005), *Call for Metropolitan Cooperation: Memorandum of Understanding from the Lille Metropolitan Area*, Lille: Agence de Développement et d'Urbanisme de Lille Métropole, La Mission Bassin Minier, La Communauté Urbaine d'Arras.

Steer Davies Gleave (2004), *High Speed Rail: International Comparisons – Final Report*, London: Commission for Integrated Transport.

Steer Davies Gleave (2008), *High Speed 2: Economic and Regeneration Impacts for Birmingham – Final Report*, London: Greengauge21 and Birmingham City Council.

SYNAPTIC (2013), *S-Map 2030: An Action Plan for Seamless Mobility in North West Europe. North West of England Case Study: Irrigating the Region (June 2013)*, London: UCL, Bartlett School of Planning, SYNAPTIC team.

Thompson, I.B. (1994), The French TGV system: progress and projects, *Geography*, 164–68.

Troin, J.-F. (1995), *Rail et Amenagement du Territoire: des Heritages aux Nouveaux de Fis*, Aix-en-Provence: Edisud.

Ureña, J.M., Menerault, P. and Garmendia, M. (2009), The high-speed rail challenge for big intermediate cities: a national, regional and local perspective, *Cities*, **26**, 266–79.

Vickerman, R., Spiekermann, K. and Wegener, M. (1999), Accessibility and economic development in Europe, *Regional Studies*, **33**, 1–15.

Wray, I. (2011), In search of strategic sites: north west England, 1990–2010, *Town Planning Review*, **82**.

21 Assessing the wider impacts of the Jubilee Line Extension in East London
Peter Jones

1. INTRODUCTION

The Jubilee Line Extension (JLE) opened in late 1999 and was the first significant addition to the London Underground network in more than 20 years (see Figure 21.1). The extension is 16km in length and has 11 stations, six of which interchange with other Underground lines, while the other five are new stations in areas near the River Thames that were not previously served by the Underground. The extension provides interchanges with all other Underground lines and with the Docklands Light Railway, and has been accompanied by the construction of three major bus interchanges.

In comparison with other proposed major rail proposals in the 1980s, the JLE did not achieve a very high benefit/cost ratio, but was prioritised by the Thatcher government as

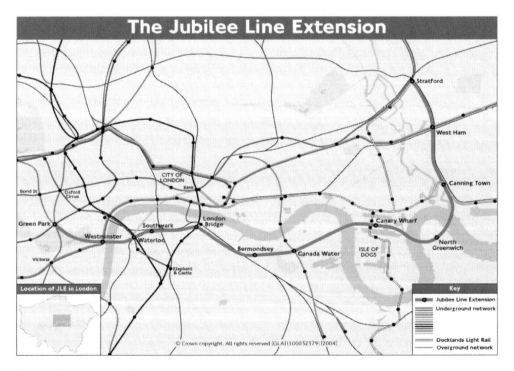

Source: JLEISU (2004a)

Figure 21.1 The location of the JLE in relation to the existing Underground network

a means of regenerating the derelict Docklands area to the east of the City of London. The JLE would assist in this regeneration by improving accessibility to the area from large parts of London, by increasing public transport capacity into the area, and by raising the image and awareness of the area. The line crosses the Thames four times, thereby reducing its physical and cultural barrier effects.

Transport for London (TfL) and the Department for Transport funded a study starting in 1997 to measure the impacts of the Jubilee Line Extension. The study was coordinated by the University of Westminster, under the overall direction of the writer, and had two main aims:

1. To understand how the extension has affected London.
2. To improve appraisal and forecasting techniques.

This chapter first describes the comprehensive monitoring and evaluation methodology that was developed for the study, before assessing the impacts of the JLE under four broad categories:

- Transport impacts and accessibility changes.
- Residential and commercial development, including impacts on land value.
- Employment and impacts on the economy.
- Impacts on incumbent and migrant residents and their travel patterns.

Finally, the chapter summarises the methodological lessons that were learnt from this exercise, and draws some general conclusions.

2.   JLE IMPACT STUDY METHODOLOGY

Considerable effort was devoted to developing a comprehensive and robust impact assessment methodology, as many previous studies of major transport investments had proved largely inconclusive. An extensive literature review was first carried out (JLEISU, 1997), to see what lessons could be learnt from previous public transport impact studies.

The impacts studied included: direct transport impacts (Knowles and Fairweather, 1994; Stokes, 1994); land-use patterns (Cervero and Landis, 1997; Grieco, 1994; Transportation Research Board, 1996); commercial and industrial property values (Dundon-Smith, 1994); place image and marketing (Crocker, 1994); retail (Bennison, 1982; Dundon-Smith, 1994; Vigar, 1995); city centre development (Townroe and Dabinett, 1994); house prices (Forrest et al., 1996; Antwi, 1995); and labour market and unemployment (Dundon-Smith, 1994; Fairweather, 1994; Gore, 1994).

This confirmed the lack of an agreed, rigorous methodology for impact studies, with very different approaches taken in the different studies regarding the scope of impacts examined. In particular, the review raised the following issues:

- The range of impacts that are considered, beyond the transport impacts. Studies varied in the degree to which they examined topics such as employment, land-use patterns, property process, social and environmental impacts.

- The spatial extent of the analysis: over what distance from stations might impacts be expected to be observed?
- Temporal coverage: at what point in the construction and operation process might impacts first be expected to be observed? Will some kinds of impacts appear more quickly than others? Given this, what is the appropriate period to use as the 'before' benchmarking period?

This last point is of particular significance: if the 'before' benchmark time period is close to the opening of the new railway line, then it might include some early anticipatory impacts (e.g., on property prices), but if it is placed much earlier then it becomes more difficult to attribute causation due to the many confounding factors that will contribute to any observed changes in the area. In general, the main challenges are to identify the counterfactual (i.e., what would have happened in the area if the line had not been built?), and to attribute causation.

Having drawn lessons from this review of literature, the main stages of the JLE impact study comprised:

- a scoping stage to establish the 'dimensions of change', in terms of the full range of expected impacts, the potential geographical sphere of influence and the time scale over which major impacts might occur;
- the identification of 'indicators of change' through which impacts could be measured over time;
- the identification of comparison areas to parts of the JLE corridor;
- identifying appropriate data sources, and specifying new survey requirements where gaps were identified in existing data sources;
- carrying out several additional 'before' surveys;
- estimating a 'baseline scenario' from existing and new survey data, representing likely future conditions in the area without the JLE;
- carrying out 'after' surveys, initially to study short-term impacts;
- analysing 'after' data to identity instances where differences have occurred and using various quantitative and qualitative data sources to attribute cause and effect, taking into account other major developments in the corridor (e.g., DLR extension to Lewisham); and
- developing an assessment framework for summarising impacts.

The study methodology included a number of novel features. In particular:

- analysis of impacts at both station catchment (c. 1km radius) and JLE corridor levels;
- use of 'reference' rather than 'control' comparison areas as the basis for determining how an area might have changed if the JLE had not been constructed; and
- beginning the measurement of change and the impact of the JLE from the time of confirmation that the line would be built, rather than just before the opening of the JLE.

Impact studies have traditionally identified 'control' areas (i.e., areas as similar as possible in character to the JLE station catchment areas), in order to remove the effects of extraneous factors from the comparisons of 'before' and 'after' data in the study area. However, given the unique characteristics of the Docklands area of London, it proved impractical to find comparable local areas in other parts of London well away from the influence of the JLE investment. To overcome this problem, the concept of the 'reference' area was developed. This is more general in extent than a control area, and may differ according to the indicator under investigation. It represents a wider area of London that is likely to be subject to similar pressures to those experienced by the relevant part of the JLE corridor. For example, the 'Inner East London area' has been used as the reference area for unemployment rates along most of the corridor, and the 'Central London Fringe area' has been used as the reference area for property pressures affecting the Isle of Dogs. For more details of the conceptual approach and assessment methodology, see JLEISU (1997).

Two distinct methods were used to identify the various dimensions of the impacts of the JLE. One was more statistical in nature and involved comparing recorded 'after conditions' in the JLE corridor with adjusted conditions from the reference areas. The other relied on modelling work to estimate what 'baseline' conditions would have been like in the JLE corridor in the post-opening period, had the line not been constructed; this required forecasts of various exogenous variables.

In order to fully explore the impacts of the JLE, 11 subject-based studies were commissioned and six surveys conducted before and after opening. Some of the key findings are summarised in the next sections of this chapter. For more comprehensive findings, see JLEISU (2004a).

3.   TYPES OF IMPACTS OF THE JLE

Patterns of Accessibility and Travel

Changes in accessibility between different areas arising from the construction of the JLE have been estimated by comparing the 2001 public transport network with the JLE (including all rail and bus services) against the equivalent network without the JLE.

Figure 21.2 shows the numbers of people living in London in 2001 reachable from each JLE station within different time bands, from 20 minutes to 60 minutes, with and without the JLE. It can be seen that the JLE substantially increases the accessibility of North Greenwich, Canada Water and Bermondsey and, to a lesser extent, Canning Town and Southwark. For example, the population within 40 minutes of North Greenwich station (which now hosts the O₂ Arena) increases by 1,348,000 from only 182,000 to 1,530,000; this is a 741 per cent increase. The increase at Canada Water is 1,374,000 (275 per cent) and at Bermondsey 1,144,000 (218 per cent).

The JLE was anticipated both to stimulate demand, due to these marked increases in accessibility, and to relieve overcrowding on parts of the existing Underground network. With the introduction of the JLE, the maximum number of people that could be carried from East London to Central London by the Underground and DLR increased by 27.5 per cent, from 35,000 to 44,650 passengers per hour (planning standard capacity). The increase in capacity was even greater from central London to the Isle of Dogs where major developments have occurred (see below), with the capacity of the JLE and DLR

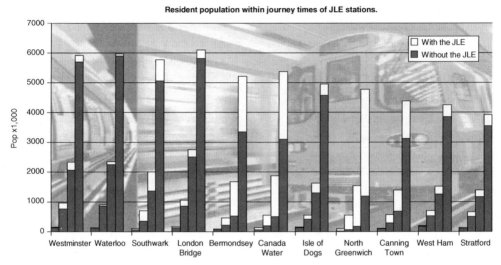

Source: JLEISU (2004a)

Figure 21.2   Population within different journey time bands from selected JLE stations

increasing by 668 per cent, from 1,730 to 13,300 passengers per hour. Subsequently, this latter capacity has been further increased by around 50 per cent, through the addition of a seventh car to the existing JLE six-car train fleet and by increasing train frequency from 24 to 30 trains per hour in the peak hours.

Early users of the JLE were asked how they would have travelled (to the same destination) before the JLE opened. The majority (54 per cent) would have used alternative Underground lines as their main mode; 14 per cent previously used National Rail services as their main mode; 21 per cent used the DLR, 7 per cent bus and 2 per cent private car. Very few JLE trips replaced previous walk/cycle trips.

Residential and Commercial Development

Analysis of planning application data (from the London Development Monitoring System) shows more interest in residential development in the core JLE catchments areas following authorisation of the JLE, than in the wider Inner East London reference area (IELRA). In absolute terms, the rate of residential dwelling construction in the JLE corridor increased from under 1,000 units per annum in the three years from 1991 to 1994 to 2,200 units per annum over the seven-year period 1994 to 2000. The proportion of residential units built in the IELRA that was in the JLE corridor doubled over these two time periods.

However, the extent to which this can be attributed to the JLE is complicated by two factors:

- fluctuations in the development market mean that an upturn in development applications would have been expected after 1993 in any case; and

- the JLE catchment areas contain a substantial proportion of the developable land in East London, and indeed the JLE alignment was selected in large part on the basis that it would open up large areas of such land for development.

The higher rates of residential applications and development in the JLE corridor through the second half of the 1990s could be associated with a 'critical mass' of development being achieved, which then generates sufficient confidence in locations for increased levels of development interest. Overcoming a negative image of an area can take several years, but the JLE may have helped in reducing the time required to bring about developer interest in the corridor.

Major commercial developments are usually longer in the formation stage due to their high costs, their requirement for flagship tenants and the difficulty of phasing, so most impacts are likely to be observed post-opening. This is particularly the case when there is no established market. The only major commercial development in the JLE corridor around the time of opening of the line was at the Canary Wharf Estate on the Isle of Dogs, which had been stimulated by the construction of the Docklands Light Railway (DLR). This was already well established prior to the JLE and is one of the largest commercial developments in the UK. However, the capacity of the transport system was a limiting factor in its development. In 1991 the estate comprised 502,000m^2; this had increased to 1.5 million m^2 in 2003, and by 2011 to over 1.9 million m^2. The JLE has increased capacity to/from the area thereby enabling in excess of an additional 1 million m^2 and a type, scale and density of development that would not have been possible without it.

Other major developments that are related to the construction of the JLE have only been proposed, or have begun construction, post opening. Examples include the Shard, at London Bridge (the tallest building in London), and the opening of the O$_2$ Arena at North Greenwich. The most notable impact, however, has been the selection of the Stratford area as the site for the 2012 Olympics, which would probably not have formed the basis of a credible bid without the JLE and its knock-on transport and land-use impacts in the local area.

An early indication of the impact of the JLE was a substantial increase in land and property prices along parts of the JLE corridor. Jones Lang LaSalle was commissioned to identify the impact of the JLE on increasing land values around two stations, Canary Wharf and Southwark (JLEISU, 2004b). For the purposes of the study it was assumed that the majority of any uplift in value would occur within 500m of stations for commercial uses and 750m for residential uses. The two stations were compared against the performance of residential, commercial, retail and industrial sectors in reference areas. There is a high variance around the estimates, but at Southwark it was estimated that the uplift in land value due to the JLE is in the region of £800 million, and at Canary Wharf in the region of £2 billion.

Population Growth in the JLE Corridor

The Census of Population indicates only marginally faster population growth in the JLE corridor than in the reference area between 1981 and1991, but a significantly faster growth was observed between 1991 and 2001, when the population in the JLE corridor grew by 31.2 per cent, compared with 10.7 per cent growth in the IELRA. Population growth has not occurred in all parts of the corridor, and it is interesting to note that the largest population increases have occurred in the station catchments where the JLE has provided access to the Underground for the first time.

Despite the larger population increases in the JLE corridor, the trends in age and ethnic structure were broadly similar to those observed in Greater London and the reference areas: the population became both 'younger' and more ethnically diverse. However, between 1991 and 2001, the extent of this structural change was greater within the JLE corridor, where the younger population, aged 0–45 years, increased by 7.0 percentage points (pp) compared with Greater London (+2.1 pp) and the IELRA (+4.3 pp.). The ethnic population of the corridor increased by 14.1 pp. compared with smaller changes in Greater London (+8.6 pp) and the IELRA (+10.6 pp.). By 2001 the population in the JLE Corridor exhibited a younger profile when compared with the reference areas but, despite significant structural change, remained less ethnically diverse. The trend towards smaller households, evident in Greater London and the IELRA, was also reflected in the household composition within the JLE corridor. Since 1971, single-person households have increased, as have single-parent households.

Historically, a high proportion of migration within the JLE corridor, as elsewhere in London, was local in nature, involving moves within the same borough or between neighbouring London boroughs. Analysis of the Household Panel Survey indicates a recent change in migration patterns; the four catchments were attracting migrants from greater distances. In 1998/9 and 2000/1, migrants locating to the catchments in the previous two years, were much less likely to have moved locally (as defined above) and more likely to have moved from further afield in London, or from outside of London. This suggests that these areas are increasingly being considered as desirable places in which to live.

However, much of the relocation by *in-migrants* appears to be 'transitory' in nature. Between one-fifth and one third of new migrants planned to relocate again within the next year, and a high proportion intended to leave the area. There was evidence of similar activity in 1998/9; examination of *out-moving* households revealed that between one-third and half had resided in the catchment for less than two years before moving.

Employment and Economic Development

A survey of employers in the JLE corridor in 2001 showed that there was a general perception that the JLE has provided better integration into the regional rail-based transport network, and so enabled firms to recruit from a wider, south-east England labour market. The JLE is also perceived to have helped change the image of the areas through which it passes, making it easier to recruit high calibre staff.

Table 21.1 considers what might have been the likely pattern of employment in the corridor had the JLE not been built, if it had grown at the same sectoral rate as the whole of the Greater London area (GLA) or the Inner East London reference area (IELRA), between 1995–8 and 1998–2000.

If it had followed the Greater London Area trend between 1995 and 1998, then in the JLE Corridor employment would have been 16,600 higher in 1998, or 23,200 higher if it had followed the IELRA trend. This suggests that no employment effect took place in advance of the JLE opening. But it may also highlight the fact that, in the absence of the

Table 21.1   Growth in employment in the JLE corridor

If Greater London growth rates:	GLA 1995–1998	Actual	Change (Actual GLA)	GLA 1998–2000	Actual	Change (Actual GLA)
	1998	1998	1998	2000	2000	2000
Primary, Manufacturing and construction	41,800	37,700	−4,100	37,100	42,800	5,700
Wholesale, retail	38,600	38,000	−600	39,400	39,100	−300
Hotels and catering	24,000	22,400	−1,600	23,800	27,100	3,300
Transport and communications	30,300	34,800	4,500	36,600	36,700	100
Financial and business	119,500	121,000	1,500	139,000	155,400	16,400
Public admin and services	127,600	111,400	−16,200	117,700	124,900	7,200
Total	381,800	365,200	−16,600	393,600	426,000	32,400
If IELRA growth rates	IELRA 1995–1998	Actual	Actual IELRA	IELRA 1995–2000	Actual	Actual IELRA
	1998	1998	1998	2000	2000	2000
Primary, manufacturing and construction	40,300	37,700	−2,600	37,800	42,800	5,000
Wholesale, retail	40,000	38,000	−2,000	39,500	39,100	−400
Hotels and catering	26,300	22,400	−3,900	25,500	27,100	1,600
Transport and communications	32,400	34,800	2,400	37,700	36,700	−1,000
Financial and business	122,700	121,000	−1,700	150,300	155,400	5,100
Public admin and services	126,700	111,400	−15,300	119,400	124,900	5,500
Total	388,400	365,200	−23,200	410,200	426,000	15,800

Source: JLEISU (2004a)

JLE, the corridor could be expected to continue to underperform relative to other parts of London.

The post-opening period is very different. This shows the JLE corridor as having 32,400 more jobs by 2000 than it would have done if it had followed the GLA growth rates of employment, or 15,800 higher had it followed IELRA growth rates of employment.

In terms of household economic activity, changes in the JLE corridor have closely mirrored those in the wider reference areas, with a large increase in the proportion of the population in employment between 1991 and 2001. In 2001, the population of the JLE corridor was marginally less likely to be in employment (59.6 per cent) compared with the GLA (63.2 per cent), but more likely than the population of the IELRA (58.8 per cent).

With the commercial emphasis in London on the financial and business sectors, it is not surprising that a high proportion of employment is found in managerial, professional and technical (MPT) occupations. Between 1991 and 2001, the proportion of employment in the MPT occupations in Greater London and the IELRA increased to 50.4 per cent from 39.6 per cent (+11 pp.). During this period, the proportion of the population employed in MPT occupations in the JLE Corridor increased by 19 pp to 50.6 per cent, thereby bringing it into line with the London average.

Differential Impacts on 'Incumbent' and 'Migrant' Populations

One of the starkest findings related to the strong differential impacts of the JLE on the existing, incumbent population and those which moved into the area. The two groups are different in composition and, generally speaking, the latter seemed to have gained more from the investment in the JLE, in many ways.

A Household Panel Survey was carried out in 1998/9 and 2000/1 in four JLE station catchment areas, and distinguished between three population groups:[1]

- Incumbent population, who were present for both survey waves.
- In-movers, to existing properties.
- New build residents, to newly constructed properties.

Their differing population characteristics are shown in Table 21.2. Migrant residents are significantly younger than the incumbent residents (with the latter having a mean age of 40). On average in-mover residents were 11 years younger (at 29 years) and new-build residents were seven years younger (at 33 years). This difference was largely due to the absence among migrants of residents over 65 years and a much-reduced proportion aged between 40–64 years. The smaller difference among the new-build residents was due to the virtual absence of children aged 0–15 years.

New-build migrants moving into the catchments areas were more likely to be from white ethnic origins (81 per cent), compared with the incumbent population (68 per cent). This is counter to the general trend observed in the Census, where a high proportion of migrants were from the ethnic minority groups. New-build migrants were twice as likely to be married or co-habiting (33 per cent) compared with incumbent households (17 per cent). Both in-mover and new-build households were less likely to be single person or single parent households.

The average equivalised household income of incumbent households increased by nearly 23 per cent between 1998/9 and 2000/1 (to £16,200), which was in line with the London average. Migrant households were likely to enjoy higher incomes and were less likely to be in receipt of benefits. The average income of in-mover households in 2000/1 was 50 per cent higher (at £24,200), while the average income of new-build households was 178 per cent higher (at £45,100). The receipt of state benefits was highest among the incumbent residents (52 per cent); in-mover (28 per cent) and new-build (9 per cent) residents were much less likely to claim benefits.

New-build households were most likely to own or be buying the property in which they lived (37 per cent), followed by incumbent households (31 per cent) and then in-movers (20 per cent). Levels of car ownership were also higher among incumbent (49 per cent) and new-build (62.1 per cent) than in-mover (39 per cent) households. Table 21.3 compares the economic profile of these three groups.

While the proportion in employment among the incumbent population remained unchanged following the opening of the JLE (50 per cent before versus 49 per cent after), this figure was 19 pp. higher among in-movers (at 68 per cent) and 34 pp higher among new-build occupants (at 83 per cent). The incumbent residents showed an increase in the proportion in managerial, professional or technical (MPT) occupations between 1998/9 and 2000/1 of 7pp, although this remained relatively low, at 36 per cent. In contrast, migrants

Table 21.2 Contrasting profiles of resident groups in the four JLE catchments

All surveyed station catchments	Staying (1998/9)	Staying (2000/1)	Out-moving (1998/9)	In-moving (2000/1)	New-build (2000/1)
Migrants making local move (%)[a]	64.9	55.4	36.9	41.5	30.6
Average age[b]	39.9	40.1	34.5	29.0	32.9
White ethnic origin (%)[c]	69.0	68.0	75.4	66.8	81.4
Married or cohabiting couple (%)	17.4	17.3	14.5	16.8	32.9
Property owned or buying with mortgage (%)	25.0	30.6	25.2	20.2	36.5
Average household income (£)[d]	13,201	16,182	21,076	24,204	45,067
Households claiming 1+ benefit (%)[e]	56.2	51.8	35.6	28.0	8.5
Car owning household (%)	49.4	49.4	52.0	39.1	62.1
Sample: Individuals (n >= 11 years)	1,746	1,918	310	347	711
Households (n)	909	909	179	179	404

Notes:
a 'Local moves' defined as moves within the same local authority: Southwark for Bermondsey and Canada Water, Tower Hamlets for Isle of Dogs and Newham for Canning Town.
b Cited average age calculated on individuals aged 11 years and older. 1998/9 survey did not collect ages of individual members aged ten years and younger. 'Staying' households were more likely to contain young persons aged 15 years and under compared with out-movers and in-movers; new-build households were least likely to contain young persons.
c Cited percentages calculated on individuals aged 11 years and older. 1998/9 survey did not collect the ethnic origin of individual members aged ten years and younger.
d Average household income calculated as McClements Equivalised Gross Income and based on responding households only; 5 per cent trimmed mean.
e Benefits including non-means-tested Child Benefit and means-tested benefits: Family Credit, Income Support, State Pension, Job Seekers Allowance and Housing Benefit.

Source: Adapted from JLEISU (2004a). Derived from JLEIS Household Survey 1998/9 and 2000/1. Quoted samples sizes relate to the absolute base; data have not been weighted. Marginally different sample sizes may apply to the presented variables according to the question specific response rate. Household sample numbers are always consistent. Individual household sample numbers vary between sample periods due to (i) inward and outward movement of individual household members and (ii) natural ageing of the population, including household members crossing the 11-year age threshold

were considerably more likely to be employed in the MPT occupations: 60 per cent of in-movers and 82 per cent of new-build occupants. Overall, the evidence suggests that the JLE has had little positive impact on employment among the incumbent populations, either in terms of higher levels or in the character of employment (occupation and industry). Instead, changes are largely the result of the different profile of the migrants. Most notably, those moving into new-build were significantly more likely to be in employment, possess higher-level qualifications and be employed in the MPT occupations.

The JLE corridor has historically suffered from particularly high unemployment rates, and the increase in employment in the corridor appears to have been of some, but only limited, benefit to local residents. In the five years from August 1996 to August 2001, recorded unemployment in the JLE corridor fell by 49 per cent (Table 21.4). However, this was less than for the Inner East London reference area (54 per cent) and considerably less than for the whole of Greater London (58 per cent) – indicating that the JLE has not been able to assist in making inroads into long-term, core unemployment levels.

Table 21.3   Economic profile of 'incumbent' and 'migrant' residents across four JLE station catchment areas

All surveyed station catchments	Staying (1998/9)	Staying (2000/1)	Out-moving (1998/9)	In-moving (2000/1)	New-build (2000/1)
Employed (%) (individuals aged 16 and older)	50.0	49.2	61.9	67.7	83.0
Employed in managerial, professional & associate professional or technical occupations (%)	28.3	35.5	47.8	59.8	82.1
Sample: Individuals (n >= 11 years)	1,746	1,918	310	347	711
Households (n)	909	909	179	179	404

Source: JLEIS Household Survey 1998/9 and 2000/1. See also notes for Table 21.2

Table 21.4   Change in unemployment among residents of the JLE corridor compared to other areas of London, August 1996 and August 2001

Area	Unemployment					
	Aug 1996	Aug 1998	Aug 2001	Growth 1996–1998 Base=1996	Growth 1998–2001 Base=1996	Growth 1996–2001 Base=1996
JLE corridor	13,260	8,950	6,720	−32.5	−16.8	−49.3
Inner East London	153,650	103,340	70,270	−32.7	−21.5	−54.3
Central London	8,310	6,170	4,450	−25.8	−20.7	−46.5
Greater London	368,850	230,490	154,660	−37.5	−20.6	−58.1

Source: Revised Annual Employment Survey Analysis, Annual Business Inquiry, NOMIS. Data not available for 1995

For London as a whole, between September 1996 and December 2000 it is estimated that 609,000 new jobs were created and unemployment fell by 214,200. This is a ratio of one less unemployed person for every three jobs created. For the 'Outer eight' JLE station catchment areas (i.e., east of London Bridge) employment increased by 42,000 between September 1995 and December 2000. In the slightly different, but equal, time period from August 1996 to August 2001, unemployment in the same area fell by 5,300. Only one less unemployed person is recorded for every eight new jobs. This shows that the link between local job creation and local unemployment reduction is by no means a direct one-to-one process. Given the positive impact of the JLE in increasing employment levels, it is disappointing that the JLE has not had more success in reducing relative unemployment levels in its catchment areas.

Table 21.5 compares levels of reported use of the JLE among these three population groups. In 2001, the highest reported levels of general use of the JLE were by new-build residents (73 per cent), followed by in-movers (60 per cent); much lower levels of use were reported by incumbent residents (37 per cent).

Table 21.5   Travel profile of resident groups across four JLE station catchment areas

All surveyed station catchments	Staying (1998/9)	Staying (2000/1)	Out-moving (1998/9)	In-moving (2000/1)	New-build (2000/1)
General use of the JLE (%)	–	36.7	–	59.6	73.1
Shopping (food) (% locally)[f]	81.1	78.4	86.1	80.6	65.1
Personal shopping (% using JLE)	–	20.6	–	38.2	42.9
Employed locally (%)[g]	30.3	28.5	19.5	14.6	16.2
Travel to work using the JLE (%)	–	30.1	–	38.6	34.2
Sample: Individuals (n >= 11 years)	1,746	1,918	310	347	711
Households (n)	909	909	179	179	404

Notes:
f 'Local shopping' defined as SE1 and SE16 for Bermondsey; SE16 for Canada Water; E14 for Canary Wharf (Isle of Dogs); E14 and E16 for Canning Town.
g 'Local employment' defined as: SE1 and SE16 for Bermondsey; SE16 for Canada Water; E14 for Canary Wharf (Isle of Dogs); E14 and E16 for Canning Town.

Source: JLEIS Household Survey 1998/9 and 2000/1. See also footnotes to Table 21.2

The focus of the weekly household food shop by incumbent and by migrant households was the local area; as a consequence, the JLE was rarely used for this purpose. However, new-build residents were less likely to use local shopping areas (65 per cent), compared with around 80 per cent among incumbent and in-mover households. The JLE was more frequently used for personal shopping by the in-movers (38 per cent) and the new-build residents (43 per cent).

There was no change in the location of employment among the incumbent population, where a relatively high proportion of residents (30 per cent), continued to be employed locally. Consequently, there was no increase in the proportion of crossing the Thames for work. In contrast, migrant residents were less likely to be employed locally (15 per cent of in-movers and 16 per cent of new-build). There was some evidence of increased cross-Thames travel among new-build residents living south of the Thames, but travel south of the river was not evident among the new-build residents living north of the Thames.

Given the pattern of employment, it was not surprising that use of the JLE for commuting was relatively low among the incumbent employed (30 per cent) and higher among the migrant populations, although not substantially so: 39 per cent among the in-mover and 34 per cent among the new-build employed.

4.   LESSONS LEARNT

The methodological decisions to use wider 'reference' rather than matched 'control' areas, to start measuring potential impacts several years in advance of the line's construction and operation, and to use qualitative as well as quantitative data to assess causation, were all vindicated.

One element of the methodology that, with the benefit of hindsight, we would recommend dropping in any future impact study was the preparation of a baseline forecast (i.e., counterfactual), in advance of the opening of the line. This proved to be a time-consuming and ineffective process. In a large and complex environment such as the JLE corridor, the best estimate of the 'without JLE' situation can only be made when all the facts are known, once the 'after' data is available. In the event, far less reliance was placed on the baseline forecasts than had originally been intended.

In a number of cases, data problems have proved to be more significant than anticipated. Recent developments in data collection and collation (e.g., UK neighbourhood statistics, GIS-referenced datasets and new tracking technologies) should simplify certain aspects of monitoring in any future study. One of the main lessons for monitoring to have emerged from the study is an enhanced understanding of the various processes of change, both with regard to their timing and the nature of their impact. In future, this knowledge should both enable more targeted collection of data, and a more realistic expectation of the extent to which various impacts are likely to manifest themselves within different time periods.

5.   CONCLUSIONS

The impacts of the JLE on London have been many and diverse, although, in practice, it has proved frustratingly difficult to attribute causation in many cases. The extent and subtleties of the impacts can only be fully appreciated by reading the more detailed technical working papers and the JLE summary report (see http://home.wmin.ac.uk/transport/jle/jle.htm), which give more details of the results of the studies and surveys specially commissioned for the JLEIS.

The JLE has raised land values and property prices in the surrounding area and has stimulated faster development than might otherwise have been expected. This impact is most clearly evident in the initial post-opening period on the Isle of Dogs, where the expansion of the initial Canary Wharf development at the time of the JLE opening has to some extent been both the cause and effect of the JLE. The need to provide adequate capacity to serve the full proposed development at Canary Wharf was one of the key reasons for constructing the JLE, and much of the recent development in the Isle of Dogs would not have happened as quickly – if at all – without the JLE. This applies even more strongly to the major expansion of development which has occurred in the decade since the JLE opened. More recently, major JLE-related development has taken place around London Bridge and Stratford Underground stations.

The general impact of the JLE on employment and business activity in London is more difficult to assess, and seems to have been more mixed. There was no change in the location of employment among the incumbent population, where a relatively high proportion of residents (30 per cent), continued to be employed locally; consequently, there was no increase in the proportion crossing the Thames for work. This group also did not benefit much from the growth in jobs. In contrast, migrant residents were more likely to be employed, but less likely to be employed locally (15 per cent of in-movers and 16 per cent of new-build). There was some evidence of increased cross-Thames travel among new-build residents living south of the Thames, but travel to south of the river was not evident among the new-build residents living north of the Thames.

We have shown that employment around JLE stations east of London Bridge has increased faster than for London as a whole, however from a relatively low base. The impact of the Canary Wharf development on the economy of London has been much more profound than the 50,000 jobs which by the start of 2003 had been created or relocated there. The existence of the Canary Wharf development demonstrated to international firms, particularly in the financial sector, that there was a potentially available and expandable supply of high quality office accommodation suitable for their needs and at lower rents than were then being charged in the City of London. Without this, London might have found it harder to sustain its predominant financial position in Europe in the face of competition from other European capitals. As such, by enabling Canary Wharf to be developed, the JLE has made a major contribution to the whole London and national economy.

The JLE passes through some of the most deprived wards in the country, and part of the intention in using the JLE as a catalyst to stimulate regeneration was to help increase the well being of the local population. There is strong evidence that the JLE has helped to increase economic activity in parts of the corridor, but the evidence on the extent to which this has benefited the local indigenous population is weak:

- The traditional local population, particularly in the Docklands and Lower Lea Valley areas, have made relatively little use of the JLE and their travel patterns have been largely unaffected by the investment.
- Local people have benefited only to a limited extent from the large increases in local employment partly attributable to the JLE. Long-term unemployment rates have dropped proportionally by no more in the station catchment areas than in comparable areas, confirming that the JLE has not helped to address these deep-seated local problems (e.g., providing employment for people who have been unemployed for a long period).

In the short term, at least, the main population groups who have benefited from the investment in the JLE have been the incoming wealthier and more highly skilled groups, who have taken up the increasing number of more highly paid jobs. They also make greater use of the JLE and, to the extent that they are home owners, directly benefit from the increases in property prices.

These may, however, be short- or medium-term phenomena. The process of regeneration may begin with an increase in property prices and more up-market developments, but its primary benefit to local residents, employees, customers and visitors lies in improving the quality of the whole urban environment and the range of local facilities provided. In the longer term, this investment may help to increase aspirations and, with appropriate provision of skills training for local people, may create new opportunities that are potentially available to all residents.

The new development that the JLE has fostered may also have acted as a safety valve, preventing even faster rises of property prices in the Inner East London housing market than would otherwise have been the case. It may also have relieved pressure on other parts of the London economy which were in danger of overheating. This would have had a beneficial effect on the whole London economy.

In identifying the effect of the JLE, it is important to note that certain impacts will manifest themselves over varying lengths of time. It is likely that the majority of journeys rerouting to take advantage of the JLE would have occurred within a relatively short time period of the JLE opening, and so were fully captured by this study. In contrast, several decades may well be required to allow the full effect of the JLE on land-use patterns (and associated changes in travel patterns) to take place, and hence allow the full impacts of the scheme to be assessed. The recent availability of the results of the 2011 Census of Population provides the opportunity to assess some of the medium-term impacts of the JLE investment.

Identifying the impacts of large-scale transport investments is a challenging exercise and one that is still relatively poorly understood. But the detailed analyses conducted as part of the JLE Impact Study has uncovered a very broad range of impacts (economic, social and environmental), with varying spatial and temporal dimensions, and differing impacts on different population groups. It would be useful to replicate these methods in other impact studies, and to use more recent data sets to look at the medium- to longer-term impacts of the line's construction.

ACKNOWLEDGEMENTS

The JLE Impact Study was co-funded by London Transport (later Transport for London) and the Department for Transport. Many consultants contributed to the findings reported here, which were specified, collated and interpreted by the staff of the JLE Impact Study Unit at the University of Westminster; other members included Tim Eyers, Rob Lane, Karen Lucas, John Paris and Tim Powell. I also gratefully acknowledge the contributions of the client team: Julia Bray, Neil Georgeson and John Willis.

NOTE

1.   Unfortunately it was not possible to interview the people who moved out of existing properties.

REFERENCES

Antwi, A. (1995), *The Impact of New Public Transport Infrastructure on House Prices: The Case of the South Yorkshire Supertram*, Sheffield: Centre for Regional and Economic Research, Sheffield Hallam University.

Bennison, D.J. (1982), *The Initial Impact of Metro on Activities Within Central Newcastle upon Tyne*, TRRL Supplementary Report 745, DoE/DoT.

Cervero, R. and Landis, J. (1997), Twenty years of the Bay Area rapid transit system: land use and development impacts, *Transportation Research A*, **31**(4), 309–33.

Crocker, S. (1994), *South Yorkshire Supertram Monitoring and Evaluation: The Impact of Infrastructure Investment on Image: Analysis of Stage One Results*, Sheffield: Centre for Regional and Economic Research, Sheffield Hallam University.

Dundon-Smith, D. (1994), *The Labour Market Survey: A Comparative Analysis of the 'Before' and 'After' Surveys*, Metrolink Impact Study WP 10, Department of Geography, University of Salford.

Fairweather, E. (1994), *The 'After' Household Survey and the Impact of Metrolink*, Metrolink Impact Study WP 11, Department of Geography, University of Salford.

Forrest, D., Glen, J. and Ward, R. (1996), The impact of a light rail system on the structure of house prices: a hedonic longitudinal study, *Journal of Transport Economics and Policy*, **30**(1), 15–29.

Gore, T. (1994), *The Labour Market Impact of Supertram: Components of an Evaluation*, Sheffield: Centre for Regional and Economic Research, Sheffield Hallam University.

Grieco, M.B. (1994), *The Impact of Transport Investment Projects upon the Inner City: A Literature Review*, Avebury: Aldershot.

JLEISU (1997), *Concepts and Methodological Framework for Assessing the Impact of the JLE*, Jubilee Line Extension Impact Study Unit, Working Paper 4, http://home.wmin.ac.uk/transport/jle/wp/WP04_Concepts_and_Methodological_Framework.pdf.

JLEISU (2004a), *JLE Summary Final Report*, Jubilee Line Extension Impact Study Unit, Working Paper 54, http://home.wmin.ac.uk/transport/jle/wp/WP54_JLE_Summary_Report_[130904].pdf.

JLEISU (2004b), *Land and Property Value Study*, Jubilee Line Extension Impact Study Unit, Working Paper 57, prepared by Jones Lang LaSalle, http://home.wmin.ac.uk/transport/jle/wp/WP57_Land_and_Property_Value_Pilot_Study.pdf.

Knowles, R. and Fairweather, E. (1994), *The 'After' Rail User Survey and the Impact of Metrolink*, Metrolink Impact Study Working Paper 12, Department of Geography, University of Salford.

Stokes, G. (1994), *The Role of Public Transport Interchange in Improving Public Transport*, PTRC 1994, Seminar E: Public Transport and Operations.

Townroe, P. and Dabinett, G. (1994), *The Evaluation of Public Transport Investment within Cities*, Sheffield: Centre for Regional and Economic Research, Sheffield Hallam University.

Transportation Research Board (1996), *Transit and Urban Form, Volume 2: Commuter and Light Rail Transit Corridors: The Land Use Connection*, TCRP Report 16, Washington, DC: National Academy Press.

Vigar, G. (1995), *South Yorkshire Supertram Monitoring and Evaluation: Retail Change and Economic Impacts*, Sheffield: Centre for Regional and Economic Research, Sheffield Hallam University.

22 The developmental impacts of the Madrid Metro Line 12 on retail activities around stations
Lucia Mejia Dorantes

1. INTRODUCTION

Firms, when making decisions about their location, tend to maximize or minimize certain objectives, which depend to some extent on the nature of the business. For example, while some industries may seek for cost minimization at their location (i.e., manufacturing firms), others may be willing to pay more due to location, in order to maximize profits (i.e., retail stores) (Erickson and Wasylenko, 1980). This is known as industrial location theory, first proposed by Albert Weber around 1940. 'Transfer oriented firms' are the ones that minimize transport costs, and 'resource and market oriented firms' the others (Beckmann, 1999; Blair and Premus, 1993). As explained by White (1975), only in a flat land, with a uniform environment of population and income, firms selling goods would be equally distributed.

Nowadays, it is widely accepted that the location of businesses depends on a combination of factors that include, among others, firm agglomeration, labour market characteristics, transportation, land market, type of firm and enhancement of environmental quality (Banister and Berechman, 2001). Agglomeration indicates that certain types of firms take advantage of being close to other firms at a particular location in urban space. If different industrial sectors are not located randomly but rather follow a profit maximizing criteria, taking advantage of physical proximity to related firms, these areas become economic poles (Feser and Sweeney, 2000; Maoh, 2005). On the other hand, authors such as Mori and Nishikimi (2002) point out that there is a process of reciprocal reinforcement between firms' agglomeration and transportation. In this respect, according to the study made by Loo (2002), people perceived that the retail sector was one of the sectors most benefited by the construction of a new infrastructure.

Researchers point out that due to agglomeration economies and the advantages of easy access, most business activities are concentrated very close to transportation stations (Cambridge Systematics et al., 1998). In the case of retail firms, researchers have proved that the location of this type of activities is importantly related to socio-economic factors; for example, income, household size, unemployment rate, consumer mobility and population density (Ingene and Yu, 1981). Moreover, it has been widely discussed that shoppers intend to optimize their travel by using multi-purpose trips (Dawson, 1980), therefore, for retail businesses, being located where people pass by is certainly an asset. Castillo-Manzano and López-Valpuesta (2009), for example, state that in the city of Seville, Metro stations had a significant positive impact on the retail market. Unfortunately, assessing the location of firms in practice is complicated since information and data are not always available at the local or regional levels (Melo and Graham, 2009; Maoh and Kanaroglou, 2007; Mejia-Dorantes et al., 2011). Therefore, literature on retail activity has been based on macro-models (Barry Mason, 1975). This study intends to shed some light on changes of market areas within a certain time span to understand how individual travel behaviour and the structure of the territory change locational patterns of retail firms with a micro-level approach.

This chapter presents the case study of the Madrid region, where five municipalities in the south-west of Madrid City are located. These towns were characterized by limited connectivity to the capital, mainly due to the lack of mass transit transportation. To rectify this situation, in 2003, a new metro line (Metrosur) was built in order to create a connection among these five municipalities and the capital city, Madrid. The new infrastructure is a circular line with six transfer stations to other metro and commuter train lines, whose objective is to provide transfers to other municipalities or to Madrid downtown. One of the main objectives of this Metro line was to promote economic activity within this region, under the expectation that improved transportation would facilitate not only the commute to Madrid but also the creation of jobs locally in these five municipalities. The subway line has been in operation for more than five years now.

The aim of this paper is twofold. On one hand, the location patterns of retail firms within the south-west region of Madrid are explored focusing on three different municipalities, and their evolution over time using spatial statistical techniques – more specifically, point pattern analysis. On the other hand, it is assessed whether the new metro line is an important characteristic for the location of retail activities using discrete choice models. The probability that a specific location is used by retail or by any other economic activity is analysed, taking into account different urban and transportation factors. To carry out this analysis, a detailed firmography database from 1998 and 2007 was used, which corresponds to more than one year prior to the construction and four years after it started operation.

The chapter is organized in the following way. The next section, after this introduction, shows the characteristics of Metrosur and the Madrid Metropolitan Area. The third section describes the methodology used. Afterwards, the fourth section describes the results. The last section discusses the results and offers the main conclusions.

2.   METROSUR AND THE MADRID METROPOLITAN AREA

The new Metro Line 12 'Metrosur' at the south-west of Madrid made it possible to connect by underground the five most important municipalities of the south of the Madrid region. These municipalities increased their population over the past decades as a response to the high land values observed in Madrid downtown. Before the opening of Line 12, the transportation system in these cities used to be focused on connecting these municipalities to the city of Madrid through both commuter trains and regional buses. The public transportation networks linking these five municipalities used to be poor, based on commuter rail or interurban buses. To go to an eastern/western municipality, people had to travel to Madrid City (north) to an interchange station to travel back to the south again, since there were no connections between these municipalities. Therefore, thanks to this Metro line, people living and/or working herein, no longer have to travel to Madrid downtown.

As shown in Figures 22.1 and 22.2, the sole connection to the Madrid Metro network

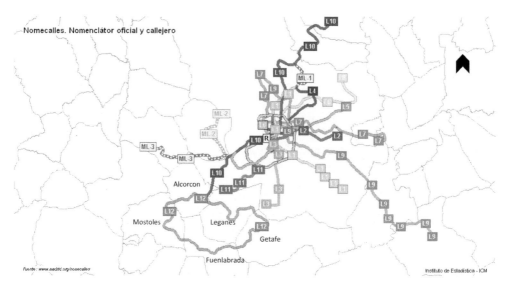

Source: Comunidad de Madrid (2011)

Figure 22.1   Map of the Madrid Metro network

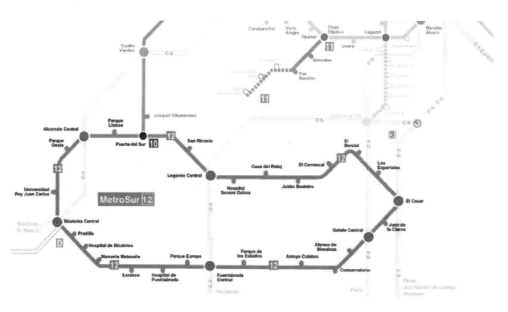

Figure 22.2   Map of Metrosur and its interchange stations

was in the municipality of Alcorcon (Puerta del Sur station, Line 10). Although other interchanges with the Madrid main Metro network were planned, none of them has been built. However, it does have six transfer stations with the commuter rail lines Cercanias (C), marked with a bigger dot in Figure 22.2.

The construction began in 2000 and it started operating in 2003. It is a circle line of around 55km, which connects the following municipalities:

- Alcorcon (A)
- Fuenlabrada (F)
- Getafe (G)
- Leganes (L)
- Mostoles (M)

Each municipality has around 200,000 inhabitants. Although each municipality has plenty of undeveloped land, it was built entirely underground. Moreover, this transport infrastructure has very high quality standards. For instance, all the stations have 115m platforms in order to have the possibility in the future to increase the number of cars to six, although only three cars per train are currently needed. It is composed of two different transport fare zones. In fact, the municipalities farthest away from Madrid (Fuenlabrada and Mostoles) have a more expensive transport fare (B2) than the other three (Alcorcon, Getafe and Leganes, which have the B1 fare), which is more expensive than the A fare, for inner locations in Madrid. The former has proved to be an issue (Mejia-Dorantes et al., 2011). The 28 Metrosur stations are daily used by more than 150,000 passengers. Each station has different levels of service as shown in Table 22.1.

One of the most important problems of those municipalities is that they are basically fringe 'dormitory' cities where most of their inhabitants commute every day to Madrid City. The rate of people living in a self-owned house is around 87 per cent in this area, compared to 82 per cent in the Madrid region (Bureau of Statistics of the Madrid Region, 2011). Consequently, jobs and business activities have been not as important as in Madrid City. Table 22.2 presents the main characteristics of the municipalities studied.

3.   METHODOLOGY

This chapter evaluates how the location of retail activities evolves throughout the years both before, and after, the inauguration of Metrosur, and it assesses if urban and transportation factors influence the decision of where to open a retail economic activity.

The theoretical background lies on the market areas, which are geographical zones where people likely to purchase a good of a firm are located. Among other things, firms consider how the location will optimize the balance between their marginal costs and revenues. As mentioned by Ingene and Yu (1981), retail activities are characterized by a high degree of competition, particularly influenced by socio-economic and accessibility conditions. They are more dependent on profit maximization, therefore, location, pricing policies and consumers' willingness to pay (based on access) all combine to generate market areas and, as a consequence, firm locational patterns (Mejia-Dorantes et al., 2012). Moreover, consumers of retail firms seek to minimize travel costs by using multipurpose trips (Barry Mason, 1975). For all these reasons, the study at micro-level of retail firms is of interest. It should be expected that additional accessibility has increased the market potential of retail activities. To test this hypothesis, this research uses two

Table 22.1   Number of passengers by station by year

TRANSFER	Municipality	Passenger getting out at station	2003	2004	2008	MS share	Total Metro
C	A	Alcorcón Central	6,314	6,881	9,372	5.29%	0.36%
	A	Parque Lisboa	4,030	5,215	4,900	3.22%	0.22%
	A	Parque Oeste	3,111	3,666	4,414	2.75%	0.19%
L10	A	Puerta del Sur	3,057	4,424	17,003	8.89%	0.61%
C	F	Fuenlabrada Central	7,792	9,619	10,869	6.08%	0.42%
	F	Hospital de Fuenlabrada	1,980	3,726	3,988	2.71%	0.19%
	F	Loranca	4,094	4,757	5,028	3.04%	0.21%
	F	Parque de los Estados	3,710	4,551	4,771	3.09%	0.21%
	F	Parque Europa	3,896	4,633	3,962	2.67%	0.18%
	G	Alonso de Mendoza	2,821	3,273	3,109	1.97%	0.13%
	G	Arroyo Culebro	1,075	1,236	1,578	0.94%	0.06%
	G	Casa del Reloj	4,433	4,293	4,601	3.21%	0.22%
	G	Conservatorio	2,175	2,521	3,469	1.90%	0.13%
	G	El Bercial	566	613	3,086	1.66%	0.11%
C	G	El Casar	2,956	3,486	4,814	2.90%	0.20%
C	G	Getafe Central	7,523	9,104	12,974	7.18%	0.49%
	G	Juan de la Cierva	7,071	7,944	8,723	5.14%	0.35%
	G	Los Espartales	2,284	2,650	2,918	1.83%	0.13%
	L	El Carrascal	3,327	3,889	5,416	3.22%	0.22%
	L	Hospital Severo Ochoa	3,253	3,888	3,994	2.52%	0.17%
	L	Julián Besteiro	4,990	5,748	5,965	3.83%	0.26%
C	L	Leganés Central	6,986	8,991	11,101	5.78%	0.40%
	L	San Nicasio	3,090	3,631	4,190	2.59%	0.18%
	M	Hospital de Móstoles	5,129	5,550	5,500	3.72%	0.25%
	M	Manuela Malasaña	537	569	971	0.62%	0.04%
C	M	Móstoles Central	8,626	9,196	11,321	6.05%	0.41%
	M	Pradillo	6,013	6,624	6,328	4.08%	0.28%
	M	Universidad Rey Juan Carlos	4,606	4,928	4,897	3.14%	0.21%
Total MetroSur			133,806	157,479	169,262	100%	6.84%

Source: CRTM (2005), Metro de Madrid (2008)

Table 22.2   Main characteristics of the municipalities studied

Municipality	Territory	Distance to the capital	GDP Per Capita (2007)	Income Per Capita (2007)	Hab with social security/1000hab (2008)
Leganes (L)	43.25 km²	11 km	18,150.00	13,745.52	274.75
Getafe (G)	78.69 km²	14 km	23,282.00	14,677.68	400.53
Fuenlabrada (F)	39.21 km²	22 km	18,622.00	12,629.03	264.40

Source: Bureau of Statistics of the Madrid Region (2011)

different approaches: a point pattern analysis and a multinomial logit model, which are described in the following sections.

The data about business activities was obtained from the Bureau of Statistics of the Region of Madrid, which contains the exact location and type of economic activity for each firm located in these municipalities. It is evaluated the evolution of retail activities in Fuenlabrada, the farthest municipality from Madrid downtown along with Leganes and Getafe over a period of ten years (1998 to 2007), from the time the construction of the Metro line was planned to four years after the inauguration of the line.

Point Pattern Analysis

Different statistical methods may be used to analyse density patterns. The point pattern analysis may be used to evaluate the distribution of events over an urban area. To analyse the retail firms' location in 1998 and 2007, the kernel estimation method for point pattern analysis was used. It generates density surfaces that show where point features are concentrated and allows the identification of zones where firms have increased or decreased their activity (Mejia-Dorantes et al., 2011). Its more simplified form is in fact the histogram, although the kernel explores the density of events at each location and over the space, as a 'moving window' (Gatrell, et al., 1996). Further information of this statistical method may be found in Cressie (1991), Gatrell et al. (1996) and Mejia-Dorantes and Martin-Ramos (2013). In this case, the outcome is a continuous surface that represents the number of retail firms per square metre and its evolution from 1998 to 2007.

Multinomial Logit Model Approach

The model assesses the opportunity that each location has to be in use by a retail firm or other types of firms, according to different independent variables presented in Table 22.3,

Table 22.3   Variables used in the specification of the logit model

Variable	Description
OC07	2 if this location is in use by a retail activity in 2007. 1 if it is in use by any other economic activity. 0 if it is vacant. The base outcome is (0)
MS	Street network distance from each possible location to the closest Metrosur station entrance, km
CBD	Street network distance from each possible location to the local downtown, km
CER	Street network distance from each possible location to the closest commuter train station (Cercanias) entrance, km
INTBUS	Street network distance from each possible location to the closest Interurban bus stop
POPD	Population density around 100m for each location, in km
STRD	Street density around 100m for each location, in km
BOV_98	Business occupation vector. It gives information related to how many business activities around 100m of each location were located in 1998
MUNIC	Categorical variable. 1 is equal to a location in Fuenlabrada, 2 for Getafe, and 3 for Leganes. The base outcome is Fuenlabrada

using the information we have for the year 2007 and 1998. Due to the lack of information regarding firms' characteristics, the analysis was carried out using a multinomial logit model. Based on the theory of firm location as a result of the optimization of profits, the model indirectly measures if a certain place maximizes business' opportunities for retail or other economic activities. It is probabilistic model where the site is the unit of analysis, and it can only have one state as an outcome. The endogenous term is a categorical variable, which takes the value of two if a certain location has a retail firm, a value of one if it has any other type of firm and zero if that location is vacant, which is the base outcome.

The probability that each establishment is occupied is defined by a utility function. Utility is assumed to be a random function due to the impossibility to measure differences in perception and all the relevant variables (Ben-Akiva and Lerman, 1985). Maddala (1986) explains that the utility Y_i for an alternative i for each establishment n may be expressed as the sum of a systematic utility and an error term.

$$Y_i^* = V_i(X_i) + \varepsilon_i \tag{1}$$

Where X_i is the vector of attributes for the ith location, and ε_i is the residual that captures the unobserved variations in the attributes of each location, and other characteristics to maximize, which are perceived by the one that makes the decision of where to locate that firm. The residuals ε_i are independently and identically distributed. Therefore,

$$Y_{kj}^* = \beta' X_{kj} + \alpha_j' Z_k + \varepsilon_i \tag{2}$$

Where Z_t are the specific characteristics of each firm and X_{kj} is the vector of values of the attributes of the jth location perceived by the kth firm. Then, the probability that a certain location is in use by a certain type of firm is:

$$P_{kj} = \frac{e^{\beta' X_{kj} + \alpha_j Z_k}}{\sum_{t=1}^{m} e^{\beta' X_{kt} + \alpha_i' Z_k}} \tag{3}$$

which is the multinomial logit model.

Real network distances were used in order to account for distances to different services. Only in the case of population density and street density vectors, Euclidean distance was used.

The spatial weight matrix of business occupation vector, BOV_98, was used to obtain the business occupation vector in 1998. It accounts for the rate of open establishments that each location has within a radius of 100m. It is a measure of geographical clustering of business to analyse agglomeration economies.

4.   RESULTS

Business Location Density

Figure 22.3 illustrates how the location of retail firms have not really changed over the years and, most importantly, that their location has not increased around metro stations.

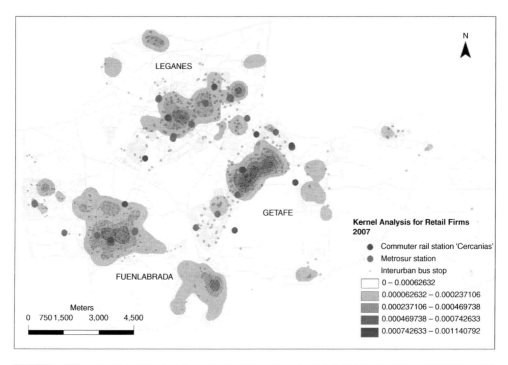

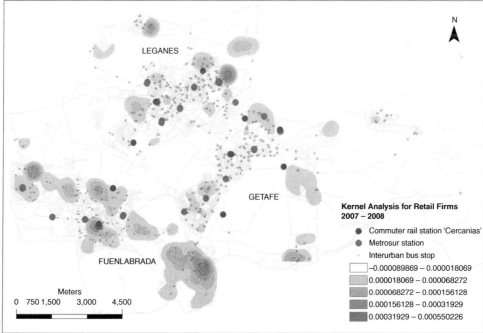

Figure 22.3   Maps of retail business density in 1998, in 2007, and the difference (from 1998 to 2007) in Fuenlabrada, Getafe and Leganes

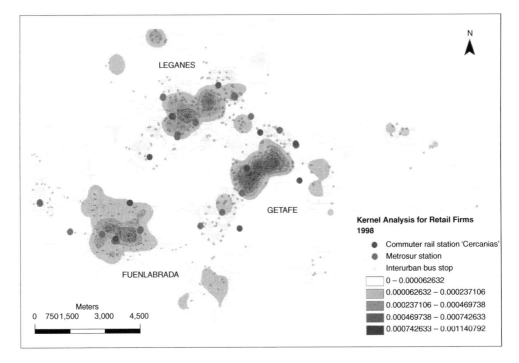

Figure 22.3   (continued)

The former is in contrast to previous analyses related to other municipalities (Mejia-Dorantes et al., 2011).

Once we have visualized their location patterns over a decade we turn our attention to the multinomial logit results in order to get more information on the behaviour of retail firms.

Multinomial Logit Model

The variable population density was taken away since, in the case of Leganes, it was not very disaggregated; therefore, it produced noise with the rest of the information. For the sake of this chapter, only the final model is presented.

The results of the estimated coefficients show that the distance to Metrosur (MS) is in both cases not significant and the sign of it implies that the probability of location is not related to the proximity to these stations. The distance to the interurban rail line, Cercanias (CER), is significant in general terms but not for the case of retail firms. The sign is negative, which would mean that it is more likely to have a firm located near a Cercanias station rather than farther away. The local downtown (CBD) is attracting retail firms although a high street density would limit the opportunities to retail stores, probably due to space constraints.

Most importantly, retail stores are especially benefited by the interaction between bus stops and their location, as show with the INTBUS variable. In both cases, the estimated coefficient is significant; the negative sign means that the probability of location of any

Table 22.4　Multinomial logit model

Number of obs = 4,2613
LR chi2(16) = 16,567.10
Log likelihood = −32,592.405

0	(base outcome)				
OC07	Coef.	t-stad	OC07	Coef.	t-stad
	1			2	
MS	0.0542	2.73 *	MS	0.2106	8.01 *
CER	−0.1035	−4.54 *	CER	−0.0432	−1.54
CBD	−0.0307	−1.31	CBD	−0.0689	−2.43 *
INTBUS	0.0281	0.41	INTBUS	−0.6799	−7.65 *
STRD	−0.0309	−26.4 *	STRD	−0.0336	−23.05 *
MUNIC			MUNIC		
Getafe	0.9109	13.23 *	*Getafe*	1.1087	13.31 *
Leganes	0.7812	11.82 *	*Leganes*	1.1379	14.25 *
BOV_98	3.7710	68.14 *	BOV_98	4.6628	69.31 *
Constant	−1.3569	−30.68 *	Constant	−2.5285	−43.77 *

Note:　* Significant at 5%

economic activity, yet principally for retail activities, increases with lower distances to bus stops.

Municipalities with a less expensive monthly ticket cost are more likely to have economic activities in their territory and, finally, the location is also strongly connected to the interrelation of more activities in previous years.

5.　DISCUSSION AND CONCLUSION

In addition to helping to evaluate the original objectives of the transportation plan, the information provided by kernel maps is useful to implement the correct measures to foster the usage of this Metro line. The kernel surfaces demonstrate spatial variations in the clustering pattern among the years. They show an increase in retail activities in certain areas, which might have been triggered by different factors. Interestingly, around most of the Metrosur stations there is no positive variation among the years. For that reason, attention should be paid and the correct measures should be implemented to foster economic activities around these stations.

The former statement is reinforced by the results brought about by the multinomial logit model. In the case of transportation, the Metrosur line seems not to be important for the location of any type of economic activity since the sign is positive. However, the commuter rail stations Cercanias, does seem to be important for the location of any economic activity. Interestingly, there seems to be a process of reciprocal reinforcement among interurban-bus stops and retail stores, which is more relevant for location than the rest of the distance variables analysed.

Thanks to the multinomial logit model, it is possible to observe that the probability of location of any type of economic activity is greater in the municipalities of Getafe and Leganes than in the municipality of Fuenlabrada. Probably this has a direct relation with the geographical location of Fuenlabrada which is the farthest from Madrid and has a more expensive monthly travel ticket than the rest of the municipalities analysed.

The results about the location of economic activities in 1998 validate the theory of agglomeration and geographic clusters of economic activities due to their economic linkages at intra-metropolitan level. The more open establishments there are around each point, the higher the probability that a certain location has to be in use by any economic activity.

The distance to the local downtown seems to be relevant, especially in the case of retail stores. Interestingly, the probability of location of an economic activity is higher with a lower road density. Probably, this result may indicate that with a higher street density, the fewer opportunities there might be for commercial areas.

The results show that the increase of accessibility brought about by the new Metro line does not imply an increase in the market areas. The former is explained by the fact that potential clients and the ones that use multipurpose trips rely more on other modes of transportation (interurban buses, Cercanias and private cars) which is verified by the limited number of users of the Metro Line 12 compared to the rest of the network. If one of the objectives of this line was to increase the number of economic activities, to compete to Madrid City, this goal has not been achieved. Moreover, results imply that a new major transport infrastructure is not a sufficient condition to boost economic activities.

This study also demonstrates that GIS tools and spatial statistics are very useful to explain and understand firms' locations and urban forms. These analyses should be used to implement the correct measures to foster the usage of a major transport infrastructure. Finally, it would be interesting to expand this research by making use of stated and revealed preference surveys in order to elicit which factors have influenced the location choice of retail firms, the characteristics of their previous location, along with hypothetical changes of their urban environment, which has also been rarely studied.

ACKNOWLEDGMENTS

The information provided by the Bureau of Statistics of the Region of Madrid to carry out this research is gratefully acknowledged.

REFERENCES

Banister, D. and Berechman, Y. (2001), Transport investment and the promotion of economic growth, *Journal of Transport Geography*, **9**(3), 209–18.
Barry Mason, J. (1975), Retail market area shape and structure: problems and prospects, in M.J. Schlinger (ed.), *Advances in Consumer Research*, Vol.2., Ann Arbor: Association for Consumer Research, pp. 173–86.
Beckmann, M.J. (1999), *Lectures on Location Theory*, New York: Springer.
Ben-Akiva, M. and Lerman, S.R. (1985), *Discrete Choice Analysis: Theory and Application to Travel Demand*, Cambridge, MA: MIT Press.

Blair, J.P. and Premus, R. (1993), Location theory, in R.D. Bingham and R. Mier (eds), *Theories of Local Economic Development: Perspectives from Across the Disciplines*, Thousand Oaks, CA: Sage, pp. 3–26.

Bureau of Statistics of the Madrid Region (2011), *Database: Municipalities' Files*.

Cambridge Systematics, Cervero, R. and Aschuer, D. (1998), *Economic Impact Analysis of Transit Investment: Guidebook for Practitioners*, TCRP Report 35, Washington, DC: National Academy Press.

Castillo-Manzano, J.I. and López-Valpuesta, L. (2009), Urban retail fabric and the metro: a complex relationship. Lessons from middle-sized Spanish cities, *Cities*, **26**(3), 141–47.

Comunidad de Madrid (2009), *Nomenclator Oficial y Callejero*, Madrid: Consejería de Economía e Innovación Tecnológica, Instituto de Estadística.

Cressie, N. (1991), *Statistics for Spatial Data*, New York: John Wiley and Sons.

CRTM (2005), Aforo y encuesta a los usuarios de la red de metro de Metrosur (Octubre-Noviembre 2004), *Tomo 5*.

Dawson, J.A. (1980), *Retail Geography*, New York and London: Taylor & Francis.

Erickson, R.A. and Wasylenko, M. (1980), Firm relocation and site selection in suburban municipalities, *Journal of Urban Economics*, **8**(1), 69–85.

Feser, E.J. and Sweeney, S.H. (2000), A test for the coincident economic and spatial clustering of business enterprises, *Journal of Geographical Systems*, **2**(4), 349–73.

Gatrell, A., Bailey, T., Diggle, P. and Rowlingson, B. (1996), Spatial point pattern analysis and its application in geographical epidemiology, *Transactions of the Institute of British Geographers*, **21**, 256–74.

Ingene, C.A. and Yu, E.S.H. (1981), Determinants of retail sales in SMSAs, *Regional Science and Urban Economics*, **11**(4), 529–47.

Loo, B.P.Y. (2002), The potential impacts of strategic highways on new town development: a case study of Route 3 in Hong Kong, *Transportation Research Part A: Policy and Practice*, **36**, 41–63.

Maddala, G.S. (1986), *Limited-dependent and Qualitative Variables in Econometrics*, Cambridge: Cambridge University Press.

Maoh, H. (2005), *Modeling Firm Demography in Urban Areas with an Application to Hamilton, Ontario: Towards an Agent-based Microsimulation Model*, ETD Collection for McMaster University.

Maoh, H. and Kanaroglou, P. (2007), Geographic clustering of firms and urban form: a multivariate analysis, *Journal of Geographical Systems*, **9**(1), 29–52.

Mejia-Dorantes, L. and Martin-Ramos, B. (2013), Mapping the firmographic mobility: a case study in a region of Madrid, *Journal of Maps*, **9**(1), 1–9.

Mejia-Dorantes, L., Paez, A. and Vassallo, J. (2011), Analysis of house prices to assess economic impacts of new public transport infrastructure: Madrid Metro Line 12, *Transport Research Record*, **2245**(1), 131–39.

Mejia-Dorantes, L., Paez, A. and Vassallo, J. (2012), Transportation infrastructure impacts on firm location: the effect of a new metro line in the suburbs of Madrid, *Journal of Transport Geography*, **22**, 236–50.

Melo, P. and Graham, D. (2009), Estimating the spatial decay of labour market interactions using data on commuting flows, *Transportation Research Record: Journal of the Transportation Research Board*, paper 09-2709.

Metro de Madrid (2008), Encuesta año 2007 'Estación de entrada-Estación de salida' a los usuarios de la red de metro, *Tomo 4: Resultados a nivel de estaciones*, **1**.

Mori, T. and Nishikimi, K. (2002), Economies of transport density and industrial agglomeration, *Regional Science and Urban Economics*, **32**(2), 167–200.

White, L.J. (1975), The spatial distribution of retail firms in an urban setting, *Regional Science and Urban Economics*, **5**(3), 325–33.

23 Bus rapid transit and buses with high levels of service: a global overview

Darío Hidalgo and Juan Carlos Muñoz

1. INTRODUCTION

Traditional public transport planning textbooks and guidelines indicate a hierarchy of transport modes according to capacity and speed (Vuchic, 2007; UN-Habitat, 2013). Buses are usually recommended for low-capacity applications; while rail, in the form of light rail transit, Metro, and regional rail are generally recommended for medium- and high-capacity applications. Nevertheless, thanks to the introduction of high-capacity bus systems, especially in Latin America and Asia, there has been a challenge to the customary approach. This chapter describes the recent history and current status of bus systems known as bus rapid transit (BRT) and buses with high level of service (BHLS), highlighting their characteristics and potential.

BRT is a flexible, rubber-tired form of rapid transit that combines stations, vehicles, services, running ways, and information technologies into an integrated system with strong identity (Levinson et al., 2003a; Hidalgo, 2012). The definition, developed in the US and extensively used in developing countries in Latin America, Africa, and Asia, is focused on the system components.

Its European counterpart, BHLS, also includes simpler priority measures to enhance operations and customer experience. BHLS is defined as an urban transport system integrating a bus or a coach and providing an increase in performance thanks to a triple optimization of: the internal characteristics of the technical and commercial offer; the integration of this offer into the whole public transport network; and the integration of this network into the urban area (Finn et al., 2011). The objectives of BRT and BHLS are to offer reliable, comfortable, and low-cost urban mobility (Wright and Hook, 2007; Finn et al. 2011).

BRT and BHLS are concepts resulting from the evolution of simple bus priority measures, such as designated busways and bus-lanes, which were proposed, and in some cases implemented, as early as 1937 throughout the world (Levinson et al., 2003b). The expression "BRT" was first used in the United States in 1966 (Wilbur Smith and Associates, 1966). The expression "BHLS" was introduced in 2007 (Finn et al. 2011).

The concepts behind BRT (and BHLS) gained popularity in Latin America after the successful upgrade of busways in Curitiba, Brazil, to full-featured BRT in 1982 and the implementation of TransMilenio in Bogotá, Colombia in 2000 (Lindau et al., 2010; Hidalgo and Gutierrez, 2013). The high performance, low cost and rapid implementation of these systems – and adaptations to Quito, Paris, Bogotá, Nantes, Amsterdam, Mexico City, Beijing, Jakarta, Los Angeles, Cleveland, Istanbul, and Guangzhou, among other cities – made the idea attractive for urban transport planners throughout the world.

As July 2014 there were about 180 cities with BRT or BHLS around the world, with

152 cities entering the list in since 2001, and at least 112 cities building, designing or planning BRT systems (BRT Global Data, 2014). BRT and BHLS are attractive options for public transport delivery, applicable to a wide variety of conditions – from low to very high passenger throughput (Muñoz and Hidalgo, 2013).

Critics of BRT and BHLS indicate that these systems are not permanent, use precious surface space, and exhibit operational and cost indicators that are inferior to rail (Light Rail Now, 2011). As no particular technology is superior to others in all aspects, it is important that BRT and BHLS are fairly analyzed in the process of selecting alternatives for transit improvements (UN-Habitat, 2013; Hensher, 1999). It is also important to indicate that BRT implementation requires strong political leadership, sound technical planning, and adequate funding levels (Hidalgo and Carrigan, 2010a, 2010b).

The concepts behind BRT and BHLS are not new, but they have only deployed extensively around the world in the past 15 years (Hidalgo, 2012; Muñoz and Hidalgo, 2013). The growth may be attributed in part to the successes of Curitiba (Lindau et al., 2010) and Bogotá (Rosenthal, 2009), and their adaptations in different parts of the world (Hidalgo and Gutierrez, 2013). In general, BRT and BHLS systems exhibit low implementation cost, rapid implementation, and high performance, with significant positive impacts (Hidalgo, 2012; Levinson et al., 2003b).

Interesting complementary trends are emerging in the BRT and BHLS industry, such as the implementation of citywide integrated bus systems, improved processes for private participation in operations, increased funding from national governments, and growth of bus manufacturers and technology providers (Hidalgo and Gutierrez, 2013). Technological developments in vehicles and information systems are also improving the quality, performance and impact of BRT (Hidalgo and Muñoz, 2014).

Despite the growth, some outstanding issues still remain: for example, BRT and BHLS do not have a single meaning and image and are often regarded as "second best" relative to rail alternatives (Muñoz and Hidalgo, 2013). Their ability to foster urban development and the use of space designated for cars are often questioned, as well as their actual costs and impacts (Gilbert, 2008). Nevertheless, rather than being considered an issue, the use of space formerly designated for cars may be considered a positive feature, as cars are thought to be the least effective means of transport (Chris, 2001; Bicycle Innovation Lab, 2011).

In addition several systems in the developing world suffer problems resulting from poor planning, implementation, and operation, due to financial, institutional and regulatory constraints (Carrigan et al., 2011). Finally, even though service reliability in BRT systems improves in comparison with buses running in mixed traffic, it still remains as a big challenge when compared with rail modes.

This chapter adapts and updates a previous publication (Hidalgo, 2012). The first section discusses the concepts of BRT and BHLS. The following sections show the history and current status of BRT in different geographical regions of the world – United States and Canada, Latin America, Europe, Australia and Oceania, and Asia; and the final section highlights some trends and needs.

2.   BRT AND BHLS COMPONENTS, CHARACTERISTICS AND IMPACTS

Components of BRT and BHLS include running ways, stations, vehicles, fare collection, intelligent transport systems (ITS), service operation plans, and branding elements. There could be different degrees of complexity for each one of these elements, resulting in varied system performance characteristics and system impacts. Performance characteristics include commercial speed, passenger capacity, service reliability, capital and operational productivity, and costs. Impacts of BRT encompass user perception, travel time, comfort, and externalities – including air pollution, noise, road safety, physical activity and urban development, and segregation, among other issues.

Advanced BRT and BHLS systems typically involve integration of the following:

- Median running ways for exclusive use of the BRT system buses, which are separated from the rest of the traffic through raised curbs (right of way A or B, according to the classification by Vuchic, 2007). Some applications have lateral (curbside) dedicated lanes, and even just bus priority. Median bus-lanes usually perform better as they have less interference.
- Stations with off-board payment and platforms with level access for boarding to the buses. Most applications in Europe and the USA have onboard ticketing, which increases dwell time and reduces speed.
- Large or higher-quality buses with multiple doors, special design features, and lower emission levels than conventional buses. Special buses with doors facing the median stations are increasingly common, reducing transferring time; some applications feature buses with doors on both sides and low entry allowing buses to operate out of the corridor (open systems).
- Use of advanced electronic ticketing systems, such as contactless fare cards, integrated to other applications.
- Several information technology applications for centralized control – such as automatic vehicle location and dispatch systems, and improved user information systems – variable message signs in stations and buses to indicate next bus and next station in real time, and provide public announcements; online and personal data appliances providing routing and schedule information, and traffic signal priority, among other applications.
- Combined service plans according to the passenger demand characteristics, including high-frequency trunk line services combined with feeder services, as well as accelerated and express bus services (for which overtaking lanes are required).
- Distinctive image differentiating running ways, stations, buses, and overall service from other bus services and transit applications in the city.
  (Levinson et al., 2003b; Diaz and Hinebaugh, 2009; Wright and Hook, 2007; Finn et al., 2011)

Few systems encompass all these components. Component mix depends on the local conditions and the service needs, as well as budgetary constraints. Table 23.1 presents suggested minimum features for different contexts (demand levels and urban conditions).

BRT and BHLS capital costs are in the range of one-tenth to one-third of comparable rail systems (Hensher, 1999; UN-Habitat, 2013). BRT costs depend on the selection of

Table 23.1   Types of bus-based transit according to transport demand needs and urban environment

Type	Main features (suggested minimum)	Throughput/ performance	Recommended context
Basic bus corridor	Median or curbside preferential lanes, onboard payment/fare validation, conventional buses	500–5,000 pphpd 12–15km/h	Low-density corridors, suburbs
Bus with high level of service (BHLS)	Preferential or dedicated lanes in congested points, advanced technology for dispatch and user information; high-quality buses; adequate integration with other modes and services and the urban environment	500–2,500+ pphpd 15–35km/h	Small urban areas, historic downtown, suburbs
Medium BRT	Dedicated lanes, preferably median lanes (single); large buses; off-board payment/ fare validation, advanced technologies for dispatch and user information	5,000–15,000 pphpd 18–23km/h	Medium-density corridors, suburb/ center connections
High-capacity BRT	Dedicated lanes (dual in the median); large stations; off-board payment/fare validation; articulated/bi-articulated buses; combined services (local, accelerated/express); real-time control and user information	15,000–45,000 pphpd 20–40km/h	High demand, dense, mixed use corridors, central city

Source: Muñoz and Hidalgo, 2013 (adapted) pphpd: passengers per hour per direction

system components and the performance requirements – higher performance systems have higher costs per kilometer than simpler systems. For instance, TransMilenio in Bogotá, which features dual lanes and large stations, had a capital cost of US$12.5 million/kilometer (infrastructure) for 45,000 passengers per hour per direction (Hidalgo and Carrigan, 2010a). The relatively simpler Metrobus, in Mexico City, with single lane and smaller stations, had a capital cost of US$3.6 million/kilometer (infrastructure) for 9,000 passengers per hour per direction (Hidalgo and Carrigan, 2010a).

It is important to recognize that side-investments, like general traffic lanes, public spaces, expropriations, and social and environmental safeguards, also have an important impact on the costs attributed to BRT corridors.

Table 23.2 presents the maximum values of some performance indicators observed in systems around the world. Observed values suggest that BRT and BHLS may be a suitable alternative for most corridors, and as such may be considered in alternatives analysis before committing the city to a given technology (Hensher, 1999; UN-Habitat, 2013).

Regarding system impacts, most systems have resulted in higher passenger demand than expected; user satisfaction is frequently high; travel times are usually reduced as a

Table 23.2   Maximum values for some performance indicators in selected BRT and BHLS systems

Performance indicator	Definition	Value	System, city	System features
Commercial speed	Distance/time as perceived by the user on board (km/h)	35km/h	Metrobüs, Istanbul, Turkey	Fully segregated bus way on expressway, stations every 1.1km
Peak section load	Passengers/hour/ direction (pphpd)	45,000 pphpd	TransMilenio, Bogotá, Colombia	Median busway, level access stations with five platforms, overtaking lanes, and combined services – local, express, seven standees per square meter, dense urban area
Infrastructure productivity	Passengers/km of bus way	35,800 pphpd	Guangzhou BRT, China	Median busway, with long station, overtaking lanes, open operation 40 routes, very dense urban area
Capital productivity	Passenger boardings/bus/ day	3,100 pphpd	Macrobús, Guadalajara, México	Median busway, overtaking lanes relatively dense, mixed-use urban area
Operational productivity	Passenger boardings/ bus-km	13.2km/h	Metrovía, Guayaquil, Ecuador	Median busway, dense urban area, very low fare (US$0.25 per trip)

Source: BRT Global Data (2014)

result of higher commercial speeds than buses in mixed traffic; reliability is increased due to the supporting infrastructure and communication technologies; and there is documentation on positive impacts for several systems regarding reduction of crashes, pollutant emissions and improved urban environments (Carrigan et al., 2013).

The high levels of demand attracted by BRT systems raise comfort concerns; most systems in developing countries use very high occupancy standards and may not be considered comfortable (Muñoz and Hidalgo, 2013). This is a result of financial restrictions that require most transit operations in developing cities to be "self-sustainable," thus preventing increasing capacity that will only be needed during the peak period. As a result, productivity levels need to be very high. Critics of BRT often cite comfort issues when comparing bus systems with rail (Light Rail Now, 2011). In summary, BRT is a victim of its own success and budget constraints limiting capacity increments.

Table 23.3   Regional distribution of BRT and BHLS as of July 2014

Regions	Passengers/day	Number of cities	Length (km)
Africa	242,000 (0.76%)	3 (1.66%)	80 (1.71%)
Asia	8,485,822 (26.92%)	36 (20%)	1,295 (27.74%)
Europe	1,785,829 (5.66%)	51 (28.33%)	799 (17.11%)
Latin America	19,685,144 (62.45%)	59 (32.77%)	1,615 (34.59%)
Northern America	891,035 (2.82%)	25 (13.88%)	785 (16.81%)
Oceania	430,041 (1.36%)	6 (3.33%)	94 (2.01%)

Source: Global BRT Data (2014)

3.   BRT AND BHLS STATUS AROUND THE WORLD

BRT and BHLS have become a component of integrated transport systems and is no longer an exotic rapid transit mode. A survey of BRT around the world (BRT Global Data, 2014) indicates that there are about 180 cities with BRT or BHLS corridors around the world, with 152 cities entering the list since 2001. The BRT and BHLS applications have not been limited to small and medium-size cities; there are advanced systems in places such as Mexico City, Rio de Janeiro, Beijing, Johannesburg, Paris, and New York City, to name some megacities. Nevertheless there is a concentration in emerging economies: 99 cities with BRT or BHLS are located in developing countries. The existing BRT and BHLS comprise about 4,668km, serving more than 31.5 million passengers per day (BRT Global Data, 2014). In 2014, more than 40 cities were expanding their corridors, and about 112 cities indicated they were building or planning BRT or BHLS.

Table 23.3 presents a regional distribution of BRT and BHLS around the world. There are systems in all continents. Latin America has one-third of the cities in the world, but concentrates almost two-thirds of the ridership. Asia has one-fifth of the cities and more than one-quarter of the kilometers. The number of users in Europe, the USA, and Canada is comparatively low in relation to the total kilometers reported. Only three cities in Africa have introduced BRT: Johannesburg and Cape Town (South Africa) and Lagos (Nigeria). The only intercontinental BRT is in Istanbul (Turkey) crossing the Bosphorus Strait.

Figure 23.1 shows the number of cities introducing BRT or BHLS since 1970, as well as the total cumulative number of cities. Most cities in the list (97) introduced BRT or BHLS in the first decade of the twenty-first century. The country with the highest number of cities introducing BRT or BHLS in the past decade is China, followed by Indonesia and the Latin American region.

BRT in the United States and Canada

Bus dedicated infrastructure was implemented in Pittsburg in 1977 and Ottawa in 1983. BRT started receiving special attention after the Federal Transit Administration sponsored a BRT conference in 1998, using Curitiba's BRT system as a model, and launched a "Demonstration Program" involving 15 cities in 1999 (Levinson et al. 2003b). The most important BRT Systems in the United States and Canada by July 2014 are presented in

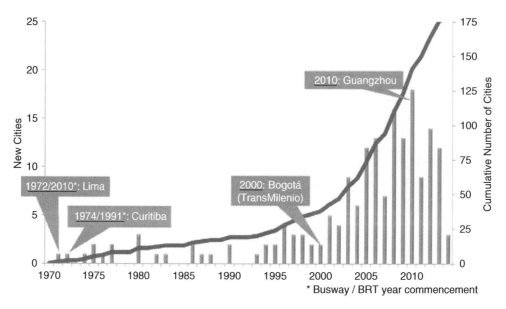

Source: BRT Global Data (2014)

Figure 23.1   Cities with BRT/BHLS 1970–2013

Table 23.4. There are 25 cities in North America (USA and Canada), covering a distance of 785km and serving about 891,000 passengers per weekday (BRT Global Data, 2014)

BRT systems in the US do not usually display full BRT features – they are not fully segregated or do not have off-board ticketing. The most advanced applications are the Orange Line (Los Angeles, California, 2007), EmX (Eugene, Oregon, 2008), and the Healthline (Cleveland, Ohio, 2009). Evaluations of these and other applications in the US are available in the FTA document *Characteristics of BRT for Decision Makers* (Diaz et al., 2009) and the National BRT Institute (2011), a federal-funded program.

In Canada, the City of Ottawa, implemented a very interesting concept, the Transitway, a fully segregated corridor with services coming in and out, allowing for direct trips without transfers. Plans to partially replace the Transitway system with light rail are underway (OC Transport, 2011). Suburban communities in Ontario also improved transit using BRT, such as York (in 2005) and Brampton (in 2010).

BRT in Latin America

BRT is a common feature of most cities in Latin America, and Curitiba, Brazil, can be considered the cradle of modern BRT (Lindau et al., 2010). The bus system there evolved from conventional buses in mixed traffic to busways, which were fitted with at-level boarding, prepayment, and articulated buses, creating the first full BRT system in the world in 1982. Later on the city introduced high capacity bi-articulated buses and the electronic fare ticketing systems.

In 2009 the Curitiba integrated bus system was upgraded again, with the introduction

Table 23.4   Most relevant BRT and BHLS systems in the United States and Canada (July 2014)

City (initial year)	Passengers/day (2013)	Number of corridors (2013)	Length (km) (2013)
Ottawa (1983)	200,000	3 Transitway	30
Winnipeg (2012)	166,000	1 RT	4
New York (2010)	106,762	2 Fordham Roadpelham Pkwy and M15 SBS 1st 2nd Ave	25
Vancouver (1996)	100,000	1 Translink	27
Pittsburgh (1977)	51,700	3 MLK East Busway, South Busway, West Busway	31
Las Vegas (2004)	35,800	3 MAX Metropolitan Area Express, SDX Strip and Downtown Express and SX Sahara Express	31
Boston (2000)	29,600	2 Silver Line (Washington St. and Waterfront)	9
York (Ontario)	35,300	5 Viva	59
Los Angeles (2005)	26,883	1 Orange Line	22
Miami (1997)	23,000	1 South Miami-Dade Busway	34
Cleveland (2009)	15,000	1 Healthline, Euclid Av.	11

Note: Other cities in the USA: Chicago, Eugene, Everett, Kansas City, Oakland, Orlando, Phoenix, San Bernardino, San Diego, Stockton, and Snohomish County; in Canada: Waterloo, Brampton, and Halifax.

Source: Global BRT Data (2014)

of the Green Line, its sixth BRT corridor, which includes the operation of 100 per cent bio-diesel articulated buses (Lindau et al., 2010). In 2010 the city also introduced capacity enhancements for one of its existing corridors, creating overpassing lanes and increasing system capacity from 13,000 to 21,000 passengers per hour per direction.

The success story of Curitiba has been replicated in several cities through the region, with adaptation to the local conditions (Hidalgo and Carrigan, 2010b). Quito replicated the Curitiba concept in 1995, with the use of electric trolleybuses to preserve the environment in its historic downtown. Bogotá expanded the concept in 2000, using very large stations with passing lanes, combined local and express services, an electronic ticketing system and centralized control, achieving extremely high peak loads – more than 45,000 passengers per hour per direction (Hidalgo et al., 2013).

The Curitiba, Quito, and Bogotá successes were then replicated, with adaptations, to 59 cities (Table 23.5). As of July 2014, there were 1,615km serving more than 19.6 million passengers per day (BRT Global Data, 2014). Latin America has one third of the world cities with BRT or BHLS, serving close to two thirds of the estimated global ridership.

*Table 23.5   Most relevant BRT and BHLS systems in Latin America and the Caribbean
(July 2014)*

City	Passengers/day	Number of corridors	Length (km)
Sao Paulo	3,164,000	10 Corredores (includes Expresso Tiradentes)	129
Rio de Janeiro	2,403,600	12 (BRS and Transoeste BRT)	78
Belo Horizonte	1,308,000	7 Corredores BHTrans	24
Bogotá, Colombia (2000)	1,980,000	8 TransMilenio	106
Recife	941,398	3 Sistema Estrutural Integrado	11
Mexico DF (2005)	855,000	5 Metrobús	105
Quito (1995)	833,095	5 Sitema Metrobus-Q	69
Buenos Aires	600.000	4 Metrobús	38
Curitiba	508,000	6 Red Integrada de Transporte RIT	81
Porto Alegre	491,600	12 Corredores	56
Cali, Colombia (2009)	490,000	5 MIO	36
Lima, Perú (1972)	350,000	1 Metropolitano	26
Santiago de Chile (2007)	340,800	14 Transantiago	91
Guayaquil (2006)	310,000	3 Metrovía	38
Guatemala (2009)	245,000	2 Transmetro	35

Note:
Other cities in Brazil: Olinda, Goiania, Mauá, Diadema, Fortaleza, João Pessoa, Niteroi, Campinas, Diadema, São Paulo, Salvador, Natal, Blumenau, Juiz de Fora Sumaré, Campo Grande, Feira de Santana, Londrina, Uberlândia, Brasília, Guarulhos, Criciúma, Santos, Caxias do Sul, Jaboatão Dos Guararapes, Sorocaba, Joinville, Maceió; Argentina: Rosario; Colombia: Barranquilla, Pereira, Bucaramanga, Medellín; Mexico: León, Chihuahua, Ecatepec, Guadalajara, Puebla, Monterrey; Panama: Panama; Uruguay: Montevideo; Venezuela; Caracas, Mérida.

Source: BRT Global Data (2014)

The highest concentration of BRT and BHLS is in Brazil with 33 cities, 114 corridors, and 814 km (BRT Global Data, 2014). Most cities in Brazil, outside Curitiba and Goiania, keep the general model of bus ways, rather than full BRT systems. There was a major upgrade of the integrated system in Sao Paulo in 2005, including an elevated fully segregated bus way – Expresso Tiradentes. Similarly, Santiago, Chile introduced a mayor reform in bus services in 2008, Transantiago, which includes several busways, and prepayment in selected stations, but keeps most fare collection off-board and has few fully segregated busways.

BHLS and BRT in Europe

European cities have preserved and enhanced their transit systems in high-capacity corridors using Metros and tramways mainly, with buses only considered in medium-capacity corridors (Heddebaut et al., 2010). Finn et al. (2011) consider that high-capacity BRT configurations do not suit the European context (lack of available space, undesirable urban cuttings, and low demand). These authors prefer the term bus with a high level of service (BHLS) rather than BRT to refer to the European applications, introduced in

Table 23.6   Most relevant BHLS in Europe as of July 2014

City (first year)	Passengers/day	Number of corridors	Length (km)
Istanbul, Turkey (2007) (extends to Asia)	750,000	1 Metrobus	52
Paris, France (1993)	89,500	3 TVM, 393 Ratp, T Zen 1	41
Hamburg, Germany (2005)	60,000	1 Metrobus Line 5	15
Nice, France (2010)	58,000	1 Ligne de Sur	n.a.
Stockholm, Sweden (1998)	57,000	4 Trunk Network	40
Edinburgh, Scotland (2004)	44,000	1 Fastlink	5
Amsterdam, the Netherlands (2002)	40,000	1 Zuidtangent	56
Utrecht, the Netherlands (2001)	40,000	2 TVM	8

Note: Other cities in France: Rouen, Caen, Lorient, Nancy, Nantes, Toulouse, La Rochelle, Maubege, Lyon, Douai, Lille; United Kingdom: Leeds, Luton, Cambridge, London, Crawley, Kent, York, Bradford, Swansea, Ipswich; The Netherlands: Almere, Eindhoven, Enshede; Germany: Essen, Overhausen; Ireland: Dublin; Portugal: Lisbon; Italy: Brescia, Prato; Czech Republic: Prague; Switzerland: Zurich; Spain: Castellón de la Plana.

Source: BRT Global Data (2014)

several cities (Table 23.6). Most applications have bus-lanes in congested areas (downtown), sharing the road with taxis and bicycles, and in few cases with lanes in expressway (high occupancy vehicle lanes in Madrid and Grenoble, Metrobüs in Istanbul).

Case studies compiled by the European Union project COST (Finn et al., 2011) indicate that BHLS corridors are well-adapted to new urban zones, small towns and medium-size conurbations. They also describe a variety of system configurations (feeder-trunk and direct services), and permit transformation into tramway systems once there is sufficient demand. Some applications used advanced vehicles, including optical or magnetic or physical guidance (e.g., Castellón de la Plana, Eindhoven, Leeds, Cambridge).

Outside the European Union the most used application is the Istanbul Metrobüs, which connects Europe and Asia in the only intercontinental BRT system. This system has central bus ways on expressway (fully segregated BRT), very long platforms, low floor buses (articulated and bi-articulated), and achieves very high commercial speed (35km/h) and peak throughput (23,000 passengers/ hour/ direction). It carries 750,000 passengers per day in a 52km corridor (BRT Global Data, 2014).

Table 23.6 shows the most relevant corridors in Europe, including Turkey. There are at least 51 cities in Europe with BHLS, 799km, serving 1.8 million passengers per day (44 per cent in Istanbul).

BRT in Asia

BRT is evolving very rapidly in several Asian countries, such as China (Fjellstrom, 2010), Indonesia (Ernst and Sutomo, 2010), India (Tiwari and Jain, 2010), and Iran. Applications are very varied, from very basic bus corridors (e.g., Delhi and Pune) to very complete systems (e.g., Ahmedabad and Teheran). Table 23.7 lists the most relevant corridors as of July 2014.

Table 23.7   Most relevant BRT and BHLS systems in Asia (July 2014)

City (First Year)	Passengers/day	Number of corridors	Length (km)
Teheran, Iran (2007)	1,800,000	8 BRT	129
Taipei, Taiwan (1996)	1,200,000	11 busways	60
Guangzhou China (2010)	843,000	1 BRT Zhongshan Avenue	22
Zhengzhou, China (2009)	650,000	1 BRT Line 1	30
Seoul, Korea (2004)	400,000	5 median busways	43
Urumqi, China (2011)	380,000	4 BRT	40
Changzhou, China (2008)	350,000	2 BRT	49
Xiamen, China (2008)	340,000	3 BRT	48
Jakarta, Indonesia (2004)	330,000	10 Transjakarta	134
Beijing, China (2004)	305,000	4 BRT	79
Hangzhou, China (2006)	260,000	1 BRT	55
Jinan, China (2008)	220,000	4 BRT	34
Ahmedabad (2009)	130,000	4 Janmarg	67
Lahore, Pakistan (2012)	130,000	1 Metro Bus	26
Pune (2006)	96,000	1 BRTS	17
Bhopal (2013)	70,000	1 Mybus	24
New Delhi (2008)	53,500	1 bus corridor	5
Indore (2013)	22,200	1	11

Note: Other cities in China: Lanzhou, Dalian, Yinchuan, Hefei, Yancheng, Zaozhuang, Lianyugang, Chongqing, Changde; Iran: Tabriz; India: Rajkot, Jaipur; Thailand: Bangkok; Japan: Kasennnuma, Nagoya; Israel: Haifa.

Source: BRT Global Data (2014)

There are at least 36 cities, 1,295km, serving 8.5 million passengers per day (BRT Global Data, 2014). Most cities started operation after 2009 and many other cities are building and planning BRT across the region.

One important advance in BRT development is the application in Guangzhou, China, which uses direct services, with large stations, overtaking lanes, and the use of advanced technologies for control and user information (Fjellstrom, 2010). This system features very high throughput (30,000 passengers per hour per direction), with a small number of transfers.

BRT in Australia and New Zealand

Australia has a long tradition of BRT, as one of the world's first systems, the Adelaide North East Busway started operation in 1986 (Currie and Delbosc, 2010). Brisbane, Melbourne, Sydney, and Auckland introduced BRT between 2001 and 2005 (Table 23.8). BRTs in Australia and New Zealand have very diverse design features, from guided busways (Adelaide) and fully grade-separated bus only roads (Brisbane, sections of Sydney), to on-street busways (Auckland) and bus-lanes (Melbourne).

According to Currie and Delbosc (2010), the BRT concept continues to be very attractive in the region with rapid increase in kilometers and ridership, especially on established systems. The authors identify risks in the provision of vehicles and accommodating high

Table 23.8   Most relevant BRT and BHLS systems in Australia and New Zealand

City (first year)	Passengers/day	Number of corridors	Length (km)
Brisbane, Australia (2001)	242,000	3 busways	23
Melbourne, Australia (2003)	36,200	4 Smartbus	233
Adelaide, Australia (1986)	23,333	1 O-Bhan	12
Auckland, New Zealand (2005)	7,200	1 North East Busway	5

Note: There are also three corridors in Sydney, 53km long.

Source: BRT Global Data (2014)

patronage growth, but highlight the cost-effectiveness. BRT development in Australia and New Zealand has exceeded rail in the past decade; nevertheless, rail has received greater attention lately. The BRT in Brisbane exhibits very advanced design features, and recently completed a downtown tunnel.

BRT in Africa

Infrastructure and service development in African cities is beginning to attract attention from the local authorities, as urbanization, motorization, and GDP grow. Governments are beginning to recognize the need for organized transit, to replace low-quality informal para-transit services (Gauthier and Weinstock, 2010).

Lagos (Nigeria) and Johannesburg (South Africa) started operations of BRT systems in 2009 while Cape Town opened in 2011. Lagos implemented a corridor on the parallel roads of an existing expressway with a length of 22km, 26 stations, and 220 buses, carrying 220,000 passengers per day. It is not considered a full BRT, as the bus-lanes are on the curb side, with some sections on mixed traffic and access to the buses requires stairs. The corridor is expected to be upgraded and extended.

Johannesburg launched a full BRT system in preparation for the football World Cup in 2009 and extended it in 2013. The system is 43km long (out of 122km planned). It connects the high-density community of Soweto with the central business district and carries 42,000 passengers per day. Cape Town completed its 15km BRT (Myciti) in 2011.

BRT systems are in planning or construction in Port Elizabeth and Pretoria (South Africa); Dar es Salaam (Tanzania) and Accra (Ghana). Other cities considering BRT include Kampala (Uganda), Nairobi (Kenya), Addis Ababa (Ethiopia), Rabat (Morocco), Bloemfontein, Ethekwini, East London, Buffalo City, Ekurhuleni, Polokwane, and Rustenburg (South Africa).

The main challenges for African cities are the creation of local capacity to oversee and operate systems, transforming the current services based on para-transit with informal operators, and funding the capital costs (infrastructure and buses).

4.   TRENDS AND NEEDS

This section describes current trends in BRT and BHLS development, particularly the growing recognition among international institutions, the social and environmental impacts, integration of advanced technologies, implementation barriers, and connections with land development.

Environmental and Social Impacts of BRT and BHLS

BRT is now recognized as an important component of sustainable mobility strategies. The most recent Global Report on Human Settlements (UN-Habitat, 2013) includes BRT, along with LRT and Metro, as a suggested component of access strategies for the growing urban population in the world. C40, a network of the world's megacities taking action to reduce greenhouse gas emissions, highlights BRT as one of the most important improvements in public transport by the member cities (C40, 2014). And the International Energy Agency suggests the construction of 25,000km of BRT before 2050 as one key action to reduce vehicle kilometers traveled and keep global temperature below a 2°C increase (IEA, 2012).

The expansion of BRT as part of integrated public transport networks requires significant efforts by cities. With adequate design, implementation, and operation, BRTs are expected to bring positive impacts beyond climate change mitigation, mainly in reduced travel times, air pollution, and traffic incidents, as well as increased personal physical activity. Moreover, ex-post evaluation of some BRT systems indicate that they result in positive re-distributional effects, i.e., net socio-economic impacts are higher to lower income segments of the society (Carrigan et al., 2013).

It is very important that systems are well integrated into the overall public transport networks and urban environments so the social and equity objectives they promise are achieved. Particular attention needs to be provided to quality of service and affordability. BRT systems in Latin America and Asia are designed for maximum productivity, and have received low ratings by users due to very high occupancy and insufficient physical coverage (Lindau et al., 2013). Discussion of additional support from funding sources different than the user fare is being considered by an increasing number of local and national authorities.

In addition, the poorest segment of the population is often priced out, as they need to spend a significant per cent of their income on transportation (see, for instance, Bocarejo and Oviedo, 2012). With the introduction of electronic payment systems, the possibility of targeted subsidies for low income population has become a reality – see, for example, the new scheme being applied in Bogotá (Rodriguez and Mehndiratta, 2014).

Advanced Technologies for BRT and BHLS

On top of global expansion, BRT and BHLS are expected to continue evolving, particularly in the application of advanced technologies for guidance, vehicle propulsion, information technologies, and headway control mechanisms (Hidalgo and Muñoz, 2014). Guidance technologies improve the performance of BRT systems by enhancing safety, improving adequate docking to passenger platforms and optimizing the use of narrow right-of-ways. Applications include mechanical, electromagnetic, and optical guidance systems.

Vehicle propulsion technologies reduce the tailpipe emissions and enhance the energy efficiency of bus systems (Cooper et al., 2013). Current propulsion technologies have advanced in reducing harmful emissions but there is still room for improvement. The introduction of new propulsion technologies – such as hybrid, plug-in hybrid, hydrogen fuel-cells, and fast-recharge battery-electric buses – is expected to greatly enhance the environmental performance of bus systems. The current issue with newer technologies is the higher capital costs associated with them; nevertheless the financial barriers are expected to be overcome over time as research and development progress.

Another area of continued improvement is the application of information technologies to BRT and BHLS systems. Information technologies enhance fare collection systems, creating flexibility and security. They also allow for improved operational planning and control, reducing uncertainty in trip-making. For instance, headway control mechanisms provide a more reliable operation, reducing waiting times, improving comfort inside the vehicles and stations, and making vehicle operations less costly (Delgado et al., 2009). Finally, information technologies will be increasingly used to boost user information and improve the passenger experience. Continued progress in this field will provide opportunities for better passenger experience.

BRT and BHLS Planning and Implementation Barriers

BRT and BHLS will continue to face planning and implementation barriers, particularly in rapidly growing cities in the developing world. Most of the barriers are related to institutional and financial frameworks, not the technical concepts behind BRT and BHLS (Lindau et al., 2013). In particular, those cities planning BRT and BHLS face institutional complexities and lack of technical capacity at the local level. Lack of coordination across municipalities and government agencies make metropolitan planning efforts difficult in several cities and result in a lack of alignment among stakeholders.

Despite progress, BRT and BHLS are still perceived by planners and decision-makers as lower-quality modes. Enhanced education and outreach is still needed. There is also the need to overcome the traditional view of traffic engineering, focused on road capacity expansions and level of service for cars, not people. BRT planning and implementation also requires enhanced community participation.

With regard to BRT and BHLS implementation, some barriers are still outstanding (Lindau et al., 2013). Most local authorities still underestimate the implementation effort. System promoters are usually optimistic regarding cost and implementation time (similar to the case of other infrastructure projects as reported by Flyvbjerg et al., 2003). BRT projects also are subject to discontinuities due to political cycles and, in some cases, advanced projects have been abandoned after a change in local elected authorities, while others have been rushed into inauguration before the end of a government term. There is also a need of national policies supporting BRT development. These issues need to be tackled for BRT and BHLS systems to continue evolving, particularly in developing cities.

5.   LAND DEVELOPMENT AND BRT

One important debate in the planning community is whether BRT influences urban development. Similar to rail systems, the influence of BRT on urban development is not obvious (Suzuki et al. 2013). Special conditions and policies need to be in place to advance transit oriented development (TOD). Suzuki et al. indicate that the urban impact of BRT in the cases of Ahmedabad, Bogotá, Guangzhou, and Ho Chi Minh City has been limited by the enabling policies – such as regulation and finance, which have not been in place. Nevertheless, the systems have very high ridership levels, resulting from relatively high densities along the transit corridors.

Regarding the impact of BRT on land prices, empirical evidence is quite limited. Cervero and Kang (2009) cite studies in Los Angeles and Bogotá. In the case of Los Angeles, they discuss small negative impacts on residential property values and small gains for commercial parcels. In the case of Bogotá, they cite appreciable land value benefits; not only from BRT itself, but from pedestrian-friendly environments near BRT bus stops. They also find that significant investment in BRT implementation in Seoul resulted in significant increase in density and land value premium for residences and varied impacts for retail and non-residential uses. They conclude that it is not the transit hardware, i.e., bus or rail, that unleash land-use changes, but the comparative travel time savings as compared with car travel. Similar studies of BRT and land development in the US show that policies to encourage redevelopment and the local public realm may be more important factors than the issue of permanence of the transit system (Thole and Samus, 2009).

REFERENCES

Bicycle Innovation Lab (2011), *The Reverse Traffic Pyramid*, www.bicycleinnovationlab.dk/?show=jpn&l=UK.
BRT Global Data (2014), *BRT Centre of Excellence and EMBARQ in partnership with IEA and SIBRT*, http://brtdata.org.
Bocarejo, S.J.P. and Oviedo, H.D.R. (2012), Transport accessibility and social inequities: a tool for identification of mobility needs and evaluation of transport investments, *Journal of Transport Geography*, **24**, 142–54.
C40 (2014), *Climate Action in Megacities Version 2.0*, www.c40.org/blog_posts/CAM2.
Carrigan, A., Hensher, D., Hidalgo, D., Mulley, C. and Muñoz, J.C. (2011), The complexity of BRT development and implementation, in VREF (ed.), *10 Years with the FUT Programme*, Göteborg: Volvo Research and Education Foundations, pp. 114–25.
Carrigan, A., King, R., Velásquez, J.M., Raifmann, M. and Duduta, N. (2013), *Social, Environmental and Economic Impacts of BRT Systems: Bus Rapid Transit Case Studies from Around the World*, EMBARQ, the Sustainable Transport and Urban Development Program of the World Resources Institute, www.embarq.org/en/social-environmental-and-economic-impacts-bus-rapid-transit.
Cervero, R. and Kang, C.D. (2011), Bus rapid transit impacts on land uses and land values in Seoul, Korea, *Transport Policy*, **18**(1), 102–16.
Chris, B. (2001), *The Green Transportation Hierarchy*, www.transalt.org/files/newsroom/magazine/012Spring/09hierarchy.html.
Cooper, E., Arioli, M., Carrigan, A. and Jain, U. (2013), Meta-analysis of transit bus exhaust emissions, *Transportation Research Record: Journal of the Transportation Research Board*, **2340**(1), 20–28.
Currie, G. and Delbosc A. (2010), Bus rapid transit in Australasia: an update on progress, *Built Environment*, **26**(3), 328–43.
Delgado, F., Muñoz, J.C., Giesen, R. and Cipriano, A. (2009), Real-time control of buses in a transit corridor based on vehicle holding and boarding limits, *Transportation Research Record: Journal of the Transportation Research Board*, **2090**(1), 59–67.
Diaz, R.B. (ed.) and Hinebaugh, D. (2009), *Characteristics of BRT for Decision Makers (CBRT)*, 2nd edn,

FTA-FL-26-7109.2009.1, Washington, DC: Federal Transit Administration, United States Department of Transportation.

Ernst, J.P. and Sutomo, H. (2010), BRT's influence on public transport improvements in Indonesian cities, *Built Environment*, **26**(3), 344–52.

Finn, B., Heddebaut, O., Kerkhof, A., Rambaud, F., Sbert-Lozano, O. and Soulas, C. (eds) (2011), *Buses with High Level of Service: Fundamental Characteristics and Recommendations for Decision Making and Research*, Cost Action TU0603, final report, October.

Fjellstrom K. (2010), Bus rapid transit in China, *Built Environment*, **26**(3), 363–74.

Flyvbjerg, B., Bruzelius, N. and Rothengatter, W. (2003), Megaprojects and Risk: An Anatomy of Ambition, Cambridge: Cambridge University Press.

Gauthier, A. and Weinstock A. (2010), Africa: transforming paratransit into BRT, *Built Environment*, **26**(3), 317–27.

Gilbert, A. (2008), Bus rapid transit: is TransMilenio a miracle cure? *Transport Reviews*, **28**(4), 439–67.

Heddebaut, O., Finn, B., Raubel, S. and Rambaud, F. (2010), The European bus with high level of service (BHLS): concept and practice, *Built Environment*, **26**(3), 307–16.

Hensher, D. (1999), A bus-based transitway or light rail? Continuing the saga on choice versus blind commitment, *Road & Transport Research*, **8**(3).

Hidalgo, D. (2012), Bus rapid transit: worldwide history of development, key systems and policy issues, *Encyclopedia of Sustainability Science and Technology*, www.springerreference.com/docs/html/chapterd-bid/308766.html.

Hidalgo, D. and Carrigan, A. (2010a), *Modernizing Public Transportation, Lessons Learned from Major Bus Improvements in Latin America and Asia*, Washington, DC: World Resources Institute, www.embarq.org/en/modernizing-public-transportation.

Hidalgo, D. and Carrigan, A. (2010b), BRT in Latin America – high capacity and performance, rapid implementation and low cost, *Built Environment*, **36**(3), 283–97.

Hidalgo, D. and Gutierrez, L. (2013), BRT around the world: explosive growth, large positive impacts and many issues outstanding, *Research in Transportation Economics*, **39**(1), 8–13.

Hidalgo, D. and Muñoz, J.C. (2014), A review of technological improvements in bus rapid transit (BRT) and buses with high level of service (BHLS), *Public Transport*, **6**(3), 185–213.

Hidalgo, D., Lleras, G. and Hernández, E. (2013), Methodology for calculating passenger capacity in bus rapid transit systems: application to the TransMilenio system in Bogotá, Colombia, *Research in Transportation Economics*, **39**(1), 139–42.

IEA (2012), *Energy Technology Perspectives 2012*, Paris: OECD.

Levinson, H., Zimmerman, S., Clinger, J., Gast, J., Rutherford S. and Bruhn, E. (2003a), *Bus Rapid Transit – Volume 2: Implementation Guidelines*, Transit Cooperative Research Program – Report 90, Vol II, Washington, DC: Transportation Research Board, National Academies.

Levinson, H., Zimmerman, S., Clinger, J., Rutherford S., Smith R.L., Cranknell, J. and Soberman, R. (2003b), *Bus Rapid Transit – Volume 1: Case Studies in Bus Rapid Transit*, Transit Cooperative Research Program – Report 90, Vol I, Washington, DC: Transportation Research Board, National Academies.

Light Rail Now (2011), *Bus Rapid Transit Analyses*, www.lightrailnow.org/facts/fa_brt.htm.

Lindau, L.A., Hidalgo, D. and Facchini, D. (2010), Curitiba, the cradle of bus rapid transit, *Built Environment*, **36**(3), 274–82.

Lindau, L.A., Hidalgo, D. and Lobo, A. (2013), *Barriers to Planning and Implementing Bus Rapid Transit Systems*, Thredbo 13, Conference Series on Regulation and Ownership of Land Transport, Oxford, September.

Muñoz, J.C. and Hidalgo, D. (2013), Workshop 2: Bus rapid transit as part of enhanced service provision, Thredbo 12, *Research in Transportation Economics*, **39**(1), 104–7.

National BRT Institute (2011), www.nbrti.org.

OC Transport (2011), *Ottawa's Light Rail Future*, www.octranspo1.com/routes/ottawas_light_rail_future.

Rodriguez, C. and Mehndiratta, S. (2014), ¿Me lleva por mil pesos? Subsidios al Transporte Público para los Pobres, http://blogs.worldbank.org/transport/es/me-lleva-por-1000-pesos-subsidios-al-transporte-p-blico-para-los-pobres.

Rosenthal, E. (2009), Buses may aid climate battle in poor cities, *The New York Times*, July 9, www.nytimes.com/2009/07/10/world/americas/10degrees.html.

Suzuki, H., Cervero, R. and Iuchi, K. (2013), *Transforming Cities with Transit: Transit and Land-use Integration for Sustainable Urban Development*, Washington, DC: World Bank.

Thole, C. and Samus, J. (2009), *Bus Rapid Transit and Development: Policies and Practices that Affect Development Around Transit*, National Bus Rapid Transit Institute, Center for Urban Transportation Research, University of South Florida, FL-26-7109-05.

Tiwari, G. and Jain D. (2010), Bus rapid transit projects in Indian cities: a status report, *Built Environment*, **26**(3), 353–62.

UN-Habitat (2013), *Planning and Design for Sustainable Urban Mobility – Global Report on Human Settlements*, Nairobi: UN-Habitat.

Vuchic, V.R. (2007), *Urban Transit Systems and Technology*, Hoboken, NJ: John Wiley & Sons.

Wilbur Smith and Associates (1966), under commission from American Automobile Manufacturers Association (H.S. Levinson, Principal Investigator), *Transportation and Parking for Tomorrow's Cities*, New Haven, CT.

Wright, L. and Hook, W. (eds) (2007), *Bus Rapid Transit Planning Guide*, 3rd edn, New York: Institute for Transportation and Development Policy.

24 The expansion of large international hub airports
Andrew R. Goetz

1. INTRODUCTION

There is no question that airports and the aviation industry play a major role in the contemporary global economy. Air passenger and cargo transport has become indispensable for global commerce, especially in tourism, trade, logistics and producer services. No other mode of transport provides such high-speed service over long distances, crossing both land and sea. Air transport provides superb accessibility between global air hubs and major spokes to facilitate economic development at these nodes and their surrounding regions. The International Air Transport Association (IATA) estimates that aviation has a global economic impact of $2.2 trillion, or about 3.5 per cent of global gross domestic product (GDP), and accounts for 56.6 million people employed in aviation and related industries (IATA, 2012).

Commercial air travel has been experiencing strong growth in demand throughout the latter half of the twentieth century, and this trend has continued, albeit somewhat less consistently, into the twenty-first century. Annual growth rates have averaged 5–6 per cent from the 1960s, but have fluctuated since 2000. Increasing GDP and disposable incomes, together with technological improvements in the speed, comfort, and safety of commercial air travel have been key factors behind the strong historical growth in aviation demand. Especially since the 1980s, rapidly increasing globalization of economic activities has been inextricably linked with air transport, as increasing globalization has been both cause and effect of increasing air travel (Goetz and Graham, 2004; Cidell, 2006). Also since the 1980s, policy shifts favouring deregulation and privatization have changed the structure of the airline industry, led to the expansion of hub-and-spoke route networks, and have contributed to stronger growth in boom periods, but also sharper declines in economically challenging periods (Banister and Berechman, 2000; Goetz and Vowles, 2009). Since 2000, the global air transport industry has experienced a series of setbacks, including fallout from the 9/11 attacks in 2001, conflicts in Afghanistan and Iraq, rapidly rising aviation fuel prices and the global economic crisis from 2008 (Graham and Goetz, 2008). Despite these debilitating events, air transport has continued to grow on average but some recent years, such as 2008–9, have experienced significant declines. Still, 20-year forecasts from the IATA continue to predict growth rates up to 5 per cent per year worldwide, and over 6 per cent for the Asia-Pacific region (IATA 2012).

The geography of global air transport is reflected in the rankings of international airports based on total passenger volume (Table 24.1). While there is a general correlation between metropolitan area population size and airport passengers, certain cities are more important in air transport provision than their populations would suggest. Cities that serve as airline hubs and international gateways, as well as important command-and-control centres of the global economy tend to have the largest air passenger activity

Table 24.1   Top 30 airports by terminal passengers handled, 2011 and 1993

Rank	2011		1993	
	Airport	Passengers (m)	Airport	Passengers (m)
1	Atlanta Hartsfield-Jackson Int'l	92.4	Chicago O'Hare Int'l	65.1
2	Beijing Capital Int'l	77.4	Dallas Fort Worth Int'l	49.7
3	London Heathrow	69.4	Los Angeles Int'l	47.8
4	Chicago O'Hare Int'l	66.6	Atlanta Hartsfield Int'l	47.7
5	Tokyo Haneda Int'l	62.2	London Heathrow	47.6
6	Los Angeles Int'l	61.8	Tokyo Haneda Int'l	41.5
7	Paris Charles de Gaulle	61.0	Denver Stapleton	32.6
8	Dallas Fort Worth Int'l	57.8	San Francisco Int'l	32.0
9	Frankfurt	56.4	Frankfurt Rheim	31.9
10	Hong Kong Chek Lap Kok Int'l	53.3	Miami Int'l	28.7
11	Denver Int'l	52.7	New York JFK Int'l	26.8
12	Jakarta Soekarno-Hatta Int'l	52.4	Newark Int'l	25.8
13	Dubai Int'l	51.0	Paris Charles de Gaulle	25.7
14	Amsterdam Schiphol	49.8	Paris Orly	25.3
15	Madrid Barajas	49.6	Hong Kong Kai Tak	24.4
16	Bangkok Suvarnabhumi	47.9	Detroit Metro Wayne Co.	24.2
17	New York JFK Int'l	47.8	Boston Logan Int'l	24.0
18	Singapore Changi	46.5	Phoenix Sky Harbor Int'l	23.5
19	Guangzhou Baiyun Int'l	45.0	Minneapolis/St. Paul Int'l	23.5
20	Las Vegas McCarran Int'l	41.4	Osaka Int'l	23.3
21	Shanghai Pudong Int'l	41.5	Seoul Kimpo Int'l	22.6
22	San Francisco Int'l	40.9	Las Vegas McCarran Int'l	22.5
23	Phoenix Sky Harbor Int'l	40.6	Honolulu Int'l	22.1
24	Houston George Bush Intercont'l	40.1	Orlando Int'l	21.5
25	Charlotte Douglas Int'l	39.0	Amsterdam Schiphol	20.8
26	Miami Int'l	38.3	Toronto Pearson Int'l	20.5
27	Munich	37.8	Houston Intercontinental	20.3
28	Kuala Lumpur Int'l	37.7	London Gatwick	20.1
29	Rome Leonardo Da Vinci Fiumicino	37.6	Tokyo Narita	20.0
30	Istanbul Ataturk Int'l	37.4	St. Louis Lambert Int'l	19.9

Source: ACI (1994, 2012)

in the world. In 2011, Atlanta Hartsfield-Jackson International, the major hub for Delta Airlines, was the largest airport in the world, serving more than 92 million passengers, followed by Beijing Capital (77 million), London Heathrow (69 million), Chicago O'Hare (67 million) and Tokyo Haneda (62 million). Of the top 30 passenger airports in 2011, 12 were located in the United States, nine in Asia-Pacific, seven in Europe and two in the Middle East. Although many US airports continue to handle increasing passenger volumes, their world rankings today are lower, indicating a relative decline. In 1993, the US accounted for the four largest, seven of the top ten, and 18 of the top 30 airports in the world. Many Asia-Pacific airports, especially those in Beijing, Hong Kong, Jakarta, Bangkok, Singapore and Guangzhou have grown substantially as a reflection of increased economic importance of the region, while European airports such as London

Heathrow, Paris Charles de Gaulle, Amsterdam Schiphol and Madrid Barajas have also experienced significant growth.

The focal point of the nexus between air transport and economic development is the airport, although the economic impacts also affect a much wider region surrounding the airport. But it is at the airport where the effects are most noticeable, in the form of employment for airport operators, airline and handling agents, air traffic control workers, concessionaires and other airport personnel (Bowen, 2010). Altogether, airports constitute a major node of employment within a metropolitan area, which can greatly affect the economic profile of the city and surrounding region, as well as creating localized impacts on transport systems and nearby neighbourhoods.

Many industries are heavily dependent on frequent and reliable air passenger and cargo transportation service, including many advanced producer services,[1] especially international banking, finance, insurance, legal services, computer services, consulting, research and development, and other business services. Many consumer service industries are also heavily dependent upon air transport, none more so than tourism and the related entertainment, recreation, lodging and restaurant industries. High-value and lighter-weight manufactured items from the medical, electronics, computer and other high-technology industries rely on the shipment of products by air. And ground transportation industries depend upon passengers and freight from the airlines as part of the global intermodal transportation system. Altogether, air transport has an effect on nearly every major industry, and touches the lives, either directly or indirectly, of nearly every person in the world.

While it is clear that aviation and airports play a major role in economic development, when viewed through the lens of sustainable development, the picture becomes somewhat more muddled. While the transportation advantages of aviation are readily apparent, the sustainability externalities, including aviation's total reliance on an increasingly expensive non-renewable resource (i.e., petroleum), together with relatively poor fuel economy (in comparison with other transport modes), and significant air pollution and greenhouse gas emissions diminish aviation's long-term economic profile. Yet initiatives in developing alternative renewable fuels and reducing harmful emissions will be helpful to maintain the important role that aviation plays in facilitating economic development.

Considering the vital role that air transport plays in the contemporary global economy, large cities are regularly confronted with important decisions about the adequacy of their airport infrastructure to accommodate current and future air transport demand. Cities, airport authorities, regional planning associations, national governments and private airport operators conduct ongoing planning activities to determine to what extent existing airport infrastructure and services are adequate and whether expansions are necessary. In regions where air transport demand is growing rapidly, such as in Asia-Pacific and parts of the Middle East, many new airports are being built. In other regions where air transport growth is more mature, such as in North America and Europe, selective expansion of existing airports tends to be the more typical course of action.

This chapter will first revisit the traditional and alternative theoretical perspectives concerning the relation between air transportation and economic development, followed by recent empirical evidence on the economic impacts of airports and air transport, including discussion of the 'aerotropolis' concept. An overview of the world's major airports, their levels of air service, expansion plans and related economic impacts comes next, followed by a case study of the development of Denver International Airport.

2.   THEORETICAL BACKGROUND: AIR TRANSPORTATION AND ECONOMIC DEVELOPMENT

Traditional Perspectives

The theoretical basis for the economic development effects of air transport can be related to its characteristics as a technologically sophisticated propulsive industry with numerous backward and forward linkages, as well as a transportation service industry that facilitates spatial interaction and the growth of other industries that rely on frequent and reliable air service.

As with other forms of transportation, air transport infrastructure facilitates expansion and improved efficiency of operations, which translates into improved services for the user. Improved technology and infrastructure should have the effect of reducing travel costs and travel time, which should then improve accessibility for users and the regions served. With improved accessibility, the opportunity for increased spatial interaction in the form of passenger and trade flow should lead to greater economic effects as measured by output, productivity, employment and lowered costs of production (Figure 24.1). With improved accessibility, there is also the potential for greater cohesion between regions, the possibility of increased economic interdependence, and further demand for transport.

Building on classical trade theory, Ullman (1956) identified three bases for spatial interaction: (1) complementarity, or the supply-demand relations between cities or

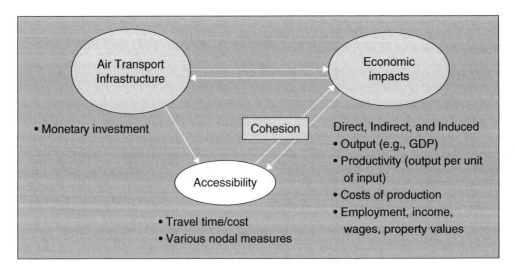

Source: Goetz (2011)

Figure 24.1   Linkages between air transport and economic growth

regions, (2) transferability, i.e., the ease of movement between places and (3) intervening opportunity, or the existence of competing alternatives that may hinder or enhance levels of spatial interaction. Transport relates directly to transferability so that, as transport linkages are established and improved, movement becomes easier and can facilitate greater levels of spatial interaction, as measured by increases in trade flow, passengers, goods and service provision, and information exchange. As spatial interaction increases, economic expansion and industrial specialization will also occur, as trade and other businesses open up new markets. Krugman (1991) has expanded on classical trade theory by specifying the effects of agglomeration economies as related to increased transport and cohesion, thus resulting in the development of specialized industrial districts and clusters.

Location theory has emphasized the important role that transport costs play in firm location decisions. Classical industrial location theory (Weber, 1929; Hoover, 1948; Isard, 1956) posits that firms will locate where transport costs are minimized, in conjunction with other location costs. Even though generalized costs of transport have decreased over time and transport accessibility has become more ubiquitous, location decisions still depend on superior access to high-quality transport. In behavioural studies of firm location, transport access is frequently cited as a key location factor (Chapman and Walker, 1991; Elgar and Miller, 2010; Markusen et al., 1986; Wilbur Smith and Associates, 2008). Transport infrastructure provides a competitive advantage to cities and regions to attract new businesses and retain existing ones. In studies of the 'New Economic Geography' (Porter, 1990; Krugman, 1991; Fujita et al., 1999) new and improved transport infrastructure facilitates agglomeration economies, technological spillovers, and core/ periphery dynamics that lead to more specialized and competitive economic clusters.

While the classical theoretical evidence for transport's effect on economic development is quite strong, there are nevertheless limits to the degree of this effect. In fact, much of the contemporary literature on this topic is clear to point out that transportation is only one of several factors that are important to economic development (Banister and Berechman, 2000; Chatman and Noland, 2011; Giuliano, 2004; Lakshmanan, 2010; Rietveld and Bruinsma, 1998; Vickerman, 2008). Transportation is usually considered to be a necessary but not sufficient condition for economic development. It is also clear that increasing investment in transport infrastructure is subject to diminishing returns (Banister, 2012). Investments in new or breakthrough technologies and networks will have more dramatic impacts than incremental investments in already established systems. Furthermore, the direction of causality is not always clear. While most studies focus on the effect of transport on economic development, it is true that increasing economic development (occurring for other reasons) will lead to a greater demand for transport. Thus, transport can be either a leading or lagging indicator of economic development (Taaffe et al., 1996; Yu et al., 2012). The role of transport investment in stimulating growth during times of economic crisis is also subject to considerable controversy (Goetz 2011; Lavee et al., 2011).

Alternative Perspectives

While most of the literature supports the hypothesis that public sector investments in transportation infrastructure result in long-term economic benefits, there are several alternative theoretical perspectives that run contrary to the prevailing view. One of these viewpoints is the limited government/free market perspective put forward by think tanks such as the Cato Institute, the Reason Foundation and the Heritage Foundation that contends most public spending (including transportation infrastructure) is wasteful, in both theory and practice. According to this view, the private sector is always more efficient, and that transportation provision should be privatized through the use of mechanisms such as tolling and congestion pricing. Another alternative viewpoint is that a better allocation of public investment in other physical infrastructure (e.g., water, electric power, communications systems) or social infrastructure (e.g., educational systems, job training) would yield greater returns than investment in transportation infrastructure.

Yet another perspective is based on the concept of sustainable development, incorporating and assessing environmental, economic and social aspects of transport investment. Based on the definition of sustainable development first proposed by the Brundtland Commission report (World Commission on Environment and Development, 1987), sustainable transport can be defined as transport that satisfies current mobility needs without compromising the ability of future generations to meet these needs. A sustainable transport system is one that provides transport and mobility with renewable fuels while minimizing emissions detrimental to the local and global environment, and preventing needless fatalities, injuries, and congestion (Black, 2010). Since approximately 95 per cent of transport today, including virtually all of aviation, is fuelled by non-renewable petroleum products, the transport sector is just now beginning to explore the use of renewable fuels (Gilbert and Perl, 2010). There is at present no practical alternative to the use of petroleum in air transport, although research and development on the use of biofuels in aviation has yielded some encouraging results. While fuel efficiency for air transport has improved greatly in recent years, especially the Airbus A380 and Boeing B787, the average aircraft in operation still uses more fuel per passenger-kilometre or ton-kilometre than most other passenger and freight transport modes. Transport also accounts for approximately 25 per cent of the world's greenhouse gas emissions attributable to human activity, mostly in the form of carbon dioxide and nitrogen oxides from fossil fuel combustion (Black, 2010). Even though aviation's contribution to total greenhouse emissions is only about 3 per cent, aviation's share has been growing faster than other transport modes and other sources at the same time as international efforts have been focused on reducing global greenhouse gas emissions (Gossling and Upham, 2009). While fatalities, injuries and congestion are at unacceptably high levels for transport overall, especially for roadways, those statistics for aviation are comparatively much better.

A viewpoint on transport's role in economic development through a sustainability lens would acknowledge the limits of transport investment in furthering development, largely as a result of environmental and social externalities (Banister and Berechman, 2000). A sustainability approach recognizes that unlimited mobility is neither possible, nor desirable, and that diminishing returns characterize transport investments. It is also useful to acknowledge that there are alternative ways to measure societal 'progress', for example, quality of life, well-being and happiness, not just the quantity of GDP. Furthermore, there are important sustainability differences among modes, and some transport modes tend to be more sustainable and thus may be more beneficial for long-term economic development. A comprehensive accounting of the sustainability of air transport reveals a mixed picture in which some dimensions (e.g., type of fuel used, fuel efficiency and pollution emissions) are problematic, while others (e.g., level of mobility provided, safety) are quite good (Goetz and Graham, 2004; Gossling and Upham, 2009; Upham et al., 2003).

3.   ECONOMIC IMPACTS OF AIRPORTS AND AIR TRANSPORT

As a specialized mode that possesses superior speed and accessibility over long distances, air transport conveys distinctive economic effects, spatially articulated through the airport. In more formal terms, the economic and employment impacts of airports and air transport can be subdivided into four categories (Banister and Berechman, 2000; Graham, 2001; York Aviation, 2004):

- **Direct effects** of air transport include employment and income generated at or near an airport which are required to perform the air transport function (Banister and Berechman, 2000; Graham, 2001). Direct jobs include airline pilots, mechanics, flight attendants, baggage handlers, check-in attendants and freight forwarders as well as airport air traffic controllers, concessionaires, parking staff and maintenance workers.
- **Indirect effects** are generated by expenditures to a chain of suppliers of goods and services needed by an airport and its tenants. Indirect effects are thus the result of backward linkages between direct airport activities and their business suppliers (Bowen, 2010). Examples of indirect activities include utility, fuel, construction, cleaning, food and retail goods suppliers (Graham, 2001).
- **Induced effects** are the result of personal spending from employees in both the direct and indirect categories. Workers at airports and their suppliers will need basic goods and services that will support additional economic activity in areas such as retail, food, transport and housing (Graham, 2001). These activities are the result of forward linkages from the airport (Bowen, 2010). The indirect and induced effects together can be referred to as 'secondary effects' (Graham, 2001).
- **Catalytic (or attracted) effects** are the wider economic impacts on a city and the surrounding region that will occur due to the generative, or magnetic, effects of air transport in attracting new business activity. It is well-recognized that in the contemporary globalized environment, frequent and reliable air services are important for much business travel as well as personal and leisure travel. Cities and regions will benefit from increased accessibility and agglomeration economies as a result of new or expanded air service. Businesses and individuals will be drawn to those locations that provide more and higher-quality air transport linkages. These spin-off effects, which are harder to measure than direct or secondary effects, are nevertheless extremely important when decisions are made regarding expansion of airports and air services. Cities and regions have been thrust into a more competitive global environment, and the provision of high-quality air transport infrastructure and services can be a decisive element in efforts to attract or retain businesses and individuals to an area.

Certain economic activities and industries possess particular characteristics that require frequent and reliable air passenger and/or cargo service. In addition to those businesses directly related to the provision of aviation services, corporate headquarters and other command-and-control nodes of the global economy tend to be concentrated in airline hubs and gateways (Bowen, 2010). Executives and managers need to conduct high-speed, long-distance travel on a regular basis and thus need access to high-quality air service. As globalization has resulted in longer supply chains and more economic linkages through-out the world, ready access to international air service has become a locational necessity for large multinational firms. When Boeing relocated its corporate headquarters from Seattle to Chicago in 2001, better air service to more international destinations was cited as a critical factor for a company that wanted to expand its international business presence.

High-technology and creative knowledge activities, especially in scientific research and development, also rely heavily upon access to air transport. Knowledge-intensive 'New Economy' industries such as computing, electronics, communications and phar-maceuticals fit this category particularly well (Bowen, 2010; Graham, 2001). The ship-ment of very high-value, low-weight and/or perishable commodities through air cargo transport has been important to these and other industries, including medical instru-mentation, electronic automotive parts and computer systems (Alkaabi and Debbage, 2011). In his book *The Work of Nations*, Reich (1999) emphasized the importance of 'symbolic-analytic' work in wealth creation, and noted that good air accessibility and a large university were the two most important catalysts in stimulating this type of economic activity. Similarly, Florida (2002, 2012) highlighted the role of the 'creative class' – knowledge workers who can create transformative innovations – in promoting economic development for cities and regions, and has noted the importance of airports, and especially high-quality passenger air transport, in attracting and retaining creative-class workers.

The wider economic effects of airports and the aviation industry can also be appre-ciated by considering the important role of aircraft manufacturers and air systems developers in national, regional and local economies. For example, Boeing and Airbus, the world's largest aircraft manufacturers together employ more than 200,000 workers in over 70 countries, with nearly 25,000 global suppliers and customers in more than 150 countries (Boeing, 2012; Airbus, 2012).

Air transport is particularly relevant to the wider travel and tourism industry, includ-ing demand for hotels, restaurants, conferences, exhibitions, package holidays, pilgrim-ages and other tours (Graham, 2001). Travel and tourism is one of the world's largest industries, contributing 9 per cent of global GDP in 2011, equal to US$6 trillion, and 255 million jobs (World Travel & Tourism Council, 2012). While it is difficult to estimate the precise role of air transport in fostering tourism, it is clear that without air transport, many countries' tourism industries would be substantially reduced. Indeed, the econo-mies of several smaller nations in the Caribbean and Pacific islands would be devastated without air transport and the tourism income that is generated. Even in larger European, American and Asian countries, tourism is a major industry and air transport typically delivers the majority of tourists to destination cities and regions (Graham, 2008).

A relatively large number of empirical studies has shown how air transport and air-ports are correlated with, or are causal factors for, growth in population, employment, and economic development (e.g., Button and Taylor, 2000; Debbage and Delk, 2001; Goetz, 1992; Irwin and Kasarda, 1991; Ivy et al., 1995; Percoco, 2010). In particular, Brueckner (2003) found that a 10 per cent increase in passenger enplanements in a metro area leads approximately to a 1 per cent increase in employment in service-related industries, while Green (2007) found that passenger boardings per capita are a powerful predictor of subsequent population and employment growth. According to Green, US hub cities experienced 9–16 per cent higher population growth and 8–13 per cent higher employment growth than US non-hub cities between 1990 and 2000. Hakfoort, Poot and Rietveld (2001) estimated the economic impact of Amsterdam's Schiphol Airport, and found that every direct job at the airport leads to approximately one other indirect or induced job. More recent studies are discovering significant tourism impacts of low-cost carrier air service in more peripheral regions of Europe and Asia (Donzelli, 2010; Chung and Whang, 2011).

At the same time, there are other examples where investment in air transport infrastructure did not result in significant economic impacts. The cases of Montreal Mirabel and China's Zhuhai Airport where actual results did not match projections (Bowen, 2010), illustrate that the 'Field of Dreams – build it and they will come' approach to airport planning and development is illusory. While the limits of transport infrastructure investment are increasingly being recognized for other transport modes, especially highways, the linkage between aviation and economic development is only just starting to be scrutinized more sceptically.

The Aerotropolis Concept

While the importance of air transport in city growth has been long recognized, the emergence of airport-focused urban development is a more recent phenomenon. Contemporary models of urban spatial structure that emphasize a more decentralized morphology of urban realms, suburban downtowns, and edge cities have explicitly incorporated the airport as an important peripheral node in the urban landscape (Garreau, 1991; Harris, 1997; Hartshorn and Muller, 1989; Vance, 1977). In most cities, the airport has typically been located away from the elite residential sector of the city and usually in the direction of a transportation/warehousing corridor with good access to radial highways and circumferential beltways. More recently, John Kasarda (2012) has popularized the concept of an 'aerotropolis' – or airport-oriented commercial, office and business development area – that relies on proximity to a major airport and the air transport accessibility it provides. Kasarda and Lindsay (2011: 174) define an aerotropolis as:

> an airport-integrated region, extending as far as sixty miles from the inner clusters of hotels, offices, distribution, and logistics facilities . . . All kinds of activities are served by and enhanced by the airport. Whether it's supply chains, whether it's enterprise networks, whether it's biosciences and pharmaceuticals and time-sensitive organic materials, the airport itself is really the nucleus of a range of 'New Economy' functions, [bolstering a city's] competitiveness, job creation, and quality of life.

Instead of being considered simply as a peripheral infrastructure function in a city, Kasarda envisions the airport as the centre of a new urban form – separate from but still connected to the traditional central business districts by highways and/or rail – emphasizing high-speed, knowledge-intensive 'New Economy' activities that would be the economic growth engine of a large urbanized region. In the idealized model, the airport and its terminals, shopping arcades, business offices, conference centres and hotels are the nucleus of the aerotropolis surrounded by logistics parks, free trade zones, wholesale merchandise marts and e-commerce fulfilment facilities. Ground transportation corridors called 'aerolanes' connect the airport with business parks, research/technology parks, industrial parks, warehouse districts, distribution centres, hotel and entertainment districts, office corridors and information-communication technology (ICT) corridors, as well as residential areas located farther away.

The aerotropolis concept has become quite popular among city politicians, economic development planners and real estate developers throughout the world. A growing number of cities have developed or are developing aerotropolis plans. Perhaps the most famous is Dubai, which has developed an integrated strategy to link the global services of Emirates Air, its hub at Dubai International Airport (13th largest in the world, based on total passengers), and the new Al Maktoum International Airport as part of the Dubai World Central aerotropolis featuring specialized free zones focused on fast-cycle logistics and aviation industries. Dubai World Central is adjacent to the Jebel Ali Seaport, the sixth largest container terminal in the world and nearby business, hotel and convention facilities, connected by motorways and a proposed high-speed rail network (Duserv Facilities Management, 2012). Singapore's Changi Airport (18th largest in the world) serves as the focal point for an aerotropolis containing the Airport Logistics Park of Singapore (ALPS), distribution centres in Changi South and Changi North, and the Loyang industrial estate featuring light manufacturing and distribution operations for high-tech, air freight dependent firms (Bowen, 2010). Significant emerging aerotropolis development can also be found in Amsterdam, Bangkok, Beijing, Dallas-Ft. Worth, Denver, Detroit, Hong Kong, Kuala Lumpur, Seoul and Shanghai, among other cities (Kasarda and Lindsay, 2011).

While the aerotropolis concept has captivated many economic development promoters and elected officials, there are nevertheless some significant concerns about it, especially regarding its sustainability. First and foremost, aerotropolis-related development relies upon the sustainability of air transport, which is problematic for the reasons already mentioned (see section 2). Second, an urban development pattern that is based on an aerotropolis is likely to be relatively low-density and extensive in its space utilization, thus contributing to increased urban sprawl as well as longer and more frequent trips made by motor vehicles, which then contribute to more energy use, atmospheric pollution and other negative externalities. Third, aerotropolis developments explicitly include residential land use and, even though its location in the aerotropolis model is farther from the airport than other land uses, there should be significant concerns about the noise impacts from airports on residences as well as other noise-sensitive activities near airports.

4.   DEVELOPMENTAL IMPACTS: DENVER INTERNATIONAL AIRPORT CASE STUDY

During the 1980s, the city of Denver, Colorado, USA decided to build a new airport to replace aging Stapleton International (located seven miles from Denver's CBD), which was experiencing rapid passenger growth but faced expansion constraints because it had become nearly surrounded by urban development. At that time, Denver Stapleton was one of the busiest airports in the world since it served as a hub to three airlines (United, Continental and Frontier) in the early years of US airline deregulation. Passenger projections indicated that Stapleton would soon exceed its capacity, resulting in congestion and delays that would stunt air transport growth and economic development in Denver and the surrounding region. The new Denver International Airport (DIA) would be located 23 miles away from Denver's CBD on a 53-square-mile site that had a full build-out capacity for 12 runways and 200 million passengers per year, thus allowing economic development opportunities to expand greatly (Dempsey et al., 1997).

While the construction of DIA was beset by numerous problems, the new airport was finally opened in 1995, and Stapleton was closed. The largest problem was the ill-fated effort to build a fully automated baggage system throughout the airport that resulted in several years of delay and significant cost overruns.[2] Originally estimated in 1988 to cost a total of $1.7 billion, the final cost for the airport grew to more than $5 billion. DIA faced other problems in its first few years such as slower-than-expected passenger growth due in part to the acquisition of Frontier by Continental Airlines (via People Express) in the late 1980s, the decision by Continental in 1994 to dismantle its hub operations in Denver, as well as overall higher airline fares because of higher rental and landing fees at the new airport. These initial setbacks limited passenger growth and the economic benefits of the new airport in its early years, though the airport itself remained profitable.

Since it opened, DIA has steadily increased its total passenger activity from 38 million in 1997 to 53 million by 2011, currently ranking as the 5th busiest airport in the US and 11th busiest in the world (Denver International Airport, 2012a). DIA has grown largely due to its role as a domestic hub airport for United Airlines and for the reconstituted low-cost Frontier Airlines, as well as being a focus city for Southwest Airlines since it restarted service to Denver in 2006. Denver is well-suited to be a domestic hub because of its geographical situation as a relatively large city in the interior US that has both centrality and intermediacy[3] between the west coast and the Midwest, south and east. Cost per passenger enplanement is down 31 per cent from 2001, from $15.28 to $10.59, which has improved DIA's competitiveness with other airports (Newmark, Knight, Frank Capital Group, 2012). DIA currently operates six runways, including one 16,000-foot runway that was specially designed for heavily laden aircraft embarking on long international flights to take off in Denver's thinner high-altitude air. Due in part to Denver's interior location, international service has thus far been limited to nonstop flights only to Canada, Mexico and a few destinations in Europe (London, Frankfurt, Reykjavik), although DIA recently announced a nonstop flight to Tokyo will be provided by United Airlines starting in March 2013.[4] It is expected that the new route to Asia will help to recruit new companies and generate more than $130 million in annual economic benefits to Denver and the surrounding region (Denver International Airport, 2012b).

The economic benefits from DIA have grown in conjunction with increasing air traffic. A 2008 study estimated direct, indirect, and induced economic impacts from DIA in the form of 217,000 jobs generating more than $7 billion in payroll, resulting in a total annual economic output of $22 billion, which was a substantial increase over previous estimates in 1998 and 2003 (Wilbur Smith and Associates, 2008). The same study found through a survey of businesses in Colorado that 72 per cent of respondents indicated that

Figure 24.2   Denver's proposed new 'Airport City'

proximity to a major commercial service airport was important to their decision to locate in Colorado. DaVita Inc., a Fortune 500 company, relocated its corporate headquarters to downtown Denver in 2009, and one of their primary reasons was high-quality air service and future rail transit access from downtown to DIA.[5]

The local area land-use around DIA has also started to become more developed since the airport opened, and recently-announced plans for a new 'Airport City' aim to develop the area around DIA into an emerging aerotropolis (Figure 24.2). Since DIA was located 23 miles north-east from downtown Denver in a quadrant of the metropolitan area that had not experienced much development, most of the land in and around DIA's 53-square-mile site remained open prairie after the new airport opened. The most active land development has since occurred in the Gateway area at the junction of Interstate Highway 70 and Pena Boulevard, the main access road into the airport.

Several mixed-use developments, offices, hotels, industrial parks, retail and residential activities have been built in the Gateway corridor, resulting in significant population growth for the adjacent Montbello and Green Valley Ranch neighbourhoods of Denver. Airport-related development has also occurred along the E-470 beltway corridor in the nearby jurisdictions of Aurora, Brighton, Commerce City and Adams County, including new office parks, new medical centres, a justice centre and a stadium for the Colorado Rapids professional soccer team (Davidson, 2006).

Closer to the airport itself, new areas for future development have been identified as part of the ambitious Airport City Denver plan announced in April 2012. Organized into Aero, Agro, Center, Logistics and Tech clusters, the plan calls for hotels, retail, renewable-energy research sites, power generating systems, agricultural sites, manufacturing and logistics activities to flank airport runways and access roads. City officials estimated the full development of the projects proposed in the plan could create 25,000 construction jobs, followed by some 30,000 jobs within the Airport City development and 40,000 elsewhere in metro Denver (Harden, 2012). Shortly after the Airport City Denver plan was announced, however, officials from Adams County, Aurora, Brighton and Commerce City objected to the aerotropolis plan because they contended it violated a 1988 intergovernmental agreement that originally allowed Denver to annex the land for the airport from Adams County and that limited potential development on the airport site (Robles, 2012). Adams County and the nearby municipalities wanted to ensure that airport-related development would also be located in their jurisdictions, and not just on the City and County of Denver airport site. Denver Mayor Michael Hancock has expressed optimism that a new agreement can be reached that would allow Denver's aerotropolis plan to move forward, but thus far no such agreement has been reached.

While city officials and consultants have been characteristically ebullient about the economic development impacts from DIA, there is nevertheless some negative fallout from the financial costs of building the airport, as well as questions about the long-term sustainability of air transport and the sprawling urban development that the airport has exacerbated. The $5 billion price tag for DIA was three times higher than original estimates, which represented a drag on the local economy especially in the airport's early years of operation. There are also concerns about the trajectory of urban growth in the Denver area wherein current regional plans call for higher-density, infill development and less reliance on single-occupant vehicle use. The location of DIA on the urban fringe has contributed to the outward extension of the urbanized area as businesses and residences have been developed at locations near the airport. Most of this development is low-density and automobile-oriented which has not contributed to the goals of current smart growth planning in the Denver area (Goetz, 2013).

5.   CONCLUSIONS

There is considerable theoretical and empirical evidence supporting the contention that airports and air transport activities are major contributors to economic development at multiple geographical scales. The high level of investment in new and expanded airport facilities in the largest cities around the world shows that city officials, airport authorities, national aviation agencies, economic development consortiums and private businesses are very supportive of airport infrastructure and believe in the role it plays in fostering economic development. The new airport building boom, especially in China and the Asia-Pacific region as well as the United Arab Emirates and other parts of the Middle East, is quite ambitious and indicative of the great potential that is related to air transport. Many cities wish to develop an 'aerotropolis' of economic activities around their airports, predicated on the expected role that airports will play in anchoring new economic growth regions of the future. According to Kasarda (2012), 'airports will shape business location and urban development in the 21st century as much as highways did in the 20th century, railroads in the 19th and seaports in the 18th'.

At the same time, some cause for scepticism is raised by concerns over the long-run sustainability of air transport. Relying exclusively on an increasingly expensive non-renewable fuel resource (petroleum) that produces undesirable global and local atmospheric emissions (carbon dioxide, nitrogen oxides), as well as local environmental externalities (noise, water pollution, land take), air transport currently does not score high on the sustainability scale. The aerotropolis concept of urban development is also subject to these same concerns. Nevertheless, the accessibility and mobility characteristics of air transport, especially its speed and geographic coverage over both land and sea, provide advantages that no other mode of transport can approach. For these reasons, air transport will continue to be a very important mode for long-distance and overseas travel. If the sustainability concerns can be addressed, then the economic development prospects for airports and air transport will be much more sanguine.

NOTES

1. Producer services are forms of service activity sold primarily to business and government clients. In contrast to retailing and consumer services that have their primary markets with households for final consumption, producer services are sold as inputs to the production process of various industries (Beyers, 2006).
2. While automated baggage systems are now a common feature in new airports, the scale and complexity of the proposed Denver system was well beyond technological capacity at that time. According to de Neufville (1994: 231–2), 'the enormous increase in complexity, that distinguishes the fully automated baggage system attempted at Denver from all others, represents much more than a simple evolution of technology. It is not just a change from a third to a fourth generation of technology, say; it is more like an attempted leap from the third to the fifth or sixth generation of baggage systems.'
3. According to Fleming and Hayuth (1994), centrality refers to the degree to which a city possesses higher-order central place characteristics, while intermediacy refers to strategic locations between important origins and destinations.
4. The Denver–Tokyo flight was intended to be served by the Boeing 787, which has experienced several fires on-board due to overheating of its lithium ion batteries, resulting in the FAA's decision to ground the plane until the problems can be fixed. The 787 service for Denver–Tokyo was initiated in May 2013.
5. The airport rail link will be completed by 2016 as part of Denver's FasTracks rail transit programme, which will result in 157 miles of light and commuter rail throughout the Denver area (Goetz et al., 2011).

REFERENCES

ACI (1994), *Annual Airport Traffic Statistics, 1993*, Geneva: Airports Council International.
ACI (2012), *Annual Airport Traffic Statistics, 2011*, Geneva: Airports Council International.
Airbus (2012), www.airbus.com/company/worldwide-presence.

Alkaabi, K.A. and Debbage, K.G. (2011), The geography of air freight: connections to US metropolitan economies, *Journal of Transport Geography*, **19**, 1517–29.

Banister, D. (2012), Transport and economic development: reviewing the evidence, *Transport Reviews*, **32**(1), 1–2.

Banister, D. and Berechman, J. (2000), *Transport Investment and Economic Development*, London: UCL Press.

Beyers, W. (2006), Producer services, in *Encyclopedia of Human Geography*, www.credoreference.com.bianca. penlib.du.edu/entry/sagehg/producer_services.

Black, W.R. (2010), *Sustainable Transportation*, New York: The Guilford Press.

Boeing (2012), http://boeing.com/stories/impact.html.

Bowen, J.T. (2010), *The Economic Geography of Air Transportation*, London: Routledge.

Brueckner, J.K. (2003), Airline traffic and urban economic development, *Urban Studies*, **40**(8), 1455–69.

Button, K. and Taylor, S. (2000), International air transportation and economic development, *Journal of Air Transport Management*, **6**, 209–22.

Chapman, K. and Walker, D.F. (1991), *Industrial Location: Principles and Policies*, Oxford: Blackwell.

Chatman, D.G. and Noland, R.B. (2011), do public transit improvements increase agglomeration economies? A review of literature and an agenda for research, *Transport Reviews*, **31**(6), 725–42.

Chung, J.Y. and Whang, T. (2011), The impact of low cost carriers on Korean Island tourism, *Journal of Transport Geography*, **19**, 1335–40.

Cidell, J. (2006), Air transportation, airports, and the discourses and practices of globalization, *Urban Geography*, **27**(7), 651–63.

Davidson, K. (2006), Prairie potential: DIA corridor will create an 'aeropolitan' of new growth and industry over next 30 years, *Colorado Construction*, **9**(8), 18–23, http://colorado.construction.com/features/archive/0604_cover.asp.

Debbage, K. and Delk, D. (2001), The geography of air passenger volume and local employment patterns by US metropolitan core area: 1973–1996, *Journal of Air Transport Management*, **7**, 159–67.

Dempsey, P.S., Goetz, A.R. and Szyliowicz, J.S. (1997), *Denver International Airport: Lessons Learned*, New York: McGraw Hill.

de Neufville, R. (1994), The baggage system at Denver: prospects and lessons, *Journal of Air Transport Management*, **1**(4), 229–36.

Denver International Airport (2012a), *Traffic Statistics*, http://business.flydenver.com/stats/traffic/index.asp.

Denver International Airport (2012b), The wait is over: Denver to Tokyo nonstop begins March 2013, *WingTips Newsletter*, **4**(6).

Donzelli, M. (2010), The effect of low-cost air transportation on the local economy: evidence from Southern Italy, *Journal of Air Transport Management*, **16**, 121–6.

Duserv Facilities Management (2010), *Dubai World Central*, www.duservefm.com/site/index.php/about-us/dubai-world-central.

Elgar, I. and Miller, E.J. (2010), How do office firms conduct their location search process? An analysis of a survey from the Greater Toronto Area, *International, Regional Science Review*, **33**, 60–85.

Fleming, D.K. and Hayuth, Y. (1994), Spatial characteristics of transportation hubs: centrality and intermediacy, *Journal of Transport Geography*, **2**(1), 3–18.

Florida, R. (2002), *The Rise of the Creative Class and How It's Transforming Work, Leisure, Community, and Everyday Life*, New York: Basic Books.

Florida, R. (2012), Airports and the wealth of cities, *The Atlantic Cities*, May 23, www.theatlanticcities.com/commute/2012/05/airports-and-wealth-cities/855.

Fujita, M., Krugman, P. and Venables, A. (1999), *The Spatial Economy*, Cambridge, MA: MIT Press.

Garreau, J. (1991), *Edge City: Life on the New Frontier*, New York: Doubleday.

Gilbert, R. and Perl, A. (2010), *Transport Revolutions: Moving People and Freight Without Oil*, Gabriola Island, BC: New Society Publishers.

Giuliano, G. (2004), Land use impacts of transportation investments: highway and transit, in S. Hanson and G. Giuliano (eds), *The Geography of Urban Transportation*, New York: The Guilford Press.

Goetz, A.R. (1992), Air passenger transportation and growth in the US urban system: 1950–1987, *Growth and Change*, **23**, 217–38.

Goetz, A.R. (2011), The global economic crisis, investment in transport infrastructure, and economic development, in K. Button and A. Reggiani (eds), *Transportation and Economic Development Challenges*, Cheltenham: Edward Elgar Publishers, pp. 41–71.

Goetz, A.R. (2013), Suburban sprawl or urban centers: tensions and contradictions of smart growth approaches in Denver, Colorado, *Urban Studies*, **50**(11), 2178–95.

Goetz, A.R. and Graham, B.J. (2004), Air transport globalization, liberalization and sustainability: post-2001 policy dynamics in the United States and Europe, *Journal of Transport Geography*, **12**, 265–76.

Goetz, A.R. and Vowles, T.M. (2009), The good, the bad, and the ugly: 30 years of US airline deregulation, *Journal of Transport Geography*, **17**(4), 251–63.

Goetz, A.R., Jonas, A.E.G. and Bhattacharjee, S. (2011), *Regional Collaboration in Transport Infrastructure Provision: The Case of Denver's FasTracks Rail Transit Program*, final report, National Center for Intermodal Transportation, University of Denver.

Gossling, S. and Upham, P. (2009), Introduction: aviation and climate change in context, in S. Gossling and P. Upham (eds), *Climate Change and Aviation: Issues, Challenges and Solutions*, London: Earthscan.

Graham, A. (2001), *Managing Airports: An International Perspective*, Oxford: Butterworth Heinemann.

Graham, B. (2008), New air services: tourism and economic development, in A. Graham, A. Papatheodorou and P. Forsyth (eds), *Aviation and Tourism: Implications for Leisure Travel*, Aldershot: Ashgate, pp. 227–38.

Graham, B. and Goetz, A.R. (2008), Global air transport, in R. Knowles, J. Shaw and I. Docherty, *Transport Geographies: Mobilities, Spaces, and Flows*, Oxford: Blackwell, pp. 137–55.

Green, R.K. (2007), Airports and economic development, *Real Estate Economics*, **35**(1), 91–112.

Hakfoort, J., Poot, T. and Rietveld, P. (2001), The regional economic impact of an airport: the case of Amsterdam Schiphol Airport, *Regional Studies*, **35**(7), 595–604.

Harden, M. (2012), Denver unveils 'Airport City' plan to guide DIA commercial development, *Denver Business Journal*, April 26, www.bizjournals.com/denver/news/2012/04/26/denver-unveils-airport-city-plan-to.html.

Harris, C.D. (1997), The nature of cities and urban geography in the last half century, *Urban Geography*, **18**(1), 15–35.

Hartshorn, T.A. and Muller, P.O. (1989), Suburban downtowns and the transformation of metropolitan Atlanta's business landscape, *Urban Geography*, **10**, 375–95.

Hoover, E. (1948), *The Location of Economic Activity*, New York: McGraw-Hill.

IATA (2012), *The Value of Aviation*, www.iata.org/events/agm/2012/Documents/2012-agm-value-of-aviation-briefing.pdf.

Irwin, M.D. and Kasarda, J.D. (1991), Air passenger linkages and employment growth in metropolitan areas, *American Sociological Review*, **56**, 524–37.

Isard, W. (1956), *Location and the Space Economy*, Cambridge, MA: MIT Press.

Ivy, R.L., Fik, T.J. and Malecki, E.J. (1995), Changes in air service connectivity and employment, *Environment & Planning A*, **27**, 165–79.

Kasarda, J.D. (2012), Aerotropolis, www.aerotropolis.com.

Kasarda, J.D. and Lindsay, G. (2011), *Aerotropolis: The Way We'll Live Next*, New York: Farrar, Straus and Giroux.

Krugman, P. (1991), *Geography and Trade*, Leuven, Belgium: Leuven University Press and Cambridge, MA: MIT Press.

Lakshmanan, T.R. (2010), The broader economic consequences of transport infrastructure investments, *Journal of Transport Geography*, **19**, 1–12.

Lavee, D., Beniad, G. and Solomon, C. (2011), The effect of investment in transportation infrastructure on the debt-to-GDP ratio, *Transport Reviews*, **31**(6), 769–89.

Markusen, A., Hall, P. and Glasmeier, A. (1986), *High Tech America: The What, How, Where, and Why of the Sunrise Industries*, Boston: Allen & Unwin.

Newmark, Knight, Frank Capital Group (2012), *DIA Porteos*, www.denveraerotropolis.com/docs/Current_Economic_Impact-n-Airport_Efficiencies_DIA_Porteos.pdf.

Percoco, M. (2010), Airport activity and local development: evidence from Italy, *Urban Studies*, **47**(11), 2427–43.

Porter, M. (1990), *The Competitive Advantage of Nations*, New York: Free Press.

Reich, R. (1999), *The Work of Nations*, New York: Alfred A. Knopf.

Rietveld, P. and Bruinsma, F. (1998), *Is Transport Infrastructure Effective? Transport Infrastructure and Accessibility: Impacts on the Space-Economy*, Berlin: Springer-Verlag.

Robles, Y. (2012), Adams County: Denver aerotropolis bigfoots prior agreement, *The Denver Post*, August 1, www.denverpost.com/breakingnews/ci_21211923/adams-county-denver-aerotropolis-big-foots-prior-agreement.

Taaffe, E.J., Gauthier, H.L. and O'Kelly, M.E. (1996), *The Geography of Transportation*, 2nd edn, Upper Saddle River: Prentice Hall.

Ullman, E.L. (1956), The Role of transportation and the bases for interaction, in W.L. Thomas (ed.), *Man's Role in Changing the Face of the Earth*, Chicago: University of Chicago Press.

Upham, P., Maughan, J., Raper, D. and Thomas, C. (eds) (2003), *Towards Sustainable Aviation*, London: Earthscan.

Vance, J.E. (1977), *The Scene of Man: The Role and Structure of the City in the Geography of Western Civilization*, New York: HarperCollins.

Vickerman, R. (2008), *Recent Evolution of Research into the Wider Economic Benefit of Transport Infrastructure Investments*, Round Table on Macro, Meso and Micro Infrastructure Planning and Assessment Tools, Paris: ECMT.

Weber, A. (1929), *Alfred Weber's Theory of the Location of Industries*, Chicago: University of Chicago Press.

Wilbur Smith and Associates, Inc. (2008), *The Economic Impact of Airports in Colorado 2008*, prepared for

Colorado Department of Transportation, Division of Aeronautics, www.coloradodot.info/programs/aeronautics/PDF_Files/2008TechReport.pdf.

World Commission on Environment and Development (1987), *Our Common Future*, Oxford: Oxford University Press.

World Travel & Tourism Council (2012), *Travel & Tourism: Economic Impact 2012, World*, www.wttc.org/site_media/uploads/downloads/world2012.pdf.

York Aviation (2004), *The Social and Economic Impact of Airports*, Geneva: ACI-Europe.

Yu, N., De Jong, M., Storm, S. and Mi, J. (2012), Transport infrastructure, spatial clusters, and regional economic growth in China, *Transport Reviews*, **32**(1): 3–28.

25 Decision-making and major transport infrastructure projects: the role of project ownership

Chantal C. Cantarelli and Bent Flyvbjerg

1. INTRODUCTION

Major projects are often defined as projects that cost more than US$1 billion (Flyvbjerg et al., 2003a). In addition to the size of the project in terms of costs, large-scale projects attract a high level of public attention or political interest because of substantial direct and indirect impacts on the community, environment, and budgets (FHWA in Capka, 2004). Overall, the main characteristics of major projects can be described by the '6Cs' of Frick (2005): colossal, captivating, costly, controversial, complex, and laden with control issues. The characteristics are interrelated; colossal projects are usually more costly and complex and can become more controversial because they often captivate more stakeholders and citizens.

A main problem in decision-making for major infrastructure projects is the high level of misinformation about costs and benefits that decision-makers face in deciding whether to build projects, and the high risks such misinformation generates. Construction cost and demand forecasts are the basis for socio-economic and environmental appraisal of transport infrastructure projects. Governments and parliaments base their decisions on incorrect information resulting in underestimated costs and overestimated benefits threatening project viability. Furthermore misinformation undermines parliament's ability to exercise democratic control (Flyvbjerg, 2008).

Let us examine the problem of inaccurate cost forecasts in more detail. There are four main concerns with cost overruns (Flyvbjerg, 2007). First, they lead to a Pareto-inefficient allocation of resources, i.e., waste. Cost forecasts are often inaccurate but the margin by which costs are incorrectly estimated (indicated by the large standard deviations of the mean) differs across projects. This may affect the ranking of projects and, as a result, decision-makers are likely to implement inferior projects. As the total budget for infrastructure investments is generally fixed, additional budget for projects that become more expensive than was initially estimated can affect the budget for other projects. Cost overruns therefore not only result in financial wastage, they may also ultimately result in fewer infrastructure projects being realized than planned. Second, cost overruns lead to delays and further cost overruns. When confronted with cost overruns, projects must often be renegotiated or reapproved, and additional efforts must be made to secure funding (Flyvbjerg et al., 2004). This inevitably takes time and consequently increases the project's costs even further. Third, cost overruns destabilize policy, planning, implementation, and operations of projects. Cost overruns can lead to continuous reapproval and unrest in the project organization and parliament. Fourth, the problem is getting bigger because projects get bigger. Needless to say, the financial consequences of cost overruns in terms of net total overrun increase with project size. Moreover, when projects become more and more expensive and still involve cost overruns, the financial consequences can become so large that it may destabilise the finances of a whole country or region. This occurred when the billion-dollar cost overrun on the 2004 Athens Olympics affected the credit rating of Greece and when revenue shortfalls hit Hong Kong's new US$20 billion Chek Lap Kok airport after it opened in 1998 (Flyvbjerg, 2007).

Throughout most of the twentieth century, much of the funding of large transport infrastructure projects came from public sources of capital (Brealey, 1996). In recent years, however, increased financial pressures on public funds, misallocation of such funds, and neoliberal ideology have led to the revival of private financing for infrastructure (Debande, 2002). More specifically, the literature gives the following reasons for increased privatization: (1) private funds may substitute for public funds when such funds are scarce, (2) involving the private sector may increase efficiency and value for money where project management capacities of private parties are superior to those found in the public sector, and (3) early involvement of private expertise may lead to better optimized and more innovative designs (Savas, 2000; Osborne, 2000; Van Ham and Koppenjan, 2001; Akintoye et al., 2003; Lobina and Hall, 2003 in Koppenjan and Leijten, 2007). However, regarding cost escalation there is, so far, little evidence that would demonstrate that private projects do indeed perform better than public ones.

The present study focuses on the accuracy of cost forecasts and the influence of ownership on cost performance. The state-of-the-art on cost overruns is described and the results of a first study on the relation between ownership and cost overruns are presented. A case study is presented to give more insight in PPP projects. The focus will be on transport infrastructure projects but comparative research shows that the issues addressed apply to a wide range of other project types, including power plants, dams, water projects, and information technology systems (Altshuler and Luberoff, 2003; Flyvbjerg et al. 2002, 2003a, 2005).

2.   INACCURACY OF COST FORECASTS

Inaccuracy in construction cost forecasts is measured as *actual costs minus forecasted costs as a percentage of forecasted costs*. An inaccuracy of zero means that the forecasted cost for the project was correct and thus equalled actual costs. Actual costs are defined as real, accounted construction costs determined at the time of project completion. Estimated costs are defined as budgeted or forecasted construction costs determined at the time of formal decision to build. This is also called the 'decision date', 'the time of the decision to proceed', or the 'go-decision' (Flyvbjerg et al., 2003a). At that moment, cost estimates were often available as data for decision-makers to make an informed decision.

One of the largest quantitative studies on cost overruns is by Flyvbjerg et al. (2002, 2003a, 2003b, 2004). The study includes 258 (land-based) transport infrastructure projects with comparable data for forecasted and actual construction costs. The projects were located in 20 nations on five continents, including both developed and developing nations. The main findings are as follows:

Table 25.1   Average cost overrun for rail, fixed links (bridges and tunnels) and roads

Type of project	Number of cases (N)	Average cost overrun (%)	Standard deviation (sd)	Level of significance, p
Rail	58	44.7	38.4	<0.001
Fixed links	33	33.8	62.4	<0.004
Road	167	20.4	29.9	<0.001

Source: Adjusted from Flyvbjerg (2008: 127)

- Cost escalation happens in almost nine out of ten projects. For a randomly selected project, the likelihood of actual costs being larger than forecast costs is 86 per cent. The likelihood of actual costs being lower than or equal to forecast cost is 14 per cent.
- Forecast costs are biased and the bias is caused by systematic underestimation.
- Costs are not only underestimated much more often than they are overestimated or correct, costs that have been underestimated are also wrong by a substantially larger margin than costs that have been overestimated.

The error of underestimating costs is significantly much more common and much larger than the error of overestimating costs. Underestimation of costs at the time of decision to build is the rule rather than the exception for transport infrastructure projects. Frequent and substantial cost escalation is the result (Flyvbjerg, 2003b).

Cost Overrun by Project Type

Table 25.1 shows the average cost overrun for rail, fixed links (bridges and tunnels) and roads.

For all project types average cost overrun is significantly different from zero. Rail projects incur the highest difference between actual and estimated costs with an average of 44.7 per cent, followed by fixed links averaging 33.8 per cent and roads with 20.4 per cent ($p < 0.001$, F-test).

Geographical Variations

Considering geographical variations in cost overrun, three geographical areas were identified: Europe, North America, and 'other geographical areas' (a group of ten developing nations plus Japan). *Table 25.2* shows the cost overruns in these three geographical areas.

For fixed links as well as road projects, cost overrun is the smallest in North America compared to Europe, with an average overrun of 25.7 per cent versus 43.4 per cent for fixed links, and an average overrun of 8.4 per cent versus 22.4 per cent for road projects. On the contrary, cost overruns for rail projects are the smallest in Europe with an average overrun of 34.2 per cent against 40.8 per cent in North America. However, the differences in average cost overrun between Europe and North America are not statistically significant for fixed links, road or rail ($p = 0.414$, $p = 0.184$, and $p = 0.510$ respectively).

Table 25.2   Cost overrun in Europe, North America and other geographical areas

Type of project	Europe			North America			Other geographical areas		
	Number of projects	Average cost overrun	SD	Number of projects	Average cost overrun	SD	Number of projects	Average cost overrun	SD
Rail	23	34.2	25.1	19	40.8	36.8	16	64.6	49.5
Fixed links	15	43.4	52.0	18	25.7	70.5	0	–	–
Road	143	22.4	24.9	24	8.4	49.4	0	–	–
Total	181	25.7	28.7	61	23.6	54.2	16	64.6	49.5

Inaccuracy Over Time

Flyvbjerg et al. (2004) further examined whether project performance, as regards cost escalation, has improved over time. Time may be measured by year of decision to build a project or by year of completion (the year operations begin). According to Flyvbjerg et al. (2003b) 'it is better to use year of decision to build rather than year of completion; the latter includes length of implementation phase, which has an influence on cost escalation, causing confounding'. However, data on the year of completion is more evident and hence more reliable. For the moment, both variables are used to measure time. Based on statistical analyses the null hypothesis that year of decision has an effect on cost overrun cannot be supported ($p = 0.22$, F-test). A test using year of completion instead of year of decision gives a similar result ($p = 0.28$, F-test).

Similar analyses have been carried out with year of decision combined with the logarithm of estimated cost as a measure of the size of projects, also split into rail, fixed links, and roads. Year of completion and logarithm of actual cost were also tried. In no case could any statistical significant result be established, neither with main effects nor with interactions (Flyvbjerg et al., 2004). Accuracy in cost forecasting has thus not improved over time. The next section will address the main explanations for cost inaccuracy in more detail.

3.   EXPLANATIONS

Three main types of explanation exist that claim to account for inaccuracy in forecasts of costs: technical, psychological, and political-economic explanations (Flyvbjerg, 2007).

Technical explanations account for cost overruns in terms of imperfect forecasting techniques, inadequate data, honest mistakes, lack of experience, etc. This is the most common type of explanation of inaccuracy in forecasts (Ascher, 1978; Flyvbjerg et al, 2002, 2005; Morris and Hough, 1987; Wachs, 1990). However, data of the large-sample study described in the previous sections do not fit the data. There are two main reasons for rejecting technical explanations of forecasting errors (Flyvbjerg et al., 2002). First, if misleading forecasts were truly caused by technical inadequacies, simple mistakes, etc., we would expect a less biased distribution of errors in cost estimates around zero, but this is not the case. Second, if imperfect techniques, inadequate data and lack of experience were main explanations of the underestimations, an improvement in forecasting accuracy over time would be expected, since errors and their sources would be recognized and addressed through the refinement of data collection, forecasting methods, etc. Again, accuracy has not improved over time. For technical explanations to be valid, they would have to explain why forecasts are so consistent in ignoring cost risks over time, location, and project type.

Psychological explanations attempt to explain biases in forecasts by a bias in the mental makeup of project promoters and forecasters. The most common psychological explanation is probably 'appraisal optimism'. According to this explanation, promoters, and forecasters are held to be overly optimistic about project outcomes in the appraisal phase, when projects are planned and decided (Fouracre et al., 1990; Mackie and Preston, 1998; Walmsley and Pickett, 1992; World Bank, 1994). An optimistic cost estimate is a low one and if appraisal optimism is a cause of cost overrun, the actual costs would be higher than the estimated costs. The systematic underestimation of costs points to the existence of appraisal optimism.

Political-economic explanations see planners and promoters as deliberately and strategically underestimating costs when forecasting the outcomes of projects. They do this in order to increase the likelihood that it is their projects, and not those of the competition, that gain approval and funding. Political-economic explanations and strategic misrepresentation account well for the systematic underestimation of costs found in the data. A strategic estimate of costs would be low, resulting in cost overrun. Optimism bias and strategic misrepresentation both involve deception, but where the latter is intentional – i.e., lying – the first is not. Optimism bias is self-deception.

Considering these three types of explanation, political-economic explanations are likely to account less for the cost overruns for privately owned projects as compared to that of publicly owned projects. Private projects are less vulnerable to the strategic behaviour that is typical in the principal–agent relationship. They do not have an incentive to provide inaccurate cost estimates because they have to bear the risk of cost overruns. The next section will present the results of a first systematic study on the role of ownership in cost overruns and examine whether private projects indeed perform better than public projects as may be expected from the above.

4.   OWNERSHIP AND COST OVERRUN

Flyvbjerg et al. (2004) tested systematically whether cost development varies with type of ownership of transport infrastructure projects. Based on a sample of 258 projects, data on ownership was established for 183 of the projects. Three types of ownership were distinguished, private ownership and two types of public ownership, namely state-owned enterprise and conventional public ownership (here called 'other public ownership'). State-owned enterprises are corporations owned by government and are typically organized according to a companies act, for instance as incorporated or limited companies with the state as sole or dominant owner. Other public ownership has a ministry typically owning the project, which appears in the public budgets (Flyvbjerg et al., 2004).

The influence of ownership on cost overruns for roads could not be analysed because all projects were of a conventional form of public ownership. For rail projects, the two

Table 25.3   Ownership and percentage cost overrun for rail

Ownership	Average cost overrun (%)			
	Number of projects	High-speed rail	Urban rail	Conventional rail
State-owned	9	88.0	35.5	–
Other public	16	15.0	53.5	29.6

Table 25.4   Ownership and percentage cost overrun for fixed links

Ownership	Number of projects	Average cost overrun (%)	Standard Deviation
Private	4	34.0	30.1
State-owned	3	110.0	71.5
Other Public	6	23.1	33.6

types of public ownership were present in the sample. *Table 25.3* shows the average cost overrun for rail projects, divided in high-speed rail, urban rail, and conventional rail.

For high-speed rail, state-owned enterprises have the highest average cost overrun with 88 per cent compared with other publicly owned projects with an average overrun of 15 per cent (p = 0.001, Welch t-test). Despite the statistical significant difference in cost performance between different types of ownership, the data are scant and from projects on different continents. It is therefore impossible to say whether the difference can be attributed to ownership alone or whether geographical location of projects also plays a role.

In contrast to high-speed rail, for urban rail, state-owned enterprises have the lowest average cost overrun with 35.5 per cent compared to other publicly owned projects with an average overrun of 53.5 per cent. However, this difference is not statistically significant (p = 0.179) and hence the difference could be due to chance.

For fixed link projects, all three types of ownership were present in the sample. *Table 25.4* shows the cost performance and ownership for fixed link projects.

The result in cost performance by ownership is quite surprising. State-owned enterprises show the poorest cost performance with an average cost overrun of 110 per cent, followed by privately owned fixed links with an average of 34 per cent and then other publicly owned projects with an average of 23.1 per cent. A standard one-way analysis of variance shows the difference in average cost overrun between ownership type to be statistically significant (p = 0.028). However, the difference in average cost overrun between privately owned and other publicly owned projects is not statistically significant (p = 0.589, non-paired t-test).

Based on these results, one cannot make firm conclusions that privately owned projects perform better than publicly owned projects, or vice versa. This is partly the consequence of the small number of privately owned projects in the sample.

However, the study showed a considerable difference in cost performance between state-owned and other publicly owned projects. This suggests that the problem in relation to cost overruns is not necessarily one of public versus private ownership but a certain kind of public ownership. Moreover, it is questioned whether it is ownership at all that makes a difference in cost performance between projects. In many publicly owned projects, private parties are involved in varying degrees. The extent of private party involvement can usually be seen by the type of contracting that is used. In a 'design, build' contract, most responsibilities lie with the public party, while in a 'design, build, finance, maintain' contract, a large extent of the responsibilities lie with the private party. Different contract types thus specify the role of private parties but with the exception of 'build, own, operate' contracts, it is typically the public sector that remains the owner. A concessionaire may be the owner during the concession period, but at the end of the concession, ownership transfers back to the public authority. The contracting type would in this respect seem a better indicator to test cost performance. The hypothesis to be tested would then be that projects with a higher level of private involvement reflected in the contracting strategy have better cost performances.

The next section will illustrate how private involvement influenced the project performance in the case of the HSL-South project, a high-speed railway line in the Netherlands.

5.   CASE STUDY: HSL-SOUTH

The HSL-South is a 125km high-speed railway line from Amsterdam to the Dutch-Belgian border, with stops at Schiphol, Rotterdam, and Breda. At the Dutch-Belgian border, the HSL-South connects with the Belgian and European network of high speed lines.

Traditionally railways in the Netherlands were placed in the hands of the state-owned monopolist, the Nederlandse Spoorwegen (NS, Dutch Railways), and construction was publicly financed and operations heavily subsidized (Teulings and Koopmans, 2004; Pickrell, 1992). For the HSL-South it was decided to follow a different contracting strategy. The project would be profit-making, the government believed, and it was therefore decided to use a public–private partnership (PPP) contracting model (Koppenjan and Leijten, 2005; Hertogh et al., 2008). Different types of contracting were used for different parts of the project. A 'design, build, finance, and maintain' contract was acquired by the Infraspeed Consortium for the superstructure (rails, sleepers, and other parts of a railway) (Priemus, 2009; Hertogh et al., 2008). ProRail, the infrastructure management company, pays €118 million per year (2000 price levels, VAT exclusive) to Infraspeed who in return has an obligation to guarantee 99 per cent track availability. The whole civil engineering substructure (foundation, earth bank, or bed supporting railroad tracks) was divided into seven 'design and construct' contracts (equivalent to 'design and build') (Priemus, 2009), which in total amounted to €2,592 million paid by the Dutch government (Hertogh et al., 2008). For the transport services an operating contract was awarded to NS Hispeed for a concession of 15 years for both domestic and international transport. For use of the infrastructure, HSA (High Speed Alliance, of which NS Hispeed is 90 per cent shareholder) pays a user fee of €148 million per year (2000 price levels, VAT exclusive). This payment will be part to cover the costs of construction, and part to compensate ProRail for the provision of capacity and traffic management, traffic control, and other administrative services.

Despite political will, private interest (and actual realized private contribution), and expected profitability, the government was confronted with extensive cost overruns. The actual costs at the time of opening in 2009 turned out to be 55 per cent higher (constant prices) than the total project budget at the time of formal decision to build in 1996.

The remainder of this section will describe how the institutional set-up, and particularly the contracting strategy and distribution of risks, led to problems of cost overruns. The case study is mainly based on the reports by the Temporary Committee Infrastructure projects (TCI, 2004), who conducted extensive research into this project.

In 1999, the Dutch government started the tender procedures for all of the HSL-South contracts at the same time. Contracting out the Green Heart tunnel proved relatively easy. This is a 9km long tunnel under the Green Heart, a protected open area between the urban conglomerations in the western part of the Netherlands. Contracting of this tunnel was successful as foreign companies participated and costs were significantly reduced due to the innovative proposals.

However, for the other contracts, the strategy to contract out the substructure turned out to be a failure; the total cost based on the offers by contractors was 43 per cent higher than the budget. Even by dividing the substructure into several contracts, increasing the number of possible candidates to get involved in the tender procedures, the anticipated competition and consequently 'good' price was not realized. This can partly be explained by the parallel contracting out of many infrastructure projects, by the collusion between market parties and by the decision to simultaneously contract out the different design and build substructure contracts. Further, the lack of competition was the result of the nature and size of the contracts that excluded foreign consortiums and small and middle-size companies (Koppenjan and Leijten, 2005: 194).

In order to lower the bids for the substructure, the government decided, among other things, to take responsibility for many of the risks that were previously allocated to potential contractors. For example, it removed the penalty clause for contractors and was now responsible for timely availability of the substructure. In this way, the government obliged itself to pay €23 million a month in case of late delivery. Further, during the project, many of the risks foreseen actually occurred, which caused a damaged relationship between client and constructors and higher costs for the government (Hertogh et al., 2008). The decision to split the project into three parts with a different contracting strategy for each part increased the interface risks for the state. It was difficult to connect the substructure to the superstructure due to the fact that the functional specifications within the separate contracts contained insufficient tolerances to deal with any innovations (Hertogh et al., 2008). The state has these interface risks and has a crucial coordinating role to manage these risks that went way beyond the government's capacity and capability (Priemus, 2009).

For the superstructure, the actual bids that were received were also higher than estimated with a difference between 50 and 80 per cent. Beside the aforementioned reasons for the higher bids in the substructure contracting, the result of the public sector comparator (PSC) may explain the difference between the estimate and actual bids. The PSC tests whether a private investment proposal offers value for money in comparison with the most efficient form of public procurement. For the HSL-South, the PSC concluded that the private implementation of the contract would cost less than public implementation. This result was an important argument to continue with private financing. The prognosis about private contributions was however based on arbitrary assumptions;

ex-ante risk analyses and adequate cost distributions were lacking. The estimate of the profitability of the projects was actually too optimistic and the PSC had been used to legitimize a choice for a 'design, build, finance and maintain' contract (Koppenjan and Leijten, 2005: 191). A group of experts declared later that the PSC value was indeed calculated 20 per cent too low (Priemus, 2009). The General Accounting Office also stated, in retrospect, that the calculations were too soft. Commitment to privatization – private involvement had been one of the objectives from the start of the project – may have been the reason for the low PSC value. There was certainly private interest but the size of the private financing and the justification thereof was flawed. Tools like the public private comparator and the public sector comparator, used to assess the value for money of PPP initiatives, prove to be easily manipulated (Pollitt, 2002; Hodge and Greve, 2005; National Audit Office, 1998, 2004).

The transport service also incurred several problems increasing the costs of the HSL-South with another €390 million. First, the value of the concession awarded to HSA was actually much lower; in other words, they were paying too much. Second, the revenues were far fewer than estimated due to the lower number of passengers; the average occupancy of the Fyra, the high-speed train service operating the Dutch HSL-South, was 15 per cent, while that of a regular service train is 29 per cent. The higher-than-estimated costs combined with the lower-than-estimated revenues resulted in serious financial problems for HSA, and would possibly have resulted in bankruptcy by mid-2012 if the government had not interfered.

Since the beginning of 2011, Schultz van Haegen, the Minister of Infrastructure and the Environment, investigated the possibilities to deal with the financial situation of HSA. This resulted in November of that year in an agreement between the minister and NS. It was decided to unite the high-speed line and the main rail network, with the guarantee from the NS that they will be guarantor for HSA in the future. This will assure the operation of high-speed trains on the HSL-South track until 2025. HSA now only has to pay about two-thirds of the original concession amount, with a total loss of earnings of about €390 million instead of €2.4 billion in the case of bankruptcy.

Three main lessons can be learned from this case study. First, private investment proposals need more thorough investigation. Privatization may be highly desired due to the reduced public funds and ex-ante evaluations may therefore include misrepresented figures. The PSC is a useful tool to measure the value of private investments but this instrument is not safe from manipulation either. Second, in consideration of private investments the market situation should be considered in parallel to ensure sufficient competition that allows efficient proposals. Third, governments should forestall taking risks back that were initially attributed to the private party. A higher price may be favourable in this respect because this entails more certainty regarding the total costs of the project.

6.   PUBLIC AND PRIVATE SECTOR ACCOUNTABILITY

From the case study presented in the previous section, it becomes clear that privatization or private involvement is no guarantee for success. On the other hand, by keeping the development and realization of a project in its own hands, a government's relationships with its contractors, project developers, industries, transport companies, and other private parties may get perverted. These actors are free to lobby for public means for infrastructure projects without having to carry any risks or contribute financially (Nijkamp and Ubbels, 1999).

Private involvement can help to identify risks more clearly and to improve the distribution of these risks to those that are best able to bear and manage them. The risks of construction and operation are typically borne by companies, while the government bears the political risks (Flyvbjerg et al., 2003a; Koppenjan and Leijten, 2007). Risk distribution was one of the major failures for the HSL-South project; the public party was eventually responsible for the delays in construction and the resulting cost overruns.

Flyvbjerg et al. (2003a) recommend involving private parties by organizing the decision-making on infrastructure projects according to the following three chronological steps:

1. The project must be defined precisely, and the conditions that are necessary for success must be fulfilled.
2. When this has been realized, private parties can be involved in such a way that they carry financial risks.
3. Only when private parties are committed will the actual decision to realize the project be taken.

In the HSL-South project, first the project decision was taken, next the conditions were assured, and finally the private parties were involved. As a result, the opportunities for private parties to influence the risks were limited; they focused their energy on covering instead of reducing risk. No integral design optimizations were realized, expensive bids were submitted, the government had to take back risks, and, finally, operational risks generated major budget overruns (Koppenjan and Leijten, 2007).

The problem of misinformation is an issue of power and profit and must be dealt with as such, using the mechanisms of transparency and accountability we commonly use in liberal democracies to mitigate rent-seeking behaviour and the misuse of power (Flyvbjerg et al., 2005). Two basic types of accountability define liberal democracies: (1) public sector accountability through transparency and public control, and (2) private sector accountability via competition and market control. Both types of accountability may be effective tools to curb planners' misrepresentation in forecasting and to promote a culture that acknowledges and deals effectively with risk.

In order to achieve public sector accountability through transparency and public control, the following would be required as practices embedded in the relevant institutions:

- National-level government should not offer discretionary grants to local infrastructure agencies for the sole purpose of building a specific type of infrastructure, for instance rail. Such grants create perverse incentives. Instead, national government should simply offer 'infrastructure grants' or 'transportation grants' to local governments and let local political officials spend the funds however they choose, but ensure that every dollar they spend on one type of infrastructure reduces their ability to fund another.

- Forecasts should be made subject to independent peer review. Where large amounts of taxpayers' money are at stake, such a review may be carried out by national or state accounting and auditing offices, like the General Accounting Office in the US or the National Audit Office in the UK, who have the independence and expertise to produce such reviews. Other types of independent review bodies may be established, for instance within national departments of finance or with relevant professional bodies.
- Forecasts should be benchmarked against comparable forecasts, for instance using reference class forecasting as described in the previous section.
- Forecasts, peer reviews, and benchmarkings should be made available to the public as they are produced, including all relevant documentation.
- Public hearings, citizen juries, and the like should be organized to allow stakeholders and civil society to voice criticism and support of forecasts. Knowledge generated in this way should be integrated in planning and decision-making.
- Scientific and professional conferences should be organized where forecasters would present and defend their forecasts in the face of colleagues' scrutiny and criticism.
- Projects with inflated benefit-cost ratios should be reconsidered and stopped if recalculated costs and benefits do not warrant implementation. Projects with realistic estimates of benefits and costs should be rewarded.
- Professional and occasionally even criminal penalties should be enforced for planners and forecasters who consistently and foreseeably produce deceptive forecasts.

An example of a professional penalty would be the exclusion from one's professional organization for violating its code of ethics. An example of a criminal penalty would be punishment as the result of prosecution before a court or similar legal body, for instance where deceptive forecasts have led to substantial mismanagement of public funds (Garett and Wachs, 1996). Malpractice in planning should be taken as seriously as it is in other professions, even if malpractice may often be difficult to prove. Failure to take malpractice seriously amounts to not taking the profession of planning seriously.

In order to achieve private sector accountability in forecasting via competition and market control, the following would be required, again as practices that are both embedded in and enforced by the relevant institutions:

- The decision to go ahead with a project should, where at all possible, be made contingent on the willingness of private financiers to participate without a sovereign guarantee for at least one-third of the total capital needs. This should be required whether projects pass the market test or not; that is, whether projects are subsidized or not or provided for reasons of social justice or not. Private lenders, shareholders, and stock market analysts would produce their own forecasts or would critically monitor existing ones. If they were wrong about the forecasts, they and their organizations would be hurt. The result would be more realistic forecasts and reduced risk.
- Full public financing or full financing with a sovereign guarantee should be avoided.

- Forecasters and their organizations must share financial responsibility for covering benefit shortfalls (and cost overruns) resulting from misrepresentation and bias in forecasting.
- The participation of risk capital should not mean that government gives up or reduces control of the project. On the contrary, it means that government can more effectively play the role it should be playing, namely as the ordinary citizen's guarantor of safety, environmental quality, risk management, and a proper use of public funds. If the institutions with responsibility for developing and building major transportation infrastructure projects would effectively implement, embed, and enforce such measures of accountability, then the misrepresentation in transportation forecasting, which is widespread today, might be mitigated. If this is not done, misrepresentation is likely to continue and the allocation of funds for transportation investments is likely to be wasteful.

7.   CONCLUSIONS AND FURTHER RESEARCH

A main problem in the decision-making of major infrastructure projects is the high level of misinformation about costs and benefits that decision-makers face in deciding whether to build the project, and the high risks such misinformation generates.

Reduced public funds and misallocation thereof were the main reasons for the revival of private financing in infrastructure planning. A first systematic study into the relation between project ownership and cost performance of transport infrastructure projects showed that the problem may not be the difference between private and public projects but a certain type of public ownership, i.e., state-owned enterprises.

This study concluded that it is not ownership in itself that matters in project performance. Ownership does not reveal which parties are responsible for construction, operation, or maintenance. For example, in publicly owned projects, even if the private sector is the key player in those phases, the performance will still be accredited to the public sector. Consequently, we cannot draw any conclusions on whether private parties' involvement results in better project performance.

Based on a case study of the HSL-South, a high-speed railway line in the Netherlands, we found that the contracting strategy and the amount of private financing are better determinants for project performance. The contracting strategy represents the extent to which private parties are responsible for the delivery of the project.

Further research on the issue of private involvement is considered particularly rewarding as it is a key issue in deciding on the institutional set-up and regulatory regime for infrastructure provision. A larger sample of transport infrastructure projects is required that allows for statistical testing. Particular tests into the extent of private money involved, either as debt of equity, and the extent to which the private party bear the risks of the project, will provide useful insights into the relation between private sector involvement and project performance. We are currently working on developing such a sample.

REFERENCES

Akintoye, A., Beck, M. and Hardcastle, C. (eds) (2003), *Public Private Partnerships: Managing Risks and Opportunities*, London: Blackwell Publishers.

Altshuler, A. and Luberoff, D. (2003), *Mega-Projects: The Changing Politics of Urban Public Investment*, Washington, DC: Brookings Institution.

Ascher, W. (1978), *Forecasting: An Appraisal for Policy-Makers and Planners*, Baltimore MD: Johns Hopkins University Press.

Brealey, R.A., Cooper, I.A. and Habib, M.A. (1996), Using project finance to fund infrastructure investments, *Journal of Applied Corporate Finance*, **9**(3), 24–38.

Capka, J.R. (2004), Megaprojects – they are a different breed, *Public Roads*, **68**(1).

Debande, O. (2002), Private Financing of transport infrastructure: an assessment of the UK experience, *Journal of Transport Economics and Policy*, **36**(3), 355–87.

Flyvbjerg, B. (2007), Policy and planning for large-infrastructure projects: problems, causes, cures, *Environment and Planning B: Planning and Design*, **34**(4), 578–97.

Flyvbjerg, B. (2008), Public planning of mega-projects: overestimation of demand and underestimation of costs, in H. Priemus, B. Flyvbjerg and B. van Wee (eds), *Decision-making on Mega-Projects: Cost-Benefit Analysis, Planning and Innovation*, Cheltenham, UK and Northampton, MA: Edward Elgar.

Flyvbjerg, B., Holm, M.K.S and Buhl, S.L. (2002), Underestimating cost in public works, error or lie? *Journal of the American Planning Association*, **68**(3), 279–95.

Flyvbjerg, B., Bruzelius, N. and Rothengatter, W. (2003a), *Megaprojects and Risk: An Anatomy of Ambition*, Cambridge: Cambridge University Press.

Flyvbjerg, B., Holm, M.K.S. and Buhl, S.L. (2003b), how common and how large are cost overruns in transport infrastructure projects? *Transport Reviews*, **23**(1), 71–88.

Flyvbjerg, B., Holm, M.K.S. and Buhl, S.L. (2004), what causes cost overrun in transport infrastructure projects? *Transport Reviews*, **24**(1), 3–18.

Flyvbjerg, B., Holm, M.K.S. and Buhl, S.L. (2005), How (in)accurate are demand forecasts in public works projects? The case of transportation, *Journal of the American Planning Association*, **71**(2), 131–46.

Fouracre, P.R., Allport, R.J. and Thomson, J.M. (1990), *The Performance and Impact of Rail Mass Transit in Developing Countries*, TRRL Research Report 278, Crowthorne: Transport and Road Research Laboratory.

Frick, K.T. (2005), *The Making and Un-making of the San Francisco–Oakland Bay Bridge: A Case in Megaproject Planning and Decision-making*, unpublished doctoral dissertation, University of California, Berkeley.

Garett, M. and Wachs, M. (1996), *Transportation Planning on Trial: The Clean Air Act and Travel Forecasting*, Thousand Oaks, CA: Sage.

Hertogh, M., Baker, S., Staal-Ong P.L. and Westerveld, E. (2008), *Managing Large Infrastructure Projects. Research on Best Practices and Lessons Learnt in Large Infrastructure Projects in Europe*, Baarn: AT Osborne BV.

Hodge, G. and Greve, C. (2005), *The Challenge of Public Private Partnerships: Learning from International Experience*, Cheltenham, UK and Northampton, MA: Edward Elgar.

Koppenjan, J. and Leijten, M. (2005), Privatising railroads: the problematic involvement of the private sector in two Dutch railway projects, *Asia Pacific Journal of Public Administration*, **27**(2), 181–99.

Koppenjan, J. and Leijten, M. (2007), How to sell a railway: lessons on the privatization of three Dutch railway projects, *European Journal of Transport and Infrastructure Research*, **7**(3), 201–22.

Mackie, P. and Preston, J. (1998), Twenty-one sources of error and bias in transport project appraisal, *Transport Policy*, **5**(1), 1–7.

Morris, P.W.G. and Hough, G.H. (1987), *The Anatomy of Major Projects: A Study of the Reality of Project Management*, New York: John Wiley.

National Audit Office (1998), *The Private Finance Initiative: The First Four Design, Finance and Operate Roads Contracts*, London: The Stationery Office.

National Audit Office (2004), *London Underground PPPs: Were They Good Deals? Report by the Comptroller and Auditor General (HC 645 Session 2003–2004)*, London: The Stationery Office.

Nijkamp, P. and Ubbels, B. (1999), How reliable are estimates of infrastructure costs? A comparative analysis, *International Journal of Transport Economics*, **26**(1), 23–53.

Osborne, S.P. (ed.) (2000), *Public-Private Partnerships: Theory and Practice in International Perspective*, London: Routledge.

Pickrell, D.H. (1992), A desire named streetcar: fantasy and fact in rail transit planning, *Journal of the American Planning Association*, **58**(2), 158–76.

Pollitt, M.G. (2002), The declining role of the state in infrastructure investments in the UK, in S.V. Berg,

M.G. Pollitt and M. Tsuji (eds), *Private Initiatives in Infrastructure. Priorities, Incentives and Performance*, Cheltenham, UK and Northampton, MA: Edward Elgar, pp. 67–100.

Priemus, H. (2009), *Contracting Public Transport Infrastructure: Recent Experience with the Dutch High Speed Line and the Amsterdam North–South Metro Line*, presentation at the 11th International Thredbo Conference on Competition and Ownership in Land Passenger Transport, 21 September, Delft University of Technology.

Savas, E.S. (2000), *Privatization and Public Private Partnerships*, New York: Chatham House Publishers/Seven Bridges Press.

TCI (2004), Onderzoek naar Infrastructuur-projecten. Reconstructie HSL-Zuid: de Besluitvorming uitvergroot TK 2004-2005, 29 283, nr. 7 Temporary Committee for Infrastructure Projects, Tweede Kamer der Staten-Generaal, The Hague: Sdu Uitgevers.

Teulings, C.N. and C.C. Koopmans (2004), *Rendement en publieke belangen. De besluitvorming bij de Betuweroute en de HSL-Zuid, Notitie ten behoeve van de Tijdelijke Commissie Infrastructuurprojecten (TCI)*, Amsterdam: SEO.

Van Ham, J.C. and Koppenjan, J.F.M. (2001), Building public private partnerships; assessing and managing risks in port development, *Public Management Review*, **3**(4), 593–616.

Wachs, M. (1990), Ethics and advocacy in forecasting for public policy, *Business and Professional Ethics Journal*, **9**(1–2), 141–57.

Walmsley, D.A. and Pickett, M.W. (1992), *The Cost and Patronage of Rapid Transit Systems Compared with Forecasts*, Research Report 352, Crowthorne: Transport Research Laboratory.

World Bank (1994), *World Development Report 1994: Infrastructure for Development*, Oxford: Oxford University Press.

26 Road pricing, impacts and cost-effectiveness
Jan Anne Annema

1. INTRODUCTION

This chapter gives an overview of impacts and the cost effectiveness of road pricing schemes in the Netherlands, and compares their effectiveness with other measures to reduce congestion such as additional road investments and traffic management measures. A broad welfare approach is used to estimate the costs and benefits and the cost-effectiveness. One question is at the forefront in this chapter: what are effective and relatively cost-effective of measures to reduce congestion?

The Dutch context related to congestion and congestion policies is briefly explained and the international scientific literature on impacts and cost-benefits of pricing measures is discussed The methodology to estimate impacts and cost-effectiveness of the Netherlands congestion measures is considered, using the numerous existing cost-benefit studies that have been carried out, especially from 2004 to 2010. The results are given from these, including a brief discussion on the uncertainty in the cost-effectiveness estimates. Finally, we discuss why relatively cost-effective pricing measures are still not being implemented in the Netherlands.

2. CONGESTION IN THE NETHERLANDS

Figure 26.1 gives the development of 'congestion' in the Netherlands in the period 1960 to 2010. In 2010 congestion in the Netherlands amounted to around 65 million vehicle travel hours lost (KIM, 2011). Congestion is actually a vague concept – in this chapter, congestion is defined as total vehicle travel hours lost on Dutch highways due to driving in jams (speeds below 50km/h) or to driving in slowed down traffic flows (speeds between 50 and 100km/h). The reference free flow speed on Dutch highways is put at 100km/h in this definition. By using this reference speed, for every vehicle on the highway with a lower speed (detected with loops) the travel hour losses are estimated.

The congestion levels in the Netherlands increased dramatically in the period 1960–2010 (Figure 26.1), also compared to other road transport negative external impact such as carbon dioxide emissions (CO_2), air pollutant emissions (nitrogen oxides, NO_x; particulate matter, PM10) and road traffic fatalities.

Since 2009, congestion levels decreased by 15 per cent (Figure 26.1). The economic crisis in 2009 and 2010 resulted in a decrease of traffic volume of 1 per cent per year, while in the period 2000–2008 there was a steady growth observable of on average 2 per cent per year (KIM, 2011). Thus, a 1 per cent traffic volume decrease resulted in a 15 per cent congestion decrease, showing the high non-linearity between traffic volume growth or decline and congestion growth or decline on Dutch highways. This phenomenon represents two sides of a coin. One side implies that a relatively small traffic volume

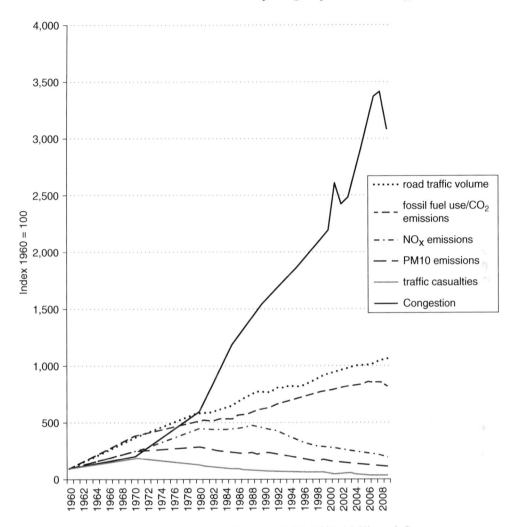

Source: Older data: CBS (2011); Wegman (2009); van den Brink (1999); McKinsey & Company (1986). Newer data: CBS (2011); van Mourik (2007); SWOV (2011); KIM (2011); PBL (2011). Beware, the before-1980 data are highly uncertain. The after-1980 data are not certain either (in all data some measurement errors will occur), but CBS (National Statistics) and the Dutch Highway Authority have gathered more systematically since then the information required to construct the trends as presented

Figure 26.1   Trends in the Netherlands road traffic volume and some road transport externalities, 1960–2010

reduction – for example, because of introducing some form of road pricing – can have relatively large impacts on congestion. However, the other is that if the economy starts growing again after 2011, and if no effective congestion measures are implemented, congestion levels can easily start rising again.

Apparently, the road capacity increase in the period 1960–2010 was not sufficient to deal with the road traffic growth on the Dutch highways in such a way that the congestion growth was turned into a congestion decrease. Nevertheless, it should be realized that the Netherlands highways were expanded to a great extent in this period. For example, from approximately 1,000 highway kilometres in 1970 to around 2,000 in 1986 (Mom and Filarski, 2008). Additionally, other measures than building extra roads were also not sufficiently effective to change the direction of the long-run congestion development (Figure 26.1). This bleak picture – at first glance – does not imply that all policies of the past to reduce congestion can be considered a failure. Annema and Vonk Noordegraaf (2009) estimated in an historic overview that between 1970 and 2008, highway expansions, traffic management measures, land-use planning and measures to increase fuel levies actually worked to reduce congestion. Without these measures, the congestion level in 2010 would have been tens of percent higher compared to the actual 2010 level. In other words, the congestion trend as depicted in Figure 26.1 is steep but without policies of the past, the line would be steeper.

One kind of policy measure that potentially could have made the congestion trend line even less steep has been debated fiercely in the past decades in the Netherlands: road pricing. According to Dutch transport historians (Mom and Filarski, 2008), already in 1965 Dutch transport engineers discussed the idea of road pricing as a means to use trunk roads more efficiently (inspired by the UK Smeed report, Smeed, 1964). Santos and Fraser (2005: 1) give the classic argument for road pricing:

> Traffic congestion arises when the volume of traffic exceeds the free-flow capacity of the link or junction, and in such cases each additional vehicle causes delay to other vehicles and suffers in turn from a slower and thus more costly journey. This negative externality creates a text-book case for a (Pigouvian) corrective tax or charge.

Around 1990, the Dutch government officially proposed for the first time road pricing in a policy document (Tweede Kamer, 1988–9). In the 1990s, some road-pricing designs were discussed politically and even some testing of portals used to register vehicles passing a corridor took place. However, public and political support were lacking and the initiatives died. Around 2004, the Minister of Transport decided to reopen the debate by appointing a committee consisting of all kinds of societal organizations: employer representatives, unions, greens, car lobby groups, freight transport employer representatives, scientists, etc. This committee was intended to try to find a common ground for road pricing. It succeeded, perhaps surprisingly. Its proposal was accepted with open arms (more or less) by the Dutch government, which decided to prepare again for road pricing in the Netherlands (see policy documents V&W, 2005 and V&W, 2008). The original proposal by the committee and the subsequent quest for even better road-pricing designs (a quest from 2005 to around 2008) resulted in large amount of studies on, among other things, impacts, costs and benefits. This chapter is much indebted to these studies. However, to already give away the final outcome of the political preparation process in the period 2006–10, in 2010 the then newly formed government decided not to implement any road pricing whatsoever. Furthermore, they also decided to stop all preparations. Why this happened is explained in more detail in the following commentary.

3. FOREIGN EXPERIENCES

In contrast, other countries and regions did implement some form of road pricing in these years. This section gives an overview of the cost-benefit ratios of these schemes. By giving this brief overview, the aim is to be able to evaluate if the Netherlands ex-ante cost-benefit estimates (CBA), presented in the next section, are sound from a methodological point of view and if the Netherlands impact estimates are more and less in agreement with the ex-post results. The brief overview is limited to cost-benefit analyses published in scientific journals. There are more CBAs on road-pricing schemes published in the grey literature but these reports could not easily be accessed or they were not published in the English or Dutch language (so the author of this chapter could not interpret them).

The first issue to note from Table 26.1 is that road pricing exists in many forms. More road charging schemes to the ones presented in Table 26.1 have been implemented such as in Singapore, Durham, Malta and so forth. For traffic impacts of these schemes see, among others, Chin, 2010; Santos and Fraser, 2005; Santos et al., 2010; Anas and Lindsey, 2011.

Second, benefits to cost ratios differ considerably. A negative outcome is shown in a study on the London charging system by Prud'homme and Bocarejo (2005), and this study has spurred much debate. Mackie (2005) argued, among others, that Prud'homme and Bocarejo (2005) underestimated the benefits of the scheme by omitting the benefits to road users in Greater London outside the city centre and by using an inappropriately low value of time. For example, Mackie states that the British value of time (VOT) for employers' business travel is €31.2 per hour (in prices of around 2003; the paper is not clear on this) while a large proportion of trips in central London (40 per cent of car trips and 50 per cent of taxi travel) is on employers' business. Prud'homme and Bocarejo (2005) used a VOT of €15.6 per hour. Also Raux (2005) criticized the Prud'homme and Bocarejo (2005) estimates by arguing that it is reasonable to apply significantly higher VOT for motorists. Additionally, Raux argued that another important factor is missed in their CBA model, namely the increase in reliability due to congestion charging. Brownstone and Small (2005) found, in evaluations of two road pricing demonstrations in southern California, that next to travel time savings improved reliability was valued quite highly by the road users.

The Stockholm congestion charging CBAs also attracted dispute. Similar to the London case, Prud'homme (now with Kopp as a co-author; Prud'homme and Kopp, 2007) estimated a negative benefit to cost ratio (Table 26.1, fifth row) for this scheme, while Eliasson (Table 26.1, sixth row) estimated a positive outcome. The main differences between the two analyses are the use of different time benefits and the amount of investments required to improve public transport in order to be able to handle the new passengers due to the congestion charging. Furthermore, debate arose on the costs of the Stockholm system to charge people and to collect the revenues (see Jansson, 2010 and Hamilton, 2010 for an overview of the debate in the Swedish press). The core of the debate is, on one hand, the unexpectedly high charging system costs (Jansson, 2010) and, on the other hand, it is the ratio between societal benefits compared to the charging system costs (and other societal costs eventually) that count (Hamilton, 2010). Hamilton even suggests that the Eliasson CBA result on the Stockholm congestion charging trial (Table 26.1, sixth row) was too pessimistic concerning system costs. Eliasson assumed

Table 26.1   Some results of road pricing CBAs

Country/city	Project	Cost-effectiveness	Benefit-cost ratio
High occupancy/toll lanes in Houston, US[a] An ex-post analysis 1998–2008	People who use an high occupancy vehicle lane with 2+ people had to pay $2 per vehicle during peak hours	±€17/lost vehicle hour gained	±1.6
London congestion charge[b] An ex-post analysis for Feb 2003–Feb 2004	Vehicles driving within the London charging zone had to pay 7.2 Euros (£5) per vehicle between 7.30h and 18.30h on weekdays	±€32/lost vehicle hour gained	±0.6
London congestion charge[c] An ex-post analysis for a £5 charge	Vehicles driving within the London charging zone had to pay €7.2 (£5) per vehicle between 7:30am and 6:30pm on weekdays	±€11/lost vehicle hour gained	±1.4
Stockholm congestion trial for 2006[d]	The costs for crossing a cordon around the inner city of Stockholm were around €1–2 depending on the time of day	±€50/lost vehicle hour gained	±0.5
Stockholm congestion trial for 2006[e]	The costs for crossing a cordon around the inner city of Stockholm were around €1–2 depending on the time of day	±€3/lost vehicle hour gained	±3
Western extension of London congestion charge for 2007[f] An ex-ante analysis	Extension included Royal Borough of Kensington and Chelsea and also area of the City of Westminster. Charge is 9.1 Euros (£8) per vehicle between 7.30h and 18.30h on weekdays	±€23–25 /lost vehicle hour gained	±0.7–0.9
Milan Ecopass, 2010[g] Preliminary CBA for the period?	Restricted zone of 8km² in centre Milan. Charge of €2–10 between 7:30am to 7:30pm dependent on engine emissions	±€5/lost vehicle hour gained	±2

Note: The studies are made in different years. Thus, the studies differ in real prices to some extent. However, the range of uncertainty in the cost effectiveness and CBA outcome is relatively high (denoted by using '±'), making corrections for using the same real prices level rather superfluous.

Source:
a   Burris and Sullivan (2006);
b   Prud'homme and Bocarejo (2005);
c   Leape (2006);
d   Prud'homme and Kopp (2007);
e   Eliasson (2008, 2009);
f   Santos and Fraser (2005);
g   Rotaris et al. (2010)

220 million Swedish crones (MSEK) annual costs (in 2005 prices, not entirely clear) while Hamilton estimates that the system is likely to operate in the 180 MSEK range from 2010.

It is not the purpose of this chapter to determine who is right or wrong. The main message of this brief overview is that the CBAs and cost effectiveness results are highly uncertain. This makes it important to carry out sensitivity analysis with input parameters used such as the VOT and system costs. The uncertainty is also reflected in the Western extension of the London congestion charge CBA. Santos and Fraser (2005) point out that their benefit-cost ratios are all below unity (as reflected in Table 26.1, seventh row). However, they continue: 'Having said that, if we use TfL's[1] [Transport for London] highest estimates of accident savings and bus benefits, the benefit-cost ratio increases to just above unity, making the scheme economically viable.'

4. THE METHODOLOGY

Before the results of the Netherlands cost-effectiveness estimates are shown, the methodology used will be explained. There are two reasons why the methodology used in this chapter is explained in some detail. First, it is, of course, customary to be as transparent as possible. Second, and more importantly, the methodology chosen may affect the outcomes considerably. In Table 26.1 in the previous section, the results of different CBAs are presented but the reader should note that part of the differences in results between the studies are caused by methodological choices. For example, the choice to take reliability improvements into account or not, or the choice for a certain VOT. Additionally, if reliability improvements have been taken into account, the inclusion method differs.

The method and assumptions used in this chapter are chiefly based on Besseling et al. (2005). The method is depicted in Figure 26.2. Besseling et al. (2005) developed the method basically to be able to carry out cost-benefit analyses (CBA) for road pricing measures. In this chapter the method is used for all policy measures considered. They are distinguished in Figure 26.2 in two main kinds: ones that lower the amount of road traffic compared to the reference case (Figure 26.2, top left) and ones that increase road capacity (Figure 26.2, top right). The method depicted in Figure 26.2 can be looked at as a kind of sieve. Every measure distinguished will be analysed using the same sieve. By doing so, it is excluded as much as possible that differences in outcomes (e.g., cost-effectiveness expressed in euros per vehicle-hour saved) are caused by methodological choices.

In the Netherlands, CBAs are made using a standardized approach based on a CBA guide (CPB and NEI, 2000). In the CBA guide, three different effects of a transport policy measure are considered: direct effect, indirect effects (additional wider economic effects) and external effects. These three kinds of policy effects will now be explained.

Direct Effects

The congestion measures studied all have implementation and/or investment costs. These initial costs are shown in Table 26.2 (in the right column). The only exception is the policy measure to increase the transport fuel levies while at the same time phasing

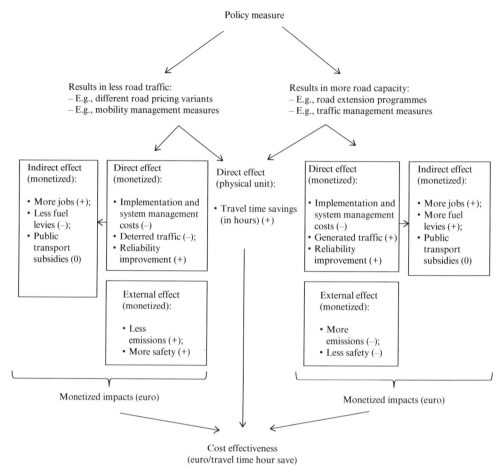

Figure 26.2   Methodology applied to estimate cost effectiveness of congestion measures

out the fixed vehicle taxes. This policy only concerns some administrative changes and involves hardly any initial investment costs. Additionally, all policy measures (again, except a fuel levy increase) have yearly management system costs. For example, road-charging schemes require relatively complicated registration and collecting systems that have to be managed constantly and that need replacement and maintenance regularly. Other direct effects of the policy measures are related to road traffic: the measures result in changes to demand and in travel time gains. These effects are estimated using transport models, such as the Dutch National Model System, LMS, or the regional models, NRM (for a description, see Gunn, 1998 or Daly, 2000).

A first direct road traffic effect of the policy measures studied in this chapter is the travel time reduction. Naturally, in the cost-effectiveness estimates, these gains will be expressed in the physical unit: travel hours saved, see Figure 26.2 (middle). A second direct road traffic effect considered is that a congestion policy measure will result in deterred traffic or in induced traffic dependent on the policy measure. Broadly speaking,

Table 26.2   Traffic volume data and monetary valuation data for 2020

Reference scenario 2020 Items	Quantities
Volumes	
● Amount car kilometres, all motives except business trips	● 151 billion km
● Amount cars, lorries and trucks kilometres, business trips	● 46 billion km
● Congestion (total travel time lost)	● 62 million vehicle hours lost
Direct effects valuation	
● Value of time (VOT), non-business trips	● €13/hour
● VOT, business trips	● €51/hour
● VOT, average all trips	● €22/hour
● Value of reliability (VOR), non-business trips	● €3.3/hour
● VOR, business trips	● €13/hour
● VOR, average all trips	● €5.5/hour
External effects valuation	
● Passenger car accident risk	● 3.0 euroct/vehicle km
● Passenger car noise	● 0.3 euroct/vehicle km
● Passenger car CO_2	● 1.0 euroct/vehicle km
● Passenger car air pollutants	● 0.8 euroct/vehicle km
● Vans, lorries, trucks (average) accident risk	● 4.5 euroct/vehicle km
● Vans, lorries, trucks (average) noise	● 1.9 euroct/vehicle km
● Vans, lorries, trucks (average) CO_2	● 5.5 euroct/vehicle km
● Vans, lorries, trucks (average) air pollutants	● 3.3 euroct/vehicle km
Indirect effects valuation	
● Maintenance costs passenger cars and vans	● 0.4 euroct/vehicle km
● Maintenance costs lorries and vans	● 10.6 euroct/vehicle km
● Extra government expenditures traveller off-peak public transport	● −11.0 euroct/passenger km
● Extra government expenditures traveller on-peak public transport	● 7.1 euroct/passenger km
● Fuel levy petrol cars and vans	● 70.0 euroct/l
● Fuel levy diesel cars, vans and light lorries	● 37.6 euroct/l
● Fuel levy diesel heavy lorries and trucks	● 36.2 euroct/l

Note: In 2010 prices

Source: Besseling et al. (2005)

the pricing policies 'force' some road users, compared to the reference scenario, to switch to another mode, to carpooling, to not taking the trip anymore or to travel at another time, and so forth. These people make room on the road for the users who decide to stay and who can 'collect', among others, the resulting travel time gains. However, for the people who make room on the roads unwillingly the policy measure results in a cost (see the (−) in Figure 26.2). On the other hand, road extension programmes and/or traffic management measures will result in more road capacity, subsequently in travel time gains and, finally, in induced traffic (e.g., Goodwin, 1996; de Jong and Gunn, 2001; Hymel et al., 2010). For these new road users, the policy measure results in a benefit ((+) in Figure 26.2). Deterred and induced traffic due to congestion measures are valued in monetary terms by using standard CBA approaches (applying the 'rule of-half'). A third direct road traffic effect distinguished is potential reliability improvement due to the measures. Unreliable travel times cause substantial costs to travellers (Peer et al., 2011). Reliability effects of congestion measures are estimated rather crudely in the method applied. It is assumed that every euro travel time benefit results in an additional €0.25 reliability gain (based on Groot et al., 2004, see Table 26.3 for the figures used). This approach is standard practice in the Netherlands because better evidence is lacking (see later discussion for some new insights).

External Impacts

The external impacts of the congestion measures considered are mainly due to the amount of deterred or induced traffic. Additionally, some positive external effects may occur because cars and heavy-duty vehicles driving in congested traffic emit more CO_2 and air pollutants per kilometre driven compared to driving in freer flows (see, for example, Barth and Boriboonsomsin, 2008). However, the traffic volume impact dominates when taking congestion measures (van Wee and van den Brink, 1999). Therefore, in the methodology applied, the external impacts are monetized using a standard number approach in which a monetary value for different transport external impacts (CO_2 emission, traffic accident risks, and so forth) are estimated per kilometre driven (based on CE, 1999; see also Table 26.3 for the numbers applied). By multiplying these numbers with the traffic volume impacts (this can either be negative or negative dependent on the type of congestion measure, Figure 26.2), the approach results in costs ($-$) or benefits ($+$).

Indirect Effects

The direct effects (travel time gains, improved reliability) might have impacts on other areas than road transport. These impacts are referred to as indirect effects in the Netherlands standardized approach (in the English literature these impacts are often denoted as 'additional wider economic impacts'). After some fierce debate between economists, in the Netherlands consensus was reached that additional indirect effects are only accepted to occur due to a policy if market imperfections can be identified or if international spillovers are convincingly shown to exist (Oosterhaven et al., 2004). In the CBA method used for four markets closely related to road transport, indirect effects are considered.

The first is the labour market. The Netherlands labour market is indeed imperfect because of unemployment benefits, labour taxes, minimum wages and centralized wage bargaining (Koopmans and Oosterhaven, 2011). Generally speaking, one could state that because of centralized wage bargaining and unemployment benefits, people in the Netherlands are not spurred very much to look for a job in another region than where they live. This is even the case when, in that other region, congestion reduces due to policies and companies there perform better economically and jobs increase. Naturally, in a perfect labour market, wages in the economically improved region would attract people to accept jobs there. In other words, in a perfect labour market, the travel time benefits of the policy would be passed through to the wider economy in the form of higher wages

Table 26.3   Overview of the 12 congestion policy measures selected

	Measure	Charging rate and other price changes	Technology assumed	Implementation costs
1	Road charge for all vehicles on all roads combined with congestion charges.	Flat rate of 3.7 euroct/km combined with congestion surcharges on certain road stretches and times of 12 euroct/km. Annual road tax is completely phased out and the new car purchase tax is decreased with 25% compared to the reference case.	On-board units (OBU) combined with Global Positioning System (GPS) and GSM Packet Radio Service (GPRS) or Dedicated Short-range Communication (DSRC).	Initial implementation costs: €2.4 billion. Yearly system management costs: €0.76 billion.
2	On specific high way sections a congestion charge has to be paid.	Rate depending on congestion levels between 5 and 22 euroct/km.	Portals with DSRC-tags.	Initial implementation costs: €0.1 billion. Yearly system management costs: €0.04 billion.
3	Road charging for all vehicles on all roads (5.7 euroct/km).	Flat rate of 5.7 euroct/km. Annual road tax and the new car purchase tax are completely phased out.	OBU combined with GPS and GPRS/DSRC.	Initial implementation costs: €2.08 billion. Yearly system management costs: €0.62 billion.
4	Road charging for all vehicles on all roads (3.4 euroct/km).	Flat rate of 3.4 euroct/km. Annual road tax is completely phased out and the new car purchase tax is decreased with 25% compared to the reference case.	OBU combined with GPS and GPRS/DSRC.	Initial implementation costs: €2.08 billion. Yearly system management costs: €0.62 billion.
5	Vehicles driving in the centres of the four large Dutch cities have to pay a daily charge.	Tariff of 7.5 euroct per day. Inhabitants receive a 90% rebate.	OBU combined with GPRS/ DSRC.	Initial implementation costs: €0.23 billion. Yearly system management costs: €0.36 billion.
6	Extra highway construction.	Additional to the reference scenario extra roads will be build costing €9 billion.	n/a.	Investment costs: €9 billion.
7	Tolls on six new roads.	Additional to the reference scenario for six new roads a toll will be imposed (tariff: €1 for cars and €3 for heavy-duty vehicles).	Portals with DSRC-tags.	Initial investment and implementation costs: €9.51 billion (€9.4 billion for new infrastructure; €0.11 billion for toll system).

Table 26.3   (continued)

	Measure	Charging rate and other price changes	Technology assumed	Implementation costs
8	Vehicles crossing a border around the centres of the four Dutch large cities have to pay a charge.	Tariff city centres inwards in the morning: €2.9 per passage.	Portals with DSRC-tags.	Yearly toll system management costs: €0.15 billion. Initial implementation costs: €0.15 billion. Yearly system management costs: €0.04 billion.
9	Fuel levy increase.	Levy increases: petrol 30 euroct/l; diesel 80 euroct/l. Annual road tax is completely phased out and the new car purchase tax is decreased with 25% compared to the reference case.	n/a.	None.
10	Public transport investments.	Additional to the reference scenario investments in public transport (improvements of existing lines and new lines) are made.	n/a.	Investment costs: €7 billion.
11	Traffic management measures.	Additional to the reference scenario investments in traffic management measures will be (extra lanes, dedicated freight traffic lanes, Dynamic Route Information Panels (DRIPs), ramp metering, etc.)	n/a.	Investment costs: €0.95 billion.
12	Road charge for heavy duty vehicles (>12 tonnes).	Road charge of €0.09 per kilometre for HDVs weighing more than 12 tons and that have not more than three axles; 10 euroct/km for HDVs weighing more than 12 tons and having four axles. Eurovignet will be phased out.	OBU combined with GPS and GPRS/DSRC.	Initial implementation costs: €0.22 billion. Yearly system management costs: €0.08 billion.

and less unemployment: no additional indirect effects would occur. However, in the imperfect market, due to, among other things, centralized wage bargaining, these wage differences cannot occur. Thus, in such a case it is fair to assume that as the congestion measures result in lower generalized costs for commuters it still can be expected that some people will be spurred to look for a job elsewhere, resulting in, among other things, structurally lower unemployment benefits expenditures. Thus, the travel time gains in the imperfect labour market are not completely passed through to the wider economy; there is some additional gain. Using model simulations, Besseling et al. (2005) assume roughly that the change in unemployment benefits expenditures are 15 per cent compared to the change in consumer surplus related to commuting. This assumption is included in the method used.

The second indirect market considered is the public transport market. This market is imperfect because government subsidies are required to balance exploitation losses. As a result of congestion measures, it can be expected that some car users will shift to public transport (pricing measures) or some public transport users will shift to the road (road extensions). Generally speaking, these impacts are not particularly high (see, for example, on some low cross-elasticities, Paulley et al., 2006), but for the sake of completeness they have been included. A shift to public transport in off-peak will lower the exploitation losses (and, thus, results in positive indirect effect). A shift to public transport in the peak will increase the exploitation losses because in that case extra capacity is needed. These shifts are valued using standard numbers for government expenditures per kilometre travelled in public transport during on-peak and off-peak (see Table 26.3).

The expenditures on management and maintenance of roads (also a market) are not paid by the road users. These expenditures are, therefore, also considered market imperfections. In the estimation method used, only maintenance expenditures are taken into account because they vary dependent on the amount of road traffic (see Table 26.3 for details).

Finally, the Netherlands transport fuel market is imperfect because of fuel levies. If a congestion measure (such as road pricing) results in less traffic, the government receives less levy revenues compared to the reference scenario. Thus, they cannot return this money to society. This is considered a welfare loss. Naturally, this reasoning works also in reverse (Figure 26.2). In Table 26.3 the details can be found. Finally, a special indirect effect related to the fuel market occurs when a measure (e.g., levy increase) results in some road users living close to the Dutch border filling their tank in Germany and Belgium instead of in the Netherlands in the reference case. This leads to welfare transfers from the Netherlands to its neighbouring countries.

Other Methodological Issues

The cost-effectiveness estimates and other impacts of the different policy measures are based on cost-benefit analyses published in public reports. In most of these reports the direct transport effects (road transport volume changes and travel time gains) are based on using the same model: the Dutch National Model System, LMS (for a description, see Gunn, 1998 or Daly, 2000). Only the direct road transport effects of the traffic management policy package and the road charge for heavy-duty vehicles are not based on these models but on rough estimates using the literature. These rough estimates are also used in this chapter. All other effects are derived from these direct effects (see methodology) by the author of this chapter using a simple spreadsheet.

Fortunately, all of the estimates in the report use the same reference scenario: the so-called European Coordination scenario (CPB, 1997), see for some basic assumptions Table 26.2 (top rows). In the different reports, different prices and discount rates were used. This has been corrected for. All prices are for 2010 and the discount rate chosen is 7 per cent (as in Besseling et al., 2005).

Finally, all estimates are carried out for one year, 2020. The reader should realize that it is assumed that the policies are implemented in the period 2005–10. Thus, the 2020 estimates represent the cost-effectiveness and impacts of the policies under study in the long run. Naturally, the 2020 estimates individually are not realistic anymore, as the period 2005–10 is gone. However, the goal of this chapter is to compare the policy options outcomes with each other. The purpose is not to give 'precise' 2020 results (if this could be done at all).

5.　COST-EFFECTIVENESS AND IMPACTS OF CONGESTION MEASURES

For 12 policy measures the cost-effectiveness and other impacts are estimated. It concerns eight road pricing variants and five other policy measures. Table 26.3 gives an overview of the 12 policy measures selected. Far more road pricing variants have been studied in the period. A rough estimation amounts to almost 100 (Besseling et al., 2005, 2008; CPB, 2005; Vervoort and Spit, 2005; Ecorys and MuConsult, 2007a, 2007b, Lebouille et al., 2007). The road pricing variants selected in this chapter are representative of the different main design choices, and they represent the most popular variants during the policy preparation phase. To be clear, measure 4 was the favourite of the Dutch Minister of Transport of the former government until the new government in 2010 cancelled the implementation of road pricing in the Netherlands. The order of the measures in Table 26.3 is chosen on purpose; the effectiveness in travel times saved decreases from top to bottom (see Figure 26.2).

In a rational-style policymaking process, it can be expected that decision-makers choose policy measures from the top left area in Figure 26.2. These are the measures, namely, which have a relatively high impact on travel time savings and are relatively cost-effective: for a 'modest' amount of euros compared to other measures where one-hour travel time can be gained. Additionally, these are measures located to the left of the heavy dotted €20 per hour travel-time saved line. With measures left of this line a travel hour can be 'bought' costing less than €20/hour while the willingness to pay for an hour of travel time savings (the average VOT, see Table 26.2) in the Netherlands in 2020 is around €20/hour. Thus, for the measures left of the €20/hour line the benefits outweigh the costs. In this favourable top-left area, three different road charging measures can be found. Two of them (measures 1 and 2) contain specific charges for places and times when congestion arises. These congestion charges turn out to be very effective. For example, in measure 2, road users have to pay €0.05–0.22 per kilometre depending on the amount of congestion on specific highway stretches.

This implies that on only 3–4 per cent of the kilometres driven in the Netherlands do kilometre charges have to be paid, making the implementation costs of this pricing option compared to the other road charging variants (which accrue to 100 per cent of kilometres driven) rather low (see Table 26.3, right column).

The two flat rate variants (measures 3 and 4) are also relatively effective and cost-effective. These flat rates became the most popular variants in the political preparation phase, because in this phase the public and political support turned increasingly out to be especially related to a notion of fairness. This notion will be discussed more elaborately in the next section. The crux is, however, that many people found it particularly fair that the Netherlands fixed vehicle taxes – taxes that have to be paid independent of the amount of kilometres driven – were transferred to taxes per kilometre driven. This process was called 'variabilization' and implied that people who drove many kilometres per year had to pay relatively more taxes and people with a more modest driving habit relatively few. In the 5.7 eurocent per kilometre flat rate, 100 per cent of all fixed taxes were variabilized. In the 3.4 eurocent per kilometre flat rate, 100 per cent of the annual road was variabilized and 25 per cent of the new car purchase tax. Here the idea was that by keeping part of the purchase tax, the government kept a policy option that they could use to influence car-buying behaviour in the direction of the purchase of more fuel-efficient cars. For example, by differentiating the purchase tax along car fuel-efficiency or CO_2 emission per kilometre driven.

For the four Dutch large cities (Amsterdam, Rotterdam, The Hague and Utrecht) two pricing variants have been studied (measures 5 and 8). The charging variant, which is quite similar to the London and Stockholm congestion charging, is relatively effective but has a negative benefit-to-cost ratio (Figure 26.2, right of the heavy dotted line). This is different compared to the corridor variant (measure 8) and some of the CBAs carried out for London and Stockholm (see section 3). The reason is twofold. First, the implementation and management costs are relatively (very) high. This is partly due to the technology chosen (perhaps cheaper options will be available in the future), but it is also due to the fact that, for four relatively small city centres, systems have to be built and managed. Second, and less importantly, the share of business trips with the high VOTs in these relatively small centres are less compared to the foreign examples as many businesses in the Netherland have moved outside the old centres. The corridor charging option (measure 8) around the four city centres is much cheaper, less effective but it has a positive benefit-to-cost ratio.

In the bottom-left area of Figure 26.2, two measures (11 and 12) can be found that are not very effective but are still cost-effective. For the traffic management measure, this is caused by the fact that they are mainly applied in the heavy congested areas, and they are relatively cheap to implement. Thus, the point of application is in the right place. However, their impact there is relatively modest. The road charge solely for HDV (measure 12) is relatively cheap to implement and maintain (Table 26.3) and has some modest impacts on travel time gains. However, these impacts are relatively low, signifying that the share of HDVs on roads is already low in the reference case. The effect of the policy option on behavioural changes in the freight market is also modest. Thus, a low share combined with a low impact results in 'low times low' impact.

Next to road pricing options, in Table 26.3 and Figure 26.2 three investments options are presented: extra highway investments (measure 6), new highways combined with tolls (measure 7) and extra public transport investments (measure 11). Extra highway investments can be relative effective in reducing congestion with a positive benefit-to-ratio (measure 11). Naturally, these extra roads are planned in the highly congested areas. Apparently, in a strongly urbanized Netherlands, many places still can be found where investing in extra road capacity is societally a profitable strategy. Nevertheless, Figure 26.2 shows that the balance between benefits and costs for the road investment strategy is somewhat shaky. The reason is that building new roads in the Netherlands (also related to its urbanized character) can turn out to be expensive because all kinds of additional measures might be required in order to minimize the burden of the highways for people living close by (tunnels, coverings, noise barriers, and so forth, may be needed). If the cost-effective estimate in measure 11 is carried out for relatively high additional cost to minimize the environmental burden of the highways, the benefit-cost ratio could turn out to be negative. This same kind of reasoning makes the measure 'new highways combined with tolls' (measure 7) in total negative concerning benefit-to-cost ratio. One of the new six tolled highways included in the estimate is a highway very close to Amsterdam connecting the new city of Almere with Schiphol Airport. This highway requires very high additional costs to minimize its environmental burden, making the overall ratio of the six combined negative. Nevertheless, the other five proposals have positive benefit-to-cost ratios, implying that investing in tolled highways can be societally a profitable strategy in the Netherlands, albeit less profitable compared to building new non-tolled highways. For public transport investments, the effects on reducing road congestion is fairly modest and the benefits do not outweigh the costs (measure 11). Also, in this case, it can be argued that the total investment package (consisting of, among other things, improving national and international rail lines and local bus and tram transport) is negative but that parts of the package are more positive. It is true that especially the local small-scale public transport investment plans turned out to be the best parts related to benefit to cost ratio (CPB et al., 1999). Nevertheless, for two reasons public transport investments are not very effective and cost-effective in reducing road congestion. First, the cross-elasticities between public transport and car use are low (see section 3). Second, investing, exploring and maintaining public transport is relatively expensive.

Finally, the fuel levy increase (measure 9) has a highly negative benefit-to-cost ratio. With this measure, the impacts were assessed if the variabilization (see measures 3 and 4) would take place using the existing fuel levies instead of introducing road charges. The resulting cost-effectiveness is very negative mainly because it is to be expected that many people living near the border will refuel in Germany and Belgium because of the resulting high fuel price differences (based on Rietveld et al., 1999). This cross-border fuelling results in relatively high welfare losses in the Netherlands (as an indirect effect) because fuel tax revenues spill over to the governments of Germany and Belgium.

Figure 26.3 shows specifically the travel time gains of the options. In the road-pricing debate, the environmental impacts also have played some role. These impacts have been included in the cost-effectiveness estimates but are now presented more clearly. Road transport CO_2 emissions reductions ($-$) or increases ($+$), compared to the reference scenario, are used as an indicator for the environmental impacts of the policy options. As shown, the fuel levy increase (measure 9) has the highest impact. Not only traffic volume is decreased considerably by this measure, the policy also results in a more fuel-efficient car fleet compared to the reference as users are strongly stimulated to buy fuel-efficient

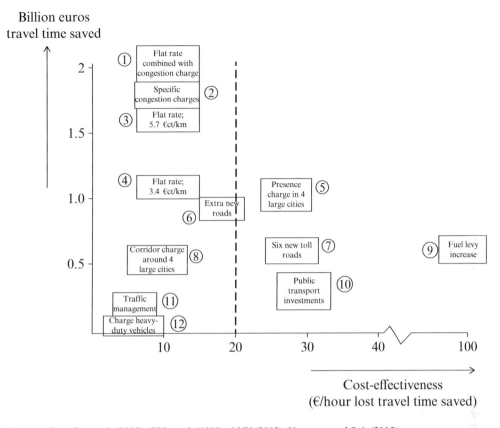

Billion euros
travel time saved

Source: Besseling et al. (2008), CPB et al. (1999), AVV (2003), Vervoort and Spit (2005)

Figure 26.3 Cost-effectiveness

cars. High positive environmental impacts are also related to the three road charging measures with a nationwide flat rate (measures 1, 3 and 4). The main reason for this is that car demand decreases considerably by these measures compared to the reference case. The specific congestion charges (measure 2), although part of the top-left area in Figures 26.2 and 26.3, have far less environmental impacts because these charges influence a relatively small part of the kilometres driven.

6. CONCLUSION AND DISCUSSION

The main conclusion is that road-pricing variants are relatively effective and cost-effective measures to reduce congestion in the Netherlands. Additionally, their benefit-to-cost ratio is positive. To come to this conclusion, many assumptions have to be made. The CBAs on road pricing schemes in the scientific literature point out that travel time impacts and the implementation and management costs of road-pricing schemes are especially uncertain. Also, in the Netherlands context, the modelled travel time gains

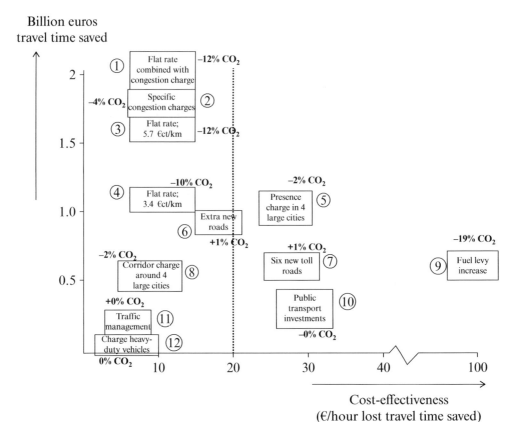

Figure 26.4   Cost-effectiveness

of pricing policies have been debated. According to Geurs and van Wee (2010) it is probable that the Dutch National Model System used overestimates these impacts. Therefore, a sensitivity analysis is carried out with 30 per cent lower travel time gains compared to the original estimate and 20 per cent higher costs. Naturally, the subsequent impacts are lower and the benefit-to-cost ratios decrease, but the conclusion is still that the road-pricing variants are effective, cost-effective and have a positive benefit-to-cost ratio. Only if additional to the 30 per cent lower travel time effects and 20 per cent higher costs it is assumed that the level of congestion in 2020 is 25 per cent lower compared to the original estimate used (the level stabilizes in this 'new' reference case on the level of around 2005), the benefit-to-cost ratios of road-pricing variants turn negative. Perhaps to pile up one setback on another is not very realistic. On the other hand, the credit and euro economic crisis in combination with a government, at the time of writing this chapter, which invests relatively high amounts of money in extra highway capacity and traffic management could indeed result in far lower congestion levels in 2020 or thereafter compared to the original reference case used in this chapter. Thus, if the Netherlands road-pricing debate is politically reopened in the future (for the reasons why it was closed, see below) it seems wise to carry out new effect estimate studies and CBAs taking the best new insights into account.

A special uncertainty relates to the reliability effects estimated. These effects were taken into account crudely in the effect studies used. Reliability improvements have a share of roughly 10–15 per cent in total road pricing measure benefits using this crude method. Thus, this benefit item cannot be neglected and adds considerably to the uncertainty of the final results. It is recommended to carry out more research in order improve the methods to incorporate travel time reliability in CBAs. One recent proposal for improved incorporation can be found in Peer et al. (2011).

Despite the positive CBA and effectiveness results for road-pricing variants, the Netherlands government in 2010 decided to abandon road pricing completely. The reason is that the political parties that ended up in the coalition government (VVD, Liberal-Conservatives, and CDA, Christian-Democrats) oppose introduction of any form of road pricing. Also the party that allows[1] the VVD-CDA government (PVV, right-wing party) strongly opposes road charging. On their website (PVV, 2010) they denote road pricing simply as 'a disastrous plan aimed at bamboozling citizens out of their money'. Furthermore, they call the OBU a 'spying device'. Although the VVD stated in their 2006 election manifesto that road charging would contribute to a more efficient use of roads (VVD, 2006), in 2010 on the official VVD website (VVD, 2009) road charging was denoted as a 'foolish' idea. Their slogan used in 2010 was: 'road pricing: no way!' The VVD opposes the idea because they think that road charging is impossibly expensive, impracticable, results only in a high tax burden and violates privacy (VVD, 2009). The CDA also favoured kilometre charging in 2006 (CDA, 2006). Although they did not change their position as radically as the VVD, they stated in 2010 that they did not support the proposal for kilometre charging anymore because it had become too complex. In summary, the political parties in power simply do not evaluate road pricing as an effective instrument to reduce congestion and/or to improve the environment. They point solely at disadvantages such as a high tax burden for road users, privacy issues and the complexity. It is clear that as long as the 2010 Netherlands government remains in power, any form of road pricing is out of the question. It is difficult to predict if and when the political debate will be opened again. This chapter shows that if this will be the case, a large knowledge base to estimate impacts, cost-effectiveness and benefit to cost ratios concerning a wide range of road pricing variants is available.

NOTE

1. This is a complicated political construction. The VVD-CDA coalition government does not have the majority in parliament. Therefore, they made an agreement with the PVV. Together with the PVV, the three parties have the majority. The agreement is that PVV supports the government on the main issues but the party is not officially part of the government and may oppose the government on particular issues.

REFERENCES

Anas, A and Lindsey, R. (2011), Reducing urban road transportation externalities: road pricing in theory and practice, *Review of Environmental Economics and Policy*, **5**(1), 66–88.

Annema, J.A. and Vonk Noordegraaf, D. (2009), De effectiviteit van filebeleid in Nederland, 1970–2008, paper for Colloquium Vervoersplanologisch Speurwerk (CVS), Antwerp.

AVV (2003), *Kosteneffectiviteit benuttingsmaatregelen (inclusief Achtergrond document) [Cost-effectiveness of Traffic Management Measures, Including Background Report]*, Rotterdam: Adviesdienst Verkeer en Vervoer, Directoraat-Generaal Rijkswaterstaat, Ministerie van Verkeer en Waterstaat.

Barth, M. and Boriboonsomsin, K. (2008), Real-world carbon dioxide impacts of traffic congestion, *Transportation Research Record: Journal of the Transportation Research Board*, **2058**, 163–71.

Besseling, P., Groot, W. and Lebouille, R. (2005), Economische analyse van verschillende vormen van prijsbeleid voor het wegverkeer, CPB Document No. 87, Centraal Planbureau, The Hague.

Besseling, P., Geurs, K., Hilbers, H., Lebouille, R. and Thissen, M. (2008), *Effecten van omzetting van de aanschafbelasting op personenauto's in een kilometerprijs [Impacts of Transferring the Car Purchase Tax into a Kilometre Charge]*, CPB document no. 166, The Hague: Centraal Planbureau.

Brownstone, D. and Small, K.A. (2005), Valuing time and reliability: assessing the evidence from road pricing demonstrations, *Transportation Research Part A*, **39**, 279–93.

Burris, M. and Sullivan, E. (2006), Benefit-cost analysis of variable pricing projects: QuickRide HOT Lanes, *Journal of Transportation Engineering*, March, pp. 183–90.

CBS (2011), *National Statistics*, www.staline.nl.

CDA (2010), Election program 'Christen Democratisch Appel' 2006, www.cda.nl/fileadmin/Organisaties/Visiegroepen/Publicaties/verkiezingsprogramma_2006.pdf.

Chin, K.-K. (2010), *The Singapore Experience: The Evolution of Technologies, Costs and Benefits, and Lessons Learnt*, discussion paper, Joint Transport Research Centre, Round Table, 4–5 February, Paris.

CPB (1997), *Economie en fysieke omgeving. Beleidsopgaven en oplossingsrichtingen 1995–2020 [Economy and Physical Environment. Policy Issues and Possible Solutions, 1995–2020]*, The Hague: Sdu Uitgevers.

CPB (2005), Enkele effecten van de Nota Mobiliteit deel III, CPB notitie 24 november 2005, Centraal Planbureau, The Hague.

CPB and NEI (2000), *Evaluatie van grote infrastructuurprojecten. Leidraad voor kosten-baten analyse, [Guide for Cost-Benefit Analysis]*, The Hague: Netherlands Bureau for Economic Policy Analysis.

CPB, RIVM, SCP and AVV (1999), *Kiezen of delen: ICES-maatregelen tegen het licht [You Cannot Have It Both Ways: ICES Policy Measures Assessed]*, document no. 103, The Hague: Centraal Planbureau.

Daly, A.J. (2000), National models, in D.A. Hensher and Button, K.J. (eds), *Handbook of Transport Modelling*, Oxford: Elsevier Science.

de Jong, G. and Gunn, H.F. (2001), Recent evidence on car cost and time elasticities of travel demand in Europe, *Journal of Transport Economics and Policy*, **35**(2), 137–60.

Ecorys and MuConsult (2007a), Overgangseffecten variabilisatie BPM, MRB en Eurovignet, Ecorys Nederland BV, Rotterdam/MuConsult, Amersfoort.

Ecorys and MuConsult (2007b), Effecten vormgeving kilometerprijs bij variabilisatie van BPM, MRB en Eurovignet, Ecorys Nederland BV, Rotterdam/MuConsult, Amersfoort.

Eliasson, J. (2008), Lessons from the Stockholm congestion charging trial, *Transport Policy*, **15**, 395–404.

Eliasson, J. (2009), A cost-benefit analysis of the Stockholm congestion charging system, *Transportation Research Part A*, **43**, 468–80.

Geurs, K. and van Wee, G.P. (2010), De kwaliteit van prognoses van de verkeerskundige effecten van de kilometerprijs, *Tijdschrift vervoerswetenschap*, **36**, 10–17.

Goodwin, P.B. (1996), Empirical evidence on induced traffic: a review and synthesis, *Transportation*, **23**, 35–54.

Groot, W., Besseling, P. and Verrips, A. (2004), *Economische toets op de Nota Mobiliteit [Economic Analysis of the National Transport Policy Plan]*, document no. 65, The Hague: Netherlands Bureau for Economic Policy Analysis.

Gunn, H.F. (1998), *An Overview of European National Models*, paper presented at the Seminar on National Transport Models, Stockholm.

Hamilton, C.J. (2011), Revisiting the cost of the Stockholm congestion charging system, *Transport Policy*, **18**, 836–47.

Hymel, K.M., Small, K.A. and Van Dender, K. (2010), Induced demand and rebound effects in road transport, *Transportation Research Part B*, **44**(10), 1220–41.

Jansson, J.O. (2010), Road pricing and parking policy, *Research in Transportation Economics*, **29**, 346–53.

KIM (2010), *Mobiliteitsbalans 2010*, The Hague: Netherlands Institute for Transport Policy Analysis.

KIM (2011), *Mobiliteitsbalans 2011*, The Hague: Netherlands Institute for Transport Policy Analysis.

Koopmans, C. and Oosterhaven, J. (2011), SCGE modelling in cost-benefit analysis: the Dutch experience, *Research in Transportation Economics*, **31**, 29–36.

Leape, J. (2006), The London Congestion Charge, *Journal of Economic Perspectives*, **4**, 157–76.

Lebouille, R., Spit, W. and Harmsen, J. (2007), Kosten en baten van varianten Anders Betalen voor Mobiliteit, Ecorys Nederland BV, Rotterdam.

Mackie, P. (2005), The London Congestion Charge: a tentative economic appraisal. A comment on the paper by Prud'homme and Bocajero, *Transport Policy*, **12**, 288–90.

McKinsey & Company (1986), *Afrekenen met Files. Samenvatting, Conclusies en Aanbevelingen [Dealing with Traffic Jams. Summary, Conclusions and Recommendations]*, Amsterdam: McKinsey & Company.

Mom, G. and Filarski, R. (2008), *Van transport naar mobiliteit. De mobiliteitsexplosie (1895–2005)*, Zutphen: Uitgeverij Walburg Press.

Oosterhaven, J., Elhorst, J.P., Koopmans, C.C. and Heyma, A. (2004), *Indirecte Effecten Infrastructuurprojecten – Aanvulling op de Leidraad OEI [Indirect Effects of Infrastructure Projects]*, The Hague: Transport and Public Work Ministry and Economic Affairs Ministry.

Paulley, N., Balcombe, R., Mackett, R., Titheridge, H., Preston, J., Wardman, M., Shires, J. and White, P. (2006), The demand for public transport: the effects of fares, quality of service, income and car ownership, *Transport Policy*, **12**, 295–306.

PBL (2011), *PBL Netherlands Environmental Assessment Agency*, www.compendiumvoordeleefomgeving.nl.

Peer, S., Koopmans, C.C. and Verhoef, E.T. (2011), Prediction of travel time variability for cost-benefit analysis, *Transportation Research Part A: Policy and Practice*, **46**(1), 79–90.

Prud'homme, R. and Bocarejo, J.P. (2005), The London Congestion Charge: a tentative economic appraisal, *Transport Policy*, **12**, 279–87.

Prud'homme, R. and Kopp, P. (2007), Le péage de Stockholm: évaluation et enseignements, *Revue Transports*, **443**, 345–59.

PVV (2010), Election program 'Partij voor de Vrijheid' 2010, www.pvv.nl/images/stories/Webversie_VerkiezingsProgrammaPVV.pdf.

Raux, C. (2005), Comments on 'The London Congestion Charge: a tentative economic appraisal' (Prud'homme and Bocajero, 2005), *Transport Policy*, **12**, 368–71.

Rietveld, P., Bruinsma, F. and van Vuuren, D. (1999), *Spatial Graduation of Fuel Taxes: Consequences for Cross-border and Domestic Fuelling*, Tinbergen Discussion paper 99-048/3.

Rotaris, L., Danielis, R., Marcucci, E. and Massiani, J. (2010), The urban road pricing scheme to curb pollution in Milan, Italy, description, impacts and preliminary cost-benefit analysis assessment, *Transportation Research Part A*, **44**(5), 359–75.

Santos, G. and Fraser, G. (2005), *Road Pricing: Lessons from London*, paper prepared for the October 2005 Panel Meeting of Economic Policy in London.

Santos, G., Behrendt, H., Maconi, L., Shirvani, T. and Teytelboym, A. (2010), Part I: externalities and economic policies in road transport, *Research in Transportation Economics*, **28**, 2–45.

Smeed, R.J. (1964), *Road Pricing: The Economic and Technical Possibilities*, London: HMSO.

SWOV (2011), *SWOV Institute for Road Safety Research*, www.swov.nl/UK/Research/Cijfers/Cijfers-UK.htm.

Tweede Kamer (1988–9), *Tweede Structuurschema Verkeer en Vervoer, deel d [Second Long Term Transport Policy Plan]*, part d, Tweede Kamer vergaderjaar 1988–9, 20 922, nrs. 1–2, s'-Gravenhage, Sdu Uitgevers.

van den Brink, R. (1999), *Verkeer en vervoer in de Milieubalans 1999 [Traffic and Transport in the 1999 National Environmental Balance]*, Bilthoven: National Institute of Public Health and the Environment.

van Mourik, H. (2007), *Verkenning autoverkeer 2012 [Forecast Car Traffic]*, The Hague: KIM Netherlands Institute for Transport Policy Analysis.

van Wee, B. and R. van den Brink (1999), Environmental impact of congestion and policies to reduce it, in OECD and European Conference of Ministers (eds), *Traffic Congestion in Europe*, report of the 110th Round Table on Transport Economics, 12–13 March 1998, Paris: OECD.

Vervoort, K. and Spit, W. (2005), *Economische toets variant 3: Betalen per kilometer vracht: Eindrapport [Economic Analysis of Variant 3: Paying Per Kilometre Freight]*, Rotterdam: Ecorys Nederland BV.

VVD (2006), Election program 'Volkspartij voor Vrijheid en Democratie' 2006, www.parlement.com/id/vhnnmt7mr5zq/vvd_en_tweede_kamerverkiezingen_2006.

VVD (2009), Election program 'Volkspartij voor Vrijheid en Democratie' 2010, www.parlement.com/9291000/d/2010_vvd_verkiezingsprogramma.pdf.

V&W (2005), *Nota Mobiliteit [Policy Document Mobility]*, The Hague: Ministerie van Verkeer en Waterstaat.

V&W (2008), *Mobiliteitsaanpak, Vlot en veilig van deur tot deur [Procedure for Mobility, Fast and Safe from Door to Door]*, The Hague: Ministerie van Verkeer en Waterstaat.

Wegman, F. (2009), Verkeersonveiligheid [Transport safety], in G.P. van Wee and J.A. Annema (eds.), *Verkeer en vervoer op hoofdlijnen [Traffic and Transport: The Main Issues]*, Bussum: Uitgeverij Coutinho.

27 Incomes, accessibility and transport poverty
Gordon Stokes

1. INTRODUCTION

Transport poverty is a notion that is difficult to define, and one that has been controversial in terms of whether a 'real' issue exists. The concept is based around the idea that low incomes and poor accessibility can lead to disproportionate spending on transport to access basic services, or lead to suppression of some trips. This chapter draws on analysis of travel behaviour and spending on transport in the United Kingdom, but the conclusion that a combination of low incomes and distance from basic services and opportunities can lead to real problems can be applied in most countries.

The chapter looks first at previous literature on social issues in transport and accessibility, followed by analyses of how simple measures of travel behaviour and accessibility vary with income and other factors. Transport need, transport poverty and transport wealth are then discussed, followed by a short discussion of how transport and development planning can help to lessen inequalities.

Those on lower incomes are much less likely to own cars, more likely to travel less and more likely to walk as their main mode of travel. There is evidence that where other transport alternatives do not exist, those on lower incomes buy cars out of 'necessity' where if alternatives were better, they would not. For those in the lowest incomes in rural areas, upwards of 30 per cent of all income is spent on travel, the bulk of which is on car travel. Households in rural areas need to spend more than those in urban areas and the bulk of the difference is due to expenditure on transport. Where alternatives to the car exist, and where facilities and services are found close to where people live, 'transport poverty' is very much lessened. The conclusion drawn is that it is important to consider issues of equity in transport provision, providing for those on low incomes by ensuring facilities are close at hand, and that public transport services are well provided for.

2. PREVIOUS WORK ON TRAVEL BEHAVIOUR AND POVERTY

The predominance of an economic and engineering approach to transport planning up until the 1990s combined with an approach to policy described as 'predict and provide' tended to assume that society was moving towards universal car ownership and that catering for growing demand was the important issue – the thinking was that if anything that could be described as 'transport poverty' did exist, car ownership and rising incomes would make it irrelevant in the future.

However, a sizeable body of research has aimed to highlight many of the equity issues in transport, dating back to the 1970s (e.g., Hillman, 1973). Since then studies have continued to raise the issue of transport inequalities, focusing on groups who are more likely to experience problems relating to mobility and accessibility, such as women (e.g., Grieco et al., 1989); children (e.g., Hillman, 1993; Cahill et al, 1996), young people (e.g., Pilling and Turner, 1998) older people (e.g., Gilhooly et al., 2002; Banister and Bowling, 2004), people with disabilities (e.g., Oxley and Richards, 1995) and certain minority ethnic groups (e.g., Rajé, 2004). Other studies have looked at affordability of car travel (e.g., Stokes, 1995).

In the early 2000s the UK Social Exclusion Unit (SEU) formally recognised that many past transport and land-use policies may have served to exacerbate existing social inequalities. The report also recommended that the life chances of low income groups and communities might be enhanced through the introduction of targeted local transport and land use measures (Social Exclusion Unit, 2003).

Studies since then have further explored the various issues of mobility, accessibility and transport provision in different contexts (e.g., Preston and Rajé, 2007; Jones and Wixey, 2005; McDonagh, 2006, looking at rural areas and Lucas et al., 2008, looking at people living in deprived areas). These have helped to develop new and improved methodologies for identifying gaps in the system of provision and have led to improved understanding of the issues.

Evidence on transport poverty has been raised more specifically in work by Smith et al. (2010) and the Commission for Rural Communities (2010). Currie and Delbosc (2013) discuss the notion of 'forced car ownership' in relation to residents on rural and semi-rural areas in Australia. A major study of fairness in transport (Sustainable Development Commission, 2011) provides a wide-ranging review of factors related to fairness and sustainability in transport and proposes new approaches to dealing with the issues. Their suggestions are returned to at the end of this chapter.

The reports of the Great Britain National Travel Survey have generally contained a section relating to social inequality (for example Section 6 – Social Inclusion and Accessibility in the 2008 report; DfT, 2009), and *Travel by Car: Availability, Income, Ethnic Group and Household Type* for the 2009 reporting (DfT, 2010). These have consistently shown lower rates of car ownership and less car use by those on lower incomes.

3. LOW INCOMES AND TRAVEL

Characteristics of Low Income People

The Great Britain National Travel Survey allows some but not all aspects relating to transport poverty to be studied. There are many social factors that relate to low income that are independent of transport. Groups much more likely to be on low incomes include children, people aged over 70, non-white people, single adults, single-parent families and those separated or widowed (Stokes and Lucas, 2011).

But factors related to mobility characteristics also show a strong correlation with low income. Those without a car are much more likely to be on low incomes. Generally we can assume that a lack of transport is a result of low income, rather than the other way round, but this is not necessarily so – for example, those self reporting 'mobility difficulties' may find their lack of travel an impediment to employment.

For all ages, people on lower incomes are more likely to report a mobility difficulty

Table 27.1   Percentage of respondents reporting a mobility difficulty by income quintile for selected age groups

	Lowest	Second	Third	Fourth	Highest	Total
20–4	4%	4%	3%	1%	1%	3%
35–9	11%	8%	4%	2%	1%	4%
50–4	27%	17%	10%	7%	4%	10%
65–9	31%	27%	20%	18%	13%	23%
80–4	49%	50%	52%	41%	41%	49%
All aged over 16	22%	21%	12%	7%	4%	13%

Source: Great Britain National Travel Survey, 2002–10

(Table 27.1). It is in the middle stages of life that the differences related to income are greatest. For example, in the 35–9 age group, 11 per cent of those in the lowest income quintile[1] have a difficulty, compared to 1 per cent for those in the highest two quintiles, while for those aged 50–4 the rates are 27 per cent compared to 4 per cent in the highest quintile – those in the lowest income quintile are more than six times more likely to report a mobility difficulty. By the age of 80–4, the differences are much less, since older age means that more 40 per cent in any age group report a difficulty. Poorer health appears to be related to income, which in turn affects mobility, although the extent to which low income 'causes' mobility difficulty and the effect to which mobility difficulty reduces the chances of higher incomes cannot be gleaned from this data.

Travel Behaviour and Income

There are several broad-brush indicators for which data is readily available that can be used to measure and compare people's travel behaviour, including whether there is a car in the household, cars per household, total distance travelled per person or trips per person. All these are inadequate in terms of showing what we might call 'transport poverty', but are indicators that show something about how much mobility people have and that can be analysed using existing surveys.

Households in low income quintiles are very much less likely to have access to a car (Table 27.2). About 56 per cent in the lowest quintile have a car available compared with 94 per cent in the two highest quintiles. But there is not a linear relationship, with 89 per cent of those in the middle income quintile having a car. The effect is that those on low

Table 27.2   Car ownership characteristics by income quintile

	Lowest	Second	Third	Fourth	Highest
People in households with one or more cars	56%	74%	88%	92%	94%
Cars per household	0.74	1.05	1.42	1.66	1.72
Cars per adult (over 17)	0.37	0.50	0.63	0.73	0.82

Source: Great Britain National Travel Survey, 2002–10

Table 27.3   *Distance travelled per person per year by economic activity and income quintile*

	Lowest	Second	Third	Fourth	Highest
Full time	6,928	7,472	8,481	10,006	12,911
Part time	5,329	6,376	7,068	8,235	10,062
Unemployed	3,900	4,939	5,621	6,797	8,513
Retired/ sick	3,621	4,276	5,449	6,256	6,811
Student	4,662	5,600	6,054	6,574	7,789
Homeworker/other	3,629	4,598	5,558	6,505	8,377
Under 16	2,909	3,889	4,447	5,360	6,270
All	4,016	5,172	6,613	8,308	10,997

Source: Great Britain National Travel Survey, 2002–10

incomes are much less likely to have a car, rather than that those on higher incomes are more likely to have one. On the other hand, cars per person and cars per adult rise in a more linear fashion with income quintile.

Distance travelled (by any mode) increases with income – while those in the lowest income quintile travel just over 4,000 miles per year, those in the highest quintile travel just under 11,000 miles, the distance rising exponentially with income quintile. Stage in life has a major effect. Being in full-time work is associated with a higher amount of travel in any income quintile (Table 27.3). An income effect is seen for all age groups and economic activity types, but is most marked for those groups of working age. For those in work, the distance travelled grows fastest at higher incomes, implying no ceiling or saturation level. Students show the least variation according to income, with retired people similarly showing less increase in distance travelled with higher incomes.

A mobility difficulty has the effect of reducing the distance travelled (Table 27.4) but as with employment status, the effect of income is greater, with no saturation level being noted – the higher the income the more a person with or without a disability will travel, implying that most disabilities need not be a limiter of travel distance if money is available.

Those in the lowest income quintile make 854 trips per year compared to the average for all incomes of about 1,000. So while they make somewhat fewer trips, the difference is not great. Some of the difference is related to economic activity status, with fewer people

Table 27.4   *Distance travelled per person per year by whether a mobility difficulty is experienced*

	Lowest	Second	Third	Fourth	Highest
With mobility disability	4,108	5,299	6,700	8,377	11,068
No disability	2,864	3,606	4,654	5,589	6,670
All	4,016	5,172	6,613	8,308	10,997

Source: Great Britain National Travel Survey, 2002–10

Table 27.5   Trips per person per year by each mode, by income quintile

	Walk	Cycle	Car Driver	Car Passenger	Bus	Rail	Taxi	Other	TOTAL Trips
Lowest	34%	2%	25%	22%	13%	1%	2%	2%	854
Second	27%	2%	35%	24%	9%	1%	1%	2%	942
Third	22%	2%	42%	24%	6%	1%	1%	2%	1,036
Fourth	19%	1%	48%	23%	4%	2%	1%	2%	1,088
Highest	17%	1%	52%	20%	3%	3%	1%	3%	1,112
All	23%	2%	41%	22%	7%	2%	1%	2%	1,009

Source: Great Britain National Travel Survey, 2002–10

Table 27.6   Miles travelled per person per year by mode and income quintile

	Walk	Cycle	Car Driver	Car Passenger	Bus	Rail	Taxi	Other	TOTAL
Lowest	224	27	1,389	1,383	439	225	39	289	4,016
Second	197	30	2,207	1,767	365	235	41	329	5,172
Third	187	41	3,329	2,070	279	331	35	341	6,613
Fourth	182	45	4,581	2,315	233	488	37	428	8,308
Highest	190	55	6,332	2,490	170	1045	56	660	10,997
Average	195	40	3,580	2,014	295	460	41	408	7,033

Source: Great Britain National Travel Survey, 2002–10

on low incomes being in work and more being retired – in general working people make more trips and retired people make fewer.

Tables 27.5 and 27.6 show the effect of income quintile on the numbers of trips and distance travelled by different modes. There is a sort of 'ceiling' whereby the average number of trips made does not rise much above 1,100 trips per year for any income group. (This is, of course, a ceiling for the average for the group as a whole – many people will be making more than 1,100 trips per year.) The main differences in the use of different modes are that lower-income people make more walking and bus journeys and very much fewer as a car driver or by rail.

The ceiling of trip rates does not apply to distance travelled or use of the car. Mileage per person increases for each income quintile group (Table 27.6) and the bulk of this increase is made up of more car driver and passenger mileage. The distances for other modes is relatively insignificant compared with car mileage. But while walking distance is insignificant (in terms of total distance travelled) for all incomes, it forms 34 per cent of trip numbers for those in the lowest income quintile.

Changes Over Time

Car ownership for the lowest income quintile has grown rapidly since 1995 with the percentage of households having a car rising from under 40 per cent to just under

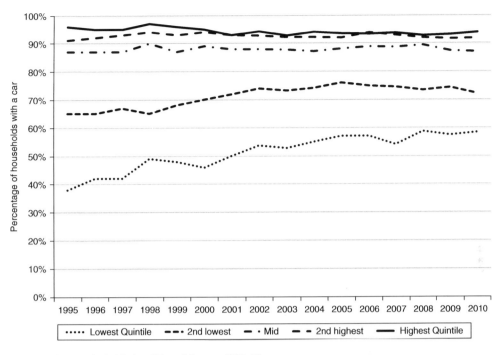

Source: Great Britain National Travel Survey, 2002–10

Figure 27.1 Percentage of households with a car by income quintile – 1995 to 2010

60 per cent, although growth was much slower during the 2000s decade. At the same time, the percentage for the two highest income groups has been stable, possibly falling but staying over 90 per cent, and only a small rise was noted for those in the second lowest income quintile (Figure 27.1).

This pattern of a tendency towards equality in travel is repeated for other measures of car use and general mobility. A pattern emerges that those with higher incomes are using cars less than they were in the 1990s with some fluctuation but a steady trend towards lower use. At the same time, those on lower incomes are becoming more reliant on cars and are much more likely to own them, although their mileage has not grown so rapidly as ownership. Recent research points to the notion of 'peak car' based on the observation that car use per person has levelled off since around 2000 (e.g., Goodwin, 2012). Some argue (e.g., Metz, 2010) that this is because, for most people, there is no further utility to be gained by travelling greater distances. At the same time, a lack of alternatives such as public transport can encourage car use among those who can little afford it. Demographic changes may also be important with increasing numbers of pensioner households having cars that they acquired when on higher incomes.

The Relative Importance of Different Factors on Travel Distance

When looking at what affects the total distance travelled for the population as a whole using regression analysis, Stokes and Lucas (2011) found that income is a major, but not overriding factor. Factors such as being retired, having a mobility difficulty and being aged under 16 have the greatest effect on reducing distance, but these are also generally associated with lower incomes. When looking at effects for those in each economic activity group, it is clear that low income is a major factor on reducing distance travelled for virtually all groups, along with being young, non-white, living in an area with a high Index of Multiple Deprivation (IMD) and having a mobility difficulty. Having children seems to have the strongest upward effect on the amount of travel.

Looking specifically at those on low incomes, a different pattern emerges. Living in a rural area has a strong upward effect on travel distance, while living in an area with a high IMD score has a strong downward effect. Being younger, non-white and having a mobility difficulty also have a reducing effect. The implication is that income is not the only major influence on travel distance, but it is one of the most important. For those on low incomes, rurality and IMD scores for the local area are of great importance – rurality increases the amount of travel while being in an area of multiple derivation reduces it.

Patterns of Behaviour for Different Sub-groups of Those on Lower Incomes

Cluster analysis by Stokes and Lucas (2011) did not provide definitive insights into the differences in behaviour between different types of lower income people. But it pointed to a large amount of variation in travel behaviour by people on low incomes, and to the existence of a large core of people on low incomes who make very little travel (about 37 per cent of those in the lowest income quintile). These people are predominantly young or old, and do not have access to a car. While a similar grouping is found by cluster analysis for all income groups, the group is much larger for low-income households and the level of trip-making is lower than for higher-income groups.

Another group notable in analysis of low-income households is much smaller and is people who can be described as 'predominantly car users' – making most of their trips by car. These people are generally working. While such 'predominantly car users' in higher-income groups use cars for all journey purposes as well as work, there is more likelihood that the low-income people in this group make very few non-work journeys. It points to a hypothesis that they need a car for their work, but do not have the resources to use it for much else than getting to and from work.

The implication is that low incomes can restrict travel, but the analysis also highlights the likely existence of 'forced' car ownership for some lower income people in work.

Summary of Travel Behaviour Related to Income

The travel behaviour of those on low incomes shows differences to those on higher incomes. At this level of analysis, many variables appear to show a continuous relationship with income – the higher the income, the greater the amount of travel, and the greater the use of motorised modes – although less the use of buses and walking. Those in the lowest income quintile are not a homogenous group displaying a paucity of travel – but that does not mean that there is not something we might call 'transport poverty' that can affect those on low incomes in conjunction with other factors.

4.   ACCESSIBILITY TO SERVICES

Accessibility has been measured in a number of ways, with the main factors used in indicators being travel time or distance to services and facilities, combined with some measure of the usefulness of that service. Indicators range from the very simple to the very complex, and there is argument about the extent to which it is better to provide a simple understandable indicator, against one that includes as much as possible and is more accurate, but more complex and less transparent. Several comprehensive reviews of accessibility measures have been written; for example, Morris et al. (1979) and Scheurer and Curtis (2004).

Here we use the simplest indicators to show relationships between access and incomes and geography. This original analysis uses indicators developed for the English Index of Multiple Deprivation (IMD) for 2010 (Communities and Local Government, 2011), and Department for Transport access to employment indicators of accessibility for small geographic areas (DfT, 2011), analysed at Lower Super Output Area level. Figure 27.2 shows how road distance to the nearest food store, general practitioner (doctor), post office and primary school varies according to the income domain used in the IMD. For

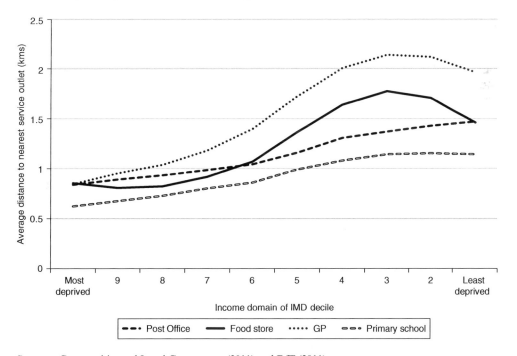

Source: Communities and Local Government (2011) and DfT (2011)

Figure 27.2   Distance to nearest service outlets by IMD decile

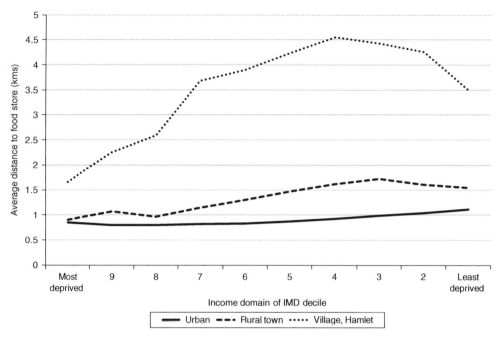

Source: Communities and Local Government (2011) and DfT (2011)

Figure 27.3   Average distance to nearest food shop by IMD decile and rurality

each service type, those in more deprived IMD areas are closest to services, but while the distance rises up to about the third least deprived deciles, it falls again for the two least deprived deciles, notably for general practitioners and food stores.

When we look at distance to food stores for urban and rural areas by IMD (see Figure 27.3 for food stores), we can see firstly that rural residents tend to live much further away from services, but that for urban areas the relationship for average local incomes is more linear. But for those in villages and hamlets there is a very marked tendency for people in the middle and towards the less deprived deciles to be more distant. Villages with local services are often the areas with the least deprivation, since they are attractive places to live with at least some services close by.

The Department for Transport produce a range of accessibility indicators for those with access to different modes of transport, and Figure 27.4 shows that rural areas of all types have very much lower accessibility by public transport to employment centres and that accessibility is not strongly influenced by IMD decile. Note that while in Figures 27.2 and 27.3 a low distance was 'good', in this case a low accessibility is not 'good'. For urban areas, those living in lower-income areas tend to have more employment within 20 minutes by public transport than those in higher-income areas. This does, however, mask variations that exist, with many of the areas with lowest incomes being in relatively inaccessible urban areas.

It is apparent that those in lower income areas tend to, on average, have better access to services, although those in the most deprived decile may have slightly worse

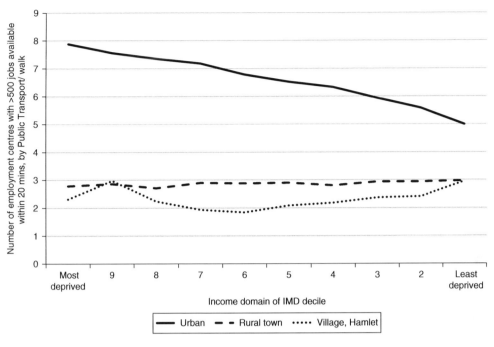

Source: Communities and Local Government (2011) and DfT (2011)

Figure 27.4   Access to employment centres by IMD decile and rurality

accessibility than those in the second and third decile. But for these simple measures it is apparent that rurality is the major determinant of distance to services and accessibility.

5.   TRANSPORT POVERTY AND TRANSPORT WEALTH

Transport Poverty

A definition of fuel poverty has been generally accepted since around 2000 as being where households need to spend more than 10 per cent of their income to keep their living areas heated to 21°C and other areas within the home to 18°C (Boardman, 2010). Calculations have been made (Centre for Sustainable Energy, 2003) using data on characteristics of houses, heating fuel availability and cost, and household incomes to calculate the percentage of people who suffer fuel poverty. Government programmes have used this definition to direct help to those likely to suffer fuel poverty (DECC 2011).

Similarly notions of housing affordability are commonplace, usually measuring the average house price for an area divided by the average income (or 'lower quartile' housing affordability that measures the same for the lower quartile house for those on a lower quartile income).

But the same consensus does not exist for transport and a measurement of transport poverty or affordability is seldom attempted. There are a number of reasons for this, but the prime difficulty relates to how we define the need for travel, which relates to the activities that a person 'needs' to carry out, and the distribution of places where they can be carried out. For some time literature has dealt with attempting to define the need for travel (e.g., Jones, 1975) without any consensus having been reached. Analysis of expenditure on transport (using the Expenditure and Food Survey) shows that those on higher incomes spend very much more on transport than those on lower incomes, which points to a large element of choice on levels of expenditure. Cars are often described as a luxury item, and certainly the status afforded to certain types of cars, and other factors means that many willingly spend much more than they 'need' to on transport (e.g., Stokes et al., 1991). For heating fuel there is much less variation in what level of heating is needed, and much less 'status' attached to different heating systems – a definition of fuel poverty can safely assume that no one would wish to spend more than 10 per cent of their income on heating, but equivalent assumptions about transport have less consensus.

The closest to a definition is probably that of Gleeson and Randolph (2002): 'Transport poverty occurs when a household is forced to consume more travel costs than it can reasonably afford, especially costs relating to motor car ownership and usage.' Dainton (2007), analysing the Expenditure and Food Survey, showed that motoring costs could cause hardship to many lower-income people, but that those in rural areas were especially hard hit.

Recent studies looking specifically at rural areas have identified groups where it can be assumed that expenditure on travel is more than one would reasonably expect – in these studies it is households on low incomes in rural areas who need to spend a high proportion of their income on transport, mainly due to a lack of alternatives to the car.

Expenditure on travel was analysed for each income quintile in urban, small town and rural settlements (Commission for Rural Communities, 2010). Table 27.7, adapted from the report, shows that those in the lowest income quintile in urban areas spent £28 per week on travel, £32 in small towns (roughly 3,000–10,000 population) but £50 per week in smaller settlements. Since the average income for this group was around £170 per week at the time of analysis, this means that nearly 30 per cent of income was being spent on transport on average. Other research in the same publication shows clearly that the extra expenditure correlates with higher levels of car ownership among those in rural areas, implying that those on low incomes generally buy cars out of necessity rather than choice. This is similar to Currie and Delbosc (2013), who use a working definition that those in low-income households who have two or more cars suffer from 'forced car ownership'.

Table 27.7   *Expenditure on transport by households in different area types, by income quintile*

	Motoring	Public transport fares	Total
Urban	£23.51	£5.02	£28.53
Rural town	£29.08	£3.22	£32.30
Village and hamlet	£43.48	£4.11	£49.59

Source: Commission for Rural Communities (2010)

Table 27.8   Extra expenditure on transport required for those in rural areas

	Rural town	Village	Hamlet
Single working adult	£15.98	£22.98	£23.99
Two pensioners	£1.99	£27.95	£33.18
Two parents/two children	£48.08	£55.35	£57.76
Single parent/one child	£19.12	£28.94	£30.18

Source: Smith et al. (2010)

Research by Smith, Davis and Hirsch (2010) calculated the extra cost that rural house-holds need to spend to maintain a standard of living regarded as acceptable using a research procedure known as 'Minimum Income Standards'. Residents of small towns and villages were regarded as needing to spend more, and the bulk of this extra spend was where a car was regarded as essential – to all the rural resident groups except pensioner households in small towns. (Groups in urban areas had not been regarded as having a car available being essential.) When costs were calculated this meant that single working adults needed to spend about £20 per week extra on transport (Table 27.8) while a house-hold with two parents and two children needed to spend more than £50 a week more.

These two pieces of research both point to the existence of problems related to expenditure needed on transport for low-income households, and the results, using very different approaches, produce comparable results. Each specifically highlights the issue in rural areas, but the implication is that anyone on a low income who finds they need a car to fulfil their travel needs is likely to spend a high proportion of their income on travel. The work on forced car ownership (Currie and Delbosc, 2013) points to the phenomenon being found for people on low incomes in suburban areas that have poor public transport. This points to a notion of transport poverty being a valid one, even if it difficult to define or measure.

Transport Wealth (or Mobility Choice)

The notion of 'transport wealth' posited here is that one has greater 'wealth' of trans-port if one has access to more choices to move around – in effect this means that those who can use two or more different modes effectively have more choice (or wealth) than those who only have access to one mode. The notion is fraught with difficulties in terms of definition and measurement. While those on lower incomes may tend to live in areas that may be better served by public transport, this may not provide the same choice of destinations as for those who have cars. And as the previous discussion has shown, the cost of running a car may not compensate for having good quality, cheap public trans-port close at hand.

In order to assess the degree to which people have access to a choice of modes, a simple indicator was created, whereby having access to a car as a main driver, being within 13 minutes' walk of a food store (and not having a mobility difficulty) and having a 15-minute bus service frequency within a six-minute walk (and no mobility difficulty) were regarded as providing that mode as a choice. The proportions of people in different income quintiles with different combinations available are shown in Figure 27.4. It can

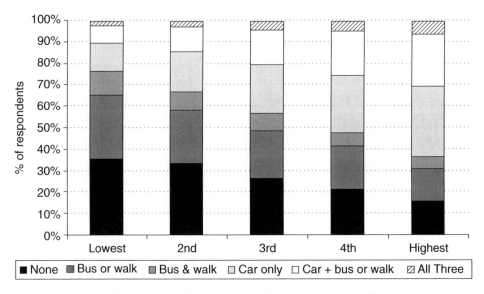

Figure 27.5   A simple indicator of transport wealth by income quintile

be seen that more in the lower-income groups have bus or walking as a single option and somewhat more have bus and walking as their options. But this is outweighed by the higher proportions in higher income quintiles having access to a car.

In order for the concept to be of any practical value it would need to assess more clearly the benefits offered by different modes in different geographic, social and economic situations.

6.   IMPLICATIONS FOR TRANSPORT PLANNING AND DEVELOPMENT

This chapter has looked at transport poverty as a combination of low incomes and a lack of accessibility. The relationship between travel behaviour and poverty is very apparent. Low-income people, on average, travel less than those on higher incomes and they are much less likely to have access to cars. But travel is not an economic 'good' where 'more is necessarily better', so a definition of transport poverty is not so straightforward.

While travel poverty is difficult to pin down, there is evidence that poorer people in rural areas (and other areas without travel alternatives) suffer through reliance on cars when they have difficulty affording them. And there is evidence that other combinations of poverty, disadvantage and exclusion can act together to limit mobility.

There is not enough analysis to identify specifics that can identify people who suffer from 'travel poverty' but the results do point to a situation where policy should address the issue. It is apparent that a minority of people have a difficulty with transport that we can loosely define as transport poverty, but that our evidence for it does not lend itself to easy measurement.

The chapter has identified an issue that needs addressing, but its focus on these particular measureable aspects has rather ignored wider issues of transport and inequality. Whether or not further analysis will lead to a readily accepted indicator of transport poverty, or whether the notion will in time find its way into transport planning and development through a wider understanding of the issues within the professions is debatable, but it is apparent that policy and practice need to accept the existence of the issue.

It would seem that there are three key principles in transport planning and development planning that need to be borne in mind to ensure transport poverty is not overlooked. These are that:

- It is important to ensure that the accessibility of services and facilities for all groups of people are assessed, along the lines of accessibility planning – but with an emphasis on ensuring accessibility is of a certain standard for those on low incomes, in rural areas, or with other characteristics that are likely to lead to transport poverty.
- New land-use development needs to be located to ensure that it will not compromise the future accessibility of those groups described above in a way that may force them into transport poverty. This is especially pertinent for housing developments that include affordable housing.
- For areas that are not close to services or that have poor public transport availability there is a need to improve public transport or provide new forms of transport supply such as car clubs and car share schemes.

The Sustainable Development Commission (2011) highlights the need to ensure that fairness is at the heart of transport planning and appraisal. It suggests a four-level hierarchy of goals for transport development. When all has been achieved from the higher-level goals, solutions can be aimed at lower-level ones. The levels (from high to low) can be summarised as:

- demand reduction – reducing the need for powered transport, by a range of measures from spatial planning to technological solutions such as telecommuting;
- modal shift to more sustainable modes and space efficient modes – for example, from private to public transport, and from motorised modes to walking and cycling;
- efficiency improvements to existing modes – behavioural change and technical interventions;
- capacity increases – should only be considered when the first three have been fully explored.

It is argued that if this hierarchy is adopted it will aid sustainability, fairness and the efficiency of transport within the economy.

With the current lack of consensus over transport poverty, it is likely that calls to take it into account will fall on deaf ears but, interestingly, climate change, peak oil and peak car may offer the best prospect for transport poverty being taken seriously. While those without cars were seen as an ever-decreasing minority and while fuel was cheap, many viewed transport poverty as a problem that would solve itself through rising incomes and universal car ownership. This can no longer be seen as the case, and policy to change travel behaviour can much more easily take transport poverty into account. We may very well be moving into an era when the most sensible transport policy solutions will also help those on the lowest incomes most.

NOTE

1. Equivalised income quintiles are used in this chapter. These relate household income to household size and structure, with the OECD method used here.

REFERENCES

Banister, D. and Bowling, A. (2004), Quality of life for the elderly: the transport dimension, *Transport Policy*, **11**, 105–15.

Boardman, B. (2010), *Fixing Fuel Poverty: Challenges and Solutions*, Sterling: Earthscan.

Cahill, M., Ruben, T. and Winn, S. (1996), *Children and Transport: Travel Patterns, Attitudes and Leisure Activities of Children in the Brighton Area*, Brighton: University of Brighton, Health and Social Policy Research Centre.

Centre for Sustainable Energy (2003), *Fuel Poverty Indicator*, www.cse.org.uk/projects/view/1109.

Commission for Rural Communities (2010), *State of the Countryside Report*, http://ruralcommunities.gov.uk/2010/07/06/state-of-the-countryside-2010.

Communities and Local Government (2011), *The English Indices of Deprivation 2010*, www.communities.gov.uk/publications/corporate/statistics/indices2010.

Currie, G. and Delbosc, A. (2013), *Exploring Trends in Forced Car Ownership in Melbourne*, Australasian Transport Research Forum 2013 Proceedings, 2–4 October, Brisbane.

Dainton, E. (2007), *The Cost of Transport and its Impact on UK Households: An Analysis of the ONS (2007) Family Spending Report*, London: RAC Foundation.

DECC (2011), *Fuel Poverty Statistics*, Department of Energy and Climate Change, www.decc.gov.uk/en/content/cms/statistics/fuelpov_stats/fuelpov_stats.aspx.

DfT (2009), *Transport Statistics Bulletin – National Travel Survey 2008*, London: Department for Transport.

DfT (2010), *Travel by Car: Availability, Income, Ethnic Group and Household Type*, London: Department for Transport, www.dft.gov.uk/pgr/statistics/datatablespublications/nts/latest/nts2009-07.pdf.

DfT (2011), *Accessibility Statistics*, London: Department for Transport www.dft.gov.uk/statistics/series/accessibility.

Gilhooly, M., Hamilton, K., O'Neill, M., Gow, J., Webster, N. and Pike, F. (2002), *Transport and Ageing: Extending Quality of Life via Public and Private Transport*, http://v-scheiner.brunel.ac.uk/bitstream/2438/1312/1/PDF%20ESRC%20Transport%20Final%20Report.pdf.

Gleeson, B. and Randolph, B. (2002), Social disadvantage and planning in the Sydney context, *Urban Policy and Research*, **20**(1), 101–7.

Goodwin, P. (2012), Three views on 'peak car', *World Transport Policy and Practice*, **17**, 8–17.

Grieco, M., Pickup, L. and Whipp, J. (1989), *Gender, Transport and Employment*, Aldershot: Gower.

Hillman, M. (1973), *Personal Mobility and Transport Policy*, London: Policy Studies Institute Broadsheet 542.

Hillman, M. (1993), *Children, Transport and the Quality of Urban Life*, London: Policy Studies Institute.

Jones, P. (1975), *Accessibility, Mobility and Travel Need: Some Problems of Definition and Measurement*, paper presented to the IBG Transport Geography Study Group conference.

Jones, P. and Wixey, S. (2005), *Measuring Accessibility as Experienced by Different Socially Disadvantaged Groups*, SAMP end of project summary report, University of Westminster, http://home.wmin.ac.uk/transport/download/SAMP_WP8_Final_Summary_Report.pdf.

Lucas, K., Tyler, S. and Christodoulou, G. (2008), *The Value of New Public Transport in Deprived Areas: Who Benefits, How and Why?* York: Joseph Rowntree Foundation.

McDonagh, J. (2006), Transport policy instruments and transport-related social exclusion in rural Republic of Ireland, *Journal of Transport Geography*, **14**(5), 355–66.

Metz, D. (2010), Saturation of demand for daily travel, *Transport Reviews*, May.

Morris, J.M., Dumble, P.L. and Wigan, M.R. (1979), Accessibility indicators for transport planning, *Australia Transportation Research Part A: General*, **13**(2), 91–109.

Oxley, P.R. and Richards, M.J. (1995), Disability and transport: a review of the personal costs of disability in relation to transport, *Transport Policy*, **2**(1), 57–65.

Pilling, A. and Turner, J. (1998), *Catching Them Young: Attitudes of Young People to Travel in Greater Manchester*, Proceedings of Universities Transport Study Groups (UTSG) Annual Conference, Dublin.

Preston, J. and Raje, F. (2007), Accessibility, mobility and transport-related social exclusion, *Journal of Transport Geography*, **15**(3), 151–60.

Rajé, F. (2004), *Transport Demand Management and Social Inclusion: The Need for Ethnic Perspectives*, Aldershot: Ashgate.

Scheurer, J. and Curtis, C. (2007), *Accessibility Measures: Overview and Practical Applications*, Curtin University Working Paper no 4.

Smith, N., Davis, A. and Hirsch, D. (2010), *A Minimum Income Standard for Rural Households*, York: Joseph Rowntree Foundation.

Social Exclusion Unit (2003), *Making the Connection: Final Report on Transport and Social Exclusion*, London: Cabinet Office.

Stokes, G. (1995), *Assessing the Effects of New Transport Policies on Rural Residents*, Transport Studies Unit, University of Oxford, TSU Ref 836.

Stokes, G. and Lucas, K. (2011), *National Travel Survey Analysis*, TSU Working Paper Series, Ref. 1053, School of Geography and the Environment, Oxford.

Stokes, G., Kenny, F. and Hallett, S. (1991), *The Love Affair with the Car – Wedlock or Deadlock*, paper presented to PTRC Summer Annual Meeting, Brighton.

Sustainable Development Commission (2011), *Fairness in a Car Dependent Society*, London: Sustainable Development Commission.

28 Development and social policy: the role of transport in social development, in the UK context
Susan Kenyon

1. INTRODUCTION

This chapter considers the role of transport in social development in the UK. Theoretical and empirical evidence is presented to support the call for transport to be recognised as a social policy, both affecting and being affected by policies that promote social development. It is shown that transport creates a need for social policies; and that social policies create a need for transport. If these needs are not met, social policies will not succeed in their social development aims. Transport is shown to influence the success of both traditional and new social policies, with a particular focus upon education, demonstrating, through a case study, an unbreakable link between transport and social development. This link is so strong that transport must now be considered to be a social policy, if social development is to be furthered in the UK. The chapter is innovative in its call for transport policy to be recognised as social policy, with the commentary offering a new perspective on the influence of transport on social development in the UK.

The chapter begins with a definition of development, before turning to define social policy. Next, there is discussion of transport and social policy. Two discourses are identified: the 'too little mobility' discourse and the 'too much mobility' discourse. The chapter then turns to a case study of education in the UK. The effects of transport on education are presented to illustrate the inextricable link between transport, social development and social policy.

2. DEVELOPMENT

Development is defined in a variety of ways by different authors in this book. Some consider urban structure and design and its relationship with travel; others examine the role of transport investment and its relationship with changes in urban development, including issues such as economic development. This chapter focuses upon the social aspects of development.

Development is an elusive concept and it is important to recognise that it is not a neutral term. This chapter necessarily eschews full discussion of the nature of and imperative for 'development', presenting instead a discussion of development as it relates to social policy in the UK. In this sense, development is seen very much from the modernisation perspective, as capitalist economic growth, with social concerns for welfare and well-being: in Rostow's terms, the stage of high mass consumption (1991). Alternatives to the modernisation perspective on development range from left-wing critiques, to

'Third World' critiques, to green critiques, as outlined in Harrison (1993), Escobar (2011) and Dobson (2007), respectively.

A growing economy is seen as an important indicator of a 'developed' society and of a society that is continuing to develop. As such, economic growth is an ideal chased by governments across the globe. However, globally, development is also now viewed more broadly. The United Nations Human Development Reports (UNHDR) indicate the extent to which countries are 'developed' through the Human Development Index (HDI), where development is measured in terms of health, education and personal income (UNDP, 2011). A range of additional data are analysed in the UNHDR, which suggest an extended concept of human development to include 'well-being', itself a nebulous term, but defined in the UNHDR as 'overall life satisfaction'. Most notably, the 2011 report talks not just of human development, but of sustainable and equitable human development, highlighting the centrality of environmental measures and equity to notions of development and well-being.

Just as the concept of development has been extended beyond the focus on economic growth at the international level, so has it at the national level. In the UK, while sustained economic growth remains a clear political priority,[1] the government has also introduced the concept of the 'Happiness Index'. The Index is predicated on the notion that a developed society is one in which individual well-being is prioritised and that, in measuring well-being, GDP is not the ideal measure. As the Prime Minister, David Cameron, states: the focus of 'development' must be 'not just on GDP but on GWB – general well-being' (cited in BBC, 2010).

Happiness and well-being are not defined by the UK government. However, we can gain an understanding of the concepts by examining the proposed indicators of happiness. This index is to include ten criteria of well-being (Table 28.1). Many of the proposed indicators lie within the scope of traditional development indicators (for example GDP, income, education, employment, health and housing), closely paralleling the Indices of Multiple Deprivation, which measure development at the local level. However, the

Table 28.1   Proposed domains for the Happiness Index alongside domains for the English Indices of Deprivation

Happiness Index	English Indices of Deprivation
Individual well-being (satisfaction with life)	
Our relationships (family, friends, community)	
Health (physical and mental)	Health deprivation and disability
What we do (work, leisure)	Employment deprivation
Where we live (housing, environment, community)	Barriers to housing and services; living environment deprivation; crime
Personal finance (income)	Income deprivation
Education and skills	Education skills and training deprivation
Governance (democracy and trust in government)	
The economy (GDP)	
The natural environment (local and global)	

Source: Beaumont (2011) and DCLG (2011)

remainder are more social measures of development, including leisure, the natural environment, social relationships and satisfaction with life.

The Happiness Index indicates the importance of the social in present concepts of development in the UK. Importantly, with the development of the Happiness Index, the government is acknowledging responsibility for social development, alongside economic development. Where social development is promoted, policies that address the social become central to government activity. The following section considers the nature and objectives of this 'social policy', demonstrating that development and social policy are inextricably linked.

3.   SOCIAL POLICY

In this chapter, social policy is defined as government policy that responds to social need and that aims to improve human welfare. Covering a range of public policies that affect the well-being of members of society, the term 'social policy' refers to a deliberate government policy intervention to influence access to economic and other goods and resources, to meet a welfare objective.

In the UK, social policy has traditionally been viewed in the context of addressing the five 'giant evils' identified by Beveridge in 1942: disease, idleness, ignorance, squalor and want. This leads to social policy to rectify need in terms of health, employment, education, housing and poverty, respectively. Traditional social policy has focused very much upon meeting basic needs to fulfil economic development objectives, linking in to the discourse around absolute poverty (Rowntree, 2001).[2] The Index of Multiple Deprivation, mentioned above, represents a focus upon these more traditional aspects of social policy. More recently, understanding of the concepts of need and welfare has been expanded to consider wider influences upon the achievement of well-being, influenced by the discourse on relative poverty (Townsend, 1979) and the expansion of the concept of development to include social development. The Happiness Index can perhaps be seen to be representative of this perspective. Cahill (1994, 2010) has pioneered this 'new social policy': social policy that looks beyond the five giants to consider modern influences upon well-being. Cahill considers the social influences of the policies and practices of communicating, viewing, shopping, working, playing – and transport.

4.   TRANSPORT AND SOCIAL POLICY

In this chapter, social policies have been defined as those that 'respond to social need and that aim to improve human welfare'. When social policy is understood in this way, transport is undeniably a social policy. In the present environment in the UK, there is a clear social need for transport to fulfil access to the opportunities, goods, services and social networks that are essential for personal and societal well-being. And transport policy has a clear role in improving human welfare by providing access to the same. When accessible transport is available, of the right quality, it directly facilitates participation in the activities that foster social development. This is demonstrated when we examine the negative impacts of too little mobility.

The 'Too Little Mobility' Discourse and Social Policy

The late 1990s/early 2000s saw a flurry of both government and academic activity in the area of transport and social exclusion in the UK. Today, an increasingly international literature demonstrates that 'inadequate mobility' can cause social exclusion and inhibit social development.[3]

As outlined above, the UK government implements a wide range of social policies in response to social need and to foster social development in the UK. However, underlying many of these policies is a need for mobility to access the assistance that the government provides. Inadequate transport to these government initiatives can directly prevent their success.

For example, for health policies to succeed in promoting and maintaining the health of the nation, service users must be able to access health services. However, low mobility has been linked to difficulties in accessing a wide range of healthcare services, including dentists, family planning, GPs and hospitals, particularly specialist services. Health can be also be affected by problems with access to other services. Poor access to healthy food shops can reinforce and perpetuate ill-health. Low mobility can influence access to sports and leisure facilities, therefore physical fitness, as can low access to non-motorised mobility. Access to social activities can also influence health outcomes. The ability to socialise helps people to cope with physical illness; and access to social activities and social networks can affect mental health.

Similarly, for employment policies to succeed in their aim of promoting full employment, employees must be able to access sites of employment. But the need for transport extends beyond this, to the need to access information about job opportunities (both formal and informal), interviews and training. Furthermore, low mobility has been linked to low pay, because it restricts travel horizons, enforcing a localised existence and thus influencing choice of employment. Mobility can also be a factor in the inability to accept overtime or employment outside of conventional hours, including shift work and part-time work; and unreliable transport can lead to late arrival at work, resulting in docked pay.

Education is a key tool for the promotion of social development in the UK, being 'at or near the heart of policies for fostering greater social integration, social mobility and national competitiveness and reducing social exclusion' (Butler and Hamnett, 2007). However, '[d]ifficulties with transport can prevent people from participating in learning or restrict their choice of the quality, subject matter or type of learning they attend' (SEU, 2003). This can affect access to education at all levels, including preschool, school, further and higher education, adult learning and job-related training (SEU, 2003). Considering school-level education, Butler and Hamnett (2007) find a strong relationship between geography and educational attainment in the UK, which may be further exacerbated by government policy on parental choice in schooling, a policy that betrays an implicit mobility dependence. Extra-curricular, informal learning opportunities – including before- and after-school homework clubs, subject-specific additional learning and sports – can influence attainment. However, pupils can be unable to attend after-school activities, because of transport constraints. With respect to post-16 education, 6 per cent of 16–24 year olds, 3 per cent of those aged 25–44 and 2 per cent aged 45–64 have turned down further education or training in the past year, because of transport difficulties (SEU, 2003).

'New' social policy areas can also be impacted by too little transport. Considering Cahill's areas of new social policy, the policies and practices of communicating, shopping and playing have all been found to have been affected by lack of access to transport. Focusing upon communicating, government social policy recognises the importance of universal access to information and communications technologies (ICTs), specifically the Internet (DCMS, n.d.). The impacts of ICTs upon transport have been much disputed, but there can be little doubt that this social policy will have implications for transport, be they substitution or enhancement (Kenyon, 2010 summarises research to date). Should it be that ICTs create a need for increased mobility, such that this social policy creates a need for transport, if this need cannot be met, not only will social policy aims be unfulfilled but further exclusion may occur.

Thus, social policies create a need for transport. When these needs are not met, the social development aims that social policies seek to meet cannot be fulfilled.

The 'Too Much Mobility' Discourse and Social Policy

The above relationship between transport and social policy highlights the role of transport in enabling the success of social policies. However, two relationships between transport and social policy are identified in this chapter. The second relationship contends that transport creates a need for social policy to address the negative social impacts of transport itself.

This 'too much mobility' discourse emerged within the sociological literature. Since the 1970s, authors including Aird (1972), Illich (1974), Flink (1975), Gorz (1979), Sachs (1992), Freund and Martin (1993), Gartman (1994), Whitelegg (1997), Paterson (2007) and Urry (2007) have identified an ideology of automobility, or a car culture, prevalent in Western societies. The negative attributes of this culture are brought to the fore by these authors, who note that this culture has created a culture of 'hypermobility' (Adams, 2000) and imposed a need for mobility for full participation in society. As Illich (1974) notes: 'Motorized vehicles create remoteness which they alone can shrink.' As car use has grown, promoted by successive UK governments in the belief that it is an essential component of economic growth, land-use patterns have changed, reducing immediate accessibility. This is borne out by statistical evidence, which highlights the increases in average journey lengths and in distances between residential location and key services (DfT, 2010). This negative effect has increasingly become part of the transport geography literature, moving gradually into the mainstream of transport studies via the sustainable transport planning agenda, which intends to move people away from car use (for example, Banister, 2005 and Goodwin, 2008).

Within this discourse, too much mobility has created a need for social policy. For example, in health, transport systems have impacts for health policy, through the health impacts of air/noise/land pollution, road traffic incidents, the decline in physical exercise and the obesogenic environment. Considering employment, one consequence of changes in land use is the movement of employment opportunities to less accessible areas (reflected in the present UK government's call for the relocation of the unemployed to sites of employment; Kite, 2010). Considering poverty, authors including ACRE (2001) highlight the deprivation by expenditure that can result from mobility, highlighting the sacrifices that are made so that mobility needs can be met. Mobility has also been linked to economic decline of geographical and social communities, linked to the flight of employment opportunities and services from the local area.

Too much mobility at the individual level may hinder access to and achievement in education. There is evidence linking transport and exclusion from school-level education, considering reduced participation in extra-curricular activities (ACRE, 2001; Carson, 2004) and the link between commute time and student achievement, related to lateness, stress and reduced time to study due to travel time. Considering further education (FE), one in five students have considered dropping out because of the cost of travel. Finally, Cahill (2010) emphasises the importance of play for children's development. However, the transport system has reduced safe spaces to play, which Cahill terms '[t]he lost world of the child friendly environment'. There are consequences for the formal education system, which must now compensate for this change in childhood development.

'New' social policy areas are also impacted by 'too much' transport. Transport has many environmental consequences, including pollution, climate change, resource depletion and land take, each of which has social implications that must be legislated for (or, more commonly, against). Fitzpatrick (2010) provides the case study of fuel poverty to illustrate the social effects of environmental change, expertly linking environmental degradation, much of which can be linked to transport, to its social policy consequences, including changes in governance and democracy. Crime has also been linked to high levels of mobility and for Barry (2002), the most significant impact of high mobility has been the impact upon social solidarity, as members of society are isolated by the individualism inherent in mass car-based mobility and, with reduced integration, less tolerant of others.

5.   CASE STUDY: HIGHER EDUCATION AND TRANSPORT[4]

Higher education (HE) is a key contributor to social development in the UK. Participation in HE has been linked to a number of benefits for the individual, including higher employment rates, higher wages and better physical and mental health among graduates, compared with non-graduates. Increased participation in HE also has societal benefits, including greater civic participation and social tolerance among graduates and better educational outcomes for the children of graduates (DIUS, 2008).

Therefore, a key social policy goal of recent UK governments has been to enable more people to participate in HE, not only by increasing, but also by widening participation in HE. Widening participation initiatives aim to increase aspiration, access to and achievement in HE (HEFCE, 2006), with the aim of enabling people from all backgrounds to achieve their full educational potential, with benefits for both the individual and society as a whole.

When governments discuss increasing access to HE, their focus is primarily upon factors such as reducing the cost of HE, tackling admissions systems that can be experienced as pejorative by non-traditional students or reducing the impact of disability upon the ability to participate and achieve. However, to be successful, students must be able to attend the site of higher education; HE must be accessible, in the purest definition of the term. Despite a history of distance learning in the UK (the Open University

Table 28.2   Similarities between the characteristics of non-traditional students and the characteristics of people experiencing mobility-related exclusion

Non-traditional students	Mobility-related exclusion
Lower socio-economic groups	Lower socio-economic groups
Non-traditional qualifications	Unknown
Minority ethnic groups	Minority ethnic groups
People with disability	People with disability
Low participation neighbourhoods	Geographical concentration of mobility-related exclusion
No history of familial attendance	Unknown
Low provision of HE in locality	Low provision of mobility and services in the locality
Potential part-timers: those in part time work and/or with caring responsibilities	Those travelling off-peak or with dependents

was established in 1971), the vast majority of UK HE students learn by being physically present at lectures and seminars, by physically visiting the library, workshop or placement.

Therefore, this policy creates transport needs. To what extent can the policy can be successful, if transport needs are not met? Table 28.2 highlights the characteristics of those who are underrepresented in HE. The table also presents the characteristics of those experiencing mobility-related exclusion. There is a high degree of similarity between the two groups. If those who are underrepresented in HE are also experiencing mobility-related exclusion, how successful can initiatives to widen participation that require physical mobility be?

To explore this question, a series of four focus groups was undertaken with current HE students at the University of Kent, a multi-site university situated primarily in the south-east of England. Two were held at the Canterbury site, which resembles that of a traditional, campus-based cathedral university; and two at the Medway site, a brownfield site housing teaching buildings only. The Medway campus is 30 miles from Canterbury, in Chatham. Established in 2004 with the specific aim of widening participation to HE, the campus aims to bring HE to the heart of one of the most deprived areas in Kent (an initiative later endorsed by the Labour government, which established the local delivery of HE as a key policy to reduce educational exclusion; DIUS, 2008).[5]

Sampling was theoretical, considering restrictions on mode choice and on participation in HE. Within this, a maximum variation sampling strategy was employed, to ensure participation of students with a wide range of characteristics. A mix of characteristics was sought in each of the focus groups, to ensure that different perspectives drawn from different experiences were heard and contrasted. Discussions lasted 1.5–2 hours and were facilitated by the author. Discussions were recorded, transcribed and anonymised. Analysis was content-focused, following a modified grounded theory approach (Corbin and Strauss, 1998). The study received ethical approval from the University of Kent.

Findings

It emerged strongly and naturally that participants experience mobility-related educational exclusion. The discussions confirmed a direct influence of inadequate mobility on access to and achievement in higher education and, therefore, a direct influence of transport upon the success of social policy that aims to widen participation in higher education. This section focuses upon the effects of mobility-related educational exclusion in four areas: academic effects, social effects, restricted choices and attrition.[6]

Academic effects of mobility-related educational exclusion
Participants reported exclusion from each of the following activities, because of inadequate transport:

- Formal teaching delivery (including lectures, workshops, seminars).
- Informal teaching delivery(for example, meetings with tutors).
- Peer learning and support.
- Placements and case visits.
- Extra-curricular academic activities (including lectures).
- On-site individual learning activities (for example, library-based research).
- Printing and submitting assignments.
- Future careers activities (including careers fairs and 'meet the employer' events).

Participants felt that exclusion from each of these activities has a clear impact upon their achievement in higher education and upon future employability.

Social effects of mobility-related educational exclusion
It would be easy to dismiss students' concerns about access to social activities. However, the social side of learning is an essential factor in preventing attrition, conferring a sense of belonging, or rootedness, within the university, so making attrition less likely (Gorard et al., 2006). Put more simply, if students are not happy, they will not complete their studies and friendships are a key to happiness. Considering Cohen and Pressman's (2004) three types of social support, emotional, informational and material support, access to each can be considered to be vital for achievement in HE. However, difficulties in accessing this social support, in maintaining/developing relationships, were attributed to mobility difficulties by many participants.

Restricted choices
Participants highlighted restricted choices, as a direct result of inadequate mobility. Restricted choices were experienced at three levels: participants could not attend the institution of their choice; take the course of their choice; or take the modules of their choice. In this sense, those without access to sufficient mobility experience a poorer university education than those with sufficient mobility. This suggests a second-class educational experience and again highlights the impossibility of success in social policy, without consideration of transport.

Attrition

The following quotation summarises the influence of mobility difficulties upon attrition, demonstrating that transport difficulties can directly cause students to abandon their studies: 'I nearly jacked in uni, no I'm not coming back, it's getting here and getting into class is such an effort when it shouldn't be, it should be easy, you should be starting your day relaxed, not fired up because it is a nightmare travelling down here . . . you get here and think, I just don't want to come here anymore' (Group 2, Medway).

6.   DISCUSSION

This case study illustrates the impact of transport upon policies to promote social development in the UK. It demonstrates how social policy creates transport needs and that, if these needs are not met, government policies cannot succeed in their social development aims.

The study focuses upon the 'too little mobility' discourse. However, the study is set within the context of the 'too much mobility' discourse, which shapes land-use and cultural/political/societal assumptions in the present-day UK. Successive UK governments have assumed a degree of mobility from non-participating students, in line with the dominant culture in the UK. The failure to perceive a role for a lack of adequate mobility in non-participation and the assumption that mobility is freely available to potential students is entirely in line with the ideology of automobility that this author suggests underlies all social policy in the UK and that, I suggest, contributes towards the failure of social policies to promote social development in this country.

The case study demonstrates the unbreakable link between transport and social policy. The study is based upon a small sample and further research with a larger sample is essential. Further research could usefully quantify these findings at a range of institutions and examine the impact of higher education upon transport. However, despite these limitations, the case study ably illustrates that social policy to widen participation cannot succeed in the face of inadequate mobility. Access to and achievement in higher education, alongside future employability, are all shown to be negatively impacted by transport.

The case study suggests that attention must be paid to accessibility in its purest term, if widening participation aims are to be achieved. However, greater mobility can itself cause social policy problems, as outlined above. If the greater mobility that is required to widen participation in HE could be achieved by walking, cycling and public transport within a compact city in which the university is accessible by these modes, this need not be negative, socially or environmentally. However, considering the reality of urban development in the UK and the characteristics of non-traditional students, this utopia is unlikely to be realised.

That social policy needs transport, but that transport creates social policy problems is a conundrum that further illustrates the need for transport to be considered as a social policy. Such integration between transport and social policy could ensure that future social policies are 'transport-proofed', with transport policies 'social policy-proofed'. The case study has considered one aspect of social policy. Further research to examine how other social policies are impacted by and impact upon transport, alongside examination of how to address these issues, is needed. Without such research, transport will continue to act as a barrier to social development in the UK.

NOTES

1. This is indicated, for example, in the present coalition government's *Business Plan*, in which growth is listed as one of three economic priorities underlying government policy (HM Treasury, 2010).
2. There are several theories as to why social policies emerged and why they continue today, in addition to the dominant argument that prioritises economic development objectives. These are expertly summarised in Mitton (2011).
3. SEU (2003) provides numerous examples of exclusion due to inadequate transport in the UK, where 'inadequate transport' includes resources at the system level (lack of a good service) and at the individual level (no money to pay for the service). This report focuses upon access to paid work, learning, healthcare, healthy food and leisure. Social opportunities are considered in Kenyon et al. (2003). Similar findings with reference to Australia are reported within Currie et al. (2007). A US perspective is provided within Lucas (2004); the Canadian perspective is considered in McCray and Brais (2007) and Spinney et al. (2009). Lundevaller (2009) considers mobility-related exclusion in Sweden; Taylor (2006) considers the effects of the same in Poland; and Ureta (2008) highlights this with respect to Chile.
4. This case study is based upon evidence first published in Kenyon (2011).
5. A full description of the University, sample details and methodology is available in Kenyon (2011).
6. Further findings, including analysis of the causes of mobility-related educational exclusion, are reported in Kenyon (2011).

REFERENCES

ACRE (2001), *Social Exclusion and Transport: The Reality of Rural Life*, Cambridge: Action for Communities in Rural England.
Adams, J. (2000), Hypermobility, *Prospect*, March.
Aird, A. (1972), *The Automotive Nightmare*, London: Hutchinson and Co.
Banister, D. (2005), *Unsustainable Transport: City Transport in the New Century*, London: Routledge.
Barry, B. (2002), Social exclusion, social isolation and the distribution of income, in J. Hills, J. LeGrand and D. Piachaud (eds), *Understanding Social Exclusion*, Oxford: Oxford University Press.
BBC (2010), Government 'planning to measure people's happiness', www.bbc.co.uk/news/uk-politics-11756049.
Beaumont, J. (2011), *Measuring National Well-being*, discussion paper on domains and measures, www.ons.gov.uk/ons/dcp171766_240726.pdf.
Butler, T. and Hamnett, C. (2007), The geography of education: introduction, *Urban Studies*, **44**(7), 1161–74.
Cahill, M. (1994), *The New Social Policy*, Oxford: Blackwell Publishers.
Cahill, M. (2010), *Transport, Environment and Society*, Berkshire: McGraw Hill.
Carson, G. (2004), *Reducing Social Exclusion by Improving Transport: Accessibility Planning and Appraisal – Some Case Studies*, Second Transport Practitioners Meeting, Birmingham, 7–8 July, London: PTRC.
Cohen, S. and Pressman, S. (2004), Stress-buffering hypothesis, in N. Anderson (ed.), *Encyclopedia of Health Behavior 2*, Thousand Oaks, CA: Sage Publications, pp. 780–82.
Corbin, J. and Strauss, A. (1998), *Basics of Qualitative Research: Techniques and Procedures for Developing Grounded Theory*, London: Sage Publications.
Currie, G., Stanley, J. and Stanley, J. (2007), *No Way To Go: Transport and Social Disadvantage in Australian Communities*, Victoria, Australia: Monash University ePress.
DCLG (2011), *The English Indices of Deprivation 2010*, www.communities.gov.uk/documents/statistics/pdf/1871208.pdf.
DCMS (n.d.), *Broadband*, Department for Culture, Media and Sport, www.culture.gov.uk/what_we_do/telecommunications_and_online/7763.aspx.
DfT (2010), *Transport Statistics Great Britain*, Department for Transport, http://webarchive.nationalarchives.gov.uk/20110218142807/dft.gov.uk/pgr/statistics/datatablespublications/tsgb.
DIUS (2008), *A New 'University Challenge'*, London: Department for Innovation, Universities and Skills.
Dobson, A. (2007), *Green Political Thought*, London: Routledge.
Escobar, A. (2011), *Encountering Development*, Princeton: Princeton University Press.

Fitzpatrick, T. (2010), *Understanding the Environment and Social Policy*, Bristol: Policy Press.

Flink, J. (1975), *The Car Culture*, Cambridge MA: MIT Press.

Freund, P. and Martin, G. (1993), *The Ecology of the Automobile*, Montreal: Black Rose Books.

Gartman, D. (1994), *Auto Opium*, London: Routledge.

Goodwin, P. (2008), Traffic jam? Policy debates after 10 years of 'sustainable' transport, in I. Docherty and J. Shaw (eds), *Traffic Jam: Ten Years of 'Sustainable' Transport in the UK*, Bristol: Policy Press, pp. 231–40.

Gorard, S., Smith, E., May, H., Thomas, L., Adnett, N. and Slack, K. (2006), *Review of Widening Participation Research: Addressing the Barriers to Participation in Higher Education*, a report to HEFCE by the University of York, Higher Education Academy and Institute for Access Studies, London: HEFCE.

Gorz, A. (1979), *Ecology as Politics*, London: Pluto.

Harrison, D. (1993), *The Sociology of Modernization and Development*, London: Routledge.

HEFCE (2006), *Widening Participation: A Review*, report to the Minister of State for Higher Education and Lifelong Learning by the Higher Education Funding Council for England, London: Higher Education Funding Council for England.

HM Treasury (2010), *Business Plan 2011–2015*, www.hm-treasury.gov.uk/d/hmt_dept_businessplan_081110.pdf.

Illich, I. (1974), *Ecology and Equity*, London: Calder and Boyers.

Kenyon, S. (2010), The impacts of Internet use upon activity participation and travel: results from a longitudinal diary-based panel study, *Transportation Research Part C*, **18**(1), 21–35.

Kenyon, S. (2011), Transport and social exclusion: access to higher education in the UK policy context, *Journal of Transport Geography*, **19**(4), 763–71.

Kenyon, S., Rafferty, J. and Lyons, G. (2003), Social exclusion and transport: a role for virtual accessibility in the alleviation of mobility-related social exclusion? *Journal of Social Policy*, **32**(3), 317–38.

Kite (2010), Coalition to tell unemployed to 'get on your bike', *The Telegraph*, www.telegraph.co.uk/news/politics/conservative/7856349/Coalition-to-tell-unemployed-to-get-on-your-bike.html.

Lucas, K. (ed.) (2004), *Running on Empty: Transport, Social Exclusion and Environmental Justice*, Bristol: Policy Press, pp. 39–54.

Lundevaller, E.H. (2009), The effect of travel cost on frequencies of shopping and recreational trips in Sweden, *Journal of Transport Geography*, **17**, 208–15.

McCray, T. and Brais, N. (2007), Exploring the role of transportation in fostering social exclusion: the use of GIS to support qualitative data, *Networks and Spatial Economics*, **7**(4), 397–412.

Mitton, L. (2011), The history and development of social policy, in J. Baldock, L. Mitton, N. Manning and S. Vickerstaff (eds), *Social Policy*, Oxford: Oxford University Press, pp. 28–51.

Paterson, M. (2007), *Automobile Politics: Ecology and Cultural Political Economy*, New York: Cambridge University Press.

Rostow, W. (1991), *The Stages of Economic Growth: A Non-communist Manifesto*, Cambridge: Cambridge University Press.

Rowntree, B.S. (2001), *Poverty: A Study of Town Life*, New York: Garland Publishing.

Sachs, W. (1992), *For Love of the Automobile: Looking Back into the History of our Desires*, Berkeley: University of California Press.

SEU (2003), *Making the Connections: Final Report on Transport and Social Exclusion*, London: Social Exclusion Unit.

Spinney, J.E.L., Scott, D.M. and Newbold, K.B. (2009), Transport mobility benefits and quality of life: a time-use perspective of elderly Canadians, *Transport Policy*, **16**(1), 1–11.

Taylor, Z. (2006), Railway closures to passenger traffic in Poland and their social consequences, *Journal of Transport Geography*, **14**, 135–51.

Townsend, P. (1979), *Poverty in the United Kingdom*, Penguin: Harmondsworth.

UNDP (2011). Human Development Report 2011: Sustainability and Equity – a Better Future for All, http://hdr.undp.org/en/reports/global/hdr2011/download.

Ureta, S. (2008), To move or not to move? Social exclusion, accessibility and daily mobility among the low-income population in Santiago, Chile, *Mobilities*, **3**(2), 269–89.

Urry, J. (2007), *Mobilities*, Bristol: Polity Press.

Whitelegg, J. (1997), *Critical Mass*, London: Pluto Press.

29 The car in the neighbourhood: residential design and social outcomes in southern Germany
Iqbal Hamiduddin

1. INTRODUCTION

The presence of traffic in the residential environment has rarely been a comfortable one. From the 'Red Flag' Act[1] (Marshall, 2005) to the creation of modern 'car-free' development, policymakers have sought to limit the physical intrusion of vehicles on civic life and to orientate the public towards more 'sustainable' modes of travel that are less energy consuming and less polluting. The innovation of design measures to protect the public against the physically and socially detrimental effects of wheeled traffic forms a strong narrative in urban planning history, extending back from the Roman cul-de-sac and notably through to the twentieth-century development of Parker and Unwin's Hampstead Garden Suburb, Stein's Radburn and Buchanan's 'environmental areas', all designed to minimise the penetration of traffic. Similarly, planners and developers have sought to reduce the need for car travel through the orientation of new residential development towards alternative modes of transport and by creating a mix of different land uses that reduce the need to travel.

But to what extent can integrated urban design and transport planning create more environmentally sustainable travel patterns among residents by reducing overall traffic, altering the behaviour of motorists in the neighbourhood and changing the spatial relationship between residents and their cars? The matter is complex, not least because of the influence of factors outside of the neighbourhood focus. Such factors include those that contribute to individual travel need, the quality of transport networks at the urban or regional scale that influence car use in meeting travel need, and the likely presence of intervening factors such as residential self-selection in contributing to patterns of travel rather than physical determinism by design. In the case of the three neighbourhood models explored in this chapter, self-selectivity was always going to be an important influence on community and mobility outcomes, because the parent cities of Freiburg and Tübingen have continued to grow because university students have settled in each city after graduation, putting severe strain on local housing markets. In both cities the new neighbourhoods represent important housing policy responses as well as opportunities to test sustainable planning and design principles.

Although the neighbourhoods seem superficially similar and although they have followed broadly similar development trajectories, important differences exist in underpinning design philosophy and detail. These differences will be explained after a brief review of the social and environmental problems posed by car-oriented planning in the next section. However, the primary purpose of the remainder of this chapter is to evaluate and compare a sample of mobility and community indicators in relation to the original underpinning philosophy and car-reduced design principles, before considering the applicability of the design concepts to other contexts. It suggests that there are few structural barriers preventing the adoption of similar approaches elsewhere.

2. THE CAR IN THE NEIGHBOURHOOD: PROBLEMS AND SOLUTIONS

The social disruption cause by traffic in residential quarters has been a problem since at least Roman times, when pavements were introduced to separate pedestrians and wheeled traffic (Southworth and Ben-Joseph, 1997), culs-de-sac appeared around Rome's forum and Caesar reportedly banned chariots from entering Pompeii at certain times of the day to give residents respite from the noise (Hass-Klau, 1990). The proliferation of the mass-production automobile accentuated problems significantly, particularly where the American grid-iron street layout meant that 'pedestrians risked a dangerous motor street crossing 20 times a mile' (Stein, 1950). But the problems posed by the car weren't purely physical. From the late 1960s a team in San Francisco led by Donald Appleyard began to map social relations in street communities in relation to levels of traffic flow (Appleyard et al., 1981). The team's findings have been replicated and confirmed since (e.g., Hart and Parkhurst, 2011). Residential streets that experience low levels of slow-moving traffic offer a more socially conducive environment where children can play, residents linger and interact with their neighbours and establish much stronger feelings of territorial 'ownership' for their street that in turn created a virtuous circle. Appleyard's team also found that households arranged themselves differently within their homes according to levels of traffic. Residents of streets that experienced high levels of traffic were more likely to orientate themselves to the rear of their buildings, to keep curtains drawn and 'cocoon' themselves inside their homes and thereby take less casual interest in activities on the street outside. The team also found that residents living in streets with high levels of traffic were much more likely to be tenants rather than homeowners, producing a considerably higher household turnover rate, leading to weaker neighbourly ties.

This new evidence served to confirm long-held views over the social intrusion of traffic on home life, and particularly the automobile, which began to dominate European societies from the 1960s as it had done in the United States almost half a century earlier. However, British planners had also begun work on remedying the problem early in the twentieth century, before motorisation came. The Garden City Movement led the way with Raymond Unwin and Barry Parker at the fore with their plan for Hampstead Garden Suburb in North London with a street network that would discourage through traffic and divert vehicles onto main thoroughfares (Southworth and Ben-Joseph, 1997); an approach that would be later recycled in a number of different forms. The crucial device employed by Unwin and Barry was to narrow the standard 35ft street carriageway – as protected by the by-law ordinance of 1875 – to just 16ft. This was set out in the 1906 Hampstead Garden Suburban Act, Section 5 of which stated that:

> Any road not exceeding 500 feet in length constructed primarily for the purpose of giving access to a group of houses in the Garden Suburb and not designed for the purposes of through traffic (known as an accommodation road), may with the consent of the local authority be exempted

from any operation of any bye-laws of the local authority relating to the width of new streets and footways.

(Hampstead Garden Suburb Trust, 1998)

Hampstead Garden Suburb provided an early model for neighbourhood traffic restraint, but it was across the Atlantic where a rapidly motorising society was causing a rethink about the place of the car in society. The forum for thinking was the Regional Planning Association of America (RPAA) – a collective loosely linked with Britain's Garden City Movement, whose architects Clarence Stein and Henry Wright created two important models for traffic restraint. The first was a small scheme at Sunnyside, New York where the 'superblock' concept was introduced – an approach in which access roads were reduced and homes clustered around culs-de-sac (Appleyard et al., 1981). Although the concept was not new – William Owen had used it in the design of the Lever Corporation's model village at Port Sunlight in the north-west of England (Hass-Klau, 1990), it represented an important departure from the traditional American grid-iron pattern and a template for Stein and Wright's second model at Radburn New Jersey. This was supposed to have been a large Garden City-scale development, but the 1929 Wall Street Crash and subsequent economic depression truncated the project prematurely. Nevertheless, a sufficiently large portion of the project was completed for it to have had a profound impact. Indeed, Raymond Unwin himself providentially commented that the scheme's design represented 'a big step in the matter of planning for the motor age and Radburn may well prove to be the basis of future planning both in America and in Europe' (Unwin, 1994: 651). Radburn embodied three important overlapping sets of ideas. The first was a development of Sunnyside's superblock template to limit the penetration of traffic into residential areas, at a much larger neighbourhood scale, and in so doing release space that could be used for other purposes. The second was the creation of a segregated pedestrian network through communal gardens and greenways created by reclaiming some of the physical space that would have been given to road carriageways and parking lots (Lee and Stabin-Nesmith, 2001). The third was in creating a social neighbourhood framework based on Clarence Perry's neighbourhood 'Scheme of Arrangement for a Family-Life Community' (Southworth and Ben-Joseph, 1997; Perry, 1929), shaped around a core containing green space and community amenities and a pattern of streets that discouraged external traffic.

Radburn's ideas have been replicated and adapted since. In Britain, the concept of neighbourhood traffic restraint and diversion became central to Alker Tripp's concept of residential and commercial 'precincts', leading eventually to pedestrianised streets and to Colin Buchanan's later concept of residential 'environmental areas', likened to 'living rooms' to contrast the 'hallway'-like movement corridors of arterial streets (Hebbert, 2005). Britain's post-war new towns incorporated Stein's segregated movement networks for pedestrians and cyclists accompanied the implementation of residential culs-de-sac and Perry's ideas to route traffic around the outside of each neighbourhood block, and for each block to become a social entity, serviced by shops and amenities within a few minutes walking.

Less flatteringly, in Britain the original Radburn concept has been almost unrecognisably adapted into a colloquially labelled 'neo-Radburn model' of suburban development based on culs-de-sac, small green areas with footpaths; patterns used to deliver low density developer-led housing, oriented towards the private car. Socially, the model has embraced growing individualism (Kunstler, 1993) and has reinforced a changing geography of social relations in which, as Webber (1964) observed, 'the place-community represents only a limited and special case of the larger genus of communities, deriving its basis from the common interests that attach to propinquity alone'. The result has been a decline in close community relations, from which the reciprocal bonds of 'social capital' develop (Putnam, 2001). As a result of the fervour for low-density suburban development, Lefebvre (1974) remarked that '[s]uburban houses and 'new towns' came close to the lowest possible 'threshold of sociability' – the point beyond which survival would be impossible because 'all social life would have disappeared'. Density has become a more recent environmental concern and the discussion over energy consumption and urban density has been covered comprehensively elsewhere (e.g., Newman and Kenworthy, 1999). Although density has been described as an integrating 'hub' for pursuing social and environmental sustainability objectives (Rogers, 1999), our understanding of broader social need – such as for natural spaces (Kaplan, 1995) indicates that the two objectives need to be separated onto different axes. Arguably the upper density 'threshold' of sociability and social 'survival' is as important as the lower, meaning that space needs to be organised in order to achieve an appropriate overall balance to achieve both social and environmental ends.

Unwin, Stein and Perry viewed the spatial organisation of traffic in the neighbourhood as the key to creating sociable neighbourhoods. Their objective was to limit the impact of the car in the neighbourhood, by restricting access through superblocks and dead ends, introducing set-backs and landscaping from carriageway space, and by creating alternative movement networks. More recently, attention has turned to the use of street space for pedestrian use and play, through legal designations such as 'home zones' that prioritise non-vehicle uses of carriageways and shared spaces where vehicles and pedestrians have to negotiate a single space; an attempt to use carriageway space to integrate rather than separate communities (CIHT, 2010: 7).

In recent decades, a combination of long-term concern over energy security and climate change and episodic energy 'crises' have focused the attention of planners towards reducing reliance on private automobile travel, both through strategies to reduce the general need to travel and specifically by the car (Banister, 2007). This outlook formed the basis of the strategies in both Freiburg and Tübingen, which will be explored in the following sections. The policy response includes both coercive ('carrot') or restrictive ('stick') physical and administrative measures to suppress car use, including the orientation of development towards high-quality public transport and mixed land uses to shorten travel distances between home, employment, education and essential life needs, and measures to limit car ownership, such as contractual restrictions, limited car parking provision and high parking charges. An extensive range of these measures to limit the car ownership, use and impact in the neighbourhood are summarised in Table 29.1.

3.   NEIGHBOURHOOD MODELS FROM SOUTHERN GERMANY

Three neighbourhood models from southern Germany are explored, consisting of Tübingen's Südstadt quarter (itself consisting of two distinctive neighbourhoods in

Table 29.1   Summary of car reduction measures

Element	Incentives ('carrot')		Preventative measures ('stick')	
	Physical	Administrative	Physical	Administrative
Ownership	Public transport proximity Mixed land uses Car share	PT user quality, coverage and cost	Parking provision (ratio)	Car parking cost Parking controls Home tenure terms
Use	Relative convenience of car alternatives Quality of pedestrian environment Cycle facilities	Public transport offer	Parking convenience (distance)	
Impact	Shared street surfaces Landscaping		Car parking location Car access restriction, e.g., pedestrianisation Urban pattern, e.g., superblocks Traffic calming, e.g., speed bumps	Speed limits Car access terms Home zones and play streets

Source: Scheurer (2001), Eastwood (2008), Melia, (2010)

Loretto and Französisch Viertel or French Quarter) and the suburbs of Vauban and Rieselfeld in Freiburg. This section introduces the underpinning concept, explores the implementation of social and environmental principles in each, and summarises the design outcomes. Besides representing 'holistic' models of sustainable planning, where the onus on the car has been reduced, the three models share some important features. First, in each case the municipal authority had control of the land prior to development. At Südstadt and Vauban, former military bases were purchased by the municipalities from the German state after the departure of troops in the early 1990s following the collapse of the Berlin Wall, while in Rieselfeld's case the site was a former sewage farm. Second, each of the three sites has used a collective self-build or Baugruppe approach to development, from approximately 10 per cent in Rieselfeld, and 25 per cent in Vauban to around 90 per cent in Südstadt (Hamiduddin and Daseking, 2014). The use of this approach accounts for the wide variety of building styles to be found in each development and also for the very strong community bonds that characterise the neighbourhoods (Hamiduddin, 2013).

Südstadt, Tübingen

Südstadt, which is nearing completion, will form a corridor of approximately 2,500 homes on the city's southern fringe along the Stuttgarter Straße, approximately 1.5km from Tübingen city centre. The scheme is formed around two distinctive quarters – Loretto

Table 29.2   Summary of key planning features in the three districts

	Vauban	Rieselfeld	Südstadt (French Quarter and Loretto)
Scale	2,300 homes	3,700 homes	2,000 homes
Overall concept	'Green' suburban quarter. Approximately half of site dedicated as 'car free' and 25% of homes delivered through group self-build.	Sustainable urban extension, built around a tram extension.	Sustainable, low car suburb with particular emphasis on small-scale and creative industries.
Public transport	Tram: all homes within 300m of stop, providing direct and reliable service to centre and to key destinations throughout city. Nearby heavy rail at St Georgen serves regional destinations. Bus services serve suburbs and outlying villages.	Tram: all homes within 400m of tram, providing direct and reliable service to centre and to key destinations throughout city. Bus services serve suburbs and outlying villages.	Bus: high-quality bus service to railway station, city centre and across the city.
Cycling	Dedicated secure and sheltered communal facilities with at least one space per home. Easy access to citywide cycle network.	Dedicated secure and sheltered communal facilities with at least one space per home. Easy access to citywide cycle network.	Dedicated secure and sheltered communal facilities with at least one space per home.
Car parking	In car-free area: 0.5 residential car parking ratio in communal edge of site car parks. On-street visitor parking on main axis. One space per home in subterranean car parks across remainder of homes.	1.5 spaces per home in communal subterranean and street parking.	Overall ratio of one space per home in communal subterranean and edge of development car parks.
Amenities	Elementary school, grocery stores, cafés and twice-weekly market. High school nearby.	Full range of schools, library, police station, medical centre, grocery stores, restaurants, cafés, twice-weekly market. Nearby zoo.	Elementary school, grocery stores, restaurants, cafés and. High school nearby.

Figure 29.1   Tübingen Südstadt – Loretto

Platz on the western side, closest to the city centre, and the French Quarter, which forms a large easterly suburb that is connected to Loretto by a narrow seam of new housing. The project was overseen by Andreas Feldtkeller, the former head of planning until 1998, who sought to create a genuine mixed-use new district emphasising small industries and the full range of local amenities that has sought to make the 'city of short distances' philosophy a practical reality. Private open space has been deliberately minimised, with a small curtilage of just one or two meters surrounding each building, and instead an emphasis has been placed on communal 'ownership' of the spaces between buildings. Boundaries between public and private space tend to be 'soft' and demarcated by landscaping rather than by hard barriers (Figure 29.1). The masterplan for the scheme was created competitively, to create a loose overall design code and a traffic concept, whilst the detail of building design was left open to each individual or Baugruppe building consortium.

Südstadt's transport framework has been influenced considerably by the thinking of Viennese traffic engineer Hermann Knoflacher in relation to two critical elements: first, a physical structure that makes public transport as convenient from the home as the private car and, second, a price structure that reflects the 'privilege' of car parking in the neighbourhood (Knoflacher, 2006, 2007). The scheme has been purposely designed to minimise the impact of the car on home life, through the application of physical restrictions including superblocks to minimise through-traffic, car-free residential blocks and public spaces and shared spaces within purely residential streets, as well as administrative measures including home zones. Car use is discouraged through a tight mix of land uses including businesses and retail to reduce overall travel and the prioritisation of high-quality bus transport and cycle facilities over car parking, which is physically separated from homes. Although high charges of approximately €25,000 for a freehold space in a communal car park makes car ownership expensive, an overall ratio of one space per home forms a comparatively low ratio for a new housing development (where two spaces per home are normal), but not excessively so.

Vauban, Freiburg

Now well-established as a model for sustainable neighbourhood planning, construction on Vauban began in the late 1990s and continues today, although the bulk of the 2,200 homes were completed by 2010. The suburb is located towards the southern edge of the city, approximately 3.5km from the city centre on the site of a former military barracks that became home to a group of environmental campaigners following the withdrawal of French troops in the early 1990s. Environmental concern has been central in the scheme's evolution. The early campaign group formed a subsequent 'Forum Vauban' community group, which entered into a dialogue with the municipal authority for the purpose of shaping development plans. The Forum's original concept was for a low-energy, car-free scheme; a concept that has been delivered in the core area of the suburb, where only temporary vehicle access is permitted and residents' car parking is available in one of two edge-of-development sites.

Like Südstadt, the physical structure of Vauban favours public transport and non-motorised modes of travel. Vehicle access restrictions into the core area of the scheme mean that traffic levels are very low, while a suite of devices – including shared street surfaces and home zones – help to minimise the social impact of residual traffic. Car use has been addressed through the implementation of a tram line into the central axis of the development means that no home is more than 300m away from a tram stop and all homes have easy access to secure cycle storage and an extensive city-wide cycle network. However, the scheme is perhaps best distinguished by the stringent terms placed on vehicle ownership within the 'car-free' core, where a space in a peripheral car park entails a payment of €18,000 (in 2012). Non-car owners can opt out by signing a car-free waiver but, unlike Südstadt, the ratio of car parking has been reduced significantly below the norm – an act that required special legal dispensation from the federal German 'garage law'.

Rieselfeld, Freiburg

Work began on the ex-urban Rieselfeld project in the early 1990s, making it the earliest of Freiburg's new housing schemes. Like Südstadt, the masterplan was conceived competitively and plans were laid down for a completed development containing approximately 4,000 homes housing 1,000 residents. The concept was for a relatively high level of self-containment through the provision of a full range of social and educational amenities

Figure 29.2   Residential street in Vauban

including an award-winning multidenominational and multifunctional church – which together with the 'Kiosk' library and community hub forms a set piece core to the district. The development also offers a full range of shops and services including a twice-weekly market in a central piazza next to the church, and provision for employment including light industry.

Rieselfeld is the least stridently 'car reduced' of the three districts, with neither the bold physical separation between car parking and homes or the high car parking levies aimed at suppressing car ownership in Südstadt and Vauban, and has a relatively high overall parking ratio of 1.5 spaces per home. But the masterplan incorporated a range of design features deliberately aimed at reducing the social impact of vehicles on homes and the need to travel by car. To reduce the impact of traffic, the scheme's grid layout creates blocks with traffic-free interiors, while approximately one-third of streets are designated as home zones and a quarter have shared street surfaces and the more heavily trafficked distributor roads contain boulevard style set-backs and land-scaping to soften the traffic impact. Like Vauban, a tram line has been integrated into the main axis in order to make public transport an attractive and convenient transport option. Similarly, all homes are equipped with secure, convenient and sheltered cycle facilities.

Figure 29.3   The 'Rieselfeld Allee' main axis

The 'City of Short Distances' Concept

The *kurze wege* concept is commonly found among municipal planning guidance across Germany and is believed to have evolved in the southerly state of Baden Württemberg (to which Freiburg and Tübingen both belong). Although the phrase implies the shortening of travel distances through the tight mixing of land uses and the creation of a permeable urban structure to favour physical travel modes, the practical application can lead to a variety of results. In relation to employment and retail, significantly different results have been produced in the new quarters of Tübingen and Freiburg. From the outset the vision for Südstadt has been for a 'creative quarter' with a high level of new employment at a ratio of approximately one job per household (Table 29.3). At Vauban and Rieselfeld the ratios are significantly lower, at approximately one job for every four households.

Much of Südstadt's new employment has been nurtured from small practical industries operating from workshops clustered both in Loretto and the French Quarter (Figure 29.4), as well as small creative practices including architecture and design studios; the embodiment of Jane Jacobs' 'creative city', which inspired the original vision (see Jacobs, 1961).

In Freiburg, retail policy has been an important vehicle for delivering the 'city of

Table 29.3   Projected levels of employment for the three completed quarters

New quarter	District population	District employment opportunities	District employment opportunities per resident	Employment opportunities per household
Vauban	5,000	600	0.12	0.25
Rieselfeld	10,000	1,000	0.1	0.27
Südstadt (Loretto and French Quarter)	6,500	2,000	0.31	1

Figure 29.4   Housing and small industries tightly mixed in the French Quarter, Tübingen

short distances' principle in urban planning, first by preventing the emergence of large edge-of-city retail developments and, second, by regulating the size of grocery stores within the city in order to produce a more dispersed pattern of retail in neighbour-hoods. Land-use ordinances have set an 800m^2 floor area limit for retail stores, with a few exceptions for 'bulky goods' such as furniture and DIY (Hildebrandt, 2008). The potential drawbacks to the approach are most obvious in narrower product ranges, but the advantages seem to be evidenced in the profusion of smaller, independent shops and a very large daily market in the city centre, and in the economic strength of the city's neighbourhoods.

Table 29.4   Population demographic structure

	Average population age	average household size	% 6–18 yr olds	% 65+ yr olds
French Quarter	31.3	1.82	14.4	3.0
Loretto	37.1	2.37	18.6	
Tübingen Avg	38.3	2.04		
Vauban		2.36	20.6	2.7
Rieselfeld		2.54	21	6.1
Freiburg Avg		1.84	10.2	16.3

4.   POLICY OUTCOMES

The purpose of this section is to present a selection of mobility and social indicators from Tübingen and Freiburg, and to explore the relationship between the data and the car reduction strategies that have been applied in the three model neighbourhoods. The data has been derived from a number of sources, consisting principally of (1) secondary data from municipal documents, (2) primary data from a comparative household questionnaire study of three neighbourhoods in Freiburg (Vauban, Rieselfeld and Haslach Gartenstadt) conducted by the author (Hamiduddin, 2013), and (3) semi-structured interviews conducted with current and former policy managers in both cities, as listed in the Acknowledgements at the end of the chapter.

Demographic Structure

The new neighbourhood schemes in Tübingen and Freiburg have younger demographic profiles than the cities to which they belong. The residential communities of each neighbourhood are characterised by a range of indicators presented in Table 29.4. Although the average overall age presents a general picture of each community, the second indicator – average household size – provides useful explanation. The larger households recorded at Loretto, Vauban and Rieselfeld correspond with a higher prevalence of families with young children – as reflected in the percentage of 6–18 year olds – whereas the large student population of the French Quarter drive down household sizes in these neighbourhoods. Tellingly, the proportion of residents aged over 65 is much smaller across all neighbourhoods, compared with Tübingen and Freiburg overall.

Whilst the demographic structures of these neighbourhoods may suggest high levels of residential self-selectivity, corresponding to processes presented elsewhere in the literature in relation to the transport orientation of new developments (e.g., Cao et al., 2008; Handy et al., 2006; Bohte et al., 2009), the heavy skewing of housing market demand towards growing populations of younger university leavers in each city means that there is little initial mystery to these patterns. However, the mode of housing delivery and the car reduced design features implemented in each of the new neighbourhoods may exert important secondary influences. In the broader context of Germany's housing market culture, where house purchasing typically occurs only once and usually to provide a

Figure 29.5   Grocery retail in Rieselfeld

Table 29.5   Car ownership

Area	Population	Homes	Vehicles	Vehicles per 1,000	Vehicles per household
Freiburg Overall	213,567	115,954	106,845	500	0.92
Vauban	**5,522**	**2,336**	**1,236**	**230**	**0.52**
Rieselfeld	**9,754**	**3,745**	**3,593**	377	**0.92**
Tübingen Overall	84,268	41,215	36,448	433	0.89
French Quarter	**2,321**	**1,275***	**594**	**256**	**0.47**
Loretto	**886**	**374**	**373**	**421**	**0.99**

Note: * Includes 600 student residences

Source: City of Freiburg (2012) and City of Tübingen (2003, 2012)

home for a young family, the Baugruppe mode of housing production used extensively in the French Quarter, Loretto and Vauban is heavily reliant on the private finance raised at this significant stage of life. However, each neighbourhood has been designed to appeal heavily to families with young children by incorporating features that reduce the objective danger posed by traffic, emphasise communal space over car parking and permit street space to be used for social purposes.

Car Ownership in Tübingen and Freiburg

Table 29.5 presents two important sets of data on car ownership from Tübingen and Freiburg: first, the density of car ownership per 1,000 head of population and, second, the ratio of car ownership per household. The former is the figure most commonly reported in official reports (e.g., City of Freiburg, 2012; Melia, 2010; City of Tübingen, 2012) and also happens to be the most flattering from an environmental point of view, but it is also misleading as it is heavily influenced by the proportion of the population that cannot drive – young children in particular. It is this factor that accounts for this contrasting account of car ownership compared with a more robust 'per household' indicator.

Vauban has the lowest density of car ownership, while Südstadt has the lowest ratio per household. Both schemes have high proportions of children and students, which account for approximately for a quarter of residents in the French Quarter. Conversely, Rieselfeld and Loretto have the highest levels of ownership at almost one vehicle per household – at and above the ratios for Freiburg and Tübingen, respectively. Although both neighbourhoods represent exemplars of sustainable urban planning, there is no particularly mystery in this pattern: both are edge of city developments where car ownership traditionally tends to be higher and both have relatively high levels of car parking. Moreover, evidence from Freiburg suggests that car ownership does not necessarily mean heavy car use, even in traditional car-oriented journeys such as shopping, as discussed in the next section.

Comparison of Work Travel in Freiburg

The household questionnaire survey asked samples of residents from three Freiburg neighbourhoods about their usual main mode of travel to work. Car ownership among survey respondents ranged from 43 per cent at Vauban (N = 92), 78 per cent at Rieselfeld (N = 95), and 74 per cent at Haslach (N = 76). The modal split, shown in Figure 29.6, is striking. Three-quarters of Vauban's residents cycle or walk to work, compared with just over half of Rieselfeld's and approximately one-third of Haslach's. Conversely, the car was the single most popular mode among Haslach's residents (38 per cent), compared with a quarter of Rieselfeld's residents and fewer than 10 per cent of Vauban's. Another feature of the findings is the relatively low level of public transport use among all residents, with a quarter of Haslach residents indicated that they used the tram, bus or train most frequently to get to work, with lower proportions of 20 per cent and 15 per cent reported from Rieselfeld and Vauban, respectively. However, these are patterns that correspond broadly with the overall modal share split for the city (Schick, 2009) whereby approximately half of residents cycle or walk, 30 per cent travel by car and around 20 per cent use public transport, of which two thirds is by tram. In other words, car ownership is a poor indicator of car use for the journey to work – an inverse relationship that may be explained by the concentration of employment within the city rather than edge of town and car-oriented developments and by the priority of access given to non-motorised modes. Freiburg was one of the first cities in Germany to pedestrianise its centre and it has recently created an entirely traffic free extended urban core with very limited parking and preferential access to cycling and public transport.

Retail Travel Patterns in Freiburg

Previous research has also indicated that Freiburg's retail policies have had a profound impact on shopping habits. In a survey of Vauban residents, Nobis (2003) found that nearly three-quarters of residents with cars used them for bulk shopping, but only 10 per cent of the same residents used their cars for their daily shopping needs. However, this study was undertaken prior to the opening of the tram service to Vauban in 2006. The 2010 household questionnaire survey found that residents across the three neighbourhoods had a tendency to use non-motorised modes, particularly walking and

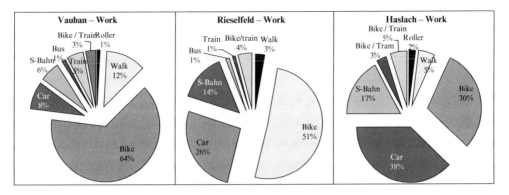

Figure 29.6   Journey to work modal share in three Freiburg neighbourhoods

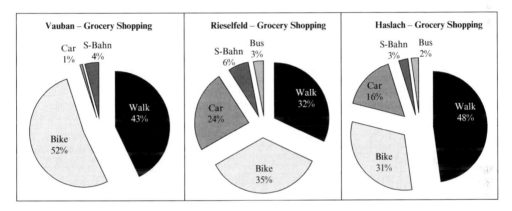

Figure 29.7   Grocery retail model share in three Freiburg neighbourhoods

cycling. Grocery shopping has a general tendency to attract high levels of automobile use, reflecting the car-oriented disposition of stores, the heavy and bulky nature of goods and the self-reinforcing weekly shopping patterns permitted by domestic storage appliances. Against this backdrop, the car-free patterns of grocery shopping recorded to a greater or lesser extent across all three of the neighbourhoods are significant. The dominance of walking and cycling indicates the effectiveness of decentralised retail policies, smaller but more frequent grocery shopping trips – which may lessen the need for domestic storage space – and a divorce between car ownership and use over a traditionally car dominant issue.

5.   CONCLUDING DISCUSSION

The following question was posed at the beginning of the chapter: to what extent can integrated urban design and transport planning create sustainable travel patterns among residents by reducing overall traffic, altering the behaviour of motorists in the neighbourhood and changing the spatial relationship between residents and their cars? From the evidence presented in this chapter, three conclusions may be drawn. First, coercive strategies have been employed in the neighbourhoods of Freiburg and Tübingen and include both obvious and subtle measures to control the factors that strongly influence travel demand and modal patterns. The more obvious measures to regulate travel demand include the encouraging of mixed land uses in each scheme and creating permeable environments for pedestrians and cyclists, and modal patterns have been influenced by the orientation of Vauban and Rieselfeld in particular towards high-quality public transport, cycling and walking routes. More subtle, however, are Freiburg's retail ordinances, which have created a distributed pattern of grocery stores and the seamless intermodal network of public transport that allows the spectrum of lifestyle needs to be met without recourse to car use. A second conclusion is that the management of traffic in the residential environment entails a complex set of relations with broader urban transport and planning policies, particularly where urban design strategies attempt to extend beyond limiting the social impact of vehicles in neighbourhoods towards strategies that attempt to coerce travel patterns away from vehicle use and discourage car ownership. The outcomes of these policies may, to an extent, be discerned from the car ownership levels at Loretto, French Quarter and Vauban particularly, but perhaps more significant are the recorded travel patterns from Vauban and Rieselfeld showing the extent to which car ownership and car use have been separated – even for traditionally heavy uses such as grocery retail. Lastly, although the demographic profile of residents in these neighbourhoods may exert an influence, such travel patterns would be untenable without the underlying structural planning that allows car reduced lifestyles to be pursued.

Questions of applicability are raised: to what extent could the experience of these neighbourhoods from two comparatively small towns of southern Germany be applied elsewhere? In the first instance the answer depends on which of three identified car reduction objectives are being pursued: social impact, car use or car ownership. In principle, the design approaches to each objective set out in Table 29.1 are broadly applicable, and the experience of Tübingen in particular demonstrates that heavy investment in public transport systems such as light rail are not necessarily needed to create reductions in car ownership in smaller cities.

ACKNOWLEDGEMENTS

The author would particularly like to thank Prof Wulf Daseking, former Director of Planning for Freiburg, and Mr Andreas Feldtkeller, former Director of Planning for Tübingen, for their time.

NOTE

1. The Locomotive Act of 1865 required all mechanical road vehicles to travel at walking speed and with a member of crew bearing a red flag 55m ahead of the vehicle.

REFERENCES

Appleyard, D., Gerson, S.M. and Lintell, M. (1981), *Liveable Streets*, Berkley, CA: UCLA Press.

Banister, D. (2007), *Transport Planning*, 2nd edn, Abingdon: Taylor & Francis.

Bohte, W., Maat, K. and van Wee, B. (2009), Measuring attitudes in research on residential self-selection and travel behaviour: a review of theories and empirical research, *Transport Reviews*, **29**(3), 325–57.

Cao, X., Mokhtarian, P.L. and Handy, S. (2008), Examining the impacts of residential self-selection on travel behaviour: a focus on empirical findings, *Transport Reviews*, **29**(3), 359–95.

CIHT (2010), *Manual for Streets 2: Wider Application of the Principles*, London: Chartered Institute of Highways and Transportation.

City of Freiburg (2012), *Demographischer Wandel in den Freiburger Stadtbezirken [Demographic Profiles in Freiburg's Districts]*, Freiburg: City of Freiburg.

City of Tübingen (2003), unpublished municipal demographic data.

City of Tübingen (2012), unpublished municipal demographic data.

Eastwood, M. (2008), *Slateford Green Transport Study*, Edinburgh: VIPRE Consultants.

Hamiduddin, I. (2013), *The Social Implications of Residential Car Reduction: Exploring Community and Mobility at the Neighbourhood Scale*, unpublished PhD thesis, University College London.

Hamiduddin, I. and Daseking, W. (2014), Community-based planning in Freiburg, Germany: the case of Vauban, in N. Gallent and D. Ciaffi (eds), *Community Action and Planning*, Abingdon: Routledge.

Hampstead Garden Suburb Trust (1998), *The Hampstead Garden Suburb Act 1906*, www.hgs.org.uk.

Handy, S., Cao, X. and Mokhtarian, P.L. (2006), Self-selection in the relationship between the built environment and walking: empirical evidence from Northern California, *Journal of the American Planning Association*, **72**(1), 55–74.

Hart, J. and Parkhurst, G. (2011), Driven to excess: impacts of motor vehicles on the quality of life of residents of three streets in Bristol, UK, *World Transport Policy & Practice*, **17**(2), 12–30.

Hass-Klau, C. (1990), *The Pedestrian and City Traffic*, London: Belhaven Press.

Hebbert, M. (2005), Engineering, urbanism and the struggle for street design, *Journal of Urban Design*, **10**(1), 39–59.

Hildebrandt, A. (2008), *Reducing Transport's GHG Emissions: Freiburg, Past Present and Future*, Freiburg: VAG.

Jacobs, J. (1961), *The Death and Life of Great American Cities*, London: Peregrine Books.

Kaplan, S. (1995), The restorative benefits of nature: toward an integrative framework, *Journal of Environmental Psychology*, **15**, 169–83.

Knoflacher, H. (2006), A new way to organize parking: the key to a successful sustainable transport system for the future, *Environment and Urbanization*, **18**(2), 387–400.

Knoflacher, H. (2007), Success and failures in urban transport planning in Europe – understanding the transport system, *Sadhana*, **32**(4), 293–307.

Kunstler, J. (1993), *The Geography of Nowhere: The Rise and Decline of America's Man-made Landscape*, New York: Simon & Schuster.

Lee, C.M. and Stabin-Nesmith, B. (2001), The continuing value of a planned community: Radburn in the evolution of suburban development, *Journal of Urban Design*, **6**(2), 151–84.

Lefebvre, H. (1974), *The Production of Space*, Oxford: Blackwell.

Marshall, S. (2005), *Streets and Street Patterns*, Abingdon: Spon.

Melia, S. (2010), *Potential for Carfree Development in the UK*, unpublished PhD thesis, UWE, Bristol.

Newman, P. and Kenworthy, J. (1999), *Sustainability and Cities: Overcoming Automobile Dependence*, Washington, DC: Island Press.

Nobis, C. (2003), The impact of car-free housing districts on mobility behaviour – case study, in E. Beriatos, C.A. Brebbia, H. Coccossis and A. Kungolos (eds), *Sustainable Planning and Development*, Southampton: WIT Press, pp. 701–20.

Perry, C. (1929), The neighborhood unit, in M. Larice and F. MacDonald (eds), *The Urban Design Reader*, 2nd edn, Abingdon: Routledge.

Putnam, R.D. (2001), *Bowling Alone: The Collapse and Revival of American Community*, New York: Simon & Schuster.

Rogers, R. (1999), *Towards an Urban Renaissance*, London: Urban Task Force.

Scheurer, J. (2001), *Car-Free Housing in European Cities*, Murdoch University, www.istp.Murdoch.edu.au/publications/projects/carfree/carfree.html.

Schick, P. (2009), *Freiburg: A Smarter Travel Town?* Freiburg City administration presentation.

Southworth, M. and Ben-Joseph, E. (1997), Streets and the shaping of towns and cities, New York: McGraw-Hill.

Stein, C. (1950), *Towards New Towns for America*, Liverpool: University of Liverpool Press.

Unwin, R. (1994), *Town Planning in Practice: An Introduction to the Art of Designing Cities and Suburbs*, Princeton, NJ: Princeton University Press.

Webber, M. (1964), *Explorations into Urban Structure*, Philadelphia: University of Pennsylvania Press.

30 Accessibility: theory and practice in the Netherlands and UK
Karst Geurs and Derek Halden

1. INTRODUCTION

Accessibility is a concept that has become central to physical planning during the past 50 years; improving accessibility is an aim that has now made its way into mainstream transport planning and policymaking throughout the world. Batty (2009) traces the origins of the concept back to the 1920s. It was used in location theory and regional economic planning, becoming important once transport planning began, mainly in North America where it was associated with transport networks and trip distribution patterns. Its conceptual basis dates back further. Hansen (1959), in his classic and much cited expose, 'How accessibility shapes land use' rolled out our first real definition: the potential for interaction (based on the notion of potential traced back to the social physics school in the nineteenth century).

Several authors have written review articles on accessibility measures, often focusing on a particular category of accessibility, such as location-based accessibility (Martín and Reggiani, 2007; Reggiani, 1998), person-based accessibility (e.g., Kwan, 1998; Pirie, 1979) or utility-based accessibility (e.g., Koenig, 1980; Niemeier, 1997). Here we use the review of Geurs and van Wee (2004), as a point of departure to look at accessibility measures from different perspectives (land use, transport, social as well as economic impacts). We also use the typology of accessibility measures developed by Halden, which classified accessibility measures according to the ways in which they had been successfully used (Halden, 2003).

In recent decades, the term 'accessibility' has marshalled renewed interest from civil engineering, geography, spatial economics and other academic fields due to its potential when delivering policies requiring cross-sector action. We have witnessed considerable progress in accessibility analysis and modelling. First, within the land-use planning perspective, there is trend towards increased spatial resolution of accessibility measurements, using transport models with detailed transport networks and increasing use of Geographic Information Systems (GIS) platforms to extract and assemble data from multiple spatial databases at fine levels of spatial resolution (e.g., see Chen et al., 2011; Kwan, 2000).

A second trend in the literature is towards disaggregated accessibility measures, largely recognising that aggregate measures fail to account for wide variation in individual behaviour and population groups at different spatial scales. Person-based accessibility, analysing accessibility at the individual level – as opposed to at zonal levels – gains traction by further understanding human activities and travel possibilities in space and time (e.g., see Ashiru et al., 2003; Dong et al., 2006; Kwan, 2000; Neutens, 2010; Schwanen and Kwan, 2008). In a fast-changing world, the travel behaviour responses are highly uncertain since new media, networks, new challenges and new ways of working mean that past trends are a poor guide to the future, so Halden highlights the benefits of a more disaggregate treatment to help manage uncertainty when making policy choices (Halden, 1996).

A third trend gives increasing attention to measuring the social dimension of transport linking accessibility concepts to social exclusion, social equity, and/or social justice (Achuthan et al., 2010; Farrington and Farrington, 2005; Páez et al., 2010; Scott and Horner, 2008). A related trend is to focus on non-motorised accessibility and related individuals' perceptions of residential environments (e.g., see Haugen, 2011; Iacono et al., 2010; Krizek, 2010). Finally, in academic accessibility studies, increasing attention is paid to measuring the spatial-economic impacts accruing from accessibility changes, ranging from analysis of utility-based accessibility measures (de Jong et al., 2007; Geurs et al., 2006, 2010) to spatial spillover effects (e.g., see Condeço-Melhorado et al., 2011; Gutiérrez et al., 2010, 2011).

In this chapter, we examine if the progress in accessibility analysis is matched with advances in the use of accessibility measures in national transport policy in the Netherlands and the UK, countries often cited as being leaders in the development of accessibility planning. Handy and Niemeier highlighted the gap between academic and practical applications of accessibility; asserting, 'It is important that accessibility measures used in practice are theoretically and behaviourally sound and that innovative approaches to measuring accessibility are made practical' (Handy and Niemeier, 1997: 1192). Here, we examine if researchers and practitioners working with these accessibility concepts in the Netherlands and the UK have heeded this advice.

This chapter is structured as follows. Section 2 reviews the accessibility measures used in Dutch transport policy and planning from the 1970s, section 3 compares the UK accessibility approach and finally section 4 presents the conclusions.

2.   ACCESSIBILITY IN DUTCH TRANSPORT POLICY

History of Accessibility Concepts Used in Dutch Transport Policy

Since the start of national transport policy there have been four major national transport policy documents. Here, we briefly describe the main policy concepts used in these documents for surface-based passenger transport. Table 30.1 summarises the main concepts.

Dutch national transport policy has focused on transport performance based indicators and targets. In each new policy document, new transport performance-based accessibility standards were developed for the main road network. Quantitative transport performance targets are mainly formulated for road networks and not for public transport or freight networks. In the 1980s, the central concept was the transport performance indicator as defined in the US *Highway Capacity Manual*. The transport performance goal in the First Transport Structure Plan (MinV&W, 1979) was to achieve a C-level of service (80–90km/h) for motorways in rural areas on working days and D/E level (50–70km/h) for motorways in metropolitan and urban areas. In the 1990s, a more advanced policy development strategy was taken based on estimations with the Dutch national transport model system (LMS) developed in the 1980s (Bovy et al., 1992). The starting point of

Table 30.1   Transport performance based concepts (passenger transport) used in the main Dutch national transport policy documents

Policy document	Indicator
First Transport Structure Plan ('SVV1', 1979)	Level-of-service (motorways)
Second Transport Structure Plan ('SVV2', 1990)	Detour factor (motorways)
	Congestion probability (motorways)
	Distance to access road (motorways)
	Capacity (motorways)
	Relative travel time (car/public transport)
	Speed (rail)
	Number of delayed trains (rail)
Mobility Policy Document ('Nota Mobiliteit', 2004)	Relative travel time between peak/off peak hours (motorways)
	Travel time reliability (motorways)
	Vehicle-hours lost (motorways)
	Punctuality (rail)
National Policy Strategy for Infrastructure and Environment ('SVIR', 2012)	Relative travel time between peak/off peak hours (motorways)
	Generalised transport cost

designing the future motorway network structure in the Second Transport Structure Plan (MinV&W, 1990) was the aim to directly connect the main 40 economic centres in the country. Detour factors were first used as a criterion (a factor of 1.2 was considered good) and, second, car drivers were to access the motorway network within 15 minutes travel time (about 10km distance) from centres of economic activities. Third, the concept of 'congestion probability' was introduced to indicate the probability of structural congestion on motorway road segments during working days. The LMS was used to estimate congestion probabilities for the year 2010 and also provided the inputs for a partial cost-benefit used to determine the 'optimal' congestion probability. A 2 per cent congestion probability was set as a policy goal for motorways that connect Rotterdam and Schiphol airport to the hinterland, and 5 per cent probability for other motorways. The SVV2 was also quite unique in setting quantified targets for reducing car use ('halving the growth in car traffic') and providing transport performance based accessibility for other modes, for example in terms of rail speed, number of delayed trains and travel time ratios between trains and cars. In the 2000s, the Mobility Policy Document (MinV&W, 2006) directed the policy aims towards 'reliable and predictable door to door travel times'. Three types of transport performance based accessibility targets were set. Firstly, a travel time reliability target was set, based on transport model estimations. By 2020, travellers should reach their destination on time in 95 per cent of cases. Second, a travel time target was set. Rush-hour travel time were not to exceed 1.5 times the off-peak journey time on motorways or twice the off-peak journey time on urban orbital roads and non-motorway roads managed by the state. This would make the average motorway rush-hour journey time over a distance of 50km 45 minutes at maximum (maximum delay 15 minutes). Third and finally, an accessibility target was defined in terms of vehicle-hours lost; the number of hours lost in 2020 should be reduced to the level of 1992. In addition, to a limited extent, quantitative accessibility objectives were also formulated for other modalities; for example, in terms of arrival reliability of trains. The national transport model system (LMS) was again used for transport analysis and a number of social cost-benefit analysis were conducted to examine the economic efficiency of road investments combined with road pricing alternatives (Besseling et al., 2005).

Current Accessibility Indicators

The current policy document, the *National Policy Strategy for Infrastructure and Environment* (MinIenM, 2012) is the first occurrence of spatial planning and transport policy being integrated in one single document. This is the result of the merger of the former Ministry of Transport and Water Management and the Ministry of Housing and Physical Planning into the Ministry of Infrastructure and Environment in 2011. However, this did not affect the main perspective on accessibility – the focus remains on infrastructure-based accessibility measures. The travel time target from the Mobility Policy document is kept as a performance-based accessibility indicator. The 'travel time reliability' indicator is replaced by a qualitative aim to achieve 'a robust and coherent mobility system'. In addition, a multimodal generalised transport cost measure was announced as a new accessibility indicator, replacing the 'vehicle hours lost' indicator. The aim of the new indicator is to give a more complete picture of the performance of different transport modes and transport networks (Hoogendoorn-Lanser et al., 2011). The indicator was announced in the SVIR and a preliminary version of the indicator was shown in the policy document (Figure 30.1). The accessibility indicator shows the generalised travel cost for car, public transport and road freight transport at the spatial scale of municipalities. This indicator expresses the transport resistance from areas to overcome the distance to particular destinations with different transport modes. The colour of the circle indicates the average accessibility of a municipality compared to all other municipalities in the Netherlands, while the size of the circle reveals the total number of journeys to this municipality. If a municipality is coloured red, this means that the average transport costs per kilometre to the municipality are high. At the moment of publication of the SVIR, a development and testing process was announced, which finished in 2014. In the first two years of the development process, several difficulties with operationalising the indicator were found. First, the out-of-pocket travel cost variables (fuel costs, parking costs, ticket cost) dominated the accessibility cost index, which as a result was not very sensitive to travel time changes. Second, comfort/quality aspects proved to be difficult to monitor and forecast. The accessibility indicator was therefore simplified into the average straight line speed of all journeys to a destination area in km/h. Accessibility for a location j (expressed in minutes per kilometre) is computed as the inverse of ratio between average travel time and average travel distances, weighted by the number of trip origins.

$$A_j = 1 / \frac{\sum_{i=1}^{n} T_{ij} t_{ij}}{\sum_{i=1}^{n} T_{ij} d_{ij}}$$

Where T_{ij} is number of trips, t_{ij} travel time and d_{ij} straight line travel distance between origin location i and destination location j. A third issue with the indicator is average

Number of arrivals per municipality

- < 50,000
- 50,000–100,000
- 100,000–150,000
- 150,000–250,000
- 250,000–350,000
- > 350,000

Accessibility indicator

Good

Bad

Source: MinIenM (2012)

Figure 30.1 Generalised travel times as the new Dutch transport performance based accessibility indicator, projection for 2030, high economic growth scenario

speeds are correlated with trip distances. In general, long(er) distance trips can be made at higher speeds than short(er) distance trips as a higher share of the distance is travelled at inter-urban networks and detour factors are lower. This would imply that the accessibility indicator is lower (negative score) in urban areas where trip distances are shorter than in suburban or rural areas (positive score). Land-use policies aiming at intensifying land use in urban areas that reduce trip distances would negatively affect the accessibility index. This was considered an unwanted effect. To correct for this effect, 'expected' travel times is used to estimate the accessibility indicator, based on a regression analysis using as the crow flies travel distances (Hoogendoorn-Lanser et al., 2013). The fourth and final issue was the difficulty in estimating the indicator as a single multimodal indicator. For example, urban regions with a high share of non-motorised transport have lower average travel speeds, which would result in a lower accessibility score. Therefore, when calculating the integral accessibility of an area for all modalities, the differences in travel speeds between modalities must be taken into account. At the moment, the new indicator is estimated for each mode separately (car, public transport, bicycle), and also different operationalisations are used for passenger and freight transport.

Discussion of Dutch Accessibility Policy

The overview of accessibility indicators used in Dutch policy documents as presented here shows that the development of accessibility indicators and goals have mainly been the result of a technical planning process. From the 1990s on, the development relied heavily on the outcomes of the projections from (different versions of) the Dutch national transport model system. In all policy documents, accessibility targets were set at such a level that some structural levels of congestion and unreliability were accepted, mainly because of financial constraints or economic efficiency reasons. Social and/or environmental arguments did not play a crucial role in the accessibility policy process. Environmental arguments did, however, play an explicit role in setting the congestion probabilities in the SVV2. As noted earlier, a partial CBA on alternatives for the 2010 motorway network was conducted, including travel time losses, traffic safety, construction and maintenance costs. The smaller the accepted congestion probability, the higher the road capacity increase and investment costs. The 'optimal' congestion probability was found to lie between 1 and 3 per cent (Rijkswaterstaat, 1987). To account for environmental impacts, not included in the CBA, and avoid infrastructure construction in natural areas, SVV2 set a 2 per cent congestion probability as the main transport performance goal for the motorways that connect Rotterdam and Schiphol airport to the hinterland, and 5 per cent probability for other motorways.

The main change in accessibility policy was the gradual move from the transport provider perspective focusing on the transport performance of single motorway road segments to a 'transport user' perspective focusing on travel time between origin and destination areas (using different transport networks and modes). The main benefit is that this approach provides an explicit link between strategic policy development and economic appraisal (CBA) at the level of infrastructure projects or programmes, in which travel time savings are the most important benefit category. Second, it allows for a (partial) comparison of accessibility levels of different transport modes.

However, the transport performance-based perspective lacks attention for individual and land-use components of accessibility that are relevant for accessibility planning. First, it does not distinguish between different types of users with different accessibility needs, such as young people, the elderly, low- or high-income groups. In the next decade, differentiating between the accessibility needs of different population groups will become more and more important, with an ageing population and population decline in several regions in the Netherlands. Keeping the current level of access to social and economic opportunities will be a major task in regions with ageing and declining populations. The social dimension has, in a sharp contract to the UK, not received much attention, if any, in the development of accessibility concepts in Dutch national transport policymaking.

Second, a transport performance indicator such as generalised travel cost is quite problematic within the context of integration of transport and land use policies and sustainability. This was already illustrated by Linneker and Spence (1992) who illustrated that inner London has the highest access costs (in terms of time and vehicle operation costs) in the UK, but also the highest level of potential accessibility to jobs, despite the high travel cost. In addition, potential accessibility measures are also better able to compare the performance of transport modes as they explicitly include the spatial distribution of activities. Access to jobs for car drivers is, for example, much higher than for public transport users not only due to the higher door-to-door travel times but also because many jobs are located in places not easily accessible by public transport. Only 16 per cent of jobs in the Netherlands are located within close proximity of public transport stops (PBL, 2012). As a result, the number of jobs that can be accessed within 60 minutes by public transport is on average a factor of 9 lower than by car compared to a factor of 3 in central urban areas (Geurs and Ritsema van Eck, 2001).

A location-based accessibility perspective did, however, not match the current accessibility paradigm of established administrative structures within the Ministry of Infrastructure and Environment. One fear was that the concept of 'potential accessibility' would not help in prioritising road investments towards the most congested locations in the country. The current accessibility indicators, despite methodological improvements, can still form a barrier towards a better integration of transport and land-use policies and development of more sustainable transport policies. In the UK, this was a major argument for adding potential accessibility as an objective in the appraisal toolkit in addition to transport performance goals (see section 4).

3. ACCESSIBILITY IN THE UK TRANSPORT POLICY

History of Accessibility Concepts Used in UK Transport Policy

The first signs of transport policy for the United Kingdom emerged in the 1950s and these policy statements sought to promote use of the car through provision of road investment. The first generation of motorways accelerated the promotion of traffic growth. The M1 was opened in 1959 and other motorways followed linking the country's major conurbations. During the 1960s there was increased emphasis on the impacts that these changes could have on people. *The Buchanan Report* identified situations where there would be a need to minimise the impacts of increased car use (Ministry of Transport, 1963) but this was largely through road design approaches rather than any assessment of travel needs.

During the 1970s and 1980s, UK research had suggested that the concept of accessibility could be usefully adopted in policy (Jones, 1981). However, UK government policy was still geared to delivering growth in traffic levels as a key part of consumerism. The principles of policy and transport appraisal were to deliver economic growth and increased taxation revenue through fuel taxes. This was founded in the belief that improved accessibility could best be delivered through greater personal mobility. However, by the 1990s, concerns were growing about the adverse impacts of increasing car traffic and it became widely recognised in transport policy statements that not all demand for travel could be met.

A popular starting point for new approaches to transport was the developing practice in securing sustainable development policy goals. Achieving sustainable development required an efficient relationship between transport supply and demand. This required a new transport planning toolkit where both supply and demand were planned. The implications of sustainable development policies for transport were explored in a joint Department of the Environment and Department for Transport Review (Ecotec, 1993). This concluded that the concept of 'potential accessibility' embraced many of the required dimensions. Requirements to plan accessibility were subsequently adopted in land-use planning policy with a planning guidance note on Transport and Planning (PPG13) being issued in draft in 1995.

During the 1990s the arguments developed for and against accessibility planning as a practical way to enhance transport planning. By the 1997 UK general election, the debate about the balance between potential accessibility and mobility in transport policy became part of election manifestos. The incoming Labour government stated in their manifesto that the 'rationale for future transport investment would be its accessibility benefit'. Accessibility policy has developed steadily since then and has become more widely integrated into the policies of many government departments. Four milestones can be distinguished. First, within transport appraisal, an explicit accessibility objective was formally introduced in 1998 within the 'new approach to appraisal' (NATA). This recognised that travel time changes due to congestion reduction represented only some aspects of accessibility change, so a more systematic treatment of spatial and social factors was required. Second, in 2003, a new cross-governmental coordinating role on accessibility was allocated to the Department for Transport (DfT). Third, from 2004 local authorities were required to set objectives to include accessibility within their local transport plans. Fourth, in 2012, NATA (now published as WebTAG) was updated to require accessibility changes for people and places to be reported explicitly when making transport investment decisions. The 2012 guidance (DfT, 2012a) gives increasing weight to economic sub-objectives such as regeneration, personal affordability and option value requiring analysis using accessibility measures to be reported for access to jobs, shops, leisure facilities, healthcare, education and other destinations.

Implementing Accessibility Planning in UK Transport Appraisal

Investment priorities in UK transport are largely established through transport appraisal requirements. The accessibility criterion was added to national transport policy objectives in 1997, as discussed above, and since then the importance of accessibility measures within appraisal has been growing under successive governments. Transport appraisal has taken a long time to change for a number of reasons. First, appraisal remains focused at growing the transport economy, rather than growing the wider economy and society, and there can be tensions between transport and non-transport policy goals. Social issues are often considered as problems to be mitigated rather than opportunities to be delivered through transport investment. Second, in NATA, the travel time-based accessibility assessments mean that mode shift from car to walking has been regarded as a negative effect from slower travel. Adding the value of access by walking radically changes transport investment priorities, so inherited commitments could appear relatively poor value if assessed differently so time has been needed for the transition in appraisal. Third, transport efficiency measures in the economic appraisal can sometimes be in conflict with accessibility measures. Sometimes reducing transport efficiency is needed to improve network coverage to deliver a wider social or economic goal outside transport. When prioritising the transport budget, one view is that transport efficiency should dominate priorities since other government departments could invest in the wider social and economic goals through partnerships on transport projects. This is discussed further below under the policy challenges.

As noted above, in 2012 very substantial changes were made to the appraisal rules so these are only now working through in practice. However the Scottish Executive developed accessibility policy and appraisal earlier than some other parts of the UK, and in 1992 launched a new transport policy document stating: 'It is not the government's policy to meet all travel demand but rather to ensure that the accessibility needs of all people and businesses, including for tourism, can be served' (Scottish Office 1992). By 2003 this had worked through into appraisal and Scottish Transport Appraisal Guidance (2003), required accessibility appraisal that described the extent to which the social needs are being served by the transport systems. The success of the Scottish approaches in delivering new types of transport investment focused at improving access to work and access to major cities, were cited by UK Ministers; for example, the reopening of the Airdrie to Bathgate and Alloa railway lines, which were both prioritised and promoted using accessibility analysis methods (LTT, 2010).

Has UK Accessibility Planning Policy Worked? Current Policy Challenges

Although in 2003 the Social Exclusion Unit (2003) recognised that accessibility was a cross-sector objective and one department needed to be responsible for delivery; in practice, accountability must always be spread across many sectors due to separate legislation governing each sector. In practice, few UK transport practitioners have perceived their role as critical in checking that health departments did not inadvertently make accessibility worse when they reorganised service delivery, or education authorities did not inadvertently build new schools in inaccessible locations, or that land-use planning authorities avoided permitting developments that would lead to the closure of local accessible services and facilities. The pressures on accessibility have continued to increase since 2003, and the transport sector has only partially checked the impacts of the changes, or organised solutions to identified problems. A senior authority staff member summed up the accountability challenge, by noting that 'nobody loses their job because accessibility gets worse, but if the potholes are not filled then there is trouble' (Derek Halden Consultancy, 2000).

Lucas (2012) asserts that the focus on accessibility planning as a methodology for achieving greater social inclusion within the system of local public transport provision came about largely in absence of any prior recognition of the academic discourse in this area. Whether there was actually an absence of interest or just a lack of structure to the debate is open to argument, but it is clear that the practice of accessibility planning was based more on experience of successful practice than in any of the theoretical indicators that had been described in the academic research. Some noted (e.g., Farrington et al.,

2004) that accessibility was a slippery concept with the abundance of models, mapping tools and indices often creating greater confusion than clarity, but it was the application of the theory that demonstrated the usefulness of the toolkit.

In an attempt to bring structure to the analysis, the UK Department for Transport (DfT), invested in a range of new analytical tools to help standardise analytical approaches. Recommendations to DfT in 2004 (Derek Halden Consultancy and University of Westminster, 2004) about how to implement accessibility planning noted that one of the main barriers to progress would be the culture and skills in the transport profession. The profession was known for its strong analytical skills and interests in specific transport modes, rather than its interest in people and their needs. Staff with people skills would be more likely to choose professions other than transport. However transport was not unique in having a better track record of operational delivery than people focus and the introduction of accessibility planning was considered to add pressure for a much needed focus on people. However, managing such culture change was a substantial undertaking, which was underestimated.

There was widespread confusion about what accessibility planning involved. The high profile given to the new policy requirements combined with the lack of training through government-funded programmes, created a gap between top-down policy pressure and bottom-up delivery support. Commercial marketing of software filled this gap in the need for more training and support. Although accessibility planning is an evidence-based approach, and modelling can be part of that, within a few years many professionals confused accessibility planning with modelling. This was also comfortable for the transport profession, reinterpreting the new requirements in terms of existing analytical skills rather than the new people and partnership focus that had been intended. Nevertheless, some authorities, particularly in rural areas where travel demand and accessibility goals can be dealt with separately more easily, have delivered highly successful programmes using multilevel, multifaceted solutions that include the participation and involvement of affected individuals and communities (Derek Halden Consultancy and Transport Advisory Service 2010).

Lucas (2012) has highlighted the difficulties authorities faced with cross-sector working. Even among highly supportive organisations, cross-sector working through accessibility planning can be perceived as threatening to established administrative structures, or simply a lower priority. However the UK experience has shown that clear public accountability for all sectors can be assisted when transport authorities prepare, publish and negotiate change using evidence of accessibility change.

The lack of funding has been a problem since much of the funding for accessibility improvements tends to come from non-transport departments. Most public service providers have statutory responsibilities for ensuring that all people can access their services with budgets to help them deliver. However most departments discharge their responsibilities by concentrating on their core values in health, social services, education, leisure services, employment services, legal services and other provision and minimising transport spending. Where possible, each public authority simply informs transport providers about the transport difficulties, or occasionally funds transport for those facing the greatest difficulties, such as the patient transport services. Accessibility planning has sought to deliver better value joint approaches but turning these shared policies into funding and resources for delivery has been more difficult.

The new approaches since 2004 for accessibility planning have sought to make it easier for employment, health, education, social services, environment and planning departments to invest more efficiently and effectively in accessibility for staff and clients. However, there is far more failure of these partnership schemes than success. Where joint cross-sector schemes have been established, it has not taken long for each sector to seek to tactically withdraw their funding in the hope that other sectors will pick up more of the cost. This race to the bottom continues to slow the rate of progress with accessibility planning, but accessibility planning remains resilient to such pressures since if government fails then public protests soon return accessibility concerns to the political agenda. Citizens demand access to services and if government cannot organise the cross-sector working to deliver then it is soon called to account.

The decision to make transport authorities responsible continues to be questioned (e.g., Lucas, 2012) and it is true that transport cannot ultimately be accountable if a land-use planning, health, education or other authority makes a decision that causes accessibility problems. Ultimate accountability must follow the more narrowly defined legislation. Declining accessibility is therefore viewed as an inevitable problem by some stakeholders, but this still leaves a gap between public expectations of accessibility and delivery. The lessons of the past 20 years in the UK are that there are few easy answers, but if mandatory annual audits of accessibility are published, then a more constructive dialogue with the public and between public authorities should deliver whatever solutions as are practical with the limitations of the polycentric power structures of a modern democracy (Halden, 2009).

UK Accessibility Statistics

There are real benefits to be obtained from clear and transparent measures of accessibility change. Practical progress has been achieved by DfT championing the cross-sector agenda through the annual publication of accessibility statistics. These statistics show:

- The travel time from each neighbourhood to 8 types of destination – major employment locations, town centres, supermarkets/grocers, hospitals, medical practices, primary schools, secondary schools and colleges.
- The choice of opportunity available from each neighbourhood based on indicators representing the number of jobs accessible, floor space of food stores, and the number of hospitals, GPs, schools and colleges.

The statistics are published online (DfT 2012b) and are mapped so that users can compare the car, walk/public transport and cycle travel times for any neighbourhood. At a national level, decisions by the Departments for Health, Work, Justice, and other departments have been influenced by accessibility statistics, and at a local level developers and local authorities making land use proposals can read off the accessibility statistics to assess compliance with policies for improved accessibility. Figure 30.2 shows the statistics for a selected neighbourhood (LSOA) with travel times by alternative modes and capped Hansen indicators of the opportunity. The reason for capping the choice indicators is that once a high level of choice has been achieved adding more choices does not increase the level of opportunity.

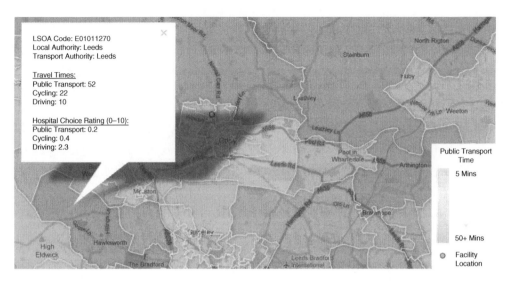

Source: Comparative statistics for one neighbourhood in Hawksworth shown (data from www.gov.uk/government/publications/accessibility-statistics-2012 and screenshot from www.loopconnections.org.uk/mapping.php)

Figure 30.2   Public transport travel times from DfT Accessibility Statistics Mapped in North West England

The national analysis is based on travel time. Time is a necessary condition for access, but is only one of many parameters. Other dimensions of access are meant to be considered in more local analyses including the personal capabilities of each group of people, and the information, comfort, physical barriers, cost and reliability of current provision. In practice the readily available time data has been used and other parameters are rarely included in the analysis. As noted earlier, this is also current practice in the Netherlands.

Accessibility is a multifaceted concept and there are many different operationalisations which show different perspectives on accessibility. As a result, attempts to measure such a complex concept with a single measure have failed. Other key points have emerged from the UK practice. Firstly, well constructed accessibility indicators avoid bias towards any mode of travel can include the impact of telecommunications networks as alternatives to travel, and can be adapted to fit a very wide range of situations. Secondly, the flexibility of the measures is their strength, but also a weakness if inappropriate indicators are used tactically to misrepresent benefits. Thirdly, policies should drive indicators not vice versa. Accessibility indicators have been widely abused in support of plans for transport schemes. SACTRA (1999), for example, found unsubstantiated claims about access to jobs to be more common than robust measures of accessibility. Transport investment should serve accessibility goals for people, not vice versa. Fourth and finally, relative accessibility for different mobility groups can usefully be used to look at inequality.

Discussion of UK Accessibility Planning

Overall, progress with the promotion of accessibility planning in the UK has been slow. Despite these problems, there is no suggestion in the UK as yet that there is another easier way of achieving the same difficult aims of cross-sector, people focused transport delivery, consistent with sustainability goals.

Yet despite the challenges of delivering complex sustainable development approaches as implemented through the major policy and appraisal changes over the past 20 years, most transport practitioners still have little incentive to plan accessibility. Accountability for people working in transport still follows much narrower structures. At the margin of transport delivery, transport authorities have achieved many successes securing access improvements and the new focus on accessibility has provided a policy framework to help embed the joint working needed to secure the changes. Research (DfT 2012c) has shown that previously roads and public transport managers had found it difficult to relate their job description to wider goals, but accessibility planning has helped to overcome these joint working problems.

4. CONCLUSIONS AND DISCUSSION

This chapter shows that accessibility planning research and practice in the Netherlands and the UK remain ambiguous about indicators and measurement. The choice of an accessibility measure (and the manner in which it is operationalised) strongly affects related results and, consequently, the forecast effects of accessibility changes on the spatial economy and social inequalities. Although accessibility measurement is ambiguous, the use of accessibility concepts to frame a cross-sector dialogue about the benefits of transport has been at least as successful as any other recent policy intervention to deliver sustainable development principles within practical transport and land-use delivery.

Dutch transport policy in the past decades focused on transport performance-based accessibility concepts. The main change in transport policy was the move from the transport provider perspective focusing on the transport performance of single motorway road segments to a 'transport user' perspective focusing on door-to-door travel time (using different transport networks and modes). A broader accessibility perspective so far does, however, not match established administrative structures within the Ministry of Infrastructure and Environment. This presents a barrier to developing cross-sector policy strategies necessary for sustainable land-use and transport systems.

The theory of accessibility planning would suggest that it is necessary to bring together different dimensions of accessibility (e.g., economic, social, cognitive and psychological) and incorporate all transport modes, user groups and travel-generating opportunities, and ensure that all providers and sectors work effectively together. These comprehensive approaches also require strong cooperation between accessibility researchers and public and private planning practitioners; enabling them to test and implement innovative practices that can be complemented by comprehensive frameworks for economic appraisal and equity impact analysis. However, closing the gap between theoretical and practical applications of accessibility concepts in the Dutch and UK policy arenas requires a clarity of accountability for access that will not be achieved quickly, involving administrative and perhaps legislative change.

The UK started to apply accessibility analysis to land-use planning in 1995 and decided that without measuring accessibility in more tangible and trackable ways, the desirable aims slip down the agenda to be replaced with single-sector goals. Recent progress has been patchy and the improvements made in accessibility measurement in the UK are not yet fully embedded in the transport appraisal practice that underpins most investment decisions. From the Dutch and UK experience, it is found that cross-sector accessibility planning is very difficult to achieve, even among highly supportive organisations. In the UK, practical progress has been achieved by championing the cross-sector agenda through the annual publication of accessibility statistics. However, the statistics are based on travel time. Other dimensions of access – including the personal capabilities of each group of people, information, comfort, physical barriers, cost and reliability of current provision – are rarely included due to a lack of data. The Dutch practice is similar, where the 2012 transport policy document announced the development of a new accessibility cost indicator that was to include travel time, costs, comfort and quality aspects. The indicator, however, proved to be difficult to monitor and forecast and was simplified to only include only travel time.

Existing successful UK and Dutch practice uses evidence of accessibility change for people. A first step to build on current successes would be to include the Hansen-based potential accessibility measure (for relevant population segments and opportunities) as an additional indicator in transport appraisal. These indicators can then be used to audit decision-making, as in much of the current accessibility planning practice. This will ensure that future land-use and transport policy strategies need to demonstrate that all modes are included and that they are integrated into the wider economy and society. How this information is then used by transport authorities, campaign groups and others to actually work towards cross-sector accessibility planning is a relevant topic for further research. The UK accessibility planning for the Olympic Games in London in 2012 might be considered best practice in this respect. The needs of each group of people were systematically considered, and by working in partnership, ways of prioritising needs were planned and delivered through a range of transport and non-transport interventions. The review of the lessons learned (TfL, 2012) shows that success depended on: making the best possible use of existing infrastructure; encouragement for people to make efficient journeys; providing bespoke services for target groups; clear accountability for the Olympic Delivery Authority discharged by working in partnership with transport authorities and transport operators; and operational delivery of the integrated approach through a transport coordination centre. This and other recent experience shows how a time-limited focus, with clear accountability, can prompt the necessary joint working and multi-sector fund assembly needed for accessibility improvements to be secured. The continued development of transport policy and planning since the 1960s is still a work in progress, and the first 40 years have taught us that the way in which accessibility is measured and understood forms an area of growing importance.

REFERENCES

Achuthan, K., Titheridge, H. and Mackett, R.L. (2010), Mapping accessibility differences for the whole journey and for socially excluded groups of people, *Journal of Maps*, **6**(1), 220–29.

Ashiru, O., Polak, J.W. and Noland, R.B. (2003), *Space-Time User Benefit and Utility Accessibility Measures for Individual Activity Schedules*, TRB2003, Washington.

Batty, M. (2009), Accessibility: in search of a unified theory, *Environment and Planning B: Planning and Design*, **36**(2), 191–4.

Besseling, P., Groot, W. and Lebouille, R. (2005), *Economische analyse van verschillende vormen van prijsbeleid voor het wegverkeer [An Economic Assessment of Various Methods of Road Pricing]*, The Hague: Netherlands Bureau for Economic Policy Analysis.

Bovy, P.H.L., Jager, J. and Gunn, H. (1992), *The Dutch National and Regional Model Systems: Principles, Scope and Applications*, Sixth WCTR Conference on Demand Traffic and Network Modelling, Pergamon, pp. 1197–208.

Chen, Y., Ravulaparthy, S., Dalal, P., Yoon, S.Y., Lei, T., Goulias, K.G., Pendyala, R.M., Bhat, C.R. and Hu, H.H. (2011), *Development of Opportunity-based Accessibility Indicators*, paper for the 90th Annual meeting of the Transportation Research Board.

Condeço-Melhorado, A., Martín, J.C. and Gutiérrez, J. (2011), Regional spillovers of transport infrastructure investment: a territorial cohesion analysis, *European Journal of Transport and Infrastructure Research*, **11**(4), 389–404.

de Jong, G., Daly, A., Pieters, M. and van der Hoorn, T. (2007), The logsum as an evaluation measure: review of the literature and new results, *Transportation Research Part A: Policy and Practice*, **41**(9), 874–89.

Derek Halden Consultancy (2000), *Review of Accessibility Measuring Techniques and their Application*, report to the Scottish Executive, Central Research Unit, www.scotland.gov.uk/Publications/2001/11/10328/File-1.

Derek Halden Consultancy and University of Westminster (2004), *Accessibility Planning: Developing and Piloting Approaches*, final report, Department for Transport, www.dhc1.co.uk/projects/accessibility_developing.pdf.

Derek Halden Consultancy and Transport Advisory Service (2010), *Sector-led Guidance on Rural Accessibility and Transport*, Improvement and Development Agency, www.idea.gov.uk.

DfT (2012a), *WebTAG: Transport Appraisal Guidance, the Accessibility Objective*, London: Department for Transport, www.dft.gov.uk/webtag/documents/expert/unit3.6.php.

DfT (2012b), *Accessibility Statistics*, www.gov.uk/government/publications/accessibility-statistics-2011.

DfT (2012c), *Accessibility Planning Policy: Evaluation and Future Direction*, final report by Atkins and University of Loughborough, www.gov.uk/government/uploads/system/uploads/attachment_data/file/3190/accessibility-planning-evaluation-report.pdf.

Dong, X., Ben-Akiva, M.E., Bowman, J.L. and Walker, J.L. (2006), Moving from trip-based to activity-based measures of accessibility, *Transportation Research Part A: Policy and Practice*, **40**(2), 163–80.

Ecotec (1993), *Reducing Transport Emissions Through Planning*, Department of the Environment and Department of Transport, London: HMSO.

Eijgenraam, C.J.J., Koopmans, C.C., Tang, P.J.G. and Verster, A.C.P. (2000), *Evaluation of Infrastructural Projects: Guide for Cost-benefit Analysis. Part I (Main Report) and Part II (Capita Selecta)*, The Hague/Rotterdam: CPB Netherlands Bureau for Economic Policy Analysis/Netherlands Economic Institute.

Farrington, J. and Farrington, C. (2005), Rural accessibility, social inclusion and social justice: towards conceptualisation, *Journal of Transport Geography*, **13**(1), 1–12.

Farrington, J., Shaw, J., Leedal, M., Maclean, M., Halden, D., Richardson, T. and Bristow, G. (2004), *Settlements, Services and Access: The Development of Policies to Promote Accessibility in Rural Areas in Great Britain*, Cardiff: Welsh Assembly Government.

Geurs, K. and Ritsema van Eck, J.R. (2001), *Accessibility Measures: Review and Applications. Evaluation of Accessibility Impacts of Land-use Transportation Scenarios, and Related Social and Economic Impacts*, RIVM report 408505 006, National Institute of Public Health and the Environment, Bilthoven.

Geurs, K. and Ritsema van Eck, J.R. (2003), Accessibility evaluation of land-use scenarios: the impact of job competition, land-use and infrastructure developments for the Netherlands, *Environment and Planning B: Planning and Design*, **30**(1), 69–87.

Geurs, K. and van Wee, B. (2004), Accessibility evaluation of land-use and transport strategies: review and research directions, *Journal of Transport Geography*, **12**, 127–40.

Geurs, K., van Wee, B. and Rietveld, P. (2006), Accessibility appraisal of integrated land-use/transport strategies: methodology and case study for the Netherlands Randstad area, *Environment and Planning B: Planning and Design*, **33**(5), 639–60.

Geurs, K., Zondag, B., de Jong, G. and de Bok, M. (2010), Accessibility appraisal of integrated land-use/

transport policy strategies: more than just adding up travel time savings, *Transportation Research Part D*, **15**, 382–93.

Gutiérrez, J., Condeço-Melhorado, A. and Martín, J.C. (2010), Using accessibility indicators and GIS to assess spatial spillovers of transport infrastructure investment, *Journal of Transport Geography*, **18**(1), 141–52.

Gutiérrez, J., Condeço-Melhorado, A., López, E. and Monzón, A. (2011), Evaluating the European added value of TEN-T projects: a methodological proposal based on spatial spillovers, accessibility and GIS, *Journal of Transport Geography*, **19**(4), 840–50.

Halden, D. (1996), Managing uncertainty in transport policy development: proceedings of the Institution of Civil Engineers, *Transport*, **117**(4), 256–62.

Halden, D. (2003), Accessibility analysis concepts and their application to transport policy, in A.D. Pearman, P.J. Mackie and J. Nellthorp (eds), Transport Projects, Programmes and Policies. Ashgate, London.

Halden D. (2009), *10 Years of Accessibility Planning – What Have we Learned?* Proceedings of the European Transport Conference, Amsterdam, www.etcproceedings.org.

Handy, S.L. and Niemeier, D.A. (1997), Measuring accessibility: an exploration of issues and alternatives, *Environment and Planning A*, **29**, 1175–94.

Hansen, W.G. (1959), How accessibility shapes land use, *Journal of American Institute of Planners*, **25**(1), 73–6.

Haugen, K. (2011), The advantage of 'near': which accessibilities matter to whom? *European Journal of Transport and Infrastructure Research*, **11**(4), 368–88.

Hoogendoorn-Lanser, S., Gordijn, H. and Schaap, N. (2011), *Bereikbaarheid anders bekeken [A Different View on Accessibility]*, The Hague: Kennisinstituut voor Mobiliteitsbeleid.

Hoogendoorn-Lanser, S., Stelling, C. and Meurs, H. (2013), De nieuwe bereikbaarheidsindicator [The new accessibility indicator], *NMagazine*, **1**, 24–7.

Iacono, M., Krizek, K.J. and El-Geneidy, A. (2010), Measuring non-motorized accessibility: issues, alternatives, and execution, *Journal of Transport Geography*, **18**(1), 133–40.

Jones, S.R. (1981), *Accessibility Measures: A Literature Review*, Crowthorne: Transport and Road Research Laboratory.

Koenig, J.G. (1980), Indicators of urban accessibility: theory and applications, *Transportation*, **9**, 145–72.

Krizek, K.J. (2010), Measuring accessibility: prescriptions for performance measures of the creative and sustainable city, *International Journal of Sustainable Development*, **13**(1–2), 149–60.

Kwan, M-P. (1998), Space-time and integral measures of individual accessibility: a comparative analysis using a point-based framework, *Geographical Analysis*, **30**(3), 191–216.

Kwan, M-P. (2000), Interactive geovisualisation of activity-travel patterns using three-dimensional geographical information systems: a methodological exploration with a large data set, *Transportation Research Part C*, **8**(4), 185–203.

Linneker, B.J. and Spence, N.A. (1992), Accessibility measures compared in an analysis of the impact of the M25 London Orbital Motorway on Britain, *Environment and Planning A*, **24**, 1137–54.

LTT (2010), Baker kneads local transport into shape for a world with less dough, *TransportXtra*, **548**, www.transportxtra.com/magazines/local_transport_today/news/?id=23220&StartRow=1.

Lucas, K. (2012), A critical assessment of accessibility planning for social inclusion, in K.T. Geurs, K. Krizek and A. Reggiani (eds), *Accessibility Analysis and Transport Planning: Challenges for Europe and North America*, Northampton, MA: Edward Elgar Publishing, pp. 228–42.

Martín, J.C. and Reggiani, A. (2007), Recent methodological developments to measure spatial interaction: synthetic accessibility indices applied to high-speed train investments, *Transport Reviews*, **27**, 551–71.

MinIenM (2012), *Structuurvisie Infrastructuur en Ruimte [National Policy Strategy for Infrastructure and Spatial Planning]*, The Hague: MinIenM.

Ministry of Transport (1963), *The Buchanan Report: Traffic in Towns*, London: HMSO.

MinV&W (1979), *Structuurschema Verkeer en Vervoer. Deel D: regeringsbeslissing [Transport Structure Plan. Part D: Government Decision]*, The Hague: Ministry of Transport, Public Works and Watermanagement.

MinV&W (1990), *Tweede Structuurschema Verkeer en Vervoer. Deel D [Second Transport Structure Plan. Part D]*, The Hague: Ministry of Transport, Public Works and Watermanagement.

MinV&W (2006), *'Nota Mobiliteit': Towards Reliable and Predictable Accessibility*, The Hague: Ministry of Transport, Public Works and Watermanagement.

Neutens, T. (2010), *Space, Time and Accessibility: Analyzing Human Activities and Travel Possibilities from a Time-geographic Perspective*, Department of Geography, University of Ghent.

Niemeier, D.A. (1997), Accessibility: an evaluation using consumer welfare, *Transportation*, **24**, 377–96.

Páez, A., Mercado, R.G., Farber, S., Morency, C. and Roorda, M. (2010), Relative accessibility deprivation indicators for urban settings: definitions and application to food deserts in Montreal, *Urban Studies*, **47**(7), 1415–38.

PBL (2011), *Nederland in 2040. Een land van Regio's [The Netherlands in 2040: A Country of Regions]*, The Hague: Netherlands Environmental Assessment Agency.

PBL (2012), *Balans van de Leefomgeving 2012 [Environmental Balance 2012]*, The Hague: Netherlands Environmental Assessment Agency.

Pirie, G.H. (1979), Measuring accessibility: a review and proposal, *Environment and Planning A*, **11**, 299–312.

Reggiani, A. (1998), Accessibility, trade and location behaviour: an introduction, in A. Reggiani (ed.), *Accessibility, Trade and Location Behaviour*, Aldershot: Ashgate.

Rijkswaterstaat (1987), *Het hoofdwegennet in 2010. Structuur en dimensionering [The Motorway Network in 2010. Structure and Dimensions]*, The Hague: Rijkswaterstaat.

Schwanen, T. and Kwan, M-P. (2008), The internet, mobile phone and space-time constraints, *GeoForum*, **39**(3), 1362–77.

Scott, D.M. and Horner, M.W. (2008), Examining the role of urban form in shaping people's accessibility to opportunities: an exploratory spatial data analysis, *Journal of Transport and Land Use*, **1**(2), 89–119.

Scottish Office (1992), *Roads Traffic and Safety*, Edinburgh: HMSO.

Scottish Transport Appraisal Guidance (2003), www.transportscotland.gov.uk/stag/home.

Social Exclusion Unit (2003), *Making the Connections: Final Report on Transport and Social Exclusion*, London: Social Exclusion Unit.

TfL (2012), Delivering Transport for the London 2012 Games, London: Transport for London, www.tfl.gov.uk.

PART IV

WIDER DIMENSIONS IN TRANSPORT AND DEVELOPMENT

31 More than A to B: cultures of mobilities and travel
Ole B. Jensen

1. INTRODUCTION

In this chapter the underpinning idea is that mobility is more than movement from A to B. Or in the language of transportation research; mobility is more than a 'derived demand'. The analytical and theoretical perspective claiming such an understanding is located within the broadly defined and cross-disciplinary 'mobilities turn' that has emerged within the social sciences during the past decade or so. The chapter will present key ideas from this field in juxtaposition to transportation research. Transport may be about movement from A to B, but 'mobilities' will take us beyond this and into the realm of culture, norms, emotions, and the like. The chapter will put emphasis on the dimensions of identity formation, social interaction, and cultural production as important but less explored areas of transportation research. However, the chapter does not claim that these cultural dimensions have been neglected all together by transportation research, nor that everything coming out of the 'mobilities turn' is new and completely unknown to transportation research. Rather the relationship is seen as a 'two-way street', where both perspectives have something to learn from each other. The chapter will illustrate this by reference to specific examples of research oscillating between urban transportation and mobilities research. Put very simply, one might say that transport research is related to how, why, and where something moves, whereas mobilities research in addition to the same set of questions would inquire into how it feels and what it means to cultures and identities that entities/things move. The movement of people, goods, and information shapes the cultures, powers, and norms that create societies and social networks. Therefore we need to add this perspective to our analysis. One way of doing so, is by engaging with the 'mobilities turn'.

The structure of the chapter is as follows: the introduction (section 1) presents the main idea behind the chapter; namely that mobilities is more than the movement from A to B. In section 2, a quick overview of key positions within transportation research and the 'mobilities turn' is presented. Due to the confinements of this chapter these are only outlined in rough contours. In particular it will be shown how the 'mobilities turn' may open up the agenda for seeing mobilities as related to issues of culture, identity formation and emotions. Section 3 presents examples of empirical research where the hallmark has been some sort of interaction between research perspectives and agendas related to transportation research as well as to mobilities research. The chapter concludes with a few pointers for future research.

2. TRANSPORT RESEARCH AND THE 'MOBILITIES TURN'

Here a quick overview of key positions within transportation research and the 'mobilities turn' is presented. The section ends arguing for a relationship of mutual understanding between transportation research and mobilities research rather than a separation and point toward the third section as evidence hereof. Elsewhere Shaw and Hesse (2010: 306) argue that the mobilities research fills a research gap in the geographical study of travel and transport, but equally pledge for mutual benefit to be gained from an open dialogue between these fields of research.

Transportation Research

One of the very early theoretical framings of transportation has actually been made by a sociologist. Thus Charles Horton Cooley's publication from 1894 'The theory of transportation' is interesting as a very early attempt to theorize transportation from the point of view of sociology. In the words of Cooley: 'We think of transportation as a movement of things – masses of any sort – from one place to another' (Cooley, 1894: 1). However, Cooley's attempt was a far cry from contemporary mobilities theory and remains an example of a very physical and economical perspective that illustrates that only within the very recent times has a more culturally and sociologically sensitive perspective been unfolding (Cooley actually criticizes the 'mechanical' understanding of transport but never manages to offer a more sociological account for cultures and norms in the publication). Transport geography was, in the 1960s and 1970s, predominantly quantitative, positivist, and law-seeking (Cresswell and Merriman, 2011: 2). Springing from such a tradition of thought, the 'rational mobile person' seemed to have been the predominant 'subject position' within transportation geography and planning. In other words, there was an underpinning assumption of the 'agent' as maximizing budgets or minimizing burdens (e.g., distance, time, costs). Perhaps time has come to include the 'non-instrumental' and even at times 'irrational mobile subject' into the frame. Not as a substitute but as a corrective to the imaginary rational mobile subject that always seeks to minimize friction of distance and optimize an economic budget in a calculative perception of time, distance, and resources. So, next to a language of 'value of time', 'friction of distance' and 'least net effort', we may need a vocabulary that opens up to how people feel and what they think and hope as they move along the vast networks of contemporary societies. The 'meaning of movement' is what concerns this sort of vocabulary as it aims to add to our basic understanding of mobilities. Goetz et al. (2009) call for bridging quantitative and qualitative transport geography and opening up towards a more critical perspective, which they identify to be the 'mobilities turn'.

Within transportation geography itself there has also been a divide between 'hard' and 'soft' or quantitative and qualitative approaches (Goetz et al., 2009) and often 'the social' has been placed as the 'black box' in the research agendas of transport research:

> transport planning and modelling mostly ignore the social dimensions of travel and broader issues of how travel and transport help to produce modern societies. Transport researchers take the demand for transport as largely given, as a black box not needing much further investigation, or as derived from the level of a society's income.
>
> (Larsen et al., 2006: 3)

To Rodrigue et al. (2009), transport geography is defined as a sub-discipline of geography, where the key concern is movement of freight, people, and information. On this background, transport geography links spatial constraints and attributes with origin, destination, extent, nature, and purpose of movements (Rodrigue et al., 2009: 7). This is a language of rational organization of moving objects in space and time. However, from 'inside' the transport research community itself we find the analysis from Banister to be very much in accordance with the critique of a preoccupation with mobility as an instrumental practice only:

> Two fundamental principles are embedded in the approach used [to transport planning], namely that travel is a derived demand and not an activity that people wish to undertake for its own sake. It is only the value of the activity at the destination that results in travel. The second principle is that people minimize their generalized costs of travel, mainly operationalized through a combination of the costs of travel and the time taken for travel.
>
> (Banister, 2008: 73)

The argument that follows from this observation is one leading towards a plea for more sustainable mobility. However, here it also serves the purpose of identifying one of the problematic underpinning assumptions; that travel is an instrumental and quantifiable practice only. Cresswell argues that if a bridge is to be built between transport and mobilities research, it might best take place in fields such as 'working on the ways in which travel time is filled with significance' (Cresswell, 2010: 5). This is very much in parallel with the argument made by Grieco and Urry when they state that:

> The importance of social synchronisation in organizing travel and transport had been largely ignored within the study of transport until the advent of the 'activity' approached developed some decades ago at the Transport Studies Unit at Oxford (Jones et al 1983). But in recent years even this approach had been critiqued for not going far enough in the insertion of the 'social; into analysing travel and transport. The importance of 'multiple mobilities' in social synchronisation and action has recently been transformed by the 'new mobilities' paradigm now developing around the world within various centres, groups, networks, conferences, journals, and book series (see Sheller and Urry 2006).
>
> (Grieco and Urry, 2011: 1)

So there are attempts to move beyond the transport/mobilities divide as it is. In light of this, we may take a closer look at the so-called 'mobilities turn'.

The 'Mobilities Turn'

This short chapter cannot possibly do justice to the 'mobilities turn' and its authors. Thus readers with an interest in more detail should consult the work of Adey (2010), Cresswell (2006), and Urry (2000, 2007) for book-length explanations and Sheller (2011), Vannini (2010), and Cresswell (2010) for review papers that all give fine overviews of the mindset and the research agenda. Urry argues in his seminal book *Sociology Beyond Societies* (2000), which in many ways was the starting point for the 'mobilities turn', that a new and mobility-oriented social science should:

- develop a sociology focusing upon movement, mobility, and contingent ordering;
- examine effects of corporeal, imagined, and virtual mobilities of people;

- consider things as 'social facts';
- embody the analysis through including the sensuous constitutions of humans and objects;
- investigate the uneven and diverse reach of networks and flows;
- examine temporal regimes and modes of dwelling and travelling;
- describe the bases of people's sense of dwelling and their dependencies upon various mobilities;
- comprehend the changing nature of citizenship, rights, and duties;
- illuminate the increased mediatization of social life and their 'imagined communities';
- investigate the changing powers and determinations of state powers;
- explain changes within states' regulating mobilities;
- interpret chaotic, unintended and non-linear social consequences of mobilities;
- explore if there is an emergent global and autopoietic system.

(Urry, 2000: 18–19, my listing)

In his later book from 2007, Urry points at five distinct forms of mobilities that must be understood relationally; corporal travel, physical movement of objects, imaginative travel, virtual travel, and communicative travel (Urry, 2007: 47). Corporal travel concerns the movement of bodies often within routinized settings (e.g., commuting, holiday, or business travel). Physical movement of objects is the pivotal locus of commodity exchange, freight, etc. The imaginative travel is the mediatized representations of mobility as, for example, in travel commercial or place branding. Virtual travel relates, for example, to the realm of Internet, with its opportunities for transcending geographical space. Finally, communicative travel is the communication and exchanges of messages across space utilizing various media. The 'mobilities turn' argues that these five forms are intertwined often in complex assemblages that interact in dynamic and non-deterministic ways. One of Urry's close collaborators in articulating the 'mobilities turn', Mimi Sheller, points at the diversity of the field in a review paper:

> Mobilities research combines social and spatial theory in new ways, and in so doing has provided a transformative nexus for bridging micro-interactional research on the phenomenology of embodiment, to cultural turn and hermeneutics, postcolonial and critical theory, macro-structural approaches to the state and political-economy, and elements of science and technology studies (STS) and new media studies.
>
> (Sheller, 2011: 1)

There is an interesting emerging institutional landscape to host these new cross-disciplinary fields of research. One key feature is the establishment of the journal *Mobilities* by John Urry, Mimi Sheller, and Kevin Hannam in 2006. Goetz et al. (2009: 327) argue that the launch of *Mobilities* was 'bringing together transport, communications, tourism, travel and migration into new theoretical discourses'. In relation to this, a number of research centres have come into existence: the Centre for Mobilities Research (CeMoRe, Lancaster), the Centre for Mobilities and Urban Studies (C-MUS, Aalborg), and the Center for Mobilities Research & Policy (mCenter, Philadelphia). Finally there are networks that accommodate this new transnational and trans-disciplinary field such as the Pan American Mobilities Network, Cosmobilities, and the Mediterranean Mobilities Network. What we are witnessing is thus an emerging intellectual infrastructure to match this new research agenda. Cresswell (2010: 4) points at the potential pitfall of the 'mobilities turn' in being too obsessed with 'the new' and overemphasizing the 'twenty-first-century high-tech hypermobility characterized by the car, the plane and mobile communication devices'. However, Vannini (2009) and others are quickly filling the gap researching 'alternative mobilities', so this is changing rapidly.

As mentioned, the 'mobilities turn' explore issues such as affect and emotion as important dimensions of the meaning of mobility. Good examples of this sort of thinking can be found in Sheller's analysis of automobility and emotions, or what she terms 'automotive emotions' (Sheller, 2004), and Nigel Thrift's arguments for affect and emotion as a vital dimension to understand the human and non-human networks and relations creating mobile sociality (Amin and Thrift, 2002; Thrift, 2008). From a research project exploring train passengers and their perception and usage of time, Watts and Lyons equally reach the point where they argue for the inclusion of affect and emotion into tools such as transport appraisals:

> For the economically modelled passenger (travelling in the course of work) nothing happens en route, everything happens before and after [. . .] Transport appraisals contests it is only concerned with the value of time saved, not with the value or nature of time spent [. . .] We propose a move to affective transport appraisal, where attention and ultimately investment in transport policy expands to include the making of travel time, as well as the simple saving of travel time.
>
> (Watts and Lyons, 2011: 106, 114, 117)

Another example of the inclusion of affect is an analysis of the eruption of Iceland's Eyjafjallajökull volcano in April 2010. In the following account, the complex relationship between disrupted global logistics and the individual's uncertainty and emotional distress precisely suggest that there were more to the closing down of international airspace as a function of the volcanic activity than simply disrupted movements from A to B:

> The volcanic activity in April 2010 in Iceland suggests that we need to pay even closer attention to the ways we engage with mobilities in emotional terms. How we may feel joy and humour as well as much deeper anxiety about the movement and friction triggered by the shaking of the regimes and systems of punctuality we take for granted in our global, cosmopolitan lifestyles . . . The key thing for me [doing field observations at an international conference during the eruption] though was the multiple strategies and coping attempts made on individual levels that clearly reflected an emotional uneasiness and discomfort amongst some of the more capable and resourceful; a conference full of global high-flying academics. The experiences thus let me to conclude that if the volcanic eruption can create so much anxiety and emotional eruption amongst resourceful and skilled social agents, it may have caused even more disruption amongst people with less ability to cope. Refugees, people who have been saving up for trips for a long time, or people depending on the openness of the flight corridors for getting home for funerals, weddings or other key events, surely must have felt much more distress than the AAG [the conference attended] attendees. In other words the AAG experience of the volcanic eruption becomes a 'critical case' of illustrating dependencies, vulnerabilities, and emotional disruption.
>
> (Jensen, 2011: 73–4)

From this short discussion of the 'mobilities turn' it hopefully becomes clear that issues of identity, culture, and social norms are as much in focus as is the physical movement of objects and humans. Much more obviously could be said here. Rather some specific examples of mobilities research will be discussed in order to specify in what ways the 'mobilities turn' may contribute to the dialogue with transportation research.

3.   CONTRIBUTIONS FROM MOBILITIES RESEARCH

There are a number of common dimensions between transport research and mobilities research that may be illustrated by the mutual interest in the five mobilities types Urry identified. Nevertheless, even though both may explore for example commuting, the latter quite swiftly will turn towards what this may mean to social networks, self-perception, organization of family life, etc. This section illustrates in more detail how these dimensions emerge within mobilities research by referring to concrete research projects.

Transportation and Urban Planning (TUP)

This was a project funded by the Danish Transportation Council and ran in the period of 1998–2004 and sponsored a smaller group of research assistants, PhD students and senior researchers. Here the reference mainly is to the publications by Næss and Jensen (2002, 2004, 2005). The key research question was to explore the relation between urban structure and transportation. The mobilities research contribution was to add a qualitative and ethnographic dimension in relation to the empirical level, and to introduce the concepts of 'transport rationales' and 'mobility cultures'. From a preliminary study in the Danish city of Frederikshavn was found that adding the qualitative dimension to the project opened up a more diverse pool of knowledge. This was taken in more elaborately in a larger study of the Greater Copenhagen region where travel diary and geocoded trip mapping added a new dimension, with qualitative research interviews focusing on the underlying norms and cultural orientations that made people choose certain modes of transport or particular routes through the city. The project opened up a tentative exploration of concepts such as 'transport rationales' and 'mobility cultures'. The former thus explored rationales such as affect, comfort, aesthetics, and perceived safety, in addition to the already well-known rationales of fastest mode, shortest route, and the like. The lesson learned from the TUP project in relation to this chapter was about exploring and adding new mobility-oriented dimensions to a rather traditional set-up of transportation research; however, not as a substitute but as an enriching perspective.

Bikeability

This project was supported by the Danish Strategic Research Council, running in the period 2010–13. It was organized in a consortium between Copenhagen University, Aalborg University, the University of Southern Denmark, the Technical University in Denmark, the Danish Cancer Society, the Danish Cyclist Federation, and two Dutch partners. In itself, this was an interesting institutional set-up where political and strategic interests met with research interests albeit in a very open and rational dialogue. From the project summary at the website it is stated that:

> This research project ... focuses on the preconditions for cycling; the possible effects of changes of the urban environment and cycling infrastructure; and methodologies for assessment of changes to existing bicycling networks based on micro-level spatially explicit data. This way the strategic focus of the project is how to enhance bike-ability of urban areas. The project will investigate, analyze and model cycling behaviour and motivation. A number of data collection and analysis methods will be taken into use, ranging from GIS based modelling and agent based simulation, to national surveys, case studies and qualitative approaches based on interviews and logbooks. Analyses will be applied on various scales from national, to neighbourhoods and individual cyclists. The achieved knowledge and the developed methods will be applicable to Danish urban and transport planning. Focus will be put on the anticipated effects on bike-ability of a) social, cultural and demographic changes of the urban population; b) changes in the urban structure (population density, amount and quality of bicycle tracks, location of facilities); c) changes of bicycle infrastructure (new paths, bridges); and d) changes to the route attributes (traffic light, separation of bicycle lanes). It is expected that the project's results will be transferable to other regions of the World where a need to enhance conditions for bicyclists is realized.
>
> (www.bikeability.dk)

In this project, more 'mainstream' transportation research was undertaken (such as traffic counting and official traffic statistics) but part of the work was anchored in the 'mobilities turn'. One such example is the 'work package' carried out by C-MUS researchers (Andrade et al., 2010, 2011). In these publications it was investigated, based on case research in three Danish cities, how bicycle infrastructure and design elements are affording (or preventing) cycling. The research is interesting in this context since it partly took into consideration very material traffic planning issues such as the height of curbs, bike lanes, and urban design issues, and related these to the everyday life mobilities and cultures of cycling (thus preparing for the development of a notion of 'mobilities design' to which we turn at the end of the chapter). In C-MUS the research under the Bikeability project drew upon earlier research into cycling with a US/Danish comparative perspective (Mikkelsen et al., 2011; Jensen, 2007). From this research, the social and cultural embedding of the cycle as a transportation technology pointed at an understanding of biking in the US as mainly either related to recreation or political statements of anti-car attitudes. These rationales are also found in Denmark, but moreover the bike is here understood as an everyday artefact and ordinary mode of transport. This is due to its deep cultural embedding as an almost unreflected everyday life practice. In both the Bikeability project and the US/DK comparative study, quantitative methods and approaches from transport research were coupled with qualitative and ethnographic approaches from the 'mobilities turn'. The contribution to transport was thus to explore the wider socio-cultural context of cycling. Furthermore, this is a key insight from the 'mobilities turn', namely that no mode of transport, infrastructure, or technology can be understood in isolation of its social and cultural context.

Staging Mobilities and 'Negotiation-in-motion'

This section is ended with an illustration of mobilities research where the focus is on the material layout, physical, and technical features as well as with the human interaction and embodied mobilities. The common focal point of these dimensions may be said to be the human and material elements and conditions assembled into a specific 'mobile situation'. Driving to work, flying out to a holiday destination, being on the run as a refugee all are concrete practices that ultimately must be understood from the vantage point of 'the situation'. This is captured by the notion of 'staging mobilities' (Jensen, 2013). The basic proposition is that mobilities are 'staged' from above by planning, regulation, and design, as well as mobile subjects 'staging' themselves from below in everyday life situations. Putting the 'mobile situation' at the centre point as:

> a process of creating lived mobility practices and the material preconditions to these. In this research contemporary urbanism is understood as highly influenced by the staged mobilities of planning, design, architecture, governance systems, technological networks as well as by the social interactions, cultural meanings and the production of social order. Staging mobilities is a socio-spatio-temporal process designing mobile lifescapes 'from above' and performed mobile engagements and interactions 'from below' . . . Staging mobilities bring a new perspective to mobilities research by documenting how the urban situation at the brink of the 21st Century must be understood from a perspective seeing 'staging' as the dominant feature of mobilities.
>
> (Jensen, 2013: 5)

The perspective of 'staging mobilities' point at dynamic lived mobilities as they manifest themselves in relation to three key themes; the physical settings, material spaces, and design; the social interactions; and the embodied performances. The perspective works on the border of transport and mobilities. The situational perspective has been used in a field study of a redesigned square and traffic junction in the city of Aalborg, Denmark. The case study was conducted in a 'shared space' type of urban environment in the city centre where it was studied how people are 'negotiating in motion' during three weeks of intense traffic counting and interaction registration in 2009. This literally meant the registration of how bikes, pedestrians, buses, vans, and cars made their way in this complex intersection in which it is not highly evident who has the right to do what. The study concluded in the following manner:

> [W]e saw from the study that to capture the ephemeral quality of such interaction we may benefit from understanding these as 'temporary congregations'. By this is meant that people meets, team up, and break up, in very volatile social interactional patterns. But these are still sufficiently enduring to make us feel the collective (as when we share the experience of missing the bus). The unsettled and socially open character of urban mobility practices furthermore makes it clear that multiple decisions needs to be made. Obviously we are aware of mode of transport and routing decisions. But also much more detailed and situational decisions such as which way to pass a person coming against us needs conceptualisation. Here we argue for the usefulness of the notion of 'negotiation in motion' to capture that the social interaction is made in a mobile space of norms, values and power. Some of these ways of encountering our 'mobile other' may be likened to an already existing repertoire of actions, mobile negotiation techniques and mobile interaction tactics. These may range from the very physical embodied 'sliding and evasion techniques' that people apply to avoid collision to the more general (and cultural specific) of the personal distance accepted for either passing or co-presence in a mobile situation (e.g. bus riding). Also we find different levels of subtleness to the way power is being displayed

in mobile interactions. We saw the almost classic 'power of speed' and the more subtle '*I pretend not to have seen you*' tactics. Here we are facing issues of 'situational and mobile power' which are highly unstable and volatile as the execution of such powers take place during motion, *in situ*, and at times even at high speed.

(Jensen, 2010: 399–400, emphasis in original)

By exploring the multiple 'negotiations in motion', the study showed how the simple acts of moving through a city are about social interaction, identities, and cultures of behavioural codes in public spaces. Two other empirical cases have been explored with the framework of 'staging mobilities' and that is the Metro in Copenhagen and the Sky Train in Bangkok (Jensen, 2013). The lesson from these empirical works is that everyday life mobility must be understood in its concrete manifestations that we find in 'mobile situations'. Such situations are complex assemblages of human and non-human entities that have much wider repercussions that simply physical displacement.

The contributions from the 'mobilities turn' to transport cannot be fully described within one chapter. Many other examples of empirical research should be consulted, other theoretical framings than the 'staging mobilities' should be explored, and different methodologies investigated. However, from this discussion it should be clear that mobilities is much more than physical movement from A to B, and that all these interesting 'side-effects' are actually important dimensions to a fuller understanding of transport.

4.   CONCLUDING REFLECTIONS

This chapter's key ambition has been to argue for the understanding of mobilities as being much more than an A-to-B movement. Mobilities have meanings and are instrumental as well as non-instrumental acts. Moreover, mobilities create cultures and affect human identities. The phenomenon of mobilities is as much about physical and functional logistics and flow, as an issue of how social subjects perceive and interact with other social subjects. Mobilities effects how social subjects understand places, and the theoretical perspective presented here opens up for empirical and theoretical research bridging the mobilities/transport divide.

Transport research may be said to carry and instrumental and functionalist bias, but much social research equally carries a blindness to the importance of space and place in general, and mobilities in particular. Furthermore, it is hardly the full picture that transportation researchers do not understand or appreciate the cultural and social aspects. But it is fair to say that such issues are not key dimensions (one exception might be Knowles et al., 2008). Much seems to indicate that there are very serious challenges awaiting both mobilities and transport research in the future with the focus on environmental issues, social equity, and global climate change (Gilbert and Perl, 2010). Thinking about future challenges of 'post-car societies', 'low carbon futures', and societal 'powering down' (Dennis and Urry, 2009; Urry 2011, 2013) calls for a more unified agenda between transport and mobilities research.

The now classic text within transportation and planning, Colin Buchanan's report *Traffic in Towns*, identified the importance of the relationship between architecture and transport. In this report, the situation of separated realms for architecture and transport is criticized and a proposal for a more holistic understanding under the name of 'traffic architecture' is made:

> There is a new and largely unexplored field of design here, but it involves abandoning the idea that urban areas must consist of buildings set alongside vehicular streets, with one design for the buildings and another for the streets. This is only a convention. If buildings and access ways are thought of together, as constituting the basic material of cities, then they can be moulded and combined in a variety of ways many of which are more advantageous than the conventional street. A useful term to describe this process is 'traffic architecture', which conveys the idea of buildings and building groups being purpose-designed for the efficient handling of traffic.
>
> (Buchanan, 1964: 67–8)

Others have pointed at this relationship between architecture, design and traffic before (Bacon, 1967; Lynch, 1981; Wall, 2005) but still the realms of analysis and intervention, planning and design have remained unconnected. Perhaps time has come for a third phase of the development. From the first identification of a need to connect traffic and architecture into 'traffic architecture' one might envision a new phase of 'mobilities design'. If Buchanan addressed the lack of integration between architecture and traffic, we might today move further toward a 'holistic' understanding by connecting architecture and traffic with what might be termed 'mobilities design':

> First of all, when we are interested in the actual and practical issues related to the staging of mobilities, it does make quite some sense to seek inspiration amongst those who are occupied with either designing these or at least reflecting upon the design of mobilities. Secondly, there is some value to the rather simple distinction between 'analysis' and 'intervention'. Needless to say there are overlaps and most intervening practitioners within design may claim to perform analysis as well. However, there are surely differences in the self-perception as well as practices between for example a sociologist analysing mobilities and an urban designer or a city planner drawing up plans and schemes for urban mobilities. Incorporating the insights from the latter group is part of the *Staging Mobilities* approach to mobilities research . . . A third point that has been coming out of this consulting of the design fields is a confirmation of the theoretical claim progressed earlier, namely that mobilities as a social and spatial practice is about much more than instrumental acts of moving from point A to point B. As we gain insights into the staging of mobilities from the vantage point of the design fields we understand that whether we are staging mobilities from above through design and planning, or from below in social interaction with fellow mobile subjects, we are engaging a field of cultural practices, social norms and identity construction.
>
> (Jensen, 2013, 191–2)

The potential of overlapping mobilities analysis and design is elaborated in more detail in Jensen (2013) but it signifies not only a change towards including architecture into the wider dimensions of design (e.g., service systems and wayfinding) but also to open up the transport dimension further towards the mobilities theme, thus including the issues of culture, norms, and identity. This will surely demand much openness among such diverse academic disciplines and professions as architecture, urban design, urban planning, traffic planning, transportation, and mobilities research. This may be a tall agenda, but given the global challenges facing urban mobilities and transport, there might be a sense of urgency facilitating such dialogue. The wider and general contribution from the 'mobilities turn' is thus partly to focus on the 'more than A to B'. Moreover, the perspective opens up for inviting mobility research and transport research into dialogue. Such a dialogue may focus on the specific situations of mobilities as well as it may include more design-oriented elements. This suggests that the cross-disciplinary interaction should be even wider if we are to comprehend the cultures of mobilities and travel of contemporary society.

REFERENCES

Adey, P. (2010), *Mobility*, London: Routledge.
Amin, A. and Thrift, N. (2002), *Cities: Reimagining the Urban*, Oxford: Polity Press.
Andrade, V., Harder, H., Jensen, O.B. and Madsen, J.O. (2010), *Bike Infrastructures*, Department Working Paper series, vol. 37, Aalborg: Department of Architecture, Design and Media Technology, Aalborg University.
Andrade, V., Jensen, O.B., Harder, H. and Madsen, J.O. (2011), Bike infrastructures and design qualities: enhancing cycling, *Danish Journal of Geoinformatics and Land Management*, **46**(1), 65–80.
Bacon, E.N. (1967), *Design of Cities*, London: Penguin.
Banister, D. (2008), The sustainable mobility paradigm, *Transport Policy*, **15**, 73–80.
Buchanan, C. (1964), *Traffic in Towns*, Harmondsworth: Penguin.
Cooley, C.H. (1894), The theory of transportation, *American Economic Association*, **XI**(3).
Cresswell, T. (2006), *On the Move: Mobility in the Modern Western World*, London: Routledge.
Cresswell, T. (2010), Mobilities I: catching up, *Progress in Human Geography*, November, 1–9.
Cresswell, T. and Merriman, P. (eds) (2011), *Geographies of Mobilities: Practices, Spaces, Subjects*, Aldershot: Ashgate.
Dennis, K. and Urry, J. (2009), *After the Car*, Cambridge: Polity.
Gilbert, R. and Perl, A. (2010), *Transport Revolutions: Moving People and Freight Without Oil*, Gabriola Island: New Society Publishers.
Goetz, A.R., Vowles, T.M. and Tierney, S. (2009), Bridging the qualitative–quantitative divide in transport geography, *The Professional Geographer*, **61**(3), 323–35.
Grieco, M. and Urry, J. (eds) (2011), *Mobilities: New Perspectives on Transport and Society*, Farnham: Ashgate.
Jensen, O.B. (2007), *Biking in the Land of the Car: Clashes of Mobility Cultures in the USA*, paper for the conference Trafikdage, Aalborg, 27–8 August.
Jensen, O.B. (2010), Negotiation in motion: unpacking a geography of mobility, *Space and Culture*, **13**(4), 389–402.
Jensen, O.B. (2011), Emotional eruptions, volcanic activity and global mobilities: a field account from a European in the US during the eruption of Eyjafjallajökull, *Mobilities*, **6**(1), 67–75.
Jensen, O.B. (2013), *Staging Mobilities*, London: Routledge.
Knowles, R., Shaw, J. and Docherty, I. (eds) (2008), *Transport Geographies: Mobilities, Flows and Space*, Oxford: Blackwell.
Larsen, J., Urry, J. and Axhausen, K. (2006), *Mobilities, Networks, Geographies*, Aldershot: Ashgate.
Lynch, K. (1981), *Good City Form*, Cambridge MA: MIT Press.
Mikkelsen, J., Smith, S. and Jensen, O.B. (2011), *Challenging the 'King of the Road': Exploring Mobility Battles Between Cars and Bikes in the USA*, paper for the 4th Nordic Geographers Meeting, Roskilde, 24–7 May.
Næss, P. and Jensen, O.B. (2002), Urban land use, mobility and theory of science: exploring the potential for critical realism in empirical research, *Journal of Environmental Policy & Planning*, **4**(4), 295–311.
Næss, P. and Jensen, O.B. (2004), Urban structure matters, even in a small town, *Journal of Environmental Planning and Management*, **47**(1), 35–57.
Næss, P. and Jensen, O.B. (2005), *Bilringene og cykelnavet. Boliglokalisering, bilafhængighed og transportadfærd i Hovedstadsområdet [Car-rings and Bike-hubs. Residential Localisation, Car Dependence and Transport Behaviour in the Greater Copenhagen Area]*, Aalborg: Aalborg University Press.
Rodrigue, J.-P., Comitois, C. and Slack, B. (2009), *The Geography of Transport Systems*, 2nd edn, London: Routledge.
Shaw, J. and Hesse, M. (2010), Transport, geography and the 'new' mobilities, *Transactions of British Geographers*, 305–12.
Sheller, M. (2004), Automotive emotions: feeling the car, *Theory, Culture & Society*, **21**(4/5), 221–42.
Sheller, M. (2011), Mobility, *Sociopedia.isa*.
Thrift, N. (2008), *Non-Representational Theory: Space. Politics. Affect*, London: Routledge.
Urry, J. (2000), *Sociology Beyond Societies: Mobilities for the Twenty-first Century*, London: Routledge.
Urry, J. (2007), *Mobilities*, Cambridge: Polity Press.
Urry, J. (2011), *Climate Change & Society*, Cambridge: Polity.

Urry, J. (2013), *Societies Beyond Oil: Oil Dregs and Social Futures*, London: Zed Books.
Vannini, P. (ed.) (2009), *The Cultures of Alternative Mobilities: Routes Less Travelled*, Farnham: Ashgate.
Vannini, P. (2010), Mobile cultures: from the sociology of transport to the study of mobilities, *Sociology Compass*, **4**(2), 111–21.
Wall, A. (2005), *Victor Gruen: From Urban Shop to City*, Barcelona: Actar.
Watts, L. and Lyons, G. (2011), Travel remedy kit: interventions into train lines and passenger times, in M. Büscher, J. Urry and K. Witchger (eds), *Mobile Methods*, London: Routledge, pp. 104–18.

32 Car-fixation, socialization, and opportunities for change
Ellen Matthies and Christian A. Klöckner

1. INTRODUCTION

Private car use – being a source of accidents, noise, and local pollution – is one of the main threats to urban quality of life (Gärling and Steg, 2007). Moreover, private car use is one of the predominant drivers of greenhouse gas emission and global warming. In order to effectively reduce the use of private cars not only does travel demand have to be reduced, but also its use must be steered to more sustainable forms of travel. A crucial factor here is the willingness of people to change their behaviour and to switch to new forms of transport.

However, can we assume that offering equal alternatives of travel is enough to make people switch to more sustainable forms of transport (e.g., use public transport or a bike)? This chapter will propose the phenomenon of 'car-fixation' as a possible explanation for the limited success of intervention programmes aimed at changing car-use patterns. The chapter will then explore how socialization processes might contribute to car-fixation, and describe how particular groups of car users are more prone to fixation than others (e.g., men more than women, rural areas more than urban) based on these mechanisms. Strategies for preventing and overcoming car-fixations that are rooted in psychological models will also be proposed.

2. PSYCHOLOGICAL APPROACHES TO EXPLAIN 'CAR-FIXATION'

When psychological research began to be interested in determinants of travel behaviour, it was natural to first turn to established psychological action models to help explain choice in this behavioural domain. The theory of planned behaviour (Ajzen, 2012), as one of the prominent candidates, has, for example, been applied several times to explain travel mode choice (e.g., Eriksson and Forward, 2011). Similarly, another example of such a theory has proven its value in several applications is the norm activation theory (Schwartz and Howard, 1981; see, e.g., Hunecke et al., 2001). Studies like these have demonstrated that variables such as intentions to use public transportation, attitudes towards travel modes, perceived control about use of different modes, personal and social norms about the behaviours in question, and problem awareness have a significant impact on mode choice. Despite this, there is an important flaw that exists in the aforementioned models pertaining to choices that are repeatedly made. These models analyse determinants of behaviour at one point in time and assume that the behaviour is under volitional control. In reality, choices are made in a historical context: what we

Good

491

decide at one point in time depends on what we decided earlier. If we were satisfied with the outcome of a mode choice we made before, why should we spend time deliberating on alternative modes and not just repeat what satisfied our needs before?

This dependency on choices made before has been referred to as a habit, a routine, or a travel-mode fixation. It has serious implications for attempts to change travel-mode choice. Most people have long histories of making travel-mode decisions, and that leads to relatively stable use patterns of particular modes for particular trips – sometimes even the same mode for all trips. These stable patterns are resistant to change to a degree that makes it difficult to influence travel behaviour by simply improving the quality of public transportation or changing peoples' attitudes or norms about the use of alternative travel modes. Several studies support the view that car users stick to their car-use routines although there are attractive and feasible alternatives (e.g., Fujii and Gärling, 2007). The theoretical concept of habit emerged when the focus shifted from singular mode choices, which can sufficiently be described with the aforementioned models, to mode choice in its historical context. It was implemented as an additional variable into both the theory of planned behaviour and the norm activation theory. Habits served as a stand-in for the stability of choice that goes beyond the mere stability of the other psychological and situational variables or, in other words, the fixation of a behaviour that even resists changes in the context or other parts of the psychological mindset. Accordingly, from a theoretical perspective, the most relevant effect that habits have in action models is that they potentially moderate the relation between intentions or personal norms and mode choice. This interaction effect has empirically been shown (e.g., Klöckner and Matthies, 2004; Verplanken et al., 1998) whereby intentions as well as personal norms lost their influence on travel-mode choice the stronger the habits to use a particular travel mode were.

In order for the construct of habit to be more than an empty 'stand-in' for unexplained stability, it also inherently requires a theoretical background that explains the mechanisms of how a habit is established and maintained, and which mediating mechanisms account for the effects that habits have on stability of choice. Notwithstanding slightly different assumptions about the theoretical nature of a habit (see below), habit researchers generally agree on the conditions that contribute to generate a habit: what is needed is the successfully repeated performance of certain behaviour in a stable context (Klöckner and Verplanken, 2012). The more often the same travel mode is chosen in the same context with a successful outcome, the stronger the link between encountering the situation itself and eliciting the same choice automatically becomes. A mental shortcut is created that links the situational cues directly to behavioural choice, bypassing deliberate decision-making, which then makes the decision-making system immune to changes in determinants of deliberate decision-making. As long as the situational cues remain stable enough and the outcome is sufficiently satisfying, choices are automatically repeated rather than deliberately changed.

Regarding the cognitive mechanisms behind this mental shortcut, two alternative – although not mutually exclusive – perspectives have been proposed in the literature: the script-based approach and the connectionist approach (Klöckner and Verplanken, 2012). The connectionist approach has its theoretical roots in research on neuronal networks. It assumes that repeated activation of neurons responsible for processing information about situational cues together with neurons connected to the choice decision, leads to a strengthened neuronal connection between the two neuron clusters (Neal et al., 2006). The more often the two clusters are co-activated, the stronger and consequently faster this connection becomes. If the connection is strong enough, the choice related neurons become activated automatically as soon as the cue processing neurons are activated. The script-based approach (Verplanken and Aarts, 1999), on the other hand, assumes that the consistent co-appearance of stable situational cues and a certain behavioural choice creates a cognitive structure that stores a blueprint of the action sequence in question. This cognitive structure is referred to as 'behavioural script'. Like a theatre script, it contains a standardized sequence of actions that is started once the initial trigger, which may be the set of situational cues or the goal of travelling to a certain destination, is encountered. Although both concepts of habit differ in their understanding of the nature of the underlying structure, the prediction they make is essentially the same: once the link or the script is established, the need for deliberate processing is dramatically reduced, automaticity takes over, and cognitive capacity is freed for other purposes. The last point also explains why habits are generally fundamental for our everyday performance: if we had to make all decisions over and over again, we would be totally overwhelmed with the effort that needed to be put into this process. Problems occur when the old decision strategy is no longer providing the best results but still good-enough results to be maintained.

It becomes apparent that the impact of travel-mode habits on mode choice may be even more subtle than as described in the previous section when the influence of strong habits in information acquisition and use in decision-making is analysed. Verplanken, Aarts, and van Knippenberg (1997) demonstrated, for instance, that people with strong bike-use habits acquired less information about the situational conditions of a particular trip before making a decision about which travel mode to use than people with weak habits. Furthermore, they are especially restrictive with information search about travel modes different from their habitualized mode. Basically, their decision strategy appears to confirm that the conditions that lead to establishing the habit in the first place are still in place and that the search is ended as soon as that is confirmed. People with strong habits limited their information search only to some crucial items belonging to the travel mode favoured by strong habit and ignored information relating to other travel modes. Attempts to increase their information search about alternatives by telling the participants that they would need to justify their decision afterwards lead to only a time limited effect. In another study, the same authors (Aarts et al., 1997) were able to show that people with strong habits not only search for less information but also use fewer pieces of information for making a decision. Generally speaking, the effect of habits seems to be that they heavily guide how much information is needed to make a decision and in which areas to look for it. The stronger a habit is, the stronger is the tendency to look only for very few pieces of information that basically help confirm previous decisions.

To summarize this section, habits seem to be a fruitful approach to explain why some people are locked into car use more than other people. If you have made a pro-car decision several times in a stable context (for example on the trip to work) it is likely that this decision becomes linked to making the trip to work. Furthermore, when being in the same situation again, the established choice is activated automatically. This reduces information search and processing about alternatives considerably and in the case of very strong habits totally.

Other authors have introduced concepts into the debate about travel mode choice that might be perceived as overlapping with 'car fixation' as proposed in this chapter. Anable (2005), for example, identified 26 per cent of participants in her survey of travel-mode change and related attitudes and beliefs as 'car addicts'. Even though other segments of the participants in her survey also showed a high amount of car use and a strong resistance towards change to other modes, car addicts are not motivated by low perceived control about behaviour change or a particular gain in joy from car driving, but by low problem awareness. Whereas Anable's segmentation approach relies on attitudes and beliefs, the concept of car-fixation that is proposed in this chapter focuses on the historical development of situation–behaviour links that can overrule attitudes, beliefs, and related constructs.

3. SOCIALIZATION AND APPROACHES TO EXPLAIN THE GENESIS OF CAR-FIXATION

Using a broad understanding, socialization refers to the processes by which children and adolescents are taught and learn the necessary skills, values, and behavioural patterns to integrate into the culture in which they live (e.g., Maccoby, 2006). According to Maccoby (2006), socialization implies that children learn 'good habits', meaning behavioural standards set by socialization agents. In this section, we wish to explore the assumption that car-fixation has its roots in a car-focused travel-mode socialization. Socialization approaches put a certain focus on so-called socialization agents; these are the persons and institutions that shape values and behaviours. According to Baslington's (2008) 'social theory of travel mode behaviour', the relevant socialization agents for travel habits are: family, school, media, and peer group. In this section we explore how socialization processes (early influences and socialization of adolescents and young adults) might contribute to car-fixation. Based on socialization mechanisms, we additionally would like to investigate if particular groups of car users are more prone to fixation than others.

Early Influences on Mode Preferences

Baslington (2008) gives an overview of empirical studies in the field of travel mode socialization. She reports that as early as at the age of seven, children are able to distinguish different modes of transportation and associate different modes of transportation with different levels of status (Meaton and Kingham, 1998). Although generally authors assume various socialization agents for travel-mode preferences (mainly parents, peer group, and media), empirical studies with children focus mainly on parents as socialization agents, and in particular on the relevance of car ownership and car use in the family. Baslington (2008) demonstrates that in car-free households a higher percentage of children could imagine living without a car in adulthood compared to children from households that own a car. Findings of other studies confirm the positive correlation between parents' car ownership and children's attitudes towards different transport modes (e.g., Cahill et al., 1996; Sandqvist, 2002).

Socialization may not be solely viewed as an intentional process driven by parents or other socialization agents, but also as a side-effect of environmental conditions and the behaviour of the social environment. Engelbert (1986) investigated the type of residential area and travel behaviour of children and reported that children living in an area with high traffic density had less autonomous travel experiences for their regular ways to kindergarten or school (using feet, bike, or bus). Johansson (2006) reports for a sample of Swedish families that parents' chauffeuring behaviour for leisure travel of their children was related to environmental factors (traffic environment and quality of foot and cycle paths) as well as to car ownership of the respective households (for an overview on school travel behaviour in various countries see McDonald, 2008).

Later Travel Socialization

Generally, as seen within socialization research, research of travel-mode choice socialization has also been mostly concerned with children's learning processes and outcomes, despite socialization being a lifelong process (Maccoby, 2006). In particular, for travel-mode socialization it is necessary to consider later stages of childhood and adolescence as well, because mode experiences undergo relevant changes in adolescence (e.g., acquisition of a driving licence). We know in general that for older children the influence of peers becomes more important, which can also be assumed for travel mode choices, particularly since we know that travel modes are relevant for status as well as have an emotional symbolic aspect. Schönhammer (1999), for example, describes the acquisition of a driver's licence as an 'initiation rite', which does not only imply the "technical' dimension of learning the necessary skills to drive a car but also the social dimension of crossing a very important threshold to adult life (Limbourg et al., 2000). As older children and adolescents travel more often and over longer distances (e.g., to school), it can be assumed that the travel experiences itself become increasingly relevant for adolescents' attitudes and preferences towards cars and other modes.

Newer Retrospective Studies

The impact of travel socialization on later travel mode choice has mostly been analysed from a projective perspective, i.e., that children were asked what travel modes they could picture themselves using later as adults (e.g., Flade et al., 2001). Empirical research on the impact of travel socialization on later mobility behaviour from an adult's perspective is rare, although this approach opens the perspective to investigate in detail via which constructs socialization takes place. Klöckner and Matthies (2004) show that habits mediate the influence of three aspects of travel-mode socialization on current car use: frequency of parents' former use of public transportation, experiencing acquisition of driver's licence as initiation to adulthood, and former multi-mobility of the peer group. Haustein, Klöckner, and Blöbaum (2009) evaluated how different aspects of travel socialization during late childhood and adolescence contributed to the explanation of travel-mode choice in young adulthood. In an online survey, three different socialization aspects were measured retrospectively: communication with parents about the environmental impact of travel mode choice at age 15, the symbolic-affective importance of driving and acquisition of a driver's licence at age 18, and multi-mobility in the peer group at age 18. Analyses revealed a significant impact of all three socialization constructs on either norms or car-use habit or both. Again, a mediator effect for habit and norms could be confirmed.

Collectively, the results of empirical travel socialization research propose that later mode choices are influenced by socialization agents and socialization environment. Based on retrospective studies, we can state that a central mediating variable is habit, but also norms are influenced by socialization (e.g., past interactions with parents, media, and peers) and are relevant for actual mode preferences (Haustein et al., 2009). In contrast to norms and preferences that are conscious entities and therefore can be reflected by individuals, habit is functioning without reflection and may therefore form a strong (unreflected) barrier to behaviour change. This makes habit a central construct in the context of car-fixation: the unreflected preference of car as travel mode. As we will present in the next section, women seem to be less fixated, which can be explained by different socialization experiences. There are also indications that people socialized in urban regions are less fixated.

Gender Differences in Travel-mode Choice and Travel-mode Socialization

Given the fact that women show different mobility behaviour than men, we now wish to reflect if the socialization processes reported above could explain gendered differences in car-fixation and mode choice. Although differences seem in part to decrease, we know that women still use public transport more often than men and reversely use cars less frequently, at least this can be said for Germany, where some of the studies on car-fixation were carried out and also still holds for the USA (Lenz et al., 2010; Crane, 2007). In 2008 in Germany, women used the car for 37 per cent of their trips, whereas men used it for 49 per cent (Lenz et al., 2010). The finding that women use public transport more frequently than men is particularly remarkable considering that those trips typically undertaken by women (i.e., shopping, accompanying children) are less convenient to manage by public transport than by car. Also recent data from the Netherlands (Olde Kalter et al., 2009) shows that, although women's travel patterns have undergone a strong shift towards individual mobility, women still spend significantly less travel time in a car compared to men and more travel time in public transport.

In an empirical study Matthies, Kuhn, and Klöckner (2002) investigated possible reasons for the differing mode choice patterns of men and women. By means of a survey among 187 inhabitants of a German city, they tested the hypothesis that women's different travel behaviour could be explained by stronger ecological norms and weaker car-use habit. In the initial step, they showed that women are more willing to reduce car use, use cars less often, and have a stronger preference for public transport. Results of multiple regression analyses confirmed the mediating relevance of norms and habit. The intention to reduce car use seemed to be mainly influenced by the ecological norm, whereas actual travel behaviour was more strongly influenced by habit. Habit was measured by response frequency measure, i.e., as salience of behavioural scripts. The weaker salience of car choices for women may in part reflect different mode choice experiences, which may stem from a restricted car access but also from different mode socialization, such as from differences in support for autonomous travel behaviour in childhood (Johansson, 2006). We also assume that gender stereotypes transferred by media and peers may play a role here. As Flade and Limbourg

(1997) have shown, boys already seem to have a stronger car orientation than girls at the age of 10–16, meaning that more boys than girls imagine themselves using cars when they are adults. We also can discern from a German study on the mobility orientation of adolescents and young adults (Hunecke et al., 2002) that male adolescents may be more car- and technique-focused than young women. In accordance with assumptions about the dual mechanism of intentional and habitual initiation of travel behaviour (Verplanken et al., 1994) in the reported study (Matthies et al., 2002), the intention to reduce car use was not determined by habit, and gender differences, for intentions could be explained by different ecological norms. Once more this can be explained by socialization, in this case by differences in environmental education of boys and girls. Furthermore, we acknowledge from a series of empirical studies that women feel more responsible for the environment and have a greater willingness to adopt an ecological lifestyle (see Torgler et al., 2008 for a study on ecological preferences of men and women in different European countries). Whenever gender differences were found in ecologically relevant everyday behaviours, women reported taking more pro-environmental action than men (Schahn and Holzer, 1990; Torgler et al., 2008).

Socialization in Urban or Rural Environment as Relevant Factor

We have ascertained that environmental conditions may be relevant for travel socialization. For children in a rural environment, we can assume that the higher prevalence of a family car in rural areas might contribute to a more car-oriented early travel-mode socialization. Additionally we would predicate that because of the better traffic situation more individual mobility is possible and children are encouraged to travel independently; for example, by bike. For later childhood and adolescence, it can be assumed that because of the negative experiences with public transport (e.g., less frequent buses or even no possibility to get to some places without a motorized vehicle), attitudes are much more in favour of car use than for public transport. Schulz (2002) reports for a sample of German adolescents that urban adolescents in fact relay more positive experiences with public transport, while in contrast adolescents from rural areas account negative experiences. Accordingly, a car-oriented mobility type is more frequent with adolescents and young adults in rural areas than in the city.

4.   STRATEGIES TO OVERCOME FIXATION

We have learned that there are different theoretical explanations for car-fixation, and these approaches might help to develop ideas for overcoming habitualized car use. Based on the assumption that habits are stabilized because the behaviour is carried out in the same situational context repeatedly (e.g., someone takes the car for the trip to work every work day, and the situation when the behaviour is initiated and carried out is the same each morning), it can be assumed that changes of the situation could lead to elaborate decision-making (e.g., Verplanken and Wood, 2006; Wood et al., 2005) and therefore mediate changes in habitual behaviour. Several intervention studies support this assumption and report lasting effects of a temporary situational change, such as temporary free tickets, significant changes of the infrastructure (road closure), or strong changes of living conditions.

Fujii and Kitamura (2003) carried out an experiment and provided 23 drivers with a one-month free bus ticket. A control group did not get the ticket. Attitudes towards car use and bus use, and frequency of using car versus bus were measured immediately before, immediately after, and one month after the intervention. The results showed that not only attitudes toward public transport were more positive after the intervention, but that the frequency of bus use increased, even one month after the intervention period. Matthies, Klöckner, and Preißner (2006) further initiated a try-out of a new travel-mode behaviour (try-out taking public transport instead of car) in a sample of 297 habitual car users. In randomly chosen experimental groups they combined a temporary gift of a free ticket (a two-week free ticket) with a plea for commitment. Participants had to report their travel mode choice for a particular, regular trip (mostly trip to work) for a period of eight weeks and a two-week follow-up period. Despite small overall effects of the interventions, it could be concluded that the free ticket initiated try-out behaviour of habitual car users and that it had long-term effects in combination with a commitment intervention.

The research group around Fujii and Gärling (Fujii et al., 2001; Fujii and Gärling, 2003) also demonstrated that a temporary disruptions of habitual behaviour, for example, by a road closure, showed lasting effects on behaviour. Similarly, after strong situational changes such as moving home, travel-mode choice behaviour seems to be more in line with attitudes towards travel modes (Verplanken et al., 1998), and interventions have been shown to be more effective (Rölle et al., 2002).

The conclusion that temporary strong changes help to break up habitual car-use behaviour or car-fixation could be explained in two ways. It could be the result of the new situational cues being so different from the old, learned cues, that the habitual behaviour is no longer triggered (connectionist approach). But also, being confronted with a strong change of the situation (e.g., by closure of a main road) might in itself temporarily increase the attention to situational factors. In this second point of view (script-based approach), even events that are not directly related to travel-mode choice situations (e.g., first parenthood) might open a 'window of change' during which habits are less effective, destabilized, and behaviour may be changed more readily.

5.   CONCLUSION

According to the reported literature and empirical findings on travel-mode socialization, it can be assumed that car-fixation may in part stem from a car-focused socialization taking place in childhood and adolescence. It can be assumed to be, on the one hand, a side-effect of unintentional parental behaviour (e.g., car ownership and mode use), and, on the other, a result of various environmental factors (e.g., traffic environment, distances, public transport infrastructure) and related travel experiences in late childhood and adolescence. Socialization theory also considers media and peer influences (Baslington, 2008). This already implies some current ideas for measures to prevent the next generation from becoming car-fixated, like training children in autonomous public transport use (e.g., install school buses or school-related travel smart programmes).

Although empirical evidence of relevance of media is not univocal, the authors suggest also to consider media campaigns that make public transport use more attractive for adolescents (e.g., the Danish 'bussen er cool' campaign).

But what about the many already 'locked in' drivers? Given the psychological background of habitualization, we cannot assume that offering equal alternatives of travel is enough to initiate new and more sustainable travel behaviour. The psychological assumptions behind car-fixation – the concept of habit – allows us to develop measures to overcome car-fixation – for example, by strong temporary changes of the situation. Additionally it can be assumed here that women are a more promising target group for travel management measures then men, because of their on-average weaker habits.

The presented theories and research results have shown that it is crucial to account for behavioural lock-ins in choice patterns created by the history of choices made before and the socialization an individual was exposed to when planning measures to change travel behaviour. A majority of people's travel-mode choices are made in everyday situations with rather stable situational or motivational conditions, which means they are relatively more automatic than deliberate. This means that any strategy that ignores the strong effects of mode fixations on information processing and the impact of intentions and norms will have a high likelihood of failure. Therefore a powerful intervention strategy, in cases where strong habits are likely to prevent change, is to either make use of windows of opportunities that open when habits are naturally weakened such as strong changes in people's lives (e.g., moving home, changing job, or becoming parents) or to disrupt the activating cues for the habits (Verplanken and Wood, 2006).

REFERENCES

Aarts, H., Verplanken, B. and van Knippenberg, A. (1997), Habit and information use in travel mode choices, *Acta Psychologica*, **96**, 1–14.

Anable, J. (2005), 'Complacent car addicts' or 'aspiring environmentalists'? Identifying travel behaviour segments using attitude theory, *Transport Policy*, **12**(1), 65–78.

Ajzen, I. (2012), The theory of planned behavior, in P.A.M. Lange, A.W. Kruglanski, and E.T. Higgins (eds), *Handbook of Theories of Social Psychology*, Vol. 1, London: Sage, pp. 438–59.

Baslington, H. (2008), Travel socialization: a social theory of travel mode behavior, *International Journal of Sustainable Transportation*, **2**, 91–114.

Cahill, M., Ruben, T. and Winn, S. (1996), *Children and Transport: Travel Patterns, Attitudes and Leisure Activities of Children in the Brighton Area*, Health and Social Policy Research Centre, Report 96/4, Faculty of Health, Department of Community Studies, University of Brighton.

Crane, R. (2007), Is there a quiet revolution in women's travel? Revisiting the gender gap in commuting, *Journal of the American Planning Association*, **73**, 298–316.

Engelbert, A. (1986), *Kinderalltag und Familienumwelt. Eine Studie über die Lebenssituation von Vorschulkindern [Children's Everyday Life and Familiar Environment: A Study on the Living Situation of Preschool Children]*, Frankfurt and New York: Campus-Verlag.

Eriksson, L. and Forward, S.E. (2011), Is the intention to travel in a pro-environmental manner and the intention to use the car determined by different factors? *Transportation Research Part D*, **16**, 372–6.

Flade, A. and Limbourg, M. (1997), *Das Hineinwachsen in die Gesellschaft [The Growing into Society]*, Darmstadt: Institut Wohnen und Umwelt.

Flade, A., Hacke, U. and Lohmann, G. (2001), Die Bedeutung des Fahrrads für Jugendliche und deren Zukunftsvorstellungen zur Fahrradnutzung [The importance of a bycicle for adolescents and their imagined future bycicle use], in A. Flade and S. Bamberg (eds), *Ansätze zur Erklärung und Beeinflussung des Mobilitätsverhaltens [Approaches to Explain and Change Mobility Behaviour]*, Darmstadt: Institut für Wohnen und Umwelt.

Fujii, S. and Gärling, T. (2003), Development of script-based travel mode choice after forced change, *Transportation Research F: Traffic Psychology and Behaviour*, **6**, 117–24.

Fujii, S. and Gärling, T. (2007), Role and acquisition of car-use habit, in T. Gärling and L. Steg (eds), *Threats to the Quality of Urban Life from Car Traffic: Problems, Causes, and Solutions*, London: Elsevier, pp. 235–50.

Fujii, S. and Kitamura, R. (2003), What does a one-month free bus ticket do to habitual drivers? *Transportation*, **30**, 81–95.

Fujii, S., Gärling, T. and Kitamura, R. (2001), Changes in drivers' perceptions and use of public transport during a freeway closure: effects of temporary structural change on cooperation in a real-life social dilemma, *Environment and Behavior*, **33**, 796–808.

Gärling, T. and Steg, L. (2007), *Threats from Car Traffic to the Quality of Urban Life: Problems, Causes, and Solutions*, Oxford: Elsevier.

Haustein, S., Klöckner, C. and Blöbaum, A. (2009), Car use of young adults: the role of travel socialization, *Transportation Research Part F: Traffic Psychology and Behaviour*, **12**, 168–78.

Hunecke, M., Blöbaum, A., Matthies, E. and Höger, R. (2001), Responsibility and environment: ecological norm orientation and external factors in the domain of travel mode choice, *Environment and Behavior*, **33**, 830–52.

Hunecke, M., Tully, C.J. and Bäumer, D. (2002), *Mobilität von Jugendlichen. Psychologische, soziologische und umweltbezogene Ergebnisse und Gestaltungsempfehlungen [Mobility of Adolescents. Psychological, Sociological and Environmental Results and Recommendations]*, Opladen: Leske + Budrich.

Johansson, M. (2006), Environment and parental factors as determinants of mode for children's leisure travel, *Journal of Environmental Psychology*, **26**, 156–69.

Klöckner, C.A. and Matthies, E. (2004), How habits interfere with norm-directed behaviour: a normative decision-making model for travel mode choice, *Journal of Environmental Psychology*, **24**, 319–27.

Klöckner, C.A. and Verplanken, B. (2012), Yesterday's habits preventing change for tomorrow? The influence of automaticity on environmental behaviour, in L. Steg, A.E. van den Berg and J.I.M. de Groot (eds), *Environmental Psychology: An Introduction*, Oxford: Wiley & Sons, pp. 197–209.

Lenz, B., Nobis, C., Köhler, K., Mehlin, M., Follmer, R., Gruschwitz, D., Jesske, B. and Quandt, S. (2010), *Mobilität in Deutschland 2008 [Mobility in Germany 2008]*, Research Report, Institut für angewandte Sozialwissenschaften (INFAS) and Deutsches Zentrum für Luft- und Raumfahrt, Bonn, Cologne, www.mobilitaet-in-deutschland.de/pdf/MiD2008_Abschlussbericht_I.pdf.

Limbourg, M., Flade, A. and Schönhartig, J. (2000), *Mobilität im Kindes- und Jugendalter [Mobility in Childhood and Adolescence]*, Opladen: Leske & Budrich.

Maccoby, E.E. (2006), Historical overview of socialization research and theory, in J.E. Grusec and P.D. Hastings (eds), *Handbook of Socialization: Theory and Research*, New York: Guilford, pp. 13–41.

Matthies, E., Kuhn, S. and Klöckner, C. (2002), Travel mode choice of women: the result of limitation, ecological norm, or weak habit? *Environment and Behavior*, **34**, 163–77.

Matthies, E., Klöckner, C.A. and Preißner, C.L. (2006), Applying a modified moral decision making model to change habitual car use: how can commitment be effective? *Applied Psychology*, **55**, 91–106.

McDonald, N. (2008), Children's mode choice for the school trip: the role of distance and school location in walking to school, *Transportation*, **35**, 23–35.

Meaton, J. and Kingham, S. (1998), Children's perceptions of transport modes: car culture in the classroom? *World Transport Policy & Practice*, **4**(2), 12–16.

Neal, D.T., Wood, W. and Quinn, J.M. (2006), Habits: a repeat performance, *Current Directions in Psychological Science*, **15**, 198–202.

Olde Kalter, M.-J., Harms, L. and Jorritsma, P. (2009), Changing travel patterns of women in the Netherlands, in Transportation Research Board of the National Acadamies (ed.), *Women's Issues in Transportation: Summary of the 4th International Conference, Vol. 2: Technical Papers*, Washington, DC: Transportation Research Board, pp. 191–202.

Rölle, D., Weber, C. and Bamberg, S. (2002), Vom Auto zum Autobus: Der Umzug als Einstieg zum Umstieg [From car to bus: moving home as an entry to switching], *Gaia*, **11**, 134–8.

Sandqvist, K. (2002), How does a family car matter? Leisure, travel and attitudes of adolescents in inner city Stockholm, *World Transport Policy & Practice*, **8**(1): 11–18.

Schahn, J. and Holzer, E. (1990), Studies of individual environmental concern: the role of knowledge, gender, and background variables, *Environment and Behavior*, **22**, 767–86.

Schönhammer, R. (1999), Auto, Geschlecht und Sex [Car, gender and sex], in C.J. Tully (ed.), *Erziehung zur Mobilität. Jugendliche in der automobilen Gesellschaft*. Frankfurt am Main: Campus, pp. 141–56.

Schulz, U. (2002), Betrachtung der ermittelten Mobilitätsstiltypen in Hinblick auf Stadt und Land [Consideration of the identified mobility types with regard to city and country], in M. Hunecke, C.J. Tully and D. Bäumer (eds), *Mobilität von Jugendlichen. Psychologische, soziologische und umweltbezogene Ergebnisse und Gestaltungsempfehlungen [Mobility of Adolescents. Psychological, Sociological and Environmental Results and Recommendations]* Opladen: Leske und Budrich, pp. 103–10.

Schwartz, S.H. and Howard, J.A. (1981), A normative decision-making model of altruism, in J.P. Rushton and R.M. Sorrentino (eds), *Altruism and Helping Behavior*, Hillsdale, NJ: Lawerence Erlbaum, pp. 89–211.

Torgler, B., García-Valiñas, M.A. and Macintyre, A. (2008), Differences in Preferences Towards the Environment: The Impact of a Gender, Age and Parental Effect, FEEM working paper no. 18, http://hdl. handle.net/10419/40684.

Verplanken, B. and Aarts, H. (1999), Habit, attitude, and planned behaviour: is habit an empty construct or an interesting case of goal directed automaticity? *European Review of Social Psychology*, **10**, 101–34.

Verplanken, B. and Wood, W. (2006), Interventions to break and create consumer habits, *Journal of Public Policy and Marketing*, **25**, 90–103.

Verplanken, B., Aarts, H. and van Knippenberg, A. (1994), Attitude versus general habit: antecedents of travel mode choice, *Journal of Applied Social Psychology*, **24**(4), 285–300.

Verplanken, B., Aarts, H. and van Knippenberg, A. (1997), Habit, information acquisition, and the process of making travel mode choices, *European Journal of Social Psychology*, **27**, 539–60.

Verplanken, B., Aarts, H., van Knippenberg, A. and Moonen, A. (1998), Habit versus planned behaviour: a field experiment, *British Journal of Social Psychology*, **37**, 111–28.

Wood, W., Quinn, J.M. and Neal, D. (2005), The power of repetition in everyday life: Habits and intentions guide action, manuscript submitted for publication.

33 Telecommunications and travel
Galit Cohen-Blankshtain

1. INTRODUCTION

The relationships between transport and information and telecommunications technologies (ICTs) have received much attention over the past four decades. As both technologies facilitate remote activities, there has been much interest in the potential substitution of tele-activities for physical travel.

However, alongside the substitution effects between transportation and ICTs, there is considerable evidence suggesting stimulation or generation effects as well. In other words, ICTs can stimulate more physical travel. Moreover, ICTs can change travel behaviour, not just the decision about the travel itself. ICTs are not considered just as possible substitutions for physical transport. They can offer tools to increase the quality of transportation networks and services. This, in turn, may have an additional, indirect effect on travel behaviour.

Bearing in mind these relationships (substitution, generation and modification) the expected effects of ICTs in the transportation system become complex and multifaceted. In addition, the rapid and continuous technological developments have challenged scientific efforts to test such relationships as research has difficulties keeping up with the developments.

The next section examines the potential for a substitution effect, followed by a review of other possible effects of ICTs on human activities in general and travel behaviour in particular.

2. ICTS AND PHYSICAL ACTIVITIES

For more than 40 years researchers and intellectuals have been hypothesizing about and trying to predict the effects of ICTs on the city and human spatial behaviour. Generally speaking, technological developments are strongly associated with human progress. Technological developments have had, and continue to have, a major impact on the way our society has evolved and they are likely to continue playing this critical role.

ICTs are a family of technologies and services used to process, store and disseminate information, facilitating the performance of information-related human activities, provided by and serving both the public at large as well as the institutional and business sectors. Since ICTs have a major impact on human life, ideas about the role of the city, its features or even the question of whether it will continue to exist have appeared in many visionary books and papers. These relationships have provided us with many metaphors that try to capture the futuristic and far-reaching consequences of ICTs on the city, the society at large and its spatial patterns. Clearly, speculations about the future and the role of the new technologies are not value free. As Geels and Smit (2000: 877) stress:

"Expectations may be biased by the broader cultural concerns of the time. People's perception of the future is often coloured by their cultural lens. Consequently, future expectations often reflect broad cultural concerns and hopes. This, to some extent, may also explain why certain future images gain widespread popularity." Thus, forecasts and speculations about the impact of ICTs in many ways reflect wishes, fears and interests.

ICTs have been identified (perhaps prematurely) as the cause of the 'death of distance' (*The Economist*, 1995). The logic behind it is the belief that if the costs of distance are nullified, the whole notion of urban entities and the need for physical movements are likely to change.

Much of the potential of ICTs to change human spatial behaviour and, as a consequence, to affect the urban form stem from the assumption that ICTs will replace the traditional transport system. Glaeser (1998) maintains that "a city is just a dense agglomeration of people and firms". Ultimately, the benefits of cities come from reduced transport costs for people, goods and ideas. Historically, the transport system has dramatically affected urban development. It has enabled city and metropolitan growth while sustaining agglomeration benefits by intensive mobility opportunities. The city has retained its agglomeration benefits although it has expanded, since the transport system has enabled proximity to the city. Thus, technologies that make distance obsolete also make the city irrelevant. The key assumption underlying such expectation is that ICT networks will replace the transport network.

The relationships between transport and telecommunications have received much attention (e.g., Hepworth and Ducatel, 1992; Mokhtarian, 1991; Nilles, 1988; Salomon, 1986; Mokhtarian and Salomon, 1997; Andreev et al., 2010; Zhu, 2012). There are several obvious reasons for this. Both technologies belong to a class of "friction reducing technologies" or "spatial technologies" (Couclelis, 1994) and have a network structure. These similarities are also evident in the similar terms that are used for both technologies such as highways and information highways, ports, traffic, navigation and congestion.

As both technologies facilitate remote activities, there is much interest in the potential substitution of tele-activities for physical travel in general (Boghani et al., 1991; Garrison and Deakin, 1988), and specifically substituting commuting travel with telecommuting (Mokhtarian, 1991; Nilles, 1988; Salomon, 1986; Mokhtarian and Salomon, 1997), shopping travel with teleshopping (Rotem-Mindali and Salomon, 2009; Salomon and Koppelman, 1992) and leisure travel with many other tele-activities and e-entertainment (Mokhtarian et al., 2006). These similarities have led scholars to measure accessibility not just with respect to mobility (physical transport) but to combine mobility options and the spatial structure, along with accessibility via ICTs modes (Shen, 1998). Thus they point out the need to integrate and incorporate transport planning and ICT policy in urban policy to enhance accessibility (Horan and Jordan, 1998; Couclelis, 2000).

The expectations that the new technologies (ICTs) would gradually replace the old technologies (transportation) led to the hypothesis that ICT networks would play the same role in the twenty-first century that streets and highways played in the twentieth century (Grant and Berqiust, 2000). Just as the car has affected the shape of urban areas, there is an expectation that ICT will change cities. The "information highway" is expected by some scholars to inherit the role of the physical highways and substitutes physical movements with electronic movements. If transport was the "maker and breaker of cities" (Clark, 1957), there were predictions that ICTs will further lift space-time constraints and decrease the importance of proximity (Negroponte, 1995).

Transport and ICT, as noted above, display many similarities. One major difference, however, is the fact that, given the time gap in their respective introductions, they are being implemented into very dissimilar backgrounds. The century of motorized transport has had a prominent role in reshaping the horse-drawn city into the metropolis of the present. ICT, on the other hand, is introduced into an entrenched automobile-dependent city. Moreover, the substitution of the horse by the automobile presents a clear case of technological substitution as they offered the same type of service. However, ICTs are far from being a perfect substitute for the car. ICTs do not substitute co-presence (Urry, 2002) and consequently its effects on cities cannot be expected to mirror the change brought about by the automobile.

Early forecasts regarding the potential of ICTs to substitute travel reflect the hopes for alternatives to the troubled transport system. Commuting trips have attracted much focus as peak-hour congestions are the main catalysts for transport investments. Therefore, telecommuting as a replacement for commuting trips was first suggested in the 1960s (NAE, 1969). In many policy and popular arenas, telecommuting was expected to provide significant transportation benefits during the 1980s and early 1990s (Handy and Mokhtarian, 1995). A 1978 study on the impact of telecommunication on transportation demand through the year 2000 estimated that telecommuting could reduce more than 10 per cent of the total urban VMT when fully implemented. A 1991 study calculated the nationwide benefits of an expected 10–20 per cent substitution of travel by telecommunications, mostly by telecommuting (Boghani et al., 1991). A 1993 study estimated that telecommuting could reduce total VMT by about 5 per cent and could save about 826 million to 1.7 billion hours in travelling by 2002. Estimations of the actual impact of telecommuting by the year 2000 suggest an aggregate impact of less than 1 per cent VMT reduction (Choo et al., 2005), and studies on the potential of telecommuting reveal a similar estimation (Mokhtarian, 1998). As Tal and Cohen-Blankshtain (2011) suggest, the overly optimistic forecasts mainly reflect the policy core-beliefs of the forecast-makers and their hopes that the potential substitution of physical travel by telecommuting will materialize. Sceptical and more critical forecasters portray a smaller potential and even smaller realization of the potential substitution (Salomon and Mokhtarian, 1997).

Although the information revolution refers mainly to the past 30 years, the expectation for substitution between travel and remote activities is much older. The telegraph and later the telephone technologies raised similar expectations. A hundred years after the telephone was invented, it was already clear that telephone use and travel had both increased dramatically, expanding contact opportunities and not substituting one for the other (Pierce, 1977; Gasper and Glaeser, 1998). It was hypothesized that the utility of telephone usage would grow with distance, as it would substitute longer physical trips. However, telephone use in urban areas is much higher than in rural areas and there are more short-distance calls than long-distance calls, rejecting the hypothesis that the tendency to use the telephone is positively correlated with distance between the parties (Sharlot and Duranton, 2006).

In contrast to the telephone, a technology that did not experience dramatic technological changes during more than a century (although there was considerable price reduction), the new ICTs are changing rapidly. Both hardware and software are rapidly developing, offering new ways to communicate and different modes of availability. It is almost impossible to generalize about the relationships between ICTs and transport from a behavioural perspective, given the large number of technologies that are included in the groups of ICTs, on the one hand, and the different human activities, on the other. Thus, much of the empirical investigation focuses on a certain technology (e.g., mobile phone, Internet) or certain activities (e.g., commuting, leisure, shopping). Empirical investigations have found that technologies have different effects on travel behaviour. For example, while mobile phones tend to complement face-to-face activities, the Internet substitutes some physical activities (Lee-Gosselin and Miranda-Moreno, 2009). However, in the past few years, the different technologies (mobile phones and Internet) have merged into smartphones, tablets and notebooks, enabling mobile Internet activities. In the year 2014, more than 78 per cent of the households in the developed world had access to internet at home, enabling various tele-activities (ITU, 2014: chart 1.10). Such technologies enable real-time, location-free coordination of face-to-face meetings and work-related projects; thus, it may diminish the role of geographical fixed nodes for planning joint activities during the day (Ling, 2004; Schwanen et al., 2008; Vilhelmson and Thulin, 2008). Mobile ICTs have facilitated the relationship with space by making it possible to rearrange activity schedules more often, and may shift behaviour towards "real-time" operation with greater flexibility in both private and professional spheres (Line et al., 2011).

The fast technological development and the rapid adoption of such technologies challenge researchers as empirical findings regarding certain technologies may no longer be relevant to the newer technologies. As behavioural research usually involves time-consuming and dedicated data collection, research findings frequently lag behind technological development and the new ways they affect human behaviour.

Bearing in mind the challenging efforts to study such a dynamic phenomenon, even studies that focus on a certain technology and a certain activity type observe complex relationships between physical activities and tele-activities according to the activity and the mode. There is evidence that telecommuters and their household members travel less (Hamer et al., 1991; Pendyala et al., 1991; Balepur et al., 1998; de Graaff, 2004) although the overall impact is less significant due to latent demand (Mokhtarian and Salomon, 2002). telecommuting may reduce the total number of trips but increase travel distance as part-time telecommuters may choose to live farther from their workplaces (Banister and Stead, 2004).Testing the effects of ICTs in commuting trips in 2001 and 2009, Zhu (2012) found that telecommuters tend to have longer one-way commute distances and durations than non-telecommuters, and the size of the effect of telecommuting was three times as large in 2009 as in 2001. This may explain the modest reduction of travelled kilometres. Stimulation effects were found also by Aguiléra (2008) as ICTs creates distant business networks.

At the aggregate level, research has found a slight decrease in total vehicle miles traveled due to telecommuting activities (Choo et al., 2005; Collantes and Mokhtarian, 2003). Teleshopping also offers a potential substitution to shopping travel but, although teleshopping activities are growing, its substitution potential is smaller compared with telecommuting. It is claimed that ICTs leads to fragmentation of the shopping process.

As a result, the combined outcome may be negative (i.e., more travel may be generated for shopping purposes; Mokhtarian, 2004).

Maintenance[1] and recreation activities are also been partly transformed into tele-activities. It was found that virtual accessibilities reduce time allocation for maintenance and recreation activities in the physical space (Donggen and Jiukun, 2011). The effect of ICTs on leisure and maintenance is mediated by gender. Women tend to conduct more maintenance activities and therefore ICTs tend to substitute some of the physical maintenance activities. No substitution effect has been found in leisure activities. On the other hand, men tend to engage in more leisure activities and there is evidence for substitution effects between physical leisure activities and virtual ones among men (Ren and Kwan, 2009).

Although analytically justified, research that focuses on just one type of activity may be misleading. As Salomon (1986) stresses: "The analysis of total human activity may lead to different conclusions from the analyses of single trip purpose." In other words, tele-activity may substitute certain physical activities but induce different activities. Such influence raises the need for holistic research regarding all human activities. These efforts have revealed stimulation effects, namely, that the use of ICTs directly induces individuals to make more trips (Srinivasan and Athuru, 2004; Wang and Law, 2007; Kenyon, 2010).

While behavioural responses to a large number of ICTs and activities can hardly be generalized due to their complex and multidirectional effects, general trends regarding the use of transport and ICTs are observed. Data regarding ICTs and transportation availability and usage suggests mutual growth of both technologies, thus supporting the stimulation hypothesis. Data shows steady growth of household Internet accessibility worldwide. In the year 2011, more than 70 per cent of the households in the developed world had access to internet, enabling various tele-activities (ITU, 2011). However, along with internet accessibility growth, there is continuous increase of car ownership (Eurostat, 2014), enabling physical movement as well.

Internet usage is rapidly increasing in addition to continuous growth of passenger kilometres that was evidenced until 2010 (BTS, 2011: Table 3–10). In 2010, for the first time, decrease in passenger kilometres was recorded. It is still not clear whether the decrease is a new trend (as was suggested by *The Economist* in 2012) or merely a reflection of the current economic recession. In both cases, we may be witnessing substitution effects.

These trends support the claim that ICTs enable an increase in human activity by offering new modes of activities. Tele-activities may substitute some of the physical activities but more than that, ICTs allow people to do more. Substitution assumes that the total number of activities will remain constant. Evidently, such an assumption should be challenged as both physical movements and tele-activities show steady growth.

3.   OTHER EFFECTS OF ICTS ON PHYSICAL TRAVEL

Although research in the past two decades focused on substitution-complementarity relationships (Aguiléra et al., 2012). A third potential effect, modification, has received less attention. Whereas substitution and complementarity have a direct effect on travel demand, modification affects travel patterns by changing destination, mode and/or route of travel, or by reducing the cost of travel. ICTs have the potential to affect the driver's utility from the trip by increasing the ability to multitask. Daily travel is conventionally treated as a disutility to be minimized – an action undertaken solely to permit the engagement in the spatially separated activities which are presumptively the real targets of interest for the traveller. While Bhat and Koppelman (1999) consider time as a constraint and an equalizer among people (we all have just 24 hours per day), Kenyon and Lyons (2007: 162) stress that:

> through the double counting of time through multitasking, this paper suggests that individuals are, in fact, able to "use" more than 24 hours in a day. Following from this, it is suggested that it is possible to increase the number of task-minutes in our days, effectively "creating" more time, through multitasking. Thus, multitasking can enable individuals to reconfigure their spatio-temporal pattern of activity participation in such a way that participation is more efficient (thereby releasing more time for additional (discretionary) activities), is of higher quality or is more fulfilling.

Since ICTs enable simultaneous tele-activities and physical movements and increase potential multitasking (Lyons and Urry, 2005), they have the potential to increase the total number of personal activities. Thus, instead of substitution between activities, we may witness stimulation effect. ICTs may free time for more travelling (e.g., telecommuters that saved the commuting trips and are willing to make trips for other purposes). They may enable activities while travelling (Lyons and Urry, 2005; Lyons et al., 2007) and may change the experience of travelling by incorporating it into our everyday tasks. Thus, ICTs can reduce travel costs.

There are conflicting arguments regarding the travel time budget and whether is it constant through the years (Metz, 2002) or increasing over time (van Wee et al., 2006). ICTs may have conflicting effects on travel time. On the one hand, ICTs may substitute travel and reduce travel time. On the other hand, ICTs may convert wasted travel time into productive time and therefore reduce travel costs and increase travel time (Kenyon and Lyons, 2007). Another modification potential concerns temporal and spatial decisions. Hamer et al. (1991) have found that teleworkers reduce 26 per cent of their peak-hour traffic by car, a much higher influence than on the reduction of total number of trips made by telecommuters (17 per cent). This shows that telecommuting has greater potential to change the time of the trip rather than eliminating the trip itself. ICTs enable more temporal flexibility (Schwanen and Kwan, 2008), meaning that, instead of substituting activities, ICTs allow people to maintain personal activities in a more relaxed space-time framework. In addition, ICTs can reduce the cost of being late, as they provide the opportunity for adjustments due to unexpected events (e.g., unexpected congestion, unexpected changes during a day, unreliable public transport service). Thus, the cost of travelling may be reduced even more, as ICTs allows to plan less "safety time belts" in order to avoid being late.

Temporal flexibility goes hand-in-hand with spatial flexibility that enables remote activities from various places. Such flexibility allows for avoiding peak-hour traffic as well as congested routes. ICTs influence not only travel behaviour but also the transport system itself. They offer tools to increase the quality of transportation networks and services. ICTs are at the heart of the development of an Intelligent Transportation System (ITS) that supports the physical transport system and enables a more efficient use of the system (Nijkamp et al., 1996; Giannopoulos and Gillespie, 1993). ITS can be divided into two categories: intelligent infrastructure systems and intelligent vehicle systems (Anagnostopoulos et al., 2006). Both have the potential to affect urban mobility directly by enhancing the transport system capacity and indirectly by affecting travel behaviour.

From an operational perspective, smart systems are developed for parking management, toll roads, public transport operation and road management. From the perspective of the users, ITS gradually incorporated in personal ICT devices enables travellers to adapt to road condition, avoid congested routes and use public transport more efficiently. The potential of ITS to increase the transport system capacity has been investigated in the past few years. For example, evaluation of ridership effects of the Chicago Transit Authority real-time bus information system in Chicago reveals that the provision of bus-tracker service does increase bus ridership, although the average increase is modest (Tang and Thakuriah, 2012). In San Francisco, evaluation of real-time parking and transit information on the Bay Area Rapid Transit (BART) indicates that only around one-third of respondents were aware of this information, and less than one-third of these people used it to make a decision whether to drive or take public transportation (Rodier and Shaheen, 2010).

ITS plays a major role in freight movements and logistic management. Developments in the field of freight resource management, freight and vehicle tracking and tracing, and front- or back-office logistic systems have dramatically improved freight movement and supply (Giannopoulos, 2004).

Taniguchi and Shimamoto (2004) identify numerous types of city logistics schemes that have either already been implemented or are proposed: advanced information systems, cooperative freight transport arrangements, public logistics terminals, load factor controls and underground freight transport organization. All schemes are supported by advanced information systems.

4.   CONCLUDING REMARKS

Can we expect decline in travelled kilometres as a result of growing ICT usage? Most of the research reviewed here suggests limiting such expectations. Empirical evidence suggests that although substitution between tele-activities and physical activity exists, both activity types continue to grow. When examining certain activities, substitution may be found, depending on type of activity, gender of the actor and other personal characteristics. However, as tele-activity releases free time for additional activities, more activities are done and the potential for additional travel increases. As a result, although we may witness a decline in some physical activities that are replaced by tele-activities (e.g., regular banking tasks, library visits), we may see an increase in other physical activities that cannot be replaced by tele-activities or that people are not willing to replace.

Although the substitution–complementarity debate was central in the ICTs–transport debate for many years, modification relationships have been overlooked. ICTs change the way we consume transport and the way we perceive travel costs and waiting time (Lyons and Urry, 2005; Watts and Urry, 2008; Edison Watkins et al., 2011). Thus, travel patterns may change, but a significant decline in total travel is unlikely. ICTs affect the time and location of our activities and, as a consequence, they affect spatial and temporal travel patterns. Although ICTs do not offer substitution to the transport system, they do offer potential reliefs and remedies to some of the negative aspects of the transport system. ITS development improves the transport system and increases its attractiveness (and, due to latent demand, contributes to further use of the system).

In the face of rapid technological developments, rapid adoption and creative use of these technologies, prediction (or even description) of their effect on travel behaviour is challenging. The information revolution affects and is being affected by changing economic structures and globalization processes. Isolating the effects of ICTs from these structural changes is not an easy task, as ICTs are embedded in human activities in various ways and directions. However, society changes much more slowly than technology. Old systems (like the transport system, the labour market or the education system) adapt slowly to technological changes and changing demand patterns. As a result, people find creative way to utilize *all* systems for their various needs. As ICTs increase the ability to multitask and enable more intensive household activity, we are witnessing an increasing use of both transport and ICTs modes with unexpected synergies between the two.

NOTE

1. Ren and Kwan (2009) defined maintenance activity as "pursuing household or personal physiological and biological needs".

REFERENCES

Aguiléra, A. (2008), Business travel and mobile workers, *Transportation Research Part A*, **42**(8), 1109–16.
Aguiléra, A., Guillot, C. and Rallet, A. (2012), Mobile ICTs and physical mobility: review and research agenda, *Transportation Research Part A*, **46**(4), 664–72.
Anagnostopoulos, C.N.E., Anagnostopoulos, I.E., Loumos, V. and Kayafas E. (2006), A license plate-recognition algorithm for intelligent transportation system applications, *IEEE Transactions on Intelligent Transportation Systems*, **7**(3), 377–92.
Andreev, P., Salomon, I. and Pliskin, N. (2010), Review: state of teleactivities, *Transportation Research Part C*, **18**, 3–20.
Balepur, P.N., Varma, K.V. and Mokhtarian, P.L. (1998), The transportation impacts of center-based telecommuting: interim findings from the Neighborhood Telecenters Project, *Transportation*, **25**(3), 287–306.
Banister, D. and Stead, D. (2004), The impact of information and communications technology on transport, *Transport Reviews*, **24**(5), 611–32.
Bhat, C.R. and Koppelman, F.S. (1999), A retrospective and prospective survey of time-use research, *Transportation*, **26**(2), 119–39.
Boghani, A., Kimble, E.W. and Spencer, E.E. (1991), *Can Telecommunications Help Solve America's Transportation Problem?* Cambridge, MA: Arthur D. Little, Inc.
BTS (2011), *National Transportation Statistics*, www.rita.dot.gov/bts/sites/rita.dot.gov.bts/files/publications/national_transportation_statistics/2011/html/table_03_10.html.
Choo, S., Mokhtarian, P.L. and Salomon, I. (2005), Does telecommuting reduce vehicle-miles traveled? An aggregate time series analysis for the US, *Transportation*, **32**(1), 37–64.
Clark, C. (1957), Transport: maker and breaker of cities, *Town Planning Review*, **28**, 237–50.
Collantes, G.O. and Mokhtarian, P.L. (2003), *Telecommuting and Residential Location: Relationships with Commute Distance Traveled for State of California Workers*, research report UCD-ITS-RR-03-16, Institute of Transportation Studies, University of California, Davis, CA, www.its.ucdavis.edu/publications/2003/UCD-ITS-RR-03-16.pdf.
Couclelis, H. (1994), Spatial technologies, *Environment and Planning B*, **21**, 142–3.

Couclelis, H. (2000), From sustainable transportation to sustainable accessibility: can we avoid a new "tragedy of the commons"? in D. Janelle and D. Hodge (eds), *Information, Place and Cyberspace: Issues in Accessibility*, Berlin: Springer-Verlag.

de Graaff, T. (2004), *On the Substitution between Telework and Travel: A Review and Application*, research memorandum 2004-16, Free University Amsterdam.

Donggen, W. and Jiukun, L. (2011), A two-level multiple discrete-continuous model of time allocation to virtual and physical activities, *Transportmetrica*, **7**(6), 395–416.

The Economist (1995), The death of distance, *The Economist* 24 September.

Edison Watkins, K., Ferris, B., Borning, A., Rutherford, G.S. and Layton, D. (2011), Where is my bus? Impact of mobile real-time information on the perceived and actual wait time of transit riders, *Transportation Research Part A*, **45**(8), 839–48.

Eurostat (2014), http://ec.europa.eu/eurostat/tgm/table.do?tab=table&init=1&language=en&pcode=tsdpc3 40&plugin=1.

Garrison, W. and Deakin, E. (1988), Travel, work, and telecommunications: a long view of the electronic revolution and its potential impacts, *Transportation Research*, **22A**(4), 239–45.

Gaspar, J. and Glaeser, E.L. (1998), Information technology and the future of cities, *Journal of Urban Economics*, **43**, 136–56.

Geels, F.W. and Smit, W.A. (2000), Failed technology futures: pitfalls and lessons from a historical survey, *Futures*, **32**, 867–85.

Giannopoulos, G.A. (2004), The application of information and communication technology in transport, *European Journal of Operational Research*, **152**, 302–20.

Giannopoulos, G.A. and Gillespie, A. (eds) (1993), *Transport and Communications Innovation in Europe*, London: Belhaven.

Glaeser, E.L. (1998), Are cities dying? *Journal of Economic Perspective*, **12**(2), 139–60.

Grant, A.E. and Berqiust, L. (2000), Telecommunications infrastructure and the city: adapting to the convergence of technology and policy, in J.M. Weeler, Y. Ayoama and B. Warf (eds), *Cities in the Telecommunications Age*, New York: Routledge, pp. 97–111.

Hamer, R., Kroes, E. and Ooststroom, H.V. (1991), Teleworking in the Netherlands: an evaluation of changes in travel behaviour, *Transportation*, **18**(4), 365–82.

Handy, S.L. and Mokhtarian, P.L. (1995), Planning for telecommuting – measurement and policy issues, *Journal of the American Planning Association*, **61**(1), 99–111.

Hepworth, M. and Ducatel, K. (1992), *Transport in the Information Age: Wheels and Wires*, Belhaven, London.

Horan, T.A. and Jordan, D.R. (1998), Integrating transportation and telecommunications planning in Santa Monica, *Journal of Urban Technology*, **5**(2), 1–20.

ITU (2014), *Measuring the Information Society Report 2014*, www.itu.int/en/ITU-D/Statistics/Documents/publications/mis2014/MIS2014_without_Annex_4.pdf.

Kenyon, S. (2010), The impacts of Internet use upon activity participation and travel: results from a longitudinal diary-based panel study, *Transportation Research Part C*, **18**, 21–35.

Kenyon, S. and Lyons, G. (2007), Introducing multitasking to the study of travel and ICT: examining its extent and assessing its potential importance, *Transportation Research Part A*, **41**(2), 161–75.

Lee-Gosselin, M. and Miranda-Moreno, L.F. (2009), What is different about urban activities of those with access to ICTs? Some early evidence from Quebec, Canada, *Journal of Transport Geography*, **17**, 104–14.

Line, T., Jain, J. and Lyons, G. (2011), The role of ICTs in everyday mobile lives, *Journal of Transport Geography*, **19**(6), 1490–99.

Ling, R. (2004), *The Mobile Connection: The Cell Phone's Impact on Society*, San Francisco, CA: Morgan Kaufmann.

Lyons, G. and Urry, J. (2005), Travel time in the information age, *Transportation Research Part A*, **39**(2–3), 257–76.

Lyons, G., Jain, J. and Holley, D. (2007), The use of travel time by rail passengers in Great Britain, *Transportation Research Part A*, **41**(1), 107–20.

Metz, D. (2002), Limitations of transport policy, *Transport Reviews*, **22**(2), 134–8.

Mokhtarian, P.L. (1991), Telecommuting and travel: state of the practice, state of the art, *Transportation*, **18**(4), 319–42.

Mokhtarian, P.L. (1998), A synthetic approach to estimating the impacts of telecommuting on travel, *Urban Studies*, **35**(2), 215–41.

Mokhtarian, P.L. (2004), A conceptual analysis of the transportation impacts of B2C e-commerce, *Transportation*, **31**(3), 257–84.

Mokhtarian, P.L. and Salomon, I. (1997), Modeling the desire to telecommute: the importance of attitudinal factors in behavioural models, *Transportation Research A*, **31**(1), 35–50.

Mokhtarian, P.L. and Salomon, I. (2002), Emerging travel patterns: do telecommunications make a difference?

in H.S. Mahmassani (ed.), *In Perpetual Motion: Travel Behaviour Research Opportunities and Application Challenges*, Oxford: Pergamon Press/Elsevier, pp. 143–82.

Mokhtarian, P.L., Salomon, I. and Handy, S. (2006), The impacts of ICT on leisure activities and travel: a conceptual exploration, *Transportation*, **33**, 263–89.

NAE (1969), *Telecommunications for Enhanced Metropolitan Function and Form*, report to the director of Telecommunications Management, National Academy of Engineering.

Negroponte, N. (1995), *Being Digital*, London: Hodder and Stoughton.

Nijkamp, P., Pepping, G. and Banister, D. (1996), *Telematics and Transport Behaviour*, Berlin: Springer-Verlag.

Nilles, J.M. (1988), Traffic reduction by telecommuting: a status review and selected bibliography, *Transportation Review*, **22A**, 301–17.

Pendyala, R.M., Goulias, K.G. and Kitamura, R. (1991), Impact of telecommuting on spatial and temporal patterns of household travel, *Transportation*, **18**(4): 383–409.

Pierce, J.R. (1977), The telephone and society in the past 100 years, in I. de Sola Pool (ed.), *The Social Impact of the Telephone*, Cambridge, MA: MIT Press.

Ren, F. and Kwan, M. (2009), The impact of the Internet on human activity–travel patterns: analysis of gender differences using multi-group structural equation models, *Journal of Transport Geography*, **17**(6), 440–50.

Rodier, C.J. and Shaheen, S.A. (2010), Transit-based smart parking: an evaluation of the San Francisco Bay area field test, *Transportation Research Part C*, **18**(2), 225–33.

Rotem-Mindali, O. and Salomon, I. (2009), Modeling consumers' purchase and delivery choices in the face of the information age, *Environment and Planning B*, **36**, 245–61.

Salomon, I. (1986), Telecommunications and travel relationships: a review, *Transportation Research A*, **20A**(3), 223–38.

Salomon, I. and Koppelman, F.S. (1992), Teleshopping or going shopping? An information acquisition perspective, *Behaviour and Information Technology*, **11**(4), 189–98.

Salomon, I. and Mokhtarian, P.L. (1997), Coping with congestion: understanding the gap between policy assumptions and behavior, *Transportation Research Part D*, **2**(2), 107–23.

Schwanen, T. and Kwan, M. (2008), The Internet, mobile phone and space-time constraints, *Geoforum*, **39**, 1362–77.

Schwanen, T., Dijst, M. and Kwan, M.P. (2008), ICTs and the decoupling of everyday activities, space and time: introduction, *Tijdschrift voor Economische en Sociale Geografie*, **99**(5), 519–27.

Sharlot, S. and Duranton, G. (2006), Cities and workplace communication: some quantitative French evidence, *Urban Studies*, **43**(8), 1365–93.

Shen, Q. (1998), Spatial technologies, accessibility, and the social construction of urban space, *Computers, Environments and Urban Systems*, **22**(5), 447–64.

Srinivasan, K.S. and Athuru, S.R. (2004), Analysis of within-household effects and between-household differences in maintenance activity allocation, *Transportation*, **32**(5), 495–521.

Tal, G. and Cohen-Blankshtain, G. (2011), understanding the role of the forecast-maker in overestimation forecasts of policy impacts: the case of travel demand management policies, *Transportation Research A*, **45**(5), 389–400.

Tang, L. and Thakuriah, P. (2012), Ridership effects of real-time bus information system: a case study in the city of Chicago, *Transportation Research Part C*, **22**, 146–61.

Taniguchi, E. and Shimamoto, H. (2004), Intelligent transportation system based dynamic vehicle routing and scheduling with variable travel times, Transportation Research Part C, **12**(3–4), 235–50.

Urry, J. (2002), Mobility and proximity, *Sociology*, **36**(2), 255–74.

van Wee, B., Rietveld, P. and Meurs, H. (2006), Is average daily travel time expenditure constant? In search of explanations for an increase in average travel time, *Journal of Transport Geography*, **14**(2), 109–22.

Wang, D. and Law, F.Y.T. (2007), Impacts of information and communication technologies (ICT) on time use and travel behavior: a structural equations analysis, *Transportation*, **34**, 513–27.

Watts, L. and Urry, J. (2008), Moving methods, travelling times, *Environment and Planning D*, **26**, 860–74.

Vilhelmson, B. and Thulin, E. (2008), Virtual mobility, time use and the place of the home, *Tijdschrift voor Economische en Sociale Geografie*, **99**(5), 602–18.

Zhu, P. (2012), Are telecommuting and personal travel complements or substitutes? *The Annals of Regional Science*, **48**, 619–39.

34 E-retailing, the network society and travel
Orit Rotem-Mindali

1. INTRODUCTION

A major trend drawing much attention is the employment of new technologies in retailing (i.e., e-commerce, e-retail, e-shopping, etc.). E-retail represents a small, but growing part of retail activities, which may have broad implications on the organization and spatial structure of retail systems, shopping patterns and city development. Such impacts depend to a great extent on consumers' response to technological changes.

An increasing use of e-commerce is hypothesized to affect mobility. As such, transport and retail geographers as well as policymakers and planners have become interested in the implications of e-commerce on travel. E-retailing involves a shift from various aspects of the traditional store format towards the introduction of electronic means of performing retail activities. E-retail encompasses three main activities: specifically, a product search activity, an online purchase function and product delivery capability. Early studies forecast that information technology would generate a revolution in the retail sector and would largely affect travel behavior (Graham and Marvin, 1996; Burt and Sparks, 2002; Wrigley et al., 2002). This is commonly attributed to the relaxation of time-space constraints in retailing and is credited to the potential of electronic applications to reduce costs of transactions, transportation and search activities. Indeed, sales in the virtual environment have grown exponentially, although the proportion of virtual shopping is still significantly smaller than that of traditional shopping. This may already hint that understanding the impact of e-commerce on travel is complex.

Conceptual studies on electronic shopping commonly distinguish four potential effects of e-retail on travel. These effects contradict each other in their potential implication on travel: substitution, complementarity, modification and neutrality (Salomon, 1985, 1986; Mokhtarian, 1990, 2002, 2004). Early studies have mainly addressed personal travel and analyzed the mobility effects of one or more of these hypotheses. This chapter will first give an introduction to retail system–consumer interactions in order to understand the overall movements of people and goods. This mobility overview will discuss the potential implications of electronic modes of retail on personal travel, by examining the existing empirical and conceptual research on the use and impacts of e-retail.

2. THE RETAIL SYSTEM IN A RAPIDLY CHANGING WORLD

Retailing is defined as the activities important to selling products to ultimate consumers. Retail activities have seen remarkable changes since the ancient market convening in the city square. Organizational structure, technology and a variety of other external social, economic and locational changes have had their impacts on the daily and less frequent interactions between consumers and retailers. Studies have considered retail as a local market activity and retail theory has evolved with a local market perspective (Severin et al., 2001). Normative spatial models such as Christaller's (1933) central place theory or spatial interaction theory, have generally focused on local market levels (Shepherd and Thomas, 1980).

Nowadays two types of retail markets can be distinguished: the traditional and the electronic retail market. The two retail markets are intertwined, but have several different characteristics. The differences between the traditional retail market and the electronic retail market are attributed to the relaxation of time-space constraints, due to the changing nature of accessibility. Accessibility is a necessary condition for traditional retail activity to take place, but not necessarily a sufficient one. It may vary from poor levels to very high levels. As retail facilities compete for customers, there is a high premium for accessibility. This is certainly the case where physical access is necessary (road network, parking, public transportation and pavements). However, where e-retailing is concerned, accessibility may not necessarily be travel-based. It is first IT-based. The different nature of accessibility that the traditional and electronic retail markets generate indicates the nature of the two markets.

The retail market is usually described using four key elements: location, income, demographics and lifestyle. A market may be contained within different geographical scales ranging from neighborhood-level to metropolitan, national and global scales. The accessibility of the electronic market largely expands its scale of its market. The level of population income and income distribution define the market size; thus again "virtual" accessibility enables the expansion of the size and distribution of potential consumers. The socio-demographic attributes of market segments, such as age and gender and the different lifestyles resulting from ethnic identity, environmentally conscious communities, etc., create sub-markets with various preferences (Jones and Simmons, 1990), which may also be affected by exposure to fads and potential activities over the virtual network.

That said, the retail system does not evolve on its own. It is driven by consumption activities, which consist of household and business acquisition processes. Retail stores attempt to provide the commodities demanded by consumers in order to maximize their profits. On that account, a continuous "race" towards keeping up with consumer demand, generated by changes taking place in the socio-demographic and economic (SED) dimensions, have impelled massive changes in the retail industry (Fernie, 1997). Some of the change in the retail systems' organizational and locational patterns can be attributed to IT. Without it, large organizations could not sustain the competition prevailing in the market, and global processes evident in recent retailing could not be realized (Fernie, 1997; *The Economist*, 2004).

Organizational structure and locational pattern are two main aspects in which retail systems have evolved. The movement from the classic city center retail outlets to the outskirts of cities is one example of locational modification of retailing. Changes, such as growing store size, planned centers and store chains, demonstrate organizational modifications. In addition, there is also evidence of an emerging trend pointing on the move away from edge-of-town large stores, which have become less profitable as fuel prices rise, and retailers have put more investment into central urban areas and smaller stores, which tend to be more profitable. These changes, together with a rise in consumption levels, associated with changes in lifestyle preferences and SED changes, have generated a dynamic retail environment.

Organizational changes can be characterized in three main groups: (1) growth in store size, (2) preference of retailers and consumers for planned shopping centers and (3) a shift towards electronic modes of retail. Changes in store size are first expressed by a move toward larger chains, reflecting economies of scale in all areas of retailing, with a decline in the number of small owner-operated and independent stores. A second trend is the introduction of new large stores (Davis and Kirby, 1980; Wrigley and Lowe, 2003; Vias, 2004). The third, which has recently been in the limelight, is the use of new technologies in retailing. This involves a shift from traditional to electronic retail activities (Mulhern, 1997; Choi and Geistfeld, 2004; Rohm and Swaminathan, 2004; Mummalaneni, 2005; Ramus and Nielsen, 2005; Wang et al., 2006). E-retail, e-tail, e-commerce and tele-shopping are all terms for electronic, mainly Internet-based, transactions (Visser and Lanzendorf, 2004). Small and medium-sized businesses (SMEs) use electronic retail platforms to achieve a competitive advantage and to enhance market position over large chain firms in the traditional market. E-retail makes it possible to reduce distribution costs and increase the market size, while enabling competitive prices (Santarelli and D'Altri, 2003; Lohrke et al., 2006; Grandon et al., 2011).

As discussed earlier, e-retail changed the meaning and the nature of accessibility to retail. When e-retail is considered, accessibility has two meanings. The first refers to physical access, namely the consumer's ability to access the retail facility, or vice versa, the retailer's access to the consumer's premises. For most product classes, physical delivery is still a necessity. The second is that of IT-based access: the telephone, computer, cellular phone, tablet and the web. Purchasing products from the Internet rather than from an offline store offers several benefits. Time-saving is one of the main advantages e-shopping presents. Yet to achieve time-saving using the Internet, a consumer must attain the skills and experience of using the web for shopping. Therefore, the more experienced a consumer is in using IT modes, the more time-effective the Internet becomes (Koivumäki et al., 2002).

3.   E-RETAIL AND THE NETWORK SOCIETY

The network society is argued to be dominated and shaped by spatial form characteristics. Castells (2010) defines it as a space of flows, in which daily activities are liberated from space and time conjugation. Accordingly, the network society may benefit from using information communication technology (ICT), since it enables activities to be fragmented; performed at different times, different locations or both (Castells, 2010; Hubers, 2013). Shopping using ICT enhances space–time flexibility, by offering the possibility to save time and to purchase anywhere, anytime (Mokhtarian, 2009). Although projections about the development of online shopping and its impacts on society were largely exaggerated (Wrigley et al., 2002), sales have grown exponentially since the mid-1990s. However, compared to total retail sales, the amount spent on e-shopping in developed countries is still relatively small: for example, an average of 7.8 percent in the Netherlands for 2009[1] (Thuiswinkel.org, 2008), 3.3 percent in the UK for 2009 (Office for National Statistics, 2011), and 4.3 percent in the USA for 2010 (computed from "Latest Quarterly E-Commerce Report" at www.census.gov/retail). Still, e-commerce represents a small but rapidly growing proportion of retail sales. Estimations regarding world Internet users suggest that there are more than two billion computer-network users around the world, reflecting world Internet penetration of about 30 percent (Lee and Tan, 2003), suggesting a large potential for increasing use of e-retail.

Nowadays, consumer e-commerce is concentrated mostly on items such as books, software, music, travel, hardware, clothing and electronics, with a growing sector of groceries (Gould and Golob, 2002; Lieber and Syverson, 2011). However, people are browsing the Internet more for information than for buying online (OECD, 2002; Teo, 2002; Forsythe and Shi, 2003; Horrigan, 2008; Rotem-Mindali, 2010). A study on the influence of the web in the US demonstrated that for every single US dollar a consumer spends online, another five to six are spent in offline purchases that are influenced by online browsing (Buderi, 2005). The Internet enables consumers to fairly easily access information about merchandise, to gather vertical information (make a comparison) at a low cost, to efficiently screen the offerings and to easily locate the lowest price for a specific item (Alba et al., 1997; Childers et al., 2001; Chiang and Dholakia, 2003; Peterson and Merino, 2003; Gupta et al., 2004). However, when Internet shopping is compared to offline store shopping, traditional store shopping, in most cases, remains preferable. The ability to touch and examine products is considered important by the typical customer. Tangibility, physical contact with a product acts as a stimulus for a purchase. In addition, personal interaction with the retailer or sales representative may generate a feeling of a more successful purchase (Mokhtarian, 2004).

Many studies have tried to isolate the reasons for the advantages and disadvantages of e-commerce as a substitute for physical retail. When e-shopping was first introduced to consumers, one of the main factors identified as contributing to a rather low adoption rate of the online shopping is trust (Grabner-Kraeuter, 2002; Visser and Lanzendorf, 2004; Hongyoun Hahn and Kim, 2009). Grabner-Kraeuter (2002) suggested that trust is not only a short-term issue, but is the most significant long-term barrier for realizing the potential of e-commerce. The reason is that buying on the Internet presents numerous risks, mainly during the transaction process. When online shopping is considered, two dimensions of perceived risk are taken into account: product risk and security risks. Product risks follow from the consumer's inability to examine products online. Security risks follow from the consumer's fear that the open Internet network allows their personal data to be compromised (Bhatnagar and Ghose, 2004).

E-commerce offers increased market activity (and efficiency) for retailers in the form of increased market access and information, and decreased operating and procurement costs. The consumers gain enhanced price competition, expanded information on goods and services and increased choice of products (Rao, 1999; Rosen and Howard, 2000; Mokhtarian, 2001).

The impacts of e-commerce as an acquisition mode are of interest in at least two contexts. First, at a somewhat theoretical level, the option of virtual access, as opposed to real travel, raises some questions with regard to the underlying reasons for why people travel. The common assumption in travel behavior modeling is that the demand for travel is a derived demand, where the demand is actually for activities that can be performed at the destination. Several studies suggest a qualification of the derived demand assumption by pointing to cases in which the activity of travel itself is the generator of a trip, or that travel constitutes an auxiliary factor (Mokhtarian and Salomon, 2001). Shopping may very well be an activity that generates a trip, or part of a trip, even when purchasing is not planned or performed. Shopping generates movements of agents (consumers, carriers) involved in these activities and generally consists of activities that may, but need not necessarily be separate activities: information-gathering, purchasing and delivery. Each activity may involve different numbers of agents as well as different types of agents that use a different transport mode in a specific timing. B2C (business to consumer) and C2C (consumer to consumer) e-commerce may decouple shopping activity and thus change the way we organize our shopping process, which has implications for mobility.

Second, since the 1990s there has been a growing body of research addressing the question of mobility. Initially, the literature has focused mainly on substitution and complementarity of travel-based and e-based options (Koppelman et al., 1991; Arnfalk, 1999; Golob and Regan, 2001; Mokhtarian and Salomon, 2002; Teo, 2002; Lenz, 2003; Visser and Lanzendorf, 2004). From the sustainable development perspective, if significant quantities of online shopping substitute for shopping-related travel, there is potential for a reduction of personal travel and its negative consequences. However, various studies have investigated the impact of Internet shopping on traditional shopping and consequent travel, criticizing these hypotheses and demonstrating that e-shopping will probably not reduce travel, and in some cases will generate more travel (Gould and Golob, 1997; Handy and Yantis, 1997; Gould et al., 1998; Zmud et al., 2001).

4.   MOBILITY EFFECTS OF E-COMMERCE

Reviewing the literature on e-shopping and mobility consequences reveals that many studies that explore the impacts of B2C and C2C e-commerce on mobility are either conceptual or review papers. Most of the literature asserts that four effects on travel may be distinguished due to e-commerce. The changes in travel behavior may result in substitution and complementarity, as well as modification and neutrality (Salomon, 1985, 1986; Mokhtarian, 1990, 2002). These four effects have provided the baseline for the development of the main hypotheses in the literature with regard to the implications of B2C and C2C e-commerce on personal travel and on freight transport.

As stated earlier, the first hypothesis has been one of the main focal themes in e-shopping research; it hypothesized that B2C and C2C e-commerce will reduce the number of shopping trips and distance travelled for shopping as consumers can conduct every stage in a shopping process without leaving their home. As such, in-store shopping will be replaced by home delivery (Dodgson et al., 2000; Golob and Regan, 2001; Nemoto et al., 2001; Sui and Rejeski, 2002; Anderson et al., 2003; Fichter, 2003; Capineri and Leinbach, 2004; Mokhtarian, 2004).

One should note that replacement of a shopping trip made on foot, by bicycle or by public transport with freight transport may not be beneficial for road congestion, energy consumption and air quality (Keskinen et al., 2001; Mokhtarian, 2004). The extent to which a shift from personal travel to freight transport is good for the environment largely depends on the modal split for shopping-related travel. In countries where many shopping trips are conducted by car (e.g., in the USA), substitution of personal travel with freight transport may be more beneficial to the environment than in countries such as the Netherlands, where many shopping trips are made by slow transportation modes (see Figure 34.1).

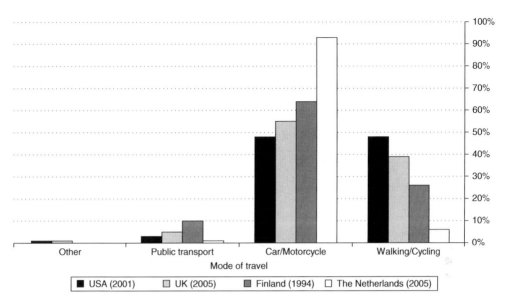

Source: US Department of Transportation (2002), Siikavirta et al. (2003), Department for Transport (2006), Ministerie van Verkeer en Waterstaat (2006)

Figure 34.1   *Share of transport modes for shopping trips in the USA, UK, Finland and the Netherlands*

Many empirical studies have found support for the hypothesis that e-shopping will substitute for personal travel. A large number of studies report figures on the number of consumers that make fewer shopping trips due to the use of computers/Internet or e-shopping. The proportion of consumers that report making fewer shopping trips differs significantly among the empirical studies: 12 percent (Sim and Koi, 2002), 20 percent (Weltevreden, 2007; Weltevreden and Van Rietbergen, 2007), 35 percent (Corpuz and Peachman, 2003), 66 percent (Dixon and Marston, 2002), 78 percent (Bhat et al., 2003). These different outcomes can be attributed to variation in the methodology, and the time and geographical context of the data collection (Weltevreden, 2007). In addition, these substitution effects also vary among products and shopping locations. For example, Tonn and Hemrick (2004) found that due to the use of email/Internet, 39 percent and 7 percent of their respondents made fewer trips to a bookstore and grocery store respectively. Research by Schellenberg (2005) revealed that approximately 25 percent of the German e-shoppers in his sample made fewer purchases in the city center and 18 percent in shopping centers at the edges of cities as a result of e-shopping. Although these studies indicate that e-shopping will lead to fewer shopping trips, they do not provide insight into the magnitude of the substitution effect, that is, the number of shopping trips or distance travelled that are replaced by e-shopping.

A smaller number of empirical studies, however, provide more insight into the (potential) number of substituted shopping trips and distance travelled for shopping. For example, Dodgson et al. (2000) predicted a decrease in the number of shopping trips by car in the UK in 2010 by 10 percent due to e-shopping. In addition, using data on online and offline shopping behavior from 2000–1, Luley et al. (2002) estimated a reduction of 0.5 percent through 5.4 percent and 0.7 percent through 6.9 percent of the daily number of shopping trips and the daily distance travelled for shopping in 2011, respectively. Another German scenario study concluded that the number of shopping trips saved by e-shopping in 2003 largely exceeded the number of generated trips (i.e., trips for information gathering, pick up and return of items), resulting in a net balance of 1.6 million substituted trips (or 7.6 million kilometers) in the Cologne region (Esser and Kurte, 2005). For 2006, they estimated a net reduction of 2.7 million shopping trips (13.2 million kilometers). According to Papola and Polydoropoulou (2006), the number of future shopping trips that are replaced with e-shopping largely differs per product category, as some products are more frequently purchased (e.g., groceries) than others (e.g., electrical appliances). However, studies rarely provide insight on the number of shopping trips that are replaced by freight transport as a result of e-shopping.

Another attribute of the shopping activity found to influence consumers' choice to shop online is product class. For search goods, the intention to shop online is higher than for experience goods, since search goods have a greater chance of success in the electronic environment (Chiang and Dholakia, 2003). Nevertheless, products are widely dissimilar within groups as well as between groups. Dissimilar products were found to produce different and even contrary results (Beatty and Smith, 1987; Bhatnagar and Ghose, 2004), therefore emphasizing the need to examine not only different product categories (e.g., search, experience and credence) but also different product classes. Belonging to a particular product class has implications for the manner in which individuals gather information, purchase and choose among alternative modes of delivery, thus having a different mobility effect (Cairns et al., 2004; Weltevreden, 2007; Rotem-Mindali and Salomon 2007). So, for example, it would not be surprising to find a sizable substitution of online shopping for store shopping if the product class is books or groceries, but projecting that substitution rate to all online shopping would clearly be inappropriate.

It should further be noted that consumer shopping efforts differ from product to product (Girard et al., 2003; Mokhtarian, 2004; Visser and Lanzendorf, 2004; Korgaonkar et al., 2006; Rotem-Mindali and Salomon, 2007). For example, search goods such as books, CDs, computers and travel are currently among the most popular products purchased online (see Weltevreden, 2007). However, in the physical world, many of these items are purchased together with other goods. As such, it is likely that when these items are delivered at home instead of purchased in-store, freight transport will increase, while the personal travel will not always decrease. On the other hand, for convenience goods such as groceries and health and personal care items, a reduction of personal travel is more probable as consumers mainly make a trip just for purchasing these items. However, convenience goods are less frequently purchased online (Weltevreden, 2007).

However, studies indicate that counteracting forces may mitigate a reduction in shopping-related travel, due to e-shopping. Specifically, many scholars contend that effects other than substitution are more likely to occur. A second hypothesis is that B2C and C2C e-commerce will have a limited or even a neutral impact on the number of shopping trips and distance travelled for shopping. Scholars give various reasons why it is reasonable to assume that many shopping trips will not be substituted with e-shopping. First, some online transactions replace purchases by other tele-modes of shopping, such as telephone or mail instead of in-store purchases (Keskinen et al., 2001; Mokhtarian, 2004). This is especially the case with purchases made from catalogue firms and service providers (e.g., insurance companies, banks, travel agencies).

Even if an online purchase replaces an in-store purchase, this need not necessarily lead to fewer (shopping) trips. Scholars contend that many shopping trips are linked with other activities, also referred to as trip-chaining (Golob and Regan, 2001; Keskinen et al., 2001; Mokhtarian, 2004; Visser and Lanzendorf, 2004). For example, people visit a shopping center on their way home from work or vice versa. Furthermore, people often make multiple purchases during a single shopping trip (Mokhtarian, 2004). As such, substitution of an in-store purchase with e-shopping does not necessarily decrease the number of shopping trips. Finally, many scholars maintain that shopping is not always a chore, but also a recreational activity, a means of social interaction. This is certainly an experience that is difficult to replace with e-shopping, which may limit substitution of in-store shopping (Graham and Marvin, 1996; Golob and Regan, 2001; Keskinen et al., 2001; Lyons, 2002; Mokhtarian, 2004).

Some studies that have found evidence for substitution also support this second hypotheses, as only a small proportion of their respondents made fewer shopping trips, while the large majority (75–88 percent) did not alter their shopping-related travel (Sim and Koi, 2002; Schellenberg, 2005; Weltevreden, 2007; Weltevreden and Van Rietbergen, 2004, 2007). Nevertheless, small effects by a very large number of persons may aggregate up to large effects on a system-wide basis (Golob and Regan, 2001).

Research by Ward (2001) supports the underlying assumption that e-shopping is more likely to poach on other home-shopping channels than on in-store shopping. He found that e-shopping and direct mail correlate to a greater degree than do e-shopping and traditional retailing or direct mail and traditional retailing. In addition, Hjorthol (2002) does not find a significant correlation between the frequency of private Internet activities (including e-shopping) and personal travel (including shopping trips).

Other studies support the conjectures that many substituted in-store purchases would have been made together with other purchases and that some shopping trips are chained with other activities. For example, Corpuz and Peachman (2003) report that 35 percent of their respondents would have taken a physical shopping trip if the Internet had not been used for the transaction. That said, approximately 45 percent of those substituted trips would have been taken along with other (shopping) trips. According to Esser and Kurte (2005), only 38 percent of all online purchases lead to a decrease in personal travel. Of the remaining shopping trips, 50 percent are multiple-purchase trips and 11 percent would have been undertaken when travelling home from work.

A third hypothesis is that e-commerce will lead to more personal (shopping) trips and/or increased lengths of shopping trips. As growing numbers of incumbent retailers develop a website as a means of marketing their business (Steinfield et al., 2001; Currah, 2002; Boschma and Weltevreden, 2005), consumers that search online for interesting products and bargains may become aware of the existence of retailers they were previously unaware of. As such, online searching may result in shopping trips that would not have occurred without the Internet, and increased trip lengths as these interesting retailers are often not located in people's home vicinity (Mokhtarian, 2004; Farag, 2006).

Furthermore, not every online order is delivered to a consumer's home, as some online orders are picked up (and paid for) at a store, a post office or a collection-and-delivery point. For example, many consumers nowadays upload their digital images to the website of a retailer and then collect and pay for the printed photographs at a store. The increasing use of e-shopping also leads to a growing amount of online purchases that are returned to the sender. A common way for consumers to do this is to return these items via a post office or a collection-and-delivery point. While some of these trips for collecting and returning goods may be chained with other activities, it is not unlikely that they also lead to more personal trips. There is also much potential for information provision to improve. ICT can assist consumers by real-time updates of where the package is; hence ensure they are home when it arrives – rather than reacting to a long-assumed window.

While it is possible that people will make more and longer (shopping) trips because of B2C e-commerce, it is even more probable that C2C e-commerce will positively affect personal travel. As growing numbers of consumers currently use the Internet to sell and/ or buy goods to/from other consumers, more personal travel is expected as many of these C2C orders will be picked up at the home of a (distant) private seller (Farag, 2006). C2C e-commerce is known for its anonymity and for the ease of registration. However, this also encompasses the risk that a product is not sent or that the quality of the item does not match the buyer's expectation (Yamamoto et al., 2004). This may stimulate self-delivery that may generate personal travel to locations that were possibly not considered prior to the introduction of C2C e-commerce and probably to longer distances (Farag, 2006). In addition, since the destinations of trips for picking up C2C orders are mainly located in residential areas, trip-chaining may be less likely as compared to picking up B2C orders.

Some studies that found evidence for substitution also found proof of an increase in personal travel due to e-shopping. For example, Bhat et al. (2003) found that 22 percent of the computer users in their sample made more shopping trips as compared to non-computer users. Furthermore, Tonn and Hemrick (2004) report that due to the use of email/Internet 14 percent and 5 percent of their respondents made more trips to the bookstore and grocery store respectively. Recall, however, that these kinds of studies do not provide insight concerning the magnitude of the mobility effects.

Other studies found a positive association between e-shopping and in-store shopping. For instance, while controlling for demographic, behavioral, attitudinal and spatial variables, Farag et al. (2005, 2006, 2007), Weltevreden and Van Rietbergen (2006), and Rotem-Mindali (2010) found that, all else being equal, the more Internet users or e-shoppers search online, the more shopping trips they make. In addition, Ferrell (2004) found that home-shopping has a positive effect on the number of shopping trips in US households. Furthermore, Wang and Law (2007) found that ICT usage generates additional time use for recreational activities and increases trip-making propensity. Although these outcomes tend to support the third hypothesis, one should be cautious about drawing this conclusion, as these studies do not have information on the frequency of in-store shopping before and after people started to search online due to the use of cross-sectional data. Moreover, Casas et al. (2001) showed that Internet shoppers make more physical shopping trips than non-Internet shoppers, but they found no significant difference in the number of physical shopping trips compared to total personal trips by Internet shoppers and non-Internet shoppers. As such, another likely conclusion from these results is that mobile persons are more likely to shop online.

5.   SUMMARY

Since new information technologies have penetrated the retail market, the consumer-retailer interactions have become much more complex, and this is true, as well, for understanding their implications. For almost two decades, transport and retail geographers have attempted to understand the implications of the use of information technologies in retail (i.e., e-shopping) on travel. Most conceptual studies have discussed the substitution, complementarity, modification and neutrality effects on travel. Empirical studies on mobility effects of e-shopping have mainly focused on either personal travel or freight transport. Moreover, studies that took into account all types of e-commerce, personal characteristics, product features, transport modes and trip-chaining have been scarce.

This chapter reviews the diverse research on e-retailing and travel. It can be concluded that understanding the impact of e-commerce on travel is complex. All hypotheses are valid to a certain extent. Thus, validity largely depends on the research methodology and the mobility effects that dominate. It is also important to emphasize that most studies do indicate that e-retailing has the potential to lead to a shift from personal travel to freight transport.

E-commerce facilitates the relaxation of the shopping-related temporal and spatial constraints. By doing so, shopping, and associated travel patterns, may be modified, through offering different modes of activity (i.e., traditional or electronic), destination, route, and/or mode of travel. E-retail offers increase efficiency and opportunities, therefore, from an urban mobility perspective, it uses the transport system more efficiently; hence, it has the potential to reduce some of the transport-related negative effects.

Then again, e-commerce may result in positive effects on the transportation system, where complementarity occurs, i.e., may induce travel kilometers. From the policy perspective, the ongoing technological progress, taking place in electronic shopping experience, together with the growth of household Internet accessibility should be accompanied with supporting and developing the freight transport in general and delivery services in particular. By coupling these efforts, substitution between personal travel and freight travel can be promoted. These diverse complex mobility effects produced by e-retail emphasize the need for a comprehensive approach, in which personal characteristics, product type, mode of transport and trip-chaining are taken into account.

NOTE

1.   The difference between the Netherlands and the other two countries is large perhaps due to different methodologies.

REFERENCES

Alba, J., Lynch, J., Weitz, B., Janiszewski, C., Lutz, R., Sawyer, A. and Wood, S. (1997), Interactive home shopping: consumer, retailer, and manufacturer incentives to participate in electronic marketplaces, *Journal of Marketing*, **61**(3), 38–53.
Anderson, W.P., Chatterjee, L. and Lakshmanan, T.R. (2003), E-commerce, transportation, and economic geography, *Growth and Change*, **34**(4), 415–32.

Arnfalk, P. (1999), *Information Technology in Pollution Prevention: Teleconferencing and Telework Used as Tools in the Reduction of Work-Related Travel*, licentiate dissertation, Lund University, Sweden.

Beatty, S.E. and Smith, S.M. (1987), External search effort – an investigation across several product categories, *Journal of Consumer Research*, **14**(1), 83–95.

Bhat, C.R., Sivakumar, A. and Axhausen, K.W. (2003), An analysis of the impact of information and communication technologies on non-maintenance shopping activities, *Transportation Research Part B*, **37**(10), 857–81.

Bhatnagar, A. and Ghose, S. (2004), Segmenting consumers based on the benefits and risks of Internet shopping, *Journal of Business Research*, **57**(12), 1352–60.

Boschma, R.A. and Weltevreden, J.W.J. (2005), B2C E-Commerce Adoption in Inner Cities: An Evolutionary Perspective, working paper 05.03, Papers in Evolutionary Economic Geography (PEEG), Utrecht University.

Buderi, R. (2005), E-commerce gets smarter, *Technology Review*, **108**(4), 54–9.

Burt, S. and Sparks, L. (2002), E-commerce and the retail process: a review, *Journal of Retailing and Consumer Services*, **10**, 275–86.

Cairns, S., Sloman, L., Newson, C., Anable, J., Kirkbride, A. and Goodwin, P. (2004), Smarter Choices: Changing the Way We Travel, London: Department for Transport.

Capineri, C. and Leinbach, T.R. (2004), Globalization, e-economy and trade, *Transport Reviews*, **24**(6), 645–63.

Casas, J., Zmud, J. and Bricka, S. (2001), *Impact of Shopping via Internet on Travel for Shopping Purposes*, 80th Annual Meeting of the Transportation Research Board, Washington, DC.

Castells, M. (2010), The space of flows, in *The Rise of the Network Society*, Oxford: Wiley-Blackwell, pp. 407–59.

Chiang, K.P. and Dholakia, R.R. (2003), Factors driving consumer intention to shop online: an empirical investigation, *Journal of Consumer Psychology*, **13**(1–2), 177–83.

Childers, T.L., Carr, C.L., Peck, J. and Carson, S. (2001), Hedonic and utilitarian motivations for online retail shopping behavior, *Journal of Retailing*, **77**(4), 511–35.

Choi, J.Y. and Geistfeld, L.V. (2004), A Cross-cultural investigation of consumer e-shopping adoption, *Journal of Economic Psychology*, **25**(6), 821–38.

Christaller, W. (1933), *Central Places in Southern Germany*, Englewood Cliffs, NJ: Prentice-Hall Inc.

Corpuz, G. and Peachman, J. (2003), *Measuring the Impacts of Internet usage on Travel Behaviour in the Sidney Household Travel Survey*, 26th Australian Transport Research Forum Conference, Wellington, New Zealand, www.atrf.info/papers/2003/18-Corpuz.pdf.

Currah, A. (2002), Behind the web store: the organisational and spatial evolution of multichannel retailing in Toronto, *Environment and Planning A*, **34**(8), 1411–41.

Davis, R.L. and Kirby, D.A. (1980), Retail organization, in J.A. Dawson (ed.), *Retail Geography*, London: Halstead Press, pp. 156–92.

Department for Transport (2006), *National Travel Survey 2005*, London: Department for Transport.

Dixon, T. and Marston, A. (2002), UK retail real estate and the effects of online shopping, *Journal of Urban Technology*, **9**(3), 19–47.

Dodgson, J., Pacey, J. and Begg, M. (2000), *Motors and Modems Revisited: The Role of Technology in Reducing Travel Demands and Traffic Congestion*, London: NERA.

The Economist (2004), A perfect market: a survey of e-commerce, *The Economist*, 15 May.

Esser, K. and Kurte, J. (2005), *B2C E-commerce: A Qualitative and Quantitative Analysis of the Consumer and Supplier Relationships and their Implications for Urban Transport (B2C-VERRA)*, Cologne: KE-Consult.

Farag, S. (2006), *E-shopping and its Interactions with In-store Shopping*, PhD thesis, Utrecht University.

Farag, S., Schwanen, T. and Dijst, M. (2005), Online searching and buying and their relationship with shopping trips empirically investigated, *Transportation Research Record*, **1926**, 242–51.

Farag, S., Krizek, K.J. and Dijst, M. (2006), E-shopping and its relationship with in-store shopping: empirical evidence from the Netherlands and the USA, *Transport Reviews*, **26**(1), 43–61.

Farag, S., Schwanen, T., Dijst, M. and Faber, J. (2007), Shopping online and/or in-store? A structural equation model of the relationships between e-shopping and in-store shopping, *Transportation Research Part A*, **41**(2), 125–41.

Fernie, J. (1997), Retail change and retail logistics in the United Kingdom: past trends and future prospects, *The Service Industries Journal*, **17**(3), 383–96.

Ferrell, C.E. (2004), *Home-based Teleshoppers and shopping Travel: Do Teleshoppers Travel Less?* The 83rd Annual Meeting of the Transportation Research Board, Washington, DC.

Fichter, K. (2003), E-commerce: sorting out the environmental consequences, *Journal of Industrial Ecology*, **6**(2), 25–41.

Forsythe, S.M. and Shi, B. (2003), Consumer patronage and risk perceptions in internet shopping, *Journal of Business Research*, **56**(11), 867–75.

Girard, T., Korgaonkar, P. and Silverblatt, R. (2003), Relationship of type of product, shopping orientations, and demographics with preference for shopping on the Internet, *Journal of Business and Psychology*, **18**(1), 101–20.

Golob, T.F. and Regan, A.C. (2001), Impacts of information technology on personal travel and commercial vehicle operations: research challenges and opportunities, *Transportation Research C*, **9**(2), 87–121.

Gould, J. and Golob, T.F. (1997), Shopping without travel or travel without shopping? An investigation of electronic home shopping, *Transport Reviews*, **17**(4), 355–76.

Gould, J. and Golob, T.F. (2002), Consumer e-commerce, virtual accessibility, and sustainable transport, W.R. Black and P. Nijkamp (eds), *Social Change and Sustainable Transport*, Indiana: Indiana University Press, pp. 279–85.

Gould, J., Golob, T.F. and Barwise, P. (1998), *Why Do People Drive to Shop? Future Travel and Telecommunications Tradeoffs*, UCI-ITS-AS-WP-98-1, Institute of Transportation Studies, University of California, Irvine.

Grabner-Kraeuter, S. (2002), The role of consumers' trust in online-shopping, *Journal of Business Ethics*, **39**(1–2), 43–50.

Graham, S. and Marvin, S. (1996), *Telecommunications and the City: Electronic Spaces, Urban Places*, London: Routledge.

Grandon, E.E., Nasco, S.A. and Mykytyn, P.P. (2011), Comparing theories to explain e-commerce adoption, *Journal of Business Research*, **64**(3): 292–98.

Gupta, A., Su, B.C. and Walter, Z. (2004), Risk profile and consumer shopping behavior in electronic and traditional channels, *Decision Support System*, **38**(3), 347–67.

Handy, S. and Yantis, T. (1997), *The Impacts of Telecommunications Technologies on Nonwork Travel Behavior*, R. R. SWUTC/97/721927-1F, Southwest Region University Transportation Center, University of Texas at Austin.

Hjorthol, R.J. (2002), The relation between daily travel and use of the home computer, *Transportation Research Part A*, **36**(5), 437–52.

Hongyoun Hahn, K. and Kim, J. (2009), The effect of offline brand trust and perceived internet confidence on online shopping intention in the integrated multi-channel context, *International Journal of Retail and Distribution Management*, **37**(2), 126–41.

Horrigan, J. (2008), *Online Shopping*, Washington, DC: Pew Internet & American Life Project, http://pewinternet.org.

Hubers, C. (2013), *Information and Communication Technologies and the Spatio-Temporal Fragmentation of Everyday Life*, PhD thesis, Utrecht University.

Jones, K. and Simmons, J. (1990), *The Retail Environment*, London: Routledge.

Keskinen, A., Delache, X., Cruddas, J., Lindjord, J.E. and Iglesias, C. (2001), *A Purchase and a Chain: Impacts of E-commerce on Transport and the Environment*, Paris: OECD/ECMT.

Koivumäki, T., Svento, R., Perttunen, J. and Oinas-Kukkonen, H. (2002), Consumer choice behavior and electronic shopping systems: a theoretical note, *Netnomics*, **4**(2), 131–44.

Koppelman, F., Salomon, I. and Proussaloglou, K. (1991), Teleshopping or store shopping? A choice model for forecasting the use of new telecommunications-based services, *Environment and Planning B: Planning and Design*, **18**, 473–89.

Korgaonkar, P., Silverblatt, R. and Girard, T. (2006), Online retailing, product classifications, and consumer preferences, *Internet Research*, **16**(3), 267–88.

Lee, K.S. and Tan, S.J. (2003), E-retailing versus physical retailing: a theoretical model and empirical test of consumer choice, *Journal of Business Research*, **56**(11), 877–85.

Lenz, B. (2003), *Will Electronic Commerce Help to Reduce Traffic in Agglomeration Areas?* TRB 82nd Annual Meeting, 12–16 January, Washington.

Lieber, E. and Syverson, C. (2011), Online vs. offline competition, in M. Peitz and J. Waldfogel (eds), *Oxford Handbook of the Digital Economy*, Oxford: Oxford University Press.

Lohrke, F.T., Franklin, G.M. and Frownfelter-Lohrke, C. (2006), The Internet as an information conduit a transaction cost analysis model of us sme internet use, *International Small Business Journal*, **24**(2), 159–78.

Luley, T., Bitzer, W. and Lenz, B. (2002), Substitution of transport through electronic commerce? A model for the Stuttgart region, *Zeitschrift für Verkehrswissenshaft*, **73**(3), 133–55.

Lyons, G. (2002), Internet: investigating new technology's evolving role, nature and effects on transport, *Transport Policy*, **9**(4), 335–46.

Ministerie van Verkeer en Waterstaat (2006), *Mobiliteitsonderzoek Nederland 2005*, The Hague: Ministerie van Verkeer en Waterstaat.

Mokhtarian, P.L. (1990), A typology of relationships between telecommunications and transportation, *Transportation Research Part A: Policy and Practice*, **24**(3), 231–42.

Mokhtarian, P.L. (2001), *The Impacts of B2c E-Commerce on Transportation and Urban Form*, prepared for the Conference on Electronic Commerce (B2c) and its Consequences for Urban Development and Transportation, University of Stuttgart.

Mokhtarian, P.L. (2002), Telecommunication and travel: the case for complementarity, *Journal of Industrial Ecology*, **6**(2), 43–57.

Mokhtarian, P.L. (2004), A conceptual analysis of the transportation impacts of B2c e-commerce, *Transportation*, **31**(3), 257–84.

Mokhtarian, P.L. (2009), Social networks and telecommunications, in R. Kitamura, T. Yoshii and T. Yamamoto (eds), *The Expanding Sphere of Travel Behaviour Research: Selected Papers from the 11th International Conference on Travel Behaviour Research*, Bingley: Emerald, pp. 429–38.

Mokhtarian, P.L. and Salomon, I. (2001), How derived is the demand for travel? Some conceptual and measurement considerations, *Transportation Research A*, **35**, 695–719.

Mokhtarian, P.L. and Salomon, I. (2002), Emerging travel patterns: do telecommunications make a difference? in H.S. Mahmassani (ed.), *Perpetual Motion: Travel Behavior Research Opportunities and Application Challenges*, London: Pergamon, pp. 143–82.

Mulhern, F.J. (1997), Retail marketing: from distribution to integration, *International Journal of Research in Marketing*, **14**(2), 103–24.

Mummalaneni, V. (2005), An empirical investigation of web site characteristics, consumer emotional states and on-line shopping behaviours, *Journal of Business Research*, **58**(4), 526–32.

Nemoto, T., Visser, J. and Yoshimoto, R. (2001), *Impacts of Information and Communication Technology on Urban Logistics System*, Paris: OECD/ECMT.

OECD (2002), *Measuring the Information Economy*, Paris: OECD Publications.

Office for National Statistics (2011), *E-commerce and ICT activity, 2010 Edition*, London: Office for National Statistics.

Papola, A. and Polydoropoulou, A. (2006), Shopping-related Travel in an ICT-rich era – a Case Study on the Impact of E-shopping on Travel Demand, 85th annual meeting of the Transportation Research Board, Washington, DC.

Peterson, R.A. and Merino, M.C. (2003), Consumer information search behavior and the Internet, *Psychology & Marketing*, **20**(2), 99–121.

Ramus, K. and Nielsen, N.A. (2005), Online grocery retailing: what do consumers think? *Internet Research*, **15**(3), 335–52.

Rao, B. (1999), The Internet and the Revolution in distribution: a cross-industry examination, *Technology in Society*, **21**(3), 287–306.

Rohm, A.J. and Swaminathan, V. (2004), A typology of online shoppers based on shopping motivations, *Journal Of Business Research*, **57**(7), 748–57.

Rosen, K.T. and Howard, A.L. (2000), E-retail: gold rush or fool's gold? *California Management Review*, **42**(3), 72–100.

Rotem-Mindali, O. (2010), E-tail versus retail: the effects on shopping related travel empirical evidence from Israel, *Transport Policy*, **17**(5), 312–22.

Rotem-Mindali, O. and Salomon, I. (2007), The impacts of e-retail on the choice of shopping trips and delivery: some preliminary findings, *Transportation Research Part A*, **41**(2), 176–89.

Rotem-Mindali, O. and Salomon, I. (2009), Modeling consumers' purchase and delivery choices in the face of the information age, *Environment and Planning B*, **36**, 245–61.

Salomon, I. (1985), Telecommunications and travel, *Journal of Transport Economics and Policy*, **19**, 219–35.

Salomon, I. (1986), Telecommunications and travel relationships: a review, *Transportation Research A*, **20**(3), 223–38.

Santarelli, E. and D'Altri, S. (2003), The diffusion of e-commerce among SMEs: theoretical implications and empirical evidence, *Small Business Economics*, **21**(3), 273–83.

Schellenberg, J. (2005), B2C e-commerce: impacts on retail structure, *Geografische Handelsforschung*, **10**.

Severin, V., Louviere, J.J. and Finn, A. (2001), The stability of retail shopping choices over time and across countries, *Journal of Retailing*, **77**(2), 185–202.

Shepherd, I.D.H. and Thomas, C.J. (1980), Urban consumer behavior, in J.A. Dawson (ed.), *Retail Geography*, London: Halstead Press, pp. 18–94.

Siikavirta, H., Punakivi, M., Kaekkainen M. and Linnanen, L. (2003), Effects of e-commerce on greenhouse gas emissions: a case study of grocery home delivery in Finland, *Journal of Industrial Ecology*, **6**(2), 83–97.

Sim, L.L. and Koi, S.M. (2002), Singapore's Internet shoppers and their impact on traditional shopping patterns, *Journal of Retailing and Consumer Services*, **9**(2), 115–24.

Steinfield, C., de Wit, D., Adelaar, T., Bruins, A., Fielt, E., Hoefsloot, M., Smit, A. and Bouwman, H. (2001), Pillars of virtual enterprise: leveraging physical assets in the new economy, *Info*, **3**(3): 203–13.

Sui, D.Z. and Rejeski, D.W. (2002), Environmental impacts of the emerging digital economy: the e-for-environment e-commerce? *Environmental Management*, **29**(2), 155–63.

Teo, T.S.H. (2002), Attitudes toward online shopping and the Internet, *Behaviour & Information Technology*, **21**(4), 259–71.

Thuiswinkel.org (2008), *Homeshopping: Research and Figures*, http://thuiswinkel.org.

Tonn, B.E. and Hemrick, A. (2004), Impacts of the use of e-mail and the Internet on personal trip-making behavior, *Social Science Computer Review*, **22**(2), 270–80.

US Department of Transportation (2002), *National Household Travel Survey 2001*, Washington, DC: US Department of Transportation.

Vias, A.C. (2004), Bigger stores, more stores, or no stores: paths of retail restructuring in rural America, *Journal of Rural Studies*, **20**(3), 303–18.

Visser, E.J. and Lanzendorf, M. (2004), Mobility and accessibility effects of B2c e-commerce: a literature review, *Tijdschrift Voor Economische En Sociale Geografie*, **95**(2), 189–205.

Wang, D. and Law, F.Y.T. (2007), Impacts of information and communication technologies (ICT) on time use and travel behavior: a structural equations analysis, *Transportation*, **34**(4), 513–27.

Wang, E.T.G., Yeh, H.Y. and Jiang, J.J. (2006), The relative weights of internet shopping fundamental objectives: effect of lifestyle differences, *Psychology & Marketing*, **23**(5), 353–67.

Ward, M.R. (2001), Will online shopping compete more with traditional retailing or catalog shopping? *Netnomics*, **3**(2), 103–17.

Weltevreden, J.W.J. (2007), Substitution or complementarity? How the Internet changes city centre shopping, *Journal of Retailing and Consumer Services*, **14**, 192–207.

Weltevreden, J.W.J. and Van Rietbergen, T. (2004), *Are Shops Disappearing?* Utrecht University, www.jesseweltevreden.com/verdwijntdewinkel.pdf.

Weltevreden, J.W.J. and Van Rietbergen, T. (2007), E-shopping versus city centre shopping: the role of perceived city centre attractiveness, *Tijdschrift Voor Economische En Sociale Geografie*, **98**(1), 68–85.

Wrigley, N. and Lowe, M. (2003), *Reading Retail: A Geographical Perspective on Retailing and Consumption Spaces*, London: Arnold.

Wrigley, N., Lowe, M. and Currah, A. (2002), Retailing and e-tailing, *Urban Geography*, **23**, 180–97.

Yamamoto, H., Ishida, K. and Ohta, T. (2004), Modeling reputation management system on online C2C market, *Computational and Mathematical Organization Theory*, **10**, 165–78.

Zmud, J., Bricka, S. and Casas, J. (2001), *Impact of Shopping Via Internet on Travel for Shopping Purposes*, Transportation Research Board, 80th Annual Meeting, January, Washington, DC.

35 Parents, children and automobility: trends, challenges and opportunities
Robyn Dowling

1. INTRODUCTION

'Automobility' is a term increasingly used to describe the travel patterns of city inhabitants in many parts of the world. As defined by scholarship within sociology and cultural studies, automobility refers to the ways in which patterns of sociability, propensities for ever-increasing personal travel, city infrastructures and economic organisations have been and are propelled by the system that pivots around the private motor vehicle (Sheller and Urry, 2007; Urry, 2004; Lucas et al., 2011). In many countries across the world, the petroleum-fuelled private car rules the spaces and rhythms of everyday life and is supported by a range of institutions and infrastructures, including transport networks like highways, traffic rules and planning frameworks (see summary in Goodwin, 2010). Automobility is particularly appropriate to the description and understanding of the contemporary travel of urban families in the developed world. Parents' and children's movements around the city are predominantly by car, and the private automobile is becoming a key tool in contemporary parenting cultures and identities. The notion of automobility hence provides the societal and intellectual scaffolding for this chapter. The chapter argues that contemporary familial travel both reproduces and challenges the hold of the automobile – and its attendant physical, social and intellectual infrastructures – in everyday life.

The chapter begins with a discussion of the key frameworks through which familial automobility can be comprehended: feminism and cultural studies. The body of the chapter provides more detail on three dimensions of familial automobility – cultures of mothering, the school run, and cars as a literal family space – emphasising the deep and myriad links between cultures of family life and the use of the private car. In recognition of the socially constructed and contested nature of automobility, and the inherent variability of cultures of parenting, the chapter ends with a number of contemporary examples in which cultures of parenting are enacted through non-automobile travel modes, and explores their significance for future familial mobility in the city.

2. FAMILIES AND MOBILITY: KEY ISSUES AND FRAMEWORKS

Mainstream transport paradigms do highlight and delineate the ways in which familial and household responsibilities shape urban travel: roles, responsibilities and expectations within families have a significant impact on how, where, why and how far people travel. Family relationships and obligations, for example, have a bearing on the direction and length of the journey to work, a preponderance of travel 'serving' others, and a focus on journeys for purposes other than work and outside the morning and afternoon peaks. This literature is not the focus of this chapter for two reasons. First, most of the detailed work on familial travel has occurred at the interstices of transport and other disciplines, such as sociology, cultural studies and feminism. These disciplines are characterised by a deep engagement with the minutiae of family life, their impact on travel patterns and the role of mobility in these patterns of daily life. It is here that links with familial cultures are most clearly enunciated. Second is the more qualitative orientation of these disciplines. While quantitative methodologies and analyses have been used to great effect in understanding familial travel (for example Schwanen, 2007; Schwanen et al., 2008), data collection techniques such as in-depth interviews, focus groups and reflective diaries, for example, are more appropriate to garnering and understanding of the place of travel in both everyday routines and their surrounding values. Other techniques have recently emerged as appropriate to understanding car-based mobility, including video and audio diaries (Laurier et al., 2008) and researchers accompanying research participants on their journeys (Middleton, 2011).

Feminist and sociological perspectives have been critical in understanding familial travel. Feminist frameworks highlight the importance of gender in travel, calling explicit attention to the importance of gender differences in the patterning and explanation of travel (Hanson, 2010; Law, 1999). Empirically, it is widely documented that there are significant gender differences in mobility, including that women, compared to men, do more chauffeuring, work closer to home and are less likely to work in occupations that require driving (for example, travelling salespeople) (Hanson 2010). The gendered nature of familial responsibilities underpins these trends. In nuclear families, commensurate with a primary breadwinner role, men are more likely to be more work-centred and have less responsibility for childcare and childrearing. Thus in men's travel in general we see a preponderance of the journey to work, travel for single- rather than multi-purpose trips, and travel into and out of the central business district in the morning and afternoon peak (Crane, 2007). Women's responsibilities for children underpin multi-purpose, cross-suburban journeys, at different times of the day and for non-work purposes (Hanson, 2010). Historically, women have been much less likely to own or have ready access to a car and hence to use their car as their primary transport mode (Hanson, 2010). This has changed over the past 20 years, where the gap between women's and men's car use has narrowed considerably (Walsh, 2008). The gendered patterning of social life is hence manifest in travel patterns.

Feminist frameworks also highlight the emotional and social attachments through which travel patterns arise. Individuals are embedded in, and shaped by, relations with others. This is especially pronounced in family life and the practices of individuals within families. Families are constituted through relations of care, relations that are intrinsically gendered. In simple terms, this means that practices of caring for others – parents and children – are one of the defining features of family life and it is the ongoing accomplishment of these tasks that produces the family as an entity. This notion of 'doing family' (West and Zimmerman, 1987; DeVault, 1994) turns attention to the ways in which relations of care adumbrate familial travel: the purpose of caring for others is a central goal of familial travel and, in turn, familial travel reproduces familial relations and identities. These include the practices and expectations of identities like mother, father, parent and child.

Cultural perspectives provide a necessary additional layer to this feminist emphasis on care and gendered identities. In general, a cultural approach involves a focus on the definitions people bring to their travel and use of different transport modes, the images and metaphors they use to understand travel, and their experiences of it. These studies envision travel as much more than a way of getting from A to B. Travel modes like the car, cycling, public transport are sites where identities – masculinity, femininity, young adulthood – are forged. Moreover, destinations are culturally meaningful – places in which practices occur and values and identities enabled. Thus relations of care and family life are embedded in beliefs and attitudes about what is 'right' or 'appropriate' – ideals of family life. Travel occurs and is valued because of its ability to accomplish notions of good parenting and associated ideals of what is valuable for children. In the next section I explicate the characteristics of contemporary cultures of parenting and their manifestation in familial automobility. The focus is on automobility not because cultures of parenting are absent in other forms of travel, but because the links between cultures of parenting and car use are increasingly strong.

3.   CULTURES OF PARENTING AND CAR USE

Contemporary cultures of parenting have a number of intersecting elements. Within the burgeoning literatures on these cultures, the following are central to understanding car use. The first is a shift away from unstructured play towards a multitude of activities as the focus of childhood. Rather than allowing children's play to be unstructured and based in and around the home and neighbourhood, structured activities outside the home are increasingly emphasised (Freeman and Quigg, 2009; Hjorthol and Fyhri, 2009b). The home and neighbourhood are less likely to be play spaces for children. These activities are valued because they are seen to give children the 'best' opportunities. This is also related to a profound sense of anxiety about urban space and society, alongside a reluctance to expose children to perceived risks. Moreover, research has shown that parents are willing to prioritise these activities, investing considerable time and monetary resources to ensure they occur (Fyhri et al., 2011). More frequent travel is the result (Hjorthol and Fyhri, 2009a).

A second element is the increasing pace of life. Contemporary life is characterised by a moral economy of time that champions speed and efficiency (Whitelegg, 1993, Tranter, 2010; Strazdins et al., 2011). Time is precious, with considerable effort of families directed at ways to protect, control and manage their time. This is manifest in a number of ways. A sense that waiting for a bus is 'wasted' time (Watts and Urry, 2008; Bissell, 2009), that children's and adults' days need to be 'full' rather than empty (i.e., nothing planned) (Hjorthol and Fyhri, 2009a), and a pervasive feeling of being harried and not having enough time (Shove, 1998). In the examples below, this sense of time is related to representations of the car as convenient. A final element is individualism. Not confined to cultures of parenting, individualism describes a prioritising of individual rather than shared needs. Within families this can be seen in an emphasis on the place of the individual within the family, as well as an emphasis on the goals of the family in contrast to a more collective goal. Thus we see the choice of activities and locations right for a specific child, often with disregard for its impact on others or consideration of sharing travel or activities. Such priorities are also encouraged by policies like school choice that enable parents to choose a school for their child regardless of geographic location (Jarvis and Alvanides, 2008).

Societies, cities and families that are shaped by, and reproduce, automobility are the broad outcome of these cultures. Frequent and spatially diverse activities of children and parents, minimal independent mobility of children, in the context of scarce time all lead to a reliance on the motor vehicle. In the rest of this section I provide three specific illustrations of these parental cultures of mobility.

4.   CULTURES OF MOTHERING AND AUTOMOBILITY IN SUBURBAN SYDNEY

Despite significant shifts over the past 30 years it remains the case that parenting in many families remains the primary responsibility of women rather than men. In work undertaken in Sydney, Australia, more than a decade ago, but with ongoing salience, I set out to understand the meanings – values, aspirations – surrounding the use of cars by suburban mothers and how this use form part of their identities as mothers, wives and workers (Dowling, 2000). This research identified the importance of cultures of mothering – clusters of beliefs, attitudes, symbols and practices attached to mothering in understanding familial automobility. Mothers' aspirations for and relationships with children, and idealised notions of 'good mothering' led them to become car-dependent.

Use of the motor vehicle was a response to perceptions of safe places and appropriate activities for children. In terms of safety, there was a common perception that Sydney is an unsafe place to live, especially for children. This meant that children were most often driven to school. Alongside these safety concerns appears to be an increased involvement and valuation of formal rather than unstructured children's activities. It was widely held that it was best for children that they be involved in a number of extracurricular activities, like sport, music and dance. Children were generally driven to these events and the description 'taxi driver' easily applied to most of the women interviewed. The activities of children not only involved increased travel, but the location of these activities also led to reliance on the car. Time, space and transport converge here. The importance of children's activities in a context where time was scarce meant that public transport was not used. These cultures of mothering had a number of other components that impacted motor vehicle use. All the women wanted to minimise travel time and keep to a schedule, goals that were more effectively managed with a motor vehicle. Women both in and out of the paid labour force were unwilling to double their travel time by using public transport. The interviews are littered with statements about the longer time it took to get places on public transport compared to in a private car. Time spent on public transport was understood as 'wasted' rather than productive.

The women interviewed did not, on the whole, approach mothering as a collective exercise. Opportunities for children and daily routines were defined individually rather than in concert with others. In particular, they were unwilling to adjust their schedules to those of public transport. Cars are an individual mode of transport, and were relied upon to manage individual routines. The second implication is that car-pooling was either not possible, or not considered. Some aspects of daily routines, like the location and starting times of employment, could not be adjusted. It was highly unlikely that a woman would be able to find someone else with exactly the same journey: 'There are people who live nearby [whom she works with] but we're all on different shifts and different schedules.' Yet even when individuals were starting from and going to the same location, ride-sharing was rare.

The perception of this group of women was that the only way to overcome potential social isolation was to not rely on others. Even if there was good public transport in their neighbourhood, or they had neighbours willing to drive them places, they would be unlikely to take up the opportunity. The car appears to be more than a response to complex time–space routines. It also offers women not in the labour force the mobility and independence they feel they need to combat potential suburban isolation. Ideas of 'good mothering', self-defined standards about what a mother should provide for her child and family in the 1990s, were all constituted through car use. Travel by car was both instigated by their desires for their children and helped materialise, or enact, these desires. The car, then, is a means to an end, a 'management tool' as depicted in Figure 35.1. And that end – good mothering – was valued so highly that many were

The Car as a Management Tool

Figure 35.1   Car as management tool

willing to make considerable sacrifices for its achievement. In relation to cars, women's own feelings about driving were defined as secondary.

5.   CARS AND THE JOURNEY TO SCHOOL

The previous example outlined the general connections between cultures of mothering, especially in suburban areas traditionally characterised by poor public transport and car use. More recent attention has turned to the component parts of these parenting and travel cultures, including the children's journey to school. As part of the decline in the independent mobility of travel, children's journeys to school are now less likely to involve active travel modes like walking and cycling and more likely to involve the car (Lang et al., 2011). Popular commentary regularly refers to the role of the 'school run' in traffic congestion – vehicular congestion around schools at starting and finishing times and also their relationship to an elongation of afternoon and morning peak travel times. The practice of driving children to school is increasing as a result of the amalgam of factors depicted in Figure 35.2. As Fyhri et al. (2011) explain, both demographic and cultural factors underpin the increasing rate of children being driven. These include greater

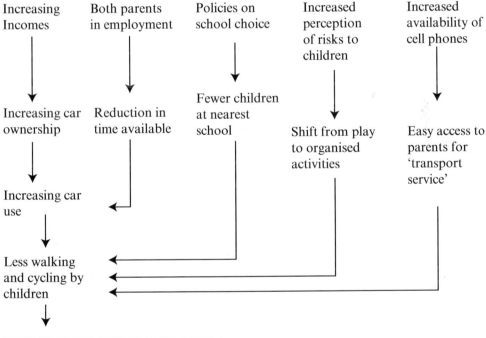

Source: Fyhri et al. (2011)

Figure 35.2   Factors underpinning driving children to school

labour force participation of mothers and higher rates of car ownership. Culturally, a key finding of recent research is that driving children to school is part of the caring work undertaken by women in families (Barker, 2011). The cultural factors outlined in the previous section are also in play: increased participation of children in organised activities; a prevailing sense of lack of time and 'busyness', and anxieties about the safety of urban spaces. In a study of the journey to school on the west coast of the United States, perceptions of safety (mainly pertaining to 'stranger danger' rather than traffic) and convenience were associated with children being driven to school (McDonald and Alborg, 2009). Individualism remains in evidence as well. In one study, the trouble of navigating school gates each morning and afternoon was derided by walkers and drivers alike. Issues such as double parking, children's safety and a feeling of stress for both parents and children in getting there on time were discussed. Nonetheless, individuals were unwilling to identify their own behaviour as contributing to the chaos; instead suggesting others' behaviour created the congestion (Lang et al., 2011). School traffic congestion is clearly an individual and collective problem, but individuals were unable to perceive or acknowledge their own role.

A prioritisation of the individual and constrains of time are also inflected in the use of mobile communications and other forms of technology in the journey to school. Consistent with other research that demonstrates that information and communication technologies (ICTs) do not replace mobility but allow greater social contact with the same amount of mobility (Line et al., 2010), mobile phones have essentially cemented familial car use. They allow familial automobility to continue to exist in the face of ongoing traffic congestion and time pressures. A recent qualitative study of mothers and their children's journeys to school found that the mobile phone was used to coordinate alternatives while in the car and/or running late, leading to the conclusion that ICTs enable women to cope with congestion rather than change their travel behaviour (Jain et al., 2011; see also Hjorthol, 2008). Car use and mobile phones are symbiotic; both valorising and enabling short planning horizons and spatial and temporal flexibility.

6.   CARS AND THE PRODUCTION OF FAMILIAL RELATIONS

A final element of familial car use from a cultural perspective relates to the journey itself. Culturally, the car is not simply a means to get from A to B, but a means in itself. In this respect, the car becomes a site in which familial relationships are enacted and families reproduced. Familial automobility, in other words, provides an interesting window onto Blunt and Dowling's (2006) conceptualisation of the home and domestic sphere as multi-scale that includes but also extends beyond the physical space of the house. The notion of the car as a management tool introduced above implies that the car is a domestic space for women. Like the home, it is in the car (sometimes through ICT, sometimes through the 'thinking space' it provides) that family (and sometimes work) arrangements are made (see Dowling, 2000; Laurier et al., 2008). For women who are mothers, the car not only facilitates the mobility required to satisfy children's spatially dispersed activities, but it also becomes a site valued for its facilitation of domestic conversations. In the Sydney study above (Dowling, 2000), and in a number of more recent studies (Barker, 2009; Laurier et al., 2008; Basmajian, 2010) the car is a conduit of familial companionship. From parents' perspectives children are 'trapped' in cars, which hence provide uninterrupted family time. Cars are sites in which children share stories of their day, without the interruptions of technology (phones, televisions, computers), other activities (homework) or other people (friends, neighbours, relatives). In this respect, cars are particular types of domestic spaces: spaces of conversation and engagement. Indeed, discussions of parenting teenagers and boys in popular psychology explicitly encourage driving children as a means to encourage communication (Lashlie, 2007)! The increasing presence of technologies such as DVD players and smartphones in cars might work against these findings, and need to be the subject of further research.

The perspective of children is increasingly important in understanding familial automobility; a number of studies are turning to children's experiences of journeys to school and their experiences of car travel. It is not only adults for whom the car is a significant social space. Barker's research with children and cars finds that cars are an important contemporary space of childhood, only surpassed by home and school (Barker, 2009: 62). For children, the car is experienced as an extension of the home and, in particular, the home as an adult-controlled space. Thus in the car children are watched over (sometimes using rear vision mirrors!), disciplined and sometimes 'forced' to share the back seat with children who are not friends. Cars are also home-like in being spaces for sibling negotiation and argumentation – in this case focused on who sits where and/or which child is entitled to the front seat. On a more positive note, cars are places in which children freely share news of their day and plan coming events. Interestingly, especially in the context of work on the increasingly technological mediation of childhood and the preponderance of activities that comprise contemporary childhood, cars are places where children get bored. On both long and short journeys, children describe having 'nothing to do' in the car. Speculatively, this may be a difference between the domestic characteristics of the car and the house. Whereas the ready availability of technology may alleviate children's boredom within the house, its absence (at least until recently) in the automobile is rendered problematic by children. Regardless of the differences, in this regime of familial automobility, cars have become domestic spaces, literally family spaces, for parents and children alike.

7.   MOVING BEYOND FAMILIES AND CARS

Cities are currently at a crossroads in relation to car use. Thoroughly embedded in urban infrastructures and design, daily routines and culturally valued lifestyles, automobility has become the biggest challenges facing countries combating anthropogenic climate change (Urry, 2008). These challenges come from diverse quarters, including but extending far beyond that of climate change. Globally, automobiles are responsible for one-fifth of energy-related CO_2 emissions (Dauvergne cited in Goodwin, 2010). They cause congestion, choking the movement of goods and people, costing Australia an estimated $9 billion in 2005 (National Transport Commission, 2011). The health and social costs of car-dependence include inactivity and obesity; premature death from car-generated air pollution; road deaths and injuries; as well as social exclusion for people who can't participate in society without a car (the aged, people under 18, those on low incomes or with mobility impairment; National Transport Commission, 2011). Likewise there are strong criticisms of the chauffeuring of children by car, including but also extending beyond the health effects of decreasing active travel of children. Declining independent mobility of children also impacts their ability to navigate streets safely as pedestrians, and car travel potentially isolates them from local communities (Barker, 2011).

Transport and urban planning policy has begun to address these concerns. In the US, UK and many countries internationally, 'Safe Routes to School' programmes have been implemented across a wide range of cities. These programs aim to promote walking and cycling to school (see McDonald et al., 2010). Similarly, in Australia the TravelSmart package of initiatives aims to help people individually reflect on their car travel and help them consider alternatives (see www.travelsmart.gov.au). Schools and businesses are also supported to develop travel plans that encourage walking and cycling. These initiatives are laudable in that they build upon, rather than ignore, the cultural underpinnings of familial car use and journeys to school. However, there is a limited evidentiary base for their successful and ongoing implementation (see, for example, the conclusions of Wen et al., 2008). Other alternatives have also emerged outside mainstream urban transport policy, in the domain of practice. In this section I provide an overview of two of these alternatives to familial automobility; that may point to some different ways of thinking about familial travel in the twenty-first century.

Carsharing

Carsharing is a phenomenon that recognises that the car is here to stay. It doesn't do away with the car altogether, but rather transforms the notion of hegemonic automobility through the ways in which cars are used, thought about and promoted. Carsharing, not to be confused with 'ride sharing' or 'car pooling,' involves a registered community using cars that are parked in dedicated car bays around the city. After becoming a member (much like a six- or 12-month gym membership), the cars can be booked (and extended) by the hour via the web or phone and accessed via smart card. Unlike traditional car rental, the vehicles in carsharing are scattered through local streets in a network, within walkable distance from most local residences and businesses.

Carsharing began in the realm of alternative economies and practices – being initiated and run by small cooperatives operating in European countries with good public transport systems, and often catering to a small group of users. However, in a number of cities, carsharing is becoming a more mainstream economic and social practice. Privately run businesses now run carsharing organisations in both the United States and the United Kingdom, including the entrance of the rental car company Hertz to the industry in 2010. Carshare members (carsharers) were initially identified as alternative or environmentally motivated. Burkhardt and Millard-Ball's (2006) research in the United States similarly finds that carsharers are likely to be social activists, innovators, or practical travellers. Yet carsharing has become a viable option for citizens in most developed cities around the world in the past five to ten years (Shaheen et al., 2009) and has a rapidly expanding presence across Asia (Shaheen and Cohen, 2007; Shaheen and Martin, 2010). It is estimated, for example, that between 2008 and 2010, carsharing membership increased by 52 per cent in the US (Botsman and Rogers, 2010). It is further estimated that by 2015, 4.4 million people in North America, and 5.5 million people in Europe, will belong to carsharing services (Botsman and Rogers, 2010: xvii).

This description of carsharing may seem at odds with familial automobility. Yet they are synchronous in a number of ways, of which two will be outlined here. The first is their utilisation of ICTs, and in particular their use of Web 2.0 technologies. Carsharing relies upon mobile and online booking systems. Smart cards connected to this booking system enable users to access the vehicle. Each car is equipped with a GPS through which cars and the kilometres travelled can be tracked, monitored and traced. This networked, accessible vehicle (Simpson, 2009) specifically exploits ICTs to reduce one element of car dependence – car ownership. It relies upon the key cultural correlates of car use – convenience (cars close to members house or workplace), flexibility (booking at any time for anytime) and individualism (each trip allows the traveller to go where they wish, when they wish), yet also recasts them through the lens of sharing ownership and access to a car. There is symmetry here between carsharing and familial relations that could be exploited by advocates of sustainable transport.

Second, carsharing is increasingly being advertised and used as a reliable transport alternative for families, especially those in inner cities. In Sydney, GoGet is the city's largest carsharing business, with an estimated 16,000 members and 600 cars scattered within a 10km radius of the central business district. A significant number of GoGet vehicles are now fitted with child restraints and are being advertised to families. The firm has been quoted in *The Sydney Morning Herald*:

> 'We've been pleasantly surprised by the uptake from families with kids and from people who had two cars but downsized to one and are using us as their second,' Mr Jeffreys said. The financial crisis had accelerated the trends 'because it's made people think really hard about whether they really need a private car.'
>
> (Munro, 2011)

Familial automobility is not opposed, but recrafted along more collaborative lines.

Walking School Buses

A second set of practice-based alternatives to familial automobility relate to the accomplishment of familial ideals like good mothering through non-car modes. Schwanen's (2011) review of women and cars alludes to some of these. In parts of Europe, for example, bicycles become part of the fabric of family life in much the same way as cars do in North America and Australia, although more often in inner cities than in suburbs more distant from CBDs. An increasingly prevalent alternative is walking school buses (WSBs). WSBs are designed to reduce the number of children being driven to school by car. As described by Kearns et al. (2003: 287):

> Walking school buses are a structured means of travel with an adult 'driver' at the front and a 'conductor' at the back. Children walk in a group along a set route picking up additional 'passengers' at specified stops along the way. They generally run regardless of weather, ensuring predictability in their operation.

Since their introduction in the late 1990s there has been a growth in the number of WSBs worldwide. They have become mainstream in transport policies like the 'Safe Routes to School' programme. WSBs explicitly confront parental safety anxieties that surround the chauffeuring of children by car. Children are escorted by an adult(s), addressing both stranger danger and traffic concerns. In not adding a journey to drop off/pick up children to a parent's commute, they also address parental time pressures. And, according to one of the few longitudinal assessments of WSBs, supervised walking 'helps to break down the social isolation often associated with automobilized family lifestyles' (Collins and Kearns, 2010: 7). Indeed, in populating streets with children and insisting that pedestrians have priority on streets, WSBs develop associations between walking and good parenting.

WSBs remain an incomplete alternative to familial automobility for a number of reasons. First, they are reliant on, and often struggle to guarantee, the work of volunteers (Kingham and Ussher, 2007). Familial routines change, especially with women's return to work as their children grow older. Attempts to recruit other social groups such as the elderly as volunteers or for token payment have been confronted with concerns about institutional and individual liability should an accident occur (McDonald and Alborg, 2009). WSBs have been more frequently established in neighbourhoods of higher socio-economic status, and more broadly the overwhelming involvement of women as volunteers (88 per cent) fails to address feminist concerns (Collins and Kearns, 2010). Nonetheless, the point to be drawn from the WSB example is the way they harness cultures of parenting in developing travel practice beyond familial automobility, and how, in turn, alternative travel constructs notions of good parenting.

8.   CONCLUSIONS

This chapter has provided an overview of the predominantly cultural literature on familial travel and its links with automobility. I have shown that gender structures family life and familial automobility in enduring ways: predominantly women rather than men coordinate and undertake the chauffeuring of children as part of their daily routine, supported by various forms of ICTs. It has also shown how cars and family life are linked through perceptions of 'good parenting': families with children value and rely upon the private automobile as a means to achieve what is defined as best for their children in a spatially elongated, temporally complex and constrained, and socially anxious context. The past five years, the chapter has argued, have seen the emergence of alternatives to, or more sustainable versions of, familial automobility that do not deny the importance of notions of good parenting. Walking school buses extend the notion of familial caring outwards to the scale of the neighbourhood and, in so doing, provide an alternative to automobility that can meet desires for good parenting. Likewise, travel modes such as carsharing do not rely on individual ownership of cars yet still provide the flexibility and convenience needed to manage complex familial routines. These examples, then, sketch possibilities for more sustainable travel futures that require thorough investigation.

REFERENCES

Barker, J. (2009), Driven to distraction? Children's experiences of car travel, *Mobilities*, **4**(1), 59–76.
Barker, J. (2011), 'Manic mums' and 'distant dads'? Gendered geographies of care and the journey to school, *Health & Place*, **17**(2), 413–21.

Basmajian, C. (2010), 'Turn on the radio, bust out a song': the experience of driving to work, *Transportation*, **37**(1), 59–84.

Bissell, D. (2009), On waiting, *Time & Society*, **18**(2–3), 410–13.

Blunt, A. and Dowling, R. (2006), *Home*, London: Routledge.

Botsman, R. and Rogers, R. (2010), *What's Mine is Yours: The Rise of Collaborative Consumption*, New York: Harper Business.

Burkhardt, J.E. and Millard-Ball, A. (2006), Who is attracted to carsharing? *Transportation Research Record*, **1986**, 98–105.

Collins, D. and Kearns, R.A. (2010), Walking school buses in the Auckland region: a longitudinal assessment, *Transport Policy*, **17**(1), 1–8.

Crane, R. (2007), Is there a quiet revolution in women's travel? Revisiting the gender gap in commuting, *Journal of the American Planning Association*, **73**(3), 298–316.

DeVault, M. (1994), *Feeding the Family: The Social Organization of Caring as Gendered Work*, Chicago: University Of Chicago Press.

Dowling, R. (2000), Cultures of mothering and car use in suburban Sydney: a preliminary investigation, *Geoforum*, **31**(3), 345–53.

Freeman, C. and Quigg, R. (2009), Commuting lives: children's mobility and energy use, *Journal of Environmental Planning and Management*, **52**(3), 393–412.

Fyhri, A., Hjorthol, R., Mackett, R.L., Fotel, T.N. and Kytta, M. (2011), Children's active travel and independent mobility in four countries: development, social contributing trends and measures, *Transport Policy*, **18**(5), 703–10.

Goodwin, K.J. (2010), Reconstructing automobility: the making and breaking of modern transportation, *Global Environmental Politics*, **10**(4), 70–75.

Hanson, S. (2010), Gender and mobility: new approaches for informing sustainability, *Gender Place and Culture*, **17**(1), 5–23.

Hjorthol, R.J. (2008), The mobile phone as a tool in family life: impact on planning of everyday activities and car use, *Transport Reviews*, **28**(3), 303–20.

Hjorthol, R. and Fyhri, A. (2009a), Do organized leisure activities for children encourage car-use? *Transportation Research Part A: Policy and Practice*, **43**(2), 209–18.

Hjorthol, R.J. and Fyhri, A. (2009b), Are we socializing our children to car use? *Sosialiserer vi våre barn til bilbruk*, **50**(2), 161–82 and 257–8.

Jain, J., Line, T. and Lyons, G. (2011), A troublesome transport challenge? Working round the school run, *Journal of Transport Geography*, **19**(6), 1608–15.

Jarvis, H. and Alvanides, S. (2008), School choice from a household resource perspective: preliminary findings from a north of England case study, *Community, Work and Family*, **11**(4), 385–403.

Kearns, R.A., Collins, D.C. and Neuwelt, P.M. (2003), The walking school bus: extending children's geographies? *Areas*, **35**(3), 285–92.

Kingham, S. and Ussher, S. (2007), An assessment of the benefits of the walking school bus in Christchurch, New Zealand, *Transportation Research Part A: Policy and Practice*, **41**(6), 502–10.

Lang, D., Collins, D. and Kearns, R. (2011), Understanding modal choice for the trip to school, *Journal of Transport Geography*, **19**(4), 509–14.

Lashlie, C. (2007), *He'll Be OK: Growing Gorgeous Boys into Good Men*, Auckland: Harper Collins Publishers New Zealand.

Laurier, E., Lorimer, H., Brown, B., Jones, O., Juhlin, O., Noble, A., Perry, M., Pica, D., Sormani, P., Strebel, I., Swan, L., Taylor, A., Watts, L. and Weilenmann, A. (2008), Driving and 'passengering': notes on the ordinary organization of car travel, *Mobilities*, **3**(1), 1–23.

Law, R. (1999), Beyond 'women and transport': towards new geographies of gender and daily mobility, *Progress in Human Geography*, **23**(4), 567–88.

Line, T., Chatterjee, K. and Lyons, G. (2010), The travel behaviour intentions of young people in the context of climate change, *Journal of Transport Geography*, **18**(2), 238–46.

Lucas, K., Blumenberg, E. and Weinberger, R. (eds) (2011), *Auto Motives: Understanding Car Use Behaviours*, Bingley: Emerald Group Publishing.

McDonald, N.C. and Alborg, A.E. (2009), Why parents drive children to school: implications for safe routes to school programs, *Journal of the American Planning Association*, **75**(3), 331–42.

McDonald, N.C., Deakin, E. and Aalborg, A.E. (2010), Influence of the social environment on children's school travel, *Preventive Medicine*, **50**(S1), S65–8.

Middleton, J. (2011), 'I'm on autopilot, I just follow the route': exploring the habits, routines, and decision- making practices of everyday urban mobilities, *Environment and Planning A*, **43**(12), 2857–77.

Munro, K. (2011), Families give the green light to car-sharing, *Sydney Morning Herald*, September 14.

National Transport Commission (2011), *Exploring the Opportunities for Forum*, discussion paper,

Smart Transport for a Growing Nation Project, September, www.ntc.gov.au/filemedia/Reports/SmarttransportNEW.pdf.

Schwanen, T. (2007), Gender differences in chauffeuring children among dual-earner families, *Professional Geographer*, **59**(4), 447–62.

Schwanen, T. (2011), Car use and gender: the case of dual-earner families in Utrecht, the Netherlands, in K. Lucas, E. Blumenberg and R. Weinberger (eds), *Auto Motives: Understanding Car Use Behaviours*, Bingley: Emerald Group Publishing.

Schwanen, T., Kwan, M.-P. and Ren, F. (2008), How fixed is fixed? Gendered rigidity of space-time constraints and geographies of everyday activities, *Geoforum*, **39**(6), 2109–21.

Shaheen, S.A. and Cohen, A.P. (2007), Growth in worldwide carsharing: an international comparison, *Transportation Research Record*, **1992**, 81–9.

Shaheen, S.A. and Martin, E. (2010), Demand for carsharing systems in Beijing, China: an exploratory study, *International Journal of Sustainable Transportation*, **4**(1), 41–55.

Shaheen, S.A., Cohen, A.P. and Chung, M.S. (2009), North American carsharing 10-year retrospective, *Transportation Research Record*, **2110**, 35–44.

Sheller, M. and Urry, J. (2000), The city and the car, *International Journal of Urban and Regional Research*, **24**(4), 737–57.

Shove, E. (1998), *Consuming Automobility*, SceneSusTech Discussion Paper, Department of Sociology, Trinity College, Dublin.

Simpson, C. (2009), Cars, climate and subjectivity: car sharing and resisting hegemonic automobile culture, *M/C Journal*, **12**(4).

Strazdins, L., Griffin, A.L., Broom, D.H., Banwell, C., Korda, R., Dixon, J., Paolucci, F. and Glover, J. (2011), Time scarcity: another health inequality? *Environment and Planning A*, **43**(3), 545–59.

Tranter, P.J. (2010), Speed kills: the complex links between transport, lack of time and urban health, *Journal of Urban Health-Bulletin of the New York Academy of Medicine*, **87**(2), 155–166.

Urry, J. (2004), The 'system' of automobility, *Theory Culture & Society*, **21**(4–5), 25–39.

Urry, J. (2008), Governance, flows, and the end of the car system? *Global Environmental Change-Human and Policy Dimensions*, **18**(3), 343–9.

Walsh, M. (2008), Gendering mobility: women, work and automobility in the United States, *History*, **93**(311), 376–95.

Watts, L. and Urry, J. (2008), Moving methods, travelling times, *Environment and Planning D: Society and Space*, **26**(5), 860–74.

Wen, L.M., Fry, D., Merom, D., Rissel, C., Dirkis, H. and Balafas, A. (2008), Increasing active travel to school: are we on the right track? A cluster randomised controlled trial from Sydney, Australia, *Preventive Medicine*, **47**(6), 612–18.

West, C. and Zimmerman, D.H. (1987), Doing gender, *Gender & Society*, **1**(2), 125–51.

Whitelegg, J. (1993), Time pollution, *Ecologist*, **23**(4), 131–4.

36 Old age and importance of the car in maintaining activity patterns in Scandinavia

Randi Hjorthol and Susanne Nordbakke

1. INTRODUCTION

Ageing of the population is occurring in many countries. In Europe the 'old-age dependency ratio' (people aged over 65 as a percentage of the population aged 20–64 years) will double in the period 2000 and 2050 according to Eurostat projections (Eurostat, 2008). In the Scandinavian countries (Denmark, Norway and Sweden), the proportion of people aged 65+ is expected to be about 25 per cent by 2050 (Eurostat, 2008). It is likely that this population will be a heterogeneous group regarding both age and other characteristics (Brunborg and Texmon, 2009).

Previous research has indicated a positive relationship between mobility measured as trip-making, out-of-home activities, access to transport and indicators of well-being and quality of life (e.g., Banister and Bowling, 2004; Mollenkopf et al., 2005; Spinney et al., 2009). For society in general, it is likely that the travel demand of the older population will have an impact on the entire transport system, i.e., in shaping the way transportation is planned, organized and managed. In Norway, about 95 per cent of the age group 35–55 years held a driving licence in 2009 (Vågane et al., 2011). In Denmark and Sweden, the proportion was a little lower, but the tendency was the same (SIKA, 2006; Kjær, 2005).

Previous research indicates that these generations will most likely retain their licence into old age (Hjorthol and Sagberg, 2000; Hakamies-Blomqvist et al., 2005). Improving health conditions, active lifestyles, increased access to a car and, for some groups, higher incomes have all created possibilities for more varied activity and extended travel than previous generations of older people had. On the other hand, a large proportion of the new generation of elderly will be in the oldest group, those 85 years of age and older, who may find it difficult getting about by car, public transport or even on foot.

Research on the mobility of older people has shown that Europeans are younger at the point they stop driving than Americans are (Hakamies-Blomqvist et al., 2004). Individuals with no driving licence or access to a car have to depend on others helping them meet their everyday activities (OECD, 2001). Car-use among older people has increased in European countries over time: in the UK (Oxley, 2000), Sweden (Krantz, 1999; Dillen, 2005), in Denmark (Magelund, 2001) and in Norway (Hjorthol, 2004; Hjorthol et al., 2010). These studies also indicate gender differences. In general, fewer women than men hold a driving licence. In Finland, Siren and Hakamies-Blomqvist (2004) found that mobility problems in the older population were significantly related to the absence of a driving licence and that older women did not have the same opportunity to drive as men did.

A British study from 1996 found the average cessation age for car-driving to be 72 years (Rabbitt et al., 1996), and in Sweden Rimmö and Hakamies-Blomqvist (2002) showed that there was a significant reduction in car-driving after the age of 75 years. Another Swedish study has indicated that women stop driving earlier than men (Dillen, 2005), just as in Finland (Siren and Hakamies-Blomqvist, 2004), the reasons cited being health, age and reduced sight (Marottoli et al., 2000). Gender, too, was a factor. Men, more than women, tend to carry on driving even if they have health problems (Freund and Szinovacz, 2002).

Marottoli et al. (1997) found that the decision to stop driving was among the strongest predictors of symptoms of depression in older people. A qualitative study from the USA of older women and driving cessation found that giving up car-driving resulted in loss of spontaneity, loss of control and fear of being a burden on the family (Bauer et al., 2003).

In this chapter, we examine the development of daily travel among older groups in Scandinavian countries in a 20-year perspective. We study the transport situation for older people today based on Norwegian data, while focusing particularly on use of the car and its role in daily transport. Finally, we address the question of the relation between welfare/well-being and significance of the car.

2.   OLDER PEOPLE'S MOBILITY IN A 20-YEAR PERSPECTIVE

Based on results from national travel surveys (NTS) in Norway, Denmark and Sweden, cohort analysis was carried out to examine the development of daily mobility among older people (Hjorthol et al., 2010). The results presented here are based on this article. The NTS go back to the beginning of the 1980s in almost the same form, and they are to a large degree comparable between countries. The Swedish data are from 1981 and 2006, the Danish data from 1984/5 and 2005/6, and the Norwegian data from 1985 and 2005. Here, we concentrate on access to a car and car-use (for more details of the data and analysis, see Hjorthol et al., 2010).

The analysis carried out is a cohort analysis. In cohort analysis, three effects can be examined: cohort, period and age effect. The cohort effect refers to the effects of being born at a specific time in history. Examining cohort effects can show how differences in socialization and experiences between different generations can vary, and how specific characteristics will follow the cohort. Intra-cohort comparisons are made by following the same cohort at different points in time. The period effect refers to effects limited to a specific period of time and applies to all cohorts. Comparisons between the same age categories at two different times are used to investigate the period effect. The age effect refers to the effects of growing older and is associated with the life span and the ageing process as such. Age effect is central in gerontology but can be hard to distinguish from the other effects because these are always so closely interrelated.

As stated in the introduction, a driving licence and having access to a car are important factors determining mode of transport. Access to a car increases freedom of choice and the opportunity to take part in all sorts of different activities.

Figure 36.1 indicates the share of different cohorts of Norwegian women who held a driving licence in 1985 (lower curve) and 2005 (upper curve). The connecting lines follow the cohorts and their development and illustrate the period effect for a given cohort.

The overall period effect is significant for all countries. In Norway, the percentage of females 40+ holding a driving licence increased from 54 to 84 per cent (p < 0.001,

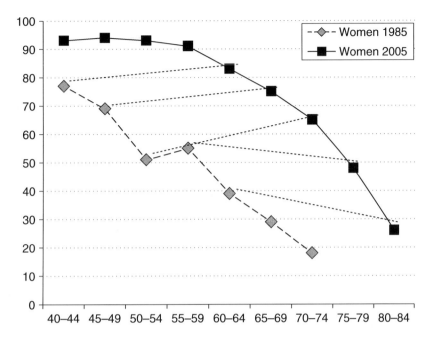

Figure 36.1 Driving licence for cohorts of Norwegian women in 1986 (N = 792) and 2005 (N = 4,884), per cent

z-test), in Denmark from 46 to 80 per cent (p < 0.001, z-test) and in Sweden from 52 to 80 per cent (p < 0.001, z-test), i.e., very similar development. The increase is found in most age groups in all three countries. The share of car licence-holding among Norwegian cohorts during this period remained very much the same. Women aged 40–44 and 50–54 in 1985 obtained a driving licence probably as a result of increased female employment, higher average incomes and increased gender equality.

In Denmark too, the driving licence level among female cohorts has been maintained during this period (25 years). The results are the same for Sweden, apart from the oldest cohort (60–64 in 1984/5), i.e., the only one in which the percentage of licence-holders has dropped (from 50 to 35 per cent at 80–84 years in 2005/6) (p < 0.001, z-test). The age differences are significant in all three countries in both years, but the levels of licence-holders are higher in 2005/6 than in 1981/5.

The general picture from these three countries is that women retain their driving licence up to a high age, with a large and significant period effect observed in all age groups. The age effect seems of less importance. The overall period effect for men in Norway is less than for women, from 94 to 96 per cent (p < 0.001, z-test). In Denmark, too, there is a significant period effect from 86 to 84 per cent (p < 0.001, z-test).

Driving licence-holders among male cohorts are reduced for the oldest during this period, while numbers for the other age groups are maintained. In Norway, there is a reduction from 97 to 88 per cent (p < 0.001) for those 64–9 years in 1985, and 80–84 years in 2005. In Denmark, the reduction is from 88 to 68 per cent (p < 0.001) among men 55–9 years in 1981 and 80–84 years in 2006, 25 years later. In Sweden, the reduction is smaller, from approximately 90 per cent in 1984/5 to 83 per cent (p < 0.05, z-test) in 2005/6 for those aged 60–64 in 1984/5. The differences by age are much less for men than for women.

While the percentages of licence-holders among Norwegian and Danish female cohorts have remained the same, and to a certain degree increased, those of their male counterparts have partly dropped, but from a much higher level of licence-holding. This is probably due to the fact that older women with a driving licence are a more 'select' group than men. Since most men in these cohorts have a licence, there are more variations in health, income and other socio-economic characteristics within the male group than among women with a licence. When holding a driving licence becomes as common for women as for men (as is virtually the case today), both the level of licence-holding and the reduction by age will probably be more like those of men in similar age groups. In the highest age groups, the different life situations of men and women often have an impact on mobility, as discussed later in relation to access to a car. The gender differences were greater in 1985 than in 2005 and in 2005/6 marked primarily after the age of 60 years. The increase in number of female car-drivers was partly a result of enhanced gender equality in the labour market and higher incomes.

Are people's travel habits retained when ageing? Shopping trips seem to be important after retirement for both women and men in all three countries. The total reduction in number of trips by age is thus primarily connected with the decline in work-related journeys (Hjorthol et al., 2010). Figure 36.2 shows the development of car-use in this period for women in Norway. There is a significant and strong increase in the number of car

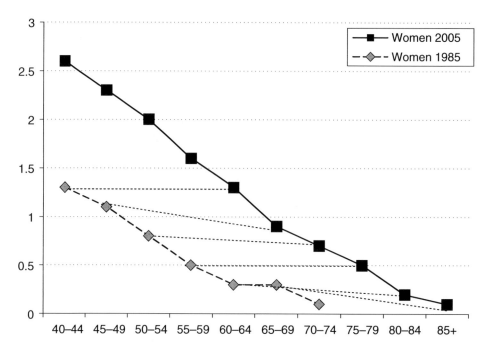

Figure 36.2   Average number of trips per day by car as driver for women in 1985 (N = 1,020) and 2005 (N = 4,883), Norway

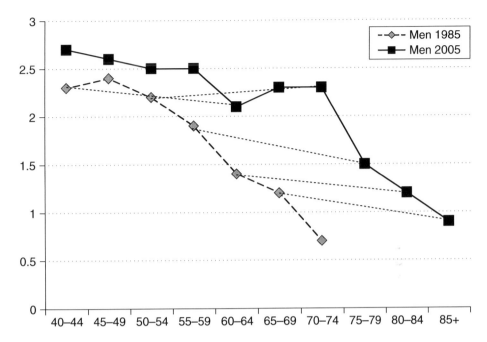

Figure 36.3 *Average number of trips per day by car as driver for men in 1985*
(N = 1,016) and 2005 (N = 4,847), Norway

trips as driver in Denmark and Norway (p < 0.01, t-test), and in all age groups (minimum p < 0.05 p < 0.01, t-test). Following the cohorts indicates stability in car-use over the lifespan. There is no significant reduction for female cohorts in Denmark and Norway.

This pattern is also found among the male groups in Norway (Figure 3), but the number of car trips is higher for men than for women. In only one of the cohorts (aged 50–54 in 1985) is there a reduced number of car trips in the period (p < 0.05, t-test). The number of car trips during the life span of Danish men is also maintained. Comparing the countries shows a lower number of car trips in Denmark than in Norway, for both men and women, corresponding to the earlier discussion about the differences between the countries.

A strong significant period effect was identified among women in regard to car-use and licence-holding. There was a marked increase in the share of women in the examined age groups holding a driving licence from 1984/5 to 2005/6 in all three countries, with most cohorts maintaining their licence up into old age. The percentages of licence-holding among some of the Norwegian cohorts have also increased during this period. This is to some extent related to the fact that the 'new' generations of women get a driving licence more readily than the older generations, but also to the fact that women in higher age groups (around 50 years) held a driving licence in this period as a result of increased female employment, higher general incomes and increased gender equality. The age differences are significant in all three countries, but the level is much higher in 2006 than in 1981/1985. Among men, the period effect is much smaller, but they started at a much higher level of licence-holding than women in all three countries.

3.   SOME CHARACTERISTICS OF THOSE WITH AND WITHOUT ACCESS TO A CAR

Access to a car, although important, is only one of several modes of travel, but what impact does it have on the total mobility of older people? And what is the difference between those who have access to a car whenever they want, and those who have neither a driving licence nor a car available? In this section we examine some of these questions and present a descriptive analysis of the results from the Norwegian national travel survey of 2009. We concentrate on two groups of older people by age, the group from 67 (retirement age in Norway) to 75 years and those over 75 years. First, we describe those within these age groups who have/do not have access to a car (Table 36.1).

Table 36.1   Socio-demographic description of older people without a driving licence and access to a car and those who have a licence and always have access to a car

Age	67–75 years		75+ years	
	No licence, no car	Licence, always available car	No licence, no car	Licence, always available car
Gender[a]				
Male	29%	54%	14%	61%
Female	71%	46%	86%	39%
Total	100%	100%	100%	100%
N	178	1,410	898	1,158
Marital status[a]				
Single	85%	24%	86%	38%
Married/cohabitant	15%	76%	14%	62%
Total	100%	100%	100%	100%
N	178	1,397	895	1,151
Education[a]				
Compulsory schooling	46%	27%	55%	33%
High school/gymnasium	32%	37%	32%	43%
University lower grade	15%	19%	9%	13%
University higher grade	7%	17%	4%	11%
Total	100%	100%	100%	100%
N	178	1,395	888	1,153
Income (individual) NOK[a, b]				
Under 200,000	50%	27%	65%	40%
200,000–299,999	41%	34%	28%	32%
300,000–399,999	7%	22%	7%	19%
400,000–499,999	2%	8%	0%	6%
500,000 +	0%	9%	0%	3%
Total	100%	100%	100%	100%
N	146	1,257	627	1,016

Notes:
a   67–74 p < 0.000, χ^2, 75+ p < 0.000, χ^2
b   100 NOK = approx. USD 18.

Table 36.2   Number and length of daily trips by age, driving licence and access to a car, Norway 2009

Age Trips per day	67–75 years		75+ years	
	No licence, no car	Licence, car always available	No licence, no car	Licence, car always available
Total number of daily trips[1]	1.25	2.84	1.19	2.23
Trips on foot[2]	0.69	0.57	0.60	0.48
Trips by cycle[3]	0.12	0.06	0.04	0.04
Trips as a driver[4]	0.00	1.80	0.00	1.39
Trips as a car passenger[5]	0.12	0.29	0.24	0.22
Trips by public transport[6]	0.29	0.10	0.28	0.08
N	178	1,410	898	1,158
Total travel distance per day km	10.1km	32.1km	5.4km	22.1km
Total time travelling per day min	42 min	66 min	24 min	53 min

Notes:
1   Between age groups $p < 0.000$ Anova. Between no car, no car and licence and available car $p < 0.000$ Anova.
2   Between age groups n.s. Anova. Between no car, no car and licence and available car $p < 0.05$ Anova.
3   Between age groups $p < 0.02$ Anova. Between no car, no car and licence and available car n.s.
4   Between age groups $p < 0.000$ Anova. Between no car, no car and licence and available car $p < 0.000$ Anova.
5   Between age groups n.s. Between no car, no car and licence and available car n.s.
6   Between age groups $p < 0.01$ Anova. Between no car, no car and licence and available car $p < 0.000$ Anova.

Table 36.1 indicates that access to a car in old age is clearly related to socio-demographic variables such as gender, marital status, education and income. Women, living alone, with low education and income have rather less access to a car than men, married or cohabitating couples and others with high income and education. The characteristics of the two groups – people with a driving licence and available car, on the one hand, and others without a car or driving licence, on the other – are quite different in regard to resources and gender, both for those 67 to 75 years and for those from 75 years and older. The average age without a licence and access to a car is 80 years, and with a licence and car is 74 years. Table 36.2 gives a very good picture of the differences in mobility of these two groups.

The group with neither a driving licence nor a car have about half as many daily trips as those with these resources. The same is found in both age groups (age has a significant impact on travel activity). In addition to trips as driver, the use of public transport differs significantly between the groups (more details on purpose of travel are given later in the chapter).

4.   CAR USE AND WELL-BEING

Previous research points to a positive relation between mobility and well-being. The question analysed in this section is whether access to a car/driving licence has an impact on well-being, which is a fuzzy concept with numerous conceptualizations (Nordbakke and Schwanen, forthcoming). In the study presented here, the link between the car/being able to drive and well-being was explored from two different angles: the first asks whether the car entails qualities that contribute to well-being. The other asks whether the car/ability to drive has an impact on participation in activities that generate well-being. These two different approaches to well-being applied to explore these questions are further described below.

The analysis is based on data from five focus group interviews carried out in 2008 and a national representative survey conducted in the fall of 2010 among 4,723 people aged 67 and above. Both data sources covered questions about daily travel, transport mode use, activity participation and the link between ability to drive/access to a car and travel and well-being. The focus groups were conducted for men and women in separate groups in two different geographical contexts: two in the rural town of Stjørdal (approximately 20,000 inhabitants) and three in Oslo (approximately 600,000 inhabitants), the capital of Norway.

For more information about the focus groups and the survey, see Hjorthol and Nordbakke (2009) and Hjorthol et al. (2011).

In What Ways Does the Car Contribute to Older People's Well-being?

In the focus groups, we asked the participants what they perceived as the most important advantages about being able to drive, in what way the car/being able to drive contributes to their well-being and how they experience/think they will feel about the loss of their driving licence. In this way we tried to identify how and why the car and ability to drive contributes to well-being.

As a point of departure for the analyses we applied a definition of well-being developed by the Norwegian psychologist Siri Næss (1974) that includes four dimensions:

1. *Being active*, in the sense of having an appetite for life, being interested in things outside oneself, having the energy to realize one's interests, not feeling tired and exhausted, having the freedom to choose, feeling in control of one's own actions, having the possibility to realize and use one's abilities.
2. *Having good interpersonal relations/relationships*, meaning having a close and whole-hearted (or warm) relationship with at least one person, having contact with other people, feeling friendship, loyalty and community/fellowship within a group (e.g., friends, neighbours, colleagues).
3. *Having self-esteem*, that is, feeling self-confident, feeling confident in one's own abilities and competence, being able to manage different tasks and challenges, feeling of being useful, feeling of satisfaction with one's own efforts.
4. *Having rich and intense experiences*, in the sense of being open to experiences of the outside world, experiencing beauty, feeling of harmony, having deep feelings of joy and satisfaction, feeling that life is rich and giving, absent of feelings of emptiness, pain and discomfort.

The focus group interviews revealed several ways in which the car and being able to drive contributes to these dimensions. This is described in the following.

Being active

Geographical setting (urban–rural) determines how important the car is for being able to travel and attend activities in daily life. The participants living in bigger cities or centrally in rural towns can manage daily life quite well without a car, but for those living in the peripheries of Stjørdal, having a car in the household or not is almost like a 'to be' or 'not to be', as there is no alternative transport. On the question concerning the day they will have to give up their driving licence, some say they will have to move to more central areas, some think they will be more dependent on others and yet others say that they will be tied to their homes:

> If they take my car (driving licence) away from me, then everything will go wrong . . . the car means everything to me, it really does.
>
> (Jarle, 76, Stjørdal)

In Stjørdal, the transport alternatives are few. The people living in the peripheries of the municipality do not have access to public transport, except for a school bus running in the morning into the centre of Stjørdal and then back again in the afternoon. To many, taxis are the only alternative, which is a too costly alternative for most.

Some participants argue that the car becomes more important with age, because walking capacity is reduced. They stress the importance of the compensatory qualities of the car that allow them to lead an active life outside their home. For those who have problems with using other means of transportation or do not have a sufficient public transport service where they live, the ability to drive gives them autonomy in the sense that they do not have to be dependent on others for transport.

The focus group interviews show that the car entails qualities beyond those of just travelling from A to B, qualities that are highly regarded independently of residential location. Being able to drive is closely associated with freedom: 'It is freedom, sitting behind the wheel, being the boss, bringing yourself from A to B' (Roar, 76, Oslo). Being free does not just mean being able to attend activities that are planned for and to transport oneself, but also the possibility of acting on impulse, choosing oneself when and where to go and when and where to stop, as described by one woman:

> You just have to fill up the tank, and then you can go wherever you want to go, to the mountains, on vacation, you just have to get into the car and go, and you can stop wherever you want.
>
> (Ruth, 71, Oslo)

Being free is also the ability to determine how long one can stay in one place:

> And then you can stay in the shopping mall for longer than you could if you ride with someone else. Then you have more time to take a closer look at things you want to buy.
>
> (Inga, 84, Stjørdal)

The freedom that a car provides, and the ability to drive, gives older people control of their lives in the sense that they can make choices and realize their purpose. The freedom to transport oneself to a desired destination means the possibility to visit family and friends and take part in leisure activities and hence for 'Having good interpersonal relations', which is another important dimension in Næss's definition of well-being.

Self-esteem and a positive self-image
Even though many of the participants who have stopped driving get lifts with family and friends for some purposes and on special occasions, most are reluctant to accept this kind of help for ordinary daily activities. Some say they cannot base their lives on their family, others say they do not want to inconvenience others. For many, reluctance to ask for help with transport relates to a desire to manage daily life for as long as possible on their own. In Oslo, they say they can manage everyday life as long as they can walk, whereas in the peripheries of Stjørdal it is all about being able to drive.

Some participants explain that being able to manage on one's own is especially important when getting older despite the view that older people are 'needy' and 'cannot manage on their own'. Being able to drive gives older people the chance to manage their daily travels on their own, something that contributes to a positive self-image, which is explained in the following:

> Interviewer: How [does this contribute to a positive self-image]?
> Torgny (76, Stjørdal): That you feel you can manage things.
> Bjørg (79, Stjørdal): Yes, that you are on your own.
> Interviewer: Is this issue with self-image more important now than when you were younger?
> Bjørg: You do not have so much to prove [when you are young].
> Interviewer: Do you have more to prove now?
> Bjørg: Yes, you want to show that you can do it, that you can manage, that you do as you please . . . When you are retired you are more on the sidelines than when you were working. I feel I have more to prove now than before. When you are retired, others pity you and think that you cannot manage. That annoys me.
> Gunvor (77, Stjørdal): I agree with you. They think you cannot manage this and that.

Many drivers help others with transport by taking their friends to activities or by helping them with transport of goods. Some pick up their grandchildren at kindergarten or at school.

> We are a group that got together to drink coffee once a week, but that was not enough, then we got two fixed days a week, and now it is three fixed days a week. Previously, there were just as many men as women. But the years have gone by. Now it is only me that sits there with a bunch of widows. I drive them all. I am so lucky that they still let me drive them. And I have the time for it.
>
> (Roald, 81, Stjørdal)

This man is not just useful to others, by giving his widow friends a lift he fills up his days providing transport and attending coffee meetings.

Having rich and intense experiences
Many experience pleasure when driving, as one man puts it: 'Driving is part of my personality, I love driving' (Roar, 76, Oslo). The driving itself, the possibility to do things on impulse and lead an active life when being able to drive can all contribute to rich and intense experiences.

But not everybody is equally fond of driving, as Peder (78) from Sjørdal puts it: 'I look at the car more as a utility article. The car is OK, it is not that. But it is perhaps more a necessary evil.'

Well-being – With and Without the Car

While the previous section explored how and in what ways the car and driving can contribute to well-being in the eyes of the older people themselves, we move on to explore the impact of the car on travel and participation in activities outside the home that can generate well-being. In this section, well-being is defined according to the theoretical framework developed by the Finnish sociologist Erik Allardt (1975), to whom well-being pertains to needs satisfaction along three dimensions:

- *To have*; the material level of living (welfare) and the need for material resources (i.e., work, education, money).
- *To love*; the non-material aspects of life and more specifically the need for social relations, such as friendship and family ties.
- *To be*; the need for self-realization, positive judgement of oneself and taking an active part in society (which might be fulfilled through, for example, education, work and friendships).

These components are partly values by themselves, partly resources (Allardt, 1975), and they are important as input in a welfare arena and as results. Employment, having a job, provides income and is at the same time often an important aspect of self-realization. Thus, employment can be seen as belonging to both having and being. Similarly, going to the cinema together with friends can belong to both 'to love' and 'to be'. The point of departure for the following analyses is that transport and travel can contribute to participation in activities outside the home where these different needs can be satisfied – and that this participation generates well-being – in terms of *having*, *loving* and *being*.

To Allardt (1975), well-being is both subjective (defined by the experiences of the individuals) and objective (defined by the objective circumstances of an individual). Hence, in the analyses we have derived needs satisfaction from both the objective circumstances of overt activity participation and people's subjective assessment of satisfaction with activity needs.

In the survey, participants were asked to state how often they attended different activities outside the home and also if there were any activities they would like to attend more often if they could and, if so, what kind of activities. Activities such as 'shopping for groceries', 'shopping for other goods', 'going to the bank or post office' and 'visits to the doctor, dentist or physiotherapist' are used as indicators of the need *to have*. 'Visits to friends and family' is the indicator of the need *to love*, and finally 'going for a walk', 'going to the gym/doing exercise (outside the home)', 'going to meetings in organizations, clubs, etc.' and 'going to the cinema, theatre, concerts, etc.' are indicators of the need *to be*.

Figure 36.4 shows participation at least once a week in different activities among drivers and non-drivers.

Only when it comes to seeing a doctor, dentist, physiotherapist, etc., do the non-drivers report a higher participation in activities; this is more evident at a monthly rating: While 33 per cent of non-drivers visit a doctor at least once a month, only 24 per cent of drivers do. This is probably related to difference in health status. In the survey, 73 per cent of the

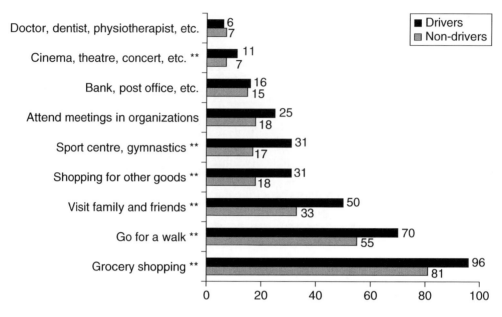

Note: ** p < 0.000 (chi-square test). The number of valid answers for drivers varies between 2,745 and 2,892 and for non-drivers between 1,047 and 1,183. Respondents answering 'not possible' are not included.

Figure 36.4   Participation in different activities at least once a week among driving licence-holders and others without a licence, per cent

drivers (N = 3,014) reported that their health was good/extremely good (self-evaluation of health status), while only 42 per cent of the non-drivers (N = 1,263) did the same.

There is no difference between the drivers and non-drivers in visiting the bank or the post office. For all other activities, the drivers report a higher degree of participation than the non-drivers. Hence, these results indicate that those with a driving licence have a higher degree of fulfilment of needs related to having, loving and being, and hence experience greater well-being. However, such a conclusion is based solely on objective measures. It might be the case that those without a driving licence have less of a need to participate in activities outside the home. To measure subjective needs satisfaction, the respondents were asked to report if there were any activities that they would like to attend more often if they could. Some of the respondents reported that a specific activity was not possible. Lack of activities in which to participate or bad health can be reasons for answering that participation in one activity is not possible. In the following, satisfaction with activity participation is explored for those who report that participation is possible.

Figure 36.5 shows the difference between drivers and non-drivers in fulfilment of activity participation.

With the exception of exercising/gymnastics outside the home, the non-drivers to a greater degree report that they would like to attend more of all the given activities than the drivers. This indicates a lower degree of satisfaction of the needs to have, to love and to be among the non-drivers and, hence, that they have a lower degree of well-being.

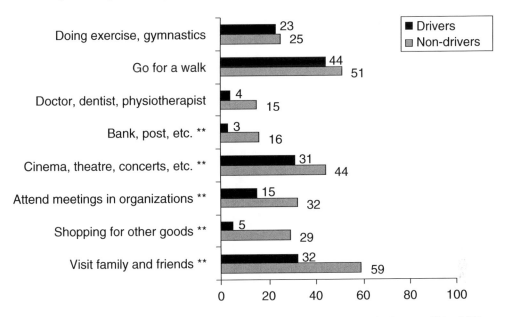

Note: ** p < 0.000 (chi-square test). The number of valid answers for drivers varies between 597 and 962 and for non-drivers between 2,081 and 2,653. Respondents answering 'not possible' are not included.

Figure 36.5 Percentage of drivers and non-drivers that report they would like to attend a given activity more often

However, having a driving licence in old age in developed countries is positively correlated with being a man (Rosenbloom, 2000; Oxley, 2000; Dillen, 2005; Hjorthol et al., 2012), lower age (Rosenbloom, 2000; Oxley, 2000; Hjorthol et al., 2012), in better health and living in a rural area (Hjorthol et al., 2012). In order to control for such confounding factors, we conducted multivariate analyses of unfilled satisfaction with grocery shopping, visits to family and friends and attending meetings in organizations, clubs, etc., activities that represent the needs to have, to love and to be, respectively. These analyses show that holding a driving licence has an independent effect on satisfaction with participation in both of these activities (see Table 36.3). These analyses confirm our above conclusion that the non-drivers have a lower degree of satisfaction of both the need to have, to love and to be and hence lower degree of well-being than the drivers.

5. LIFE AFTER THE CAR

Næss's approach to well-being to a great degree captures the psychological benefits of driving and different needs (also captured with Allardt's approach). In the survey, people who had given up their driving licence were asked to answer a range of statements about changes in life in this regard. These claims are meant to reflect the psychological benefits of the car and the link between a car/driving licence and satisfaction of different needs, which are imputed here from activity participation (Table 36.4).

Table 36.3   *Would like to do more grocery shopping, to make more visits to friends and family and to attend more meetings in organizations, clubs, etc. (logistic regression)*

	Would like to do more grocery shopping*			Would like to make more visits to friends and family**			Would like to attend more meetings in organizations, clubs, etc.***		
	B	Sig.	Exp(B)	B	Sig.	Exp(B)	B	Sig.	Exp(B)
Age	.064	.000	1.066	.024	.000	1.025	.030	.000	1.031
Man[1]	−.244	.125	.783	−.056	.476	.945	−.166	.109	.847
Driving licence[2]	−1.414	.000	.243	−.846	.000	.429	−.722	.000	.486
Place of residence[3]		.131			.142			.304	
The four largest cities in Norway (Oslo/Bergen/Trondheim/Stavanger)	−.468	.012	.626	−.232	.024	.793	−.153	.243	.859
The surrounding municipalities of the four largest cities	−.224	.273	.799	−.176	.113	.839	−.138	.325	.871
The six next largest cities in Norway	−.361	.118	.697	−.149	.229	.862	−.267	.098	.766
Smaller towns	−.169	.370	.844	−.024	.819	.977	−.258	.060	.773
Poor health[4]	1.341	.000	3.823	.952	.000	2.590	1.133	.000	3.106
Constant	6.461	.000	.002	1.628	.001	.196	3.077	.000	.046

Notes: Reference values:
1   Women.
2   Do not have a driving licence.
3   Densely populated areas.
4   Do not have health problems (self-reported).
   *   N = 3,399 ('not possible' (N = 230) not included), Nagelkerke R square = 0.237.
  **   N = 3,395 ('not possible' (N = 156) not included), Nagelkerke R square = 0.107.
 ***   N = 3,003 ('not possible' (N = 501) not included), Nagelkerke R square = 0.105.

The most important consequences relate to reductions in freedom, independence, pleasure of driving and control of life. These are relatively greater than the effect on actual travel and participation in activities (that can generate well-being). Still, many experience problems with travel and activity participation, especially with leisure activities in the evening (68 per cent), and almost two out of three even report difficulties with grocery shopping. Women to a higher degree report that loss of their driving licence had no effect on their travel, while more men than women report that they have lost the possibility to help others with transport. More men than women report that they miss driving itself because they found it pleasurable. Apart from these differences between men and women, there are no other significant differences in how they experience the consequences of giving up their driving licence.

Table 36.4   Consequences of giving up the driving licence: percentages of men and women, respectively, agreeing with a given claim (the number of valid answers varies between 111 and 160 for men and 239 and 410 for women)

	Men	Women	Total	N	p
It has had no influence on my travels, I travel by other mode of transport	46	57	54	449	0.045
It has become more difficult to get to the doctor, physiotherapist and dentist	59	52	54	461	n.s.
It has become more difficult to participate in leisure activities in daytime	66	56	59	407	n.s.
It has become more difficult to shop for groceries	67	59	62	490	n.s.
It has become more difficult to participate in leisure activities in the evenings	67	69	68	440	n.s.
I miss the car, it gave me a sense of control in life	78	67	70	460	n.s.
I took great pleasure in driving and now I miss it	83	70	74	457	0.007
I have lost the possibility to help others with transport	87	75	79	350	0.046
I have the lost the possibility to go when and where I want	86	78	80	465	n.s.
I have become more dependent on others for transport	81	84	83	570	n.s.

Note: The final column gives the *p*-values for significant chi square tests. 'n.s.' = not significant (*p* > 0.05).

6.   SUMMARY AND CONCLUSION

Cohort analysis of older generations indicates that the share of licence-holding in the period from the beginning of the 1980s to 2005/6 of different generations of women in Denmark, Norway and Sweden has remained the same or slightly increased. The general picture in these three countries is that women retain their licence up to a high age, but not quite as high as the men do. In this period, however, the level of licence-holders among all women in these age groups has increased. Car-use increased significantly for all groups of women in the period. The three younger cohorts' car-use habits remained static throughout the period, their driving just as much (number of trips) at an age of 65–79 years as when 40–54. The same pattern is found among the male groups, although the number of car trips is higher for men than for women. This cohort analysis indicates that social context and historical period are important considerations when studying the development of older people's travel patterns. Age itself is not enough. The descriptive statistics from the Norwegian Travel Survey 2009 illustrate the social distribution of licenced drivers and car ownership. Gender, marital status, age, education and income are all variables that impact on access to transport resources.

Our focus group interviews show that the car contributes to well-being along many different dimensions beyond that of transport from A to B: to a sense of freedom and independence, to the possibility to act on impulse, to be in control of life and a positive self-image. Moreover, driving itself is pleasurable. The survey shows that the emotional experiences along these dimensions are greater than the practical implications experienced on travel and other activities when giving up driving. Nevertheless, the majority experience problems with travel and activity participation when they are unable to drive.

When comparing those with and without a driving licence, we also find significant differences in needs satisfaction – measured in terms of (overt) participation in activities and subjective satisfaction with activity participation. We conclude this study by suggesting that the car entails dimensions that contribute to well-being beyond simply transport from A to B, i.e., to greater well-being in terms of needs satisfaction and activity participation.

These results indicate both the positive impact the car has on older people and the social inequity in access to this resource and consequences this might have for older people. Even though availability of a car is increasing among older people, there will still be a need for transport supply catering for drivers and non-drivers alike. There is a clear indication of gender effects when it comes to the different aspects of transport. Older women will be the group in most need of adjusted supply, irrespective of where they live. But the problems and demands will be more articulated and severe in rural than in urban areas, as we have seen in this study. The quality of public transport supply varies between urban and rural areas, and a considerable number of older people, especially those over 80, have problems using it (Hjorthol, 2012). As shown in this study, mobility and being able to carry out everyday activities are central aspects of the welfare and quality of life of older people. Adjusted public transport, special transport services and comprehensive land-use and transport planning to reduce distances are important in the mobility of older people, especially those who do not drive. Refresher courses for older drivers have had a positive effect in Norway (Levin et al., 2012). Rather than banning older people from driving altogether, an evaluation of their ability to drive could be made, and a restricted driving licence issued would be a step in the right direction for securing their mobility. For older people this would be significant in their taking part in different welfare arenas and would give them more freedom and control of everyday life.

REFERENCES

Allardt, E. (1975), *Att Ha At Älska At Vara – Om välfärd i Norden*, Lund: Argos förlag AB.
Banister, D. and Bowling, A. (2004), Quality of life for the elderly: the transport dimension, *Transport Policy*, **11**, 105–15.
Bauer, M.J., Rottunda, S. and Adler, G. (2003), Older women and driving cessation, *Qualitative Social Work*, **2**, 309–25.
Brunborg, H. and Texmon, I. (2009), *Befolkningsframskrivning 2009–2060*, Økonomiske analyser 4/2009, Statistics Norway, Oslo.
Dillen, J. (2005), *Äldre personers resvanor och aktiviteter. Resultat från undersökningar med personer i alderen 65 år och äldre*, Stockholm: Transek AB.
Eurostat (2008), *Population and Social Conditions*, Statistics in Focus, European Commission.
Freund, B. and Szinovacz, M. (2002), Effects of cognition on driving involvement among the oldest old: variations by gender and alternative transportation opportunities, *Gerontologist*, **42**(5), 621–33.
Hakamies-Blomqvist, L., Sirén, A. and Davidse, R. (2004), *Older Drivers: A Review*, VTI rapport 497A. VTI, Linlöping. Statens väg-och transportforskningsinstitut, Linköping.
Hakamies-Blomqvist, L., Henriksson, P., Anund, A. and Sörensen, G. (2005), *Fyrtiotalisterna som framtida äldre trafikanter*, VTI, Linköping, Statens väg-och transportforskningsinstitut, Linköping.
Hjorthol, R. (2004), Kan utviklingen i mobilitet og reisevaner fortelle noe om likestilling?' *Kvinner, køn og forskning*, **13**(1), 18–30.
Hjorthol, R. (2012), Transport resources, mobility and unmet transport needs in old age, *Ageing and Society*, available on CJO 2012 doi:10.1017/ SO144686X12000517.
Hjorthol, R. and Nordbakke, S. (2008), *Bilens betydning for eldre gruppers velferd og livskvalitet*, TØI-rapport 1000/2008, Oslo: Transportøkonomisk institutt.

Hjorthol, R. and Sagberg, F. (2000), Introductory report: Norway, in S. Rosenbloom (ed.), *Transport and Aging of the Population*, Paris: Economic Research Centre.

Hjorthol, R., Levin, L. and Sirén, A. (2010), Mobility in different generations of older persons: the development of daily travel in different cohorts in Denmark, Norway and Sweden, *Journal of Transport Geography*, **18**, 624–33.

Hjorthol, R., Nordbakke, S., Vågane, L., Levin, L., Sirén, A. and Ulleberg, P. (2011), *Eldres mobilitet og velferd – utvikling, reisebehov og tiltak*, TØI-rapport 1179/2011, Oslo: Transportøkonomisk institutt.

Hjorthol, R., Nordbakke, S. and Vågane, L. (2012), Transportbehov og transportressurser blant eldre [Transport need and transport resources among older people], *Tidsskrift for velferdsforskning*, **15**(1), 37–52.

Kjær, M.R. (2005), *Ædre bilister – mobilitet og risiko i trafikken*, Notat 1/2005, Danish Transport Research Institute, Lyngby.

Krantz, L.-G. (1999), *Rörlighetens mångfald och förändring. Befolkningens dagliga resande i Sverige 1978 og 1996*, Gothenburg: Handelshögskolan vid Göteborgs Universitet.

Levin, L., Ulleberg, P., Siren, A. and Hjorthol, R. (2012), *Measures to Enhance Mobility Among Older People in Scandinavia: A Literature Review of Best Practice*, VTI rapport 749 A, Linköping: VTI.

Magelund, L. (2001), *Eldres Automobilitet*, Transportrådets nyhetsbrev nr. 4, Copenhagen.

Marottoli, R.A., Mendes, C.F., Glass, T.A., Williams, C.S., Cooney, L.M., Berkman, L.F. and Tinetti, M.E. (1997), Driving cessation and increased depressive symptoms: prospective evidence from the New Haven EPESE, *Journal of American Geriatrics Society*, **45**, 202–6.

Marottoli, R.A., Mendes, C.F., Glass, T.A. and Williams, C.S. (2000), Consequences of driving cessation: decreased out-of-home activity levels, *Journal of Gerontology: Social Sciences*, **55**(6), 334–40.

Mollenkopf, H., Marcellini, F., Ruoppila, I., Széman, Z. and Tacken, M. (2005), *Enhancing Mobility in Later Life: Personal Coping, Environmental Resources and Technical Support: The Out-of-home Mobility of Older Adults in Urban and Rural Regions in Five European Countries*, Amsterdam: IOS Press.

Næss, S. (1974), *Psykologiske aspekter ved livskvalitet. Om begrepet "indre livskvalitet" som mål for sosialpolitikken og et forsøk på å operasjonalisere begrepet*, INAS arbeidsrapport nr. 11, Oslo.

Nordbakke, S. and Schwanen, T. (forthcoming), *Wellbeing and Mobility: A Theoretical Framework and Literature Review Focusing on Older People*.

OECD (2001), *Ageing and Transport: Mobility Needs and Safety Issues*, Paris: Organisation for Economic Co-operation and Development.

Oxley, P. (2000), Introductory report: Great Britain, in S. Rosenbloom (ed.). *Transport and Aging of the Population*, Paris: Economic Research Centre.

Rabbitt, P., Carmichael, A., Jones, S. and Holland, C. (1996), *When and Why Older People Give Up Driving*, the University of Manchester, AA Foundation for Road Safety Research, Manchester.

Rimmö, P.-A. and Hakamies-Blomqvist, L. (2002), Older drivers' aberrant driving behaviour, impaired activity, and health as reasons for self-imposed driving limitations, *Transportation Research Part F*, **5**, 47–62.

Rosenbloom, S. (2000), *Transport and Aging of the Population*, Paris: Economic Research Centre.

SIKA (2006), *KOM Den nationella kommunikationsvaneundersökningen*, SIKA rapport 2006:23, Statens institut för kommunikationsanalys, Stockholm.

Siren, A. and Hakamies-Blomqvist, L. (2004), Private car as the grand equaliser? Demographic factors and mobility in Finnish men and women aged 65+, *Transportation Research Part F*, **7**, 107–18.

Spinney, J.E.L., Scott, D.M. and Newbold, K.B. (2009), Transport mobility benefits and quality of life: a time-use perspective of elderly Canadians, *Transport Policy*, **16**(1), 1–11.

Vågane, L., Brechan, I. and Hjorthol, R. (2011), *Den nasjonale reisevaneundersøkelsen 2009 – nøkkelrapport*, TØI report 1130/2011, Institute of Transport Economics, Oslo.

37 Ageing populations and travel
Gamze Dane, Anna Grigolon, Soora Rasouli, Harry Timmermans and Dujuan Yang

1. INTRODUCTION

The effectiveness of sustainable transport policies ultimately depends on the response of different lifecycle groups to these policies. This chapter is concerned with one such life-cycle group: the elderly. They are also known in the literature as 'solitary survivors' or 'mature' groups (Wells and Gubar, 1966; Lawson, 1991; Fodness, 1992). It is an interest-ing group for a variety of reasons. First, the elderly need to adjust to changing needs and a shifting institutional context. After retirement they may have more discretionary time, they may be empty-nesters, although their household caring tasks may perhaps be substi-tuted by grandparenting tasks. The new generation of elderly is said to have accumulated more wealth and resources (e.g., Spinney et al., 2009). Moreover, in general, their health is better than that of previous generations of elderly, giving them more opportunities to stay active and travel (Ziegler and Schwanen, 2011). On the other hand, they are less flex-ible in adjusting to changes, i.e., diminishing public urban facilities and transportation resources (e.g., Rosenbloom, 2001; Collia et al., 2003; Hildebrand, 2003). These consid-erations suggest they are more likely to continue travelling, with detrimental effects on sustainable transport policy ambitions.

Little empirical evidence is, however, known about the travel behaviour of the elderly. This chapter summarises results of our previous analyses and activity-travel behaviour of this lifecycle group and adds the results of some new analyses that were specifically conducted for this chapter. To put the analyses in a coherent theoretical perspective, results are described and interpreted in the activity-based approach.

The activity-based approach has given a new impetus to the analysis of travel behav-iour in the transportation research community. Although the literature suggests that the definition of an activity-based perspective varies considerably, in this research the approach articulates a series of shifting views and corresponding new concepts that have been widely used to understand activity-travel patterns of individuals and households in time and space. First, it has been realised that (most) travel is induced by the needs and desires of individuals and households to participate in various kinds of activities. Because activity locations are scattered in space, logically, travel is required to reach these locations and become engaged in the activities. Moreover, the choice of activity location, transport mode and activity duration co-vary with the nature of the activity. Second, the activity-based approach has added the temporal dimension to travel behaviour analysis, blending travel behaviour and time-use research. Research started to investigate the timing and duration of activity participation and related travel at a high level of temporal resolution. Third, realising that some travel decisions are made at the household level or even at the level of social networks as opposed to the individual level, the approach has implied a shift in focus from individual travel behaviour to travel behaviour of households and larger decision-making units such as members of social networks. Finally, due to the influence of time geography concepts in activity-based analysis (Timmermans et al., 2002), it has been realised that overt travel behaviour does not only reflect individual preferences but also various kinds of constraints that prohibit individuals and households to fully realise their preferences. The availability and quality of travel options is a key component of the quality of life, especially for constrained lifecycle groups such as the elderly and working couples (Banister and Bowling, 2004). Among these, in addition to time and budget constraints, coupling and space-time constraints are highly relevant, influencing the possibilities and ways in which people (can) organise their activities and travel in time and space across different time horizons.

Thus, the combination of these ideas, notions and concepts has resulted in much richer theoretical frameworks to analyse and model travel behaviour. Fundamental to this knowledge accumulation is the understanding that these triggers, motivators and constraints of activity participation and corresponding travel vary for different lifecycle groups and segments in the population. This is the very reason why we opt using the central concepts and perspectives of activity-based analysis to describe and interpret various aspects of the travel behaviour of the Dutch elderly.

The chapter has two separate but related levels of generalisation. We start with pure descriptive analyses of the space-time behaviour of the elderly. The value of this analysis concerns an understanding of the behaviour of this lifecycle group. By their very nature, pure descriptive data are not very informative and useful when the goal is to assess the effects of sustainable policy decisions. For such policy analyses, a modelling approach that, in generalising descriptive results, goes beyond descriptive analysis is required. Thus, we complement the descriptive analyses by an examination of the challenges this segment poses in *modelling* activity-travel patterns. One might argue that modelling challenges are independent of specific socio-demographic groups. However, heterogeneity in behaviour among the elderly may be higher, while in addition their different context may lead to significant differences in their activity-travel patterns. The segment of elderly is highly relevant for policy analysis and model applications as many Western societies are rapidly aging. It not only leads to the question how to predict future activity-travel patterns of the elderly, but also begs the question of the uncertainty of the travel forecasts involved.

The aim of this chapter is thus to provide some more insight into the travel behaviour of the elderly, using Dutch datasets about time-use and travel. The activity-based perspective is used to guide the analyses. Various facets of activity-travel patterns of the elderly will be compared against national averages. To position these findings in a wider overall perspective, findings will be compared with the results of similar studies conducted in other countries, based on a literature review. Consistent with current developments in activity-based analysis, different temporal perspectives will be analysed. That is, we will examine vacation travel behaviour and analyse daily activity-travel patterns of these groups. In addition to the common focus on activity participation, timing, duration and transport mode, we will also analyse expenditure patterns of the elderly. After these analytical perspectives, the second part of the chapter will focus on modelling challenges and model applications.

Table 37.1   Overview of the datasets

	MON 2009	CVTO 2008	CVO 2009
Focus	Daily travel	Leisure	Vacation
Sample size	28,600 households	12,162 trips	16,774 trips
Definition	Includes all activities (regardless of duration)	All activities undertaken for leisure purposes, at least one hour out of home and without overnight	Stay outside the home for recreation or pleasure for at least one night
Categories	1. Compulsory (school and work) 2. Maintenance (shopping, delivery goods) 3. Leisure (social or recreational trip, tours or hiking)	1. Outside recreation 2. Water recreation 3. Sporting 4. Visiting sport event 5. Wellness and beauty 6. Attraction visit 7. Event visit 8. Fun shopping 9. Culture 10. Going out 11. Hobbies, courses, etc.	1. Destination 2. Transport mode 3. Accommodation 4. Travel party 5. Duration 6. Season

2.   DATA

Three different databases were used for the analysis reported in the present chapter, as shown in Table 37.1. Analysis of activity-travel patterns is based on the MON dataset, the Dutch overall Travel Survey. It records the data of 28,600 households and consists of out-of-home activity-travel data with almost equal frequencies for every month, except September, October and November, for which the number of responses is higher. Besides household, individual and transportation ownership information, the survey includes one-day activity-travel diary data, collected for all household members on a designated diary day. Respondents provided information about all trips made on a designated day and about the activities conducted at trip destinations. In line with an activity-based approach, trip information includes start time, end time, trip purpose, origin, destination, activity type at the destination, activity duration and transport mode.

For the purpose of analysis, travel purposes were classified into three broad categories: compulsory (school and work-related trips), maintenance (shopping, delivery goods), and leisure (social or recreational trip, tours or hiking). Transport modes were classified into three categories: car (car driver or car passenger), public transport (bus, train, tram/metro) and slow modes (bike or walking).

Data on leisure activities were based on the 2008 CVTO (Continu Vrije Tijds Onderzoek) dataset, a national-level survey conducted by the Dutch Board of Tourism and Conventions and TNS NIPO. This survey collects information on leisure activity episodes that the individual participated in over the course of a week. Only the activities that are conducted for one hour or more are included in the dataset. A wide range of activities is collected, which can be clustered into 11 activities, as shown in Table 37.1. The data is representative of the Dutch population and includes information about expenditures for various kinds of activities (direct costs of activity) such as consumptions during the activity, entrance fee, money spent in the shops, etc. and the expenditure of travel for these activities. The data do not include subscription, contribution and membership costs.

The episode-level information collected in the dataset includes the kind of activity, start time, duration of the activity and travel, expenditure for the activity and travel, location of the activity and travel distance to the activity. In addition, data on individual and household socio-demographics are collected. It is also important to highlight that CVTO considers leisure activities the ones undertaken for at least one hour away from home while the MON dataset includes all activities, regardless of the duration of them.

In the context of vacation travel activities, data were derived from the 2009 CVO panel (Continu Vakantie Onderzoek), organised by the NBTC-NIPO Research. The dataset involving 6,721 respondents contains numerous socio-demographic and trip-related variables organised in several categories. From a total of 16,774 trips made by all respondents in 2009, 23.6 per cent of the vacation trips were made by the elderly.

3.   DESCRIPTORS OF TRAVEL BEHAVIOUR

The group of the elderly was further classified into three age brackets: 60–64 years, 65–74 years and older than 74 years of age. This distinction is motivated by the fact that the first bracket consists of a mixture of retired and non-retired people. The age of 65 is currently the official retirement age in the Netherlands. The last bracket is used to identify the oldest segments. The MON data include respectively 2,681, 3,523 and 2,123 cases for these brackets. Activity-travel patterns of these groups were analysed for the following choice facets: activity participation, transport mode and travel distance for different activities and start time of activities.

Table 37.2 shows differences between the elderly in their participation duration in compulsory, maintenance and leisure activities. As expected, the engagement in compulsory activities as expressed in total out of home activity duration is highest for the 60–64 year group, reflecting their work activities. With increasing age, this duration decreases for compulsory activities. In contrast, maintenance and leisure activities are highest for the 65–74 group. Thus it seems that after retirement, engagement shifts to these kind of activities, bus total amount of time spent on these activities decreases as people grow

Table 37.2   Out-of-home activity duration per person per day by age groups (in minutes)

Activity type	60–64	65–74	75+	Overall sample average
Compulsory	99.16	38.19	27.46	279.19
Maintenance	42.03	79.39	60.59	47.12
Leisure	67.24	121.03	99.90	72.85

Source: MON 2009

Table 37.3 Number of trips per person by travel mode per day

Activity type	Travel mode	60–64	65–74	75+	Overall sample
Compulsory	Car	0.523	0.304	0.194	0.423
	Bike	0.177	0.094	0.066	0.232
	On foot	0.063	0.060	0.081	0.082
	PT	0.119	0.032	0.063	0.173
	Others	0.016	0.011	0.012	0.019
Total		0.899	0.501	0.416	0.929
Maintenance	Car	0.595	0.620	0.544	0.199
	Bike	0.416	0.456	0.343	0.118
	On foot	0.191	0.239	0.280	0.075
	PT	0.069	0.116	0.081	0.022
	Others	0.015	0.025	0.049	0.008
Total		1.286	1.457	1.297	0.422
Leisure	Car	0.702	0.733	0.537	0.848
	Bike	0.374	0.389	0.212	0.488
	On foot	0.511	0.520	0.536	0.329
	PT	0.113	0.135	0.182	0.215
	Others	0.024	0.025	0.074	0.037
Total		1.724	1.803	1.540	1.917

Source: MON 2009

older. Yet Table 37.2 also demonstrates that the elderly, on average, stay active in conducting activities out of home.

Table 37.3 shows the number of trips induced by involvement in the activities categorised by different modes. It shows that number of trips by car for compulsory activities is the highest and reduces fast with increasing age. This decrease is partly substituted by more walking trips. For maintenance and leisure activities, differences among age groups are much smaller. Compared with the sample average, the number of maintenance trips made by the elderly is generally much higher.

Another interesting and relevant descriptor is the average travel time and travel distance for different kinds of activities. Tables 37.4 and 37.5 show that travel time and travel distance by car is highest for compulsory activities, but reduces rapidly with increasing age. Differences between the age groups are much smaller for maintenance and leisure activities, suggesting that these groups do not differ that much in their travel behaviour. Compared to the sample average, travel time by all transport mode for compulsory activities is lower but travel distance by car and public transport mode are higher than the sample average. For maintenance and leisure activities, both travel time and travel distances are higher than the average.

Tables 37.6 and 37.7 shows the average travel time and travel distance by male and female age groups. Consistent with previous findings, males travel more than females both in terms of time and distance for compulsory activities. There is small difference between male and female groups for maintenance and leisure trips, but the data still indicate that females on average stay more responsible for maintenance activities.

Table 37.4   Average daily travel time per person for different activities (in minutes)

Activity type	Travel time	60–64	65–74	75+	Overall sample
Compulsory	Car	13.97	6.91	3.73	23.10
	Bike	2.44	1.26	0.82	6.62
	On foot	0.53	0.58	0.77	1.21
	PT	7.54	1.52	2.33	20.39
	Others	0.34	0.16	0.13	1.28
Maintenance	Car	9.36	10.39	7.55	6.79
	Bike	4.64	5.101	3.86	2.69
	On foot	2.17	2.64	2.98	1.42
	PT	3.44	5.76	3.25	2.51
	Others	0.23	0.35	0.59	0.26
Leisure	Car	21.22	22.22	14.21	11.50
	Bike	9.46	9.61	5.29	5.05
	On foot	10.19	9.87	9.11	5.79
	PT	10.27	13.29	13.94	5.05
	Others	0.83	0.85	1.57	1.34
Total		96.69	90.57	70.19	94.99

Source: MON 2009

Table 37.5   Average daily travel distance per person for different activities (in kilometres)

Activity type	Travel distance	60–64	65–74	75+	Overall sample
Compulsory	Car	104.13	42.29	19.87	85.40
	Bike	5.26	2.41	1.54	7.01
	On foot	0.44	0.45	0.54	0.52
	PT	46.92	5.23	6.61	18.21
	Others	2.33	0.52	0.13	6.54
Maintenance	Car	51.30	56.62	31.85	17.43
	Bike	9.12	9.38	7.02	2.45
	On foot	1.74	2.06	2.27	0.58
	PT	14.15	35.06	7.43	1.87
	Others	0.42	1.18	0.81	0.39
Leisure	Car	175.43	175.89	93.58	48.14
	Bike	20.45	19.47	9.75	4.70
	On foot	7.85	7.73	7.15	1.86
	PT	113.46	141.95	91.64	7.39
	Others	5.59	4.41	2.38	28.75
Total		558.67	504.69	282.63	231.24

Source: MON 2009

Table 37.6   Average daily travel time per person by gender (in minutes)

Activity type	Travel time	Male				Female			
		60–64	65–74	75+	Overall sample	60–64	65–74	75+	Overall sample
Compulsory	Car	21.15	9.45	4.89	29.98	6.69	4.49	2.71	16.42
	Bike	2.94	1.55	1.01	6.75	1.93	1.01	0.66	6.50
	On foot	0.65	0.59	0.72	1.09	0.41	0.56	0.82	1.32
	PT	9.29	0.72	1.77	20.54	5.75	2.28	2.81	20.25
	Others	0.43	0.26	0.09	1.81	0.25	0.07	0.18	0.76
Maintenance	Car	9.67	12.20	9.27	6.34	9.05	8.67	6.04	7.23
	Bike	3.33	4.59	4.14	1.99	5.96	5.58	3.61	3.36
	On foot	1.88	2.26	2.46	1.12	2.47	3.01	3.45	1.71
	PT	2.31	4.06	3.26	1.54	4.59	7.37	3.24	3.44
	Others	0.16	0.41	0.41	0.20	0.31	0.31	0.75	0.32
Leisure	Car	21.23	23.57	16.52	11.70	21.23	20.93	12.16	11.31
	Bike	10.36	11.24	8.11	5.36	8.55	8.07	2.82	4.75
	On foot	10.70	10.41	9.75	5.35	9.68	9.36	8.53	6.21
	PT	6.83	9.84	12.81	3.72	13.75	16.57	14.95	6.34
	Others	1.05	0.55	1.51	1.34	0.62	1.14	1.63	1.34
Total		102.01	91.73	76.74	98.82	91.31	89.47	64.41	91.28

Source: MON 2009

Table 37.7   Average daily travel distance per person by gender (in kilometres)

Activity type	Travel distance	Male				Female			
		60–64	65–74	75+	Overall sample	60–64	65–74	75+	Overall sample
Compulsory	Car	164.56	60.22	24.83	110.79	42.94	25.29	15.49	60.79
	Bike	6.64	3.04	1.81	7.32	3.87	1.81	1.29	6.70
	On foot	0.55	0.47	0.53	0.47	0.33	0.42	0.55	0.57
	PT	66.56	2.68	6.28	19.03	27.03	7.65	6.89	17.42
	Others	3.92	0.82	0.08	11.14	0.72	0.23	0.17	2.09
Maintenance	Car	56.46	70.91	39.02	16.53	46.07	43.07	25.54	18.30
	Bike	6.57	8.78	7.31	1.81	11.69	9.95	6.76	3.07
	On foot	1.54	1.77	1.89	0.45	1.94	2.34	2.61	0.70
	PT	9.16	26.73	8.34	1.27	19.21	42.95	6.63	2.45
	Others	0.38	1.37	0.67	0.29	0.46	0.99	0.94	0.48
Leisure	Car	173.42	191.71	110.02	51.20	177.46	160.89	79.07	45.18
	Bike	24.27	24.12	15.09	5.37	16.59	15.05	5.04	4.06
	On foot	8.15	8.21	7.66	1.75	7.55	7.27	6.71	1.97
	PT	48.31	173.51	86.42	6.46	179.46	112.01	96.25	8.30
	Others	8.03	2.36	2.91	32.72	3.11	6.35	1.93	24.90
Total		578.58	576.78	312.91	266.58	538.51	436.32	255.92	196.98

Source: MON 2009

Table 37.8   Average start time of travel by activity type

Activity type	60–64	65–74	75+	Overall sample average
Compulsory	9:48	11:24	11:50	10:10
Maintenance	12:04	11:47	11:51	12:52
Leisure	12:55	12:31	12:47	13:29

Source: MON 2009

Table 37.9   Comparison of activity duration, expenditure, value of activity and travel expenditure for out-of-home leisure activities

Sample	Activity duration (min)	Activity expenditure (€)	Activity expenditure per unit time (€/min)	Travel expenditure (€)
Elderly	199	19.90	0.10	2.90
60–64	199	16.70	0.08	3.20
65–74	202	21.50	0.11	2.80
75+	192	20.40	0.11	2.70
Overall sample	198	19.50	0.10	2.60

Source: CVTO 2008

Table 37.8 shows the average start time by age groups. It is interesting to see that with age increasing, people start compulsory activities later and later. Except the 60–64 group, the other two groups are both later than average. In contrast, in the case of maintenance and leisure activities, ageing people start earlier than the sample average and especially the 65–74 group starts earliest.

Expenditure and time-use related to leisure activities
The previous database (MON) contains information about three types of activities: compulsory, maintenance and leisure. Zooming in on leisure activities, this section analyses differences between elderly age groups in relation to both out-of-home leisure activities (such as going to a restaurant or to a green park) and vacation trips (domestic or trips to abroad). Starting with out-of-home leisure activities, the CVTO data was analysed. Table 37.9 shows the average activity duration, activity expenditure, value of activity per unit time and average travel expenditure by the elderly and overall. The results indicate that the averages for elderly sample do not differ substantially from the overall averages.

Time spent on out-of-home leisure activities for people aged more than 75 years is less than the overall average. Moreover, the average activity expenditure show that people aged between 60 and 64 years spend less money on leisure out-of-home activities compared to the other age categories of the elderly and the overall average. In addition, the value of activity per unit time indicates that the value of activity increases for people aged more than 65 years. Furthermore, the average travel expenditure shows that the people aged between 60 and 64 years spend more money on travel compared to the

Table 37.10 *Comparison of elderly and overall sample for all out-of-home different types of leisure activity categories*

Activity type	Elderly				Overall sample			
	Duration (min)	Activity (€)	(€/min)	Travel (€)	Duration (min)	Activity (€)	(€/min)	Travel (€)
Outside recreation	220	6.7	0.03	4.4	211	6.6	0.03	4.7
Water recreation	178	5.9	0.03	1.2	181	5.0	0.03	1.8
Sporting	201	4.0	0.02	1.6	178	5.3	0.03	1.6
Visiting sport event	220	4.2	0.02	3.2	233	8.4	0.04	2.9
Wellness and beauty	170	26.6	0.16	2.5	206	28	0.14	3.1
Attraction visit	226	9.6	0.04	3.1	243	9.9	0.04	2.7
Event visit	293	15.1	0.05	4.9	302	19.9	0.07	5.1
Fun shopping	155	48.7	0.31	2.2	160	44.5	0.28	2.1
Culture	259	18.9	0.07	4.9	244	16.1	0.07	3.3
Going out	208	20.6	0.10	3.3	208	20.2	0.10	2.5
Hobbies, courses, etc.	200	4.1	0.02	2.3	209	4.9	0.02	2.2

Source: CVTO 2008

other age categories. However, the difference for average travel expenditure is not high between the age categories. Table 37.10 shows the average activity duration, average activity expenditure, value of activity and average travel expenditures for each leisure out-of-home activity categories according to the elderly and overall sample. At this level, some differences start to appear.

Table 37.11 shows the same averages as Table 37.10, but now focuses on each elderly age group. The duration of wellness and beauty, hobbies/courses and attraction visit activities is highest for people aged between 60 and 64, while the duration of outside recreation, water recreation, sporting, sport event visit and fun shopping activities is highest for age group 65–74. Finally, the duration of event visit, culture and going out activities is highest for people aged 75 or older. Interestingly, the duration of sports activity for all categories of elderly is higher than the national sample average. Moreover, the duration of cultural activities for all age categories of elderly is also higher than the national sample. In contrast, the duration of wellness and beauty, hobbies/courses, and event visit activities for all age categories of elderly is lower than the national sample.

The expenditure of water recreation activity is the highest for age group 60–64 years. In addition, age group 65–74 years spend more on outside recreation, sporting, wellness and beauty, attraction visit, event visit, hobbies/courses and fun shopping activities compared to the other age groups. Moreover, the expenditure of sport event visit, culture and going out activities is highest for people aged more than 75 years. The results indicate that the expenditure of sporting, sport event visit, hobbies/courses and event visit activities for all age categories of elderly is lower than the national sample.

The value of travel does not differ excessively between the age categories except fun shopping activity where the value of this activity for people aged between 60 and 64 years is less than other age categories. Furthermore, the value of hobbies/courses and event visit activity is the same for all age categories. In addition to this, the results indicate that

Table 37.11   *Activity duration, expenditure, value of activity and travel expenditure for all out-of-home leisure activities*

Activities	Age group	Duration (min)	Activity (€)	(€/min)	Travel (€)
Outside recreation	60–64	215	5.0	0.02	5.2
	65–74	226	8.3	0.04	4.1
	75+	211	4.9	0.02	4.0
Water recreation	60–64	156	8.3	0.05	1.3
	65–74	206	5.9	0.03	1.5
	75+	110	3.3	0.03	0.5
Sporting	60–64	183	3.2	0.02	1.5
	65–74	212	4.9	0.02	1.7
	75+	194	2.8	0.01	1.6
Visiting sport event	60–64	206	4.1	0.02	1.8
	65–74	229	4.0	0.02	3.6
	75+	227	5.1	0.02	5.5
Wellness and beauty	60–64	188	27.9	0.15	4.9
	65–74	168	28.6	0.17	1.1
	75+	136	17	0.13	1.1
Attraction visit	60–64	249	7.6	0.03	3.2
	65–74	204	11.1	0.05	3.2
	75+	232	10.3	0.04	2.7
Event visit	60–64	292	13.5	0.05	5.0
	65–74	293	16.4	0.06	5.2
	75+	295	14.6	0.05	4.1
Fun shopping	60–64	156	39.4	0.25	2.4
	65–74	163	55.2	0.34	2.0
	75+	135	46.3	0.34	2.3
Culture	60–64	258	13.0	0.05	6.1
	65–74	246	19.8	0.08	5.0
	75+	279	22.6	0.08	3.6
Going out	60–64	203	20.4	0.10	4.3
	65–74	199	18.1	0.09	2.9
	75+	229	25.3	0.11	2.9
Hobbies, courses, etc.	60–64	208	3.9	0.02	1.8
	65–74	203	4.7	0.02	2.5
	75+	183	3.2	0.02	2.4

Source: CVTO 2008

the value of sporting, event visit and sport event visit activities for all age categories of elderly is lower than the national sample.

The travel expenditure of outside recreation, wellness and beauty, fun shopping, culture and going out for age category 60–64 years is higher than other age categories. Moreover, the travel expenditure of water recreation, sporting, hobbies/courses, and event visit for people aged between 65 and 74 years is the highest. In addition to this, the travel expenditure of attraction visit activity for age groups 60–64 and 65–74 years is higher than age group 75+. Furthermore, the results indicate that the travel expenditure

Table 37.12   Shares between vacation variables (in per cent)

Variables	Levels	60–64	65–74	75+	Overall sample
Destination	Abroad	47	46	49	49
	Domestic	53	54	51	51
Transport mode	Airplane	13	16	14	16
	Bus	4	5	7	3
	Car	77	73	72	75
	Other	2	1	3	2
	Train	4	4	4	4
Accommodation	Camping	28	21	17	26
	Hostel	2	3	2	4
	Hotel	30	36	38	28
	Own house	10	12	10	9
	Rented house	26	26	29	31
	Other	3	2	3	2
Travel party	Alone	10	11	13	7
	With partner	39	47	37	27
	Group only 16+	23	21	21	20
	Group 15–	9	8	6	31
	Other	20	13	23	15
Season	Autumn	23	25	25	20
	Spring	28	29	30	26
	Winter	15	13	11	15
	Summer	34	33	34	38
Duration	Short (1–3 nights)	18	17	19	22
	Medium (4–9 nights)	52	51	49	49
	Long (10+ nights)	30	32	32	29

Source: CVO 2009

of sport event visits for people aged more than 75 years is the highest. The results also exhibit that the travel expenditure of water recreation activity for all age categories of elderly is lower than the national sample while the travel expenditure of culture and going out activities is higher than the national sample.

In relation to vacation travel, Table 37.12 shows the results of the analyses of the CVO data. In general there are no significant differences between vacation choices of the elderly groups in relation to the overall sample. Domestic trips are slightly more preferred than trips to abroad. Car is the most used transport mode for vacation trips. Hotel, camping and rented house are the most popular accommodation types. However, most elderly respondents indicated to travel with their partner, whereas the total population indicates to travel with groups with people aged less than 15 years-old, i.e., travelling with members of the family. Travelling in the winter is the least popular for all groups. Medium-sized vacations, with duration between four and nine nights, are the most popular between elderly respondents and the overall sample.

The comparison of the results of average expenditure per day between elderly age groups in relation to leisure activities (CVTO database) and vacations trips (CVO database)

Table 37.13 *Comparison of expenditures (in euros) between leisure and vacation*
activities

		60–64	65–74	75+	Overall sample
Leisure activities	Outside recreation	10.20	12.40	8.90	11.30
(CVTO 2008)	Water recreation	9.60	7.40	3.80	6.80
	Sporting	4.70	6.60	4.40	6.90
	Visiting sport event	5.90	7.60	10.60	11.30
	Wellness and beauty	32.80	29.70	18.10	31.10
	Attraction visit	10.80	14.30	13.0	12.60
	Event visit	18.50	21.60	18.70	25.0
	Fun shopping	41.80	57.20	48.60	46.60
	Culture	19.10	24.80	26.20	19.40
	Going out	24.70	21.0	28.20	22.70
	Other hobbies/courses	5.70	7.20	5.60	7.10
Vacations	Short (1–3 nights)	109.60	112.20	116.20	116.60
(CVO 2009)	Medium (4–9 nights)	109.80	114.80	129.10	131.60
	Long (10+ nights)	107.30	108.80	112.80	123.30

are shown in Table 37.13. For the age group 60–64, water recreation and wellness and beauty exhibit higher expenditures than the other groups, including the overall sample. Age group 65–74 spend more on outside recreation, attraction visit, fun shopping and hobbies/courses. The elderly older than 75 years of age spend more on culture and going out. The overall sample exhibits higher expenditures than the other groups for self sporting, visiting sport event and event visit. Regarding vacations, the overall sample spent more on short holidays, medium and long vacations. However, when comparing the elderly group only, respondents older than 75 years of age spend more on vacation trips than the other groups. Comparing these results with the expenditure on leisure activities, it seems that the 75+ group is more prone to spend on culture, going out and on more expensive vacations.

4. FROM DESCRIPTION TO POLICY ASSESSMENTS

The results of these descriptive analyses offer interesting insights into current travel behaviour of the elderly. However, these results need generalisation if the aim of the study shifts from description and understanding to forecasting and policy assessment. It is no surprise that due to the rapidly increasing importance of the ageing society in a variety of policy domains, several recent studies have formulated scenarios and applied comprehensive models of activity-travel behaviour to simulate future demand of the elderly. An exemplary study is Arentze et al. (2008), who applied the Albatross model system (Arentze and Timmermans, 2000, 2004, 2005) to a series of economic, demographic and globalisation policy scenarios. The simulated effect on the total number of activities (per capita) was negative but small. In contrast, substantial shifts were simulated in the distribution of activities across activity types. Work activities and business activities (per capita) decreased considerably in all scenarios. Bring/get activities also decreased strongly. On the other hand, in particular shopping, service related and social activities showed an increase. Simulated effects also showed that aging coincides with a decreasing share of activities starting before 10am, while the shares of activities starting in off-peak episodes tend to increase. Effects on trip-chaining behavior are small, while the predicted effects on transport mode depended on the specific scenario.

Maoh et al. (2009) conducted a similar study. They found an increase in the number of trips and mobility levels of elderly in the Hamilton Metropolitan Area, Canada. Their findings are consistent with earlier Canadian research (Newbold et al., 2005) where a cohort analysis found that white older Canadians make fewer trips than those on the workforce, their number of car trips increased between 1986 and 1998 as the population aged.

While this and related studies show the relevance of the use of these activity-based models of travel demand, modelling the behavior of the elderly causes extra challenges. As long as the travel behavior of the group of interest is relatively stable, estimated relationships that make up the model can be used to predict or simulate their future behavior assuming these relationships are time invariant. In the present study and many others, however, some of the estimated parameters were changed, blurring the difference between empirical models and serious games. Not only is the input data, derived from the scenarios uncertain, the parameters of the model are also uncertain.

Under such circumstances, it is critical to complete descriptive and model-based policy scenarios assessments with formal uncertainty analysis. It should be realised in this context that the current generation of activity-based model is stochastic in nature. Consequently, to differentiate model uncertainty from pure policy effects, formal uncertainty analysis to such policy scenario applications of models of travel demand are required (Rasouli and Timmermans, 2012). To support this contention, an uncertainty analysis of travel behavior of the elderly was conducted applying the Albatross model to the Rotterdam region, the Netherlands. More specifically, a 10 per cent fraction of the synthetic population, consisting of 41,668 persons and 27,961 households, was randomly selected. For each sampled individual of this fraction, the Albatross model was run 50 times. In each run, the action state of the 28 decision trees of the model was determined using Monte Carlo draws. These runs result in a probability distribution of each facet of the simulated activity-travel patterns and the associated performance indicators. Using distance travelled per day per person for various activities as an example, results indicated that the average distance travelled by elderly is 15.54km, with a standard deviation of 0.35. The coefficient of variation is 2.24. Similar statistics for dual-earner households (the most extreme group) and the overall mean are respectively 1.6 (average distance travelled for dual-earner households: 33.9km; standard deviation distance travelled for dual earner households: 0.53) and 0.9 (average distance travelled: 25.62km; standard deviation distance travelled: 0.234). Thus, the application of this activity-based model indicates that the results of descriptive analyses of activity-travel patterns of elderly can be generalised to develop a model of travel demand. However, results also demonstrate that uncertainty in forecasts and policy assessments of the travel behavior of the elderly travel behavior is much higher than uncertainty in average travel behavior and much higher compared to uncertainty of the travel behaviour of dual-earner households.

5. CONCLUSIONS AND DISCUSSION

The chapter has reported some main results of descriptive analyses of daily activity-travel patterns, corresponding expenditures and vacation behaviour of the segment of the elderly in the Netherlands. The elderly represent a highly interesting group for travel behaviour analysis because many Western societies are rapidly ageing and the activity-travel patterns of this segment thus make up a considerable part of especially non-work related travel. It is not surprising, therefore, that the elderly have been subject of many similar analyses in other countries and that models have been applied assess travel behaviour impacts of policy scenarios related to the future development of this group.

This chapter has added new descriptive and modelling results to this rapidly growing literature on activity and mobility patterns of the elderly. Compared to other similar studies, we have opted for a broader perspective by not only analysing daily activity-travel patterns, but also examining expenditure patterns and vacation patterns. On the other hand, we only examined general activity-travel and did not focus on specific activities. Further results on specific activities for Dutch elderly can be found in van den Berg et al. (2011) on social activities and Kemperman and Timmermans (2006, 2009) on active activities and transport modes.

Results of the analyses suggest that the elderly may not differ that much from other groups in terms of their activity-travel behavior. For maintenance and leisure activities, both travel time and travel distances are slight higher than the overall average. Comparing different kinds of activities, travel time and travel distance of ageing people by car is higher for compulsory activities, but these mobility indicators decrease rapidly with increasing age. The start time of activities of the aging population is later than average, except for maintenance activities.

These results indicate that the behaviour of the elderly does not differ substantially from the overall average in terms of the duration of and expenditure on leisure activities (out-of-home and vacation trips). An important finding is that different elderly age groups show different patterns for duration and expenditure on each out-of-home leisure activities. This is also the main cause of the higher uncertainty in model-based policy assessments. These different patterns in behaviour between age groups of the elderly can be largely understood in terms of the constraints (a key concept in an activity-based perspective) acting on agendas. As constraints and commitments (work) are relaxed activity-travel patterns become more flexible and tend to shift to off-peak hours. This finding seems to be generalisable to other countries. For example, Karimi et al. (2012) found that the main difference between elderly and non-elderly people was caused by the difference in share of mandatory activities. While both cohorts exhibit very similar behaviour in their choice of activity duration, their time-of-day choice is very different. Our finding related to the shifting choice of choice mode with increasing age has been also been found by Grégoire and Morency (2012) in Quebec, Canada, and Andrews et al. (2012) and Sikder and Pinjari (2012) in the United States.

Because the elderly are a heterogeneous segment of the population, we also reflected on implications for forecasting and supported our contentions with an indicative uncertainty analysis of a large computational process model of activity-travel behaviour for the elderly. Implications of sustainable transport are mixed. On the one hand, higher mobility will increase vehicle miles travelled of the Dutch population. On the other hand, shifting start time may imply that high congestion during peak-hours may be reduced. To qualify such expectations, model applications and uncertainty analysis are required.

REFERENCES

Andrews, G., Susilo, Y., Parkhurst, G. and Shaw, J. (2012), Exploring the *Impact of Zero-fare Transportation Policies on Demand for Elderly Bus Travel*, paper presented at the 91st Annual Meeting of the Transportation Research Board, Washington, DC.

Arentze, T.A. and Timmermans, H.J.P. (2000), *Albatross: A Learning-Based Transportation Oriented Simulation System*, Eindhoven: EIRASS.

Arentze, T.A. and Timmermans, H.J.P. (2004), A learning-based transportation oriented simulation system, *Transportation Research Record*, **38**, 613–33.

Arentze, T.A. and Timmermans, H.J.P. (2005), *Albatross 2.0: Learning-Based Transportation Oriented Simulation System*, Eindhoven: EIRASS.

Arentze, T.A., Timmermans, H.J.P., Jorritsma, P. and Kalter, M.J.O. (2008), More gray hair – but for whom? Scenario-based simulations of elderly activity travel patterns in 2020, *Transportation*, **35**, 613–27.

Banister, D. and Bowling, A. (2004), Quality of life for the elderly: the transport dimension, *Transport Policy*, **11**(2), 105–15.

Collia, D.V., Sharp, J. and Giesbrecht, L. (2003), The 2001 overall household travel survey: a look into the travel patterns of older Americans, *Journal of Safety Research*, **34**, 461–70.

Fodness, D. (1992), The impact of family life cycle on the vacation decision-making process, *Journal of Travel Research*, **31**(2), 8–13.

Grégoire, J. and Morency, C. (2012), *Exploring Changes Affecting the Travel Behaviors of Seniors*, paper presented at the 91st Annual Meeting of the Transportation Research Board, Washington, DC.

Hildebrand, E.D. (2003), Dimensions in elderly travel behaviour: a simplified activity-based model using lifestyle clusters, *Transportation*, **30**, 285–306.

Karimi, B., Rashidi, T.H., Mohammadian, A. and Sturm, K. (2012), *Young-old Elderly and Baby Boomers: An Explanatory Analysis on Activity Duration, Time-of-day Choice, and Planning Time Horizons*, paper presented at the 91st Annual Meeting of the Transportation Research Board, Washington, DC.

Kemperman, A.D.A.M. and Timmermans, H.J.P. (2006), Heterogeneity in urban park use of aging visitors: a latent class analysis, *Leisure Sciences*, **28**, 57–71.

Kemperman, A.D.A.M. and Timmermans, H.J.P. (2009), Influences of built environment on walking and cycling by latent segments of aging population, *Transportation Research Record*, **2134**. 1–9.

Lawson, R. (1991), Patterns of tourist expenditures and types of vacation across the family life cycle, *Journal of Travel Research*, **29**(4), 12–18.

Maoh, D., Kanaroglou, P., Scott, D., Paez, A. and Newbold, B. (2009), IMPACT: an integrated GIS-based model for simulating the consequences of demographic changes and population ageing on transportation, *Computers, Environment and Urban Systems*, **33**(3), 200–10.

Newbold, K.B., Scott, D.M., Spinney, J.E.L., Kanaroglou, P. and Páez, A. (2005), Travel behavior within Canada's older population: a cohort analysis, *Journal of Transport Geography*, **13**, 340–51.

Rasouli, S. and Timmermans, H.J.P. (2012), Uncertainty in travel demand forecasting, *Transportation Letters*, **4**, 55–73.

Rosenbloom, S. (2001), Sustainability and automobility among the elderly: an interoverall assessment, *Transportation*, **28**, 375–408.

Sikder, S. and Pinjari, A.R. (2012), *Immobility Levels and Mobility Preferences among Elderly in the United States: Evidence from the 2009 National Household Travel Survey (NHTS)*, paper presented at the 91st Annual Meeting of the Transportation Research Board, Washington, DC.

Spinney, J.E.L., Scott, D.M. and Newbold, K.B. (2009), Transport mobility benefits and quality of life: a time-use perspective of elderly Canadians, *Transport Policy*, **16**(1), 1–11.

Timmermans, H.J.P., Arentze, T.A. and Joh, C.H. (2002), Analysing space-time behaviour: new approaches to old problems, *Progress in Human Geography*, **26**, 175–90.

van den Berg, P., Arentze, T.A. and Timmermans, H.J.P. (2011), Estimating social travel demand of senior citizens in the Netherlands, *Journal of Transport Geography*, **19**, 323–31.

Wells, W. and Gubar, G. (1966), Life cycle concept in marketing research, *Journal of Marketing Research*, **3**(4), 355–63.

Ziegler, F. and Schwanen, T. (2011), I like to go out to be energised by different people: an exploratory analysis of mobility and wellbeing in later life, *Ageing and Society*, **31**, 758–81.

38 Investigating urban oil vulnerability
Jago Dodson, Neil Sipe and Terry Li

1. INTRODUCTION

This chapter describes and discusses the problem of combined volatile petroleum prices and varying housing mortgage cost pressures with household socio-economic patterns and urban structure within a large, dispersed city region. The chapter addresses two prominent economic phenomena witnessed in the past decade that have impacted on urban transport systems. The first phenomenon has been the sharp increase and uncertainty in global oil prices from 2004 onwards and that marked a departure from relatively consistent and modest prices experienced during the previous two decades. This global petroleum price growth increased vehicular fuel costs in most countries and spurred concerns about their impact on households. As of mid-2013, global oil prices remain volatile having risen to record highs in 2008 followed by a precipitous plunge at the onset of the global financial crisis before gradually increasing to settle around US$110 per barrel. The second significant urban phenomenon during this period was marked inflation in house prices in many urban housing markets and the subsequent plateauing or decline within these markets due to the global financial crisis (GFC). The global credit market failures witnessed as a result of the GFC have been tied to domestic mortgage lending in a number of countries. This weakness has reduced the vitality of housing markets in many nations, including Australia. The household sector faces considerable ongoing stress from high housing debts and from continuing doubts about the scale and ultimate effect of the global financial crisis on international banking systems and on national economic performance, welfare provision and fiscal sustainability.

The problems of volatile fuel prices and high levels of housing debt pose major questions for urban systems over both short- and long-term timescales. The transport systems of many cities, especially those of advanced new world Anglophone nations, are highly car-dependent (Newman and Kenworthy, 1999). Sustained high and volatile transport fuel prices can exacerbate the impact of automobile reliant transport and compound household distress. In most Australasian and North American contexts the dominant urban form is suburban comprising largely individual detached dwellings held via owner occupied tenure – typically mortgage-funded – among a wider array of dispersed land uses. The current configuration of this spatial pattern is intimately connected to automobile use. Suburban housing systems that have been spatially organised around inexpensive petroleum fuels will confront a difficult adjustment in a costlier fuel environment and that will occur in combination with ongoing global economic and financial dysfunction, not to mention other transition processes such as carbon constraint. Likewise, a smooth shift to alternative vehicle fuel and technology types is not assured. Improving the methods through which these problems are understood so that new perspectives, analyses and solutions can be generated is a pressing question for urban scholars.

This chapter investigates the problem of oil and mortgage vulnerability using

Brisbane, Australia as a case study. The chapter has three main objectives. First it details the problem of long run petroleum availability and the ongoing prospects for a highly constrained global petroleum supply environment. The chapter examines these questions in the context of Brisbane, a highly car-dependent dispersed city in South East Queensland, Australia, which is broadly representative of similar urban settlements in Australia and North America. The Brisbane case study demonstrates how oil vulnerability can be identified at the local scale, using methods for this purpose developed by the authors over the past decade. This is then appraised in the context of changing urban planning policy and practice in south-east Queensland, which includes deliberate – albeit weak – attempts to address problems of oil supply vulnerability. The chapter concludes with some observations about the understanding of urban household transport oil vulnerability and broader prospects under increasingly challenging oil supply scenarios.

2.　OIL CONSTRAINT

The past ten years have seen a marked divergence in global oil prices from historical patterns. Although the apparent new baseline price of US$100 per barrel is no longer a topic of daily commentary, it is significant because it marks a divergence from the prevailing prices of the previous two decades. An array of causal factors underpins the growth and variability in global oil prices since 2004, of which we offer only a brief summary here. A key factor was rapid global economic growth in the early to mid-2000s that included new demand from rapidly developing nations, including China, India, Indonesia and Brazil. A number of production constraints and disruptions affected oil supplies in the 2000s, including declines in North Sea production and the removal of Iraqi oil production. Geopolitical tensions have also played a role, including ongoing fears about the relationship between Iran as a major oil producer and other nations, such as the US and Israel. In addition the past decade has seen mounting fears over the longer-term sustainability of global petroleum resources in the face of continuing demand for oil. A number of observers have argued that the world has already passed or will soon face a 'peak' in global oil production followed by irreversible declines in petroleum production (Heinberg, 2003; Campbell, 2005; Government Accountability Office, 2007; IEA, 2008). The question of petroleum depletion has been widely debated and some consolidation around a pessimistic view. The IEA's chief economic analyst, Fatih Birol, for example, admitted that 'we are expecting that in three or four years' time the production of conventional oil will come to a plateau, and start to decline' (quoted in Monbiot, 2008). Fantazzini, Höök and Angelantoni (2011) present data that shows a plateau of global oil production in 2004 despite growing demand. A raft of public and government groups have all acknowledged the likelihood of much higher future oil prices (Volvo, 2008; ITPOES, 2010; Joint Forces Command, 2010; Lloyds, 2010). While the debate over the timing of an oil production peak remains unsettled, higher oil prices are already having a negative impact (Hamilton, 2009). Even non-conventional sources of petroleum such as tar sands and oil shale may add to global oil production this is unlikely to result in lower long-term prices. In addition the carbon emissions generated in the production of these non-conventional fuels are likely to pose further constraints and cost on their substitution for conventional petroleum. Thus the nature and degree of impacts on economic and social patterns, that pose the critical questions for cities, their urban transport systems and for those who study them, is also uncertain.

3. AUSTRALIA'S CITIES

Australian cities are highly exposed to the cost effects of oil price growth. The impacts of higher fuel prices are transmitted directly to households via their use of, and wider reliance upon, automobiles for urban travel. Australian petrol prices increased from AU$0.85 per litre in 2004 to well above AU$1.60 per litre by mid-2008 and in mid-2013 remained at around AU$1.55 per litre. Although all motor vehicle users are exposed to higher transport fuel costs, the majority of such users are situated in the middle and outer suburbs of Australia's five largest cities – Sydney, Melbourne, Brisbane, Perth and Adelaide – which contain approximately half of the national population. As a result of car-based post-WWII suburbanisation, Australia's five largest cities, including Sydney, represent collectively the largest national cluster of major car-dependent urban regions outside the United States (Newman and Kenworthy, 1999).

Australian households are particularly exposed to high oil prices because there is a close relationship between global oil prices and the fuel prices seen at the petrol bowser in Australia. Australia levies excise on motor vehicle fuel at a much lower rate than many jurisdictions, especially those in Europe. In Australia, fuel excise accounts for just 38 per cent of fuel prices placing the country fourth lowest in a 2006 international survey of the OECD countries (Australian Treasury, 2006: xxviii). High taxation on motor vehicle fuels has the effect of reducing automobile reliance by making alternatives more competitive (Gusdorf and Hallegatte, 2007) and serves as a proxy for high global prices. Thus, Australia's low fuel excise provides a much weaker price signal to Australian households to adjust their levels of car dependence compared to high fuel price jurisdictions. And Australian households are partly protected by the relative strength of Australia's currency and overall economy; just 15.6 per cent of Australian household income each week is spent on transport (ABS, 2011), which includes all transport activity, such as air flights, not just motor vehicles.

Notwithstanding broad automobile dependence in Australian cities, such patterns of car dependence in Australian cities are uneven, however, with inner areas typically less affected than middle or outer suburban zones. For example, in Sydney, Australia's largest city, for which good data is available, residents of the inner east use private vehicles for around 57 per cent and 55 per cent of travel. By contrast those in Sydney's north-west and south-west suburban fringe areas rely on private vehicles for 79 per cent of their travel (Department of Planning, 2006). Total travel distances by automobile are also uneven. Households in Sydney's north-west and south-west report average daily 'vehicle kilometres travelled' (VKT) of 27km and 30km, respectively, compared to those in the inner east and inner west who travelled on average only 12km and 13km, respectively (Department of Planning, 2006).

Motor vehicle ownership also tends to be higher in outer suburban zones and lower in inner urban localities. The rate of motor vehicle ownership in Sydney's inner urban areas is on average 1.16 motor vehicles per household whereas those in the outer suburban north-west or south-west have average ownership levels of 1.78 and 1.73 vehicles per household respectively. If high daily VKTs signal high marginal operational transport costs due to motor vehicle reliance then high ownership levels imply high capital and opportunity costs. Petrol is not the only cost of owning and operating a motor vehicle – purchase and opportunity costs of finance, interest costs on car loans and ongoing registration, maintenance and insurance costs are all upfront factors that impose costs on households.

Differential spatial patterns of vehicle ownership and use Australian cities also reflect the uneven distribution of high-quality public transport services and infrastructure. Public transport in Australian cities is generally of good quality near the historic commercial core but declines in quality, density and frequency with increasing distance (Mees, 2000) from the central city. Other than Melbourne, Australia's major cities substituted buses for trams in the 1950s and 1960s but such services have not been extended at a rate sufficient to match urban growth. Buses in more recently developed peripheral suburban zones are often privately operated, modestly funded, weakly integrated and poorly connected to metropolitan rail systems (Mees, 2000). An effect of such differences is a core and middle suburban area well-served by public transport but that is surrounded by an inadequately served outer suburban periphery. Access to high-quality public transport, especially that which is able to provide an alternative to the motor car for urban travel, therefore, is a key dimension of socio-economic opportunity and inclusion. This has considerable relevance to questions of suburban oil vulnerability given that public transport is the main alternative to motor vehicle use, especially for longer trips.

4.   MAPPING PETROLEUM FUTURES

The recognition that global petroleum supplies are likely to become increasingly constrained in future, whether due to depletion of the resource or to greater demand than is able to be supplied at low prices, holds considerable implications for metropolitan areas that are dependent on petroleum for their travel. Australian cities, and particularly the extensive suburban zones they contain, are potentially highly exposed to the impacts of higher oil prices. Understanding the dimensions and distribution of this problem, the potential impact on urban households and the necessary planning and policy steps to resolve this issue is a key question for governments and urban scholars.

To better understand the problem of oil vulnerability, particularly its socio-economic dimensions, we have applied a selection of analytical methods to the Australian city of Brisbane, which is located within the wider south-east Queensland (SEQ) region. Brisbane and the SEQ region provide an ideal case study zone for investigating oil vulnerability. The SEQ region has experienced high levels of population growth since the early 1970s with 3.05 million residents in 2012. Although the region has a strong urban core in the form of the Brisbane city centre, which is served by both rail and busway networks, the wider region is polycentric and dispersed. Many of the major sub-regional settlements such as the Gold Coast City to the south-east – Australia's sixth largest city and second largest municipality – and the Sunshine Coast to the north saw most of their development occur around the automobile and with limited transport and land-use integration. Travel within the SEQ region is heavily dominated by and dependent on the motor vehicle. Travel survey data reveals a mode share for the automobile of 78.9 per cent for the journey to work in 2006 (BITRE, 2013). and a marginally higher 80 per cent for all journeys (Queensland Transport, 2005). Levels of car use are spatially differentiated, however, within the SEQ region. As with the other major cities, the inner suburbs near the Brisbane CBD that are served by good quality historical networks – such as the bus lines that replaced earlier trams – exhibit relatively higher rates of public transport use whereas outer suburban zones where public transport is less well provisioned and organised tend to have relatively higher rates of automobile use. The Sunshine Coast and Gold Coast are almost completely reliant on the car, which caters to 87 per cent of travel in each city (SCRC, 2012; GCCC, 2012).

5.   METHODS FOR INVESTIGATING AUSTRALIAN OIL VULNERABILITY

As oil prices began rising in the mid-2000s we began to consider how rising prices might play out across Australia's major cities, including Brisbane and south-east Queensland. Our concern was to understand how the growth in overall oil prices would impact across the uneven socio-spatial geography within each of Australia's major cities. We identified a clear gap in the contemporary literature on automobile dependence and urban socio-spatial structure. Although problems of overall comparative metropolitan automobile dependence were well understood (Newman and Kenworthy, 1999), the way such patterns were internally differentiated within cities was much less frequently addressed. The literature on transport disadvantage and public transport accessibility offered a proximate indicator of car dependence but these were often city-specific. In addition, considerable social scientific effort had been expended over time investigating socio-spatial differences within cities, especially following the industrial restructuring experienced in many advanced nations since the 1970s. Thus we were concerned to ensure that the differences concealed within average city-level automobile dependence figures would be representative at the local scale. Such a focus would also potentially ensure that any policy response to the effects of higher oil prices on households – such as improved local public transport – could be closely targeted to areas of greatest need.

Although the structure of the patterning differs from examples elsewhere, such as the UK or USA, Australian cities do exhibit sharp socio-spatial differentials. Wealthy households tend to be located in inner and middle zones near to the highly concentrated CBDs where the highest value employment is found and where public transport is of relatively high quality. Less affluent households, by contrast, tend to locate in outer and fringe suburban areas where provision of infrastructure is less adequate. To understand this differential impact we coined the term 'oil vulnerability', which refers to the socio-economic exposure of households to rising oil and motor vehicle fuel prices, based on their socio-economic status, car-dependence and access to alternatives.

We hypothesised that the distributional impact of higher oil prices would be greater for lower-income households with high levels of car dependence and relatively poorer access to alternative travel modes such as public transport. In turn we sought to identify where the likely highly oil vulnerable households were located in Australian cities at very local scales so policymakers and planners could respond to the long-term problem of oil price growth. At the time we began this work there were few methods or datasets that could depict such patterns at a fine spatial level of detail without the need for construction of bespoke databases and with intensive labour demands. We elected to use Australian Bureau of Statistics Census data to construct indices of oil vulnerability. The selection of Australian Census data was further motivated by the similarity of Census data in other jurisdictions, particularly the USA, Canada and United Kingdom, which would enable the potential future development of comparable appraisals for other cities (see Sipe and Dodson, 2013). We initially constructed two indexes termed the VIPER and the VAMPIRE (see below). Because they use Australian Census data at the local neighbourhood scale, both measures enable very detailed spatial resolution of the distribution of oil vulnerability patterns. We consider this detailed local differentiation readily compensates for the efficient measure of oil vulnerability using census variables, as discussed below. Following the VIPER and VAMPIRE work, we then sought to improve the acuity of the measures used, by including motor vehicle fleet and fuel efficiency datasets in our analysis, which provide additional information on the cost burden of motor vehicle travel within different parts of cities. This latter work is set out in a subsequent section.

The VIPER

The Vulnerability Index for Petroleum Expenses and Risks (VIPER) was constructed to measure broad socio-economic vulnerability to oil price growth (see Dodson and Sipe, 2007). The index is composed of two key sets of variables at the level of the Census Collectors District (CCD). Each CCD contains approximately 200 households. Socio-economic vulnerability is incorporated by using the Australian Bureau of Statistics' (ABS) Socio Economic Index for Areas (SEIFA), which is a composite measure of disadvantage constructed by the bureau from a range of census variables. Transport exposure to higher oil price costs is measured by combining two variables: the proportion of households in a given CCD who have two or more motor vehicles and the proportion of work journeys taken (JTW) by CCD residents by motor vehicle. Together the two sets of variables depict the combination of relative social disadvantage and relative reliance on motor vehicles. The VIPER index involved combining the two variable sets into a single index, which then was used to map relative oil vulnerability at the CCD level. A detailed prescription for the VIPER index is provided in Dodson and Sipe (2007). In summary, this involved constructing a composite measure of oil vulnerability at the CCD level based on a combination of percentage values for the three variables. The existing literature offered little insight into which of the variables should be given greatest weight, so we used a 50 per cent split between the SEIFA index and the combined motor vehicle ownership and JTW levels. This provided a single value for each CCD following which all CCDs within the metropolitan region were ranked and assigned high to low oil vulnerability weightings according to 10th, 25th, 50th, 75th and 90th percentile bands for very high, high, medium, low and very low vulnerability. These band categories were then mapped giving a very high resolution depiction of the problem.

The VIPER map for Brisbane reveals distinct patterns in the spatial distribution of oil vulnerability across the city. It is clear that inner urban locations are broadly less vulnerable to the socio-economic impacts of higher fuel prices than those in outer urban areas. This is likely due to two factors. First, households in inner urban areas close to

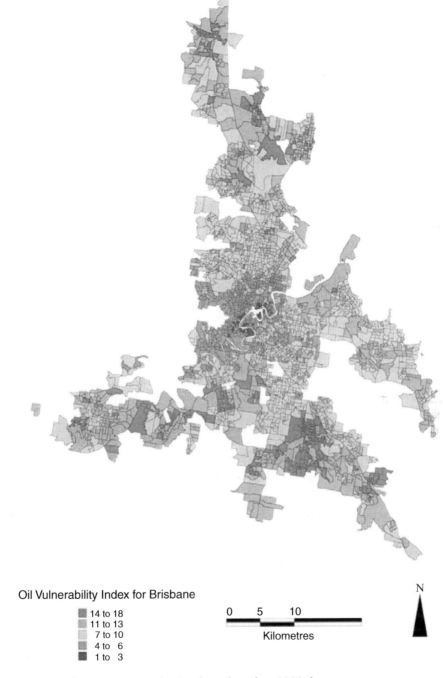

Oil Vulnerability Index for Brisbane

14 to 18
11 to 13
7 to 10
4 to 6
1 to 3

0   5   10

Kilometres

N

Figure 38.1   The VIPER map for Brisbane based on 2001 data

the high-value employment CBD tend to have higher incomes than those in middle and outer zones – a pattern that is both reinforced by and reflected in the steep house price gradients in Australian cities. Second, these households have good access to the higher-quality bus and rail networks within the inner and middle zones, which permit a higher proportion of travel to be taken by public transport. This in turn contributes to lesser dependence on automobiles for work journeys and a reduced imperative towards motor vehicle ownership. In contrast, those in outer and fringe suburban areas, particularly where these are remote from heavy rail lines, tend to have lower incomes, reinforced by housing markets, poorer access to good quality public transport, particularly for circumferential (i.e., non-CBD) travel and a concomitant higher reliance on automobiles with higher rates of vehicle ownership. Overall the VIPER demonstrates that the socio-spatial structure of Brisbane acts to differentiate households on the basis of relative oil vulnerability. The consequences of this differentiation mean that the cost burden of higher global oil prices, as measured by VIPER, is likely to fall hardest upon those who are already most socio-economically stressed. The configuration of urban structure and transport patterns is clearly socio-economically regressive in Brisbane (and in other major Australian cities).

The VAMPIRE

The Vulnerability Assessment for Mortgage Petroleum and Inflation Risk and Expenses (VAMPIRE) index seeks to identify the relative distribution of *oil and mortgage vulnerability*, arising from a combination of higher fuel prices, socio-economic stress and housing mortgage interest rate costs (see Dodson and Sipe, 2008). At the time we began our investigations in the mid-2000s Australia was experiencing a marked house price boom and mortgage interest rates had become topics of considerable public interest. The Reserve Bank of Australia (RBA) is responsible for setting the official interest rate that is closely connected to retail mortgage rates. The RBA is required to keep inflation within a 2–3 percentage point band and tends to raise official interest rates to prevent consumer price inflation due to excessively cheap credit. Yet oil price increases are also inflationary, both directly via fuel prices, as well as systemically via second round economic effects. Accordingly there was a risk that higher oil prices would be accompanied by both increases to mortgage interest rates as well as increased overall price inflation. The distribution of households with mortgages is different to those on just modest incomes; in Australian cities, mortgagee households tend to be located in more recently developed areas, particularly the outer and fringe suburbs of the major cities where large-scale greenfield development occurs. As a result, transport fuel and housing cost pressures were expected to generate household stress in a spatially different way to those represented by the VIPER. We termed this latter phenomenon 'oil and mortgage vulnerability' to be measured via the VAMPIRE index.

The VAMPIRE was constructed using ABS Census variables relevant to the vulnerability factors: motor vehicle ownership and reliance on automobiles for work travel, the proportion of households with mortgages in a given area, and relative household income. Despite a literature search, we were unable to find research revealing the appropriate weighting of such factors, so these were combined on a equal thirds weighting, with the transport variables combined as per the VIPER but with the mortgage and income variables as stand-alone thirds. As per the VIPER index, the VAMPIRE construction was undertaken at the CCD level with the three variables initially combined in order to provide single value for each CCD. All the CCDs within the metropolitan region were then ranked and assigned high to low oil vulnerability weightings consistent with 10th, 25th, 50th, 75th and 90th percentile bands for very high, high, medium, low and very low vulnerability. We then mapped these band categories to generate very high spatial resolution depiction of the problem. We prepared a VAMPIRE index for each of Australia's major cities, including Brisbane.

Household oil and mortgage vulnerability in Brisbane is clearly spatially differentiated. As with the VIPER index, inner urban areas tend to be less vulnerable on this measure, likely due to the higher proportion of households who do not have mortgages, the typically higher incomes among this group and the relatively better access to higher-quality public transport networks in these areas. In contrast, many outer and fringe areas have high levels of vulnerability to higher oil prices combined with income and inflation effects. These are typically areas with very high rates of car dependence, where development is more recent and poorly served by public transport, and where house prices have allocated mortgagee households with lower incomes. Like the VIPER, the VAMPIRE reveals a regressive urban structure in Brisbane whereby those most socio-economically vulnerable to higher oil prices are those least able to afford higher costs and with least availability of alternative transport modes such as public transport.

Both the VIPER and the VAMPIRE indexes demonstrate that the relative household oil vulnerability they measure is highly unevenly distributed in Brisbane, which our research shows is also the case in other major Australian cities. In general inner and middle zones with relatively good public transport access and house price structures that exclude lower-income groups are less vulnerable to the impact of higher oil prices than outer and fringe suburban locations where the poor provision of public transport and relatively cheaper housing tends to concentrate highly car dependent households on modest or low incomes. Some important differences were notable between the VIPER and VAMPIRE indexes. The VIPER tended to reveal high levels of socio-economic oil vulnerability in places where poor households were concentrated, particularly renter households. In contrast the VAMPIRE tended to highlight the oil vulnerability of mortgagee households who typically located in relatively more affluent zones than the VIPER households, often including new residential estates on the urban fringe.

6. PLANNING RESPONSE AND STRATEGY

The attempt to understand spatial patterns of oil vulnerability implies a concern for their socio-economic consequences. Although increasingly our research was motivated in part by the inherently interesting questions that higher oil prices pose for Australian cities, we were also concerned to see a policy response that could avoid, remedy or mitigate the effects of higher oil prices particularly for lower-income households. At the time our work was initially published in both academic and public venues in the mid-2000s, public concern about rising oil prices had begun to develop.

In Queensland, advocacy from an array of civic groups began to highlight problems of petroleum depletion and oil vulnerability. At the political level, the Queensland State

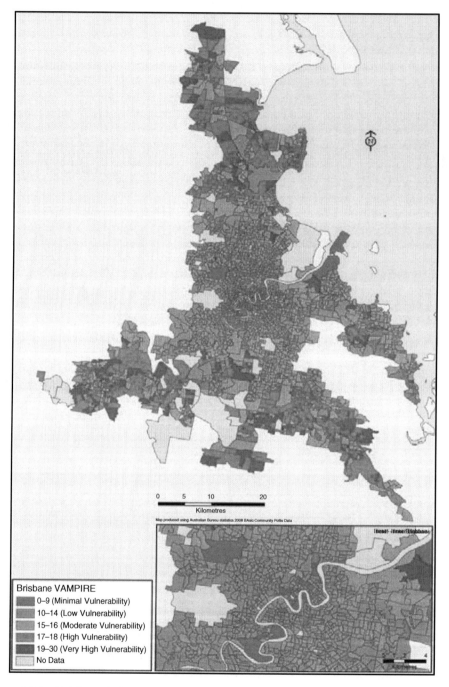

Figure 38.2   Brisbane VAMPIRE map

Minister of Environment and Sustainability took interest in the problem and began to advocate for attention to the problem. The Premier responded to this collective advocacy by establishing a Queensland Oil Vulnerability taskforce, which was tasked with providing an advisory report on the problem. The Oil Vulnerability Taskforce (2007) identified petroleum depletion and higher fuel costs as a major challenge for Queensland if early depletion scenarios were realised. The report was, however, somewhat ambivalent on the impacts of petroleum depletion; with large coal reserves Queensland was considered to be well-positioned economically to become a major liquid fuel supplier once global oil prices reached the point where coal-to-liquid production became cost-effective. The greatest problem, the Oil Vulnerability Taskforce surmised, was to ensure the distributional effects, particularly those impacting on car-dependent suburbia, were managed, to avoid social dislocation. The Queensland government determined to release the research materials prepared by the taskforce and prepared a public information document on oil vulnerability issues, but at that time did not undertake any deliberate policy steps to address the problem. Much of the impetus was lost following the 2011 election when the Minister for Sustainability, Andrew McNamara, who had been a major petroleum risk advocate within government, left office.

At the municipal level, the Brisbane City Council, which is SEQ's and Australia's largest municipality and covers most of our VIPER and VAMPIRE case study area, determined that oil vulnerability questions were sufficiently important that it commissioned its own taskforce to appraise the issue along with climate change questions. This decision was in part influenced by our presentation of the VIPER and VAMPIRE indexes to a Council Committee. The Energy and Climate Taskforce report was released in late 2007 and agreed that petroleum constraint was likely to become a problem that would require deliberate policy response. The report was surprisingly extensive in its recommendations on both climate and oil vulnerability challenges advocating a raft of actions to reduce Brisbane's exposure to climate change and oil depletion (BCC, 2007). The transport components of this mix included dramatically increased support for public transport and active travel accompanied by private motor vehicle and petroleum fuel demand constraint. In responding to the Taskforce, the Brisbane City Council (i.e., the Lord Mayor with a majority of councillors) declined to adopt most of these recommendations, preferring to leave any oil depletion adaptation response to individual choices. As a result, little substantive change has been made to the way council operations or the planning and management of Brisbane's land-uses and transport mix have been undertaken.

SEQRP 2009

Regional scale planning in the SEQ region has begun to address oil vulnerability issues, partly in response to the research and advocacy we have undertaken, which is partly described in this chapter. Statutory regional planning was instituted in 2005 and reviewed in 2009. This update came after the sharp mid-2000s rise in global oil prices and the surge in global interest in climate change following the UK Stern Report. Although urban growth management is the dominant concern of the 2009 SEQRP, the plan includes surprisingly substantive consideration of climate matters and an unusually explicit engagement with 'oil price vulnerability'. The climate change elements of the SEQRP include a number of measures with an energy vulnerability dimension, including those relating to design guidelines to make new developments more energy efficient, reducing transport fuel consumption, and enabling renewable energy generation. The substantive oil vulnerability content of the SEQRP is found in a section titled 'Responding to oil supply vulnerability'. The discussion within this section is clear about the possibility of petroleum depletion suggesting that:

> Most of the world is now dependent on a diminishing number of oil-producing countries for their oil needs. Current rates of global oil production are predicted to decline within the next five years.
>
> (DIP, 2009b: 46)

The policies offered to address this challenge are also surprisingly explicit:

1. Manage risks and reduce impacts on people, economic sectors and areas from the effects of oil supply vulnerability.
2. Design Development Areas to encourage walking, cycling and public transport use to get to local shopping facilities and employment locations, and early provision of public transport services.
3. Ensure transport infrastructure and service investment actively reduces oil dependence, particularly for trips that could be undertaken by public or active transport.
4. Reduce the length of trips and dependence on oil by localising access to goods, services and employment opportunities.

> (DIP, 2009b: 46)

The first two policies are general objectives but Policies 3 and 4 suggest a firmer policy direction. Policy 3, which aims to reduce oil dependence via transport investment, would have major implications for metropolitan land-use and transport planning if it was pursued intently. Current engineering technology and investment practices that expand road capacity would need to stop, given clear scientific evidence that such provision leads to automobile and thus petroleum dependence (Newman, 1991; SACTRA, 1994; Goodwin, 1996; Luk and Chung, 1997; Zeibots, 2005). Assiduous application of this policy would mean abandoning almost all the major road projects proposed in the SEQ Infrastructure Plan, which accompanies the SEQ Regional Plan, and are budgeted at AU\$49.8 billion over the 2009–2031 period (DIP, 2009a). The abandonment of such schemes is very unlikely given that wider planning and fiscal policy is actively supporting them (Dodson, 2009; Gleeson and Steele, 2009). In addition, the oil price vulnerability policies within the SEQRP imply the need to direct investment to oil vulnerable areas. Yet the majority of the transport infrastructure identified within the SEQ Infrastructure Plan is directed to the least oil vulnerable zones, such as the \$15 billion central Brisbane Inner City Rail project and the Northern Busway and Eastern Busway projects estimated at \$2.6 billion and \$3.63 billion, respectively. Redressing the extensive oil vulnerability in outer suburban zones, identified by the VIPER or VAMPIRE indexes, is not seriously proposed by either the SEQRP or the SEQIP.

That the SEQRP includes a dedicated section on 'oil price vulnerability' places it ahead of other the metropolitan plans the other four major Australian cities. While such inclusion is laudable, their passage through to implementation appears highly unlikely.

Motor Vehicle Fuel and Technology Transitions

One of the responses we have had to our work is the proposition that the expectation of higher global oil prices will initiate a transition to electric vehicles that do not rely on petroleum fuels. The past decade has seen a number of car companies produce hybrid electric vehicles, such as Toyota's Prius. Other companies, such as Chevrolet and Tesla Motors have released all-electric vehicles, while electric buses are beginning to be adopted in some jurisdictions. It has been proposed to us that cities no longer need fear higher oil prices because a transition away from internal combustion vehicle will resolve the kinds of problems we identified in our VAMPIRE analysis.

In contrast to such optimistic sentiments we became concerned that similar socio-economic processes to those apparent in the VIPER and VAMPIRE studies may occur in any transition within the private motor vehicle fleet, such that a convenient story of smooth technology transition would overlook many regressive effects due to urban socio-spatial structure. To illustrate this problem we undertook further work to understand the fuel efficiency of the private motor vehicle fleet in Brisbane (see Li et al., 2013). This work has been methodologically much more intensive than our VIPER and VAMPIRE studies, so we have provided only a summary version here. The key task was to create datasets linking vehicle fuel efficiency with household socio-economic status. To do this we linked Queensland government motor vehicle registration unit record data for Brisbane with the federal government's Green Vehicle dataset (DIT, 2012) on fuel efficiency by make and model, and then combined this with journey to work and socio-economic data from the ABS Census. In our analysis, current high vehicle fuel efficiency, including hybrids, served as a proxy for future electric vehicles. This is justified on the basis that new fuel-efficient vehicles typically command a premium in new vehicle prices. Our analysis built a rich picture of how the spatial distribution of fuel efficiency in the contemporary vehicle fleet intersects with suburban socio-spatial patterns, using Brisbane as a case study.

In general, inner urban areas tend to own newer, smaller, more fuel-efficient vehicles than those in outer suburban areas, whose vehicles tend to be older, larger and less fuel-efficient. We also found that the average commuting distance increases with distance from the CBD while average fuel efficiency of vehicles declines. In essence, therefore, outer suburban residents travel further, in less efficient vehicles, than more centrally situated households. Outer suburban residents are also likely to be on relatively lower incomes than those closer to the centre. The result is that households in outer suburbs often experience comparatively weaker socio-economic status and typically face a greater energy-cost burden for transport. For example, one-third of the most disadvantaged suburbs in greater Brisbane also display the most energy-intensive motor vehicle use, as measured by our analysis (Li et al., 2013). A socially equitable transition to highly fuel-efficient or electric vehicles ought to favour those with the highest current exposure to high fuel prices. Yet our findings suggest this is unlikely to happen.

Outer suburban groups also own the oldest vehicles in the fleet, which tend to be second-hand and cheaper, which also contributes to poor fuel-efficiency and higher transport costs. The newest most fuel-efficient vehicles are typically purchased by wealthier inner-urban households. Yet their higher incomes and relatively lower average journey to work vehicle kilometres travelled mean they have less objective need for such advantage. Such patterns applied to electric vehicles suggest their high cost and novelty status means they will also be taken up proportionally more by this more advantaged group. And any subsidies offered encourage such uptake will also primarily advantage the wealthy.

The implication of our analysis is that the intersection of new fuel and vehicle technology costs with the social and travel patterns in Australian cities mean that suburban households face continued socio-economic stress even as these new vehicles become more widely adopted in Australian cities. Although perhaps over the long term, hybrid and electric vehicles do offer an alternative to internal combustion cars a number of barriers, such as the small scale of the sector, doubts about range and performance, plus low standardisation of charging and ancillary infrastructure mean their uptake has greatly lagged behind some of the more lofty aspirations of their proponents. Further, the reductions in fuel excise revenue they herald are likely to stress government revenue streams, whether for road or public transport infrastructure. Such vehicles thus currently offer little respite from rising fuel costs.

7.   CONCLUSIONS

The world's petroleum energy future remains highly uncertain. An array of economic and technical factors will influence future volumes of petroleum production, the quantity of petroleum demanded by consumers and, ultimately, the price paid by petroleum users. The larger body of evidence, however, suggests that oil prices are unlikely to decline in the long run and will more likely increase, possibly markedly. The large car-dependent urban regions that predominate human settlements in Australasia, North America and increasingly in parts of Europe and Asia will face problems of adaptation and adjustment to a higher oil price future.

The impact of higher oil prices will be unevenly felt in many urban areas due to socio-spatial differences in household wealth and income and due to uneven distribution of alternative infrastructures such as public transport, or support for active travel modes. The work we have undertaken over the past eight years has sought to illuminate these problems to show where the areas of greatest risk from higher oil prices are located so that planners may better respond, preferably proactively, to the problems that are likely to be faced. We are, however, somewhat sanguine about the possibility of a comprehensive, systematically effective response. The attempts to ameliorate or mitigate the problem to date in Brisbane, or elsewhere in Australia, have been at best minimal, and similar jurisdictions in North America have also been slow to respond, if at all. Even allowing new vehicle types to take the place of petroleum-powered vehicles is unlikely to be a socially neutral response. Dependence on petroleum fuel for transport remains a major risk factor in the vulnerability of many cities that will need to be addressed, perhaps soon.

REFERENCES

ABS (2011), *Household Expenditure Survey, Australia: Summary of Results 2009–2010*, Cat No. 6530.0, Canberra: Australian Bureau of Statistics.

Australian Treasury (2006), *International Comparison of Australia's Taxes*, Canberra: Australian Government.

BITRE (2013), *Population Growth, Jobs Growth, and Commuting Flows in South East Queensland*, Canberra: Bureau of Transport and Regional Economics, Department of Infrastructure and Transport.

Campbell, C. (2005), *Oil Crisis*, London: Multi-Science Publishing.

Department of Planning (2006), *Transport and Population Data Centre Statistics for the Subregional Planning Process*, Sydney: New South Wales Government.

DIP (2009a), *South East Queensland Infrastructure Plan and Program 2009–2026*, Brisbane: Department of Infrastructure and Planning.

DIP (2009b), *South East Queensland Regional Plan 2009–2031*, Brisbane, Department of Infrastructure and Planning.

DIT (2012), *Green Vehicle Guide Dataset*, Canberra: Department of Infrastructure and Transport.

Dodson, J. (2009), The 'infrastructure turn' in Australian metropolitan spatial planning, *International Planning Studies*, **14**(2), 109–23.

Dodson, J. and Sipe, N. (2007), Oil vulnerability in the Australian city: assessing socio-economic risks from higher urban fuel prices, *Urban Studies*, **44**, 37–62.

Dodson, J. and Sipe, N. (2008), Shocking the suburbs: urban location, homeownership and oil vulnerability in the Australian city, *Housing Studies*, **23**(3), 377–401.

Fantazzini, D., Höök, M. and Angelantoni, A. (2011), Global oil risks in the early 21st century, *Energy Policy*, **39**(12), 7865–73.

Gleeson, B. and Steele, W. (2009), *The Bellwether Zone? Planning Infrastructure in South-East Queensland*, 4th National Conference on the State of Australian Cities, University of Western Australia, Perth, 27–30 November.

Goodwin, P. (1996), Empirical evidence on induced traffic, *Transportation*, **23**(1), 35–54.

Government Accountability Office (2007), *Crude Oil: Uncertainty about Future Oil Supply Makes It Important to Develop a Strategy for Addressing a Peak and Decline in Oil Production*, Washington, DC: United States Government.

Gusdorf, F. and Hallegatte, S. (2007), Compact or spread-out cities: urban planning, taxation, and the vulnerability to transportation shocks, *Energy Policy*, **35**, 4826–38.

Hamilton, J. (2009), *Causes and Consequences of the Oil Shock of 2007–08*, Washington, DC: Brookings Institution.

Heinberg, R. (2003), *The Party's Over: Oil, War and The Fate of Industrial Societies*, Gabriola Island, BC: New Society Publishers.

IEA (2008), *World Energy Outlook 2008*, Paris: International Energy Agency and Organisation for Economic Co-operation and Development.

ITPOES (2010), *The Oil Crunch: A Wake-up Call for the UK Economy*, ITPOES Second Report, London: UK Industry Taskforce on Peak Oil & Energy Security.

Joint Forces Command (2010), *Joint Operating Environment 2010*, Washington, DC: US Department of Defence.

Li, T., Sipe, N. and Dodson, J. (2013), Investigating private motorised travel and vehicle fleet efficiency: using new data and methods to reveal socio-spatial patterns in Brisbane, Australia, *Geographical Research*, **51**(3), 269–78.

Lloyds (2010), *Sustainable Energy Security: Strategic Risks and Opportunities for Business*, London: Lloyds and Chatham House.

Luk, J. and Chung, E. (1997), *Induced Demand and Road Investment*, AR299, Melbourne: Australian Road Research Board.

Mees, P. (2000a), *Rethinking Public Transport in Sydney*, UFP Issues Paper 5, Urban Frontiers Program Issues Papers, Sydney: Urban Frontiers Program, University of Western Sydney.

Mees, P. (2000b), *A Very Public Solution: Transport in the Dispersed City*, Melbourne: Melbourne University Press.

Monbiot, G. (2008), When will the oil run out? *The Guardian*.

Newman, P. (1991), Cities and oil dependence, *Cities*, August, 170–73.

Newman, P. and Kenworthy, J. (1999), *Sustainability and Cities: Overcoming Automobile Dependence*, Washington, DC: Island Press.

Queensland Government (2007), *Queensland's Vulnerability to Rising Oil Prices: Taskforce Report*, Brisbane: Queensland Government.

Queensland Transport (2005), *Smart Travel Choices for South East Queensland: A Transport Green Paper*, Brisbane: Queensland Government.

SACTRA (1994), *Trunk Roads and the Generation of Traffic*, London: HMSO.

Sipe, N. and Dodson, J. (2013), Oil vulnerability in the American city, in J. Renne and B. Fields (eds), *Transport Beyond Oil: Policy Choices for a Multimodal Future*, Washington, DC: Island Press.

Volvo (2008), *Future Fuels for Commercial Vehicles*, Goteborg: AB Volvo.

Zeibots, M. (2005), *The relationship Between Increases in Motorway Capacity And Declines in Urban Rail Passenger Journeys: A Case Study of Sydney's M4 Motorway and Western Sydney Rail Lines*, 28th Australasian Transport Research Forum, Sydney, NSW, Transport and Population Data Centre, NSW Department of Planning.

39 Troublesome leisure travel: counterproductive sustainable transport policies
Erling Holden and Kristin Linnerud

1. INTRODUCTION

The level and growth of passenger transportation – or travel – represents a major challenge to environmentally sustainable development (EEA, 2002; OECD, 2000, 2002). Among a number of environmental consequences, climate change, air pollution and excess energy consumption are the most important.

In developed countries, leisure travel constitutes a major and growing share of total travel. In the EU, for example, leisure travel accounts for approximately one-third of all trips (EEA, 2008). A survey of travel in Norway (Denstadli et al., 2006) suggests that leisure trips are responsible for more than half of total CO_2 emissions from travel because leisure trips tend to be longer and use more energy-consuming modes of transportation than everyday trips. Banister et al. (2000) projected that over the next 20 years, more people will spend more time on leisure activities because of an ageing population in OECD countries. Much of this increased leisure travel could involve long-distance air travel because more people have the means, time and desire to see the world (Gössling, 2010).

Meanwhile, research on sustainable passenger transport has mainly focused on everyday travel. Among the driving forces for everyday travel are globalization, lifestyles and individual travel preferences, demographic trends, household structure, economic growth and household income, urban sprawl, and specialization in education and labour (Banister, 2005; Banister et al., 2000; Tengström, 1999; Black, 2003; Geenhuizen et al., 2002; Salomon and Mokhtarian, 2002).

Although the above-mentioned driving forces may also influence the demand for leisure travel, we generally lack a deeper understanding of which factors affect leisure travel decisions and the sustainability of leisure travel (e.g., see Black and Nijkamp, 2002; Holden, 2007). Leisure travel is usually undertaken by choice, not by necessity. This distinction is important for policymakers because they can explore policies for reducing the need for or length of necessary trips or for enhancing alternatives to driving (Handy et al., 2005), but they may confront greater problems in reducing the amount of leisure travel because this kind of travel may be valued in its own right.

User requirements are also different for leisure travel and everyday commuting. Commuters require timeliness and predictability, but leisure trips are often less time critical. They may involve a greater load (baggage) as well as travel to and in areas with less-developed or unfamiliar public transportation systems. Lifestyle and psychological factors are also crucial in explaining demand for leisure travel, and leisure travel choices are linked to peoples' expression of identity. Thus, designing efficient, sustainable and comprehensive transportation policies requires an understanding of how leisure travel differs from other types of travel.

As has been true with research, sustainable passenger transport policies have been directed more towards everyday travel and not leisure travel. Some policies have been tailored to reduce energy use and emissions related to everyday travel; for instance, by building more compact cities to reduce the average distances of necessary trips. Such policies, however, may have little or no impact on leisure travel. In addition, some policy instruments are not applied widely enough to encompass important aspects of leisure travel. For example, the success of reducing greenhouse gas emissions in tourism will depend critically on policy and practice changes in the aviation sector, but this sector so far has not successfully been included in binding policy agreements (Scott et al., 2010).

More surprisingly, under some circumstances, some policies that aim at reducing the negative impacts of everyday travel may have the opposite effect on leisure travel. That is, while people respond to these policies by consuming less energy on everyday travel, they consume even more energy on leisure travel, thus reducing the effectiveness in terms of meeting the goals of a sustainable transportation sector and reduced greenhouse gas emissions.

In this chapter, we present three well-established sustainable transport policies – developing more compact cities, building pro-environment awareness and attitudes, and promoting growth of information and communication technologies – designed to reduce emissions from everyday travel and show that these policies may also be associated with increased emissions from leisure travel. Moreover we suggest mechanisms to explain why a given policy may produce these contradictory effects. Finally, we examine the policy implications of the results and discuss further research.

2.   THE CONTRADICTORY RESULTS OF SELECTED POLICIES

Compact Cities

The main principle in the theory of compact cities is high-density development close to or within the city core, with a mixture of housing, workplaces, and shops. The supporters of compact cities (e.g., Newman and Kenworthy, 1989; Elkin et al., 1991; McLaren, 1992; Sherlock, 1991; Næss, 2006; Geurs and van Wee, 2006) claim that they result in the least energy-intensive everyday travel pattern, thereby reducing greenhouse gas emissions. The question we raise is whether the reduced amount of everyday travel is counterbalanced by increased leisure travel.

Most empirical studies confirm that urban form affects everyday travel behaviour. Newman and Kenworthy (1989) explored the relationship between urban density and transport-related energy consumption in 32 cities in North America. They found that the gasoline consumption per capita was significantly lower in compact cities. Although Newman and Kenworthy (1989) have been criticized on methodological grounds (e.g., Rodriguez et al., 2006), later analysis (e.g., Holtzclaw et al., 2002; Cervero and Kockelman, 1997; Kitamura et al., 1997; Holden, 2004; Holden and Norland, 2005; Næss, 2006) arrived at similar conclusions, even when controlling for socio-economic, socio-demographic, and attitudinal variables. In a recent review of the literature,

Rickwood et al. (2008: 57) concluded that "there is clear evidence from both intra- and inter-city comparisons that higher density, transit oriented cities have lower per-capita transport energy use".

It is possible, however, that people live in city centres because they prefer to travel less, not that they travel less because they live in city centres. Recently, this "self-selection" bias has been given more emphasis when designing empirical models of the relationship between the built environment and the frequency of regular non-work travels (e.g., Boarnet and Sarmiento, 1998; Boarnet and Crane, 2000; Cao et al., 2009). Cao et al. (2009) found that, although residential preferences and travel attitudes significantly influenced the frequency of auto, public transportation and non-motorized trips, neighbourhood characteristics retained a separate influence on behaviour after controlling for self-selection. Thus, it seems that a compact city structure causes lower energy consumption on everyday travel, even after accounting for self-selection bias.

These studies did not, however, examine the effect compact cities have on leisure travel. Titheridge et al. (2000) claimed that the relationship between non-work travel, especially long-distance leisure travel, and urban form has been neglected, but a few empirical studies have been conducted (e.g., Tillberg, 2002; Schlich and Axhausen, 2002; Holden and Norland, 2005; Næss, 2006). These show that although residents in densely populated areas travel less in their everyday life, they do sometimes travel more in their leisure time.

Næss (2006) undertook a comprehensive quantitative and qualitative analysis of households' travel behaviour in the Copenhagen Metropolitan Area. In a multiple regression analysis, he regressed each dependent travel-behaviour variable on land-use, socio-economic, socio-demographic, and attitudinal variables. When controlling for the location of the residence relative to city centre Copenhagen and lower order centres, he found the following significant indications of compensatory travel on weekends among respondents living in dense local areas (Næss, 2006: 206): longer average distance travelled by cars, a lower proportion of public transportation use (by distance travelled) and fewer trips made on foot. Moreover, he found a correlation between city-centre living and the likelihood of making holiday trips by plane.

Holden and Norland (2005) and Holden and Linnerud (2011) conducted quantitative studies of households' travel behaviour in the Greater Oslo region in Norway. They regressed each of the dependent variables – everyday travel and leisure travel by plane – on land-use characteristics as well as socio-economic, socio-demographic and attitudinal variables. However, the regression models in Holden and Linnerud (2011) paid more attention to the relation between attitudes and behaviour. The results showed that the energy consumption for everyday travel increases significantly with distance from residence to the city centre and to the local sub-centre, whereas energy consumption for long-distance leisure travel by plane increases significantly with housing density in residential areas and with lack of access to a private yard.

Three mechanisms may explain the contradictory result found in these studies. First, people who live in densely populated areas may undertake longer trips in their leisure time to compensate for lack of access to a private yard and local greenery. In in-depth interviews, Tillberg (2002) and Næss (2006) found some support for the hypothesis that residents of densely populated areas may compensate for a lack of access to private yards and local greenery by taking longer weekend trips by car. The residents may also spend less time gardening and maintaining a single family home. Holden and Norland (2005) and Holden and Linnerud (2011) showed that residents having access to a private yard use significantly less energy for long-distance leisure travel by both car and plane than do residents without such access. Taken together, these studies suggest that access to private yards and local greenery reduces the amount of leisure travel – both by car and by plane.

Second, people may budget approximately fixed amounts of time and money to travel. If people do have a fixed budget and if living in a compact city means saving time and money on everyday travel, more money and time will be used on leisure travel – and vice versa. The assumption of fixed budgets of time and money devoted to travel was originally put forward by Zahavi (1981) and was further explored by Marchetti (1993, 1994). Based upon time-use and travel surveys from numerous cities and countries throughout the world, Schafer and Victor (2000) estimated that a person spends an average of 1.1 hours per day travelling and devotes a predictable fraction of income to travel. They also showed that these time and money budgets, as an average taken at a regional and national level, have been relatively stable over space and time. However, this remains an area of contested points, and while a review by Metz (2008) concludes that travel time budgets are constant, a review by Mokhtarian and Chen (2004) concludes that they are not, except, perhaps, at the most aggregate level.

The underlying mechanisms explaining the regularities in travel budgets are not well understood, but demand theory may provide some insight. A reduction in the price of a normal good will have two effects: (1) a decrease in price of one good relative to others results in a rise in demand for the cheaper good and (2) income saved results in an increase of demand for all goods. The first impact is emphasized by, for example, Crane (2000) who argued that, if compact cities results in less time spent per trip, people will undertake more everyday trips. However, we think it is likely that major parts of everyday travel (such as commuting to a job) are bounded with respect to distance and frequency, and that they therefore are less sensitive to changes in cost (time or money). If so, the income effect dominates, and reductions in time or money consumed on everyday travel may result in increased time and money spent on leisure travel. This is especially the case if consumers divide their total budget into separate sub-budgets, implying a separate travel budget, as suggested by the Mental Accounting Theory (Thaler, 1999).

Third, we cannot rule out that the contradictory result in these studies is at least in part a result of self-selection bias. That is, decisions on where to live and where to travel may be simultaneously determined by values and preferences not included in the model. Also decisions on whether to have a yard or whether to buy a car may be determined by the same values and preferences that determine travel behaviour. If so, including these households and land-use characteristics as right-hand variables in regression models of travel behaviour will result in biased coefficients.

Næss (2006) believes self-selection bias to be the main explanation behind the apparent correlation between urban form and leisure-time travel. He states,

> this [more flights by residents living close to central Copenhagen] is hardly a causal influence of residential location. A possible, yet speculative explanation is that an 'urban' and cosmopolitan lifestyle, prevalent in particular among young students and academics, contributes both to an increased propensity for flights and a preference for inner-city living.
>
> (Næss, 2006: 221).

Like Næss, we find it plausible that values and preferences influence both our housing and leisure travel decisions. However, the causation may also work the other way around; over time, a compact city may facilitate and foster an urban and cosmopolitan lifestyle, which includes a propensity for leisure travel flights. The interrelations between the different variables are complex, and further research is needed involving careful model specification, more sophisticated estimation techniques (e.g., the instrument variable technique) and in-depth interviews.

Pro-environment Attitudes

Authorities can use information-based policies to influence people's attitudes and knowledge and thereby influence people to choose more environmentally friendly transportation technology and pattern and amounts of transportation. If these policies are successful, one could expect that people with pro-environment attitudes would make everyday and leisure travel choices that would contribute to lower emissions. The question we raise is whether people with pro-environment attitudes compensate for reduced everyday travel with increased leisure travel.

Pieters (1988), Ronis et al. (1989), Thøgersen (1999), Moisander and Uusitalo (1994), Ajzen (2005) and Holden (2008) discussed the conditions necessary for environmental attitudes to successfully direct household energy and transportation consumption. They concluded that attitude-behaviour consistency improves when attitudes directly relate to the travel decision that should be changed, when attitudes are developed under direct experience and when environmentally friendly travel options are easily accessible when travel choices are made.

Few empirical studies of travel behaviour and land-use characteristics, however, have included data on environmental attitudes in the list of explanatory variables (e.g., see Kitamura et al., 1997; Næss, 2006; Holden and Linnerud, 2011; Barr et al., 2010, 2011). Kitamura et al. (1997) examined the effects of attitudinal characteristics on the number and proportions of everyday trips by mode of transportation for residents of five San Francisco Bay Area neighbourhoods. Attitudinal variables were drawn from survey responses designed to elicit opinions on the environment, driving, public transportation and related questions. The dependent variables were regressed on land-use, socio-economic, socio-demographic and attitudinal variables. Although each block of variables offered some significant explanatory power to the models, the attitudinal variables explained the highest proportion of the variation in the data. For everyday travel, they found that the pro-environment variable significantly increased the number and proportion of non-motorized trips and significantly reduced the proportion of auto trips.

Holden and Linnerud (2011) analysed the impact of attitudes on travel behaviour by constructing three pro-environmental indicators that differ with respect to how directly the attitudes relate to the travel decision that should be changed: an index for general pro-environmental attitudes; a dummy variable for membership of one or more environmental non-governmental organizations (NGOs); and an index for specific pro-environmental attitudes related to transport. They draw three conclusions on the basis of the results. First, while general environmental attitudes are poor predictors of travel behaviour, specific transport environmental attitudes are significantly correlated with travel behaviour. These results are in accordance with the attitude-behaviour consistency theories referred to above.

Second, respondents who express concern for the environmental consequences of transportation have significantly lower household energy consumption related to everyday travel compared to other people. For example, respondents who very much agreed with all three pro-environment transport-specific statements (an index value of 15) consumed an average of 1,008 kWh less on everyday travel as compared to respondents who very much disagreed with the statements (an index value of 3). Third, and most surprisingly, respondents who have a high score on the transport-related environmental attitude factor travel more by plane for leisure than do others. For example, respondents with an index score of 15 consumed an average of 1,188kWh more on leisure travel by plane as compared with respondents with a score of 3. Thus, whereas "green" individuals to some extent comply with their green attitudes (e.g., by using public transportation in their everyday lives), their attitude and behaviour are not consistent when travelling for leisure.

Barr et al. (2011) draw similar conclusions on the inconsistency between pro-environmental attitudes and leisure travel behaviour. They defined three lifestyle groups based on respondents' environmental behaviours in a UK survey among households. They found that those with higher levels of environmental commitment in and around the home also tended to be those who flew furthest and most frequently thus failing to transfer these activities to their holiday environments.

As with compact cities, these results may be partly a result of self-selection bias. That is, preferences and values not included in the models may affect both people's environmental awareness and their preferences for travel to distant locations. For example, people who are interested in distant cultures and concerned about global issues simultaneously may be concerned about climate change and have a strong preference for leisure travel by plane. This conflict of interest (environmental concerns and preference for long leisure travel by plane) may be solved in a moral accounting context, in which long leisure travel by plane may be justified or offset by environmental contributions in other parts of a household's consumption. This line of reasoning is similar to and extends the fixed time and money budget line of reasoning presented above.

Some support for the moral accounting explanation is found in Holden (2001, 2007), who used in-depth interviews of Norwegians to study the relationships between environmental attitudes and household consumption. The interviews revealed three mechanisms that influence whether individuals behave in an environmentally friendly way: a desire to project an environmentally friendly image (being a "hero"), a sense of powerlessness (being a "victim") and a desire to indulge oneself (being a "villain"). Holden suggests that the sense of powerlessness is related to running a home and everyday travel and that the desire to indulge oneself dominates during leisure hours. Consequently, "other consumption" (e.g., food and clothing) becomes the primary way one projects an environmentally friendly image. From our perspective, the important point is that the third mechanism, in particular, influences long-distance leisure travel by plane.

Thus, while green individuals strive to act in an environmentally responsible manner in their everyday lives, they seem to have a conflicting need to cast aside their environmental concerns when travelling for leisure. Many respondents indicated that they have a desire to indulge themselves in some situations – to free themselves from the constraints involved in environmentally friendly behaviour. Moreover, they seem to feel that they do their fair share for the environment in their non-leisure time and that they therefore should not have to continue behaving environmentally responsibly during their leisure activities.

A qualitative study by Barr et al. (2010) shows similar evidence that actions for sustainability are heavily contextualized by the sites in which they are performed. They find that social practices in a domestic setting are relatively easily adapted to accommodate environmental behaviours, yet in tourism settings embedded practices of leisure are often highly consumptive and imbued with important symbolic value that makes adaptations problematic. In interviews addressing environmental behaviours in a touristic setting, particularly in response to climate change, many argued that "a holiday is a holiday", contesting the view that spaces of leisure and tourism were appropriate sites in which to be environmentally conscious.

Information and Communication Technology (ICT)

The interaction between ICT and personal activities and related travel has been an important theme in transportation research in recent years.[1] From the evidence provided by these studies, it is apparent that this interaction is highly complex and that there is no clear-cut evidence as to whether ICT use is neutral to, increases or decreases total travel demand. There are, however, some findings that suggest that although ICT may reduce the need for everyday travel, it may stimulate the demand for leisure travel.

Salomon (1986) classified the direct[2] impacts of ICT on travel: substitution (ICT replaces travel), complementarity (ICT generates new activities that result in increased travel), modification (travel is modified in different ways, such as choice of different travel modes and trip timing, trip chaining and activity sequencing) and neutrality (no effect on travel). Using this classification, Andreev et al. (2010) reviewed about 100 studies on the impacts of ICT on personal activities and travel and concluded: "Of the four major direct impacts of ICT on travel, i.e. substitution, complementarity, modification and neutrality, substitution has been the most prevalent impact for telecommuting, with complementarity most prevalent impact for teleshopping and teleleisure" (Andreev et al., 2010: 3).

Telecommuting is the most studied activity. According to Andreev et al. (2010: 10): "It is safe to say, in general, that in the short term telecommuting leads to reduction of the various travel characteristics (e.g., vehicle kilometres, passenger kilometres, morning-peak hours, emission and number of commuting trips). In the long term, however, telecommuting impacts are still blurred." Teleleisure can be defined as the use of ICT to enable leisure activities (including leisure travel). Investigation of the impacts of teleleisure remains the most understudied issue in teleactivities studies (Mokhtarian et al., 2006; Andreev et al., 2010). A few empirical studies have been carried out, however, and some did not find a substitution effect (e.g., Handy and Yantis, 1997; Krizek et al., 2005) and others found complementary impacts (Hjorthol, 2002; Senbil and Kitamura, 2003; Wang and Law, 2007). Thus, there appears to be some support for the claim that ICT currently results in decreased travel related to mandatory personal activities (e.g., work) and increased travel related to discretionary activities (e.g., leisure travel).

If, as previously stated, people have a fixed time and income budget related to travel, we would expect that saved money and time on everyday travel resulting from ICT enables more use of money and time on leisure travel. As pointed out by Banister and Stead (2004: 613), "even if there are reductions in one set of transport-related activities (e.g., the journey to work), there may be compensating increases elsewhere as the car is now available during the day for other uses (e.g., for shopping and social activities) or for other users". Early empirical support for such compensatory mechanisms between work and non-work travel can be found in Henderson and Mokhtarian (1996), Gould and Golob (1997) and Balepur et al. (1998). For example, Henderson and Mokhtarian (1996) observed a considerable reduction in commute-related travel and a slight increase in non-work travel as a result of telecommuting. Gould and Golob (1997) found that people working exclusively at home spend significantly more time shopping on work days than people who work away from home.

Although ICT may be a substitute for work travel (moving information rather than people), it may be a complement for leisure travel by plane. That is, ICT may influence the demand for flights, for example, through using the Internet to provide last-minute deals to sell excess capacity, particularly for flights, hotels and holiday packages. Apart from the cost savings on marketing, companies can build up a profile of that market and adapt their products to meet the perceived requirements of the customer. Banister and Stead (2004: 624) stated: "The potential increase in travel is immense, as people take more overseas holidays and cheap trips to see friends, sites or other destinations. It has facilitated new ownership patterns of second homes in the Sunbelt of Europe and the ability to regularly reach them for long weekends." In a similar fashion, Gössling and Nilsson (2010) illustrated how frequent flyer programmes, facilitated by the use of ICT, may work as an institutionalized framework for high mobility by rewarding and thus increasing interest in aeromobility.

On the other hand, ICT is to an increasing extent used to facilitate public transportation and thus reduces the emissions from everyday travel. One of the greatest obstacles in convincing people to use surface-bound public transportation systems is the real or perceived inconvenience in travelling from point A to point B, which usually involves covering some distance by foot and the coordination of different modes of transportation. In Gössling (2010) a solution to this coordination problem, involving the use of iPhone, is suggested. The idea is based upon a public transportation initiative called Dutch 9292, which includes a database with schedules for all Dutch public transportation systems. Another initiative is WISETRIP, which includes multi-modal door-to-door solutions for journeys involving international travel.[3] These examples illustrate how ICT can be used to stimulate an environmentally friendly change of transport mode.

3.   CONCLUSION

Our main finding is that well-known policies aimed at reducing energy consumption and CO_2 emissions of everyday travel may have the opposite effect on leisure travel. We examined studies related to three sustainable transport policies – developing more compact cities, fostering pro-environment attitudes and promoting the use of ICT – and found that they may facilitate more use of public transportation and reduce trip distances in everyday life, but they may also directly or indirectly stimulate leisure travel.

The main reason for this unintended side-effect is that the policies are not directed towards the main objective – reducing CO_2 emissions from all travel. Instead, they are tailored to achieve an intermediate objective, which almost always is targeted at everyday transportation. For instance, the intermediate objective of a city planner may be to reduce average trip length for cars or other vehicles. But reducing the distance travelled also affects the cost of travelling and the quality of life in a city, which in turn may influence the demand for leisure travel.

Several mechanisms may contribute to this result. People seem to have relatively fixed money and time budgets for travel, and the time and money saved on everyday travel are then consumed on leisure travel. In addition, a given policy may stimulate substitutes to everyday travel and complements to leisure travel. And, finally, people seem to find it difficult to align their behaviour with their environmental attitudes during their leisure time. They, therefore, may keep a moral account, and long-distance leisure trips may be justified or offset by environmental contributions in other parts of a household's consumption. More descriptive research is needed in this area to test whether and why such compensation mechanisms exist. More generally, there is still a lack of knowledge of the complex relation between everyday and leisure travel.

As the understanding of these relationships and mechanisms deepens, policymaking must change. According to economic theory, the optimal strategy would be to apply policies that directly target the problem of emissions from transportation. This implies setting a price on CO_2 emissions on all modes of transportation – including aviation. A widely applied emission price would create incentives for reducing travel volumes as well as choosing environmentally friendly technologies, travel patterns and modes. Moreover, it would promote development of city infrastructures, ICT solutions and attitudes in which the emissions from both everyday and leisure activities would be considered and reduced. This emission price could be implemented as a global tax on fuels differentiated to reflect the amount of CO_2 emissions (similar to the system introduced in Sweden and Norway in 1991) or by a global quota system (similar to the EU Emission Trading System).

However, a widely applied emission price of the required level may not be publically or politically acceptable. While the cost is clearly visible, the benefits are not. Also, public acceptance may be especially lacking for decreasing desirable travels, like leisure-time travels, as compared to necessary travels, like work-related travels (Mokhtarian, 2005; Holden, 2007). And policymakers may view leisure-time travels as less economically productive than work-related travels and, thus, less relevant for policy making (Andreev et al., 2010).

Thus, a carefully designed policy mix is needed, in which a CO_2 price is complemented by other instruments. Since traditional sustainable transport policy measures may be less relevant to leisure travel, these must be improved and complemented with other policy measures to achieve comprehensive sustainable travel. Three ideas worth considering are the following.

- First, limits to urban density: decentralized concentration of smaller cities or polycentric development within larger cities could be promoted. While offering good opportunities for developing an affordable and well-functioning public transport system that may lead to lower energy consumption for everyday travel, it also avoids some of the disadvantages caused by extreme densities and may reduce the incentives for long-distance journeys by plane.

- Second, attitudes to leisure travel: the public could be informed about the environmental consequences of leisure-time journeys, especially by plane. In-depth interviews reveal that people generally are not aware of the negative environmental consequences of leisure-time journeys (Holden, 2008). Tailored information campaigns may alter leisure travel behaviour. And increased environmental awareness could give the political legitimacy to levy taxes on emissions from such journeys.
- Finally, ICT and leisure travel choice: the use of ICT could be promoted to facilitate environmentally friendly modes of transport in people's leisure time. For instance, multimodal journey planners involving international travel could be developed along the same lines as the WISETRIP project funded by the EU Seventh framework programme – although, for each journey, the total emissions should be given, enabling the traveller to choose the most environmentally friendly option.

NOTES

1. See, for example, *Transportation Research Part A*, **41** (2007) and *Transportation Research Part C*, **18** (2010).
2. Banister and Stead (2004) also noted longer-term, more subtle indirect and direct effects of technology innovation on travel.
3. www.wisetrip-eu.org.

REFERENCES

Ajzen, I. (2005), *Attitudes, Personality and Behaviour*, 2nd edn, Buckingham: Open University Press.
Andreev, P., Salomon, I. and Pliskin, N. (2010), Review: state of teleactivities, *Transportation Research Part C*, **18**, 2–20.
Balepur, P.N., Varma, K.V. and Mokhtarian, P.L. (1998), Transportation impacts of center-based telecommuting: interim findings from the neighborhood telecenters project, *Transportation*, **25**, 287–306.
Banister, D. (2005), *Unsustainable Transport*, London: Routledge.
Banister, D. and Stead, D. (2004), Impact of ICT on transport, *Transport Reviews*, **24**, 611–32.
Banister, D., Stead, D., Steen, P., Akerman, J., Dreborg, K., Nijkamp, P. and Schleicher-Tappeser, R. (2000), *European Transport Policy and Sustainable Mobility*, London and New York: Spon Press.
Barr, S., Shaw, G., Coles, T.E. and Prillwitz, J. (2010), 'A holiday is a holiday': practicing sustainability home and away, *Journal of Transport Geography*, **18**, 474–81.
Barr, S., Shaw, G. and Coles, T. (2011), Times for (un)sustainability? Challenges and opportunities for developing behaviour change policy: a case-study of consumers at home and away, *Global Environmental Change*, **21**(4), 1234–44.
Black, W.R. (2003), *Transportation: A Geographical Analysis*, London and New York: The Guilford Press.
Black, W.R. and Nijkamp, P. (eds) (2002), *Social Change and Sustainable Transport*, Bloomington, IN: Indiana University Press.
Boarnet, M.G. and Crane, R. (2000), *Travel by Design: The Influence of Urban Form on Travel*, New York: Oxford University Press.
Boarnet, M.G. and Sarmiento, S. (1998), Can land use policy really affect travel behaviour? *Urban Studies*, **35**, 1155–69.
Cao, J., Mokhtarian, P.L. and Handy, S.L. (2009), The relationship between the built environment and nonwork travel: a case study of Northern California, *Transportation Research Part A*, **43**, 548–59.
Cervero, R. and Kockelman, K. (1997), Travel demand and the 3Ds: density, diversity, and design, *Transportation Research Part D*, **2**, 199–219.

Crane, R. (2000), The influence of urban form on travel: an interpretive review, *Journal of Planning Literature*, **15**, 3–23.

Denstadli, J.M., Engebretsen, Ø., Hjorthol, R. and Vågane, L. (2006), *2005 Norwegian Travel Survey – Key Results*, Report no. 844/2006, Institute of Transport Economics, Oslo.

EEA (2002), *Energy and Environment in the European Union*, environmental issue report 31, Copenhagen: European Environment Agency.

EEA (2008), *Beyond Transport Policy: Exploring and Managing the External Drivers of Transport Demand*, technical report 12, Copenhagen: European Environment Agency.

Elkin, T., McLaren, D. and Hillman, M. (1991), Reviving the City: Towards Sustainable Urban Development, London: Friends of the Earth.

Geenhuizen, M., van, Nijkamp, P. and Black, W.R. (2002), Social change and sustainable transport: a manifesto on transatlantic research opportunities, W.R. Black and P. Nijkamp (eds), *Social Change and Sustainable Transport*, Bloomington: Indiana University Press, pp. 3–16.

Geurs, K.T. and van Wee, B. (2006), Ex-post evaluation of thirty years of compact urban development in the Netherlands, *Urban Studies*, **43**, 139–60.

Gössling, S. (2010), *Carbon Management in Tourism: Mitigating the Impacts on Climate Change*, London: Routledge.

Gössling, S. and Nilsson, J.H. (2010), Frequent flyer programmes and the reproduction of aeromobility, *Environment and Planning A*, **42**, 241–52.

Gould, J. and Golob, T. (1997), Shopping without travel or travel without shopping? An investigation of electronic home shopping, *Transport Reviews*, **17**, 355–76.

Handy, S. and Yantis, T. (1997), The Impacts of Telecommunications Technologies on Nonwork Travel Behavior, R.R. SWUTC/97/721927-1F, Southwest Region University Transportation Center, The University of Texas at Austin.

Handy, S., Weston, L. and Mokhtarian, P.L. (2005), Driving by choice or necessity? *Transportation Research A*, **39**, 183–203.

Henderson, D.K. and Mokhtarian, P.L. (1996), Impacts of center-based telecommuting on travel and emissions: analysis of the Puget sound demonstration project, *Transportation Research D*, **1**, 25–49.

Hjorthol, R.J. (2002), The relation between daily travel and use of the home computer, *Transportation Research Part A*, **36**, 437–52.

Holden, E. (2001), *Housing as Basis for Sustainable Consumption*, PhD thesis, Norwegian University of Science and Technology, Norway.

Holden, E. (2004), Ecological footprints and sustainable urban form, *Journal of Housing and the Built Environment*, **19**, 91–109.

Holden, E. (2007), *Achieving Sustainable Mobility: Everyday and Leisure-time Travel in the EU*, Aldershot: Ashgate.

Holden, E. (2008), Green attitudes and sustainable household consumption of energy and transport: six conditions that improve attitude-behaviour consistency, in S. Bergmann, T. Hoff, and T. Sager (eds), *Spaces of Mobility*, London: Equinox Publishing, pp. 59–80.

Holden, E. and Linnerud, K. (2011), Troublesome leisure travel: the contradictions of three sustainable transport policies, *Urban Studies*, **48**(14), 3087–106.

Holden, E. and Norland, I.T. (2005), Three challenges for the compact city as a sustainable urban form: household consumption of energy and transport in eight residential areas in the Greater Oslo region, *Urban Studies*, **42**, 2145–66.

Holtzclaw, J., Clear, R., Dittmar, H., Goldstein, D. and Haas, P. (2002), Location efficiency: neighbourhood and socio-economic characteristics determine auto ownership and use – studies in Chicago, Los Angeles and San Francisco, *Transportation Planning and Technology*, **25**, 1–27.

Kitamura, R., Mokhtarian, P.L. and Laidet, L. (1997), A micro-analysis of land use and travel in five neighborhoods in the San Francisco Bay area, *Transportation*, **24**, 125–8.

Krizek, K.J., Li, Y. and Handy, S.L. (2005), ICT as a substitute for non-work travel: a direct examination, TRB 2005 Annual Meeting (CD-ROM).

Marchetti, C. (1993), *On Mobility*, final status report, contract no. 4672-92-03 ED ISP A, IIASA, Laxenburg, Austria.

Marchetti, C. (1994), Anthropological invariants in travel behaviour, *Technological Forecasting and Social Change*, **47**, 75–88.

McLaren, D. (1992), Compact or dispersed? Dilution is no solution, *Built Environment*, **18**, 268–84.

Metz, D. (2008), The myth of travel time saving, *Transport Reviews*, **28**, 321–36.

Moisander, J. and Uusitalo, L. (1994), Attitude-behaviour inconsistency: limitations of the reasoned action approach in predicting behaviour from pro-environmental attitudes, in G. Antonides and W.F van Raaij (eds), *IAREP/SABE Conference*, Rotterdam, 10–13 July, pp. 560–79.

Mokhtarian, P.L. (2005), Travel as a desired end, not just a means, *Transportation Research Part A*, **39**, 93–6.

Mokhtarian, P.L. and Chen, C. (2004), TTB or not TTB, that is the question: a review and analysis of the empirical literature on travel time (and money) budgets, *Transportation Research Part A*, **38**, 643–75.

Mokhtarian, P.L., Handy, S. and Salomon, I. (2006), The impacts of ICT on leisure activities and travel: a conceptual exploration, *Transportation*, **33**, 263–89.

Næss, P. (2006), *Urban Structure Matters*, Abingdon and New York: Routledge.

Newman, P. and Kenworthy, J. (1989), *Cities and Automobile Dependence: An International Sourcebook*, Aldershot: Gower Publications.

OECD (2000), *Environmentally Sustainable Transport: Futures, Strategies and Best Practices*, Paris: Organisation for Economic Co-operation and Development.

OECD (2002), *Towards Sustainable Household Consumption? Trends and Policies in OECD Countries*, Paris: Organisation for Economic Co-operation and Development.

Pieters, R. (1988), Attitude-behaviour relationships, W.F. van Raaij, G.M. van Veldhoven and K.-E. Wärneryd (eds), *Handbook of Economic Psychology*, Dordrecht: Kluwer Academic Publishers, pp. 144–204.

Rickwood, P., Glazebrook, G. and Searle, G. (2008), Urban structure and energy: a review, *Urban Policy and Research*, **26**, 57–81.

Rodriguez, D.A., Targa, F. and Aytur, S.A. (2006), Transport implications of urban containment policies: a study of the largest twenty-five US metropolitan areas, *Urban Studies*, **43**, 1879–97.

Ronis, D.L., Yates, J.F. and Kirscht, J.P. (1989), Attitudes, decisions, and habits as determinants of repeated behaviour: attitude structure and function, in A.R. Pratkanis, S.J. Breckler and A.G. Greenwald (eds), *Attitude Structure and Function*, Hillsdale, NJ: Lawrence Erlbaum, pp. 213–39.

Salomon, I. (1986), Telecommunications and travel relations: a review, *Transportation Research Part A*, **20**, 223–38.

Salomon, I. and Mokhtarian, P.L. (2002), Driven to travel: the identification of mobility-inclined market segments, in W.R. Black and P. Nijkamp (eds), *Social Change and Sustainable Transport*, Bloomington, IN: Indiana University Press, pp. 173–80.

Schafer, A. and Victor, D.G. (2000), The future mobility of the world population, *Transportation Research Part A*, **34**, 171–205.

Schlich, R. and Axhausen, K.W. (2002), *Wohnumfeld und Freizeitverkehr – eine Unthersuchung zur Fluchttheorie*, Arbeitsberichte Verkher-und Raumplanung 155, Zurich: EHT/IVT.

Scott, D., Peeters, P. and Gössling, S. (2010), Can tourism deliver its 'aspirational' emission reduction targets? *Journal of Sustainable Tourism*, **18**(3), 393–408.

Senbil, M. and Kitamura, R. (2003), *Simultaneous Relationships between Telecommunications and Activities*, Tenth International Conference on Travel Behaviour Research, Lucerne.

Sherlock, H. (1991), *Cities are Good for Us*, London: Paladin.

Tengström, E. (1999), Towards Environmental Sustainability? A Comparative Study of Danish, Dutch and Swedish Transport Policies in a European Context, Aldershot: Ashgate.

Thaler, R. (1999), Mental accounting matters, *Journal of Behavioural Decision Making*, **12**, 183–206.

Thøgersen, J. (1999), *Making Ends Meet: A Synthesis of Results and Implications of a Research Programme*, working paper no. 99-1, Department of Marketing, Aarhus School of Business.

Tillberg, K. (2002), Residential location and daily mobility patterns: a Swedish case study of households with children, in W.R. Black and P. Nijkamp (eds), *Social Change and Sustainable Transport*, Bloomington, IN: Indiana University Press, pp. 165–72.

Titheridge, H., Haal, S. and Banister, D. (2000), Assessing the sustainability of urban development policies, in K. Williams, E. Burton and M. Jenks (eds), *Achieving Sustainable Urban Form*, London: E. & F.N. Spon, pp. 149–59.

Wang, D. and Law, F. (2007), Impacts of information and communication technologies (ICT) on time use and travel behaviour: a structural equations analysis, *Transportation*, **34**, 513–27.

Zahavi, Y. (1981), *The UMOT-Urban Interactions*, DOT-RSPA-DBP 10/7, Washington, DC: US Department of Transportation.

40 The future of transport and development in the new millennium: the inescapable implications of climate change
Mayer Hillman

1. INTRODUCTION

Governments around the world acting on behalf of their populations now face a dire predicament. Carbon dioxide emissions in the global atmosphere have reached a dangerous level of concentration and are predicted to go on rising considerably into the foreseeable future. Temperature and sea-level increases and changes in weather patterns are beginning to shrink the habitable land mass on which a burgeoning future population, forecast to be more than a third higher than it is now, will have to live. One of the most eminent US climate scientists, James Hansen (Hansen et al., 2008), has warned of the danger of the concentration of these emissions exceeding 350ppmv (parts per million by volume): at present, they exceed 390ppmv and are well on the way to an irreversible tipping point. Fairly recently, temperatures around the world were calculated to be seriously unsafe if the global temperature were to exceed a rise of 2°C above the pre-Industrial Revolution level. A rise of up to 5°C later this century is now predicted by the Intergovernmental Panel on Climate Change (IPCC, 2013). The fact that these figures are global averages, with countries in more extreme latitudes likely to experience even sharper rises, provide even more disturbing grounds for concern.

Evidence of this process is reflected in the growing acidification of the oceans, and disturbing warning signs that these, together with other carbon sinks, may no longer be able to absorb roughly half of the emissions from our continuing burning of fossil fuels that they have done until recently. It is reflected too in the loss of the volume of sea ice in the Arctic and in methane release from tundra regions in northern latitudes such as parts of Siberia. These changes, on a scale never witnessed before in such a short period of human history, are part of a feedback mechanism that will inevitably accelerate the process of climate change – and yet are not comprehensively incorporated into the modelling process currently used to provide the figures determining government policy on the speed and rate of reduction of carbon emissions (Meyer, 2013). Their inclusion can only result in seeing the IPCC's predictions to be woeful underestimates.

A major cause of these alarming changes is the spreading and intensifying addiction to fossil fuel-based lifestyles around the world. Even a major reversal of current policies in relevant sectors of the economy, such as transport, will be unable to prevent ecological catastrophe on such a scale as to gravely prejudice the survival and quality of life of human beings and other species on the planet.

2.   PROSPECTS FOR FUTURE GENERATIONS

Hillman (2011) has observed that no other aggregation of human behaviour in recorded history can begin to match the appalling legacy we are bequeathing to future generations by our near-total failure to face up to the implications of climate change. It would be difficult to fault the prediction that most, if not all, the following outcomes will prove correct:

- regions of the world becoming uninhabitable at an accelerating rate leading in due course to hundreds of millions of ecological migrants having to seek refuge in countries around the world that have been relatively spared the worst depredations of climate change yet whose populations will be highly unlikely to welcome them;
- extensive water and food shortages in many countries;
- catastrophic loss of life and likely wars of survival;
- widespread decrease of species diversity and genetic variability;
- declining proportion of some of the planet's existing finite mineral reserves remaining;
- imposition on thousands of future generations an absolute need to prevent radioactive waste from nuclear-based electricity generation plants leaking from its repositories;
- grave risk of nuclear war owing to the proliferation of weapons-applicable fissile material;
- huge financial debts owing to this generation's unwillingness to live within its means;
- a world in which news of the consequences of our abject failure to meet the challenge of climate change gets progressively and inescapably grimmer.

3.   THE RESPONSE FROM ALL SECTORS OF SOCIETY

We do not seem prepared to reverse the process that seems almost certain to have this lamentable outcome. We are loathe even to contemplate the changes that must be made, especially those entailing a very substantial and speedy reduction in our fossil fuel-based activities. Encouraging statements are made by politicians, professional institutions and religious leaders giving the impression that they are aware of the gravity of the situation: in urging the public and especially government to act more responsibly as current stewards of the planet, in their professed commitment to the cause of equity and social justice, and in promoting the adoption of sustainable strategies to ensure worldwide delivery of low-carbon economies.

However, when attempts are made to translate these worthy objectives into practice, the statements made in proposing them seem unlikely to deliver them. Authoritative predictions for the future from the US Energy Information Administration (2011) indicate that global energy consumption will continue to rise, with more than a 50 per cent increase by 2035. The statements could be interpreted as little more than empty rhetoric, a judgement supported by reference to the fact that those questioning the sufficiency of current efforts are typically dismissed as theoreticians incapable of understanding human nature and political reality, as 'holier than thou' kill-joys, or as concealing a hidden left-wing agenda.

Forecasts in the UK Department for Transport publications (DfT, 2011) suggest that hope of light at the tunnel's end is being cast into doubt: first, by the absence of any indication that even affluent populations' demand for high energy-based activities in the transport sector, is by any means satiated (this is especially true in aviation and maritime transport, which have so far escaped adequate inclusion in international agreements on the curtailment of emissions); second, by ignoring the contribution of the process of globalization that extends supply chains and thereby generally generates the need for more fossil fuel use: third, by the sharply rising Third World populations' understandable aspiration to follow the West's lead in adopting high-energy lifestyles; fourth, by the disturbing inadequacy of the government's carbon reduction targets; and, finally, by reasonable doubts that even these will be met.

From this perspective, a reappraisal of the relevance of climate change to current transport and planning decisions has to be undertaken. The implications are far more significant than may be initially apparent. Every domain of policy that is directly or indirectly related to the extent of the energy-intensiveness of our lifestyles must be evaluated by reference to factors that could substantially affect it. The overriding consideration must be to relate it to the impact of climate change on the future habitability of the planet and the quality of life of its population. The contribution each proposed change would make in terms of adding carbon emissions to the planet's capacity to safely absorb them must be incorporated into calculations on the subject. Focusing in particular on every area of fossil-fuel dependent activity that cannot be categorized as absolutely essential will inevitably demonstrate why, as a matter of urgency, a massive reduction in emissions must be achieved and then maintained until such time as advances in technology have hopefully enabled renewable energy to largely replace the current, largely fossil fuel-based energy mix.

4. MISLEADING JUDGEMENTS INFORMING PUBLIC POLICY

A strong case exists for seriously challenging many widely endorsed assumptions underpinning public policy at present. As a consequence, the transition to decreasingly fossil fuel-dependent lifestyles has been rendered increasingly difficult to be achieved in the rapidly declining time available to do so. One obvious explanation for this is that one of the major functions of government is seen to be to cater for as much public demand as possible – without regard to the consequences then running counter to the necessity of adopting and then delivering very low carbon-based patterns of activity.

Appropriate decisions to cater for future transport activity are exemplars of this process. These indicate that there is little, if any, awareness of the critical contradiction between investing large sums of public money to meet the growing demand for high-speed long-distance travel by road, rail and air, while at the same time seeking to limit the devastating consequences of climate change. The inescapable fact remains that the planet's atmosphere only has a finite *non-negotiable* capacity to safely absorb further fossil-fuel burning – which is the overriding reason for rejecting out of hand so-called 'improvements' to the transport infrastructure, such as HS2, Crossrail and expansion of airport capacity in the south-east of England. It may be that those who propose policies such as these are in denial of the irrefutable scientific evidence on this, or think it insufficiently relevant to promoting economic growth, the policy that is so wholeheartedly supported by all the main political policies.

These outcomes can be laid at the door of those subscribing to the many questionable assumptions – close to tenets of faith – that continue to stand in the way of making a speedy transfer to lifestyles, practices and patterns of development that will assuredly deliver very low-carbon footprints. Sadly, those who choose to deny the significance of climate change have wide support, as the public would clearly prefer scientists to be proved wrong in their predictions on this subject and, therefore, hope that the need for the urgent adoption of a strategy to deliver such footprints will prove unnecessary. These assumptions include a near-absolute confidence on key aspects of decision-making in this century.

Raising the Standard of Living

The public has been led to believe that it has a right to ever-rising improvements in its material standards and life choices. Statements of all the main political parties give a strong impression that such a future is possible without the need for the major behavioural changes that the public would clearly prefer not to make. People are seen to have an inalienable right well into the future to engage in environmentally damaging activities. It is assumed that high dependence on car use between home and places of work, education, shopping and leisure cannot be questioned if there are no acceptable less damaging alternative means of reaching these destinations. This holds true even more so in relation to flying, especially where it is thought that a fair fare based on the 'polluter pays' principle is being paid. However, a major explanation for the disastrous outcome of these lines of thinking is that it is judged perfectly reasonable for individuals to decide where and how to travel entirely from a 'self-interest' perspective, with little, if any, regard to the effects on other people's quality of life, on community health, on the physical environment and, by no means least, on accelerating climate change. Of course, as the effects are worse where decisions lead to more carbon-intensive journeys over longer distances and at higher and therefore more energy-intensive speeds, there can be no justification for the most relevant institutions and the media to continue to be allowed to fail alerting the public to the largely inescapable links of these patterns of activity with climate change.

Economic growth is seen to be the primary way of improving the public's welfare and quality of life. To escape the damaging effects of the current worldwide recession, every effort must be made to return to it – and it will have the further benefit of generating more employment.

However, it is as if the limit on the degree to which the powerful link between GDP and greenhouse gas emissions can be sufficiently de-coupled owing to the existence of some easily adopted means of de-coupling. No doubt for that reason, at their annual conferences, all three of the main political parties in the UK regularly affirm their belief that the primary aim of government must be to return speedily to economic growth.

Promoting Economic Growth

It is seen as unnecessary for the sectoral components of growth to be differentiated according to their contribution to climate change and, as a consequence, that an adequate response to climate change does not have, nor must be allowed, to limit economic growth.

However, in the absence of grounds for such a judgement, the implication is that a stratagem will assuredly be found in due course for making compatible the goals of ever-rising economic growth into the foreseeable future and protection of the global environment from irreversible climate change.

Valuing Externalities

Taxation can be deployed to ensure that the 'polluter pays principle' is applied sufficiently effectively to allow for a realistic price to be set to cover all the costs of emitting carbon dioxide into the atmosphere. That price, it is argued, then frees the market to work in its most efficient way.

However, this requires attaching a realistic monetary value that adequately compensates for the impacts of the emissions over the 100 years that they remain in the atmosphere. At present, no value is given to cover some unquantifiable but nevertheless huge short and long-term adverse effects, such as the rise in food prices following a switch from agricultural land being used for biofuels rather than food crops, and the mass migration and resettlement of ecological refugees fleeing their homes to escape the effects of climate change.

Dependence on Fossil Fuels

Against a background of the numerous opportunities for energy saving, it is presumed that the major contributions that science and technology can make to finding cost-effective ways of reducing the amount of fossil fuels used that would otherwise be needed for continuing the pursuit of economic growth will prove adequate. These include using them more efficiently; burying underground the carbon dioxide from their combustion; investing more in renewable sources of energy, such as, solar, wind and wave power and bioenergy; more advanced techniques based on less carbon-intensive electricity generation; and identifying relatively low-carbon alternative fuels, such as shale gas and tar sands. Implicit in this approach is the view, based on sparse evidence, that, in time, these practices will lead to a sufficient reduction of emissions and that the public, industry and commerce can be motivated to deliver it voluntarily, encouraged by better information, subsidies, offers of grants, exhortation and legislation.

However, many of these developments aimed at making a marked contribution to reducing dependence on fossil fuels and carbon emissions are being reappraised in the light of recent outcomes of research and development. They include carbon capture and storage owing to the fact that the House of Commons Environmental Audit Committee (2008) stated that it has not been proven technically or commercially viable – Macalister and Carrington (2011) reported that its flagship project was 'close to collapse'; shale gas, owing to dangers of the leakage of methane – a particularly lethal greenhouse gas (Anderson 2011); oil from tar sands proving too carbon-intensive and unacceptable on environmental grounds, as reported in an issue of Scientific American in 2001; biomass as being too land-intensive as reported by the European Biofuels Technology Platform (2011); and, in the case of nuclear-based electricity, too risky, as cited by Hillman (in Hillman and Tindale, 2009). Analytical evaluation of some of these installations has concluded that they are far too expensive, especially in a time of economic recession, and Macalister and Carrell (2011) have reported the likely withdrawal of a major utility company's involvement in a UK nuclear programme.

Reducing Greenhouse Gas Emissions

Modest reductions in greenhouse gas emissions on the principle that 'every little bit counts' are welcomed as indicative of a process that can eventually lead to sufficient reductions. It is also implied that, in a democratic society, only an atmospheric concentration of carbon dioxide can be chosen that is acceptable to a majority of the electorate. Associated with this is the inference that there is both sufficient time left for this stage to be reached and that the necessary funds can be found for its delivery.

However, the safe level of concentration cannot be negotiated as it ignores the fact noted earlier that the safe level to which we must adapt is fixed. Moreover, time to reach that level is regrettably unavailable: the deteriorating condition of the planet is far too advanced to allow for the near-universal recognition of the unsustainability of a largely 'business-as-usual' strategy – as well as acceptance of the moral responsibility of citizens to act in light of this.

Carbon emissions from the transport sector overall are still rising alarmingly. In the light of this, efforts continue to be directed to enabling the car to remain the mainstay of personal travel: this can be seen in recent years in impressive improvements in the energy-efficiency of vehicles enabling less fuel to be needed; in the promotion of car-sharing, car clubs and economical ways of driving, and in research on alternative fuels such as electricity generated from shale gas and bioenergy.

Although considerable improvements have been made in the past three decades in increasing the energy efficiency of cars, that has not led to an equivalent reduction in emissions from them owing to the fact that many more households are now car-owning or multi-car-owning.

Rail transport is seen as a relatively low-carbon emitter and this, therefore, with all-political party support, is cited to justify the case for heavily subsidizing train fares and, for instance, providing vast sums of public money for the construction of a high-speed rail system from London to Birmingham and, later, further north. Indeed, in support for its case, the UK coalition government has claimed that HS2 will attract significant numbers of travellers from flying and motoring. To this has been added the view that its construction will aid the competitiveness of the UK business community and thereby 'help to fulfil our ambitions for economic growth and a low carbon economy'. Allied to this is exaggeration of public transport's role as the way out of the impasse created by growing car use.

However, such a view ignores the fact that the energy efficiency of cars has improved in the past three decades to such an extent that fuel consumption per person kilometre is now often lower by car than by train. This is especially true if the fuel used on a journey to and from a station at either end of the rail journey is factored into the calculation. Moreover, there is every indication that recent improvements in the car's fuel consumption are set to continue in future. In addition, rail travel is principally associated with long-distance journeys (nearly three times as long, on average, as car journeys) – a factor all too frequently excluded from inter-modal comparisons. Moreover, the fact is overlooked that most current car mileage was not previously made by public transport. This error then results in chasing an ephemeral objective – the belief that the situation can be reversed by sufficiently high investment in promoting rail travel.

Deterrents to Reducing Emissions Sufficiently and In Time

Public policy to limit damage from climate change is aimed at identifying the most effective policies and practices that encourage individuals and industry to switch to lower carbon lifestyles.

However, the essential behavioural changes that must be made may take several decades to bring about. Moreover, it is common knowledge that even a public properly informed of the essentiality of making these changes is not necessarily prepared to do so. Although public opinion polls, at least in Europe, such as those reported in a European Commission publication, indicate that climate change is a real cause for concern and one greater than concern about the economic recession, governments in a democracy are expected to 'get in step with public opinion' (The Guardian, 2011). Yet, there is little evidence that that public even in the European Community is prepared to act other than to take modest steps to that end: carbon dioxide emissions from within the EU have risen rather than fallen to meet agreed targets for their reduction in the last few years.

Consideration of the Claims of Future Generations

A future can be reasonably anticipated in which most people, once adequately educated about climate change, and the processes contributing to it, will be prepared to voluntarily escape their addictions to longer and faster travel and forego the associated high fossil fuel-based lifestyles.

However, it is totally unrealistic to expect many individuals, communities or indeed countries to act unilaterally when others are not doing so. Nor is it realistic to expect a significant proportion of individuals or businesses to impose on themselves a self-denying ordinance of personal rationing. To be effective, it would require the rationing to be mandatory.

It is thought that the world's population is better-off if more fossil fuel reserves are found to feed its increasingly energy-dependent lifestyles, as the rising demand for them can then be more readily met. In addition, if more can be found, it puts to a later date the perceived need for strong effective steps to be taken to cut down on emissions.

However, this comforting thought overlooks the fact that the more reserves that are found, the more will be burned, thereby adding to the concentration of greenhouse gases into an already dangerously overloaded global atmosphere. Allied to this is the concern, increasingly expressed, that we are using the planet's reserves of oil at such a rate that there will be little left within 40 years or so. It is clear from this perspective that the 'we' relates to the availability of oil solely for our generation. What about the claims of future generations? They may well have more essential applications for it when compared with the frivolous way in which we are using it now (long-distance car commuting, international events entailing participants having to fly long distances, stag parties in Prague, skiing in the Rockies, a beach holiday in Muscat or an around-the-world cruise). Insofar as presumably decision-makers wish that life on earth should continue to be enjoyed for hundreds if not thousands of years into the future, surely the claims of future generations should be factored into the calculations showing at current levels of consumption what is being left for them?

5.   THE IMPLICATIONS FOR FUTURE DEVELOPMENTS

The time is over for engaging in these distorting lines of reasoning and wishful thinking. They have led to considerable public investment in transport systems that almost exclusively cater for lifestyles with rising rather than sharply declining dependence on fossil fuels.

The providers of retailing, hospitals and leisure activities have exploited the benefits of economies of scale by increasing the size of outlets while reducing their number, in the knowledge that an increasing proportion of their customers or clients have access to a car, and they can largely ignore the personal and public costs of doing so. In a chapter of a book published in 1996, Hillman highlighted the fact that to enable access to and from ever more distant destinations, changes in the built environment, particularly in suburban, urban fringe and rural locations, have resulted in patterns of activity that cannot realistically and sustainably be served without a car and in which only a small minority of journeys is possible by non-motorized means.

Indeed, it is almost as if, in decisions over the past few decades, there has been a conspiracy to do the opposite of what we so obviously should have done. The effect of this can be seen in the lowering quality of life of those without a car. The physical outcome of policy can no longer be allowed to be largely antithetical to the process of making such changes to our lifestyles and to restructuring existing urban areas and other patterns of settlement so that they effectively promote self-sufficiency, sustainability, conviviality, quality of life improvements and, most particularly, very low-carbon community activities.

Concern for the future in this domain of public policy would appear to be wholly justified by changes taking place in countries such as India, where the annual growth rate of car ownership has reached 9 per cent. Yet the factors that appear to account for the political failure to face reality and institute measures that will ensure the speedy adoption of very low-carbon lifestyles inevitably point to the need for a much diminished role for the car.

The exponential growth of towns and cities has only been made possible by exploiting, with seemingly gay abandon, the planet's finite reserves of fossil fuels and ignored the finite limits of the global atmosphere to safely absorb more greenhouse gases. It is salutary to reflect on the fact that at a time when it is widely agreed that carbon emissions have to be drastically reduced, in the transport sector, rail travel is heavily subsidized as is, indirectly, both car travel and flying because the ecological damage they cause is hardly – if at all – covered in their costs of travel.

The same holds true in relation to most overseas travel, whether for business, tourism or for social reasons. The fact must be faced that, as some destinations can only be reached by air, this must not be cited in justification of rejecting the inevitable logic, namely that this form of travel must be hugely curtailed.

6. THE ONLY STRATEGY WITH ANY PROSPECT OF SUCCESS

What are the implications of this depressing diagnosis of our predicament and is there a way out? It is often argued that every available measure will have to be deployed to achieve the desired outcome. However, there is a complementary approach that will assuredly – not just hopefully – deliver success and provide the essential framework within which the contribution of each measure can be evaluated. Such an approach obviously has to reflect the fact that it is not possible to respond sufficiently effectively to climate change in the absence of a global agreement on the method to be used to share the planet's finite assets, especially that of a safe atmospheric concentration of greenhouse gases.

Based on the principles of precaution and equity set out in the United Nations Framework Convention on Climate Change, this is the Global Commons Institute's (GCI) proposal first put forward by Meyer (2000) and fast gaining support internationally – Contraction & Convergence (C&C) (see, for instance, the Global Commons Institute website: www.gci.org.uk). Indeed, the last Archbishop of Canterbury stated that 'C&C thinking appears utopian only if we refuse to contemplate the alternatives honestly' (Williams, 2006).

It requires the imposition of a global cap on greenhouse gases and, given the finite capacity of the planet's atmosphere to safely absorb further gases noted earlier, sharing them on an equal per capita basis between the world's populations. This is surely the only moral, politically practical and therefore realistic course of action to take. The fact that no one has a right to more than their fair share means that this will ensure that everyone's personal responsibility to limit their use of fossil fuels is not just an aspiration but an imperative within which they will live. In the application of equal per capita shares as the principle of allocation, there must be a minimum of exceptions or extenuating circumstances, such as more units for those living in colder countries owing to higher heating bills in the winter or for those living in hotter countries owing to the higher costs of air conditioning.

Only governments have the authority and power to take the necessary steps at the level of individual and corporate decision-making to set this process in train by taking immediate steps to reach an international agreement on the massive switch to very low-carbon lifestyles. Therefore, C&C's national manifestation will be in the form of a Personal Carbon Allowance (PCA), that is an equal per capita 'ration' allocated by each government, with an annual phased reduction to a scientifically determined extent down to the agreed level of global carbon emissions. Initially, the annual allowance would cover the principal fossil fuel-based activities used in the home – heating, hot water, power and lighting – and transport. In its later more sophisticated form, the ration would include household food, consumer durables, and so on, with an allocation for each product calculated on its 'cradle-to-grave' carbon content.

The allowances would act as a parallel currency to real money, as well as creating an ecologically virtuous circle. A key feature is buying and selling: a 'conserver gains' principle would replace the conventional 'polluter pays' principle. Those who lead less energy-intensive lives and those who invest in energy efficiency and energy renewables are unlikely to use all their allowance. They will then not only spend less on fuel but also have the added incentive of increasing their incomes by selling their unused units. But the cost of buying these units will rise annually in line with the reduction of the allowance as it will be determined by the availability of the surplus set against the demand for it. The process will act in a way that encourages individuals to adopt green practices far more effectively than they would through regulation, pricing, exhortation or appeals to conscience.

Since Hillman and Fawcett (2004) first set down this concept in some detail, a number of related studies have been undertaken on it and proposals put forward for its adoption. Many of these have been reported and reviewed in a special issue of an academic journal edited by Fawcett and Parag (2010). This publication focused comprehensively on the range of researchers discussing various aspects of personal carbon trading. They include research by Prescott, Starkey and Anderson (2005) at the Tyndall Centre for Climate Change Research; several other projects at the Institute of Public Policy Research (Monbiot, 2006); the Environmental Change Institute at Oxford University (Bottrill, 2008; Fawcett et al., 2008); the Royal Society of Arts (Prescott, 2008) and the Lean Economy Institute (Fleming and Chamberlin, 2011).

A particularly influential study by Roberts and Thumim (2006), commissioned by the then Labour administration to explore the feasibility of per capita carbon rationing, concluded that it should not be pursued at present for two reasons. First, it was judged to be 'ahead of its time' and would not be accepted by the general public and, second, in practice, its costs of administration would be prohibitive. These could be seen as remarkable assertions, given that the government and its advisers in the policy area of climate change have repeatedly stressed the grave consequences of climate change and therefore the need for urgent action, and that, when it was judged by government at the beginning of World War II that a serious food shortage was in prospect, rationing was immediately introduced, without the 'smart' technological advances available now for an initiative in a time of equivalent global crisis attributable to shortage. No suggestions were made at the time for the price mechanism to be applied to deal with the problem of demand exceeding supply – and there were no demonstrations in Trafalgar Square!

Not only does C&C offer the only prospect of ensuring that the worst effects of climate change are avoided, but a range of other highly desirable outcomes will follow in its wake. Hillman (2006b) drew attention to the public health benefits likely to stem from people recognizing that more cycling and walking not only enables them to live more easily within their carbon allowance but also delivers improvement in their physical fitness and general health. In 1992, he had also referred to the lowered demand on the NHS that would follow.

Policy on social justice will be enormously advanced and personal and national budgets will be driven by economy. As the ration is reduced each year, down to the ecologically safe level, demand for fossil fuel-dependent products and activities will fall away, easing considerably the problems associated with the scarcity of fossil fuels and security of their supply.

The populations of the developing world will be the main beneficiaries as they will become the recipients of transfer payments at the level of the individual far more equitably and justifiably, and on a far larger scale, than from technology transfer or charitable aid from affluent countries. These beneficiaries will almost certainly use the revenue from this source to improve the quality of their lives to ensure that this part of their income is maintained. It is highly unlikely that the monies received would be used by adopting energy-intensive lifestyles as the effect of that would be to 'kill the goose that laid the golden egg'!

There will be a demographic benefit too as the sharing of the global gases that can be safely emitted into the atmosphere will be made according to each country's population in the first year of C&C's adoption. If any country's population rises thereafter, its share will fall, and vice-versa. In this way, it will be able to be used to influence population numbers.

There can be no denying that managing the transition to very low-carbon lifestyles in the developed world will not be easy. Most aspects of life and nearly all sectors of the economy will be profoundly affected. The outcome of the introduction of an annual carbon ration down to the very low level that must be achieved is unpredictable. No one can realistically predetermine to what extent units will be used for transport purposes, such as car travel, in the face of the competing claims on it for heating, hot water, lighting, power and so on. However, it can be stated emphatically that the future of fossil fuel-based activities can only be realistically predicted by considering how individuals will respond to the inevitable introduction of the annual sharply declining carbon allowance.

Consider the consequences for future transport demand: at present, the average individual's annual emissions in the UK just for car and public transport are about three times the amount that can be allowed for the total of an individual's fossil fuel uses for a year (roughly equivalent to one round flight from London to New York!). Against this background, Hillman (2007a) has highlighted the strong possibility that activities entailing long-distance travel by any means other than perhaps sailing, will fall dramatically, and therefore that all transport policy, practice and high-cost transport infrastructure projects already sanctioned to meet the largely unconstrained growth in demand, will need to be critically reappraised. On the other hand, provision for the inevitable huge growth in demand for low-carbon (and incidentally very low-cost) green travel – cycling, walking and bus – and, complementing this, for local, short-distance patterns of provision, will replace it.

It is very likely that most forms of motorized travel, especially those such as rail that are associated with relatively long-distance journeys, will decline sharply rather than continue to rise. The bus may be the exception owing to the fact that it only caters for short-distance trips, and is generally very economical in fuel used per passenger kilometre. The same holds true, though to a lesser extent, for the coach in spite of the fact that, in the main, it caters for longer trips.

Changes in land-use and transport planning infrastructure in favour of compact urban developments will logically follow, with high levels of investment – albeit at much lower costs – needed for urban planning changes and for the considerable increase in provision for walking and cycling and public transport running on renewable energy so that the great majority of travel is short-distance and carbon free. The process of rationing would naturally promote such investment as public demand for energy-intensive travel declines sharply.

7.   WHAT CAN WE DO?

How is our failure as individuals to make the changes from our current lifestyles to be reversed? Hillman (2007a) has argued that a widespread programme of public education on the links between carbon emissions and our energy-profligate lifestyles is needed, so that it becomes obvious to voters that there is no alternative to the government introducing carbon rationing. More recently, he has emphasized that we must learn very quickly to come to terms with the implications of the irrefutable evidence of ecological decline and therefore the significant behavioural changes that must be made to limit the rate of that decline (Hillman, 2007b).

At the personal level, it is self-evident that we will be far more motivated if we are aware of the extent of our personal contribution to the problem. To do so simply requires the completion of a carbon dioxide emissions self-audit, such as ones designed by Hillman (2006a) and DEFRA (2001). The resulting total is likely to be telling particularly when it is compared with the annual total with the world's current annual per capita emissions of just over 4 tonnes, the average of the UK population of about 12 tonnes (of which the household car accounts for more than a quarter), and the average of well under 1 tonne for much of the current populations of India, Africa and Bangladesh.

Among the numerous logical consequences of curtailing emissions will be the inclusion in applications to a local authority for planning permission of a carbon footprint calculation covering both the constructional process and annual emissions from the development. At the same time, and for the same reason, there will be increasing pressure to reject applications for low-density developments given their association with higher levels of car ownership and car mileage.

There can be no escape from four unarguable truths, and the logical reaction to them in behavioural terms that can be drawn from stopping to deny both their existence and their relevance to policy. First, insofar as we know that our own patterns of fossil fuel-dependent activities are making matters worse, we are all complicit to varying degrees. Second, 'doing something' can only be interpreted as representing meaningful progress if it results in an essential target being met on time for, otherwise, it can easily delay and make more difficult our coming to terms with the inadequacy of the steps being taken. For instance, the EU target of providing 15 per cent of its member states' energy requirements from renewables by 2020 implies that the great majority will still be coming from burning fossil fuels, thereby still adding to the concentration of greenhouse gas emissions in the years beyond that date. Third, unfortunately, there is much in the pipeline stemming from past and therefore unavoidable patterns of activity. Finally, all of us, without exception, have a responsibility to make the necessary changes to limit the damage through changes in our personal and working lives. In particular, professions such as that of transport and urban planning, have a critical part to play.

8. CONCLUSIONS

Given the urgency of the situation, the implications of failure to limit carbon emissions to the fair equal share for each individual dictated by the planet's finite capacity to absorb the emissions safely are dire. We cannot continue passing the buck between individuals, industry and government. We must stop pretending or implying through our decisions that the harm that we are causing is either unavoidable or only marginal and that we have as much time as is needed to get it right. The carbon dioxide emissions that we are now adding to the atmosphere will affect the climate for well over 100 years. We cannot go on deceiving ourselves that the essential reduction to a much lower overall level of emissions can be achieved in the absence of everyone being subject to a mandatory requirement not to exceed their fair share. It is wishful thinking to believe that it can be achieved on a voluntary basis.

The only strategy with any prospect of success in delivering the degree of reduction that is essential is the one based on C&C and PCAs. Although it is very difficult to predict how people will use their annual allowance given all the claims on it, it is very likely that demand for car travel and developments that are dependent on it will fall dramatically, that rail travel will be limited and air travel will be exceedingly rare.

It is indefensible to reach decisions that will inevitably prejudice the prospects for future generations enjoying life on earth as we have been able to do. The longer we procrastinate, the greater the certainty of environmental degradation, social upheaval and economic chaos. While the challenge is immense, it is essential that it is met. The time is long over for denial that apocalyptic disaster is inevitable unless we take drastic steps immediately to reduce substantially further burning of the world's fossil fuel reserves. If the measuring template were in place, every year's delay could be seen to leave in its wake both the loss of biodiversity, quality of life and, in all likelihood, the loss of actual life on an alarming scale.

Responding to climate change is ultimately a moral choice. We can no longer proceed as if we have a right to turn a blind eye to the damage we are causing. What will we do in the decades ahead when justifiably challenged by our children and grandchildren on our woeful failure to have acted in time? The accumulation of irrefutable evidence on climate change will make it progressively unacceptable to attempt to excuse ourselves either by claiming that 'we did not know' the consequences of our actions or, in many respects even more reprehensibly, by just pleading guilty – and even joking about it.

It is incumbent on us all to be involved now by coming to terms with the fact that the role of transport and other sectors of our fossil fuel-based economies must be heavily reduced. Otherwise we are wittingly condoning insufficient action. In all conscience, we must not bequeath a dying planet to the next generation. We are heading inexorably in that direction.

REFERENCES

The contents of this chapter draw heavily on its author's articles in *Environmental Law and Management*, **23**, 2011, and in *World Transport Policy and Practice*, **17**(4), 2012.

Anderson, K. (2011), *Environmental and Climate Change Impacts of Shale Gas*, Manchester: Tyndall Centre for Climate Change Research, University of Manchester.

Bottrill, C. (2008), *Understanding Domestic Tradable Quotas and Personal Carbon Allowances*, Oxford: Environmental Change Institute, University of Oxford.

DEFRA (2001), *Guidelines for Greenhouse Gas Conversion Factors for Company Reporting*, London: Department for Environment, Food and Rural Affairs.

DfT (2011), *Transport Statistics Great Britain, Rail Trends, Great Transport and UK Aviation Forecasts*, London: Department for Transport.

European Biofuels Technology Platform (2011), *Biofuels and Sustainability Issues*, Gülzow: European Biofuels Technology Platform.

European Commission (2011), *Eurobarometer 372, Climate Change*, October.

Fawcett, T. and Parag, Y. (eds) (2010), *Climate Policy*, **10**(4).

Fawcett, T., Bottrill, C., Boardman, B. and Lye, G. (2008), *Trialling Personal Carbon Allowances*, UKERC research report, Institute for Public Policy Research.

Fleming, D. and Chamberlin, S. (2011), *Tradable Energy Quotas: A Policy Framework for Peak oil and Climate Change*, London: The Lean Economy Connection.

The Guardian (2011), Letter from T. Benn, Cabinet Minister in a former Labour administration, and others, *The Guardian*, 6 October.

Hansen, J., Sato, M., Kharecha, P., Beerling, D., Berner, R., Masson-Delmotte, V., Pagani, M., Raymo, M., Royer, D.L. and Zachos, J.C. (2008), Target atmospheric CO_2: where should humanity aim? *Open Atmospheric Science Journal*, **2**, 217–31.

Hillman, M. (1992), *Cycling: Towards Health and Safety*, a report for the British Medical Association, Oxford: Oxford University Press.

Hillman, M. (1996), In favour of the compact city, in M. Jenks, E. Burton and K. Williams (eds), *The Compact City: A Sustainable Urban Form*, London: E. and F.N. Spon.

Hillman, M. (2006a), *Watching Your Figure*, questionnaire designed for the BBC.

Hillman, M. (2006b), Personal carbon allowances, *British Medical Journal*, **332**, 387–8.

Hillman, M. (2007a), Carbon rationing: the only realistic strategy, in *Climate Action*, London: Sustainable Development International and United Nations Environment Programme.

Hillman, M. (2007b), Afterword: Where do we go from here? in D. Cromwell and M. Levene (eds), *Surviving Climate Change: The Struggle to Avert Global Catastrophe*, London: Pluto Press.

Hillman, M. (2011), Climate change: quo vadis et quis custodiet? *Environmental Law and Management*, **23**(1), 30–4.

Hillman, M. and Fawcett, T. (2004), *How We Can Save the Planet*, London: Penguin Books.

Hillman, M. and Tindale, S. (2009), *Nuclear Power: For and Against*, website@psi.org.uk.

House of Commons Environmental Audit Committee (2008), *Carbon Capture and Storage*, Report of Session 2007–08.

IPCC (2013), *Fifth Assessment Report, Summary for Policy Makers*, Intergovernmental Panel on Climate Change

Macalister, T. and Carrell, S. (2011), RWE reviews involvement in UK nuclear programme, *The Guardian*, 7 October.

Macalister, T. and Carrington, D. (2011), *The Guardian*, 6 October.

Meyer, A. (2000), *Contraction & Convergence: The Global Solution to Climate Change*, Schumacher briefing no. 5, Totnes: Green Books for the Schumacher Society.

Meyer, A. (2013), http://www.gci.org.uk/CBAT.html.

Monbiot, G. (2006), *Heat: How We Can Stop the Planet Burning*, London: Penguin Books.

Prescott, M. (2008), *A Persuasive Climate: Personal Trading and Changing Lifestyles*, London: Royal Society for the Encouragement of Arts, Manufactures and Commerce.

Prescott, M., Starkey, R. and Anderson, K. (2005), *Domestic Tradable Quotas: A Policy Instrument for Reducing Greenhouse-gas Emissions from Energy Use*, technical report, Tyndall Centre for Climate Change Research.

Roberts, S. and Thumim, J. (2006), *A Rough Guide to Individual Carbon Trading: the Ideas, the Issues and the Next Steps*, Bristol: Centre for Sustainable Energy, University of Bristol.
Scientific American (2011), Report on EU climate chief's concerns about pollution from extracting oil from tar sands, *Scientific American*, October 27.
US Energy Information Administration (2011), *International Energy Outlook Report*, Number: DOE/EIA-0484, September.
Williams, R. (2006), *Changing the Myths We Live*, lecture.

41 The value of transition management for sustainable transport
Harry Geerlings and Flor Avelino

1. INTRODUCTION

Transport has many positive characteristics, both for the individual user as well as for society as a whole. This explains why the transport sector, for more then a century now, has experienced an unprecedented growth. This growth can be characterized as an evolutionary process and is evident in both the transport of passengers and goods. At the same time, transport has undesired side-effects. There are serious concerns related to emissions (at the regional, national and global level), safety, health issues and resource management, and the almost unlimited demand for transport cannot always be facilitated by construction of new infrastructure, which leads to congestion. These concerns have been raised since the 1960s and are encompassed in the concepts of sustainability.

Governments and other stakeholders are generally aware that policy measures are needed to find a balance between accessibility and sustainability. This is an enormous challenge, and the question arises how this can be realized. Evolving within the framework of policymaking, a new approach has been introduced that deals with these new challenges: 'transition management'. Transition management can be considered as an innovative management strategy to overcome barriers and to support public decision-makers and private actors to influence complex societal transformation processes towards a certain desirable direction, in this case a more sustainable transport system.

This chapter deals with the theory of transition management and is structured as follows. Section 2 addresses the need for (more) sustainable transport. This is not an easy task, as sustainable development distinguishes several sometimes seemingly opposing goals, which hence makes it a very difficult task to find synergy between these different goals. In section 3, the concepts of transition theory and transition management are discussed. Attention is given to the conceptual framework, as well as to its application in practice. An overview is provided of how transition theory has developed, how it emerged in the policy arena, and how transition management is operationalized in mobility policy and innovation projects on sustainable mobility. In section 4, this approach is illustrated by a concrete case of the Rotterdam port expansion, which focuses on opportunities to reach a (more) sustainable transport system despite a significant growth of container transport. Finally, in section 5, conclusions are drawn and we discuss what transition management can mean for sustainable transport.

2.   THE SEARCH FOR SUSTAINABLE TRANSPORT

Transport plays a crucial role in modern societies. Over the past century, the transport sector is characterized by an unprecedented growth. This growth can be observed in both passenger and freight transport, and this trend occurs all over the world. However, the success of the transport sector is having a profoundly negative impact in several domains. Initially, the emphasis was placed on the impacts of emissions (e.g., PM, SO_2, HC and NO_2) on health and safety, but in recent years a new concern has been added to the political agenda: climate change and the reduction of carbon dioxide (CO_2) emissions. Moreover, there are various spatial, economic and social issues (Zijlstra and Avelino, 2012). The dominance of road transport in both passenger and freight transport, are related to (sub)urbanization, urban sprawl and zoning (Dupuy, [1995] 2008; Zijlstra, 2009), and social problems, such as exclusion, isolation, alienation and the loss of social capital (Dupuy, 1999; CEC, 2011).

The concern for the environmental burden caused by human action has been studied for many years and is reflected in numerous reports and policy documents. In 1987, the World Commission for Environment and Development (WCED) introduced the concept of sustainable development in their report *Our Common Future* (WCED, 1987). Even today, there is no universally accepted definition of sustainable development, nor is there one of sustainable transport. Sustainable development distinguishes several sometimes seemingly opposing goals, which hence makes it a very difficult task to find synergy between these different goals. We approach sustainability as an essentially contested notion; it is intrinsically complex, normative, subjective, and ambiguous (Kasemir et al., 2003), and inherently context-specific (Grin, 2004). It is one of those concepts that 'inevitably involve endless disputes about their proper uses on the part of their users', and 'to engage in such disputes is itself to engage in politics' (Lukes, [1974] 2002: 45). In other words, the concept of sustainable development implies that it is a dynamic concept with different degrees of interpretation. Although there is no agreed upon definition of sustainability, there is consensus among many researcher that the concept of sustainable development is not about a 'technological fix' or merely physical conditions, but that it requires organizational challenges, socio-political change and political willingness (Geerlings, 1999; Meadowcroft, 1999, 2009; Banister, 2008; Geerlings et al., 2009a).

There is a general awareness among governments and other stakeholders that new approaches and policy measures are needed to find a balance between accessibility and sustainability. Evolving within the framework of policymaking, one of these new approaches is 'transition management'.

3.   TRANSITION STUDIES, TRANSITION MANAGEMENT AND ITS APPLICATION TO TRANSPORT

Transition studies refers to a field of research that focuses on 'transitions', generally defined as non-linear processes of social change in which a societal system is structurally transformed (Grin et al., 2010; Markard et al., 2012). A 'sustainability transition' generally refers to a 'radical transformation towards a sustainable society as a response to a number of persistent problems confronting contemporary modern societies' (Grin et al., 2010). One of the central premises in transition studies is that persistent problems are symptoms of unsustainable societies, and that dealing with these persistent problems in order to enable more sustainable systems, requires transitions and system innovations. Transition research has its intellectual roots in innovation studies as found in social studies of technology (Rip and Kemp, 1998). While originally the focus was on transitions in socio-technical systems (e.g., mobility, energy, agriculture), recent developments have broadened the focus towards societal systems more generally (e.g., regions, sectors) and to 'reflexive' governance for sustainable development (Voss et al., 2009). Analytically, the understanding of transition processes can be distinguished from the understanding of how actors (can) influence transition processes: the first object of study is referred to as transition dynamics or transition theory, the latter as transition management (Rotmans et al., 2001; Loorbach, 2007). In this section, we give a short overview of the conceptual frameworks of both transition theory and transition management, and we discuss how this has been applied to the transport sector.

Transition Theory and its Application to Transport

The primary object of study concerns societal systems at the level of sectors or regions. This systemic perspective requires a holistic view that acknowledges the interaction between human and non-human aspects. The influence on societal systems is not only economic, ecological and technological, but also social, cultural, institutional and political. Social actors within these systems are reflexive and as such shape and influence the dynamics of the system they inhabit. But as societal systems are complex, these systems have a functional dynamic of their own that no actor can control. While a system innovation refers to transformations within specific subsystems, a transition transcends individual systems and comprises various system innovations at different scale-levels and over a long-term period of time.

In order to analyse transition dynamics, different levels in time and (functional) aggregation are distinguished, resulting in the 'multi-phase', 'multi-level' and 'multi-pattern' frameworks (Grin et al., 2010; Geels et al., 2012). The multi-level framework (MLP) is one of the most central concepts in transition studies (Geels and Kemp, 2000; Geels, 2005). The MLP distinguishes between different levels of functional aggregation; landscape (macro-level, regime (meso-level) and niches (micro-level).

The landscape refers to the surroundings of a particular societal system under study, where one sees exogenous macro-trends with a relatively slow progress. Specific definitions of the regime have been altered and broadened over the years. Rip and Kemp (1998) first defined a technological regime in terms of rules, engineering practices and process technologies as embedded in institutions and infrastructures. Geels (2004) defined a socio-technical regime as consisting of 'cognitive, regulative and normative rules' that 'account for the stability and lock-in of socio-technical systems'. In the meantime, Loorbach (2007) defines a societal regime as 'a dominant set of structure, culture and practices'. Regardless of differing definitions, the notion of the regime essentially refers to the most 'dominant' societal constellation that 'dominates' the stable functioning of a societal system and defends the status quo (Avelino, 2011). Niches, on the other hand, refer to those constellations in which non-conformism and innovation can develop. These niches are also part of the societal system, but able to deviate

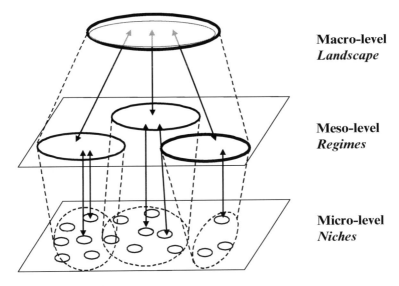

Macro-level
Landscape

Meso-level
Regimes

Micro-level
Niches

Figure 41.1   Multi-level framework

from the dominant structures, cultures and practices within that system. As the regime dominates the societal system, a necessary condition for a transition to occur is that a regime is either transformed or replaced by a new regime, under pressure of landscape developments that provide opportunities for new niche-innovations. In this interaction between regime, niches and landscape, various 'phases', 'patterns' and 'pathways' are distinguished, which serve to construct different narratives on how transition processes develop, and to describe and analyse empirical observations (De Haan and Rotmans, 2011).

Various researchers have applied the analytical frameworks of transition research to study the transport sector and transitions to sustainable mobility (Geels, 2005; Hoogma et al., 2002; Dijk, 2010). An interesting overview of socio-technical transition analyses specifically applied on sustainable transport can be found in Geels et al. (2012).

Governance Model Transition Management

Based on the transition concepts discussed earlier, a governance model has been developed that aims to 'resolve persistent problems in societal systems'; transition management. The underlying assumption is that full control and management of these problems is not possible, but that one can 'manage' these problems in terms of adjusting, adapting and influencing the societal system by organizing a joint searching and learning process, focused on 'long-term sustainable solutions' (Rotmans et al., 2001). Although transition management can be used as a descriptive and analytical framework to study how actors (attempt to) influence transition processes, it has so far mostly gained attention as a prescriptive governance model. Transition management is presented as 'a new mode of governance for sustainable development' (Loorbach, 2007) that 'tries to utilize the opportunities for transformation that are present in an existing system' by 'joining in with ongoing dynamics rather than forcing changes, (Rotmans et al., 2001).

In transition studies, sustainable development is approached as a concept that is intrinsically complex, normative, subjective and ambiguous, and inherently context-specific (see section 2). Even though there is no agreed upon definition of sustainability, there are still some basic features that characterize the concept; it is an intergenerational phenomenon, it operates at multiple scale levels and it covers social-cultural, economic and ecological dimensions (Avelino and Rotmans, 2011). The paradigm of integrated sustainability assessment (Weaver et al., 2008), argues that the study of sustainable development requires integrated systems analysis embedded in a participatory process context, thus involving both 'interdisciplinary' and 'trans-disciplinary' research. The aim of transition management is to organize such a participatory process, in which actors from various backgrounds explore what sustainability means for their particular context.

These aims are captured in a 'cyclical process model' (TM-cycle, see Figure 41.2),

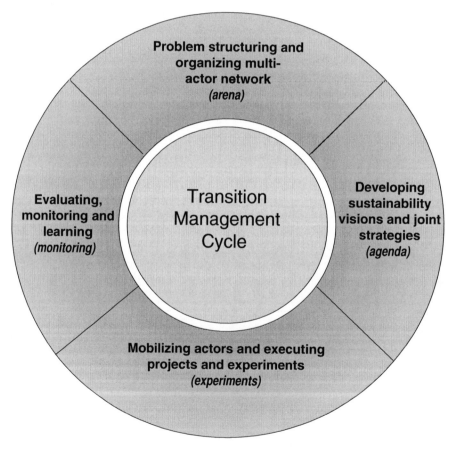

Source: Loorbach (2007, slightly adapted)

Figure 41.2   The TM-cycle

which serves to organize a participatory stakeholder-process that is primarily aimed at envisioning, learning, and experimenting, including the following activities: (1) problem structuring, establishment of a transition arena and envisioning; (2) developing coalitions, transition agendas, transition images and related transition paths; (3) establishing and carrying out transition experiments and mobilizing transition networks; and (4) monitoring, evaluating and learning lessons from the experiments and, 'based on these, adjust vision, agenda and coalitions' (Loorbach, 2007). In the past few years, different elements of the TM-cycle have been developed, applied, and researched; transition experiments (Van der Bosch, 2010), transition monitoring (Diepenmaat and Taanman, 2009), several participatory tools such as integrated system analysis (Loorbach, 2007), transition scenarios (Sondeijker, 2009) and urban transition management (Nevens et al., 2013).

A central element in transition management concerns the set-up of a so-called transition arena: 'a multi-actor governance instrument [that] intends to stimulate and coordinate innovation through creating shared (new) problem definitions and shared long-term goals', consisting of 'a virtual arena, an open and dynamic network in which different perspectives, different expectations, and different agendas are confronted, discussed and aligned where possible' (Loorbach, 2007). The overall principle is to focus primarily on 'frontrunners': individuals that are 'ahead' with developing new structures, cultures and practices. These frontrunners need not necessarily be 'niche players', they can also be 'enlightened regime players', i.e., individuals who operate within a regime context, but use this position to develop or facilitate niches and alter existing structures.

Although the prescriptive transition management model ideally starts of with a 'transition arena' and sets up 'transition experiments' after a long-term goal and 'transition paths' have been formulated, there is no fixed sequence in these transition management activities: they are carried out 'partially and completely in sequence, in parallel and in random sequence' (Loorbach, 2007). Transition management is also used to 'build on existing projects and experiments to transition these by broadening and scaling-up and (re)defining visions' (Loorbach, 2007). Specific 'transitioning instruments' to 'transition' ongoing (innovation) projects have also been developed, studied and experimented with (Avelino, 2009, 2011; Van den Bosch, 2010).

Application of Transition Management in the (Dutch) Transport Sector

The transition management model has gained much attention from policymakers, managers and other practitioners in the past few years, particularly in the Netherlands. It has been applied in multiple policy contexts, and to various programmes and projects (Kemp and Rotmans, 2009). In 2001, the concepts of 'transition' and 'transition management' were introduced in the 4th Dutch National Environmental Policy Plan (Ministerie voor Volkshuisvesting, Ruimtelijke Ordening en Milieu, 2001), was presented as 'a strategy to deal with environmental degradation by stimulating sustainable development as a specific aim of policy making' (Avelino, 2011). Moreover, in 2003, the Dutch government decided to grant subsidies to 'strengthen the Dutch knowledge economy in its innovative and societal needs', by improving the 'knowledge infrastructure' in fields that have a specific societal relevance. The 'transition to sustainable mobility' was one of the four 'necessary transitions' mentioned in the 4th Dutch National Environmental Policy Plan in 2001. Subsequently, 'transition to sustainable mobility' emerged as a combination of words that has been increasingly used throughout the Netherlands.

A particular case worth mentioning here concerns the Transumo programme. Transumo is an abbreviation for 'TRANsition to SUstainable MObility'. Its main ambition was 'to accelerate/encourage the transition to sustainable mobility' by establishing a new knowledge-infrastructure (Avelino, 2011). For this end, it facilitated over many organizations from public, private and knowledge sectors to collaborate in applied research projects on sustainable transport. The programme was started in 2004 and finalized at the end of 2009. Transumo operationalized its transformative ambition through the development and dissemination of 'trans- and interdisciplinary' knowledge, through conferences, meetings, workshops, websites and numerous publications (articles, books, reports, brochures, websites, etc.) (Avelino, 2011).

Sustainable mobility was an explicit orientation for the Transumo programme. Even though Transumo's approach differed from the prescriptive transition management cycle in numerous aspects, it did make a rather elaborate effort to apply transition management in the form of 'transitioning' (Avelino, 2011). Transumo did such 'transitioning' in several projects and, in fact, the very concept of transitioning and subsequent 'transitioning instruments' were for a great part developed and researched on the basis of Transumo activities (Avelino, 2011). In that sense, Transumo did not only 'apply' transition management, but actually played a significant role in developing it. This is in itself is in line with the reflexivity principle of transition management; an approach that aims to adapt, develop and renew itself, based on co-production between research and practice (Kemp and Rotmans, 2009).

In the next section, we elaborate on one of the Transumo projects in the area of the sea port extension in Rotterdam, and we discuss how the concept of transition management was applied in that context.

4.   THE TRANSUMO-A15 EXPERIMENT

The theory about sustainable transport and transition management was applied to practice, in a Dutch transition experiment named 'From Maasvlakte to the Hinterland: Sustainable Freight Transport as Challenge', or the 'A15-project' in short. The A15 is a national highway that connects the port with the hinterland. In the A15-project, more than 250 stakeholders, including both public and private organizations, the Port Authority, research organizations, local government and pressure groups participated in order to meet the challenge of finding sustainable solutions for accessibility and environmental problems in the Rotterdam port region from 2020 and onwards. This was considered a relevant issue due to port expansion and the increase of container flows from 10 million containers a year in the year 2005 to around 30 million containers in the year 2030. The A15 is the main transport vein from the Port of Rotterdam to the hinterland, but suffers increasingly from congestion as a result of the ongoing transport and traffic growth. Furthermore, the surrounding (urban) environment suffers from air pollution and noise. The participants in this joint project considered a wide range of technical and organizational measures and the transition process needed for the regional mobility system in order to tackle the accessibility and sustainability challenges ahead.

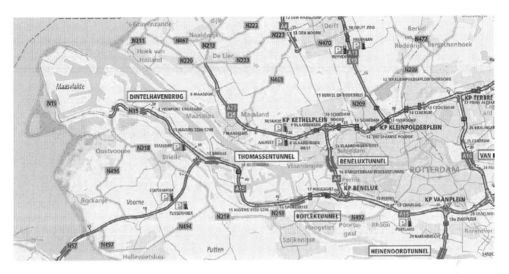

Source: Geerlings et al. (2009a)

Figure 41.3   *Map of the current Rotterdam port area and its surrounding road network*

In the following sections, attention is paid to two main questions: (1) how the project dealt with sustainability issues and (2) how transition management was dealt with. For both questions four observations are presented. But first the case of the port extension will be introduced.

A Complex Relationship: The Port and the A15 Motorway

The Rotterdam port area (Figure 41.3), an area of major economic importance for the Netherlands, is Europe's largest logistic and industrial hub (Port of Rotterdam, 2011) and about 5 per cent of the national employment, and about 10 per cent of the GDP is generated in this region. The 'Maasvlakte' is the name of the latest port and industrial zone extension area, built on reclaimed land in the region of the port of Rotterdam. It was created because more space was needed in the Europoort, the complex of ports and industrial areas that was built in the 1960s between the city of Rotterdam and the North Sea. The port of Rotterdam is still growing and, from an economic perspective, it is seen as important that this ongoing growth of the port is facilitated. However, the handling capacity of the port is bounded by the transport capacity of the available infrastructure and the connections with the hinterland; there is a latest enlargement of 400km^2, called Maasvlakte-2. This new area was available from 2013 onwards and it is expected that the number of containers handled in the port of Rotterdam can further increase from 11 million containers a year in 2009 to 33 million containers in the year 2030.

In the port of Rotterdam there are five major transport modalities: road, rail, coastal and inland shipping, and pipeline. Most freight is transported to the hinterland by road, but increasing congestion lengthens travel time considerably. This not only increases the transport costs of transporters and shippers, but also has a negative impact on the international competition position of the port. As well as longer travel time and congestion, there are also impacts on the regional environment. Air pollution and noise put pressure on the quality of life in the region. In the neighbourhood of the A15 motorway that runs from the Maasvlakte eastwards, there are several urban areas that suffer from pollution and noise. In the short term, between 2010 and 2015 a large-scale road expansion from two to three lanes was planned for busiest parts of the highway (Geerlings et al., 2009b). However, this extra capacity will only be a temporary solution. The ongoing expansion of the road capacity with additional lanes is not considered a sustainable solution in the long run: in the light of the expected growth in transport it enhances capacity only temporarily. Apart from that, traffic is expected to increase further, as the expansion of the port area will generate extra transport.

The additional area of Maasvlakte-2 will provide increased growth possibilities for the port and, hence, increased transport. Furthermore, the extra infrastructure will probably attract latent transport (Geerlings et al., 2009b), which means that more sustainable solutions are needed. One could think of many different solutions, such as the modal shift policy (e.g., more rail transport and inland shipping), increasing the efficiency of existing infrastructure, the introduction of new technology, logistical innovations, organizational innovations and better cooperation. The combined issues at play in the port area lead to a high degree of complexity in the decision-making processes and complicate the determination of future directions. Actors have to make decisions under great uncertainty, while many other actors are also making strategic decisions and choices (Ostrom, 1990). The port is hence a good example of an area with complex problems (or 'wicked' problems) (see, for instance, Rittel and Webber, 1973).

How the A15-project Dealt with Sustainability

Retaining the principle of sustainability
In order to comply with the 'people-planet-profit-balance', participants emphasized the 'side-effects' of economic optimization that are indirectly beneficial for the planet and people. 'Increasing efficiency' and 'combining freight loads' primarily leads to cost reduction and the speeding up of traffic flows (good for profit). It does, however, also lead to 'less transport' (in terms of less kilometres), and therefore also to 'less noise' (i.e., good for people), and 'less emissions' (i.e., good for the planet). In this way, the goals of accessibility and economic optimization were framed in terms of sustainability. However, the concept of sustainability was also used in a more profound manner and went beyond strategic framing (Avelino, 2011).

The ostensible paradox between accessibility and sustainability
The Transumo-A15 project started with a strong focus on economic performance and the importance of accessibility for the competitive position of the port of Rotterdam. Through the introduction of transition management, another discussion on sustainability was triggered, which went beyond the issue of economic performance. Interestingly, the concepts of 'accessibility' and 'sustainability' were often posed as opposites in meetings, and participants had a tendency to categorize one another in terms of 'those that cared more about accessibility' and 'those that cared more about sustainability' (Bressers et al., 2012). A participant in the project stated that there were many discussions in the steering group on the goal of the project, and the concession they found was to frame

accessibility as a 'goal' and sustainability as a 'condition'. The member of the steering group argued that conditions were actually more important than goals, for 'a goal is flexible, while conditions are hard' (Avelino, 2011).

At the start of the project it was agreed that accessibility and sustainability would receive equal attention in the research, but soon the priority came to lie on accessibility 'within the boundaries of environmental conditions'. At the end of the project it turned out that the restriction was unnecessary, because it was expected that environmental conditions would, in the long-term, no longer form any problem. A conclusion that comes forth from the project is that there is no reason to make sustainability secondary to accessibility, but that a proactive sustainability policy can be set up to which transport developments can be adapted. As such it was a new insight that 'accessibility' and 'sustainability' did not contradict one another and that sustainability was not just about legally imposed environmental restrictions. In this sense, the A15-project challenged government and business actors in the A15-region to take up sustainability as an ambition and opportunity, rather than confining it to environmental restrictions that 'threaten' the economic position of the port (Avelino, 2011).

Openness for innovative solutions
The participants in the A15-project explored and discussed many possible solutions to deal with the problems in the A15 region. The investigated solutions included dynamic traffic management, night distribution, innovative public transport, inland terminals for short-sea shipping and new infrastructural works. The combined package of these measures applied to road, rail and water. Although the initial result looked promising, in the process of being formulated in a 'deliverable', it appeared that this 'package of solutions' was not innovative enough and that there was a lack of strategies on how to implement these solutions. Consequently a second round was initiated, aiming to give more attention to environmental aspects and innovation. The results of this new trajectory were presented as Deliverable D15 (Kuipers et al., 2007) under the three keywords 'dynamic', 'sustainable' and 'daring'. Even though the results were not optimal, it became clear that they could provide a substantial contribution. The concept of sustainability became more and more accepted as a challenge to be achieved.

Adapting to the dynamic social context
A project that deals with transitions and sustainability is inherently dealing with normative and subjective notions that are contested and dependent on the context in which they are applied. During the period that this project was running (2006–9), a broader trend manifested itself, namely an increasing interest for the phenomena of climate change. Initially, the representatives of the business community were not willing to address the issue of greenhouse effects. But this perception changed when the abstract notion of climate change was translated into new, more concrete issues and business opportunities such as bio-based economy, electric vehicles, etc. For policymakers, it meant that sustainability could lead to concrete actions and that the concept became more embedded at national and regional levels. For the A15-project, this was an unexpected development that supported those participants who argued that sustainability should be considered as being at least as important as accessibility.

How the A15-project Applied Transition Management

Transition management as source for inspiration

One of the general observations in the A15-project relates to the excessive use of transition terminology. The project documents (proposals, plans and reports) were filled with the terms 'transition management', 'system innovation' and 'transition to sustainable mobility'. During the actual meetings, however, these words were used much less, and sometimes not at all (Avelino, 2011). Transumo provided a format in which project documents had to be delivered (Lohuis et al, 2008). The participants had to specify how their project would contribute, or had contributed, to the transition to sustainable mobility, which system innovations were involved and how transition management was applied. Although the A15-project could not afford to apply a full-fledged transition management process with the use of a 'transition arena', room was made for an 'alternative transition trajectory', which resulted in the 'innovation impulse' that consisted of two sessions. This innovation impulse was inspired by transition management, as far as possible given the time constraints (Avelino et al., 2011).

Transition management as a structure for the processes

With regard to the regular trajectory of the A15-project, there was a clear application of some of the more fundamental, underlying principles of transition management. The first principle was the advocacy for a proactive attitude by new governance networks and regional coalitions, involving different sectors (business, local government, research) – rather than solely relying on government to solve public sector problems. The second principle was an inter- and trans-disciplinary approach, and in a combination of qualitative and quantitative research to identify the problems at hand. The third principle could be found in the acknowledgement of uncertainty and complexity with regard to future developments, and the resulting recommendation to be prepared for an uncertain future through adaptive strategies that combined 'flexible and dynamic measures'; for example, not to let the accessibility of the port entirely depend on the construction of specific infrastructure such as the A4-road, but to experiment with a variety of alternative measures (e.g., road pricing, transport avoidance, mobility management, infrastructure for other modalities, etc.).

Flexible project architecture

It was clear from the beginning that, to give sustainability an equal value as accessibility in the project, a well-defined and flexible project design was necessary. The researchers in the consortium (who mainly came from the academic world and specialized consultants) were responsible for collecting the data and analysing it by means of document reviews, statistics, traffic modelling, interviewing, and collecting, analysing and applying quantitative data (with regard to traffic and environmental effects in the A15 region) in traffic models and scenarios. But there were also 'open' meetings, to which 'outsiders' were invited to identify possible solutions in close cooperation with the 250 stakeholders in order to deal with the problems and make recommendations based on these possible solutions. These open meetings provided a forum in which the 'insiders' presented their vision for the future, project results and 'deliverables', and the 'outsiders' were asked to react, comment, discuss and give input with regard to a specific theme (Bressers et al., 2012). Furthermore, the A15 project was flexible in the sense that the process architecture was continuously reconsidered and adapted depending on new developments and needs. After each round, the process and results so far were evaluated, and a new set of activities were started. The alternative trajectory/innovation impulse and the thematic working groups were not planned beforehand, but incorporated in the ongoing process in interaction with new actors involved in the project. The outcomes of these new activities were integrated with ongoing activities and synthesized in final reports.

Recognizing the challenges

In the final publications and meetings of the Transumo program, the A15-project was characterized by outsiders and participants as a unique project with an interesting consortium, providing substantive results and an innovative process approach inspired by transition management (Avelino, 2011). A remaining question is to what extent the project will contribute to a transition to a sustainable region, where a dynamic port and a future-proof industrial complex become a natural part of the region. In a concluding report, the participants of the A15-project identified three main barriers for a transition to a sustainable region. First, it is very difficult to achieve breakthroughs; even if certain innovative solutions are embraced enthusiastically by stakeholders, it remains difficult to up-scale and mainstream them. Second, many important stakeholders seem to be captured in locked-in visions on port and business development. Related to this, it is difficult to find leaders of change in such a context (the so-called 'frontrunners' in transition management). Third, there are a number of participants who act upon fulfilling the minimum requirements, rather than striving for maximum results. This lead to a situation in which some parties are satisfied with an outcome 'as good as', instead of acting according to the ambition to be 'better than'.

5.   CONCLUSIONS

In the field of transport, there is a general awareness that new approaches are needed to come to a (more) sustainable transport system. The need for more sustainable transport is relevant on different levels (local, regional and global), but the spatial-temporal characteristics of the impacts differ very strongly. The challenge is to develop a proactive methodology that addresses the economic (profit), environmental (planet) and social (people) objectives in a coherent strategy, while also inviting for prospective and long-term thinking. Moreover, it is necessary to recognize the need for cooperation and interaction between the government, private firms and civil society to fulfil the changing needs of society.

A Transition to Sustainable Transport: Lessons Learned

Based on theoretical insights and practical experiments the following recommendations for a transition towards sustainable transport can be presented.

Transitions require coercion and encouragement
Given the large uncertainties about the future, a rich and flexible package of measures should be in place to safeguard sustainable transport on corridor such as the A15. The challenge is to link the different investment horizons of businesses and governments, in order to prevent too much ad hoc and marginal investment in sustainable transport. And equally important: to make non-coercive and non-binding agreements to help companies to push their creativity and to stimulate entrepreneurship in the right direction.

Accessibility and sustainability planning should be future-proof
Sustainable transport should be strongly supported by two pillars: (1) a forward-looking strategy and understanding of future needs to safeguard accessibility, and (2) an assessment of this strategy against strict criteria of sustainable transport. Stakeholders should be aware that these long-term goals should be reached in a context of fragmentation, short-term agendas and mechanisms of regional institutional practices with many locked-ins. For example, the planning of traffic and transport, environment and quality of life quite often takes place in separate arenas that act with their own logic. However, things seem to be changing as we observe how ambitions of sustainable transport are increasingly connected to ambitions in the field of sustainable economy, sustainable land use and sustainable working and living environment in concrete agreements. Thus, any agreement on the construction of new infrastructure should be coupled with the ambitions on sustainable transport.

No robust infrastructure without flexible packages of measures
Investing in infrastructure is an important contribution to improving the accessibility and robustness of the traffic system. Significant investments in new infrastructure (e.g., tunnels and highways), should be appraised together with developing tools for traffic, transport and mobility for the longer term. This is true even at the highest growth scenarios for the transport. A strategy without additional infrastructure delivers a higher risk given the limited robustness of the system.

The solution is a combination of technology and 'orgware'
New technology (logistics concepts, information systems, fuel, etc.) requires new arrangements (coalitions, agreements, mandates, rules) and vice versa: new arrangements call for new technology. This requires vision, decisiveness and precision for the stakeholders involved in transport development. The biggest challenge for a transition to a sustainable transport system is not only to develop new technology (the techware), but also to develop new governance arrangements (the orgware). This involves new contracts, coalition models and institutional arrangements in the relationship between shippers, freight forwarders, shipping companies, terminal operators and transport companies, market players and governments that are dealing with different levels of government, citizens and road-users.

Transition Management in Practice: Final Reflection

Transition management can be seen as a governance model for sustainable development, as a specific policy discourse and as a field of academic research. The theoretical concept of transitions refers to a transformation process in which society changes in a fundamental way over a generation or more. Transition management can be considered as a governance approach that makes the future more clearly manifest in current decisions, by adopting longer time-frames, exploring alternative trajectories, and opening avenues for system innovation (as well as system improvement).

The basic premise of transition management in both theory and practice, is that sustainable development requires transitions: non-linear processes of social change in which a societal system is structurally transformed. In order to describe processes of change in these complex societal systems, different levels in time and aggregation are distinguished, resulting in various conceptual frameworks such as the multi-level perspective (MLP). Such complex system perspective forms the theoretical basis of transition management.

An important hypothesis in transition theory is that fundamental change only breaks through if developments at the macro-, meso- and micro-level reinforce each other, and if developments within different domains come together at a particular scale level. A transition then is the result of a mixture of long-term, slow developments and short-term, fast developments and it aims to foster learning about system innovations and to bring together many actors (technologists, designers, governments, business and citizens) to work on sustainability transitions, taking on board criticisms that ecological modernization is often too much supply- and technology-oriented and that it neglects issues of lifestyle and values.

The concept of transition management is being applied in various sectors, such as the energy sector, agriculture, water management and the transport sector. The experiment of the Transumo A15-project demonstrates the multiple challenges that transition management faces in practice. In the case of the Transumo A15-project, transition management has provided clear insights on how to deal with the challenge of sustainable mobility. Transition management can be considered as a governance approach that makes the future more clearly manifest in current decisions, by adopting longer time-frames, exploring alternative trajectories and opening avenues for system innovation (as well as system improvement). It is shown that these insights, based on the theory of transition management, provide a new basis for understanding the complexities of the challenges that the transport sector is presently facing, and gives a new impulse to the search for a more sustainable transport system.

REFERENCES

Avelino, F. (2009), Empowerment and the challenge of applying transition management to ongoing projects, *Policy Sciences*, **42**(4), 369–90.

Avelino, F. (2011), *Power in Transition: Empowering Discourses on Sustainability Transitions*, PhD thesis, Erasmus University Rotterdam.

Avelino, F. and Rotmans, J. (2011), A dynamic conceptualization of power for sustainability research, *Journal of Cleaner Production*, **19**(8), 796–804.

Avelino, F., Bressers, N. and Kemp, R. (2011), Transition management as new policy making for sustainable mobility, in H. Geerlings, Y. Shiftan and D. Stead (eds), *Transition Towards Sustainable Mobility: The Role of Instruments, Individuals and Institutions*, Hampshire: Ashgate.

Banister, D. (2008), The sustainable mobility paradigm, *Transport Policy*, **15**(2), 73–80.

Bressers, N., Avelino, F. and Geerlings, H. (2012), Short- versus long-term and other dichotomies: applying transition management in the A15-project, in H. Geerlings, Y. Shiftan and D. Stead (eds), *Transition towards Sustainable Mobility: the Role of Instruments, Individuals and Institutions*, Hampshire: Ashgate.

CEC (2011), *Roadmap to a Single European Transport Area: Towards a Competitive and Resource-efficient Transport System*, White Paper COM (2011) 144, Luxembourg: Office for Official Publications of the European Community.

De Haan, J. and Rotmans, R. (2011), Patterns in transitions: understanding complex chains of change, *Technological Forecasting & Social Change*, **78**(1), 90–102.

Diepenmaat, H. and Taanman, M. (2009), *Grip op maatschappelijke transitie: Transitiemonitoring*, Rotterdam: DRIFT/EUR.

Dijk, M. (2010), *Innovation in Car Mobility: Co-evolution of Demand and Supply Under Sustainability Pressures*, PhD thesis, Centre for Integrated Assessment and Sustainable development (ICIS), Maastricht University.

Dupuy, G. (1999), From the 'magic circle' to 'automobile dependence': measurements and political implications, *Transport Policy*, **6**(1), 1–17.

Dupuy, G. ([1995] 2008), The automobile system: a territorial adapter, in J. van Schaick and I.T. Klassen (ed.), *Urban Networks, Network Urbanism*, Amsterdam: Techne Press, pp. 121–37.

Geels, F. (2004), From sectoral systems of innovation to socio-technical systems. insights about dynamics and change from sociology and institutional theory, *Research Policy*, **33**, 897–920.

Geels, F. (2005), *Technological Transitions and System Innovations: A Co-evolutionary and Socio-Technical Analysis*, Cheltenham: Edward Elgar.

Geels, F. and Kemp, R. (2000), *Transities vanuit Sociotechnisch perspecief*, Maastricht: MERIT.

Geels, F., Kemp, R., Dudley, G. and Lyons, G. (eds) (2012), *Automobility in Transition? A Socio-Technical Analysis of Sustainable Transport*, New York: Routledge.

Geerlings, H. (1999), *Meeting the Challenge of Sustainable Mobility; the Role of Technological Innovations*, Heidelberg/Berlin: Springer Verlag.

Geerlings, H., Lohuis, J., Wiegmans, B. and Willemsen, A. (2009a), A renaissance in understanding technology dynamics? The emerging concept of transition management, *Transport Planning & Technology*, **32**(5), 401–22.

Geerlings, H., van Meijeren, J., Soeterbroek, F., Huybregts, R., Kuipers, B., Kul, H., Smaal, M. and Vonk Noordegraaf, D. (2009b), *Deliverable D 25: Synthese: resultaten en aanbevelingen van 3 jaar studie*, Erasmus University, Rotterdam.

Grin, J. (2004), De politiek van omwenteling met beleid, inaugural speech, Amsterdam: Vossiuspers.

Grin, J., Rotmans, J. and Schot, J. (2010), *Transitions to Sustainable Development: New Directions in the Long Term Transformative Change*, New York: Routledge.

Hoogma, R., Kemp, R., Schot, J. and Truffer, B. (2002), *Experimenting for Sustainable Transport Futures: The Approach of Strategic Niche Management*, London: E.F. & N. Spon.

Kasemir, B., Jäger, J., Jeager, C.C. and Gardner, M.T. (2003), *Public Participation in Sustainability Science: A Handbook*, Cambridge: Cambridge University Press.

Kemp, R. and Rotmans, J. (2009), Transitioning policy: co-production of a new strategic framework for energy innovation policy in the Netherlands, *Policy Sciences*, **42**, 303–22.

Kuipers, B., van Rooijen, T. and Vonk Noordegraaf, D.M. (2007), *Deliverable D15 Uitwerking Maatregelenpakket 2: 3D 'Duurzaam, dynamisch en gedurfd'-concept*, Rotterdam/Delft.

Lohuis, J., Bouma, I., Avelino, F., Bressers, N., Vonk Noordegraaf, D., Soeterbroek, F. and Geerlings, H. (2008), *Deliverable 16-Uitkomsten van de innovatie-impuls*, Erasmus University, Rotterdam.

Loorbach, D. (2007), *Transition Management: New Mode of Governance for Sustainable Development*, Utrecht: International Books.

Lukes, S. ([1974] 2002), Power: a radical view, in M. Haugaard (ed.), *Power: A Reader*, Manchester: Manchester University Press.

Markard, J., Raven, R. and Truffer, B. (2012), Sustainability transitions: an emerging field of research and its prospects, *Research Policy*, **41**(6), 955–67.

Meadowcroft, J. (1999), The politics of sustainable development: emergent arenas and challenges for political science, *International Political Science Review*, **20**, 219–37.

Meadowcroft, J. (2009), What about the politics? Sustainable development, transition management, and long term energy transitions, *Policy Sciences*, **42**(4), 323–40.

Ministerie voor Volkshuisvesting, Ruimtelijke Ordening en Milieu (2001), *Vierde Nationaal Milieubeleidsplan [4th Dutch National Environmental Policy Plan]*, The Hague: Staatsuitgeverij.

Ostrom, E. (1990), *Governing the Commons: The Evolution of Institutions for Collective Action*, Cambridge: Cambridge University Press.

Nevens, F., Frantzeskaki, N., Loorbach, D. and Gorissen, L. (2013), Urban Transition Labs: co-creating transformative action for sustainable cities, *Journal of Cleaner Production*, **50**, 111–22.

Port of Rotterdam (2011), *Port Compass: Direct the Future, Start Today*, Rotterdam: Rotterdam Port Authority.

Rip, A. and Kemp, R. (1998), Technological change, in S. Rayner and E.L. Malone (eds), *Human Choice and Climate Change*, Columbus, OH: Battelle Press, pp. 327–99.

Rittel, H.W.J. and Webber, M.M. (1973), Dilemmas in a general theory of planning, *Policy Sciences*, **4**(2), 155–69.

Rotmans, J. (2005), *Societal Innovation: Between Dream and Reality Lies Complexity*, inaugural address, Rotterdam: Erasmus Research Institute of Management.

Rotmans, J., Kemp, R. and van Asselt, M. (2001), More evolution than revolution: transition management in public policy, *The Journal of Futures Studies, Strategic Thinking and Policy*, **3**(1), 15–32.

Sondeijker, S. (2009), *Imagining Sustainability: Methodological Building Blocks for Transition Scenarios*, PhD thesis, Erasmus University, Rotterdam.

Van den Bosch, S. (2010), *Transition Experiments: Exploring Societal Changes Towards Sustainability*, PhD Thesis, Erasmus University, Rotterdam.

Voss, J-P., Smith, A. and Grin, J. (2009), Designing long-term policy: rethinking transition management, *Policy Sciences*, **42**(4), 275–302.

WCED (1987), *Our Common Future*, Oxford: Oxford University Press.

Weaver, P., Jäger, J. and Rotmans, J. (2008), Integrated sustainability assessment: concept, process and tools, *Journal of Innovation and Sustainable Development*, **3**(1), 1–162.

Zijlstra, T. (2009), *Autoafhankelijkheid: over 'auto'-centrisch denken bij ontwerpers en planners*, Master's thesis, Technical University of Eindhoven.

Zijlstra, T. and Avelino, F. (2012), A socio-spatial perspective on the car regime, in F. Geels, R. Kemp, G. Dudley and G. Lyons (eds), *Automobility in Transition? A Socio-Technical Analysis of Sustainable Transport*, New York: Routledge.

42 The regional tram-train of Kassel, Germany: how regional responsibility leads to local success

Helmut Holzapfel and Rainer Meyfahrt

1. THE ORIGIN OF THE REGIOTRAM IDEA

The German city of Kassel (population approximately 200,000) is located 150km north of Frankfurt. It is the centre of a rurally oriented region with some 700,000 inhabitants. Directly adjacent to the city of Kassel are located independent municipalities and cities with a population of approximately 100,000 inhabitants. In the 1960s, the city assumed a peripheral position in the Federal Republic of Germany and in Europe. The border of the former German Democratic Republic (GDR) was only 50km distant and transport connections to the east hardly existed. Economic development stagnated over a long period. Kassel was significantly destroyed in the Second World War. The reconstruction of the city was conducted on the basis of concepts that derived from modernist notions of architecture and city planning prevalent in the period from 1950 to 1970. This involved the construction of wide streets and an entirely new urban layout for the city. The historic old city was not reconstructed. From today's perspective, these concepts appear excessively automobile-friendly and difficult to integrate with contemporary ideas regarding sustainable urban development.[1]

Around 1970, the public transport system entered a period of crisis.[2] The city had a tram system originating from the beginning of the development of the city's transport system. The first electric trams were already in operation at the beginning of the 1900s and the network was continually expanded from that time onwards. However, because of the post-war automobile-oriented development of the city mentioned above, the tram system began to be called into question around 1970. Existing tram lines were taken out of operation. After a further line was shut down in 1971, an intensive discussion developed regarding the possible shutdown of the entire system. Transport into the surrounding countryside of the city was provided by bus companies owned by the Deutsche Bahn or state government. Cooperation between these entities did not occur.

By 1977, the classic tram system in Kassel seemed to be reaching an end. A vehicle inventory revealed the system was technically and economically outmoded. With high deficits, a bad image and the failure to react to the changing distribution of settlement in the region, these combined factors gave rise to the logical proposal from the transport companies to transfer further tram lines to bus services. In this regard, the city transport company was following the model of decommissioning branch lines in the system pursued by the Deutsche Bundesbahn on a national level. In the Kassel region, this represented a particularly high percentage of the existing lines. The most important causes of this decommissioning policy (in addition to the mistaken expectation that soon public transport would not be necessary in any case) was the growing discrepancy between the changing settlement structures and the existing rail networks, which had not been changed for decades. In smaller metropolitan areas such as the Kassel region, rail networks are particularly endangered as the problems resulting from individual transport are less pressing and the rate of automobile use among the population is in any case quite high.

In a common initiative arising from union members, citizens and Kassel University (which had been founded in 1971), protest to these ideas arose and a counter-proposal was developed.[3] This was a plan for the expansion of the tram system, which gained growing support and was increasingly implemented with the necessary political majorities. From 1981 onwards, the Green Party became a formidable power in the Kassel City Parliament, with a strong influence on the development of public transport. The Social Democrats, with a strong position in Kassel, also ultimately decided to support the retention of the system. The development of the tram network now began to receive significant support from the city authorities and important concepts were provided from the university in Kassel. In these concepts were the first suggestions to extend the tram network into the surrounding countryside to serve neighbouring municipalities. The idea would be to use the existing rail network of the state-owned railway Deutsche Bahn for the tram service.

The central prerequisites for the "renaissance of the tram" in Kassel were, on the one hand, changes in the political situation and the dominant actors and, on the other, organizational changes in the legislation governing the railways in Germany – the possibilities and limitations of which will be discussed in greater detail below. In Kassel, it was initially various individuals who worked or were educated at the local university, and who were then in the position to introduce important changes while occupying management positions in the local public transport company (Kasseler Verkehrs-Gesellschaft, KVG) or the regional public transport authority (Nordhessischer Verkehrs-Verbund, NVV) (Meyfahrt and Beinhauer, 1995).

As a consequence, the plans for the modernization and expansion of the tram system in Kassel became a success story. The system was developed step by step. New, customer-friendly tram vehicles were acquired. Modern forms of marketing were put into practice and more and more customers began to use the tram (Lührman and Meyfahrt, 1994). The plans to make use of tram vehicles on rail lines and to provide service to the environs of the city of Kassel, in a better form than was provided at the time with locomotive driven trains, proved to be realistic. In the city of Karlsruhe in southern Germany, a similar model had been developed in a research project starting in 1983. Since 1992, trams operated on the rail lines to the neighbouring city of Bretten. This was far more economical and attractive as a service than the locomotive-driven train service. In Kassel, this idea was improved through the use of low-floor trams that were accessible to the disabled. Some of these were additionally equipped with diesel motors (bivalent operation) making it possible to use rail lines that did not have overhead lines for electric power. Operation of trams on rail lines began in 1995. Starting in 2006, the first trams began to serve the larger region and in August 2007 a new connection between the tram network and the railway system was brought into use through the construction of a tunnel at Kassel's old main railway station. Since this time it has been possible for passengers from the surrounding region of Kassel to travel to their destinations in the city centre without having to transfer. As a "brand" the terms for "region" and "tram" were combined, and the system has been marketed as the "RegioTram".

Nordhessischer VerkehrsVerbund
Area & Key Figures

▶ 1.050.000 inhabitants, one third in

the Kassel conurbation

▶ 7,000 km² area

▶ 4,840 stations and stops

▶ 280.000 passengers per day
(Tram 37%, Urban Bus 18%,
Regional Train 9%, Regional Bus 36%)

▶ € 65 M revenues from passenger fares

▶ competent local authority for integrates public passenger transport services
(rail, tram, bus)

Figure 42.1   Nordhessischer Verkehrs-Verbund area and key figures

In the space of 30 years, a complete reversal in transport infrastructure policy (including the implementation of the new policy) had taken place. As already indicated, this development was made possible not only through changes among the concerned actors in the system, but also through political changes in the local government and in the railway policy of the German government at the federal level. In the years 1990–2000 in Germany a gradual process of "regionalisation" of the responsibilities for public transport and particularly for rail transport took place. This development was facilitated in particular by the "Act for Regionalisation of Public Transport" (Regionalisierungsgesetz, RegG) enacted on 27 December 1993. Responsibility for the planning, the fare system and the design of transport offerings was transferred to regional institutions. It is a central thesis of this article that good local public transport service for cities and regions can create distinctive economic, social and ecological benefits, but that these benefits can only come to fruition through sufficient attention and promotion of the specific local and regional interests of a particular area. We will show that, despite some changes in relevant legislation in Germany, there still are considerable disadvantages for the regions and the interests represented there and that the current planning procedures in Germany do not yet incorporate local aspects and concerns sufficiently. Nonetheless, the example of Kassel shows what can be accomplished and what can be transferred to other situations on an international basis. In the following remarks, it will be shown how a local initiative was able to succeed, but how this initiative was repeatedly impeded and limited by central powers (in Germany, the federal government and the state-owned Deutsche Bahn AG).

2. A REGIONAL TRANSPORT SYSTEM FINDING A SPACE BETWEEN LOCAL AND CENTRAL INTERESTS

The basic idea of the RegioTram Nordhessen is the connection of the tram system of the central city of Kassel with the railway network of the urban centre's more rural environs. The connection at the former main station in Kassel creates a total network that is similar to the city train networks of larger metropolitan regions (S-Bahn) and which is viewed by the customers as a single entity. The enhanced attractiveness of this system should ensure that it is possible even in a relatively thinly populated rural region to provide service at an attractive interval of 30 minutes, that the centre and the periphery can be effectively connected and that these transport offerings can be provided on a good economical basis.

A special feature of the RegioTram network of North Hesse is the multiplicity of operating and traction systems in use, the inclusion of several network operators as well as the involvement of regional corporations in the financing of the system.

The degree and manner of participation of the regional authorities is distinctly different in the various network components:

- co-financing of the infrastructure necessary for the system (connection at the main station, system interchange points, etc.) by the various districts and the city of Kassel;

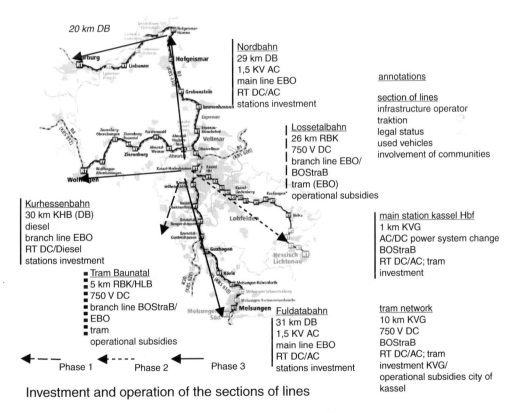

Investment and operation of the sections of lines

Figure 42.2   Investment and operation of the sections of lines

- co-financing of new RegioTram stations by the affected municipalities;
- operating subsidies from the townships for the Lossetalbahn line;
- overall organisation by transport association of the North Hesse districts and the city of Kassel;
- operating subsidies in accordance with the German Regionalisation Act by the state of Hesse via the NVV;
- subsidies for the contingency costs for infrastructure in the Lossetalbahn line through the NVV.

The realisation of the tram-train projects in North Hesse occurred in three phases, which featured considerable differences in the planning and realisation process depending on the participating actors as well as distinct differences in manner of operation deriving from differing operational models.

Phase 1 involved the extension of the tram to Baunatal (1995) making use of existing railway infrastructure and conventional tram vehicles. Planning and operation have been realised cooperatively by a tram transport company and a railway transport company through a shared subsidiary (Regionalbahn Kassel GmbH, RBK). The cooperation takes place in the areas of infrastructure, vehicles and personnel. The initiative for this common effort came from the involved transport companies, the financing of the necessary investments and the operation was sponsored by the affected townships. The operation and the contingency financing of the infrastructure received additional financing by the transport association (Meyfahrt and Beinhauer, 1993).

Phase 2 comprised the reactivation of the Lossetalbahn line, which had been decommissioned in 1986, with newly laid tram segments for better servicing of the relevant city and village centres (2001–6). The initiative came from the involved city transport companies. The affected communities were included from the beginning in the planning and decision-making process. The RBK acquired the line from the Deutsche Bahn for one Deutschmark, as a decommissioned line had to be handed over to a new operator on this basis in accordance with the current law of the time. The line now operates using tram vehicles which are specially equipped for railway branch lines in accordance with the Eisenbahn-Bau und Betriebsordnung (EBO, Railway Construction and Operations Ordinance). The RBK financed the new construction and the vehicles (with subsidies coming from the federal Municipal Transport Financing Act); the municipalities and the NVV subsidise the operation; the NVV also subsidises the contingency costs for the infrastructure while the RBK bears the revenue risk. The complete planning and construction process as well as the operation were handled locally which has allowed decisions to be made quickly and efficiently (Meyfahrt and Beinhauer, 2001).

Phase 3 was based on the successes in extending the network realised in the first two phases and has established a basis for a comprehensive development of the track network in the Kassel region through the connection of the tram and railway networks at the Main Station in Kassel (2007). In this case the local municipal transport companies again provided preliminary planning work, but the decisive initiative came from the transport association and thus from the regional authority. The Deutsche Bahn and its various subsidiaries, DB Netz, DB Station and Service, DB Energie, DB Regio, as well as diverse real estate companies of the Deutsche Bahn, were important actors in the project but had no local connections and were not particularly interested in the undertakings. The affected municipalities were only partially involved in the project and were represented by the districts. The planning and decision process was strongly influenced by the decision process connected with EU regulation 1370/2009, which was taking place at the same time (EU regulation no. 1370–2009 of the European Parliament and of the Council dated 23 October 2007 concerning public transport services on rail and street and for the repeal of EEC regulations nos. 119/69 and 1107/70 of the Council). There were recurrent conflicts regarding the self-provision of services and legal questions regarding competition regulations and awarding of contracts. The result was a complicated combination of different actors with various responsibilities and risks to be borne. The overall risk – investment and operation – is carried by the transport association and thus by the regional authority. The transport companies have no influence on the decision-making process. The regional authority for its part has no influence on the monopoly prices set by the Deutsche Bahn infrastructure companies, which make up an increasing portion of the running costs of the system (Meyfahrt, 2002).

In addition to the multiple process-based and organisational aspects that had to be regulated, technical solutions also had to be found for connections between the railway and the tram systems. This has involved using all the familiar two-system solutions for vehicles and infrastructure use.

An analysis and comparison of the various tram-train planning, decision and realisation processes as well as the actual operation of the system in North Hesse is thus of particular interest in connection with the tram-train idea. The necessary investment of €200 million for a region of approximately 700,000 inhabitants was only possible on the basis of two legal prerequisites: the federal Municipal Transport Financing Act (Gemeindeverkehrsfinanzierungsgesetz, GVFG), which provides a formal basis for requesting investment subsidies from the federal government for local investors, and the federal Regionalisation Act, which makes ongoing subsidies available to the local authorities for local rail-based commuter transport in their respective areas. This made the local investment portion of approximately 25 per cent manageable, and the redirection of regionalisation funds from the railway to the tram-train segment allowed the operation of the system without additional burdens. Both of these laws, which served as prerequisites for the new system, are currently in jeopardy in Germany. The Municipal Transport Financing Act will be discontinued in the course of the federalism reform. The funds made available through the Regionalisation Act are currently increased annually by 1.5 per cent; at the same time, the Deutsche Bahn is increasing its track and station costs by 3 per cent per year according to their planning figures. And in North Hesse the station costs have increased by 40 per cent in the past two years. The track and station costs thus make up 40 per cent of the total costs of the RegioTram.

The results of the comparison of the various planning and operating conditions found in North Hesse point to three problem areas that are not only of local significance and represent more general structural problems.

Different Interests of Local, Regional, National and Transnational Institutions

Tram-train systems connect tram networks with railway networks (see Salmerón i Bosch, 2012). Tram networks are oriented to local requirements and serve local transport needs. Railway networks provide regional and long-distance transport. The differing interests and needs of local and long-distance transport are reflected in the responsible authorities, institutions, network operators and transport companies.

Tram-train systems only provide local and regional transport and are initiated at the local level. An intelligent linking of existing infrastructure elements requires detailed knowledge of the local structures at all levels. Nationally centralised institutions cannot bring this knowledge to bear. Successful project realisation is only possible when local interests can directly participate and are prepared to contribute part of the financing.

At an operational level, local needs are also of prime importance.[4] The connection with local feeder systems, particularly in the bus segment, the integration of local and regional fare price systems, and overall quality control must be in place prior to the connection with long-distance transport system.

This prioritisation of local interests and needs stands in contradiction to the region that controls the railway network. The following factors are of particular significance:

- The predominance of faster regional transport over slower local transport. The result is difficulties in integrating tram-train schedules with the local tram schedules.
- The complex and expensive administrative apparatus of the Deutsche Bahn, which is broken into numerous individual companies making it difficult to reach decisions and creating additional costs.
- The lack of locally competent personnel at the Deutsche Bahn. The Deutsche Bahn has very few specialists operating at the local level and their individual companies with differing regional responsibilities have to first find a way to coordinate among themselves.
- The minor economic significance of any particular tram-train project in comparison to the Deutsche Bahn's own major projects. This has the effect that the central organs of the Deutsche Bahn companies give precedence to their own larger undertakings.
- The supervisory and approval authorities of the Deutsche Bahn (Federal Railway Authority (Eisenbahnbundesamt) and the Federal Network Agency (Bundesnetzagentur)) have no local knowledge.

The internal standards of the Deutsche Bahn do not take the interests of tram-train projects into account. The configuration of new stations must be decided in elaborate proceedings and implemented often in opposition to the Deutsche Bahn Station and Service authority (e.g., platform height, weather protection, seating arrangements, passenger information).

The following considerations are of particular significance for the local interests:

- The knowledge of the local situation and history of the infrastructure. This allows the utilisation of existing resources and the establishment of optimal connection points.
- The agreement and realisation of projects in local decision-making bodies requires local knowledge and local presence of planners and responsible parties.
- The financing of projects must typically be supplemented by contributions from

the regional authorities. Political identification with the pending projects makes it possible to achieve ongoing subsidies for operation of the new systems.

- Local supervisory and approval authorities have easier access to files and to local actors in the planning process, which results in faster decisions.
- Local infrastructure owners can do their own planning without failing to comply with contracting regulations. This makes a more direct realisation and interaction between planning and operation possible.
- Effective quality control in realisation and operation is in the direct interest of the local institutions and thus is simpler and more economical.

The described difficulties and differences between central and local interests cannot be avoided in an objective sense. In many cases, however, it is possible to take local interests better into account through the selection of alternatives. In the RegioTram project this involved the establishment of the central station and the connection at the Main Station by the local Kassel transport company (KVG); with the Lossetal line it entailed the acquisition of the line from the Deutsche Bahn and the operation of the infrastructure by the RBK.

At a second level, local and regional interests collided with one another in the tram network. Regional interests, represented by the North Hesse Transport Association (NVV) were focussed on an optimal connection between the centre and the periphery; the local interests of the city of Kassel were not so clearly formulated.

Parallel to the general discussion of the RegioTram concept, the city of Kassel prepared a draft paper for discussion regarding new concepts for the inner city. The draft proposed the removal of the tram line from the Königsstrasse (the main commercial street of the city) and bringing the tram and the RegioTram onto a city ring around the central pedestrian area (see Kassel City Administration, 2000). The aim of this proposal was an "urban development improvement" of the Königsstrasse to create a "boulevard" and the stimulation of the adjacent city areas. After a survey of the citizens conducted in conjunction with the local elections in 2001, the idea of removal of the tram line was replaced by the aim of reducing tram exposure on Königsstrasse. The RegioTram played no significant role in the formulation of this aim. The political actors, the media and portions of the public assumed that public transport users could be expected to walk the necessary distances from the city ring into the central pedestrian area. This would, however, contradict a central goal of the RegioTram concept, namely to provide direct access to the inner city. The planning authorities of the city continue to refuse to recognise this contradiction in their own planning activities.

The economic consequences of this refusal do not have to be borne by the city of Kassel because the NVV as the relevant authority has the sole financial responsibility. However, the city formulates the same position regarding running the tram lines through the Königsstrasse – the negative consequences for the revenues of the KVG are to be borne indirectly by itself.

The Monopolies of the National Railway Infrastructure Companies

First and foremost, tram-train projects should result in a better use of existing infrastructure or – with relatively small investments – allow massive improvements in the transport offerings and in the profitability of operation. They thus depend directly on the readiness of infrastructure owners to cooperate and participate.

The track infrastructure is owned by three different companies: Deutsche Bahn AG, Hessische Landesbahn GmbH (HLB) and the Kasseler Verkehrs-Gesellschaft AG (KVG) as well as their subsidiaries. The transport association, as the authority for the regional rail transport, only has indirect influence over the KVG and the HLB. The Lord Mayor of Kassel is a member of the supervisory boards of the NVV and the KVG; representatives of the state of Hesse in the supervisory board of the NVV have a right to issue instructions in the HLB. The Deutsche Bahn is entirely independent of local and state (as opposed to federal) bodies. Even the influence of the federal government of Germany as an owner of the Deutsche Bahn is very limited in accordance with stock corporation law.

Through local interests and institutional connections, the NVV, KVG and HLB took on the RegioTram project as the central public transport project in North Hesse and promoted it accordingly. For the infrastructure companies of the Deutsche Bahn the project was not seen as an "in-house" project; "outside" interests brought the project to them. The Deutsche Bahn infrastructure companies are 100 per cent financed through fees for network use, train stations and other infrastructure-based revenues. For investments in the networks and train stations through third-party funding (in this case the regional authorities and Municipal Transport Financing Act subsidies), they nonetheless demand positive results from the profitability calculations as a prerequisite for their approval of the investments. This dependency of local investments on centrally made decisions may make sense, but the Deutsche Bahn's demand that the NVV place a guaranteed order for long-term train service in accordance with the profitability calculation that had been made is not justifiable.

No tram-train project can be realised without the involvement of the Deutsche Bahn infrastructure companies. In this situation, it must be noted that the monopoly situation of the Deutsche Bahn is not subject to political control. For the Deutsche Bahn, the only relevant factor is its own economic advantage. The local actors must acquiesce to the wishes of the Deutsche Bahn if they want to have their project realised. Of major significance in this regard is the fact that the Deutsche Bahn infrastructure companies can set the conditions and the prices for network use autonomously and thus there is a considerable potential for discrimination.

The price model of the Deutsche Bahn network is based on "trains" that are billed for the number of kilometres they travel within a component of the network.[5] The length of the train is not considered in this calculation. Thus an ICE train or freight train of great length is treated exactly like a RegioTram vehicle of 35m. Likewise the weight of the trains is not considered, with the exception of heavy freight trains over 3,000 tons. Up to this point, all trains including a 60-ton RegioTram are treated identically. As far as signalling and network management are concerned, the equal treatment is justified – in all cases trains are dispatched and dealt with. But the difference in the level of use and wear on the tracks occurring with a RegioTram or a 3,000-ton freight train is, of course, very large.

The systemisation and improved efficiency in network use achieved through coordinated scheduling is not rewarded by granting price discounts; rather it is penalised by a factor of 1.65, making freight trains that do not run according to a coordinated schedule less expensive in comparison. A conversion of the prices on the basis of transported tons

Table 42.1   *A conversion of the prices on the basis of transported tons or of passenger seats per train on the Kassel–Hofgeismar line*

	Price/ton	Price/passenger seat
RegioTram single traction	0,071 €	0,053 €
Freight train up to 3000 t	0,001 €	–
ICE	0,005 €	0,007 €

Note: Track prices of the DB Netz AG 2012.

or of passenger seats per train shows the shifting of the cost burden to local passenger transport (on the line Kassel–Hofgeismar):

Tram-train systems depend on transport intervals of maximum 30 minutes and on this basis make use of smaller units. Halving the interval between scheduled trains doubles the track fees. If, instead of this, double traction was used once an hour, the track fees would remain the same. This again shows the orientation of the track price system to the requirements of long-distance transport. The higher revenues gained through the use of a local tram-train system do not, however, result in any particular benefit for the overall system as they result in only a marginal increase in the overall income of the DB network.

In a local network such as the Lossetalbahn line, these effects can be avoided and do not result in additional costs. The track fees of the Lossetalbahn must cover the track costs of the RBK as the concerned infrastructure provider as with the DB network. With a halving of the interval between trains the total income would increase so significantly that the kilometre prices could be reduced. The comparison of track costs between the Lossetalbahn and main lines of the DB also shows the positive effects of direct attribution of subsidies to the supported lines: a RegioTram trip to Hofgeismar on the DB network costs approximately €148 in track and station fees; a trip of the same length to Hessisch Lichtenau on the Lossetalbahn line costs €55.

The price system of DB Station and Service was fundamentally changed in 2011.[6] How the Deutsche Bahn is calculating its costs remains entirely opaque to the regional authority. It is disclosed that seven different train station categories have been established according to their significance. For each category, the costs are determined for each regional authority and a corresponding price is set. For the categorisation of train stations a system is used that considers the number of platform edges, the maximum length of the platforms, the number of travelling passengers, the number of train stops, the service and the technical solutions providing step-free access for the disabled.

In the NVV, 80 per cent of the stations fall in Category 6. These are stops for which the Deutsche Bahn in the basic service provides no clock, no seating possibility and no weather protection – entirely unacceptable facilities for tram-train service.

Nonetheless the prices for the NVV in the past two years have increased by over 40 per cent – with no possibility of influencing the situation at the local level. The terms of use specified by the Deutsche Bahn[7] make reference to exceptional rights of termination. However, given the monopoly situation, this seems merely a cynical remark to those dependent on their services.

In this regard, there is also not a basis for attributing costs and revenues to the tram-train project. Subsidies paid for the new stations and increased revenues resulting from

Table 42.2　The development of prices for a stop at a RegioTram station, the Main Station in Kassel or Kassel Wilhelmshöhe

	Station category 6	Main Station Kassel	Long-distance Station KS-Wilhelmshöhe
2005	€2.32–2.37	€4.65	€15.81
2010	€2.42–2.98	€5.64	€14.63
2011	€4.00	€22.64	€22.64
2012	€4.33	€25.32	€25.32

Note:　Station price list DB Station & Service AG, 2005–12.

the more frequent service do not benefit the prices for the RegioTram stations but rather all of the stations in the concerned category. However, at least in this instance the money stays within the regional authorities. The prices for a stop at a RegioTram station or at the Main Station in Kassel or Kassel Wilhelmshöhe have developed as shown in Table 42.2.

As with the track fees, the station fees do not depend on the type of train. Only as regards the factor of train length is the stop of an ICE train at the Wilhelmshöhe station charged more than that of a RegioTram by a factor of 1.2–3 times. At other RegioTram stops, if station buildings are still to be found they are typically locked. More often than not they are in a state of disrepair – whether they are owned by the Deutsche Bahn AG, one of its real estate companies or have been sold to a so-called property user. The purchase of train stations by the local municipality is the only way to positively influence the condition of a train station and its surroundings. But such purchases usually are infeasible owing to the price notions of the Deutsche Bahn.

A unified "user interface" for bus, tram, tram-train and train service is necessary to facilitate effective use of the various systems and their connections. This has been achieved at the level of the NVV. The Deutsche Bahn, which has bundled its sales activities in the DB Sales (DB Vertrieb), also insists here on the recognition of its conditions in a monopolistic fashion. The recognition of the DB fares is established. The sale of DB tickets beyond the area covered by the NVV in the ticket machines on the RegioTrams has not been possible to put into place because of the unacceptable conditions imposed by the DB Sales, in particular the excessive sales costs of approximately 18 per cent of the sales price (as opposed to approximately 8 per cent for NVV fares). The creation of a non-discriminatory sales system with end-to-end integration remains a task for the future.

The Competitive Environment and EU Regulations

Rules and regulations pertaining to competition and fair award of contracts have a large influence on passenger rail service. The demanded principle of open bidding for planning and construction work and for the operation of rail transport services is "simple" when there are similar conditions in many locations and at all times thus creating a genuine "market" and allowing the determination of a fair price. Tram-train systems fulfil these requirements only in some areas.

That the vehicles for a tram-train project must be newly acquired and are in practice unusable in any other situation cannot be avoided in the typical request for tenders occurring in the context of local passenger rail service. These vehicles must remain in the business field of the regional ordering authority. Only in a second tender process can the vehicles be made available to other competitors.

In the area of infrastructure, depot and repair facilities are necessary that are customised for the vehicles in use. These facilities are bound to the location of the system; particularly in the tram network alternative or additional locations can hardly be found. It makes no sense to construct new depot and repair facilities every 8–15 years as is often specified in the general bidding regulations. These problems exist in principle in the railway segment as well, but in larger networks there are more alternatives. In tram-train systems therefore the infrastructure composed of vehicles, repair and depot facilities must be primarily allocated to the (local) monopoly actor.

Open competitive bidding processes also make little sense for staffing purposes. Vehicle crews need double qualifications in the train and tram areas. In the local labour force of a given tram-train system, there will thus be approximately as many qualified drivers as are required for such a system. With a new tender, the new company must either formally take on all the current drivers as personnel or train new drivers or assume that all or most of the drivers will change over to the winner of the tender on their own.

Contracting authorities in tram-train systems thus find themselves dealing mainly with companies that are acting as a monopoly provider or have considerable advantages as the existing provider. It therefore seems sensible to use a system that relies on direct award of contracts to local tram operators or to a cooperative entity composed of the tram operator and railway company. The new EU regulation 1370/2009 (see above) makes this possible in the tram area and in the railway area. The issue of direct award of contracts in the tram-train area has not been legally clarified. Typically no single contracting authority has sufficient control in the whole area of such a system.

The respective interpretations and realisations of the EU competition regulations (in Germany the Public Transport Act (PBefG) enacted 26 June 2013) tend to impede tram-train projects more than promote them. All of the existing projects were realised in a very freely regulated competitive situation or before the current regulations were formulated or in field in which the regulations were circumvented in some creative manner.

3.   SUCCESS AND FUTURE PERSPECTIVES

In Kassel we find a true success story in the tram-train area but the limits of what is possible are also to be observed. One thing is certain: it is possible to establish a closely coordinated rail system that provides good local connections and is oriented to the regional interests with the currently available technical possibilities – even in an area typified by more rural structures around a medium-sized city in Europe. A system of this sort provides significant benefits for a region, particularly in view of the costs for automobile transport which will surely rise in future. Such a rail system can provide the central city (in this case Kassel) as well as the smaller municipalities in the surrounding area considerable advantages: It can strengthen the functions of the central city (e.g., education, administration, higher quality shopping); it can at least ensure the accessibility of central transport nodes (hub connections, in the case of Kassel the central train station for long-distance ICE rail service Kassel-Wilhelmshöhe); and it can promote the touristic traffic to the smaller municipalities in the area around a central city.

The positive effects of public transport can be seen in Kassel for example in the case of the university which is located close to the centre of the city. It has developed to have 22,000 students and approximately 2,500 employees without the construction of new, large-scale parking facilities. The great majority of the students make use of the public transport system and the tram and the RegioTram play an important role in the localities of the surrounding area. Without the retention and the development of the tram system and the newly established connections throughout the region, it would only be possible to have such a university location outside of the urban centre (with the attendant parking facilities and traffic load) or with a considerable demolition of existing residential areas in the city. A regional rail system can thus provide significant ecological and social benefits.

The Kassel region has weathered the economic crises of recent years considerably better than comparable regions in Germany. Good public transport access within the region is certainly only one factor (among many) that has influenced this development, but it has definitely contributed to the success of the region.

The more closely coordinated network structure and improvement of internal accessibility provided by a system of tram-trains can help to preserve many advantages of the system of the "European city", even in areas of medium size with rural surroundings, and in a future where economic challenges and uncertainty are to be expected. A large selection of institutions and facilities remain accessible within the region without the use of the automobile thereby ensuring good social communication and adaptability to developments which today cannot be exactly foreseen.

It is important to keep in mind that a region can make its own decisions about the type of transport accessibility it wants to have. In the case described here there was a "time window" in Germany in the period of 1990 to 2000 that enabled better control over finances and the regulatory situation at a local level. Today it is to be feared that these conditions are changing.

It can be seen in the example of Kassel, and also in wider Germany, a true shifting of the authority and particularly the control over financial resources to the regions did not occur. The Deutsche Bahn, which belongs to the federal state, continues to have considerable advantages both financially and institutionally which are evident in the preferential treatment afforded to the long-distance transport that it continues to provide in Germany in a nearly exclusively monopolistic situation. The regional administration of transport must in many cases (e.g., with train stations) simply accept the conditions imposed by the Deutsche Bahn. This can have the result that necessary measures that would serve to increase the attractiveness of local transport cannot be realised. For cities and regions to achieve an overarching transport planning in their areas, a comprehensive planning of mobility development will be necessary that also includes parameters such as settlement and population development. Such an approach is of great importance to provide an effective means of dealing with challenges of the coming decades such as the growing expense of transport and the general ageing of the population.

Integrated regional transport concepts that take account of the regional interests in the public transport sector are necessary in Europe. Such concepts can make the regions of Europe fit for a future in which the automobile need not play the same role that it does today. The example of Kassel shows how it is possible to achieve regional and urban control over one sector of public transport and how this can result in significant benefits even in less central locations. It also shows, however, that there is still much to be done to make the most of such progress and to accomplish this in a context where the existing interests and advantages of the central rail system predominate.

Main Actors and Legislation Shaping Regional Transport in North Hesse

Deutsche Bahn (DB): By far the largest train operating company in Germany, state-owned. The company is split into several subsidiaries. The company owns almost the entire rail network in Germany; train operating companies, such as DB Regio, Cantus or Metronom, must pay for the use of network and stations.

NVV (Nordhessischer Verkehrs-Verbund): Regional transport authority that organises the supply of regional public transport in North Hesse with the exception of long-distance rail transport, which is organised by the Deutsche Bahn.

KVG (Kasseler Verkehrs-Gesellschaft): Kassel's local tram and bus company.

Eisenbahn-Bau- und Betriebsordnung (EBO) (Railway Construction and Operations Ordinance): Federal rules for construction and operation of railways in Germany.

Straßenbahn-Bau- und Betriebsordnung (BOStrab) (Tram Construction and Operations Ordinance): Federal rules of construction and operation of trams in Germany.

Gemeindeverkehrsfinanzierungsgesetz (GVFG) (Municipal Transport Financing Act): Federal funding for local public and individual traffic investment, (normally 60–75 per cent).

Regionalisierungsgesetz (RegG) (Regionalisation Act): Federal legislation enacted in 1996 that directs federal funding to various state and regional authorities for providing public transport at the regional level.

NOTES

1. About the history of Kassel, see Güntzel (2012).
2. This is described in Holzapfel (2012: 136).
3. See Gesamthochschule Kassel, "Die Straßenbahn muß bleiben: Stellungnahme des Fachbereichs Stadt- und Landschaftsplanung", special edition of the newspaper *Der Monolith*, 1977.
4. About the need for localism and regionalism, see Holzapfel (2010).
5. The Network Statement and the Terms and Conditions Governing Usage of Service Installations Operated by DB Netz AG (SNB) is issued annually.
6. See Stationspreissystem SPS11, DB Station & Service AG, Central Sales Office, Berlin, 2 November 2012, with an explanation of the pricing.
7. Infrastructure Terms of Use for Passenger Train Stations are issued annually by DB Station & Service AG, Central Sales (LSVP).

REFERENCES

Güntzel, R. (2012), *The Demigod's City: A Short History of Kassel*, Marburg: Tectum Verlag.

Holzapfel, H. (2010), Urbanisation and the need for sustainable development: everywhere and nowhere, *World Transport Policy & Practice*, **16**(2).

Holzapfel, H. (2012), The city that came out of the shadows, *Town & Country Planning*, March, 252–3.

Kassel City Administration (2000), *Kassel im Dialog, Entwurf eines Leitbildes für die Entwicklung der Innenstadt*, Kassel: Kassel City Administration.

Lührman, H. and Meyfahrt, R. (1994), Entwicklungslinien des ÖPNV in Kassel, *Der Städtetag*, January, 50–55.

Meyfahrt, R. (2002), Tram-train revives Kassel Network, *Railway Gazette International*, December, 779–80.

Meyfahrt, R. and Beinhauer, M. (1993), Straßenbahn und Eisenbahn auf der Neubaustrecke Kassel-Baunatal, *Der Nahverkehr*, **12**, 18–23.

Meyfahrt, R. and Beinhauer, M. (1995), Von der Kooperation zum Verbund, *Der Nahverkehr*, May, 44–9.

Meyfahrt, R. and Beinhauer, M. (2001), Mit der Tram ins Lossetal, *Der Nahverkehr*, **6**, 40–61.

Salmerón i Bosch, C. (2012), The Tram-trains of Europe: A New Regional Mobility for Europe, Barcelona: Terminus.

43 The making of European transport policy
Dominic Stead

> Europe's transport dilemmas were not created yesterday,
> nor will they be solved tomorrow.
> (Ross 1998: xiv)

1. INTRODUCTION – THE ORIGINS AND DEVELOPMENT OF THE COMMON TRANSPORT POLICY (CTP)

The objective of a common transport policy dates back more than five decades to the treaty establishing the European Economic Community (EEC) – the Treaty of Rome, which was signed in 1957. Transport was in fact one of the main areas of common policy of the treaty: ten articles in the treaty were devoted to transport (more than the number of articles concerning agriculture). Certain ideas behind a common transport policy can even be traced further back in time. The Treaty of Paris (1951), for example, which established the European Coal and Steel Community (the forerunner to the EEC), contained a chapter on transport (Table 43.1). Nevertheless, despite being a common area

Table 43.1   Transport in the treaties

Treaty	Signed	In force	Effect on transport policy
Treaty of Paris (TECSC)	April 1951	January 1952	Non-discrimination in carriage of coal and steel
Treaty of Rome (TEC)	March 1957	January 1958	First outline of common transport policy
Single European Act (SEA)	February 1986	July 1987	Extends qualified majority voting to air and sea transport; first mention of environment action
Treaty on European Union (TEU)	February 1992	November 1993	Adds safety to transport title; makes provision for infrastructure (TENs); requires environmental protection to be integrated into other policies
Treaty of Amsterdam (TA)	October 1997	May 1999	Further reinforcement of environment provisions
Treaty of Lisbon	December 2007	December 2009	Gives more emphasis to combatting climate change as an EU policy objective; pushes energy issues more firmly into the EU policy domain

Source: Based on Stevens (2004)

of policy for more than 50 years and featuring in all key European treaties, European transport policy developed relatively slowly, especially before the mid-1980s, which is generally considered to be a turning point in European transport policy-making (Giorgi and Schmidt, 2002; Jensen, 2008; Kerwer and Teutsch, 2001; Lyons, 2000; Rothacher, 2005; Stevens, 2004). Before this time, many member states were unwilling to relinquish control of national transport markets (Lyons, 2000) and had very different views about the role of transport policy vis-à-vis the economy and society (Aspinwall, 1999; Stevens, 2004). Many authors therefore refer to two distinct phases in the development of European transport policy (i.e., 1950s to the mid-1980s and mid-1980s onwards).[1] Both periods cover a similar duration (around three decades) but the policy focus and the level of activity in the policy sector are both very different in these two periods.

Phase 1: The 1950s to the Mid-1980s

The first phase of community initiatives, from the late 1950s until the mid-1980s, was primarily aimed at establishing Community standards, harmonizing member states' regulations on transport and establishing common conditions for transport services (Jensen, 2008: 133). In the 1960s, a detailed transport policy programme was developed but this soon proved unacceptable to many member states from a range of political ideologies (Kerwer and Teutsch, 2001). For some member states, the proposals were considered too liberal; for others the proposals were judged to be too incompatible with their existing situation (Kerwer and Teutsch, 2001). According to Stevens (2004: p.60), the Commission had high ambitions for an overarching common transport policy in the 1960s but these ambitions 'were blocked at every turn'. By the early 1970s, as a consequence of these experiences, the European Commission switched to a more pragmatic approach to transport policy (Erdmenger, 1983), where many transport-related issues were pursued separately in order to find solutions in specific areas (and specific modes). Consequently, progress with the development of a European Common Transport Policy (CTP) was slow, incremental and piecemeal (Lyons, 2000; Kerwer and Teutsch, 2001).

Slow progress in the development of a European Common Transport Policy up to the mid-1980s was primarily due to the inability to reconcile the opposing interests and regulatory approaches of the member states under the condition of unanimity voting in the European Council (Kerwer and Teutsch, 2001). At the outset, the CTP was hampered by contrasting regulatory approaches and conflicting economic interests of the member states. Of the six founding members of the European Economic Community (EEC), France, Germany and Italy, with national policy regimes characterized by a high degree of state intervention in transport markets, were traditionally sceptical of a liberal transport regime at the European level. These countries viewed transport policy as a means to accomplish regional, industrial and social policy goals. The Netherlands, in contrast, was a pronounced support of a liberal approach to European transport policy, seeing benefits for Dutch transport industries under a more deregulated system. Another explanation for slow progress in the development of the CTP is that, because various international bodies and agreements on transport already existed (e.g., European Conference of Ministers of Transport; International Air Transport Association; International Civil Aviation Organization; International Maritime Organization; International Road Federation; International Union of Railways), the development of a European common transport policy was not always regarded as an absolute necessity (Kerwer and Teutsch, 2001).

Phase 2: The Mid-1980s Onwards

According to authors such as Aspinwall (1999) and Stevens (2004), the foundations of contemporary common transport policy were laid between 1985 and 1992 under the impetus of the single market programme. The late 1980s and early 1990s saw the introduction of a raft of measures as the European Single Market was established. Policies shifted from standardization (harmonization) to liberalization (Giorgi and Schmidt, 2002; Jensen, 2008), and a number of transport sectors were targeted for liberalization (e.g., shipping, air, rail, road haulage). In addition, European funding was granted for a number of new transport infrastructure projects from the late via 1980s onwards via the Structural Funds, especially the European Regional Development Fund, which became more available to transport projects after reforms in 1988 (Giorgi and Schmidt, 2002).

The mid-1980s also heralded the first appearance of European environmental policy, which had important implications for transport policy. The 1986 Single European Act contained new articles on the environment, allowing the Community 'to preserve, protect and improve the quality of the environment, to contribute towards protecting human health, and to ensure a prudent and rational utilization of natural resources' in cases when action at the Community level is more appropriate than at the level of individual member states according to the principle of subsidiarity (taking decisions at the lowest appropriate level).[2] In June 1990, one of the conclusions of the European Council was that 'the environmental risks inherent in greater production and in increased demand for transport, energy and infrastructure [due to the completion of the internal market] must be countered and environmental considerations must be fully and effectively integrated into these and all other policy areas'. Two years later, the Treaty on the European Union (1992) enhanced the position of environmental policy in relation to transport and other sectoral policies (stipulating that 'environmental protection requirements must be integrated into the definition and implementation of other Community policies'), and brought transport safety and transport infrastructure into the Treaty, thereby extending the scope of the European Community in transport policy (Stevens, 2004).

The mid-1980s marked the beginning of policymaking in various new areas of European transport policy as illustrated by the three examples presented below. The first of these is concerned with bringing together transport and sustainable development, or the pursuit of 'sustainable mobility' as it is often termed in European policy documents. The second example focuses on the development of European transport infrastructure, primarily via the Trans-European Transport Network, while the third example concerns the evolution of European policy on urban transport, specifically in the context of subsidiarity. The development paths of policy in each of these three areas are discussed below.

2. THE PURSUIT OF SUSTAINABLE MOBILITY

The 1990 report *Transport in a Fast Changing Europe* (produced by the Transport 2000 Plus Working Group at the request of the European Commission) is credited as one of the first documents to introduce the concept of sustainable mobility in the area of European transport policy (Jensen, 2008). Shortly after this time, and closely coinciding with the Earth Summit in Rio de Janeiro and the signing of the Treaty on the European Union, the Commission produced a number of documents focusing specifically on the relationship between transport and the environment including a communication on the impact of transport on the environment and a White Paper on the future development of the Common Transport Policy, both of which were published in 1992 and shared a number of the same themes on transport and sustainable development (Lyons, 2000). Notably, the two documents also contained reference to sustainable mobility in their subtitles.[3] These documents signalled the intention to give more emphasis to environmental issues in determining the content of the common transport policy (Stevens, 2004). Although the Commission continued to develop its transport policies on a pragmatic modal basis long after 1992, with a strong emphasis on measures required to buttress the single market (Stevens, 2004), there was a noticeable shift in the rationale for transport policies away from market-led statements about completing the internal market and towards more environmentally and socially motivated arguments.

The introduction of the concept of sustainable mobility arguably brought environmental issues from the periphery to the centre of transport policy, at least on paper, although there were concerns that the concept acted more 'as a lubricant to the very development it was meant to challenge' (the ever increasing movement of people and goods) rather than putting a brake on unsustainable transport trends (Gudmundsson and Höjer, 1996: 269). The concept highlights a key dilemma of European transport policy, namely how to reconcile the free movement of people and goods, one of the one of basic pillars of the European Union, while at the same time protecting the environment and improving the health and safety of citizens. 'Sustainable' and 'mobility' reflect the two frequently competing aims of European transport policy. As such, the concept of sustainable mobility is in certain senses an oxymoron: mobility is not sustainable, certainly if mobility is motorized. This has led to debates whether it would be more appropriate to use the concept of accessibility (the ability to carry out activities, which may or may not imply movement) rather than mobility (which generally implies physical movement) when referring to sustainability (see for example Vivier, 2001).

The Treaty of Amsterdam, signed in 1997, further reinforced the position of European environmental policy by giving the Parliament increased powers to influence transport policy as a result of extended co-decision procedures for measures concerning transport and the environment (Lyons, 2000). As such, this treaty is considered by some to be a major milestone in the development of EU transport policy (e.g. Lyons, 2000). Around this time, various EU institutions certainly began to focus more closely on how to integrate environmental protection into other Community objectives including transport (Lyons, 2000). Around the same time (1998), the Commission issued a communication on transport and CO_2 emissions (prompted by a joint Council of Transport and Environment Ministers, convened during the British Presidency of the European Union) in which the transport sector's contribution to rising levels of carbon dioxide in the atmosphere transport was made abundantly clear. The communication also highlighted that the growth in transport CO_2 emissions, if left unchecked, 'would make it extremely difficult to achieve the CO_2 emission reduction target agreed at Kyoto'. The joint Council of Transport and Environment Ministers also marked the start of a 'third wave' of the integration of environmental issues into other areas of European policy (1998–2002), under the process launched by the European Council at their meeting in Cardiff in June 1998 – the Cardiff Process (for a more detailed discussion, see Jordan et al, 2008).

In 2001, a new White Paper on European transport policy (entitled *European Transport Policy for 2010: Time to Decide*) was published, setting out a ten-year strategy for European transport policy. Some months earlier, the European sustainable development strategy had identified three headline objectives for transport but these objectives received little prominence in the new White Paper. In fact, the White Paper had no clearly stated objectives: what it did have were strategies, sub-strategies and policy aims (Stead, 2001). A modal approach to transport policy still seemed to predominate, which can, for example, be seen from the document's policy aims. This is not so dissimilar to Stevens' summary of the situation in the 1980s, in which European transport policy was essentially 'a patchwork of . . . mildly useful mono-modal initiatives' (Stevens, 2004: 60).[4] Reference to sustainable mobility was noticeably missing (although the White Paper did include several references to sustainable development). My own summary of the document at the time was that it 'reads like a collection of separate contributions from different sections within the European Commission which have been written in the absence of a common vision for European transport policy' and that, compared to the previous White Paper in 1992, 'it is really the emphasis that has changed rather than the content' (Stead, 2001: 417–18). Schmidt and Giorgi (2001) took a similar view, stating that the White Paper contained few 'new' priorities.

Growing tensions between sustainability and mobility were explicitly recognized in the 2006 mid-term review of the 2001 Transport White Paper, stating, for example, that 'efforts to achieve the goals of meeting growing mobility needs and strict environmental standards are beginning to show signs of friction' (CEC, 2006: 8). Meanwhile, the concept of sustainable mobility, absent from the 2001 White Paper, made a return to the policy agenda in this 2006 document. Three years later, sustainable development was one of the main concepts in the 2009 communication on future directions for European transport policy (CEC, 2009a). This communication paved the way for a new ten-year strategy document on European transport policy (in the form of a White Paper), which was published in 2011, entitled *Roadmap to a Single European Transport Area – Towards a Competitive and Resource Efficient Transport System* (CEC, 2011a).[5] The White Paper recognized that the current transport system is not sustainable and stated that, in the long term, 'it is clear that transport cannot develop along the same path' (CEC, 2011a: 4). After stating that the EU needs to reduce 2050 greenhouse gas emissions by 80–95 per cent below 1990 levels, the document set out a 60 per cent reduction target for the transport sector between 1990 and 2050, arguing that 'deeper cuts can be achieved in other sectors of the economy' (CEC, 2011a: 3). In the medium-term, the White Paper committed itself to an interim goal of reducing these emissions in 2030 by 20 per cent of their 2008 level. However, as the White Paper itself acknowledged, this would mean that greenhouse gas emissions from transport in 2030 are still 8 per cent above the 1990 level, due to 'the substantial increase in transport emissions over the past two decades' (CEC, 2011a: 3). This underlines the magnitude of change required to achieve the long-term emission targets for transport, particularly since the White Paper explicitly stated that '[c]urbing mobility is not an option' (CEC, 2011a: 5).

So the general conception of sustainable mobility in the Commission does not therefore appear to imply any reduction in transport demand: a technological fix approach prevails.

3.   THE DEVELOPMENT OF THE TRANS-EUROPEAN TRANSPORT NETWORK (TEN-T)

One of the main ideas behind developing the Trans-European Transport Network (TEN-T) was to underpin and strengthen the creation of the internal market and to reinforce economic and social cohesion. The objective was to integrate national networks and modes of transport, link peripheral regions of the European Union to the centre, and improve safety and efficiency. The development of the TEN-T originates from the Maastricht Treaty (1992), although references to the need for a trans-European transport network can be found in lobbying material from the 1980s produced by the European Round Table of Industrialists (ERT). In fact, the ERT is generally acclaimed to be the initiator of the TEN-T: Gardner (1991: 48), for example, states that the ERT is 'the spiritual progenitor of the 1992 process and the single most powerful business group in Europe'. According to Endo (1999), the ERT is one of the few pressure groups able to actually change EU policy. The beginnings of the TEN-T policy can be traced to a 1984 report by the ERT (*Missing Links*), which proposed three major European transport infrastructure projects: (1) EuroRoute – a Channel link between England and France; (2) Scanlink – a plan to fill in the road and rail gaps between Norway, Sweden, Denmark and Northern Germany; and (3) a trans-European network of high-speed trains. The report also made recommendations for more investment of private capital in infrastructure development. Having defined infrastructure problems in terms of missing international infrastructure links, the ERT then sought to set the agenda for action and in 1991 called for a better network of roads (especially to overcome Alpine and Pyrenean 'barriers'), high-speed railways and air terminals in an influential report entitled *Missing Networks – A European Challenge*. Some of Europe's largest automobile and oil companies, including Fiat, Daimler Benz, Petrofina, Pirelli, Total and Volvo, were represented on the working group behind these ERT reports (Richardson, 1997). According to Richardson (1997), the ERT's 1991 report was a blueprint for the TEN-T proposals introduced in the 1992 Transport White Paper, which was published just a few months later.[6]

The formal decision to develop the TEN-T was made by the European Parliament and Council in 1996. Since then, the plans for the network have undergone several revisions as a result of the expansion of the European Union and budgetary changes (Table 43.2). The guidelines for the development of the trans-European transport network, adopted in 1996, provide the general reference framework for the implementation of the transport network and for identifying projects of common interest. A list of 14 major infrastructure projects (the 'Essen projects') was included in the 1996 guidelines as the first priorities to be completed before 2010. In 2001, the TEN-T guidelines were amended in various respects, including greater emphasis on the multimodal dimension of the TEN-T by bringing seaports and inland ports fully into the network. The guidelines were amended again in 2004, primarily in order to take account of substantial enlargement of the EU in the same year, and the expected changes in traffic flows as a result.[7] The 2004 guidelines contained a list of 30 priority projects of European interest: the original 14 Essen projects plus an additional 16 projects to be completed by 2020. Many of the new projects extended into the 'new' member states of the EU. More than half of these 30 projects concern rail transport (17 projects), another four concern road transport, four are multi-modal in nature, three concern water transport, one concerns air transport project and one concerns global navigation and positioning project (Galileo). In 2005, the relaunched Lisbon strategy presented the TEN-T was as a key element for increasing economic competitiveness and employment. Since 2006, the responsibility for implementing and managing the TEN-T programme (on behalf of the European Commission) rests with the Trans-European Transport Network Executive Agency (TEN-T EA).

With a budget of hundreds of billions of euros, Balanya et al. (2000) claim that the European TEN policy represents the largest infrastructure programme in the world. In general, TEN-T projects are funded to a major extent by national governments but they also receive funding through various Community financial instruments (e.g., Cohesion Funds in eligible countries and European Regional Development Funds) as well as loans from the European Investment Bank. Peters (2003) argues that, whilst

Table 43.2 *Chronology of the development of the Trans-European Transport Network (TEN-T)*

1990	Commission adopts first action plan on trans-European networks (transport, energy and telecommunications).
1993	TENs given legal base in Maastricht Treaty.
1994	Essen European Council endorses list of 14 TEN-T 'specific' projects, drawn up by a group chaired by then Commission Vice-President Henning Christophersen.
1995	Financial regulation for TEN-T support adopted.
1996	Adoption of TEN-T guidelines.
2001	Extension of TEN-T guidelines to port infrastructure (seaports, inland ports and intermodal terminals) adopted.
2003	A group chaired by former Commission Vice-President Karel Van Miert proposes new priority projects and calls for new means of funding.
2004	Revised guidelines and financial regulation adopted, with a list of 30 priority projects (including the original 14) and a higher maximum funding rate of 20% in certain cases.
2005	Nomination of the first six European coordinators.
2005	A group chaired by former Commission Vice-President Loyola de Palacio proposes axes linking TEN-T to neighbouring countries outside the EU.
2006	Trans-European Transport Network Executive Agency (TEN-T EA) established to provide technical and financial management of the TEN-T projects.
2009	European Commission review of the TEN-T policy (published as a Green Paper: COM(2009)44), including the formation of expert groups to discuss details of the TEN-T Policy Review.
2010	Publication of EU guidelines for the development of the Trans-European Transport Network. Public consultation exercise on TEN-T planning and implementation.
2011	Announcement of the 'Connecting Europe Facility': additional funding to finance projects that 'fill the missing links in Europe's energy, transport and digital backbone'.[8]

the majority of the priority projects concern rail and the fact that more than half of the TEN-T special budget line went towards rail, European financial support for TEN-T projects is nevertheless skewed towards road transport, particularly under the more sizeable Cohesion Funds and ERDF budgets. Consequently, the TEN-T policy has aroused opposition on environmental grounds, namely that it merely promotes road use at the expense of parallel modes (rail), thus undercutting sustainability objectives (Ross, 1998). It has also been controversial because of relatively low economic impacts (Netherlands Environmental Assessment Agency and Stockholm Resilience Centre, 2009) and high environmental impacts, particularly on biodiversity, associated with the development of infrastructure along some parts of the network (Byron and Arnold, 2008; EEA, 2006; Rothacher, 2005). In addition, the TEN-T policy has been criticized because it does not provide an effective contribution to the EU's climate change objectives (Netherlands Environmental Assessment Agency and Stockholm Resilience Centre, 2009) and increases the demand for transport by adding new routes and increasing the speed of travel (see, for example, Adams, 2005). As a consequence, there has been (and continues to be) a substantial amount of environmental resistance to the TEN-T policy, both at the transnational level and in individual member states of the EU (van der Heijden, 2006). However, the strength of this resistance is often limited, partly due to the primacy of economic arguments in many policy debates (especially in many of the newer EU member states) and partly due to the fragmentation of argumentation and action among the environmental movement (van der Heijden, 2006).

According to many observers, the TEN-T policy essentially represents a collection of nationally or regionally important infrastructure projects. Even the European Commission's own review of the TEN-T policy acknowledges that the planning of the network 'has not been driven by genuine European objectives' (CEC, 2009b: 5). Stephenson (2010) contends that the principle of subsidiarity, enshrined in the Maastricht Treaty, has meant that political decisions about TEN-T infrastructure have not just involved national governments but have also brought regional and local authorities, private/public partnerships, construction companies and service operators into the decision-making process. The EU's role on the other hand has been mainly limited to acting as a catalyst to the process by identifying the common European interest of projects and acting as a facilitator in negotiations (Stephenson, 2010).

4.   THE EVOLUTION OF EUROPEAN POLICY ON URBAN TRANSPORT

In line with the principle of subsidiarity, many competences for making transport policy within Europe are mainly national or sub-national. In many cases, competences are multi-level, whereby powers and responsibilities are shared between different levels of government. Although not numerous, various examples of European policies or initiatives can be found that exert some influence on national and local transport policies in member states. European policy on urban transport is one example. The argument for European policies in this field is that cities generate much of the EU's GDP and creating a high-quality urban environment will enhance Europe's potential for economic growth and job creation – a key priority of the Lisbon Strategy and the Europe 2020 Strategy (the successor of the Lisbon Strategy).

The urban dimension of EU transport policy started to receive attention in the mid-1990s with the publication of the Green Paper on the Citizens' Network in 1995 (CEC, 1995), a discussion paper on public transport and its contribution to social and environmental goals.[9] The Green Paper argued that, while developing integrated solutions to passenger transport problems is primarily a task for national, and local and regional authorities, there are nevertheless areas where action at a Community level is important. Sharing information and spreading know-how about best practices and state-of-the-art technologies were identified as two ways in which action could be taken at the European level. Similar statements were made in the 2001 Transport White Paper concerning the role of European intervention in urban transport policies. Regulatory initiatives to encourage the use of diversified energy in transport were also highlighted as possible measures, although the White Paper was wary of encroaching into the territory of lower levels of administration (and infringing the principle of subsidiarity), stating:

> Even if the subsidiarity principle dictates that responsibility for urban transport lies mainly with the national and local authorities, the ills besetting transport in urban areas and spoiling the quality of life cannot be ignored . . . The subsidiarity principle allows the European Union to take initiatives, including regulatory initiatives, to encourage the use of diversified energy in transport. On the other hand, the Union cannot use regulation as a means of imposing alternative solutions to the car in towns and cities.
>
> (CEC, 2001a: 85)

Recognizing the limitations of European policy on urban transport, the 2001 White Paper restricted itself to promoting good practice. So, despite a fairly lengthy section of text on the issue, the only specific measures on urban transport contained in the White Paper were the support (with a certain amount of Community funding) and the promotion of innovative and clean transport in pioneering towns and cities and the identification and dissemination of best practice in urban transport (primarily supported by the European CIVITAS initiative, which provides support for European cities in testing and implementing innovative and integrated strategies that address energy, transport and environmental objectives).

The issue of urban transport was considered in further detail in 2004 in a preparatory document preceding the Thematic Strategy on the Urban Environment. As well as outlining various actions to promote good practice in urban transport policy (similar to those in the 2001 White Paper), the document also signalled the intention to require sustainable urban transport plans in all European towns and cities above a certain size. According to the document: 'the Commission believes that a requirement [for sustainable urban transport plans in European towns and cities] could now be set at EU level' (CEC, 2004: 17). However, by the time the Thematic Strategy on the Urban Environment was published in 2006, the intention to introduce this new requirement for sustainable urban transport plans had become an intention to issue guidance on sustainable urban transport plans (with some best practice examples): European policy on urban transport issues had again been brought back down to identifying and disseminating examples of best practice. The idea of urban transport plans (termed urban mobility plans) reappeared in the 2011 Transport White Paper, although again only as a proposal for action: to 'examine the possibility of a European support framework for a progressive implementation of Urban Mobility Plans in European cities' (CEC, 2011a: 26), suggesting that the European-wide introduction of urban transport plans had not come any closer since they were first discussed in policy in 2004 (see above). Again, the issue of competence (and subsidiarity) appeared to stand in the way of action at the European level, since urban mobility plans are 'elaborated under local, regional and national institutional arrangements' (CEC, 2011b: 91). The Commission therefore only sees a role for itself in encouraging 'the necessary coordination by providing improved forums for discussion . . . [and] continuing to facilitate the exchange of best practices' (CEC, 2011b: 91).

The mid-term review of the Transport White Paper, also published in 2006, contained no new proposals in the area of urban transport policy (and made no reference to sustainable urban transport plans). Seemingly rather unsure of its position in this area of policy, it announced the intention to publish a Green Paper (in 2007) on urban transport in order 'to identify potential European added value to action at local level' (CEC, 2006: 14). What emerged in 2007 however was a document that primarily set out a series of questions and issues, rather than any new policy instruments or solutions: it provided very little clarity about the precise future role of the European Union in urban mobility policy, or the potential added value of European activities in this policy area (Stead, 2007). The Green Paper ended by promising an action plan to identify 'possible actions at the EU, national, regional, and local levels' and 'the appropriate instruments for each action' (CEC, 2007: 23) – promises that could easily be described by cynics as little more than policy procrastination. The fact that the action plan for urban mobility was delayed by a year (and did not appear until the second half of 2009) only served to prove the point for those looking to confirm the procrastination view. Critics also suggested that the delay was linked to concerns about Barroso's reappointment as European President and worries about causing disputes on the issue of subsidiarity in member states, especially in Germany (which was in the process of preparing for regional and general elections in June and September 2009 respectively) where the principle of subsidiarity has already sparked a major row between the German federal government and the Länder.

In short, various attempts have been made to develop European policies to address urban transport issues in some way. The majority of activity in this area has, however, been limited to the identification and exchange of good practice, since many other actions are deemed to infringe the principle of subsidiarity. Even the exchange of good practice at the European level is controversial, despite the commonly encountered assumption that good practices (or best practices) are equally applicable and effective in another setting. The large number and diversity of European member states, all with substantial differences in governance, administrative cultures and professional capacities (particularly since EU enlargement in 2004 and 2007), have raised doubts about the validity of the assumption that there are common solutions, especially between dissimilar situations (Stone, 1999; Stead et al., 2010; Stead, 2012).

5. CONCLUSIONS

Transport was one of main areas of common policy when the European Economic Community was first established. Since then, the development of European transport policy has witnessed two main phases. The first phase (up to the mid-1980s) is characterized by the slow, incremental, piecemeal development of policy (mainly standardization policy) where European member states had little appetite and shared few common aims for transport policy. The second phase (mid-1980s onwards) is characterized by a raft of liberalization policies paving the way for the European Single Market. New competences for European environmental policy focused attention to the environmental impacts of transport policy and gave rise to the concept of sustainable mobility. This period also saw the emergence of the TEN-T policy, which was seen as another way of supporting and strengthening the European Single Market (in addition to liberalization policies). The TEN-T policy does not sit easily with the concept of sustainable mobility. There are clear tensions between these two dimensions of European transport policy and these are likely to remain in the future. There are also clear tensions between attempts to address urban transport problems through European policy and the concept of subsidiarity. The consequence of this tension is that few specific policies have been developed in this area: action has been mainly restricted to information sharing and demonstration projects, whose impacts on policy change at the local level are limited. In the past decade, there has been little appetite for reducing the demand for transport demand in European policy because of the dominance of the Lisbon Agenda (the predecessor of the EU 2020 Strategy), which placed great emphasis on economic growth and job creation: managing transport demand was generally perceived as a potential brake on achieving these objectives.

European transport policy is made in the context of multilevel governance, where powers and responsibilities are shared between a variety of decision-making levels and actors. According to the principle of subsidiarity, the competence for many decisions on transport policy is the national or sub-national level rather than the European level. Consequently, the EU has a limited remit for developing transport policy. Most of the remit is related to creating conditions for a free and open market within the European Union, such as the harmonization of driving times for hauliers, vehicle safety standards and emission limits for vehicles. The principle of subsidiarity frequently occurs in European transport policy statements, and there is a clear interest but also a wariness about European intervention in certain areas of transport policy (e.g., urban transport).

Whilst the origins of European transport policy can be traced to the Treaty of Rome and even further back in time, it was a policy area in which relatively little activity occurred until the mid-1980s. There were high ambitions before this time for an overarching common transport policy but various initiatives were blocked along the way. Consequently, progress on developing a common transport policy was slow and mainly sectoral (i.e., modal) up this point: the main thrust of policies was standardization and harmonization. By the mid-1980s, a clear change in policy emphasis occurred, primarily as a consequence of efforts to achieve the internal market: the liberalization of transport became a key focus for European transport policy. New European competence for environmental policy marked a further shift in common transport policy, where the external costs of mobility (including social and environmental impacts) became more important, and the concept of sustainable mobility was born. The 1990s also saw the genesis of the Trans-European Network Policy, whose objective was to create the physical infrastructure (not just for transport but also for telecommunications, electricity and gas networks) to allow all regions in Europe, central and peripheral alike, to participate in the single market. More recently still, the Treaty of Lisbon gives more emphasis to combatting climate change as an EU policy objective and pushes energy issues more firmly into the EU policy domain.

Alongside various changes in policy objectives and instruments over time, there has been (and remains) an 'uncomfortable disjunction between stated and actual goals, or rather between a stated menu of balanced aims and a de facto hierarchy of policy priorities' (Ross, 1998: 222). While contemporary European transport policy statements often advocate the balancing of the three key objectives of growth, cohesion and sustainability, it is growth objectives that are almost always primary and the objectives of cohesion and sustainability secondary (Ross, 1998), especially since the launch of the Lisbon Strategy in 2000 (succeeded by the EU 2020 Strategy in 2010), which essentially prioritized economic growth and competitiveness above other policy objectives.[10] At the relaunch of the Lisbon Strategy in 2005 (a year after the largest single expansion of the European Union[11]), President Barroso famously declared his priority to tend to the economy as a 'sick child' (European Commission, 2005b), which resulted in European transport policies being reframed towards safeguarding the relatively high levels of employment in the transport sector and maintaining its contribution to economic growth, in preference to policies for tighter environmental protection and/or greater social cohesion. This leads to conflicts and tensions between transport policy and other areas of policymaking at the European level, such as European environment policy (see, for example, Richardson, 1997).

While European transport policymaking primarily takes place within a triangle of relationships between the European Commission, the Council of Ministers and the European Parliament, a number of other European institutions also shape policy, notably the European Council and the European Court of Justice (Stevens, 2004). Beyond these European institutions (and the governments of the member states) that shape European transport policy, a host of other actors representing all the different interests affected by transport policy also exert their influence on policy, especially business interests due to the importance of the transport sector to the European economy (a fact that is often mentioned in European transport strategy). The operation of these powerful interests generally takes place out of the public's view and occurs by means of informal lobbying and marketing, leading Ross (1998: 124) to conclude that, 'for all the current fears about a powerful Eurocracy in Brussels, much of the real driving force has been powerful industry interests operating from below'. The influence of these less visible actors in EU transport policymaking should not be underestimated or overlooked.

NOTES

1. Most accounts of the development of the Common Transport Policy refer to the mid-1980s as the turning point in European transport policy-making (see for example Aspinwall, 1999; Jensen, 2008; Lyons, 2000; Stevens, 2004). Giorgi and Schmidt (2002) distinguish three separate periods of policymaking thereafter

(the latter part of the 1980s, the 1990s and 2000 and beyond), broadly corresponding with the publication of the White Paper on Completing the Single Market in 1985 and the White Papers on transport policy in 1992 and 2001 (see below for more detail about these documents).

2. Stevens (2004) argues that the environmental principles contained in the Single European Act and the Treaty on the European Union can be traced back as far as the first Environmental Action Programme of 1973.

3. The 1992 communication on the impact of transport on the environment was sub-titled 'A Community strategy for sustainable mobility' while the 1992 White Paper on the future development of the Common Transport Policy had the sub-title 'A global approach to the construction of a Community framework for sustainable mobility'.

4. Note that Stevens' own assessment of the 2001 White Paper is much more positive about the nature of policy shift than my view. He describes the content of the White Paper as a 'bold, comprehensive and coherent programme, such as have not been seen since the 1960s' (Stevens, 2004: 65). One of his main concerns is 'how much of the programme advocated in the White Paper will attract sufficient support in the Council and the Parliament to be put into effect'.

5. Note that the 2009 Green Paper on future directions for European transport policy is distinct from the 2009 Green Paper on the Trans-European Transport Network (see below).

6. The ERT was particularly active in promoting its views on European infrastructure policy from the mid-1980s to the early 1990s. The ERT Working Group on infrastructure was chaired by Pehr Gyllenhammar (from Volvo) from 1984 to 1988 and by Umberto Agnelli (from Fiat) from 1988 to 1992. More recently, the ERT has been more active in promoting its views on various issues that have implications for transport policy such as competition policy, competitiveness, foreign economic relations, societal changes, energy and climate.

7. 10 new countries joined the EU in 2004 (Cyprus, Czech Republic, Estonia, Hungary, Latvia, Lithuania, Malta, Poland, Slovakia and Slovenia), followed by another two in 2007 (Bulgaria and Romania).

8. More than 60 per cent of the 'Connecting Europe Facility' budget (€31.7 billion) was earmarked for transport infrastructure projects (European Commission, 2011).

9. This is in contrast to the fact that, three years earlier, urban transport issues did not feature very strongly in the 1992 White Paper on future development of the common transport policy (CEC, 1992).

10. Freund and Martin (1993: 129) note that 'social needs (i.e. energy efficiency, reduced pollution, democratic transport) are decidedly inferior to private economic imperatives in the development of transport infrastructures'.

11. The accession of ten new member states in 2004 was the largest ever wave of expansion of the European Union in terms of the increase in physical area, number of states and population.

REFERENCES

Adams, J. (2005), Hypermobility: a challenge to governance, in C. Lyall and J. Tait (eds), *New Modes of Governance: Developing an Integrated Policy Approach to Science, Technology, Risk and the Environment*, Aldershot: Ashgate, pp. 123–38.

Aspinwall, M. (1999), Planes, trains and automobiles: transport governance in the European Union, in B. Kohler-Koch and R. Eising (eds), *The Transformation of Governance in the European Union*, London: Routledge, pp. 119–34.

Balanya, B., Doherty, A., Hoedeman, O., Ma'amit, A. and Wesselius, E. (2000), *Europe Inc. Regional and Global Restructuring and the Rise of Corporate Power*, London: Pluto Press.

Byron, H. and Arnold, L. (2008), *TEN-T and Natura 2000: The Way Forward: An Assessment of the Potential Impact of the TEN-T Priority Projects on Natura 2000*, Sandy: RSPB, www.birdlife.org/eu/EU_policy/Ten_T.

CEC (1992), *The Future Development of the Common Transport Policy: A Global Approach to the Construction of a Community Framework for Sustainable Mobility*, White Paper COM(92)494, Luxembourg: Office for Official Publications of the European Communities, www.europa.eu/legislation_summaries/environment/air_pollution/l28063_en.htm.

CEC (1995), *The Citizens' Network: Fulfilling the Potential of Public Passenger Transport in Europe*, Green Paper COM(95)601, Luxembourg: Office for Official Publications of the European Communities, www.europa.eu/documentation/official-docs/green-papers/index_en.htm.

CEC (2001a), *European Transport Policy for 2020: Time to Decide*, White Paper COM(2001)370, Luxembourg: Office for Official Publications of the European Communities, www.europa.eu/documentation/official-docs/white-papers/index_en.htm.

CEC (2001b), *A Sustainable Europe for a Better World: A European Union Strategy for Sustainable Development*, Communication of the European Commission COM(2001)264, Luxembourg: Office for Official Publications of the European Communities, www.ec.europa.eu/environment/eussd.

CEC (2004), *Towards a Thematic Strategy on the Urban Environment*, communication from the Commission to the Council, the European Parliament, the European Economic and Social Committee and the Committee of the Regions COM(2004)60, Luxembourg: Office for Official Publications of the European Communities, www.ec.europa.eu/environment/urban/towards_com.htm.

CEC (2006), *Keep Europe moving – Sustainable Mobility For Our Continent*, mid-term review of the European Commission's 2001 Transport White Paper COM(2006)314, Luxembourg: Office for Official Publications of the European Communities, www.ec.europa.eu/transport/strategies/2006_keep_europe_moving_en.htm.

CEC (2007), Towards a New Culture for Urban Mobility, Green Paper COM(2007)551, Luxembourg: Office for Official Publications of the European Communities, www.europa.eu/documentation/official-docs/green-papers/index_en.htm.

CEC (2009a), A Sustainable Future for Transport: Towards an Integrated, Technology-led and User Friendly System, Communication from the Commission. COM(2009)279, Luxembourg: Office for Official Publications of the European Communities, www.ec.europa.eu/transport/strategies/2009_future_of_transport_en.htm.

CEC (2009b), *TEN-T: A Policy Review. Towards a Better Integrated Trans-European Transport Network at the Service of the Common Transport Policy*, Green Paper COM(2009)44, Luxembourg: Office for Official Publications of the European Communities, www.ec.europa.eu/transport/infrastructure/consultations/2009_04_30_ten_t_green_paper_en.htm.

CEC (2011a), Roadmap to a Single European Transport Area – Towards a Competitive and Resource Efficient Transport System, White Paper COM(2011)144, Luxembourg: Office for Official Publications of the European Communities, www.ec.europa.eu/transport/strategies/2011_white_paper_en.htm.

CEC (2011b), Roadmap to a Single European Transport Area – Towards a Competitive and Resource Efficient Transport System, Commission staff working document accompanying the White Paper SEC(2011)391, Luxembourg: Office for Official Publications of the European Communities, www.ec.europa.eu/transport/strategies/2011_white_paper_en.htm.

EEA (2006), *Urban Sprawl in Europe: The Ignored Challenge*, EEA Report No. 10/2006, Copenhagen: European Environment Agency, www.eea.europa.eu/publications/eea_report_2006_10.

Endo, K. (1999), *The Presidency of the European Commission under Jacques Delors: The Politics of Shared Leadership*, Basingstoke: Macmillan.

Erdmenger, J. (1983), *The European Community transport policy: Towards a Common Transport Policy*, Aldershot: Gower.

European Commission (2005a), *Trans-European Transport Network: TEN-T Priority Axes and Projects 2005*, Brussels: Directorate General for Energy and Transport, European Commission, www.ec.europa.eu/transport/infrastructure/maps/30_priority_axes_en.htm.

European Commission (2005b), *Working Together for Growth and Jobs: A New Start for the Lisbon Strategy*, speech by José Manuel Barroso at the Conference of Presidents, European Parliament, SPEECH/05/67, 2 February 2005, Brussels: European Commission, www.europa.eu/rapid/pressReleasesAction.do?reference=SPEECH/05/67.

European Commission (2011), *Connecting Europe Facility: Commission Adopts Plan for €50 Billion Boost to European Networks*, European Commission Press Release IP/11/1200, 19 October, Brussels: European Commission, www.europa.eu/rapid/pressReleasesAction.do?reference=IP/11/1200.

European Council (2006), *Review of the EU Sustainable Development Strategy (EU SDS) – Renewed Strategy*, DOC 10917/06, Brussels: Council of the European Union, www.ec.europa.eu/environment/eussd.

Freund, P.E.S. and Martin, G.T. (1993), *The Ecology of the Automobile*, Montreal: Black Rose.

Gardner, J.N. (1991), *Effective Lobbying in the European Community*, Deventer/ Boston: Kluwer.

Geerlings, H. and Stead, D. (2003), The integration of land use planning, transport and environment in European policy and research, *Transport Policy*, **10**(3), 187–96.

Giorgi, L. and Schmidt, M. (2002), European transport policy – a historical and forward looking perspective, *German Policy Studies*, **2**(4), 1–19.

Gudmundsson, H. and Höjer, M. (1996), Sustainable development principles and their implications for transport, *Ecological Economics*, **19**(3), 269–82.

Güller, P. (1996), Urban travel in east and west: key problems and a framework for action, in ECMT (ed.), *Sustainable Transport in Central and Eastern European Cities*, Paris: ECMT, pp. 16–43.

Hamer, M. (1987), *Wheels Within Wheels: A Study of the Road Lobby*, London: Routledge.

Jensen, A. (2008), The institutionalisation of European transport policy from a mobility perspective, in T.U. Thomsen, L.D. Nielsen and H. Gudmundsson (eds), *Social Perspectives on Mobility*, Aldershot: Ashgate, pp. 127–54.

Jordan, A., Schout, A. and Unfried, M. (2008), The European Union, in A. Jordan and A. Lenschow (eds),

Innovation in Environmental Policy? Integrating the Environment for Sustainability, Cheltenham: Edward Elgar, pp. 159–79.

Kerwer, D. and Teutsch, M. (2001), Transport policy in the European Union, in A. Héritier, D. Kerwer, C. Knill, D. Lehmkuhl, T. Teutsch and A.C. Douillet (eds), *Differential Europe: The European Union Impact on National Policymaking*, Lanham, MD/Boulder, CO/New York/Oxford: Rowman & Littlefield, pp. 23–56.

Lyons, P.K. (2000), *Transport Policies of the European Union*, Elstead: EC Inform, www.pikle.co.uk/eci/TransCont.html.

Netherlands Environmental Assessment Agency and Stockholm Resilience Centre (2009), *Getting into the Right Lane for 2050*, PBL publication 500150001, Bilthoven/The Hague: PBL, www.pbl.nl/nl/publicaties/2009/Getting-into-the-Right-Lane-for-2050.html.

Peters, D. (2003), Cohesion, polycentricity, missing links and bottlenecks: conflicting spatial storylines for pan-European transport investments, *European Planning Studies*, **11**(3), 317–39.

Richardson, T. (1997), The Trans-European Transport Network: environmental policy integration in the European Union, *European Urban and Regional Studies*, **4**(4), 333–46.

Ross, J.F.L. (1998), *Linking Europe: Transport Policies and Politics in the European Union*, Westport, CT/London: Praeger.

Rothacher, A. (2005), *Uniting Europe: Journey between Gloom and Glory*, London: Imperial College Press.

Schmidt, M. and Giorgi, L. (2001), Successes, failures and prospects for the Common Transport Policy, *Innovation: The European Journal of Social Science Research*, **14**(4), 293–313.

Stead, D. (2001), The European Transport White Paper, *European Journal of Transport and Infrastructure Research*, **1**(4), 415–18.

Stead, D. (2007), The European Green Paper on Urban Mobility, *European Journal of Transport and Infrastructure Research*, **7**(4), 353–8.

Stead, D. (2012), Best practices and policy transfer in spatial planning, *Planning Practice and Research*, **27**(1), 103–16.

Stead, D., de Jong, M. and Reinholde, I. (2010), West-east policy transfer in Europe: the case of urban transport policy, in P. Healey and R. Upton (eds), *Crossing Borders: International Exchange and Planning Practices*, London: Routledge, pp. 173–90.

Stephenson, P. (2010), The role of working groups of commissioners in co-ordinating policy implementation: the case of trans-European networks (TENs), *Journal of Common Market Studies*, **48**(3), 709–36.

Stevens, H. (2004), *Transport Policy in the European Union*, Basingstoke: Palgrave Macmillan.

Stone, D. (1999), Learning lessons and transferring policy across time, space and disciplines, *Politics*, **19**(1), 51–9.

van der Heijden, H.A.B. (2006), Environmentalism and Trans-European Transport Networks, *International Journal of Urban and Regional Research*, **30**(1), 23–37.

Vivier, J. (2001), Mobility and accessibility – complementary or contradictory objectives, *Public Transport International*, **50**(5), 4–11.

44 Understanding process: can transport research come to terms with temporality?
Tim Schwanen

1. PRACTISING PROCESS

In many different ways the chapters in this book highlight the reciprocal relations of transport with material landscapes, economic systems, social structures and cultures. The contributions acknowledge the dynamic character of those relations, and some explicitly examine changes over time in them. Evidently, then, that thinking about transport and development must be framed in terms of temporality, or as irreversible processes with directionality in which past, present and future are implicated (Adam, 2008).

As a topic, temporality thus defined has always been at the heart of transport analysis. After all, the point of the predict-and-provide approach to transport planning that emerged after World War II across the Global North was to facilitate the expansion of car use and the infrastructures facilitating this (Owens, 1995). Additionally, the current commitment to sustainable and low-carbon mobility is all about academics contributing to systemic change in existing transport systems in light of concerns over climate change, energy security and social injustice (Givoni and Banister, 2013). Examples of more specific events in the history of transport analysis that attest to the importance of temporality include the emergence of the first studies of induced demand (Downs, 1962; Goodwin, 1996), individuals' travel habits (Goodwin, 1977; Banister, 1978) and, more recently, adaptation to climate change (Changdon, 1996; Jonkeren, 2009). There has, however, been little critical reflection on how process itself has been thought and practised in the transport research community.

It is difficult to make general claims about how process is practised across the preceding chapters and the transport literature more generally. Two key procedures can nonetheless be identified. The first of these is to draw inferences from information on one or several points in time. It is not uncommon for transport researchers to draw conclusions about processes from cross-sectional data. Think, for instance, of studies that examine the relation between population density and car use in a sample of neighbourhoods or cities at a single point in time and, on the basis of their findings, conclude that densification will reduce car use. Such a claim may be attractive to policymakers but also rests on a problematic assumption, namely that the observed relation for a group of spatial units at a given moment is equal to the trajectory that a single unit will follow through time. If this were true, we would live in an a-temporal world of closed systems, with very simple cause-and-effect relationships and no room for the unexpected and novelty.

Analysis becomes more robust when inferences about processes are drawn from data at two or more moments in time in conjunction with practices of interpolation. Panel studies of travel behaviour provide an obvious example of this technique. They have been undertaken at least since the 1980s (Kitamura, 1990) and this collection also includes examples. Another example is the use of repeated cross-sectional data. Yet, drawing inferences from data at multiple points in time is not without problems either. The concern is that time is reduced to 'a series of salami slices' or disconnected 'nows' (Crang, 2005: 208); it becomes impossible to understand how in a given present the past and future are enfolded. As a result, it becomes unclear how past and future condition and shape the present. These problems are exacerbated by the tendency to assume more or less smooth transitions between data points: if the value of the phenomenon of interest at t_1 is higher (lower) than at t_0, researchers are inclined to interpret the change as one of more or less gradual increase (decrease), and similar values at both points in time are taken to indicate stability. Nonetheless, anything could have happened and all sorts of irregularities in the patterns under study may have occurred during the gaps between the data points. In fact, without recourse to empirical information, the tendency to smoothen amounts to 'doing' philosophy. It is an instance of ontological politics (Mol, 1999) – the active shaping of reality in some ways and not others to facilitate particular motives (including the desire to keep analysis tractable).

The second key procedure through which transport researchers deal with process in methods for making the future actionable in the present (e.g., simulation modelling, scenario analysis) is to specify a set of rules that are assumed to be stable across space and time and use these either to extrapolate from past and current states and developments into the future, or – as in backcasting (Dreborg, 1996; Hickman and Banister, 2007) – to work backwards from imagined futures to the present. The term 'rules' is used in a broad sense here; it can refer to the relations between phenomena or processes captured in mathematical formulas, algorithms or heuristics. What matters here is that the existence of fairly concrete, stable rules is taken as given. More than this, their existence is necessary: together with the assumption that elements and categories like individuals, trip or transport mode maintain their identity and persist through time, the stability of rules is required for change to occur. On one level, these assumptions of stability are entirely with (Western) common sense, but on another they mean that change is a mere derivative: process is only possible by virtue of the anterior forms of permanence. This way of thinking and practicing process has deep roots in Western philosophy: it is a variant of the separation of eternity from time, permanence from flux, stability from change – as well as the privileging of the first over the second term in each pair – that can be found in the philosophies of Plato, Aristotle and Descartes and many others (PR: 209).

Considering the knowledge they have helped to generate about the dynamics that link transport to material landscapes, economic systems, social structures and cultures, it is beyond doubt that the above two key procedures for practising process are helpful and productive. Yet, as manifestations of particular ontological politics, they might also have less benign consequences. By enacting process and temporality in one particular manner they have also side-lined alternatives, thus limiting our knowledge of the interactions between transport and development. In the remainder of this chapter, the outlined key procedures are suspended and the philosophy of Alfred North Whitehead is drawn upon to think about process and temporality in the transport context in other ways. The specific motivations for the selection of Whitehead are explained below. For now it suffices to say that Whitehead was a 'philosopher of becoming' (Connolly, 2011) who needs to be placed in a lineage of thinkers that also encompasses Henri Bergson, William James and John Dewey before World War II; Gilles Deleuze between 1950 and 1990; and Bruno

Latour, Isabelle Stengers, Donna Haraway, Brian Massumi and William Connolly more recently. For all their differences these thinkers are united in rethinking temporality and process.

Below some of Whitehead's ideas will be outlined, followed by an exploration of how they can be used to think differently about process using the relations between urban structure and travel as a case study.

2.   WHY WHITEHEAD?

Like all intellectual labour, Whitehead's philosophy cannot be understood without due consideration of the space-time context in which it emerged. Whitehead was an English mathematician-turned-philosopher whose most important philosophical works were published in the 1920s and 1930s – a time when philosophers and scientists were grappling with the consequences of the Darwinian, Einsteinian and quantum revolutions that had fundamentally altered the way the world was understood. For Whitehead the advances in physics implied that the whole world had to be understood in terms of energy and activity:

> [I]n the modern concept the group of agitations which we term matter is fused into its environment. There is no possibility of a detached, self-contained local existence . . . the environment with its peculiarities seeps into the group-agitation which we term matter, and group-agitations extend their character to the environment.
>
> (MT: 138)

> There are no essentially self-contained activities within limited regions. These passive geometrical relationships between substrata passively occupying regions have passed out of the picture. Nature is a theatre for the interrelations of activities. *All things change, the activities and their interrelations.*
>
> (MT: 140, emphasis added)

This meant, among other things, that the fallacy of 'simple location' (AI: 157) had to be avoided: a 'thing' – a car, a person, the competency required for cycling, a pro-environmental attitude, and so forth – cannot be assigned to a specifiable point in space and time.

Yet Whitehead also felt that 'fragments of older doctrines' prevented philosophers and scholars from grasping activity, interrelations and process. Those older doctrines consisted of both the common-sense Newtonian perspective on space and time as static containers in which events unfold in a mechanistic and Newtonian fashion, and the philosophical heritage of Descartes and Hume. These thinkers had etched dualism – the distinction of mind and body, thought and thing, subject and object, public and private, etc. – and the supremacy of conscious sense-perception for knowledge acquisition onto Western thinking, with profound consequences: on Whitehead's view they made it impossible to understand the processes by which body, soul and the world are interconnected and the whole is in the part and vice versa.

Dualistic thinking, the privileging of conscious perception through sight and the fallacy of simple location share one common characteristic. They are all versions of the *fallacy of misplaced concreteness* (SMW: 58) – i.e., the substitution of abstractions for the concrete happenings of the world such that those happenings become more rather than less difficult to understand. Whitehead was not against abstraction as such. In fact, he was adamant that thought is impossible without abstraction. The advantage of working with a restricted number of abstractions is that:

> You can confine your thoughts to clear-cut definite things, with clear-cut definite relations. Accordingly, if you have a logical head, you can deduce a variety of conclusions respecting the relationships between these abstract entities. Furthermore, if the abstractions are *well-founded*, that is to say, if they do not abstract from everything that is important in experience, the scientific thought that confines itself to these abstractions will arrive at a variety of important truths.
>
> (SMW: 59, emphasis added)

Problems emerge, however, if abstractions are less well-founded and things that (potentially) matter to the phenomena under study are omitted from the abstraction. It is then 'of the utmost importance to be vigilant in critically revising your *modes* of abstraction' (SMW: 59, emphasis in original). His philosophy could be understood as an ambitious yet fallible attempt to correct – or at least provide alternatives for – the misplaced concretenesses that had become ingrained into thought in the 1920s and 1930s.

The observation that Whitehead's philosophy is firmly situated in the philosophical and scientific problems of the early twentieth century may raise concerns about using his ideas some 80 years later – at a time when insights from evolutionary and complexity theories have become deeply ingrained into popular perception, and the limits of human vision as a source of knowledge acquisition are widely appreciated. Irrespective of the revaluation of his thought in philosophy and social theory in this millennium (Latour, 2005; Halewood, 2008; Haraway, 2003; Shaviro, 2009; Stengers, [2002] 2011), there are four sets of reasons why his philosophy is surprisingly germane to contemporary transport research. One is that the fallacies of simple location and misplaced concreteness continue to haunt contemporary research into transport and related systems; this will be elaborated below with regard to the built environment and travel behaviour interface.

Second, Whitehead offers an interesting perspective on questions of indeterminacy and uncertainty with regard to how transport systems evolve over time. In a way his philosophy anticipated contemporary concerns over 'deep uncertainties' (Walker et al., 2010), and particularly those situations in which analysts cannot enumerate which futures are more likely to unfold because they do not fully understand – or cannot agree on – the causal mechanisms and functional relationships between the phenomena or processes being studied. Transport research and planning are historically ill-equipped to deal with such uncertainties but the latter pervade attempts to bring about systemic sustainability transitions in contemporary transport systems. Rather than ignore deep uncertainties, transport researchers and planners could also draw on the humanities and social sciences to strengthen styles of adaptive policymaking (Marchau et al., 2010) that appreciate those uncertainties.

A third reason for paying attention to Whitehead's philosophy now is its inclusiveness: it allows temporality, and reality more generally, to be enacted in more diverse ways than contemporary transport studies tend to do. As elaborated below, this is because Whitehead sought to keep permanence and flux, stability and change mutually implicated rather than to privilege one over the other. Finally, Whitehead was a positive philosopher: he was not simply in the business of critique or deconstruction but offered his audiences numerous new concepts and modes of thought, inviting them to embark on their own adventures of ideas. In response to what he understood as fallacies in thought, Whitehead developed his own speculative, coherent and fallible scheme about how the world evolves. Detailed discussions are available in Rose (2002) and Stengers ([2002] 2011) but his scheme highlights creativity, local self-organisation and indeterminacy. At its heart lies the claim that everything is an *event*; the world consists of events and nothing more.

3.   PROCESS ACCORDING TO WHITEHEAD

Whitehead famously illustrated the centrality of the event with reference to Cleopatra's Needle on London's Victoria Embankment. This appears to be a stable, static object.

> [B]ut a physicist who looks on that part of the life of nature as a dance of electrons, will tell you that it has lost some molecules and gains others, and even the plain man can see that it gets dirtier and is occasionally washed.
>
> (CN: 136)

At every moment it is actively happening as a fresh creation so that thing and event are one and the same. In the technical language of *Process and Reality* – Whitehead's magnum opus – the Needle is a society of *actual occasions*.[1] A society is a set of actual occasions, held together by a characteristic that is common to all of them and that they inherited from the past or acquired by a common process (PR: 34). We as human beings are all societies of actual occasions but so are plants, rocks, electrons, cars, neighbourhoods, as well as knowledge of a public transport timetable or the habit to cycle to work. The concept of society is scale independent and does not respect any distinction between the human and non-human, although there are different grades of complexity and creativity – with societies involving humans at the apex. The term event is related to society; it denotes a set of actual occasions that are interrelated in physical space or time and has a single actual occasion as its limiting type (PR: 73).

Evidently, then, the actual occasion is a foundational concept in Whitehead's scheme. It is the process whereby an entity becomes. It unites the two senses of process he derives from John Locke: *concrescence* and *transmission* (PR: 210). The former is the process whereby multiple elements become one through a range of operations. Concrescence consists of three phases: reception, prehension and satisfaction. The 'input' to a given actual occasion is formed by the whole universe of past actual occasions, concurrent actual occasions and eternal objects (see below). These are received and subsequently 'prehended'. At this stage selections are made in the received elements. There are 'negative prehensions' or elements being excluded, while other elements are included into the concrescent actual occasion. Such inclusions are known as 'positive prehensions' or feelings.[2] The purpose of the phase of prehension is to create a unity from the received multiplicity; exactly how this is done is unique to each actual occasion. When true unity has been created, the stage of satisfaction has been reached and the actual occasion perishes immediately: 'Once an occasion happens, it is already over, already dead' (Shaviro, 2009: 19). It has lost its vitality and is an objective datum to be used in subsequent processes of concrescence. In this way the forces of creativity and self-organisation are perpetually passed on and order and identities are transmitted across actual occasions. What for conscious sense-perception by human beings appears stable over time – Cleopatra's Needle, the persistent car use of a 'complacent car addict' (Anable, 2005), decision rules like utility maximisation or elimination-by-aspects (Tversky, 1972) or the inverse correlation between population density and energy consumption in transport – is in Whitehead's cosmos the result of transmission with actual occasion t inheriting something from actual occasions $t_{-1}, t_{-2}, \ldots, t_{-n}$.

However, endurance and continuity are possible up to a degree only: with each perishing and concrescence a new unity has been created as a result of positive and negative prehensions. A person never encounters the same Needle twice as both the obelisk and she herself will have changed. After all, a person is 'the succession of [actual occasions], extending from birth to the present moment' (MT: 163) and her experience at a specific moment is a concrescence of her antecedent occasions as well as her physical body and the world. In light of this togetherness, Whitehead argued for a particular understanding of causality. Rather than the – at least among mainstream transport researchers' – common-sense idea derived from Hume ([1739] 1985) that, under certain conditions, an antecedent x can be said to cause a posterior y if x and y co-vary with sufficient regularity, he posited a doctrine of mutual immanence: 'each [actual] occasion presupposes the antecedent world as active in its own nature' as this makes possible the transference of relative continuity and the transmission of social order from occasion to occasion.

Whitehead's scheme also stands out in its treatment of potentiality, and this is where *eternal objects* become relevant. The eternal object is a difficult concept; it is best defined as 'pure potential' (PR: 23). Eternal objects exist but cannot be grasped or known directly. They are therefore real but not actual and can only be known indirectly through the ways they are integrated – Whitehead uses the term 'ingressed' – into actual occasions. Consider 'redness':

> You cannot know what is red by merely thinking of redness. You can only find red things by adventuring amid physical experiences in *this* actual world.
>
> (PR: 256, emphasis in original)

The experience of colour hints at the existence of an eternal object, and the same is true when numbers, shapes, moral qualities, tactile sensations like roughness, physical fundamentals like gravity, or emotions like anger and love are sensed (Shaviro, 2009). Anything, Whitehead writes, 'whose conceptual recognition does not involve a necessary reference to any definitive actual entities of the temporal world' (PR: 44) is an eternal object. Eternal objects are akin to universals in other philosophical schemes (e.g., Plato's Forms) but there is an important difference: they are by nature passive, neutral and powerless. They do not directly shape the actual world, only through ingression in actual occasions.

Eternal objects perform multiple functions in Whitehead's scheme but two will be highlighted here. The first of these is to put novelty, indeterminacy and uncertainty centre-stage. At some point in the concrescence of an actual occasion all eternal objects ingress it. Because they embody potentiality the point of this ingression is to imply 'alternatives, contingencies, situations that could have been otherwise' (Shaviro, 2009: 41). In subsequent stages of a concrescence, the mechanisms of positive and negative prehension decide if and how transmission will be affected and change relative to previous actual occasions will occur. Hence, a concrescence is an exhaustion of potentiality and uncertainty, a movement from indeterminacy to complete determination at the time of satisfaction.

Second, eternal objects help to avoid the perils of dualism. Whitehead's insistence on the passivity of eternal objects creates a balance between the universal and the specific, the general and the particular. It is not a given that the former term in each pair prevails – as in nomothetic conceptions of science – but neither is the latter term to be celebrated to the detriment of the former. The challenge is to keep them mutually implicated, and this also holds for the dualisms at the heart of temporality – i.e., stability and change, and permanence and flux.[3] Unlike Plato, Aristotle, Descartes and many others, Whitehead wanted to avoid separating these pairs and privileging one term over the other:

> [P]ermanence can be snatched only out of flux; and the passing moment can find its adequate intensity only by its submission to permanence. Those who disjoin the two elements can find no interpretation of patent facts.
>
> (PR: 338)

This makes Whitehead's scheme neutral and inclusive: it does not require us to favour stability over change or vice versa. It thus enables a different ontological politics and permits more diverse ways of bringing reality into being than other philosophical frameworks, including those taken for granted in transport research.

4.   THINKING WITH WHITEHEAD

This is not to say that 'thinking with Whitehead' (Stengers, [2002] 2011) is easy or straightforward. There is a gulf that separates his philosophy from academic research, not least because the former is much speculative. More than offering a plausible account of how the world is, its function is to provide the philosophical means to explore process and the full potentiality of what societies of actual occasions might become. Moreover, many of Whitehead's concepts and claims diverge radically from the ideas that underlie the techniques, methods and procedures routinely used in transport research. What, for instance, is to be made of regression analysis when the fallacy of simple location must be avoided and causality is understood in terms of mutual immanence? Nonetheless, in this section the literature on the links between urban structure and travel behaviour is read through a Whiteheadian lens to explore what new modes of thought this can generate.

Modes of Abstraction

The first point to make is that there will always be some effect of urban structure on how people travel; claims or hypotheses to the contrary are incomprehensible to those who think with Whitehead. After all, the environment seeps into a person's behaviour and corporeal body, and an act is always a series of concrescences in each of which the many – including the actual occasions out of which the built environment emerges – become one. The question, then, is how the actual occasions from which the built environment emerges become part of travel events, and how the former are prehended.

A transport researcher's response might well refer to the 7Ds articulated by Ewing and

Cervero (2010) – i.e., density, diversity and design plus destination accessibility, destination to transit, demand management and demographics. In Whitehead's scheme these Ds would all classify as eternal objects, meaning they cannot be direct causes of (changes in) travel behaviour. This is because, for Whitehead, everything in the actual world is referable to actual occasions (PR: 244) and eternal objects are always passive and cannot explain anything of their own; everything depends on how they ingress in actual occasions. In fact, the idea of (changes in) density levels as a result of residential moves or urban planning interventions causing (changes in) travel patterns is an instance of the fallacy of misplaced concreteness.

Moreover, there are good reasons to believe that density, diversity and so forth are inadequate abstractions for understanding changes in travel behaviour, even if a longitudinal study design is used. This is primarily because (numerical) indicators of density stifle the concrete happenings, activity and energy of which neighbourhoods or urban areas consist. They may thus underestimate the level of heterogeneity and fluctuation over time, thereby favouring permanence over flux. The point about stifling is obvious when night-time populations of spatial units are derived from censuses or administrative registers to construct density measures that are subsequently linked to indicators of the travel behaviour of residents or visitors, most of which occurs between 6:00am and 10:00pm. This disregard for diurnal cycles has been criticised before in slightly different contexts (Goodchild and Janelle, 1984; Kwan, 2012) but the problem extends to more granular scales of time: the character of a neighbourhood or city changes from moment to moment. Another reason why indicators of density and other Ds are flawed is that what they measure – population (or segments thereof), (types of) buildings, (types of) employment, (types of) land uses, (types of) roads, etc. – is too undifferentiated. Such measures cannot articulate the singularity of spatial units like neighbourhoods or buffer zones around individuals over a period of time, no matter how brief the latter is.

In other words, new modes of abstraction need to be developed if (dynamics in) the relations between urban structure and travel behaviour are to be understood. Previous work has provided useful suggestions in this regard: Kwan (2012) advocates the use of much more detailed and dynamic representations of the contexts people move through over the course of out-of-home journeys, and Andrews et al. (2012) argue with regard to walking and cycling that analysts should consider the precise character of the movement activities (e.g., whether people walk to reach a destination as efficiently as possible, walk a dog, jog, play, use mobility aids, etc.) that people undertake, their perceptive and cognitive concerns, and how all of this interacts with the physical, socio-cultural and socio-political features of the places they traverse. Further work is nonetheless required and would benefit from analysing concrescences and transmissions in a range of settings and circumstances. How are inherited and other elements prehended? What is passed on and how, if at all, is it transformed?

Concrescence and Prehension

Large parts of *Process and Reality* are devoted to elaborations of how concrescence unfolds, and it is beyond this chapter to explore the details. Suffice it to say that the middle stage of prehension is the critical part, and that this phase is more or less complex depending on the sort of society to which an actual occasion belongs. It is often much more elaborate in 'human' societies than in, say, a rock. Nevertheless, in all cases prehension involves three common factors (PR: 23): the actual occasion of which the prehension is an element ('subject'); the datum that is prehended ('object'); and the subjective form ('feeling'), which is how the subject prehends the datum.

Both Whitehead himself and more recent commentators (e.g. Shaviro, 2009) have likened the subjective form to an affective tone. It emerges as part of a concrescence rather than preceding the latter. The subjective form determines the complexity of the prehension, and comes in many species, including emotions, valuation, purposes, aversions and consciousness (PR: 23). For Whitehead, cognition and consciousness are special and unusual cases of feeling that arise only in a late, derivative phase of prehension. This implies, contra conventional theories of travel behaviour, that:

> [t]hose elements of our experience which stand out clearly and distinctly in our consciousness are not its basic facts; they are derivative modifications which arise in the process.
>
> (PR: 162)

This claim concurs not only 'with the plain facts of experience [that] consciousness flickers' (PR: 267) but also with the 'rule of thumb among cognitive scientists that unconscious thought is 95 per cent of all thought – and that may be a serious underestimate' (Norretranders, 1998: 127, in Thrift, 2007). Whitehead reverses the widely assumed order of cognition and affect in humans (PR: 175; Shaviro, 2009): rather than cognition steering perception – one form of prehension among many – to generate emotions, prehension is first of all an affectation of one's body by the datum. This affectation – the coming into being of Whitehead's subjective form – may trigger emotions, intuitive action and on rare occasions deliberative thought. This is why he writes that:

> The brain is continuous with the body, and the body is continuous with the rest of the natural world. Human experience is an act of self-origination including the whole of nature, limited to the perspective of a focal region within the body, but not necessarily pre-existing in any fixed coordination with a definitive part of the brain.
>
> (AI: 225)

According to *Process and Reality*, the datum ('object') that is prehended consists, first, of the actual world and, second, of the realm of eternal objects. In the case of a person taking a trip, the former would imply the infrastructures, buildings and other materialities that make up the physical environment; its socio-cultural and socio-political features; his/her bodily capacities, skills and cognitive knowledge; the behaviours of other travellers; and many other perished and objectified actual occasions. The list of eternal objects eligible for ingression is equally extensive and would include efficiency, least effort, safety, comfort, inconvenience, social status, moral environmental awareness, punctuality, pleasure, pain, anger and so forth. Prehension of the actual world and eternal objects means that what used to be public ('object') becomes private ('subject'). It could be said that the datum 'flows into' and affects the actual occasions making up the traveller's body/mind. In this the datum gets appropriated, excluded, transformed and synthesised so that ultimately a new subject, behaviour (e.g., undertaking a trip to a destination, use of a particular transport mode, staying where one is, etc.) and actual world emerge as output and datum for subsequent actual occasions.

This process – and therefore the role of urban structure[4] – is unique at every occasion, for two reasons. One is that the inputs – the actual world, including urban structure, and the subject – are never the same. The other is that, due to the difference in inputs, a novel subjective form comes into being with each actual occasion, allowing the eternal objects to be ingressed, transformed and synthesised in new ways as well. As a result, potentials like density, compactness, frustration, joy and so forth – all of which are passive and powerless as eternal objects – can be included and, in ingressed form, affect travel behaviour in differ ways. More generally, in Whitehead's cosmos the effects of urban structure at t_0 operate in two ways, via actual occasions at t_{-1} and via the ingression of eternal objects at t_0. Because the subjective form is specific to t_n, an earlier quote from Whitehead can be amended into the phrase 'all things *can* change, the activities and their interrelations'.

Three sets of the implications follow from this for transport research. One concerns the use of the key procedures for dealing with process outlined at the beginning of this chapter and will be discussed in the final section. The second is that future research on the links between urban structure and transport would benefit from focusing on the human body – a society that has remained woefully overlooked in transport research. Focusing on bodies is productive because of their centrality to prehension. The human body is the locus where affectation and feelings occur and where energy and activity are transmitted and transformed through biochemical and neurological processes. At the same time, decades of social science demonstrate that human bodies cannot be reduced to physical processes. They are also socially constructed and therefore gendered, racialised, sexualised, aged and otherwise differentiated (Butler, 1993; Laws, 1995). Such social construction is likely to shape how a human body can be affected (Connolly, 2011), and so what subjective forms may appear in the actual occasions of which it consists. This means that analysing the nexus of transport and (built) environment purely through continuous monitoring of neuro-chemical fluctuations in human bodies, such as stress or hormone levels and brain activity, would constitute another fallacy of misplaced concreteness.

A mode of abstraction that is less likely to omit potentially important aspects of embodiment is offered by recent developments of Deleuze's (1988) understanding of bodies in terms of what they can do.[5] For Deleuze a body can only be defined as 'composed of an infinite number of particles' held together by 'relations of motion and rest, of speeds and slownesses between particles' and the 'capacity for affecting and being affected'.[6] This way of thinking foregrounds how and what a body can do and become when it uses transport systems where it encounters land-use configurations, other people, discourses about gender, age and so forth. One benefit of thinking about bodies in terms of capacities to affect and be affected is that it allows researchers to focus on thresholds in prehension. Multiple thresholds can be identified with regard to actual occasions from which travel behaviour emerges, but perhaps the most significant threshold pertains to the moment that bodily affectations become so intense that they impel people to think about changing their travel behaviour. This, after all, is the moment when intervention through deliberative thought in the trajectory of actual occasions becomes a possibility.

One such intervention – and a rather drastic form in light of the centrality of a person's home location to his/her everyday life and that of one's household members – is residential self-selection. This is conventionally understood as choosing a residential location that allows people to travel in the way they like, and in empirical research often boils down to the question whether any statistically significant effect of (changes in) built environment indicators on (changes in) travel behaviour remains when (changes in) attitudes have been taken into account. For those who think with Whitehead this is to commit the fallacy of misplaced concreteness once more. Attitudes are events – series of actual occasions in each of which eternal objects have ingressed and subjective forms have emerged from bodily affections. They may endure in almost identical form over time but fluctuation is quite likely. For Whitehead, the use of attitudes to explain where people live and how they travel would put the cart before the horse. Rather than such cognitive constructs as attitudes shaping affects, the more direct cause of behaviour is the bodily affectation. From the latter the subjective form emerges that transforms the datum, including previously constructed attitudes, into a new set of outputs. The latter encompass, among others, behaviour, attitudes and urban structure.

The third implication is implicit in the previous and pertains to Whitehead's emphasis on the continuity of body, mind and world. This continuity renders problematic travel behaviour studies' conventional focus on the individual as a self-contained unit and sovereign initiator of behaviour. This is yet another situation in which the fallacy of misplaced concreteness lurks. With the conventional take on a person as the body-and-mind-contained-within-the-skin also comes the risk of sideling the ways in which s/he is intimately entwined with other humans and broader society. Such abstracting from the always-already socialised nature of human behaviour may result in inflated correlations between urban structure and travel behaviour indicators in quantitative research, and hence exaggerated expectations among researchers and policymakers about behavioural changes brought about by densification, increased accessibility and so forth. To reduce the risk of inflated correlations and expectation, researchers should give due consideration to the continuity of body, mind and world. This can also be done through a range of other analytical approaches apart from the Whitehead framework outlined here; examples include practice theory (Shove, 2003; Watson, 2012) and recent work on mobility habits (Bissell, 2010, 2013; Schwanen et al. 2012b).

5.   PRACTISING PROCESS (REPRISE)

Thinking with Whitehead about the land use–travel behaviour nexus means losing the built environment and attitudes as direct causes of behaviour but also gaining much in return. Three understandings stand out in this regard: the importance of modes of abstraction; the centrality of bodies and their affectations, which can only be understood if the continuity of body, mind and world is appreciated; and the idea that in transmission all things can and often do change, the activities and their interrelations. This last understanding leads us back to the second key procedure for dealing with process that I introduced at the beginning of this chapter. One implication of Whitehead's philosophy is that the assumption of stable concrete rules through which transport futures can be made actionable in the present is tricky. The centrality of the subjective form to prehension indicates, first, that rules matter and, second, that if-then rules, decision rules and other operations through which events are interrelated are not somehow 'outside' process as pre-existing phenomena; they emerge along the way. Making a priori assumptions about the nature of rules is an entirely acceptable abstraction in situations where hereditary transmission will produce minimal change in rules. There can, however, be no hard guarantee that such assumptions are appropriate as there always is the potential of becoming otherwise: one never knows in advance how concrescence will develop. Indeterminacy and deep uncertainty (Walker et al., 2010) are central to the analysis of temporality and should be appreciated rather than ignored.

The gulf separating Whitehead's philosophy from transport research practice must be appreciated. Still, it can be argued that transport researchers need to be more critical and reflexive regarding rules. The use in some advanced simulation models of rules to select rules depending on the situation (Arentze et al., 2001) is an important first step that allows for flexibility and recognises uncertainty in how processes unfold. It nonetheless still assumes that the identity of the rules can be known a priori. A new research programme is therefore needed. Rather than determining what the rules are, this programme should explore their potentiality – i.e., what they can *become* through concrescence and transmission. Grasping all potentialities won't be possible but careful ethnographic observation in real time of how rules emerge as situations unfold will allow researchers to develop at least a sense of those potentialities. Following Adey and Anderson's (2011) studies of how decisions unfold during exercises in UK Civil Contingencies, researchers could simulate real-life situations whereby people – travellers, planners, infrastructure operators, etc. – have to respond to unfolding events in which information is limited, contradictory and changing over time. Alternatives could be to redevelop the Household Activity-Travel Simulator (HATS) (Jones, 1979) and driving simulators, or the deployment of virtual reality experiments. The space of possibility with regard to the character of rules derived from the proposed research programme could then be fed into modelling research and different sorts of scenario analysis.

Whitehead's philosophy also deepens understanding of the limitations of drawing inferences from data at two points in time – the first procedure of dealing with process outlined at the beginning of this chapter. Drawing on Whitehead means that time is not reduced to a series of salami slices, for two reasons: past, present and future are always tightly interwoven in a concrescence; and datum, prehension and satisfaction cannot be accorded a simple location in chronological time. This, in combination with the imbrication of actual occasions in each other, makes transmission both feasible and understandable. Using data on transport at multiple points in time interrupts the interweaving of past, present and future and creates gaps where chains of transmission can no longer be traced. Given that both activities and their interrelations can and often do change, anything can indeed have happened. If researchers want to avoid the conventional ontological politics regarding those gaps, they need to trade panel and repeated cross-sectional research designs for approaches that preserve a greater part of hereditary transmission. Multi-week time-space diaries or GPS tracking are potentially suitable for this but raise a host of other problems: respondent burden, privacy issues and cost become intractable if these methods are deployed continuously on the scale of months or years. An alternative way of interrogating the potentialities for hereditary transmission on longer time scales would be to re-develop narrative analysis in which the researcher and participants retrospectively co-construct life histories and time-lines (Davies, 1996; Kwan and Ding, 2008).

All research practices and methods are partial. They all select and leave out something:

'[y]ou cannot think without abstractions' (SMW: 59). In a way, then, it is unfair to criticise research by drawing on a speculative philosophical scheme. Mere criticism is nonetheless not the point of this chapter. Much as Whitehead's philosophy is 'the critic of abstractions' (SMW: 59) inviting readers to embark on their own adventure of ideas, it hopes to spark into being new ways of understanding and practicing temporality in transport research by raising awareness about what is taken for granted and directing attention towards potentiality. The obstacles ahead are not insignificant but the prospect of stability and change and permanence and flux becoming mutually implicated in transport research is well worth the risk.

LIST OF ABBREVIATIONS

AI   *Adventures of Ideas* (Whitehead [1933] 1967)
CN   *The Concept of Nature* (Whitehead [1920] 2007)
MT   *Modes of Thought* (Whitehead [1938] 1968)
PR   *Process and Reality* (Whitehead [1929] 1978)
SMW   *Science and the Modern World* (Whitehead [1925] 1967)

NOTES

1. Whitehead's terms always have different meanings than those with which readers are familiar. Their purpose is to induce new thinking by turning 'what is socially given . . . into a potential for many diverging adventures' (Stengers, 2005: 54).
2. The implication is that Whitehead distributes affect throughout the world; it is no longer the preserve of humans or living organisms. This idea has more recently been picked up and developed by Deleuze (1988) and thinkers influenced by him (Massumi, 2002; Thrift, 2007).
3. In many ways these pairs are synonyms but in this chapter only the change/stability pair is used in situations where a reference point is implied and reference is made to chronological or extensive time. The permanence/flux pair is here used in a more general sense; it also pertains to Bergson's (1911) duration – intensive time in which no states can be identified.
4. Here this term is not limited to physical form, land use or even urban development. It rather refers to the always-already entangled physical-social-cultural-political world.
5. See, for instance, Abrahamsson and Simpson (2011), Colls (2011) and Schwanen et al. (2012a).
6. This understanding suggests that the human or animal body is only one of many varieties of bodies: a molecule, a tool, a population, a sentence and a language are other manifestations. Part of the appeal of Deleuze's definition is that it enables analysts to circumvent the fallacy of simple location.

REFERENCES

Abrahamsson, S. and Simpson, P. (2011), The limits of the body: boundaries, capacities, thresholds, *Social & Cultural Geography*, **12**, 331–8.
Adam, B. (2008), Of timespaces, futurescapes and timeprints, www.cardiff.ac.uk/socsi/futures/conf_ba_lueneberg170608.pdf.
Adey, P. and Anderson, B. (2011), Event and anticipation: UK Civil Contingencies and the space-times of decision, *Environment and Planning A*, **43**, 2878–99.
Anable, J. (2005), 'Complacent car addicts' or 'aspiring environmentalists'? Identifying travel behaviour segments using attitude theory, *Transport Policy*, **12**, 65–78.
Andrews, G.J., Hall, E., Evans, B. and Colls, R. (2012), Moving beyond walkability: on the potential of health geography, *Social Science and Medicine*, **75**, 1925–32.

Arentze, T., Hofman, F. and Timmermans, H. (2001), Deriving rules from activity diary data: a learning algorithm and results of computer experiments, *Journal of Geographical Systems*, **3**, 325–46.

Banister, D. (1978), The influence of habit formation on modal choice – a heuristic model, *Transportation*, **7**, 19–33.

Bergson, H. (1911), *Creative Evolution*, New York: Henry Holt & Co.

Bissell, D. (2010), Vibrating materialities: mobility–body–technology relations, *Area*, **42**, 479–86.

Bissell, D. (2013), Habit displaced: the disruption of skilful performance, *Geographical Research*, **51**, 120–29.

Butler, J. (1993), *Bodies that Matter: On the Discursive Limits of Sex*, New York: Routledge.

Changdon, S.A. (1996), Effects of summer precipitation on urban transportation, *Climatic Change*, **32**, 481–94.

Colls, R. (2011), Feminism, bodily difference and non-representational theories, *Transactions of the Institute of British Geographers*, **37**, 430–45.

Connolly, W.E. (2011), *A World of Becoming*, Durham, NC: Duke University Press.

Crang, M. (2005), Time:space, in P. Cloke and Johnston, R. (eds), *Spaces of Geographical Thought*, London: Sage, pp. 199–220.

Davies, K. (1996), Capturing women's lives: a discussion of time and methodological issues, *Women's Studies International Forum*, **19**, 579–88.

Deleuze, G. (1988), *Spinoza: Practical Philosophy*, San Francisco: City Light Books.

Downs, A. (1962), The law of peak-hour expressway congestion, *Traffic Quarterly*, **16**, 393–409.

Dreborg, K.H. (1996), Essence of backcasting, *Futures*, **28**, 813–28.

Ewing, R. and Cervero, R. (2010), Travel and the built environment: a meta-analysis, *Journal of the Association of American Planners*, **76**, 265–94.

Givoni, M. and Banister, D. (2013), *Moving Towards Low Carbon Mobility*, Cheltenham: Edward Elgar.

Goodchild, M.F. and Janelle, D.G. (1984), The city around the clock: space-time patterns of urban ecological structure, *Environment and Planning A*, **16**, 807–20.

Goodwin, P.B. (1977), Habit and hysteresis in mode choice, *Urban Studies*, **14**, 95–8.

Goodwin, P.B. (1996), Empirical evidence on induced traffic: a review and synthesis, *Transportation*, **23**, 35–54.

Halewood, M. (2008), Introduction to special section on A. N. Whitehead, *Theory, Culture & Society*, **25**, 1–14.

Haraway, D. (2003), *The Companion Species Manifesto: Dogs, People, and Significant Otherness*, Chicago: Prickly Paradigm Press.

Hickman, R. and Banister, D. (2007), Looking over the horizon: transport and reduced CO_2 emissions in the UK by 2030, *Transport Policy*, **14**, 377–87.

Hume, D. ([1739] 1985), *A Treatise of Human Nature*, London: Penguin Classics.

Jones, P. (1979), 'HATS': a technique for investigating household decisions, *Environment and Planning A*, **11**, 59–70.

Jonkeren, O.E. (2009), *Adaptation to Climate Change in Inland Waterway Transport*, Amsterdam: Thela Thesis and Tinbergen Institute, Free University.

Kitamura, R. (1990), Panel analysis in transportation planning: an overview, *Transportation Research A: General*, **24**, 401–15.

Kwan, M.P. (2012), The uncertain geographic context problem, *Annals of the Association of American Geographers*, **102**, 958–68.

Kwan, M.P. and Ding, G. (2008), Geo-narrative: extending geographic information systems for narrative analysis in qualitative and mixed-method research, *The Professional Geographer*, **60**, 443–65.

Latour, B. (2005), What is given in experience? *Boundary*, **2**(32), 223–37.

Laws, G. (1995), Theorizing ageism: lessons from postmodernism and feminism, *The Gerontologist*, **35**, 112–18.

Marchau, V.A.W.J., Walker, W.E. and van Wee, G.P. (2010), Dynamic adaptive transport policies for handling deep uncertainty, *Technological Forecasting and Social Change*, **77**, 940–50.

Massumi, B. (2002), *Parables for the Virtual: Movement, Affect, Sensation*, Durham, NC: Duke University Press.

Mol, A. (1999), Ontological politics: a word and some questions, in J. Law and J. Hassard (eds), *Actor Network Theory and After*, Oxford: Blackwell, pp. 74–89.

Owens, S. (1995), From 'predict and provide' to 'predict and prevent'? Pricing and planning in transport policy, *Transport Policy*, **2**, 43–9.

Rose, P. (2002), *On Whitehead*, Belmont, CA: Wadsworth.

Schwanen, T., Hardill, I. and Lucas, S. (2012a), Spatialities of ageing: the co-construction and co-evolution of old age and space, *Geoforum*, **43**, 1291–95.

Schwanen, T., Banister, D. and Anable, J. (2012b), Rethinking habits and their role in behaviour change: the case of low-carbon mobility, *Journal of Transport Geography*, **24**, 522–32.

Shaviro, S. (2009), *Without Criteria: Kant, Whitehead, Deleuze, and Aesthetics*, Cambridge, MA: MIT Press.

Shove, E. (2003), *Comfort, Cleanliness and Convenience: The Social Organization of Normality*, Oxford: Berg.

Stengers, I. ([2002] 2011), *Thinking with Whitehead: A Free and Wild Creation of Concepts*, Cambridge, MA: Harvard University Press.

Stengers, I. (2005),Whitehead's account of the sixth day, *Configurations*, **13**, 35–55.

Thrift, N. (2007), *Non-representational Theory: Space, Politics, Affect*, Abingdon: Routledge.

Tversky, A. (1972), Elimination by aspects: a theory of choice, *Psychological Review*, **79**, 281–99.

Walker, W.E., Marchau, V. and Swanson, D. (2010), Addressing deep uncertainty using adaptive policies: introduction to section 2, *Technological Forecasting and Social Change*, **77**, 917–23.

Watson, M. (2012), How theories of practice can inform transition to a decarbonised transport system, *Journal of Transport Geography*, **24**, 488–96.

Whitehead, A.N. ([1920] 2007), *The Concept of Nature*, Charleston, SC: Bibliobazaar.

Whitehead, A.N. ([1929] 1978), *Process and Reality*, corrected edition, New York: The Free Press.

Whitehead, A.N. ([1925] 1967), *Science and the Modern World*, New York: The Free Press.

Whitehead, A.N. ([1933] 1967), *Adventure of Ideas*, New York: The Free Press.

Whitehead, A.N. ([1938] 1968), *Modes of Thought*, New York: The Free Press.

PART V

SUMMARY AND CONCLUSIONS

45 Transport and development – what next?
David Banister, David Bonilla, Moshe Givoni and Robin Hickman

1. INTRODUCTION

The relationships between transport and development have become a central part of transport thinking, particularly in the cities of the developed countries. These cities already have a high level of connectivity with dense street patterns, roads and public transport systems that can accommodate most traffic under normal conditions. The quality of that transport network has been seen to be central to the economic success of cities and in making them an attractive centre for investment. Increasingly, the transport benefits of new infrastructure investment have been enhanced by the wider economic benefits brought about through agglomeration economies, labour market benefits (better employment opportunities) and other multiplier effects. In the rapidly growing cities in the developing world, there is still the need for new infrastructure to accommodate the huge increases in demand arising from population growth and from increased wealth. Yet in time, even these 'new cities' will have to limit new investment as demand for travel always seems to exceed the means to provide for that demand. Questions are now being raised in all cities about what is a sufficient amount of infrastructure and whether issues of demand management and capacity management should become the central concerns of decision-makers rather than continuing to follow the supply-led future.

This edited collection has addressed these fundamental concerns, about how much transport infrastructure is sufficient for cities. Development is seen as a much wider concept here that embraces social, environmental and spatial issues, as well as the economic implications. The three main parts of the book are structured around these important factors that place development within the concept of well-being rather than growth. Issues relating to consumption and economic growth are important elements for development, but in this book the concern is also over the equally important issues of resources, accessibility, location, community design, health, the spatial implications of development, linking public transport to local development, poverty and inequality, social policy, cultural aspects, open and green spaces, the impacts of technology, demographics, sustainable transport, climate change and politics. When discussing transport and development, all these factors are central to the realities of the debates, and the diversity of issues and interpretations that can be made for a rich and comprehensive understanding of the different pathways that have been followed.

This concluding chapter brings together many of these interesting and important issues by sketching out a vision of cities and change, through looking backwards and forwards, before setting out an agenda for the future. Development is seen as a multifaceted process that provides a fundamental rationale for cities and regions, and it is argued that transport plays a key role in facilitating the success brought about by development.

Transport supports the development of new and existing cities, but it can also act as a barrier to development, and additional demand for travel is often a consequence of development. Every city is different and the pathways followed both start and end at different points, but there are many underlying commonalities relating to economic success and stability, employment and trade, innovation, research and education, as well as social inclusions, clean air and health, governance and a high quality of life. The problems facing cities also have common elements relating to the need for housing, affordability and accessibility, security and safety, climate change and investment (including infrastructure). Although cities, regions and locations all have underlying commonalities and problems, each one is very different, and these differences have been brought out in the individual chapters of the book. The richness and diversity is something to be treasured and valued, and this in turn makes it difficult to come to any form of overall synthesis in this concluding chapter.

2.   CITIES AND CHANGE

Cities are undergoing a renaissance with a huge growth in urban population, and the emergence of the 'megacity' (over 10 million population), the 'metacity' (over 20 million population) and the 'metacity regions' (with a total population over 80 million). Examples of metacity regions can be seen in Japan (Tokyo to Nagoya and Osaka), in China (Pearl River Delta), and in Brazil (Sao Paulo to Rio de Janeiro). In 1900, about 13 per cent of the global population was urban, but by 2000 this figure was 47 per cent, and the 50 per cent threshold was reached in 2007 when 3.3 billion people were 'urban'. By 2030, the figure will exceed 60 per cent (four billion), and by 2050 nearly 70 per cent (six billion) of the global population (nine billion) will be living in urban areas. This enormous growth will be fuelled by natural growth, longer lives and migration into the city, and the dynamics of urbanization will also change as the population will be young and active. Cities will provide the main sources of employment in manufacturing and service provision. But in addition, they will also provide the new growth in the knowledge economy and in the networked society. Cities will continue to drive the global economy, as well as being centres of innovation, creativity and wealth.

The traditional notions of work, as being construed by a 35-hour week and by 40 years of commitment to one employer, has already effectively been transformed. The new forms of work are much more flexible, with people moving around between different jobs, with hours to suit their own needs, and with time taken out to learn new skills or to raise a family – at least for increasing parts of the working population. Gender barriers are being broken down and home-working becomes much more common, as both work and leisure are becoming increasingly organized around the Internet in its many manifestations. The cities that adapt to this new knowledge and network based environment are the ones that will prosper, with tradition counting for less as labour becomes ever more mobile. In addition to being the centres of work, cities will retain their positions as centres of government, finance, education and culture, as this is where decisions will be made that affect the next stages in the increasingly globalized markets.

Multinational companies may still influence many aspects of life, but it is likely that governance may change, as decision-making revolves increasingly around the power of the Internet, and coalitions that are formed to address particular challenges (e.g., climate change or social equity issues). Because of the greater transparency brought about by web-based transactions, there is a much greater flexibility in decision-making and a strong movement against big government. It is unclear how many of these potential conflicts of interest between governments, multinational companies and society in general will actually be resolved.

Within this ever-evolving landscape of change, and as cities restructure themselves to this new set of challenges brought about by the latest technological revolution, it is clear that social and environmental issues will continue to need careful attention. Cities are dependent on all people being able to engage in the opportunities that are presented, but there is still likely to be homelessness, crime and poverty, so social priorities are central to the 'successful' planning of cities, as are the needs to address energy, pollution, water, waste management and climate change.

At present, cities account for 75 per cent of the global energy consumption and nearly 80 per cent of greenhouse gas (GHG) emissions come from cities burning fossil fuels, and many of the world's great cities are located on the coast and on river estuaries, making them vulnerable to floods and sea-level rises. Of the 29 megacities[1] (2013), 20 are coastal or on major rivers (under 100ft above sea level). In certain countries, a high proportion of the total population are at risk of flooding, including Bangladesh (46 per cent of the population), Egypt (38 per cent of the population) and Vietnam (55 per cent of the population). Cities are robust and durable, and in the past they have lasted longer than many countries, but this stability might change in the future, as extreme weather events become more frequent and of a much greater intensity. Much of the infrastructure in cities was designed and built more than 100 years ago, and it needs reconstruction, and new fibre optic networks are required for high-speed access to the Internet. It is here that transport has a key role to play in the city, both in terms of the need for people to get together for work, leisure, social, educational and cultural activities, but also to enable the city itself to work. This would include the movement of freight around the city, and the support necessary for the efficient operation of the energy, waste and delivery businesses. Physical movement and distribution are still central to the operation of the city, as not every activity or transaction can be undertaken electronically. As Colin Clark (1958: 237) stated more than 50 years ago: 'A system of transport is a necessity, which like the respiratory system of the body, we take entirely for granted as long as it is working well – our imagination just fails to tell us what would happen if it broke down.'

Megacities have grown and will continue to grow at a much faster rate than the provision of new infrastructure and housing, and this situation is having a deleterious impact on the quality of life through sprawl, congestion and pollution, through poor-quality housing and poverty, and through the need for more reliable energy supply, clean water and sanitation. The potential global risk is of increasing poverty and social inequality, which may in turn lead to social unrest and higher rates of disease and crime. Although the role of good governance and urban planning may be reduced, it is important to see development as investment in the future of the city, and to maintain and enhance the quality of the built environment is key to which cities emerge as the new centres of innovation and affluence. Although it has been acknowledged that all cities are different, the narrative given in the next two sections is generic and it traces some of the commonalities between cities from all parts of the world.

3.   THE RETROSPECTIVE VIEW

Cities of Low Mobility

Before 1960, many cities had low levels of car ownership and movement was depend-ent on walking, cycling and public transport. These relatively slow forms of transport limited the growth of cities, but it must be realized that it was the introduction of public transport that permitted the initial expansion of cities – London provides a good example. In 1801, 87 per cent London's population was located in the inner area (20 per cent of the total area – 1,500km²), amounting to 0.957 million out of a total population of 1.1 million, and this was before the advent of public transport. By 1901, 70 per cent of the population (4.5 million out of 6.5 million) was still located in the inner area, even though decentralization had been facilitated by rail, tram and bus. In 2001, 45 per cent of the population (7.2 million) were in the inner area, and now (2013) about 40 per cent of the population are in the inner area, and 60 per cent in the outer area (80 per cent of area). The car has only been influential in this process since the 1970s.

In his study of the London rail network development, Levinson (2008) found positive feedback between population density and network density over the period 1871–2001, where additional stations in the periphery on the underground and overground rail net-works encouraged suburbanization and relocation, as land was cheap. In the centre of London, more expensive land was increasingly being used for commercial development and the population moved out, and the concept of commuting was created. This pattern has been replicated globally, and it reflects the classic location theory that location is influenced by rent levels (declining from the city centre) and transport costs (rising from the city centre) (Alonso, 1964).

Cities for Cars and High Levels of Mobility

Mobility levels increased with the mass production of the car and cheap energy, and more than any other consumer durable, it has come to represent prosperity and a modern notion of development. This period was marked by high levels of investment in the infrastructure, the expansion of cities, new towns and the ethos of predict and provide dominated (Banister, 2002: 25). There was a divergence of thinking between the US and Europe. In the US, where land was cheap and available, with few constraints on development, suburbia grew with single family units, low densities and large land plots, and accessibility was provided by the car. In Europe, less land was available and there were stronger controls on development, and a desire for higher densities, at least among planners and other urban modernists, and this allowed for a stronger role for public transport to provide accessibility (Banister, 2012).

The reconstruction and extension of cities was not universally supported, and influ-ential arguments raged about the nature of community and whether it could be created, or whether it could only be destroyed (Jacobs, 1961). Urban renewal could only come from mixed-use developments and maintaining the vitality of existing neighbourhoods, designed around local movement and the small scale. These arguments centred on social capital. In terms of urban development, this meant that cities were constructed at medium densities with lively neighbourhoods that encouraged mixed communities (all ages, ethnicities and classes) leading to lower levels of crime, and fostering innovation, creativity and employment.

Cities for Sustainable Mobility

It was only in the early 1970s, following the release of *Silent Spring, The Limits to Growth, Energy and Equity* and other similar publications (Carson, 1962; Meadows et al., 1972; Illich, 1974) that environmental quality became a major political concern. Even then the concern was mainly over the local environmental quality, including some pollutants, air quality, noise and community severance, but not issues relating to carbon or the future of oil. The oil crisis of 1973 was quickly forgotten, and oil's low cost and abundance continued to dominate the debate at the expense of concerns over security of supply, resource depletion and carbon.

It has only been in the past 20 years, since the World Summit in Rio (1992) and the climate agreement in Kyoto (1997), that global warming has become a major concern of science and policy. It took more than seven years for the Kyoto Protocol to be ratified (February 2005). Since that time there has been frenetic activity in examining how sustainability can be placed at the centre of transport in urban areas, so that the twin axes of development (economic and social) can be balanced against the third axis (environmental). These three 'pillars of sustainability' have been at the heart of the debates on future urban form and sustainable transport (Perrels et al., 2008).

Part II of this book draws on some of the academic debate that has been important to practice – with the protagonists arguing that urban structure plays an important role in generating particular travel patterns, with a range of built environment characteristics considered (such as density, mixed use, accessibility, etc.). There has been some limited critique, mainly from the perspective of individual choice, and also the ineffectiveness of governments to deliver neighbourhoods of 'appropriate' design. In the main, policy development (in the EU at least) has followed the 'compact city' approach that argues for medium (and high) built densities, enabling efficient public transport and thresholds to support concentrations of economic activity, services and facilities (CEC, 1992). Mixed-use environments and good public open spaces are important, with urban containment policies implemented through the demarcation of a growth boundary or urban edge. Compaction or higher building densities help cut the volume of traffic in urban areas, and this was seen by the EU as the main means to provide cities with environmental and quality of life benefits.

This rather 'simplistic' view of development failed to recognize the complexity of choices about travel, but it does not negate these arguments, as there may be strong accessibility reasons for co-location of services/facilities and homes (Breheny, 1992). The current thinking in the EU is for 'smart, sustainable and inclusive growth' (EU, 2010), but the terminology is rarely clearly defined, and compact city planning is still central to reducing the intensity of individual car use and for developing higher quality public transport connectivity between the city and its functional urban agglomeration. Policy implementation has often been weak, and urban development, particularly on the edge of the larger urban areas, or in the smaller urban centres, has (perhaps perversely) followed the dispersal route, with the compact city approach gaining little traction. Many of the complexities and nuances explored in the academic debate are not followed at the level of practice.

Cities for People

Other issues such as agglomeration and a concern over the appropriate forms of governance have become more important, while parallel movements such as 'New Urbanism' have examined similar principles at the local neighbourhood scale. Local neighbourhoods are seen as being composed of 'fine-grained, mixed-use, mixed housing types, compact form, an attractive public realm, pedestrian-friendly streetscapes, defined centres and edges, and varying transport options' (Grant, 2006: 8). This means that a wide range of facilities are grouped together around key public transport facilities and intersections to maximize accessibility by efficient forms of transport (e.g., walk and cycle, as well as public transport), but there is a concern that these types of development are not diverse or dynamic, as they are only attractive to certain types of people; and as there is not sufficient good quality housing in attractive urban neighbourhoods, the cost of living in these locations is often expensive.

Within the context of transport, the new urbanism is linked to transit-oriented developments (TODs), where higher densities and better public transport access are traded off against the greater flexibility of the car. In some situations, TODs can reduce car use per capita among its residents by half and save households around 20 per cent of their income as they have lower levels of car ownership (Cervero, 2008) and the ecological footprint of cities can be reduced. People travel shorter distances when they move into neighbourhoods with higher accessibility (Krizek, 2003), with median distance increasing from 3.2km in the more accessible neighbourhoods to 8.1km in less accessible neighbourhoods. Street connectivity is also important here as it can reduce distances for slow modes, but culs-de-sac are also popular with residents even though they tend to extend travel distances. Main Street programmes in the US (and more recently in the UK) are intended to revitalize town centres by restricting access at certain times and to create vibrant communities day and night (Handy, 2004). Other initiatives to encourage urban living include extensive pedestrianization, the closure of residential streets, gated communities and even the removal of freeways (e.g., the Embarcadero Freeway in San Francisco).

Transport has had a fundamental impact on urban development, and this pathway from public transport-oriented cities through the car-dominated city and the more recent concerns over the social and environmental factors has been replicated in nearly all cities, but at different times and in different ways. Part III of this book examines the spatial impacts of transport investment, again drawing on the rich debate concerning the different types of modes and impacts that be seen. The impacts of public transport, of varying forms, are perhaps most well-explored. But again, there is little agreement as to the 'likely' impacts of investments, with effects largely determined by context, macro and micro economic trends, the associated planning strategy and other factors.

Two themes have emerged from this retrospective view on the arguments over the roles and relationships between transport and development. One is that people are and should be at the centre of the debate, and not subject to arbitrary standards about levels of density and very physical interpretations of land use and planning. Related to this is the need to consider urbanity, where the function of urban living is to increase the means by which people can interact with each other and feel a sense of belonging through engagement with the full range of urban organizations and institutions. Second, the more recent debate on the importance of the environment has given a new impetus to the need for higher density forms of living, as the global population increases and as the proportion living in urban areas increases from 50 per cent (2008) to 70 per cent (2050). City living must provide the location in which most people live, as it makes the most efficient use of available land and it allows for the greatest economies of scale and scope, and it should also be less dependent on non-renewable resources.

There also seems to be a basic dilemma between the 'desirable city' that is a clear aspiration for many politicians and other visionaries, and the difficulty or impossibility of getting there. The consequence of viewing development only in a narrow economic sense means that many of the negative aspects are strengthened in the interests of growth and getting there faster. So the quality of the urban environment may deteriorate through congestion, social unrest, high housing costs, poor levels of air pollution and resource scarcity, with transport contributing to some of these factors and all these coming from pursuing development for its own sake. It is only when there is a realization that quality does not need to be sacrificed and that it is possible to move towards the 'desirable city' without having to pass through the deterioration in the quality of urban living that real progress will be made.

4.   REFLECTIONS AND PROSPECTS

In a 2009 UN Habitat report, eight sustainability directions were identified so that cities can address sustainable urban development in an integrated way (UN Habitat, 2009: 129). The three energy themes cover the use of renewable energy, carbon neutral investments that improve energy efficiency, and distributed local electricity and water systems. Three other themes reflect the need for cities to move toward more local production (biofuels, food and fibres, and biodiversity), eco-efficient strategies for industry (to include waste and recycling), and the means to improve the housing stock. The two final themes are most relevant here, as they reflect the importance of place strategies and transport. The 'sense of place' strategies promote the human dimension as driving all the other strategies. This can be assisted by local economic development strategies, by place-based engagement approaches to all planning and development processes, and by the innovative use of 'sustainability credits', or complementary currencies, to implement local sustainability innovations as development bonuses. The sustainable transport strategies include quality fast transit along each main corridor, dense TODs built around each station, pedestrian and bicycle strategies for each centre and TOD (with cycle links across the city), the plug-in infrastructure for electric vehicles as they emerge, cycling and pedestrian infrastructure as an integrated part of all street planning, and a green wall growth boundary around the city preventing further urban encroachment.

This report concludes that 'there is some agreement that an equitable and sustainable city will have the following spatial features: higher densities but low-rise; mixed uses; public transport based; spatial integration; a defined and protected open space system; and an urban edge to prevent sprawl' (UN Habitat, 2009: 219). There is an awareness

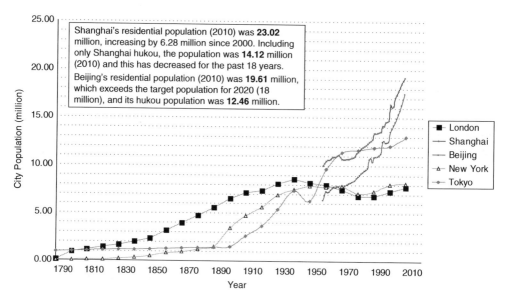

Figure 45.1   Population growth in London, New York, Tokyo, Beijing and Shanghai

that this ideal may be far easier to achieve in developed countries, where there is much greater institutional capacity to bring about compliance with the supporting organizations, processes and enforcement necessary to carry out the intentions. But the report is optimistic in that it still sees the achievement of these principles in different contexts as a worthwhile goal. The UN Habitat contribution is the realization that there is more to development than economic growth, and that the equitable and sustainable city should be given as much importance in the priorities of decision-makers, but that the institutional capacity may need to be strengthened.

In the rapidly growing cities of the developing world, both the speed and scale of change are unprecedented, and this requires strong institutional and governance structures as well as substantial infrastructure investment funds. For example, Figure 45.1 shows the growth in population of five world cities, illustrating the recent (since 1960) surge in the populations of Beijing and Shanghai, with each of their populations more than doubling from high base populations of 7.3 million and 10.5 million respectively. Even at that time, they were larger than London was in 2000 or New York was in 1990. Looking back over time, it can be seen that London has followed a steady path of population increase, reaching 1 million in 1805, 5 million in 1885 and peaking at 8.6 million in 1940. New York's population growth pattern is similar to that now being experienced in China, as it was also subject to mass inward migration. The population in New York reached 1 million in 1875, but from 1890 it rose from 1.5 million to 7.5 million in 1940, a five times increase over a 50-year period. Tokyo has also grown by more than six times, from 2 million in 1900 to 13 million by 2010, but over a longer period. The patterns of population growth and migration in the Chinese cities are not new, even though the speed and scale of change is substantially larger.

Such an argument is promoting an explicitly social dimension to the more central thinking behind the new economic geography (Krugman, 1991), where increasing returns to scale promote concentration of activity, and where transport costs are seen to be important in determining market structure, under conditions of imperfect competition. Central to the case is factor mobility, where knowledge, information and labour are instrumental in determining the spatial patterns of development (Krugman, 2011). The desire for urban living and the opportunities that it offers are central to the attraction of the city, as well as the sound economic reasons for clustering and concentration. To some extent this reasoning also counters Storper's concerns over the need to include knowledge and information spillovers, and other intangibles to fully explain the complexity of the processes taking place (Storper, 2011).

There is a strong economic rationale behind this urbanization process, and it is consistent with resource availability and the export-led manufacturing, it provides an extreme example of Krugman's (1991) core-periphery model, with industrial clustering and localization, together with specialization and higher levels of productivity. In addition, the larger cities have attracted the best-educated workers and more international investment, and there also seems to be network benefits arising from better communications and transport infrastructure. These agglomeration economies occur when the different agencies (firms and workers) benefit from being in close proximity to each other, and good quality transport can help strengthen these agglomeration economies as the connectivity in the spatial economy is improved, and this in turn may again lead to higher output productivity (Graham, 2007).

Climate change (as manifest by the increased frequency and intensity of extreme weather events) may imply the submersion, washing away and buckling of roads and other infrastructures (Meyer, 2010), while the rising price and constrained supply of oil-based fuels may make certain trips unaffordable or impossible. Parts of cities – for example, along the coast or inland waterways, neighbourhoods that can only be reached by car or where the car is the basic way of getting around – may become virtually inaccessible, and these effects may be propagated throughout whole cities. These detrimental effects impact on the attractiveness and the viability of the city, with consequential reductions in output and competitiveness. In addition, insurance premiums will increase both in flooding-prone neighbourhoods and more generally. If significant numbers of people or firms decide to leave certain parts of an urban area, land values and prices may fall, imposing significant financial risks to private individuals, corporate investors, public authorities (local and central) and others.

For urban areas to thrive in the future, resilience needs to be developed to address transport-related vulnerabilities at the city level and at the transport system level. Additionally, integral or 'expanded' assessments (Jaroszweski et al., 2010) of city-level risks and vulnerabilities are required, which consider both climate change and oil scarcity simultaneously as part of coupled human/environment systems that are complex and multi-scalar (i.e., ranging from the globe to the individual). Vulnerability is here understood as the degree of susceptibility of a system (e.g., a city, transport network, the daily travel/activity pattern of an individual) and its lack of ability to cope with the adverse effects of events associated with climate change and oil scarcity. Vulnerability is a function of the exposure of a transport system to (and its sensitivity to) those events, and its adaptive capacities to respond to them (Koetse and Rietveld, 2009; Changa et al., 2011). Transport and urban planning research with regard to climate change is growing rapidly but it tends to focus on mitigation rather than vulnerability and adaptation (IPCC, 2014a, 2014b).

Part IV of this book refers to the 'wider dimensions' that need to be addressed in the research field – the psychological and sociological determinants of travel; the value often perceived within travel; the existence of norms, habits and values; the role of ICT and its relation to physical travel; the heterogeneous nature of the population; and the appropriate forms of governance in defining and responding to societal goals. All of these areas influence the urban structure and travel and transport investment and spatial impact relationships – and often they are poorly understood.

In many ways the message of this chapter is optimistic, in that many cities in Europe are becoming more sustainable, at least in transport terms in their everyday activities as more than 50 per cent of trips are made by walking and cycling. Public transport plays an important role for travel over longer distances, and in many cases the role for the car is being questioned. But, if the trends are considered closely, then huge challenges still remain – in the travel that remains largely car-dependent beyond the main urban centres, in the huge growth in international communication and physical travel – and much of this remains carbon-intensive and highly socially inequitable in terms of access. Quality of life and urban living are seen as being the main driving forces in the greening of everyday travel, with high quality low carbon mobility options often possible. To some extent cities in the USA and Canada are following the same pathway, but it is more difficult here as distances are much greater, and the alternative low carbon infrastructure is not an attractive option to the car. More opportunities are being taken to concentrate development and to build at higher densities through mixed use and balanced approaches – but often there is much disagreement over the policy approach and the progress is agonisingly slow. Technology may also have a key role to play here through greater efficiency in car design, through new forms of ownership (leasing and car sharing), and through reducing the need to travel by adopting new working and social patterns of activity (Banister, 2013). Social and work-based networking offer immense possibilities to again change the nature of physical movements and other forms of communication so that flexibility is maintained within the transport system.

The growth in the megacities present new possibilities and problems, with key questions being raised as to whether the solutions used can be adapted and applied elsewhere. Part of the problem relates to the scale and rate of change, but part to the speed at which the land-use planning system can adapt to the requirements that are now being placed on it. For example, much of the traditional thinking is to provide a built environment and transport system that will last at least 100 years, and investment decisions are made on that basis, examining all the costs and benefits and discounting them over 30 or 60 years. The new agenda requires a far quicker decision process and far greater flexibility to be included in any major decision, as land values, land uses and travel patterns are all changing over a much shorter period of time, as industrialization moves into service-based and knowledge-based futures. The cloudy definition of sustainability has not helped in research or practice – with the term representing many things to many people. Perhaps a wider understanding of 'development' as a means to achieve well-being at the individual and societal levels will give further clarity in direction. We hope this book brings together much of the interesting debate from the past 30 years – and offers us a basis for moving our research and practice forward. Transport, as ever, has an important role to play in promoting the sustainable city, including greater well-being in life. The huge growth in the urban population at the urban scale, with much of it yet to be designed, offers us many opportunities – and we should seek to grasp them.

NOTE

1. Megacities (over 10 million population) in rank order (2013): Tokyo, Guangzhou, Shanghai, Jakarta, Seoul, Delhi, Mexico City, Karachi, Manila, New York City, Sao Paulo, Mumbai, Beijing, Los Angeles, Osaka, Dhaka, Cairo, Kolkata, London, Buenos Aires, Bangkok, Istanbul, Lagos, Tehran, Rio de Janeiro, Shenzhen, Moscow, Paris, Tianjin. The top 12 are metacities (over 20 million population). The figures are not entirely comparable as truly comparative data is not available (http://en.wikipedia.org/wiki/Megacity).

REFERENCES

Alonso, W. (1964), *Location and Land Use*, Cambridge, MA: Harvard University Press.

Banister, D. (2002), *Transport Planning*, London: Routledge.

Banister, D. (2012), Assessing the reality: transport and land use planning to achieve sustainability, *The Journal of Transport and Land Use*, **5**(3), 1–14.

Banister, D. (2013), *Scanning the Transport Horizon*, paper prepared for the Foresights Futures Programme, Government Office for Science, revised version.

Breheny, M. (ed.) (1992), The Compact City, special issue of *Built Environment*, **18**(4), 659–74.

Carson, R. (1962), *Silent Spring*, London: Hamish Hamilton.

CEC (1992), *Sustainable Mobility: Impact of Transport on the Environment*, COM92(46), Brussels: Commission of the European Communities.

Cervero, R. (2008), *Effects of TOD on Housing, Parking and Travel*, Transit Cooperative Research Program Report 128, Federal Transit Administration, Washington, DC.

Changa, H., Lafrenza, M. and Junga, I.W. (2011), Potential impacts of climate change on flood-induced travel disruptions: a case study of Portland, Oregon, USA, *Annals of the Association of American Geographers*, **100**, 938–52.

Clark, C. (1958), Transport: maker and breaker of cities, *Town Planning Review*, **28**(4), 237–50.

EU (2010), *A Strategy for Smart, Sustainable and Inclusive Growth*, COM (2010) 2020, Brussels: European Union.

Graham, D.J. (2007), Agglomeration, productivity and transport investment, *Journal of Transport Economics and Policy*, **41**(3), 317–43.

Grant, J. (2006), *Planning the Good Community: New Urbanism in Theory and Practice*, London and New York: Routledge.

Handy, S. (2004), *Accessibility v Mobility-enhancing Strategies for Addressing Automobile Dependence in the US*, paper presented at the ECMT round table on Transport and Spatial Policies: The Role of Regulatory and Fiscal Incentives, RT124, Paris, November 2002, 49–85.

Illich, I. (1974), *Energy and Equity*, London: Calder & Boyars.

IPCC (2014a), *Impacts, Adaptation and Vulnerability*, report of Working Group II, Yokohama, Japan.

IPCC (2014b), *Mitigation of Climate Change*, report of Working Group III, Berlin, Germany.

Jacobs, J. (1961), *The Death and Life of the Great American Cities*, New York: Random House.

Jaroszweski, D., Chapman, L. and Petts, J. (2010), Assessing the potential impact of climate change on transportation: the need for an interdisciplinary approach, *Journal of Transport Geography*, **18**, 331–5.

Koetse, M.J. and Rietveld, P. (2009), The impact of climate change and weather on transport: an overview of empirical findings, *Transportation Research D*, **14**, 205–21.

Krizek, K.J. (2003), Residential relocation and changes in urban travel: does neighbourhood scale urban form matter, *Journal of the American Planning Association*, **69**(3), 265–81.

Krugman, P. (1991), Increasing returns in economic geography, *Journal of Political Economy*, **99**, 483–99.

Krugman, P. (2011), The new economic geography, now middle aged, *Regional Studies* **45**(1), 1–7.

Levinson, D. (2008), Density and dispersion: the co-development of land use and rail in London, *Journal of Economic Geography*, **8**(1), 55–77.

Meadows, D.H., Meadows, D.L., Randers, J. and Behrens, W.W. (1972), *The Limits to Growth*, New York: Universe Books.

Meyer, M.D. (2010), Greenhouse gas and climate change assessment: framing the transportation research agenda, *Journal of the American Planning Association*, **76**, 402–12.

Perrels, A., Himanen, V. and Lee-Gosseling, M. (eds) (2008), *Building Blocks for Sustainable Transport: Obstacles, Trends, Solutions*, Bingley: Emerald.

Storper, M. (2011), From retro to avant-garde: a commentary on Paul Krugman's 'The new economic geography, now middle aged', *Regional Studies*, **45**(1), 9–15.

UN Habitat (2009), *Planning Sustainable Cities, Global Report on Human Settlements*, London: Earthscan.

Index